414   £2.60

England's Test Cricketers 1877–1996

England's Test Cricketers
1877–1996

JASON WOOLGAR

ROBERT HALE • LONDON

ISBN 0 7090 6018 1

Robert Hale Limited
Clerkenwell House
Clerkenwell Green
London EC1R 0HT

2 4 6 8 10 9 7 5 3 1

Printed and bound by
Mackays of Chatham

Contents

Foreword

When David Gower presented me with my first cap in August 1989 a part of my dreams and ambitions had been realized. To be given my first cap by, and play in the same side as, a player I had admired as a boy was a great thrill. My father then told me that the easiest part was getting there, the hard part was staying there. To date I have represented England 62 times in Test matches and I hope there are many more to come.

During my initial involvement with the England team one experienced campaigner confided in me 'that you play your first Test match for love and the rest for money'. It was a disillusioning comment at the time and one indicative of a team being thrashed by an Australian side showing more pride and passion.

I have always remembered that comment and have never tried to play as if money was the motivating force. To represent your country is a proud achievement for anyone and it should be cherished as such in the short time it lasts. Any other way and the public would surely see through it and condemn it.

This book is a statistical record of England's 582 Test match cricketers. Naturally, there are many great and illustrious names in England's past. Whilst I am never one to wallow in yesteryear it could probably be said that the last time England was indisputably the best team in world cricket was the late 1950s. At present we may not be able to emulate them, but the future always brings gratuities and there can be no better place to start than with the visiting Australians in 1997, in what will surely be a fascinating year.

I have never previously placed too much store by statistics as cricket is a game that has so much more to offer. They do, however, afford a cricketer an opportunity to look back over a career fulfilled or otherwise. And if in a small way they add to the understanding of a player's achievements or greatness or a team's successes or failures they are more than worth the space afforded them.

Michael Atherton

Introduction

It is true to say that I would have preferred this book to have been an uninterrupted parade of England's finest talents and the subsequent triumphs they so gloriously achieved. To some extent this is the case as I have included every single cricketer to represent England at Test level and among them are obviously some of the world's greatest players.

Unfortunately, for a writer of my generation (I first started watching Test cricket in 1977) the majority of these great players seem lost in the very distant past and the highs which they obtained have, all too commonly, been engulfed in a sea of ineptitude and mediocrity.

The reasons for this are of course numerous and have been well chronicled if not resolved. I am only one of a legion of cricket followers, both professional and otherwise, who have already written and discussed at great length the problems that currently trouble our beloved game and this is perhaps not the forum for each of the various arguments to be taken a great deal further. Having said this there are two areas which greatly affect the current England Test side which this book highlights to such a degree they are, if not inescapable, then certainly difficult to ignore.

The first concerns our beleaguered Test match selectors. Although it is all too easy to lay most of England's ills at their door it became very apparent, very quickly, when researching this book, that our selectors have changed little over the last century. I had always imagined that our selection policies, at best erratic at worst hysterical, were a sad feature of modern times, born as a result of continued embarrassing defeats. Although the latter does still apply to some degree little appears to have changed during the last 120 years with every failure resulting in an apoplexy of axe-wielding and the continuation of a self-propagating nightmare. In fact to some degree the selectors have expressed a remarkable consistency in inconsistency, resulting in the fact that of the 582 players to have represented England in Test matches an incredible 373 (64.08%) have played ten or less matches with 74 having made only two appearances and a further 83 having played just once. After speaking to many players both past and present, it is perhaps not surprising that even the more talented of them have struggled under the constant pressure of the selectors' self-imposed Damoclean sword.

The second and slightly more worrying area of concern (considering that the first will probably never be addressed), which this book highlights, is England's failure to produce a genuine world-class performer within the last 15-20 years. This is not said to denigrate the current crop of players nor is it pure conjecture on my part, it is more a matter of record. England have not had either a batsman capable of maintaining a Test career average of 50 or more since the late Ken Barrington or a bowler of taking 200 Test wickets since Ian Botham. When you note that Barrington first played in the mid 1950s and that Botham made his debut more than 20 years ago it can be seen just how acute the problem has become.

We have of course still produced some tremendous players during recent years, many capable of great performances and again many of sufficient ability to merit selection for other international sides, always a benchmark of quality. However, none would be the greatest player in the world's strongest teams, certainly not the catalyst that England are currently lacking.

In the most simplistic terms the foundations of a successful team are built along the following lines; one or two batsmen averaging 50 or more with the remainder maintaining averages within the 40s; two or three bowlers capable of taking 150-250 wickets, preferably at least one a spin bowler, although not always necessary as per the West Indies; a good all-rounder or two and a capable wicket-keeper batsman. As I have already stated this is over-simplifying matters, however when you look at the strongest teams both in world cricket today and throughout history most contain the majority of the above. Whereas in England in very recent years we have, at best, been able to produce three or four reasonably talented batsmen and a world class wicket-keeper who, selectors please note, can bat.

While a batsman with a superior average can often be dispensed with, wicket-taking bowlers cannot and it is our inability to produce these and therefore consistently dismiss sides twice that continues to thwart us. A lack of such bowlers is further accentuated by the absence of a top quality all-rounder, a player capable of providing the selectors with considerably more options and some much needed variety. England have, until recently at least, been fortunate in this department being able to call upon both Tony Greig and Ian Botham. It is a sad fact, however, that were it not for Botham's seamless replacement of the almost equally talented Greig, and his subsequent heroics, England's failings would certainly have been exposed a great deal sooner.

Although these and other problems will continue, the debates will no doubt rage for only as long as it takes England to unearth a player of genuine world-class ability, capable of galvanizing a moderately talented team into an exceptional one and thereby thinly papering over the extensive cracks that will continue to blight our game at international level.

As far as the players that have actually represented England are concerned, as you will be able to gather from Michael Atherton's candid foreword, playing for your country means considerably more to some than others. Although it can only be hoped that the vast majority of the players featured herein have taken great pride in wearing the blue cap it is still surprising, to me at least, the number of whom have refused to play for England either due to a preference to concentrate instead on business careers, or a refusal to undertake the more arduous tours. Some, most surprisingly of all, have even withdrawn from matches as a result of pay disputes.

With this is mind I could easily have entitled this book the good the bad and the downright indifferent but instead I leave you to make up your own minds. The facts are before you, 582 Test match careers, many of which survive even the closest scrutiny, many more which unfortunately do not. Some of the enclosed are undoubtedly lucky to feature, particularly those whose only first-class matches were of the Test variety, others were incredibly unfortunate not to have done so with far greater frequency. Of course there will always be players of such talent that their giant strides belittle those around them, this is not a new phenomenon nor is it uniquely English.

For every Hutton and Hammond there will always be a dozen less gifted individuals and it is probably true to say that the vast majority of England's Test match achievements have been contributed by no more than 10% of their players. Although statistically this is relatively easy to prove, for example 418 (70.6%) of England's 592 Test match centuries have been scored by 38 players (6.52%), statistics, as politicians have taught us, can be used to form almost any required interpretation and can never quite tell the complete story. Individual heroics will often be overlooked, as will injuries and solitary poor performances which have often limited or even ended careers. However, they are a more than useful guide and are able to conjure evocative and lasting memories. For me every entry represents a match or innings, every innings a shot or delivery of those that have played the greatest of games at the highest of levels.

Jason Wooolgar
London, November 1996

Acknowledgements

As fitting in such circumstances I have below acknowledged the great debt I owe to a large number of people, all of whom have made this book possible. In addition I would like to collectively mention the many previous cricket writers, historians and statisticians who have made sense of a myriad of information compiled over 120 years. It is these great students of the game that have enabled the latter generations to produce books of this kind.

I am indebted to the following individuals and organizations who provided me with valuable assistance:

Philip Bailey, Robert Brooke, Bill Frindall, Richard Lockwood, The Test and County Cricket Board, The Australian Cricket Board, The International Cricket Council, The Association of Cricket Statisticians and Historians.

All of the publications listed below were consulted and I am most grateful to the authors and publishers of each.

The Wisden Book Of Test Cricket Volume I 1877–1977 – Bill Frindall
The Wisden Book Of Test Cricket Volume II 1977–1989 – Bill Frindall
World Cricketers A Biographical Dictionary – Christopher Martin-Jenkins
Who's Who Of Cricketers – Philip Bailey, Philip Thorn and Peter Wynne-Thomas
The Cricketers' Who's Who (various years)
ACS International Cricket Year Book (various years)
The Cricketer International (various editions)
The Cricketer Quarterly (various editions)
Cricket Statistics System – Gordon Vince

I would also like to thank John Welch for his efforts and also my publishers for their support, in particular Susan Hale for her continued assistance.

Finally, on a personal note I would like to express my sincere gratitude to my family, particularly Kim Sykes and Elaine Woolgar, for not only painstakingly checking every draft, but also for their patience and tolerance when the pressure in creating such a book took an obvious toll.

Notes and Abbreviations

The most important aspect in compiling a book of this kind is to ensure that all material is accurate and comprehensible. I have therefore attempted to convey the information in the most accessible manner possible, the majority of which is self-explanatory. However I have made some slight departures from previous works and have noted these below.

For the sake of uniformity I have not recorded each player's teams in exact chronological order as many overlap and this can create confusion. I have instead listed them as follows: first of all either of the first-class universities followed by county teams and then any foreign sides, be they at domestic or international level. Finally, I have recorded the dates that each player has appeared for England, these dates comprise the actual first and last year a player has appeared for the national team and do not include tour dates i.e. if a player made his first appearance in March 1990 this is listed as 1990 and not 1989/90.

As far as the record section is concerned I have intentionally not included every minor and obscure record, instead choosing to concentrate on the major areas of achievement which I feel will be of maximum interest to the vast majority of cricket enthusiasts and which have not previously been reviewed in such detail.

My biggest departure in this field concerns century partnerships which are generally listed for two batsmen only. As far as I am concerned partnerships are for each particular wicket regardless of the number of batsmen used to create them. If therefore a batsman has been forced to retire and a combination of three have produced a century stand then it is included. I realize that this will not meet with total agreement and have therefore carefully highlighted each such occurrence.

I have also included strike rates for each of the bowlers as well as introducing dismissals, catches and stumpings records per match for the wicket-keepers and fielders. These are entitled DPM, CPM, and SPM respectively.

As the number of deliveries per over has differed between countries throughout the years I have also listed below the exact number of balls bowled per over for each country during any given period.

Australia
1876/77 – 1887/88	4
1891/92 – 1920/21	6
1924/25	8
1928/29 – 1932/33	6
1936/37 – 1978/79	8
1979/80 – present	6

England
1880 – 1888	4
1890 – 1899	5
1902 – 1938	6
1939	8
1946 – present	6

South Africa
1888/89	4
1891/92 – 1898/99	5
1902/03 – 1935/36	6
1938/39 – 1957/58	8
1961/62 – 1969/70	6

West Indies
1929/30 – present	6

New Zealand
1929/30 – 1967/68	6
1968/69 – 1978/79	8
1979/80 – present	6

India
1933/34 – present	6

Pakistan
1954/55 – 1972/73	6
1974/75 – 1977/78	8
1978/79 – present	6

Sri Lanka
1981/82 – present	6

Zimbabwe
1992/93 – present	6

All records, for all sections of the book, encompass the 1996 English season and are therefore complete up to and including the Third Test between England and Pakistan at the Oval in August 1996.

Player Profiles

R.ABEL

Full Name: Robert Abel (known as Bobby)
Born: 30/11/1857, Rotherhithe, Surrey
Died: 10/12/1936, Stockwell, London
Teams: Surrey 1881-1904, England 1888-1902
Matches: 13 (Won 7, Drew 0, Lost 6)
Right-hand opening/middle order batsman – Off break bowler

No	Date	Opposition	Venue	R	Bat	C
1	16/07/1888	Australia	Lord's	L	3	1
					8	
2	13/08/1888	Australia	The Oval	W	70	
						1
3	30/08/1888	Australia	Old Trafford	W	0	
						1
4	12/03/1889	South Africa	Port Elizabeth	W	46	3
					23*	
5	25/03/1889	South Africa	Cape Town	W	120	1
6	01/01/1892	Australia	Melbourne	L	32	
					28	1
7	29/01/1892	Australia	Sydney	L	132*	2
					1	
8	24/03/1892	Australia	Adelaide	W	24	1
9	22/06/1896	Australia	Lord's	W	94	
					4	
10	16/07/1896	Australia	Old Trafford	L	26	
					13	
11	10/08/1896	Australia	The Oval	W	26	
					21	1
12	03/07/1902	Australia	Bramall Lane	L	38	1
					8	
13	24/07/1902	Australia	Old Trafford	L	6	
					21	

Batting & Fielding

Mat	Inns	N/O	Runs	H/S	Avg	100s	50s	Cat
13	22	2	744	132*	37.20	2	2	13

C.A.ABSOLOM

Full Name: Charles Alfred Absolom (known as Charlie)
Born: 07/06/1846, Blackheath, Kent
Died: 30/07/1889, Port-of-Spain, Trinidad
Teams: Cambridge University 1866-69, Kent 1868-79, England 1879
Matches: 1 (Won 0, Drew 0, Lost 1)
Right-hand opening/middle order batsman – Right-arm medium bowler

No	Date	Opposition	Venue	R	Bat	C
1	02/01/1879	Australia	Melbourne	L	52	
					6	

Batting & Fielding

Mat	Inns	N/O	Runs	H/S	Avg	100s	50s	Cat
1	2	0	58	52	29.00	0	1	0

J.P.AGNEW

Full Name: Jonathan Philip Agnew (known as Jon)
Born: 04/04/1960, Macclesfield, Cheshire
Team: Leicestershire 1978-90, England 1984-85
Matches: 3 (Won 0, Drew 2, Lost 1)
Right-hand lower order batsman – Right-arm fast bowler

No	Date	Opposition	Venue	R	Bat	C		Bowling		
1	09/08/1984	West Indies	The Oval	L	5		12	3	46	0
					2*		14	1	51	2
2	23/08/1984	Sri Lanka	Lord's	D	1*		32	3	123	2
							11	3	54	0
3	01/08/1985	Australia	Old Trafford	D	2*		14	0	65	0
							9	2	34	0

Batting & Fielding

Mat	Inns	N/O	Runs	H/S	Avg	100s	50s	Cat
3	4	3	10	5	10.00	0	0	0

Bowling

Balls	Runs	Wkts	Avg	Best	5WI	10WM	S/R
552	373	4	93.25	2-51	0	0	138.00

D.A.ALLEN

Full Name: David Arthur Allen
Born: 29/10/1935, Horfield, Bristol
Teams: Gloucestershire 1953-72, England 1960-66
Matches: 39 (Won 9, Drew 24, Lost 6)
Right-hand middle/lower order batsman – Off break bowler

No	Date	Opposition	Venue	R	Bat	C	Bowling			
1	06/01/1960	West Indies	Bridgetown	D	10		43	12	82	0
2	28/01/1960	West Indies	Port-of-Spain	W	10*		5	0	9	0
					16	1	31	13	57	3
3	17/02/1960	West Indies	Kingston	D	30*		28	10	57	1
					17*		9	4	19	0
4	09/03/1960	West Indies	Georgetown	D	55		42	11	75	3
					1*					
5	25/03/1960	West Indies	Port-of-Spain	D	7		24	1	61	2
					25		15	2	57	0
6	21/07/1960	South Africa	Old Trafford	D	0		19.5	6	58	4
					14*		7	4	5	0
7	18/08/1960	South Africa	The Oval	D	0		28	15	36	0
					12*	1	2	1	2	0
8	08/06/1961	Australia	Edgbaston	D	11		24	4	88	2
9	06/07/1961	Australia	Headingley	W	5*		28	12	45	1
							14	6	30	2
10	27/07/1961	Australia	Old Trafford	L	42					
					10		38	25	58	4
11	17/08/1961	Australia	The Oval	D	22*					
					42*		30	6	133	4
12	21/10/1961	Pakistan	Lahore (2)	W	40		33	14	67	2
						1	22	13	51	3
13	11/11/1961	India	Bombay (2)	D	0		39	21	54	3
						2	11	5	12	0
14	01/12/1961	India	Kanpur	D	12		43	17	88	1
15	13/12/1961	India	Delhi	D			47	18	87	4
16	30/12/1961	India	Calcutta	L	15		34	13	67	5
					7		43.2	16	95	4
17	10/01/1962	India	Madras (2)	L	34		51.3	20	116	3
					21	1	33	11	64	1
18	19/01/1962	Pakistan	Dacca	D	0		40.3	13	94	2
						1	23.1	11	30	5
19	02/02/1962	Pakistan	Karachi (1)	D	1		27	14	51	1
							35	19	42	0
20	31/05/1962	Pakistan	Edgbaston	W	79*		32	16	62	2
							36	16	73	3
21	21/06/1962	Pakistan	Lord's	W	2		15	6	41	1
22	05/07/1962	Pakistan	Headingley	W	62		9	6	14	0
							24	11	47	3
23	16/08/1962	Pakistan	The Oval	W			22	9	33	1
							27	14	52	1
24	15/02/1963	Australia	Sydney	D	14	1	43	15	87	2
							19	11	26	3
25	06/06/1963	West Indies	Old Trafford	L	5		57	22	122	2
					1		0.1	0	1	0
26	20/06/1963	West Indies	Lord's	D	2		10	3	35	1
					4*		21	7	50	1
27	04/06/1964	Australia	Trent Bridge	D	21		16	8	22	1
					3					
28	04/12/1964	South Africa	Durban (2)	W			19.5	5	41	5
							47	15	99	2

No	Date	Opposition	Venue	R	Bat	C	O	M	R	W
29	23/12/1964	South Africa	Johannesburg (3)	D	2		39	19	45	1
							49	17	87	4
30	01/01/1965	South Africa	Cape Town	D	22		40	14	79	2
							17	6	27	0
31	12/02/1965	South Africa	Port Elizabeth	D	38*	1	44	13	80	3
32	10/12/1965	Australia	Brisbane (2)	D	3		39	12	108	0
33	30/12/1965	Australia	Melbourne	D	2		20	4	55	2
						1	18	3	48	1
34	07/01/1966	Australia	Sydney	W	50*		19	5	42	2
							20	8	47	4
35	28/01/1966	Australia	Adelaide	L	2		21	1	103	0
					5*					
36	25/02/1966	New Zealand	Christchurch	D	88		40	14	80	0
							19	15	8	1
37	04/03/1966	New Zealand	Dunedin	D	9		27.4	9	68	2
							33	17	46	4
38	11/03/1966	New Zealand	Auckland	D	7*		47.5	12	123	5
							23.3	7	34	1
39	02/06/1966	West Indies	Old Trafford	L	37		31.1	8	104	2
					1					

Batting & Fielding

Mat	Inns	N/O	Runs	H/S	Avg	100s	50s	Cat
39	51	15	918	88	25.50	0	5	10

Bowling

Balls	Runs	Wkts	Avg	Best	5WI	10WM	S/R
11297	3779	122	30.97	5-30	4	0	92.59

G.O.B.ALLEN

Full Name: Sir George Oswald Browning Allen, CBE (known as Gubby)
Born: 31/07/1902, Bellevue Hill, Sydney
Died: 29/11/1989, St John's Wood, London
Teams: Cambridge University 1922-23, Middlesex 1921-50, England 1930-48
Matches: 25 (Won 10, Drew 7, Lost 8)
England Captain: 11 times 1936-48 (Won 4, Drew 2, Lost 5) **Toss:** 6-5
Right-hand middle order batsman – Right-arm fast bowler

No	Date	Opposition	Venue	R	Bat	C	O	M	R	W
1	27/06/1930	Australia	Lord's	L	3		34	7	115	0
					57					
2	27/06/1931	New Zealand	Lord's	D	122		15	2	45	1
							25	8	47	2
3	29/07/1931	New Zealand	The Oval	W			13	7	14	5
						1	13	4	23	0
4	15/08/1931	New Zealand	Old Trafford	D						
5	02/12/1932	Australia	Sydney	W	19	2	15	1	65	0
						1	9	5	13	1
6	30/12/1932	Australia	Melbourne	L	30		17	3	41	2
					23	1	12	1	44	2
7	13/01/1933	Australia	Adelaide	W	15	1	23	4	71	4
					15	1	17.2	5	50	4
8	10/02/1933	Australia	Brisbane (2)	W	13		24	4	83	2
							17	3	44	3
9	23/02/1933	Australia	Sydney	W	48		25	1	128	1
						1	11.4	2	54	2
10	24/03/1933	New Zealand	Christchurch	D			20	5	46	2
							4.1	1	5	0
11	31/03/1933	New Zealand	Auckland	D	12		5	2	11	0
							3	1	4	0
12	24/06/1933	West Indies	Lord's	W	16		6	1	13	2
							11	2	33	1
13	06/07/1934	Australia	Old Trafford	D	61		31	3	113	
							6	0	23	1
14	18/08/1934	Australia	The Oval	L	19		34	5	170	4
					26	2	16	2	63	0
15*	27/06/1936	India	Lord's	W	13		17	7	35	5
							18	1	43	5
16*	25/07/1936	India	Old Trafford	D	1		14	3	39	2
							19	2	96	0

No	Date	Opposition	Venue	R	Bat	C	O	M	R	W
17*	15/08/1936	India	The Oval	W	13	1	12	3	37	1
							20	3	80	7
18*	04/12/1936	Australia	Brisbane (2)	W	35		16	2	71	3
					68		6	0	36	5
19*	18/12/1936	Australia	Sydney	W	9	1	5.7	1	19	3
						1	19	4	61	1
20*	01/01/1937	Australia	Melbourne	L	0*	1	12	2	35	1
					11	1	23	2	84	2
21*	29/01/1937	Australia	Adelaide	L	11	2	16	0	60	2
					9		14	1	61	0
22*	26/02/1937	Australia	Melbourne	L	0		17	0	99	0
					7					
23*	11/02/1948	West Indies	Port-of-Spain	D	36		16	0	82	0
					2		4.2	0	21	1
24*	03/03/1948	West Indies	Georgetown	L	0*	1	2.4	0	5	1
					20	1				
25*	27/03/1948	West Indies	Kingston	L	23		20	1	83	1
					13		2	0	14	0

Batting & Fielding

Mat	Inns	N/O	Runs	H/S	Avg	100s	50s	Cat
25	33	2	750	122	24.19	1	3	20

Bowling

Balls	Runs	Wkts	Avg	Best	5WI	10WM	S/R
4386	2379	81	29.37	7-80	5	1	54.14

M.J.C.ALLOM

Full Name: Maurice James Carrick Allom
Born: 23/03/1906, Northwood, Middlesex
Died: 08/04/1995, Shipbourne, Tonbridge, Kent
Teams: Cambridge University 1926-28, Surrey 1927-37, England 1930-31
Matches: 5 (Won 1, Drew 4, Lost 0)
Right-hand lower order batsman – Right-arm fast medium bowler

No	Date	Opposition	Venue	R	Bat	C	O	M	R	W
1	10/01/1930	New Zealand	Christchurch	W	4*		19	4	38	5
							15	6	17	3
2	24/01/1930	New Zealand	Wellington	D	2		28	4	73	1
							6	1	21	0
3	14/02/1930	New Zealand	Auckland	D			6	4	3	0
4	21/02/1930	New Zealand	Auckland	D	8*		26.1	5	42	4
5	16/01/1931	South Africa	Durban (2)	D			25	4	44	0
							11	0	27	1

Batting & Fielding

Mat	Inns	N/O	Runs	H/S	Avg	100s	50s	Cat
5	3	2	14	8*	14.00	0	0	0

Bowling

Balls	Runs	Wkts	Avg	Best	5WI	10WM	S/R
817	265	14	18.92	5-38	1	0	58.35

P.J.W.ALLOTT

Full Name: Paul John Walter Allott
Born: 14/09/1956, Altrincham, Cheshire
Teams: Lancashire 1978-91, Wellington 1985/86-86/87, England 1981-85
Matches: 13 (Won 4, Drew 5, Lost 4)
Right-hand lower order batsman – Right-arm fast medium bowler

No	Date	Opposition	Venue	R	Bat	C	O	M	R	W
1	13/08/1981	Australia	Old Trafford	W	52*		6	1	17	2
					14		17	3	71	2
2	13/01/1982	India	Madras (1)	D	6		31	4	135	0
3	17/02/1982	Sri Lanka	Colombo (1)	W	3		13	4	44	0

No	Date	Opposition	Venue	R	Bat	C		Bowling		
4	10/06/1982	India	Lord's	W	41*		4	1	15	0
						1	17	3	51	1
5	08/07/1982	India	The Oval	D	3	1	24	4	69	1
							4	1	12	0
6	12/07/1984	West Indies	Headingley	L	3	1	26.5	7	61	6
					4		7	2	24	0
7	26/07/1984	West Indies	Old Trafford	L	26		28	9	76	3
					14					
8	09/08/1984	West Indies	The Oval	L	16	1	17	7	25	3
					4		26	1	96	2
9	23/08/1984	Sri Lanka	Lord's	D	0		36	7	89	1
							1	0	2	0
10	13/06/1985	Australia	Headingley	W	12		22	3	74	2
							17	4	57	0
11	27/06/1985	Australia	Lord's	L	1*		30	4	70	1
					0		7	4	8	1
12	11/07/1985	Australia	Trent Bridge	D	7		18	4	55	1
13	01/08/1985	Australia	Old Trafford	D	7		13	1	29	0
							6	2	4	0

Batting & Fielding

Mat	Inns	N/O	Runs	H/S	Avg	100s	50s	Cat
13	18	3	213	52*	14.20	0	1	4

Bowling

Balls	Runs	Wkts	Avg	Best	5WI	10WM	S/R
2225	1084	26	41.69	6-61	1	0	85.57

L.E.G.AMES

Full Name: Leslie Ethelbert George Ames, CBE (known as Les)
Born: 03/12/1905, Elham, Kent
Died: 27/02/1990, Canterbury, Kent
Teams: Kent 1926-51, England 1929-39
Matches: 47 (Won 15, Drew 21, Lost 11)
Right-hand middle order batsman – Wicket-keeper

No	Date	Opposition	Venue	R	Bat	C	St	B
1+	17/08/1929	South Africa	The Oval	D	0	2		4
2+	11/01/1930	West Indies	Bridgetown	D	16			6
					44*	1		20
3+	01/02/1930	West Indies	Port-of-Spain	W	42	1		4
					105	2	1	8
4+	21/02/1930	West Indies	Georgetown	L	31	2	2	3
					3		1	9
5+	03/04/1930	West Indies	Kingston	D	149	1		19
					27		1	17
6+	27/06/1931	New Zealand	Lord's	L	137	1	1	2
					17*			23
7+	29/07/1931	New Zealand	The Oval	W	41	3		2
								6
8+	15/08/1931	New Zealand	Old Trafford	D				
9+	25/06/1932	India	Lord's	W	65			5
					6			5
10+	02/12/1932	Australia	Sydney	W	0	3		12
						1		12
11+	30/12/1932	Australia	Melbourne	L	4			5
					2	2		3
12+	13/01/1933	Australia	Adelaide	W	3	1		2
					69			4
13+	10/02/1933	Australia	Brisbane (2)	W	17	1	2	5
					14*			13
14+	23/02/1933	Australia	Sydney	W	4			13
								4
15+	24/03/1933	New Zealand	Christchurch	D	103			3
								0
16	31/03/1933	New Zealand	Auckland	D	26			
17+	24/06/1933	West Indies	Lord's	W	83*			3
								1

No	Date	Opposition	Venue	R	Bat	C	St	B
18+	22/07/1933	West Indies	Old Trafford	D	47	1		0
						1	1	8
19+	12/08/1933	West Indies	The Oval	W	37	2	2	1
						4		0
20+	08/06/1934	Australia	Trent Bridge	L	7	2		4
					12	2		22
21+	22/06/1934	Australia	Lord's	W	120	1		1
						1		6
22+	06/07/1934	Australia	Old Trafford	D	72	1		20
								1
23+	20/07/1934	Australia	Headingley	D	9	1		8
					8			
24+	18/08/1934	Australia	The Oval	L	33*	2		4
25+	08/01/1935	West Indies	Bridgetown	W	8		2	0
								4
26	24/01/1935	West Indies	Port-of-Spain	L	2			
					6	1		
27+	14/02/1935	West Indies	Georgetown	D	0			4
					5*		1	9
28+	14/03/1935	West Indies	Kingston	L	126			8
					17			
29+	15/06/1935	South Africa	Trent Bridge	D	17	1		4
								0
30	29/06/1935	South Africa	Lord's	L	5			
					8	1		
31+	13/07/1935	South Africa	Headingley	D	0			8
					13		1	14
32+	17/08/1935	South Africa	The Oval	D	148*	3		6
							2	6
33+	04/12/1936	Australia	Brisbane (2)	W	24	2		4
					9			0
34+	18/12/1936	Australia	Sydney	W	29			1
						1		0
35+	01/01/1937	Australia	Melbourne	L	3	1	2	2
					19	1		6
36+	29/01/1937	Australia	Adelaide	L	52	2		0
					0	3		10
37+	26/02/1937	Australia	Melbourne	L	19	3		1
					11			
38+	26/06/1937	New Zealand	Lord's	D	5	1		4
					20	1		4
39+	24/07/1937	New Zealand	Old Trafford	W	16*	1	2	4
					39	1		7
40+	14/08/1937	New Zealand	The Oval	D	6*	1		2
						1		4
41+	10/06/1938	Australia	Trent Bridge	D	46	2		10
								5
42+	24/06/1938	Australia	Lord's	D	83			1
					6			
43+	24/12/1938	South Africa	Johannesburg (1)	D	42		1	5
					3*			0
44+	31/12/1938	South Africa	Cape Town	D	115		1	2
						1		1
45+	20/01/1939	South Africa	Durban (2)	W	27*	1		1
						3		7
46+	18/02/1939	South Africa	Johannesburg (1)	D	34	1		5
					17			
47+	03/03/1939	South Africa	Durban (2)	D	84	2		2
					17*			5

Batting & Fielding

Mat	Inns	N/O	Runs	H/S	Avg	100s	50s	Cat	St	Byes
47	72	12	2434	149	40.56	8	7	74	23	444

D.L.AMISS

Full Name: Dennis Leslie Amiss, MBE
Born: 07/04/1943, Harborne, Birmingham
Teams: Warwickshire 1960-87, England 1966-77
Matches: 50 (Won 18, Drew 19, Lost 13)
Right-hand opening batsman – Left-arm slow bowler

No	Date	Opposition	Venue	R	Bat	C
1	18/08/1966	West Indies	The Oval	W	17	
2	22/06/1967	India	Lord's	W	29	1
						1
3	13/07/1967	India	Edgbaston	W	5	2
					45	
4	24/08/1967	Pakistan	The Oval	W	26	
					3*	
5	06/06/1968	Australia	Old Trafford	L	0	
					0	
6	03/06/1971	Pakistan	Edgbaston	D	4	
					22	
7	17/06/1971	Pakistan	Lord's	D	19*	1
8	08/07/1971	Pakistan	Headingley	W	23	
					56	
9	22/07/1971	India	Lord's	D	9	1
					0	1
10	20/12/1972	India	Delhi	W	46	
					9	
11	30/12/1972	India	Calcutta	L	11	
					1	1
12	12/01/1973	India	Madras (1)	L	15	
					8	
13	02/03/1973	Pakistan	Lahore (2)	D	112	
					16	
14	16/03/1973	Pakistan	Hyderabad	D	158	
					0	
15	24/03/1973	Pakistan	Karachi (1)	D	99	2
					21*	
16	07/06/1973	New Zealand	Trent Bridge	W	42	
					138*	
17	21/06/1973	New Zealand	Lord's	D	9	
					53	
18	05/07/1973	New Zealand	Headingley	W	8	
19	26/07/1973	West Indies	The Oval	L	29	
					15	
20	09/08/1973	West Indies	Edgbaston	D	56	1
					86*	
21	23/08/1973	West Indies	Lord's	L	35	1
					10	
22	02/02/1974	West Indies	Port-of-Spain	L	6	
					174	
23	16/02/1974	West Indies	Kingston	D	27	
					262*	
24	06/03/1974	West Indies	Bridgetown	D	12	
					4	
25	22/03/1974	West Indies	Georgetown	D	118	
26	30/03/1974	West Indies	Port-of-Spain	W	44	
					16	
27	06/06/1974	India	Old Trafford	W	56	
					47	
28	20/06/1974	India	Lord's	W	188	
29	04/07/1974	India	Edgbaston	W	79	
30	25/07/1974	Pakistan	Headingley	D	13	
					8	
31	08/08/1974	Pakistan	Lord's	D	2	1
					14*	
32	22/08/1974	Pakistan	The Oval	D	183	
33	29/11/1974	Australia	Brisbane (2)	L	7	1
					25	
34	26/12/1974	Australia	Melbourne	D	4	
					90	
35	04/01/1975	Australia	Sydney	L	12	
					37	
36	25/01/1975	Australia	Adelaide	L	0	
					0	
37	08/02/1975	Australia	Melbourne	W	0	1
						1

No	Date	Opposition	Venue	R	Bat	C
38	20/02/1975	New Zealand	Auckland	W	19	2
						1
39	28/02/1975	New Zealand	Christchurch	D	164*	
40	10/07/1975	Australia	Edgbaston	L	4	
					5	
41	31/07/1975	Australia	Lord's	D	0	1
					10	
42	12/08/1976	West Indies	The Oval	L	203	
					16	
43	17/12/1976	India	Delhi	W	179	
44	01/01/1977	India	Calcutta	W	35	
					7*	
45	14/01/1977	India	Madras (1)	W	4	
					46	
46	28/01/1977	India	Bangalore	L	82	
					0	1
47	11/02/1977	India	Bombay (3)	D	50	
					14	
48	12/03/1977	Australia	Melbourne	L	4	
					64	1
49	16/06/1977	Australia	Lord's	D	4	
					0	1
50	07/07/1977	Australia	Old Trafford	W	11	1
					28*	

Batting & Fielding

Mat	Inns	N/O	Runs	H/S	Avg	100s	50s	Cat
50	88	10	3612	262*	46.30	11	11	24

K.V.ANDREW

Full name: Keith Vincent Andrew
Born: 15/12/1929, Greenacres, Oldham, Lancashire
Teams: Northamptonshire 1953-66, England 1954-63
Matches: 2 (Won 0, Drew 0, Lost 2)
Right-hand lower order batsman – Wicket-keeper

No	Date	Opposition	Venue	R	Bat	C	St	B
1+	26/11/1954	Australia	Brisbane (2)	L	6			11
					5			
2+	06/06/1963	West Indies	Old Trafford	L	3*	1		3
					15			0

Batting & Fielding

Mat	Inns	N/O	Runs	H/S	Avg	100s	50s	Cat	St	Byes
2	4	1	29	15	9.66	0	0	1	0	14

R.APPLEYARD

Full Name: Robert Appleyard (known as Bob)
Born: 27/06/1924, Wibsey, Bradford, Yorkshire
Teams: Yorkshire 1950-58, England 1954-56
Matches: 9 (Won 7, Drew 2, Lost 0)
Right-hand lower order batsman – Right-arm medium or off break bowler

No	Date	Opposition	Venue	R	Bat	C	Bowling			
1	01/07/1954	Pakistan	Trent Bridge	W			17	5	51	5
							30.4	8	72	2
2	17/12/1954	Australia	Sydney	W	8		7	1	32	0
					19*		6	1	12	1
3	31/12/1954	Australia	Melbourne	W	1*		11	3	38	2
					6		4	1	17	1
4	28/01/1955	Australia	Adelaide	W	10*		23	7	58	3
						2	12	7	13	3
5	25/02/1955	Australia	Sydney	D		2	16	2	54	1
6	11/03/1955	New Zealand	Dunedin	W	0*		7	3	16	0
							7	2	19	2
7	25/03/1955	New Zealand	Auckland	W	6		16	4	38	3
							6	3	7	4

No	Date	Opposition	Venue	R	Bat	C		Bowling	
8	09/06/1955	South Africa	Trent Bridge	W	0*		28	9 46	2
							19	4 32	0
9	07/06/1956	Australia	Trent Bridge	D	1*		11	4 17	2
							19	6 32	0

Batting & Fielding

Mat	Inns	N/O	Runs	H/S	Avg	100s	50s	Cat
9	9	6	51	19*	17.00	0	0	4

Bowling

Balls	Runs	Wkts	Avg	Best	5WI	10WM	S/R
1596	554	31	17.87	5-51	1	0	51.48

A.G.ARCHER

Full Name: Alfred German Archer
Born: 06/12/1871, Richmond, Surrey
Died: 15/07/1935, Seaford, Sussex
Teams: Worcestershire 1900-01, England 1899
Matches: 1 (Won 1, Drew 0, Lost 0)
Right-hand lower order batsman – Wicket-keeper

No	Date	Opposition	Venue	R	Bat	C
1	01/04/1899	South Africa	Cape Town	W	7	
					24*	

Batting & Fielding

Mat	Inns	N/O	Runs	H/S	Avg	100s	50s	Cat
1	2	1	31	24*	31.00	0	0	0

T.ARMITAGE

Full Name: Thomas Armitage (known as Tom)
Born: 25/04/1848, Walkley, Sheffield, Yorkshire
Died: 21/09/1922, Pullman, Chicago, USA
Teams: Yorkshire 1872-79, England 1877
Matches: 2 (Won 1, Drew 0, Lost 1)
Right-hand opening/middle order batsman – Right-arm medium or underhand lob bowler

No	Date	Opposition	Venue	R	Bat	C		Bowling	
1	15/03/1877	Australia	Melbourne	L	9		3	0 15	0
					3				
2	31/03/1877	Australia	Melbourne	W	21				

Batting & Fielding

Mat	Inns	N/O	Runs	H/S	Avg	100s	50s	Cat
2	3	0	33	21	11.00	0	0	0

Bowling

Balls	Runs	Wkts	Avg	Best	5WI	10WM	S/R
12	15	0	–	0-15	0	0	–

E.G.ARNOLD

Full Name: Edward George Arnold (known as Ted)
Born: 07/11/1876, Exmouth, Devon
Died: 25/10/1942, Worcester
Teams: Worcestershire 1899-1913, London County 1900, England 1903-07
Matches: 10 (Won 5, Drew 3, Lost 2)
Right-hand middle order batsman – Right-arm fast medium bowler

No	Date	Opposition	Venue	R	Bat	C		Bowling	
1	11/12/1903	Australia	Sydney	W	27		32	7 76	4
						1	28	2 93	2
2	15/01/1904	Australia	Adelaide	L	23*		27	4 93	3
					1		19	3 74	0
3	26/02/1904	Australia	Sydney	W	0	1	15.3	5 28	4
					0		12	3 42	2
4	05/03/1904	Australia	Melbourne	L	0		18	4 46	1
					19	2	8	3 23	2

No	Date	Opposition	Venue	R	Bat	C	\	Bowling	\	\
5	29/05/1905	Australia	Trent Bridge	W	2*		11	2	39	1
						1	4	2	7	0
6	15/06/1905	Australia	Lord's	D	7*		7	3	13	1
7	24/07/1905	Australia	Old Trafford	W	25		14	2	53	2
						1	15	5	35	2
8	14/08/1905	Australia	The Oval	D	40		9	0	50	0
					0		9	2	17	1
9	01/07/1907	South Africa	Lord's	D	4		22	7	37	5
							13	2	41	0
10	29/07/1907	South Africa	Headingley	W	0	1	4	1	11	0
					12	1	13	7	10	1

Batting & Fielding

Mat	Inns	N/O	Runs	H/S	Avg	100s	50s	Cat
10	15	3	160	40	13.33	0	0	8

Bowling

Balls	Runs	Wkts	Avg	Best	5WI	10WM	S/R
1683	788	31	25.41	5-37	1	0	54.29

G.G.ARNOLD

Full Name: Geoffrey Graham Arnold (known as Geoff)
Born: 03/09/1944, Earlsfield, Surrey
Teams: Surrey 1963-77, Sussex 1978-82, Orange Free State 1976/77, England 1967-75
Matches: 34 (Won 13, Drew 13, Lost 8)
Right-hand lower order batsman – Right-arm fast medium bowler

No	Date	Opposition	Venue	R	Bat	C	\	Bowling	\	\
1	10/08/1967	Pakistan	Trent Bridge	W	14		17	5	35	3
						1	5	3	5	0
2	24/08/1967	Pakistan	The Oval	W	59		29	9	58	5
							17	5	49	0
3	21/08/1969	New Zealand	The Oval	W	1	2	8	2	13	0
							10	3	17	0
4	08/06/1972	Australia	Old Trafford	W	1		25	4	62	4
					0*		20	2	59	1
5	27/07/1972	Australia	Headingley	W	1*		9.5	2	28	2
							6	1	17	2
6	10/08/1972	Australia	The Oval	L	22		35	11	87	3
					4		15	5	26	1
7	20/12/1972	India	Delhi	W	12		23.4	7	45	6
							20.4	6	46	3
8	12/01/1973	India	Madras (1)	L	17		23.1	12	34	3
					0		4	1	11	0
9	25/01/1973	India	Kanpur	D	45		35	10	72	1
							7	3	15	1
10	06/02/1973	India	Bombay (2)	D	27		21	3	64	3
							3	0	13	0
11	02/03/1973	Pakistan	Lahore (2)	D	0		43	10	95	2
					3*		4	1	12	0
12	16/03/1973	Pakistan	Hyderabad	D	8		24	2	78	1
					19*					
13	24/03/1973	Pakistan	Karachi (1)	D	2		19	2	69	0
							15	2	52	0
14	07/06/1973	New Zealand	Trent Bridge	W	1		18	8	23	2
					10*		53	15	131	5
15	21/06/1973	New Zealand	Lord's	D	8*		41	6	108	1
					23*					
16	05/07/1973	New Zealand	Headingley	W	26		27	8	62	3
							22	11	27	5
17	26/07/1973	West Indies	The Oval	L	4		39	10	113	5
					4		18.1	7	49	3
18	09/08/1973	West Indies	Edgbaston	D	24		37	13	74	3
						1	20	1	43	4
19	23/08/1973	West Indies	Lord's	L	5	1	35	6	111	0
					1					
20	06/03/1974	West Indies	Bridgetown	D	12	1	26	5	91	1
					2*					
21	22/03/1974	West Indies	Georgetown	D	1		10	5	17	0
22	30/03/1974	West Indies	Port-of-Spain	W	6		8	0	27	0
					13		5.3	1	13	1

No	Date	Opposition	Venue	R	Bat	C		Bowling	
23	20/06/1974	India	Lord's	W	5	1	24.5	6	81	1
							8	1	19	4
24	04/07/1974	India	Edgbaston	W			14	3	43	3
							19	3	61	2
25	25/07/1974	Pakistan	Headingley	D	1		31.5	8	67	3
							23.1	11	36	3
26	08/08/1974	Pakistan	Lord's	D	10		8	1	32	0
							15	3	37	1
27	22/08/1974	Pakistan	The Oval	D	2		37	5	106	1
						1	6	0	22	2
28	13/12/1974	Australia	Perth	L	1		27	1	129	2
					4		1.7	0	15	1
29	04/01/1975	Australia	Sydney	L	3*		29	7	86	5
					14		22	3	78	1
30	25/01/1975	Australia	Adelaide	L	0		12.2	3	42	1
					0		20	1	71	1
31	08/02/1975	Australia	Melbourne	W	0		6	2	24	0
							23	6	83	3
32	20/02/1975	New Zealand	Auckland	W			20	4	69	1
							6	1	31	0
33	28/02/1975	New Zealand	Christchurch	D			25	5	80	3
34	10/07/1975	Australia	Edgbaston	L	0*	1	33	3	91	3
					6*					

Batting & Fielding

Mat	Inns	N/O	Runs	H/S	Avg	100s	50s	Cat
34	46	11	421	59	12.02	0	1	9

Bowling

Balls	Runs	Wkts	Avg	Best	5WI	10WM	S/R
7650	3254	115	28.29	6-45	6	0	66.52

J.ARNOLD

Full Name: John Arnold (known as Johnny)
Born: 30/11/1907, Cowley, Oxford
Died: 04/04/1984, Southampton, Hampshire
Teams: Hampshire 1929-50, England 1931
Matches: 1 (Won 0, Drew 1, Lost 0)
Right-hand opening batsman – Right-arm slow bowler

No	Date	Opposition	Venue	R	Bat	C
1	27/06/1931	New Zealand	Lord's	D	0	
					34	

Batting & Fielding

Mat	Inns	N/O	Runs	H/S	Avg	100s	50s	Cat
1	2	0	34	34	17.00	0	0	0

W.E.ASTILL

Full Name: William Ewart Astill (known as Ewart)
Born: 01/03/1888, Ratby, Leicestershire
Died: 10/02/1948, Stoneygate, Leicester
Teams: Leicestershire 1906-39, England 1927-30
Matches: 9 (Won 3, Drew 3, Lost 3)
Right-hand middle/lower order batsman – Right-arm slow medium bowler

No	Date	Opposition	Venue	R	Bat	C		Bowling	
1	24/12/1927	South Africa	Johannesburg (1)	W	7		8	4	11	0
							6	0	17	0
2	31/12/1927	South Africa	Cape Town	W	25		8	0	32	1
					9	1	29	11	48	3
3	21/01/1928	South Africa	Durban (2)	D	40	1	3	1	8	0
						1	24	6	41	2
4	28/01/1928	South Africa	Johannesburg (1)	L	3	1	11	0	55	2
					17		3.2	1	10	1
5	04/02/1928	South Africa	Durban (2)	L	1		36	10	99	3
					0		2	0	9	0
6	11/01/1930	West Indies	Bridgetown	D	1		9	1	19	1
						1	30	10	72	0

No	Date	Opposition	Venue	R	Bat	C		Bowling		
7	01/02/1930	West Indies	Port-of-Spain	W	19		24.2	6	58	4
					14	1	20	3	34	0
8	21/02/1930	West Indies	Georgetown	L	0		28	3	92	0
					5		43	17	70	4
9	03/04/1930	West Indies	Kingston	D	39	1	33	12	73	3
					10		46	13	108	1

Batting & Fielding

Mat	Inns	N/O	Runs	H/S	Avg	100s	50s	Cat
9	15	0	190	40	12.66	0	0	7

Bowling

Balls	Runs	Wkts	Avg	Best	5WI	10WM	S/R
2182	856	25	34.24	4-58	0	0	87.28

M.A.ATHERTON

Full Name: Michael Andrew Atherton (known as Mike)
Born: 23/03/1968, Manchester, Lancashire
Teams: Cambridge University 1987-89, Lancashire 1987-96, England 1989-96
Matches: 62 (Won 13, Drew 24, Lost 25)
England Captain: 35 times 1993-96 (Won 8, Drew 14, Lost 13) **Toss:** 16-19
Right-hand opening batsman – Leg break bowler

No	Date	Opposition	Venue	R	Bat	C		Bowling		
1	10/08/1989	Australia	Trent Bridge	L	0		7	0	24	0
					47					
2	24/08/1989	Australia	The Oval	D	12	1	1	0	10	0
					14					
3	07/06/1990	New Zealand	Trent Bridge	D	151					
4	21/06/1990	New Zealand	Lord's	D	0		1	1	0	0
					54					
5	05/07/1990	New Zealand	Edgbaston	W	82	1	9	5	17	0
					70	2				
6	26/07/1990	India	Lord's	W	8					
					72	1	1	0	11	0
7	09/08/1990	India	Old Trafford	D	131	1	16	3	68	0
					74		4	0	22	0
8	23/08/1990	India	The Oval	D	7	1	7	0	60	1
					86					
9	23/11/1990	Australia	Brisbane (2)	L	13	2				
					15		2	0	16	0
10	26/12/1990	Australia	Melbourne	L	0		2	1	3	0
					4	2	3	0	14	0
11	04/01/1991	Australia	Sydney	D	105	1	5	0	28	0
					3*		3	1	9	0
12	25/01/1991	Australia	Adelaide	D	0					
					87					
13	01/02/1991	Australia	Perth	L	27					
					25					
14	06/06/1991	West Indies	Headingley	W	2					
					6	1				
15	20/06/1991	West Indies	Lord's	D	5	1				
16	04/07/1991	West Indies	Trent Bridge	L	32					
					4					
17	25/07/1991	West Indies	Edgbaston	L	16	1				
					1					
18	08/08/1991	West Indies	The Oval	W	0					
					13					
19	02/07/1992	Pakistan	Old Trafford	D	0	1				
						2				
20	23/07/1992	Pakistan	Headingley	W	76	1				
					5	1				
21	06/08/1992	Pakistan	The Oval	L	60					
					4					
22	19/02/1993	India	Bombay (3)	L	37	2				
					11					
23	13/03/1993	Sri Lanka	Colombo (2)	L	13	1				
					2					
24	03/06/1993	Australia	Old Trafford	L	19					
					25					

No	Date	Opposition	Venue	R	Bat	C	Bowling			
25	17/06/1993	Australia	Lord's	L	80					
					99					
26	01/07/1993	Australia	Trent Bridge	D	11					
					9	1				
27	22/07/1993	Australia	Headingley	L	55					
					63					
28*	05/08/1993	Australia	Edgbaston	L	72					
					28					
29*	19/08/1993	Australia	The Oval	W	50					
					42					
30*	19/02/1994	West Indies	Kingston	L	55					
					28					
31*	17/03/1994	West Indies	Georgetown	L	144	1				
					0					
32*	25/03/1994	West Indies	Port-of-Spain	L	48					
					0					
33*	08/04/1994	West Indies	Bridgetown	W	85	2				
					15					
34*	16/04/1994	West Indies	St John's	D	135					
35*	02/06/1994	New Zealand	Trent Bridge	W	101					
						1				
36*	16/06/1994	New Zealand	Lord's	D	28					
					33					
37*	30/06/1994	New Zealand	Old Trafford	D	111	1				
38*	21/07/1994	South Africa	Lord's	L	20					
					8					
39*	04/08/1994	South Africa	Headingley	D	99	1				
					17					
40*	18/08/1994	South Africa	The Oval	W	0					
					63					
41*	25/11/1994	Australia	Brisbane (2)	L	54					
					23					
42*	24/12/1994	Australia	Melbourne	L	44	1				
					25					
43*	01/01/1995	Australia	Sydney	D	88					
					67					
44*	26/01/1995	Australia	Adelaide	W	80	2				
					14					
45*	03/02/1995	Australia	Perth	L	4					
					8	1				
46*	08/06/1995	West Indies	Headingley	L	81					
					17	1				
47*	22/06/1995	West Indies	Lord's	W	21					
					9					
48*	06/07/1995	West Indies	Edgbaston	L	0					
					4					
49*	27/07/1995	West Indies	Old Trafford	W	47					
					22					
50*	10/08/1995	West Indies	Trent Bridge	D	113	1				
					43					
51*	24/08/1995	West Indies	The Oval	D	36	1				
					95					
52*	16/11/1995	South Africa	Centurion	D	78					
53*	30/11/1995	South Africa	Johannesburg (3)	D	9					
					185*					
54*	14/12/1995	South Africa	Durban (2)	D	2					
55*	26/12/1995	South Africa	Port Elizabeth	D	72	1				
					34					
56*	02/01/1996	South Africa	Cape Town	L	0	1				
					10					
57*	06/06/1996	India	Edgbaston	W	33	2				
					53*					
58*	20/06/1996	India	Lord's	D	0					
					17					
59*	04/07/1996	India	Trent Bridge	D	160					
60*	25/07/1996	Pakistan	Lord's	L	12					
					64					
61*	08/08/1996	Pakistan	Headingley	D	12	3	7	1	20	1
62*	22/08/1996	Pakistan	The Oval	L	31					
					43					

Batting & Fielding

Mat	Inns	N/O	Runs	H/S	Avg	100s	50s	Cat
62	114	3	4627	185*	41.68	10	29	44

Bowling

Balls	Runs	Wkts	Avg	Best	5WI	10WM	S/R
408	302	2	151.00	1-20	0	0	204.00

C.W.J.ATHEY

Full Name: Charles William Jeffrey Athey (known as Bill)
Born: 27/09/1957, Middlesbrough, Yorkshire
Teams: Yorkshire 1976-83, Gloucestershire 1984-92, Sussex 1993-96, England 1980-88
Matches: 23 (Won 2, Drew 15, Lost 6)
Right-hand middle order batsman – Off break bowler

No	Date	Opposition	Venue	R	Bat	C
1	28/08/1980	Australia	Lord's	D	9 1	1
2	27/03/1981	West Indies	St John's	D	2 1	1
3	10/04/1981	West Indies	Kingston	D	3 1	
4	19/06/1986	India	Headingley	L	32 8	
5	03/07/1986	India	Edgbaston	D	0 38	
6	24/07/1986	New Zealand	Lord's	D	44 16	
7	07/08/1986	New Zealand	Trent Bridge	L	55 6	2
8	21/08/1986	New Zealand	The Oval	D	17	1
9	14/11/1986	Australia	Brisbane (2)	W	76 1	
10	28/11/1986	Australia	Perth	D	96 6	1
11	12/12/1986	Australia	Adelaide	D	55 12	
12	26/12/1986	Australia	Melbourne	W	21	1
13	10/01/1987	Australia	Sydney	L	5 31	1
14	04/06/1987	Pakistan	Old Trafford	D	19	
15	18/06/1987	Pakistan	Lord's	D	123	
16	02/07/1987	Pakistan	Headingley	L	4 26	2
17	23/07/1987	Pakistan	Edgbaston	D	0 14*	
18	25/11/1987	Pakistan	Lahore (2)	L	5 2	
19	07/12/1987	Pakistan	Faisalabad	D	27 20	
20	16/12/1987	Pakistan	Karachi (1)	D	26 12	
21	29/01/1988	Australia	Sydney	D	37	1 1
22	12/02/1988	New Zealand	Christchurch	D	22 19	1
23	21/07/1988	West Indies	Headingley	L	16 11	

Batting & Fielding

Mat	Inns	N/O	Runs	H/S	Avg	100s	50s	Cat
23	41	1	919	123	22.97	1	4	13

W.ATTEWELL

Full Name: William Attewell (known as Dick)
Born: 12/06/1861, Keyworth, Nottinghamshire
Died: 11/06/1927, Long Eaton, Derbyshire
Teams: Nottinghamshire 1881-99, England 1884-1892
Matches: 10 (Won 6, Drew 0, Lost 4)
Right-hand lower order batsman – Right-arm medium bowler

No	Date	Opposition	Venue	R	Bat	C		Bowling		
1	12/12/1884	Australia	Adelaide	W	12*	1	50	23	48	1
							18	10	26	0
2	01/01/1885	Australia	Melbourne	W	30		61	35	54	2
							5	2	7	0
3	20/02/1885	Australia	Sydney	L	14		71	47	53	4
					0	1	58	36	54	2
4	14/03/1885	Australia	Sydney	L	1	2	18	13	22	0
					1*		3	1	4	0
5	21/03/1885	Australia	Melbourne	W	0		5	1	18	1
						1	36.1	22	24	3
6	10/02/1888	Australia	Sydney	W	7*					
					10*	1	4.2	2	4	1
7	21/07/1890	Australia	Lord's	W	0*	1	32	15	42	4
						1	42.2	22	54	1
8	01/01/1892	Australia	Melbourne	L	8		21.1	11	28	1
					24		61	32	51	2
9	29/01/1892	Australia	Sydney	L	0	1	31	20	25	1
					0		46	24	43	1
10	24/03/1892	Australia	Adelaide	W	43*					
							34	10	69	3

Batting & Fielding

Mat	Inns	N/O	Runs	H/S	Avg	100s	50s	Cat
10	15	6	150	43*	16.66	0	0	9

Bowling

Balls	Runs	Wkts	Avg	Best	5WI	10WM	S/R
2850	626	27	23.18	4-42	0	0	105.55

R.J.BAILEY

Full Name: Robert John Bailey (known as Rob)
Born: 28/10/1963, Biddulph, Staffordshire
Teams: Northamptonshire 1982-96, England 1988-90
Matches: 4 (Won 0, Drew 1, Lost 3)
Right-hand middle order batsman – Off break bowler

No	Date	Opposition	Venue	R	Bat	C
1	04/08/1988	West Indies	The Oval	L	43	
					3	
2	23/03/1990	West Indies	Port-of-Spain	D	0	
					0	
3	05/04/1990	West Indies	Bridgetown	L	17	
					6	
4	12/04/1990	West Indies	St John's	L	42	
					8	

Batting & Fielding

Mat	Inns	N/O	Runs	H/S	Avg	100s	50s	Cat
4	8	0	119	43	14.87	0	0	0

T.E.BAILEY

Full Name: Trevor Edward Bailey
Born: 03/12/1923, Westcliff-on-Sea, Essex
Teams: Cambridge University 1947-48, Essex 1946-67, England 1949-59
Matches: 61 (Won 24, Drew 20, Lost 17)
Right-hand middle order batsman – Right-arm fast medium bowler

No	Date	Opposition	Venue	R	Bat	C		Bowling		
1	11/06/1949	New Zealand	Headingley	D	12		32.3	6	118	6
							9	0	51	0

No	Date	Opposition	Venue	R	Bat	C	O	M	R	W
2	25/06/1949	New Zealand	Lord's	D	93		33	3	136	0
					6*					
3	23/07/1949	New Zealand	Old Trafford	D	72*		30.2	5	84	6
							16	0	71	1
4	13/08/1949	New Zealand	The Oval	D	36		26.1	7	72	3
							11	1	67	0
5	08/06/1950	West Indies	Old Trafford	W	82*		10	2	28	1
					33	1	3	1	9	0
6	12/08/1950	West Indies	The Oval	L	18		34.2	9	84	2
					12					
7	01/12/1950	Australia	Brisbane (2)	L	1*		12	4	28	3
					7	2	7	2	22	4
8	22/12/1950	Australia	Melbourne	L	12		17.1	5	40	4
					0	2	15	3	47	2
9	05/01/1951	Australia	Sydney	L	15					
					0*					
10	23/02/1951	Australia	Melbourne	W	5		9	1	29	0
							15	3	32	1
11	17/03/1951	New Zealand	Christchurch	D	134*		30	9	51	2
12	24/03/1951	New Zealand	Wellington	W	29		11	2	18	2
						1	14.2	1	43	3
13	07/06/1951	South Africa	Trent Bridge	L	3		45	13	102	0
					11		2	0	10	0
14	26/07/1951	South Africa	Headingley	D	95		17	4	48	0
							1	0	8	0
15	11/06/1953	Australia	Trent Bridge	D	13	1	44	14	75	2
							5	1	28	0
16	25/06/1953	Australia	Lord's	D	2	1	16	2	55	0
					71		10	4	24	0
17	09/07/1953	Australia	Old Trafford	D	27		26	4	83	1
						1				
18	23/07/1953	Australia	Headingley	D	7		22	4	71	3
					38		6	1	9	1
19	15/08/1953	Australia	The Oval	W	64		14	3	42	1
20	15/01/1954	West Indies	Kingston	L	28*		16	4	36	0
					15*	1	20	4	46	1
21	06/02/1954	West Indies	Bridgetown	L	28		22	6	63	1
					4		12	1	48	0
22	24/02/1954	West Indies	Georgetown	W	49		5	0	13	0
							22	9	41	2
23	17/03/1954	West Indies	Port-of-Spain	D	46	1	32	7	104	0
							12	2	20	2
24	30/03/1954	West Indies	Kingston	W	23		16	7	34	7
							25	11	54	1
25	10/06/1954	Pakistan	Lord's	D	3		3	2	1	0
							6	2	13	1
26	01/07/1954	Pakistan	Trent Bridge	W	36*		3	0	18	0
27	22/07/1954	Pakistan	Old Trafford	D	42					
28	26/11/1954	Australia	Brisbane (2)	L	88	1	26	1	140	3
					23					
29	17/12/1954	Australia	Sydney	W	0		17.4	3	59	4
					6		6	0	21	0
30	31/12/1954	Australia	Melbourne	W	30		9	1	33	0
					24*		3	0	14	0
31	28/01/1955	Australia	Adelaide	W	38	1	12	3	39	3
					15					
32	25/02/1955	Australia	Sydney	D	72					
33	11/03/1955	New Zealand	Dunedin	W	0		12.2	6	19	2
							8	4	9	0
34	25/03/1955	New Zealand	Auckland	W	18	2	13	2	34	0
35	09/06/1955	South Africa	Trent Bridge	W	49	1	5	2	8	0
							17	8	21	2
36	23/06/1955	South Africa	Lord's	W	13		16	2	56	1
					22					
37	07/07/1955	South Africa	Old Trafford	L	44		37	8	102	1
					38*					
38	21/07/1955	South Africa	Headingley	L	9		16	7	23	1
					8		40.5	11	97	3

No	Date	Opposition	Venue	R	Bat	C		Bowling		
39	13/08/1955	South Africa	The Oval	W	0		5	1	6	1
					1		6	1	15	0
40	07/06/1956	Australia	Trent Bridge	D	14	2	3	1	8	0
							9	3	16	0
41	21/06/1956	Australia	Lord's	L	32	2	34	12	72	2
					18	1	24.5	8	64	4
42	12/07/1956	Australia	Headingley	W	33*	1	7			
							7	2	13	0
43	26/07/1956	Australia	Old Trafford	W	20		4	3	4	0
							20	8	31	0
44	24/12/1956	South Africa	Johannesburg (3)	W	16	1	15	5	33	3
					10		15.4	6	20	5
45	01/01/1957	South Africa	Cape Town	W	34		11	5	13	0
					28	1				
46	25/01/1957	South Africa	Durban (2)	D	80		17	3	38	1
					18					
47	15/02/1957	South Africa	Johannesburg (3)	L	13	1	21	3	54	3
					1		13	4	12	2
48	01/03/1957	South Africa	Port Elizabeth	L	41		25	12	23	3
					18		24.7	5	39	2
49	30/05/1957	West Indies	Edgbaston	D	1	1	34	11	80	0
50	20/06/1957	West Indies	Lord's	W	1	1	21	8	44	7
						1	22	6	54	4
51	04/07/1957	West Indies	Trent Bridge	D	3*		28	9	77	1
							12	3	22	0
52	22/08/1957	West Indies	The Oval	W	0					
53	05/06/1958	New Zealand	Edgbaston		2		20	9	17	2
					6*	2	20	9	23	2
54	19/06/1958	New Zealand	Lord's	W	17		1	0	4	0
						1	5	1	7	1
55	03/07/1958	New Zealand	Headingley	W			3	0	7	0
							3	2	3	0
56	21/08/1958	New Zealand	The Oval	D	14		14	3	32	2
57	05/12/1958	Australia	Brisbane (2)	L	27		13	2	35	3
					68		5	1	21	0
58	31/12/1958	Australia	Melbourne	L	48		16	0	50	0
					14					
59	09/01/1959	Australia	Sydney	D	8		5	0	19	0
					25					
60	30/01/1959	Australia	Adelaide	L	4	1	22	2	91	1
					6					
61	13/02/1959	Australia	Melbourne	L	0		14	2	43	0
					0					

Batting & Fielding

Mat	Inns	N/O	Runs	H/S	Avg	100s	50s	Cat
61	91	14	2290	134*	29.74	1	10	32

Bowling

Balls	Runs	Wkts	Avg	Best	5WI	10WM	S/R
9712	3856	132	29.21	7-34	5	1	73.57

D.L.BAIRSTOW

Full Name: David Leslie Bairstow
Born: 01/09/1951, Horton, Bradford, Yorkshire
Teams: Yorkshire 1970-90, Griqualand West 1976/77-77/78, England 1979-81
Matches: 4 (Won 0, Drew 3, Lost 1)
Right-hand middle order batsman – Wicket-keeper

No	Date	Opposition	Venue	R	Bat	C	St	B
1+	30/08/1979	India	The Oval	D	9	3		2
					59			11
2+	07/08/1980	West Indies	Headingley	D	40	2		2
					9*			
3+	28/08/1980	Australia	Lord's	D	6	1	1	1
						1		1
4+	13/03/1981	West Indies	Bridgetown	L	0	4		4
					2	1		3

Batting & Fielding

Mat	Inns	N/O	Runs	H/S	Avg	100s	50s	Cat	St	Byes
4	7	1	125	59	20.83	0	1	12	1	24

A.H.BAKEWELL

Full Name: Alfred Harry Bakewell (known as Fred)
Born: 02/11/1908, Walsall, Staffordshire
Died: 23/01/1983, Westbourne, Dorset
Teams: Northamptonshire 1928-36, England 1931-35
Matches: 6 (Won 3, Drew 3, Lost 0)
Right-hand opening batsman – Right-arm bowler

No	Date	Opposition	Venue	R	Bat	C		Bowling		
1	27/06/1931	New Zealand	Lord's	D	9					
					27					
2	29/07/1931	New Zealand	The Oval	W	40					
3	12/08/1933	West Indies	The Oval	W	107	2				
4	10/02/1934	India	Madras (1)	W	85					
					4					
5	27/07/1935	South Africa	Old Trafford	D	63	1				
					54		3	0	8	0
6	17/08/1935	South Africa	The Oval	D	20					

Batting & Fielding

Mat	Inns	N/O	Runs	H/S	Avg	100s	50s	Cat
6	9	0	409	107	45.44	1	3	3

Bowling

Balls	Runs	Wkts	Avg	Best	5WI	10WM	S/R
18	8	0	–	0-8	0	0	–

J.C.BALDERSTONE

Full Name: John Christopher Balderstone (known as Chris)
Born: 16/11/1940, Longwood, Huddersfield, Yorkshire
Teams: Yorkshire 1961-69, Leicestershire 1971-86, England 1976
Matches: 2 (Won 0, Drew 0, Lost 2)
Right-hand opening/middle order batsman – Left-arm slow bowler

No	Date	Opposition	Venue	R	Bat	C		Bowling		
1	22/07/1976	West Indies	Headingley	L	35					
					4					
2	12/08/1976	West Indies	The Oval	L	0					
					0	1	16	0	80	1

Batting & Fielding

Mat	Inns	N/O	Runs	H/S	Avg	100s	50s	Cat
2	4	0	39	35	9.75	0	0	1

Bowling

Balls	Runs	Wkts	Avg	Best	5WI	10WM	S/R
96	80	1	80.00	1-80	0	0	96.00

R.W.BARBER

Full Name: Robert William Barber (known as Bob)
Born: 26/09/1935, Withington, Manchester, Lancashire
Teams: Cambridge University 1955-57, Lancashire 1954-62, Warwickshire 1963-69, England 1960-68
Matches: 28 (Won 8, Drew 14, Lost 6)
Left-hand opening batsman – Leg break and googly bowler

No	Date	Opposition	Venue	R	Bat	C		Bowling		
1	09/06/1960	South Africa	Edgbaston	W	5		6	0	26	0
					4		10	2	29	1
2	21/10/1961	Pakistan	Lahore (2)	W	6		40	4	124	3
					39*		20.5	6	54	3
3	11/11/1961	India	Bombay (2)	D	19	2	22	5	74	1
					31	1	13	2	42	0

No	Date	Opposition	Venue	R	Bat	C		Bowling		
4	01/12/1961	India	Kanpur	D	69*					
					10					
5	13/12/1961	India	Delhi	D			25	3	103	1
6	30/12/1961	India	Calcutta	L	12	1	3	0	17	0
					6		2	0	9	0
7	10/01/1962	India	Madras (2)	L	16		14	0	70	2
					21					
8	19/01/1962	Pakistan	Dacca	D	86		11	8	12	0
9	02/02/1962	Pakistan	Karachi (1)	D	23		14	1	44	1
						1	41	7	117	3
10	13/08/1964	Australia	The Oval	D	24		6	1	23	0
					29					
11	04/12/1964	South Africa	Durban (2)	W	74	1	14	1	48	2
						1	6	2	8	0
12	23/12/1964	South Africa	Johannesburg (3)	D	97		14	1	33	1
							2	0	12	0
13	01/01/1965	South Africa	Cape Town	D	58	1				
						1	1	0	2	0
14	22/01/1965	South Africa	Johannesburg (3)	D	61					
						2				
15	27/05/1965	New Zealand	Edgbaston	W	31		3	2	7	2
					51	1	45	15	132	4
16	17/06/1965	New Zealand	Lord's	W	13		8	2	24	0
					34		28	10	57	3
17	08/07/1965	New Zealand	Headingley	W	13	1	2	0	2	0
							14	7	14	0
18	22/07/1965	South Africa	Lord's	D	56	1	10.3	3	30	2
					12		25	5	60	1
19	05/08/1965	South Africa	Trent Bridge	L	41		9	3	39	0
					1	1	3	0	20	0
20	26/08/1965	South Africa	The Oval	D	40					
					22		13	1	44	0
21	10/12/1965	Australia	Brisbane (2)	D	5		5	0	42	0
					34					
22	30/12/1965	Australia	Melbourne	D	48	1	6	1	24	0
					0*		17	0	87	1
23	07/01/1966	Australia	Sydney	W	185	1	2.1	1	2	1
						1	5	0	16	0
24	28/01/1966	Australia	Adelaide	L	0		4	0	30	0
					19					
25	11/02/1966	Australia	Melbourne	D	17	1	16	0	60	1
					20					
26	04/08/1966	West Indies	Headingley	L	6		14	2	55	1
					55					
27	18/08/1966	West Indies	The Oval	W	36		15	3	49	3
						2	22.1	2	78	2
28	06/06/1968	Australia	Old Trafford	L	20		11	0	56	2
					46		10	1	31	1

Batting & Fielding

Mat	Inns	N/O	Runs	H/S	Avg	100s	50s	Cat
28	45	3	1495	185	35.59	1	9	21

Bowling

Balls	Runs	Wkts	Avg	Best	5WI	10WM	S/R
3426	1806	42	43.00	4-132	0	0	81.57

W.BARBER

Full Name: Wilfred Barber (known as Wilf)
Born: 18/04/1901, Cleckheaton, Yorkshire
Died: 10/09/1968, Bradford, Yorkshire
Teams: Yorkshire 1926-47, England 1935
Matches: 2 (Won 0, Drew 2, Lost 0)
Right-hand opening/middle order batsman – Right-arm fast medium bowler

No	Date	Opposition	Venue	R	Bat	C		Bowling		
1	13/07/1935	South Africa	Headingley	D	24	1				
					14		0.2	0	0	1
2	27/07/1935	South Africa	Old Trafford	D	1					
					44					

Batting & Fielding

Mat	Inns	N/O	Runs	H/S	Avg	100s	50s	Cat
2	4	0	83	44	20.75	0	0	1

Bowling

Balls	Runs	Wkts	Avg	Best	5WI	10WM	S/R
2	0	1	0.00	1-0	0	0	2.00

G.D.BARLOW

Full Name: Graham Derek Barlow
Born: 26/03/1950, Folkestone, Kent
Teams: Middlesex 1969-86, England 1976-77
Matches: 3 (Won 2, Drew 1, Lost 0)
Left-hand opening/middle order batsman – Right-arm medium bowler

No	Date	Opposition	Venue	R	Bat	C
1	17/12/1976	India	Delhi	W	0	
2	01/01/1977	India	Calcutta	W	4	
					7*	
3	16/06/1977	Australia	Lord's	D	1	
					5	

Batting & Fielding

Mat	Inns	N/O	Runs	H/S	Avg	100s	50s	Cat
3	5	1	17	7*	4.25	0	0	0

R.G.BARLOW

Full Name: Richard Gorton Barlow (known as Dick)
Born: 28/05/1851, Barrow Bridge, Bolton, Lancashire
Died: 31/07/1919, Stanley Park, Blackpool, Lancashire
Teams: Lancashire 1871-91, England 1881-87
Matches: 17 (Won 8, Drew 4, Lost 5)
Right-hand opening batsman- Left-arm medium bowler

No	Date	Opposition	Venue	R	Bat	C	Bowling			
1	31/12/1881	Australia	Melbourne	D	0		23	13	22	0
					33					
2	17/02/1882	Australia	Sydney	L	31		8	4	8	0
					62	1	4	1	6	0
3	03/03/1882	Australia	Sydney	L	4					
					8					
4	10/03/1882	Australia	Melbourne	D	16	1	15	6	25	0
					56					
5	28/08/1882	Australia	The Oval	L	11		31	22	19	5
					0		13	5	27	0
6	30/12/1882	Australia	Melbourne	L	10	2	20	6	37	0
					28		4	2	6	0
7	19/01/1883	Australia	Melbourne	W	14		22	18	9	1
							31	6	67	3
8	26/01/1883	Australia	Sydney	W	28	1	47.1	31	52	1
					24		34.2	20	40	7
9	17/02/1883	Australia	Sydney	L	2	2	48	21	88	3
					20	1	37.1	20	44	0
10	10/07/1884	Australia	Old Trafford	D	6		8	3	18	0
					14*					
11	21/07/1884	Australia	Lord's	W	38	1	20	6	44	0
							21	8	31	1
12	11/08/1884	Australia	The Oval	D	0		50	22	72	0
					21*					
13	05/07/1886	Australia	Old Trafford	W	38*	2	23	15	19	1
					30	1	52	34	44	7
14	19/07/1886	Australia	Lord's	W	12		6	3	7	0
							25	20	12	2
15	12/08/1886	Australia	The Oval	W	3	1				
							14	8	13	0
16	28/01/1887	Australia	Sydney	W	2	1	35	23	25	3
					4		13	6	20	0
17	25/02/1887	Australia	Sydney	W	34					
					42*		9	2	12	0

Batting & Fielding

Mat	Inns	N/O	Runs	H/S	Avg	100s	50s	Cat
17	30	4	591	62	22.73	0	2	14

Bowling

Balls	Runs	Wkts	Avg	Best	5WI	10WM	S/R
2456	767	34	22.55	7-40	3	0	72.23

S.F.BARNES

Full Name: Sydney Francis Barnes
Born: 19/04/1873, Smethwick, Staffordshire
Died: 26/12/1967, Chadsmoor, Staffordshire
Teams: Warwickshire 1894-96, Lancashire 1899-1903, England 1901-14
Matches: 27 (Won 13, Drew 5, Lost 9)
Right-hand lower order batsman – Right-arm fast medium or slow bowler

No	Date	Opposition	Venue	R	Bat	C	Bowling			
1	13/12/1901	Australia	Sydney	W	26*	1	35.1	9	65	5
						1	16	2	74	1
2	01/01/1902	Australia	Melbourne	L	1		16.1	5	42	6
					0		64	17	121	7
3	17/01/1902	Australia	Adelaide	L	5		7	0	21	0
4	03/07/1902	Australia	Bramall Lane	L	7		20	9	49	6
					5		12	4	50	1
5	13/12/1907	Australia	Sydney	L	1		22	3	74	1
					11		30	7	63	2
6	01/01/1908	Australia	Melbourne	W	14		17	7	30	0
					38*		27.4	4	72	5
7	10/01/1908	Australia	Adelaide	L	12		27	8	60	3
					8		42	9	83	3
8	07/02/1908	Australia	Melbourne	L	3		23	11	37	1
					22*		35	13	69	1
9	21/02/1908	Australia	Sydney	L	1	1	22.4	6	60	7
					11		27	6	78	1
10	01/07/1909	Australia	Headingley	L	1		25	12	37	1
					1		35	16	63	6
11	26/07/1909	Australia	Old Trafford	D	0		27	9	56	5
						1	22.3	5	66	1
12	09/08/1909	Australia	The Oval	D	0		19	3	57	2
							27	7	61	2
13	15/12/1911	Australia	Sydney	L	9	1	35	5	107	3
					14		30	8	72	1
14	30/12/1911	Australia	Melbourne	W	1		23	9	44	5
							32.1	7	96	3
15	12/01/1912	Australia	Adelaide	W	2*		23	4	71	3
						1	46.4	7	105	5
16	09/02/1912	Australia	Melbourne	W	0		29.1	4	74	5
							20	6	47	2
17	23/02/1912	Australia	Sydney	W	5		19	2	56	3
					4		39	12	106	4
18	10/06/1912	South Africa	Lord's	W	0*	1	13	3	25	5
							34	9	85	6
19	24/06/1912	Australia	Lord's	D			31	10	74	0
20	08/07/1912	South Africa	Headingley	W	0	2	22	7	52	6
					15*		21.2	5	63	4
21	29/07/1912	Australia	Old Trafford	D	1*					
22	12/08/1912	South Africa	The Oval	W	8		21	10	28	5
							16.4	4	29	8
23	19/08/1912	Australia	The Oval	W	7	1	27	15	30	5
					0		4	1	18	0
24	13/12/1913	South Africa	Durban (1)	W	0	1	19.4	1	57	5
							25	11	48	5
25	26/12/1913	South Africa	Johannesburg (1)	W	0*		26.5	9	56	8
							38.4	7	103	9
26	01/01/1914	South Africa	Johannesburg (1)	W	5		16	3	26	3
					0		38	8	102	5
27	14/02/1914	South Africa	Durban (1)	D	4*		29.5	7	56	7
						1	32	10	88	7

Batting & Fielding

Mat	Inns	N/O	Runs	H/S	Avg	100s	50s	Cat
27	39	9	242	38*	8.06	0	0	12

Bowling

Balls	Runs	Wkts	Avg	Best	5WI	10WM	S/R
7873	3106	189	16.43	9-103	24	7	41.65

W.BARNES

Full Name: William Barnes (known as Billy)
Born: 27/05/1852, Sutton-in-Ashfield, Nottinghamshire
Died: 24/03/1899, Mansfield Woodhouse, Nottinghamshire
Teams: Nottinghamshire 1875-94, England 1880-90
Matches: 21 (Won 13, Drew 2, Lost 6)
Right-hand middle order batsman – Right-arm fast medium bowler

No	Date	Opposition	Venue	R	Bat	C		Bowling		
1	06/09/1880	Australia	The Oval	W	28	2				
					5		8.3	3	17	1
2	28/08/1882	Australia	The Oval	L	5	1				
					2		12	5	15	1
3	30/12/1882	Australia	Melbourne	L	26		30	11	51	2
					2*		13	8	6	1
4	19/01/1883	Australia	Melbourne	W	32	1	23	7	32	2
						1	3	1	4	0
5	26/01/1883	Australia	Sydney	W	2		13	6	22	1
					3					
6	17/02/1883	Australia	Sydney	L	2		10	2	33	0
					20		16	5	22	0
7	10/07/1884	Australia	Old Trafford	D	0	1	19	10	25	1
					8					
8	11/08/1884	Australia	The Oval	D	19		52	25	81	2
9	12/12/1884	Australia	Adelaide	W	134		14	2	37	0
					28*		31	10	51	3
10	01/01/1885	Australia	Melbourne	W	58	2	50	27	50	3
						3	38.3	26	31	6
11	20/02/1885	Australia	Sydney	L	0					
					5	1				
12	14/03/1885	Australia	Sydney	L	50	1	35.3	17	61	4
					20		9	3	15	1
13	21/03/1885	Australia	Melbourne	W	74		28	12	47	2
14	19/07/1886	Australia	Lord's	W	58		14.3	7	25	3
							10	5	18	1
15	12/08/1886	Australia	The Oval	W	3		7	4	10	0
16	28/01/1887	Australia	Sydney	W	0		22.1	16	19	2
					32	1	46	29	28	6
17	16/07/1888	Australia	Lord's	L	3		6	0	17	0
					1	1				
18	13/08/1888	Australia	The Oval	W	62		16	9	18	2
							29	16	32	5
19	30/08/1888	Australia	Old Trafford	W	24					
20	21/07/1890	Australia	Lord's	W	9		6	2	16	1
						2	6	3	10	1
21	11/08/1890	Australia	The Oval	W	5					
					5					

Batting & Fielding

Mat	Inns	N/O	Runs	H/S	Avg	100s	50s	Cat
21	33	2	725	134	23.38	1	5	19

Bowling

Balls	Runs	Wkts	Avg	Best	5WI	10WM	S/R
2289	793	51	15.54	6-28	3	0	44.88

C.J.BARNETT

Full Name: Charles John Barnett (known as Charlie)
Born: 03/07/1910, Fairview, Cheltenham, Gloucestershire
Died: 28/05/1993, Stroud, Gloucestershire
Teams: Gloucestershire 1927-48, England 1933-48
Matches: 20 (Won 10, Drew 5, Lost 5)
Right-hand opening/middle order batsman – Right-arm medium bowler

No	Date	Opposition	Venue	R	Bat	C	Bowling			
1	12/08/1933	West Indies	The Oval	W	52					
						2				
2	15/12/1933	India	Bombay (1)	W	33	2	1	1	1	0
					17*					
3	05/01/1934	India	Calcutta	D	8					
					0	1	2	0	7	0
4	10/02/1934	India	Madras (1)	W	4	2				
					26	1	1	0	1	0
5	15/08/1936	India	The Oval	W	43					
					32*					
6	04/12/1936	Australia	Brisbane (2)	W	69	1				
					26					
7	18/12/1936	Australia	Sydney	W	57					
8	01/01/1937	Australia	Melbourne	L	11					
					23	1				
9	29/01/1937	Australia	Adelaide	L	129					
					21		5	1	15	0
10	26/02/1937	Australia	Melbourne	L	18					
					41					
11	26/06/1937	New Zealand	Lord's	D	5					
					83*					
12	24/07/1937	New Zealand	Old Trafford	W	62					
					12					
13	14/08/1937	New Zealand	The Oval	D	13	1				
					21					
14	10/06/1938	Australia	Trent Bridge	D	126	1	0	10	0	
15	24/06/1938	Australia	Lord's	D	18	2				
					12					
16	22/07/1938	Australia	Headingley	L	30					
					29	1				
17	21/06/1947	South Africa	Lord's	W	33	1				
18	05/07/1947	South Africa	Old Trafford	W	5		8	3	11	0
					19*	1	5	1	12	0
19	26/07/1947	South Africa	Headingley	W	6					
20	10/06/1948	Australia	Trent Bridge	L	8					
					6					

Batting & Fielding

Mat	Inns	N/O	Runs	H/S	Avg	100s	50s	Cat
20	35	4	1098	129	35.41	2	5	14

Bowling

Balls	Runs	Wkts	Avg	Best	5WI	10WM	S/R
256	93	0	–	0-1	0	0	–

K.J.BARNETT

Full Name: Kim John Barnett
Born: 17/07/1960, Stoke-on-Trent, Staffordshire
Teams: Derbyshire 1979-96, Boland 1982/83-87/88, England 1988-89
Matches: 4 (Won 1, Drew 1, Lost 2)
Right-hand opening batsman – Leg break bowler

No	Date	Opposition	Venue	R	Bat	C	Bowling			
1	25/08/1988	Sri Lanka	Lord's	W	66					
					0	1				
2	08/06/1989	Australia	Headingley	L	80		6	0	32	0
					34					
3	22/06/1989	Australia	Lord's	L	14					
					3					
4	06/07/1989	Australia	Edgbaston	D	10					

Batting & Fielding

Mat	Inns	N/O	Runs	H/S	Avg	100s	50s	Cat
4	7	0	207	80	29.57	0	2	1

Bowling

Balls	Runs	Wkts	Avg	Best	5WI	10WM	S/R
36	32	0	–	0-32	0	0	–

F.BARRATT

Full Name: Fred Barratt
Born: 12/04/1894, Annesley, Nottinghamshire
Died: 29/01/1947, Standard Hill, Nottingham
Teams: Nottinghamshire 1914-31, England 1929-30
Matches: 5 (Won 2, Drew 3, Lost 0)
Right-hand lower order batsman – Right-arm fast bowler

No	Date	Opposition	Venue	R	Bat	C		Bowling	
1	27/07/1929	South Africa	Old Trafford	W	2*	1	10	4	8	1
							20	7	30	1
2	10/01/1930	New Zealand	Christchurch	W	4		4	1	8	0
						1	9	2	16	1
3	24/01/1930	New Zealand	Wellington	D	5		33	4	87	0
4	14/02/1930	New Zealand	Auckland	D			12	3	26	1
5	21/02/1930	New Zealand	Auckland	D	17		37	12	60	1

Batting & Fielding

Mat	Inns	N/O	Runs	H/S	Avg	100s	50s	Cat
5	4	1	28	17	9.33	0	0	2

Bowling

Balls	Runs	Wkts	Avg	Best	5WI	10WM	S/R
750	235	5	47.00	1-8	0	0	150.00

K.F.BARRINGTON

Full Name: Kenneth Frank Barrington (known as Ken)
Born: 24/11/1930, Reading, Berkshire
Died: 14/03/1981, Needham's Point, Bridgetown, Barbados
Teams: Surrey 1953-68, England 1955-68
Matches: 82 (Won 31, Drew 39, Lost 12)
Right-hand middle order batsman – Leg break bowler

No	Date	Opposition	Venue	R	Bat	C		Bowling	
1	09/06/1955	South Africa	Trent Bridge	W	0				
2	23/06/1955	South Africa	Lord's	W	34				
					18				
3	04/06/1959	India	Trent Bridge	W	56	1			
4	18/06/1959	India	Lord's	W	80				
5	02/07/1959	India	Headingley	W	80				
						1			
6	23/07/1959	India	Old Trafford	W	87	1	14	3	36	3
					46	1	27	4	75	2
7	20/08/1959	India	The Oval	W	8	1	6	0	24	0
8	06/01/1960	West Indies	Bridgetown	D	128		18	3	60	1
9	28/01/1960	West Indies	Port-of-Spain	W	121	1	16	10	15	0
					49	1	25.5	13	34	2
10	17/02/1960	West Indies	Kingston	D	16		21	7	38	1
					4		4	4	0	0
11	09/03/1960	West Indies	Georgetown	D	27		6	2	22	0
					0				
12	25/03/1960	West Indies	Port-of-Spain	D	69		8	0	21	0
					6		8	2	27	1
13	23/06/1960	South Africa	Lord's	W	24				

No	Date	Opposition	Venue	R	Bat	C	Bowling			
14	07/07/1960	South Africa	Trent Bridge	W	80					
					1*	3	1	5	0	
15	21/07/1960	South Africa	Old Trafford	D	76					
					35					
16	18/08/1960	South Africa	The Oval	D	1					
					10					
17	08/06/1961	Australia	Edgbaston	D	21	1				
					48*					
18	22/06/1961	Australia	Lord's	L	4	2				
					66					
19	06/07/1961	Australia	Headingley	W	6					
20	27/07/1961	Australia	Old Trafford	L	78	1				
					5					
21	17/08/1961	Australia	The Oval	D	53					
					83					
22	21/10/1961	Pakistan	Lahore (2)	W	139		6	0	25	0
					6					
23	11/11/1961	India	Bombay (2)	D	151*	1				
					52*		3	0	18	0
24	01/12/1961	India	Kanpur	D	21					
					172					
25	13/12/1961	India	Delhi	D	113*		9	1	39	0
26	30/12/1961	India	Calcutta	L	14					
					3	1				
27	10/01/1962	India	Madras (2)	L	20					
					48					
28	19/01/1962	Pakistan	Dacca	D	84	1	11	1	39	0
							21	13	17	0
29	31/05/1962	Pakistan	Edgbaston	W	9	1	2	2	0	0
30	21/06/1962	Pakistan	Lord's	W	0					
							1	0	8	0
31	05/07/1962	Pakistan	Headingley	W	1	1				
						1	1	0	4	0
32	16/08/1962	Pakistan	The Oval	W	50*					
							2	0	10	0
33	30/11/1962	Australia	Brisbane (2)	D	78	1	12	3	44	1
					23					
34	29/12/1962	Australia	Melbourne	W	35	2	6	0	23	0
					0*		5	0	22	0
35	11/01/1963	Australia	Sydney	L	35	1	8	0	43	0
					21					
36	25/01/1963	Australia	Adelaide	D	63					
					132*	2				
37	15/02/1963	Australia	Sydney	D	101					
					94		8	3	22	0
38	23/02/1963	New Zealand	Auckland	W	126		12	4	38	0
						1				
39	01/03/1963	New Zealand	Wellington	W	76		2.3	1	1	1
						3	11	3	32	3
40	15/03/1963	New Zealand	Christchurch	W	47	1	5	0	18	0
					45					
41	06/06/1963	West Indies	Old Trafford	L	16					
					8					
42	20/06/1963	West Indies	Lord's	D	80	1				
					60					
43	04/07/1963	West Indies	Edgbaston	W	9					
					1	1				
44	25/07/1963	West Indies	Headingley	L	25	1				
					32					
45	22/08/1963	West Indies	The Oval	L	16					
					28					
46	10/01/1964	India	Madras (2)	D	80		4	0	23	0
							2	0	6	0
47	04/06/1964	Australia	Trent Bridge	D	22	2				
					33					
48	18/06/1964	Australia	Lord's	D	5					
49	02/07/1964	Australia	Headingley	L	29					
					85	1				
50	23/07/1964	Australia	Old Trafford	D	256					
							1	0	4	0
51	13/08/1964	Australia	The Oval	D	47					
					54*					

No	Date	Opposition	Venue	R	Bat	C	Bowling			
52	04/12/1964	South Africa	Durban (2)	W	148*					
						1				
53	23/12/1964	South Africa	Johannesburg (3)	D	121		4	0	29	0
54	01/01/1965	South Africa	Cape Town	D	49					
					14*		3.1	1	4	3
55	22/01/1965	South Africa	Johannesburg (3)	D	93					
					11					
56	12/02/1965	South Africa	Port Elizabeth	D	72	2				
57	27/05/1965	New Zealand	Edgbaston	W	137					
						1	5	0	25	0
58	08/07/1965	New Zealand	Headingley	W	163					
						2				
59	22/07/1965	South Africa	Lord's	D	91	2				
					18	1				
60	05/08/1965	South Africa	Trent Bridge	L	1					
					1					
61	26/08/1965	South Africa	The Oval	D	18	1				
					73	1				
62	10/12/1965	Australia	Brisbane (2)	D	53	1				
					38					
63	30/12/1965	Australia	Melbourne	D	63					
						2	7.4	0	47	2
64	07/01/1966	Australia	Sydney	W	1					
65	28/01/1966	Australia	Adelaide	L	60					
					102					
66	11/02/1966	Australia	Melbourne	D	115					
					32*					
67	02/06/1966	West Indies	Old Trafford	L	5					
					30					
68	16/06/1966	West Indies	Lord's	D	19					
					5					
69	08/06/1967	India	Headingley	W	93	1				
					46		9	1	38	0
70	22/06/1967	India	Lord's	W	97					
71	13/07/1967	India	Edgbaston	W	75					
					13	1				
72	27/07/1967	Pakistan	Lord's	D	148	1	11	1	29	1
					14	1	13	2	23	2
73	10/08/1967	Pakistan	Trent Bridge	W	109*					
						1				
74	24/08/1967	Pakistan	The Oval	W	142					
					13*		8	2	29	0
75	19/01/1968	West Indies	Port-of-Spain	D	143		18	6	44	1
							15	0	69	1
76	08/02/1968	West Indies	Kingston	D	63					
					13		6	1	14	0
77	29/02/1968	West Indies	Bridgetown	D	17	1	8	1	29	1
							4	0	17	0
78	14/03/1968	West Indies	Port-of-Spain	W	48	1	10	2	41	1
79	28/03/1968	West Indies	Georgetown	D	4		18	4	43	1
					0					
80	20/06/1968	Australia	Lord's	D	75					
							2	0	12	1
81	11/07/1968	Australia	Edgbaston	D	0	1				
82	25/07/1968	Australia	Headingley	D	49	1				
					46*	1	6	1	14	0

Batting & Fielding

Mat	Inns	N/O	Runs	H/S	Avg	100s	50s	Cat
82	131	15	6806	256	58.67	20	35	58

Bowling

Balls	Runs	Wkts	Avg	Best	5WI	10WM	S/R
2715	1300	29	44.82	3-4	0	0	93.62

V.A.BARTON

Full Name: Victor Alexander Barton
Born: 06/10/1867, Hound, Netley, Hampshire
Died: 23/03/1906, Belle Vue, Southampton, Hampshire
Teams: Kent 1889-90, Hampshire 1895-1902, England 1892
Matches: 1 (Won 1, Drew 0, Lost 0)
Right-hand middle order batsman – Right-arm medium bowler

No	Date	Opposition	Venue	R	Bat	C
1	19/03/1892	South Africa	Cape Town	W	23	

Batting & Fielding

Mat	Inns	N/O	Runs	H/S	Avg	100s	50s	Cat
1	1	0	23	23	23.00	0	0	0

W.BATES

Full Name: Willie Bates (known as Billy)
Born: 19/11/1855, Lascelles Hall, Huddersfield, Yorkshire
Died: 08/01/1900, Lepton, Yorkshire
Teams: Yorkshire 1877-87, England 1881-87
Matches: 15 (Won 7, Drew 2, Lost 6)
Right-hand middle order batsman – Off break bowler

No	Date	Opposition	Venue	R	Bat	C		Bowling		
1	31/12/1881	Australia	Melbourne	D	58		41	20	43	2
					47		13	3	43	2
2	17/02/1882	Australia	Sydney	L	4		72	43	52	4
					5	1	24	11	37	1
3	03/03/1882	Australia	Sydney	L	1	1	38	17	67	3
					2		24.3	13	43	1
4	10/03/1882	Australia	Melbourne	D	23		28.1	14	49	3
					52*					
5	30/12/1882	Australia	Melbourne	L	28		21	7	31	1
					11		13.1	7	22	0
6	19/01/1883	Australia	Melbourne	W	55	1	26.2	14	28	7
							33	14	74	7
7	26/01/1883	Australia	Sydney	W	17	1	45	20	55	1
					4					
8	17/02/1883	Australia	Sydney	L	9	1	15	6	24	1
					48*	1	39	19	52	2
9	12/12/1884	Australia	Adelaide	W	18		24.1	10	31	5
							9	3	26	0
10	01/01/1885	Australia	Melbourne	W	35		17	11	17	0
						1				
11	20/02/1885	Australia	Sydney	L	12		6	2	6	0
					31		20	10	24	5
12	14/03/1885	Australia	Sydney	L	64	1	17	5	44	0
					1					
13	21/03/1885	Australia	Melbourne	W	61					
						1				
14	28/01/1887	Australia	Sydney	W	8		21	9	19	1
					24		17	11	8	0
15	25/02/1887	Australia	Sydney	W	8					
					30		26	13	26	4

Batting & Fielding

Mat	Inns	N/O	Runs	H/S	Avg	100s	50s	Cat
15	26	2	656	64	27.33	0	5	9

Bowling

Balls	Runs	Wkts	Avg	Best	5WI	10WM	S/R
2364	821	50	16.42	7-28	4	1	47.28

G.BEAN

Full Name: George Bean
Born: 07/03/1864, Sutton-in-Ashfield, Nottinghamshire
Died: 16/03/1923, Mansfield, Nottinghamshire
Teams: Nottinghamshire 1885, Sussex 1886-1898, England 1892
Matches: 3 (Won 1, Drew 0, Lost 2)
Right-hand opening/middle order batsman – Right-arm medium bowler

No	Date	Opposition	Venue	R	Bat	C
1	01/01/1892	Australia	Melbourne	L	50	
					3	
2	29/01/1892	Australia	Sydney	L	19	1
					4	
3	24/03/1892	Australia	Adelaide	W	16	2
						1

Batting & Fielding

Mat	Inns	N/O	Runs	H/S	Avg	100s	50s	Cat
3	5	0	92	50	18.40	0	1	4

A.V.BEDSER

Full Name: Alec Victor Bedser, OBE
Born: 04/07/1918, Reading, Berkshire
Teams: Surrey 1939-60, England 1946-55
Matches: 51 (Won 14, Drew 20, Lost 17)
Right-hand lower order batsman – Right-arm fast medium bowler

No	Date	Opposition	Venue	R	Bat	C		Bowling	
1	22/06/1946	India	Lord's	W	30		29.1	11	49	7
							32.1	3	96	4
2	20/07/1946	India	Old Trafford	D	8	2	26	9	41	4
						1	25	4	52	7
3	17/08/1946	India	The Oval	D			32	6	60	2
4	29/11/1946	Australia	Brisbane (2)	L	0	1	41	5	159	2
					18					
5	13/12/1946	Australia	Sydney	L	14		46	7	153	1
					3*					
6	01/01/1947	Australia	Melbourne	D	27*		31	4	99	3
					25		34.3	4	176	3
7	31/01/1947	Australia	Adelaide	D	2	2	30	6	97	3
					3		15	1	68	0
8	28/02/1947	Australia	Sydney	L	10*		27	7	49	2
					4		22	4	75	2
9	21/03/1947	New Zealand	Christchurch	D	8*	1	39	5	95	4
10	07/06/1947	South Africa	Trent Bridge	D	7		57.1	14	106	3
					2		14	3	31	1
11	21/06/1947	South Africa	Lord's	W	0	1	26	1	76	0
							14	6	20	0
12	10/06/1948	Australia	Trent Bridge	L	22		44.2	12	113	3
					3*		14.3	4	46	2
13	24/06/1948	Australia	Lord's	L	9		43	14	100	4
					9	1	34	6	112	1
14	08/07/1948	Australia	Old Trafford	D	37		36	12	81	4
							19	12	27	0
15	22/07/1948	Australia	Headingley	L	79		31.2	4	92	3
					17		21	2	56	0
16	14/08/1948	Australia	The Oval	L	0		31.2	9	61	1
					0					
17	16/12/1948	South Africa	Durban (2)	W	11		13.5	2	39	4
					1*	1	18	5	51	2
18	27/12/1948	South Africa	Johannesburg (2)	D	12		22	6	42	1
							17	4	51	1
19	01/01/1949	South Africa	Cape Town	D	16		34	5	92	0
						1	7	0	40	0
20	12/02/1949	South Africa	Johannesburg (2)	D	1		24	3	81	2
					19		17	0	54	1
21	05/03/1949	South Africa	Port Elizabeth	W	33	1	38	9	61	4
					1		16	3	43	1
22	11/06/1949	New Zealand	Headingley	D	20	1	22	8	56	0
						2	9	1	26	0
23	13/08/1949	New Zealand	The Oval	D	0	1	31	6	74	4
							23	4	59	3
24	24/06/1950	West Indies	Lord's	L	5		40	14	60	3
					0		44	16	80	1
25	20/07/1950	West Indies	Trent Bridge	L	13		48	9	127	5
					2		11	1	35	0
26	12/08/1950	West Indies	The Oval	L	0		38	9	75	2
					0					

No	Date	Opposition	Venue	R	Bat	C	Bowling			
27	01/12/1950	Australia	Brisbane (2)	L		1	16.5	4	45	4
					0		6.5	2	9	3
28	22/12/1950	Australia	Melbourne	L	4*	1	19	3	37	4
					14*		16.3	2	43	2
29	05/01/1951	Australia	Sydney	L	3	2	43	4	107	4
					4					
30	02/02/1951	Australia	Adelaide	L	7		26	4	74	3
					0	1	25	6	62	0
31	23/02/1951	Australia	Melbourne	W	11		22	5	46	5
							20.3	4	59	5
32	17/03/1951	New Zealand	Christchurch	D	5		41	10	83	1
33	24/03/1951	New Zealand	Wellington	W	28		19	6	21	0
						1	24	10	34	1
34	07/06/1951	South Africa	Trent Bridge	L	0*		63	18	122	3
					0		22.4	8	37	6
35	21/06/1951	South Africa	Lord's	W	26*		8	5	7	0
							24	8	53	2
36	05/07/1951	South Africa	Old Trafford	W	30*		32.3	10	58	7
							24.2	8	54	5
37	26/07/1951	South Africa	Headingley	D	8	1	58	14	113	2
							4	1	5	0
38	16/08/1951	South Africa	The Oval	W	2		19.3	6	36	2
							19.5	6	32	3
39	05/06/1952	India	Headingley	W	7		33	13	38	2
							21	9	32	2
40	19/06/1952	India	Lord's	W	3	1	33	8	62	2
							36	13	60	2
41	17/07/1952	India	Old Trafford	W	17		11	4	19	2
							15	6	27	5
42	14/08/1952	India	The Oval	D			14.5	4	41	5
43	11/06/1953	Australia	Trent Bridge	D	2		38.3	16	55	7
							17.2	7	44	7
44	25/06/1953	Australia	Lord's	D	1		42.4	8	105	5
							31.5	8	77	3
45	09/07/1953	Australia	Old Trafford	D	10		45	10	115	5
							4	1	14	2
46	23/07/1953	Australia	Headingley	D	0*		28.5	2	95	6
					3*		17	1	65	1
47	15/08/1953	Australia	The Oval	W	22*	1	29	3	88	3
							11	2	24	0
48	01/07/1954	Pakistan	Trent Bridge	W			21	8	30	2
							30	11	83	2
49	22/07/1954	Pakistan	Old Trafford	D	22*		15.5	4	36	3
							8	5	9	3
50	26/11/1954	Australia	Brisbane (2)	L	5	1	37	4	131	1
					5					
51	07/07/1955	South Africa	Old Trafford	L	1		31	2	92	2
					3		10	1	61	2

Batting & Fielding

Mat	Inns	N/O	Runs	H/S	Avg	100s	50s	Cat
51	71	15	714	79	12.75	0	1	26

Bowling

Balls	Runs	Wkts	Avg	Best	5WI	10WM	S/R
15918	5876	236	24.89	7-44	15	5	67.44

J.E.BENJAMIN

Full Name: Joseph Emmanuel Benjamin (known as Joey)
Born: 02/02/1961, Christ Church, St Kitts
Teams: Warwickshire 1988-91, Surrey 1992-96, England 1994
Matches: 1 (Won 1, Drew 0, Lost 0)
Right-hand lower order batsman – Right-arm fast medium bowler

No	Date	Opposition	Venue	R	Bat	C	Bowling			
1	18/08/1994	South Africa	The Oval	W	0		17	2	42	4
							11	1	38	0

Batting & Fielding

Mat	Inns	N/O	Runs	H/S	Avg	100s	50s	Cat
1	1	0	0	0	0.00	0	0	0

Bowling

Balls	Runs	Wkts	Avg	Best	5WI	10WM	S/R
168	80	4	20.00	4-42	0	0	42.00

M.R.BENSON

Full Name: Mark Richard Benson
Born: 06/07/1958, Shoreham-by-Sea, Sussex
Teams: Kent 1980-96, England 1986
Matches: 1 (Won 0, Drew 1, Lost 0)
Left-hand opening batsman – Off break bowler

No	Date	Opposition	Venue	R	Bat	C
1	03/07/1986	India	Edgbaston	D	21	
					30	

Batting & Fielding

Mat	Inns	N/O	Runs	H/S	Avg	100s	50s	Cat
1	2	0	51	30	25.50	0	0	0

R.BERRY

Full Name: Robert Berry (known as Bob)
Born: 29/01/1926, West Gorton, Manchester, Lancashire
Teams: Lancashire 1948-54, Worcestershire 1955-58, Derbyshire 1959-62, England 1950
Matches: 2 (Won 1, Drew 0, Lost 1)
Left-hand lower order batsman – Left-arm slow bowler

No	Date	Opposition	Venue	R	Bat	C		Bowling		
1	08/06/1950	West Indies	Old Trafford	W	0	2	31.5	13	63	5
					4*		26	12	53	4
2	24/06/1950	West Indies	Lord's	L	2		19	7	45	0
					0*		32	15	67	0

Batting & Fielding

Mat	Inns	N/O	Runs	H/S	Avg	100s	50s	Cat
2	4	2	6	4*	3.00	0	0	2

Bowling

Balls	Runs	Wkts	Avg	Best	5WI	10WM	S/R
653	228	9	25.33	5-63	1	0	72.55

M.P.BICKNELL

Full Name: Martin Paul Bicknell
Born: 14/01/1969, Guildford, Surrey
Teams: Surrey 1986-96, England 1993
Matches: 2 (Won 0, Drew 0, Lost 2)
Right-hand lower order batsman – Right-arm fast medium bowler

No	Date	Opposition	Venue	R	Bat	C	Bowling		
1	22/07/1993	Australia	Headingley	L	12		50	8	155	1
					0				
2	05/08/1993	Australia	Edgbaston	L	14		34	9	99	3
					0		3	0	9	0

Batting & Fielding

Mat	Inns	N/O	Runs	H/S	Avg	100s	50s	Cat
2	4	0	26	14	6.50	0	0	0

Bowling

Balls	Runs	Wkts	Avg	Best	5WI	10WM	S/R
522	263	4	65.75	3-99	0	0	130.50

J.G.BINKS

Full Name: James Graham Binks (known as Jimmy)
Born: 05/10/1935, Hull, Yorkshire
Teams: Yorkshire 1955-69, England 1964
Matches: 2 (Won 0, Drew 2, Lost 0)
Right-hand lower order batsman – Wicket-keeper

No	Date	Opposition	Venue	R	Bat	C	St	B
1+	21/01/1964	India	Bombay (2)	D	10	3		2
					55			0
2+	29/01/1964	India	Calcutta	D	13	5		0
					13			7

Batting & Fielding

Mat	Inns	N/O	Runs	H/S	Avg	100s	50s	Cat	St	Byes
2	4	0	91	55	22.75	0	1	8	0	9

M.C.BIRD

Full Name: Morice Carlos Bird
Born: 25/03/1888, St Michael's Hamlet, Liverpool, Lancashire
Died: 09/12/1933, Broadstone, Dorset
Teams: Lancashire 1907, Surrey 1909-21, England 1910-14
Matches: 10 (Won 6, Drew 1, Lost 3)
Right-hand middle order batsman – Right-arm medium bowler

No	Date	Opposition	Venue	R	Bat	C		Bowling	
1	01/01/1910	South Africa	Johannesburg (1)	L	4		1	1	0	0
					5		4	1	11	3
2	21/01/1910	South Africa	Durban (1)	L	1		3	2	3	0
					42		7	3	10	1
3	26/02/1910	South Africa	Johannesburg (1)	W	20					
					45		1	1	0	0
4	07/03/1910	South Africa	Cape Town	L	57		1	0	3	1
					11		1	0	5	0
5	11/03/1910	South Africa	Cape Town	W	0					
					0	1	3	0	12	0
6	13/12/1913	South Africa	Durban (1)	W	61					
7	26/12/1913	South Africa	Johannesburg (1)	W	1		4	1	15	0
8	01/01/1914	South Africa	Johannesburg (1)	W	1					
					20*		2	1	2	0
9	14/02/1914	South Africa	Durban (1)	D	8					
						1	6	1	21	0
10	27/02/1914	South Africa	Port Elizabeth	W	4	3				
							11	1	38	3

Batting & Fielding

Mat	Inns	N/O	Runs	H/S	Avg	100s	50s	Cat
10	16	1	280	61	18.66	0	2	5

Bowling

Balls	Runs	Wkts	Avg	Best	5WI	10WM	S/R
264	120	8	15.00	3-11	0	0	33.00

J.BIRKENSHAW

Full Name: Jack Birkenshaw
Born: 13/11/1940, Rothwell, Yorkshire
Teams: Yorkshire 1958-60, Leicestershire 1961-80, Worcestershire 1981, England 1973-74
Matches: 5 (Won 1, Drew 4, Lost 0)
Right-hand middle/lower order batsman – Off break bowler

No	Date	Opposition	Venue	R	Bat	C		Bowling	
1	25/01/1973	India	Kanpur	D	64		20	6	42	1
							25	5	66	2
2	06/02/1973	India	Bombay (2)	D	36		23	2	67	2
					12		12	1	52	0
3	24/03/1973	Pakistan	Karachi (1)	D	21	1	31	5	89	1
							18.3	5	57	5
4	22/03/1974	West Indies	Georgetown	D	0		22	7	41	1
5	30/03/1974	West Indies	Port-of-Spain	W	8	2	8	1	31	0
					7		10	1	24	1

Batting & Fielding

Mat	Inns	N/O	Runs	H/S	Avg	100s	50s	Cat
5	7	0	148	64	21.14	0	1	3

Bowling

Balls	Runs	Wkts	Avg	Best	5WI	10WM	S/R
1017	469	13	36.07	5-57	1	0	78.23

R.J.BLAKEY

Full Name: Richard John Blakey
Born: 15/01/1967, Huddersfield, Yorkshire
Teams: Yorkshire 1985-96, England 1993
Matches: 2 (Won 0, Drew 0, Lost 2)
Right-hand middle order batsman – Wicket-keeper

No	Date	Opposition	Venue	R	Bat	C	St	B
1+	11/02/1993	India	Madras (1)	L	0	1		0
					6			
2+	19/02/1993	India	Bombay (3)	L	1	1		5
					0			

Batting & Fielding

Mat	Inns	N/O	Runs	H/S	Avg	100s	50s	Cat	St	Byes
2	4	0	7	6	1.75	0	0	2	0	5

Hon.I.F.W.BLIGH

Full Name: Hon.Ivo Francis Walter Bligh (later the eighth Earl of Darnley)
Born: 13/03/1859, Westminster, London
Died: 10/04/1927, Puckle Hill House, Shorne, Kent
Teams: Cambridge University 1878-81, Kent 1877-83, England 1882-83
Matches: 4 (Won 2, Drew 0, Lost 2)
England Captain: 4 times 1882-83 (Won 2, Drew 0, Lost 2) **Toss:** 3-1
Right-hand opening batsman

No	Date	Opposition	Venue	R	Bat	C
1*	30/12/1882	Australia	Melbourne	L	0	
					3	
2*	19/01/1883	Australia	Melbourne	W	0	
						2
3*	26/01/1883	Australia	Sydney	W	13	1
					17*	2
4*	17/02/1883	Australia	Sydney	L	19	1
					10	1

Batting & Fielding

Mat	Inns	N/O	Runs	H/S	Avg	100s	50s	Cat
4	7	1	62	19	10.33	0	0	7

C.BLYTHE

Full Name: Colin Blythe (known as Charlie)
Born: 30/05/1879, Deptford, Kent
Died: 08/11/1917, near Passchendaele, Belgium
Teams: Kent 1899-1914, England 1901-10
Matches: 19 (Won 5, Drew 4, Lost 10)
Right-hand lower order batsman – Left-arm slow bowler

No	Date	Opposition	Venue	R	Bat	C	Bowling		
1	13/12/1901	Australia	Sydney	W	20		16	8	26	3
							13	5	30	4
2	01/01/1902	Australia	Melbourne	L	4		16	2	64	4
					0*		31	7	85	1
3	17/01/1902	Australia	Adelaide	L	2	1	11	3	54	1
					10*		41	16	66	0
4	14/02/1902	Australia	Sydney	L	4		37	17	57	1
					8		6	0	23	1
5	28/02/1902	Australia	Melbourne	L	0*		9	2	29	1
					5*		13	3	36	2
6	03/07/1905	Australia	Headingley	D	0		8	0	36	1
							24	11	41	3
7	02/01/1906	South Africa	Johannesburg (1)	L	17	1	16	5	33	3
					0		28	12	50	1
8	06/03/1906	South Africa	Johannesburg (1)	L	12		25	6	66	1
					0		4.5	3	7	0

No	Date	Opposition	Venue	R	Bat	C		Bowling			
9	10/03/1906	South Africa	Johannesburg (1)	L	3*		26	8	72	2	
					7		31	6	96	1	
10	24/03/1906	South Africa	Cape Town	W	27		32	13	68	6	
						1	28.5	10	50	5	
11	30/03/1906	South Africa	Cape Town	L	1	1	35	11	106	2	
					11*						
12	01/07/1907	South Africa	Lord's	D	4*		8	3	18	2	
							21	5	56	2	
13	29/07/1907	South Africa	Headingley	W	5*		15.5	1	59	8	
					4*		22.4	9	40	7	
14	19/08/1907	South Africa	The Oval	D	10	1	20.3	5	61	5	
					0		12.3	3	36	2	
15	13/12/1907	Australia	Sydney	L	5		12	1	33	0	
					15	1	19	5	55	1	
16	27/05/1909	Australia	Edgbaston	W	1		23	6	44	6	
							24	3	58	5	
17	26/07/1909	Australia	Old Trafford	D	1		20.3	5	63	5	
							24	5	77	2	
18	07/03/1910	South Africa	Cape Town	L	1*		15	7	26	0	
					4*		20	7	38	2	
19	11/03/1910	South Africa	Cape Town	W	2*		18	5	46	7	
							30	13	58	3	

Batting & Fielding

Mat	Inns	N/O	Runs	H/S	Avg	100s	50s	Cat
19	31	12	183	27	9.63	0	0	6

Bowling

Balls	Runs	Wkts	Avg	Best	5WI	10WM	S/R
4546	1863	100	18.63	8-59	9	4	45.46

J.H.BOARD

Full Name: John Henry Board (known as Jack)
Born: 23/02/1867, Clifton, Bristol
Died: 15/04/1924, on board the SS Kenilworth Castle en route from South Africa
Teams: Gloucestershire 1891-1914, London County 1900-1904, Hawke's Bay 1910/11-14/15, England 1899-1906
Matches: 6 (Won 3, Drew 0, Lost 3)
Right-hand middle order batsman – Wicket-keeper

No	Date	Opposition	Venue	R	Bat	C	St	B
1+	14/02/1899	South Africa	Johannesburg (1)	W	29	1	1	5
					17	1		4
2+	01/04/1899	South Africa	Cape Town	W	0		1	4
					6			5
3+	02/01/1906	South Africa	Johannesburg (1)	L	9*	2		9
					7			6
4+	06/03/1906	South Africa	Johannesburg (1)	L	0		1	9
					2	1		2
5+	24/03/1906	South Africa	Cape Town	W	0	2		20
					14*			0
6+	30/03/1906	South Africa	Cape Town	L	20	1		12
					4			

Batting & Fielding

Mat	Inns	N/O	Runs	H/S	Avg	100s	50s	Cat	St	Byes
6	12	2	108	29	10.80	0	0	8	3	76

J.B.BOLUS

Full Name: John Brian Bolus (known as Brian)
Born: 31/01/1934, Whitkirk, Leeds, Yorkshire
Teams: Yorkshire 1956-62, Nottinghamshire 1963-72, Derbyshire 1973-75, England 1963-64
Matches: 7 (Won 0, Drew 5, Lost 2)
Right-hand opening batsman – Left-arm medium bowler

No	Date	Opposition	Venue	R	Bat	C	Bowling
1	25/07/1963	West Indies	Headingley	L	14		
					43		
2	22/08/1963	West Indies	The Oval	L	33		
					15	1	

No	Date	Opposition	Venue	R	Bat	C		Bowling	
3	10/01/1964	India	Madras (2)	D	88				
					22	1			
4	21/01/1964	India	Bombay (2)	D	25				
					57				
5	29/01/1964	India	Calcutta	D	39				
					35				
6	08/02/1964	India	Delhi	D	58				
7	15/02/1964	India	Kanpur	D	67				
							3	0 16	0

Batting & Fielding

Mat	Inns	N/O	Runs	H/S	Avg	100s	50s	Cat
7	12	0	496	88	41.33	0	4	2

Bowling

Balls	Runs	Wkts	Avg	Best	5WI	10WM	S/R
18	16	0	–	0-16	0	0	–

M.W.BOOTH

Full Name: Major William Booth
Born: 10/12/1886, Lowtown, Pudsey, Yorkshire
Died: 01/07/1916, near La Cigny, France
Teams: Yorkshire 1908-14, England 1913-14
Matches: 2 (Won 2, Drew 0, Lost 0)
Right-hand middle order batsman – Right-arm fast medium bowler

No	Date	Opposition	Venue	R	Bat	C		Bowling	
1	13/12/1913	South Africa	Durban (1)	W	14		10	0 38	2
2	27/02/1914	South Africa	Port Elizabeth	W	32		18	3 43	1
							24	5 49	4

Batting & Fielding

Mat	Inns	N/O	Runs	H/S	Avg	100s	50s	Cat
2	2	0	46	32	23.00	0	0	0

Bowling

Balls	Runs	Wkts	Avg	Best	5WI	10WM	S/R
312	130	7	18.57	4-49	0	0	44.57

B.J.T.BOSANQUET

Full Name: Bernard James Tindal Bosanquet
Born: 13/10/1877, Bulls Cross, Enfield, Middlesex
Died: 12/10/1936, Wykehurst, Ewhurst, Surrey
Teams: Oxford University 1898-1900, Middlesex 1898-1919, England 1903-05
Matches: 7 (Won 3, Drew 2, Lost 2)
Right-hand middle order batsman – Leg-break & googly bowler (previously right-arm fast)

No	Date	Opposition	Venue	R	Bat	C		Bowling	
1	11/12/1903	Australia	Sydney	W	2		13	0 52	2
					1*	1	23	1 100	1
2	15/01/1904	Australia	Adelaide	L	10		30.1	4 95	3
					10	2	15.5	0 73	4
3	26/02/1904	Australia	Sydney	W	12		2	1 5	0
					7		15	1 51	6
4	05/03/1904	Australia	Melbourne	L	16		4	0 27	0
					4	1			
5	29/05/1905	Australia	Trent Bridge	W	27	1	7	0 29	0
					6	2	32.4	2 107	8
6	15/06/1905	Australia	Lord's	D	6	1			
					4*				
7	03/07/1905	Australia	Headingley	D	20	1	4	0 29	0
					22*		15	1 36	1

Batting & Fielding

Mat	Inns	N/O	Runs	H/S	Avg	100s	50s	Cat
7	14	3	147	27	13.36	0	0	9

Bowling

Balls	Runs	Wkts	Avg	Best	5WI	10WM	S/R
970	604	25	24.16	8-107	2	0	38.80

I.T.BOTHAM

Full Name: Ian Terence Botham, OBE
Born: 24/11/55 – Oldfield, Heswall, Cheshire
Teams: Somerset 1974-86, Worcestershire 1987-91, Durham 1992-93, Queensland 1987/88, England 1977-92
Matches: 102 (Won 33, Drew 37, Lost 32)
England Captain: 12 times 1980-81 (Won 0, Drew 8, Lost 4) **Toss:** 6-6
Right-hand middle order batsman – Right-arm fast medium bowler

No	Date	Opposition	Venue	R	Bat	C	Bowling			
1	28/07/1977	Australia	Trent Bridge	W	25	1	20	5	74	5
							25	5	60	0
2	11/08/1977	Australia	Headingley	W	0		11	3	21	5
							17	3	47	0
3	10/02/1978	New Zealand	Wellington	L	7	1	12.6	2	27	2
					19		9.3	3	13	2
4	24/02/1978	New Zealand	Christchurch	W	103		24.7	6	73	5
					30*	3	7	1	38	3
5	04/03/1978	New Zealand	Auckland	D	53		34	4	109	5
						1	13	1	51	0
6	01/06/1978	Pakistan	Edgbaston	W	100	1	15	4	52	1
							17	3	47	0
7	15/06/1978	Pakistan	Lord's	W	108	1	5	2	17	0
						1	20.5	8	34	8
8	29/06/1978	Pakistan	Headingley	D	4	1	18	2	59	4
9	27/07/1978	New Zealand	The Oval	W	22		22	7	58	1
					19		2	2	46	3
10	10/08/1978	New Zealand	Trent Bridge	W	8		21	9	34	6
						2	24	7	59	3
11	24/08/1978	New Zealand	Lord's	W	21		38	13	101	6
							18.1	4	39	5
12	01/12/1978	Australia	Brisbane (2)	W	49		12	1	40	3
							26	5	95	3
13	15/12/1978	Australia	Perth	W	11		11	2	46	0
					30	1	11	1	54	0
14	29/12/1978	Australia	Melbourne	L	22		20.1	4	68	3
					10	1	15	4	41	3
15	06/01/1979	Australia	Sydney	W	59	3	28	3	87	2
					6	2				
16	27/01/1979	Australia	Adelaide	W	74		11.4	0	42	4
					7		14	4	37	1
17	10/02/1979	Australia	Sydney	W	23	2	9.7	1	57	4
						2				
18	12/07/1979	India	Edgbaston	W	33	3	26	4	86	2
							29	8	70	5
19	02/08/1979	India	Lord's	D	36	1	19	9	35	5
					35		13	80	1	
20	16/08/1979	India	Headingley	D	137	2	13	3	39	0
21	30/08/1979	India	The Oval	D	38	2	28	7	65	4
					0	2	29	5	97	3
22	14/12/1979	Australia	Perth	L	15		35	9	78	6
					18		45.5	14	98	5
23	04/01/1980	Australia	Sydney	L	27		17	7	29	4
					0	1	23.3	12	43	0
24	01/02/1980	Australia	Melbourne	L	8	2	39.5	15	105	3
					119*		12	5	18	1
25	15/02/1980	India	Bombay (3)	W	114		22.5	7	58	6
							26	7	48	7
26*	05/06/1980	West Indies	Trent Bridge	L	57	1	20	6	50	3
					4		16.4	6	48	1
27*	19/06/1980	West Indies	Lord's	D	8		37	7	145	3
28*	10/07/1980	West Indies	Old Trafford	D	8	1	20	6	64	3
					35					
29*	24/07/1980	West Indies	The Oval	D	9		18.2	8	47	2
					4					
30*	07/08/1980	West Indies	Headingley	D	37		19	8	31	1
					7					
31*	28/08/1980	Australia	Lord's	D	0		22	2	89	0
							9.2	1	43	1
32*	13/02/1981	West Indies	Port-of-Spain	L	0	2	28	6	113	2
					16					

No	Date	Opposition	Venue	R	Bat	C			Bowling	
33*	13/03/1981	West Indies	Bridgetown	L	26	2	25.1	5	77	4
					1		29	5	102	3
34*	27/03/1981	West Indies	St John's	D	1		37	6	127	4
					1					
35*	10/04/1981	West Indies	Kingston	D	13	1	26.1	9	73	2
					16					
36*	18/06/1981	Australia	Trent Bridge	L	1	1	16.5	6	34	2
					33		10	1	34	1
37*	02/07/1981	Australia	Lord's	D	0		26	8	71	2
					0	1	8	3	10	1
38	16/07/1981	Australia	Headingley	W	50	1	39.2	11	95	6
					149*	1	7	3	14	1
39	30/07/1981	Australia	Edgbaston	W	26	1	20	1	64	1
					3	1	14	9	11	5
40	13/08/1981	Australia	Old Trafford	W	0	3	6.2	1	28	3
					118	1	36	16	86	2
41	27/08/1981	Australia	The Oval	D	3	2	47	13	125	6
					16	1	42	9	128	4
42	27/11/1981	India	Bombay (3)	L	7		28	6	72	4
					29		22.3	3	61	5
43	09/12/1981	India	Bangalore	D	55		47	9	137	2
44	23/12/1981	India	Delhi	D	66		41	6	122	2
45	01/01/1982	India	Calcutta	D	58		27	8	63	2
					31	1	11	3	26	0
46	13/01/1982	India	Madras (1)	D	52		31	10	83	1
						2	8	1	29	0
47	30/01/1982	India	Kanpur	D	142		25	6	67	1
48	17/02/1982	Sri Lanka	Colombo (1)	W	13		12.5	1	28	3
							12	1	37	0
49	10/06/1982	India	Lord's	W	67		19.4	3	46	5
							31.5	7	103	1
50	24/06/1982	India	Old Trafford	D	128		19	4	86	1
51	08/07/1982	India	The Oval	D	208	1	19	2	73	2
							4	0	12	0
52	29/07/1982	Pakistan	Edgbaston	W	2		24	1	86	2
					0		21	7	70	4
53	12/08/1982	Pakistan	Lord's	L	31		44	8	148	3
					69		7	0	30	0
54	26/08/1982	Pakistan	Headingley	W	57		24.5	9	70	4
					4	1	30	8	74	5
55	12/11/1982	Australia	Perth	D	12		40	10	121	2
					0		6	1	17	0
56	26/11/1982	Australia	Brisbane (2)	L	40		22	1	105	3
					15	1	15.5	1	70	0
57	10/12/1982	Australia	Adelaide	L	35	3	36.5	5	112	4
					58		10	2	45	1
58	26/12/1982	Australia	Melbourne	W	27		18	3	69	1
					46		25.1	4	80	2
59	02/01/1983	Australia	Sydney	D	5	2	30	8	75	4
					32	3	10	0	35	1
60	14/07/1983	New Zealand	The Oval	W	15	2	16	2	62	4
					26		4	0	17	0
61	28/07/1983	New Zealand	Headingley	L	38		26	9	81	0
					4		0.1	0	4	0
62	11/08/1983	New Zealand	Lord's	W	8	1	20.4	6	50	4
					61		7	2	20	1
63	25/08/1983	New Zealand	Trent Bridge	W	103		14	4	33	1
					27		25	4	73	0
64	20/01/1984	New Zealand	Wellington	D	138		27.4	8	59	5
						1	36	6	137	1
65	03/02/1984	New Zealand	Christchurch	L	18	1	17	1	88	1
					0					
66	10/02/1984	New Zealand	Auckland	D	70	1	29	10	70	0
67	02/03/1984	Pakistan	Karachi (1)	L	22	2	30	5	90	2
					10	2				
68	14/06/1984	West Indies	Edgbaston	L	64		34	7	127	1
					38					
69	28/06/1984	West Indies	Lord's	L	30		27.4	6	103	8
					81		20.1	2	117	0

No	Date	Opposition	Venue	R	Bat	C	Bowling O	M	R	W
70	12/07/1984	West Indies	Headingley	L	45	2	7	0	45	0
					14					
71	26/07/1984	West Indies	Old Trafford	L	6	1	29	5	100	2
					1					
72	09/08/1984	West Indies	The Oval	L	14	1	23	8	72	5
					54	1	22.3	2	103	3
73	23/08/1984	Sri Lanka	Lord's	D	6		29	6	114	1
							27	6	90	6
74	13/06/1985	Australia	Headingley	W	60	2	29.1	8	86	3
					12		33	7	107	4
75	27/06/1985	Australia	Lord's	L	5		24	2	109	5
					85		15	0	49	2
76	11/07/1985	Australia	Trent Bridge	D	38	1	34.2	3	107	3
77	01/08/1985	Australia	Old Trafford	D	20	1	23	4	79	4
							15	3	50	0
78	15/08/1985	Australia	Edgbaston	W	18	1	27	1	108	1
							14.1	2	52	3
79	29/08/1985	Australia	The Oval	W	12	1	20	3	64	3
						2	17	3	44	3
80	21/02/1986	West Indies	Kingston	L	15		19	4	67	2
					29					
81	07/03/1986	West Indies	Port-of-Spain	L	2	1	9.4	0	68	1
					1					
82	21/03/1986	West Indies	Bridgetown	L	14	2	24	3	80	1
					21					
83	03/04/1986	West Indies	Port-of-Spain	L	38	1	24.1	3	71	5
					25		3	0	24	0
84	11/04/1986	West Indies	St John's	L	10		40	6	147	2
					13		15	0	78	0
85	21/08/1986	New Zealand	The Oval	D	59*		25	4	75	3
							1	0	7	0
86	14/11/1986	Australia	Brisbane (2)	W	138		16	1	58	2
							12	0	34	1
87	28/11/1986	Australia	Perth	D	0	3	22	4	72	1
					6	1	7.2	4	13	0
88	26/12/1986	Australia	Melbourne	W	29	3	16	4	41	5
							7	1	19	0
89	10/01/1987	Australia	Sydney	L	16	2	23	10	42	0
					0	1	3	0	17	0
90	04/06/1987	Pakistan	Old Trafford	D	48		14	7	29	1
91	18/06/1987	Pakistan	Lord's	D	6					
92	02/07/1987	Pakistan	Headingley	L	26					
					24					
93	23/07/1987	Pakistan	Edgbaston	D	37	1	48	13	121	1
					6	1	20.3	3	66	2
94	06/08/1987	Pakistan	The Oval	D	34	1	52	7	217	3
					51*					
95	06/07/1989	Australia	Edgbaston	D	46	1	26	5	75	1
						1				
96	27/07/1989	Australia	Old Trafford	L	0		24	6	63	2
					4					
97	10/08/1989	Australia	Trent Bridge	L	12	1	30	4	103	0
98	08/08/1991	West Indies	The Oval	W	31	3	11	4	27	1
					4*		16	4	40	2
99	22/08/1991	Sri Lanka	Lord's	W	22		10	3	26	1
						2	6	2	15	0
100	06/02/1992	New Zealand	Wellington	D	15	1	14	4	53	1
					1		8	1	23	2
101	04/06/1992	Pakistan	Edgbaston	D			19	6	52	0
102	18/06/1992	Pakistan	Lord's	L	2	2	5	2	9	0
					6					

Batting & Fielding

Mat	Inns	N/O	Runs	H/S	Avg	100s	50s	Cat
102	161	6	5200	208	33.54	14	22	120

Bowling

Balls	Runs	Wkts	Avg	Best	5WI	10WM	S/R
21815	10878	383	28.40	8-34	27	4	56.95

M.P.BOWDEN

Full Name: Montague Parker Bowden (known as Monty)
Born: 01/11/1865, Stockwell, Surrey
Died: 19/02/1892, near Umtali (formerly Laurencedale), Mashonaland, Rhodesia
Teams: Surrey 1883-88, Transvaal 1889/90, England 1889
Matches: 2 (Won 2, Drew 0, Lost 0)
England Captain: Once 1889 (Won 1, Drew 0, Lost 0) **Toss:** 1-0
Right-hand middle order batsman & Wicket-keeper

No	Date	Opposition	Venue	R	Bat	C
1	12/03/1889	South Africa	Port Elizabeth	W	0	
						1
2*	25/03/1889	South Africa	Cape Town	W	25	

Batting & Fielding

Mat	Inns	N/O	Runs	H/S	Avg	100s	50s	Cat
2	2	0	25	25	12.50	0	0	1

W.E.BOWES

Full Name: William Eric Bowes (known as Bill)
Born: 25/07/1908, Elland, Yorkshire
Died: 04/09/1987, Otley, Yorkshire
Teams: Yorkshire 1929-47, England 1932-46
Matches: 15 (Won 5, Drew 7, Lost 3)
Right-hand lower order batsman – Right-arm fast medium bowler

No	Date	Opposition	Venue	R	Bat	C		Bowling		
1	25/06/1932	India	Lord's	W	7		30	13	49	4
							14	5	30	2
2	30/12/1932	Australia	Melbourne	L	4*		19	2	50	1
					0*		4	0	20	0
3	31/03/1933	New Zealand	Auckland	D			19	5	34	6
							2	0	4	0
4	22/06/1934	Australia	Lord's	W	10*		31	5	98	3
							14	4	24	1
5	20/07/1934	Australia	Headingley	D	0		50	13	142	6
6	18/08/1934	Australia	The Oval	L			38	2	164	4
					2		11.3	3	55	5
7	15/06/1935	South Africa	Trent Bridge	D			22	9	31	0
							4	3	2	0
8	13/07/1935	South Africa	Headingley	D	0*		29	5	62	2
							19	9	31	2
9	27/07/1935	South Africa	Old Trafford	D	0*	1	36	7	100	5
							15	1	34	0
10	17/08/1935	South Africa	The Oval	D			40.4	7	112	3
							13	2	40	2
11	22/07/1938	Australia	Headingley	L	3		35.4	6	79	3
					0		11	0	35	0
12	20/08/1938	Australia	The Oval	W			19	3	49	5
							10	3	25	2
13	24/06/1939	West Indies	Lord's	W			28.4	5	86	3
						1	19	7	44	1
14	22/07/1939	West Indies	Old Trafford	D			17.4	4	33	6
							5	0	13	1
15	22/06/1946	India	Lord's	W	2		25	7	64	1
							4	1	9	0

Batting & Fielding

Mat	Inns	N/O	Runs	H/S	Avg	100s	50s	Cat
15	11	5	28	10*	4.66	0	0	2

Bowling

Balls	Runs	Wkts	Avg	Best	5WI	10WM	S/R
3655	1519	68	22.33	6-33	6	0	53.75

E.H.BOWLEY

Full Name: Edward Henry Bowley (known as Ted)
Born: 06/06/1890, Leatherhead, Surrey
Died: 09/07/1974, Winchester, Hampshire
Teams: Sussex 1912-34, Auckland 1926/27-28/29, England 1929-30
Matches: 5 (Won 2, Drew 3, Lost 0)
Right-hand opening batsman – Leg break bowler

No	Date	Opposition	Venue	R	Bat	C		Bowling	
1	13/07/1929	South Africa	Headingley	W	31				
					46		4	1 7	0
2	27/07/1929	South Africa	Old Trafford	W	13	1			
3	24/01/1930	New Zealand	Wellington	D	9		5	0 32	0
					2	1	5	0 19	0
4	14/02/1930	New Zealand	Auckland	D	109				
5	21/02/1930	New Zealand	Auckland	D	42		28	6 58	0

Batting & Fielding

Mat	Inns	N/O	Runs	H/S	Avg	100s	50s	Cat
5	7	0	252	109	36.00	1	0	2

Bowling

Balls	Runs	Wkts	Avg	Best	5WI	10WM	S/R
252	116	0	–	0-7	0	0	–

G.BOYCOTT

Full Name: Geoffrey Boycott, OBE (known as Geoff)
Born: 21/10/1940, Fitzwilliam, Yorkshire
Teams: Yorkshire 1962-86, Northern Transvaal 1971/72, England 1964-82
Matches: 108 (Won 35, Drew 53, Lost 20)
England Captain: 4 Times 1978 (Won 1, Drew 2, Lost 1) **Toss:** 3-1
Right-hand opening batsman – Right-arm medium bowler

No	Date	Opposition	Venue	R	Bat	C		Bowling	
1	04/06/1964	Australia	Trent Bridge	D	48				
2	02/07/1964	Australia	Headingley	L	38				
					4				
3	23/07/1964	Australia	Old Trafford	D	58		1	0 3	0
4	13/08/1964	Australia	The Oval	D	30				
					113				
5	04/12/1964	South Africa	Durban (2)	W	73				
6	23/12/1964	South Africa	Johannesburg (3)	D	4				
							5	3 3	0
7	01/01/1965	South Africa	Cape Town	D	15				
					1*		20	5 47	3
8	22/01/1965	South Africa	Johannesburg (3)	D	5		8	1 25	0
					76*				
9	12/02/1965	South Africa	Port Elizabeth	D	117	1	26	7 69	1
					7	1	2	0 13	1
10	27/05/1965	New Zealand	Edgbaston	W	23				
					44*				
11	17/06/1965	New Zealand	Lord's	W	14				
					76				
12	22/07/1965	South Africa	Lord's	D	31				
					28				
13	05/08/1965	South Africa	Trent Bridge	L	0				
					16		26	10 60	0
14	10/12/1965	Australia	Brisbane (2)	D	45		4	0 16	0
					63*				
15	30/12/1965	Australia	Melbourne	D	51				
					5*		9	0 32	2
16	07/01/1966	Australia	Sydney	W	84		3	1 8	0
						1			
17	28/01/1966	Australia	Adelaide	L	22		7	3 33	0
					12				
18	11/02/1966	Australia	Melbourne	D	17				
					1				

No	Date	Opposition	Venue	R	Bat	C	Bowling
19	25/02/1966	New Zealand	Christchurch	D	4, 4		12 6 30 0
20	04/03/1966	New Zealand	Dunedin	D	5	2	
21	16/06/1966	West Indies	Lord's	D	60, 25		
22	30/06/1966	West Indies	Trent Bridge	L	0, 71		
23	04/08/1966	West Indies	Headingley	L	12, 14		
24	18/08/1966	West Indies	The Oval	W	4		
25	08/06/1967	India	Headingley	W	246*		
26	13/07/1967	India	Edgbaston	W	25, 6	2	
27	10/08/1967	Pakistan	Trent Bridge	W	15, 1*		
28	19/01/1968	West Indies	Port-of-Spain	D	68		
29	08/02/1968	West Indies	Kingston	D	17, 0		
30	29/02/1968	West Indies	Bridgetown	D	90		
31	14/03/1968	West Indies	Port-of-Spain	W	62, 80*		
32	28/03/1968	West Indies	Georgetown	D	116, 30	1	
33	06/06/1968	Australia	Old Trafford	L	35, 11	1	
34	20/06/1968	Australia	Lord's	D	49		
35	11/07/1968	Australia	Edgbaston	D	36, 31		
36	12/06/1969	West Indies	Old Trafford	W	128, 1*		
37	26/06/1969	West Indies	Lord's	D	23, 106		
38	10/07/1969	West Indies	Headingley	W	12, 0		
39	24/07/1969	New Zealand	Lord's	W	0, 47		
40	07/08/1969	New Zealand	Trent Bridge	D	0		
41	21/08/1969	New Zealand	The Oval	W	46, 8		
42	27/11/1970	Australia	Brisbane (2)	D	37, 16	1	
43	11/12/1970	Australia	Perth	D	70, 50		1 0 7 0
44	09/01/1971	Australia	Sydney	W	77, 142*	1	
45	21/01/1971	Australia	Melbourne	D	12, 76*		
46	29/01/1971	Australia	Adelaide	D	58, 119*	2	
47	17/06/1971	Pakistan	Lord's	D	121*		
48	08/07/1971	Pakistan	Headingley	W	112, 13		
49	22/07/1971	India	Lord's	D	3, 33	1	
50	08/06/1972	Australia	Old Trafford	W	8, 47		
51	22/06/1972	Australia	Lord's	L	11, 6		
52	07/06/1973	New Zealand	Trent Bridge	W	51, 1		
53	21/06/1973	New Zealand	Lord's	D	61, 92		
54	05/07/1973	New Zealand	Headingley	W	115	1	
55	26/07/1973	West Indies	The Oval	L	97, 30	1	

No	Date	Opposition	Venue	R	Bat	C	Bowling			
56	09/08/1973	West Indies	Edgbaston	D	56*	1				
57	23/08/1973	West Indies	Lord's	L	4					
					15					
58	02/02/1974	West Indies	Port-of-Spain	L	6	1				
					93					
59	16/02/1974	West Indies	Kingston	D	68					
					5					
60	06/03/1974	West Indies	Bridgetown	D	10					
					13					
61	22/03/1974	West Indies	Georgetown	D	15					
62	30/03/1974	West Indies	Port-of-Spain	W	99	1				
					112					
63	06/06/1974	India	Old Trafford	W	10					
					6	1				
64	28/07/1977	Australia	Trent Bridge	W	107					
					80*					
65	11/08/1977	Australia	Headingley	W	191					
66	25/08/1977	Australia	The Oval	D	39					
					25*					
67	14/12/1977	Pakistan	Lahore (2)	D	63		3	0	4	0
68	02/01/1978	Pakistan	Hyderabad	D	79					
					100*					
69*	18/01/1978	Pakistan	Karachi (1)	D	31					
					56					
70*	10/02/1978	New Zealand	Wellington	L	77					
					1	2				
71*	24/02/1978	New Zealand	Christchurch	W	8					
					26					
72*	04/03/1978	New Zealand	Auckland	D	54					
73	10/08/1978	New Zealand	Trent Bridge	W	131					
74	24/08/1978	New Zealand	Lord's	W	24					
					4					
75	01/12/1978	Australia	Brisbane (2)	W	13					
					16					
76	15/12/1978	Australia	Perth	W	77					
					23	1				
77	29/12/1978	Australia	Melbourne	L	1					
					38					
78	06/01/1979	Australia	Sydney	W	8					
					0					
79	27/01/1979	Australia	Adelaide	W	6					
					49					
80	10/02/1979	Australia	Sydney	W	19		1	0	6	0
					13	1				
81	12/07/1979	India	Edgbaston	W	155		5	1	8	0
82	02/08/1979	India	Lord's	D	32					
						1				
83	16/08/1979	India	Headingley	D	31		2	2	0	0
84	30/08/1979	India	The Oval	D	35					
					125					
85	14/12/1979	Australia	Perth	L	0	1				
					99*					
86	04/01/1980	Australia	Sydney	L	8					
					18					
87	01/02/1980	Australia	Melbourne	L	44					
					7	1				
88	15/02/1980	India	Bombay (3)	W	22					
					43*					
89	05/06/1980	West Indies	Trent Bridge	L	36					
					75					
90	19/06/1980	West Indies	Lord's	D	8		7	2	11	0
					49*					
91	10/07/1980	West Indies	Old Trafford	D	5					
					86					
92	24/07/1980	West Indies	The Oval	D	53					
					5					

No	Date	Opposition	Venue	R	Bat	C		Bowling		
93	07/08/1980	West Indies	Headingley	D	4					
					47					
94	28/08/1980	Australia	Lord's	D	62					
					128*					
95	13/02/1981	West Indies	Port-of-Spain	L	30					
					70					
96	13/03/1981	West Indies	Bridgetown	L	0					
					1	1				
97	27/03/1981	West Indies	St John's	D	38	1	3	2	5	0
					104*					
98	10/04/1981	West Indies	Kingston	D	40					
					12					
99	18/06/1981	Australia	Trent Bridge	L	27	2				
					4					
100	02/07/1981	Australia	Lord's	D	17					
					60					
101	16/07/1981	Australia	Headingley	W	12		3	2	2	0
					46					
102	30/07/1981	Australia	Edgbaston	W	13					
					29					
103	13/08/1981	Australia	Old Trafford	W	10					
					37					
104	27/08/1981	Australia	The Oval	D	137					
					0					
105	27/11/1981	India	Bombay (3)	L	60	1				
					3					
106	09/12/1981	India	Bangalore	D	36	1				
					50					
107	23/12/1981	India	Delhi	D	105					
					34*					
108	01/01/1982	India	Calcutta	D	18					
					6					

Batting & Fielding

Mat	Inns	N/O	Runs	H/S	Avg	100s	50s	Cat
108	193	23	8114	246*	47.72	22	42	33

Bowling

Balls	Runs	Wkts	Avg	Best	5WI	10WM	S/R
944	382	7	54.57	3-47	0	0	134.85

W.M.BRADLEY

Full Name: Walter Morris Bradley (known as Bill)
Born: 02/01/1875, Sydenham, London
Died: 19/06/1944, Wandsworth Common, London
Teams: Kent 1895-1903, London County 1903, England 1899
Matches: 2 (Won 0, Drew 2, Lost 0)
Right-hand lower order batsman – Right-arm fast bowler

No	Date	Opposition	Venue	R	Bat	C	Bowling			
1	17/07/1899	Australia	Old Trafford	D	23*		33	13	67	5
							46	16	82	1
2	14/08/1899	Australia	The Oval	D	0		29	12	52	0
							17	8	32	0

Batting & Fielding

Mat	Inns	N/O	Runs	H/S	Avg	100s	50s	Cat
2	2	1	23	23*	23.00	0	0	0

Bowling

Balls	Runs	Wkts	Avg	Best	5WI	10WM	S/R
625	233	6	38.83	5-67	1	0	104.16

L.C.BRAUND

Full Name: Leonard Charles Braund (known as Len)
Born: 18/10/1875, Clewer, Berkshire
Died: 23/12/1955, Putney Common, London
Teams: Surrey 1896-98, Somerset 1899-1920, London County 1900-04, England 1901-08
Matches: 23 (Won 7, Drew 4, Lost 12)
Right-hand middle order batsman – Leg break bowler

No	Date	Opposition	Venue	R	Bat	C		Bowling		
1	13/12/1901	Australia	Sydney	W	58	2	15	4	40	2
							28.4	8	61	5
2	01/01/1902	Australia	Melbourne	L	2*	2				
					25	1	53.2	17	114	1
3	17/01/1902	Australia	Adelaide	L	103*	1	46	9	143	3
					17	1	25	5	79	0
4	14/02/1902	Australia	Sydney	L	17	2	60	25	118	4
					0		15	2	55	0
5	28/02/1902	Australia	Melbourne	L	32	1	10	2	33	1
					2	2	26.1	4	95	5
6	29/05/1902	Australia	Edgbaston	D	14	1	1	0	1	0
						1	5	0	14	1
7	12/06/1902	Australia	Lord's	D						
8	03/07/1902	Australia	Bramall Lane	L	0	4	13	4	34	2
					9	1	12	0	58	0
9	24/07/1902	Australia	Old Trafford	L	65		9	0	37	0
					3	1	11	3	22	0
10	11/08/1902	Australia	The Oval	W	22		16.5	5	29	2
					2		9	1	15	2
11	11/12/1903	Australia	Sydney	W	102	1	26	9	39	0
					0		12	2	56	0
12	01/01/1904	Australia	Melbourne	W	20	1	5	0	20	0
					3	2				
13	15/01/1904	Australia	Adelaide	L	13		13	1	49	0
					25	1	21	6	57	2
14	26/02/1904	Australia	Sydney	W	39	1	11	2	27	0
					19		16	3	24	0
15	05/03/1904	Australia	Melbourne	L	5	3	28.5	6	81	8
					0		4	1	6	1
16	01/07/1907	South Africa	Lord's	D	104		7	4	10	1
							4	0	26	0
17	29/07/1907	South Africa	Headingley	W	1	1				
					0	1				
18	19/08/1907	South Africa	The Oval	D	18					
					34		1	0	5	0
19	13/12/1907	Australia	Sydney	L	30	4	17	2	74	2
					32*		7	2	14	0
20	01/01/1908	Australia	Melbourne	W	49	1	16	5	41	0
					30		18	2	68	0
21	10/01/1908	Australia	Adelaide	L	0		9	1	26	1
					47		23	3	85	2
22	07/02/1908	Australia	Melbourne	L	4	1	12	3	42	0
					10	1	7	0	48	0
23	21/02/1908	Australia	Sydney	L	31	1				
					0		20	3	64	0

Batting & Fielding

Mat	Inns	N/O	Runs	H/S	Avg	100s	50s	Cat
23	41	3	987	104	25.97	3	2	39

Bowling

Balls	Runs	Wkts	Avg	Best	5WI	10WM	S/R
3803	1810	47	38.51	8-81	3	0	80.91

J.M.BREARLEY

Full Name: John Michael Brearley, OBE (known as Mike)
Born: 28/04/1942, Harrow, Middlesex
Teams: Cambridge University 1961-64, Middlesex 1961-83, England 1976-81
Matches: 39 (Won 21, Drew 12, Lost 6)
England Captain: 31 Times 1977-81 (Won 18, Drew 9, Lost 4) **Toss:** 13-18
Right-hand opening/middle order batsman – Right-arm medium bowler

No	Date	Opposition	Venue	R	Bat	C
1	03/06/1976	West Indies	Trent Bridge	D	0	
					17	1
2	17/06/1976	West Indies	Lord's	D	40	
					13	
3	17/12/1976	India	Delhi	W	5	
4	01/01/1977	India	Calcutta	W	5	
						2

No	Date	Opposition	Venue	R	Bat	C
5	14/01/1977	India	Madras (1)	W	59 29	2 3
6	28/01/1977	India	Bangalore	L	4 4	1 1
7	11/02/1977	India	Bombay (3)	D	91 18	
8	12/03/1977	Australia	Melbourne	L	12 43	1
9*	16/06/1977	Australia	Lord's	D	9 49	2
10*	07/07/1977	Australia	Old Trafford	W	6 44	1
11*	28/07/1977	Australia	Trent Bridge	W	15 81	2 1
12*	11/08/1977	Australia	Headingley	W	0	1
13*	25/08/1977	Australia	The Oval	D	39 4	
14*	14/12/1977	Pakistan	Lahore (2)	D	23	
15*	02/01/1978	Pakistan	Hyderabad	D	17 74	2 1
16*	01/06/1978	Pakistan	Edgbaston	W	38	1 1
17*	15/06/1978	Pakistan	Lord's	W	2	2
18*	29/06/1978	Pakistan	Headingley	D	0	2
19*	27/07/1978	New Zealand	The Oval	W	2 11	1 1
20*	10/08/1978	New Zealand	Trent Bridge	W	50	2
21*	24/08/1978	New Zealand	Lord's	W	33 8*	1
22*	01/12/1978	Australia	Brisbane (2)	W	6 13	1
23*	15/12/1978	Australia	Perth	W	17 0	1
24*	29/12/1978	Australia	Melbourne	L	1 0	1
25*	06/01/1979	Australia	Sydney	W	17 53	
26*	27/01/1979	Australia	Adelaide	W	2 9	1
27*	10/02/1979	Australia	Sydney	W	46 20*	
28*	12/07/1979	India	Edgbaston	W	24	1
29*	02/08/1979	India	Lord's	D	12	1 1
30*	16/08/1979	India	Headingley	D	15	1
31*	30/08/1979	India	The Oval	D	34 11	2 1
32*	14/12/1979	Australia	Perth	L	64 11	1
33*	04/01/1980	Australia	Sydney	L	7 19	2
34*	01/02/1980	Australia	Melbourne	L	60* 10	
35*	15/02/1980	India	Bombay (3)	W	5	1
36*	16/07/1981	Australia	Headingley	W	10 14	
37*	30/07/1981	Australia	Edgbaston	W	48 13	
38*	13/08/1981	Australia	Old Trafford	W	2 3	1
39*	27/08/1981	Australia	The Oval	D	0 51	2 1

Batting & Fielding

Mat	Inns	N/O	Runs	H/S	Avg	100s	50s	Cat
39	66	3	1442	91	22.88	0	9	52

W.BREARLEY

Full Name: Walter Brearley
Born: 11/03/1876, Bolton, Lancashire
Died: 13/01/1937, Marylebone, London
Teams: Lancashire 1902-11, London County 1904, England 1905-12
Matches: 4 (Won 2, Drew 1, Lost 1)
Right-hand lower order batsman – Right-arm fast bowler

No	Date	Opposition	Venue	R	Bat	C		Bowling		
1	24/07/1905	Australia	Old Trafford	W	0		17	3	72	4
							14	3	54	4
2	14/08/1905	Australia	The Oval	D	11*		31.1	8	110	5
							11	2	41	1
3	01/07/1909	Australia	Headingley	L	6		14.1	1	42	2
						4*	24.1	6	36	1
4	10/06/1912	South Africa	Lord's	W	0					
							6	2	4	0

Batting & Fielding

Mat	Inns	N/O	Runs	H/S	Avg	100s	50s	Cat
4	5	2	21	11*	7.00	0	0	0

Bowling

Balls	Runs	Wkts	Avg	Best	5WI	10WM	S/R
705	359	17	21.11	5-110	1	0	41.47

D.V.BRENNAN

Full Name: Donald Vincent Brennan (known as Don)
Born: 10/02/1920, Eccleshill, Yorkshire
Died: 09/01/1985, Ilkley, Yorkshire
Teams: Yorkshire 1947-53, England 1951
Matches: 2 (Won 1, Drew 1, Lost 0)
Right-hand lower order batsman – Wicket-keeper

No	Date	Opposition	Venue	R	Bat	C	St	B
1+	26/07/1951	South Africa	Headingley	D	16			1
								0
2+	16/08/1951	South Africa	The Oval	W	0		1	11
								11

Batting & Fielding

Mat	Inns	N/O	Runs	H/S	Avg	100s	50s	Cat	St	Byes
2	2	0	16	16	8.00	0	0	0	1	23

J.BRIGGS

Full Name: John Briggs (known as Johnny)
Born: 03/10/1862, Sutton-in-Ashfield, Nottinghamshire
Died: 11/01/1902, Heald Green, Cheadle, Cheshire
Teams: Lancashire 1879-1900, England 1884-99
Matches: 33 (Won 19, Drew 2, Lost 12)
Right-hand middle/lower order batsman – Left-arm slow bowler

No	Date	Opposition	Venue	R	Bat	C		Bowling		
1	12/12/1884	Australia	Adelaide	W	1					
2	01/01/1885	Australia	Melbourne	W	121	1				
							8	3	13	0
3	20/02/1885	Australia	Sydney	L	3					
					1					
4	14/03/1885	Australia	Sydney	L	3					
					5					
5	21/03/1885	Australia	Melbourne	W	43	2				
6	05/07/1886	Australia	Old Trafford	W	1					
					2*					
7	19/07/1886	Australia	Lord's	W	0		34	22	29	5
						1	38.1	17	45	6
8	12/08/1886	Australia	The Oval	W	53	1	30	17	28	3
							32	19	30	3
9	28/01/1887	Australia	Sydney	W	5		14	5	25	1
					33		7	5	7	1

No	Date	Opposition	Venue	R	Bat	C		Bowling	
10	25/02/1887	Australia	Sydney	W	17		20	6 34	0
					16	1	22	9 31	3
11	10/02/1888	Australia	Sydney	W	0				
					14	1			
12	16/07/1888	Australia	Lord's	L	17		21	8 26	3
					0		4	1 9	1
13	13/08/1888	Australia	The Oval	W	0		37	24 25	5
							6	3 7	0
14	30/08/1888	Australia	Old Trafford	W	22*		9	4 17	1
							7.1	2 10	2
15	12/03/1889	South Africa	Port Elizabeth	W	0		37	21 39	4
						1	27	14 34	2
16	25/03/1889	South Africa	Cape Town	W	6		19.1	11 17	7
							14.2	5 11	8
17	01/01/1892	Australia	Melbourne	L	41		3	1 13	0
					4		21	9 26	1
18	29/01/1892	Australia	Sydney	L	28		10	2 24	0
					12	1	32.4	8 69	4
19	24/03/1892	Australia	Adelaide	W	39		21.5	4 49	6
							28	7 87	6
20	14/08/1893	Australia	The Oval	W	0		14.3	5 34	5
							35	6 114	5
21	24/08/1893	Australia	Old Trafford	D	2		42	18 81	4
							28.3	11 64	2
22	14/12/1894	Australia	Sydney	W	57		25	4 96	0
					42	2	11	2 25	3
23	29/12/1894	Australia	Melbourne	W	5		13.5	2 26	2
					31		12	0 49	0
24	11/01/1895	Australia	Adelaide	L	12		8	2 34	1
					0		19	3 57	2
25	01/02/1895	Australia	Sydney	L	11	1	22	4 65	4
					6				
26	01/03/1895	Australia	Melbourne	W	0		23.4	5 46	2
							16	3 37	1
27	16/07/1896	Australia	Old Trafford	L	0		40	18 99	2
					16		18	8 24	1
28	13/12/1897	Australia	Sydney	W	1		20	7 42	1
							22	3 86	2
29	01/01/1898	Australia	Melbourne	L	46*		40	10 96	3
					12				
30	14/01/1898	Australia	Adelaide	L	14		63	26 128	1
					0*				
31	29/01/1898	Australia	Melbourne	L	21*		17	4 38	1
					23		6	1 31	0
32	26/02/1898	Australia	Sydney	L	0		17	4 39	1
					29		5	1 25	0
33	29/06/1899	Australia	Headingley	D			30	11 53	3

Batting & Fielding

Mat	Inns	N/O	Runs	H/S	Avg	100s	50s	Cat
33	50	5	815	121	18.11	1	2	12

Bowling

Balls	Runs	Wkts	Avg	Best	5WI	10WM	S/R
5332	2094	118	17.74	8-11	9	4	45.18

B.C.BROAD

Full Name: Brian Christopher Broad (known as Chris)
Born: 29/09/1957, Knowle, Bristol
Teams: Gloucestershire 1979-94, Nottinghamshire 1984-91, Orange Free State 1985/86, England 1984-88
Matches: 25 (Won 2, Drew 13, Lost 10)
Left-hand opening batsman – Right-arm medium bowler

No	Date	Opposition	Venue	R	Bat	C	Bowling
1	28/06/1984	West Indies	Lord's	L	55		
					0		
2	12/07/1984	West Indies	Headingley	L	32	1	
					2		
3	26/07/1984	West Indies	Old Trafford	L	42		
					21		
4	09/08/1984	West Indies	The Oval	L	4		
					39		

No	Date	Opposition	Venue	R	Bat	C		Bowling	
5	23/08/1984	Sri Lanka	Lord's	D	86				
6	14/11/1986	Australia	Brisbane (2)	W	8	1			
					35*	1			
7	28/11/1986	Australia	Perth	D	162	2			
					16				
8	12/12/1986	Australia	Adelaide	D	116	1			
					15*				
9	26/12/1986	Australia	Melbourne	W	112				
10	10/01/1987	Australia	Sydney	L	6				
					17				
11	18/06/1987	Pakistan	Lord's	D	55				
12	02/07/1987	Pakistan	Headingley	L	8				
					4				
13	23/07/1987	Pakistan	Edgbaston	D	54				
					30				
14	06/08/1987	Pakistan	The Oval	D	0				
					42				
15	25/11/1987	Pakistan	Lahore (2)	L	41	1			
					13				
16	07/12/1987	Pakistan	Faisalabad	D	116				
					14		1	0 4	0
17	16/12/1987	Pakistan	Karachi (1)	D	7				
					13				
18	29/01/1988	Australia	Sydney	D	139	1			
19	12/02/1988	New Zealand	Christchurch	D	114				
					20				
20	25/02/1988	New Zealand	Auckland	D	9				
21	03/03/1988	New Zealand	Wellington	D	61				
22	02/06/1988	West Indies	Trent Bridge	D	54				
					16				
23	16/06/1988	West Indies	Lord's	L	0				
					1				
24	08/06/1989	Australia	Headingley	L	37				
					7	1			
25	22/06/1989	Australia	Lord's	L	18	1			
					20				

Batting & Fielding

Mat	Inns	N/O	Runs	H/S	Avg	100s	50s	Cat
25	44	2	1661	162	39.54	6	6	10

Bowling

Balls	Runs	Wkts	Avg	Best	5WI	10WM	S/R
6	4	0	–	0-4	0	0	–

W.BROCKWELL

Full Name: William Brockwell (known as Bill)
Born: 21/01/1865, Kingston-upon-Thames, Surrey
Died: 30/06/1935, Richmond, Surrey
Teams: Surrey 1886-1903, London County 1901-03, Kimberley 1889/90, England 1893-1899
Matches: 7 (Won 3, Drew 2, Lost 2)
Right-hand opening batsman – Right-arm fast medium bowler

No	Date	Opposition	Venue	R	Bat	C		Bowling	
1	24/08/1893	Australia	Old Trafford	D	11		3	0 17	0
						1			
2	14/12/1894	Australia	Sydney	W	49		22	7 78	1
					37	1			
3	29/12/1894	Australia	Melbourne	W	0				
					21	1	14	3 33	3
4	11/01/1895	Australia	Adelaide	L	12		20	13 30	1
					24	1	10	1 50	0
5	01/02/1895	Australia	Sydney	L	1	1	5	1 25	0
					17				
6	01/03/1895	Australia	Melbourne	W	5		6	1 22	0
					5				
7	17/07/1899	Australia	Old Trafford	D	20		6	2 18	0
						1	15	3 36	0

Batting & Fielding

Mat	Inns	N/O	Runs	H/S	Avg	100s	50s	Cat
7	12	0	202	49	16.83	0	0	6

Bowling

Balls	Runs	Wkts	Avg	Best	5WI	10WM	S/R
582	309	5	61.80	3-33	0	0	116.40

H.R.BROMLEY-DAVENPORT

Full Name: Hugh Richard Bromley-Davenport
Born: 18/08/1870, Capesthorne Hall, Chelford, Cheshire
Died: 23/05/1954, South Kensington, London
Teams: Cambridge University 1892-93, Middlesex 1896-98, England 1896-99
Matches: 4 (Won 4, Drew 0, Lost 0)
Right-hand lower order batsman – Left-arm fast bowler

No	Date	Opposition	Venue	R	Bat	C		Bowling		
1	13/02/1896	South Africa	Port Elizabeth	W	26		12	2	46	2
					7		7	1	23	1
2	02/03/1896	South Africa	Johannesburg (1)	W	84		3	0	13	0
3	21/03/1896	South Africa	Cape Town	W	7					
							9	3	16	1
4	14/02/1899	South Africa	Johannesburg (1)	W	4					
					0	1				

Batting & Fielding

Mat	Inns	N/O	Runs	H/S	Avg	100s	50s	Cat
4	6	0	128	84	21.33	0	1	1

Bowling

Balls	Runs	Wkts	Avg	Best	5WI	10WM	S/R
155	98	4	24.50	2-46	0	0	38.75

D.BROOKES

Full Name: Dennis Brookes
Born: 29/10/1915, Kippax, Leeds, Yorkshire
Teams: Northamptonshire 1934-59, England 1948
Matches: 1 (Won 0, Drew 1, Lost 0)
Right-hand opening batsman – Right-arm medium bowler

No	Date	Opposition	Venue	R	Bat	C
1	21/01/1948	West Indies	Bridgetown	D	10	
					7	1

Batting & Fielding

Mat	Inns	N/O	Runs	H/S	Avg	100s	50s	Cat
1	2	0	17	10	8.50	0	0	1

A.BROWN

Full Name: Alan Brown
Born: 17/10/1935, Rainworth, Nottinghamshire
Teams: Kent 1957-70, England 1961
Matches: 2 (Won 1, Drew 1, Lost 0)
Right-hand lower order batsman – Right-arm fast medium bowler

No	Date	Opposition	Venue	R	Bat	C		Bowling		
1	21/10/1961	Pakistan	Lahore (2)	W	3*		15.5	3	44	0
							14	4	27	3
2	11/11/1961	India	Bombay (2)	D		1	19	2	64	0
							5	0	15	0

Batting & Fielding

Mat	Inns	N/O	Runs	H/S	Avg	100s	50s	Cat
2	1	1	3	3*	–	0	0	1

Bowling

Balls	Runs	Wkts	Avg	Best	5WI	10WM	S/R
323	150	3	50.00	3-27	0	0	107.66

D.J.BROWN

Full Name: David John Brown (also known as Big Dave)
Born: 30/01/1942, Walsall, Staffordshire
Teams: Warwickshire 1961-82, England 1965-69
Matches: 26 (Won 8, Drew 16, Lost 2)
Right-hand lower order batsman – Right-arm fast medium bowler

No	Date	Opposition	Venue	R	Bat	C	Bowling			
1	22/07/1965	South Africa	Lord's	D	1	1	24	9	44	3
					5		21	11	30	3
2	26/08/1965	South Africa	The Oval	D	0		22	4	63	0
							23	3	63	2
3	10/12/1965	Australia	Brisbane (2)	D	3		21	4	71	3
4	07/01/1966	Australia	Sydney	W	1		17	1	63	5
							11	2	32	1
5	28/01/1966	Australia	Adelaide	L	1		28	4	109	1
					0					
6	11/02/1966	Australia	Melbourne	D	12		31	3	134	1
7	25/02/1966	New Zealand	Christchurch	D	44		30	3	80	3
						1	4	2	6	1
8	11/03/1966	New Zealand	Auckland	D	0		18	6	32	1
							8.1	3	8	1
9	02/06/1966	West Indies	Old Trafford	L	14		28	4	84	0
					10					
10	22/06/1967	India	Lord's	W	5		18	3	61	3
					5		5	2	10	0
11	13/07/1967	India	Edgbaston	W	3		11	6	17	3
					29*		2	1	1	0
12	19/01/1968	West Indies	Port-of-Spain	D	22*		22	3	65	2
							14	4	27	3
13	08/02/1968	West Indies	Kingston	D	14		13	1	34	1
					0		33	9	65	2
14	29/02/1968	West Indies	Bridgetown	D	1		32	10	66	2
							11	0	61	1
15	14/03/1968	West Indies	Port-of-Spain	W	0		27	2	107	3
							10	2	33	0
16	20/06/1968	Australia	Lord's	D			14	5	42	5
						1	19	9	40	0
17	11/07/1968	Australia	Edgbaston	D	0		13	2	44	1
							6	1	15	0
18	25/07/1968	Australia	Headingley	D	14		35	4	99	2
							27	5	79	0
19	22/08/1968	Australia	The Oval	W	2		22	5	63	3
					1	2	8	3	19	1
20	21/02/1969	Pakistan	Lahore (2)	D	7		14	0	43	3
					44*		15	4	47	2
21	28/02/1969	Pakistan	Dacca	D	4	1	23	8	51	3
							6	1	18	0
22	06/03/1969	Pakistan	Karachi (1)	D	25*					
23	12/06/1969	West Indies	Old Trafford	W	15		13	1	39	4
							22	3	59	3
24	26/06/1969	West Indies	Lord's	D	1		38	8	99	3
							9	3	25	0
25	10/07/1969	West Indies	Headingley	W	12		7.3	2	13	2
					34		21	8	53	2
26	24/07/1969	New Zealand	Lord's	W	11*	1	12	5	17	0
					7		5	3	6	0

Batting & Fielding

Mat	Inns	N/O	Runs	H/S	Avg	100s	50s	Cat
26	34	5	342	44*	11.79	0	0	7

Bowling

Balls	Runs	Wkts	Avg	Best	5WI	10WM	S/R
5098	2237	79	28.31	5-42	2	0	64.53

F.R.BROWN

Full Name: Frederick Richard Brown, MBE (known as Freddie)
Born: 16/12/1910, Lima, Peru
Died: 24/07/1991, Ramsbury, Wiltshire
Teams: Cambridge University 1930-31, Surrey 1931-48, Northamptonshire 1949-53, England 1931-53
Matches: 22 (Won 8, Drew 8, Lost 6)
England Captain: 15 Times 1949-51 (Won 5, Drew 4, Lost 6) **Toss:** 3-12
Right-hand middle order batsman – Right-arm medium or leg break and googly bowler

No	Date	Opposition	Venue	R	Bat	C	Bowling			
1	29/07/1931	New Zealand	The Oval	W			29	12	52	2
						1	16	6	38	1
2	15/08/1931	New Zealand	Old Trafford	D						
3	25/06/1932	India	Lord's	W	1		25	7	48	1
					29		14	1	54	2
4	24/03/1933	New Zealand	Christchurch	D	74	1	19	10	34	1
5	31/03/1933	New Zealand	Auckland	D	13		2	0	19	0
6	24/07/1937	New Zealand	Old Trafford	W	1	1	22.4	4	81	3
					57		5	0	14	1
7*	23/07/1949	New Zealand	Old Trafford	D	22	1	18	4	43	0
						1	21	3	71	2
8*	13/08/1949	New Zealand	The Oval	D	21		5	1	14	0
						2	10	0	29	0
9*	12/08/1950	West Indies	The Oval	L	0		21	4	74	1
					15					
10*	01/12/1950	Australia	Brisbane (2)	L	4		11	0	63	2
					17					
11*	22/12/1950	Australia	Melbourne	L	62		9	0	28	1
					8		12	2	26	4
12*	05/01/1951	Australia	Sydney	L	79		44	4	153	4
					18					
13*	02/02/1951	Australia	Adelaide	L	16	1	3	0	24	0
							3	1	14	1
14*	23/02/1951	Australia	Melbourne	W	6	1	18	4	49	5
						2	9	1	32	1
15*	17/03/1951	New Zealand	Christchurch	D	62	2	15.2	3	34	1
16*	24/03/1951	New Zealand	Wellington	W	47	1	6	1	10	1
					10*	1	1	0	1	0
17*	07/06/1951	South Africa	Trent Bridge	L	29		34	11	74	2
					7	1				
18*	21/06/1951	South Africa	Lord's	W	1	1				
						2				
19*	05/07/1951	South Africa	Old Trafford	W	42	1				
20*	26/07/1951	South Africa	Headingley	D	2		38	10	107	3
							11	2	26	0
21*	16/08/1951	South Africa	The Oval	W	1	1	20	10	31	2
					40		13	5	20	0
22	25/06/1953	Australia	Lord's	D	22		25	7	53	0
					28	1	27	4	82	4

Batting & Fielding

Mat	Inns	N/O	Runs	H/S	Avg	100s	50s	Cat
22	30	1	734	79	25.31	0	5	22

Bowling

Balls	Runs	Wkts	Avg	Best	5WI	10WM	S/R
3260	1398	45	31.06	5-49	1	0	72.44

G.BROWN

Full Name: George Brown
Born: 06/10/1887, Cowley, Oxfordshire
Died: 03/12/1964, Winchester, Hampshire
Teams: Hampshire 1908-33, England 1921-23
Matches: 7 (Won 2, Drew 3, Lost 2)
Left-hand opening/middle order batsman – Wicket-keeper – Right-arm medium bowler

No	Date	Opposition	Venue	R	Bat	C	St	B
1+	02/07/1921	Australia	Headingley	L	57	1		16
					46			10

No	Date	Opposition	Venue	R	Bat	C	St	B
2+	23/07/1921	Australia	Old Trafford	D	31			22
3+	13/08/1921	Australia	The Oval	D	32	1	2	6
					84			
4+	23/12/1922	South Africa	Johannesburg (1)	L	22	2		5
					1		1	14
5+	01/01/1923	South Africa	Cape Town	W	10*	1		14
					0			15
6+	09/02/1923	South Africa	Johannesburg (1)	D	0	1		11
						1		16
7+	16/02/1923	South Africa	Durban (2)	W	15*	1		14
					1	1		11

Batting & Fielding

Mat	Inns	N/O	Runs	H/S	Avg	100s	50s	Cat	St	Byes
7	12	2	299	84	29.90	0	2	9	3	154

J.T.BROWN

Full Name: John Thomas Brown (known as Jack)
Born: 20/08/1869, Great Driffield, Yorkshire
Died: 04/11/1904, Pimlico, Westminster, London
Teams: Yorkshire 1889-1904, England 1894-1899
Matches: 8 (Won 4, Drew 1, Lost 3)
Right-hand opening batsman – Leg break bowler

No	Date	Opposition	Venue	R	Bat	C		Bowling		
1	14/12/1894	Australia	Sydney	W	22					
					53					
2	29/12/1894	Australia	Melbourne	W	0	1				
					37	1				
3	11/01/1895	Australia	Adelaide	L	39*	1				
					2	1				
4	01/02/1895	Australia	Sydney	L	20*	1				
					0					
5	01/03/1895	Australia	Melbourne	W	30					
					140					
6	22/06/1896	Australia	Lord's	W	9					
					36					
7	16/07/1896	Australia	Old Trafford	L	22	1				
					19					
8	29/06/1899	Australia	Headingley	D	27					
					14*	1	7	0	22	0

Batting & Fielding

Mat	Inns	N/O	Runs	H/S	Avg	100s	50s	Cat
8	16	3	470	140	36.15	1	1	7

Bowling

Balls	Runs	Wkts	Avg	Best	5WI	10WM	S/R
35	22	0	–	0-22	0	0	–

S.J.E.BROWN

Full Name: Simon John Emmerson Brown
Born: 29/06/1969, Cleadon, Co Durham
Teams: Northamptonshire 1987-91, Durham 1992-96, England 1996
Matches: 1 (Won 0, Drew 0, Lost 1)
Right-hand lower order batsman – Left-arm fast medium bowler

No	Date	Opposition	Venue	R	Bat	C		Bowling		
1	25/07/1996	Pakistan	Lord's	L	1	1	17	2	78	1
					10*		16	2	60	1

Batting & Fielding

Mat	Inns	N/O	Runs	H/S	Avg	100s	50s	Cat
1	2	1	11	10*	11.00	0	0	1

Bowling

Balls	Runs	Wkts	Avg	Best	5WI	10WM	S/R
198	138	2	69.00	1-60	0	0	99.00

C.P.BUCKENHAM

Full Name: Claude Percival Buckenham
Born: 16/01/1876, Herne Hill, Surrey
Died: 23/02/1937, Dundee, Angus, Scotland
Teams: Essex 1899-1914, England 1910
Matches: 4 (Won 1, Drew 0, Lost 3)
Right-hand middle/lower order batsman – Right-arm fast bowler

No	Date	Opposition	Venue	R	Bat	C		Bowling		
1	01/01/1910	South Africa	Johannesburg (1)	L	0		19	1	77	3
					1		39	5	110	4
2	21/01/1910	South Africa	Durban (1)	L	16		27	4	51	2
					3		31	4	94	3
3	26/02/1910	South Africa	Johannesburg (1)	W	1	1	31	2	115	5
							23	4	73	0
4	07/03/1910	South Africa	Cape Town	L	5	1	20	3	61	3
					17		7	2	12	1

Batting & Fielding

Mat	Inns	N/O	Runs	H/S	Avg	100s	50s	Cat
4	7	0	43	17	6.14	0	0	2

Bowling

Balls	Runs	Wkts	Avg	Best	5WI	10WM	S/R
1182	593	21	28.23	5-115	1	0	56.28

A.R.BUTCHER

Full Name: Alan Raymond Butcher
Born: 07/01/1954 – Croydon, Surrey
Teams: Surrey 1972-86, Glamorgan 1987-92, England 1979
Matches: 1 (Won 0, Drew 1, Lost 0)
Left-hand opening batsman – Left-arm medium/slow bowler

No	Date	Opposition	Venue	R	Bat	C		Bowling		
1	30/08/1979	India	The Oval	D	14					
					20		2	0	9	0

Batting & Fielding

Mat	Inns	N/O	Runs	H/S	Avg	100s	50s	Cat
1	2	0	34	20	17.00	0	0	0

Bowling

Balls	Runs	Wkts	Avg	Best	5WI	10WM	S/R
12	9	0	–	0-9	0	0	–

R.O.BUTCHER

Full Name: Roland Orlando Butcher
Born: 14/10/1953, East Point, St Philip, Barbados
Teams: Middlesex 1974-90, Barbados 1974/75, Tasmania 1982/83, England 1981
Matches: 3 (Won 0, Drew 2, Lost 1)
Right-hand middle order batsman – Right-arm medium bowler

No	Date	Opposition	Venue	R	Bat	C
1	13/03/1981	West Indies	Bridgetown	L	17	
					2	1
2	27/03/1981	West Indies	St John's	D	20	2
3	10/04/1981	West Indies	Kingston	D	32	
					0	

Batting & Fielding

Mat	Inns	N/O	Runs	H/S	Avg	100s	50s	Cat
3	5	0	71	32	14.20	0	0	3

H.J.BUTLER

Full Name: Harold James Butler
Born: 12/03/1913, Clifton, Nottingham
Died: 17/07/1991, Lenton, Nottingham
Teams: Nottinghamshire 1933-54, England 1947-48
Matches: 2 (Won 1, Drew 1, Lost 0)
Right-hand lower order batsman – Right-arm fast medium bowler

No	Date	Opposition	Venue	R	Bat	C	Bowling			
1	26/07/1947	South Africa	Headingley	W			28	15	34	4
							24	9	32	3
2	11/02/1948	West Indies	Port-of-Spain	D	15*	1	32	4	122	3
					0		8	2	27	2

Batting & Fielding

Mat	Inns	N/O	Runs	H/S	Avg	100s	50s	Cat
2	2	1	15	15*	15.00	0	0	1

Bowling

Balls	Runs	Wkts	Avg	Best	5WI	10WM	S/R
552	215	12	17.91	4-34	0	0	46.00

H.R.BUTT

Full Name: Henry Rigden Butt (known as Harry)
Born: 27/12/1865, Sands End, Fulham, Middlesex
Died: 21/12/1928, West Hill, Hastings, Sussex
Teams: Sussex 1890-1912, England 1896
Matches: 3 (Won 3, Drew 0, Lost 0)
Right-hand lower order batsman – Wicket-keeper

No	Date	Opposition	Venue	R	Bat	C	St	B
1+	13/02/1896	South Africa	Port Elizabeth	W	1			2
					0			0
2+	02/03/1896	South Africa	Johannesburg (1)	W	8*	1		0
3+	21/03/1896	South Africa	Cape Town	W	13			5
							1	2

Batting & Fielding

Mat	Inns	N/O	Runs	H/S	Avg	100s	50s	Cat	St	Byes
3	4	1	22	13	7.33	0	0	1	1	9

A.R.CADDICK

Full Name: Andrew Richard Caddick (known as Andy)
Born: 21/11/1968, Christchurch, New Zealand
Teams: Somerset 1991-96, England 1993-96
Matches: 9 (Won 1, Drew 3, Lost 5)
Right-hand lower order batsman – Right-arm fast medium bowler

No	Date	Opposition	Venue	R	Bat	C	Bowling			
1	03/06/1993	Australia	Old Trafford	L	7		15	4	38	0
					25	2	20	3	79	1
2	17/06/1993	Australia	Lord's	L	21		38	5	120	0
					0*					
3	01/07/1993	Australia	Trent Bridge	D	15		22	5	81	1
					12		16	6	32	3
4	22/07/1993	Australia	Headingley	L	9		42	5	138	0
					12					
5	19/02/1994	West Indies	Kingston	L	3		29	5	94	3
					29*		6	1	19	1
6	25/03/1994	West Indies	Port-of-Spain	L	6		19	5	43	0
					1	1	26	5	65	6
7	08/04/1994	West Indies	Bridgetown	W	8		24	2	92	0
							17	3	63	5
8	16/04/1994	West Indies	St John's	D	22	1	47.2	8	158	3
							2	1	11	0
9	08/08/1996	Pakistan	Headingley	D	4		40.2	6	113	3
							17	4	52	3

Batting & Fielding

Mat	Inns	N/O	Runs	H/S	Avg	100s	50s	Cat
9	15	2	174	29*	13.38	0	0	4

Bowling

Balls	Runs	Wkts	Avg	Best	5WI	10WM	S/R
2284	1198	29	41.31	6-65	2	0	78.75

Hon.F.S.G.CALTHORPE

Full Name: Hon.Frederick Somerset Gough Calthorpe (known as Freddie)
Born: 27/05/1892, Kensington, London
Died: 19/11/1935, Worplesdon, Surrey
Teams: Cambridge University 1912-14 & 1919, Sussex 1911-12, Warwickshire 1919-30, England 1930
Matches: 4 (Won 1, Drew 2, Lost 1)
England Captain: 4 Times 1930 (Won 1, Drew 2, Lost 1) **Toss:** 2-2
Right-hand middle order batsman – Right-arm medium bowler

No	Date	Opposition	Venue	R	Bat	C		Bowling	
1*	11/01/1930	West Indies	Bridgetown	D	40	1	4	0	14	0
							20	7	38	1
2*	01/02/1930	West Indies	Port-of-Spain	W	12					
					0	1				
3*	21/02/1930	West Indies	Georgetown	L	15		6	0	23	0
					49	1				
4*	03/04/1930	West Indies	Kingston	D	5					
					8		4	1	16	0

Batting & Fielding

Mat	Inns	N/O	Runs	H/S	Avg	100s	50s	Cat
4	7	0	129	49	18.42	0	0	3

Bowling

Balls	Runs	Wkts	Avg	Best	5WI	10WM	S/R
204	91	1	91.00	1-38	0	0	204.00

D.J.CAPEL

Full Name: David John Capel
Born: 06/02/1963, Northampton
Teams: Northamptonshire 1981-96, Eastern Province 1985/86-86/87, England 1987-90
Matches: 15 (Won 1, Drew 8, Lost 6)
Right-hand middle order batsman – Right-arm medium bowler

No	Date	Opposition	Venue	R	Bat	C		Bowling	
1	02/07/1987	Pakistan	Headingley	L	53		18	1	64	0
					28					
2	25/11/1987	Pakistan	Lahore (2)	L	0		3	0	28	0
					0					
3	07/12/1987	Pakistan	Faisalabad	D	1		7	1	23	0
					2					
4	16/12/1987	Pakistan	Karachi (1)	D	98		3	0	8	1
					24					
5	29/01/1988	Australia	Sydney	D	21		6	3	13	2
							17	4	38	1
6	12/02/1988	New Zealand	Christchurch	D	11	1	10	2	32	0
					0		13	5	16	0
7	25/02/1988	New Zealand	Auckland	D	5	2	26.2	4	57	2
							21	4	40	1
8	03/03/1988	New Zealand	Wellington	D			39	7	129	2
9	30/06/1988	West Indies	Old Trafford	L	1	1	12	2	38	1
					0					
10	04/08/1988	West Indies	The Oval	L	16		7	0	21	0
					12		3	0	20	0
11	24/08/1989	Australia	The Oval	D	4		16	2	66	1
					17		8	0	35	1
12	24/02/1990	West Indies	Kingston	W	5	1	13	4	31	2
							15	1	50	0
13	23/03/1990	West Indies	Port-of-Spain	D	40		15	2	53	1
					17*		13	3	30	0

No	Date	Opposition	Venue	R	Bat	C		Bowling		
14	05/04/1990	West Indies	Bridgetown	L	2		24	5	88	3
					6	1	16	1	66	1
15	12/04/1990	West Indies	St John's	L	10		28	1	118	2
					1					

Batting & Fielding

Mat	Inns	N/O	Runs	H/S	Avg	100s	50s	Cat
15	25	1	374	98	15.58	0	2	6

Bowling

Balls	Runs	Wkts	Avg	Best	5WI	10WM	S/R
2000	1064	21	50.66	3-88	0	0	95.23

A.W.CARR

Full Name: Arthur William Carr
Born: 21/05/1893, Mickleham, Surrey
Died: 07/02/1963, West Witton, Yorkshire
Teams: Nottinghamshire 1910-34, England 1922-29
Matches: 11 (Won 3, Drew 7, Lost 1)
England Captain: 6 times 1926-29 (Won 1, Drew 5, Lost 0) **Toss:** 3-3
Right-hand middle order batsman – Right-arm medium bowler

No	Date	Opposition	Venue	R	Bat	C
1	23/12/1922	South Africa	Johannesburg (1)	L	27	
					27	
2	01/01/1923	South Africa	Cape Town	W	42	1
					6	
3	18/01/1923	South Africa	Durban (2)	D	7	
					2*	
4	09/02/1923	South Africa	Johannesburg (1)	D	63	
					6	
5	16/02/1923	South Africa	Durban (2)	W	14	
					5	
6*	12/06/1926	Australia	Trent Bridge	D		
7*	26/06/1926	Australia	Lord's	D		1
8*	10/07/1926	Australia	Headingley	D	13	
9*	24/07/1926	Australia	Old Trafford	D		
10*	27/07/1929	South Africa	Old Trafford	W	10	
11*	17/08/1929	South Africa	The Oval	D	15	1

Batting & Fielding

Mat	Inns	N/O	Runs	H/S	Avg	100s	50s	Cat
11	13	1	237	63	19.75	0	1	3

D.B.CARR

Full Name: Donald Bryce Carr, OBE
Born: 28/12/1926, Wiesbaden, Germany
Teams: Oxford University 1948-51, Derbyshire 1946-63, England 1951-52
Matches: 2 (Won 0, Drew 1, Lost 1)
England Captain: Once 1952 (Won 0, Drew 0, Lost 1) **Toss:** 1-0
Right-hand middle order batsman – Left-arm slow bowler

No	Date	Opposition	Venue	R	Bat	C		Bowling		
1	02/11/1951	India	Delhi	D	14		16	4	56	0
					76					
2*	06/02/1952	India	Madras (1)	L	40		19	2	84	2
					5					

Batting & Fielding

Mat	Inns	N/O	Runs	H/S	Avg	100s	50s	Cat
2	4	0	135	76	33.75	0	1	0

Bowling

Balls	Runs	Wkts	Avg	Best	5WI	10WM	S/R
210	140	2	70.00	2-84	0	0	105.00

D.W.CARR

Full Name: Douglas Ward Carr
Born: 17/03/1872, Cranbrook, Kent
Died: 23/03/1950, Salcombe Hill, Sidmouth, Devon
Teams: Kent 1909-14, England 1909
Matches: 1 (Won 0, Drew 1, Lost 0)
Right-hand lower order batsman – Googly bowler (previously right-arm medium)

No	Date	Opposition	Venue	R	Bat	C	Bowling		
1	09/08/1909	Australia	The Oval	D	0		34	2 146	5
							35	1 136	2

Batting & Fielding

Mat	Inns	N/O	Runs	H/S	Avg	100s	50s	Cat
1	1	0	0	0	0.00	0	0	0

Bowling

Balls	Runs	Wkts	Avg	Best	5WI	10WM	S/R
414	282	7	40.28	5-146	1	0	59.14

T.W.CARTWRIGHT

Full Name: Thomas William Cartwright
Born: 22/07/1935, Alderman's Green, Coventry, Warwickshire
Teams: Warwickshire 1952-69, Somerset 1970-76, Glamorgan 1977, England 1964-65
Matches: 5 (Won 1, Drew 3, Lost 1)
Right-hand middle order batsman – Right-arm medium bowler

No	Date	Opposition	Venue	R	Bat	C	Bowling		
1	23/07/1964	Australia	Old Trafford	D	4		77	32 118	2
2	13/08/1964	Australia	The Oval	D	0		62	23 110	3
3	22/01/1965	South Africa	Johannesburg (3)	D	9	2	55	18 97	1
					8*		24	6 99	1
4	27/05/1965	New Zealand	Edgbaston	W	4		7	3 14	2
							12	6 12	0
5	05/08/1965	South Africa	Trent Bridge	L	1*		31.3	9 94	6
					0				

Batting & Fielding

Mat	Inns	N/O	Runs	H/S	Avg	100s	50s	Cat
5	7	2	26	9	5.20	0	0	2

Bowling

Balls	Runs	Wkts	Avg	Best	5WI	10WM	S/R
1611	544	15	36.26	6-94	1	0	107.40

A.P.F.CHAPMAN

Full Name: Arthur Percy Frank Chapman (known as Percy)
Born: 03/09/1900, The Mount, Reading, Berkshire
Died: 16/09/1961, Alton, Hampshire
Teams: Cambridge University 1920-22, Kent 1924-38, England 1924-31
Matches: 26 (Won 12, Drew 9, Lost 5)
England Captain: 17 Times 1926-31 (Won 9, Drew 6, Lost 2) **Toss:** 9-8
Left-hand middle order batsman – Left-arm slow bowler (previously left-arm medium)

No	Date	Opposition	Venue	R	Bat	C	Bowling		
1	14/06/1924	South Africa	Edgbaston	W	8				
						1			
2	28/06/1924	South Africa	Lord's	W					
3	19/12/1924	Australia	Sydney	L	13	2	0 10	0	
					44	1	3	1 10	0
4	01/01/1925	Australia	Melbourne	L	28	1			
					4*				
5	16/01/1925	Australia	Adelaide	L	26				
					58				
6	13/02/1925	Australia	Melbourne	W	12	1			
7	12/06/1926	Australia	Trent Bridge	D					
8	26/06/1926	Australia	Lord's	D	50*				

No	Date	Opposition	Venue	R	Bat	C	Bowling
9	10/07/1926	Australia	Headingley	D	15		
					42*		
10*	14/08/1926	Australia	The Oval	W	49		
					19		
11*	23/06/1928	West Indies	Lord's	W	50		
						1	
12*	21/07/1928	West Indies	Old Trafford	W	3*	1	
13*	11/08/1928	West Indies	The Oval	W	5	4	
14*	30/11/1928	Australia	Brisbane (1)	W	50	1	
					27	3	
15*	14/12/1928	Australia	Sydney	W	20		
						2	
16*	29/12/1928	Australia	Melbourne	W	24		
					5		
17*	01/02/1929	Australia	Adelaide	W	39	1	
					0	1	
18*	13/06/1930	Australia	Trent Bridge	W	52	1	
					29	1	
19*	27/06/1930	Australia	Lord's	L	11	1	
					121	1	
20*	11/07/1930	Australia	Headingley	D	45	2	
21*	25/07/1930	Australia	Old Trafford	D	1	1	
22*	24/12/1930	South Africa	Johannesburg (1)	L	28		
					11		
23*	01/01/1931	South Africa	Cape Town	D	0	1	
					4		
24*	16/01/1931	South Africa	Durban (2)	D			
						2	
25*	13/02/1931	South Africa	Johannesburg (1)	D	5		
					3		
26*	21/02/1931	South Africa	Durban (2)	D	24	1	
						3	

Batting & Fielding

Mat	Inns	N/O	Runs	H/S	Avg	100s	50s	Cat
26	36	4	925	121	28.90	1	5	32

Bowling

Balls	Runs	Wkts	Avg	Best	5WI	10WM	S/R
40	20	0	–	0-10	0	0	–

H.R.J.CHARLWOOD

Full Name: Henry Rupert James Charlwood
Born: 19/12/1846, Horsham, Sussex
Died: 06/06/1888, Scarborough, Yorkshire
Teams: Sussex 1865-82, England 1877
Matches: 2 (Won 1, Drew 0, Lost 1)
Right-hand middle order batsman – Lob bowler

No	Date	Opposition	Venue	R	Bat	C
1	15/03/1877	Australia	Melbourne	L	36	
					13	
2	31/03/1877	Australia	Melbourne	W	14	
					0	

Batting & Fielding

Mat	Inns	N/O	Runs	H/S	Avg	100s	50s	Cat
2	4	0	63	36	15.75	0	0	0

W.CHATTERTON

Full Name: William Chatterton
Born: 27/12/1861, Thornsett, Derbyshire
Died: 19/03/1913, Flowery Field, Hyde, Cheshire
Teams: Derbyshire 1882-1902, England 1892
Matches: 1 (Won 1, Drew 0, Lost 0)
Right-hand middle order batsman – Right-arm slow bowler

No	Date	Opposition	Venue	R	Bat	C
1	19/03/1892	South Africa	Cape Town	W	48	

Batting & Fielding

Mat	Inns	N/O	Runs	H/S	Avg	100s	50s	Cat
1	1	0	48	48	48.00	0	0	0

J.H.CHILDS

Full Name: John Henry Childs
Born: 15/08/1951, Lipson, Plymouth, Devon
Teams: Gloucestershire 1975-84, Essex 1985-1996, England 1988
Matches: 2 (Won 0, Drew 0, Lost 2)
Left-hand lower order batsman – Left-arm slow bowler

No	Date	Opposition	Venue	R	Bat	C		Bowling		
1	30/06/1988	West Indies	Old Trafford	L	2*		40	12	91	1
					0*					
2	04/08/1988	West Indies	The Oval	L	0*	1	6	1	13	1
					0*		40	16	79	1

Batting & Fielding

Mat	Inns	N/O	Runs	H/S	Avg	100s	50s	Cat
2	4	4	2	2*	–	0	0	1

Bowling

Balls	Runs	Wkts	Avg	Best	5WI	10WM	S/R
516	183	3	61.00	1-13	0	0	172.00

S.CHRISTOPHERSON

Full Name: Stanley Christopherson
Born: 11/11/1861, Kidbrooke, Blackheath, Kent
Died: 06/04/1949, St John's Wood, London
Teams: Kent 1883-90, England 1884
Matches: 1 (Won 1, Drew 0, Lost 0)
Right-hand lower order batsman – Right-arm fast bowler

No	Date	Opposition	Venue	R	Bat	C		Bowling		
1	21/07/1884	Australia	Lord's	W	17		26	10	52	1
							8	3	17	0

Batting & Fielding

Mat	Inns	N/O	Runs	H/S	Avg	100s	50s	Cat
1	1	0	17	17	17.00	0	0	0

Bowling

Balls	Runs	Wkts	Avg	Best	5WI	10WM	S/R
136	69	1	69.00	1-52	0	0	136.00

E.W.CLARK

Full Name: Edward Winchester Clark (known as Nobby)
Born: 09/08/1902, Elton, Huntingdonshire
Died: 28/04/1982, West Winch, King's Lynn, Norfolk
Teams: Northamptonshire 1922-47, England 1929-34
Matches: 8 (Won 3, Drew 4, Lost 1)
Left-hand lower order batsman – Left-arm fast bowler

No	Date	Opposition	Venue	R	Bat	C		Bowling		
1	17/08/1929	South Africa	The Oval	D	7		36	8	79	3
2	22/07/1933	West Indies	Old Trafford	D	0		40	8	99	4
							15	1	64	2
3	12/08/1933	West Indies	The Oval	W	8*		8	3	16	3
							21	10	54	2
4	15/12/1933	India	Bombay (1)	W	1		13	3	41	1
							19	5	69	3
5	05/01/1934	India	Calcutta	D	10		26	8	39	3
							19.3	4	50	3
6	10/02/1934	India	Madras (1)	W	4*		15	4	37	0
							8	2	27	0

No	Date	Opposition	Venue	R	Bat	C	Bowling			
7	06/07/1934	Australia	Old Trafford	D	2*		40	9	100	1
							4	1	16	0
8	18/08/1934	Australia	The Oval	L	2*		37.2	4	110	2
					2*		20	1	98	5

Batting & Fielding

Mat	Inns	N/O	Runs	H/S	Avg	100s	50s	Cat
8	9	5	36	10	9.00	0	0	0

Bowling

Balls	Runs	Wkts	Avg	Best	5WI	10WM	S/R
1931	899	32	28.09	5-98	1	0	60.34

J.C.CLAY

Full Name: John Charles Clay (known as Johnny)
Born: 18/03/1898, Bonvilston, Glamorgan
Died: 11/08/1973, St Hilary, near Cowbridge, Glamorgan
Teams: Glamorgan 1921-49, Wales 1923-26, England 1935
Matches: 1 (Won 0, Drew 1, Lost 0)
Right-hand lower order batsman – Off break bowler (previously right-arm fast medium)

No	Date	Opposition	Venue	R	Bat	C	Bowling			
1	17/08/1935	South Africa	The Oval	D		1	14	1	30	0
							18	6	45	0

Batting & Fielding

Mat	Inns	N/O	Runs	H/S	Avg	100s	50s	Cat
1	0	–	–	–	–	–	–	1

Bowling

Balls	Runs	Wkts	Avg	Best	5WI	10WM	S/R
192	75	0	–	0-30	0	0	–

D.B.CLOSE

Full Name: Dennis Brian Close, CBE (known as Brian)
Born: 24/02/1931, Rawdon, Leeds, Yorkshire
Teams: Yorkshire 1949-70, Somerset 1971-77, England 1949-76
Matches: 22 (Won 10, Drew 6, Lost 6)
England Captain: 7 Times 1966-67 (Won 6, Drew 1, Lost 0) **Toss:** 4-3
Left-hand opening/middle order batsman – Right-arm medium or off break bowler

No	Date	Opposition	Venue	R	Bat	C	Bowling			
1	23/07/1949	New Zealand	Old Trafford	D	0		25	12	39	1
							17	2	46	0
2	22/12/1950	Australia	Melbourne	L	0		6	1	20	1
					1	1	1	0	8	0
3	13/08/1955	South Africa	The Oval	W	32					
					15					
4	30/05/1957	West Indies	Edgbaston	D	15					
					42	1	2	1	8	0
5	20/06/1957	West Indies	Lord's	W	32	1				
6	02/07/1959	India	Headingley	W	27	1	5	1	18	1
						3	11	0	35	4
7	27/07/1961	Australia	Old Trafford	L	33	1				
					8	1	8	1	33	0
8	06/06/1963	West Indies	Old Trafford	L	30		10	2	31	0
					32					
9	20/06/1963	West Indies	Lord's	D	9	1	9	3	21	0
					70					
10	04/07/1963	West Indies	Edgbaston	W	55					
					13					
11	25/07/1963	West Indies	Headingley	L	0	1				
					56					
12	22/08/1963	West Indies	The Oval	L	46					
					4		6	0	36	0
13*	18/08/1966	West Indies	The Oval	W	4		9	2	21	1
						1	3	1	7	0
14*	08/06/1967	India	Headingley	W	22*		3	3	0	0
						2	21	5	48	2

No	Date	Opposition	Venue	R	Bat	C		Bowling		
15*	22/06/1967	India	Lord's	W	7					
							15	5	28	2
16*	13/07/1967	India	Edgbaston	W	26					
					47		21.4	7	68	4
17*	27/07/1967	Pakistan	Lord's	D	4	1	6	3	10	0
					36	2	8	5	13	0
18*	10/08/1967	Pakistan	Trent Bridge	W	41		3	0	12	0
						2	4	1	11	1
19*	24/08/1967	Pakistan	The Oval	W	6	1	5	1	15	0
					8		1	0	4	1
20	03/06/1976	West Indies	Trent Bridge	D	2	2				
					36*					
21	17/06/1976	West Indies	Lord's	D	60					
					46	1				
22	08/07/1976	West Indies	Old Trafford	L	2					
					20	1				

Batting & Fielding

Mat	Inns	N/O	Runs	H/S	Avg	100s	50s	Cat
22	37	2	887	70	25.34	0	4	24

Bowling

Balls	Runs	Wkts	Avg	Best	5WI	10WM	S/R
1212	532	18	29.55	4-35	0	0	67.33

L.J.COLDWELL

Full Name: Leonard John Coldwell (known as Len)
Born: 10/01/1933, Newton Abbot, Devon
Died: 06/08/1996, Teignmouth, Devon
Teams: Worcestershire 1955-69, England 1962-64
Matches: 7 (Won 4, Drew 2, Lost 1)
Right-hand lower order batsman – Right-arm fast medium bowler

No	Date	Opposition	Venue	R	Bat	C		Bowling		
1	21/06/1962	Pakistan	Lord's	W	0*		14	2	25	3
							41	13	85	6
2	16/08/1962	Pakistan	The Oval	W			28	11	53	3
							23	4	60	1
3	29/12/1962	Australia	Melbourne	W	1		17	2	58	2
							25	2	60	0
4	11/01/1963	Australia	Sydney	L	2*		15	1	41	1
					0					
5	23/02/1963	New Zealand	Auckland	W		1	27	9	66	1
							5	2	4	1
6	04/06/1964	Australia	Trent Bridge	D	0*		22	3	48	3
					0*					
7	18/06/1964	Australia	Lord's	D	6*		23	7	51	1
							19	4	59	0

Batting & Fielding

Mat	Inns	N/O	Runs	H/S	Avg	100s	50s	Cat
7	7	5	9	6*	4.50	0	0	1

Bowling

Balls	Runs	Wkts	Avg	Best	5WI	10WM	S/R
1668	610	22	27.72	6-85	1	0	75.81

D.C.S.COMPTON

Full Name: Denis Charles Scott Compton, CBE
Born: 23/05/1918, Hendon, Middlesex
Teams: Middlesex 1936-58, Holkar 1944/45, Europeans 1944/45-45/46, England 1937-57
Matches: 78 (Won 25, Drew 32, Lost 21)
Right-hand middle order batsman – Left-arm slow bowler

No	Date	Opposition	Venue	R	Bat	C		Bowling		
1	14/08/1937	New Zealand	The Oval	D	65					
						1	6	0	34	2
2	10/06/1938	Australia	Trent Bridge	D	102	1				
						1				
3	24/06/1938	Australia	Lord's	D	6	1				
					76*					

No	Date	Opposition	Venue	R	Bat	C		Bowling		
4	22/07/1938	Australia	Headingley	L	14					
					15					
5	20/08/1938	Australia	The Oval	W	1	1				
6	24/06/1939	West Indies	Lord's	W	120	1				
							3	0	8	0
7	22/07/1939	West Indies	Old Trafford	D	4					
					34*					
8	19/08/1939	West Indies	The Oval	D	21		5	1	20	0
					10*					
9	22/06/1946	India	Lord's	W	0					
10	20/07/1946	India	Old Trafford	D	51		4	0	18	0
					71*		3	1	5	0
11	17/08/1946	India	The Oval	D	24*	1	5	0	15	0
12	29/11/1946	Australia	Brisbane (2)	L	17		6	0	20	0
					15					
13	13/12/1946	Australia	Sydney	L	5	1	6	0	38	0
					54					
14	01/01/1947	Australia	Melbourne	D	11					
					14	1				
15	31/01/1947	Australia	Adelaide	D	147		3	0	12	0
					103*					
16	28/02/1947	Australia	Sydney	L	17	1				
					76	1	1.2	0	8	0
17	21/03/1947	New Zealand	Christchurch	D	38					
18	07/06/1947	South Africa	Trent Bridge	D	65		2	1	6	0
					163		4	0	14	0
19	21/06/1947	South Africa	Lord's	W	208		21	11	32	2
							32	10	46	2
20	05/07/1947	South Africa	Old Trafford	W	115	1	7	1	27	0
					6		17	2	58	1
21	26/07/1947	South Africa	Headingley	W	30		4	0	9	0
						1	2	0	10	0
22	16/08/1947	South Africa	The Oval	D	53		11	4	31	0
					113		4	0	30	0
23	10/06/1948	Australia	Trent Bridge	L	19		5	0	24	0
					184					
24	24/06/1948	Australia	Lord's	L	53					
					29		3	0	11	0
25	08/07/1948	Australia	Old Trafford	D	145*	1				
					0		9	3	18	0
26	22/07/1948	Australia	Headingley	L	23		3	0	15	0
					66	1	15	3	82	1
27	14/08/1948	Australia	The Oval	L	4		2	0	6	0
					39					
28	16/12/1948	South Africa	Durban (2)	W	72	2	2	0	5	0
					28	2	16	11	11	1
29	27/12/1948	South Africa	Johannesburg (2)	D	114		10	0	34	1
							13	3	31	0
30	01/01/1949	South Africa	Cape Town	D	1	1	25.2	3	70	5
					51*		3	1	7	0
31	12/02/1949	South Africa	Johannesburg (2)	D	24		4	0	19	0
					25	1	9	2	35	0
32	05/03/1949	South Africa	Port Elizabeth	W	49	2	7	0	39	0
					42	1	9	0	57	0
33	11/06/1949	New Zealand	Headingley	D	114	1	8	2	23	1
					26		1	0	5	0
34	25/06/1949	New Zealand	Lord's	D	116	1	7	0	33	1
					6					
35	23/07/1949	New Zealand	Old Trafford	D	25		6	0	28	1
							8	0	28	1
36	13/08/1949	New Zealand	The Oval	D	13		2	0	6	1
						1	1	0	3	0
37	12/08/1950	West Indies	The Oval	L	44		7	2	21	0
					11					
38	01/12/1950	Australia	Brisbane (2)	L	3					
					0					
39	05/01/1951	Australia	Sydney	L	0		6	1	14	0
					23					
40	02/02/1951	Australia	Adelaide	L	5	1	1	0	11	0
					0		4.6	1	18	1

No	Date	Opposition	Venue	R	Bat	C		Bowling		
41	23/02/1951	Australia	Melbourne	W	11	1				
					11*	1				
42	17/03/1951	New Zealand	Christchurch	D	79		4	0	21	0
							2	0	10	0
43	24/03/1951	New Zealand	Wellington	W	10	1				
					18					
44	07/06/1951	South Africa	Trent Bridge	L	112	1	2	0	7	0
					5					
45	21/06/1951	South Africa	Lord's	W	79					
						1	2	0	13	0
46	26/07/1951	South Africa	Headingley	D	25		1	0	4	0
							7	1	16	0
47	16/08/1951	South Africa	The Oval	W	73		1	0	5	0
					18					
48	05/06/1952	India	Headingley	W	14		7	1	20	0
					35*	1				
49	19/06/1952	India	Lord's	W	6					
					4*	1	2	0	10	0
50	11/06/1953	Australia	Trent Bridge	D	0	1				
51	25/06/1953	Australia	Lord's	D	57	1				
					33		3	0	21	1
52	09/07/1953	Australia	Old Trafford	D	45	1				
53	23/07/1953	Australia	Headingley	D	0					
					61					
54	15/08/1953	Australia	The Oval	W	16					
					22*	1				
55	15/01/1954	West Indies	Kingston	L	12		2	1	5	0
					2					
56	06/02/1954	West Indies	Bridgetown	L	13		5	0	29	0
					93		1	0	13	0
57	24/02/1954	West Indies	Georgetown	W	64		3	1	6	0
						1				
58	17/03/1954	West Indies	Port-of-Spain	D	133	2	8.4	1	40	2
							7	0	51	0
59	30/03/1954	West Indies	Kingston	W	31					
						1				
60	10/06/1954	Pakistan	Lord's	D	0	1				
							13	2	36	1
61	01/07/1954	Pakistan	Trent Bridge	W	278	1				
						1				
62	22/07/1954	Pakistan	Old Trafford	D	93	1				
63	12/08/1954	Pakistan	The Oval	L	53	1				
					29					
64	26/11/1954	Australia	Brisbane (2)	L	2*					
					0					
65	31/12/1954	Australia	Melbourne	W	4					
					23					
66	28/01/1955	Australia	Adelaide	W	44					
					34*					
67	25/02/1955	Australia	Sydney	D	84					
68	09/06/1955	South Africa	Trent Bridge	W	27					
						1				
69	23/06/1955	South Africa	Lord's	W	20					
					69					
70	07/07/1955	South Africa	Old Trafford	L	158					
					71					
71	21/07/1955	South Africa	Headingley	L	61					
					26					
72	13/08/1955	South Africa	The Oval	W	30					
					30					
73	23/08/1956	Australia	The Oval	D	94					
					35*					
74	24/12/1956	South Africa	Johannesburg (3)	W	5					
					32					
75	01/01/1957	South Africa	Cape Town	W	58					
					64		2	1	3	0
76	25/01/1957	South Africa	Durban (2)	D	16					
					19		1	0	5	0
77	15/02/1957	South Africa	Johannesburg (3)	L	42					
					1					
78	01/03/1957	South Africa	Port Elizabeth	L	0					
					5					

Batting & Fielding

Mat	Inns	N/O	Runs	H/S	Avg	100s	50s	Cat
78	131	15	5807	278	50.06	17	28	49

Bowling

Balls	Runs	Wkts	Avg	Best	5WI	10WM	S/R
2716	1410	25	56.40	5-70	1	0	108.64

C.COOK

Full Name: Cecil Cook (known as Sam)
Born: 23/08/1921, Tetbury, Gloucestershire
Teams: Gloucestershire 1946-64, England 1947
Matches: 1 (Won 0, Drew 1, Lost 0)
Right-hand lower order batsman – Left-arm slow bowler

No	Date	Opposition	Venue	R	Bat	C		Bowling		
1	07/06/1947	South Africa	Trent Bridge	D	0		21	4	87	0
					4		9	0	40	0

Batting & Fielding

Mat	Inns	N/O	Runs	H/S	Avg	100s	50s	Cat
1	2	0	4	4	2.00	0	0	0

Bowling

Balls	Runs	Wkts	Avg	Best	5WI	10WM	S/R
180	127	0	–	0-40	0	0	–

G.COOK

Full Name: Geoffrey Cook (known as Geoff)
Born: 09/10/1951, Middlesbrough, Yorkshire
Teams: Northamptonshire 1971-90, Eastern Province 1978/79-80/81, England 1982-83
Matches: 7 (Won 3, Drew 4, Lost 0)
Right-hand opening batsman – Left-arm slow bowler

No	Date	Opposition	Venue	R	Bat	C		Bowling		
1	17/02/1982	Sri Lanka	Colombo (1)	W	11	2				
					0	1				
2	10/06/1982	India	Lord's	W	4	2				
					10	2	1	0	4	0
3	24/06/1982	India	Old Trafford	D	66	1				
4	08/07/1982	India	The Oval	D	50					
					8					
5	12/11/1982	Australia	Perth	D	1	1	4	2	16	0
					7					
6	26/12/1982	Australia	Melbourne	W	10					
					26					
7	02/01/1983	Australia	Sydney	D	8					
					2		2	1	7	0

Batting & Fielding

Mat	Inns	N/O	Runs	H/S	Avg	100s	50s	Cat
7	13	0	203	66	15.61	0	2	9

Bowling

Balls	Runs	Wkts	Avg	Best	5WI	10WM	S/R
42	27	0	–	0-4	0	0	–

N.G.B.COOK

Full Name: Nicholas Grant Billson Cook (known as Nick)
Born: 17/06/1956, Leicester
Teams: Leicestershire 1978-85, Northamptonshire 1986-96, England 1983-89
Matches: 15 (Won 2, Drew 6, Lost 7)
Right-hand lower order batsman – Left-arm slow bowler

No	Date	Opposition	Venue	R	Bat	C		Bowling		
1	11/08/1983	New Zealand	Lord's	W	16	1	26	11	35	5
					5		27.2	9	90	3

No	Date	Opposition	Venue	R	Bat	C		Bowling		
2	25/08/1983	New Zealand	Trent Bridge	W	4	2	32	14	63	5
					26		50	22	87	4
3	20/01/1984	New Zealand	Wellington	D	7	1	23	11	43	1
							66.3	26	153	3
4	02/03/1984	Pakistan	Karachi (1)	L	9		30	12	65	6
					5		14	8	18	5
5	12/03/1984	Pakistan	Faisalabad	D	1*		54	14	133	2
							16	6	38	0
6	19/03/1984	Pakistan	Lahore (2)	D	3		46	12	117	1
							18.3	2	73	0
7	14/06/1984	West Indies	Edgbaston	L	2		38	6	127	1
					9					
8	12/07/1984	West Indies	Headingley	L	1		9	1	29	1
					0		9	2	27	2
9	26/07/1984	West Indies	Old Trafford	L	13	1	39	6	114	1
					0					
10	25/11/1987	Pakistan	Lahore (2)	L	10		31	10	87	3
					5					
11	07/12/1987	Pakistan	Faisalabad	D	2		20.3	10	37	2
							9	3	15	1
12	16/12/1987	Pakistan	Karachi (1)	D	2		33	12	56	1
					14					
13	27/07/1989	Australia	Old Trafford	L	0*		28	6	85	2
					5		4.5	0	18	0
14	10/08/1989	Australia	Trent Bridge	L	2*		40	10	91	3
					7*					
15	24/08/1989	Australia	The Oval	D	31		25	5	78	0
							6	2	10	0

Batting & Fielding

Mat	Inns	N/O	Runs	H/S	Avg	100s	50s	Cat
15	25	4	179	31	8.52	0	0	5

Bowling

Balls	Runs	Wkts	Avg	Best	5WI	10WM	S/R
4174	1689	52	32.48	6-65	4	1	80.26

G.A.COPE

Full Name: Geoffrey Alan Cope (known as Geoff)
Born: 23/02/1947, Burmantofts, Leeds, Yorkshire
Teams: Yorkshire 1966-80, England 1977-78
Matches: 3 (Won 0, Drew 3, Lost 0)
Right-hand lower order batsman – Off break bowler

No	Date	Opposition	Venue	R	Bat	C		Bowling		
1	14/12/1977	Pakistan	Lahore (2)	D	0	1	39	6	102	3
							3	0	7	0
2	02/01/1978	Pakistan	Hyderabad	D	22		14	6	49	2
							24	9	42	2
3	18/01/1978	Pakistan	Karachi (1)	-	D	18		28	8	77	1

Batting & Fielding

Mat	Inns	N/O	Runs	H/S	Avg	100s	50s	Cat
3	3	0	40	22	13.33	0	0	1

Bowling

Balls	Runs	Wkts	Avg	Best	5WI	10WM	S/R
864	277	8	34.62	3-102	0	0	108.00

W.H.COPSON

Full Name: William Henry Copson (known as Bill)
Born: 27/04/1908, Stonebroom, Derbyshire
Died: 13/09/1971, Clay Cross, Derbyshire
Teams: Derbyshire 1932-50, England 1939-47
Matches: 3 (Won 1, Drew 2, Lost 0)
Right-hand lower order batsman – Right-arm fast medium bowler

No	Date	Opposition	Venue	R	Bat	C		Bowling		
1	24/06/1939	West Indies	Lord's	W			24	2	85	5
						1	16.4	2	67	4
2	22/07/1939	West Indies	Old Trafford	D			9	2	31	2
							3	1	2	1

No	Date	Opposition	Venue	R	Bat	C		Bowling		
3	16/08/1947	South Africa	The Oval	D	6		27	13	46	3
							30	11	66	0

Batting & Fielding

Mat	Inns	N/O	Runs	H/S	Avg	100s	50s	Cat
3	1	0	6	6	6.00	0	0	1

Bowling

Balls	Runs	Wkts	Avg	Best	5WI	10WM	S/R
762	297	15	19.80	5-85	1	0	50.80

D.G.CORK

Full Name: Dominic Gerald Cork
Born: 07/08/1971, Newcastle-under-Lyme, Staffordshire
Teams: Derbyshire 1990-96, England 1995-96
Matches: 16 (Won 3, Drew 9, Lost 4)
Right-hand middle/lower order batsman – Right-arm fast medium bowler

No	Date	Opposition	Venue	R	Bat	C		Bowling		
1	22/06/1995	West Indies	Lord's	W	30		22	4	72	1
					23		19.3	5	43	7
2	06/07/1995	West Indies	Edgbaston	L	4		22	5	69	4
					16					
3	27/07/1995	West Indies	Old Trafford	W	56*	1	20	1	86	4
							23.5	2	111	4
4	10/08/1995	West Indies	Trent Bridge	D	31		36	9	110	2
					4		5	1	25	1
5	24/08/1995	West Indies	The Oval	D	33		36	3	145	3
6	16/11/1995	South Africa	Centurion	D	13					
7	30/11/1995	South Africa	Johannesburg (3)	D	8		32	7	84	5
							31.3	6	78	4
8	14/12/1995	South Africa	Durban (2)	D	23*		27	12	64	0
9	26/12/1995	South Africa	Port Elizabeth	D	1		43.2	12	113	4
						1	26.3	5	63	3
10	02/01/1996	South Africa	Cape Town	L	16		25	6	60	3
					8		4	0	23	0
11	06/06/1996	India	Edgbaston	W	4		20.1	5	61	4
							19	5	40	2
12	20/06/1996	India	Lord's	D	0		42.3	10	112	2
					1					
13	04/07/1996	India	Trent Bridge	D	32*	1	32	6	124	1
						1	7	0	32	1
14	25/07/1996	Pakistan	Lord's	L	3		28	6	100	2
					3		24	4	86	3
15	08/08/1996	Pakistan	Headingley	D	26	1	37	6	113	5
						1	16	2	49	1
16	22/08/1996	Pakistan	The Oval	L	0	1	23	5	71	1
					26		3	0	15	0

Batting & Fielding

Mat	Inns	N/O	Runs	H/S	Avg	100s	50s	Cat
16	23	3	361	56*	18.05	0	1	7

Bowling

Balls	Runs	Wkts	Avg	Best	5WI	10WM	S/R
3752	1949	67	29.08	7-43	3	0	56.00

W.L.CORNFORD

Full Name: Walter Latter Cornford (known as Tich)
Born: 25/12/1900, Hurst Green, Sussex
Died: 06/02/1964, Elm Grove, Brighton, Sussex
Teams: Sussex 1921-47, England 1930
Matches: 4 (Won 1, Drew 3, Lost 0)
Right-hand lower order batsman – Wicket-keeper

No	Date	Opposition	Venue	R	Bat	C	St	B
1+	10/01/1930	New Zealand	Christchurch	W	6	1		7
							1	9
2+	24/01/1930	New Zealand	Wellington	D	10	2	1	17
								1
3+	14/02/1930	New Zealand	Auckland	D				0
4+	21/02/1930	New Zealand	Auckland	D	18	2	1	31
					2			

Batting & Fielding

Mat	Inns	N/O	Runs	H/S	Avg	100s	50s	Cat	St	Byes
4	4	0	36	18	9.00	0	0	5	3	65

R.M.H.COTTAM

Full Name: Robert Michael Henry Cottam (known as Bob)
Born: 16/10/1944, Cleethorpes, Lincolnshire
Teams: Hampshire 1963-71, Northamptonshire 1972-76, England 1969-72
Matches: 4 (Won 1, Drew 2, Lost 1)
Right-hand lower order batsman – Right-arm fast medium bowler

No	Date	Opposition	Venue	R	Bat	C	Bowling			
1	21/02/1969	Pakistan	Lahore (2)	D	4*		22.2	5	50	4
						1	13	1	35	2
2	28/02/1969	Pakistan	Dacca	D	4	1	27.1	6	52	2
							30	17	43	1
3	20/12/1972	India	Delhi	W	3		23	5	66	2
							7	1	18	0
4	30/12/1972	India	Calcutta	L	3		23	6	45	3
					13		5	0	18	0

Batting & Fielding

Mat	Inns	N/O	Runs	H/S	Avg	100s	50s	Cat
4	5	1	27	13	6.75	0	0	2

Bowling

Balls	Runs	Wkts	Avg	Best	5WI	10WM	S/R
903	327	14	23.35	4-50	0	0	64.50

Hon.C.J.COVENTRY

Full Name: Hon.Charles John Coventry
Born: 26/02/1867, Marylebone, London
Died: 02/06/1929, Earl's Croome, Worcestershire
Teams: England 1889
Matches: 2 (Won 2, Drew 0, Lost 0)
Right-hand lower order batsman

No	Date	Opposition	Venue	R	Bat	C
1	12/03/1889	South Africa	Port Elizabeth	W	12	
2	25/03/1889	South Africa	Cape Town	W	1*	

Batting & Fielding

Mat	Inns	N/O	Runs	H/S	Avg	100s	50s	Cat
2	2	1	13	12	13.00	0	0	0

N.G.COWANS

Full Name: Norman George Cowans
Born: 17/04/1961, Enfield, St Mary, Jamaica
Teams: Middlesex 1980-93, Hampshire 1994-95, England 1982-85
Matches: 19 (Won 7, Drew 6, Lost 6)
Right-hand lower order batsman – Right-arm fast bowler

No	Date	Opposition	Venue	R	Bat	C	Bowling			
1	12/11/1982	Australia	Perth	D	4		13	2	54	0
					36	1	3	1	15	0
2	26/11/1982	Australia	Brisbane (2)	L	10		6	0	36	0
					5		9	1	31	1
3	26/12/1982	Australia	Melbourne	W	3		16	0	69	2
					10	1	26	6	77	6

No	Date	Opposition	Venue	R	Bat	C	Bowling			
4	02/01/1983	Australia	Sydney	D	0*	1	21	3	67	1
							13	1	47	1
5	14/07/1983	New Zealand	The Oval	W	3		19	3	60	1
							11	2	41	0
6	28/07/1983	New Zealand	Headingley	L	0		28	8	88	3
					10		5	0	23	0
7	11/08/1983	New Zealand	Lord's	W	1*		9	1	30	0
					1		11	1	36	2
8	25/08/1983	New Zealand	Trent Bridge	W	7		21	8	74	3
					0		21	2	95	3
9	03/02/1984	New Zealand	Christchurch	L	4		14	2	52	3
					7					
10	10/02/1984	New Zealand	Auckland	D	21	1	36	11	98	2
					2		1		4	0
11	02/03/1984	Pakistan	Karachi (1)	L	1*	1	12	3	34	0
					0*	1	2.3	1	10	0
12	19/03/1984	Pakistan	Lahore (2)	D	3*		29	5	89	2
					3		14	2	42	5
13	26/07/1984	West Indies	Old Trafford	L	0	1	19	2	76	0
					14					
14	28/11/1984	India	Bombay (3)	L	0		28	6	109	2
					0		5	2	18	1
15	12/12/1984	India	Delhi	W	0*		20	5	70	0
							13	2	43	2
16	31/12/1984	India	Calcutta	D	1		41	12	103	3
							4	1	6	0
17	13/01/1985	India	Madras (1)	W		1	12.5	3	39	2
						1	15	1	73	2
18	31/01/1985	India	Kanpur	D	9		36	9	115	2
							7	0	51	0
19	13/06/1985	Australia	Headingley	W	22*		20	4	78	1
							13	2	50	1

Batting & Fielding

Mat	Inns	N/O	Runs	H/S	Avg	100s	50s	Cat
19	29	7	175	36	7.95	0	0	9

Bowling

Balls	Runs	Wkts	Avg	Best	5WI	10WM	S/R
3452	2003	51	39.27	6-77	2	0	67.68

C.S.COWDREY

Full Name: Christopher Stuart Cowdrey (known as Chris)
Born: 20/10/1957, Farnborough, Kent
Teams: Kent 1977-91, Glamorgan 1992, England 1984-88
Matches: 6 (Won 2, Drew 2, Lost 2)
England Captain: Once 1988 (Won 0, Drew 0, Lost 1) **Toss:** 0-1
Right-hand middle order batsman – Right-arm medium bowler

No	Date	Opposition	Venue	R	Bat	C	Bowling			
1	28/11/1984	India	Bombay (3)	L	13	1	5	0	30	1
					14					
2	12/12/1984	India	Delhi	W	38					
3	31/12/1984	India	Calcutta	D	27	1	2	0	15	0
							4	0	10	0
4	13/01/1985	India	Madras (1)	W	3*	1	19	1	65	2
						2	5	0	26	0
5	31/01/1985	India	Kanpur	D	1		21	1	103	1
							5	0	39	0
6*	21/07/1988	West Indies	Headingley	L	0		2	0	8	0
					5		3.3	0	13	0

Batting & Fielding

Mat	Inns	N/O	Runs	H/S	Avg	100s	50s	Cat
6	8	1	101	38	14.42	0	0	5

Bowling

Balls	Runs	Wkts	Avg	Best	5WI	10WM	S/R
399	309	4	77.25	2-65	0	0	99.75

M.C.COWDREY

Full Name: Sir Michael Colin Cowdrey (known as Colin)
Born: 24/12/1932, Bangalore, India
Teams: Oxford University 1952-54, Kent 1950-76, England 1954-75
Matches: 114 (Won 43, Drew 50, Lost 21)
England Captain: 27 times 1959-69 (Won 8, Drew 15, Lost 4) **Toss:** 17-10
Right-hand middle order batsman – Leg break bowler

No	Date	Opposition	Venue	R	Bat	C	Bowling
1	26/11/1954	Australia	Brisbane (2)	L	40 10	2	
2	17/12/1954	Australia	Sydney	W	23 54	1	
3	31/12/1954	Australia	Melbourne	W	102 7	1	
4	28/01/1955	Australia	Adelaide	W	79 4		
5	25/02/1955	Australia	Sydney	D	0		
6	11/03/1955	New Zealand	Dunedin	W	42 0*	1	
7	25/03/1955	New Zealand	Auckland	W	22		
8	07/07/1955	South Africa	Old Trafford	L	1 50		
9	07/06/1956	Australia	Trent Bridge	D	25 81		
10	21/06/1956	Australia	Lord's	L	23 27	1	
11	12/07/1956	Australia	Headingley	W	0		
12	26/07/1956	Australia	Old Trafford	W	80	1 1	
13	23/08/1956	Australia	The Oval	D	0 8		
14	24/12/1956	South Africa	Johannesburg (3)	W	59 6	3	
15	01/01/1957	South Africa	Cape Town	W	101 61	1	
16	25/01/1957	South Africa	Durban (2)	D	6 24	1 1	
17	15/02/1957	South Africa	Johannesburg (3)	L	8 55	1 2	
18	01/03/1957	South Africa	Port Elizabeth	L	3 8		
19	30/05/1957	West Indies	Edgbaston	D	4 154	1	
20	20/06/1957	West Indies	Lord's	W	152	2	
21	04/07/1957	West Indies	Trent Bridge	D	55		
22	25/07/1957	West Indies	Headingley	W	68	1 2	
23	22/08/1957	West Indies	The Oval	W	2	1 1	
24	05/06/1958	New Zealand	Edgbaston	W	81 70		
25	19/06/1958	New Zealand	Lord's	W	65	1 1 1	
26	03/07/1958	New Zealand	Headingley	W		2 1	
27	21/08/1958	New Zealand	The Oval	D	25	1	
28	05/12/1958	Australia	Brisbane (2)	L	13 28	1	
29	31/12/1958	Australia	Melbourne	L	44 12		
30	09/01/1959	Australia	Sydney	D	34 100*	1	
31	30/01/1959	Australia	Adelaide	L	84 8	1	1.3 0 9 0
32	13/02/1959	Australia	Melbourne	L	22 46	3	

No	Date	Opposition	Venue	R	Bat	C	Bowling			
33	27/02/1959	New Zealand	Christchurch	W	15	1				
34	14/03/1959	New Zealand	Auckland	D	5	1				
35	04/06/1959	India	Trent Bridge	W	5	1				
36	18/06/1959	India	Lord's	W	34 / 63*					
37	02/07/1959	India	Headingley	W	160	1 / 2				
38*	23/07/1959	India	Old Trafford	W	67 / 9	1				
39*	20/08/1959	India	The Oval	W	6	1 / 1				
40	06/01/1960	West Indies	Bridgetown	D	30 / 16*					
41	28/01/1960	West Indies	Port-of-Spain	W	18 / 5					
42	17/02/1960	West Indies	Kingston	D	114 / 97		1	0	4	0
43*	09/03/1960	West Indies	Georgetown	D	65 / 27					
44*	25/03/1960	West Indies	Port-of-Spain	D	119 / 0	1	1	0	15	0
45*	09/06/1960	South Africa	Edgbaston	W	3 / 0	1				
46*	23/06/1960	South Africa	Lord's	W	4	2				
47*	07/07/1960	South Africa	Trent Bridge	W	67 / 27	2				
48*	21/07/1960	South Africa	Old Trafford	D	20 / 25		1	0	4	0
49*	18/08/1960	South Africa	The Oval	D	11 / 155	1 / 1				
50*	08/06/1961	Australia	Edgbaston	D	13 / 14					
51*	22/06/1961	Australia	Lord's	L	16 / 7					
52	06/07/1961	Australia	Headingley	W	93 / 22	2 / 2				
53	17/08/1961	Australia	The Oval	D	0 / 3					
54	31/05/1962	Pakistan	Edgbaston	W	159	1 / 2	1	0	1	0
55	21/06/1962	Pakistan	Lord's	W	41 / 20	3				
56*	05/07/1962	Pakistan	Headingley	W	7	1				
57	16/08/1962	Pakistan	The Oval	W	182	1 / 1				
58	30/11/1962	Australia	Brisbane (2)	D	21 / 9					
59	29/12/1962	Australia	Melbourne	W	113 / 58*	2				
60	11/01/1963	Australia	Sydney	L	85 / 8					
61	25/01/1963	Australia	Adelaide	D	13 / 32	2 / 1				
62	15/02/1963	Australia	Sydney	D	2 / 53					
63	23/02/1963	New Zealand	Auckland	W	86					
64	01/03/1963	New Zealand	Wellington	W	128*	1				
65	15/03/1963	New Zealand	Christchurch	W	43 / 35*					
66	06/06/1963	West Indies	Old Trafford	L	4 / 12					
67	20/06/1963	West Indies	Lord's	D	4 / 19*	3 / 3				
68	29/01/1964	India	Calcutta	D	107 / 13*	2 / 1				
69	08/02/1964	India	Delhi	D	151					

No	Date	Opposition	Venue	R	Bat	C	Bowling
70	15/02/1964	India	Kanpur	D	38	1	5 0 34 0
71	04/06/1964	Australia	Trent Bridge	D	32 33		
72	18/06/1964	Australia	Lord's	D	10		
73	13/08/1964	Australia	The Oval	D	20 93*	2	
74	27/05/1965	New Zealand	Edgbaston	W	85		
75	17/06/1965	New Zealand	Lord's	W	119 4*		
76	08/07/1965	New Zealand	Headingley	W	13	2	
77	22/07/1965	South Africa	Lord's	D	29 37	1	
78	05/08/1965	South Africa	Trent Bridge	L	105 20	2 1	
79	26/08/1965	South Africa	The Oval	D	58 78*	1	
80	30/12/1965	Australia	Melbourne	D	104	1	
81	07/01/1966	Australia	Sydney	W	0	2 2	
82	28/01/1966	Australia	Adelaide	L	38 35		
83	11/02/1966	Australia	Melbourne	D	79 11*		
84	25/02/1966	New Zealand	Christchurch	D	0 21	1 1	
85	04/03/1966	New Zealand	Dunedin	D	89*		
86	11/03/1966	New Zealand	Auckland	D	59 27		
87	02/06/1966	West Indies	Old Trafford	L	12 69	1	
88*	16/06/1966	West Indies	Lord's	D	9 5		
89*	30/06/1966	West Indies	Trent Bridge	L	96 32	1 1	
90*	04/08/1966	West Indies	Headingley	L	17 12		
91	10/08/1967	Pakistan	Trent Bridge	W	14 2*		
92	24/08/1967	Pakistan	The Oval	W	16 9	1	
93*	19/01/1968	West Indies	Port-of-Spain	D	72	1	1 0 1 0
94*	08/02/1968	West Indies	Kingston	D	101 0		
95*	29/02/1968	West Indies	Bridgetown	D	1	1	
96*	14/03/1968	West Indies	Port-of-Spain	W	148 71		
97*	28/03/1968	West Indies	Georgetown	D	59 82	1	
98*	06/06/1968	Australia	Old Trafford	L	4 11	1	
99*	20/06/1968	Australia	Lord's	D	45	3	
100*	11/07/1968	Australia	Edgbaston	D	104		
101*	22/08/1968	Australia	The Oval	W	16 35	1	
102*	21/02/1969	Pakistan	Lahore (2)	D	100 12		
103*	28/02/1969	Pakistan	Dacca	D	7		
104*	06/03/1969	Pakistan	Karachi (1)	D	14		
105	27/11/1970	Australia	Brisbane (2)	D	28	2	1 0 10 0 2 0 8 0
106	11/12/1970	Australia	Perth	D	40 1		3 0 18 0

No	Date	Opposition	Venue	R	Bat	C	Bowling
107	21/01/1971	Australia	Melbourne	D	13	1	
108	05/03/1971	New Zealand	Auckland	D	54		
					45		
109	03/06/1971	Pakistan	Edgbaston	D	16	1	
					34		
110	13/12/1974	Australia	Perth	L	22		
					41		
111	26/12/1974	Australia	Melbourne	D	35	1	
					8		
112	04/01/1975	Australia	Sydney	L	22		
					1		
113	25/01/1975	Australia	Adelaide	L	26	1	
					3		
114	08/02/1975	Australia	Melbourne	W	7		
						1	

Batting & Fielding

Mat	Inns	N/O	Runs	H/S	Avg	100s	50s	Cat
114	188	15	7624	182	44.06	22	38	120

Bowling

Balls	Runs	Wkts	Avg	Best	5WI	10WM	S/R
119	104	0	–	0-1	0	0	–

A.COXON

Full Name: Alexander Coxon (known as Alec)
Born: 18/01/1916, Huddersfield, Yorkshire
Teams: Yorkshire 1945-50, England 1948
Matches: 1 (Won 0, Drew 0, Lost 1)
Right-hand lower order batsman – Right-arm fast medium bowler

No	Date	Opposition	Venue	R	Bat	C	Bowling		
1	24/06/1948	Australia	Lord's	L	19	35	10	90	2
					0	28	3	82	1

Batting & Fielding

Mat	Inns	N/O	Runs	H/S	Avg	100s	50s	Cat
1	2	0	19	19	9.50	0	0	0

Bowling

Balls	Runs	Wkts	Avg	Best	5WI	10WM	S/R
378	172	3	57.33	2-90	0	0	126.00

J.CRANSTON

Full Name: James Cranston
Born: 09/01/1859, Bordesley, Birmingham
Died: 10/12/1904, Bristol
Teams: Gloucestershire 1876-99, England 1890
Matches: 1 (Won 1, Drew 0, Lost 0)
Left-hand middle order batsman

No	Date	Opposition	Venue	R	Bat	C
1	11/08/1890	Australia	The Oval	W	16	
					15	1

Batting & Fielding

Mat	Inns	N/O	Runs	H/S	Avg	100s	50s	Cat
1	2	0	31	16	15.50	0	0	1

K.CRANSTON

Full Name: Kenneth Cranston (known as Ken)
Born: 20/10/1917, Aigburth, Liverpool, Lancashire
Teams: Lancashire 1947-48, England 1947-48
Matches: 8 (Won 2, Drew 3, Lost 3)
England Captain: Once 1948 (Won 0, Drew 1, Lost 0) **Toss:** 0-1
Right-hand middle order batsman – Right-arm medium bowler

No	Date	Opposition	Venue	R	Bat	C		Bowling		
1	05/07/1947	South Africa	Old Trafford	W	23		34	12	64	2
2	26/07/1947	South Africa	Headingley	W	3	1	11.1	3	24	1
							7	3	12	4
3	16/08/1947	South Africa	The Oval	D	45		9	2	25	2
					0		21	3	61	2
4*	21/01/1948	West Indies	Bridgetown	D	2		15	4	29	0
					8		13	3	31	1
5	11/02/1948	West Indies	Port-of-Spain	D	7		7	1	29	1
					6		3	0	18	0
6	03/03/1948	West Indies	Georgetown	L	24		25	5	78	4
					32		2	0	11	0
7	27/03/1948	West Indies	Kingston	L	13					
					36					
8	22/07/1948	Australia	Headingley	L	10	2	14	1	51	0
					0		7.1	0	28	1

Batting & Fielding

Mat	Inns	N/O	Runs	H/S	Avg	100s	50s	Cat
8	14	0	209	45	14.92	0	0	3

Bowling

Balls	Runs	Wkts	Avg	Best	5WI	10WM	S/R
1010	461	18	25.61	4-12	0	0	56.11

J.F.CRAPP

Full Name: John Frederick Crapp (known as Jack)
Born: 14/10/1912, St Columb Major, Cornwall
Died: 13/02/1981, Knowle, Somerset
Teams: Gloucestershire 1936-56, England 1948-49
Matches: 7 (Won 1, Drew 4, Lost 2)
Left-hand middle order batsman

No	Date	Opposition	Venue	R	Bat	C
1	08/07/1948	Australia	Old Trafford	D	37	1
					19*	1
2	22/07/1948	Australia	Headingley	L	5	2
					18	
3	14/08/1948	Australia	The Oval	L	0	2
					9	
4	27/12/1948	South Africa	Johannesburg (2)	D	56	
5	01/01/1949	South Africa	Cape Town	D	35	1
					54	
6	12/02/1949	South Africa	Johannesburg (2)	D	51	
					5	
7	05/03/1949	South Africa	Port Elizabeth	W	4	
					26*	

Batting & Fielding

Mat	Inns	N/O	Runs	H/S	Avg	100s	50s	Cat
7	13	2	319	56	29.00	0	3	7

J.N.CRAWFORD

Full Name: John Neville Crawford (known as Jack)
Born: 01/12/1886, Cane Hill, Surrey
Died: 02/05/1963, Epsom, Surrey
Teams: Surrey 1904-21, South Australia 1909/10-1913/14, Otago 1914/15, Wellington 1917/18, England 1906-08
Matches: 12 (Won 2, Drew 2, Lost 8)
Right-hand middle order batsman – Right-arm medium or off break bowler

No	Date	Opposition	Venue	R	Bat	C		Bowling		
1	02/01/1906	South Africa	Johannesburg (1)	L	44		7	1	14	2
					43	1	17	4	49	0
2	06/03/1906	South Africa	Johannesburg (1)	L	23		11	1	44	2
					6		2	1	4	0
3	10/03/1906	South Africa	Johannesburg (1)	L	4		13	1	51	0
					34	1	4	0	17	0
4	24/03/1906	South Africa	Cape Town	W	36*		13.3	3	28	1
					4	1	15	5	46	1
5	30/03/1906	South Africa	Cape Town	L	74	3	18	3	69	3
					13					

No	Date	Opposition	Venue	R	Bat	C		Bowling			
6	01/07/1907	South Africa	Lord's	D	22			8	1	20	0
								4	0	19	0
7	19/08/1907	South Africa	The Oval	D	2	1		11	2	33	0
					2			6	3	14	0
8	13/12/1907	Australia	Sydney	L	31			5	1	14	0
					5	1		8	2	33	2
9	01/01/1908	Australia	Melbourne	W	16			29	1	79	5
					10			33	6	125	3
10	10/01/1908	Australia	Adelaide	L	62			14	0	65	1
					7			45.5	4	113	3
11	07/02/1908	Australia	Melbourne	L	1	2		23.5	3	48	5
					0			25	5	72	3
12	21/02/1908	Australia	Sydney	L	6	3		18	4	52	3
					24*			36	10	141	5

Batting & Fielding

Mat	Inns	N/O	Runs	H/S	Avg	100s	50s	Cat
12	23	2	469	74	22.33	0	2	13

Bowling

Balls	Runs	Wkts	Avg	Best	5WI	10WM	S/R
2203	1150	39	29.48	5-48	3	0	56.48

J.P.CRAWLEY

Full Name: John Paul Crawley
Born: 21/09/1971, Maldon, Essex
Teams: Cambridge University 1991-92, Lancashire 1990-96, England 1994-96
Matches: 12 (Won 3, Drew 6, Lost 3)
Right-hand middle order batsman – Right-arm medium bowler

No	Date	Opposition	Venue	R	Bat	C
1	21/07/1994	South Africa	Lord's	L	9	1
					7	1
2	04/08/1994	South Africa	Headingley	D	38	2
					0	
3	18/08/1994	South Africa	The Oval	W	5	
4	01/01/1995	Australia	Sydney	D	72	
5	26/01/1995	Australia	Adelaide	W	28	1
					71	
6	03/02/1995	Australia	Perth	L	0	
					0	
7	27/07/1995	West Indies	Old Trafford	W	8	1
					15*	1
8	10/08/1995	West Indies	Trent Bridge	D	14	2
					11	
9	24/08/1995	West Indies	The Oval	D	50	
					2	
10	14/12/1995	South Africa	Durban (2)	D		1
11	08/08/1996	Pakistan	Headingley	D	53	
12	22/08/1996	Pakistan	The Oval	L	106	1
					19	

Batting & Fielding

Mat	Inns	N/O	Runs	H/S	Avg	100s	50s	Cat
12	19	1	508	106	28.22	1	4	11

R.D.B.CROFT

Full Name: Robert Damien Bale Croft
Born: 25/05/1970, Morriston, Glamorgan
Teams: Glamorgan 1989-96, England 1996
Matches: 1 (Won 0, Drew 0, Lost 1)
Right-hand middle/lower order batsman – Off break bowler

No	Date	Opposition	Venue	R	Bat	C		Bowling			
1	22/08/1996	Pakistan	The Oval	L	5*	1		47	10	116	2
					6			0.4	0	9	0

Batting & Fielding

Mat	Inns	N/O	Runs	H/S	Avg	100s	50s	Cat
1	2	1	11	6	11.00	0	0	1

Bowling

Balls	Runs	Wkts	Avg	Best	5WI	10WM	S/R
286	125	2	62.50	2-116	0	0	143.00

T.S.CURTIS

Full Name: Timothy Stephen Curtis (known as Tim)
Born: 15/01/1960, Chislehurst, Kent
Teams: Cambridge University 1983, Worcestershire 1979-96, England 1988-89
Matches: 5 (Won 0, Drew 1, Lost 4)
Right-hand opening batsman – Leg break bowler

No	Date	Opposition	Venue	R	Bat	C	Bowling			
1	21/07/1988	West Indies	Headingley	L	12	1				
					12					
2	04/08/1988	West Indies	The Oval	L	30	1				
					15					
3	06/07/1989	Australia	Edgbaston	D	41					
							3	0	7	0
4	27/07/1989	Australia	Old Trafford	L	22	1				
					0					
5	10/08/1989	Australia	Trent Bridge	L	2					
					6					

Batting & Fielding

Mat	Inns	N/O	Runs	H/S	Avg	100s	50s	Cat
5	9	0	140	41	15.55	0	0	3

Bowling

Balls	Runs	Wkts	Avg	Best	5WI	10WM	S/R
18	7	0	–	0-7	0	0	–

W.R.CUTTELL

Full Name: Willis Robert Cuttell (known as Robert)
Born: 13/09/1864, Sheffield, Yorkshire
Died: 09/12/1929, Nelson, Lancashire
Teams: Lancashire 1896-1906, England 1899
Matches: 2 (Won 2, Drew 0, Lost 0)
Right-hand middle/lower order batsman – Right-arm slow medium leg break bowler

No	Date	Opposition	Venue	R	Bat	C	Bowling			
1	14/02/1899	South Africa	Johannesburg (1)	W	19		17	5	42	2
					21	2	32	24	17	3
2	01/04/1899	South Africa	Cape Town	W	7		8	3	14	1
					18					

Batting & Fielding

Mat	Inns	N/O	Runs	H/S	Avg	100s	50s	Cat
2	4	0	65	21	16.25	0	0	2

Bowling

Balls	Runs	Wkts	Avg	Best	5WI	10WM	S/R
285	73	6	12.16	3-17	0	0	47.50

E.W.DAWSON

Full Name: Edward William Dawson (known as Eddie)
Born: 13/02/1904, Paddington, London
Died: 04/06/1979, Idmiston, Wiltshire
Teams: Cambridge University 1924-27, Leicestershire 1922-34, England 1928-30
Matches: 5 (Won 1, Drew 3, Lost 1)
Right-hand opening batsman

No	Date	Opposition	Venue	R	Bat	C
1	04/02/1928	South Africa	Durban (2)	L	14	
					9	

No	Date	Opposition	Venue	R	Bat	C
2	10/01/1930	New Zealand	Christchurch	W	7	
					10	
3	24/01/1930	New Zealand	Wellington	D	44	
					7	
4	14/02/1930	New Zealand	Auckland	D	23	
5	21/02/1930	New Zealand	Auckland	D	55	
					6	

Batting & Fielding

Mat	Inns	N/O	Runs	H/S	Avg	100s	50s	Cat
5	9	0	175	55	19.44	0	1	0

H.DEAN

Full Name: Harry Dean
Born: 13/08/1884, Burnley, Lancashire
Died: 12/03/1957, Garstang, Lancashire
Teams: Lancashire 1906-21, England 1912
Matches: 3 (Won 2, Drew 1, Lost 0)
Left-hand lower order batsman – Left-arm fast medium bowler

No	Date	Opposition	Venue	R	Bat	C	Bowling		
1	24/06/1912	Australia	Lord's	D			29	10	49	2
2	08/07/1912	South Africa	Headingley	W	2*	1	12.3	1	41	3
					8		8	3	15	2
3	19/08/1912	Australia	The Oval	W	0*		16	7	29	0
					0	1	9	2	19	4

Batting & Fielding

Mat	Inns	N/O	Runs	H/S	Avg	100s	50s	Cat
3	4	2	10	8	5.00	0	0	2

Bowling

Balls	Runs	Wkts	Avg	Best	5WI	10WM	S/R
447	153	11	13.90	4-19	0	0	40.63

P.A.J.DEFREITAS

Full Name: Phillip Anthony Jason DeFreitas (known as Phil)
Born: 18/02/1966 – Scotts Head, Dominica
Teams: Leicestershire 1985-88, Lancashire 1989-1993, Derbyshire 1994-96, England 1986-95
Matches: 44 (Won 10, Drew 16, Lost 18)
Right-hand middle/lower order batsman – Right-arm fast medium bowler

No	Date	Opposition	Venue	R	Bat	C	Bowling		
1	14/11/1986	Australia	Brisbane (2)	W	40	1	16	5	32	2
							17	2	62	3
2	28/11/1986	Australia	Perth	D	11		24	4	67	1
					15		13.4	2	47	0
3	12/12/1986	Australia	Adelaide	D	4*		32	4	128	1
							16	5	36	1
4	26/12/1986	Australia	Melbourne	W	7		11	1	30	0
							12	1	44	1
5	04/06/1987	Pakistan	Old Trafford	D	11		12	4	36	1
6	25/11/1987	Pakistan	Lahore (2)	L	5		29	7	84	1
					15					
7	16/12/1987	Pakistan	Karachi (1)	D	12		23.5	3	86	5
					6					
8	12/02/1988	New Zealand	Christchurch	D	4		22	6	39	2
					16		19	6	26	1
9	03/03/1988	New Zealand	Wellington	D		1	50.1	21	110	1
10	02/06/1988	West Indies	Trent Bridge	D	3		27	5	93	2
11	30/06/1988	West Indies	Old Trafford	L	15		35	5	81	1
					0					
12	04/08/1988	West Indies	The Oval	L	18	2	13	4	33	0
					0		17	2	46	0
13	08/06/1989	Australia	Headingley	L	1		45.3	8	140	2
					21		18	2	76	1

No	Date	Opposition	Venue	R	Bat	C	Bowling			
14	05/04/1990	West Indies	Bridgetown	L	24		29.5	5	99	2
					0		22	2	69	3
15	12/04/1990	West Indies	St John's	L	21	1	27	4	74	1
					0					
16	07/06/1990	New Zealand	Trent Bridge	D	14		22	6	53	5
							2	2	0	1
17	21/06/1990	New Zealand	Lord's	D	38		35.4	1	122	0
18	26/12/1990	Australia	Melbourne	L	3		25	5	69	2
					0		16	3	46	0
19	25/01/1991	Australia	Adelaide	D	45		26.2	6	56	4
					19*		23	6	61	1
20	01/02/1991	Australia	Perth	L	5		16.5	2	57	2
					5		6.2	0	29	1
21	06/06/1991	West Indies	Headingley	W	15		17.1	5	34	4
					3		21	4	59	4
22	20/06/1991	West Indies	Lord's	D	29	1	31	6	93	2
					3		3	2	1	1
23	04/07/1991	West Indies	Trent Bridge	L	8		31.1	9	67	3
					55*		11	3	29	0
24	25/07/1991	West Indies	Edgbaston	L	10		25.3	9	40	2
					7		13	2	54	3
25	08/08/1991	West Indies	The Oval	W	7		13	6	38	1
							20	9	42	2
26	22/08/1991	Sri Lanka	Lord's	W	1		26	8	70	7
							22	8	45	1
27	18/01/1992	New Zealand	Christchurch	W	7*		32.4	16	54	2
							23	6	54	0
28	30/01/1992	New Zealand	Auckland	W	1		16	2	53	2
					0		27	11	62	4
29	06/02/1992	New Zealand	Wellington	D	3		8	4	12	0
30	04/06/1992	Pakistan	Edgbaston	D			33	6	121	4
31	18/06/1992	Pakistan	Lord's	L	3		26	8	58	3
					0					
32	19/02/1993	India	Bombay (3)	L	11	2	20	4	75	0
					12					
33	03/06/1993	Australia	Old Trafford	L	5	1	23	8	46	1
					7		24	1	80	1
34	02/06/1994	New Zealand	Trent Bridge	W	51*		23	4	94	4
							22.3	4	71	5
35	16/06/1994	New Zealand	Lord's	D	11		35	8	102	3
					3		16	0	63	3
36	30/06/1994	New Zealand	Old Trafford	D	69		17	2	61	3
						1	30	6	60	3
37	21/07/1994	South Africa	Lord's	L	20	1	18	5	67	0
					1		14	3	43	0
38	04/08/1994	South Africa	Headingley	D	15		29.1	6	89	4
							14	3	41	1
39	18/08/1994	South Africa	The Oval	W	37		26.2	5	93	4
						1	12	3	25	0
40	25/11/1994	Australia	Brisbane (2)	L	7		31	8	102	2
					11		22	1	74	2
41	24/12/1994	Australia	Melbourne	L	14		23	4	66	2
					0	1	26	2	70	1
42	26/01/1995	Australia	Adelaide	W	21		20	3	70	2
					88		11	3	31	0
43	03/02/1995	Australia	Perth	L	0		29	8	91	3
					0	1	22	10	54	1
44	08/06/1995	West Indies	Headingley	L	23		23	3	82	2
					1		4	0	33	0

Batting & Fielding

Mat	Inns	N/O	Runs	H/S	Avg	100s	50s	Cat
44	68	5	934	88	14.82	0	4	14

Bowling

Balls	Runs	Wkts	Avg	Best	5WI	10WM	S/R
9838	4700	140	33.57	7-70	4	0	70.27

M.H.DENNESS

Full Name: Michael Henry Denness (known as Mike)
Born: 01/12/1940, Bellshill, Lanarkshire, Scotland
Teams: Kent 1962-76, Essex 1977-80, Scotland 1959-67, England 1969-75
Matches: 28 (Won 8, Drew 13, Lost 7)
England Captain: 19 times 1974-75 (Won 6, Drew 8, Lost 5) **Toss:** 9-10
Right-hand opening/middle order batsman – Right-arm medium or off break bowler

No	Date	Opposition	Venue	R	Bat	C
1	21/08/1969	New Zealand	The Oval	W	2	1
					55*	2
2	20/12/1972	India	Delhi	W	16	
					35	
3	30/12/1972	India	Calcutta	L	21	
					32	
4	12/01/1973	India	Madras (1)	L	17	
					76	1
5	25/01/1973	India	Kanpur	D	31	1
6	06/02/1973	India	Bombay (2)	D	29	1
7	02/03/1973	Pakistan	Lahore (2)	D	50	1
					68	
8	16/03/1973	Pakistan	Hyderabad	D	8	
					0	
9	24/03/1973	Pakistan	Karachi (1)	D	47	1
						2
10*	02/02/1974	West Indies	Port-of-Spain	L	9	2
					44	
11*	16/02/1974	West Indies	Kingston	D	67	2
					28	
12*	06/03/1974	West Indies	Bridgetown	D	24	
					0	
13*	22/03/1974	West Indies	Georgetown	D	42	
14*	30/03/1974	West Indies	Port-of-Spain	W	13	
					4	1
15*	06/06/1974	India	Old Trafford	W	26	
					45*	
16*	20/06/1974	India	Lord's	W	118	2
17*	04/07/1974	India	Edgbaston	W	100	
18*	25/07/1974	Pakistan	Headingley	D	9	1
					44	
19*	08/08/1974	Pakistan	Lord's	D	20	
						1
20*	22/08/1974	Pakistan	The Oval	D	18	1
						1
21*	29/11/1974	Australia	Brisbane (2)	L	6	1
					27	
22*	13/12/1974	Australia	Perth	L	2	
					20	
23*	26/12/1974	Australia	Melbourne	D	8	1
					2	2
24*	25/01/1975	Australia	Adelaide	L	51	
					14	
25*	08/02/1975	Australia	Melbourne	W	188	1
						1
26*	20/02/1975	New Zealand	Auckland	W	181	
27*	28/02/1975	New Zealand	Christchurch	D	59*	
28*	10/07/1975	Australia	Edgbaston	L	3	1
					8	

Batting & Fielding

Mat	Inns	N/O	Runs	H/S	Avg	100s	50s	Cat
28	45	3	1667	188	39.69	4	7	28

D.DENTON

Full Name: David Denton
Born: 04/07/1874, Thornes, Wakefield, Yorkshire
Died: 16/02/1950, Thornes, Wakefield, Yorkshire
Teams: Yorkshire 1894-1920, England 1905-10
Matches: 11 (Won 3, Drew 1, Lost 7)
Right-hand middle order batsman – Right-arm fast medium bowler

No	Date	Opposition	Venue	R	Bat	C
1	03/07/1905	Australia	Headingley	D	0	
					12	
2	02/01/1906	South Africa	Johannesburg (1)	L	0	
					34	
3	06/03/1906	South Africa	Johannesburg (1)	L	1	
					4	2
4	10/03/1906	South Africa	Johannesburg (1)	L	4	1
					61	2
5	24/03/1906	South Africa	Cape Town	W	34	
					20	
6	30/03/1906	South Africa	Cape Town	L	4	
					10	
7	01/01/1910	South Africa	Johannesburg (1)	L	28	1
					26	
8	21/01/1910	South Africa	Durban (1)	L	0	
					6	
9	26/02/1910	South Africa	Johannesburg (1)	W	104	
					24	
10	07/03/1910	South Africa	Cape Town	L	0	
					10	
11	11/03/1910	South Africa	Cape Town	W	26	2
					16*	

Batting & Fielding

Mat	Inns	N/O	Runs	H/S	Avg	100s	50s	Cat
11	22	1	424	104	20.19	1	1	8

J.G.DEWES

Full Name: John Gordon Dewes
Born: 11/10/1926, North Latchford, Cheshire
Teams: Cambridge University 1948-50, Middlesex 1948-56, England 1948-50
Matches: 5 (Won 0, Drew 0, Lost 5)
Left-hand opening batsman – Right-arm medium bowler

No	Date	Opposition	Venue	R	Bat	C
1	14/08/1948	Australia	The Oval	L	1	
					10	
2	20/07/1950	West Indies	Trent Bridge	L	0	
					67	
3	12/08/1950	West Indies	The Oval	L	17	
					3	
4	01/12/1950	Australia	Brisbane (2)	L	1	
					9	
5	22/12/1950	Australia	Melbourne	L	8	
					5	

Batting & Fielding

Mat	Inns	N/O	Runs	H/S	Avg	100s	50s	Cat
5	10	0	121	67	12.10	0	1	0

E.R.DEXTER

Full Name: Edward Ralph Dexter (known as Ted)
Born: 15/05/1935, Milan, Italy
Teams: Cambridge University 1956-58, Sussex 1957-68, England 1958-68
Matches: 62 (Won 23, Drew 29, Lost 10)
England Captain: 30 times 1961-64 (Won 9, Drew 14, Lost 7) **Toss:** 13-17
Right-hand middle order batsman – Right-arm medium bowler

No	Date	Opposition	Venue	R	Bat	C		Bowling	
1	24/07/1958	New Zealand	Old Trafford	W	52		5	0 23	0

No	Date	Opposition	Venue	R	Bat	C	Bowling			
2	09/01/1959	Australia	Sydney	D	1					
					11					
3	13/02/1959	Australia	Melbourne	L	0					
					6					
4	27/02/1959	New Zealand	Christchurch	W	141					
							1	0	3	0
5	14/03/1959	New Zealand	Auckland	D	1		19	8	23	3
6	23/07/1959	India	Old Trafford	W	13		3	0	3	0
					45		12	2	33	1
7	20/08/1959	India	The Oval	W	0		16	7	24	2
							7	1	11	0
8	06/01/1960	West Indies	Bridgetown	D	136*		37.4	11	85	2
9	28/01/1960	West Indies	Port-of-Spain	W	77					
					0					
10	17/02/1960	West Indies	Kingston	D	25		6	3	7	2
					16		12	3	38	0
11	09/03/1960	West Indies	Georgetown	D	39	1	5	0	20	0
					110					
12	25/03/1960	West Indies	Port-of-Spain	D	76		4	1	20	1
					47					
13	09/06/1960	South Africa	Edgbaston	W	52		1	0	4	0
					26		6	4	4	0
14	23/06/1960	South Africa	Lord's	W	56					
							4	0	17	2
15	07/07/1960	South Africa	Trent Bridge	W	3					
					0		6	2	12	0
16	21/07/1960	South Africa	Old Trafford	D	38		17	5	41	0
					22					
17	18/08/1960	South Africa	The Oval	D	28		30	5	79	3
					16		0.2	0	0	0
18	08/06/1961	Australia	Edgbaston	D	10	1	5	1	22	0
					180					
19	22/06/1961	Australia	Lord's	L	27		24	7	56	3
					17					
20	06/07/1961	Australia	Headingley	W	28					
						1				
21	27/07/1961	Australia	Old Trafford	L	16		6.4	2	16	3
					76		20	4	61	3
22	17/08/1961	Australia	The Oval	D	24		24	2	68	0
					0					
23*	21/10/1961	Pakistan	Lahore (2)	W	20		7	1	26	0
					66*	1	7	2	10	1
24*	11/11/1961	India	Bombay (2)	D	85		12	4	25	1
					27		4	0	15	0
25*	01/12/1961	India	Kanpur	D	2		31	5	84	2
					126*					
26*	13/12/1961	India	Delhi	D	45*		2	0	11	0
27*	30/12/1961	India	Calcutta	L	57		29	7	83	0
					62					
28*	10/01/1962	India	Madras (2)	L	2		5	0	22	1
					3	2				
29*	19/01/1962	Pakistan	Dacca	D	12		28	12	34	0
						1	5	4	1	0
30*	02/02/1962	Pakistan	Karachi (1)	D	205	1	18.2	4	48	2
						1	32	9	86	3
31*	31/05/1962	Pakistan	Edgbaston	W	72		12	6	23	0
							7	2	16	0
32*	21/06/1962	Pakistan	Lord's	W	65		12	3	41	1
					32*		15	4	44	0
33	05/07/1962	Pakistan	Headingley	W	20		9.1	3	10	4
						1	8	1	24	1
34*	26/07/1962	Pakistan	Trent Bridge	D	85					
							7	0	25	1
35*	16/08/1962	Pakistan	The Oval	W	172					
						1	6	1	16	0
36*	30/11/1962	Australia	Brisbane (2)	D	70	2	10	0	46	1
					99		16	0	78	2
37*	29/12/1962	Australia	Melbourne	W	93		6	1	10	0
					52		9	2	18	1
38*	11/01/1963	Australia	Sydney	L	32					
					11		3.2	0	27	0

No	Date	Opposition	Venue	R	Bat	C	Bowling			
39*	25/01/1963	Australia	Adelaide	D	61		23	1	94	3
					10		17	0	65	3
40*	15/02/1963	Australia	Sydney	D	47		7	1	24	1
					6		4	1	11	0
41*	23/02/1963	New Zealand	Auckland	W	7	1	9	4	20	0
						1				
42*	01/03/1963	New Zealand	Wellington	W	31		1	0	2	0
43*	15/03/1963	New Zealand	Christchurch	W	46	1	9	3	8	0
					10		2	2	18	0
44*	06/06/1963	West Indies	Old Trafford	L	73		12	4	16	0
					35					
45*	20/06/1963	West Indies	Lord's	D	70		20	6	41	0
					2					
46*	04/07/1963	West Indies	Edgbaston	W	29		20	5	38	4
					57		3	1	7	1
47*	25/07/1963	West Indies	Headingley	L	8		23	4	68	1
					10	1	2	0	15	0
48*	22/08/1963	West Indies	The Oval	L	29		6	1	8	0
					27		9	1	34	1
49*	04/06/1964	Australia	Trent Bridge	D	9					
					68					
50*	18/06/1964	Australia	Lord's	D	2	1	7	1	16	2
						1	3	0	5	0
51*	02/07/1964	Australia	Headingley	L	66		19	5	40	0
					17		3	0	9	0
52*	23/07/1964	Australia	Old Trafford	D	174	1	4	0	12	0
53*	13/08/1964	Australia	The Oval	D	23	1	13	1	36	1
					25					
54	04/12/1964	South Africa	Durban (2)	W	28	1				
						2				
55	23/12/1964	South Africa	Johannesburg (3)	D	172		4	0	16	0
						1	8	0	33	1
56	01/01/1965	South Africa	Cape Town	D	61		2	0	10	0
							17	3	64	1
57	22/01/1965	South Africa	Johannesburg (3)	D	38		6	0	30	0
					0					
58	12/02/1965	South Africa	Port Elizabeth	D	40					
					5*					
59	27/05/1965	New Zealand	Edgbaston	W	57	1				
					0*		5	1	18	1
60	17/06/1965	New Zealand	Lord's	W	62		8	2	27	0
					80*					
61	25/07/1968	Australia	Headingley	D	10	1	7	0	25	0
					38		1	0	3	0
62	22/08/1968	Australia	The Oval	W	21	1				
					28					

Batting & Fielding

Mat	Inns	N/O	Runs	H/S	Avg	100s	50s	Cat
62	102	8	4502	205	47.89	9	27	29

Bowling

Balls	Runs	Wkts	Avg	Best	5WI	10WM	S/R
5317	2306	66	34.93	4-10	0	0	80.56

G.R.DILLEY

Full Name: Graham Roy Dilley
Born: 18/05/1959, Dartford, Kent
Teams: Kent 1977-86, Worcestershire 1987-92, Natal 1985/86, England 1979-89
Matches: 41 (Won 2, Drew 24, Lost 15)
Left-hand lower order batsman – Right-arm fast bowler

No	Date	Opposition	Venue	R	Bat	C	Bowling			
1	14/12/1979	Australia	Perth	L	38*		18	1	47	2
					16		18	3	50	1
2	04/01/1980	Australia	Sydney	L	22*		5	1	13	0
					4	1	12	0	33	0
3	10/07/1980	West Indies	Old Trafford	D	0		28	7	47	3

No	Date	Opposition	Venue	R	Bat	C	Bowling			
4	24/07/1980	West Indies	The Oval	D	1		23	6	57	4
					1					
5	07/08/1980	West Indies	Headingley	D	0	1	23	6	79	4
6	13/02/1981	West Indies	Port-of-Spain	L	0		28	4	73	0
					1*					
7	13/03/1981	West Indies	Bridgetown	L	0		23	7	51	3
					7*		25	3	111	1
8	27/03/1981	West Indies	St John's	D	2		25	5	99	2
9	10/04/1981	West Indies	Kingston	D	1*		28.4	6	116	4
10	18/06/1981	Australia	Trent Bridge	L	34		20	7	38	3
					13		11.1	4	24	4
11	02/07/1981	Australia	Lord's	D	7*		30	8	106	3
					27*		7.5	1	18	2
12	16/07/1981	Australia	Headingley	W	13		27	4	78	2
					56	1	2	0	11	0
13	27/11/1981	India	Bombay (3)	L	0		13	1	47	4
					9		18	5	61	1
14	09/12/1981	India	Bangalore	D	52		24	4	75	0
15	13/01/1982	India	Madras (1)	D	8		31	4	87	1
							5	1	13	0
16	30/01/1982	India	Kanpur	D	1	1	14	2	67	1
17	28/07/1983	New Zealand	Headingley	L	0	1	17	4	36	0
					15		8	2	16	0
18	12/03/1984	Pakistan	Faisalabad	D	2*		28	6	101	3
							9	0	41	2
19	05/06/1986	India	Lord's	L	4	1	34	7	146	4
					2*		10	3	28	2
20	19/06/1986	India	Headingley	L	10		24.2	7	54	3
					2		17	2	71	1
21	24/07/1986	New Zealand	Lord's	D	17		35.1	9	82	4
							6	3	5	1
22	21/08/1986	New Zealand	The Oval	D			28.2	4	92	4
23	14/11/1986	Australia	Brisbane (2)	W	0		25.4	7	68	5
						1	19	6	47	1
24	28/11/1986	Australia	Perth	D			24.4	4	79	4
							15	1	53	1
25	12/12/1986	Australia	Adelaide	D	0		32	3	111	1
							21	8	38	1
26	10/01/1987	Australia	Sydney	L	4*		23.5	5	67	2
					2*		15	4	48	1
27	18/06/1987	Pakistan	Lord's	D	17					
28	02/07/1987	Pakistan	Headingley	L	1*		33	7	89	1
					0					
29	23/07/1987	Pakistan	Edgbaston	D	2		35	6	92	5
							18	3	53	2
30	06/08/1987	Pakistan	The Oval	D	0*	2	47.3	10	154	6
31	16/12/1987	Pakistan	Karachi (1)	D	0*		21	2	102	1
					0*					
32	29/01/1988	Australia	Sydney	D	13		19.1	4	54	3
							13	1	48	0
33	12/02/1988	New Zealand	Christchurch	D	7*		24.5	9	38	6
					2		18	5	32	2
34	25/02/1988	New Zealand	Auckland	D	8*		28	9	60	5
							23	9	44	2
35	03/03/1988	New Zealand	Wellington	D			11	1	36	0
36	02/06/1988	West Indies	Trent Bridge	D	2	1	34	5	101	1
37	16/06/1988	West Indies	Lord's	L	0		23	6	55	5
					28		27	6	73	4
38	30/06/1988	West Indies	Old Trafford	L	14		28.1	4	99	4
					4					
39	21/07/1988	West Indies	Headingley	L	8		20	5	59	1
					2*		4	0	16	0
40	22/06/1989	Australia	Lord's	L	7		34	3	141	2
					24		10	2	27	1
41	06/07/1989	Australia	Edgbaston	D	11*		31	3	123	2
							10	4	27	0

Batting & Fielding

Mat	Inns	N/O	Runs	H/S	Avg	100s	50s	Cat
41	58	19	521	56	13.35	0	2	10

Bowling

Balls	Runs	Wkts	Avg	Best	5WI	10WM	S/R
8192	4107	138	29.76	6-38	6	0	59.36

A.E.DIPPER

Full Name: Alfred Ernest Dipper (known as Alf)
Born: 09/11/1885, Apperley, Gloucestershire
Died: 07/11/1945, Lambeth, London
Teams: Gloucestershire 1908-32, England 1921
Matches: 1 (Won 0, Drew 0, Lost 1)
Right-hand opening batsman – Right-arm medium bowler

No	Date	Opposition	Venue	R	Bat	C
1	11/06/1921	Australia	Lord's	L	11	
					40	

Batting & Fielding

Mat	Inns	N/O	Runs	H/S	Avg	100s	50s	Cat
1	2	0	51	40	25.50	0	0	0

G.H.G.DOGGART

Full Name: George Hubert Graham Doggart (known as Hubert)
Born: 18/07/1925, Earl's Court, London
Teams: Cambridge University 1948-50, Sussex 1948-61, England 1950
Matches: 2 (Won 1, Drew 0, Lost 1)
Right-hand middle order batsman – Off break bowler

No	Date	Opposition	Venue	R	Bat	C
1	08/06/1950	West Indies	Old Trafford	W	29	1
					22	1
2	24/06/1950	West Indies	Lord's	L	0	
					25	1

Batting & Fielding

Mat	Inns	N/O	Runs	H/S	Avg	100s	50s	Cat
2	4	0	76	29	19.00	0	0	3

B.L.D'OLIVEIRA

Full Name: Basil Lewis D'Oliveira, OBE
Born: 04/10/1931, Signal Hill, Cape Town, South Africa
Teams: Worcestershire 1964-80, England 1966-72
Matches: 44 (Won 17, Drew 21, Lost 6)
Right-hand middle order batsman – Right-arm medium or off break bowler

No	Date	Opposition	Venue	R	Bat	C		Bowling		
1	16/06/1966	West Indies	Lord's	D	27		14	5	24	1
							25	7	46	1
2	30/06/1966	West Indies	Trent Bridge	L	76		30	14	51	2
					54		34	8	77	2
3	04/08/1966	West Indies	Headingley	L	88		19	3	52	0
					7					
4	18/08/1966	West Indies	The Oval	W	4	1	21	7	35	1
						1	17	4	44	1
5	08/06/1967	India	Headingley	W	109	1	9	4	29	1
					24*	1	11	5	22	0
6	22/06/1967	India	Lord's	W	33		15	6	38	2
						2				
7	27/07/1967	Pakistan	Lord's	D	59	1	15	7	17	0
					81*					
8	10/08/1967	Pakistan	Trent Bridge	W	7		18	9	27	1
9	24/08/1967	Pakistan	The Oval	W	3	1	17	6	41	0
						1				
10	19/01/1968	West Indies	Port-of-Spain	D	32	1	27	13	49	1
							5	2	21	0

No	Date	Opposition	Venue	R	Bat	C	O	M	R	W
11	08/02/1968	West Indies	Kingston	D	0	2				
					13*		32	12	51	2
12	29/02/1968	West Indies	Bridgetown	D	51		19	5	36	0
							4	0	19	0
13	14/03/1968	West Indies	Port-of-Spain	W	0		15	2	62	0
					12*					
14	28/03/1968	West Indies	Georgetown	D	27		8	1	27	0
					2		8	0	28	0
15	06/06/1968	Australia	Old Trafford	L	9	1	25	11	38	1
					87*		5	3	7	1
16	22/08/1968	Australia	The Oval	W	158		4	2	3	0
					9		5	4	1	1
17	21/02/1969	Pakistan	Lahore (2)	D	26	3	8	2	28	1
					5					
18	28/02/1969	Pakistan	Dacca	D	114*		8	1	15	0
						1	9	2	12	0
19	06/03/1969	Pakistan	Karachi (1)	D	16					
20	12/06/1969	West Indies	Old Trafford	W	57	1				
							9	2	29	1
21	26/06/1969	West Indies	Lord's	D	0		26	10	46	0
					18		15	2	45	2
22	10/07/1969	West Indies	Headingley	W	48		15	8	27	1
					39		10	3	22	0
23	24/07/1969	New Zealand	Lord's	W	37					
					12		8	3	6	1
24	07/08/1969	New Zealand	Trent Bridge	D	45	1	25	9	40	1
					5		5	0	8	0
25	21/08/1969	New Zealand	The Oval	W	1		1	0	4	0
							14	9	19	0
26	27/11/1970	Australia	Brisbane (2)	D	57		16	2	63	0
							7	5	7	0
27	11/12/1970	Australia	Perth	D	8	1	17	1	41	1
					31		4	2	5	0
28	09/01/1971	Australia	Sydney	W	0	1	9	2	20	2
					56	1	7	3	16	0
29	21/01/1971	Australia	Melbourne	D	117		22	6	71	1
30	29/01/1971	Australia	Adelaide	D	47					
					5		15	4	28	0
31	12/02/1971	Australia	Sydney	W	1		12	2	24	0
					47	1	5	1	15	2
32	25/02/1971	New Zealand	Christchurch	W	100		3	1	2	0
33	05/03/1971	New Zealand	Auckland	D	58					
					5					
34	03/06/1971	Pakistan	Edgbaston	D	73		38	17	78	2
					22					
35	17/06/1971	Pakistan	Lord's	D			10	5	22	1
36	08/07/1971	Pakistan	Headingley	W	74		36	18	46	3
					72	2	15	7	16	2
37	22/07/1971	India	Lord's	D	4		15	7	20	0
					30					
38	05/08/1971	India	Old Trafford	D	12		24	11	40	2
					23*		3	2	1	0
39	19/08/1971	India	The Oval	L	2	1	7	5	5	1
					17		9	3	17	0
40	08/06/1972	Australia	Old Trafford	W	23		6	1	13	1
					37	1	16	4	23	1
41	22/06/1972	Australia	Lord's	L	32		17	5	48	1
					3		8	3	14	1
42	13/07/1972	Australia	Trent Bridge	D	29	1	18	5	41	1
					50*		7	0	12	0
43	27/07/1972	Australia	Headingley	W	12		2	1	8	0
						1				
44	10/08/1972	Australia	The Oval	L	4		9	4	17	0
					43					

Batting & Fielding

Mat	Inns	N/O	Runs	H/S	Avg	100s	50s	Cat
44	70	8	2484	158	40.06	5	15	29

Bowling

Balls	Runs	Wkts	Avg	Best	5WI	10WM	S/R
5706	1859	47	39.55	3-46	0	0	121.40

H.E.DOLLERY

Full Name: Horace Edgar Dollery (known as Tom)
Born: 14/10/1914, Reading, Berkshire
Died: 20/01/1987, Edgbaston, Birmingham
Teams: Warwickshire 1934-55, Wellington 1950/51, England 1947-50
Matches: 4 (Won 1, Drew 2, Lost 1)
Right-hand middle order batsman

No	Date	Opposition	Venue	R	Bat	C
1	07/06/1947	South Africa	Trent Bridge	D	9	
					17	
2	24/06/1948	Australia	Lord's	L	0	
					37	
3	08/07/1948	Australia	Old Trafford	D	1	
4	08/06/1950	West Indies	Old Trafford	W	8	1
					0	

Batting & Fielding

Mat	Inns	N/O	Runs	H/S	Avg	100s	50s	Cat
4	7	0	72	37	10.28	0	0	1

A.DOLPHIN

Full Name: Arthur Dolphin
Born: 24/12/1885, Wilsden, Yorkshire
Died: 23/10/1942, Lilycroft, Heaton, Bradford, Yorkshire
Teams: Yorkshire 1905-27, Patiala 1926/27, England 1921
Matches: 1 (Won 0, Drew 0, Lost 1)
Right-hand lower order batsman – Wicket-keeper

No	Date	Opposition	Venue	R	Bat	C	St	B
1+	11/02/1921	Australia	Melbourne	L	1	1		1
					0			5

Batting & Fielding

Mat	Inns	N/O	Runs	H/S	Avg	100s	50s	Cat	St	Byes
1	2	0	1	1	0.50	0	0	1	0	6

J.W.H.T.DOUGLAS

Full Name: John William Henry Tyler Douglas (known as Johnny)
Born: 03/09/1882, Clapton, London
Died: 19/12/1930, near Laeso Trindel Lightship, Denmark
Teams: Essex 1901-28, London County 1903-04, England 1911-25
Matches: 23 (Won 9, Drew 4, Lost 10)
England Captain: 18 times 1911-24 (Won 8, Drew 2, Lost 8) **Toss:** 7-11
Right-hand middle order batsman – Right-arm fast medium bowler

No	Date	Opposition	Venue	R	Bat	C	Bowling			
1*	15/12/1911	Australia	Sydney	L	0		24	5	62	1
					32	1	21	3	50	4
2*	30/12/1911	Australia	Melbourne	W	9		15	4	33	1
							10	0	38	0
3*	12/01/1912	Australia	Adelaide	W	35		7	2	7	1
							29	10	71	2
4*	09/02/1912	Australia	Melbourne	W	0					
							17.5	6	46	5
5*	23/02/1912	Australia	Sydney	W	18	1	7	0	14	1
					8		9	0	34	0
6	19/08/1912	Australia	The Oval	W	18					
					24	3				
7*	13/12/1913	South Africa	Durban (1)	W	119		8	2	19	2
							2	1	2	0
8*	26/12/1913	South Africa	Johannesburg (1)	W	3		2	0	11	0
							6	0	27	0

No	Date	Opposition	Venue	R	Bat	C	O	M	R	W
9*	01/01/1914	South Africa	Johannesburg (1)	W	30		7	2	16	0
					77	1	13.4	2	34	2
10*	14/02/1914	South Africa	Durban (1)	D	0	1	7	0	31	0
					7		14	1	51	1
11*	27/02/1914	South Africa	Port Elizabeth	W	30		5.4	2	14	4
							9	1	34	1
12*	17/12/1920	Australia	Sydney	L	21		3	0	14	0
					7		26	3	79	2
13*	31/12/1920	Australia	Melbourne	L	15		24	1	83	2
					9					
14*	14/01/1921	Australia	Adelaide	L	60	1	24	6	69	2
					32		19	2	61	0
15*	11/02/1921	Australia	Melbourne	L	50		4	0	17	0
					60		5	1	13	0
16*	25/02/1921	Australia	Sydney	L	32*		16	0	84	2
					68					
17*	28/05/1921	Australia	Trent Bridge	L	11		13	2	34	2
					13					
18*	11/06/1921	Australia	Lord's	L	34		9	1	53	2
					14		6	0	23	0
19	02/07/1921	Australia	Headingley	L	75	1	20	3	80	3
					8		11	0	38	0
20	23/07/1921	Australia	Old Trafford	D			5	2	3	1
21	13/08/1921	Australia	The Oval	D	21*		30	2	117	3
22*	26/07/1924	South Africa	Old Trafford	D			8	2	20	0
23	01/01/1925	Australia	Melbourne	L	8		19.5	0	95	1
					14		4	0	9	0

Batting & Fielding

Mat	Inns	N/O	Runs	H/S	Avg	100s	50s	Cat
23	35	2	962	119	29.15	1	6	9

Bowling

Balls	Runs	Wkts	Avg	Best	5WI	10WM	S/R
2812	1486	45	33.02	5-46	1	0	62.48

P.R.DOWNTON

Full Name: Paul Rupert Downton
Born: 04/04/1957, Farnborough, Kent
Teams: Kent 1977-79, Middlesex 1980-91, England 1981-88
Matches: 30 (Won 5, Drew 8, Lost 17)
Right-hand middle order batsman – Wicket-keeper

No	Date	Opposition	Venue	R	Bat	C	St	B
1+	13/02/1981	West Indies	Port-of-Spain	L	4	1		0
					5			
2+	27/03/1981	West Indies	St John's	D	13	2		1
3+	10/04/1981	West Indies	Kingston	D	0	3		0
					26*			
4+	18/06/1981	Australia	Trent Bridge	L	8	1		4
					3	1		1
5+	14/06/1984	West Indies	Edgbaston	L	33			6
					56			
6+	28/06/1984	West Indies	Lord's	L	23*	2		0
					4			4
7+	12/07/1984	West Indies	Headingley	L	17	1		0
					27			
8+	26/07/1984	West Indies	Old Trafford	L	0	3		4
					24			
9+	09/08/1984	West Indies	The Oval	L	16	1		1
					10	3		0
10+	23/08/1984	Sri Lanka	Lord's	D	10	2		2
						1		5
11+	28/11/1984	India	Bombay (3)	L	37*	1		4
					62		1	2
12+	12/12/1984	India	Delhi	W	74	3	1	1
						2		6
13+	31/12/1984	India	Calcutta	D	6*	1		0
								0

No	Date	Opposition	Venue	R	Bat	C	St	B
14+	13/01/1985	India	Madras (1)	W	3*	3		0
						2		1
15+	31/01/1985	India	Kanpur	D	1	2		9
								0
16+	13/06/1985	Australia	Headingley	W	54	2		0
						3		4
17+	27/06/1985	Australia	Lord's	L	21	1		0
					0			0
18+	11/07/1985	Australia	Trent Bridge	D	0	2		6
19+	01/08/1985	Australia	Old Trafford	D	23	2	1	0
								1
20+	15/08/1985	Australia	Edgbaston	W	0*	3		0
						1		1
21+	29/08/1985	Australia	The Oval	W	16	1		0
						4		4
22+	21/02/1986	West Indies	Kingston	L	2	1		2
					3			0
23+	07/03/1986	West Indies	Port-of-Spain	L	8	1	2	0
					5			0
24+	21/03/1986	West Indies	Bridgetown	L	11	1		2
					26			
25+	03/04/1986	West Indies	Port-of-Spain	L	7	3		0
					11*			0
26+	11/04/1986	West Indies	St John's	L	5			2
					13			4
27+	05/06/1986	India	Lord's	L	5			0
					29	1		1
28+	02/06/1988	West Indies	Trent Bridge	D	16*	3		6
29+	16/06/1988	West Indies	Lord's	L	11	3		0
					27	3		0
30+	30/06/1988	West Indies	Old Trafford	L	24			0
					6			

Batting & Fielding

Mat	Inns	N/O	Runs	H/S	Avg	100s	50s	Cat	St	Byes
30	48	8	785	74	19.62	0	4	70	5	84

N.F.DRUCE

Full Name: Norman Frank Druce (known as Frank)
Born: 01/01/1875, Denmark Hill, London
Died: 27/10/1954, Milford on Sea, Hampshire
Teams: Cambridge University 1894-97, Surrey 1895-97, England 1897-98
Matches: 5 (Won 1, Drew 0, Lost 4)
Right-hand middle order batsman

No	Date	Opposition	Venue	R	Bat	C
1	13/12/1897	Australia	Sydney	W	20	2
						2
2	01/01/1898	Australia	Melbourne	L	44	
					15	
3	14/01/1898	Australia	Adelaide	L	24	
					27	
4	29/01/1898	Australia	Melbourne	L	24	
					16	1
5	26/02/1898	Australia	Sydney	L	64	
					18	

Batting & Fielding

Mat	Inns	N/O	Runs	H/S	Avg	100s	50s	Cat
5	9	0	252	64	28.00	0	1	5

A.DUCAT

Full Name: Andrew Ducat (known as Andy or Andy 'Mac'Ducat)
Born: 16/02/1886, Brixton, London
Died: 23/07/1942, Lord's Cricket Ground, St John's Wood, London
Teams: Surrey 1906-31, England 1921
Matches: 1 (Won 0, Drew 0, Lost 1)
Right-hand middle order batsman – Right-arm slow bowler

No	Date	Opposition	Venue	R	Bat	C
1	02/07/1921	Australia	Headingley	L	3	
					2	1

Batting & Fielding

Mat	Inns	N/O	Runs	H/S	Avg	100s	50s	Cat
1	2	0	5	3	2.50	0	0	1

G.DUCKWORTH

Full Name: George Duckworth
Born: 09/05/1901, Warrington, Lancashire
Died: 05/01/1966, Warrington, Lancashire
Teams: Lancashire 1923-38, England 1924-36
Matches: 24 (Won 10, Drew 10, Lost 4)
Right-hand lower order batsman – Wicket-keeper

No	Date	Opposition	Venue	R	Bat	C	St	B
1+	26/07/1924	South Africa	Old Trafford	D				8
2+	11/08/1928	West Indies	The Oval	W	7*	1		2
						1		6
3+	30/11/1928	Australia	Brisbane (1)	W	5*			1
						1		0
4+	14/12/1928	Australia	Sydney	W	39*	1		4
					2*			5
5+	29/12/1928	Australia	Melbourne	W	3	3		4
					0*	2	1	6
6+	01/02/1929	Australia	Adelaide	W	5	2		0
					1	1		9
7+	08/03/1929	Australia	Melbourne	L	12	3		6
					9			12
8+	15/06/1929	South Africa	Edgbaston	D	11*			6
								9
9+	29/06/1929	South Africa	Lord's	D	8*	1	1	9
							1	2
10+	13/07/1929	South Africa	Headingley	W	21	1	1	0
						1	1	6
11+	27/07/1929	South Africa	Old Trafford	W		1	1	0
						2	2	13
12+	13/06/1930	Australia	Trent Bridge	W	4	1	1	4
					14*	1		17
13+	27/06/1930	Australia	Lord's	L	18		1	6
					0	1		1
14+	11/07/1930	Australia	Headingley	D	33	2		5
15+	25/07/1930	Australia	Old Trafford	D	0*	1		23
16+	16/08/1930	Australia	The Oval	L	3	4		22
					15			
17+	24/12/1930	South Africa	Johannesburg (1)	L	0*	1		12
					4	2		16
18+	01/01/1931	South Africa	Cape Town	D	0			8
19+	16/01/1931	South Africa	Durban (2)	D		4		5
						1		8
20+	31/03/1933	New Zealand	Auckland	D	6*		1	9
								0
21+	27/07/1935	South Africa	Old Trafford	D	2	1		3
								6
22+	27/06/1936	India	Lord's	W	2		1	4
						2		4
23+	25/07/1936	India	Old Trafford	D	10*	2		1
							1	9
24+	15/08/1936	India	The Oval	W		2		8
						1		3

Batting & Fielding

Mat	Inns	N/O	Runs	H/S	Avg	100s	50s	Cat	St	Byes
24	28	12	234	39*	14.62	0	0	45	15	282

K.S.DULEEPSINHJI

Full Name: Kumar Shri Duleepsinhji (Prince Duleepsinhji, known as Duleep)
Born: 13/06/1905, Sarodar, India
Died: 05/12/1959, Bombay, India
Teams: Cambridge University 1925-28, Sussex 1924-32, Hindus 1928/29, England 1929-31
Matches: 12 (Won 2, Drew 8, Lost 2)
Right-hand middle order batsman – Leg break bowler

No	Date	Opposition	Venue	R	Bat	C		Bowling		
1	15/06/1929	South Africa	Edgbaston	D	12					
					1		1	0	7	0
2	10/01/1930	New Zealand	Christchurch	W	49	2				
					33*	1				
3	24/01/1930	New Zealand	Wellington	D	40	2				
					56*	1				
4	14/02/1930	New Zealand	Auckland	D	117					
5	21/02/1930	New Zealand	Auckland	D	63	1				
6	27/06/1930	Australia	Lord's	L	173					
					48					
7	11/07/1930	Australia	Headingley	D	35					
					10					
8	25/07/1930	Australia	Old Trafford	D	54	2				
9	16/08/1930	Australia	The Oval	L	50					
					46					
10	27/06/1931	New Zealand	Lord's	D	25					
					11					
11	29/07/1931	New Zealand	The Oval	W	109					
						1				
12	15/08/1931	New Zealand	Old Trafford	D	63					

Batting & Fielding

Mat	Inns	N/O	Runs	H/S	Avg	100s	50s	Cat
12	19	2	995	173	58.52	3	5	10

Bowling

Balls	Runs	Wkts	Avg	Best	5WI	10WM	S/R
6	7	0	–	0-7	0	0	–

F.J.DURSTON

Full Name: Frederick John Durston (known as Jack)
Born: 11/07/1893, Clophill, Bedfordshire
Died: 08/04/1965, Norwood Green, Southall, Middlesex
Teams: Middlesex 1919-33, England 1921
Matches: 1 (Won 0, Drew 0, Lost 1)
Right-hand lower order batsman – Right-arm fast bowler

No	Date	Opposition	Venue	R	Bat	C		Bowling		
1	11/06/1921	Australia	Lord's	L	6*		24.1	2	102	4
					2		9.3	0	34	1

Batting & Fielding

Mat	Inns	N/O	Runs	H/S	Avg	100s	50s	Cat
1	2	1	8	6*	8.00	0	0	0

Bowling

Balls	Runs	Wkts	Avg	Best	5WI	10WM	S/R
202	136	5	27.20	4-102	0	0	40.40

M.A.EALHAM

Full Name: Mark Alan Ealham
Born: 27/08/1969, Willesborough, Kent
Teams: Kent 1989-96, England 1996
Matches: 2 (Won 0, Drew 1, Lost 1)
Right-hand middle order batsman – Right-arm medium bowler

No	Date	Opposition	Venue	R	Bat	C		Bowling	
1	04/07/1996	India	Trent Bridge	D	51		29	9 90	2
							14	5 21	4
2	25/07/1996	Pakistan	Lord's	L	25		21	4 42	1
					5	1	16	4 39	0

Batting & Fielding

Mat	Inns	N/O	Runs	H/S	Avg	100s	50s	Cat
2	3	0	81	51	27.00	0	1	1

Bowling

Balls	Runs	Wkts	Avg	Best	5WI	10WM	S/R
480	192	7	27.42	4-21	0	0	68.57

P.H.EDMONDS

Full Name: Philippe-Henri Edmonds (known as Phil)
Born: 08/03/1951, Lusaka, Northern Rhodesia
Teams: Cambridge University 1971-73, Middlesex 1971-92, Eastern Province 1975/76, England 1975-87
Matches: 51 (Won 16, Drew 24, Lost 11)
Right-hand middle/lower order batsman – Left-arm slow bowler

No	Date	Opposition	Venue	R	Bat	C		Bowling	
1	14/08/1975	Australia	Headingley	D	13*		20	7 28	5
					8		17	4 64	1
2	28/08/1975	Australia	The Oval	D	4		38	7 118	0
					7		6.1	2 14	0
3	02/01/1978	Pakistan	Hyderabad	D	4	3	24	2 75	3
						2	30	6 95	0
4	18/01/1978	Pakistan	Karachi (1)	D	6		33	7 66	7
5	10/02/1978	New Zealand	Wellington	L	4		3	1 7	0
					11	3	1	0 4	0
6	24/02/1978	New Zealand	Christchurch	W	50	4	34	11 38	4
						1	6	2 22	2
7	04/03/1978	New Zealand	Auckland	D	8	1	10	2 23	0
							45	15 107	3
8	01/06/1978	Pakistan	Edgbaston	W	4*		4	2 2	0
							26	10 44	4
9	15/06/1978	Pakistan	Lord's	W	36*	1	8	6 6	4
							12	4 21	0
10	29/06/1978	Pakistan	Headingley	D	1*		11	2 22	0
11	27/07/1978	New Zealand	The Oval	W	28	1	17	2 41	0
							34.1	23 20	4
12	10/08/1978	New Zealand	Trent Bridge	W	6		15.4	5 21	2
						1	33.1	15 44	4
13	24/08/1978	New Zealand	Lord's	W	5	2	12	3 19	0
14	01/12/1978	Australia	Brisbane (2)	W	1		1	1 0	0
						1	12	1 27	0
15	12/07/1979	India	Edgbaston	W			26	11 60	2
						1	17	6 37	0
16	02/08/1979	India	Lord's	D	20		2	1 1	0
							45	18 62	2
17	16/08/1979	India	Headingley	D	18		28	8 59	1
18	30/08/1979	India	The Oval	D	16		5	1 17	0
					27*		38	11 87	1
19	10/06/1982	India	Lord's	W	64		2	1 5	0
							15	6 39	0
20	24/06/1982	India	Old Trafford	D	12		37	12 94	3
21	08/07/1982	India	The Oval	D	14	1	35.2	11 89	3
							13	5 34	0
22	14/07/1983	New Zealand	The Oval	W	12		2	0 19	0
					43*		40.1	16 101	3
23	28/07/1983	New Zealand	Headingley	L	8		45	14 101	1
					0	1			
24	28/11/1984	India	Bombay (3)	L	48		33	6 82	1
					8		8	3 21	1
25	12/12/1984	India	Delhi	W	26		44.2	16 83	2
							44	24 60	4

No	Date	Opposition	Venue	R	Bat	C	Bowling			
26	31/12/1984	India	Calcutta	D	8		47	22	72	3
							4	3	2	
27	13/01/1985	India	Madras (1)	W	36		6	1	33	0
							41.5	13	119	2
28	31/01/1985	India	Kanpur	D	49		48	16	112	1
29	27/06/1985	Australia	Lord's	L	21	1	25.4	5	85	2
					1	1	16	5	35	1
30	11/07/1985	Australia	Trent Bridge	D	12		66	18	155	2
31	01/08/1985	Australia	Old Trafford	D	1	1	15.1	4	40	4
						1	54	12	122	1
32	15/08/1985	Australia	Edgbaston	W		3	20	4	47	1
						1	15	9	13	2
33	29/08/1985	Australia	The Oval	W	12		14	2	52	2
34	21/02/1986	West Indies	Kingston	L	5*	1	21	6	53	0
					7					
35	07/03/1986	West Indies	Port-of-Spain	L	3*	1	30	5	98	2
					13		12.3	3	24	1
36	21/03/1986	West Indies	Bridgetown	L	4		29	2	85	0
					4					
37	05/06/1986	India	Lord's	L	7*	1	22	7	41	1
					7		11	2	51	1
38	03/07/1986	India	Edgbaston	D	18		24	7	55	1
					10		28	11	31	4
39	24/07/1986	New Zealand	Lord's	D	6	2	42	10	97	4
					9*		5	0	18	0
40	07/08/1986	New Zealand	Trent Bridge	L	0	1	28	11	52	2
					20		4	1	16	0
41	21/08/1986	New Zealand	The Oval	D			22	10	29	2
42	14/11/1986	Australia	Brisbane (2)	W	9*	1	12	6	12	1
							24	8	46	0
43	28/11/1986	Australia	Perth	D			21	4	55	2
							27	13	25	1
44	12/12/1986	Australia	Adelaide	D	13		52	14	134	2
						1	29	7	63	1
45	26/12/1986	Australia	Melbourne	W	19					
							19.4	5	45	3
46	10/01/1987	Australia	Sydney	L	3		34	5	79	3
					0		43	16	79	2
47	04/06/1987	Pakistan	Old Trafford	D	23*		7	5	2	1
48	18/06/1987	Pakistan	Lord's	D	17*					
49	02/07/1987	Pakistan	Headingley	L	0	1	25	10	59	1
					0*					
50	23/07/1987	Pakistan	Edgbaston	D	24*	1	24.3	12	50	1
					0	1	4	1	11	1
51	06/08/1987	Pakistan	The Oval	D	2		32	8	97	0

Batting & Fielding

Mat	Inns	N/O	Runs	H/S	Avg	100s	50s	Cat
51	65	15	875	64	17.50	0	2	42

Bowling

Balls	Runs	Wkts	Avg	Best	5WI	10WM	S/R
12028	4273	125	34.18	7-66	2	0	96.22

J.H.EDRICH

Full Name: John Hugh Edrich, MBE
Born: 21/06/1937, Blofield, Norfolk
Teams: Surrey 1958-78, England 1963-76
Matches: 77 (Won 22, Drew 43, Lost 12)
England Captain: Once 1975 (Won 0, Drew 0, Lost 1) **Toss:** 0-1
Left-hand opening batsman – Right-arm medium bowler

No	Date	Opposition	Venue	R	Bat	C	Bowling
1	06/06/1963	West Indies	Old Trafford	L	20	1	
					38		
2	20/06/1963	West Indies	Lord's	D	0	1	
					8		

No	Date	Opposition	Venue	R	Bat	C	Bowling			
3	22/08/1963	West Indies	The Oval	L	25 12					
4	08/02/1964	India	Delhi	D	41					
5	15/02/1964	India	Kanpur	D	35	1	4	1	17	0
6	18/06/1964	Australia	Lord's	D	120					
7	02/07/1964	Australia	Headingley	L	3 32					
8	23/07/1964	Australia	Old Trafford	D	6	1				
9	08/07/1965	New Zealand	Headingley	W	310*					
10	22/07/1965	South Africa	Lord's	D	0 7*	1				
11	10/12/1965	Australia	Brisbane (2)	D	32 37					
12	30/12/1965	Australia	Melbourne	D	109	1 1				
13	07/01/1966	Australia	Sydney	W	103					
14	28/01/1966	Australia	Adelaide	L	5 1	1				
15	11/02/1966	Australia	Melbourne	D	85 3	1				
16	25/02/1966	New Zealand	Christchurch	D	2 2					
17	04/03/1966	New Zealand	Dunedin	D	36		1	0	6	0
18	11/03/1966	New Zealand	Auckland	D						
19	18/08/1966	West Indies	The Oval	W	35	1				
20	08/06/1967	India	Headingley	W	1 22					
21	22/06/1967	India	Lord's	W	12	1				
22	19/01/1968	West Indies	Port-of-Spain	D	25					
23	08/02/1968	West Indies	Kingston	D	96 6	1				
24	29/02/1968	West Indies	Bridgetown	D	146					
25	14/03/1968	West Indies	Port-of-Spain	W	32 29	1				
26	28/03/1968	West Indies	Georgetown	D	0 6	1 1				
27	06/06/1968	Australia	Old Trafford	L	49 38	1				
28	20/06/1968	Australia	Lord's	D	7					
29	11/07/1968	Australia	Edgbaston	D	88 64					
30	25/07/1968	Australia	Headingley	D	62 65	1				
31	22/08/1968	Australia	The Oval	W	164 17					
32	21/02/1969	Pakistan	Lahore (2)	D	54 8					
33	28/02/1969	Pakistan	Dacca	D	24 12*					
34	06/03/1969	Pakistan	Karachi (1)	D	32					
35	12/06/1969	West Indies	Old Trafford	W	58 9*	2				
36	26/06/1969	West Indies	Lord's	D	7 1	1				
37	10/07/1969	West Indies	Headingley	W	79 15					
38	24/07/1969	New Zealand	Lord's	W	16 115					
39	07/08/1969	New Zealand	Trent Bridge	D	155					

No	Date	Opposition	Venue	R	Bat	C	Bowling
40	21/08/1969	New Zealand	The Oval	W	68	1	
					22		
41	27/11/1970	Australia	Brisbane (2)	D	79		
42	11/12/1970	Australia	Perth	D	47		
					115*		
43	09/01/1971	Australia	Sydney	W	55	1	
					12	1	
44	21/01/1971	Australia	Melbourne	D	9	2	
					74*		
45	29/01/1971	Australia	Adelaide	D	130	1	
					40		
46	12/02/1971	Australia	Sydney	W	30		
					57		
47	25/02/1971	New Zealand	Christchurch	W	12	1	
					2		
48	05/03/1971	New Zealand	Auckland	D	1	1	
					24		
49	03/06/1971	Pakistan	Edgbaston	D	0		
					15		
50	17/06/1971	Pakistan	Lord's	D	37	1	
51	08/07/1971	Pakistan	Headingley	W	2	2	
					33	1	
52	22/07/1971	India	Lord's	D	18		
					62	1	
53	05/08/1971	India	Old Trafford	D	0	1	
					59		
54	19/08/1971	India	The Oval	L	41		
					0		
55	08/06/1972	Australia	Old Trafford	W	49	1	
					26		
56	22/06/1972	Australia	Lord's	L	10		
					6		
57	13/07/1972	Australia	Trent Bridge	D	37		
					15		
58	27/07/1972	Australia	Headingley	W	45		
					4		
59	10/08/1972	Australia	The Oval	L	8		
					18		
60	06/06/1974	India	Old Trafford	W	7		
					100*		
61	20/06/1974	India	Lord's	W	96		
62	04/07/1974	India	Edgbaston	W			
						1	
63	25/07/1974	Pakistan	Headingley	D	9		
					70		
64	08/08/1974	Pakistan	Lord's	D	40		
65	22/08/1974	Pakistan	The Oval	D	25		
66	29/11/1974	Australia	Brisbane (2)	L	48		
					6		
67	26/12/1974	Australia	Melbourne	D	49		
					4		
68*	04/01/1975	Australia	Sydney	L	50		
					33*		
69	08/02/1975	Australia	Melbourne	W	70	1	
						1	
70	20/02/1975	New Zealand	Auckland	W	64		
						2	
71	28/02/1975	New Zealand	Christchurch	D	11	1	
72	10/07/1975	Australia	Edgbaston	L	34		
					5		
73	31/07/1975	Australia	Lord's	D	9		
					175		
74	14/08/1975	Australia	Headingley	D	62		
					35		
75	28/08/1975	Australia	The Oval	D	12	1	
					96		
76	03/06/1976	West Indies	Trent Bridge	D	37	1	
					76*		
77	08/07/1976	West Indies	Old Trafford	L	8		
					24		

Batting & Fielding

Mat	Inns	N/O	Runs	H/S	Avg	100s	50s	Cat
77	127	9	5138	310*	43.54	12	24	43

Bowling

Balls	Runs	Wkts	Avg	Best	5WI	10WM	S/R
30	23	0	–	0-6	0	0	–

W.J.EDRICH

Full Name: William John Edrich (known as Bill)
Born: 26/03/1916, Lingwood, Norfolk
Died: 24/04/1986, Whitehill Court, Chesham, Buckinghamshire
Teams: Middlesex 1937-58, England 1938-55
Matches: 39 (Won 10, Drew 19, Lost 10)
Right-hand middle order batsman – Right-arm fast medium bowler

No	Date	Opposition	Venue	R	Bat	C		Bowling		
1	10/06/1938	Australia	Trent Bridge	D	5					
							13	2	39	1
2	24/06/1938	Australia	Lord's	D	0		4	2	5	0
					10		5.2	0	27	2
3	22/07/1938	Australia	Headingley	L	12		3	0	13	0
					28	1				
4	20/08/1938	Australia	The Oval	W	12	1	10	2	55	1
						2				
5	24/12/1938	South Africa	Johannesburg (1)	D	4	1	9	0	44	0
					10		3	0	7	0
6	31/12/1938	South Africa	Cape Town	D	0	1	5	1	15	0
							3	1	5	0
7	20/01/1939	South Africa	Durban (2)	W			4	0	9	1
						1	7	2	16	1
8	18/02/1939	South Africa	Johannesburg (1)	D	6		4	0	11	0
9	03/03/1939	South Africa	Durban (2)	D	1		9	2	29	0
					219	1	6	1	18	0
10	17/08/1946	India	The Oval	D			19.2	4	68	4
11	29/11/1946	Australia	Brisbane (2)	L	16		25	2	107	3
					7					
12	13/12/1946	Australia	Sydney	L	71		26	3	79	3
					119					
13	01/01/1947	Australia	Melbourne	D	89		10.3	2	50	3
					13		18	1	86	0
14	31/01/1947	Australia	Adelaide	D	17		20	3	88	0
					46		7	2	25	0
15	28/02/1947	Australia	Sydney	L	60		7	0	34	0
					24	1	2	0	14	0
16	21/03/1947	New Zealand	Christchurch	D	42		11	2	35	1
17	07/06/1947	South Africa	Trent Bridge	D	57		20	8	56	1
					50		4	0	8	0
18	21/06/1947	South Africa	Lord's	W	189	1	9	1	22	0
						3	13	5	31	3
19	05/07/1947	South Africa	Old Trafford	W	191		35.1	9	95	4
					22*		22.4	4	77	4
20	26/07/1947	South Africa	Headingley	W	43		17	4	46	3
							14	2	35	1
21	10/06/1948	Australia	Trent Bridge	L	18	1	18	1	72	0
					13		4	0	20	0
22	24/06/1948	Australia	Lord's	L	5		8	0	43	1
					2	1	2	0	11	0
23	08/07/1948	Australia	Old Trafford	D	32		7	3	27	1
					53		2	0	8	0
24	22/07/1948	Australia	Headingley	L	111	2	3	0	19	0
					54					
25	14/08/1948	Australia	The Oval	L	3	1	9	1	38	1
					28					
26	11/06/1949	New Zealand	Headingley	D	36	3	9	2	18	2
					70		2	0	13	0
27	25/06/1949	New Zealand	Lord's	D	9	2	4	0	16	0
					31					
28	23/07/1949	New Zealand	Old Trafford	D	78		4	1	8	0
							5	0	26	0

No	Date	Opposition	Venue	R	Bat	C	Bowling
29	13/08/1949	New Zealand	The Oval	D	100	3	3 0 16 0
						1	
30	08/06/1950	West Indies	Old Trafford	W	7	2	1 4 0
					71	3	1 10 0
31	24/06/1950	West Indies	Lord's	L	8		16 4 30 0
					8	1	13 2 37 0
32	09/07/1953	Australia	Old Trafford	D	6	2	
33	23/07/1953	Australia	Headingley	D	10	1	
					64		
34	15/08/1953	Australia	The Oval	W	21	2	
					55*	1	
35	10/06/1954	Pakistan	Lord's	D	4	1	
36	26/11/1954	Australia	Brisbane (2)	L	15	3	0 28 0
					88		
37	17/12/1954	Australia	Sydney	W	10		
					29	1	
38	31/12/1954	Australia	Melbourne	W	4		
					13	1	
39	28/01/1955	Australia	Adelaide	W	21	1	
					0		

Batting & Fielding

Mat	Inns	N/O	Runs	H/S	Avg	100s	50s	Cat
39	63	2	2440	219	40.00	6	13	39

Bowling

Balls	Runs	Wkts	Avg	Best	5WI	10WM	S/R
3234	1693	41	41.29	4-68	0	0	78.87

H.ELLIOTT

Full Name: Harry Elliott
Born: 02/11/1891, Scarcliffe, Derbyshire
Died: 02/02/1976, Derby
Teams: Derbyshire 1920-47, England 1928-34
Matches: 4 (Won 3, Drew 0, Lost 1)
Right-hand lower order batsman – Wicket-keeper

No	Date	Opposition	Venue	R	Bat	C	St	B
1+	04/02/1928	South Africa	Durban (2)	L	1			1
					3			3
2+	21/07/1928	West Indies	Old Trafford	W	6			10
						2		1
3+	15/12/1933	India	Bombay (1)	W	37*	1	1	2
						3		4
4+	10/02/1934	India	Madras (1)	W	14	1		1
						1	2	10

Batting & Fielding

Mat	Inns	N/O	Runs	H/S	Avg	100s	50s	Cat	St	Byes
4	5	1	61	37*	15.25	0	0	8	3	32

R.M.ELLISON

Full Name: Richard Mark Ellison
Born: 21/09/1959, Willesborough, Ashford, Kent
Teams: Kent 1981-93, Tasmania 1986-87, England 1984-86
Matches: 11 (Won 3, Drew 2, Lost 6)
Left-hand middle/lower order batsman – Right-arm medium bowler

No	Date	Opposition	Venue	R	Bat	C	Bowling
1	09/08/1984	West Indies	The Oval	L	20*		18 3 34 2
					13		26 7 60 3
2	23/08/1984	Sri Lanka	Lord's	D	41		28 6 70 1
					1	1	7 0 36
3	28/11/1984	India	Bombay (3)	L	1		18 3 85 0
					0		
4	12/12/1984	India	Delhi	W	10		26 6 66 4
							7 1 20 0

No	Date	Opposition	Venue	R	Bat	C	O	M	R	W
5	31/12/1984	India	Calcutta	D	1		53	14	117	0
							1	0	1	0
6	15/08/1985	Australia	Edgbaston	W			31.5	9	77	6
						1	9	3	27	4
7	29/08/1985	Australia	The Oval	W	3		18	5	35	2
							17	3	46	5
8	21/02/1986	West Indies	Kingston	L	9		33	12	78	5
					11					
9	07/03/1986	West Indies	Port-of-Spain	L	4		18	3	58	0
					36		3	1	12	0
10	11/04/1986	West Indies	St John's	L	6		24.3	3	114	2
					16		4	0	32	0
11	05/06/1986	India	Lord's	L	12		29	11	63	1
					19		6	0	17	0

Batting & Fielding

Mat	Inns	N/O	Runs	H/S	Avg	100s	50s	Cat
11	16	1	202	41	13.46	0	0	2

Bowling

Balls	Runs	Wkts	Avg	Best	5WI	10WM	S/R
2264	1048	35	29.94	6-77	3	1	64.68

J.E.EMBUREY

Full Name: John Ernest Emburey
Born: 20/08/1952, Peckham, London
Teams: Middlesex 1973-95, Northamptonshire 1996, Western Province 1982/83-83/84, England 1978-95
Matches: 64 (Won 15, Drew 28, Lost 21)
England Captain: 2 times 1988 (Won 0, Drew 0, Lost 2) **Toss:** 1-1
Right-hand middle/lower order batsman – Off break bowler

No	Date	Opposition	Venue	R	Bat	C	O	M	R	W
1	24/08/1978	New Zealand	Lord's	W	2	2	26.1	12	39	2
							3	2	1	0
2	29/12/1978	Australia	Melbourne	L	0	1	14	1	44	0
					7*		21.2	12	30	3
3	06/01/1979	Australia	Sydney	W	0	1	29	10	57	1
					14	1	17.2	7	46	4
4	27/01/1979	Australia	Adelaide	W	4	1	12	7	13	2
					42	1	9	5	16	0
5	10/02/1979	Australia	Sydney	W	0	1	18	3	48	2
							24	4	52	4
6	15/02/1980	India	Bombay (3)	W	8					
7	10/07/1980	West Indies	Old Trafford	D	3		10.3	1	20	3
					28*					
8	24/07/1980	West Indies	The Oval	D	24		23	12	38	2
					2					
9	07/08/1980	West Indies	Headingley	D	13*	2	6	0	25	1
10	28/08/1980	Australia	Lord's	D	3		38	9	104	1
							9	2	35	0
11	13/02/1981	West Indies	Port-of-Spain	L	17*	1	52	16	124	5
					1					
12	13/03/1981	West Indies	Bridgetown	L	0		18	4	45	0
					9		24	7	57	0
13	27/03/1981	West Indies	St John's	D	10	1	35	12	85	0
14	10/04/1981	West Indies	Kingston	D	1		56	23	108	2
15	02/07/1981	Australia	Lord's	D	31		25	12	35	2
							21	10	24	0
16	30/07/1981	Australia	Edgbaston	W	3		26.5	12	43	4
					37*	1	22	10	40	2
17	13/08/1981	Australia	Old Trafford	W	1		4	0	16	1
					57		49	9	107	2
18	27/08/1981	Australia	The Oval	D	0		23	2	58	0
					5*		23	3	76	1
19	27/11/1981	India	Bombay (3)	L	0					
					1		13	2	35	2
20	01/01/1982	India	Calcutta	D	1	1	24	11	44	2
							30	11	62	2
21	30/01/1982	India	Kanpur	D	2		32	7	81	0

No	Date	Opposition	Venue	R	Bat	C	Bowling			
22	17/02/1982	Sri Lanka	Colombo (1)	W	0	1	19	3	55	0
							25	9	33	6
23	13/06/1985	Australia	Headingley	W	21		6	1	23	2
							43.4	14	82	5
24	27/06/1985	Australia	Lord's	L	33	1	19	3	57	0
					20		8	4	24	1
25	11/07/1985	Australia	Trent Bridge	D	16*	1	55	15	129	3
26	01/08/1985	Australia	Old Trafford	D	31*		24	7	41	2
						1	51	17	99	4
27	15/08/1985	Australia	Edgbaston	W			9	2	21	0
							13	5	19	1
							1	0	1	0
28	29/08/1985	Australia	The Oval	W	9		19	7	48	1
							1	0	1	0
29	07/03/1986	West Indies	Port-of-Spain	L	0		27	5	78	5
					14		10	1	36	2
30	21/03/1986	West Indies	Bridgetown	L	0		38	7	96	1
					35*					
31	03/04/1986	West Indies	Port-of-Spain	L	8		27	10	62	3
					0					
32	11/04/1986	West Indies	St John's	L	7*		37	11	93	2
					0		14	0	83	1
33	05/06/1986	India	Lord's	L	7	1	27	13	28	1
					1					
34	19/06/1986	India	Headingley	L	0	2	17	4	45	1
					1		7	3	9	0
35	03/07/1986	India	Edgbaston	D	38		18.5	7	40	2
					27*	1	7	1	19	0
36	07/08/1986	New Zealand	Trent Bridge	L	8		42.5	17	87	2
					75		6	1	15	1
37	21/08/1986	New Zealand	The Oval	D	9*		31	15	39	1
38	14/11/1986	Australia	Brisbane (2)	W	8		34	11	66	0
							42.5	14	80	5
39	28/11/1986	Australia	Perth	D	5*		43	9	110	2
					4*		28	11	41	1
40	12/12/1986	Australia	Adelaide	D	49		46	11	117	1
							22	6	50	0
41	26/12/1986	Australia	Melbourne	W	22		4	0	16	0
						1	20	5	43	2
42	10/01/1987	Australia	Sydney	L	69	1	30	4	62	0
					22	1	46	15	78	7
43	04/06/1987	Pakistan	Old Trafford	D	19	1	16	3	28	0
44	18/06/1987	Pakistan	Lord's	D	12					
45	23/07/1987	Pakistan	Edgbaston	D	58	1	26	7	48	0
					20	1	4	1	3	0
46	06/08/1987	Pakistan	The Oval	D	53		61	10	143	0
47	25/11/1987	Pakistan	Lahore (2)	L	0		48	16	109	3
					38*					
48	07/12/1987	Pakistan	Faisalabad	D	15		21	8	49	3
					10*		2	0	3	0
49	16/12/1987	Pakistan	Karachi (1)	D	70		53	24	90	1
					74*					
50	29/01/1988	Australia	Sydney	D	23	2	30	10	57	0
							38	5	98	1
51	12/02/1988	New Zealand	Christchurch	D	42		4	3	2	0
					19		10	4	16	0
52	25/02/1988	New Zealand	Auckland	D	45		17	7	28	1
							57	24	91	1
53	03/03/1988	New Zealand	Wellington	D			45.5	10	99	1
54	02/06/1988	West Indies	Trent Bridge	D	0		16	4	95	2
55*	16/06/1988	West Indies	Lord's	L	7	2	6	2	17	1
					30	1	15	1	62	0
56*	30/06/1988	West Indies	Old Trafford	L	1		25	7	54	0
					8					
57	25/08/1988	Sri Lanka	Lord's	W	0	`	2	1	4	0
							18	9	34	1
58	22/06/1989	Australia	Lord's	L	0		42	12	88	4
					36*		3	0	8	0

No	Date	Opposition	Venue	R	Bat	C	Bowling			
59	06/07/1989	Australia	Edgbaston	D	26		29	5	61	2
							20	8	37	0
60	27/07/1989	Australia	Old Trafford	L	5		45	9	118	1
					64		13	3	30	1
61	19/02/1993	India	Bombay (3)	L	12		59	14	144	2
					1					
62	13/03/1993	Sri Lanka	Colombo (2)	L	1*		34	6	117	2
					59		14	2	48	2
63	05/08/1993	Australia	Edgbaston	L	55*		39	9	119	2
					37		18	4	31	1
64	27/07/1995	West Indies	Old Trafford	W	8	1	10	2	33	0
							20	5	49	0

Batting & Fielding

Mat	Inns	N/O	Runs	H/S	Avg	100s	50s	Cat
64	96	20	1713	75	22.53	0	10	34

Bowling

Balls	Runs	Wkts	Avg	Best	5WI	10WM	S/R
15391	5646	147	38.40	7-78	6	0	104.70

G.M.EMMETT

Full Name: George Malcolm Emmett
Born: 02/12/1912, Agra, India
Died: 18/12/1976, Knowle, Somerset
Teams: Gloucestershire 1936-59, England 1948
Matches: 1 (Won 0, Drew 1, Lost 0)
Right-hand opening batsman – Left-arm slow bowler

No	Date	Opposition	Venue	R	Bat	C
1	08/07/1948	Australia	Old Trafford	D	10	
					0	

Batting & Fielding

Mat	Inns	N/O	Runs	H/S	Avg	100s	50s	Cat
1	2	0	10	10	5.00	0	0	0

T.EMMETT

Full Name: Thomas Emmett (known as Tom)
Born: 03/09/1841, Halifax, Yorkshire
Died: 30/06/1904, Leicester
Teams: Yorkshire 1866-88, England 1877-82
Matches: 7 (Won 1, Drew 2, Lost 4)
Left-hand middle/lower order batsman – Left-hand fast round-arm bowler

No	Date	Opposition	Venue	R	Bat	C	Bowling			
1	15/03/1877	Australia	Melbourne	L	8		12	7	13	0
					9	3				
2	31/03/1877	Australia	Melbourne	W	48	1				
					8		13	6	23	0
3	02/01/1879	Australia	Melbourne	L	0		59	31	68	7
					24*					
4	31/12/1881	Australia	Melbourne	D	5		35	12	61	2
					6	1	16	11	19	0
5	17/02/1882	Australia	Sydney	L	10	2	6	2	24	0
					9		6	3	17	0
6	03/03/1882	Australia	Sydney	L	4		16	6	37	0
					2	1				
7	10/03/1882	Australia	Melbourne	D	27	1	19	14	22	0

Batting & Fielding

Mat	Inns	N/O	Runs	H/S	Avg	100s	50s	Cat
7	13	1	160	48	13.33	0	0	9

Bowling

Balls	Runs	Wkts	Avg	Best	5WI	10WM	S/R
728	284	9	31.55	7-68	1	0	80.88

A.J.EVANS

Full Name: Alfred John Evans (known as John)
Born: 01/05/1889, Newtown, Hampshire
Died: 18/09/1960, Marylebone, London
Teams: Oxford University 1909-12, Hampshire 1908-20, Kent 1921-28, England 1921
Matches: 1 (Won 0, Drew 0, Lost 1)
Right-hand middle order batsman – Right-arm fast medium bowler

No	Date	Opposition	Venue	R	Bat	C
1	11/06/1921	Australia	Lord's	L	4	
					14	

Batting & Fielding

Mat	Inns	N/O	Runs	H/S	Avg	100s	50s	Cat
1	2	0	18	14	9.00	0	0	0

T.G.EVANS

Full Name: Thomas Godfrey Evans, CBE (known as Godfrey)
Born: 18/08/1920, Finchley, Middlesex
Teams: Kent 1939-67, England 1946-59
Matches: 91 (Won 36, Drew 30, Lost 25)
Right-hand middle/lower order batsman – Wicket-keeper

No	Date	Opposition	Venue	R	Bat	C	St	B
1+	17/08/1946	India	The Oval	D				1
2+	13/12/1946	Australia	Sydney	L	5	1		0
					9			
3+	01/01/1947	Australia	Melbourne	D	17	2		0
					0*	2		14
4+	31/01/1947	Australia	Adelaide	D	0	2		16
					10*			0
5+	28/02/1947	Australia	Sydney	L	29	1		7
					20	1		4
6+	21/03/1947	New Zealand	Christchurch	D	21*	2		10
7+	07/06/1947	South Africa	Trent Bridge	D	2		1	7
					74	1		1
8+	21/06/1947	South Africa	Lord's	W	16		2	0
								3
9+	05/07/1947	South Africa	Old Trafford	W	27	1		3
								5
10+	26/07/1947	South Africa	Headingley	W	6*	2		0
						1		4
11+	16/08/1947	South Africa	The Oval	D	45	2		3
					39*	2	1	12
12+	21/01/1948	West Indies	Bridgetown	D	26	1		0
						2	1	6
13+	11/02/1948	West Indies	Port-of-Spain	D	30	1		2
					21	1		0
14+	03/03/1948	West Indies	Georgetown	L	1	1		0
					37			0
15+	27/03/1948	West Indies	Kingston	L	9			11
					4			0
16+	10/06/1948	Australia	Trent Bridge	L	12	2		9
					50			0
17+	24/06/1948	Australia	Lord's	L	9	1	1	3
					24*	1	1	22
18+	08/07/1948	Australia	Old Trafford	D	34	2		5
								0
19+	22/07/1948	Australia	Headingley	L	3		1	9
					47*			6
20+	14/08/1948	Australia	The Oval	L	1	2	1	4
					8			
21+	16/12/1948	South Africa	Durban (2)	W	0	3		3
					4			1
22+	27/12/1948	South Africa	Johannesburg (2)	D	18	1	2	4
								9
23+	01/01/1949	South Africa	Cape Town	D	27		1	1
						1	2	0
24+	11/06/1949	New Zealand	Headingley	D	27	3		2
								1
25+	25/06/1949	New Zealand	Lord's	D	5	1		16

No	Date	Opposition	Venue	R	Bat	C	St	B
26+	23/07/1949	New Zealand	Old Trafford	D	12		1 2	3 2
27+	13/08/1949	New Zealand	The Oval	D	17	3 1	1	0 10
28+	08/06/1950	West Indies	Old Trafford	W	104 15	1	1 2	0 4
29+	24/06/1950	West Indies	Lord's	L	8 2	1 1	2	10 0
30+	20/07/1950	West Indies	Trent Bridge	L	32 63		1	2 0
31+	01/12/1950	Australia	Brisbane (2)	L	16 5	2		5 0
32+	22/12/1950	Australia	Melbourne	L	49 2	2 2		4 10
33+	05/01/1951	Australia	Sydney	L	23* 14	1		3
34+	02/02/1951	Australia	Adelaide	L	13 21	2 1		2 7
35+	23/02/1951	Australia	Melbourne	W	1	1		2 2
36+	17/03/1951	New Zealand	Christchurch	D	19	2	1	16 0
37+	24/03/1951	New Zealand	Wellington	W	13			3 30
38+	07/06/1951	South Africa	Trent Bridge	L	5 0	1 1	1	3 4
39+	21/06/1951	South Africa	Lord's	W	0	1		0 11
40+	05/07/1951	South Africa	Old Trafford	W	2	1		0 13
41+	05/06/1952	India	Headingley	W	66	2	1 2	1 0
42+	19/06/1952	India	Lord's	W	104		1	7 29
43+	17/07/1952	India	Old Trafford	W	71	1		0 8
44+	14/08/1952	India	The Oval	D	1	1		0
45+	11/06/1953	Australia	Trent Bridge	D	8	2		2 0
46+	25/06/1953	Australia	Lord's	D	0 11*	1	1	4 8
47+	09/07/1953	Australia	Old Trafford	D	44*	2 1	1 2	6 0
48+	23/07/1953	Australia	Headingley	D	25 1	1	1	4 3
49+	15/08/1953	Australia	The Oval	W	28	4		4 11
50+	15/01/1954	West Indies	Kingston	L	10 0	1		9 10
51+	06/02/1954	West Indies	Bridgetown	L	10 5	1	1	0 4
52+	24/02/1954	West Indies	Georgetown	W	19	1 1		8 2
53+	30/03/1954	West Indies	Kingston	W	28	1		0 4
54+	10/06/1954	Pakistan	Lord's	D	25		1	4 0
55+	01/07/1954	Pakistan	Trent Bridge	W	4	1 2		9 4
56+	22/07/1954	Pakistan	Old Trafford	D	31			4 2
57+	12/08/1954	Pakistan	The Oval	L	0 3	3		0 3
58+	17/12/1954	Australia	Sydney	W	3 4	1 2		5 0
59+	31/12/1954	Australia	Melbourne	W	20 22	2 3		7 1
60+	28/01/1955	Australia	Adelaide	W	37 6*	2 1		3 4
61+	25/02/1955	Australia	Sydney	D	10	1 1		10 0
62+	11/03/1955	New Zealand	Dunedin	W	0	1	1	5 7

No	Date	Opposition	Venue	R	Bat	C	St	B
63+	25/03/1955	New Zealand	Auckland	W	0	2		3
								0
64+	09/06/1955	South Africa	Trent Bridge	W	12	1		1
						1		8
65+	23/06/1955	South Africa	Lord's	W	20	3	1	6
					14	3		11
66+	07/07/1955	South Africa	Old Trafford	L	0	1		15
					36			
67+	07/06/1956	Australia	Trent Bridge	D	0			0
					8*			10
68+	21/06/1956	Australia	Lord's	L	0	2	1	0
					20	4		2
69+	12/07/1956	Australia	Headingley	W	40	1		4
								7
70+	26/07/1956	Australia	Old Trafford	W	47		1	0
								12
71+	23/08/1956	Australia	The Oval	D	0			6
								1
72+	24/12/1956	South Africa	Johannesburg (3)	W	20	1	1	1
					30	2		2
73+	01/01/1957	South Africa	Cape Town	W	62	4		1
					1	1		0
74+	25/01/1957	South Africa	Durban (2)	D	0	1	1	0
					10			5
75+	15/02/1957	South Africa	Johannesburg (3)	L	7	2		0
					8	1		4
76+	01/03/1957	South Africa	Port Elizabeth	L	5	3		0
					21	3		1
77+	30/05/1957	West Indies	Edgbaston	D	14	1		1
					29*			7
78+	20/06/1957	West Indies	Lord's	W	82	1		2
						3		4
79+	04/07/1957	West Indies	Trent Bridge	D	26*	3		5
						4		2
80+	25/07/1957	West Indies	Headingley	W	10			0
						1		0
81+	22/08/1957	West Indies	The Oval	W	40			0
						1	1	4
82+	05/06/1958	New Zealand	Edgbaston	W	2	2		0
					0			0
83+	19/06/1958	New Zealand	Lord's	W	11			0
								0
84+	03/07/1958	New Zealand	Headingley	W		1		0
								6
85+	24/07/1958	New Zealand	Old Trafford	W	3	2		4
						1		5
86+	21/08/1958	New Zealand	The Oval	D	12			0
						1		2
87+	05/12/1958	Australia	Brisbane (2)	L	4	2		4
					4			2
88+	31/12/1958	Australia	Melbourne	L	4	2		0
					11		1	0
89+	30/01/1959	Australia	Adelaide	L	4	1		2
					0			
90+	04/06/1959	India	Trent Bridge	W	73	1		5
								0
91+	18/06/1959	India	Lord's	W	0	1		0
						1	1	0

Batting & Fielding

Mat	Inns	N/O	Runs	H/S	Avg	100s	50s	Cat	St	Byes
91	133	14	2439	104	20.49	2	8	173	46	697

A.E.FAGG

Full Name: Arthur Edward Fagg
Born: 18/06/1915, Chartham, Kent
Died: 13/09/1977, Tunbridge Wells, Kent
Matches: 5 (Won 3, Drew 2, Lost 0)
Teams: Kent 1932-57, England 1936-39
Right-hand opening batsman – Occasional right-arm medium bowler

No	Date	Opposition	Venue	R	Bat	C
1	25/07/1936	India	Old Trafford	D	39	
2	15/08/1936	India	The Oval	W	8	1
					22	1
3	04/12/1936	Australia	Brisbane (2)	W	4	
					27	2
4	18/12/1936	Australia	Sydney	W	11	
5	22/07/1939	West Indies	Old Trafford	D	7	1
					32	

Batting & Fielding

Mat	Inns	N/O	Runs	H/S	Avg	100s	50s	Cat
5	8	0	150	39	18.75	0	0	5

N.H.FAIRBROTHER

Full Name: Neil Harvey Fairbrother
Born: 09/09/1963, Warrington, Lancashire
Teams: Lancashire 1982-96, England 1987-93
Matches: 10 (Won 1, Drew 6, Lost 3)
Left-hand middle order batsman – Left-arm medium bowler

No	Date	Opposition	Venue	R	Bat	C	Bowling			
1	04/06/1987	Pakistan	Old Trafford	D	0	1				
2	16/12/1987	Pakistan	Karachi (1)	D	3					
					1					
3	25/02/1988	New Zealand	Auckland	D	1					
							2	0	9	0
4	03/03/1988	New Zealand	Wellington	D		2				
5	07/06/1990	New Zealand	Trent Bridge	D	19					
6	21/06/1990	New Zealand	Lord's	D	2	1				
					33*					
7	05/07/1990	New Zealand	Edgbaston	W	2					
					3					
8	29/01/1993	India	Calcutta	L	17					
					25					
9	11/02/1993	India	Madras (1)	L	83					
					9					
10	13/03/1993	Sri Lanka	Colombo (2)	L	18					
					3					

Batting & Fielding

Mat	Inns	N/O	Runs	H/S	Avg	100s	50s	Cat
10	15	1	219	83	15.64	0	1	4

Bowling

Balls	Runs	Wkts	Avg	Best	5WI	10WM	S/R
12	9	0	–	0-9	0	0	–

F.L.FANE

Full Name: Frederick Luther Fane (known as Freddie)
Born: 27/04/1875, Curragh Camp, Co Kildare, Ireland
Died: 27/11/1960, Kelvedon Hatch, Brentwood, Essex
Teams: Oxford University 1896-98, Essex 1895-1922, London County 1901, England 1906-10
Matches: 14 (Won 4, Drew 0, Lost 10)
England Captain: 5 times 1907-10 (Won 2, Drew 0, Lost 3) **Toss:** 3-2
Right-hand opening batsman

No	Date	Opposition	Venue	R	Bat	C
1	02/01/1906	South Africa	Johannesburg (1)	L	1	
					3	1
2	06/03/1906	South Africa	Johannesburg (1)	L	8	
					65	
3	10/03/1906	South Africa	Johannesburg (1)	L	143	
					7	1
4	24/03/1906	South Africa	Cape Town	W	9	
					66*	

No	Date	Opposition	Venue	R	Bat	C
5	30/03/1906	South Africa	Cape Town	L	30 / 10	
6*	13/12/1907	Australia	Sydney	L	2 / 33	
7*	01/01/1908	Australia	Melbourne	W	13 / 50	1
8*	10/01/1908	Australia	Adelaide	L	48 / 0	
9	21/02/1908	Australia	Sydney	L	0 / 46	
10	01/01/1910	South Africa	Johannesburg (1)	L	23 / 0	
11	21/01/1910	South Africa	Durban (1)	L	6 / 6	1
12	26/02/1910	South Africa	Johannesburg (1)	W	39 / 17	
13*	07/03/1910	South Africa	Cape Town	L	14 / 37	1
14*	11/03/1910	South Africa	Cape Town	W	6	1

Batting & Fielding

Mat	Inns	N/O	Runs	H/S	Avg	100s	50s	Cat
14	27	1	682	143	26.23	1	3	6

K.FARNES

Full Name: Kenneth Farnes (known as Ken)
Born: 08/07/1911, Leytonstone, Essex
Died: 20/10/1941, Chipping-Warden, Oxfordshire
Teams: Cambridge University 1931-33, Essex 1930-39, England 1934-39
Matches: 15 (Won 4, Drew 6, Lost 5)
Right-hand lower order batsman – Right-arm fast bowler

No	Date	Opposition	Venue	R	Bat	C	Bowling			
1	08/06/1934	Australia	Trent Bridge	L	1 / 0		40.2 / 25	10 / 3	102 / 77	5 / 5
2	22/06/1934	Australia	Lord's	W	1		12 / 4	3 / 2	43 / 6	0 / 0
3	08/01/1935	West Indies	Bridgetown	W	5		15 / 9	4 / 2	40 / 23	4 / 1
4	14/03/1935	West Indies	Kingston	L	5 / 0		24	4	72	1
5	29/01/1937	Australia	Adelaide	L	0* / 7*		20.6 / 24	1 / 2	71 / 89	3 / 2
6	26/02/1937	Australia	Melbourne	L	0* / 0	1	28.5	5	96	6
7	10/06/1938	Australia	Trent Bridge	D			37 / 24	11 / 2	106 / 78	4 / 0
8	24/06/1938	Australia	Lord's	D	5*		43 / 13	6 / 3	135 / 51	3 / 0
9	22/07/1938	Australia	Headingley	L	2 / 7		26 / 11.3	3 / 4	77 / 17	4 / 1
10	20/08/1938	Australia	The Oval	W			13 / 12.1	2 / 1	54 / 63	1 / 4
11	24/12/1938	South Africa	Johannesburg (1)	D	0		23 / 7	1 / 3	87 / 17	1 / 0
12	31/12/1938	South Africa	Cape Town	D	1*		13 / 8	3 / 1	37 / 23	0 / 1
13	20/01/1939	South Africa	Durban (2)	W			13 / 28.2	1 / 8	29 / 80	4 / 3
14	18/02/1939	South Africa	Johannesburg (1)	D	4		26	7	64	2
15	03/03/1939	South Africa	Durban (2)	D	20		46 / 22.1	9 / 2	108 / 74	1 / 4

Batting & Fielding

Mat	Inns	N/O	Runs	H/S	Avg	100s	50s	Cat
15	17	5	58	20	4.83	0	0	1

Bowling

Balls	Runs	Wkts	Avg	Best	5WI	10WM	S/R
3932	1719	60	28.65	6-96	3	1	65.53

W.FARRIMOND

Full Name: William Farrimond (known as Bill)
Born: 23/05/1903, Daisy Hill, Lancashire
Died: 15/11/1979, Westhoughton, Bolton, Lancashire
Teams: Lancashire 1924-45, England 1931-35
Matches: 4 (Won 0, Drew 2, Lost 2)
Right-hand middle order batsman – Wicket-keeper

No	Date	Opposition	Venue	R	Bat	C	St	B
1+	13/02/1931	South Africa	Johannesburg (1)	D	28			6
								6
2+	21/02/1931	South Africa	Durban (2)	D	35	1		0
					9		2	8
3+	24/01/1935	West Indies	Port-of-Spain	L	16	1		2
					2			3
4+	29/06/1935	South Africa	Lord's	L	13	1		1
					13	1		3

Batting & Fielding

Mat	Inns	N/O	Runs	H/S	Avg	100s	50s	Cat	St	Byes
4	7	0	116	35	16.57	0	0	5	2	29

P.G.H.FENDER

Full Name: Percy George Herbert Fender
Born: 22/08/1892, Balham, London
Died: 15/06/1985, Exeter, Devon
Teams: Sussex 1910-13, Surrey 1914-35, England 1921-29
Matches: 13 (Won 4, Drew 5, Lost 4)
Right-hand middle order batsman – Right-arm medium leg break bowler

No	Date	Opposition	Venue	R	Bat	C	Bowling			
1	14/01/1921	Australia	Adelaide	L	2	1	12	0	52	1
					42		22	0	105	1
2	11/02/1921	Australia	Melbourne	L	3		32	3	122	5
					59		13.2	2	39	0
3	25/02/1921	Australia	Sydney	L	2	2	20	1	90	5
					40		1	0	2	0
4	23/07/1921	Australia	Old Trafford	D	44*		15	6	30	2
5	13/08/1921	Australia	The Oval	D	0		19	3	82	0
					6					
6	23/12/1922	South Africa	Johannesburg (1)	L	0	1	7	1	17	1
					9	2	12	0	64	0
7	01/01/1923	South Africa	Cape Town	W	3	1	14	4	29	4
					2	1	20	3	52	1
8	18/01/1923	South Africa	Durban (2)	D	60		29	7	72	1
9	09/02/1923	South Africa	Johannesburg (1)	D	44		20	4	78	2
					9	1	17	2	60	0
10	16/02/1923	South Africa	Durban (2)	W	1	2	11	3	25	1
					0	1	11	3	21	0
11	14/06/1924	South Africa	Edgbaston	W	36					
							17	5	56	0
12	28/06/1924	South Africa	Lord's	W		1	9	1	45	1
							14	5	25	1
13	15/06/1929	South Africa	Edgbaston	D	6	1	32	10	64	2
					12		15.4	3	55	1

Batting & Fielding

Mat	Inns	N/O	Runs	H/S	Avg	100s	50s	Cat
13	21	1	380	60	19.00	0	2	14

Bowling

Balls	Runs	Wkts	Avg	Best	5WI	10WM	S/R
2178	1185	29	40.86	5-90	2	0	75.10

J.J.FERRIS

Full Name: John James Ferris (known as J.J.)
Born: 21/05/1867, Sydney, New South Wales, Australia
Died: 17/11/1900, Addington, Durban, South Africa
Teams: Gloucestershire 1892-95, New South Wales 1886/87-97/98, South Australia 1895/96, Australia 1887-90, England 1892
Matches: 1 (Won 1, Drew 0, Lost 0), 8 (Won 1, Drew 0, Lost 7)
Left-hand lower order batsman – Left-arm medium or slow bowler

No	Date	Opposition	Venue	R	Bat	C		Bowling		
1	19/03/1892	South Africa	Cape Town	W	16		29.2	11	54	6
							25	16	37	7

For Australia

No	Date	Opposition	Venue	R	Bat	C		Bowling		
1	28/01/1887	England	Sydney	L	1		17.3	7	27	4
					0*		61	30	76	5
2	25/02/1887	England	Sydney	L	1	1	45	16	71	5
					2		60	33	69	4
3	10/02/1888	England	Sydney	L	0		47	25	60	4
					5		16	4	43	2
4	16/07/1888	England	Lord's	W	14		21	13	19	3
					20*	1	23	11	26	5
5	13/08/1888	England	The Oval	L	13*		35.2	15	73	1
					16					
6	30/08/1888	England	Old Trafford	L	0*		40	20	49	2
					3					
7	21/07/1890	England	Lord's	L	8	1	40	17	55	2
					8	1	25	11	42	2
8	11/08/1890	England	The Oval	L	6		25	14	25	4
					1		23	8	49	5

Batting & Fielding

Mat	Inns	N/O	Runs	H/S	Avg	100s	50s	Cat	
1	1	0	16	16	16.00	0	0	0	(England)
8	16	4	98	20*	8.16	0	0	4	(Australia)
9	17	4	114	20*	8.76	0	0	4	(Total)

Bowling

Balls	Runs	Wkts	Avg	Best	5WI	10WM	S/R	
272	91	13	7.00	7-37	2	1	20.92	(England)
2030	684	48	14.25	5-26	4	0	42.29	(Australia)
2302	775	61	12.70	7-37	6	1	37.73	(Total)

A.FIELDER

Full Name: Arthur Fielder
Born: 19/07/1877, Plaxtol, Tonbridge, Kent
Died: 30/08/1949, Lambeth, London
Teams: Kent 1900-14, England 1904-08
Matches: 6 (Won 2, Drew 0, Lost 4)
Right-hand lower order batsman – Right-arm fast bowler

No	Date	Opposition	Venue	R	Bat	C		Bowling		
1	01/01/1904	Australia	Melbourne	W	1	1				
					4	1				
2	15/01/1904	Australia	Adelaide	L	6		7	0	33	0
					14*		25	11	51	1
3	13/12/1907	Australia	Sydney	L	1*		30.2	4	82	6
					6		27.3	4	88	3
4	01/01/1908	Australia	Melbourne	W	6*		27.5	4	77	2
					18*		27	6	74	1
5	10/01/1908	Australia	Adelaide	L	0*		27.5	5	80	4
					1		23	3	81	1
6	07/02/1908	Australia	Melbourne	L	1	2	22	3	54	4
					20		31	2	91	4

Batting & Fielding

Mat	Inns	N/O	Runs	H/S	Avg	100s	50s	Cat
6	12	5	78	20	11.14	0	0	4

Bowling

Balls	Runs	Wkts	Avg	Best	5WI	10WM	S/R
1491	711	26	27.34	6-82	1	0	57.34

L.B.FISHLOCK

Full Name: Laurence Barnard Fishlock (Laurie)
Born: 02/01/1907, Battersea, London
Died: 25/06/1986, Sutton, Surrey
Teams: Surrey 1931-52, England 1936-47
Matches: 4 (Won 1, Drew 2, Lost 1)
Left-hand opening batsman – Left-arm slow bowler

No	Date	Opposition	Venue	R	Bat	C
1	25/07/1936	India	Old Trafford	D	6	
2	15/08/1936	India	The Oval	W	19*	
3	17/08/1946	India	The Oval	D	8	
4	28/02/1947	Australia	Sydney	L	14	1
					0	

Batting & Fielding

Mat	Inns	N/O	Runs	H/S	Avg	100s	50s	Cat
4	5	1	47	19*	11.75	0	0	1

J.A.FLAVELL

Full Name: John Alfred Flavell (known as Jack)
Born: 15/05/1929, Wall Heath, Staffordshire
Teams: Worcestershire 1949-67, England 1961-64
Matches: 4 (Won 0, Drew 2, Lost 2)
Left-hand lower order batsman – Right-arm fast medium bowler

No	Date	Opposition	Venue	R	Bat	C		Bowling		
1	27/07/1961	Australia	Old Trafford	L	0*		22	8	61	1
					0*		29.4	4	65	2
2	17/08/1961	Australia	The Oval	D	14		31	5	105	2
3	04/06/1964	Australia	Trent Bridge	D			16	3	28	1
					7		4.2	0	11	1
4	02/07/1964	Australia	Headingley	L	5		29	5	97	0
					5					

Batting & Fielding

Mat	Inns	N/O	Runs	H/S	Avg	100s	50s	Cat
4	6	2	31	14	7.75	0	0	0

Bowling

Balls	Runs	Wkts	Avg	Best	5WI	10WM	S/R
792	367	7	52.42	2-65	0	0	113.14

K.W.R.FLETCHER

Full Name: Keith William Robert Fletcher, OBE
Born: 20/05/1944, Worcester
Teams: Essex 1962-88, England 1968-1982
Matches: 59 (Won 16, Drew 29, Lost 14)
England Captain: 7 times 1981-82 (Won 1, Drew 5, Lost 1) **Toss:** 5-2
Right-hand middle order batsman – Leg break bowler

No	Date	Opposition	Venue	R	Bat	C		Bowling		
1	25/07/1968	Australia	Headingley	D	0					
					23*					
2	21/02/1969	Pakistan	Lahore (2)	D	20	1				
					83	1	8	2	31	0
3	28/02/1969	Pakistan	Dacca	D	16					
4	06/03/1969	Pakistan	Karachi (1)	D	38					
5	24/07/1969	New Zealand	Lord's	W	9					
					7	1				
6	07/08/1969	New Zealand	Trent Bridge	D	31	1	3	1	14	0
7	27/11/1970	Australia	Brisbane (2)	D	34					
							9	1	48	1

No	Date	Opposition	Venue	R	Bat	C	Bowling			
8	11/12/1970	Australia	Perth	D	22		1	0	4	0
					0		4	0	18	0
9	09/01/1971	Australia	Sydney	W	23	2				
					8		1	0	6	0
10	29/01/1971	Australia	Adelaide	D	80					
					5		4	0	16	0
11	12/02/1971	Australia	Sydney	W	33					
					20	1	1	0	9	0
12	25/02/1971	New Zealand	Christchurch	W	4	2				
					2	1				
13	05/08/1971	India	Old Trafford	D	1					
					28*					
14	19/08/1971	India	The Oval	L	1	1				
					0					
15	27/07/1972	Australia	Headingley	W	5					
16	20/12/1972	India	Delhi	W	2					
					0	1				
17	30/12/1972	India	Calcutta	L	16					
					5	3				
18	12/01/1973	India	Madras (1)	L	97*					
					21					
19	25/01/1973	India	Kanpur	D	58	1				
20	06/02/1973	India	Bombay (2)	D	113	1				
21	02/03/1973	Pakistan	Lahore (2)	D	55					
					12					
22	16/03/1973	Pakistan	Hyderabad	D	78	1	3	0	22	0
					21					
23	24/03/1973	Pakistan	Karachi (1)	D	54					
					1*	1				
24	07/06/1973	New Zealand	Trent Bridge	W	17					
					8					
25	21/06/1973	New Zealand	Lord's	D	25	1				
					178					
26	05/07/1973	New Zealand	Headingley	W	81	1				
27	26/07/1973	West Indies	The Oval	L	11					
					5					
28	09/08/1973	West Indies	Edgbaston	D	52					
					44*					
29	23/08/1973	West Indies	Lord's	L	68					
					86*					
30	02/02/1974	West Indies	Port-of-Spain	L	4	1				
					0		0.5	0	5	0
31	06/03/1974	West Indies	Bridgetown	D	37	1				
					129*					
32	22/03/1974	West Indies	Georgetown	D	41					
33	30/03/1974	West Indies	Port-of-Spain	W	6	1				
					45	3				
34	06/06/1974	India	Old Trafford	W	123*					
35	20/06/1974	India	Lord's	W	15	1				
36	04/07/1974	India	Edgbaston	W	51*					
37	25/07/1974	Pakistan	Headingley	D	11	1				
					67*	1				
38	08/08/1974	Pakistan	Lord's	D	8					
39	22/08/1974	Pakistan	The Oval	D	122					
40	29/11/1974	Australia	Brisbane (2)	L	17	1				
					19	1				
41	13/12/1974	Australia	Perth	L	4	1				
					0					
42	04/01/1975	Australia	Sydney	L	24					
					11					
43	25/01/1975	Australia	Adelaide	L	40					
					63					
44	08/02/1975	Australia	Melbourne	W	146					

No	Date	Opposition	Venue	R	Bat	C	Bowling			
45	20/02/1975	New Zealand	Auckland	W	216	2				
						3				
46	28/02/1975	New Zealand	Christchurch	D						
47	10/07/1975	Australia	Edgbaston	L	6	2				
					51					
48	14/08/1975	Australia	Headingley	D	8					
					14					
49	17/12/1976	India	Delhi	W	8					
						1				
50	28/01/1977	India	Bangalore	L	10					
					1	1				
51	11/02/1977	India	Bombay (3)	D	14					
					58*	2				
52	12/03/1977	Australia	Melbourne	L	4	1				
					1	1				
53*	27/11/1981	India	Bombay (3)	L	15	1				
					3					
54*	09/12/1981	India	Bangalore	D	25	1				
					12*					
55*	23/12/1981	India	Delhi	D	51	1				
56*	01/01/1982	India	Calcutta	D	69	1				
					60*		3	1	6	1
57*	13/01/1982	India	Madras (1)	D	3					
							1	0	9	0
58*	30/01/1982	India	Kanpur	D	14	1	2	1	5	0
59*	17/02/1982	Sri Lanka	Colombo (1)	W	45	1				
					0*	2				

Batting & Fielding

Mat	Inns	N/O	Runs	H/S	Avg	100s	50s	Cat
59	96	14	3272	216	39.90	7	19	54

Bowling

Balls	Runs	Wkts	Avg	Best	5WI	10WM	S/R
285	193	2	96.50	1-6	0	0	142.50

W.FLOWERS

Full Name: Wilfred Flowers (birth registered as W.Flowers)
Born: 07/12/1856, Calverton, Nottinghamshire
Died: 01/11/1926, Carlton, Nottingham
Teams: Nottinghamshire 1877-96, England 1884-93
Matches: 8 (Won 5, Drew 1, Lost 2)
Right-hand middle order batsman – Off break bowler

No	Date	Opposition	Venue	R	Bat	C	Bowling			
1	12/12/1884	Australia	Adelaide	W	15		10	1	27	0
					7		16	4	27	0
2	01/01/1885	Australia	Melbourne	W	5	1	29	12	46	2
					11		6	11	0	
3	20/02/1885	Australia	Sydney	L	24		46	24	46	5
					56		20	14	19	0
4	14/03/1885	Australia	Sydney	L	14		14	5	27	1
					7		3.3	2	3	0
5	21/03/1885	Australia	Melbourne	W	16		9	6	9	0
							21	7	34	3
6	28/01/1887	Australia	Sydney	W	2					
					14					
7	25/02/1887	Australia	Sydney	W	37	1	8	3	9	2
					18		13	5	17	0
8	17/07/1893	Australia	Lord's	D	35		11	3	21	1
					4					

Batting & Fielding

Mat	Inns	N/O	Runs	H/S	Avg	100s	50s	Cat
8	14	0	254	56	18.14	0	1	2

Bowling

Balls	Runs	Wkts	Avg	Best	5WI	10WM	S/R
858	296	14	21.14	5-46	1	0	61.28

F.G.J.FORD

Full Name: Francis Gilbertson Justice Ford
Born: 14/12/1866, Paddington, London
Died: 07/02/1940, Burwash, Sussex
Teams: Cambridge University 1887-90, Middlesex 1886-99, England 1894-95
Matches: 5 (Won 3, Drew 0, Lost 2)
Left-hand middle order batsman – Left-arm slow bowler

No	Date	Opposition	Venue	R	Bat	C		Bowling		
1	14/12/1894	Australia	Sydney	W	30	2	11	2	47	1
					48					
2	29/12/1894	Australia	Melbourne	W	9	1				
					24		6	2	7	0
3	11/01/1895	Australia	Adelaide	L	21		8	2	19	0
					14	1	6	0	33	0
4	01/02/1895	Australia	Sydney	L	0		2	0	14	0
					11					
5	01/03/1895	Australia	Melbourne	W	11	1	2	0	9	0

Batting & Fielding

Mat	Inns	N/O	Runs	H/S	Avg	100s	50s	Cat
5	9	0	168	48	18.66	0	0	5

Bowling

Balls	Runs	Wkts	Avg	Best	5WI	10WM	S/R
210	129	1	129.00	1-47	0	0	210.00

F.R.FOSTER

Full Name: Frank Rowbotham Foster
Born: 31/01/1889, Deritend, Birmingham
Died: 03/05/1958, Northampton
Teams: Warwickshire 1908-14, England 1911-12
Matches: 11 (Won 8, Drew 2, Lost 1)
Right-hand middle order batsman – Left-arm fast medium bowler

No	Date	Opposition	Venue	R	Bat	C		Bowling		
1	15/12/1911	Australia	Sydney	L	56	1	29	6	105	2
					21		31.3	5	92	5
2	30/12/1911	Australia	Melbourne	W	9		16	2	52	1
							38	9	91	6
3	12/01/1912	Australia	Adelaide	W	71		26	9	36	5
							49	15	103	1
4	09/02/1912	Australia	Melbourne	W	50		22	2	77	4
						1	19	3	38	3
5	23/02/1912	Australia	Sydney	W	15		16	0	55	1
					4		30.1	7	43	4
6	10/06/1912	South Africa	Lord's	W	11	2	13.1	7	16	5
							27	10	54	3
7	24/06/1912	Australia	Lord's	D	20	1	36	18	42	2
8	08/07/1912	South Africa	Headingley	W	30		16	7	29	0
					0	2	23	4	51	2
9	29/07/1912	Australia	Old Trafford	D	13		1	0	3	0
10	12/08/1912	South Africa	The Oval	W	8	2	6	2	15	0
						1	7	2	19	1
11	19/08/1912	Australia	The Oval	W	19	1	2	0	5	0
					3*					

Batting & Fielding

Mat	Inns	N/O	Runs	H/S	Avg	100s	50s	Cat
11	15	1	330	71	23.57	0	3	11

Bowling

Balls	Runs	Wkts	Avg	Best	5WI	10WM	S/R
2447	926	45	20.57	6-91	4	0	54.37

N.A.FOSTER

Full Name: Neil Alan Foster
Born: 06/05/1962, Colchester, Essex
Teams: Essex 1980-93, England 1983-93
Matches: 29 (Won 3, Drew 13, Lost 13)
Right-hand lower order batsman – Right-arm fast medium bowler

No	Date	Opposition	Venue	R	Bat	C	Bowling			
1	11/08/1983	New Zealand	Lord's	W	10		16	5	40	0
					3	1	12	0	35	1
2	20/01/1984	New Zealand	Wellington	D	10		24	9	60	1
						1	37	12	91	2
3	10/02/1984	New Zealand	Auckland	D	18*		30	8	78	1
4	12/03/1984	Pakistan	Faisalabad	D		1	30	7	109	1
							5	1	10	1
5	19/03/1984	Pakistan	Lahore (2)	D	6		32	8	67	5
					0		15	4	44	0
6	28/06/1984	West Indies	Lord's	L	6		6	2	13	0
					9*		12	0	69	0
7	13/01/1985	India	Madras (1)	W	5		23	2	104	6
							28	8	59	5
8	31/01/1985	India	Kanpur	D	8		36	8	123	3
9	27/06/1985	Australia	Lord's	L	3		23	1	83	1
					0					
10	21/03/1986	West Indies	Bridgetown	L	0		19	0	76	3
					0					
11	03/04/1986	West Indies	Port-of-Spain	L	0		24	3	68	2
					14		2.5	0	15	0
12	11/04/1986	West Indies	St John's	L	10		28	5	86	2
					0*		10	0	40	0
13	03/07/1986	India	Edgbaston	D	17		41	9	93	3
					0		22	9	48	1
14	24/07/1986	New Zealand	Lord's	D	8		25	6	56	0
							3	1	13	1
15	04/06/1987	Pakistan	Old Trafford	D	8		15	3	34	1
16	18/06/1987	Pakistan	Lord's	D	21					
17	02/07/1987	Pakistan	Headingley	L	9		46.2	15	107	8
					22					
18	23/07/1987	Pakistan	Edgbaston	D	29	1	37	8	107	2
							27	7	59	4
19	06/08/1987	Pakistan	The Oval	D	4		12	3	32	0
20	25/11/1987	Pakistan	Lahore (2)	L	39		23	6	58	2
					1					
21	07/12/1987	Pakistan	Faisalabad	D	0		18	4	42	4
					0		3	0	4	0
22	29/01/1988	Australia	Sydney	D	19	1	19	6	27	2
							15	6	27	0
23	21/07/1988	West Indies	Headingley	L	8*	1	32.2	6	98	3
					0		7	1	36	0
24	04/08/1988	West Indies	The Oval	L	7		16	2	64	5
					34		18	3	52	1
25	25/08/1988	Sri Lanka	Lord's	W	14*		21	5	51	3
							33	10	98	2
26	08/06/1989	Australia	Headingley	L	2*	1	46	14	109	3
					1*		19	4	65	1
27	22/06/1989	Australia	Lord's	L	16		45	7	129	3
					4		18	3	39	3
28	27/07/1989	Australia	Old Trafford	L	39		34	12	74	2
					6		5	2	5	0
29	17/06/1993	Australia	Lord's	L	16		30	4	94	0
					20					

Batting & Fielding

Mat	Inns	N/O	Runs	H/S	Avg	100s	50s	Cat
29	45	7	446	39	11.73	0	0	7

Bowling

Balls	Runs	Wkts	Avg	Best	5WI	10WM	S/R
6261	2891	88	32.85	8-107	5	1	71.14

R.E.FOSTER

Full Name: Reginald Erskine Foster (known as Tip)
Born: 16/04/1878, Malvern, Worcestershire
Died: 13/05/1914, Brompton, Kensington, London
Teams: Oxford University 1897-1900, Worcestershire 1899-1912, England 1903-07
Matches: 8 (Won 4, Drew 2, Lost 2)
England Captain: 3 times 1907 (Won 1, Drew 2, Lost 0) **Toss:** 3-0
Right-hand middle order batsman – Right-arm fast bowler

No	Date	Opposition	Venue	R	Bat	C
1	11/12/1903	Australia	Sydney	W	287	2
					19	
2	01/01/1904	Australia	Melbourne	W	49*	
3	15/01/1904	Australia	Adelaide	L	21	
					16	
4	26/02/1904	Australia	Sydney	W	19	2
					27	1
5	05/03/1904	Australia	Melbourne	L	18	2
					30	1
6*	01/07/1907	South Africa	Lord's	D	8	1
7*	29/07/1907	South Africa	Headingley	W	0	
					22	2
8*	19/08/1907	South Africa	The Oval	D	51	1
					35	1

Batting & Fielding

Mat	Inns	N/O	Runs	H/S	Avg	100s	50s	Cat
8	14	1	602	287	46.30	1	1	13

A.J.FOTHERGILL

Full Name: Arnold James Fothergill
Born: 26/08/1854, Newcastle upon Tyne, Northumberland
Died: 01/08/1932, Newcastle upon Tyne, Northumberland
Teams: Somerset 1882-84, England 1889
Matches: 2 (Won 2, Drew 0, Lost 0)
Left-hand lower order batsman – Left-arm fast medium bowler

No	Date	Opposition	Venue	R	Bat	C		Bowling		
1	12/03/1889	South Africa	Port Elizabeth	W	32		24	15	15	1
							18.1	11	19	4
2	25/03/1889	South Africa	Cape Town	W	1		24	12	26	2
							14	4	30	1

Batting & Fielding

Mat	Inns	N/O	Runs	H/S	Avg	100s	50s	Cat
2	2	0	33	32	16.50	0	0	0

Bowling

Balls	Runs	Wkts	Avg	Best	5WI	10WM	S/R
321	90	8	11.25	4-19	0	0	40.12

G.FOWLER

Full Name: Graeme Fowler
Born: 20/04/1957, Accrington, Lancashire
Teams: Lancashire 1979-92, Durham 93-94, England 1982-85
Matches: 21 (Won 5, Drew 6, Lost 10)
Left-hand opening batsman – Right-arm medium bowler

No	Date	Opposition	Venue	R	Bat	C	Bowling
1	26/08/1982	Pakistan	Headingley	W	9	1	
					86		
2	26/11/1982	Australia	Brisbane (2)	L	7		
					83		
3	10/12/1982	Australia	Adelaide	L	11		
					37		
4	26/12/1982	Australia	Melbourne	W	4	1	
					65		
5	14/07/1983	New Zealand	The Oval	W	1		
					105		

No	Date	Opposition	Venue	R	Bat	C		Bowling		
6	28/07/1983	New Zealand	Headingley	L	9					
					19					
7	03/02/1984	New Zealand	Christchurch	L	4					
					10					
8	10/02/1984	New Zealand	Auckland	D	0					
9	12/03/1984	Pakistan	Faisalabad	D	57					
							1	0	3	0
10	19/03/1984	Pakistan	Lahore (2)	D	58	1				
					19					
11	14/06/1984	West Indies	Edgbaston	L	0					
					7					
12	28/06/1984	West Indies	Lord's	L	106	1				
					11					
13	12/07/1984	West Indies	Headingley	L	10					
					50	1				
14	26/07/1984	West Indies	Old Trafford	L	38					
					0					
15	09/08/1984	West Indies	The Oval	L	31	1				
					7					
16	23/08/1984	Sri Lanka	Lord's	D	25	1				
							1	1	0	8	0
17	28/11/1984	India	Bombay (3)	L	28					
					55					
18	12/12/1984	India	Delhi	W	5	1				
					29					
19	31/12/1984	India	Calcutta	D	49	1		1	1	0	0
20	13/01/1985	India	Madras (1)	W	201					
					2					
21	31/01/1985	India	Kanpur	D	69					

Batting & Fielding

Mat	Inns	N/O	Runs	H/S	Avg	100s	50s	Cat
21	37	0	1307	201	35.32	3	8	10

Bowling

Balls	Runs	Wkts	Avg	Best	5WI	10WM	S/R
18	11	0	–	0-0	0	0	–

A.R.C.FRASER

Full Name: Angus Robert Charles Fraser
Born: 08/08/1965, Billinge, Lancashire
Teams: Middlesex 1984-96, England 1989-96
Matches: 32 (Won 8, Drew 14, Lost 10)
Right-hand lower order batsman – Right-arm fast medium bowler

No	Date	Opposition	Venue	R	Bat	C		Bowling		
1	06/07/1989	Australia	Edgbaston	D	12		33	8	63	4
							12	0	29	0
2	27/07/1989	Australia	Old Trafford	L	2		36.5	4	95	3
					3		10	0	28	0
3	10/08/1989	Australia	Trent Bridge	L	29		52.3	18	108	2
					1					
4	24/02/1990	West Indies	Kingston	W	2*		20	8	28	5
							14	5	31	1
5	23/03/1990	West Indies	Port-of-Spain	D	11		13.1	2	41	3
							24	4	61	2
6	26/07/1990	India	Lord's	W			39.1	9	104	5
							22	7	39	3
7	09/08/1990	India	Old Trafford	D	1		35	5	124	5
							21	3	81	1
8	23/08/1990	India	The Oval	D	0		42	17	112	2
9	23/11/1990	Australia	Brisbane (2)	L	1		21	6	33	3
					0		14	2	49	0
10	26/12/1990	Australia	Melbourne	L	24		39	10	82	6
					0		20	4	33	1
11	25/01/1991	Australia	Adelaide	D	2	1	23	6	48	0
							26	3	66	1
12	19/08/1993	Australia	The Oval	W	28		26.4	4	87	5
					13	1	19.1	5	44	3

No	Date	Opposition	Venue	R	Bat	C	Bowling			
13	17/03/1994	West Indies	Georgetown	L	0*		29	5	85	2
					0					
14	25/03/1994	West Indies	Port-of-Spain	L	8*		24	9	49	4
					0*	2	25	6	71	0
15	08/04/1994	West Indies	Bridgetown	W	3		28.5	7	75	8
							17	7	40	0
16	16/04/1994	West Indies	St John's	D	0		43	4	121	2
							2	1	2	0
17	02/06/1994	New Zealand	Trent Bridge	W	8	1	21	10	40	2
							23	8	53	2
18	16/06/1994	New Zealand	Lord's	D	10		36	9	102	2
					2		15	0	50	0
19	30/06/1994	New Zealand	Old Trafford	D	10		12	3	17	0
							19	7	34	1
20	21/07/1994	South Africa	Lord's	L	3		24.5	7	72	3
					1	1	23	5	62	2
21	04/08/1994	South Africa	Headingley	D	6		31	5	92	2
							7	2	19	0
22	01/01/1995	Australia	Sydney	D	27		11	1	26	2
							25	3	73	5
23	26/01/1995	Australia	Adelaide	W	7		28.5	6	95	3
					5		12	1	37	1
24	03/02/1995	Australia	Perth	L	9		32	11	84	1
					5		21	3	74	2
25	22/06/1995	West Indies	Lord's	W	1		33	13	66	5
					2*		25	9	57	0
26	06/07/1995	West Indies	Edgbaston	L	0*		31	7	93	2
					1*					
27	27/07/1995	West Indies	Old Trafford	W	4		16.2	5	45	4
							19	5	53	2
28	10/08/1995	West Indies	Trent Bridge	D	0		17.3	6	77	1
					4		6	1	17	1
29	24/08/1995	West Indies	The Oval	D	10*	1	40	6	155	1
30	16/11/1995	South Africa	Centurion	D	4*					
31	30/11/1995	South Africa	Johannesburg (3)	D	0		20	5	69	0
							29	6	84	3
32	02/01/1996	South Africa	Cape Town	L	5*		17	10	34	1
					1					

Batting & Fielding

Mat	Inns	N/O	Runs	H/S	Avg	100s	50s	Cat
32	46	10	265	29	7.36	0	0	7

Bowling

Balls	Runs	Wkts	Avg	Best	5WI	10WM	S/R
7967	3509	119	29.48	8-75	8	0	66.94

A.P.FREEMAN

Full Name: Alfred Percy Freeman (known as Tich)
Born: 17/05/1888, Lewisham, London
Died: 28/01/1965, Bearsted, Kent
Teams: Kent 1914-36, England 1924-29
Matches: 12 (Won 6, Drew 2, Lost 4)
Right-hand lower order batsman – Leg break and googly bowler

No	Date	Opposition	Venue	R	Bat	C	Bowling			
1	19/12/1924	Australia	Sydney	L	0		49	11	124	2
					50*	1	37	4	134	3
2	16/01/1925	Australia	Adelaide	L	6*		18	0	107	1
					24		17	1	94	2
3	31/12/1927	South Africa	Cape Town	W	7		29	12	58	4
					0*		22	7	66	3
4	21/01/1928	South Africa	Durban (2)	D	3		16.3	3	44	1
							33	3	122	3
5	28/01/1928	South Africa	Johannesburg (1)	L	9*		3	0	18	1
					4		13	2	34	1
6	04/02/1928	South Africa	Durban (2)	L	0*		16	2	57	1
					1	1				
7	23/06/1928	West Indies	Lord's	W	1		18.3	5	40	2
							21.1	10	37	4

No	Date	Opposition	Venue	R	Bat	C	Bowling			
8	21/07/1928	West Indies	Old Trafford	W	0		33.4	18	54	5
							18	5	39	5
9	11/08/1928	West Indies	The Oval	W	19		27	8	85	2
						1	21.4	4	47	4
10	13/07/1929	South Africa	Headingley	W	15		32.3	6	115	7
							35	7	92	3
11	27/07/1929	South Africa	Old Trafford	W			32	12	71	7
							39.4	13	100	5
12	17/08/1929	South Africa	The Oval	D	15	1	49	9	169	0

Batting & Fielding

Mat	Inns	N/O	Runs	H/S	Avg	100s	50s	Cat
12	16	5	154	50*	14.00	0	1	4

Bowling

Balls	Runs	Wkts	Avg	Best	5WI	10WM	S/R
3732	1707	66	25.86	7-71	5	3	56.54

B.N.FRENCH

Full Name: Bruce Nicholas French
Born: 13/08/1959, Warsop, Nottinghamshire
Teams: Nottinghamshire 1976-95, England 1986-88
Matches: 16 (Won 0, Drew 13, Lost 3)
Right-hand middle/lower order batsman – Wicket-keeper

No	Date	Opposition	Venue	R	Bat	C	St	B
1+	19/06/1986	India	Headingley	L	8	2		0
					5	1		4
2+	03/07/1986	India	Edgbaston	D	8	3		3
					1	3		1
3+	24/07/1986	New Zealand	Lord's	D	0*			0
								0
4+	07/08/1986	New Zealand	Trent Bridge	L	21	1		0
					12*			0
5+	21/08/1986	New Zealand	The Oval	D		2		1
								0
6+	04/06/1987	Pakistan	Old Trafford	D	59	2		9
7+	18/06/1987	Pakistan	Lord's	D	42			
8+	23/07/1987	Pakistan	Edgbaston	D	0	1		4
					1*			0
9+	06/08/1987	Pakistan	The Oval	D	1	1		2
10+	25/11/1987	Pakistan	Lahore (2)	L	38*		1	18
					9			
11+	07/12/1987	Pakistan	Faisalabad	D	2	3		0
								4
12+	16/12/1987	Pakistan	Karachi (1)	D	31	4		0
					0			
13+	29/01/1988	Australia	Sydney	D	47	4		0
								3
14+	12/02/1988	New Zealand	Christchurch	D	7	4		2
					3	1		6
15+	25/02/1988	New Zealand	Auckland	D	13	4		1
						2		8
16+	03/03/1988	New Zealand	Wellington	D				0

Batting & Fielding

Mat	Inns	N/O	Runs	H/S	Avg	100s	50s	Cat	St	Byes
16	21	4	308	59	18.11	0	1	38	1	66

C.B.FRY

Full Name: Charles Burgess Fry (also known as C.B.)
Born: 25/04/1872, West Croydon, Surrey
Died: 07/09/1956, Child's Hill, Hampstead, London
Teams: Oxford University 1892-95, Sussex 1894-1908, Hampshire 1909-21, London County 1900-02, Europeans 1921/22, England 1896-1912
Matches: 26 (Won 9, Drew 14, Lost 3)
England Captain: 6 times 1912 (Won 4, Drew 2, Lost 0) **Toss:** 4-2
Right-hand opening/middle order batsman – Right-arm fast medium bowler

No	Date	Opposition	Venue	R	Bat	C	Bowling
1	13/02/1896	South Africa	Port Elizabeth	W	43		
					15		
2	02/03/1896	South Africa	Johannesburg (1)	W	64		
						1	
3	01/06/1899	Australia	Trent Bridge	D	50	1	
					9		
4	15/06/1899	Australia	Lord's	L	13	1	
					4		
5	29/06/1899	Australia	Headingley	D	38	1	
						1	
6	17/07/1899	Australia	Old Trafford	D	9		
					4		
7	14/08/1899	Australia	The Oval	D	60	1	
8	29/05/1902	Australia	Edgbaston	D	0	1	2 1 3 0
						1	
9	12/06/1902	Australia	Lord's	D	0		
10	03/07/1902	Australia	Bramall Lane	L	1		
					4		
11	15/06/1905	Australia	Lord's	D	73	1	
					36*		
12	03/07/1905	Australia	Headingley	D	32		
					30		
13	24/07/1905	Australia	Old Trafford	W	17	2	
14	14/08/1905	Australia	The Oval	D	144	1	
					16		
15	01/07/1907	South Africa	Lord's	D	33		
						1	
16	29/07/1907	South Africa	Headingley	W	2	1	
					54		
17	19/08/1907	South Africa	The Oval	D	129		
					3		
18	27/05/1909	Australia	Edgbaston	W	0		
					35*		
19	01/07/1909	Australia	Headingley	L	1	1	
					7		
20	09/08/1909	Australia	The Oval	D	62		
					35*		
21*	10/06/1912	South Africa	Lord's	W	29		
22*	24/06/1912	Australia	Lord's	D	42		
23*	08/07/1912	South Africa	Headingley	W	10		
					7		
24*	29/07/1912	Australia	Old Trafford	D	19		
25*	12/08/1912	South Africa	The Oval	W	9		
26*	19/08/1912	Australia	The Oval	W	5	1	
					79	1	

Batting & Fielding

Mat	Inns	N/O	Runs	H/S	Avg	100s	50s	Cat
26	41	3	1223	144	32.18	2	7	17

Bowling

Balls	Runs	Wkts	Avg	Best	5WI	10WM	S/R
10	3	0	–	0-3	0	0	–

J.E.R.GALLIAN

Full Name: Jason Edward Riche Gallian
Born: 25/06/1971, Manly, Sydney, New South Wales, Australia
Teams: Oxford University 1992-93, Lancashire 1990-96, England 1995
Matches: 3 (Won 0, Drew 2, Lost 1)
Right-hand opening/middle order batsman – Right-arm medium bowler

No	Date	Opposition	Venue	R	Bat	C	Bowling
1	06/07/1995	West Indies	Edgbaston	L	7		
					0		

No	Date	Opposition	Venue	R	Bat	C	Bowling			
2	24/08/1995	West Indies	The Oval	D	0	1	12	1	56	0
					25					
3	26/12/1995	South Africa	Port Elizabeth	D	14	2	0	6	0	
					28					

Batting & Fielding

Mat	Inns	N/O	Runs	H/S	Avg	100s	50s	Cat
3	6	0	74	28	12.33	0	0	1

Bowling

Balls	Runs	Wkts	Avg	Best	5WI	10WM	S/R
84	62	0	–	0-6	0	0	–

M.W.GATTING

Full Name: Michael William Gatting, OBE (known as Mike)
Born: 06/06/1957, Kingsbury, Middlesex
Teams: Middlesex 1975-96, England 1978-1995
Matches: 79 (Won 15, Drew 38, Lost 26)
England Captain: 23 times 1986-88 (Won 2, Drew 16, Lost 5) **Toss:** 14-9
Right-hand middle order batsman – Right-arm medium bowler

No	Date	Opposition	Venue	R	Bat	C	Bowling			
1	18/01/1978	Pakistan	Karachi (1)	D	5	2				
					6					
2	04/03/1978	New Zealand	Auckland	D	0	1				
							1	0	1	0
3	19/06/1980	West Indies	Lord's	D	18					
4	10/07/1980	West Indies	Old Trafford	D	33					
					56					
5	24/07/1980	West Indies	The Oval	D	48	1				
					15					
6	07/08/1980	West Indies	Headingley	D	1					
					1					
7	28/08/1980	Australia	Lord's	D	12	1				
					51*					
8	13/03/1981	West Indies	Bridgetown	L	2	1				
					0					
9	18/06/1981	Australia	Trent Bridge	L	52					
					15	1				
10	02/07/1981	Australia	Lord's	D	59	1				
					16					
11	16/07/1981	Australia	Headingley	W	15					
					1	2				
12	30/07/1981	Australia	Edgbaston	W	21					
					39	1				
13	13/08/1981	Australia	Old Trafford	W	32					
					11	1	3	1	13	0
14	27/08/1981	Australia	The Oval	D	53	1				
					56	1				
15	09/12/1981	India	Bangalore	D	29					
16	23/12/1981	India	Delhi	D	5					
17	01/01/1982	India	Calcutta	D	0					
					2*					
18	13/01/1982	India	Madras (1)	D	0					
							1	0	4	0
19	30/01/1982	India	Kanpur	D	32					
20	29/07/1982	Pakistan	Edgbaston	W	17					
					5					
21	12/08/1982	Pakistan	Lord's	L	32*	1				
					7					
22	26/08/1982	Pakistan	Headingley	W	25	1	8	2	17	0
					25	1	2	1	4	0
23	11/08/1983	New Zealand	Lord's	W	81					
					15	1				
24	25/08/1983	New Zealand	Trent Bridge	W	14	2	5	2	8	0
					11	1	2	1	5	0
25	20/01/1984	New Zealand	Wellington	D	19	2				
							8	4	14	1
26	03/02/1984	New Zealand	Christchurch	L	19*	2	0	14	0	
					0					

No	Date	Opposition	Venue	R	Bat	C	Bowling			
27	02/03/1984	Pakistan	Karachi (1)	L	26 4					
28	12/03/1984	Pakistan	Faisalabad	D	75	2	3 2	0 0	17 18	1 0
29	19/03/1984	Pakistan	Lahore (2)	D	0 53	1 3				
30	28/06/1984	West Indies	Lord's	L	1 29	2				
31	28/11/1984	India	Bombay (3)	L	15 136	7		0	20	0
32	12/12/1984	India	Delhi	W	26 30*	1	2 1	0 0	5 3	0 0
33	31/12/1984	India	Calcutta	D	48	1	2	1	1	0
34	13/01/1985	India	Madras (1)	W	207 10*	2				
35	31/01/1985	India	Kanpur	D	62 41*		1	0	7	0
36	13/06/1985	Australia	Headingley	W	53 12					
37	27/06/1985	Australia	Lord's	L	14 75*					
38	11/07/1985	Australia	Trent Bridge	D	74 35*		1	0	2	0
39	01/08/1985	Australia	Old Trafford	D	160		4	0	14	0
40	15/08/1985	Australia	Edgbaston	W	100*					
41	29/08/1985	Australia	The Oval	W	4					
42	11/04/1986	West Indies	St John's	L	15 1	2				
43	05/06/1986	India	Lord's	L	0 40	1				
44*	19/06/1986	India	Headingley	L	13 31*	2				
45*	03/07/1986	India	Edgbaston	D	183* 26		2	0	10	0
46*	24/07/1986	New Zealand	Lord's	D	2 26	2				
47*	07/08/1986	New Zealand	Trent Bridge	L	17 4					
48*	21/08/1986	New Zealand	The Oval	D	121					
49*	14/11/1986	Australia	Brisbane (2)	W	61 12	1	1 2	0 0	2 2	0 0
50*	28/11/1986	Australia	Perth	D	14 70		5	3	3	0
51*	12/12/1986	Australia	Adelaide	D	100 0		9 2	1 1	22 4	0 0
52*	26/12/1986	Australia	Melbourne	W	40	2	1	0	4	0
53*	10/01/1987	Australia	Sydney	L	0 96	2	1 2	0 2	2 0	0 0
54*	04/06/1987	Pakistan	Old Trafford	D	42					
55*	18/06/1987	Pakistan	Lord's	D	43					
56*	02/07/1987	Pakistan	Headingley	L	8 9	1	9	3	16	0
57*	23/07/1987	Pakistan	Edgbaston	D	124 8	1	3	0	6	0
58*	06/08/1987	Pakistan	The Oval	D	61 150*		10	2	18	0
59*	25/11/1987	Pakistan	Lahore (2)	L	0 23					
60*	07/12/1987	Pakistan	Faisalabad	D	79 8					
61*	16/12/1987	Pakistan	Karachi (1)	D	18 0	1				
62*	29/01/1988	Australia	Sydney	D	13					
63*	12/02/1988	New Zealand	Christchurch	D	8 23					

No	Date	Opposition	Venue	R	Bat	C	Bowling			
64*	25/02/1988	New Zealand	Auckland	D	42					
							17	4	40	1
65*	03/03/1988	New Zealand	Wellington	D	33*		6	1	21	1
66*	02/06/1988	West Indies	Trent Bridge	D	5	1				
					29					
67	30/06/1988	West Indies	Old Trafford	L	0					
					4					
68	22/06/1989	Australia	Lord's	L	0					
					22					
69	29/01/1993	India	Calcutta	L	33					
					81					
70	11/02/1993	India	Madras (1)	L	2					
					19					
71	19/02/1993	India	Bombay (3)	L	23	1				
					61					
72	13/03/1993	Sri Lanka	Colombo (2)	L	29	1				
					18	1				
73	03/06/1993	Australia	Old Trafford	L	4	1				
					23	1				
74	17/06/1993	Australia	Lord's	L	5					
					59					
75	25/11/1994	Australia	Brisbane (2)	L	10	1				
					13					
76	24/12/1994	Australia	Melbourne	L	9					
					25					
77	01/01/1995	Australia	Sydney	D	0	1				
78	26/01/1995	Australia	Adelaide	W	117					
					0	1				
79	03/02/1995	Australia	Perth	L	0					
					8					

Batting & Fielding

Mat	Inns	N/O	Runs	H/S	Avg	100s	50s	Cat
79	138	14	4409	207	35.55	10	21	59

Bowling

Balls	Runs	Wkts	Avg	Best	5WI	10WM	S/R
752	317	4	79.25	1-14	0	0	188.00

L.H.GAY

Full Name: Leslie Hewitt Gay
Born: 24/03/1871, Brighton, Sussex
Died: 01/11/1949, Salcombe Hill, Sidmouth, Devon
Teams: Cambridge University 1891-93, Somerset 1894, Hampshire 1900, England 1894
Matches: 1 (Won 1, Drew 0, Lost 0)
Right-hand lower order batsman – Wicket-keeper

No	Date	Opposition	Venue	R	Bat	C	St	B
1+	14/12/1894	Australia	Sydney	W	33	1		8
					4	2	1	2

Batting & Fielding

Mat	Inns	N/O	Runs	H/S	Avg	100s	50s	Cat	St	Byes
1	2	0	37	33	18.50	0	0	3	1	10

G.GEARY

Full Name: George Geary
Born: 09/07/1893, Barwell, Leicestershire
Died: 06/03/1981, Leicester
Teams: Leicestershire 1912-38, England 1924-34
Matches: 14 (Won 8, Drew 4, Lost 2)
Right-hand lower order batsman – Right-arm fast medium bowler

No	Date	Opposition	Venue	R	Bat	C	Bowling			
1	26/07/1924	South Africa	Old Trafford	D			11	5	21	0
2	10/07/1926	Australia	Headingley	D	35*	1	41	5	130	2

No	Date	Opposition	Venue	R	Bat	C	Bowling			
3	14/08/1926	Australia	The Oval	W	9	1	27	8	43	0
					1	2	6.3	2	15	1
4	24/12/1927	South Africa	Johannesburg (1)	W	3	1	27.3	7	70	7
							27	9	60	5
5	31/12/1927	South Africa	Cape Town	W	0	1	23	2	50	0
					1					
6	14/12/1928	Australia	Sydney	W	66		18	5	35	5
					8		31.4	11	55	2
7	29/12/1928	Australia	Melbourne	W	1		31.5	4	83	3
					4*		30	4	94	2
8	01/02/1929	Australia	Adelaide	W	3		12	3	32	0
					6	1	16	2	42	1
9	08/03/1929	Australia	Melbourne	L	4	2	81	36	105	5
					3		20	5	31	1
10	27/07/1929	South Africa	Old Trafford	W	31*	2	22.3	13	18	2
							37	18	50	2
11	17/08/1929	South Africa	The Oval	D	12*		49	15	121	3
12	11/07/1930	Australia	Headingley	D	0		35	10	95	1
13	08/06/1934	Australia	Trent Bridge	L	53		43	8	101	3
					0		23	5	46	1
14	22/06/1934	Australia	Lord's	W	9	1	22	4	56	0
						1				

Batting & Fielding

Mat	Inns	N/O	Runs	H/S	Avg	100s	50s	Cat
14	20	4	249	66	15.56	0	2	13

Bowling

Balls	Runs	Wkts	Avg	Best	5WI	10WM	S/R
3810	1353	46	29.41	7-70	4	1	82.82

P.A.GIBB

Full Name: Paul Antony Gibb
Born: 11/07/1913, Brandsby, Yorkshire
Died: 07/12/1977, Guildford, Surrey
Matches: 8 (Won 2, Drew 5, Lost 1)
Teams: Cambridge University 1935-38, Yorkshire 1935-46, Essex 1951-56, Scotland 1934-38, England 1938-46
Right-hand opening/middle order batsman – Wicket-keeper

No	Date	Opposition	Venue	R	Bat	C	St	B
1	24/12/1938	South Africa	Johannesburg (1)	D	93			
					106			
2	31/12/1938	South Africa	Cape Town	D	58			
3	20/01/1939	South Africa	Durban (2)	W	38			
4	18/02/1939	South Africa	Johannesburg (1)	D	9			
					45			
5	03/03/1939	South Africa	Durban (2)	D	4			
					120			
6+	22/06/1946	India	Lord's	W	60	1	1	10
								10
7+	20/07/1946	India	Old Trafford	D	24			10
					0	1		5
8+	29/11/1946	Australia	Brisbane (2)	L	13	1		5
					11			

Batting & Fielding

Mat	Inns	N/O	Runs	H/S	Avg	100s	50s	Cat	St	Byes
8	13	0	581	120	44.69	2	3	3	1	40

N.GIFFORD

Full Name: Norman Gifford, MBE
Born: 30/03/1940, Ulverston, Lancashire
Teams: Worcestershire 1960-82, Warwickshire 1983-88, England 1964-73
Matches: 15 (Won 3, Drew 9, Lost 3)
Left-hand lower order batsman – Left-arm slow bowler

No	Date	Opposition	Venue	R	Bat	C		Bowling		
1	18/06/1964	Australia	Lord's	D	5		12	6	14	2
							17	9	17	1
2	02/07/1964	Australia	Headingley	L	1*		34	15	62	2
					1	1	20	5	47	0
3	17/06/1971	Pakistan	Lord's	D		1	12	6	13	1
4	08/07/1971	Pakistan	Headingley	W	3*		53.4	26	69	3
					2*		34	14	51	2
5	22/07/1971	India	Lord's	D	17	1	45.3	14	84	4
					7*		19	4	43	4
6	05/08/1971	India	Old Trafford	D	8					
7	08/06/1972	Australia	Old Trafford	W	15					
					0		3	0	29	0
8	22/06/1972	Australia	Lord's	L	3	1	11	4	20	0
					16*					
9	13/07/1972	Australia	Trent Bridge	D	16		5	1	18	1
						1	15	1	49	0
10	12/01/1973	India	Madras (1)	L	19	1	34	15	64	3
					3*		7.5	2	22	0
11	25/01/1973	India	Kanpur	D			8	2	17	0
12	16/03/1973	Pakistan	Hyderabad	D	24	1	52	16	111	3
13	24/03/1973	Pakistan	Karachi (1)	D	4*		46	12	99	2
						1	29	9	55	5
14	07/06/1973	New Zealand	Trent Bridge	W	25*					
							17	7	35	0
15	21/06/1973	New Zealand	Lord's	D	8		39	6	107	0
					2*					

Batting & Fielding

Mat	Inns	N/O	Runs	H/S	Avg	100s	50s	Cat
15	20	9	179	25*	16.27	0	0	8

Bowling

Balls	Runs	Wkts	Avg	Best	5WI	10WM	S/R
3084	1026	33	31.09	5-55	1	0	93.45

A.E.R.GILLIGAN

Full Name: Arthur Edward Robert Gilligan
Born: 23/12/1894, Denmark Hill, London
Died: 05/09/1976, Mare Hill, Pulborough, Sussex
Teams: Cambridge University 1919-20, Surrey 1919, Sussex 1920-32, England 1922-25
Matches: 11 (Won 5, Drew 1, Lost 5)
England Captain: 9 times 1924-25 (Won 4, Drew 1, Lost 4) **Toss:** 2-7
Right-hand middle/lower order batsman – Right-arm fast medium bowler

No	Date	Opposition	Venue	R	Bat	C		Bowling		
1	23/12/1922	South Africa	Johannesburg (1)	L	18		7	1	23	0
					7	1	20	3	69	3
2	16/02/1923	South Africa	Durban (2)	W	4		23	7	35	3
					39*		36	10	78	3
3*	14/06/1924	South Africa	Edgbaston	W	13		6.3	4	7	6
							28	6	83	5
4*	28/06/1924	South Africa	Lord's	W			31	7	70	3
						1	24	6	54	2
5*	12/07/1924	South Africa	Headingley	W	28		10	3	27	1
							18	7	37	0
6*	16/08/1924	South Africa	The Oval	D	36		16	5	44	0
7*	19/12/1924	Australia	Sydney	L	1		23	0	92	1
					1		27	6	114	2

No	Date	Opposition	Venue	R	Bat	C		Bowling		
8*	01/01/1925	Australia	Melbourne	L	17*	1	26	1	114	3
					0		11	2	40	0
9*	16/01/1925	Australia	Adelaide	L	9		7.7	1	17	1
					31					
10*	13/02/1925	Australia	Melbourne	W	0		6	1	24	0
							7	0	26	1
11*	27/02/1925	Australia	Sydney	L	5		13	1	46	1
					0*		15	2	46	1

Batting & Fielding

Mat	Inns	N/O	Runs	H/S	Avg	100s	50s	Cat
11	16	3	209	39*	16.07	0	0	3

Bowling

Balls	Runs	Wkts	Avg	Best	5WI	10WM	S/R
2404	1046	36	29.05	6-7	2	1	66.77

A.H.H.GILLIGAN

Full Name: Alfred Herbert Harold Gilligan (known as Harold)
Born: 29/06/1896, Denmark Hill, London
Died: 05/05/1978, Stroud Common, Shamley Green, Surrey
Teams: Sussex 1919-31, England 1930
Matches: 4 (Won 1, Drew 3, Lost 0)
England Captain: 4 times 1930 (Won 1, Drew 3, Lost 0) **Toss:** 1-3
Right-hand opening/middle order batsman – Leg break bowler

No	Date	Opposition	Venue	R	Bat	C
1*	10/01/1930	New Zealand	Christchurch	W	10	
					4	
2*	24/01/1930	New Zealand	Wellington	D	32	
3*	14/02/1930	New Zealand	Auckland	D		
4*	21/02/1930	New Zealand	Auckland	D	25	

Batting & Fielding

Mat	Inns	N/O	Runs	H/S	Avg	100s	50s	Cat
4	4	0	71	32	17.75	0	0	0

H.GIMBLETT

Full Name: Harold Gimblett
Born: 19/10/1914, Bicknoller, Somerset
Died: 30/03/1978, Dewlands Park, Verwood, Dorset
Teams: Somerset 1935-54, England 1936-39
Matches: 3 (Won 2, Drew 1, Lost 0)
Right-hand opening batsman – Right-arm medium bowler

No	Date	Opposition	Venue	R	Bat	C
1	27/06/1936	India	Lord's	W	11	
					67*	
2	25/07/1936	India	Old Trafford	D	9	
3	24/06/1939	West Indies	Lord's	W	22	1
					20	

Batting & Fielding

Mat	Inns	N/O	Runs	H/S	Avg	100s	50s	Cat
3	5	1	129	67*	32.25	0	1	1

C.GLADWIN

Full Name: Clifford Gladwin (known as Cliff)
Born: 03/04/1916, Doe Lea, Derbyshire
Died: 09/04/1988, Chesterfield, Derbyshire
Teams: Derbyshire 1939-58, England 1947-49
Matches: 8 (Won 3, Drew 5, Lost 0)
Right-hand lower order batsman – Right-arm fast medium bowler

No	Date	Opposition	Venue	R	Bat	C	Bowling			
1	05/07/1947	South Africa	Old Trafford	W	16		50	24	58	2
							16	6	28	1
2	16/08/1947	South Africa	The Oval	D	51*	1	16	2	39	0
							16	5	33	0
3	16/12/1948	South Africa	Durban (2)	W	0*		12	3	21	3
					7*		7	3	15	0
4	27/12/1948	South Africa	Johannesburg (2)	D	23		20	6	29	1
							16	5	37	0
5	01/01/1949	South Africa	Cape Town	D	17*		30	7	51	1
							10	2	27	0
6	12/02/1949	South Africa	Johannesburg (2)	D	19		24	7	43	2
					7*		16	6	39	1
7	05/03/1949	South Africa	Port Elizabeth	W	10	1	30.5	6	70	3
					15		6	2	14	0
8	25/06/1949	New Zealand	Lord's	D	5		28	5	67	1

Batting & Fielding

Mat	Inns	N/O	Runs	H/S	Avg	100s	50s	Cat
8	11	5	170	51*	28.33	0	1	2

Bowling

Balls	Runs	Wkts	Avg	Best	5WI	10WM	S/R
2129	571	15	38.06	3-21	0	0	141.93

T.W.J.GODDARD

Full Name: Thomas William John Goddard (known as Tom)
Born: 01/10/1900, Gloucester
Died: 22/05/1966, Gloucester
Teams: Gloucestershire 1922-52, England 1930-39
Matches: 8 (Won 1, Drew 7, Lost 0)
Right-hand lower order batsman – Off break bowler (previously right-arm fast)

No	Date	Opposition	Venue	R	Bat	C	Bowling			
1	25/07/1930	Australia	Old Trafford	D			32.1	14	49	2
2	24/07/1937	New Zealand	Old Trafford	W	4*		18	5	48	0
					1*		14.4	5	29	6
3	14/08/1937	New Zealand	The Oval	D			10	2	25	0
							18	8	41	2
4	24/12/1938	South Africa	Johannesburg (1)	D	0*		27	5	54	3
							11	3	31	0
5	31/12/1938	South Africa	Cape Town	D			38	15	64	3
							11	1	68	1
6	18/02/1939	South Africa	Johannesburg (1)	D	8		18	2	65	1
7	22/07/1939	West Indies	Old Trafford	D		1	4	0	43	2
							4.6	1	15	1
8	19/08/1939	West Indies	The Oval	D	0	1	12	1	56	1

Batting & Fielding

Mat	Inns	N/O	Runs	H/S	Avg	100s	50s	Cat
8	5	3	13	8	6.50	0	0	3

Bowling

Balls	Runs	Wkts	Avg	Best	5WI	10WM	S/R
1563	588	22	26.72	6-29	1	0	71.04

G.A.GOOCH

Full Name: Graham Alan Gooch
Born: 23/07/1953, Whipps Cross, Leytonstone, Essex
Teams: Essex 1973-96, Western Province 1982/83-1983/84, England 1975-95
Matches: 118 (Won 32, Drew 44, Lost 42)
England Captain: 34 times 1988-93 (Won 10, Drew 12, Lost 12) **Toss:** 16-18
Right-hand opening batsman – Right-arm medium bowler

No	Date	Opposition	Venue	R	Bat	C	Bowling
1	10/07/1975	Australia	Edgbaston	L	0	1	
					0		
2	31/07/1975	Australia	Lord's	D	6		
					31	1	

No	Date	Opposition	Venue	R	Bat	C	Bowling			
3	15/06/1978	Pakistan	Lord's	W	54					
						1				
4	29/06/1978	Pakistan	Headingley	D	20	1				
5	27/07/1978	New Zealand	The Oval	W	0					
					91*					
6	10/08/1978	New Zealand	Trent Bridge	W	55	1				
7	24/08/1978	New Zealand	Lord's	W	2		10	0	29	0
					42*					
8	01/12/1978	Australia	Brisbane (2)	W	2	1	1	0	1	0
					2					
9	15/12/1978	Australia	Perth	W	1	2				
					43	1				
10	29/12/1978	Australia	Melbourne	L	25					
					40					
11	06/01/1979	Australia	Sydney	W	18	1	5	1	14	0
					22	1				
12	27/01/1979	Australia	Adelaide	W	1					
					18					
13	10/02/1979	Australia	Sydney	W	74	1				
						2				
14	12/07/1979	India	Edgbaston	W	83	2				
						2				
						2	6	3	8	0
15	02/08/1979	India	Lord's	D	10		10	5	16	1
							2	0	8	0
16	16/08/1979	India	Headingley	D	4	1	3	1	2	0
17	30/08/1979	India	The Oval	D	79		2	0	6	0
					31	1	2	0	9	0
18	04/01/1980	Australia	Sydney	L	18	1	11	4	16	2
					4		8	2	20	0
19	01/02/1980	Australia	Melbourne	L	99					
					51					
20	15/02/1980	India	Bombay (3)	W	8		4	2	3	0
					49*	1				
21	05/06/1980	West Indies	Trent Bridge	L	17		7	2	11	1
					27		2	1	2	0
22	19/06/1980	West Indies	Lord's	D	123	2	7	1	26	0
					47					
23	10/07/1980	West Indies	Old Trafford	D	2	2				
					26					
24	24/07/1980	West Indies	The Oval	D	83	1	1	0	2	0
					0					
25	07/08/1980	West Indies	Headingley	D	14		8	3	18	2
					55					
26	28/08/1980	Australia	Lord's	D	8		8	3	16	0
					16					
27	13/02/1981	West Indies	Port-of-Spain	L	41		2	0	3	0
					5					
28	13/03/1981	West Indies	Bridgetown	L	26	2	2	0	13	0
					116					
29	27/03/1981	West Indies	St John's	D	33		2	2	0	0
					83					
30	10/04/1981	West Indies	Kingston	D	153	1	8	3	20	0
					3					
31	18/06/1981	Australia	Trent Bridge	L	10					
					6					
32	02/07/1981	Australia	Lord's	D	44		10	4	28	0
					20					
33	16/07/1981	Australia	Headingley	W	2					
					0					
34	30/07/1981	Australia	Edgbaston	W	21					
					21					
35	13/08/1981	Australia	Old Trafford	W	10	1				
					5					
36	27/11/1981	India	Bombay (3)	L	2					
					1					
37	09/12/1981	India	Bangalore	D	58	1				
					40					
38	23/12/1981	India	Delhi	D	71	1	8.1	1	12	2
					20*					
39	01/01/1982	India	Calcutta	D	47	1	6	1	10	0
					63	1	2	0	4	0

No	Date	Opposition	Venue	R	Bat	C	Bowling			
40	13/01/1982	India	Madras (1)	D	127		9	2	27	0
							8	2	24	0
41	30/01/1982	India	Kanpur	D	58					
42	17/02/1982	Sri Lanka	Colombo (1)	W	22					
					31	1				
43	13/06/1985	Australia	Headingley	W	5		21	4	57	2
					28	1	9	3	21	0
44	27/06/1985	Australia	Lord's	L	30	1	3	1	11	0
					17					
45	11/07/1985	Australia	Trent Bridge	D	70	1	8.2	2	13	0
					48					
46	01/08/1985	Australia	Old Trafford	D	74					
47	15/08/1985	Australia	Edgbaston	W	19					
48	29/08/1985	Australia	The Oval	W	196	1				
49	21/02/1986	West Indies	Kingston	L	51	1	2	1	6	0
					0					
50	07/03/1986	West Indies	Port-of-Spain	L	2	2				
					43	1				
51	21/03/1986	West Indies	Bridgetown	L	53	1				
					11					
52	03/04/1986	West Indies	Port-of-Spain	L	14					
					0					
53	11/04/1986	West Indies	St John's	L	51	1	5	2	21	1
					51					
54	05/06/1986	India	Lord's	L	114					
					8	1				
55	19/06/1986	India	Headingley	L	8	2	6	0	19	1
					5		7	2	12	0
56	03/07/1986	India	Edgbaston	D	0	2				
					40					
57	24/07/1986	New Zealand	Lord's	D	18	2	13	6	23	1
					183					
58	07/08/1986	New Zealand	Trent Bridge	L	18	1	2	2	0	1
					17					
59	21/08/1986	New Zealand	The Oval	D	32	3	4	1	15	0
60	25/11/1987	Pakistan	Lahore (2)	L	12	1				
					15					
61	07/12/1987	Pakistan	Faisalabad	D	28	2				
					65		2	1	4	0
62	16/12/1987	Pakistan	Karachi (1)	D	12					
					93					
63	02/06/1988	West Indies	Trent Bridge	D	73	2				
					146					
64	16/06/1988	West Indies	Lord's	L	44	1				
					16					
65	30/06/1988	West Indies	Old Trafford	L	27					
					1					
66	21/07/1988	West Indies	Headingley	L	9	1				
					50					
67*	04/08/1988	West Indies	The Oval	L	9	2				
					84					
68*	25/08/1988	Sri Lanka	Lord's	W	75	2				
					36	1				
69	08/06/1989	Australia	Headingley	L	13		9	1	31	0
					68					
70	22/06/1989	Australia	Lord's	L	60	2	6	2	9	0
					0	1				
71	06/07/1989	Australia	Edgbaston	D	8	1				
							14	5	30	1
72	27/07/1989	Australia	Old Trafford	L	11					
					13					
73	24/08/1989	Australia	The Oval	D	0		2	1	2	0
					10					
74*	24/02/1990	West Indies	Kingston	W	18					
					8	1				
75*	23/03/1990	West Indies	Port-of-Spain	D	84					
					18*	1				
76*	07/06/1990	New Zealand	Trent Bridge	D	0	2				

No	Date	Opposition	Venue	R	Bat	C		Bowling		
77*	21/06/1990	New Zealand	Lord's	D	85 / 37		13	7	25	0
78*	05/07/1990	New Zealand	Edgbaston	W	154 / 30	1				
79*	26/07/1990	India	Lord's	W	333 / 123	1 / 1	6	3	26	1
80*	09/08/1990	India	Old Trafford	D	116 / 7	2				
81*	23/08/1990	India	The Oval	D	85 / 88		12	1	44	0
82*	26/12/1990	Australia	Melbourne	L	20 / 58					
83*	04/01/1991	Australia	Sydney	D	59 / 54	2	14	3	46	1
84*	25/01/1991	Australia	Adelaide	D	87 / 117	1 / 2	9	2	23	1
85*	01/02/1991	Australia	Perth	L	13 / 18	1				
86*	06/06/1991	West Indies	Headingley	W	34 / 154*	1 / 2				
87*	20/06/1991	West Indies	Lord's	D	37		2	0	3	0
88*	04/07/1991	West Indies	Trent Bridge	L	68 / 13					
89*	25/07/1991	West Indies	Edgbaston	L	45 / 40		6	1	11	0
90*	08/08/1991	West Indies	The Oval	W	60 / 29	1 / 2				
91*	22/08/1991	Sri Lanka	Lord's	W	38 / 174					
92	18/01/1992	New Zealand	Christchurch	W	2					
93*	30/01/1992	New Zealand	Auckland	W	4 / 114					
94*	06/02/1992	New Zealand	Wellington	D	30 / 11					
95*	04/06/1992	Pakistan	Edgbaston	D	8		10	5	9	0
96*	18/06/1992	Pakistan	Lord's	L	69 / 13					
97*	02/07/1992	Pakistan	Old Trafford	D	78	1	18	2	39	3
							16	5	30	2
98*	23/07/1992	Pakistan	Headingley	W	135 / 37		6	3	11	0
							1	0	5	0
99*	06/08/1992	Pakistan	The Oval	L	20 / 24	1				
100*	29/01/1993	India	Calcutta	L	17 / 18	1				
101*	19/02/1993	India	Bombay (3)	L	4 / 8					
102*	03/06/1993	Australia	Old Trafford	L	65 / 133					
103*	17/06/1993	Australia	Lord's	L	12 / 29		9	1	26	0
104*	01/07/1993	Australia	Trent Bridge	D	38 / 120					
105*	22/07/1993	Australia	Headingley	L	59 / 26		16	5	40	0
106	05/08/1993	Australia	Edgbaston	L	8 / 48					
107	19/08/1993	Australia	The Oval	W	56 / 79	2				
108	02/06/1994	New Zealand	Trent Bridge	W	210					
109	16/06/1994	New Zealand	Lord's	D	13 / 0		5	1	13	0
110	30/06/1994	New Zealand	Old Trafford	D	0	2 / 1	2	0	13	0
111	21/07/1994	South Africa	Lord's	L	20 / 28	1				
112	04/08/1994	South Africa	Headingley	D	23 / 27		3	0	9	0
113	18/08/1994	South Africa	The Oval	W	8 / 33					

No	Date	Opposition	Venue	R	Bat	C	Bowling			
114	25/11/1994	Australia	Brisbane (2)	L	20		9	2	20	1
					56		3	2	5	0
115	24/12/1994	Australia	Melbourne	L	15					
					2					
116	01/01/1995	Australia	Sydney	D	1					
					29		7	1	27	0
117	26/01/1995	Australia	Adelaide	W	47		5	0	22	0
					34					
118	03/02/1995	Australia	Perth	L	37		1	1	0	0
					4					

Batting & Fielding

Mat	Inns	N/O	Runs	H/S	Avg	100s	50s	Cat
118	215	6	8900	333	42.58	20	46	103

Bowling

Balls	Runs	Wkts	Avg	Best	5WI	10WM	S/R
2655	1069	23	46.47	3-39	0	0	115.43

D.GOUGH

Full Name: Darren Gough
Born: 18/09/1970, Barnsley, Yorkshire
Teams: Yorkshire 1989-96, England 1994-95
Matches: 12 (Won 2, Drew 5, Lost 5)
Right-hand lower order batsman – Right-arm fast medium bowler

No	Date	Opposition	Venue	R	Bat	C	Bowling			
1	30/06/1994	New Zealand	Old Trafford	D	65		16.3	2	47	4
							31.2	5	105	2
2	21/07/1994	South Africa	Lord's	L	12		28	6	76	4
					0*		19.3	5	46	4
3	04/08/1994	South Africa	Headingley	D	27		37	3	153	2
							10	5	15	0
4	18/08/1994	South Africa	The Oval	W	42*		19	1	85	0
							9	1	39	1
5	25/11/1994	Australia	Brisbane (2)	L	17*	2	32	7	107	4
					10		23	3	78	2
6	24/12/1994	Australia	Melbourne	L	20		26	9	60	4
					0	1	25	6	59	3
7	01/01/1995	Australia	Sydney	D	51	1	18.5	4	49	6
							28	4	72	1
8	08/06/1995	West Indies	Headingley	L	0	1	5	1	24	1
					29					
9	22/06/1995	West Indies	Lord's	W	11	1	27	2	84	2
					20		20	0	79	3
10	06/07/1995	West Indies	Edgbaston	L	1		18	3	68	0
					12					
11	16/11/1995	South Africa	Centurion	D	0					
12	30/11/1995	South Africa	Johannesburg (3)	D	2		15	2	64	0
						1	12	2	48	0

Batting & Fielding

Mat	Inns	N/O	Runs	H/S	Avg	100s	50s	Cat
12	18	3	319	65	21.26	0	2	7

Bowling

Balls	Runs	Wkts	Avg	Best	5WI	10WM	S/R
2521	1358	43	31.58	6-49	1	0	58.62

A.R.GOVER

Full Name: Alfred Richard Gover (known as Alf)
Born: 29/02/1908, Woodcote, Epsom, Surrey
Teams: Surrey 1928-47, England 1936-46
Matches: 4 (Won 0, Drew 4, Lost 0)
Right-hand lower order batsman – Right-arm fast bowler

No	Date	Opposition	Venue	R	Bat	C	Bowling			
1	25/07/1936	India	Old Trafford	D			15	2	39	0
							20	2	61	0
2	26/06/1937	New Zealand	Lord's	D	2*		22	8	49	2
							18	7	27	1
3	14/08/1937	New Zealand	The Oval	D		1	28	3	85	3
							12	1	42	1
4	17/08/1946	India	The Oval	D			21	3	56	1

Batting & Fielding

Mat	Inns	N/O	Runs	H/S	Avg	100s	50s	Cat
4	1	1	2	2*	–	0	0	1

Bowling

Balls	Runs	Wkts	Avg	Best	5WI	10WM	S/R
816	359	8	44.87	3-85	0	0	102.00

D.I.GOWER

Full Name: David Ivon Gower, OBE
Born: 01/04/1957, Tunbridge Wells, Kent
Teams: Leicestershire 1975-89, Hampshire 1990-93, England 1978-92
Matches: 117 (Won 32, Drew 43, Lost 42)
England Captain: 32 times 1982-89 (Won 5, Drew 9, Lost 18) **Toss:** 14-18
Left-hand middle order batsman – Off break bowler

No	Date	Opposition	Venue	R	Bat	C	Bowling
1	01/06/1978	Pakistan	Edgbaston	W	58		
2	15/06/1978	Pakistan	Lord's	W	56		
3	29/06/1978	Pakistan	Headingley	D	39		
4	27/07/1978	New Zealand	The Oval	W	111		
					11		
5	10/08/1978	New Zealand	Trent Bridge	W	46		
6	24/08/1978	New Zealand	Lord's	W	71		
					46		
7	01/12/1978	Australia	Brisbane (2)	W	44		
					48*		
8	15/12/1978	Australia	Perth	W	102		
					12		
9	29/12/1978	Australia	Melbourne	L	29		
					49	1	
10	06/01/1979	Australia	Sydney	W	7		
					34		
11	27/01/1979	Australia	Adelaide	W	9		
					21	2	
12	10/02/1979	Australia	Sydney	W	65	1	
13	12/07/1979	India	Edgbaston	W	200*		
14	02/08/1979	India	Lord's	D	82		
						1	
15	16/08/1979	India	Headingley	D	0		
16	30/08/1979	India	The Oval	D	0		
					7	1	
17	14/12/1979	Australia	Perth	L	17		
					23	1	
18	04/01/1980	Australia	Sydney	L	3	1	
					98*		
19	01/02/1980	Australia	Melbourne	L	0	1	
					11		
20	15/02/1980	India	Bombay (3)	W	16		
21	05/06/1980	West Indies	Trent Bridge	L	20	1	
					1		
22	28/08/1980	Australia	Lord's	D	45		
					35		
23	13/02/1981	West Indies	Port-of-Spain	L	48	1	
					27		
24	13/03/1981	West Indies	Bridgetown	L	17		
					54		
25	27/03/1981	West Indies	St John's	D	32	1	
					22		
26	10/04/1981	West Indies	Kingston	D	22		
					154*		
27	18/06/1981	Australia	Trent Bridge	L	26	1	
					28		
28	02/07/1981	Australia	Lord's	D	27	1	
					89		

No	Date	Opposition	Venue	R	Bat	C	Bowling			
29	16/07/1981	Australia	Headingley	W	24 / 9					
30	30/07/1981	Australia	Edgbaston	W	0 / 23					
31	13/08/1981	Australia	Old Trafford	W	23 / 1	1				
32	27/11/1981	India	Bombay (3)	L	5 / 20					
33	09/12/1981	India	Bangalore	D	82 / 34*					
34	23/12/1981	India	Delhi	D	0					
35	01/01/1982	India	Calcutta	D	11 / 74					
36	13/01/1982	India	Madras (1)	D	64					
37	30/01/1982	India	Kanpur	D	85	1	1 / 1	0 / 0	1 / 1	0 / 1
38	17/02/1982	Sri Lanka	Colombo (1)	W	89 / 42*	3 / 1				
39	10/06/1982	India	Lord's	W	37 / 14*	1				
40	24/06/1982	India	Old Trafford	D	9					
41	08/07/1982	India	The Oval	D	47 / 45	1				
42	29/07/1982	Pakistan	Edgbaston	W	74 / 13	1				
43*	12/08/1982	Pakistan	Lord's	L	29 / 0					
44	26/08/1982	Pakistan	Headingley	W	74 / 7	1				
45	12/11/1982	Australia	Perth	D	72 / 28					
46	26/11/1982	Australia	Brisbane (2)	L	18 / 34					
47	10/12/1982	Australia	Adelaide	L	60 / 114	2				
48	26/12/1982	Australia	Melbourne	W	18 / 3					
49	02/01/1983	Australia	Sydney	D	70 / 24	2				
50	14/07/1983	New Zealand	The Oval	W	11 / 25	1 / 1				
51	28/07/1983	New Zealand	Headingley	L	9 / 112*	1				
52	11/08/1983	New Zealand	Lord's	W	108 / 34	1				
53	25/08/1983	New Zealand	Trent Bridge	W	72 / 33	1 / 1				
54	20/01/1984	New Zealand	Wellington	D	33	2				
55	03/02/1984	New Zealand	Christchurch	L	2 / 8					
56	10/02/1984	New Zealand	Auckland	D	26					
57	02/03/1984	Pakistan	Karachi (1)	L	58 / 57					
58*	12/03/1984	Pakistan	Faisalabad	D	152					
59*	19/03/1984	Pakistan	Lahore (2)	D	9 / 173*	3				
60*	14/06/1984	West Indies	Edgbaston	L	10 / 12	1				
61*	28/06/1984	West Indies	Lord's	L	3 / 21					
62*	12/07/1984	West Indies	Headingley	L	2 / 43	1				
63*	26/07/1984	West Indies	Old Trafford	L	4 / 57*					
64*	09/08/1984	West Indies	The Oval	L	12 / 7	1				
65*	23/08/1984	Sri Lanka	Lord's	D	55	1				

No	Date	Opposition	Venue	R	Bat	C		Bowling		
66*	28/11/1984	India	Bombay (3)	L	13 2	1 1				
67*	12/12/1984	India	Delhi	W	5	1				
68*	31/12/1984	India	Calcutta	D	19	1	3	0	13	0
69*	13/01/1985	India	Madras (1)	W	18	1				
70*	31/01/1985	India	Kanpur	D	78 32*	1				
71*	13/06/1985	Australia	Headingley	W	17 5	1				
72*	27/06/1985	Australia	Lord's	L	86 22					
73*	11/07/1985	Australia	Trent Bridge	D	166 17					
74*	01/08/1985	Australia	Old Trafford	D	47	1				
75*	15/08/1985	Australia	Edgbaston	W	215	1 2				
76*	29/08/1985	Australia	The Oval	W	157	1				
77*	21/02/1986	West Indies	Kingston	L	16 9					
78*	07/03/1986	West Indies	Port-of-Spain	L	66 47	1				
79*	21/03/1986	West Indies	Bridgetown	L	66 23	1				
80*	03/04/1986	West Indies	Port-of-Spain	L	10 22					
81*	11/04/1986	West Indies	St John's	L	90 21	1				
82*	05/06/1986	India	Lord's	L	18 8					
83	03/07/1986	India	Edgbaston	D	49 26	2				
84	24/07/1986	New Zealand	Lord's	D	62 3	1 2	1	0	1	0
85	07/08/1986	New Zealand	Trent Bridge	L	71 26		0.0	0	4	0
86	21/08/1986	New Zealand	The Oval	D	131					
87	14/11/1986	Australia	Brisbane (2)	W	51 15*					
88	28/11/1986	Australia	Perth	D	136 48					
89	12/12/1986	Australia	Adelaide	D	38					
90	26/12/1986	Australia	Melbourne	W	7	1				
91	10/01/1987	Australia	Sydney	L	72 37					
92	04/06/1987	Pakistan	Old Trafford	D	22					
93	18/06/1987	Pakistan	Lord's	D	8					
94	02/07/1987	Pakistan	Headingley	L	10 55	1				
95	23/07/1987	Pakistan	Edgbaston	D	61 18					
96	06/08/1987	Pakistan	The Oval	D	28 34	1				
97	02/06/1988	West Indies	Trent Bridge	D	18 88*					
98	16/06/1988	West Indies	Lord's	L	46 1	1				
99	30/06/1988	West Indies	Old Trafford	L	9 34					
100	21/07/1988	West Indies	Headingley	L	13 2	1				
101*	08/06/1989	Australia	Headingley	L	26 34					
102*	22/06/1989	Australia	Lord's	L	57 106					

No	Date	Opposition	Venue	R	Bat	C	Bowling
103*	06/07/1989	Australia	Edgbaston	D	8		
104*	27/07/1989	Australia	Old Trafford	L	35	1	
					15		
105*	10/08/1989	Australia	Trent Bridge	L	11	2	
					5		
106*	24/08/1989	Australia	The Oval	D	79	1	
					7		
107	26/07/1990	India	Lord's	W	40		
					32*		
108	09/08/1990	India	Old Trafford	D	38		
					16		
109	23/08/1990	India	The Oval	D	8		
					157*		
110	23/11/1990	Australia	Brisbane (2)	L	61		
					27		
111	26/12/1990	Australia	Melbourne	L	100		
					0		
112	04/01/1991	Australia	Sydney	D	123		
					36	1	
113	25/01/1991	Australia	Adelaide	D	11		
					16		
114	01/02/1991	Australia	Perth	L	28*		
					5		
115	02/07/1992	Pakistan	Old Trafford	D	73	1	
116	23/07/1992	Pakistan	Headingley	W	18*		
					31*		
117	06/08/1992	Pakistan	The Oval	L	27		
					1		

Batting & Fielding

Mat	Inns	N/O	Runs	H/S	Avg	100s	50s	Cat
117	204	18	8231	215	44.25	18	39	74

Bowling

Balls	Runs	Wkts	Avg	Best	5WI	10WM	S/R
36	20	1	20.00	1-1	0	0	36.00

E.M.GRACE

Full Name: Dr Edward Mills Grace
Born: 28/11/1841, Downend, Bristol
Died: 20/05/1911, Park House, Thornbury, Gloucestershire
Teams: Gloucestershire 1870-96, England 1880
Matches: 1 (Won 1, Drew 0, Lost 0)
Right-hand opening batsman – Right-arm lob bowler (previously right-hand fast round-arm)

No	Date	Opposition	Venue	R	Bat	C
1	06/09/1880	Australia	The Oval	W	36	
					0	1

Batting & Fielding

Mat	Inns	N/O	Runs	H/S	Avg	100s	50s	Cat
1	2	0	36	36	18.00	0	0	1

G.F.GRACE

Full Name: George Frederick Grace (known as Fred)
Born: 13/12/1850, Downend, Bristol
Died: 22/09/1880, Basingstoke, Hampshire
Teams: Gloucestershire 1870-80, England 1880
Matches: 1 (Won 1, Drew 0, Lost 0)
Right-hand middle order batsman – Right-hand fast round-arm bowler

No	Date	Opposition	Venue	R	Bat	C
1	06/09/1880	Australia	The Oval	W	0	2
					0	

Batting & Fielding

Mat	Inns	N/O	Runs	H/S	Avg	100s	50s	Cat
1	2	0	0	0	0.00	0	0	2

W.G.GRACE

Full Name: Dr William Gilbert Grace (known as W.G.)
Born: 18/07/1848, Downend, Bristol
Died: 23/10/1915, Mottingham, Kent
Teams: Gloucestershire 1870-99, Kent 1877, London County 1900-04, England 1880-99
Matches: 22 (Won 13, Drew 4, Lost 5)
England Captain: 13 times 1888-89 (Won 8, Drew 2, Lost 3) **Toss:** 4-9
Right-hand opening batsman – Right-hand medium round-arm bowler

No	Date	Opposition	Venue	R	Bat	C		Bowling		
1	06/09/1880	Australia	The Oval	W	152	1	1.1	0	2	1
					9*		28	10	66	2
2	28/08/1882	Australia	The Oval	L	4	2				
					32	2				
3	10/07/1884	Australia	Old Trafford	D	8	2	11	10	2	1
					31					
4	21/07/1884	Australia	Lord's	W	14	2	7	4	13	1
5	11/08/1884	Australia	The Oval	D	19	1	24	14	23	1
6	05/07/1886	Australia	Old Trafford	W	8		9	3	21	1
					4	2	1	0	1	0
7	19/07/1886	Australia	Lord's	W	18	2				
8	12/08/1886	Australia	The Oval	W	170	2				
						2				
9	16/07/1888	Australia	Lord's	L	10	1				
					24	2				
10*	13/08/1888	Australia	The Oval	W	1	1				
11*	30/08/1888	Australia	Old Trafford	W	38	1				
						3				
12*	21/07/1890	Australia	Lord's	W	0	1				
					75*		14	10	12	2
13*	11/08/1890	Australia	The Oval	W	0					
					16					
14*	01/01/1892	Australia	Melbourne	L	50	1				
					25	1				
15*	29/01/1892	Australia	Sydney	L	26	2				
					5	3	16	2	34	0
16*	24/03/1892	Australia	Adelaide	W	58					
						2				
17*	14/08/1893	Australia	The Oval	W	68					
						1				
18*	24/08/1893	Australia	Old Trafford	D	40	1				
					45					
19*	22/06/1896	Australia	Lord's	W	66					
					7		6	1	14	0
20*	16/07/1896	Australia	Old Trafford	L	2		7	3	11	0
					11					
21*	10/08/1896	Australia	The Oval	W	24					
					9					
22*	01/06/1899	Australia	Trent Bridge	D	28		20	8	31	0
					1	1	2	0	6	0

Batting & Fielding

Mat	Inns	N/O	Runs	H/S	Avg	100s	50s	Cat
22	36	2	1098	170	32.29	2	5	39

Bowling

Balls	Runs	Wkts	Avg	Best	5WI	10WM	S/R
666	236	9	26.22	2-12	0	0	74.00

T.W.GRAVENEY

Full Name: Thomas William Graveney, OBE (known as Tom)
Born: 16/06/1927, Riding Mill, Northumberland
Teams: Gloucestershire 1948-60, Worcestershire 1961-70, Queensland 1969/70-71/72, England 1951-69
Matches: 79 (Won 36, Drew 29, Lost 14)
England Captain: Once 1968 (Won 0, Drew 1, Lost 0) **Toss:** 0-1
Right-hand middle order batsman – Leg break bowler

No	Date	Opposition	Venue	R	Bat	C	Bowling			
1	05/07/1951	South Africa	Old Trafford	W	15					
2	14/12/1951	India	Bombay (2)	D	175					
					25*					
3	30/12/1951	India	Calcutta	D	24					
					21		1	0	9	0
4	12/01/1952	India	Kanpur	W	6	1				
					48*					
5	06/02/1952	India	Madras (1)	L	39					
					25					
6	05/06/1952	India	Headingley	W	71					
					20*					
7	19/06/1952	India	Lord's	W	73					
8	17/07/1952	India	Old Trafford	W	14	2				
9	14/08/1952	India	The Oval	D	13					
10	11/06/1953	Australia	Trent Bridge	D	22					
						2				
11	25/06/1953	Australia	Lord's	D	78					
					2	1				
12	09/07/1953	Australia	Old Trafford	D	5					
13	23/07/1953	Australia	Headingley	D	55					
					3	1				
14	15/08/1953	Australia	The Oval	W	4					
15	15/01/1954	West Indies	Kingston	L	16	2				
					34					
16	06/02/1954	West Indies	Bridgetown	L	15	1				
					64*					
17	24/02/1954	West Indies	Georgetown	W	0					
					33*	2				
18	17/03/1954	West Indies	Port-of-Spain	D	92	1	3	0	26	0
					0*		5	0	33	0
19	30/03/1954	West Indies	Kingston	W	11					
					0	2				
20	01/07/1954	Pakistan	Trent Bridge	W	84					
						1				
21	22/07/1954	Pakistan	Old Trafford	D	65					
						1				
22	12/08/1954	Pakistan	The Oval	L	1					
					0	1				
23	17/12/1954	Australia	Sydney	W	21	2				
					0					
24	25/02/1955	Australia	Sydney	D	111					
						2	6	0	34	1
25	11/03/1955	New Zealand	Dunedin	W	41					
					32*					
26	25/03/1955	New Zealand	Auckland	W	13					
						2				
27	09/06/1955	South Africa	Trent Bridge	W	42	1				
						2				
28	23/06/1955	South Africa	Lord's	W	15	1				
					60					
29	07/07/1955	South Africa	Old Trafford	L	0	2				
					1					
30	21/07/1955	South Africa	Headingley	L	10					
					36					
31	13/08/1955	South Africa	The Oval	W	13					
					42	2				
32	07/06/1956	Australia	Trent Bridge	D	8					
					10*		6	3	6	0
33	21/06/1956	Australia	Lord's	L	5					
					18	1				
34	20/06/1957	West Indies	Lord's	W	0	1				
35	04/07/1957	West Indies	Trent Bridge	D	258					
					28*		5	2	14	0
36	25/07/1957	West Indies	Headingley	W	22					
37	22/08/1957	West Indies	The Oval	W	164					

No	Date	Opposition	Venue	R	Bat	C	Bowling			
38	05/06/1958	New Zealand	Edgbaston	W	7 19	1				
39	19/06/1958	New Zealand	Lord's	W	37	1				
40	03/07/1958	New Zealand	Headingley	W	31					
41	24/07/1958	New Zealand	Old Trafford	W	25					
42	05/12/1958	Australia	Brisbane (2)	L	19 36	2				
43	31/12/1958	Australia	Melbourne	L	0 3	1				
44	09/01/1959	Australia	Sydney	D	33 22	1				
45	30/01/1959	Australia	Adelaide	L	41 53*					
46	13/02/1959	Australia	Melbourne	L	19 54	1				
47	27/02/1959	New Zealand	Christchurch	W	42	1				
48	14/03/1959	New Zealand	Auckland	D	46	1				
49	31/05/1962	Pakistan	Edgbaston	W	97	1 2				
50	21/06/1962	Pakistan	Lord's	W	153	3				
51	05/07/1962	Pakistan	Headingley	W	37	1				
52	26/07/1962	Pakistan	Trent Bridge	D	114	1				
53	29/12/1962	Australia	Melbourne	W	41	1	3	1	10	0
54	25/01/1963	Australia	Adelaide	D	22 36*	2				
55	15/02/1963	Australia	Sydney	D	14 3	3	4	0	24	0
56	16/06/1966	West Indies	Lord's	D	96 30*					
57	30/06/1966	West Indies	Trent Bridge	L	109 32	1				
58	04/08/1966	West Indies	Headingley	L	8 19	1				
59	18/08/1966	West Indies	The Oval	W	165	3				
60	08/06/1967	India	Headingley	W	59 14					
61	22/06/1967	India	Lord's	W	151	1				
62	13/07/1967	India	Edgbaston	W	10 17	1				
63	27/07/1967	Pakistan	Lord's	D	81 30	1				
64	10/08/1967	Pakistan	Trent Bridge	W	28					
65	24/08/1967	Pakistan	The Oval	W	77					
66	19/01/1968	West Indies	Port-of-Spain	D	118	3 1				
67	08/02/1968	West Indies	Kingston	D	30 21	1				
68	29/02/1968	West Indies	Bridgetown	D	55	2				
69	14/03/1968	West Indies	Port-of-Spain	W	8 2	1				
70	28/03/1968	West Indies	Georgetown	D	27 0	1				
71	06/06/1968	Australia	Old Trafford	L	2 33	1				
72	20/06/1968	Australia	Lord's	D	14	1				
73	11/07/1968	Australia	Edgbaston	D	96 39*					
74*	25/07/1968	Australia	Headingley	D	37 41	1 1				

No	Date	Opposition	Venue	R	Bat	C	Bowling			
75	22/08/1968	Australia	The Oval	W	63					
					12					
76	21/02/1969	Pakistan	Lahore (2)	D	13					
					12		6	0	11	0
77	28/02/1969	Pakistan	Dacca	D	46					
78	06/03/1969	Pakistan	Karachi (1)	D	105					
79	12/06/1969	West Indies	Old Trafford	W	75	1				

Batting & Fielding

Mat	Inns	N/O	Runs	H/S	Avg	100s	50s	Cat
79	123	13	4882	258	44.38	11	20	80

Bowling

Balls	Runs	Wkts	Avg	Best	5WI	10WM	S/R
260	167	1	167.00	1-34	0	0	260.00

T.GREENHOUGH

Full Name: Thomas Greenhough (known as Tommy)
Born: 09/11/1931, Cronkey Shaw, Rochdale, Lancashire
Teams: Lancashire 1951-66, England 1959-60
Matches: 4 (Won 3, Drew 1, Lost 0)
Right-hand lower order batsman – Leg break and googly bowler

No	Date	Opposition	Venue	R	Bat	C	Bowling			
1	04/06/1959	India	Trent Bridge	W	0		26	7	58	1
							23	5	48	2
2	18/06/1959	India	Lord's	W	0*		16	4	35	5
							18.1	8	31	2
3	20/08/1959	India	The Oval	W	2		29	11	36	2
						1	27	12	47	2
4	18/08/1960	South Africa	The Oval	D	2		44	17	99	2
							5	2	3	0

Batting & Fielding

Mat	Inns	N/O	Runs	H/S	Avg	100s	50s	Cat
4	4	1	4	2	1.33	0	0	1

Bowling

Balls	Runs	Wkts	Avg	Best	5WI	10WM	S/R
1129	357	16	22.31	5-35	1	0	70.56

A.GREENWOOD

Full Name: Andrew Greenwood
Born: 20/08/1847, Cowmes, Huddersfield
Died: 12/02/1889, Huddersfield, Yorkshire
Teams: Yorkshire 1869-80, England 1877
Matches: 2 (Won 1, Drew 0, Lost 1)
Right-hand opening/middle order batsman

No	Date	Opposition	Venue	R	Bat	C
1	15/03/1877	Australia	Melbourne	L	1	1
					5	
2	31/03/1877	Australia	Melbourne	W	49	
					22	1

Batting & Fielding

Mat	Inns	N/O	Runs	H/S	Avg	100s	50s	Cat
2	4	0	77	49	19.25	0	0	2

A.W.GREIG

Full Name: Anthony William Greig
Born: 06/10/1946, Queenstown, South Africa
Teams: Sussex 1966-78, Border 1965/66-69/70, Eastern Province 1970/71-71/72, England 1972-77
Matches: 58 (Won 17, Drew 24, Lost 17)
England Captain: 14 times 1975-77 (Won 3, Drew 6, Lost 5) **Toss:** 6-8
Right-hand middle order batsman – Right-arm medium or off break bowler

No	Date	Opposition	Venue	R	Bat	C	Bowling			
1	08/06/1972	Australia	Old Trafford	W	57	1	7	1	21	1
					62	1	19.2	7	53	4
2	22/06/1972	Australia	Lord's	L	54	2	29	6	74	1
					3		3	0	17	0
3	13/07/1972	Australia	Trent Bridge	D	7	1	38.4	9	88	2
					36*		12	1	46	0
4	27/07/1972	Australia	Headingley	W	24	1	10	1	25	0
5	10/08/1972	Australia	The Oval	L	16	2	18	9	25	0
					29		25.3	10	49	2
6	20/12/1972	India	Delhi	W	68*	3	23	8	32	2
					40*	2	6	1	16	0
7	30/12/1972	India	Calcutta	L	29		9	1	13	1
					67		19.5	9	24	5
8	12/01/1973	India	Madras (1)	L	17	1	12	1	35	0
					5	1				
9	25/01/1973	India	Kanpur	D	8	1	29	11	40	1
						1	10	7	6	1
10	06/02/1973	India	Bombay (2)	D	148		22	7	62	0
							13	7	19	1
11	02/03/1973	Pakistan	Lahore (2)	D	41	1	29.2	5	86	4
					72	1	6	0	28	2
12	16/03/1973	Pakistan	Hyderabad	D	36		13	2	39	0
					64					
13	24/03/1973	Pakistan	Karachi (1)	D	48		20	1	76	0
						1	10	2	26	0
14	07/06/1973	New Zealand	Trent Bridge	W	2		10.4	0	33	4
					139		45.1	10	101	3
15	21/06/1973	New Zealand	Lord's	D	63	1				
					12					
16	05/07/1973	New Zealand	Headingley	W	0		13	4	29	1
							6	1	22	0
17	26/07/1973	West Indies	The Oval	L	38		30.3	6	81	2
					0	1	8	1	22	0
18	09/08/1973	West Indies	Edgbaston	D	27	2	26	3	84	0
							7.4	0	35	2
19	23/08/1973	West Indies	Lord's	L	44	2	33	2	180	3
					13					
20	02/02/1974	West Indies	Port-of-Spain	L	37		17	3	60	0
					20	1	2	1	4	0
21	16/02/1974	West Indies	Kingston	D	45	1	49	14	102	3
					14					
22	06/03/1974	West Indies	Bridgetown	D	148	2	46	2	164	6
					25					
23	22/03/1974	West Indies	Georgetown	D	121	1	24	8	57	2
24	30/03/1974	West Indies	Port-of-Spain	W	19	1	36.1	10	86	8
					1	1	33	7	70	5
25	06/06/1974	India	Old Trafford	W	53		5	1	18	0
							25.1	8	35	3
26	20/06/1974	India	Lord's	W	106		21	4	63	1
27	04/07/1974	India	Edgbaston	W		1	3	0	11	0
						1	16	3	49	2
28	25/07/1974	Pakistan	Headingley	D	37	2	11	4	14	1
					12	4	9	3	23	1
29	08/08/1974	Pakistan	Lord's	D	9	2	8.5	4	23	3
						2	19	6	55	1
30	22/08/1974	Pakistan	The Oval	D	32	1	25	5	92	2
							7	1	15	0
31	29/11/1974	Australia	Brisbane (2)	L	110	1	16	2	70	1
					2		13	2	60	0
32	13/12/1974	Australia	Perth	L	23	1	9	0	69	1
					32					
33	26/12/1974	Australia	Melbourne	D	28	1	24	2	63	2
					60		18	2	56	4
34	04/01/1975	Australia	Sydney	L	9	2	22.7	2	104	4
					54		12	1	64	0
35	25/01/1975	Australia	Adelaide	L	19	2	10	0	63	0
					20	2	2	0	9	0
36	08/02/1975	Australia	Melbourne	W	89	2	8.7	1	35	1
						1	31.7	7	88	4
37	20/02/1975	New Zealand	Auckland	W	51		26	4	98	5
							15	3	51	5

No	Date	Opposition	Venue	R	Bat	C	Bowling			
38	28/02/1975	New Zealand	Christchurch	D		1	9	1	27	2
39	10/07/1975	Australia	Edgbaston	L	8		15	2	43	1
					7					
40*	31/07/1975	Australia	Lord's	D	96	1	15	5	47	1
					41		26	6	82	2
41*	14/08/1975	Australia	Headingley	D	51	1	3	0	14	0
					49		9	3	20	0
42*	28/08/1975	Australia	The Oval	D	17	2	24	5	107	3
					15		5	2	9	1
43*	03/06/1976	West Indies	Trent Bridge	D	0	1	27	4	82	1
							1	0	16	0
44*	17/06/1976	West Indies	Lord's	D	6					
					20	1	14	3	42	2
45*	08/07/1976	West Indies	Old Trafford	L	9	2	8	1	24	0
					3		2	0	8	0
46*	22/07/1976	West Indies	Headingley	L	116	1	10	2	57	0
					76*	1				
47*	12/08/1976	West Indies	The Oval	L	12		34	5	96	2
					1		2	0	11	0
48*	17/12/1976	India	Delhi	W	25	1				
							40	11	84	2
49*	01/01/1977	India	Calcutta	W	103	2				
							10	0	27	2
50*	14/01/1977	India	Madras (1)	W	54		4	1	4	0
					41					
51*	28/01/1977	India	Bangalore	L	2	1	18	5	44	2
					31		23	2	74	0
52*	11/02/1977	India	Bombay (3)	D	76		22	6	64	3
					10	1	14	3	39	1
53*	12/03/1977	Australia	Melbourne	L	18	3				
					41	1	14	3	66	2
54	16/06/1977	Australia	Lord's	D	5					
					91					
55	07/07/1977	Australia	Old Trafford	W	76	2	13	4	37	1
						1	12	6	19	1
56	28/07/1977	Australia	Trent Bridge	W	11	1	15	4	35	1
					0	2	9	2	24	1
57	11/08/1977	Australia	Headingley	W	43	1	20	7	64	2
						2	8	2	17	1
58	25/08/1977	Australia	The Oval	D	0					

Batting & Fielding

Mat	Inns	N/O	Runs	H/S	Avg	100s	50s	Cat
58	93	4	3599	148	40.43	8	20	87

Bowling

Balls	Runs	Wkts	Avg	Best	5WI	10WM	S/R
9802	4541	141	32.20	8-86	6	2	69.51

I.A.GREIG

Full Name: Ian Alexander Greig
Born: 08/12/1955, Queenstown, South Africa
Teams: Cambridge University 1977-79, Sussex 1980-85, Surrey 1987-91, Border 1974/75-79/80, Griqualand West 1975/76, England 1982
Matches: 2 (Won 1, Drew 0, Lost 1)
Right-hand middle order batsman – Right-arm medium bowler

No	Date	Opposition	Venue	R	Bat	C	Bowling			
1	29/07/1982	Pakistan	Edgbaston	W	14		14.2	3	53	4
					7		4	1	19	0
2	12/08/1982	Pakistan	Lord's	L	3		13	2	42	0
					2					

Batting & Fielding

Mat	Inns	N/O	Runs	H/S	Avg	100s	50s	Cat
2	4	0	26	14	6.50	0	0	0

Bowling

Balls	Runs	Wkts	Avg	Best	5WI	10WM	S/R
188	114	4	28.50	4-53	0	0	47.00

B.A.F.GRIEVE

Full Name: Basil Arthur Firebrace Grieve
Born: 28/05/1864, Kilburn, Middlesex
Died: 19/11/1917, Eastbourne, Sussex
Team: England 1889
Matches: 2 (Won 2, Drew 0, Lost 0)
Right-hand lower order batsman – Right-arm medium bowler

No	Date	Opposition	Venue	R	Bat	C
1	12/03/1889	South Africa	Port Elizabeth	W	14*	
					12*	
2	25/03/1889	South Africa	Cape Town	W	14	

Batting & Fielding

Mat	Inns	N/O	Runs	H/S	Avg	100s	50s	Cat
2	3	2	40	14*	40.00	0	0	0

S.C.GRIFFITH

Full Name: Stewart Cathie Griffith, CBE (known as Billy)
Born: 16/06/1914, Wandsworth, London
Died: 07/04/1993, Felpham, Sussex
Teams: Cambridge University 1934-36, Surrey 1934, Sussex 1937-54, England 1948-49
Matches: 3 (Won 1, Drew 2, Lost 0)
Right-hand lower order batsman – Wicket-keeper

No	Date	Opposition	Venue	R	Bat	C	St	B
1	11/02/1948	West Indies	Port-of-Spain	D	140			
					4			
2+	12/02/1949	South Africa	Johannesburg (2)	D	8	3		4
								7
3+	05/03/1949	South Africa	Port Elizabeth	W	5	1		2
					0	1		6

Batting & Fielding

Mat	Inns	N/O	Runs	H/S	Avg	100s	50s	Cat	St	Byes
3	5	0	157	140	31.40	1	0	5	0	19

G.GUNN

Full Name: George Gunn
Born: 13/06/1879, Hucknall Torkard, Nottinghamshire
Died: 29/06/1958, Tylers Green, Cuckfield, Sussex
Teams: Nottinghamshire 1902-32, England 1907-30
Matches: 15 (Won 6, Drew 2, Lost 7)
Right-hand opening batsman – Right-arm bowler

No	Date	Opposition	Venue	R	Bat	C	Bowling			
1	13/12/1907	Australia	Sydney	L	119	1				
					74					
2	01/01/1908	Australia	Melbourne	W	15					
					0					
3	10/01/1908	Australia	Adelaide	L	65					
					11	2				
4	07/02/1908	Australia	Melbourne	L	13	1				
					43					
5	21/02/1908	Australia	Sydney	L	122*	1				
					0	2				
6	14/06/1909	Australia	Lord's	L	1					
					0					
7	15/12/1911	Australia	Sydney	L	4					
					62	1				
8	30/12/1911	Australia	Melbourne	W	10					
					43	2				
9	12/01/1912	Australia	Adelaide	W	29	1				
					45					
10	09/02/1912	Australia	Melbourne	W	75	1				
11	23/02/1912	Australia	Sydney	W	52	1				
					61					
12	11/01/1930	West Indies	Bridgetown	D	35					
					29		2	0	8	0

No	Date	Opposition	Venue	R	Bat	C	Bowling
13	01/02/1930	West Indies	Port-of-Spain	W	1		
					23	1	
14	21/02/1930	West Indies	Georgetown	L	11		
					45		
15	03/04/1930	West Indies	Kingston	D	85		
					47	1	

Batting & Fielding

Mat	Inns	N/O	Runs	H/S	Avg	100s	50s	Cat
15	29	1	1120	122*	40.00	2	7	15

Bowling

Balls	Runs	Wkts	Avg	Best	5WI	10WM	S/R
12	8	0	–	0-8	0	0	–

J.R.GUNN

Full Name: John Richmond Gunn
Born: 19/07/1876, Hucknall Torkard, Nottinghamshire
Died: 21/08/1963, Basford, Nottingham
Teams: Nottinghamshire 1896-1925, London County 1904, England 1901-05
Matches: 6 (Won 2, Drew 0, Lost 4)
Left-hand middle order batsman – Left-arm medium or slow bowler

No	Date	Opposition	Venue	R	Bat	C		Bowling	
1	13/12/1901	Australia	Sydney	W	21		5	0	27	0
2	01/01/1902	Australia	Melbourne	L	0					
					2		6	1	13	0
3	17/01/1902	Australia	Adelaide	L	24	1	42	14	76	5
					5		38	14	88	3
4	14/02/1902	Australia	Sydney	L	0*		16	5	48	1
					13*		8.3	1	17	2
5	28/02/1902	Australia	Melbourne	L	8	1	17	6	38	4
					4	1	28	11	53	2
6	29/05/1905	Australia	Trent Bridge	W	8		6	2	27	1

Batting & Fielding

Mat	Inns	N/O	Runs	H/S	Avg	100s	50s	Cat
6	10	2	85	24	10.62	0	0	3

Bowling

Balls	Runs	Wkts	Avg	Best	5WI	10WM	S/R
999	387	18	21.50	5-76	1	0	55.50

W.GUNN

Full Name: William Gunn (known as Billy)
Born: 04/12/1858, St Anne's, Nottingham
Died: 29/01/1921, Nottingham
Teams: Nottinghamshire 1880-1904, England 1887-99
Matches: 11 (Won 7, Drew 3, Lost 1)
Right-hand middle order batsman – Right-arm slow bowler

No	Date	Opposition	Venue	R	Bat	C
1	28/01/1887	Australia	Sydney	W	0	
					4	1
2	25/02/1887	Australia	Sydney	W	9	1
					10	2
3	16/07/1888	Australia	Lord's	L	2	1
					8	
4	30/08/1888	Australia	Old Trafford	W	15	
5	21/07/1890	Australia	Lord's	W	14	
					34	
6	11/08/1890	Australia	The Oval	W	32	
					1	
7	17/07/1893	Australia	Lord's	D	2	
					77	
8	14/08/1893	Australia	The Oval	W	16	
9	24/08/1893	Australia	Old Trafford	D	102*	
					11	

No	Date	Opposition	Venue	R	Bat	C
10	22/06/1896	Australia	Lord's	W	25	
					13*	
11	01/06/1899	Australia	Trent Bridge	D	14	
					3	

Batting & Fielding

Mat	Inns	N/O	Runs	H/S	Avg	100s	50s	Cat
11	20	2	392	102*	21.77	1	1	5

N.E.HAIG

Full Name: Nigel Esme Haig
Born: 12/12/1887, Kensington, London
Died: 27/10/1966, Eastbourne, Sussex
Teams: Middlesex 1912-34, England 1921-30
Matches: 5 (Won 1, Drew 2, Lost 2)
Right-hand middle order batsman – Right-arm fast medium bowler

No	Date	Opposition	Venue	R	Bat	C		Bowling		
1	11/06/1921	Australia	Lord's	L	3		20	4	61	2
					0		3	0	27	0
2	11/01/1930	West Indies	Bridgetown	D	47	1	10	4	27	0
							20	4	40	1
3	01/02/1930	West Indies	Port-of-Spain	W	5		8	1	33	1
					5		21	8	33	2
4	21/02/1930	West Indies	Georgetown	L	4	1	23	7	61	1
					0		10	1	44	2
5	03/04/1930	West Indies	Kingston	D	28	2	30	10	73	3
					34		26	15	49	1

Batting & Fielding

Mat	Inns	N/O	Runs	H/S	Avg	100s	50s	Cat
5	9	0	126	47	14.00	0	0	4

Bowling

Balls	Runs	Wkts	Avg	Best	5WI	10WM	S/R
1026	448	13	34.46	3-73	0	0	78.92

S.HAIGH

Full Name: Schofield Haigh
Born: 19/03/1871, Berry Brow, Huddersfield, Yorkshire
Died: 27/02/1921, Taylor Hill, Huddersfield, Yorkshire
Teams: Yorkshire 1895-1913, England 1899-1912
Matches: 11 (Won 3, Drew 3, Lost 5)
Right-hand middle/lower order batsman – Right-arm fast medium bowler

No	Date	Opposition	Venue	R	Bat	C		Bowling		
1	14/02/1899	South Africa	Johannesburg (1)	W	2*		30	5	101	3
					1		12	5	20	2
2	01/04/1899	South Africa	Cape Town	W	0	1	27	4	88	3
					25	1	11.4	6	11	6
3	15/06/1905	Australia	Lord's	D	14	1	12	3	40	2
4	03/07/1905	Australia	Headingley	D	11		11	5	19	1
							14	4	36	1
5	02/01/1906	South Africa	Johannesburg (1)	L	23	1				
					0		1	0	9	0
6	06/03/1906	South Africa	Johannesburg (1)	L	3		19.2	4	64	4
					0*					
7	10/03/1906	South Africa	Johannesburg (1)	L	0	2	15	2	50	0
					16		24	5	72	1
8	24/03/1906	South Africa	Cape Town	W	0		19	8	38	1
						2	2	0	12	0
9	30/03/1906	South Africa	Cape Town	L	1		6	1	18	0
					2					
10	14/06/1909	Australia	Lord's	L	1*		19	5	41	0
					5					
11	29/07/1912	Australia	Old Trafford	D	9		6	4	3	0

Batting & Fielding

Mat	Inns	N/O	Runs	H/S	Avg	100s	50s	Cat
11	18	3	113	25	7.53	0	0	8

Bowling

Balls	Runs	Wkts	Avg	Best	5WI	10WM	S/R
1294	622	24	25.91	6-11	1	0	53.91

C.HALLOWS

Full Name: Charles Hallows (known as Charlie)
Born: 04/04/1895, Little Lever, Lancashire
Died: 10/11/1972, Bolton, Lancashire
Teams: Lancashire 1914-32, England 1921-28
Matches: 2 (Won 1, Drew 1, Lost 0)
Left-hand opening batsman – Left-arm slow bowler

No	Date	Opposition	Venue	R	Bat	C
1	23/07/1921	Australia	Old Trafford	D	16*	
2	23/06/1928	West Indies	Lord's	W	26	

Batting & Fielding

Mat	Inns	N/O	Runs	H/S	Avg	100s	50s	Cat
2	2	1	42	26	42.00	0	0	0

W.R.HAMMOND

Full Name: Walter Reginald Hammond (known as Wally)
Born: 19/06/1903, Buckland, Dover, Kent
Died: 01/07/1965, Kloof, Durban, South Africa
Teams: Gloucestershire 1920-51, South African Air Force 1942-43, England 1927-47
Matches: 85 (Won 29, Drew 38, Lost 18)
England Captain: 20 times 1938-47 (Won 4, Drew 13, Lost 3) **Toss:** 12-8
Right-hand middle order batsman – Right-arm fast medium bowler

No	Date	Opposition	Venue	R	Bat	C	O	M	R	W
1	24/12/1927	South Africa	Johannesburg (1)	W	51		8	2	21	0
							21.2	9	36	5
2	31/12/1927	South Africa	Cape Town	W	43		17	4	53	3
					14	3	30	13	50	2
3	21/01/1928	South Africa	Durban (2)	D	90		16	3	54	0
					1*	1	16	2	37	0
4	28/01/1928	South Africa	Johannesburg (1)	L	28		22	4	62	3
					25	1	9	3	20	1
5	04/02/1928	South Africa	Durban (2)	L	66	1	12	2	41	0
					3		10	2	25	1
6	23/06/1928	West Indies	Lord's	W	45					
						2	15	6	20	1
							6	2	16	0
7	21/07/1928	West Indies	Old Trafford	W	63					
						3	6	0	23	1
							8	0	40	1
8	11/08/1928	West Indies	The Oval	W	3	3	4	2	4	0
						1	15	5	38	0
9	30/11/1928	Australia	Brisbane (1)	W	44		1	0	2	0
					28		5	0	18	0
10	14/12/1928	Australia	Sydney	W	251		9	0	43	0
11	29/12/1928	Australia	Melbourne	W	200		8	4	19	1
					32		16	6	30	0
12	01/02/1929	Australia	Adelaide	W	119*		9	1	32	0
					177	1	14	3	21	0
13	08/03/1929	Australia	Melbourne	L	38		16	3	31	1
					16		26	8	53	3
14	15/06/1929	South Africa	Edgbaston	D	18		22	12	25	0
					138*		3	0	19	0
15	29/06/1929	South Africa	Lord's	D	8		8	3	19	1
					5					
16	13/07/1929	South Africa	Headingley	W	65	2	8	2	13	0
					0		7	0	19	0
17	17/08/1929	South Africa	The Oval	D	17					
					101*	1				
18	13/06/1930	Australia	Trent Bridge	W	8	1				
					4	3	29	5	74	0
19	27/06/1930	Australia	Lord's	L	38	1	35	8	82	1
					32		4.2	1	6	0
20	11/07/1930	Australia	Headingley	D	113		17	3	46	1
					35					

No	Date	Opposition	Venue	R	Bat	C	Bowling			
21	25/07/1930	Australia	Old Trafford	D	3		21	6	24	2
22	16/08/1930	Australia	The Oval	L	13		42	12	70	1
					60					
23	24/12/1930	South Africa	Johannesburg (1)	L	49	2				
					63		25	5	63	4
24	01/01/1931	South Africa	Cape Town	D	57		10	2	27	0
					65					
25	16/01/1931	South Africa	Durban (2)	D	136*					
						1	11	6	9	2
26	13/02/1931	South Africa	Johannesburg (1)	D	75	1	28	6	50	1
					15	3	11	2	27	0
27	21/02/1931	South Africa	Durban (2)	D	29	1	19	6	36	2
					28	1	5	0	28	0
28	27/06/1931	New Zealand	Lord's	D	7	3	10.3	5	8	1
					46		21	2	50	1
29	29/07/1931	New Zealand	The Oval	W	100*	2	1	0	10	
30	15/08/1931	New Zealand	Old Trafford	D	16					
31	25/06/1932	India	Lord's	W	35		4	0	15	0
					12	2	5.3	3	9	3
32	02/12/1932	Australia	Sydney	W	112	1	14.2	0	34	1
							15	6	37	2
33	30/12/1932	Australia	Melbourne	L	8	1	10	3	21	0
					23		10.5	2	21	3
34	13/01/1933	Australia	Adelaide	W	2		17.4	4	30	1
					85		9	3	27	0
35	10/02/1933	Australia	Brisbane (2)	W	20	1	23	5	61	2
					14	2	10	4	18	0
36	23/02/1933	Australia	Sydney	W	101	1	8	0	32	0
					75*		3	0	10	0
37	24/03/1933	New Zealand	Christchurch	D	227	2	2	0	2	0
38	31/03/1933	New Zealand	Auckland	D	336*		3	0	11	0
							2	0	6	0
39	24/06/1933	West Indies	Lord's	W	29	1				
40	22/07/1933	West Indies	Old Trafford	D	34	1	5	0	27	0
						2				
41	12/08/1933	West Indies	The Oval	W	11					
42	08/06/1934	Australia	Trent Bridge	L	25	2	13	4	29	0
					16	3	12	5	25	1
43	22/06/1934	Australia	Lord's	W	2	1	4	1	6	0
						2	13	0	38	1
44	06/07/1934	Australia	Old Trafford	D	4		28.3	6	111	3
						1	2	1	2	0
45	20/07/1934	Australia	Headingley	D	37		29	5	82	0
					20					
46	18/08/1934	Australia	The Oval	L	15		12	0	53	0
					43	3	7	1	18	1
47	08/01/1935	West Indies	Bridgetown	W	43	1				
					29*		1	0	1	0
48	24/01/1935	West Indies	Port-of-Spain	L	1		14	5	28	0
					9		10	0	17	0
49	14/02/1935	West Indies	Georgetown	D	47					
						1	1			
50	14/03/1935	West Indies	Kingston	L	11					
					34					
51	15/06/1935	South Africa	Trent Bridge	D	28	1				
52	29/06/1935	South Africa	Lord's	L	27	1	5.3	3	8	2
					27	1	14.4	4	26	1
53	13/07/1935	South Africa	Headingley	D	63	2	12	6	13	1
					87*	1	7	4	10	1
54	27/07/1935	South Africa	Old Trafford	D	29		17	2	49	1
					63*		5	0	15	0
55	17/08/1935	South Africa	The Oval	D	65	1	9	2	25	0
56	25/07/1936	India	Old Trafford	D	167	1	9	1	34	0
							12	2	19	1
57	15/08/1936	India	The Oval	W	217		8	2	17	0
					5*		7	0	24	0

No	Date	Opposition	Venue	R	Bat	C		Bowling		
58	04/12/1936	Australia	Brisbane (2)	W	0	1	4	0	12	0
					25	1				
59	18/12/1936	Australia	Sydney	W	231*		4	0	6	0
							15.7	3	29	3
60	01/01/1937	Australia	Melbourne	L	32		5.3	0	16	2
					51		22	3	89	0
61	29/01/1937	Australia	Adelaide	L	20		6	0	30	2
					39	3	15.2	1	57	5
62	26/02/1937	Australia	Melbourne	L	14		16	1	62	0
					56					
63	26/06/1937	New Zealand	Lord's	D	140	1	6	2	12	0
64	24/07/1937	New Zealand	Old Trafford	W	33		15	5	27	1
					0		6	1	18	0
65	14/08/1937	New Zealand	The Oval	D	31		7	1	25	1
							11	3	19	2
66*	10/06/1938	Australia	Trent Bridge	D	26	1	19	7	44	0
						2	12	6	15	0
67*	24/06/1938	Australia	Lord's	D	240	1				
					2	1				
68*	22/07/1938	Australia	Headingley	L	76	2				
					0					
69*	20/08/1938	Australia	The Oval	W	59	1	2	0	8	0
70*	24/12/1938	South Africa	Johannesburg (1)	D	24		10	3	27	0
					58		6	3	13	1
71*	31/12/1938	South Africa	Cape Town	D	181		9	0	25	0
72*	20/01/1939	South Africa	Durban (2)	W	120	3	2	1	2	0
						2	3	0	11	1
73*	18/02/1939	South Africa	Johannesburg (1)	D	1		7	1	19	1
					61*					
74*	03/03/1939	South Africa	Durban (2)	D	24		14	4	34	0
					140	1	9	1	30	0
75*	24/06/1939	West Indies	Lord's	W	14					
					30*	1				
76*	22/07/1939	West Indies	Old Trafford	D	22	2				
					32	1				
77*	19/08/1939	West Indies	The Oval	D	43	1				
					138					
78*	22/06/1946	India	Lord's	W	33					
						2				
79*	20/07/1946	India	Old Trafford	D	69		1	0	3	0
					8					
80*	17/08/1946	India	The Oval	D	9*					
81*	29/11/1946	Australia	Brisbane (2)	L	32	1				
					23					
82*	13/12/1946	Australia	Sydney	L	1	1				
					37					
83*	01/01/1947	Australia	Melbourne	D	9	2				
					26	1				
84*	31/01/1947	Australia	Adelaide	D	18	1				
					22					
85*	21/03/1947	New Zealand	Christchurch	D	79	1				

Batting & Fielding

Mat	Inns	N/O	Runs	H/S	Avg	100s	50s	Cat
85	140	16	7249	336*	58.45	22	24	110

Bowling

Balls	Runs	Wkts	Avg	Best	5WI	10WM	S/R
7969	3138	83	37.80	5-36	2	0	96.01

J.H.HAMPSHIRE

Full Name: John Harry Hampshire
Born: 10/02/1941, Thurnscoe, Yorkshire
Teams: Yorkshire 1961-81, Leicestershire 1980/81, Derbyshire 1982-84, Tasmania 1967/68-78/79, England 1969-75
Matches: 8 (Won 3, Drew 4, Lost 1)
Right-hand middle order batsman – Leg break bowler

No	Date	Opposition	Venue	R	Bat	C
1	26/06/1969	West Indies	Lord's	D	107	2
					5	1
2	10/07/1969	West Indies	Headingley	W	1	
					22	1
3	29/01/1971	Australia	Adelaide	D	55	
					3	
4	12/02/1971	Australia	Sydney	W	10	
					24	2
5	25/02/1971	New Zealand	Christchurch	W	40	
					51*	
6	05/03/1971	New Zealand	Auckland	D	9	1
					0	
7	10/08/1972	Australia	The Oval	L	42	1
					20	
8	14/08/1975	Australia	Headingley	D	14	1
					0	

Batting & Fielding

Mat	Inns	N/O	Runs	H/S	Avg	100s	50s	Cat
8	16	1	403	107	26.86	1	2	9

H.T.W.HARDINGE

Full Name: Harold Thomas William Hardinge (known as Wally)
Born: 25/02/1886, Greenwich, London
Died: 08/05/1965, Tenison Road, Cambridge
Teams: Kent 1902-33, England 1921
Matches: 1 (Won 0, Drew 0, Lost 1)
Right-hand opening batsman – Left-arm slow bowler

No	Date	Opposition	Venue	R	Bat	C
1	02/07/1921	Australia	Headingley	L	25	
					5	

Batting & Fielding

Mat	Inns	N/O	Runs	H/S	Avg	100s	50s	Cat
1	2	0	30	25	15.00	0	0	0

J.HARDSTAFF SNR

Full Name: Joseph Hardstaff Senior (known as Joe)
Born: 09/11/1882, Kirkby-in-Ashfield, Nottinghamshire
Died: 02/04/1947, Nuncargate, Nottinghamshire
Teams: Nottinghamshire 1902-24, England 1907-08
Matches: 5 (Won 1, Drew 0, Lost 4)
Right-hand middle order batsman – Right-arm fast medium bowler

No	Date	Opposition	Venue	R	Bat	C
1	13/12/1907	Australia	Sydney	L	12	
					63	
2	01/01/1908	Australia	Melbourne	W	12	
					19	
3	10/01/1908	Australia	Adelaide	L	61	
					72	
4	07/02/1908	Australia	Melbourne	L	8	1
					39	
5	21/02/1908	Australia	Sydney	L	17	
					8	

Batting & Fielding

Mat	Inns	N/O	Runs	H/S	Avg	100s	50s	Cat
5	10	0	311	72	31.10	0	3	1

J.HARDSTAFF JNR

Full Name: Joseph Hardstaff Junior (known as Young Joe)
Born: 03/07/1911, Nuncargate, Nottinghamshire
Died: 01/01/1990, Worksop, Nottinghamshire
Teams: Nottinghamshire 1930-55, Services in India 1943/44-44/45, Europeans 1944/45, Auckland 1948/49-49/50, England 1935-48
Matches: 23 (Won 7, Drew 9, Lost 7)
Right-hand middle order batsman – Right-arm medium bowler

No	Date	Opposition	Venue	R	Bat	C
1	13/07/1935	South Africa	Headingley	D	10 0	
2	27/06/1936	India	Lord's	W	2	1
3	25/07/1936	India	Old Trafford	D	94	1
4	04/12/1936	Australia	Brisbane (2)	W	43 20	1
5	18/12/1936	Australia	Sydney	W	26	
6	01/01/1937	Australia	Melbourne	L	3 17	1
7	29/01/1937	Australia	Adelaide	L	20 43	
8	26/02/1937	Australia	Melbourne	L	83 1	
9	26/06/1937	New Zealand	Lord's	D	114 64	
10	24/07/1937	New Zealand	Old Trafford	W	58 11	
11	14/08/1937	New Zealand	The Oval	D	103	
12	22/07/1938	Australia	Headingley	L	4 11	
13	20/08/1938	Australia	The Oval	W	169*	1
14	24/06/1939	West Indies	Lord's	W	3*	1
15	22/07/1939	West Indies	Old Trafford	D	76 1	1
16	19/08/1939	West Indies	The Oval	D	94	
17	22/06/1946	India	Lord's	W	205*	
18	20/07/1946	India	Old Trafford	D	5 0	
19	31/01/1947	Australia	Adelaide	D	67 9	
20	21/01/1948	West Indies	Bridgetown	D	98 0	
21	03/03/1948	West Indies	Georgetown	L	3 63	1
22	27/03/1948	West Indies	Kingston	L	9 64	1
23	10/06/1948	Australia	Trent Bridge	L	0 43	

Batting & Fielding

Mat	Inns	N/O	Runs	H/S	Avg	100s	50s	Cat
23	38	3	1636	205*	46.74	4	10	9

LORD HARRIS

Full Name: Hon.George Robert Canning Harris (4th Lord Harris from 1872)
Born: 03/02/1851, St Anne's, Trinidad
Died: 24/03/1932, Belmont, Faversham, Kent
Teams: Oxford University 1871-74, Kent 1870-1911, England 1879-84
Matches: 4 (Won 2, Drew 1, Lost 1)
England Captain: 4 times 1879-84 (Won 2, Drew 1, Lost 1) **Toss:** 2-2
Right-hand middle order batsman – Right-hand fast round-arm bowler

No	Date	Opposition	Venue	R	Bat	C		Bowling	
1*	02/01/1879	Australia	Melbourne	L	33 36	3	0	14	0
2*	06/09/1880	Australia	The Oval	W	52	1			
3*	21/07/1884	Australia	Lord's	W	4				
4*	11/08/1884	Australia	The Oval	D	14 6*	1	5	1	15	0

Batting & Fielding

Mat	Inns	N/O	Runs	H/S	Avg	100s	50s	Cat
4	6	1	145	52	29.00	0	1	2

Bowling

Balls	Runs	Wkts	Avg	Best	5WI	10WM	S/R
32	29	0	–	0-14	0	0	–

J.C.HARTLEY

Full Name: John Cabourn Hartley
Born: 15/11/1874, Lincoln
Died: 08/03/1963, Woodhall Spa, Lincolnshire
Teams: Oxford University 1895-97, Sussex 1895-98, England 1906
Matches: 2 (Won 0, Drew 0, Lost 2)
Right-hand lower order batsman – Leg break bowler

No	Date	Opposition	Venue	R	Bat	C		Bowling		
1	10/03/1906	South Africa	Johannesburg (1)	L	0	1	19	1	62	1
					9	1	7	1	31	0
2	30/03/1906	South Africa	Cape Town	L	6		6	0	22	0
					0					

Batting & Fielding

Mat	Inns	N/O	Runs	H/S	Avg	100s	50s	Cat
2	4	0	15	9	3.75	0	0	2

Bowling

Balls	Runs	Wkts	Avg	Best	5WI	10WM	S/R
192	115	1	115.00	1-62	0	0	192.00

LORD HAWKE

Full Name: Hon.Martin Bladen Hawke (7th Lord Hawke from 1887)
Born: 16/08/1860, Willingham Rectory, Gainsborough, Lincolnshire
Died: 10/10/1938, West End, Edinburgh, Scotland
Teams: Cambridge University 1882-85, Yorkshire 1881-1911, England 1896-99
Matches: 5 (Won 5, Drew 0, Lost 0)
England Captain: 4 times 1896-99 (Won 4, Drew 0, Lost 0) **Toss:** 4-0
Right-hand middle order batsman

No	Date	Opposition	Venue	R	Bat	C
1	13/02/1896	South Africa	Port Elizabeth	W	0	
					30	
2*	02/03/1896	South Africa	Johannesburg (1)	W	4	
						1
3*	21/03/1896	South Africa	Cape Town	W	12*	
						2
4*	14/02/1899	South Africa	Johannesburg (1)	W	0	
					5	
5*	01/04/1899	South Africa	Cape Town	W	1	
					3	

Batting & Fielding

Mat	Inns	N/O	Runs	H/S	Avg	100s	50s	Cat
5	8	1	55	30	7.85	0	0	3

E.G.HAYES

Full Name: Ernest George Hayes (known as Ernie)
Born: 06/11/1876, Peckham, London
Died: 02/12/1953, West Dulwich, London
Teams: Surrey 1896-1919, London County 1903, Leicestershire 1926, England 1906-12
Matches: 5 (Won 2, Drew 1, Lost 2)
Right-hand middle order batsman – Leg break bowler

No	Date	Opposition	Venue	R	Bat	C		Bowling		
1	02/01/1906	South Africa	Johannesburg (1)	L	20					
					3		9	1	28	1
2	10/03/1906	South Africa	Johannesburg (1)	L	35					
					11*					

No	Date	Opposition	Venue	R	Bat	C		Bowling		
3	24/03/1906	South Africa	Cape Town	W	0	1				
					0					
4	09/08/1909	Australia	The Oval	D	4		4	0	10	0
					9		2	0	14	0
5	12/08/1912	South Africa	The Oval	W	4	1				

Batting & Fielding

Mat	Inns	N/O	Runs	H/S	Avg	100s	50s	Cat
5	9	1	86	35	10.75	0	0	2

Bowling

Balls	Runs	Wkts	Avg	Best	5WI	10WM	S/R
90	52	1	52.00	1-28	0	0	90.00

F.C.HAYES

Full Name: Frank Charles Hayes
Born: 06/12/1946, Preston, Lancashire
Teams: Lancashire 1970-84, England 1973-76
Matches: 9 (Won 1, Drew 3, Lost 5)
Right-hand middle order batsman – Right-arm medium bowler

No	Date	Opposition	Venue	R	Bat	C
1	26/07/1973	West Indies	The Oval	L	16	
					106*	1
2	09/08/1973	West Indies	Edgbaston	D	29	1
					0	
3	23/08/1973	West Indies	Lord's	L	8	
					0	
4	02/02/1974	West Indies	Port-of-Spain	L	12	
					8	2
5	16/02/1974	West Indies	Kingston	D	10	
					0	
6	22/03/1974	West Indies	Georgetown	D	6	
7	30/03/1974	West Indies	Port-of-Spain	W	24	
					0	
8	08/07/1976	West Indies	Old Trafford	L	0	1
					18	
9	22/07/1976	West Indies	Headingley	L	7	2
					0	

Batting & Fielding

Mat	Inns	N/O	Runs	H/S	Avg	100s	50s	Cat
9	17	1	244	106*	15.25	1	0	7

T.W.HAYWARD

Full Name: Thomas Walter Hayward (known as Tom)
Born: 29/03/1871, Cambridge
Died: 19/07/1939, Cambridge
Teams: Surrey 1893-1914, England 1896-1909
Matches: 35 (Won 14, Drew 9, Lost 12)
Right-hand opening batsman – Right-arm medium bowler

No	Date	Opposition	Venue	R	Bat	C		Bowling		
1	13/02/1896	South Africa	Port Elizabeth	W	30		3	1	7	1
					6	2	2	2	0	1
2	02/03/1896	South Africa	Johannesburg (1)	W	122					
							4	1	21	0
3	21/03/1896	South Africa	Cape Town	W	31	1				
						1				
4	22/06/1896	Australia	Lord's	W	12*					
					13	1	11	3	44	0
5	10/08/1896	Australia	The Oval	W	0		2	0	17	0
					13	1				
6	13/12/1897	Australia	Sydney	W	72		3	1	11	0
						1	5	1	16	0
7	01/01/1898	Australia	Melbourne	L	23		9	4	23	1
					33					
8	14/01/1898	Australia	Adelaide	L	70		8	1	36	0
					1					

No	Date	Opposition	Venue	R	Bat	C	O	M	R	W
9	29/01/1898	Australia	Melbourne	L	22	1	10	4	24	0
					25		10	4	24	2
10	26/02/1898	Australia	Sydney	L	47		4	0	12	0
					43		3	0	18	1
11	01/06/1899	Australia	Trent Bridge	D	0	2	3	0	14	0
					28		6	2	16	0
12	15/06/1899	Australia	Lord's	L	1	1	6	0	25	0
					77					
13	29/06/1899	Australia	Headingley	D	40*					
							10	1	45	2
14	17/07/1899	Australia	Old Trafford	D	130					
							3	1	10	0
15	14/08/1899	Australia	The Oval	D	137	1				
							11	3	38	1
16	13/12/1901	Australia	Sydney	W	69					
17	01/01/1902	Australia	Melbourne	L	0					
					12	1				
18	17/01/1902	Australia	Adelaide	L	90					
					47	1	7	0	28	0
19	14/02/1902	Australia	Sydney	L	41					
					12					
20	28/02/1902	Australia	Melbourne	L	19		16	9	22	4
					15		22	4	63	1
21	11/08/1902	Australia	The Oval	W	0					
					7					
22	11/12/1903	Australia	Sydney	W	15					
					91					
23	01/01/1904	Australia	Melbourne	W	58					
					0	1				
24	15/01/1904	Australia	Adelaide	L	20					
					67					
25	26/02/1904	Australia	Sydney	W	18					
					52					
26	05/03/1904	Australia	Melbourne	L	0					
27	29/05/1905	Australia	Trent Bridge	W	5	1				
					47					
28	15/06/1905	Australia	Lord's	D	16					
					8					
29	03/07/1905	Australia	Headingley	D	26	2				
					60					
30	24/07/1905	Australia	Old Trafford	W	82					
31	14/08/1905	Australia	The Oval	D	59					
					2					
32	01/07/1907	South Africa	Lord's	D	21					
33	29/07/1907	South Africa	Headingley	W	24	1				
					15					
34	19/08/1907	South Africa	The Oval	D	0					
					3					
35	14/06/1909	Australia	Lord's	L	16					
					6					

Batting & Fielding

Mat	Inns	N/O	Runs	H/S	Avg	100s	50s	Cat
35	60	2	1999	137	34.46	3	12	19

Bowling

Balls	Runs	Wkts	Avg	Best	5WI	10WM	S/R
887	514	14	36.71	4-22	0	0	63.35

A.HEARNE

Full Name: Alec Hearne
Born: 22/07/1863, Ealing, Middlesex
Died: 16/05/1952, Beckenham, Kent
Teams: Kent 1884-1906, England 1892
Matches: 1 (Won 1, Drew 0, Lost 0)
Right-hand middle order batsman – Right-arm slow bowler

No	Date	Opposition	Venue	R	Bat	C
1	19/03/1892	South Africa	Cape Town	W	9	
						1

Batting & Fielding

Mat	Inns	N/O	Runs	H/S	Avg	100s	50s	Cat
1	1	0	9	9	9.00	0	0	1

F.HEARNE

Full Name: Frank Hearne
Born: 23/11/1858, Ealing, Middlesex
Died: 14/07/1949, Mowbray, Cape Town, South Africa
Teams: Kent 1879-89, Western Province 1889/90-1903/04, South Africa 1892-96, England 1889
Matches: 2 (Won 2, Drew 0, Lost 0), 4 (Won 0, Drew 0, Lost 4)
Right-hand opening batsman – Right-hand fast round-arm bowler

No	Date	Opposition	Venue	R	Bat	C		Bowling	
1	12/03/1889	South Africa	Port Elizabeth	W	27	1			
2	25/03/1889	South Africa	Cape Town	W	20				

For South Africa

No	Date	Opposition	Venue	R	Bat	C		Bowling	
1	19/03/1892	England	Cape Town	L	24		12.2	0	40	2
					23				
2	13/02/1896	England	Port Elizabeth	L	23				
					5				
3	02/03/1896	England	Johannesburg (1)	L	0	1			
					16				
4	21/03/1896	England	Cape Town	L	0	1			
					30				

Batting & Fielding

Mat	Inns	N/O	Runs	H/S	Avg	100s	50s	Cat	
2	2	0	47	27	23.50	0	0	1	(England)
4	8	0	121	30	15.12	0	0	2	(South Africa)
6	10	0	168	30	16.80	0	0	3	(Total)

Bowling

Balls	Runs	Wkts	Avg	Best	5WI	10WM	S/R	
62	40	2	20.00	2-40	0	0	31.00	(Total)

G.G.HEARNE

Full Name: George Gibbons Hearne
Born: 07/07/1856, Ealing, Middlesex
Died: 13/02/1932, Denmark Hill, London
Teams: Kent 1875-95, England 1892
Matches: 1 (Won 1, Drew 0, Lost 0)
Left-hand middle/lower order batsman – Left-hand medium round-arm bowler

No	Date	Opposition	Venue	R	Bat	C
1	19/03/1892	South Africa	Cape Town	W	0	

Batting & Fielding

Mat	Inns	N/O	Runs	H/S	Avg	100s	50s	Cat
1	1	0	0	0	0.00	0	0	0

J.T.HEARNE

Full Name: John Thomas Hearne (known as Jack or Old Jack)
Born: 03/05/1867, Chalfont St Giles, Buckinghamshire
Died: 17/04/1944, Chalfont St Giles, Buckinghamshire
Teams: Middlesex 1888-1923, England 1892-99
Matches: 12 (Won 4, Drew 3, Lost 5)
Right-hand lower order batsman – Right-arm medium or off break bowler

No	Date	Opposition	Venue	R	Bat	C		Bowling		
1	19/03/1892	South Africa	Cape Town	W	40	1	8	2	12	1
2	22/06/1896	Australia	Lord's	W	11					
							36	14	76	5
3	16/07/1896	Australia	Old Trafford	L	18		28	11	53	0
					9		24	13	22	0
4	10/08/1896	Australia	The Oval	W	8		26.1	10	41	6
					1		13	8	19	4

No	Date	Opposition	Venue	R	Bat	C	Bowling			
5	13/12/1897	Australia	Sydney	W	17		20.1	7	42	5
							38	8	99	4
6	01/01/1898	Australia	Melbourne	L	1		36	6	94	1
					0					
7	14/01/1898	Australia	Adelaide	L	0		44.1	15	94	2
					4					
8	29/01/1898	Australia	Melbourne	L	0	2	35.4	13	98	6
					4*		7	3	19	0
9	26/02/1898	Australia	Sydney	L	2*		21	9	40	1
					3*		15	5	52	1
10	01/06/1899	Australia	Trent Bridge	D	4*		59	28	71	4
							29	10	70	1
11	29/06/1899	Australia	Headingley	D	3		23	5	69	1
							31.3	12	50	4
12	17/07/1899	Australia	Old Trafford	D	1		10	6	7	0
						1	47	26	54	3

Batting & Fielding

Mat	Inns	N/O	Runs	H/S	Avg	100s	50s	Cat
12	18	4	126	40	9.00	0	0	4

Bowling

Balls	Runs	Wkts	Avg	Best	5WI	10WM	S/R
2976	1082	49	22.08	6-41	4	1	60.73

J.W.HEARNE

Full Name: John William Hearne (known as Jack or Young Jack)
Born: 11/02/1891, Hillingdon, Middlesex
Died: 14/09/1965, West Drayton, Middlesex
Teams: Middlesex 1909-36, England 1911-26
Matches: 24 (Won 12, Drew 5, Lost 7)
Right-hand middle order batsman – Leg break & googly bowler

No	Date	Opposition	Venue	R	Bat	C	Bowling			
1	15/12/1911	Australia	Sydney	L	76	1	10	1	44	1
					43		13	2	51	0
2	30/12/1911	Australia	Melbourne	W	114		1	0	8	0
					12*		1	0	5	0
3	12/01/1912	Australia	Adelaide	W	12		2	0	6	0
					2		10	0	61	0
4	09/02/1912	Australia	Melbourne	W	0	2	1	0	4	0
						1	3	0	17	0
5	23/02/1912	Australia	Sydney	W	4					
					18					
6	24/06/1912	Australia	Lord's	D	21*		12	1	31	0
7	08/07/1912	South Africa	Headingley	W	45					
					35		2	0	5	1
8	29/07/1912	Australia	Old Trafford	D	9					
9	12/08/1912	South Africa	The Oval	W	20	1				
					5*	1				
10	19/08/1912	Australia	The Oval	W	1					
					14					
11	01/01/1914	South Africa	Johannesburg (1)	W	27	2	16	4	49	5
					0		14	2	58	1
12	14/02/1914	South Africa	Durban (1)	D	2					
					8*		11	0	46	0
13	27/02/1914	South Africa	Port Elizabeth	W	32		9	2	34	1
						1	12	4	30	0
14	17/12/1920	Australia	Sydney	L	14		34	8	77	3
					57		42	7	124	1
15	31/12/1920	Australia	Melbourne	L		1	14	0	38	0
16	02/07/1921	Australia	Headingley	L	7	1	5	0	21	0
					27					
17	28/06/1924	South Africa	Lord's	W			18	3	35	1
							19	4	35	1
18	12/07/1924	South Africa	Headingley	W	20					
					23*		19	3	54	1
19	16/08/1924	South Africa	The Oval	D	35		23	3	90	3

No	Date	Opposition	Venue	R	Bat	C	O	M	R	W
20	19/12/1924	Australia	Sydney	L	7		12.1	3	28	1
					0		25	2	88	0
21	01/01/1925	Australia	Melbourne	L	9		13	1	69	0
					23	1	29	5	84	4
22	13/02/1925	Australia	Melbourne	W	44	1	19.3	1	77	3
					20			0	76	1
23	27/02/1925	Australia	Sydney	L	16		7	0	33	0
					24		22	0	84	2
24	12/06/1926	Australia	Trent Bridge	D						

Batting & Fielding

Mat	Inns	N/O	Runs	H/S	Avg	100s	50s	Cat
24	36	5	806	114	26.00	1	2	13

Bowling

Balls	Runs	Wkts	Avg	Best	5WI	10WM	S/R
2926	1462	30	48.73	5-49	1	0	97.53

E.E.HEMMINGS

Full Name: Edward Ernest Hemmings (known as Eddie)
Born: 20/02/1949, Leamington Spa, Warwickshire
Teams: Warwickshire 1966-78, Nottinghamshire 1979-92, Sussex 1993-96, England 1982-91
Matches: 16 (Won 3, Drew 9, Lost 4)
Right-hand lower order batsman – Off break bowler (previously right-arm medium)

No	Date	Opposition	Venue	R	Bat	C	O	M	R	W
1	29/07/1982	Pakistan	Edgbaston	W	2	1	24	5	56	2
					19	1	10	4	27	1
2	12/08/1982	Pakistan	Lord's	L	6		20	3	53	0
					14		2.1	0	13	0
3	26/11/1982	Australia	Brisbane (2)	L	15*		33.3	6	81	0
					18		29	9	43	2
4	10/12/1982	Australia	Adelaide	L	0	1	48	17	96	1
					0		4	1	5	0
5	02/01/1983	Australia	Sydney	D	29		27	10	68	3
					95		47	16	116	3
6	07/12/1987	Pakistan	Faisalabad	D	1*		18	5	35	1
							7	3	16	0
7	29/01/1988	Australia	Sydney	D	8*		22	3	53	3
							52	15	107	0
8	03/03/1988	New Zealand	Wellington	D			45	15	107	0
9	10/08/1989	Australia	Trent Bridge	L	38		33	9	81	0
					35					
10	07/06/1990	New Zealand	Trent Bridge	D	13*		19	6	47	1
							2	2	0	0
11	21/06/1990	New Zealand	Lord's	D	0		30	13	67	2
12	05/07/1990	New Zealand	Edgbaston	W	20		27.3	10	58	6
					0		29	13	43	1
13	26/07/1990	India	Lord's	W	20		20	3	109	2
							21	2	79	2
14	09/08/1990	India	Old Trafford	D	19		29.2	8	74	2
							31	10	75	3
15	23/08/1990	India	The Oval	D	51		36	3	117	2
16	04/01/1991	Australia	Sydney	D	0	1	32	7	105	3
							41	9	94	3

Batting & Fielding

Mat	Inns	N/O	Runs	H/S	Avg	100s	50s	Cat
16	21	4	383	95	22.52	0	2	5

Bowling

Balls	Runs	Wkts	Avg	Best	5WI	10WM	S/R
4437	1825	43	42.44	6-58	1	0	103.18

E.H.HENDREN

Full Name: Elias Henry Hendren (known as Patsy)
Born: 05/02/1889, Turnham Green, Middlesex
Died: 04/10/1962, Tooting Bec, London
Teams: Middlesex 1907-37, England 1920-35
Matches: 51 (Won 16, Drew 17, Lost 18)
Right-hand middle order batsman – Right-arm slow bowler

No	Date	Opposition	Venue	R	Bat	C	Bowling			
1	17/12/1920	Australia	Sydney	L	28	1				
					56					
2	31/12/1920	Australia	Melbourne	L	67					
					1					
3	14/01/1921	Australia	Adelaide	L	36					
					51	1				
4	11/02/1921	Australia	Melbourne	L	30					
					32					
5	25/02/1921	Australia	Sydney	L	5	1				
					13					
6	28/05/1921	Australia	Trent Bridge	L	0					
					7					
7	11/06/1921	Australia	Lord's	L	0					
					10					
8	14/06/1924	South Africa	Edgbaston	W	74					
						1				
9	28/06/1924	South Africa	Lord's	W	50*					
10	12/07/1924	South Africa	Headingley	W	132	1				
11	26/07/1924	South Africa	Old Trafford	D						
12	16/08/1924	South Africa	The Oval	D	142					
13	19/12/1924	Australia	Sydney	L	74*	1				
					9	1				
14	01/01/1925	Australia	Melbourne	L	32					
					18					
15	16/01/1925	Australia	Adelaide	L	92		5.1	0	27	1
					4	2				
16	13/02/1925	Australia	Melbourne	W	65	1				
17	27/02/1925	Australia	Sydney	L	10					
					10					
18	12/06/1926	Australia	Trent Bridge	D						
19	26/06/1926	Australia	Lord's	D	127*					
20	10/07/1926	Australia	Headingley	D	0	1				
					4*					
21	24/07/1926	Australia	Old Trafford	D	32*	1				
22	14/08/1926	Australia	The Oval	W	8					
					15					
23	11/08/1928	West Indies	The Oval	W	14					
						1				
24	30/11/1928	Australia	Brisbane (1)	W	169					
					45					
25	14/12/1928	Australia	Sydney	W	74					
						1				
26	29/12/1928	Australia	Melbourne	W	19	1				
					45					
27	01/02/1929	Australia	Adelaide	W	13					
					11	1				
28	08/03/1929	Australia	Melbourne	L	95					
					1					
29	15/06/1929	South Africa	Edgbaston	D	70					
					8*					
30	29/06/1929	South Africa	Lord's	D	43					
					11	2				
31	13/07/1929	South Africa	Headingley	W	0					
					5					
32	27/07/1929	South Africa	Old Trafford	W	12					

No	Date	Opposition	Venue	R	Bat	C		Bowling		
33	11/01/1930	West Indies	Bridgetown	D	80	1				
					36*	1				
34	01/02/1930	West Indies	Port-of-Spain	W	77	2				
					205*					
35	21/02/1930	West Indies	Georgetown	L	56					
					123	1				
36	03/04/1930	West Indies	Kingston	D	61	1				
					55					
37	13/06/1930	Australia	Trent Bridge	W	5					
					72					
38	27/06/1930	Australia	Lord's	L	48					
					9					
39	24/12/1930	South Africa	Johannesburg (1)	L	8					
					3	1				
40	01/01/1931	South Africa	Cape Town	D	93					
					86					
41	16/01/1931	South Africa	Durban (2)	D						
42	13/02/1931	South Africa	Johannesburg (1)	D	64	1				
					45	1				
43	21/02/1931	South Africa	Durban (2)	D	30					
44	08/06/1934	Australia	Trent Bridge	L	79					
					3					
45	22/06/1934	Australia	Lord's	W	13					
						2				
46	06/07/1934	Australia	Old Trafford	D	132	1				
							1	0	4	0
47	20/07/1934	Australia	Headingley	D	29					
					42					
48	08/01/1935	West Indies	Bridgetown	W	3	1				
					20					
49	24/01/1935	West Indies	Port-of-Spain	L	41	2				
					11					
50	14/02/1935	West Indies	Georgetown	D	38					
					38*					
51	14/03/1935	West Indies	Kingston	L	40					
					11					

Batting & Fielding

Mat	Inns	N/O	Runs	H/S	Avg	100s	50s	Cat
51	83	9	3525	205*	47.63	7	21	33

Bowling

Balls	Runs	Wkts	Avg	Best	5WI	10WM	S/R
47	31	1	31.00	1-27	0	0	47.00

M.HENDRICK

Full Name: Michael Hendrick (known as Mike)
Born: 22/10/1948, Darley Dale, Derbyshire
Teams: Derbyshire 1969-81, Nottinghamshire 1982-84, England 1974-81
Matches: 30 (Won 12, Drew 12, Lost 6)
Right-hand lower order batsman – Right-arm fast medium bowler

No	Date	Opposition	Venue	R	Bat	C		Bowling		
1	06/06/1974	India	Old Trafford	W		1	20	4	57	3
						2	17	1	39	1
2	20/06/1974	India	Lord's	W	1*		18	4	46	3
						1	1	0	2	0
3	04/07/1974	India	Edgbaston	W			14.2	1	28	4
							14.4	4	43	3
4	25/07/1974	Pakistan	Headingley	D	1*		26	4	91	2
							18	6	39	3
5	08/08/1974	Pakistan	Lord's	D	6	2	9	2	36	1
							15	4	29	0
6	29/11/1974	Australia	Brisbane (2)	L	4		19	3	64	2
					0		13	2	47	0
7	26/12/1974	Australia	Melbourne	D	8*		2.6	1	8	0
					0*					
8	28/02/1975	New Zealand	Christchurch	D		2	20	2	89	2
9	03/06/1976	West Indies	Trent Bridge	D	5	2	24	7	59	1
						1	7	2	22	0

No	Date	Opposition	Venue	R	Bat	C		Bowling	
10	08/07/1976	West Indies	Old Trafford	L	0		14	1	48	2
					0*		24	4	63	1
11	28/07/1977	Australia	Trent Bridge	W	1	3	21.2	6	46	2
						1	32	14	56	2
12	11/08/1977	Australia	Headingley	W	4	1	15.3	2	41	4
							22.5	6	54	4
13	25/08/1977	Australia	The Oval	D	15		37	5	93	2
14	10/02/1978	New Zealand	Wellington	L	0		17	2	46	0
					0		10	2	16	2
15	10/08/1978	New Zealand	Trent Bridge	W	7	1	15	9	18	1
							20	7	30	1
16	24/08/1978	New Zealand	Lord's	W	12		28	14	39	1
						2				
17	15/12/1978	Australia	Perth	W	7*		14	1	39	2
					1		8	3	11	2
18	29/12/1978	Australia	Melbourne	L	6*	1	23	3	50	3
					0	1	14	4	25	1
19	06/01/1979	Australia	Sydney	W	10		24	4	50	2
					7	1	10	3	17	2
20	27/01/1979	Australia	Adelaide	W	0*		19	1	45	2
					3*		14	6	19	3
21	10/02/1979	Australia	Sydney	W	0		12	2	21	1
							7	3	22	1
22	12/07/1979	India	Edgbaston	W			24.1	9	36	2
						1	20.4	8	45	4
23	02/08/1979	India	Lord's	D			15	7	15	2
							25	12	56	0
24	16/08/1979	India	Headingley	D	0		14	6	13	1
25	30/08/1979	India	The Oval	D	0	1	22.3	7	38	3
							8	2	15	0
26	05/06/1980	West Indies	Trent Bridge	L	7*		19	4	69	1
					2*	1	14	5	40	1
27	19/06/1980	West Indies	Lord's	D	10*		11	2	32	0
28	28/08/1980	Australia	Lord's	D	5		30	6	67	1
							15	4	53	0
29	18/06/1981	Australia	Trent Bridge	L	6*		20	7	43	2
					0*		20	7	33	0
30	27/08/1981	Australia	The Oval	D	0*		31	8	63	0
							29.2	6	82	4

Batting & Fielding

Mat	Inns	N/O	Runs	H/S	Avg	100s	50s	Cat
30	35	15	128	15	6.40	0	0	25

Bowling

Balls	Runs	Wkts	Avg	Best	5WI	10WM	S/R
6208	2248	87	25.83	4-28	0	0	71.35

C.HESELTINE

Full Name: Christopher Heseltine
Born: 26/11/1869, South Kensington, London
Died: 13/06/1944, Walhampton, Lymington, Hampshire
Teams: Hampshire 1895-1904, England 1896
Matches: 2 (Won 2, Drew 0, Lost 0)
Right-hand lower order batsman – Right-arm fast bowler

No	Date	Opposition	Venue	R	Bat	C		Bowling	
1	02/03/1896	South Africa	Johannesburg (1)	W	0	1	9	0	29	0
						1	16.2	3	38	5
2	21/03/1896	South Africa	Cape Town	W	18	1	6	0	17	0

Batting & Fielding

Mat	Inns	N/O	Runs	H/S	Avg	100s	50s	Cat
2	2	0	18	18	9.00	0	0	3

Bowling

Balls	Runs	Wkts	Avg	Best	5WI	10WM	S/R
157	84	5	16.80	5-38	1	0	31.40

G.A.HICK

Full Name: Graeme Ashley Hick
Born: 23/05/1966, Salisbury, Rhodesia
Teams: Worcestershire 1984-96, Northern Districts 1987/88-88/89, Queensland 1990/91, Zimbabwe 1983/84-85/86, England 1991-96
Matches: 46 (Won 10, Drew 17, Lost 19)
Right-hand middle order batsman – Off break bowler

No	Date	Opposition	Venue	R	Bat	C	Bowling			
1	06/06/1991	West Indies	Headingley	W	6	2				
					6					
2	20/06/1991	West Indies	Lord's	D	0		18	4	77	2
						1				
3	04/07/1991	West Indies	Trent Bridge	L	43	1	5	0	18	0
					0					
4	25/07/1991	West Indies	Edgbaston	L	19	2	1	1	0	0
					1	2				
5	18/01/1992	New Zealand	Christchurch	W	35	2	3	0	11	0
							14	8	11	0
6	30/01/1992	New Zealand	Auckland	W	30	2				
					4		1	1	0	0
7	06/02/1992	New Zealand	Wellington	D	43		69	27	126	4
					22					
8	04/06/1992	Pakistan	Edgbaston	D	51		13	1	46	0
9	18/06/1992	Pakistan	Lord's	L	13					
					11	2				
10	02/07/1992	Pakistan	Old Trafford	D	22	1	3	0	17	0
						1	2	2	0	0
11	23/07/1992	Pakistan	Headingley	W	1	4				
						2				
12	29/01/1993	India	Calcutta	L	1	4	12.5	5	19	3
					25		6	1	9	2
13	11/02/1993	India	Madras (1)	L	64	1	29	2	77	1
					0					
14	19/02/1993	India	Bombay (3)	L	178		29	3	97	2
					47					
15	13/03/1993	Sri Lanka	Colombo (2)	L	68		8	0	27	0
					26		2	0	11	0
16	03/06/1993	Australia	Old Trafford	L	34					
					22		9	1	20	0
17	17/06/1993	Australia	Lord's	L	20		8	3	21	0
					64					
18	19/08/1993	Australia	The Oval	W	80					
					36		8	3	11	0
19	19/02/1994	West Indies	Kingston	L	23		21	4	55	1
					96		3	1	2	0
20	17/03/1994	West Indies	Georgetown	L	33		20	1	61	0
					5					
21	25/03/1994	West Indies	Port-of-Spain	L	40		3	1	5	0
					6					
22	08/04/1994	West Indies	Bridgetown	W	34	2				
					59	1	4	2	3	1
23	16/04/1994	West Indies	St John's	D	20		18	3	61	0
							8	2	11	0
24	02/06/1994	New Zealand	Trent Bridge	W	18	4				
							14	6	12	1
25	16/06/1994	New Zealand	Lord's	D	58	1	2	0	9	0
					37		2	2	0	0
26	30/06/1994	New Zealand	Old Trafford	D	20	1				
						2				
27	21/07/1994	South Africa	Lord's	L	38		10	5	22	1
					11		24	14	38	1
28	04/08/1994	South Africa	Headingley	D	25		1	0	8	0
					110		6	3	6	0
29	18/08/1994	South Africa	The Oval	W	39	2	5	1	13	0
					81*		2	0	11	0
30	25/11/1994	Australia	Brisbane (2)	L	3	3	4	0	22	0
					80		2	1	1	0
31	24/12/1994	Australia	Melbourne	L	23	3	2	0	9	0
					2		3	2	5	0
32	01/01/1995	Australia	Sydney	D	2	2				
					98*	1	5	0	21	0

No	Date	Opposition	Venue	R	Bat	C	Bowling			
33	08/06/1995	West Indies	Headingley	L	18	1	4	0	15	1
					27					
34	22/06/1995	West Indies	Lord's	W	13					
					67	1				
35	06/07/1995	West Indies	Edgbaston	L	3					
					3					
36	10/08/1995	West Indies	Trent Bridge	D	118*	2	4	1	11	0
					7					
37	24/08/1995	West Indies	The Oval	D	96	1	10	3	38	0
					51*					
38	16/11/1995	South Africa	Centurion	D	141					
39	30/11/1995	South Africa	Johannesburg (3)	D	6		15	1	38	1
					4	1	15	3	35	0
40	14/12/1995	South Africa	Durban (2)	D	31*	1	2	0	5	0
41	26/12/1995	South Africa	Port Elizabeth	D	62		12	1	32	0
					11*	1				
42	02/01/1996	South Africa	Cape Town	L	2	1				
					36		1.4	0	7	0
43	06/06/1996	India	Edgbaston	W	8					
						1	4	1	12	0
44	20/06/1996	India	Lord's	D	1		2	0	8	0
					6					
45	04/07/1996	India	Trent Bridge	D	20	1	4	1	8	0
							9	4	23	0
46	25/07/1996	Pakistan	Lord's	L	4	1	6	0	26	1
					4		7	2	16	0

Batting & Fielding

Mat	Inns	N/O	Runs	H/S	Avg	100s	50s	Cat
46	80	6	2672	178	36.10	4	15	62

Bowling

Balls	Runs	Wkts	Avg	Best	5WI	10WM	S/R
2973	1247	22	56.68	4-126	0	0	135.13

K.HIGGS

Full Name: Kenneth Higgs (known as Ken)
Born: 14/01/1937, Kidsgrove, Staffordshire
Teams: Lancashire 1958-69, Leicestershire 1972-86, England 1965-68
Matches: 15 (Won 4, Drew 7, Lost 4)
Left-hand lower order batsman – Right-arm fast medium bowler

No	Date	Opposition	Venue	R	Bat	C	Bowling			
1	26/08/1965	South Africa	The Oval	D	2		24	4	47	4
							41.1	10	96	4
2	10/12/1965	Australia	Brisbane (2)	D	4		30	6	102	2
3	25/02/1966	New Zealand	Christchurch	D	8*	1	30	6	51	3
							9	7	5	4
4	04/03/1966	New Zealand	Dunedin	D	0*	1	20	6	29	3
							13	7	12	2
5	11/03/1966	New Zealand	Auckland	D	0		28	13	33	2
							28	11	27	3
6	02/06/1966	West Indies	Old Trafford	L	1		31	5	94	3
					5					
7	16/06/1966	West Indies	Lord's	D	13		33	9	91	6
							34	5	82	2
8	30/06/1966	West Indies	Trent Bridge	L	5		25.4	3	71	4
					4		38	6	109	3
9	04/08/1966	West Indies	Headingley	L	49		43	11	94	4
					7					
10	18/08/1966	West Indies	The Oval	W	63	1	17	4	52	1
							15	6	18	1
11	08/06/1967	India	Headingley	W			14	8	19	0
							24	3	71	1
12	27/07/1967	Pakistan	Lord's	D	14		39	12	81	3
					1		6	3	6	0
13	10/08/1967	Pakistan	Trent Bridge	W	0*		19	12	35	4
							6	1	8	2
14	24/08/1967	Pakistan	The Oval	W	7		29	10	61	3
							20	7	58	5

No	Date	Opposition	Venue	R	Bat	C		Bowling		
15	06/06/1968	Australia	Old Trafford	L	2	1	35.3	11	80	2
					0		23	8	41	0

Batting & Fielding

Mat	Inns	N/O	Runs	H/S	Avg	100s	50s	Cat
15	19	3	185	63	11.56	0	1	4

Bowling

Balls	Runs	Wkts	Avg	Best	5WI	10WM	S/R
4112	1473	71	20.74	6-91	2	0	57.91

A.HILL

Full Name: Allen Hill
Born: 14/11/1843, Newton, Kirkheaton, Huddersfield, Yorkshire
Died: 28/08/1910, Leyland, Lancashire
Teams: Yorkshire 1871-82, England 1877
Matches: 2 (Won 1, Drew 0, Lost 1)
Right-hand lower order batsman – Right-hand round-arm fast bowler

No	Date	Opposition	Venue	R	Bat	C		Bowling		
1	15/03/1877	Australia	Melbourne	L	35*	1	23	10	42	1
					0		14	6	18	1
2	31/03/1877	Australia	Melbourne	W	49		27	12	27	4
					17*		21	9	43	1

Batting & Fielding

Mat	Inns	N/O	Runs	H/S	Avg	100s	50s	Cat
2	4	2	101	49	50.50	0	0	1

Bowling

Balls	Runs	Wkts	Avg	Best	5WI	10WM	S/R
340	130	7	18.57	4-27	0	0	48.57

A.J.L.HILL

Full Name: Arthur James Ledger Hill
Born: 26/07/1871, Bassett, Hampshire
Died: 06/09/1950, Sparsholt House, Hampshire
Teams: Cambridge University 1890-93, Hampshire 1895-1921, England 1896
Matches: 3 (Won 3, Drew 0, Lost 0)
Right-hand middle order batsman – Lob bowler (previously right-arm fast medium)

No	Date	Opposition	Venue	R	Bat	C		Bowling		
1	13/02/1896	South Africa	Port Elizabeth	W	25					
					37					
2	02/03/1896	South Africa	Johannesburg (1)	W	65					
						1				
3	21/03/1896	South Africa	Cape Town	W	124					
							8	4	8	4

Batting & Fielding

Mat	Inns	N/O	Runs	H/S	Avg	100s	50s	Cat
3	4	0	251	124	62.75	1	1	1

Bowling

Balls	Runs	Wkts	Avg	Best	5WI	10WM	S/R
40	8	4	2.00	4-8	0	0	10.00

M.J.HILTON

Full Name: Malcolm Jameson Hilton
Born: 02/08/1928, Chadderton, Lancashire
Died: 08/07/1990, Oldham, Lancashire
Teams: Lancashire 1946-61, England 1950-52
Matches: 4 (Won 1, Drew 1, Lost 2)
Right-hand lower order batsman – Left-arm slow bowler

No	Date	Opposition	Venue	R	Bat	C		Bowling		
1	12/08/1950	West Indies	The Oval	L	3		41	12	91	0
					0					
2	26/07/1951	South Africa	Headingley	D	9*	1	61.3	18	176	3
					10		5	17	0	

No	Date	Opposition	Venue	R	Bat	C		Bowling		
3	12/01/1952	India	Kanpur	W	10		22.5	10	32	4
							32	11	61	5
4	06/02/1952	India	Madras (1)	L	0		40	9	100	2
					15					

Batting & Fielding

Mat	Inns	N/O	Runs	H/S	Avg	100s	50s	Cat
4	6	1	37	15	7.40	0	0	1

Bowling

Balls	Runs	Wkts	Avg	Best	5WI	10WM	S/R
1244	477	14	34.07	5-61	1	0	88.85

G.H.HIRST

Full Name: George Herbert Hirst
Born: 07/09/1871, Kirkheaton, Yorkshire
Died: 10/05/1954, Lindley, Huddersfield, Yorkshire
Teams: Yorkshire 1891-1929, Europeans 1921/22, England 1897-1909
Matches: 24 (Won 8, Drew 8, Lost 8)
Right-hand middle order batsman – Left-arm fast medium bowler

No	Date	Opposition	Venue	R	Bat	C		Bowling		
1	13/12/1897	Australia	Sydney	W	62		28	7	57	0
							13	3	49	0
2	01/01/1898	Australia	Melbourne	L	0	2	25	1	89	1
					3					
3	14/01/1898	Australia	Adelaide	L	85		22	6	62	1
					6					
4	26/02/1898	Australia	Sydney	L	44		4	1	14	0
					7	1	7	0	33	0
5	01/06/1899	Australia	Trent Bridge	D	6	1	24	9	42	1
							11	4	20	0
6	29/05/1902	Australia	Edgbaston	D	48		11	4	15	3
							9	6	10	0
7	12/06/1902	Australia	Lord's	D						
8	03/07/1902	Australia	Bramall Lane	L	8		15	1	59	0
					0	2	10	1	40	0
9	11/08/1902	Australia	The Oval	W	43		29	5	77	5
					58*		5	1	7	1
10	11/12/1903	Australia	Sydney	W	0		24	8	47	2
					60*		29	1	79	0
11	01/01/1904	Australia	Melbourne	W	7	1	8	1	33	1
					4	1	14.4	4	38	2
12	15/01/1904	Australia	Adelaide	L	58		15	1	58	2
					44	1	13	1	36	1
13	26/02/1904	Australia	Sydney	W	25		13	1	36	0
					18		12.5	2	32	2
14	05/03/1904	Australia	Melbourne	L	0		19	6	44	0
					1	1	16.5	4	48	5
15	03/07/1905	Australia	Headingley	D	35	1	7	1	37	1
					40*	1	10	2	26	1
16	24/07/1905	Australia	Old Trafford	W	25		2	0	12	0
							7	2	19	0
17	14/08/1905	Australia	The Oval	D	5	1	23	6	86	3
							9	2	32	1
18	01/07/1907	South Africa	Lord's	D	7		18	7	35	1
							16	8	26	1
19	29/07/1907	South Africa	Headingley	W	17	1	9	3	22	1
					2	1	9	2	21	1
20	19/08/1907	South Africa	The Oval	D	4	1	22	7	39	3
					16		13	1	42	3
21	27/05/1909	Australia	Edgbaston	W	15	2	23	8	28	4
							23.5	4	58	5
22	14/06/1909	Australia	Lord's	L	31		26.5	2	83	3
					1		8	1	28	0
23	01/07/1909	Australia	Headingley	L	4		26	6	65	2
					0		17	3	39	1
24	26/07/1909	Australia	Old Trafford	D	1		7	0	15	0
							12	3	32	1

Batting & Fielding

Mat	Inns	N/O	Runs	H/S	Avg	100s	50s	Cat
24	38	3	790	85	22.57	0	5	18

Bowling

Balls	Runs	Wkts	Avg	Best	5WI	10WM	S/R
3967	1770	59	30.00	5-48	3	0	67.23

J.W.HITCH

Full Name: John William Hitch (known as Bill or Billitch)
Born: 07/05/1886, Radcliffe, Lancashire
Died: 07/07/1965, Rumney, Cardiff, Glamorgan
Teams: Surrey 1907-25, England 1911-21
Matches: 7 (Won 4, Drew 2, Lost 1)
Right-hand lower order batsman – Right-arm fast bowler

No	Date	Opposition	Venue	R	Bat	C	Bowling			
1	30/12/1911	Australia	Melbourne	W	0*		7	0	37	1
							5	0	21	0
2	12/01/1912	Australia	Adelaide	W	0		2	1	2	1
						1	11	0	69	1
3	23/02/1912	Australia	Sydney	W	4	1	9	0	31	2
					4		6	1	23	0
4	29/07/1912	Australia	Old Trafford	D	4					
5	12/08/1912	South Africa	The Oval	W	0*	1				
						1				
6	17/12/1920	Australia	Sydney	L	3		10	0	37	0
					19		8	0	40	0
7	13/08/1921	Australia	The Oval	D	18		19	3	65	2
					51*					

Batting & Fielding

Mat	Inns	N/O	Runs	H/S	Avg	100s	50s	Cat
7	10	3	103	51*	14.71	0	1	4

Bowling

Balls	Runs	Wkts	Avg	Best	5WI	10WM	S/R
462	325	7	46.42	2-31	0	0	66.00

J.B.HOBBS

Full Name: Sir John Berry Hobbs (known as Jack)
Born: 16/12/1882, Cambridge
Died: 21/12/1963, Hove, Sussex
Teams: Surrey 1905-34, England 1908-30
Matches: 61 (Won 28, Drew 11, Lost 22)
Right-hand opening batsman – Right-arm medium bowler

No	Date	Opposition	Venue	R	Bat	C	Bowling			
1	01/01/1908	Australia	Melbourne	W	83					
					28					
2	10/01/1908	Australia	Adelaide	L	26					
					23*					
3	07/02/1908	Australia	Melbourne	L	57					
					0					
4	21/02/1908	Australia	Sydney	L	72					
					13	1	7	3	13	0
5	27/05/1909	Australia	Edgbaston	W	0					
					62*	1				
6	14/06/1909	Australia	Lord's	L	19					
					9					
7	01/07/1909	Australia	Headingley	L	12					
					30					
8	01/01/1910	South Africa	Johannesburg (1)	L	89		6	1	20	0
					35		6	2	16	0
9	21/01/1910	South Africa	Durban (1)	L	53	1	5	2	5	0
					70		2	0	5	0
10	26/02/1910	South Africa	Johannesburg (1)	W	11					
					93*					
11	07/03/1910	South Africa	Cape Town	L	1					
					0					

No	Date	Opposition	Venue	R	Bat	C	O	Bowling M	R	W
12	11/03/1910	South Africa	Cape Town	W	187		4 / 8	0 / 3	11 / 19	0 / 1
13	15/12/1911	Australia	Sydney	L	63 / 22	1				
14	30/12/1911	Australia	Melbourne	W	6 / 126*	1 / 1				
15	12/01/1912	Australia	Adelaide	W	187 / 3	1				
16	09/02/1912	Australia	Melbourne	W	178					
17	23/02/1912	Australia	Sydney	W	32 / 45					
18	10/06/1912	South Africa	Lord's	W	4		11	2	36	0
19	24/06/1912	Australia	Lord's	D	107					
20	08/07/1912	South Africa	Headingley	W	27 / 55	1				
21	29/07/1912	Australia	Old Trafford	D	19					
22	12/08/1912	South Africa	The Oval	W	68 / 9*					
23	19/08/1912	Australia	The Oval	W	66 / 32					
24	13/12/1913	South Africa	Durban (1)	W	82					
25	26/12/1913	South Africa	Johannesburg (1)	W	23	1				
26	01/01/1914	South Africa	Johannesburg (1)	W	92 / 41					
27	14/02/1914	South Africa	Durban (1)	D	64 / 97					
28	27/02/1914	South Africa	Port Elizabeth	W	33 / 11*					
29	17/12/1920	Australia	Sydney	L	49 / 59	1				
30	31/12/1920	Australia	Melbourne	L	122 / 20					
31	14/01/1921	Australia	Adelaide	L	18 / 123		7	2	16	0
32	11/02/1921	Australia	Melbourne	L	27 / 13					
33	25/02/1921	Australia	Sydney	L	40 / 34	1				
34	02/07/1921	Australia	Headingley	L						
35	14/06/1924	South Africa	Edgbaston	W	76					
36	28/06/1924	South Africa	Lord's	W	211	2				
37	12/07/1924	South Africa	Headingley	W	31 / 7	1				
38	16/08/1924	South Africa	The Oval	D	30					
39	19/12/1924	Australia	Sydney	L	115 / 57		2	0	13	0
40	01/01/1925	Australia	Melbourne	L	154 / 22					
41	16/01/1925	Australia	Adelaide	L	119 / 27		3	0	11	0
42	13/02/1925	Australia	Melbourne	W	66					
43	27/02/1925	Australia	Sydney	L	0 / 13					
44	12/06/1926	Australia	Trent Bridge	D	19*					
45	26/06/1926	Australia	Lord's	D	119					
46	10/07/1926	Australia	Headingley	D	49 / 88					
47	24/07/1926	Australia	Old Trafford	D	74					
48	14/08/1926	Australia	The Oval	W	37 / 100					
49	21/07/1928	West Indies	Old Trafford	W	53					

No	Date	Opposition	Venue	R	Bat	C		Bowling	
50	11/08/1928	West Indies	The Oval	W	159				
51	30/11/1928	Australia	Brisbane (1)	W	49				
					11				
52	14/12/1928	Australia	Sydney	W	40				
53	29/12/1928	Australia	Melbourne	W	20				
					49				
54	01/02/1929	Australia	Adelaide	W	74				
					1				
55	08/03/1929	Australia	Melbourne	L	142				
					65				
56	17/08/1929	South Africa	The Oval	D	10				
					52				
57	13/06/1930	Australia	Trent Bridge	W	78	1			
					74				
58	27/06/1930	Australia	Lord's	L	1	1			
					19				
59	11/07/1930	Australia	Headingley	D	29	1			
					13				
60	25/07/1930	Australia	Old Trafford	D	31				
61	16/08/1930	Australia	The Oval	L	47				
					9				

Batting & Fielding

Mat	Inns	N/O	Runs	H/S	Avg	100s	50s	Cat
61	102	7	5410	211	56.94	15	28	17

Bowling

Balls	Runs	Wkts	Avg	Best	5WI	10WM	S/R
376	165	1	165.00	1-19	0	0	376.00

R.N.S.HOBBS

Full Name: Robin Nicholas Stuart Hobbs
Born: 08/05/1942, Chippenham, Wiltshire
Teams: Essex 1961-75, Glamorgan 1979-81, England 1967-71
Matches: 7 (Won 4, Drew 3, Lost 0)
Right-hand lower order batsman – Leg break & googly bowler

No	Date	Opposition	Venue	R	Bat	C		Bowling		
1	08/06/1967	India	Headingley	W		1	22.2	9	45	3
							45.2	13	100	1
2	22/06/1967	India	Lord's	W	7					
							6	1	16	0
3	13/07/1967	India	Edgbaston	W	15*	1	6.3	1	25	3
					2	2	32	10	73	2
4	27/07/1967	Pakistan	Lord's	D	1*	1	35	16	46	1
					1*		16	9	28	0
5	19/01/1968	West Indies	Port-of-Spain	D	2		15	1	34	1
						1	13	2	44	1
6	06/03/1969	Pakistan	Karachi (1)	D						
7	08/07/1971	Pakistan	Headingley	W	6	1	20	5	48	0
					0	1	4	0	22	0

Batting & Fielding

Mat	Inns	N/O	Runs	H/S	Avg	100s	50s	Cat
7	8	3	34	15*	6.80	0	0	8

Bowling

Balls	Runs	Wkts	Avg	Best	5WI	10WM	S/R
1291	481	12	40.08	3-25	0	0	107.58

W.E.HOLLIES

Full Name: William Eric Hollies (known as Eric)
Born: 05/06/1912, Old Hill, Staffordshire
Died: 16/04/1981, Chinley, Derbyshire
Teams: Warwickshire 1932-57, England 1935-50
Matches: 13 (Won 4, Drew 6, Lost 3)
Right-hand lower order batsman – Leg break & googly bowler

No	Date	Opposition	Venue	R	Bat	C	Bowling			
1	08/01/1935	West Indies	Bridgetown	W			16	4	36	2
2	14/02/1935	West Indies	Georgetown	D	1*		26	7	50	7
							5	2	17	0
3	14/03/1935	West Indies	Kingston	L	1*		46	11	114	1
					6					
4	07/06/1947	South Africa	Trent Bridge	D	0*		55.2	16	123	5
					18*		9	1	33	0
5	21/06/1947	South Africa	Lord's	W			28	10	52	2
							20	7	32	0
6	05/07/1947	South Africa	Old Trafford	W	5	1	23	8	42	1
							14	4	49	1
7	14/08/1948	Australia	The Oval	L	0		56	14	131	5
					0					
8	11/06/1949	New Zealand	Headingley	D	0*		25	6	57	0
							11	3	33	0
9	25/06/1949	New Zealand	Lord's	D			58	18	133	5
10	23/07/1949	New Zealand	Old Trafford	D	0		18	8	29	0
							26	6	52	2
11	13/08/1949	New Zealand	The Oval	D	1*		20	7	51	1
							17	6	30	2
12	08/06/1950	West Indies	Old Trafford	W	0		33	13	70	3
					3		35.2	11	63	5
13	20/07/1950	West Indies	Trent Bridge	L	2*	1	43.4	8	134	2
					0		7	6	1	0

Batting & Fielding

Mat	Inns	N/O	Runs	H/S	Avg	100s	50s	Cat
13	15	8	37	18*	5.28	0	0	2

Bowling

Balls	Runs	Wkts	Avg	Best	5WI	10WM	S/R
3554	1332	44	30.27	7-50	5	0	80.77

E.R.T.HOLMES

Full Name: Errol Reginald Thorold Holmes
Born: 21/08/1905, Calcutta, India
Died: 16/08/1960, Marylebone, London
Teams: Oxford University 1925-27, Surrey 1924-55, England 1935
Matches: 5 (Won 1, Drew 1, Lost 3)
Right-hand middle order batsman – Right-arm fast medium bowler

No	Date	Opposition	Venue	R	Bat	C	Bowling			
1	08/01/1935	West Indies	Bridgetown	W	0	1				
					6					
2	24/01/1935	West Indies	Port-of-Spain	L	85*	2	3	1	10	1
					0*					
3	14/02/1935	West Indies	Georgetown	D	2					
							3	1	16	1
4	14/03/1935	West Indies	Kingston	L	0		8	0	40	0
					3					
5	29/06/1935	South Africa	Lord's	L	10	1				
					8		4	2	10	0

Batting & Fielding

Mat	Inns	N/O	Runs	H/S	Avg	100s	50s	Cat
5	9	2	114	85*	16.28	0	1	4

Bowling

Balls	Runs	Wkts	Avg	Best	5WI	10WM	S/R
108	76	2	38.00	1-10	0	0	54.00

P.HOLMES

Full Name: Percy Holmes
Born: 25/11/1886, Oakes, Huddersfield, Yorkshire
Died: 03/09/1971, Marsh, Huddersfield, Yorkshire
Teams: Yorkshire 1913-33, England 1921-32
Matches: 7 (Won 3, Drew 1, Lost 3)
Right-hand opening batsman – Right-arm medium bowler

No	Date	Opposition	Venue	R	Bat	C
1	28/05/1921	Australia	Trent Bridge	L	30	
					8	
2	24/12/1927	South Africa	Johannesburg (1)	W	0	
					15*	
3	31/12/1927	South Africa	Cape Town	W	9	
					88	1
4	21/01/1928	South Africa	Durban (2)	D	70	
					56	
5	28/01/1928	South Africa	Johannesburg (1)	L	1	
					63	
6	04/02/1928	South Africa	Durban (2)	L	0	2
					0	
7	25/06/1932	India	Lord's	W	6	
					11	

Batting & Fielding

Mat	Inns	N/O	Runs	H/S	Avg	100s	50s	Cat
7	14	1	357	88	27.46	0	4	3

L.HONE

Full Name: Leland Hone
Born: 30/01/1853, Dublin, Ireland
Died: 31/12/1896, St Stephen's Green, Dublin, Ireland
Teams: MCC 1878-80, England 1879
Matches: 1 (Won 0, Drew 0, Lost 1)
Right-hand middle order batsman – Occasional wicket-keeper

No	Date	Opposition	Venue	R	Bat	C	St	B
1+	02/01/1879	Australia	Melbourne	L	7	2		19
					6			0

Batting & Fielding

Mat	Inns	N/O	Runs	H/S	Avg	100s	50s	Cat	St	Byes
1	2	0	13	7	6.50	0	0	2	0	19

J.L.HOPWOOD

Full Name: John Leonard Hopwood (known as Len)
Born: 30/10/1903, Newton Hyde, Cheshire
Died: 15/06/1985, Denton, Lancashire
Teams: Lancashire 1923-39, England 1934
Matches: 2 (Won 0, Drew 2, Lost 0)
Right-hand opening/middle order batsman – Left-arm medium bowler

No	Date	Opposition	Venue	R	Bat	C	Bowling			
1	06/07/1934	Australia	Old Trafford	D	2		38	20	46	0
							9	5	16	0
2	20/07/1934	Australia	Headingley	D	8		30	7	93	0
					2*					

Batting & Fielding

Mat	Inns	N/O	Runs	H/S	Avg	100s	50s	Cat
2	3	1	12	8	6.00	0	0	0

Bowling

Balls	Runs	Wkts	Avg	Best	5WI	10WM	S/R
462	155	0	–	0-16	0	0	–

A.N.HORNBY

Full Name: Albert Neilson Hornby (also known as Monkey)
Born: 10/02/1847, Blackburn, Lancashire
Died: 17/12/1925, Parkfield, Wardle, Nantwich, Cheshire
Teams: Lancashire 1867-99, England 1879-84
Matches: 3 (Won 0, Drew 1, Lost 2)
England Captain: 2 times 1982-84 (Won 0, Drew 1, Lost 1) **Toss:** 1-1
Right-hand opening batsman – Right & Left-arm bowler

No	Date	Opposition	Venue	R	Bat	C		Bowling		
1	02/01/1879	Australia	Melbourne	L	2		7	7	0	1
					4					
2*	28/08/1882	Australia	The Oval	L	2					
					9					
3*	10/07/1884	Australia	Old Trafford	D	0					
					4					

Batting & Fielding

Mat	Inns	N/O	Runs	H/S	Avg	100s	50s	Cat
3	6	0	21	9	3.50	0	0	0

Bowling

Balls	Runs	Wkts	Avg	Best	5WI	10WM	S/R
28	0	1	0.00	1-0	0	0	28.00

M.J.HORTON

Full Name: Martin John Horton
Born: 21/04/1934, Worcester
Teams: Worcestershire 1952-66, Northern Districts 1967/68-70/71, England 1959
Matches: 2 (Won 2, Drew 0, Lost 0)
Right-hand opening batsman – Off break bowler

No	Date	Opposition	Venue	R	Bat	C		Bowling		
1	04/06/1959	India	Trent Bridge	W	58		5	0	15	0
						1	19	11	20	0
2	18/06/1959	India	Lord's	W	2		15.4	7	24	2
						1				

Batting & Fielding

Mat	Inns	N/O	Runs	H/S	Avg	100s	50s	Cat
2	2	0	60	58	30.00	0	1	2

Bowling

Balls	Runs	Wkts	Avg	Best	5WI	10WM	S/R
238	59	2	29.50	2-24	0	0	119.00

N.D.HOWARD

Full Name: Nigel David Howard
Born: 18/05/1925, Gee Cross, Hyde, Cheshire
Died: 31/05/1979, Douglas, Isle of Man
Teams: Lancashire 1946-53, England 1951-52
England Captain: 4 times 1951-52 (Won 1, Drew 3, Lost 0) **Toss:** 2-2
Right-hand opening/middle order batsman

No	Date	Opposition	Venue	R	Bat	C
1*	02/11/1951	India	Delhi	D	13	
					9	
2*	14/12/1951	India	Bombay (2)	D	20	1
						2
3*	30/12/1951	India	Calcutta	D	23	1
					20*	
4*	12/01/1952	India	Kanpur	W	1	

Batting & Fielding

Mat	Inns	N/O	Runs	H/S	Avg	100s	50s	Cat
4	6	1	86	23	17.20	0	0	4

H.HOWELL

Full Name: Henry Howell (known as Harry)
Born: 29/11/1890, Hockley, Birmingham
Died: 09/07/1932, Selly Oak, Birmingham
Teams: Warwickshire 1913-28, England 1920-24
Matches: 5 (Won 0, Drew 1, Lost 4)
Right-hand lower order batsman – Right-arm fast bowler

No	Date	Opposition	Venue	R	Bat	C		Bowling		
1	31/12/1920	Australia	Melbourne	L	5		37	5	142	3
					0*					

No	Date	Opposition	Venue	R	Bat	C		Bowling		
2	14/01/1921	Australia	Adelaide	L	2		26	1	89	0
					4*		34	6	115	4
3	11/02/1921	Australia	Melbourne	L	0*		17	2	86	0
					0*		10	1	36	0
4	28/05/1921	Australia	Trent Bridge	L	0*		9	3	22	0
					4*					
5	16/08/1924	South Africa	The Oval	D	20			5	69	0

Batting & Fielding

Mat	Inns	N/O	Runs	H/S	Avg	100s	50s	Cat
5	8	6	15	5	7.50	0	0	0

Bowling

Balls	Runs	Wkts	Avg	Best	5WI	10WM	S/R
918	559	7	79.85	4-115	0	0	131.14

R.HOWORTH

Full Name: Richard Howorth (known as Dick)
Born: 26/04/1909, Bacup, Lancashire
Died: 02/04/1980, Worcester
Teams: Worcestershire 1933-51, Europeans 1944/45, England 1947-48
Matches: 5 (Won 0, Drew 3, Lost 2)
Left-hand middle/lower order batsman – Left-arm slow bowler

No	Date	Opposition	Venue	R	Bat	C		Bowling		
1	16/08/1947	South Africa	The Oval	D	23	1	39	16	64	3
					45*	1	37	12	85	3
2	21/01/1948	West Indies	Bridgetown	D	14		30	8	68	1
					16		41	8	124	6
3	11/02/1948	West Indies	Port-of-Spain	D	14		32	3	76	2
					14		1	0	2	0
4	03/03/1948	West Indies	Georgetown	L	4		23	4	58	0
					2		9	0	25	1
5	27/03/1948	West Indies	Kingston	L	12*		40	10	106	3
					1		4	0	27	0

Batting & Fielding

Mat	Inns	N/O	Runs	H/S	Avg	100s	50s	Cat
5	10	2	145	45*	18.12	0	0	2

Bowling

Balls	Runs	Wkts	Avg	Best	5WI	10WM	S/R
1536	635	19	33.42	6-124	1	0	80.84

J.HUMPHRIES

Full Name: Joseph Humphries (known as Joe)
Born: 19/05/1876, Stonebroom, Derbyshire
Died: 07/05/1946, Chesterfield, Derbyshire
Teams: Derbyshire 1899-1914, England 1908
Matches: 3 (Won 1, Drew 0, Lost 2)
Right-hand lower order batsman – Wicket-keeper

No	Date	Opposition	Venue	R	Bat	C	St	B
1+	01/01/1908	Australia	Melbourne	W	6	1		0
					16	1		12
2+	10/01/1908	Australia	Adelaide	L	7	2		3
					1			20
3+	07/02/1908	Australia	Melbourne	L	3*			1
					11	3		7

Batting & Fielding

Mat	Inns	N/O	Runs	H/S	Avg	100s	50s	Cat	St	Byes
3	6	1	44	16	8.80	0	0	7	0	43

J.HUNTER

Full Name: Joseph Hunter (known as Joe)
Born: 03/08/1855, Scarborough, Yorkshire
Died: 04/01/1891, Rotherham, Yorkshire
Teams: Yorkshire 1878-88, England 1884-85
Matches: 5 (Won 3, Drew 0, Lost 2)
Right-hand lower order batsman – Wicket-keeper

No	Date	Opposition	Venue	R	Bat	C	St	B
1+	12/12/1884	Australia	Adelaide	W	1	2		7
							1	7
2+	01/01/1885	Australia	Melbourne	W	39*			3
						2		0
3+	20/02/1885	Australia	Sydney	L	13	2	2	3
					5*			1
4+	14/03/1885	Australia	Sydney	L	13			5
					4			0
5+	21/03/1885	Australia	Melbourne	W	18	2		5
								5

Batting & Fielding

Mat	Inns	N/O	Runs	H/S	Avg	100s	50s	Cat	St	Byes
5	7	2	93	39*	18.60	0	0	8	3	36

N.HUSSAIN

Full Name: Nasser Hussain
Born: 28/03/1968, Madras, India
Teams: Essex 1987-96, England 1990-96
Matches: 12 (Won 3, Drew 4, Lost 5)
Right-hand middle order batsman – Leg break bowler

No	Date	Opposition	Venue	R	Bat	C
1	24/02/1990	West Indies	Kingston	W	13	
						1
2	05/04/1990	West Indies	Bridgetown	L	18	
					0	
3	12/04/1990	West Indies	St John's	L	35	
					34	
4	01/07/1993	Australia	Trent Bridge	D	71	
					47*	
5	22/07/1993	Australia	Headingley	L	15	
					18*	
6	05/08/1993	Australia	Edgbaston	L	3	1
					0	
7	19/08/1993	Australia	The Oval	W	30	1
					0	
8	06/06/1996	India	Edgbaston	W	128	
					19	1
9	20/06/1996	India	Lord's	D	36	1
					28	
10	04/07/1996	India	Trent Bridge	D	107*	1
11	08/08/1996	Pakistan	Headingley	D	48	
12	22/08/1996	Pakistan	The Oval	L	12	1
					51	

Batting & Fielding

Mat	Inns	N/O	Runs	H/S	Avg	100s	50s	Cat
12	21	3	713	128	39.61	2	2	7

K.L.HUTCHINGS

Full Name: Kenneth Lotherington Hutchings
Born: 07/12/1882, Southborough, Kent
Died: 03/09/1916, Ginchy, France
Teams: Kent 1902-12, England 1907-09
Matches: 7 (Won 1, Drew 2, Lost 4)
Right-hand middle order batsman – Right-arm fast bowler

No	Date	Opposition	Venue	R	Bat	C	Bowling			
1	13/12/1907	Australia	Sydney	L	42	1				
					17					
2	01/01/1908	Australia	Melbourne	W	126	1				
					39	1				
3	10/01/1908	Australia	Adelaide	L	23	2	2	1	5	1
					0	2	7	0	34	0
4	07/02/1908	Australia	Melbourne	L	8					
					3		2	0	24	0

No	Date	Opposition	Venue	R	Bat	C		Bowling	
5	21/02/1908	Australia	Sydney	L	13	1			
					2				
6	26/07/1909	Australia	Old Trafford	D	9	1			
7	09/08/1909	Australia	The Oval	D	59				
							4	0	18	0

Batting & Fielding

Mat	Inns	N/O	Runs	H/S	Avg	100s	50s	Cat
7	12	0	341	126	28.41	1	1	9

Bowling

Balls	Runs	Wkts	Avg	Best	5WI	10WM	S/R
90	81	1	81.00	1-5	0	0	90.00

L.HUTTON

Full Name: Sir Leonard Hutton (known as Len)
Born: 23/06/1916, Fulneck, Pudsey, Yorkshire
Died: 06/09/1990, Norbiton, Kingston-upon-Thames, Surrey
Teams: Yorkshire 1934-55, England 1937-55
Matches: 79 (Won 27, Drew 32, Lost 20)
England Captain: 23 times 1952-55 (Won 11, Drew 8, Lost 4) **Toss:** 7-16
Right-hand opening batsman – Leg break bowler

No	Date	Opposition	Venue	R	Bat	C		Bowling		
1	26/06/1937	New Zealand	Lord's	D	0					
					1		2	1	4	0
2	24/07/1937	New Zealand	Old Trafford	W	100					
					14					
3	14/08/1937	New Zealand	The Oval	D	12	1	2	0	7	0
						1	2.4	1	4	1
4	10/06/1938	Australia	Trent Bridge	D	100					
5	24/06/1938	Australia	Lord's	D	4					
					5	1				
6	20/08/1938	Australia	The Oval	W	364					
7	31/12/1938	South Africa	Cape Town	D	17					
8	20/01/1939	South Africa	Durban (2)	W	31	1				
9	18/02/1939	South Africa	Johannesburg (1)	D	92	1				
					32					
10	03/03/1939	South Africa	Durban (2)	D	38					
					55	1	1	0	10	0
11	24/06/1939	West Indies	Lord's	W	196	1				
					16	1				
12	22/07/1939	West Indies	Old Trafford	D	13	1				
					17					
13	19/08/1939	West Indies	The Oval	D	73		7	0	45	1
					165*					
14	22/06/1946	India	Lord's	W	7					
					22*					
15	20/07/1946	India	Old Trafford	D	67					
					2					
16	17/08/1946	India	The Oval	D	25					
17	29/11/1946	Australia	Brisbane (2)	L	7					
					0					
18	13/12/1946	Australia	Sydney	L	39					
					37					
19	01/01/1947	Australia	Melbourne	D	2	1				
					40		3	0	28	0
20	31/01/1947	Australia	Adelaide	D	94					
					76					
21	28/02/1947	Australia	Sydney	L	122*					
22	07/06/1947	South Africa	Trent Bridge	D	17	1				
					9		2	0	15	0
23	21/06/1947	South Africa	Lord's	W	18					
					13*					
24	05/07/1947	South Africa	Old Trafford	W	12	1				
					24	2				

No	Date	Opposition	Venue	R	Bat	C	Bowling			
25	26/07/1947	South Africa	Headingley	W	100					
					32*					
26	16/08/1947	South Africa	The Oval	D	83					
					36	1	2	0	14	0
27	03/03/1948	West Indies	Georgetown	L	31					
					24					
28	27/03/1948	West Indies	Kingston	L	56					
					60	3				
29	10/06/1948	Australia	Trent Bridge	L	3	1				
					74	1				
30	24/06/1948	Australia	Lord's	L	20	3				
					13					
31	22/07/1948	Australia	Headingley	L	81					
					57		4	1	30	0
32	14/08/1948	Australia	The Oval	L	30					
					64					
33	16/12/1948	South Africa	Durban (2)	W	83					
					5					
34	27/12/1948	South Africa	Johannesburg (2)	D	158					
						1				
35	01/01/1949	South Africa	Cape Town	D	41	1				
					87					
36	12/02/1949	South Africa	Johannesburg (2)	D	2					
					123					
37	05/03/1949	South Africa	Port Elizabeth	W	46					
					32					
38	11/06/1949	New Zealand	Headingley	D	101					
					0		3	0	23	0
39	25/06/1949	New Zealand	Lord's	D	23	1				
					66					
40	23/07/1949	New Zealand	Old Trafford	D	73					
							1	1	0	0
41	13/08/1949	New Zealand	The Oval	D	206	1				
42	08/06/1950	West Indies	Old Trafford	W	39					
					45					
43	24/06/1950	West Indies	Lord's	L	35	1				
					10					
44	12/08/1950	West Indies	The Oval	L	202*	1				
					2					
45	01/12/1950	Australia	Brisbane (2)	L	8*	2				
					62*					
46	22/12/1950	Australia	Melbourne	L	12	2				
					40					
47	05/01/1951	Australia	Sydney	L	62					
					9					
48	02/02/1951	Australia	Adelaide	L	156*	1				
					45	1				
49	23/02/1951	Australia	Melbourne	W	79	2				
					60*	1				
50	17/03/1951	New Zealand	Christchurch	D	28					
							3	0	7	0
51	24/03/1951	New Zealand	Wellington	W	57					
					29					
52	07/06/1951	South Africa	Trent Bridge	L	63					
					11	1				
53	21/06/1951	South Africa	Lord's	W	12	2				
					12*					
54	05/07/1951	South Africa	Old Trafford	W	27	2				
					98*					
55	26/07/1951	South Africa	Headingley	D	100					
56	16/08/1951	South Africa	The Oval	W	28	1				
					27	2				
57*	05/06/1952	India	Headingley	W	10					
					10					
58*	19/06/1952	India	Lord's	W	150					
					39*	1				
59*	17/07/1952	India	Old Trafford	W	104	1				
60*	14/08/1952	India	The Oval	D	86	1				
61*	11/06/1953	Australia	Trent Bridge	D	43					
					60*	1				

No	Date	Opposition	Venue	R	Bat	C		Bowling		
62*	25/06/1953	Australia	Lord's	D	145 5					
63*	09/07/1953	Australia	Old Trafford	D	66	1				
64*	23/07/1953	Australia	Headingley	D	0 25	1				
65*	15/08/1953	Australia	The Oval	W	82 17	1				
66*	15/01/1954	West Indies	Kingston	L	24 56					
67*	06/02/1954	West Indies	Bridgetown	L	72 77	1				
68*	24/02/1954	West Indies	Georgetown	W	169					
69*	17/03/1954	West Indies	Port-of-Spain	D	44 30*		6	0	43	0
70*	30/03/1954	West Indies	Kingston	W	205					
71*	10/06/1954	Pakistan	Lord's	D	0					
72*	12/08/1954	Pakistan	The Oval	L	14 5					
73*	26/11/1954	Australia	Brisbane (2)	L	4 13					
74*	17/12/1954	Australia	Sydney	W	30 28	2				
75*	31/12/1954	Australia	Melbourne	W	12 42					
76*	28/01/1955	Australia	Adelaide	W	80 5					
77*	25/02/1955	Australia	Sydney	D	6		0.6	0	2	1
78*	11/03/1955	New Zealand	Dunedin	W	11 3					
79*	25/03/1955	New Zealand	Auckland	W	53	1				

Batting & Fielding

Mat	Inns	N/O	Runs	H/S	Avg	100s	50s	Cat
79	138	15	6971	364	56.67	19	33	57

Bowling

Balls	Runs	Wkts	Avg	Best	5WI	10WM	S/R
260	232	3	77.33	1-2	0	0	86.66

R.A.HUTTON

Full Name: Richard Anthony Hutton
Born: 06/09/1942, Pudsey, Yorkshire
Teams: Cambridge University 1962-64, Yorkshire 1962-74, Transvaal 1975/76, England 1971
Matches: 5 (Won 1, Drew 3, Lost 1)
Right-hand middle order batsman – Right-arm fast medium bowler

No	Date	Opposition	Venue	R	Bat	C		Bowling		
1	17/06/1971	Pakistan	Lord's	D	58*	1	16	5	36	2
2	08/07/1971	Pakistan	Headingley	W	28 4	2 1	41 6	8 0	72 18	3 0
3	22/07/1971	India	Lord's	D	20 0	1 1	24 3	8 0	38 12	2 0
4	05/08/1971	India	Old Trafford	D	15	1	14 7	3 1	35 16	1 1
5	19/08/1971	India	The Oval	L	81 13*	1 1	12	2	30	0

Batting & Fielding

Mat	Inns	N/O	Runs	H/S	Avg	100s	50s	Cat
5	8	2	219	81	36.50	0	2	9

Bowling

Balls	Runs	Wkts	Avg	Best	5WI	10WM	S/R
738	257	9	28.55	3-72	0	0	82.00

J.IDDON

Full Name: John Iddon
Born: 08/01/1902, Mawdesley, Lancashire
Died: 17/04/1946, Madeley, Staffordshire
Teams: Lancashire 1924-45, England 1935
Matches: 5 (Won 1, Drew 2, Lost 2)
Right-hand middle order batsman – Left-arm slow bowler

No	Date	Opposition	Venue	R	Bat	C	Bowling			
1	08/01/1935	West Indies	Bridgetown	W	14*					
2	24/01/1935	West Indies	Port-of-Spain	L	73					
					0					
3	14/02/1935	West Indies	Georgetown	D	0					
4	14/03/1935	West Indies	Kingston	L	54		7	1	24	0
					0					
5	15/06/1935	South Africa	Trent Bridge	D	29		4	2	3	0

Batting & Fielding

Mat	Inns	N/O	Runs	H/S	Avg	100s	50s	Cat
5	7	1	170	73	28.33	0	2	0

Bowling

Balls	Runs	Wkts	Avg	Best	5WI	10WM	S/R
66	27	0	–	0-3	0	0	–

A.P.IGGLESDEN

Full Name: Alan Paul Igglesden
Born: 08/10/1964, Farnborough, Kent
Teams: Kent 1986-96, England 1989-94
Matches: 3 (Won 0, Drew 1, Lost 2)
Right-hand lower order batsman – Right-arm fast medium bowler

No	Date	Opposition	Venue	R	Bat	C	Bowling			
1	24/08/1989	Australia	The Oval	D	2*	1	24	2	91	2
							13	1	55	1
2	19/02/1994	West Indies	Kingston	L	3*		24	5	53	1
					0		7	0	36	1
3	17/03/1994	West Indies	Georgetown	L	0		24.3	3	94	1
					1*					

Batting & Fielding

Mat	Inns	N/O	Runs	H/S	Avg	100s	50s	Cat
3	5	3	6	3*	3.00	0	0	1

Bowling

Balls	Runs	Wkts	Avg	Best	5WI	10WM	S/R
555	329	6	54.83	2-91	0	0	92.50

J.T.IKIN

Full Name: John Thomas Ikin (known as Jack)
Born: 07/03/1918, Bignall End, Staffordshire
Died: 15/09/1984, Bignall End, Staffordshire
Teams: Lancashire 1939-57, England 1946-55
Matches: 18 (Won 5, Drew 7, Lost 6)
Left-hand middle order batsman – Leg break & googly bowler

No	Date	Opposition	Venue	R	Bat	C	Bowling			
1	22/06/1946	India	Lord's	W	16	1				
						1	10	1	43	1
2	20/07/1946	India	Old Trafford	D	2	2	2	0	11	0
					29*	1				
3	29/11/1946	Australia	Brisbane (2)	L	0		2	0	24	0
					32					
4	13/12/1946	Australia	Sydney	L	60	1	3	0	15	0
					17					
5	01/01/1947	Australia	Melbourne	D	48					
					5					

No	Date	Opposition	Venue	R	Bat	C	Bowling
6	31/01/1947	Australia	Adelaide	D	21	2	0 9 0
					1		
7	28/02/1947	Australia	Sydney	L	0	2	
					0	1	
8	21/03/1947	New Zealand	Christchurch	D	45		
9	21/01/1948	West Indies	Bridgetown	D	3	2	16 3 38 1
						2	12 1 48 0
10	11/02/1948	West Indies	Port-of-Spain	D	21	1	20 5 60 0
					19		
11	03/03/1948	West Indies	Georgetown	L	7		5 2 22 0
					24		
12	27/03/1948	West Indies	Kingston	L	5		19 0 69 1
					3		2 0 15 0
13	07/06/1951	South Africa	Trent Bridge	L	1	1	
					33	2	
14	21/06/1951	South Africa	Lord's	W	51	2	
					4*	2	
15	05/07/1951	South Africa	Old Trafford	W	22	3	
					38	2	
16	17/07/1952	India	Old Trafford	W	29	1	
						2	
17	14/08/1952	India	The Oval	D	53	1	
18	13/08/1955	South Africa	The Oval	W	17	1	
					0		

Batting & Fielding

Mat	Inns	N/O	Runs	H/S	Avg	100s	50s	Cat
18	31	2	606	60	20.89	0	3	31

Bowling

Balls	Runs	Wkts	Avg	Best	5WI	10WM	S/R
572	354	3	118.00	1-38	0	0	190.66

R.ILLINGWORTH

Full Name: Raymond Illingworth CBE (known as Ray)
Born: 08/06/1932, Pudsey, Yorkshire
Teams: Yorkshire 1951-83, Leicestershire 1969-78, England 1958-73
Matches: 61 (Won 29, Drew 25, Lost 7)
England Captain: 31 times 1969-73 (Won 12, Drew 14, Lost 5) **Toss:** 15-16
Right-hand middle order batsman – Off break bowler

No	Date	Opposition	Venue	R	Bat	C	Bowling
1	24/07/1958	New Zealand	Old Trafford	W	3*		28 9 39 1
							17 9 20 2
2	23/07/1959	India	Old Trafford	W	21		16 10 16 2
					47*	3	39 13 63 1
3	20/08/1959	India	The Oval	W	50	2	1 0 2 0
							29 10 43 1
4	06/01/1960	West Indies	Bridgetown	D	5		47 9 106 0
5	28/01/1960	West Indies	Port-of-Spain	W	10		7 3 8 0
					41*		28 14 38 0
6	17/02/1960	West Indies	Kingston	D	17	1	30 13 46 2
					6		13 4 35 0
7	09/03/1960	West Indies	Georgetown	D	4		43 11 72 0
					9		
8	25/03/1960	West Indies	Port-of-Spain	D	0		12 4 25 0
							16 3 53 2
9	09/06/1960	South Africa	Edgbaston	W	1		17 11 15 3
					16		24 6 57 3
10	23/06/1960	South Africa	Lord's	W	0*		
							1 1 0 0
11	07/07/1960	South Africa	Trent Bridge	W	37		
						1	19 9 33 0
12	21/07/1960	South Africa	Old Trafford	D	22*		11 2 35 0
					5		5 3 6 0
13	08/06/1961	Australia	Edgbaston	D	15	2	44 12 110 2
14	22/06/1961	Australia	Lord's	L	13	1	11.3 5 16 1
					0	2	

No	Date	Opposition	Venue	R	Bat	C	O	M	R	W
15	16/08/1962	Pakistan	The Oval	W	2*		13	5	27	0
							21	9	54	1
16	25/01/1963	Australia	Adelaide	D	12		20	3	85	1
							5	1	23	0
17	15/02/1963	Australia	Sydney	D	27		5	1	15	0
					18		10	5	8	0
18	23/02/1963	New Zealand	Auckland	W	20		1	0	5	0
						2	18	7	34	4
19	01/03/1963	New Zealand	Wellington	W	46	1				
						1	27	14	34	1
20	15/03/1963	New Zealand	Christchurch	W	2					
21	08/07/1965	New Zealand	Headingley	W			28	14	42	4
							7	0	28	0
22	30/06/1966	West Indies	Trent Bridge	L	0	1	8	1	21	0
					4		25	7	82	0
23	18/08/1966	West Indies	The Oval	W	3		15	7	40	2
							15	9	22	2
24	08/06/1967	India	Headingley	W		1	22	11	31	3
					12*		58	26	100	4
25	22/06/1967	India	Lord's	W	4	1	2	2	0	1
							22.3	12	29	6
26	13/07/1967	India	Edgbaston	W	2		7	4	14	2
					10		43	13	92	4
27	27/07/1967	Pakistan	Lord's	D	4		31	14	48	2
					9		15	11	10	1
28	11/07/1968	Australia	Edgbaston	D	27	1	22	10	37	3
							5.2	2	4	0
29	25/07/1968	Australia	Headingley	D	6		29	15	47	1
							51	22	87	6
30	22/08/1968	Australia	The Oval	W	8		48	15	87	2
					10		28	18	29	1
31*	12/06/1969	West Indies	Old Trafford	W	21	1	6	2	23	0
						1	30	12	52	1
32*	26/06/1969	West Indies	Lord's	D	113	1	16	4	39	0
					9*	1	27	9	66	3
33*	10/07/1969	West Indies	Headingley	W	1					
					19		14	5	38	1
34*	24/07/1969	New Zealand	Lord's	W	53	2	22	8	37	4
					0		18	9	24	0
35*	07/08/1969	New Zealand	Trent Bridge	D	33		12	4	15	2
							2	0	3	1
36*	21/08/1969	New Zealand	The Oval	W	4	1	32.3	13	55	3
							15	9	20	0
37*	27/11/1970	Australia	Brisbane (2)	D	8	1	11	1	47	0
							18	11	19	1
38*	11/12/1970	Australia	Perth	D	34	2	13	2	43	1
					29		4	2	12	0
39*	09/01/1971	Australia	Sydney	W	25		14	3	59	1
					53		9	5	9	0
40*	21/01/1971	Australia	Melbourne	D	41		13	0	59	2
41*	29/01/1971	Australia	Adelaide	D	24	1	5	2	14	1
					48*		14	7	32	0
42*	12/02/1971	Australia	Sydney	W	42		11	3	16	1
					29		20	7	39	3
43*	25/02/1971	New Zealand	Christchurch	W	36		6	3	12	0
						2	17	5	45	0
44*	05/03/1971	New Zealand	Auckland	D	0		18	4	45	0
					22					
45*	03/06/1971	Pakistan	Edgbaston	D	1		26	5	72	3
					1					
46*	17/06/1971	Pakistan	Lord's	D			7	6	1	0
47*	08/07/1971	Pakistan	Headingley	W	20		28	14	31	0
					45		26	11	58	3
48*	22/07/1971	India	Lord's	D	33	3	25	12	43	0
					20		16	2	33	2
49*	05/08/1971	India	Old Trafford	D	107		7	2	16	0
50*	19/08/1971	India	The Oval	L	11	1	34.3	12	70	5
					4		36	15	40	0
51*	08/06/1972	Australia	Old Trafford	W	26*	1				
					14					

No	Date	Opposition	Venue	R	Bat	C	Bowling			
52*	22/06/1972	Australia	Lord's	L	30	1	7	2	13	1
					12					
53*	13/07/1972	Australia	Trent Bridge	D	24*					
							15	4	41	1
54*	27/07/1972	Australia	Headingley	W	57	3	21	11	32	2
						1	19.1	5	32	2
55*	10/08/1972	Australia	The Oval	L	0		17	4	53	1
					31		8.5	2	26	0
56*	07/06/1973	New Zealand	Trent Bridge	W	8					
					3	1	21	7	31	0
57*	21/06/1973	New Zealand	Lord's	D	3		39	12	87	0
					22					
58*	05/07/1973	New Zealand	Headingley	W	65		6	0	20	0
							2	1	1	0
59*	26/07/1973	West Indies	The Oval	L	27		15	3	43	0
					40		24	8	50	3
60*	09/08/1973	West Indies	Edgbaston	D	27		32	19	37	1
							26	6	67	1
61*	23/08/1973	West Indies	Lord's	L	0		31.4	3	114	1
					13					

Batting & Fielding

Mat	Inns	N/O	Runs	H/S	Avg	100s	50s	Cat
61	90	11	1836	113	23.24	2	5	45

Bowling

Balls	Runs	Wkts	Avg	Best	5WI	10WM	S/R
11934	3807	122	31.20	6-29	3	0	97.81

R.K.ILLINGWORTH

Full Name: Richard Keith Illingworth
Born: 23/08/1963, Greengates, Bradford, Yorkshire
Teams: Worcestershire 1982-96, Natal 1988/89, England 1991-95
Matches: 9 (Won 1, Drew 4, Lost 4)
Right-hand lower order batsman – Left-arm slow bowler

No	Date	Opposition	Venue	R	Bat	C	Bowling			
1	04/07/1991	West Indies	Trent Bridge	L	13	1	33	8	110	3
					13		2	0	5	0
2	25/07/1991	West Indies	Edgbaston	L	0*		17	2	75	1
					5*		4.4	0	23	0
3	08/06/1995	West Indies	Headingley	L	17*	1	24	9	50	1
					10*		3	0	31	0
4	22/06/1995	West Indies	Lord's	W	16*		7	2	18	0
					4	1	7	4	9	0
5	06/07/1995	West Indies	Edgbaston	L	0		8	4	11	1
					0					
6	10/08/1995	West Indies	Trent Bridge	D	8*		51	21	96	4
					14*					
7	16/11/1995	South Africa	Centurion	D	0					
8	14/12/1995	South Africa	Durban (2)	D			29	12	37	3
9	26/12/1995	South Africa	Port Elizabeth	D	28		39.5	8	105	3
						2	22	7	45	3

Batting & Fielding

Mat	Inns	N/O	Runs	H/S	Avg	100s	50s	Cat
9	14	7	128	28	18.28	0	0	5

Bowling

Balls	Runs	Wkts	Avg	Best	5WI	10WM	S/R
1485	615	19	32.36	4-96	0	0	78.15

M.C.ILOTT

Full Name: Mark Christopher Ilott
Born: 27/08/1970, Watford, Hertfordshire
Teams: Essex 1988-96, England 1993-95
Matches: 5 (Won 0, Drew 3, Lost 2)
Right-hand lower order batsman – Left-arm fast medium bowler

No	Date	Opposition	Venue	R	Bat	C		Bowling		
1	01/07/1993	Australia	Trent Bridge	D	6		34	8	108	3
							18	5	44	1
2	22/07/1993	Australia	Headingley	L	0*		51	11	161	3
					4					
3	05/08/1993	Australia	Edgbaston	L	3		24	4	85	1
					15		2	0	14	0
4	14/12/1995	South Africa	Durban (2)	D			15	3	48	3
5	26/12/1995	South Africa	Port Elizabeth	D	0*		29.4	7	82	1

Batting & Fielding

Mat	Inns	N/O	Runs	H/S	Avg	100s	50s	Cat
5	6	2	28	15	7.00	0	0	0

Bowling

Balls	Runs	Wkts	Avg	Best	5WI	10WM	S/R
1042	542	12	45.16	3-48	0	0	86.83

D.J.INSOLE

Full Name: Douglas John Insole, CBE (known as Doug)
Born: 18/04/1926, Clapton, London
Teams: Cambridge University 1947-49, Essex 1947-63, England 1950-57
Matches: 9 (Won 3, Drew 2, Lost 4)
Right-hand middle order batsman – Right-arm medium bowler

No	Date	Opposition	Venue	R	Bat	C
1	20/07/1950	West Indies	Trent Bridge	L	21	1
					0	
2	21/07/1955	South Africa	Headingley	L	3	
					47	
3	12/07/1956	Australia	Headingley	W	5	
4	24/12/1956	South Africa	Johannesburg (3)	W	1	1
					29	3
5	01/01/1957	South Africa	Cape Town	W	29	
					3*	
6	25/01/1957	South Africa	Durban (2)	D	13	1
					110*	
7	15/02/1957	South Africa	Johannesburg (3)	L	47	
					68	2
8	01/03/1957	South Africa	Port Elizabeth	L	4	
					8	
9	30/05/1957	West Indies	Edgbaston	D	20	
					0	

Batting & Fielding

Mat	Inns	N/O	Runs	H/S	Avg	100s	50s	Cat
9	17	2	408	110*	27.20	1	1	8

R.C.IRANI

Full Name: Ronald Charles Irani (known as Ronnie)
Born: 26/10/1971, Leigh, Lancashire
Teams: Lancashire 1990-93, Essex 1994-96, England 1996
Matches: 2 (Won 1, Drew 1, Lost 0)
Right-hand middle order batsman – Right-arm medium bowler

No	Date	Opposition	Venue	R	Bat	C		Bowling		
1	06/06/1996	India	Edgbaston	W	34		7	4	22	1
							2	0	21	0
2	20/06/1996	India	Lord's	D	1		12	3	31	1
					41					

Batting & Fielding

Mat	Inns	N/O	Runs	H/S	Avg	100s	50s	Cat
2	3	0	76	41	25.33	0	0	0

Bowling

Balls	Runs	Wkts	Avg	Best	5WI	10WM	S/R
126	74	2	37.00	1-22	0	0	63.00

R.D.JACKMAN

Full Name: Robin David Jackman
Born: 13/08/1945, Simla, India
Teams: Surrey 1966-82, Western Province 1971/72, Rhodesia 1972/73-79/80, England 1981-82
Matches: 4 (Won 1, Drew 1, Lost 2)
Right-hand lower order batsman – Right-arm fast medium bowler

No	Date	Opposition	Venue	R	Bat	C	Bowling		
1	13/03/1981	West Indies	Bridgetown	L	7		22	4	65	3
					7		25	5	76	2
2	10/04/1981	West Indies	Kingston	D	0		26.2	6	57	1
3	12/08/1982	Pakistan	Lord's	L	0		36	5	110	4
					17		4	0	22	0
4	26/08/1982	Pakistan	Headingley	W	11		37	14	74	3
							28	11	41	1

Batting & Fielding

Mat	Inns	N/O	Runs	H/S	Avg	100s	50s	Cat
4	6	0	42	17	7.00	0	0	0

Bowling

Balls	Runs	Wkts	Avg	Best	5WI	10WM	S/R
1070	445	14	31.78	4-110	0	0	76.42

Hon.F.S.JACKSON

Full Name: Rt Hon.Sir Frank Stanley Jackson (also known as Francis Stanley Jackson)
Born: 21/11/1870, Allerton Hall, Chapel Allerton, Leeds, Yorkshire
Died: 09/03/1947, Knightsbridge, London
Teams: Cambridge University 1890-93, Yorkshire 1890-1907, England 1893-1905
Matches: 20 (Won 6, Drew 10, Lost 4)
England Captain: 5 times 1905 (Won 2, Drew 3, Lost 0) **Toss:** 5-0
Right-hand middle order batsman – Right-arm fast medium bowler

No	Date	Opposition	Venue	R	Bat	C	Bowling		
1	17/07/1893	Australia	Lord's	D	91		5	1	10	0
					5					
2	14/08/1893	Australia	The Oval	W	103					
						2	11	3	33	0
3	22/06/1896	Australia	Lord's	W	44	1	11	5	28	0
					18	1	16	6	34	0
4	16/07/1896	Australia	Old Trafford	L	18	1				
					1	1				
5	10/08/1896	Australia	The Oval	W	45					
					2	1				
6	01/06/1899	Australia	Trent Bridge	D	8		11	3	27	0
					0		26	8	57	3
7	15/06/1899	Australia	Lord's	L	73		18	6	31	0
					37					
8	29/06/1899	Australia	Headingley	D	9		5	1	18	0
							11	6	13	1
9	17/07/1899	Australia	Old Trafford	D	44		3.3	1	9	1
					14*		18	8	36	0
10	14/08/1899	Australia	The Oval	D	118		14	7	39	0
							13	2	54	0
11	29/05/1902	Australia	Edgbaston	D	53	1				
							4	2	7	0
12	12/06/1902	Australia	Lord's	D	55*					
13	03/07/1902	Australia	Bramall Lane	L	3	1	5.1	1	11	1
					14		17	2	60	3
14	24/07/1902	Australia	Old Trafford	L	128		11	0	58	0
					7					
15	11/08/1902	Australia	The Oval	W	2	1	20	4	66	2
					49		4	3	7	0
16*	29/05/1905	Australia	Trent Bridge	W	0		14.5	2	52	5
					82*	1	5	3	6	0
17*	15/06/1905	Australia	Lord's	D	29		15	0	50	4
					0					
18*	03/07/1905	Australia	Headingley	D	144*		4	0	10	1
					17		8	2	10	0

No	Date	Opposition	Venue	R	Bat	C		Bowling	
19*	24/07/1905	Australia	Old Trafford	W	113		7	0 26	2
							5	0 20	0
20*	14/08/1905	Australia	The Oval	D	76		9	1 27	1
					31				

Batting & Fielding

Mat	Inns	N/O	Runs	H/S	Avg	100s	50s	Cat
20	33	4	1415	144*	48.79	5	6	10

Bowling

Balls	Runs	Wkts	Avg	Best	5WI	10WM	S/R
1587	799	24	33.29	5-52	1	0	66.12

H.L.JACKSON

Full Name: Herbert Leslie Jackson (known as Les)
Born: 05/04/1921, Whitwell, Derbyshire
Teams: Derbyshire 1947-63, England 1949-61
Matches: 2 (Won 1, Drew 1, Lost 0)
Right-hand lower order batsman – Right-arm fast bowler

No	Date	Opposition	Venue	R	Bat	C		Bowling	
1	23/07/1949	New Zealand	Old Trafford	D	7*		27	11 47	2
							12	3 25	1
2	06/07/1961	Australia	Headingley	W	8		31	11 57	2
						1	13	5 26	2

Batting & Fielding

Mat	Inns	N/O	Runs	H/S	Avg	100s	50s	Cat
2	2	1	15	8	15.00	0	0	1

Bowling

Balls	Runs	Wkts	Avg	Best	5WI	10WM	S/R
498	155	7	22.14	2-26	0	0	71.14

J.A.JAMESON

Full Name: John Alexander Jameson
Born: 30/06/1941, Byculla, Bombay, India
Teams: Warwickshire 1960-76, England 1971-74
Matches: 4 (Won 0, Drew 3, Lost 1)
Right-hand opening batsman – Right-arm medium or off break bowler

No	Date	Opposition	Venue	R	Bat	C		Bowling	
1	05/08/1971	India	Old Trafford	D	15				
					28				
2	19/08/1971	India	The Oval	L	82				
					16				
3	16/02/1974	West Indies	Kingston	D	23		7	2 17	1
					38				
4	06/03/1974	West Indies	Bridgetown	D	3				
					9				

Batting & Fielding

Mat	Inns	N/O	Runs	H/S	Avg	100s	50s	Cat
4	8	0	214	82	26.75	0	1	0

Bowling

Balls	Runs	Wkts	Avg	Best	5WI	10WM	S/R
42	17	1	17.00	1-17	0	0	42.00

D.R.JARDINE

Full Name: Douglas Robert Jardine
Born: 23/10/1900, Malabar Hill, Bombay, India
Died: 18/06/1958, Montreux, Switzerland
Teams: Oxford University 1920-23, Surrey 1921-33, England 1928-34
Matches: 22 (Won 15, Drew 5, Lost 2)
England Captain: 15 times 1931-34 (Won 9, Drew 5, Lost 1) **Toss:** 7-8
Right-hand middle order batsman – Leg break bowler

No	Date	Opposition	Venue	R	Bat	C	Bowling			
1	23/06/1928	West Indies	Lord's	W	22	1				
						1				
2	21/07/1928	West Indies	Old Trafford	W	83					
						1				
3	30/11/1928	Australia	Brisbane (1)	W	35	1				
					65*					
4	14/12/1928	Australia	Sydney	W	28					
5	29/12/1928	Australia	Melbourne	W	62	3	1	0	10	0
					33					
6	01/02/1929	Australia	Adelaide	W	1					
					98					
7	08/03/1929	Australia	Melbourne	L	19					
					0					
8*	27/06/1931	New Zealand	Lord's	D	38	1				
					0*					
9*	29/07/1931	New Zealand	The Oval	W	7*	1				
10*	15/08/1931	New Zealand	Old Trafford	D	28*					
11*	25/06/1932	India	Lord's	W	79	1				
					85*	1				
12*	02/12/1932	Australia	Sydney	W	27					
13*	30/12/1932	Australia	Melbourne	L	1	1				
					0					
14*	13/01/1933	Australia	Adelaide	W	3	1				
					56	1				
15*	10/02/1933	Australia	Brisbane (2)	W	46	1				
					24	2				
16*	23/02/1933	Australia	Sydney	W	18	2				
					24	1				
17*	24/03/1933	New Zealand	Christchurch	D	45					
18*	24/06/1933	West Indies	Lord's	W	21					
19*	22/07/1933	West Indies	Old Trafford	D	127					
20*	15/12/1933	India	Bombay (1)	W	60					
						1				
21*	05/01/1934	India	Calcutta	D	61	3				
						2				
22*	10/02/1934	India	Madras (1)	W	65					
					35*					

Batting & Fielding

Mat	Inns	N/O	Runs	H/S	Avg	100s	50s	Cat
22	33	6	1296	127	48.00	1	10	26

Bowling

Balls	Runs	Wkts	Avg	Best	5WI	10WM	S/R
6	10	0	–	0-10	0	0	–

P.W.JARVIS

Full Name: Paul William Jarvis
Born: 29/06/1965, Redcar, Yorkshire
Teams: Yorkshire 1981-93, Sussex 1994-96, England 1988-93
Matches: 9 (Won 0, Drew 4, Lost 5)
Right-hand lower order batsman – Right-arm fast medium bowler

No	Date	Opposition	Venue	R	Bat	C	Bowling			
1	12/02/1988	New Zealand	Christchurch	D	14		21	8	43	2
					10*		17	7	30	1
2	25/02/1988	New Zealand	Auckland	D	10		33	9	74	2
							27	7	54	1
3	02/06/1988	West Indies	Trent Bridge	D	6		18.1	1	63	2
4	16/06/1988	West Indies	Lord's	L	7		13	2	47	0
					29*		26	3	107	4
5	22/06/1989	Australia	Lord's	L	6		31	3	150	1
					5		9.2	0	38	0

No	Date	Opposition	Venue	R	Bat	C		Bowling		
6	06/07/1989	Australia	Edgbaston	D	22		23	4	82	0
							6	1	20	1
7	29/01/1993	India	Calcutta	L	4		27	5	72	2
					6		5.2	1	23	0
8	11/02/1993	India	Madras (1)	L	8	1	28	7	72	2
					2					
9	13/03/1993	Sri Lanka	Colombo (2)	L	0		25.5	1	76	3
					3	1	8	2	14	0

Batting & Fielding

Mat	Inns	N/O	Runs	H/S	Avg	100s	50s	Cat
9	15	2	132	29*	10.15	0	0	2

Bowling

Balls	Runs	Wkts	Avg	Best	5WI	10WM	S/R
1912	965	21	45.95	4-107	0	0	91.04

R.O.JENKINS

Full Name: Roland Oliver Jenkins (known as Roly)
Born: 24/11/1918, Rainbow Hill, Worcester
Died: 22/07/1996, Worcester
Teams: Worcestershire 1938-58, England 1948-52
Matches: 9 (Won 4, Drew 3, Lost 2)
Right-hand middle/lower order batsman – Leg break & googly bowler

No	Date	Opposition	Venue	R	Bat	C		Bowling		
1	16/12/1948	South Africa	Durban (2)	W	5		14	3	50	1
					22		22.3	6	64	3
2	27/12/1948	South Africa	Johannesburg (2)	D	4		21.4	3	88	3
							19	3	54	0
3	01/01/1949	South Africa	Cape Town	D	1		11	1	46	1
							9	0	48	4
4	12/02/1949	South Africa	Johannesburg (2)	D	25		8	1	39	1
							9	2	26	0
5	05/03/1949	South Africa	Port Elizabeth	W	29		15	2	53	3
						1	4	0	27	0
6	24/06/1950	West Indies	Lord's	L	4	1	35.2	6	116	5
					4		59	13	174	4
7	20/07/1950	West Indies	Trent Bridge	L	39	1	13	0	73	1
					6*		11	1	46	0
8	05/06/1952	India	Headingley	W	38		27	6	78	1
						1	13	2	50	4
9	19/06/1952	India	Lord's	W	21		7.3	1	26	1
							10	1	40	0

Batting & Fielding

Mat	Inns	N/O	Runs	H/S	Avg	100s	50s	Cat
9	12	1	198	39	18.00	0	0	4

Bowling

Balls	Runs	Wkts	Avg	Best	5WI	10WM	S/R
2118	1098	32	34.31	5-116	1	0	66.18

G.L.JESSOP

Full Name: Gilbert Laird Jessop
Born: 19/05/1874, Cheltenham, Gloucestershire
Died: 11/05/1955, Fordington, Dorset
Teams: Cambridge University 1896-99, Gloucestershire 1894-1914, London County 1900-03, England 1899-1912
Matches: 18 (Won 7, Drew 4, Lost 7)
Right-hand middle order batsman – Right-arm fast bowler

No	Date	Opposition	Venue	R	Bat	C		Bowling		
1	15/06/1899	Australia	Lord's	L	51		37.1	10	105	3
					4		6	0	19	0
2	13/12/1901	Australia	Sydney	W	24	1	1	0	4	0
						1				
3	01/01/1902	Australia	Melbourne	L	27					
					32		1	0	9	0
4	17/01/1902	Australia	Adelaide	L	1		7	0	19	0
					16		24.4	9	41	2

No	Date	Opposition	Venue	R	Bat	C		Bowling		
5	14/02/1902	Australia	Sydney	L	0		26	5	68	4
					15		7	0	23	0
6	28/02/1902	Australia	Melbourne	L	35		1	0	13	0
					16					
7	29/05/1902	Australia	Edgbaston	D	6	2				
8	12/06/1902	Australia	Lord's	D						
9	03/07/1902	Australia	Bramall Lane	L	12					
					55		4	0	15	0
10	11/08/1902	Australia	The Oval	W	13		6	2	11	0
					104					
11	29/05/1905	Australia	Trent Bridge	W	0	1	7	2	18	1
							1	0	1	0
12	01/07/1907	South Africa	Lord's	D	93	1	2	0	8	0
13	29/07/1907	South Africa	Headingley	W	0					
					10					
14	19/08/1907	South Africa	The Oval	D	2	2				
					11					
15	27/05/1909	Australia	Edgbaston	W	22	1				
						1				
16	01/07/1909	Australia	Headingley	L						
17	10/06/1912	South Africa	Lord's	W	3					
						1				
18	08/07/1912	South Africa	Headingley	W	16					
					1					

Batting & Fielding

Mat	Inns	N/O	Runs	H/S	Avg	100s	50s	Cat
18	26	0	569	104	21.88	1	3	11

Bowling

Balls	Runs	Wkts	Avg	Best	5WI	10WM	S/R
742	354	10	35.40	4-68	0	0	74.20

A.O.JONES

Full Name: Arthur Owen Jones
Born: 16/08/1872, Shelton, Nottinghamshire
Died: 21/12/1914, Dunstable, Bedfordshire
Teams: Cambridge University 1892-93, Nottinghamshire 1892-1914, London County 1901, England 1899-1909
Matches: 12 (Won 3, Drew 2, Lost 7)
England Captain: 2 times 1908 (Won 0, Drew 0, Lost 2) **Toss:** 1-1
Right-hand opening batsman – Leg break bowler

No	Date	Opposition	Venue	R	Bat	C		Bowling		
1	14/08/1899	Australia	The Oval	D	31	2	30	12	73	3
							12	2	43	0
2	13/12/1901	Australia	Sydney	W	9					
						1				
3	01/01/1902	Australia	Melbourne	L	0					
					6	2	1	0	2	0
4	17/01/1902	Australia	Adelaide	L	5					
					11					
5	14/02/1902	Australia	Sydney	L	15	1				
					6					
6	28/02/1902	Australia	Melbourne	L	10	2				
					28					
7	29/05/1905	Australia	Trent Bridge	W	4	2				
					30					
8	15/06/1905	Australia	Lord's	D	1	1				
					5					
9*	07/02/1908	Australia	Melbourne	L	3	1				
					31	1				
10*	21/02/1908	Australia	Sydney	L	0					
					34	1				
11	27/05/1909	Australia	Edgbaston	W	28					
						1				
12	14/06/1909	Australia	Lord's	L	8		2	0	15	0
					26					

Batting & Fielding

Mat	Inns	N/O	Runs	H/S	Avg	100s	50s	Cat
12	21	0	291	34	13.85	0	0	15

Bowling

Balls	Runs	Wkts	Avg	Best	5WI	10WM	S/R
228	133	3	44.33	3-73	0	0	76.00

I.J.JONES

Full Name: Ivor Jeffrey Jones (known as Jeff)
Born: 10/12/1941, Dafen, Carmarthenshire
Teams: Glamorgan 1960-68, England 1964-68
Matches: 15 (Won 2, Drew 11, Lost 2)
Right-hand lower order batsman – Left-arm fast medium bowler

No	Date	Opposition	Venue	R	Bat	C	Bowling		
1	21/01/1964	India	Bombay (2)	D	5		13	0	48	0
							11	1	31	0
2	30/12/1965	Australia	Melbourne	D	1		24	4	92	3
							20	1	92	1
3	07/01/1966	Australia	Sydney	W	16		20	6	51	2
							7	0	35	0
4	28/01/1966	Australia	Adelaide	L	0*		29	3	118	6
					8					
5	11/02/1966	Australia	Melbourne	D	4*		29	1	145	3
6	25/02/1966	New Zealand	Christchurch	D	0		28.4	9	71	4
							7	3	13	0
7	04/03/1966	New Zealand	Dunedin	D			26	11	46	3
							15	4	32	2
8	11/03/1966	New Zealand	Auckland	D	0	1	21	4	52	2
							25	9	28	3
9	02/06/1966	West Indies	Old Trafford	L	0*		28	6	100	0
					0*					
10	16/06/1966	West Indies	Lord's	D	0*		21	3	64	1
							25	2	95	0
11	19/01/1968	West Indies	Port-of-Spain	D	2		19	5	63	3
							15	3	32	1
12	08/02/1968	West Indies	Kingston	D	0*		14.1	4	39	2
							30	4	90	3
13	29/02/1968	West Indies	Bridgetown	D	1*	1	21.1	3	56	1
							11	3	53	0
14	14/03/1968	West Indies	Port-of-Spain	W	1	1	29	1	108	2
							11	2	20	0
15	28/03/1968	West Indies	Georgetown	D	0*	1	31	5	114	1
					0*		17	1	81	1

Batting & Fielding

Mat	Inns	N/O	Runs	H/S	Avg	100s	50s	Cat
15	17	9	38	16	4.75	0	0	4

Bowling

Balls	Runs	Wkts	Avg	Best	5WI	10WM	S/R
3546	1769	44	40.20	6-118	1	0	80.59

H.JUPP

Full Name: Henry Jupp (known as Harry)
Born: 19/11/1841, Dorking, Surrey
Died: 08/04/1889, Bermondsey, London
Teams: Surrey 1862-81, England 1877
Matches: 2 (Won 1, Drew 0, Lost 1)
Right-hand opening batsman – Wicket-keeper – Right-hand round-arm fast bowler

No	Date	Opposition	Venue	R	Bat	C
1	15/03/1877	Australia	Melbourne	L	63	
					4	
2	31/03/1877	Australia	Melbourne	W	0	
					1	2

Batting & Fielding

Mat	Inns	N/O	Runs	H/S	Avg	100s	50s	Cat
2	4	0	68	63	17.00	0	1	2

V.W.C.JUPP

Full Name: Vallance William Crisp Jupp
Born: 27/03/1891, Burgess Hill, Sussex
Died: 09/07/1960, Spratton, Northamptonshire
Teams: Sussex 1909-22, Northamptonshire 1923-38, England 1921-28
Matches: 8 (Won 3, Drew 2, Lost 3)
Right-hand middle order batsman – Off break bowler (previously right-arm fast medium)

No	Date	Opposition	Venue	R	Bat	C		Bowling		
1	28/05/1921	Australia	Trent Bridge	L	8	1	5	0	14	1
					15		3.1	0	13	0
2	02/07/1921	Australia	Headingley	L	14		18	2	70	2
					28	1	13	2	45	2
3	23/12/1922	South Africa	Johannesburg (1)	L	1		21	6	59	4
					33		31	7	87	3
4	01/01/1923	South Africa	Cape Town	W	12		9	3	18	2
					38	1	11	3	23	0
5	18/01/1923	South Africa	Durban (2)	D	16	1	22.4	6	70	2
6	09/02/1923	South Africa	Johannesburg (1)	D	7		15	5	36	3
					10*		12	3	39	0
7	23/06/1928	West Indies	Lord's	W	14		23	9	37	4
							15	4	66	3
8	21/07/1928	West Indies	Old Trafford	W	12	1	18	5	39	2

Batting & Fielding

Mat	Inns	N/O	Runs	H/S	Avg	100s	50s	Cat
8	13	1	208	38	17.33	0	0	5

Bowling

Balls	Runs	Wkts	Avg	Best	5WI	10WM	S/R
1301	616	28	22.00	4-37	0	0	46.46

W.W.KEETON

Full Name: William Walter Keeton (known as Walter)
Born: 30/04/1905, Shirebrook, Derbyshire
Died: 10/10/1980, Forest Town, Nottinghamshire
Teams: Nottinghamshire 1926-52, England 1934-39
Matches: 2 (Won 0, Drew 2, Lost 0)
Right-hand opening batsman

No	Date	Opposition	Venue	R	Bat	C
1	20/07/1934	Australia	Headingley	D	25	
					12	
2	19/08/1939	West Indies	The Oval	D	0	
					20	

Batting & Fielding

Mat	Inns	N/O	Runs	H/S	Avg	100s	50s	Cat
2	4	0	57	25	14.25	0	0	0

A.S.KENNEDY

Full Name: Alexander Stuart Kennedy (known as Alex)
Born: 24/01/1891, Edinburgh, Scotland
Died: 15/11/1959, Langdown, Hythe, Southampton, Hampshire
Teams: Hampshire 1907-36, England 1922-23
Matches: 5 (Won 2, Drew 2, Lost 1)
Right-hand opening/middle order batsman – Right-arm medium bowler

No	Date	Opposition	Venue	R	Bat	C		Bowling		
1	23/12/1922	South Africa	Johannesburg (1)	L	41*	2	20.4	5	37	4
					0	1	41.3	9	132	4
2	01/01/1923	South Africa	Cape Town	W	2		18	10	24	1
					11*		35.2	13	58	4
3	18/01/1923	South Africa	Durban (2)	D	8	1	39	14	88	5
4	09/02/1923	South Africa	Johannesburg (1)	D	16	1	24	5	68	3
							27.5	7	70	3
5	16/02/1923	South Africa	Durban (2)	W	14		25	9	46	2
					1		49.1	19	76	5

Batting & Fielding

Mat	Inns	N/O	Runs	H/S	Avg	100s	50s	Cat
5	8	2	93	41*	15.50	0	0	5

Bowling

Balls	Runs	Wkts	Avg	Best	5WI	10WM	S/R
1683	599	31	19.32	5-76	2	0	54.29

D.KENYON

Full Name: Donald Kenyon, MBE (known as Don)
Born: 15/05/1924, Wordsley, Staffordshire
Teams: Worcestershire 1946-67, England 1951-55
Matches: 8 (Won 2, Drew 5, Lost 1)
Right-hand opening batsman – Right-arm medium bowler

No	Date	Opposition	Venue	R	Bat	C
1	02/11/1951	India	Delhi	D	35	
					6	
2	14/12/1951	India	Bombay (2)	D	21	1
					2	
3	30/12/1951	India	Calcutta	D	3	
					0	
4	11/06/1953	Australia	Trent Bridge	D	8	
					16	1
5	25/06/1953	Australia	Lord's	D	3	
					2	
6	09/06/1955	South Africa	Trent Bridge	W	87	
7	23/06/1955	South Africa	Lord's	W	1	
					2	2
8	07/07/1955	South Africa	Old Trafford	L	5	1
					1	

Batting & Fielding

Mat	Inns	N/O	Runs	H/S	Avg	100s	50s	Cat
8	15	0	192	87	12.80	0	1	5

E.T.KILLICK

Full Name: Rev Edgar Thomas Killick (known as Tom)
Born: 09/05/1907, Fulham, London
Died: 18/05/1953, Northampton
Teams: Cambridge University 1927-30, Middlesex 1926-39, England 1929
Matches: 2 (Won 0, Drew 2, Lost 0)
Right-hand opening batsman

No	Date	Opposition	Venue	R	Bat	C
1	15/06/1929	South Africa	Edgbaston	D	31	
					23	
2	29/06/1929	South Africa	Lord's	D	3	1
					24	1

Batting & Fielding

Mat	Inns	N/O	Runs	H/S	Avg	100s	50s	Cat
2	4	0	81	31	20.25	0	0	2

R.KILNER

Full Name: Roy Kilner
Born: 17/10/1890, Low Valley, Wombwell, Yorkshire
Died: 05/04/1928, Kendray, Barnsley, Yorkshire
Teams: Yorkshire 1911-27, England 1924-26
Matches: 9 (Won 2, Drew 5, Lost 2)
Left-hand middle order batsman – Left-arm slow bowler

No	Date	Opposition	Venue	R	Bat	C	Bowling			
1	14/06/1924	South Africa	Edgbaston	W	59	1				
							22	10	40	0
2	26/07/1924	South Africa	Old Trafford	D			12	6	19	0

No	Date	Opposition	Venue	R	Bat	C	Bowling			
3	16/01/1925	Australia	Adelaide	L	6		56	7	127	4
					24	1	22.1	7	51	4
4	13/02/1925	Australia	Melbourne	W	74	1	13	1	29	3
							16	3	41	2
5	27/02/1925	Australia	Sydney	L	24		38	4	97	4
						1	34	13	54	0
6	12/06/1926	Australia	Trent Bridge	D						
7	26/06/1926	Australia	Lord's	D		1	34.5	11	70	4
							22	2	49	0
8	10/07/1926	Australia	Headingley	D	36		37	6	106	2
9	24/07/1926	Australia	Old Trafford	D	9*	2	28	12	51	1

Batting & Fielding

Mat	Inns	N/O	Runs	H/S	Avg	100s	50s	Cat
9	8	1	233	74	33.28	0	2	6

Bowling

Balls	Runs	Wkts	Avg	Best	5WI	10WM	S/R
2368	734	24	30.58	4-51	0	0	98.66

J.H.KING

Full Name: John Herbert King
Born: 16/04/1871, Lutterworth, Leicestershire
Died: 18/11/1946, Denbigh
Teams: Leicestershire 1895-1925, England 1909
Matches: 1 (Won 0, Drew 0, Lost 1)
Left-hand middle order batsman – Left-arm medium bowler

No	Date	Opposition	Venue	R	Bat	C	Bowling			
1	14/06/1909	Australia	Lord's	L	60		27	5	99	1
					4					

Batting & Fielding

Mat	Inns	N/O	Runs	H/S	Avg	100s	50s	Cat
1	2	0	64	60	32.00	0	1	0

Bowling

Balls	Runs	Wkts	Avg	Best	5WI	10WM	S/R
162	99	1	99.00	1-99	0	0	162.00

S.P.KINNEIR

Full Name: Septimus Paul Kinneir (known as Paul)
Born: 13/05/1871, Corsham, Wiltshire
Died: 16/10/1928, Birmingham
Teams: Warwickshire 1898-1914, England 1911
Matches: 1 (Won 0, Drew 0, Lost 1)
Left-hand opening batsman – Left-arm slow bowler

No	Date	Opposition	Venue	R	Bat	C
1	15/12/1911	Australia	Sydney	L	22	
					30	

Batting & Fielding

Mat	Inns	N/O	Runs	H/S	Avg	100s	50s	Cat
1	2	0	52	30	26.00	0	0	0

A.E.KNIGHT

Full Name: Albert Ernest Knight
Born: 08/10/1872, Leicester
Died: 25/04/1946, Edmonton, Middlesex
Teams: Leicestershire 1895-1912, London County 1903-04, England 1904
Matches: 3 (Won 2, Drew 0, Lost 1)
Right-hand middle order batsman

No	Date	Opposition	Venue	R	Bat	C
1	01/01/1904	Australia	Melbourne	W	2	
					0	

No	Date	Opposition	Venue	R	Bat	C
2	26/02/1904	Australia	Sydney	W	70*	
					9	
3	05/03/1904	Australia	Melbourne	L	0	1
					0	

Batting & Fielding

Mat	Inns	N/O	Runs	H/S	Avg	100s	50s	Cat
3	6	1	81	70*	16.20	0	1	1

B.R.KNIGHT

Full Name: Barry Rolfe Knight
Born: 18/02/1938, Chesterfield, Derbyshire
Teams: Essex 1955-66, Leicestershire 1967-69, England 1961-69
Matches: 29 (Won 7, Drew 20, Lost 2)
Right-hand middle order batsman – Right-arm fast medium bowler

No	Date	Opposition	Venue	R	Bat	C	Bowling			
1	01/12/1961	India	Kanpur	D	12	1	36	11	80	2
2	13/12/1961	India	Delhi	D			24.3	5	72	2
3	30/12/1961	India	Calcutta	L	12		18	3	61	0
					39*		7	2	18	2
4	10/01/1962	India	Madras (2)	L	19		14	2	62	2
					33		4	0	12	0
5	19/01/1962	Pakistan	Dacca	D	10		29	13	52	1
						1	14	6	19	0
6	02/02/1962	Pakistan	Karachi (1)	D	6		19	4	66	4
							17	3	43	1
7	26/07/1962	Pakistan	Trent Bridge	D	14		17	1	38	4
							21	6	48	0
8	16/08/1962	Pakistan	The Oval	W	3		9	5	11	1
						1	11	3	33	1
9	30/11/1962	Australia	Brisbane (2)	D	0	1	17.5	2	65	3
					4*		14	1	63	0
10	23/02/1963	New Zealand	Auckland	W	125		10.4	2	23	2
							10	2	13	0
11	01/03/1963	New Zealand	Wellington	W	31		21	8	32	3
						1	4	1	7	1
12	15/03/1963	New Zealand	Christchurch	W	32	1	23	5	39	2
					20*		10	3	38	1
13	10/01/1964	India	Madras (2)	D	6		27	7	73	1
					7		7	1	22	0
14	21/01/1964	India	Bombay (2)	D	12		20	3	53	2
						1	13	2	28	2
15	29/01/1964	India	Calcutta	D	13		13.2	5	39	1
							4	0	33	0
16	08/02/1964	India	Delhi	D	21		11	0	46	0
							8	1	47	0
17	15/02/1964	India	Kanpur	D	127		1	0	4	0
							2	0	12	0
18	30/12/1965	Australia	Melbourne	D	1		26.5	2	84	4
							21	4	61	2
19	11/02/1966	Australia	Melbourne	D	13		36.2	4	105	2
20	04/03/1966	New Zealand	Dunedin	D	12		32	14	41	2
						2	3	1	3	0
21	11/03/1966	New Zealand	Auckland	D	25	1	16	7	40	0
					13*		18	9	21	1
22	16/06/1966	West Indies	Lord's	D	6		21	0	63	2
						1	30	3	106	2
23	20/06/1968	Australia	Lord's	D	27*	1	10.4	5	16	3
							16	9	35	0
24	11/07/1968	Australia	Edgbaston	D	6		14	2	34	1
					1					
25	12/06/1969	West Indies	Old Trafford	W	31		2	0	11	0
							12	3	15	2
26	26/06/1969	West Indies	Lord's	D	0		38	11	65	1
					1*		27.5	6	78	0
27	10/07/1969	West Indies	Headingley	W	7		22	5	63	4
					27		18.2	4	47	2

No	Date	Opposition	Venue	R	Bat	C	Bowling			
28	24/07/1969	New Zealand	Lord's	W	29		10	3	20	0
					49		3	1	5	0
29	07/08/1969	New Zealand	Trent Bridge	D	18*	2	18.5	4	44	2
							4	0	14	0

Batting & Fielding

Mat	Inns	N/O	Runs	H/S	Avg	100s	50s	Cat
29	38	7	812	127	26.19	2	0	14

Bowling

Balls	Runs	Wkts	Avg	Best	5WI	10WM	S/R
5377	2223	70	31.75	4-38	0	0	76.81

D.J.KNIGHT

Full Name: Donald John Knight
Born: 12/05/1894, Sutton, Surrey
Died: 05/01/1960, Marylebone, London
Teams: Oxford University 1914 & 1919, Surrey 1911-37, England 1921
Matches: 2 (Won 0, Drew 0, Lost 2)
Right-hand opening batsman

No	Date	Opposition	Venue	R	Bat	C
1	28/05/1921	Australia	Trent Bridge	L	8	1
					38	
2	11/06/1921	Australia	Lord's	L	7	
					1	

Batting & Fielding

Mat	Inns	N/O	Runs	H/S	Avg	100s	50s	Cat
2	4	0	54	38	13.50	0	0	1

N.V.KNIGHT

Full Name: Nicholas Verity Knight (known as Nick)
Born: 28/11/1969, Watford, Hertfordshire
Teams: Essex 1991-94, Warwickshire 1995-96, England 1995-96
Matches: 6 (Won 2, Drew 2, Lost 2)
Left-hand opening/middle order batsman – Right-arm medium bowler

No	Date	Opposition	Venue	R	Bat	C
1	27/07/1995	West Indies	Old Trafford	W	17	2
					13	2
2	10/08/1995	West Indies	Trent Bridge	D	57	1
					2	
3	06/06/1996	India	Edgbaston	W	27	3
					14	1
4	25/07/1996	Pakistan	Lord's	L	51	
					1	
5	08/08/1996	Pakistan	Headingley	D	113	
6	22/08/1996	Pakistan	The Oval	L	17	
					8	1

Batting & Fielding

Mat	Inns	N/O	Runs	H/S	Avg	100s	50s	Cat
6	11	0	320	113	29.09	1	2	10

A.P.E.KNOTT

Full Name: Alan Philip Eric Knott
Born: 09/04/1946, Belvedere, Kent
Teams: Kent 1964-85, Tasmania 1969/70, England 1967-81
Matches: 95 (Won 29, Drew 46, Lost 20)
Right-hand middle order batsman – Wicket-keeper

No	Date	Opposition	Venue	R	Bat	C	St	B
1+	10/08/1967	Pakistan	Trent Bridge	W	0	3		0
						4		0
2+	24/08/1967	Pakistan	The Oval	W	28	2		5
						3	1	1

No	Date	Opposition	Venue	R	Bat	C	St	B
3+	14/03/1968	West Indies	Port-of-Spain	W	69*	1		0
								1
4+	28/03/1968	West Indies	Georgetown	D	7	2		0
					73*	1		1
5+	06/06/1968	Australia	Old Trafford	L	5	2		0
					4	1		2
6+	20/06/1968	Australia	Lord's	D	33	2		0
								0
7+	11/07/1968	Australia	Edgbaston	D	4			1
					4*			0
8+	25/07/1968	Australia	Headingley	D	4	1		0
						1	3	13
9+	22/08/1968	Australia	The Oval	W	28	3	1	4
					34	1		0
10+	21/02/1969	Pakistan	Lahore (2)	D	52	2		8
					30			3
11+	28/02/1969	Pakistan	Dacca	D	2	3		4
						1		0
12+	06/03/1969	Pakistan	Karachi (1)	D	96*			
13+	12/06/1969	West Indies	Old Trafford	W	0		1	0
						1		4
14+	26/06/1969	West Indies	Lord's	D	53	2		5
					11	1		4
15+	10/07/1969	West Indies	Headingley	W	44	1		0
					31	4		0
16+	24/07/1969	New Zealand	Lord's	W	8	1		4
					10	3		5
17+	07/08/1969	New Zealand	Trent Bridge	D	15	2		1
								0
18+	21/08/1969	New Zealand	The Oval	W	21		1	0
						3	1	3
19+	27/11/1970	Australia	Brisbane (2)	D	73	3		7
						3	1	4
20+	11/12/1970	Australia	Perth	D	24	3		5
					30*			4
21+	09/01/1971	Australia	Sydney	W	6			0
					21*	3		2
22+	21/01/1971	Australia	Melbourne	D	19			10
						2		8
23+	29/01/1971	Australia	Adelaide	D	7	4		0
						1		2
24+	12/02/1971	Australia	Sydney	W	27	3	1	0
					15	1	1	2
25+	05/03/1971	New Zealand	Auckland	D	101			7
					96			0
26+	03/06/1971	Pakistan	Edgbaston	D	116			6
					4*			
27+	17/06/1971	Pakistan	Lord's	D		4		0
28+	08/07/1971	Pakistan	Headingley	W	10	4		6
					7	2	1	17
29+	22/07/1971	India	Lord's	D	67	2		7
					24	1	1	0
30+	05/08/1971	India	Old Trafford	D	41	4		1
						1		0
31+	19/08/1971	India	The Oval	L	90			6
					1	2		6
32+	08/06/1972	Australia	Old Trafford	W	18	2		1
					1	2		0
33+	22/06/1972	Australia	Lord's	L	43	2		0
					12	1		0
34+	13/07/1972	Australia	Trent Bridge	D	0	3		4
								0
35+	27/07/1972	Australia	Headingley	W	0	2		0
						3		0
36+	10/08/1972	Australia	The Oval	L	92	1		0
					63	1		0
37+	20/12/1972	India	Delhi	W	4	2		0
						1	1	8
38+	30/12/1972	India	Calcutta	L	35	1		0
					2	2		8
39+	12/01/1973	India	Madras (1)	L	10	1		6
					13	1		0

No	Date	Opposition	Venue	R	Bat	C	St	B
40+	25/01/1973	India	Kanpur	D	40	1		1
								5
41+	06/02/1973	India	Bombay (2)	D	56			4
					8	2		0
42+	02/03/1973	Pakistan	Lahore (2)	D	29			1
					34			0
43+	16/03/1973	Pakistan	Hyderabad	D	71	2		14
					63*			
44+	24/03/1973	Pakistan	Karachi (1)	D	2			4
						2		0
45+	07/06/1973	New Zealand	Trent Bridge	W	49	4		8
					2	1		0
46+	21/06/1973	New Zealand	Lord's	D	0	3		0
					0			
47+	05/07/1973	New Zealand	Headingley	W	21	2		5
						2		1
48+	26/07/1973	West Indies	The Oval	L	4*	1		1
					5	2		2
49+	09/08/1973	West Indies	Edgbaston	D	0			0
						4		0
50+	23/08/1973	West Indies	Lord's	L	21			1
					5			
51+	02/02/1974	West Indies	Port-of-Spain	L	7	3		3
					21			0
52+	16/02/1974	West Indies	Kingston	D	39			16
					6			
53+	06/03/1974	West Indies	Bridgetown	D	87			3
					67			
54+	22/03/1974	West Indies	Georgetown	D	61			6
55+	30/03/1974	West Indies	Port-of-Spain	W	33*	1		11
					44			9
56+	06/06/1974	India	Old Trafford	W	0	2		3
						4	1	1
57+	20/06/1974	India	Lord's	W	26	2		4
						3		0
58+	04/07/1974	India	Edgbaston	W		3		1
						1		0
59+	25/07/1974	Pakistan	Headingley	D	35	3		0
					5	2		0
60+	08/08/1974	Pakistan	Lord's	D	83			0
								0
61+	22/08/1974	Pakistan	The Oval	D	9	1		6
						1		5
62+	29/11/1974	Australia	Brisbane (2)	L	12	2		0
					19	2		1
63+	13/12/1974	Australia	Perth	L	51	3	1	7
					18			0
64+	26/12/1974	Australia	Melbourne	D	52	3		2
					4	1		6
65+	04/01/1975	Australia	Sydney	L	82	2		0
					10			0
66+	25/01/1975	Australia	Adelaide	L	5	1		4
					106*	2		0
67+	08/02/1975	Australia	Melbourne	W	5	3		2
						3		9
68+	20/02/1975	New Zealand	Auckland	W	29*	2		5
						1		0
69+	28/02/1975	New Zealand	Christchurch	D				3
70+	10/07/1975	Australia	Edgbaston	L	14	2		1
					38			
71+	31/07/1975	Australia	Lord's	D	69	1		0
					22*			4
72+	14/08/1975	Australia	Headingley	D	14			0
					31			4
73+	28/08/1975	Australia	The Oval	D	9	1		0
					64			0
74+	03/06/1976	West Indies	Trent Bridge	D	9	2		0
								0
75+	17/06/1976	West Indies	Lord's	D	17	1		2
					4			3
76+	08/07/1976	West Indies	Old Trafford	L	1			0
					14			5

No	Date	Opposition	Venue	R	Bat	C	St	B
77+	22/07/1976	West Indies	Headingley	L	116	1		1
					2			4
78+	12/08/1976	West Indies	The Oval	L	50	1	1	1
					57			4
79+	17/12/1976	India	Delhi	W	75	1		0
						2		3
80+	01/01/1977	India	Calcutta	W	2	1		0
						2		2
81+	14/01/1977	India	Madras (1)	W	45	1		0
					11	1		5
82+	28/01/1977	India	Bangalore	L	29	3		8
					81*	1		1
83+	11/02/1977	India	Bombay (3)	D	24	1	1	0
					1		1	4
84+	12/03/1977	Australia	Melbourne	L	15	1		4
					42	3		0
85+	16/06/1977	Australia	Lord's	D	8	2		0
					8			0
86+	07/07/1977	Australia	Old Trafford	W	39	4		0
								0
87+	28/07/1977	Australia	Trent Bridge	W	135	1		4
					2			1
88+	11/08/1977	Australia	Headingley	W	57	2		0
						2		1
89+	25/08/1977	Australia	The Oval	D	6	1		1
90+	05/06/1980	West Indies	Trent Bridge	L	6	3		1
					7	3		0
91+	19/06/1980	West Indies	Lord's	D	9	1		1
92+	10/07/1980	West Indies	Old Trafford	D	2	3		2
					6			
93+	24/07/1980	West Indies	The Oval	D	3	1		0
					3			
94+	13/08/1981	Australia	Old Trafford	W	13	2		0
					59	3		0
95+	27/08/1981	Australia	The Oval	D	36			4
					70*	1		1

Batting & Fielding

Mat	Inns	N/O	Runs	H/S	Avg	100s	50s	Cat	St	Byes
95	149	15	4389	135	32.75	5	30	250	19	422

N.A.KNOX

Full Name: Neville Alexander Knox
Born: 10/10/1884, Clapham, London
Died: 03/03/1935, Southborough, Surbiton, Surrey
Teams: Surrey 1904-10, England 1907
Matches: 2 (Won 1, Drew 1, Lost 0)
Right-hand lower order batsman – Right-arm fast bowler

No	Date	Opposition	Venue	R	Bat	C		Bowling		
1	29/07/1907	South Africa	Headingley	W	8		3	0	13	1
					5					
2	19/08/1907	South Africa	The Oval	D	8*		10	2	39	2
					3		8	0	53	0

Batting & Fielding

Mat	Inns	N/O	Runs	H/S	Avg	100s	50s	Cat
2	4	1	24	8*	8.00	0	0	0

Bowling

Balls	Runs	Wkts	Avg	Best	5WI	10WM	S/R
126	105	3	35.00	2-39	0	0	42.00

J.C.LAKER

Full Name: James Charles Laker (known as Jim)
Born: 09/02/1922, Frizinghall, Bradford, Yorkshire
Died: 23/04/1986, Putney, London
Teams: Surrey 1946-59, Essex 1962-64, Auckland 1951/52, England 1948-59
Matches: 46 (Won 19, Drew 15, Lost 12)
Right-hand lower order batsman – Off break bowler

No	Date	Opposition	Venue	R	Bat	C	Bowling O	M	R	W
1	21/01/1948	West Indies	Bridgetown	D	2		37	9	103	7
							30	12	95	2
2	11/02/1948	West Indies	Port-of-Spain	D	55 24		36	10	108	2
3	03/03/1948	West Indies	Georgetown	L	10 6		36	11	94	2
							9	1	34	2
4	27/03/1948	West Indies	Kingston	L	6 6*	1	36.4	5	103	3
							2	0	11	0
5	10/06/1948	Australia	Trent Bridge	L	63 4		55	14	138	4
6	24/06/1948	Australia	Lord's	L	28 0		7	3	17	0
							31.2	6	111	2
7	22/07/1948	Australia	Headingley	L	4 15*		30	8	113	3
							32	11	93	0
8	13/08/1949	New Zealand	The Oval	D	0		3	0	11	0
							29	6	78	4
9	08/06/1950	West Indies	Old Trafford	W	4 40		17	5	43	0
							14	4	43	1
10	05/07/1951	South Africa	Old Trafford	W	27		27	7	47	1
							19	3	42	3
11	16/08/1951	South Africa	The Oval	W	6 13*	1	37	12	64	4
							28	8	55	6
12	05/06/1952	India	Headingley	W	15		22.3	9	39	4
						1	13	4	17	0
13	19/06/1952	India	Lord's	W	23*	1	12	5	21	0
							39	15	102	4
14	17/07/1952	India	Old Trafford	W	0		2	0	7	0
						1				
15	14/08/1952	India	The Oval	D	6*		2	0	3	0
16	09/07/1953	Australia	Old Trafford	D	5		17	3	42	1
							9	5	11	2
17	23/07/1953	Australia	Headingley	D	10 48		9	1	33	0
							2	0	17	1
18	15/08/1953	Australia	The Oval	W	1		5	0	34	1
							16.5	2	75	4
19	06/02/1954	West Indies	Bridgetown	L	1 0		30.1	6	81	4
							30	13	62	0
20	24/02/1954	West Indies	Georgetown	W	27		21	11	32	2
							36	18	56	2
21	17/03/1954	West Indies	Port-of-Spain	D	7*	1	50	8	154	2
22	30/03/1954	West Indies	Kingston	W	9	1	4	1	13	0
						1	50	27	71	4
23	10/06/1954	Pakistan	Lord's	D	13*		22	12	17	1
							10.2	5	22	1
24	13/08/1955	South Africa	The Oval	W	2 12		23	13	28	2
							37.4	18	56	5
25	07/06/1956	Australia	Trent Bridge	D	9*		29.1	11	58	4
							30	19	29	2
26	21/06/1956	Australia	Lord's	L	12 4		29.1	10	47	3
							7	3	17	0
27	12/07/1956	Australia	Headingley	W	5		29	10	58	5
							41.3	21	55	6
28	26/07/1956	Australia	Old Trafford	W	3		16.4	4	37	9
							51.2	23	53	10
29	23/08/1956	Australia	The Oval	D	4		32	12	80	4
							18	14	8	3
30	24/12/1956	South Africa	Johannesburg (3)	W	0 3*		21	10	33	1
							2	1	5	1
31	01/01/1957	South Africa	Cape Town	W	0		28	8	65	1
							14.1	9	7	2
32	25/01/1957	South Africa	Durban (2)	D	0* 6		12	1	47	0
						1	18	7	29	2
33	15/02/1957	South Africa	Johannesburg (3)	L	17 5		15	3	49	1
							7	1	26	1
34	01/03/1957	South Africa	Port Elizabeth	L	6 3*		14	1	37	1
							14	5	26	1
35	30/05/1957	West Indies	Edgbaston	D	7		54	17	119	4
							24	20	13	2
36	04/07/1957	West Indies	Trent Bridge	D		1	62	27	101	3
							43	14	98	1
37	25/07/1957	West Indies	Headingley	W	1		17	4	24	2
							6.2	1	16	1

No	Date	Opposition	Venue	R	Bat	C	Bowling
38	22/08/1957	West Indies	The Oval	W	10*		23 12 39 3
							17 4 38 2
39	05/06/1958	New Zealand	Edgbaston	W	11*		5 2 9 1
						1	9 4 14 1
40	19/06/1958	New Zealand	Lord's	W	1	1	12 6 13 4
							13 8 24 1
41	03/07/1958	New Zealand	Headingley	W			22 11 17 5
							36 23 27 3
42	21/08/1958	New Zealand	The Oval	D	15		14 3 44 1
							20 10 25 1
43	05/12/1958	Australia	Brisbane (2)	L	13		10.1 3 15 2
					15		17 3 39 1
44	31/12/1958	Australia	Melbourne	L	22*		12 1 47 0
					3		4 1 7 1
45	09/01/1959	Australia	Sydney	D	2		46 9 107 5
							8 3 10 2
46	13/02/1959	Australia	Melbourne	L	2		30.5 4 93 4
					5*		

Batting & Fielding

Mat	Inns	N/O	Runs	H/S	Avg	100s	50s	Cat
46	63	15	676	63	14.08	0	2	12

Bowling

Balls	Runs	Wkts	Avg	Best	5WI	10WM	S/R
12027	4101	193	21.24	10-53	9	3	62.31

A.J.LAMB

Full Name: Allan Joseph Lamb
Born: 20/06/1954, Langebaanweg, Cape Province, South Africa
Teams: Northamptonshire 1978-95, Western Province 1972/73-81/82, Orange Free State 1987/88, England 1982-92
Matches: 79 (Won 21, Drew 26, Lost 32)
England Captain: 3 times 1990 (Won 0, Drew 0, Lost 3) **Toss:** 2-1
Right-hand middle order batsman – Right-arm medium bowler

No	Date	Opposition	Venue	R	Bat	C	Bowling
1	10/06/1982	India	Lord's	W	9		
					37*		
2	24/06/1982	India	Old Trafford	D	9		
3	08/07/1982	India	The Oval	D	107		
					45		
4	29/07/1982	Pakistan	Edgbaston	W	6		
					5		
5	12/08/1982	Pakistan	Lord's	L	33	1	
					0		
6	26/08/1982	Pakistan	Headingley	W	0		
					4		
7	12/11/1982	Australia	Perth	D	46	2	
					56		1 1 0 0
8	26/11/1982	Australia	Brisbane (2)	L	72		
					12	1	
9	10/12/1982	Australia	Adelaide	L	82		
					8		
10	26/12/1982	Australia	Melbourne	W	83	1	
					26		
11	02/01/1983	Australia	Sydney	D	0	1	
					29		
12	14/07/1983	New Zealand	The Oval	W	24	1	
					102*	1	
13	28/07/1983	New Zealand	Headingley	L	58		
					28	1	
14	11/08/1983	New Zealand	Lord's	W	17	4	
					4	2	
15	25/08/1983	New Zealand	Trent Bridge	W	22		
					137*	1	
16	20/01/1984	New Zealand	Wellington	D	13		
						1	
17	03/02/1984	New Zealand	Christchurch	L	11		
					9		
18	10/02/1984	New Zealand	Auckland	D	49		

No	Date	Opposition	Venue	R	Bat	C	Bowling			
19	02/03/1984	Pakistan	Karachi (1)	L	4 / 20	2				
20	12/03/1984	Pakistan	Faisalabad	D	19	2				
21	19/03/1984	Pakistan	Lahore (2)	D	29 / 6					
22	14/06/1984	West Indies	Edgbaston	L	15 / 13	1				
23	28/06/1984	West Indies	Lord's	L	23 / 110					
24	12/07/1984	West Indies	Headingley	L	100 / 3					
25	26/07/1984	West Indies	Old Trafford	L	100* / 9					
26	09/08/1984	West Indies	The Oval	L	12 / 1	2				
27	23/08/1984	Sri Lanka	Lord's	D	107	1	1	0	6	0
28	28/11/1984	India	Bombay (3)	L	9 / 1	3				
29	12/12/1984	India	Delhi	W	52 / 37*	3				
30	31/12/1984	India	Calcutta	D	67		1	0	6	1
31	13/01/1985	India	Madras (1)	W	62	2 / 1				
32	31/01/1985	India	Kanpur	D	13					
33	13/06/1985	Australia	Headingley	W	38 / 31*	2				
34	27/06/1985	Australia	Lord's	L	47 / 9	1 / 2				
35	11/07/1985	Australia	Trent Bridge	D	17					
36	01/08/1985	Australia	Old Trafford	D	67	1	1	0	10	0
37	15/08/1985	Australia	Edgbaston	W	46	1				
38	29/08/1985	Australia	The Oval	W	1					
39	21/02/1986	West Indies	Kingston	L	49 / 13		0.0	0	1	0
40	07/03/1986	West Indies	Port-of-Spain	L	62 / 40	1 / 1				
41	21/03/1986	West Indies	Bridgetown	L	5 / 6					
42	03/04/1986	West Indies	Port-of-Spain	L	36 / 11					
43	11/04/1986	West Indies	St John's	L	1 / 1	1				
44	05/06/1986	India	Lord's	L	6 / 39	2				
45	19/06/1986	India	Headingley	L	10 / 10					
46	21/08/1986	New Zealand	The Oval	D	0					
47	14/11/1986	Australia	Brisbane (2)	W	40 / 9	1				
48	28/11/1986	Australia	Perth	D	0 / 2	1	1	1	0	0
49	12/12/1986	Australia	Adelaide	D	14 / 9*	1				
50	26/12/1986	Australia	Melbourne	W	43					
51	10/01/1987	Australia	Sydney	L	24 / 3	3				
52	02/06/1988	West Indies	Trent Bridge	D	0 / 6*					
53	16/06/1988	West Indies	Lord's	L	10 / 113					
54	30/06/1988	West Indies	Old Trafford	L	33 / 9					
55	21/07/1988	West Indies	Headingley	L	64* / 19					

No	Date	Opposition	Venue	R	Bat	C	Bowling
56	25/08/1988	Sri Lanka	Lord's	W	63		
					8	1	
57	08/06/1989	Australia	Headingley	L	125		
					4		
58	24/02/1990	West Indies	Kingston	W	132		
59	23/03/1990	West Indies	Port-of-Spain	D	32	3	
					25	2	
60*	05/04/1990	West Indies	Bridgetown	L	119	1	
					10		
61*	12/04/1990	West Indies	St John's	L	37	1	
					35		
62	07/06/1990	New Zealand	Trent Bridge	D	0		
63	21/06/1990	New Zealand	Lord's	D	39		
					84*		
64	05/07/1990	New Zealand	Edgbaston	W	2		
					4	2	
65	26/07/1990	India	Lord's	W	139		
					19		
66	09/08/1990	India	Old Trafford	D	38		
					109		
67	23/08/1990	India	The Oval	D	7	2	
					52		
68*	23/11/1990	Australia	Brisbane (2)	L	32		
					14		
69	25/01/1991	Australia	Adelaide	D	0	1	
					53		
70	01/02/1991	Australia	Perth	L	91	1	
					5		
71	06/06/1991	West Indies	Headingley	W	11	2	
					0	2	
72	20/06/1991	West Indies	Lord's	D	1	3	
73	04/07/1991	West Indies	Trent Bridge	L	13		
					29		
74	25/07/1991	West Indies	Edgbaston	L	9		
					25		
75	18/01/1992	New Zealand	Christchurch	W	93	1	
76	30/01/1992	New Zealand	Auckland	W	13		
					60	1	
77	06/02/1992	New Zealand	Wellington	D	30		
					142		
78	04/06/1992	Pakistan	Edgbaston	D	12		
79	18/06/1992	Pakistan	Lord's	L	30		
					12		

Batting & Fielding

Mat	Inns	N/O	Runs	H/S	Avg	100s	50s	Cat
79	139	10	4656	142	36.09	14	18	75

Bowling

Balls	Runs	Wkts	Avg	Best	5WI	10WM	S/R
30	23	1	23.00	1-6	0	0	30.00

JAMES LANGRIDGE

Full Name: James Langridge (known as Jim)
Born: 10/07/1906, Chailey, Sussex
Died: 10/09/1966, Withdean, Brighton, Sussex
Teams: Sussex 1924-53, Auckland 1927/28, England 1933-46
Matches: 8 (Won 4, Drew 3, Lost 1)
Left-hand middle order batsman – Left-arm slow bowler

No	Date	Opposition	Venue	R	Bat	C	Bowling			
1	22/07/1933	West Indies	Old Trafford	D	9		9	1	23	0
						2	17	4	56	7
2	12/08/1933	West Indies	The Oval	W	22	1				
							7	1	23	0
3	15/12/1933	India	Bombay (1)	W	31		17	4	42	3
							16	7	32	1

No	Date	Opposition	Venue	R	Bat	C		Bowling		
4	05/01/1934	India	Calcutta	D	70		17	7	27	0
							10	4	19	0
5	10/02/1934	India	Madras (1)	W	1		6	1	9	1
					46		24	5	63	5
6	29/06/1935	South Africa	Lord's	L	27	1	13	3	27	2
					17		10	4	19	0
7	27/06/1936	India	Lord's	W	19	2	4	1	9	0
8	17/08/1946	India	The Oval	D			29	9	64	0

Batting & Fielding

Mat	Inns	N/O	Runs	H/S	Avg	100s	50s	Cat
8	9	0	242	70	26.88	0	1	6

Bowling

Balls	Runs	Wkts	Avg	Best	5WI	10WM	S/R
1074	413	19	21.73	7-56	2	0	56.52

W.LARKINS

Full Name: Wayne Larkins
Born: 22/11/1953, Roxton, Bedfordshire
Teams: Northamptonshire 1972-91, Durham 1992-95, Eastern Province 1982/83-83/84, England 1980-91
Matches: 13 (Won 2, Drew 6, Lost 5)
Right-hand opening batsman – Right-arm medium bowler

No	Date	Opposition	Venue	R	Bat	C
1	01/02/1980	Australia	Melbourne	L	25	1
					3	
2	15/02/1980	India	Bombay (3)	W	0	
3	10/07/1980	West Indies	Old Trafford	D	11	1
					33	
4	24/07/1980	West Indies	The Oval	D	7	
					0	
5	07/08/1980	West Indies	Headingley	D	9	1
					30	
6	27/08/1981	Australia	The Oval	D	34	
					24	
7	24/02/1990	West Indies	Kingston	W	46	1
					29*	2
8	23/03/1990	West Indies	Port-of-Spain	D	54	
					7	1
9	05/04/1990	West Indies	Bridgetown	L	0	
					0	
10	12/04/1990	West Indies	St John's	L	30	
					10	
11	23/11/1990	Australia	Brisbane (2)	L	12	
					0	
12	26/12/1990	Australia	Melbourne	L	64	
					54	
13	04/01/1991	Australia	Sydney	D	11	1
					0	

Batting & Fielding

Mat	Inns	N/O	Runs	H/S	Avg	100s	50s	Cat
13	25	1	493	64	20.54	0	3	8

J.D.F.LARTER

Full Name: John David Frederick Larter (known as David)
Born: 24/04/1940, Inverness, Scotland
Teams: Northamptonshire 1960-69, England 1962-65
Matches: 10 (Won 5, Drew 4, Lost 1)
Right-hand lower order batsman – Right-arm fast medium bowler

No	Date	Opposition	Venue	R	Bat	C		Bowling		
1	16/08/1962	Pakistan	The Oval	W			25	4	57	5
							21.1	0	88	4
2	23/02/1963	New Zealand	Auckland	W			26	12	51	3
							14.1	3	26	4

No	Date	Opposition	Venue	R	Bat	C	Bowling			
3	01/03/1963	New Zealand	Wellington	W			14	2	52	0
						2	7	1	18	0
4	15/03/1963	New Zealand	Christchurch	W	2		21	5	59	0
							23	8	32	3
5	10/01/1964	India	Madras (2)	D	2*		19	2	62	0
							11	3	33	0
6	21/01/1964	India	Bombay (2)	D	0		10.3	2	35	2
						1	5	0	13	0
7	29/01/1964	India	Calcutta	D	0		18	4	61	1
						1	8	0	27	2
8	08/07/1965	New Zealand	Headingley	W			28.1	6	66	4
							22	10	54	2
9	22/07/1965	South Africa	Lord's	D	0*		26	10	47	0
							17	2	67	1
10	05/08/1965	South Africa	Trent Bridge	L	2	1	17	6	25	1
					10		29	7	68	5

Batting & Fielding

Mat	Inns	N/O	Runs	H/S	Avg	100s	50s	Cat
10	7	2	16	10	3.20	0	0	5

Bowling

Balls	Runs	Wkts	Avg	Best	5WI	10WM	S/R
2172	941	37	25.43	5-57	2	0	58.70

H.LARWOOD

Full Name: Harold Larwood
Born: 14/11/1904, Nuncargate, Nottinghamshire
Died: 22/07/1995, Sydney, Australia
Teams: Nottinghamshire 1924-38, Europeans 1936/37, England 1926-33
Matches: 21 (Won 13, Drew 5, Lost 3)
Right-hand lower order batsman – Right-arm fast bowler

No	Date	Opposition	Venue	R	Bat	C	Bowling			
1	26/06/1926	Australia	Lord's	D			32	2	99	2
							15	3	37	1
2	14/08/1926	Australia	The Oval	W	0		34	11	82	3
					5	1	14	3	34	3
3	23/06/1928	West Indies	Lord's	W	17*	1	15	4	27	1
4	11/08/1928	West Indies	The Oval	W	32		21	6	46	2
						2	14	3	41	3
5	30/11/1928	Australia	Brisbane (1)	W	70		14.4	4	32	6
					37	4	7	0	30	2
6	14/12/1928	Australia	Sydney	W	43		26.2	4	77	3
							35	5	105	1
7	29/12/1928	Australia	Melbourne	W	0		37	3	127	3
							16	3	37	1
8	01/02/1929	Australia	Adelaide	W	3	1	37	6	92	1
					5	1	20	4	60	0
9	08/03/1929	Australia	Melbourne	L	4		34	7	83	1
					11		32.1	5	81	0
10	15/06/1929	South Africa	Edgbaston	D	6		42.4	17	57	5
							11	6	12	0
11	29/06/1929	South Africa	Lord's	D	35		20	4	65	1
					9		12	3	17	1
12	13/07/1929	South Africa	Headingley	W	0		17	4	35	1
13	13/06/1930	Australia	Trent Bridge	W	18		15	8	12	1
					7		5	1	9	1
14	11/07/1930	Australia	Headingley	D	10*	2	33	3	139	1
15	16/08/1930	Australia	The Oval	L	19	1	48	6	132	1
					9					
16	15/08/1931	New Zealand	Old Trafford	D						
17	02/12/1932	Australia	Sydney	W	0		31	5	96	5
							18	4	28	5
18	30/12/1932	Australia	Melbourne	L	9		20.3	2	52	2
					4		15	2	50	2
19	13/01/1933	Australia	Adelaide	W	3*		25	6	55	3
					8		19	3	71	4

No	Date	Opposition	Venue	R	Bat	C		Bowling		
20	10/02/1933	Australia	Brisbane (2)	W	23		31	7	101	4
						1	17.3	3	49	3
21	23/02/1933	Australia	Sydney	W	98	1	32.2	10	98	4
							11	0	44	1

Batting & Fielding

Mat	Inns	N/O	Runs	H/S	Avg	100s	50s	Cat
21	28	3	485	98	19.40	0	2	15

Bowling

Balls	Runs	Wkts	Avg	Best	5WI	10WM	S/R
4969	2212	78	28.35	6-32	4	1	63.70

M.N.LATHWELL

Full Name: Mark Nicholas Lathwell
Born: 26/12/1971, Bletchley, Buckinghamshire
Teams: Somerset 1991-96, England 1993
Matches: 2 (Won 0, Drew 1, Lost 1)
Right-hand opening batsman – Right-arm medium bowler

No	Date	Opposition	Venue	R	Bat	C
1	01/07/1993	Australia	Trent Bridge	D	20	
					33	
2	22/07/1993	Australia	Headingley	L	0	
					25	

Batting & Fielding

Mat	Inns	N/O	Runs	H/S	Avg	100s	50s	Cat
2	4	0	78	33	19.50	0	0	0

D.V.LAWRENCE

Full Name: David Valentine Lawrence (also known as Syd)
Born: 28/01/1964, Gloucester
Teams: Gloucestershire 1981-92, England 1988-92
Matches: 5 (Won 3, Drew 1, Lost 1)
Right-hand lower order batsman – Right-arm fast bowler

No	Date	Opposition	Venue	R	Bat	C		Bowling		
1	25/08/1988	Sri Lanka	Lord's	W	4		15	4	37	1
							21	5	74	2
2	04/07/1991	West Indies	Trent Bridge	L	4		24	2	116	2
					34		12.2	0	61	1
3	08/08/1991	West Indies	The Oval	W	9		16	1	67	2
							25.5	4	106	5
4	22/08/1991	Sri Lanka	Lord's	W	3		15.1	3	61	2
							23	7	83	2
5	06/02/1992	New Zealand	Wellington	D	6		27	7	67	1
							2.1	1	4	0

Batting & Fielding

Mat	Inns	N/O	Runs	H/S	Avg	100s	50s	Cat
5	6	0	60	34	10.00	0	0	0

Bowling

Balls	Runs	Wkts	Avg	Best	5WI	10WM	S/R
1089	676	18	37.55	5-106	1	0	60.50

E.LEADBEATER

Full Name: Edric Leadbeater (known as Eddie)
Born: 15/08/1927, Lockwood, Huddersfield, Yorkshire
Teams: Yorkshire 1949-56, Warwickshire 1957-58, England 1951
Matches: 2 (Won 0, Drew 2, Lost 0)
Right-hand lower order batsman – Leg break & googly bowler

No	Date	Opposition	Venue	R	Bat	C		Bowling		
1	14/12/1951	India	Bombay (2)	D	2		11	2	38	1
						1	14.1	4	62	0
2	30/12/1951	India	Calcutta	D	38	2	15	2	64	1
							8	0	54	0

Batting & Fielding

Mat	Inns	N/O	Runs	H/S	Avg	100s	50s	Cat
2	2	0	40	38	20.00	0	0	3

Bowling

Balls	Runs	Wkts	Avg	Best	5WI	10WM	S/R
289	218	2	109.00	1-38	0	0	144.50

H.W.LEE

Full Name: Henry William Lee (known as Harry)
Born: 26/10/1890, Marylebone, London
Died: 21/04/1981, Westminster, London
Teams: Middlesex 1911-34, Cooch Behar's XI 1917/18, England to India 1918/19, England 1931
Matches: 1 (Won 0, Drew 1, Lost 0)
Right-hand opening batsman – Right-arm slow medium or off break bowler

No	Date	Opposition	Venue	R	Bat	C
1	13/02/1931	South Africa	Johannesburg (1)	D	18	
					1	

Batting & Fielding

Mat	Inns	N/O	Runs	H/S	Avg	100s	50s	Cat
1	2	0	19	18	9.50	0	0	0

W.S.LEES

Full Name: Walter Scott Lees
Born: 25/12/1875, Sowerby Bridge, Yorkshire
Died: 10/09/1924, West Hartlepool, Co Durham
Teams: Surrey 1896-1911, London County 1903, England 1906
Matches: 5 (Won 1, Drew 0, Lost 4)
Right-hand lower order batsman – Right-arm fast medium bowler

No	Date	Opposition	Venue	R	Bat	C		Bowling		
1	02/01/1906	South Africa	Johannesburg (1)	L	11	1	23.1	10	34	5
					1*		33	10	74	3
2	06/03/1906	South Africa	Johannesburg (1)	L	25*		26	13	47	1
					4		4	0	16	1
3	10/03/1906	South Africa	Johannesburg (1)	L	6	1	31.3	7	78	6
					3		26	6	85	3
4	24/03/1906	South Africa	Cape Town	W	5		27	12	42	1
							14	5	27	4
5	30/03/1906	South Africa	Cape Town	L	9*		24.4	6	64	2
					2					

Batting & Fielding

Mat	Inns	N/O	Runs	H/S	Avg	100s	50s	Cat
5	9	3	66	25*	11.00	0	0	2

Bowling

Balls	Runs	Wkts	Avg	Best	5WI	10WM	S/R
1256	467	26	17.96	6-78	2	0	48.30

G.B.LEGGE

Full Name: Geoffrey Bevington Legge
Born: 26/01/1903, Bromley, Kent
Died: 21/11/1940, Brampford Speke, Devon
Teams: Oxford University 1925-26, Kent 1924-31, England 1927-30
Matches: 5 (Won 2, Drew 3, Lost 0)
Right-hand middle order batsman – Leg break bowler

No	Date	Opposition	Venue	R	Bat	C		Bowling		
1	24/12/1927	South Africa	Johannesburg (1)	W	0					
2	10/01/1930	New Zealand	Christchurch	W	36					
						1				
3	24/01/1930	New Zealand	Wellington	D	39					
					9					
4	14/02/1930	New Zealand	Auckland	D	19*		5	0	34	0

No	Date	Opposition	Venue	R	Bat	C	Bowling			
5	21/02/1930	New Zealand	Auckland	D	196					
					0					

Batting & Fielding

Mat	Inns	N/O	Runs	H/S	Avg	100s	50s	Cat
5	7	1	299	196	49.83	1	0	1

Bowling

Balls	Runs	Wkts	Avg	Best	5WI	10WM	S/R
30	34	0	–	0-34	0	0	–

C.F.H.LESLIE

Full Name: Charles Frederick Henry Leslie
Born: 08/12/1861, Westminster, London
Died: 12/02/1921, Mayfair, Westminster, London
Teams: Oxford University 1881-83, Middlesex 1881-86, England 1882-83
Matches: 4 (Won 2, Drew 0, Lost 2)
Right-hand middle order batsman – Right-arm fast bowler

No	Date	Opposition	Venue	R	Bat	C	Bowling			
1	30/12/1882	Australia	Melbourne	L	4		11	1	31	3
					4					
2	19/01/1883	Australia	Melbourne	W	54					
3	26/01/1883	Australia	Sydney	W	0					
					8					
4	17/02/1883	Australia	Sydney	L	17		5	2	11	1
					19	1	8	7	2	0

Batting & Fielding

Mat	Inns	N/O	Runs	H/S	Avg	100s	50s	Cat
4	7	0	106	54	15.14	0	1	1

Bowling

Balls	Runs	Wkts	Avg	Best	5WI	10WM	S/R
96	44	4	11.00	3-31	0	0	24.00

J.K.LEVER

Full Name: John Kenneth Lever, MBE (also known as J.K.)
Born: 24/02/1949, Stepney, London
Teams: Essex 1967-89, Natal 1982/83-1984/85, England 1976-86
Matches: 21 (Won 6, Drew 10, Lost 5)
Right-hand lower order batsman – Left-arm fast medium bowler

No	Date	Opposition	Venue	R	Bat	C	Bowling			
1	17/12/1976	India	Delhi	W	53		23	6	46	7
						1	13.4	6	24	3
2	01/01/1977	India	Calcutta	W	2	1	22	2	57	2
						1	3	0	12	0
3	14/01/1977	India	Madras (1)	W	23		19.5	2	59	5
					2		6.5	0	18	2
4	28/01/1977	India	Bangalore	L	20*		17	2	48	1
					11		9	1	28	1
5	11/02/1977	India	Bombay (3)	D	7	1	17.4	4	43	3
					4	1	17.4	6	46	2
6	12/03/1977	Australia	Melbourne	L	11		12	1	36	2
					4		21	1	95	2
7	16/06/1977	Australia	Lord's	D	8		19	5	61	1
					3	1	5	2	4	0
8	07/07/1977	Australia	Old Trafford	W	10		25	8	60	3
						1	4	1	11	0
9	25/08/1977	Australia	The Oval	D	3		22	6	61	1
10	14/12/1977	Pakistan	Lahore (2)	D	0	1	16	1	47	2
							3	0	13	1
11	02/01/1978	Pakistan	Hyderabad	D	4		16.6	7	41	1
					0*		20	2	62	0
12	18/01/1978	Pakistan	Karachi (1)	D	33*		12	4	32	0
13	04/03/1978	New Zealand	Auckland	D	1		34	5	96	3
							17	4	59	2

No	Date	Opposition	Venue	R	Bat	C		Bowling	
14	15/12/1978	Australia	Perth	W	14		7	0	20	1
					10		8.1	2	28	4
15	02/08/1979	India	Lord's	D	6*		9.5	3	29	1
							24	7	69	1
16	01/02/1980	Australia	Melbourne	L	22	1	53	15	111	4
					12		7.4	3	18	0
17	15/02/1980	India	Bombay (3)	W	21		23	3	82	1
						1	20.1	2	65	3
18	05/06/1980	West Indies	Trent Bridge	L	15	1	20	2	76	1
					4		8	2	25	0
19	09/12/1981	India	Bangalore	D	1		36	9	100	5
20	23/12/1981	India	Delhi	D	2		37	7	104	2
21	19/06/1986	India	Headingley	L	0*		30	4	102	2
					0		23	5	64	4

Batting & Fielding

Mat	Inns	N/O	Runs	H/S	Avg	100s	50s	Cat
21	31	5	306	53	11.76	0	1	11

Bowling

Balls	Runs	Wkts	Avg	Best	5WI	10WM	S/R
4433	1951	73	26.72	7-46	3	1	60.72

P.LEVER

Full Name: Peter Lever (also known as Plank)
Born: 17/09/1940, Todmorden, Yorkshire
Teams: Lancashire 1960-76, Tasmania 1971/72, England 1970-75
Matches: 17 (Won 6, Drew 10, Lost 1)
Right-hand lower order batsman – Right-arm fast medium bowler

No	Date	Opposition	Venue	R	Bat	C		Bowling	
1	11/12/1970	Australia	Perth	D	2	2	21	3	78	1
							5	2	10	1
2	09/01/1971	Australia	Sydney	W	36		8.6	1	31	2
						1	11	1	24	1
3	21/01/1971	Australia	Melbourne	D	19	1	25	6	79	0
							12	1	53	0
4	29/01/1971	Australia	Adelaide	D	5	1	17.1	2	49	4
							17	4	49	0
5	12/02/1971	Australia	Sydney	W	4		14.6	3	43	3
					17		12	2	23	1
6	25/02/1971	New Zealand	Christchurch	W	4		5	4	1	0
							15	3	30	1
7	05/03/1971	New Zealand	Auckland	D	64		19	3	43	0
					0		2	0	6	0
8	03/06/1971	Pakistan	Edgbaston	D	47	2	38	7	126	1
9	17/06/1971	Pakistan	Lord's	D			16	3	38	2
10	08/07/1971	Pakistan	Headingley	W	19		31	9	65	1
					8		3.3	1	10	3
11	05/08/1971	India	Old Trafford	D	88*		26	4	70	5
							7	3	14	0
12	13/07/1972	Australia	Trent Bridge	D	9		26	8	61	1
							19	3	76	0
13	29/11/1974	Australia	Brisbane (2)	L	4	2	16	1	53	0
					14		18	4	58	0
14	08/02/1975	Australia	Melbourne	W	6*		11	2	38	6
							16	1	65	3
15	20/02/1975	New Zealand	Auckland	W			20	4	75	0
							11.5	0	37	2
16	28/02/1975	New Zealand	Christchurch	D		1	18	2	66	1
17	31/07/1975	Australia	Lord's	D	4	1	15	0	83	2
							20	5	55	0

Batting & Fielding

Mat	Inns	N/O	Runs	H/S	Avg	100s	50s	Cat
17	18	2	350	88*	21.87	0	2	11

Bowling

Balls	Runs	Wkts	Avg	Best	5WI	10WM	S/R
3571	1509	41	36.80	6-38	2	0	87.09

H.D.G.LEVESON-GOWER

Full Name: Sir Henry Dudley Gresham Leveson-Gower (also known as Shrimp)
Born: 08/05/1873, Titsey Place, Surrey
Died: 01/02/1954, Kensington, London
Teams: Oxford University 1893-96, Surrey 1895-1920, England 1910
Matches: 3 (Won 1, Drew 0, Lost 2)
England Captain: 3 times 1910 (Won 1, Drew 0, Lost 2) **Toss:** 0-3
Right-hand middle order batsman – Leg break bowler

No	Date	Opposition	Venue	R	Bat	C
1*	01/01/1910	South Africa	Johannesburg (1)	L	17	1
					31	
2*	21/01/1910	South Africa	Durban (1)	L	6*	
					23	
3*	26/02/1910	South Africa	Johannesburg (1)	W	6	
					12*	

Batting & Fielding

Mat	Inns	N/O	Runs	H/S	Avg	100s	50s	Cat
3	6	2	95	31	23.75	0	0	1

W.H.V.LEVETT

Full Name: William Howard Vincent Levett (known as Hopper)
Born: 25/01/1908, Goudhurst, Kent
Died: 01/12/1995, Hastings, Sussex
Teams: Kent 1930-47, England 1934
Matches: 1 (Won 0, Drew 1, Lost 0)
Right-hand lower order batsman – Wicket-keeper

No	Date	Opposition	Venue	R	Bat	C	St	B
1+	05/01/1934	India	Calcutta	D	5			5
					2*	3		10

Batting & Fielding

Mat	Inns	N/O	Runs	H/S	Avg	100s	50s	Cat	St	Byes
1	2	1	7	5	7.00	0	0	3	0	15

A.R.LEWIS

Full Name: Anthony Robert Lewis (known as Tony)
Born: 06/07/1938, Uplands, Swansea, Glamorgan
Teams: Cambridge University 1960-62, Glamorgan 1955-74, England 1972-73
Matches: 9 (Won 2, Drew 5, Lost 2)
England Captain: 8 times 1972-73 (Won 1, Drew 5, Lost 2) **Toss:** 3-5
Right-hand middle order batsman – Leg break bowler

No	Date	Opposition	Venue	R	Bat	C
1*	20/12/1972	India	Delhi	W	0	
					70*	
2*	30/12/1972	India	Calcutta	L	4	
					3	
3*	12/01/1973	India	Madras (1)	L	4	
					11	
4*	25/01/1973	India	Kanpur	D	125	
5*	06/02/1973	India	Bombay (2)	D	0	
					17*	
6*	02/03/1973	Pakistan	Lahore (2)	D	29	
					74	
7*	16/03/1973	Pakistan	Hyderabad	D	7	
					21	
8*	24/03/1973	Pakistan	Karachi (1)	D	88	
9	07/06/1973	New Zealand	Trent Bridge	W	2	
					2	

Batting & Fielding

Mat	Inns	N/O	Runs	H/S	Avg	100s	50s	Cat
9	16	2	457	125	32.64	1	3	0

C.C.LEWIS

Full Name: Clairmonte Christopher Lewis (known as Chris)
Born: 14/02/1968, Georgetown, Guyana
Teams: Leicestershire 1987-91, Nottinghamshire 1992-95, Surrey 1996, England 1990-96
Matches: 32 (Won 10, Drew 7, Lost 15)
Right-hand middle order batsman – Right-arm fast medium bowler

No	Date	Opposition	Venue	R	Bat	C		Bowling		
1	05/07/1990	New Zealand	Edgbaston	W	32		19	5	51	1
					1		22	3	76	3
2	26/07/1990	India	Lord's	W		1	24	3	108	1
						1	8	1	26	2
3	09/08/1990	India	Old Trafford	D	3	1	13	1	61	1
						1	20	3	86	1
4	23/11/1990	Australia	Brisbane (2)	L	20	1	9	0	29	3
					14		6	0	29	0
5	25/07/1991	West Indies	Edgbaston	L	13	2	35	10	111	6
					65		16	7	45	0
6	08/08/1991	West Indies	The Oval	W	47*		3	1	10	0
						1	25	12	35	0
7	22/08/1991	Sri Lanka	Lord's	W	11	1	10	5	29	0
							18	4	31	2
8	18/01/1992	New Zealand	Christchurch	W	70		30	9	69	1
							22	3	66	2
9	30/01/1992	New Zealand	Auckland	W	33		21	5	31	5
					23		27	4	83	2
10	04/06/1992	Pakistan	Edgbaston	D	24		33	3	116	0
11	18/06/1992	Pakistan	Lord's	L	2		29	7	76	1
					15	1	16	3	43	3
12	02/07/1992	Pakistan	Old Trafford	D	55	1	24	5	90	2
							17	5	46	3
13	23/07/1992	Pakistan	Headingley	W	0		23	6	48	2
							16	3	55	0
14	06/08/1992	Pakistan	The Oval	L	4	2	30	8	70	1
					14					
15	29/01/1993	India	Calcutta	L	21	2	23	5	64	0
					16		3	1	5	0
16	11/02/1993	India	Madras (1)	L	0		11	1	40	1
					117					
17	19/02/1993	India	Bombay (3)	L	49	1	42	9	114	2
					3					
18	13/03/1993	Sri Lanka	Colombo (2)	L	22	1	31	5	66	4
					45		8	1	21	1
19	03/06/1993	Australia	Old Trafford	L	9	1	13	2	44	0
					43		9	0	43	0
20	17/06/1993	Australia	Lord's	L	0		36	5	151	2
					0					
21	19/02/1994	West Indies	Kingston	L	8	1	26	4	82	2
					21		3	0	6	0
22	17/03/1994	West Indies	Georgetown	L	17	1	28	1	110	3
					24					
23	25/03/1994	West Indies	Port-of-Spain	L	9		25.2	3	61	4
					6		27.5	6	71	3
24	08/04/1994	West Indies	Bridgetown	W	0		17	2	60	1
					10		8.2	1	23	1
25	16/04/1994	West Indies	St John's	D	75*		33	1	140	0
26	26/01/1995	Australia	Adelaide	W	10		18	1	81	2
					7		13	4	24	4
27	03/02/1995	Australia	Perth	L	40	2	31.5	8	73	3
					11	1	16	0	71	2
28	06/06/1996	India	Edgbaston	W	0		18	2	44	2
							22.4	6	72	5
29	20/06/1996	India	Lord's	D	31		40	11	101	3
					26*					
30	04/07/1996	India	Trent Bridge	D	21		37	10	89	3
						1	14	4	50	2

No	Date	Opposition	Venue	R	Bat	C		Bowling		
31	08/08/1996	Pakistan	Headingley	D	9		32	4	100	0
						1	16	3	52	1
32	22/08/1996	Pakistan	The Oval	L	5		23	3	112	0
					4					

Batting & Fielding

Mat	Inns	N/O	Runs	H/S	Avg	100s	50s	Cat
32	51	3	1105	117	23.02	1	4	25

Bowling

Balls	Runs	Wkts	Avg	Best	5WI	10WM	S/R
6852	3490	93	37.52	6-111	3	0	73.67

M.LEYLAND

Full Name: Morris Leyland (known as Maurice)
Born: 20/07/1900, New Park, Harrogate, Yorkshire
Died: 01/01/1967, Scotton Banks, Harrogate, Yorkshire
Teams: Yorkshire 1920-47, Patiala 1926/27, England 1928-38
Matches: 41 (Won 15, Drew 15, Lost 11)
Left-hand middle order batsman – Left-arm slow bowler

No	Date	Opposition	Venue	R	Bat	C		Bowling		
1	11/08/1928	West Indies	The Oval	W	0		3	0	6	1
2	08/03/1929	Australia	Melbourne	L	137		3	0	11	0
					53*					
3	15/06/1929	South Africa	Edgbaston	D	3					
4	29/06/1929	South Africa	Lord's	D	73	1	5	2	9	0
					102					
5	13/07/1929	South Africa	Headingley	W	45	1				
					0		3	0	19	0
6	27/07/1929	South Africa	Old Trafford	W	55					
7	17/08/1929	South Africa	The Oval	D	16	1	9	4	25	0
8	11/07/1930	Australia	Headingley	D	44		11	0	44	0
					1*					
9	25/07/1930	Australia	Old Trafford	D	35		8	2	17	0
10	16/08/1930	Australia	The Oval	L	3		16	7	34	0
					20					
11	24/12/1930	South Africa	Johannesburg (1)	L	29					
					15					
12	01/01/1931	South Africa	Cape Town	D	52		30	6	91	3
					28					
13	16/01/1931	South Africa	Durban (2)	D	31*					
							9	1	32	0
14	13/02/1931	South Africa	Johannesburg (1)	D	91		4	0	11	0
					46					
15	21/02/1931	South Africa	Durban (2)	D	8					
16	02/12/1932	Australia	Sydney	W	0					
						1				
17	30/12/1932	Australia	Melbourne	L	22					
					19					
18	13/01/1933	Australia	Adelaide	W	83					
					42	1				
19	10/02/1933	Australia	Brisbane (2)	W	12					
					86					
20	23/02/1933	Australia	Sydney	W	42					
					0					
21	24/06/1933	West Indies	Lord's	W	1					
22	08/06/1934	Australia	Trent Bridge	L	6	1	1	0	5	0
					18					
23	22/06/1934	Australia	Lord's	W	109		4	1	10	0
24	06/07/1934	Australia	Old Trafford	D	153					
25	20/07/1934	Australia	Headingley	D	16		5	0	20	0
					49*					

No	Date	Opposition	Venue	R	Bat	C		Bowling	
26	18/08/1934	Australia	The Oval	L	110		3	0 20	0
					17				
27	08/01/1935	West Indies	Bridgetown	W	3	2			
					2				
28	24/01/1935	West Indies	Port-of-Spain	L	0		9	1 31	0
					18		13	3 41	1
29	14/02/1935	West Indies	Georgetown	D	13		2	0 12	0
					0				
30	15/06/1935	South Africa	Trent Bridge	D	69		7	2 18	0
31	29/06/1935	South Africa	Lord's	L	18				
					4				
32	27/07/1935	South Africa	Old Trafford	D	53				
					37		12	4 28	0
33	17/08/1935	South Africa	The Oval	D	161				
							7	2 15	0
34	27/06/1936	India	Lord's	W	60				
						1			
35	15/08/1936	India	The Oval	W	26		2	0 5	0
							3	0 19	0
36	04/12/1936	Australia	Brisbane (2)	W	126	1			
					33	1			
37	18/12/1936	Australia	Sydney	W	42				
38	01/01/1937	Australia	Melbourne	L	17				
					111*				
39	29/01/1937	Australia	Adelaide	L	45	1			
					32		2	0 6	0
40	26/02/1937	Australia	Melbourne	L	7		3	0 26	0
					28				
41	20/08/1938	Australia	The Oval	W	187		3.1	0 11	1
						1	5	0 19	0

Batting & Fielding

Mat	Inns	N/O	Runs	H/S	Avg	100s	50s	Cat
41	65	5	2764	187	46.06	9	10	13

Bowling

Balls	Runs	Wkts	Avg	Best	5WI	10WM	S/R
1103	585	6	97.50	3-91	0	0	183.83

A.F.A.LILLEY

Full Name: Arthur Frederick Augustus Lilley (known as Dick)
Born: 28/11/1866, Holloway Head, Birmingham
Died: 17/11/1929, Sandy Park, Brislington, Bristol
Teams: Warwickshire 1894-1911, London County 1900-01, England 1896-1909
Matches: 35 (Won 11, Drew 12, Lost 12)
Right-hand middle order batsman – Wicket-keeper – Occasional right-arm medium bowler

No	Date	Opposition	Venue	R	Bat	C	St	B	Bowling		
1+	22/06/1896	Australia	Lord's	W	0	2		1			
						2		7			
2+	16/07/1896	Australia	Old Trafford	L	65*	2		6	5	1 23	1
					19	3		0			
3+	10/08/1896	Australia	The Oval	W	2			8			
					6			2			
4+	15/06/1899	Australia	Lord's	L	19*	4		0			
					12			0			
5+	29/06/1899	Australia	Headingley	D	55	2	1	2			
						2		17			
6+	17/07/1899	Australia	Old Trafford	D	58	2		14			
						1		14			
7+	14/08/1899	Australia	The Oval	D	37	1		5			
						1		7			
8+	13/12/1901	Australia	Sydney	W	84		1	1			
						3	1	5			
9+	01/01/1902	Australia	Melbourne	L	6	2	1	6			
					0	1		7			
10+	17/01/1902	Australia	Adelaide	L	10			2			
					21			9			
11+	14/02/1902	Australia	Sydney	L	40	2		7			
					0	1		0			

No	Date	Opposition	Venue	R	Bat	C	St	B	Bowling
12+	28/02/1902	Australia	Melbourne	L	41	1		7	
					9	1		3	
13+	29/05/1902	Australia	Edgbaston	D	2	2	1	3	
								0	
14+	12/06/1902	Australia	Lord's	D					
15+	03/07/1902	Australia	Bramall Lane	L	8	1		3	
					9	1		0	
16+	24/07/1902	Australia	Old Trafford	L	7	3		5	
					4	1		1	
17+	11/08/1902	Australia	The Oval	W	0	2		5	
					16	1		7	
18+	11/12/1903	Australia	Sydney	W	4	2		0	
						2	1	10	
19+	01/01/1904	Australia	Melbourne	W	4	1		0	
					0	1		0	
20+	15/01/1904	Australia	Adelaide	L	28	1	1	7	
					0	1	1	8	
21+	26/02/1904	Australia	Sydney	W	24	1			
					6	1	3	10	
22+	05/03/1904	Australia	Melbourne	L	6*	1		4	
					0	1		1	
23+	29/05/1905	Australia	Trent Bridge	W	37	1	1	16	
						2		4	
24+	15/06/1905	Australia	Lord's	D	0	1		3	
25+	03/07/1905	Australia	Headingley	D	11	2		4	
							1	11	
26+	24/07/1905	Australia	Old Trafford	W	28			9	
								4	
27+	14/08/1905	Australia	The Oval	D	17				
28+	01/07/1907	South Africa	Lord's	D	48	2		9	
								15	
29+	29/07/1907	South Africa	Headingley	W	3	2	2	3	
					0			3	
30+	19/08/1907	South Africa	The Oval	D	42	1	1	3	
					9*			5	
31+	27/05/1909	Australia	Edgbaston	W	0			0	
						1		7	
32+	14/06/1909	Australia	Lord's	L	47	3		16	
					25*	1		4	
33+	01/07/1909	Australia	Headingley	L	4*	2		0	
					2	2		15	
34+	26/07/1909	Australia	Old Trafford	D	26*			6	
								9	
35+	09/08/1909	Australia	The Oval	D	2*			1	
							1	4	

Batting & Fielding

Mat	Inns	N/O	Runs	H/S	Avg	100s	50s	Cat	St	Byes
35	52	8	903	84	20.52	0	4	70	22	346

Bowling

Balls	Runs	Wkts	Avg	Best	5WI	10WM	S/R
25	23	1	23.00	1-23	0	0	25.00

JAMES LILLYWHITE

Full Name: James Lillywhite Junior (known as Jim)
Born: 23/02/1842, Westhampnett, Sussex
Died: 25/10/1929, Westerton, Chichester, Sussex
Teams: Sussex 1862-83, England 1877
Matches: 2 (Won 1, Drew 0, Lost 1)
England Captain: 2 times 1877 (Won 1, Drew 0, Lost 1) **Toss:** 0-2
Left-hand lower order batsman – Left-arm slow medium bowler

No	Date	Opposition	Venue	R	Bat	C		Bowling		
1*	15/03/1877	Australia	Melbourne	L	10		14	5	19	1
					4		1	0	1	1
2*	31/03/1877	Australia	Melbourne	W	2*	1	29	17	36	2
							41	15	70	4

Batting & Fielding

Mat	Inns	N/O	Runs	H/S	Avg	100s	50s	Cat
2	3	1	16	10	8.00	0	0	1

Bowling

Balls	Runs	Wkts	Avg	Best	5WI	10WM	S/R
340	126	8	15.75	4-70	0	0	42.50

D.LLOYD

Full Name: David Lloyd
Born: 18/03/1947, Accrington, Lancashire
Teams: Lancashire 1965-83, England 1974-75
Matches: 9 (Won 2, Drew 4, Lost 3)
Left-hand opening/middle order batsman – Left-arm slow bowler

No	Date	Opposition	Venue	R	Bat	C		Bowling	
1	20/06/1974	India	Lord's	W	46		2	0	4	0
2	04/07/1974	India	Edgbaston	W	214*				
						1			
3	25/07/1974	Pakistan	Headingley	D	48	1			
					9				
4	08/08/1974	Pakistan	Lord's	D	23				
					12*	3			
5	22/08/1974	Pakistan	The Oval	D	4		2	0	13	0
6	13/12/1974	Australia	Perth	L	49	2			
					35				
7	26/12/1974	Australia	Melbourne	D	14	1			
					44	1			
8	04/01/1975	Australia	Sydney	L	19				
					26	2			
9	25/01/1975	Australia	Adelaide	L	4				
					5				

Batting & Fielding

Mat	Inns	N/O	Runs	H/S	Avg	100s	50s	Cat
9	15	2	552	214*	42.46	1	0	11

Bowling

Balls	Runs	Wkts	Avg	Best	5WI	10WM	S/R
24	17	0	–	0-4	0	0	–

T.A.LLOYD

Full Name: Timothy Andrew Lloyd (known as Andy)
Born: 05/11/1956, Oswestry, Shropshire
Teams: Warwickshire 1977-92, Orange Free State 1978/79, England 1984
Matches: 1 (Won 0, Drew 0, Lost 1)
Left-hand middle order batsman – Right-arm medium bowler

No	Date	Opposition	Venue	R	Bat	C
1	14/06/1984	West Indies	Edgbaston	L	10*	

Batting & Fielding

Mat	Inns	N/O	Runs	H/S	Avg	100s	50s	Cat
1	1	1	10	10*	–	0	0	0

P.J.LOADER

Full Name: Peter James Loader
Born: 25/10/1929, Wallington, Surrey
Teams: Surrey 1951-63, Western Australia 1963/64, England 1954-58
Matches: 13 (Won 6, Drew 1, Lost 6)
Right-hand lower order batsman – Right-arm fast bowler

No	Date	Opposition	Venue	R	Bat	C		Bowling	
1	12/08/1954	Pakistan	The Oval	L	8*	18	5	35	3
					5	16	6	26	0
2	21/07/1955	South Africa	Headingley	L	0*	19	7	52	4
					0*	29	9	67	0

No	Date	Opposition	Venue	R	Bat	C	Bowling			
3	01/01/1957	South Africa	Cape Town	W	10		21	5	33	2
							7	2	11	0
4	25/01/1957	South Africa	Durban (2)	D	1		25	6	79	2
					3		8	2	21	1
5	15/02/1957	South Africa	Johannesburg (3)	L	13		23	3	78	1
					7		13	3	33	0
6	01/03/1957	South Africa	Port Elizabeth	L	0*		20	3	35	3
					0		4	3	1	0
7	25/07/1957	West Indies	Headingley	W	1	1	20.3	9	36	6
							14	2	50	3
8	22/08/1957	West Indies	The Oval	W	0		7	4	12	1
							3	2	2	0
9	05/06/1958	New Zealand	Edgbaston	W	17		21.3	6	37	1
							23	11	40	3
10	19/06/1958	New Zealand	Lord's	W	4	1	4	2	6	0
							9	6	7	2
11	03/07/1958	New Zealand	Headingley	W			5	2	10	0
							13	7	14	0
12	05/12/1958	Australia	Brisbane (2)	L	6*		19	4	56	4
					0*		9	1	27	0
13	31/12/1958	Australia	Melbourne	L	1		27.2	4	97	3
					0		5	1	13	0

Batting & Fielding

Mat	Inns	N/O	Runs	H/S	Avg	100s	50s	Cat
13	19	6	76	17	5.84	0	0	2

Bowling

Balls	Runs	Wkts	Avg	Best	5WI	10WM	S/R
2662	878	39	22.51	6-36	1	0	68.25

G.A.R.LOCK

Full Name: Graham Anthony Richard Lock (known as Tony)
Born: 05/07/1929, Limpsfield, Surrey
Died: 29/03/1995, Perth, Australia
Teams: Surrey 1946-63, Leicestershire 1965-67, Western Australia 1962/63-70/71,
England 1952-68
Matches: 49 (Won 19, Drew 17, Lost 13)
Right-hand lower order batsman – Left-arm slow medium bowler

No	Date	Opposition	Venue	R	Bat	C	Bowling			
1	17/07/1952	India	Old Trafford	W	1*	2				
							9.3	2	36	4
2	14/08/1952	India	The Oval	D		1	6	5	1	0
3	23/07/1953	Australia	Headingley	D	9	3	23	9	53	1
					8		8	1	48	1
4	15/08/1953	Australia	The Oval	W	4		9	2	19	1
							21	9	45	5
5	15/01/1954	West Indies	Kingston	L	4		41	14	76	3
					0		14	2	36	2
6	06/02/1954	West Indies	Bridgetown	L	0*		41	9	116	1
					0		33	7	100	0
7	24/02/1954	West Indies	Georgetown	W	13	1	27.5	7	60	2
							25	11	41	1
8	17/03/1954	West Indies	Port-of-Spain	D	10		63	14	178	2
							10	2	40	1
9	30/03/1954	West Indies	Kingston	W	4	2	15	6	31	1
						1	27	16	40	1
10	07/07/1955	South Africa	Old Trafford	L	19*		64	24	121	2
					17		7	2	23	1
11	21/07/1955	South Africa	Headingley	L	17		6	1	20	1
					7	1	42	13	88	1
12	13/08/1955	South Africa	The Oval	W	18	1	22	11	39	4
					1		33	14	62	4
13	07/06/1956	Australia	Trent Bridge	D	0	2	36	16	61	3
						1	22	11	23	1
14	12/07/1956	Australia	Headingley	W	21		27.1	11	41	4
						1	40	23	40	3
15	26/07/1956	Australia	Old Trafford	W	25*	1	14	3	37	1
						2	55	30	69	0

No	Date	Opposition	Venue	R	Bat	C	Bowling			
16	23/08/1956	Australia	The Oval	D	0	1	25	10	49	2
						2	18.1	11	17	1
17	01/03/1957	South Africa	Port Elizabeth	L	14		11	5	21	1
					12		15	6	17	1
18	30/05/1957	West Indies	Edgbaston	D	0	1	34.4	15	55	0
						1	27	19	31	3
19	25/07/1957	West Indies	Headingley	W	20	1	14	6	23	0
							1	0	6	1
20	22/08/1957	West Indies	The Oval	W	17	1	21.4	12	28	5
							16	7	20	6
21	05/06/1958	New Zealand	Edgbaston	W	4		2	2	0	0
							8.3	3	25	3
22	19/06/1958	New Zealand	Lord's	W	23*	1	11.3	7	17	5
						1	12.3	8	12	4
23	03/07/1958	New Zealand	Headingley	W			18.1	13	14	4
							35.2	20	51	7
24	24/07/1958	New Zealand	Old Trafford	W	7		33	12	61	1
						1	24	11	35	7
25	21/08/1958	New Zealand	The Oval	D	25	2	13	6	19	2
						1	18	11	20	1
26	05/12/1958	Australia	Brisbane (2)	L	5		10	4	17	0
					1		14.7	5	37	1
27	31/12/1958	Australia	Melbourne	L	5		17	2	54	0
					6		3.1	1	11	0
28	09/01/1959	Australia	Sydney	D	21	1	43.2	9	130	4
					11*		11	4	23	0
29	30/01/1959	Australia	Adelaide	L	2		25	0	96	0
					9		2	0	8	0
30	27/02/1959	New Zealand	Christchurch	W	15	3	26	15	31	5
						1	28.2	13	53	6
31	14/03/1959	New Zealand	Auckland	D			20.3	12	29	2
32	22/06/1961	Australia	Lord's	L	5		26	13	48	0
					1					
33	06/07/1961	Australia	Headingley	W	30	1	29	5	68	2
							10	1	32	0
34	17/08/1961	Australia	The Oval	D	3		42	14	102	1
					0					
35	11/11/1961	India	Bombay (2)	D	23	1	45	22	74	4
					22*		16	9	33	1
36	01/12/1961	India	Kanpur	D	49	1	44	15	93	3
37	13/12/1961	India	Delhi	D			40	15	83	1
38	30/12/1961	India	Calcutta	L	2*	1	36	19	63	2
					1	1	46	15	111	4
39	10/01/1962	India	Madras (2)	L	0	2	40	13	106	1
					11		39.3	16	65	6
40	19/01/1962	Pakistan	Dacca	D	4	2	73	24	155	4
							42	23	70	4
41	02/02/1962	Pakistan	Karachi (1)	D	0*	1	14	8	25	1
						1	37	16	86	1
42	31/05/1962	Pakistan	Edgbaston	W		1	19	8	37	2
							36	14	80	3
43	21/06/1962	Pakistan	Lord's	W	7		14	1	78	0
44	26/07/1962	Pakistan	Trent Bridge	D		1	14	5	19	0
							15	4	27	1
45	04/07/1963	West Indies	Edgbaston	W	1	1	2	1	5	0
					56	1				
46	25/07/1963	West Indies	Headingley	L	53	1	28.4	9	54	3
					1	1	7.1	0	54	1
47	22/08/1963	West Indies	The Oval	L	4	2	29	6	65	1
					0	1	25	8	52	1
48	14/03/1968	West Indies	Port-of-Spain	W	3	1	32	3	129	1
49	28/03/1968	West Indies	Georgetown	D	89		28	7	61	2
					2	1	9	1	22	1

Batting & Fielding

Mat	Inns	N/O	Runs	H/S	Avg	100s	50s	Cat
49	63	9	742	89	13.74	0	3	59

Bowling

Balls	Runs	Wkts	Avg	Best	5WI	10WM	S/R
13147	4451	174	25.58	7-35	9	3	75.55

W.H.LOCKWOOD

Full Name: William Henry Lockwood (known as Bill)
Born: 25/03/1868, Old Radford, Nottinghamshire
Died: 26/04/1932, Old Radford, Nottinghamshire
Teams: Nottinghamshire 1886-87, Surrey 1889-1904, England 1893-1902
Matches: 12 (Won 5, Drew 4, Lost 3)
Right-hand middle/lower order batsman – Right-arm fast bowler

No	Date	Opposition	Venue	R	Bat	C	Bowling			
1	17/07/1893	Australia	Lord's	D	22		45	11	101	6
					0					
2	14/08/1893	Australia	The Oval	W	10	1	19	9	37	4
							29	7	96	4
3	14/12/1894	Australia	Sydney	W	18		3	2	1	0
					29		16	3	40	0
4	29/12/1894	Australia	Melbourne	W	3*		5	0	17	1
					33*		25	5	60	0
5	11/01/1895	Australia	Adelaide	L	0	2	8	2	33	1
					1		15	2	71	1
6	01/02/1895	Australia	Sydney	L			8.2	3	22	1
7	01/03/1895	Australia	Melbourne	W	5	1	27	7	72	1
							16	7	24	0
8	14/08/1899	Australia	The Oval	D	24		40.3	17	71	7
							15	7	33	0
9	29/05/1902	Australia	Edgbaston	D	52*					
10	12/06/1902	Australia	Lord's	D						
11	24/07/1902	Australia	Old Trafford	L	7		20.1	5	48	6
					0		17	5	28	5
12	11/08/1902	Australia	The Oval	W	25		24	2	85	1
					2		20	6	45	5

Batting & Fielding

Mat	Inns	N/O	Runs	H/S	Avg	100s	50s	Cat
12	16	3	231	52*	17.76	0	1	4

Bowling

Balls	Runs	Wkts	Avg	Best	5WI	10WM	S/R
1970	884	43	20.55	7-71	5	1	45.81

G.A.LOHMANN

Full Name: George Alfred Lohmann
Born: 02/06/1865, Campden Hill, Kensington, London
Died: 01/12/1901, Worcester, Cape Province, South Africa
Teams: Surrey 1884-96, Western Province 1894/95-96/97, England 1886-96
Matches: 18 (Won 15, Drew 0, Lost 3)
Right-hand lower order batsman – Right-arm fast medium bowler

No	Date	Opposition	Venue	R	Bat	C	Bowling			
1	05/07/1886	Australia	Old Trafford	W	32	2	23	9	41	1
						1	5	3	14	0
2	19/07/1886	Australia	Lord's	W	7*		7	3	21	0
						1	14	9	11	0
3	12/08/1886	Australia	The Oval	W	7		30.2	17	36	7
						1	37	14	68	5
4	28/01/1887	Australia	Sydney	W	17		21	12	30	3
					3		24	11	20	3
5	25/02/1887	Australia	Sydney	W	2		25	12	35	8
					6		40	16	52	2
6	10/02/1888	Australia	Sydney	W	12		19	13	17	5
					0		32	18	35	4
7	16/07/1888	Australia	Lord's	L	2	3	20	9	28	2
					0	1	14	4	33	4
8	13/08/1888	Australia	The Oval	W	62*	2	29.3	21	21	1
						1	6	4	11	0

No	Date	Opposition	Venue	R	Bat	C		Bowling		
9	30/08/1888	Australia	Old Trafford	W	0	1	17	9	31	1
							8	3	20	3
10	21/07/1890	Australia	Lord's	W	19		21	10	43	0
						1	29	19	28	3
11	11/08/1890	Australia	The Oval	W	3	2	32.2	19	34	3
					2		21	8	32	3
12	01/01/1892	Australia	Melbourne	L	3	1	28	14	40	0
					0	2	39	15	53	2
13	29/01/1892	Australia	Sydney	L	10	1	43.2	18	58	8
					15		51	14	84	2
14	24/03/1892	Australia	Adelaide	W	0	1	21	8	46	3
							6	2	8	1
15	13/02/1896	South Africa	Port Elizabeth	W	0	1	15.4	6	38	7
					0		9.4	5	7	8
16	02/03/1896	South Africa	Johannesburg (1)	W	2	2	14.2	6	28	9
					1		17	4	43	3
17	21/03/1896	South Africa	Cape Town	W	8	2	24	9	42	7
							23	8	45	1
18	22/06/1896	Australia	Lord's	W	1		11	6	13	3
						1	22	6	39	0

Batting & Fielding

Mat	Inns	N/O	Runs	H/S	Avg	100s	50s	Cat
18	26	2	213	62*	8.87	0	1	28

Bowling

Balls	Runs	Wkts	Avg	Best	5WI	10WM	S/R
3821	1205	112	10.75	9-28	9	5	34.11

F.A.LOWSON

Full Name: Frank Anderson Lowson
Born: 01/07/1925, Bradford, Yorkshire
Died: 08/09/1984, Pool-in-Wharfdale, Yorkshire
Teams: Yorkshire 1949-58, England 1951-55
Matches: 7 (Won 2, Drew 3, Lost 2)
Right-hand opening batsman – Off break bowler

No	Date	Opposition	Venue	R	Bat	C
1	26/07/1951	South Africa	Headingley	D	58	1
2	16/08/1951	South Africa	The Oval	W	0	
					37	1
3	02/11/1951	India	Delhi	D	4	
					68	
4	14/12/1951	India	Bombay (2)	D	5	
					22	
5	12/01/1952	India	Kanpur	W	26	
					12	2
6	06/02/1952	India	Madras (1)	L	1	
					7	
7	21/07/1955	South Africa	Headingley	L	5	
					0	1

Batting & Fielding

Mat	Inns	N/O	Runs	H/S	Avg	100s	50s	Cat
7	13	0	245	68	18.84	0	2	5

A.P.LUCAS

Full Name: Alfred Perry Lucas (known as Bunny)
Born: 20/02/1857, Westminster, London
Died: 12/10/1923, Great Waltham, Essex
Teams: Cambridge University 1875-78, Surrey 1874-82, Middlesex 1883-88, Essex 1894-1907, England 1879-84
Matches: 5 (Won 2, Drew 1, Lost 2)
Right-hand opening batsman – Right-hand round-arm slow bowler

No	Date	Opposition	Venue	R	Bat	C		Bowling		
1	02/01/1879	Australia	Melbourne	L	6		18	6	31	0
					13					

No	Date	Opposition	Venue	R	Bat	C		Bowling		
2	06/09/1880	Australia	The Oval	W	55					
					2	1	12	7	23	0
3	28/08/1882	Australia	The Oval	L	9					
					5					
4	10/07/1884	Australia	Old Trafford	D	15*					
					24					
5	21/07/1884	Australia	Lord's	W	28					

Batting & Fielding

Mat	Inns	N/O	Runs	H/S	Avg	100s	50s	Cat
5	9	1	157	55	19.62	0	1	1

Bowling

Balls	Runs	Wkts	Avg	Best	5WI	10WM	S/R
120	54	0	–	0-23	0	0	–

B.W.LUCKHURST

Full Name: Brian William Luckhurst
Born: 05/02/1939, Sittingbourne, Kent
Teams: Kent 1958-85, England 1970-74
Matches: 21 (Won 6, Drew 10, Lost 5)
Right-hand opening batsman – Left-arm slow bowler

No	Date	Opposition	Venue	R	Bat	C		Bowling		
1	27/11/1970	Australia	Brisbane (2)	D	74					
					20*	1				
2	11/12/1970	Australia	Perth	D	131	1				
					19					
3	09/01/1971	Australia	Sydney	W	38	1				
					5					
4	21/01/1971	Australia	Melbourne	D	109	2				
5	12/02/1971	Australia	Sydney	W	0					
					59					
6	25/02/1971	New Zealand	Christchurch	W	10	1				
					29*	1				
7	05/03/1971	New Zealand	Auckland	D	14					
					15		2	0	6	0
8	03/06/1971	Pakistan	Edgbaston	D	35	1				
					108*					
9	17/06/1971	Pakistan	Lord's	D	46					
					53*					
10	08/07/1971	Pakistan	Headingley	W	0					
					0	1				
11	22/07/1971	India	Lord's	D	30	1				
					1					
12	05/08/1971	India	Old Trafford	D	78					
					101					
13	19/08/1971	India	The Oval	L	1					
					33		2	0	9	1
14	08/06/1972	Australia	Old Trafford	W	14					
					0	1				
15	22/06/1972	Australia	Lord's	L	1					
					4	1	0.5	0	5	0
16	13/07/1972	Australia	Trent Bridge	D	23					
					96	1				
17	27/07/1972	Australia	Headingley	W	18					
					12*					
18	09/08/1973	West Indies	Edgbaston	D	12					
					42	1	4	2	12	0
19	23/08/1973	West Indies	Lord's	L	1					
					12					
20	29/11/1974	Australia	Brisbane (2)	L	1					
					3					
21	13/12/1974	Australia	Perth	L	27					
					23					

Batting & Fielding

Mat	Inns	N/O	Runs	H/S	Avg	100s	50s	Cat
21	41	5	1298	131	36.05	4	5	14

Bowling

Balls	Runs	Wkts	Avg	Best	5WI	10WM	S/R
57	32	1	32.00	1-9	0	0	57.00

Hon.A.LYTTELTON

Full Name: Hon.Alfred Lyttelton
Born: 07/02/1857, Westminster, London
Died: 05/07/1913, Marylebone, London
Teams: Cambridge University 1876-79, Middlesex 1877-87, England 1880-84
Matches: 4 (Won 2, Drew 1, Lost 1)
Right-hand middle order batsman – Wicket-keeper – Occasional right-hand under-arm bowler

No	Date	Opposition	Venue	R	Bat	C	St	B	Bowling			
1+	06/09/1880	Australia	The Oval	W	11*			9				
					13			7				
2+	28/08/1882	Australia	The Oval	L	2			1				
					12	1		6				
3+	21/07/1884	Australia	Lord's	W	31			5				
								1				
4+	11/08/1884	Australia	The Oval	D	8	1		7	12	5	19	4
					17							

Batting & Fielding

Mat	Inns	N/O	Runs	H/S	Avg	100s	50s	Cat	St	Byes
4	7	1	94	31	15.66	0	0	2	0	36

Bowling

Balls	Runs	Wkts	Avg	Best	5WI	10WM	S/R
48	19	4	4.75	4-19	0	0	12.00

G.G.MACAULAY

Full Name: George Gibson Macaulay
Born: 07/12/1897, Thirsk, Yorkshire
Died: 13/12/1940, Sullom Voe, Shetland Islands
Teams: Yorkshire 1920-35, England 1923-33
Matches: 8 (Won 4, Drew 4, Lost 0)
Right-hand lower order batsman – Right-arm medium bowler (previously right-arm fast)

No	Date	Opposition	Venue	R	Bat	C	Bowling			
1	01/01/1923	South Africa	Cape Town	W	19	1	13	5	19	2
					1*	1	37	11	64	5
2	18/01/1923	South Africa	Durban (2)	D	3*		29	8	55	1
					2					
3	09/02/1923	South Africa	Johannesburg (1)	D	1*		27	5	80	2
						1	17	6	27	1
4	16/02/1923	South Africa	Durban (2)	W	0	1	20	5	42	3
					1	1	18	6	39	2
5	12/07/1924	South Africa	Headingley	W	0*		11.3	2	23	1
							27	8	60	1
6	10/07/1926	Australia	Headingley	D	76		32	8	123	1
7	24/06/1933	West Indies	Lord's	W	9		18	7	25	1
							20	6	57	4
8	22/07/1933	West Indies	Old Trafford	D			14	2	48	0

Batting & Fielding

Mat	Inns	N/O	Runs	H/S	Avg	100s	50s	Cat
8	10	4	112	76	18.66	0	1	5

Bowling

Balls	Runs	Wkts	Avg	Best	5WI	10WM	S/R
1701	662	24	27.58	5-64	1	0	70.87

J.C.W.MACBRYAN

Full Name: John Crawford William MacBryan
Born: 22/07/1892, Box, Wiltshire
Died: 14/07/1983, Cambridge
Teams: Cambridge University 1919-20, Somerset 1911-31, England 1924
Matches: 1 (Won 0, Drew 1, Lost 0)
Right-hand middle order batsman

No	Date	Opposition	Venue	R	Bat	C
1	26/07/1924	South Africa	Old Trafford	D		

Batting & Fielding

Mat	Inns	N/O	Runs	H/S	Avg	100s	50s	Cat
1	0	–	–	–	–	–	–	0

M.J.MCCAGUE

Full Name: Martin John McCague
Born: 24/05/1969, Larne, Co Antrim, Ireland
Teams: Kent 1991-96, Western Australia 1990/91-91/92, England 1993-94
Matches: 3 (Won 0, Drew 1, Lost 2)
Right-hand lower order batsman – Right-arm fast bowler

No	Date	Opposition	Venue	R	Bat	C		Bowling		
1	01/07/1993	Australia	Trent Bridge	D	9	1	32.3	5	121	4
							19	6	58	0
2	22/07/1993	Australia	Headingley	L	0		28	2	115	0
					11					
3	25/11/1994	Australia	Brisbane (2)	L	1		19.2	4	96	2
					0					

Batting & Fielding

Mat	Inns	N/O	Runs	H/S	Avg	100s	50s	Cat
3	5	0	21	11	4.20	0	0	1

Bowling

Balls	Runs	Wkts	Avg	Best	5WI	10WM	S/R
593	390	6	65.00	4-121	0	0	98.83

J.E.MCCONNON

Full Name: James Edward McConnon (known as Jim or Mac)
Born: 21/06/1922, Burnopfield, Co Durham
Teams: Glamorgan 1950-61, England 1954
Matches: 2 (Won 0, Drew 1, Lost 1)
Right-hand lower order batsman – Off break bowler

No	Date	Opposition	Venue	R	Bat	C		Bowling		
1	22/07/1954	Pakistan	Old Trafford	D	5*	4	13	5	19	3
2	12/08/1954	Pakistan	The Oval	L	11		9	2	35	0
					2		14	5	20	1

Batting & Fielding

Mat	Inns	N/O	Runs	H/S	Avg	100s	50s	Cat
2	3	1	18	11	9.00	0	0	4

Bowling

Balls	Runs	Wkts	Avg	Best	5WI	10WM	S/R
216	74	4	18.50	3-19	0	0	54.00

C.P.MCGAHEY

Full Name: Charles Percy McGahey (known as Charlie)
Born: 12/02/1871, Hackney, London
Died: 10/01/1935, Whipps Cross, Leytonstone, Essex
Teams: Essex 1894-1921, London County 1901-04, England 1902
Matches: 2 (Won 0, Drew 0, Lost 2)
Right-hand middle order batsman – Leg break bowler

No	Date	Opposition	Venue	R	Bat	C
1	14/02/1902	Australia	Sydney	L	18	
					13	
2	28/02/1902	Australia	Melbourne	L	0	
					7	1

Batting & Fielding

Mat	Inns	N/O	Runs	H/S	Avg	100s	50s	Cat
2	4	0	38	18	9.50	0	0	1

G.MACGREGOR

Full Name: Gregor MacGregor
Born: 31/08/1869, Merchiston, Edinburgh, Scotland
Died: 20/08/1919, Marylebone, London
Teams: Cambridge University 1888-91, Middlesex 1892-1907, Scotland 1905, England 1890-93
Matches: 8 (Won 4, Drew 2, Lost 2)
Right-hand lower order batsman – Wicket-keeper

No	Date	Opposition	Venue	R	Bat	C	St	B
1+	21/07/1890	Australia	Lord's	W	0		2	0
						1		0
2+	11/08/1890	Australia	The Oval	W	1	2		0
					2*			7
3+	01/01/1892	Australia	Melbourne	L	9*	1		5
					16	1		0
4+	29/01/1892	Australia	Sydney	L	3	1		6
					12			6
5	24/03/1892	Australia	Adelaide	W	31			
6+	17/07/1893	Australia	Lord's	D	5*	3		15
7+	14/08/1893	Australia	The Oval	W	5	3		5
								18
8+	24/08/1893	Australia	Old Trafford	D	12	2		5
							1	4

Batting & Fielding

Mat	Inns	N/O	Runs	H/S	Avg	100s	50s	Cat	St	Byes
8	11	3	96	31	12.00	0	0	14	3	71

A.J.W.MCINTYRE

Full Name: Arthur John William McIntyre
Born: 14/05/1918, Kennington, London
Teams: Surrey 1938-63, England 1950-55
Matches: 3 (Won 0, Drew 0, Lost 3)
Right-hand middle/lower order batsman – Wicket-keeper – Leg break bowler

No	Date	Opposition	Venue	R	Bat	C	St	B
1+	12/08/1950	West Indies	The Oval	L	4	3		5
					0			
2	01/12/1950	Australia	Brisbane (2)	L	1	1		
					7			
3+	21/07/1955	South Africa	Headingley	L	3	2		0
					4	2		8

Batting & Fielding

Mat	Inns	N/O	Runs	H/S	Avg	100s	50s	Cat	St	Byes
3	6	0	19	7	3.16	0	0	8	0	13

F.A.MACKINNON

Full Name: Francis Alexander MacKinnon of Mackinnon
Born: 09/04/1848, Paddington, London
Died: 27/02/1947, Drumduan Forres, Morayshire, Scotland
Teams: Cambridge University 1870, Kent 1875-85, England 1879
Matches: 1 (Won 0, Drew 0, Lost 1)
Right-hand middle order batsman

No	Date	Opposition	Venue	R	Bat	C
1	02/01/1879	Australia	Melbourne	L	0	
					5	

Batting & Fielding

Mat	Inns	N/O	Runs	H/S	Avg	100s	50s	Cat
1	2	0	5	5	2.50	0	0	0

A.C.MACLAREN

Full Name: Archibald Campbell MacLaren (known as Archie)
Born: 01/12/1871, Whalley Range, Manchester, Lancashire
Died: 17/11/1944, Warfield Park, Bracknell, Berkshire
Teams: Lancashire 1890-1914, England 1894-1909
Matches: 35 (Won 10, Drew 9, Lost 16)
England Captain: 22 times 1897-1909 (Won 4, Drew 7, Lost 11) **Toss:** 11-11
Right-hand opening batsman – Right-arm fast bowler

No	Date	Opposition	Venue	R	Bat	C
1	14/12/1894	Australia	Sydney	W	4	
					20	1
2	29/12/1894	Australia	Melbourne	W	0	
					15	
3	11/01/1895	Australia	Adelaide	L	25	
					35	
4	01/02/1895	Australia	Sydney	L	1	
					0	
5	01/03/1895	Australia	Melbourne	W	120	1
					20*	
6	16/07/1896	Australia	Old Trafford	L	0	
					15	
7	10/08/1896	Australia	The Oval	W	20	2
					6	
8*	13/12/1897	Australia	Sydney	W	109	
					50*	
9*	01/01/1898	Australia	Melbourne	L	35	
					38	
10	14/01/1898	Australia	Adelaide	L	14	
					124	
11	29/01/1898	Australia	Melbourne	L	8	
					45	
12*	26/02/1898	Australia	Sydney	L	65	1
					0	
13*	15/06/1899	Australia	Lord's	L	4	
					88*	
14*	29/06/1899	Australia	Headingley	D	9	
						1
15*	17/07/1899	Australia	Old Trafford	D	8	1
					6	
16*	14/08/1899	Australia	The Oval	D	49	
17*	13/12/1901	Australia	Sydney	W	116	
						1
18*	01/01/1902	Australia	Melbourne	L	13	1
					1	1
19*	17/01/1902	Australia	Adelaide	L	67	1
					44	
20*	14/02/1902	Australia	Sydney	L	92	2
					5	
21*	28/02/1902	Australia	Melbourne	L	25	
					49	2
22*	29/05/1902	Australia	Edgbaston	D	9	
23*	12/06/1902	Australia	Lord's	D	47*	
24*	03/07/1902	Australia	Bramall Lane	L	31	
					63	1
25*	24/07/1902	Australia	Old Trafford	L	1	1
					35	
26*	11/08/1902	Australia	The Oval	W	10	1
					2	2
27	29/05/1905	Australia	Trent Bridge	W	2	
					140	
28	15/06/1905	Australia	Lord's	D	56	
					79	
29	24/07/1905	Australia	Old Trafford	W	14	1
30	14/08/1905	Australia	The Oval	D	6	1
					6	
31*	27/05/1909	Australia	Edgbaston	W	5	2
32*	14/06/1909	Australia	Lord's	L	7	1
					24	

No	Date	Opposition	Venue	R	Bat	C
33*	01/07/1909	Australia	Headingley	L	17	
					1	1
34*	26/07/1909	Australia	Old Trafford	D	16	
						2
35*	09/08/1909	Australia	The Oval	D	15	
					1	1

Batting & Fielding

Mat	Inns	N/O	Runs	H/S	Avg	100s	50s	Cat
35	61	4	1931	140	33.87	5	8	29

J.E.P.MCMASTER

Full Name: Joseph Emile Patrick McMaster
Born: 16/03/1861, Gilford, Co.Down, Ireland
Died: 07/06/1929, London
Teams: England 1889
Matches: 1 (Won 1, Drew 0, Lost 0)
Right-hand lower order batsman

No	Date	Opposition	Venue	R	Bat	C
1	25/03/1889	South Africa	Cape Town	W	0	

Batting & Fielding

Mat	Inns	N/O	Runs	H/S	Avg	100s	50s	Cat
1	1	0	0	0	0.00	0	0	0

J.W.H.MAKEPEACE

Full Name: Joseph William Henry Makepeace (known as Harry)
Born: 22/08/1881, Middlesbrough, Yorkshire
Died: 19/12/1952, Spital, Bebington, Cheshire
Teams: Lancashire 1906-30, England 1920-21
Matches: 4 (Won 0, Drew 0, Lost 4)
Right-hand opening batsman – Leg break bowler

No	Date	Opposition	Venue	R	Bat	C
1	31/12/1920	Australia	Melbourne	L	4	
					4	
2	14/01/1921	Australia	Adelaide	L	60	
					30	
3	11/02/1921	Australia	Melbourne	L	117	
					54	
4	25/02/1921	Australia	Sydney	L	3	
					7	

Batting & Fielding

Mat	Inns	N/O	Runs	H/S	Avg	100s	50s	Cat
4	8	0	279	117	34.87	1	2	0

D.E.MALCOLM

Full Name: Devon Eugene Malcolm
Born: 22/02/1963, Kingston, Jamaica
Teams: Derbyshire 1984-96, England 1989-96
Matches: 36 (Won 8, Drew 12, Lost 16)
Right-hand lower order batsman – Right-arm fast bowler

No	Date	Opposition	Venue	R	Bat	C		Bowling		
1	10/08/1989	Australia	Trent Bridge	L	9		44	2	166	1
					5					
2	24/02/1990	West Indies	Kingston	W	0		16	4	49	1
							21.3	2	77	4
3	23/03/1990	West Indies	Port-of-Spain	D	0*		20	2	60	4
							26.2	4	77	6
4	05/04/1990	West Indies	Bridgetown	L	12		33	6	142	0
					4	1	10	0	46	0
5	12/04/1990	West Indies	St John's	L	0*		34.5	3	126	4
					1*					
6	07/06/1990	New Zealand	Trent Bridge	D	4*		19	7	48	2
							7	2	22	0
7	21/06/1990	New Zealand	Lord's	D	0*		43	14	94	5

No	Date	Opposition	Venue	R	Bat	C	Bowling			
8	05/07/1990	New Zealand	Edgbaston	W	0		25	7	59	3
					0		24.4	8	46	5
9	26/07/1990	India	Lord's	W			25	1	106	1
							10	0	65	2
10	09/08/1990	India	Old Trafford	D	13		26	3	96	1
							14	5	59	1
11	23/08/1990	India	The Oval	D	15*		35	7	110	2
12	23/11/1990	Australia	Brisbane (2)	L	5		17	2	45	1
					0*		9	5	22	0
13	26/12/1990	Australia	Melbourne	L	6		25.5	4	74	2
					1		23	7	52	1
14	04/01/1991	Australia	Sydney	D			45	12	128	4
							6	1	19	2
15	25/01/1991	Australia	Adelaide	D	2		38	7	104	2
							21	0	87	1
16	01/02/1991	Australia	Perth	L	7		30	4	94	3
					6		9	0	40	0
17	06/06/1991	West Indies	Headingley	W	5*		14	0	69	0
					4		6.4	0	26	1
18	20/06/1991	West Indies	Lord's	D	0	1	19	3	76	1
							2.5	0	9	1
19	18/06/1992	Pakistan	Lord's	L	0	1	15.5	1	70	4
					0		15	2	42	1
20	02/07/1992	Pakistan	Old Trafford	D	4		31	3	117	3
							12	2	57	0
21	06/08/1992	Pakistan	The Oval	L	2		29	6	94	5
					0					
22	29/01/1993	India	Calcutta	L	4*		24	3	67	3
					0		6	1	16	0
23	11/02/1993	India	Madras (1)	L	0*		27	7	8	0
					0					
24	13/03/1993	Sri Lanka	Colombo (2)	L	13		25	7	60	0
					8*		3	1	11	0
25	19/08/1993	Australia	The Oval	W	0*		26	5	86	3
					0*		20	3	84	3
26	19/02/1994	West Indies	Kingston	L	6		23	3	113	3
					18		5	1	19	0
27	02/06/1994	New Zealand	Trent Bridge	W			17.4	5	45	2
							10	2	39	0
28	18/08/1994	South Africa	The Oval	W	4		25	5	81	1
						1	16.3	2	57	9
29	24/12/1994	Australia	Melbourne	L	11*		28.3	4	78	1
					0		22	3	86	0
30	01/01/1995	Australia	Sydney	D	29		13	4	34	2
							21	4	75	1
31	26/01/1995	Australia	Adelaide	W	0		26	5	78	3
					10*		16.1	3	39	4
32	03/02/1995	Australia	Perth	L	0*		31	6	93	0
					0	1	23.3	3	105	2
33	08/06/1995	West Indies	Headingley	L	0		7.3	0	48	2
					5		4	0	12	0
34	24/08/1995	West Indies	The Oval	D	10		39	7	160	3
35	30/11/1995	South Africa	Johannesburg (3)	D	0*		22	5	62	4
							13	2	65	2
36	02/01/1996	South Africa	Cape Town	L	1		20	6	56	2
					0*		2	0	12	0

Batting & Fielding

Mat	Inns	N/O	Runs	H/S	Avg	100s	50s	Cat
36	53	18	224	29	6.40	0	0	5

Bowling

Balls	Runs	Wkts	Avg	Best	5WI	10WM	S/R
7922	4441	122	36.40	9-57	5	2	64.93

N.A.MALLENDER

Full Name: Neil Alan Mallender
Born: 13/08/1961, Kirk Sandall, Yorkshire
Teams: Northamptonshire 1980-86, Somerset 1987-94, Northamptonshire 1995-96, Otago 1983/84, England 1992
Matches: 2 (Won 1, Drew 0, Lost 1)
Right-hand lower order batsman – Right-arm fast medium bowler

No	Date	Opposition	Venue	R	Bat	C	Bowling		
1	23/07/1992	Pakistan	Headingley	W	1		23	7	72	3
							23	7	50	5
2	06/08/1992	Pakistan	The Oval	L	4		28.5	6	93	2
					3					

Batting & Fielding

Mat	Inns	N/O	Runs	H/S	Avg	100s	50s	Cat
2	3	0	8	4	2.66	0	0	0

Bowling

Balls	Runs	Wkts	Avg	Best	5WI	10WM	S/R
449	215	10	21.50	5-50	1	0	44.90

F.G.MANN

Full Name: Francis George Mann, CBE (known as George)
Born: 06/09/1917, Byfleet, Surrey
Teams: Cambridge University 1938-39, Middlesex 1937-54, England 1948-49
Matches: 7 (Won 2, Drew 5, Lost 0)
England Captain: 7 times 1948-49 (Won 2, Drew 5, Lost 0) **Toss:** 5-2
Right-hand middle order batsman

No	Date	Opposition	Venue	R	Bat	C
1*	16/12/1948	South Africa	Durban (2)	W	19	
					13	2
2*	27/12/1948	South Africa	Johannesburg (2)	D	7	
3*	01/01/1949	South Africa	Cape Town	D	44	1
4*	12/02/1949	South Africa	Johannesburg (2)	D	17	
					16	
5*	05/03/1949	South Africa	Port Elizabeth	W	136*	
					2	
6*	11/06/1949	New Zealand	Headingley	D	38	
					49*	
7*	25/06/1949	New Zealand	Lord's	D	18	
					17	

Batting & Fielding

Mat	Inns	N/O	Runs	H/S	Avg	100s	50s	Cat
7	12	2	376	136*	37.60	1	0	3

F.T.MANN

Full Name: Francis Thomas Mann (known as Frank)
Born: 03/03/1888, Winchmore Hill, Middlesex
Died: 06/10/1964, Milton-Lilbourne, Wiltshire
Teams: Cambridge University 1908-11, Middlesex 1909-31, England 1922-23
Matches: 5 (Won 2, Drew 2, Lost 1)
England Captain: 5 times 1922-23 (Won 2, Drew 2, Lost 1) **Toss:** 3-2
Right-hand middle order batsman – Right-arm slow bowler

No	Date	Opposition	Venue	R	Bat	C
1*	23/12/1922	South Africa	Johannesburg (1)	L	4	
					28*	1
2*	01/01/1923	South Africa	Cape Town	W	4	1
					45	
3*	18/01/1923	South Africa	Durban (2)	D	84	
4*	09/02/1923	South Africa	Johannesburg (1)	D	34	1
					59	
5*	16/02/1923	South Africa	Durban (2)	W	8	1
					15	

Batting & Fielding

Mat	Inns	N/O	Runs	H/S	Avg	100s	50s	Cat
5	9	1	281	84	35.12	0	2	4

V.J.MARKS

Full Name: Victor James Marks (known as Vic)
Born: 25/06/1955, Middle Chinnock, Somerset
Teams: Oxford University 1975-78, Somerset 1975-89, Western Australia 1986/87, England 1982-84
Matches: 6 (Won 2, Drew 3, Lost 1)
Right-hand middle order batsman – Off break bowler

No	Date	Opposition	Venue	R	Bat	C		Bowling	
1	26/08/1982	Pakistan	Headingley	W	7		5	0 23	0
					12*		2	1 8	1
2	14/07/1983	New Zealand	The Oval	W	4				
					2		43	20 78	3
3	10/02/1984	New Zealand	Auckland	D	6		40.2	9 115	3
4	02/03/1984	Pakistan	Karachi (1)	L	5		13	4 40	0
					1		12	5 23	1
5	12/03/1984	Pakistan	Faisalabad	D	83		27	9 59	1
							8	2 26	1
6	19/03/1984	Pakistan	Lahore (2)	D	74		20	4 59	1
					55		10	0 53	0

Batting & Fielding

Mat	Inns	N/O	Runs	H/S	Avg	100s	50s	Cat
6	10	1	249	83	27.66	0	3	0

Bowling

Balls	Runs	Wkts	Avg	Best	5WI	10WM	S/R
1082	484	11	44.00	3-78	0	0	98.36

C.S.MARRIOTT

Full Name: Charles Stowell Marriott (also known as Father)
Born: 14/09/1895, Heaton Moor, Lancashire
Died: 13/10/1966, Dollis Hill, Middlesex
Teams: Cambridge University 1920-21, Lancashire 1919-21, Kent 1924-37, England 1933
Matches: 1 (Won 1, Drew 0, Lost 0)
Right-hand lower order batsman – Leg break & googly bowler

No	Date	Opposition	Venue	R	Bat	C		Bowling	
1	12/08/1933	West Indies	The Oval	W	0		11.5	2 37	5
						1	29.2	6 59	6

Batting & Fielding

Mat	Inns	N/O	Runs	H/S	Avg	100s	50s	Cat
1	1	0	0	0	0.00	0	0	1

Bowling

Balls	Runs	Wkts	Avg	Best	5WI	10WM	S/R
247	96	11	8.72	6-59	2	1	22.45

F.MARTIN

Full Name: Frederick Martin
Born: 12/10/1861, Dartford, Kent
Died: 13/12/1921, Dartford, Kent
Teams: Kent 1885-99, England 1890-1892
Matches: 2 (Won 2, Drew 0, Lost 0)
Left-hand lower order batsman – Left-arm medium bowler

No	Date	Opposition	Venue	R	Bat	C		Bowling	
1	11/08/1890	Australia	The Oval	W	1		27	9 50	6
							30.2	12 52	6
2	19/03/1892	South Africa	Cape Town	W	13	1			
						1	24.3	9 39	2

Batting & Fielding

Mat	Inns	N/O	Runs	H/S	Avg	100s	50s	Cat
2	2	0	14	13	7.00	0	0	2

Bowling

Balls	Runs	Wkts	Avg	Best	5WI	10WM	S/R
410	141	14	10.07	6-50	2	1	29.28

J.W.MARTIN

Full Name: John William Martin (known as Jack)
Born: 16/02/1917, Catford, London
Died: 04/01/1987, Woolwich, London
Teams: Kent 1939-53, England 1947
Matches: 1 (Won 0, Drew 1, Lost 0)
Right-hand lower order batsman – Right-arm fast bowler

No	Date	Opposition	Venue	R	Bat	C		Bowling		
1	07/06/1947	South Africa	Trent Bridge	D	0		36	4	111	1
					26		9	2	18	0

Batting & Fielding

Mat	Inns	N/O	Runs	H/S	Avg	100s	50s	Cat
1	2	0	26	26	13.00	0	0	0

Bowling

Balls	Runs	Wkts	Avg	Best	5WI	10WM	S/R
270	129	1	129.00	1-111	0	0	270.00

P.J.MARTIN

Full Name: Peter James Martin
Born: 15/11/1968, Accrington, Lancashire
Teams: Lancashire 1989-96, England 1995-96
Matches: 7 (Won 1, Drew 3, Lost 3)
Right-hand lower order batsman – Right-arm fast medium

No	Date	Opposition	Venue	R	Bat	C		Bowling		
1	08/06/1995	West Indies	Headingley	L	2	1	27	9	48	1
					19		8	2	49	1
2	22/06/1995	West Indies	Lord's	W	29	1	23	5	65	2
					1	1	7	0	30	0
3	06/07/1995	West Indies	Edgbaston	L	1	1	19	5	49	1
					0					
4	14/12/1995	South Africa	Durban (2)	D		1	27	9	60	4
5	26/12/1995	South Africa	Port Elizabeth	D	4		33	9	79	1
							17	8	39	3
6	02/01/1996	South Africa	Cape Town	L	0		24	9	37	3
					9		4	2	3	0
7	20/06/1996	India	Lord's	D	4		34	10	70	1
					23					

Batting & Fielding

Mat	Inns	N/O	Runs	H/S	Avg	100s	50s	Cat
7	11	0	92	29	8.36	0	0	5

Bowling

Balls	Runs	Wkts	Avg	Best	5WI	10WM	S/R
1338	529	17	31.11	4-60	0	0	78.70

J.R.MASON

Full Name: John Richard Mason (known as Jack)
Born: 26/03/1874, Blackheath, Kent
Died: 15/10/1958, Cooden Beach, Sussex
Teams: Kent 1893-1914, England 1897-98
Matches: 5 (Won 1, Drew 0, Lost 4)
Right-hand middle order batsman – Right-arm fast medium bowler

No	Date	Opposition	Venue	R	Bat	C		Bowling		
1	13/12/1897	Australia	Sydney	W	6	1	2	1	8	1
					32		2	0	10	0
2	01/01/1898	Australia	Melbourne	L	3		11	1	33	1
					3					
3	14/01/1898	Australia	Adelaide	L	11		11	2	41	0
					0					
4	29/01/1898	Australia	Melbourne	L	30	1				
					26		4	1	10	0
5	26/02/1898	Australia	Sydney	L	7	1	13	7	20	0
					11		11	1	27	0

Batting & Fielding

Mat	Inns	N/O	Runs	H/S	Avg	100s	50s	Cat
5	10	0	129	32	12.90	0	0	3

Bowling

Balls	Runs	Wkts	Avg	Best	5WI	10WM	S/R
324	149	2	74.50	1-8	0	0	162.00

A.D.G.MATTHEWS

Full Name: Austin David George Matthews
Born: 03/05/1904, Penarth, Glamorgan
Died: 29/07/1977, Penrhyn Bay, Llandudno, Caernarvonshire
Teams: Northamptonshire 1927-36, Glamorgan 1937-47, England 1937
Matches: 1 (Won 0, Drew 1, Lost 0)
Right-hand lower order batsman – Right-arm fast medium bowler

No	Date	Opposition	Venue	R	Bat	C		Bowling		
1	14/08/1937	New Zealand	The Oval	D	2*	1	22	6	52	1
							8	2	13	1

Batting & Fielding

Mat	Inns	N/O	Runs	H/S	Avg	100s	50s	Cat
1	1	1	2	2*	–	0	0	1

Bowling

Balls	Runs	Wkts	Avg	Best	5WI	10WM	S/R
180	65	2	32.50	1-13	0	0	90.00

P.B.H.MAY

Full Name: Peter Barker Howard May, CBE
Born: 31/12/1929, The Mount, Reading, Berkshire
Died: 27/12/1994, Liphook, Hampshire
Teams: Cambridge University 1950-52, Surrey 1950-63, England 1951-61
Matches: 66 (Won 33, Drew 18, Lost 15)
England Captain: 41 times 1955-61 (Won 20, Drew 11, Lost 10) **Toss:** 26-15
Right-hand middle order batsman

No	Date	Opposition	Venue	R	Bat	C
1	26/07/1951	South Africa	Headingley	D	138	
2	16/08/1951	South Africa	The Oval	W	33	1
					0	
3	05/06/1952	India	Headingley	W	16	1
					4	
4	19/06/1952	India	Lord's	W	74	
					26	
5	17/07/1952	India	Old Trafford	W	69	
						1
6	14/08/1952	India	The Oval	D	17	1
7	11/06/1953	Australia	Trent Bridge	D	9	
8	15/08/1953	Australia	The Oval	W	39	
					37	
9	15/01/1954	West Indies	Kingston	L	31	
					69	
10	06/02/1954	West Indies	Bridgetown	L	7	
					62	
11	24/02/1954	West Indies	Georgetown	W	12	
					12	
12	17/03/1954	West Indies	Port-of-Spain	D	135	
					16	
13	30/03/1954	West Indies	Kingston	W	30	
					40*	
14	10/06/1954	Pakistan	Lord's	D	27	
15	01/07/1954	Pakistan	Trent Bridge	W	0	1
16	22/07/1954	Pakistan	Old Trafford	D	14	
17	12/08/1954	Pakistan	The Oval	L	26	
					53	2
18	26/11/1954	Australia	Brisbane (2)	L	1	1
					44	

No	Date	Opposition	Venue	R	Bat	C
19	17/12/1954	Australia	Sydney	W	5	
					104	
20	31/12/1954	Australia	Melbourne	W	0	
					91	
21	28/01/1955	Australia	Adelaide	W	1	4
					26	
22	25/02/1955	Australia	Sydney	D	79	1
23	11/03/1955	New Zealand	Dunedin	W	10	
					13	
24	25/03/1955	New Zealand	Auckland	W	48	
						1
25*	09/06/1955	South Africa	Trent Bridge	W	83	2
						1
26*	23/06/1955	South Africa	Lord's	W	0	
					112	
27*	07/07/1955	South Africa	Old Trafford	L	34	
					117	1
28*	21/07/1955	South Africa	Headingley	L	47	1
					97	1
29*	13/08/1955	South Africa	The Oval	W	3	
					89*	1
30*	07/06/1956	Australia	Trent Bridge	D	73	
31*	21/06/1956	Australia	Lord's	L	63	
					53	
32*	12/07/1956	Australia	Headingley	W	101	
33*	26/07/1956	Australia	Old Trafford	W	43	
34*	23/08/1956	Australia	The Oval	D	83*	2
					37*	1
35*	24/12/1956	South Africa	Johannesburg (3)	W	6	
					14	
36*	01/01/1957	South Africa	Cape Town	W	8	1
					15	1
37*	25/01/1957	South Africa	Durban (2)	D	2	
					2	
38*	15/02/1957	South Africa	Johannesburg (3)	L	61	
					0	
39*	01/03/1957	South Africa	Port Elizabeth	L	24	
					21	
40*	30/05/1957	West Indies	Edgbaston	D	30	
					285*	1
41*	20/06/1957	West Indies	Lord's	W	0	1
						1
42*	04/07/1957	West Indies	Trent Bridge	D	104	1
43*	25/07/1957	West Indies	Headingley	W	69	
44*	22/08/1957	West Indies	The Oval	W	1	1
45*	05/06/1958	New Zealand	Edgbaston	W	84	
					11	
46*	19/06/1958	New Zealand	Lord's	W	19	1
						2
47*	03/07/1958	New Zealand	Headingley	W	113*	
						1
48*	24/07/1958	New Zealand	Old Trafford	W	101	
49*	21/08/1958	New Zealand	The Oval	D	9	
50*	05/12/1958	Australia	Brisbane (2)	L	26	
					4	
51*	31/12/1958	Australia	Melbourne	L	113	1
					17	
52*	09/01/1959	Australia	Sydney	D	42	
					92	
53*	30/01/1959	Australia	Adelaide	L	37	
					59	
54*	13/02/1959	Australia	Melbourne	L	11	
					4	
55*	27/02/1959	New Zealand	Christchurch	W	71	
						1

No	Date	Opposition	Venue	R	Bat	C
56*	14/03/1959	New Zealand	Auckland	D	124*	
57*	04/06/1959	India	Trent Bridge	W	106	
						2
58*	18/06/1959	India	Lord's	W	9	1
					33*	1
59*	02/07/1959	India	Headingley	W	2	
						1
60*	06/01/1960	West Indies	Bridgetown	D	1	
61*	28/01/1960	West Indies	Port-of-Spain	W	0	
					28	
62*	17/02/1960	West Indies	Kingston	D	9	
					45	
63	22/06/1961	Australia	Lord's	L	17	
					22	
64*	06/07/1961	Australia	Headingley	W	26	
					8*	
65*	27/07/1961	Australia	Old Trafford	L	95	
					0	
66*	17/08/1961	Australia	The Oval	D	71	
					33	

Batting & Fielding

Mat	Inns	N/O	Runs	H/S	Avg	100s	50s	Cat
66	106	9	4537	285*	46.77	13	22	42

M.P.MAYNARD

Full Name: Matthew Peter Maynard
Born: 21/03/1966, Oldham, Lancashire
Teams: Glamorgan 1985-96, Northern Districts 1990/91-91/92, England 1988-94
Matches: 4 (Won 1, Drew 0, Lost 3)
Right-hand middle order batsman – Right-arm medium bowler

No	Date	Opposition	Venue	R	Bat	C
1	04/08/1988	West Indies	The Oval	L	3	
					10	
2	05/08/1993	Australia	Edgbaston	L	0	
					10	
3	19/08/1993	Australia	The Oval	W	20	1
					9	1
4	19/02/1994	West Indies	Kingston	L	35	1
					0	

Batting & Fielding

Mat	Inns	N/O	Runs	H/S	Avg	100s	50s	Cat
4	8	0	87	35	10.87	0	0	3

C.P.MEAD

Full Name: Charles Philip Mead (known as Phil)
Born: 09/03/1887, Battersea, London
Died: 26/03/1958, Boscombe, Hampshire
Teams: Hampshire 1905-36, England 1911-28
Matches: 17 (Won 10, Drew 5, Lost 2)
Left-hand middle order batsman – Left-arm slow bowler

No	Date	Opposition	Venue	R	Bat	C
1	15/12/1911	Australia	Sydney	L	0	
					25	
2	30/12/1911	Australia	Melbourne	W	11	
						1
3	12/01/1912	Australia	Adelaide	W	46	1
					2*	
4	09/02/1912	Australia	Melbourne	W	21	
						1
5	13/12/1913	South Africa	Durban (1)	W	41	
6	26/12/1913	South Africa	Johannesburg (1)	W	102	

No	Date	Opposition	Venue	R	Bat	C			
7	01/01/1914	South Africa	Johannesburg (1)	W	0				
					86				
8	14/02/1914	South Africa	Durban (1)	D	31				
					1				
9	27/02/1914	South Africa	Port Elizabeth	W	117				
10	23/07/1921	Australia	Old Trafford	D	47				
11	13/08/1921	Australia	The Oval	D	182*				
12	23/12/1922	South Africa	Johannesburg (1)	L	1				
					49				
13	01/01/1923	South Africa	Cape Town	W	21				
					31				
14	18/01/1923	South Africa	Durban (2)	D	181				
15	09/02/1923	South Africa	Johannesburg (1)	D	38				
					0				
16	16/02/1923	South Africa	Durban (2)	W	66	1			
					5				
17	30/11/1928	Australia	Brisbane (1)	W	8				
					73				

Batting & Fielding

Mat	Inns	N/O	Runs	H/S	Avg	100s	50s	Cat
17	26	2	1185	182*	49.37	4	3	4

W.MEAD

Full Name: Walter Mead
Born: 01/04/1868, Clapton, London
Died: 18/03/1954, Shelley, Ongar, Essex
Teams: Essex 1894-1913, London County 1904, England 1899
Matches: 1 (Won 0, Drew 0, Lost 1)
Right-hand lower order batsman – Right-arm slow medium off and leg break bowler

No	Date	Opposition	Venue	R	Bat	C		Bowling			
1	15/06/1899	Australia	Lord's	L	7	1		53	24	91	1
					0						

Batting & Fielding

Mat	Inns	N/O	Runs	H/S	Avg	100s	50s	Cat
1	2	0	7	7	3.50	0	0	1

Bowling

Balls	Runs	Wkts	Avg	Best	5WI	10WM	S/R
265	91	1	91.00	1-91	0	0	265.00

W.E.MIDWINTER

Full Name: William Evans Midwinter (known as Billy)
Born: 19/06/1851, St Briavels, Gloucestershire
Died: 03/12/1890, Yarra Bend, Kew, Melbourne, Victoria, Australia
Teams: Gloucestershire 1877-82, Victoria 1874/75-86/87, Australia 1877-87, England 1881-82
Matches: 4 (Won 0, Drew 2, Lost 2), 8 (Won 2, Drew 2, Lost 4)
Right-hand middle order batsman – Right-hand round-arm medium bowler

No	Date	Opposition	Venue	R	Bat	C		Bowling			
1	31/12/1881	Australia	Melbourne	D	36			39	21	50	2
					4						
2	17/02/1882	Australia	Sydney	L	4			34	16	43	1
					8			18	8	23	1
3	03/03/1882	Australia	Sydney	L	12	1		62	25	75	2
					10	2					
4	10/03/1882	Australia	Melbourne	D	21	2		41	9	81	4

For Australia

1	15/03/1877	England	Melbourne	W	5			54	23	78	5
					17	1		19	7	23	1
2	31/03/1877	England	Melbourne	L	31			21	8	30	1
					12			13.1	6	25	1
3	17/02/1883	England	Sydney	W	10			47	24	50	2
					8*			23	13	21	2

No	Date	Opposition	Venue	R	Bat	C	Bowling			
4	10/07/1884	England	Old Trafford	D	37	1				
5	21/07/1884	England	Lord's	L	3		13	2	29	0
					6					
6	11/08/1884	England	The Oval	D	30	1	31	16	41	1
							3	0	15	0
7	28/01/1887	England	Sydney	L	0	2				
					10		4	1	10	0
8	25/02/1887	England	Sydney	L	1		3	1	2	0
					4		6	3	9	1

Batting & Fielding

Mat	Inns	N/O	Runs	H/S	Avg	100s	50s	Cat	
4	7	0	95	36	13.57	0	0	5	(England)
8	14	1	174	37	13.38	0	0	5	(Australia)
12	21	1	269	37	13.45	0	0	10	(Total)

Bowling

Balls	Runs	Wkts	Avg	Best	5WI	10WM	S/R	
776	272	10	27.20	4-81	0	0	77.60	(England)
949	333	14	23.78	5-78	1	0	67.78	(Australia)
1725	605	24	25.20	5-78	1	0	71.87	(Total)

C.MILBURN

Full Name: Colin Milburn
Born: 23/10/1941, Burnopfield, Co Durham
Died: 28/02/1990, Newton Aycliffe, Co Durham
Teams: Northamptonshire 1960-74, Western Australia 1966/67-68/69, England 1966-69
Matches: 9 (Won 2, Drew 4, Lost 3)
Right-hand opening batsman – Right-arm medium bowler

No	Date	Opposition	Venue	R	Bat	C
1	02/06/1966	West Indies	Old Trafford	L	0	
					94	
2	16/06/1966	West Indies	Lord's	D	6	1
					126*	1
3	30/06/1966	West Indies	Trent Bridge	L	7	
					12	
4	04/08/1966	West Indies	Headingley	L	29*	
					42	
5	13/07/1967	India	Edgbaston	W	40	
					15	2
6	27/07/1967	Pakistan	Lord's	D	3	1
					32	
7	20/06/1968	Australia	Lord's	D	83	
8	22/08/1968	Australia	The Oval	W	8	1
					18	1
9	06/03/1969	Pakistan	Karachi (1)	D	139	

Batting & Fielding

Mat	Inns	N/O	Runs	H/S	Avg	100s	50s	Cat
9	16	2	654	139	46.71	2	2	7

A.M.MILLER

Full Name: Audley Montague Miller
Born: 19/10/1869, Brentry, Westbury-on-Trym, Gloucestershire
Died: 26/06/1959, Clifton, Bristol
Teams: MCC 1896-1903, England 1896
Matches: 1 (Won 1, Drew 0, Lost 0)
Right-hand middle order batsman – Right-arm medium bowler

No	Date	Opposition	Venue	R	Bat	C
1	13/02/1896	South Africa	Port Elizabeth	W	4*	
					20*	

Batting & Fielding

Mat	Inns	N/O	Runs	H/S	Avg	100s	50s	Cat
1	2	2	24	20*	–	0	0	0

G.MILLER

Full Name: Geoffrey Miller (known as Geoff)
Born: 08/09/1952, Chesterfield, Derbyshire
Teams: Derbyshire 1973-90, Essex 1987-89, Natal 1983/84, England 1976-84
Matches: 34 (Won 15, Drew 10, Lost 9)
Right-hand middle order batsman – Off break bowler

No	Date	Opposition	Venue	R	Bat	C	O	M	R	W
1	12/08/1976	West Indies	The Oval	L	36		27	4	106	1
					24					
2	07/07/1977	Australia	Old Trafford	W	6		10	3	18	2
							9	2	24	1
3	28/07/1977	Australia	Trent Bridge	W	13					
							5	2	5	0
4	14/12/1977	Pakistan	Lahore (2)	D	98*	1	37	10	102	3
							10	4	24	0
5	02/01/1978	Pakistan	Hyderabad	D	5	1	9	0	57	0
							2	0	8	0
6	18/01/1978	Pakistan	Karachi (1)	D	11		14	0	71	1
					3					
7	10/02/1978	New Zealand	Wellington	L	24					
					4					
8	24/02/1978	New Zealand	Christchurch	W	89	1				
						1				
9	04/03/1978	New Zealand	Auckland	D	15	1	1	1	0	0
							30	10	99	3
10	01/06/1978	Pakistan	Edgbaston	W	48					
						1	12	4	19	2
11	15/06/1978	Pakistan	Lord's	W	0					
							9	3	9	0
12	29/06/1978	Pakistan	Headingley	D	18*		9	3	22	0
13	27/07/1978	New Zealand	The Oval	W	0	1	25	10	31	2
							34	19	35	2
14	10/08/1978	New Zealand	Trent Bridge	W	4		6	1	14	0
							6	3	10	0
15	01/12/1978	Australia	Brisbane (2)	W	27					
							34	12	52	2
16	15/12/1978	Australia	Perth	W	40		16	6	31	1
					25		7	4	21	3
17	29/12/1978	Australia	Melbourne	L	7		19	6	35	3
					1		14	5	39	2
18	06/01/1979	Australia	Sydney	W	4		13	2	37	1
					17		20	7	38	3
19	27/01/1979	Australia	Adelaide	W	31					
					64		18	3	36	2
20	10/02/1979	Australia	Sydney	W	18		9	3	13	1
						1	27.1	6	44	5
21	12/07/1979	India	Edgbaston	W	63*		11	3	18	0
							9	1	27	0
22	02/08/1979	India	Lord's	D	62	1				
							17	6	37	0
23	16/08/1979	India	Headingley	D	27		32	13	52	2
24	14/12/1979	Australia	Perth	L	25		11	2	30	0
					8	1	10	0	36	0
25	13/02/1981	West Indies	Port-of-Spain	L	3	1	18	4	42	1
					8					
26	24/06/1982	India	Old Trafford	D	98		16	4	51	1
27	29/07/1982	Pakistan	Edgbaston	W	47	1	2	1	1	0
					5		7.4	1	26	2
28	12/11/1982	Australia	Perth	D	30		33	11	70	4
					0		4	3	8	0
29	26/11/1982	Australia	Brisbane (2)	L	0		19.3	4	35	1
					60		3	0	10	0
30	10/12/1982	Australia	Adelaide	L	7		14	2	33	0
					17					
31	26/12/1982	Australia	Melbourne	W	10		15	5	44	3
					14	1	16	6	30	1
32	02/01/1983	Australia	Sydney	D	34	2	17	7	34	1
					21*		49.3	12	133	3
33	14/06/1984	West Indies	Edgbaston	L	22	1	15	1	83	1
					11					

No	Date	Opposition	Venue		R	Bat	C			Bowling	
34	28/06/1984	West Indies	Lord's		L	0	1	2	0	14	0
						9		11	0	45	0

Batting & Fielding

Mat	Inns	N/O	Runs	H/S	Avg	100s	50s	Cat
34	51	4	1213	98*	25.80	0	7	17

Bowling

Balls	Runs	Wkts	Avg	Best	5WI	10WM	S/R
5149	1859	60	30.98	5-44	1	0	85.81

F.W.MILLIGAN

Full Name: Frank William Milligan
Born: 19/03/1870, Farnborough, Hampshire
Died: 31/03/1900, Ramathlabama, South Africa
Teams: Yorkshire 1894-98, England 1899
Matches: 2 (Won 2, Drew 0, Lost 0)
Right-hand middle/lower order batsman – Right-arm fast bowler

No	Date	Opposition	Venue		R	Bat	C			Bowling	
1	14/02/1899	South Africa	Johannesburg (1)		W	11		7	0	29	0
						8					
2	01/04/1899	South Africa	Cape Town		W	1		2	2	0	0
						38	1				

Batting & Fielding

Mat	Inns	N/O	Runs	H/S	Avg	100s	50s	Cat
2	4	0	58	38	14.50	0	0	1

Bowling

Balls	Runs	Wkts	Avg	Best	5WI	10WM	S/R
45	29	0	–	0-0	0	0	–

G.MILLMAN

Full Name: Geoffrey Millman (known as Geoff)
Born: 02/10/1934, Bedford
Teams: Nottinghamshire 1957-65, England 1961-62
Matches: 6 (Won 2, Drew 2, Lost 2)
Right-hand opening/middle order batsman – Wicket-keeper – Occasional off break bowler

No	Date	Opposition	Venue		R	Bat	C	St	B
1+	30/12/1961	India	Calcutta		L	0	1		2
						4	2	2	0
2+	10/01/1962	India	Madras (2)		L	32*	1		4
						14	2		6
3+	19/01/1962	Pakistan	Dacca		D	3*			4
									5
4+	02/02/1962	Pakistan	Karachi (1)		D	0	2		2
							1		8
5+	31/05/1962	Pakistan	Edgbaston		W		1		8
							1		1
6+	21/06/1962	Pakistan	Lord's		W	7	1		1
							1		6

Batting & Fielding

Mat	Inns	N/O	Runs	H/S	Avg	100s	50s	Cat	St	Byes
6	7	2	60	32*	12.00	0	0	13	2	47

C.A.MILTON

Full Name: Clement Arthur Milton (known as Arthur)
Born: 10/03/1928, Bedminster, Somerset
Teams: Gloucestershire 1948-74, England 1958-59
Matches: 6 (Won 3, Drew 2, Lost 1)
Right-hand opening batsman – Right-arm medium bowler

No	Date	Opposition	Venue		R	Bat	C		Bowling
1	03/07/1958	New Zealand	Headingley		W	104*	2		

No	Date	Opposition	Venue	R	Bat	C	Bowling			
2	21/08/1958	New Zealand	The Oval	D	36	2				
							4	2	12	0
3	05/12/1958	Australia	Brisbane (2)	L	5					
					17	1				
4	09/01/1959	Australia	Sydney	D	8					
					8					
5	04/06/1959	India	Trent Bridge	W	9					
6	18/06/1959	India	Lord's	W	14					
					3					

Batting & Fielding

Mat	Inns	N/O	Runs	H/S	Avg	100s	50s	Cat
6	9	1	204	104*	25.50	1	0	5

Bowling

Balls	Runs	Wkts	Avg	Best	5WI	10WM	S/R
24	12	0	–	0-12	0	0	

A.MITCHELL

Full Name: Arthur Mitchell (also known as Ticker)
Born: 13/09/1902, Baildon Green, Yorkshire
Died: 25/12/1976, Bradford, Yorkshire
Teams: Yorkshire 1922-45, England 1933-36
Matches: 6 (Won 3, Drew 3, Lost 0)
Right-hand middle order batsman – Right-arm slow bowler

No	Date	Opposition	Venue	R	Bat	C	Bowling			
1	15/12/1933	India	Bombay (1)	W	5	2				
					9					
2	05/01/1934	India	Calcutta	D	47					
3	10/02/1934	India	Madras (1)	W	25	1				
					28	2				
4	13/07/1935	South Africa	Headingley	D	58	1				
					72		1	0	4	0
5	17/08/1935	South Africa	The Oval	D	40	1				
6	27/06/1936	India	Lord's	W	14	1				
					0	1				

Batting & Fielding

Mat	Inns	N/O	Runs	H/S	Avg	100s	50s	Cat
6	10	0	298	72	29.80	0	2	9

Bowling

Balls	Runs	Wkts	Avg	Best	5WI	10WM	S/R
6	4	0	–	0-4	0	0	–

F.MITCHELL

Full Name: Frank Mitchell
Born: 13/08/1872, Market Weighton, Yorkshire
Died: 11/10/1935, Blackheath, Kent
Teams: Cambridge University 1894-97, Yorkshire 1894-1904, London County 1901,
Transvaal 1902/03-03/04, South Africa 1912, England 1899
Matches: 2 (Won 2, Drew 0, Lost 0), 3 (Won 0, Drew 0, Lost 3)
Right-hand middle order batsman – Right-arm medium bowler

No	Date	Opposition	Venue	R	Bat	C
1	14/02/1899	South Africa	Johannesburg (1)	W	28	1
					1	
2	01/04/1899	South Africa	Cape Town	W	18	
					41	1

For South Africa

No	Date	Opposition	Venue	R	Bat	C
1*	27/05/1912	Australia	Old Trafford	L	11	
					0	
2*	10/06/1912	England	Lord's	L	1	
					1	
3*	15/07/1912	Australia	Lord's	L	12	
					3	

Batting & Fielding

Mat	Inns	N/O	Runs	H/S	Avg	100s	50s	Cat	
2	4	0	88	41	22.00	0	0	2	(England)
3	6	0	28	12	4.66	0	0	0	(South Africa)
5	10	0	116	41	11.60	0	0	2	(Total)

T.B.MITCHELL

Full Name: Thomas Bignall Mitchell (known as Tommy)
Born: 04/09/1902, Creswell, Derbyshire
Died: 27/01/1996, Hickleton, Doncaster, Yorkshire
Teams: Derbyshire 1928-39, England 1933-35
Matches: 5 (Won 1, Drew 2, Lost 2)
Right-hand lower order batsman – Leg break & googly bowler

No	Date	Opposition	Venue	R	Bat	C		Bowling		
1	10/02/1933	Australia	Brisbane (2)	W	0		16	5	49	2
						1	5	0	11	1
2	31/03/1933	New Zealand	Auckland	D			18	1	49	1
3	08/06/1934	Australia	Trent Bridge	L	1*		21	4	62	1
					4		13	2	46	0
4	20/07/1934	Australia	Headingley	D	9		23	1	117	0
5	29/06/1935	South Africa	Lord's	L	5*		20	3	71	1
					1		33	5	93	2

Batting & Fielding

Mat	Inns	N/O	Runs	H/S	Avg	100s	50s	Cat
5	6	2	20	9	5.00	0	0	1

Bowling

Balls	Runs	Wkts	Avg	Best	5WI	10WM	S/R
894	498	8	62.25	2-49	0	0	111.75

N.S.MITCHELL-INNES

Full Name: Norman Stewart Mitchell-Innes
Born: 07/09/1914, Calcutta, India
Teams: Oxford University 1934-37, Somerset 1931-49, Scotland 1937, England 1935,
Matches: 1 (Won 0, Drew 1, Lost 0)
Right-hand middle order batsman – Right-arm medium bowler (previously right-arm fast)

No	Date	Opposition	Venue	R	Bat	C
1	15/06/1935	South Africa	Trent Bridge	D	5	

Batting & Fielding

Mat	Inns	N/O	Runs	H/S	Avg	100s	50s	Cat
1	1	0	5	5	5.00	0	0	0

A.W.MOLD

Full Name: Arthur Webb Mold
Born: 27/05/1863, Middleton Cheney, Northamptonshire
Died: 29/04/1921, Middleton Cheney, Northamptonshire
Teams: Lancashire 1889-1901, England 1893
Matches: 3 (Won 1, Drew 2, Lost 0)
Right-hand lower order batsman – Right-arm fast bowler

No	Date	Opposition	Venue	R	Bat	C		Bowling		
1	17/07/1893	Australia	Lord's	D	0		20.1	7	44	3
2	14/08/1893	Australia	The Oval	W	0*		4	0	12	0
							23	8	73	1
3	24/08/1893	Australia	Old Trafford	D	0		28	11	48	1
						1	23	6	57	2

Batting & Fielding

Mat	Inns	N/O	Runs	H/S	Avg	100s	50s	Cat
3	3	1	0	0*	0.00	0	0	1

Bowling

Balls	Runs	Wkts	Avg	Best	5WI	10WM	S/R
491	234	7	33.42	3-44	0	0	70.14

L.J.MOON

Full Name: Leonard James Moon
Born: 09/02/1878, Kensington, London
Died: 23/11/1916, near Karasouli, Salonica, Greece
Teams: Cambridge University 1897-1900, Middlesex 1899-1909, England 1906
Matches: 4 (Won 1, Drew 0, Lost 3)
Right-hand opening batsman – Wicket-keeper

No	Date	Opposition	Venue	R	Bat	C	St	B
1	06/03/1906	South Africa	Johannesburg (1)	L	30			
					0			
2+	10/03/1906	South Africa	Johannesburg (1)	L	36	1		10
					15			9
3	24/03/1906	South Africa	Cape Town	W	33	1		
					28			
4	30/03/1906	South Africa	Cape Town	L	7	2		
					33			

Batting & Fielding

Mat	Inns	N/O	Runs	H/S	Avg	100s	50s	Cat	St	Byes
4	8	0	182	36	22.75	0	0	4	0	19

F.MORLEY

Full Name: Frederick Morley
Born: 16/12/1850, Sutton-in-Ashfield, Nottinghamshire
Died: 28/09/1884, Sutton-in-Ashfield, Nottinghamshire
Teams: Nottinghamshire 1872-83, England 1880-83
Matches: 4 (Won 3, Drew 0, Lost 1)
Left-hand lower order batsman – Left-arm fast bowler

No	Date	Opposition	Venue	R	Bat	C		Bowling		
1	06/09/1880	Australia	The Oval	W	2	2	32	9	56	5
							61	30	90	3
2	19/01/1883	Australia	Melbourne	W	0*		23	16	13	0
						2	2	0	7	0
3	26/01/1883	Australia	Sydney	W	2*		34	16	47	4
					0		35	19	34	2
4	17/02/1883	Australia	Sydney	L	0		44	25	45	2
					2		12	9	4	0

Batting & Fielding

Mat	Inns	N/O	Runs	H/S	Avg	100s	50s	Cat
4	6	2	6	2*	1.50	0	0	4

Bowling

Balls	Runs	Wkts	Avg	Best	5WI	10WM	S/R
972	296	16	18.50	5-56	1	0	60.75

H.MORRIS

Full Name: Hugh Morris
Born: 05/10/1963, Canton, Cardiff, Glamorgan
Teams: Glamorgan 1981-96, England 1991
Matches: 3 (Won 2, Drew 0, Lost 1)
Left-hand opening batsman – Right-arm medium bowler

No	Date	Opposition	Venue	R	Bat	C
1	25/07/1991	West Indies	Edgbaston	L	3	
					1	
2	08/08/1991	West Indies	The Oval	W	44	
					2	1
3	22/08/1991	Sri Lanka	Lord's	W	42	1
					23	1

Batting & Fielding

Mat	Inns	N/O	Runs	H/S	Avg	100s	50s	Cat
3	6	0	115	44	19.16	0	0	3

J.E.MORRIS

Full Name: John Edward Morris
Born: 01/04/1964, Crewe, Cheshire
Teams: Derbyshire 1982-93, Durham 1994-96, Griqualand West 1988/89, England 1990
Matches: 3 (Won 1, Drew 2, Lost 0)
Right-hand middle order batsman – Right-arm medium bowler

No	Date	Opposition	Venue	R	Bat	C
1	26/07/1990	India	Lord's	W	4*	2
						1
2	09/08/1990	India	Old Trafford	D	13	
					15*	
3	23/08/1990	India	The Oval	D	7	
					32	

Batting & Fielding

Mat	Inns	N/O	Runs	H/S	Avg	100s	50s	Cat
3	5	2	71	32	23.66	0	0	3

J.B.MORTIMORE

Full Name: John Brian Mortimore
Born: 14/05/1933, Southmead, Bristol
Teams: Gloucestershire 1950-75, England 1959-64
Matches: 9 (Won 3, Drew 5, Lost 1)
Right-hand lower order batsman – Off break bowler

No	Date	Opposition	Venue	R	Bat	C	Bowling		
1	13/02/1959	Australia	Melbourne	L	44*		11	1	41	1
					11					
2	27/02/1959	New Zealand	Christchurch	W	11		22	8	40	1
							21	10	27	1
3	14/03/1959	New Zealand	Auckland	D	9		4	1	24	0
4	02/07/1959	India	Headingley	W	7		8	3	24	0
							18.4	6	36	3
5	23/07/1959	India	Old Trafford	W	29		13	6	46	0
					7		16	6	29	1
6	10/01/1964	India	Madras (2)	D	0		38	7	110	0
					73*		15	3	41	2
7	08/02/1964	India	Delhi	D	21	1	38	13	74	3
						1	32	11	52	0
8	15/02/1964	India	Kanpur	D	19	1	48	31	39	1
							23	14	28	0
9	23/07/1964	Australia	Old Trafford	D	12		49	13	122	0

Batting & Fielding

Mat	Inns	N/O	Runs	H/S	Avg	100s	50s	Cat
9	12	2	243	73*	24.30	0	1	3

Bowling

Balls	Runs	Wkts	Avg	Best	5WI	10WM	S/R
2162	733	13	56.38	3-36	0	0	166.30

A.E.MOSS

Full Name: Alan Edward Moss
Born: 14/11/1930, Tottenham, Middlesex
Teams: Middlesex 1950-63, England 1954-60
Matches: 9 (Won 5, Drew 3, Lost 1)
Right-hand lower order batsman – Right-arm fast medium bowler

No	Date	Opposition	Venue	R	Bat	C	Bowling		
1	15/01/1954	West Indies	Kingston	L	0		26	5	84	1
					16		10	0	30	1
2	07/06/1956	Australia	Trent Bridge	D			4	3	1	0
3	04/06/1959	India	Trent Bridge	W	11		24	11	33	2
							12	7	13	0

No	Date	Opposition	Venue	R	Bat	C	Bowling			
4	18/06/1959	India	Lord's	W	26		14	5	31	0
							23	10	30	2
5	02/07/1959	India	Headingley	W		1	22	11	30	2
							6	3	10	1
6	06/01/1960	West Indies	Bridgetown	D	4		47	14	116	0
7	25/03/1960	West Indies	Port-of-Spain	D	1		34	3	94	2
							4	0	16	1
8	23/06/1960	South Africa	Lord's	W			10.3	0	35	4
							14	1	41	1
9	07/07/1960	South Africa	Trent Bridge	W	3*		10	3	26	1
							15.4	3	36	3

Batting & Fielding

Mat	Inns	N/O	Runs	H/S	Avg	100s	50s	Cat
9	7	1	61	26	10.16	0	0	1

Bowling

Balls	Runs	Wkts	Avg	Best	5WI	10WM	S/R
1657	626	21	29.80	4-35	0	0	78.90

M.D.MOXON

Full Name: Martyn Douglas Moxon
Born: 04/05/1960, Stairfoot, Barnsley, Yorkshire
Teams: Yorkshire 1981-96, Griqualand West 1982/83-83/84, England 1986-89
Matches: 10 (Won 0, Drew 6, Lost 4)
Right-hand opening batsman – Right-arm medium bowler

No	Date	Opposition	Venue	R	Bat	C	Bowling			
1	24/07/1986	New Zealand	Lord's	D	74					
					5					
2	07/08/1986	New Zealand	Trent Bridge	L	9	1				
					23					
3	06/08/1987	Pakistan	The Oval	D	8	3	6	2	27	0
					15					
4	29/01/1988	Australia	Sydney	D	40					
						1				
5	12/02/1988	New Zealand	Christchurch	D	1	2				
					27					
6	25/02/1988	New Zealand	Auckland	D	99	2				
							2	0	3	0
7	03/03/1988	New Zealand	Wellington	D	81*					
8	16/06/1988	West Indies	Lord's	L	26	1				
					14					
9	30/06/1988	West Indies	Old Trafford	L	0					
					15					
10	10/08/1989	Australia	Trent Bridge	L	0					
					18					

Batting & Fielding

Mat	Inns	N/O	Runs	H/S	Avg	100s	50s	Cat
10	17	1	455	99	28.43	0	3	10

Bowling

Balls	Runs	Wkts	Avg	Best	5WI	10WM	S/R
48	30	0	–	0-3	0	0	–

A.D.MULLALLY

Full Name: Alan David Mullally
Born: 12/07/1969, Southend-on-Sea, Essex
Teams: Hampshire 1988, Leicestershire 1990-96, Western Australia 1987/88-89/90,
Victoria 1990-91, England 1996
Matches: 6 (Won 1, Drew 3, Lost 2)
Right-hand lower order batsman – Left-arm fast medium bowler

No	Date	Opposition	Venue	R	Bat	C	Bowling			
1	06/06/1996	India	Edgbaston	W	14*		22	7	60	3
							15	4	43	2

No	Date	Opposition	Venue	R	Bat	C		Bowling		
2	20/06/1996	India	Lord's	D	0*		39	14	71	3
					0*					
3	04/07/1996	India	Trent Bridge	D	1		40	12	88	2
							13	3	36	2
4	25/07/1996	Pakistan	Lord's	L	0		24	8	44	3
					6		30.2	9	70	1
5	08/08/1996	Pakistan	Headingley	D	9*		41	10	99	2
							15	2	43	0
6	22/08/1996	Pakistan	The Oval	L	24		37.1	7	97	3
					0		3	0	24	1

Batting & Fielding

Mat	Inns	N/O	Runs	H/S	Avg	100s	50s	Cat
6	9	4	54	24	10.80	0	0	0

Bowling

Balls	Runs	Wkts	Avg	Best	5WI	10WM	S/R
1677	675	22	30.68	3-44	0	0	76.22

T.A.MUNTON

Full Name: Timothy Alan Munton (known as Tim)
Born: 30/07/1965, Melton Mowbray, Leicestershire
Teams: Warwickshire 1985-96, England 1992
Matches: 2 (Won 1, Drew 1, Lost 0)
Right-hand lower order batsman – Right-arm fast medium bowler

No	Date	Opposition	Venue	R	Bat	C		Bowling		
1	02/07/1992	Pakistan	Old Trafford	D	25*		30	6	112	1
							17	6	26	0
2	23/07/1992	Pakistan	Headingley	W	0		10.3	3	22	2
							10	0	40	1

Batting & Fielding

Mat	Inns	N/O	Runs	H/S	Avg	100s	50s	Cat
2	2	1	25	25*	25.00	0	0	0

Bowling

Balls	Runs	Wkts	Avg	Best	5WI	10WM	S/R
405	200	4	50.00	2-22	0	0	101.25

W.L.MURDOCH

Full Name: William Lloyd Murdoch (known as Billy)
Born: 18/10/1854, Sandhurst, Australia
Died: 18/02/1911, Melbourne, Victoria, Australia
Teams: Sussex 1893-99, London County 1901-04, New South Wales 1875/76-93/94, Australia 1877-90, England 1892
Matches: 1 (Won 1, Drew 0, Lost 0), 18 (Won 6, Drew 4, Lost 8)
Right-hand opening/middle order batsman – Wicket-keeper

No	Date	Opposition	Venue	R	Bat	C	St	B
1	19/03/1892	South Africa	Cape Town	W	12			
							1	7

For Australia

No	Date	Opposition	Venue	R	Bat	C	St	B
1	31/03/1877	England	Melbourne	L	3			
					8	1		
2	02/01/1879	England	Melbourne	W	4			
					4*			
3*	06/09/1880	England	The Oval	L	0			
					153*			
4*	31/12/1881	England	Melbourne	D	39			
					22*			
5*+	17/02/1882	England	Sydney	W	10	1	1	0
					49			
6*	03/03/1882	England	Sydney	W	6			
					4			
7*	10/03/1882	England	Melbourne	D	85	1		
8*	28/08/1882	England	The Oval	W	13			
					29	1		

No	Date	Opposition	Venue	R	Bat	C	St	B
9*	30/12/1882	England	Melbourne	W	48			
					33*			
10*	19/01/1883	England	Melbourne	L	19*			
					17			
11*	26/01/1883	England	Sydney	L	19	1		
					0	1		
12*	17/02/1883	England	Sydney	W	0	1		
					17	3		
13*	10/07/1884	England	Old Trafford	D	28			
14*	21/07/1884	England	Lord's	L	10			
					17			
15*	11/08/1884	England	The Oval	D	211	1		
16*	12/12/1884	England	Adelaide	L	5			
					7			
17*	21/07/1890	England	Lord's	L	9			
					19			
18*	11/08/1890	England	The Oval	L	2	2		
					6			

Batting & Fielding

Mat	Inns	N/O	Runs	H/S	Avg	100s	50s	Cat	St	B	
1	1	0	12	12	12.00	0	0	0	1	7	(Eng)
18	33	5	896	211	32.00	2	1	13	1	0	(Aus)
19	34	5	908	211	31.31	2	1	13	2	7	(Tot)

J.T.MURRAY

Full Name: John Thomas Murray, MBE
Born: 01/04/1935, North Kensington, London
Teams: Middlesex 1952-75, England 1961-67
Matches: 21 (Won 9, Drew 9, Lost 3)
Right-hand lower order batsman – Wicket-keeper – Right-arm medium bowler

No	Date	Opposition	Venue	R	Bat	C	St	B
1+	08/06/1961	Australia	Edgbaston	D	16	1		8
2+	22/06/1961	Australia	Lord's	L	18	2		1
					25	2		0
3+	06/07/1961	Australia	Headingley	W	6	1	1	7
						2		0
4+	27/07/1961	Australia	Old Trafford	L	24	3		4
					4	4		6
5+	17/08/1961	Australia	The Oval	D	27	2		10
					40			
6+	21/10/1961	Pakistan	Lahore (2)	W	4	3		4
						2		9
7+	11/11/1961	India	Bombay (2)	D	8			33
					2			4
8+	01/12/1961	India	Kanpur	D	2		1	2
					9*			
9+	13/12/1961	India	Delhi	D				2
10+	05/07/1962	Pakistan	Headingley	W	29	1		8
						1		0
11+	26/07/1962	Pakistan	Trent Bridge	D		4		2
						1		0
12+	16/08/1962	Pakistan	The Oval	W		3		0
					14*			4
13+	11/01/1963	Australia	Sydney	L	0	1		10
					3*			
14+	23/02/1963	New Zealand	Auckland	W	9*	2		5
								2
15	12/02/1965	South Africa	Port Elizabeth	D	4			
					8*			
16+	04/03/1966	New Zealand	Dunedin	D	50	4		4
								10
17+	18/08/1966	West Indies	The Oval	W	112	1		1
						2		1
18+	08/06/1967	India	Headingley	W		1		0
					4	1		10
19+	22/06/1967	India	Lord's	W	7	6		2
								11

No	Date	Opposition	Venue	R	Bat	C	St	B
20+	13/07/1967	India	Edgbaston	W	77		1	4
					4	1		5
21+	27/07/1967	Pakistan	Lord's	D	0	1		1
					0			1

Batting & Fielding

Mat	Inns	N/O	Runs	H/S	Avg	100s	50s	Cat	St	Byes
21	28	5	506	112	22.00	1	2	52	3	171

W.NEWHAM

Full Name: William Newham (known as Billy)
Born: 12/12/1860, Shrewsbury, Shropshire
Died: 26/06/1944, Portslade, Brighton, Sussex
Teams: Sussex 1881-1905, England 1888
Matches: 1 (Won 1, Drew 0, Lost 0)
Right-hand middle order batsman

No	Date	Opposition	Venue	R	Bat	C
1	10/02/1888	Australia	Sydney	W	9	
					17	

Batting & Fielding

Mat	Inns	N/O	Runs	H/S	Avg	100s	50s	Cat
1	2	0	26	17	13.00	0	0	0

P.J.NEWPORT

Full Name: Philip John Newport (known as Phil)
Born: 11/10/1962, High Wycombe, Buckinghamshire
Teams: Worcestershire 1982-96, Boland 1987/88, England 1988-91
Matches: 3 (Won 1, Drew 0, Lost 2)
Right-hand lower order batsman – Right-arm fast medium bowler

No	Date	Opposition	Venue	R	Bat	C		Bowling	
1	25/08/1988	Sri Lanka	Lord's	W	26		21	4	77	3
							26.3	7	87	4
2	08/06/1989	Australia	Headingley	L	36	1	39	5	153	2
					8		5	2	22	0
3	01/02/1991	Australia	Perth	L	0		14	0	56	1
					40*		6	0	22	0

Batting & Fielding

Mat	Inns	N/O	Runs	H/S	Avg	100s	50s	Cat
3	5	1	110	40*	27.50	0	0	1

Bowling

Balls	Runs	Wkts	Avg	Best	5WI	10WM	S/R
669	417	10	41.70	4-87	0	0	66.90

M.S.NICHOLS

Full Name: Morris Stanley Nichols (also known as Stan)
Born: 06/10/1900, Stondon Massey, Essex
Died: 26/01/1961, Newark, Nottinghamshire
Teams: Essex 1924-39, England 1930-39
Matches: 14 (Won 4, Drew 9, Lost 1)
Left-hand middle order batsman – Right-arm fast bowler

No	Date	Opposition	Venue	R	Bat	C		Bowling	
1	10/01/1930	New Zealand	Christchurch	W	21	2	17	5	28	4
							14.3	6	23	2
2	24/01/1930	New Zealand	Wellington	D	78*		20	5	66	0
					3*		9	1	22	1
3	14/02/1930	New Zealand	Auckland	D	1*		5	0	18	0
4	21/02/1930	New Zealand	Auckland	D	75		19	4	45	1
					7*					
5	25/07/1930	Australia	Old Trafford	D	7*		21	5	33	2
6	12/08/1933	West Indies	The Oval	W	49		10	1	36	1
							14	3	51	2

No	Date	Opposition	Venue	R	Bat	C		Bowling	
7	15/12/1933	India	Bombay (1)	W	2	1	23.2	8	53	3
						2	23.5	7	55	5
8	05/01/1934	India	Calcutta	D	13	2	28	6	78	3
						1	20	6	48	1
9	10/02/1934	India	Madras (1)	W	1	1	12	3	30	1
					8	1	6	1	23	0
10	15/06/1935	South Africa	Trent Bridge	D	13*	1	23.5	9	35	6
							5	1	14	1
11	29/06/1935	South Africa	Lord's	L	10		21	5	47	2
					7*		18	4	64	1
12	13/07/1935	South Africa	Headingley	D	4		21.4	4	58	3
					2		22	5	65	0
13	17/08/1935	South Africa	The Oval	D	30		23	3	79	0
							5	1	20	0
14	19/08/1939	West Indies	The Oval	D	24		34	4	161	2

Batting & Fielding

Mat	Inns	N/O	Runs	H/S	Avg	100s	50s	Cat
14	19	7	355	78*	29.58	0	2	11

Bowling

Balls	Runs	Wkts	Avg	Best	5WI	10WM	S/R
2565	1152	41	28.09	6-35	2	0	62.56

A.S.M.OAKMAN

Full Name: Alan Stanley Myles Oakman
Born: 20/04/1930, Hastings, Sussex
Teams: Sussex 1947-68, England 1956
Matches: 2 (Won 2, Drew 0, Lost 0)
Right-hand middle order batsman – Off break bowler

No	Date	Opposition	Venue	R	Bat	C		Bowling	
1	12/07/1956	Australia	Headingley	W	4	1			
						1			
2	26/07/1956	Australia	Old Trafford	W	10	2			
						3	8	3	21	0

Batting & Fielding

Mat	Inns	N/O	Runs	H/S	Avg	100s	50s	Cat
2	2	0	14	10	7.00	0	0	7

Bowling

Balls	Runs	Wkts	Avg	Best	5WI	10WM	S/R
48	21	0	–	0-21	0	0	–

T.C.O'BRIEN

Full Name: Sir Timothy Carew O'Brien (known as Tim or Timmy)
Born: 05/11/1861, Dublin, Ireland
Died: 09/12/1948, Ramsey, Isle of Man
Teams: Oxford University 1884-85, Middlesex 1881-98, Ireland 1902-07, England 1884-96
Matches: 5 (Won 3, Drew 1, Lost 1)
England Captain: Once 1896 (Won 1, Drew 0, Lost 0) **Toss:** 0-1
Right-hand middle order batsman – Left-arm bowler

No	Date	Opposition	Venue	R	Bat	C
1	10/07/1884	Australia	Old Trafford	D	0	
					20	
2	16/07/1888	Australia	Lord's	L	0	1
					4	
3*	13/02/1896	South Africa	Port Elizabeth	W	17	1
					16	1
4	02/03/1896	South Africa	Johannesburg (1)	W	0	1
5	21/03/1896	South Africa	Cape Town	W	2	

Batting & Fielding

Mat	Inns	N/O	Runs	H/S	Avg	100s	50s	Cat
5	8	0	59	20	7.37	0	0	4

J.O'CONNOR

Full Name: Jack O'Connor
Born: 06/11/1897, Cambridge
Died: 22/02/1977, Buckhurst Hill, Essex
Teams: Essex 1921-39, England 1929-30
Matches: 4 (Won 1, Drew 3, Lost 0)
Right-hand middle order batsman – Leg break & off break bowler

No	Date	Opposition	Venue	R	Bat	C		Bowling	
1	29/06/1929	South Africa	Lord's	D	0				
					11				
2	11/01/1930	West Indies	Bridgetown	D	37		10	0	31	1
						2			
3	01/02/1930	West Indies	Port-of-Spain	W	30				
					21		4	1	9	0
4	03/04/1930	West Indies	Kingston	D	51		2	2	0	0
					3		11	3	32	0

Batting & Fielding

Mat	Inns	N/O	Runs	H/S	Avg	100s	50s	Cat
4	7	0	153	51	21.85	0	1	2

Bowling

Balls	Runs	Wkts	Avg	Best	5WI	10WM	S/R
162	72	1	72.00	1-31	0	0	162.00

C.M.OLD

Full Name: Christopher Middleton Old (known as Chris)
Born: 22/12/1948, Middlesbrough, Yorkshire
Teams: Yorkshire 1966-82, Warwickshire 1983-85, Northern Transvaal 1981/82-82/83,
England 1972-81
Matches: 46 (Won 17, Drew 20, Lost 9)
Left-hand lower order batsman – Right-arm fast medium bowler

No	Date	Opposition	Venue	R	Bat	C		Bowling		
1	30/12/1972	India	Calcutta	L	33*	1	26	7	72	2
					17*		21	6	43	4
2	12/01/1973	India	Madras (1)	L	4	1	20	4	51	0
					9		9	3	19	2
3	25/01/1973	India	Kanpur	D	4	1	24	5	69	4
						1	11	3	28	0
4	06/02/1973	India	Bombay (2)	D	28	1	21.2	2	78	3
							3	1	11	0
5	02/03/1973	Pakistan	Lahore (2)	D	0		27	2	98	0
					17*					
6	21/06/1973	New Zealand	Lord's	D	7		41.5	7	113	5
					7					
7	05/07/1973	New Zealand	Headingley	W	34		20	4	71	4
							14	1	41	2
8	09/08/1973	West Indies	Edgbaston	D	0		30	3	86	3
							14	0	65	1
9	02/02/1974	West Indies	Port-of-Spain	L	11		20.4	2	89	3
					3		3	0	18	0
10	16/02/1974	West Indies	Kingston	D	2		23	6	72	2
					19					
11	06/03/1974	West Indies	Bridgetown	D	1		28	4	102	0
					0					
12	22/03/1974	West Indies	Georgetown	D	14		13	3	32	0
13	06/06/1974	India	Old Trafford	W	12		16	0	46	1
							16	7	20	4
14	20/06/1974	India	Lord's	W	3		21	6	67	4
							8	3	21	5
15	04/07/1974	India	Edgbaston	W		1	13	0	43	1
							15	3	52	3
16	25/07/1974	Pakistan	Headingley	D	0		21	4	65	3
					10*		17	0	54	3
17	08/08/1974	Pakistan	Lord's	D	41	1	5	0	17	0
							14	1	39	2
18	22/08/1974	Pakistan	The Oval	D	65	1	29.3	3	143	0
							2	0	6	1
19	13/12/1974	Australia	Perth	L	7		22.6	3	85	3
					43					

No	Date	Opposition	Venue	R	Bat	C	Bowling			
20	08/02/1975	Australia	Melbourne	W	0		11	0	50	3
							18	1	75	0
21	20/02/1975	New Zealand	Auckland	W	9*	1	7	3	17	1
22	10/07/1975	Australia	Edgbaston	L	13	1	33	7	111	2
					7					
23	14/08/1975	Australia	Headingley	D	5	1	11	3	30	1
					10		17	5	61	1
24	28/08/1975	Australia	The Oval	D	25*	1	28	7	74	3
					0	1	2	0	7	0
25	03/06/1976	West Indies	Trent Bridge	D	33		34.3	7	80	3
						1	10	0	64	1
26	17/06/1976	West Indies	Lord's	D	19	1	10	0	58	1
					13		14	4	46	1
27	17/12/1976	India	Delhi	W	15		12.5	0	28	2
							4	2	6	0
28	01/01/1977	India	Calcutta	W	52	1	20	5	37	2
							12	4	38	3
29	14/01/1977	India	Madras (1)	W	2		13	4	19	2
					4	2	5	1	11	0
30	28/01/1977	India	Bangalore	L	9		12	0	43	0
					13	1	10	4	19	1
31	12/03/1977	Australia	Melbourne	L	3		12	4	39	3
					2		27.6	2	104	4
32	16/06/1977	Australia	Lord's	D	9	1	35	10	70	2
					0		14	0	46	2
33	07/07/1977	Australia	Old Trafford	W	37	1	20	3	57	1
							8	1	26	0
34	14/12/1977	Pakistan	Lahore (2)	D	2		21	7	63	1
							4	0	18	0
35	10/02/1978	New Zealand	Wellington	L	10		30	11	54	6
					9		9	2	32	1
36	24/02/1978	New Zealand	Christchurch	W	8		14	4	55	0
					1		7	4	9	1
37	01/06/1978	Pakistan	Edgbaston	W	5		22.4	6	50	7
						1	25	12	38	1
38	15/06/1978	Pakistan	Lord's	W	0		10	3	26	1
							15	4	36	0
39	29/06/1978	Pakistan	Headingley	D			41.4	22	41	4
40	27/07/1978	New Zealand	The Oval	W	16		20	7	43	1
							5	2	13	0
41	01/12/1978	Australia	Brisbane (2)	W	29*		9.7	1	24	2
							17	1	60	2
42	07/08/1980	West Indies	Headingley	D	6		28.5	9	64	2
43	28/08/1980	Australia	Lord's	D	24*		35	9	91	3
							20	6	47	3
44	13/02/1981	West Indies	Port-of-Spain	L	1		16	4	49	1
					0					
45	16/07/1981	Australia	Headingley	W	0		43	14	91	0
					29		9	1	21	1
46	30/07/1981	Australia	Edgbaston	W	11*		21	8	44	3
					23		11	4	19	1

Batting & Fielding

Mat	Inns	N/O	Runs	H/S	Avg	100s	50s	Cat
46	66	9	845	65	14.82	0	2	22

Bowling

Balls	Runs	Wkts	Avg	Best	5WI	10WM	S/R
8858	4020	143	28.11	7-50	4	0	61.94

N.OLDFIELD

Full Name: Norman Oldfield (known as Buddy)
Born: 05/05/1911, Dukinfield, Cheshire
Died: 19/04/1996, Cleveleys, Blackpool
Teams: Lancashire 1935-39, Northamptonshire 1948-54, England 1939
Matches: 1 (Won 0, Drew 1, Lost 0)
Right-hand opening batsman

No	Date	Opposition	Venue	R	Bat	C
1	19/08/1939	West Indies	The Oval	D	80	
					19	

Batting & Fielding

Mat	Inns	N/O	Runs	H/S	Avg	100s	50s	Cat
1	2	0	99	80	49.50	0	1	0

D.E.V.PADGETT

Full Name: Douglas Ernest Vernon Padgett (known as Doug)
Born: 20/07/1934, Dirk Hill, Bradford, Yorkshire
Teams: Yorkshire 1951-1971, England 1960
Matches: 2 (Won 0, Drew 2, Lost 0)
Right-hand opening/middle order batsman – Right-arm medium bowler

No	Date	Opposition	Venue	R	Bat	C		Bowling	
1	21/07/1960	South Africa	Old Trafford	D	5				
					2		2	0 8	0
2	18/08/1960	South Africa	The Oval	D	13				
					31				

Batting & Fielding

Mat	Inns	N/O	Runs	H/S	Avg	100s	50s	Cat
2	4	0	51	31	12.75	0	0	0

Bowling

Balls	Runs	Wkts	Avg	Best	5WI	10WM	S/R
12	8	0	–	0-8	0	0	–

G.A.E.PAINE

Full Name: George Alfred Edward Paine
Born: 11/06/1908, Paddington, London
Died: 30/03/1978, Solihull, Warwickshire
Teams: Middlesex 1926, Warwickshire 1929-47, England 1935
Matches: 4 (Won 1, Drew 1, Lost 2)
Right-hand lower order batsman – Left-arm slow bowler

No	Date	Opposition	Venue	R	Bat	C		Bowling		
1	08/01/1935	West Indies	Bridgetown	W		2	9	3	14	3
					2	2	1	1	0	0
2	24/01/1935	West Indies	Port-of-Spain	L	4		26	6	85	2
					14		42	10	109	3
3	14/02/1935	West Indies	Georgetown	D	49	1	33	7	63	2
					18		7	0	28	2
4	14/03/1935	West Indies	Kingston	L	0		56	12	168	5
					10*					

Batting & Fielding

Mat	Inns	N/O	Runs	H/S	Avg	100s	50s	Cat
4	7	1	97	49	16.16	0	0	5

Bowling

Balls	Runs	Wkts	Avg	Best	5WI	10WM	S/R
1044	467	17	27.47	5-168	1	0	61.41

L.C.H.PALAIRET

Full Name: Lionel Charles Hamilton Palairet
Born: 27/05/1870, Broughton East, Grange-over-Sands, Lancashire
Died: 27/03/1933, Exmouth, Devon
Teams: Oxford University 1890-93, Somerset 1891-1909, England 1902
Matches: 2 (Won 1, Drew 0, Lost 1)
Right-hand opening batsman – Right-arm medium bowler

No	Date	Opposition	Venue	R	Bat	C
1	24/07/1902	Australia	Old Trafford	L	6	1
					17	1
2	11/08/1902	Australia	The Oval	W	20	
					6	

Batting & Fielding

Mat	Inns	N/O	Runs	H/S	Avg	100s	50s	Cat
2	4	0	49	20	12.25	0	0	2

C.H.PALMER

Full Name: Charles Henry Palmer, CBE
Born: 15/05/1919, Old Hill, Staffordshire
Teams: Worcestershire 1938-49, Leicestershire 1950-59, Europeans 1945/46, England 1954
Matches: 1 (Won 0, Drew 0, Lost 1)
Right-hand middle order batsman – Right-arm medium or slow bowler

No	Date	Opposition	Venue	R	Bat	C		Bowling		
1	06/02/1954	West Indies	Bridgetown	L	22					
					0		5	1	15	0

Batting & Fielding

Mat	Inns	N/O	Runs	H/S	Avg	100s	50s	Cat
1	2	0	22	22	11.00	0	0	0

Bowling

Balls	Runs	Wkts	Avg	Best	5WI	10WM	S/R
30	15	0	–	0-15	0	0	–

K.E.PALMER

Full Name: Kenneth Ernest Palmer (known as Ken)
Born: 22/04/1937, Winchester, Hampshire
Teams: Somerset 1955-69, England 1965
Matches: 1 (Won 0, Drew 1, Lost 0)
Right-hand middle order batsman – Right-arm fast medium bowler

No	Date	Opposition	Venue	R	Bat	C		Bowling		
1	12/02/1965	South Africa	Port Elizabeth	D	10		35	6	113	1
							28	1	76	0

Batting & Fielding

Mat	Inns	N/O	Runs	H/S	Avg	100s	50s	Cat
1	1	0	10	10	10.00	0	0	0

Bowling

Balls	Runs	Wkts	Avg	Best	5WI	10WM	S/R
378	189	1	189.00	1-113	0	0	378.00

P.H.PARFITT

Full Name: Peter Howard Parfitt
Born: 08/12/1936, Billingford, Fakenham, Norfolk
Teams: Middlesex 1956-72, England 1961-72
Matches: 37 (Won 11, Drew 20, Lost 6)
Left-hand middle order batsman – Off break bowler

No	Date	Opposition	Venue	R	Bat	C		Bowling		
1	30/12/1961	India	Calcutta	L	21	2				
					46	2				
2	10/01/1962	India	Madras (2)	L	25		11	2	22	1
					33	3	11	3	24	1
3	19/01/1962	Pakistan	Dacca	D	9					
						1	8	3	14	0
4	02/02/1962	Pakistan	Karachi (1)	D	111	1				
						1	3	2	4	0
5	31/05/1962	Pakistan	Edgbaston	W	101*		2	1	2	0
						2				
6	21/06/1962	Pakistan	Lord's	W	16					
7	05/07/1962	Pakistan	Headingley	W	119					
8	26/07/1962	Pakistan	Trent Bridge	D	101*					
							1	0	5	0
9	16/08/1962	Pakistan	The Oval	W	3	2				
						1				

No	Date	Opposition	Venue	R	Bat	C	Bowling			
10	30/11/1962	Australia	Brisbane (2)	D	80 4					
11	11/01/1963	Australia	Sydney	L	0 28					
12	23/02/1963	New Zealand	Auckland	W	131*					
13	01/03/1963	New Zealand	Wellington	W	0					
14	15/03/1963	New Zealand	Christchurch	W	4 31	1 3 2				
15	29/01/1964	India	Calcutta	D	4	1	34	16	71	2
16	08/02/1964	India	Delhi	D	67		5 19	2 3	7 81	0 1
17	15/02/1964	India	Kanpur	D	121		30 27	12 7	61 68	1 1
18	18/06/1964	Australia	Lord's	D	20	2 2				
19	02/07/1964	Australia	Headingley	L	32 6	1				
20	23/07/1964	Australia	Old Trafford	D	12					
21	13/08/1964	Australia	The Oval	D	3	2				
22	04/12/1964	South Africa	Durban (2)	W	0					
23	23/12/1964	South Africa	Johannesburg (3)	D	52		2 4	0 2	6 6	0 0
24	01/01/1965	South Africa	Cape Town	D	44	1	8 19	0 4	28 74	0 1
25	22/01/1965	South Africa	Johannesburg (3)	D	122* 22	1				
26	12/02/1965	South Africa	Port Elizabeth	D	0	2				
27	17/06/1965	New Zealand	Lord's	W	11	1				
28	08/07/1965	New Zealand	Headingley	W	32		6	2	25	1
29	05/08/1965	South Africa	Trent Bridge	L	18 86	1 1				
30	26/08/1965	South Africa	The Oval	D	24 46					
31	25/02/1966	New Zealand	Christchurch	D	54 46*		3 6	0 3	14 5	0 2
32	04/03/1966	New Zealand	Dunedin	D	4	1 1				
33	11/03/1966	New Zealand	Auckland	D	3 30		17 2	6 0	30 9	1 0
34	26/06/1969	West Indies	Lord's	D	4 39		1	0	8	0
35	13/07/1972	Australia	Trent Bridge	D	0 46	4				
36	27/07/1972	Australia	Headingley	W	2 0*	1				
37	10/08/1972	Australia	The Oval	L	51 18		2	0	10	0

Batting & Fielding

Mat	Inns	N/O	Runs	H/S	Avg	100s	50s	Cat
37	52	6	1882	131*	40.91	7	6	42

Bowling

Balls	Runs	Wkts	Avg	Best	5WI	10WM	S/R
1326	574	12	47.83	2-5	0	0	110.50

C.W.L.PARKER

Full Name: Charles Warrington Leonard Parker (known as Charlie)
Born: 14/10/1882, Prestbury, Gloucestershire
Died: 11/07/1959, Cranleigh, Surrey
Teams: Gloucestershire 1903-35, England 1921
Matches: 1 (Won 0, Drew 1, Lost 0)
Right-hand lower order batsman – Left-arm slow bowler

No	Date	Opposition	Venue	R	Bat	C		Bowling		
1	23/07/1921	Australia	Old Trafford	D	3*		28	16	32	2

Batting & Fielding

Mat	Inns	N/O	Runs	H/S	Avg	100s	50s	Cat
1	1	1	3	3*	–	0	0	0

Bowling

Balls	Runs	Wkts	Avg	Best	5WI	10WM	S/R
168	32	2	16.00	2-32	0	0	84.00

P.W.G.PARKER

Full Name: Paul William Giles Parker
Born: 15/01/1956, Bulawayo, Rhodesia
Teams: Cambridge University 1976-78, Sussex 1976-91, Durham 1992-93, Natal 1980/81, England 1981
Matches: 1 (Won 0, Drew 1, Lost 0)
Right-hand middle order batsman – Right-arm medium or leg break bowler

No	Date	Opposition	Venue	R	Bat	C
1	27/08/1981	Australia	The Oval	D	0	
					13	

Batting & Fielding

Mat	Inns	N/O	Runs	H/S	Avg	100s	50s	Cat
1	2	0	13	13	6.50	0	0	0

W.G.A.PARKHOUSE

Full Name: William Gilbert Anthony Parkhouse (known as Gilbert)
Born: 12/10/1925, Swansea, Glamorgan
Teams: Glamorgan 1948-64, England 1950-59
Matches: 7 (Won 3, Drew 0, Lost 4)
Right-hand opening batsman – Right-arm medium bowler

No	Date	Opposition	Venue	R	Bat	C
1	24/06/1950	West Indies	Lord's	L	0	
					48	
2	20/07/1950	West Indies	Trent Bridge	L	13	
					69	
3	22/12/1950	Australia	Melbourne	L	9	1
					28	
4	05/01/1951	Australia	Sydney	L	25	
					15	
5	24/03/1951	New Zealand	Wellington	W	2	1
					20	
6	02/07/1959	India	Headingley	W	78	1
7	23/07/1959	India	Old Trafford	W	17	
					49	

Batting & Fielding

Mat	Inns	N/O	Runs	H/S	Avg	100s	50s	Cat
7	13	0	373	78	28.69	0	2	3

C.H.PARKIN

Full Name: Cecil Harry Parkin
Born: 18/02/1886, Eaglescliffe, Co Durham
Died: 15/06/1943, Cheetham Hill, Manchester, Lancashire
Teams: Yorkshire 1906, Lancashire 1914-26, England 1920-24
Matches: 10 (Won 1, Drew 2, Lost 7)
Right-hand lower order batsman – Right-arm slow off break & leg break bowler

No	Date	Opposition	Venue	R	Bat	C		Bowling		
1	17/12/1920	Australia	Sydney	L	4*		26.5	5	58	1
					4		35.3	5	102	3
2	31/12/1920	Australia	Melbourne	L	4		27	0	116	2
					9					

No	Date	Opposition	Venue	R	Bat	C		Bowling		
3	14/01/1921	Australia	Adelaide	L	12		20	2	60	5
					17		40	8	109	2
4	11/02/1921	Australia	Melbourne	L	10		22	5	64	1
					4		12	2	46	1
5	25/02/1921	Australia	Sydney	L	9		19	1	83	1
					36		9	1	32	0
6	11/06/1921	Australia	Lord's	L	0	2	20	5	72	2
					11		9	0	31	1
7	02/07/1921	Australia	Headingley	L	5*	1	20.1	0	106	4
					4		20	0	91	1
8	23/07/1921	Australia	Old Trafford	D			29.4	12	38	5
					23					
9	13/08/1921	Australia	The Oval	D			23	4	82	3
					23					
10	14/06/1924	South Africa	Edgbaston	W	8*					
							16	5	38	0

Batting & Fielding

Mat	Inns	N/O	Runs	H/S	Avg	100s	50s	Cat
10	16	3	160	36	12.30	0	0	3

Bowling

Balls	Runs	Wkts	Avg	Best	5WI	10WM	S/R
2095	1128	32	35.25	5-38	2	0	65.46

J.H.PARKS

Full Name: James Horace Parks (known as Jim)
Born: 12/05/1903, Haywards Heath, Sussex
Died: 21/11/1980, Cuckfield, Sussex
Teams: Sussex 1924-39, Canterbury 1946/47, England 1937
Matches: 1 (Won 0, Drew 1, Lost 0)
Right-hand opening/middle order batsman – Right-arm slow medium bowler

No	Date	Opposition	Venue	R	Bat	C		Bowling		
1	26/06/1937	New Zealand	Lord's	D	22		11	3	26	2
					7		10	6	10	1

Batting & Fielding

Mat	Inns	N/O	Runs	H/S	Avg	100s	50s	Cat
1	2	0	29	22	14.50	0	0	0

Bowling

Balls	Runs	Wkts	Avg	Best	5WI	10WM	S/R
126	36	3	12.00	2-26	0	0	42.00

J.M.PARKS

Full Name: James Michael Parks (known as Jim)
Born: 21/10/1931, Haywards Heath, Sussex
Teams: Sussex 1949-72, Somerset 1973-76, England 1954-68
Matches: 46 (Won 9, Drew 29, Lost 8)
Right-hand middle order batsman – Wicket-keeper – Leg break bowler

No	Date	Opposition	Venue	R	Bat	C	St	B	Bowling
1	22/07/1954	Pakistan	Old Trafford	D	15				
						1			
2+	25/03/1960	West Indies	Port-of-Spain	D	43	1	1	6	
					101*	1	1	0	
3+	09/06/1960	South Africa	Edgbaston	W	35	1		2	
					4	1		7	
4+	23/06/1960	South Africa	Lord's	W	3	3		0	
						3		0	
5+	07/07/1960	South Africa	Trent Bridge	W	16	1		4	
						4		0	
6+	21/07/1960	South Africa	Old Trafford	D	36	2		1	
					20			3	
7+	18/08/1960	South Africa	The Oval	D	23			6	
					17	1		0	
8+	20/06/1963	West Indies	Lord's	D	35			10	
					17	3		5	
9+	04/07/1963	West Indies	Edgbaston	W	12			0	
					5	3		0	

No	Date	Opposition	Venue	R	Bat	C	St	B	Bowling
10+	25/07/1963	West Indies	Headingley	L	22	2		4	
					57	1		0	
11+	22/08/1963	West Indies	The Oval	L	19	1		0	
					23			4	
12+	10/01/1964	India	Madras (2)	D	27	1		1	
					30	2	1	0	
13	21/01/1964	India	Bombay (2)	D	1				
					40*				
14	29/01/1964	India	Calcutta	D	30				
						1			
15+	08/02/1964	India	Delhi	D	32	1		0	
								5	
16+	15/02/1964	India	Kanpur	D	51*	2	1	5	
								5	6 0 43 1
17+	04/06/1964	Australia	Trent Bridge	D	15	2		0	
					19	1		0	
18+	18/06/1964	Australia	Lord's	D	12			8	
								8	
19+	02/07/1964	Australia	Headingley	L	68	1	1	1	
					23			1	
20+	23/07/1964	Australia	Old Trafford	D	60	1		1	
								0	
21+	13/08/1964	Australia	The Oval	D	10			4	
22+	04/12/1964	South Africa	Durban (2)	W	108*			4	
						1		9	
23+	23/12/1964	South Africa	Johannesburg (3)	D	26			0	
						1		4	
24+	01/01/1965	South Africa	Cape Town	D	59	2		5	
						2		1	
25+	22/01/1965	South Africa	Johannesburg (3)	D	0	2		0	
					10			0	
26+	12/02/1965	South Africa	Port Elizabeth	D	35			10	
								1	
27+	27/05/1965	New Zealand	Edgbaston	W	34	1		1	
						1		1	
28+	17/06/1965	New Zealand	Lord's	W	2	2	1	17	
						3		3	
29+	08/07/1965	New Zealand	Headingley	W		3		8	
								5	
30+	22/07/1965	South Africa	Lord's	D	32		1	0	
					7	2		4	
31+	05/08/1965	South Africa	Trent Bridge	L	6	2	1	4	
					44*			0	
32+	26/08/1965	South Africa	The Oval	D	42			0	
								1	
33+	10/12/1965	Australia	Brisbane (2)	D	52	2		0	
34+	30/12/1965	Australia	Melbourne	D	71	2		2	
							1	1	
35+	07/01/1966	Australia	Sydney	W	13	3	2	7	
								3	
36+	28/01/1966	Australia	Adelaide	L	49	4		4	
					16				
37+	11/02/1966	Australia	Melbourne	D	89	1		6	
38+	25/02/1966	New Zealand	Christchurch	D	30	5		7	
					4*	3		2	3 1 8 0
39+	11/03/1966	New Zealand	Auckland	D	38	1		2	
					45*	2		2	
40+	02/06/1966	West Indies	Old Trafford	L	43	1		8	
					11				
41+	16/06/1966	West Indies	Lord's	D	91	3		2	
					0	2		0	
42+	30/06/1966	West Indies	Trent Bridge	L	11	2		3	
					7			0	
43+	04/08/1966	West Indies	Headingley	L	2	1		1	
					16				
44+	19/01/1968	West Indies	Port-of-Spain	D	42	1		4	
								0	
45+	08/02/1968	West Indies	Kingston	D	3	3		12	
					3	2		33	
46+	29/02/1968	West Indies	Bridgetown	D	0	2		1	
						1		8	

Batting & Fielding

Mat	Inns	N/O	Runs	H/S	Avg	100s	50s	Cat	St	Byes
46	68	7	1962	108*	32.16	2	9	103	11	275

Bowling

Balls	Runs	Wkts	Avg	Best	5WI	10WM	S/R
54	51	1	51.00	1-43	0	0	54.00

NAWAB OF PATAUDI

Full Name: Nawab of Pataudi Senior (Iftikhar Ali Khan)
Born: 16/03/1910, Pataudi, India
Died: 05/01/1952, New Delhi, India
Teams: Oxford University 1928-31, Worcestershire 1932-38, Patiala 1931/32,
Western India States 1943/44, Southern Punjab 1945/46, India 1946, England 1932-34
Matches: 3 (Won 1, Drew 0, Lost 2), 3 (Won 0, Drew 2, Lost 1)
Right-hand middle order batsman

No	Date	Opposition	Venue	R	Bat	C
1	02/12/1932	Australia	Sydney	W	102	
2	30/12/1932	Australia	Melbourne	L	15	
					5	
3	08/06/1934	Australia	Trent Bridge	L	12	
					10	

For India

No	Date	Opposition	Venue	R	Bat	C
1*	22/06/1946	England	Lord's	L	9	
					22	
2*	20/07/1946	England	Old Trafford	D	11	
					4	
3*	17/08/1946	England	The Oval	D	9	

Batting & Fielding

Mat	Inns	N/O	Runs	H/S	Avg	100s	50s	Cat	
3	5	0	144	102	28.80	1	0	0	(England)
3	5	0	55	22	11.00	0	0	0	(India)
6	10	0	199	102	19.90	1	0	0	(Total)

M.M.PATEL

Full Name: Minal Mahesh Patel (known as Min)
Born: 07/07/1970, Bombay, India
Teams: Kent 1989-96, England 1996
Matches: 2 (Won 1, Drew 1, Lost 0)
Right-hand lower order batsman – Left-arm slow bowler

No	Date	Opposition	Venue	R	Bat	C		Bowling		
1	06/06/1996	India	Edgbaston	W	18		2	0	14	0
							8	3	18	0
2	04/07/1996	India	Trent Bridge	D	27	2	24	2	101	1
							12	3	47	0

Batting & Fielding

Mat	Inns	N/O	Runs	H/S	Avg	100s	50s	Cat
2	2	0	45	27	22.50	0	0	2

Bowling

Balls	Runs	Wkts	Avg	Best	5WI	10WM	S/R
276	180	1	180.00	1-101	0	0	276.00

E.PAYNTER

Full Name: Edward Paynter (known as Eddie)
Born: 05/11/1901, Oswaldtwistle, Lancashire
Died: 05/02/1979, Keighley, Yorkshire
Teams: Lancashire 1926-45, England 1931-39
Matches: 20 (Won 8, Drew 11, Lost 1)
Left-hand opening/middle order batsman – Right-arm medium bowler

No	Date	Opposition	Venue	R	Bat	C
1	15/08/1931	New Zealand	Old Trafford	D	3	
2	25/06/1932	India	Lord's	W	14	
					54	
3	13/01/1933	Australia	Adelaide	W	77	
					1*	
4	10/02/1933	Australia	Brisbane (2)	W	83	
					14*	
5	23/02/1933	Australia	Sydney	W	9	
6	24/03/1933	New Zealand	Christchurch	D	0	
7	31/03/1933	New Zealand	Auckland	D	36	
8	26/06/1937	New Zealand	Lord's	D	74	1
9	24/07/1937	New Zealand	Old Trafford	W	33	
					7	
10	10/06/1938	Australia	Trent Bridge	D	216*	1
						1
11	24/06/1938	Australia	Lord's	D	99	
					43	1
12	22/07/1938	Australia	Headingley	L	28	
					21*	
13	20/08/1938	Australia	The Oval	W	0	
14	24/12/1938	South Africa	Johannesburg (1)	D	117	
					100	
15	31/12/1938	South Africa	Cape Town	D	1	1
16	20/01/1939	South Africa	Durban (2)	W	243	
17	18/02/1939	South Africa	Johannesburg (1)	D	40	
					15	
18	03/03/1939	South Africa	Durban (2)	D	62	1
					75	1
19	24/06/1939	West Indies	Lord's	W	34	
					32*	
20	22/07/1939	West Indies	Old Trafford	D	9	
					0	

Batting & Fielding

Mat	Inns	N/O	Runs	H/S	Avg	100s	50s	Cat
20	31	5	1540	243	59.23	4	7	7

E.PEATE

Full Name: Edmund Peate (known as Ted)
Born: 02/03/1855, Holbeck, Leeds, Yorkshire
Died: 11/03/1900, Newlay, Horsforth, Yorkshire
Teams: Yorkshire 1879-87, England 1881-86
Matches: 9 (Won 2, Drew 4, Lost 3)
Left-hand lower order batsman – Left-arm slow bowler

No	Date	Opposition	Venue	R	Bat	C		Bow	ling	
1	31/12/1881	Australia	Melbourne	D	4*		59	24	64	1
					2		11	5	22	0
2	17/02/1882	Australia	Sydney	L	1*		52	28	53	1
					1*		20	12	22	0
3	03/03/1882	Australia	Sydney	L	11*		45	24	43	5
					8*		25	18	14	3
4	10/03/1882	Australia	Melbourne	D	13		20	6	38	1
5	28/08/1882	Australia	The Oval	L	0		38	24	31	4
					2		21	9	40	4
6	10/07/1884	Australia	Old Trafford	D	2		49	25	62	3
					8*					
7	21/07/1884	Australia	Lord's	W	8*		40	14	85	6
							16	4	34	0
8	11/08/1884	Australia	The Oval	D	4*	1	63	25	99	2
9	05/07/1886	Australia	Old Trafford	W	6		19	7	30	0
							46	25	45	1

Batting & Fielding

Mat	Inns	N/O	Runs	H/S	Avg	100s	50s	Cat
9	14	8	70	13	11.66	0	0	2

Bowling

Balls	Runs	Wkts	Avg	Best	5WI	10WM	S/R
2096	682	31	22.00	6-85	2	0	67.61

I.A.R.PEEBLES

Full Name: Ian Alexander Ross Peebles
Born: 20/01/1908, Aberdeen, Scotland
Died: 27/02/1980, Speen, Buckinghamshire
Teams: Oxford University 1930, Middlesex 1928-48, Scotland 1937, England 1927-31
Matches: 13 (Won 3, Drew 7, Lost 3)
Right-hand lower order batsman – Leg break & googly bowler

No	Date	Opposition	Venue	R	Bat	C		Bowling	
1	24/12/1927	South Africa	Johannesburg (1)	W	2*		12	5 22	0
							7	1 25	0
2	31/12/1927	South Africa	Cape Town	W	3*		14	3 27	0
					6		12.1	4 26	1
3	21/01/1928	South Africa	Durban (2)	D	18*		16	3 69	3
							11	2 29	1
4	28/01/1928	South Africa	Johannesburg (1)	L	26		12	0 48	0
					7				
5	25/07/1930	Australia	Old Trafford	D	6		55	9 150	3
6	16/08/1930	Australia	The Oval	L	3*		71	8 204	6
					0*				
7	24/12/1930	South Africa	Johannesburg (1)	L	0		14	2 43	4
					13*		7	0 41	0
8	01/01/1931	South Africa	Cape Town	D	7*	1	28	2 95	0
					0				
9	13/02/1931	South Africa	Johannesburg (1)	D	3		38.5	10 63	6
					2		27	6 86	1
10	21/02/1931	South Africa	Durban (2)	D	2*	1	27.4	3 67	4
							25	4 71	3
11	27/06/1931	New Zealand	Lord's	D	0		26	3 77	5
						1	42.4	6 150	4
12	29/07/1931	New Zealand	The Oval	W		1	12	3 35	0
						1	22	4 63	4
13	15/08/1931	New Zealand	Old Trafford	D					

Batting & Fielding

Mat	Inns	N/O	Runs	H/S	Avg	100s	50s	Cat
13	17	8	98	26	10.88	0	0	5

Bowling

Balls	Runs	Wkts	Avg	Best	5WI	10WM	S/R
2882	1391	45	30.91	6-63	3	0	64.04

R.PEEL

Full Name: Robert Peel (known as Bobby)
Born: 12/02/1857, Churwell, Leeds, Yorkshire
Died: 12/08/1941, Morley, Leeds, Yorkshire
Teams: Yorkshire 1882-97, England 1884-1896
Matches: 20 (Won 12, Drew 1, Lost 7)
Left-hand middle/lower order batsman – Left-arm slow bowler

No	Date	Opposition	Venue	R	Bat	C		Bowling	
1	12/12/1884	Australia	Adelaide	W	4		41	15 68	3
						1	40.1	15 51	5
2	01/01/1885	Australia	Melbourne	W	5		102.1	56 78	3
							44	26 45	3
3	20/02/1885	Australia	Sydney	L	8*	1	32	13 51	0
					3	1	20	10 24	1
4	14/03/1885	Australia	Sydney	L	17*		31	12 53	1
					0		9	4 16	1
5	21/03/1885	Australia	Melbourne	W	0	1	41	26 28	3
						2	30	16 37	1
6	10/02/1888	Australia	Sydney	W	3		18.3	9 18	5
					9		33	14 40	5

No	Date	Opposition	Venue	R	Bat	C		Bowling	
7	16/07/1888	Australia	Lord's	L	8		21	7	36	4
					4		10.2	3	14	4
8	13/08/1888	Australia	The Oval	W	25		8	4	14	1
							28.2	13	49	4
9	30/08/1888	Australia	Old Trafford	W	11		26.2	17	31	7
							16	4	37	4
10	21/07/1890	Australia	Lord's	W	16		24	11	28	3
							43	23	59	3
11	01/01/1892	Australia	Melbourne	L	19		43	23	54	3
					6	1	16.5	7	25	2
12	29/01/1892	Australia	Sydney	L	20					
					6		35	13	49	1
13	24/03/1892	Australia	Adelaide	W	83	1				
						2				
14	17/07/1893	Australia	Lord's	D	12	1	22	12	36	0
					0*					
15	14/12/1894	Australia	Sydney	W	4	1	53	14	140	2
					17	1	30	9	67	6
16	29/12/1894	Australia	Melbourne	W	6		14	4	21	1
					53		40.1	9	77	4
17	11/01/1895	Australia	Adelaide	L	0		16	1	43	0
					0	2	34	6	96	4
18	01/02/1895	Australia	Sydney	L	0		24	5	74	3
					0					
19	01/03/1895	Australia	Melbourne	W	73	1	48	13	114	4
					15*	1	46	16	89	3
20	10/08/1896	Australia	The Oval	W	0		20	9	30	2
					0		12	5	23	6

Batting & Fielding

Mat	Inns	N/O	Runs	H/S	Avg	100s	50s	Cat
20	33	4	427	83	14.72	0	3	17

Bowling

Balls	Runs	Wkts	Avg	Best	5WI	10WM	S/R
5216	1715	102	16.81	7-31	6	2	51.13

F.PENN

Full Name: Frank Penn
Born: 07/03/1851, Lewisham, London
Died: 26/12/1916, Bifrons, Patrixbourne, Kent
Teams: Kent 1875-81, England 1880
Matches: 1 (Won 1, Drew 0, Lost 0)
Right-hand middle order batsman – Right-hand round-arm slow bowler

No	Date	Opposition	Venue	R	Bat	C		Bowling	
1	06/09/1880	Australia	The Oval	W	23					
					27*		3	1	2	0

Batting & Fielding

Mat	Inns	N/O	Runs	H/S	Avg	100s	50s	Cat
1	2	1	50	27*	50.00	0	0	0

Bowling

Balls	Runs	Wkts	Avg	Best	5WI	10WM	S/R
12	2	0	–	0-2	0	0	–

R.T.D.PERKS

Full Name: Reginald Thomas David Perks (known as Reg)
Born: 04/10/1911, Hereford
Died: 22/11/1977, Worcester
Teams: Worcestershire 1930-55, England 1939
Matches: 2 (Won 0, Drew 2, Lost 0)
Left-hand lower order batsman – Right-arm fast medium bowler

No	Date	Opposition	Venue	R	Bat	C		Bowling	
1	03/03/1939	South Africa	Durban (2)	D	2*		41	5	100	5
							32	6	99	1
2	19/08/1939	West Indies	The Oval	D	1*	1	30.5	6	156	5

Batting & Fielding

Mat	Inns	N/O	Runs	H/S	Avg	100s	50s	Cat
2	2	2	3	2*	–	0	0	1

Bowling

Balls	Runs	Wkts	Avg	Best	5WI	10WM	S/R
829	355	11	32.27	5-100	2	0	75.36

H.PHILIPSON

Full Name: Hylton Philipson (name registered as Hilton)
Born: 08/06/1866, Tynemouth, Northumberland
Died: 04/12/1935, Westminster, London
Teams: Oxford University 1887-89, Middlesex 1895-98, England 1892-95
Matches: 5 (Won 3, Drew 0, Lost 2)
Right-hand middle/lower order batsman – Wicket-keeper

No	Date	Opposition	Venue	R	Bat	C	St	B
1+	24/03/1892	Australia	Adelaide	W	1			5
							1	3
2+	29/12/1894	Australia	Melbourne	W	1	2		0
					30			5
3+	11/01/1895	Australia	Adelaide	L	7	1		2
					1	1		7
4+	01/02/1895	Australia	Sydney	L	4	1	2	3
					9			
5+	01/03/1895	Australia	Melbourne	W	10*	2		3
						1		5

Batting & Fielding

Mat	Inns	N/O	Runs	H/S	Avg	100s	50s	Cat	St	Byes
5	8	1	63	30	9.00	0	0	8	3	33

A.C.S.PIGOTT

Full Name: Anthony Charles Shackleton Pigott (known as Tony)
Born: 04/06/1958, Fulham, London
Teams: Sussex 1978-93, Surrey 1994-96, Wellington 1982/83-83/84, England 1984
Matches: 1 (Won 0, Drew 0, Lost 1)
Right-hand lower order batsman – Right-arm fast medium bowler

No	Date	Opposition	Venue	R	Bat	C		Bowling		
1	03/02/1984	New Zealand	Christchurch	L	4		17	7	75	2
					8*					

Batting & Fielding

Mat	Inns	N/O	Runs	H/S	Avg	100s	50s	Cat
1	2	1	12	8*	12.00	0	0	0

Bowling

Balls	Runs	Wkts	Avg	Best	5WI	10WM	S/R
102	75	2	37.50	2-75	0	0	51.00

R.PILLING

Full Name: Richard Pilling (known as Dick)
Born: 11/08/1855, Old Warden, Bedfordshire
Died: 28/03/1891, Old Trafford, Manchester, Lancashire
Teams: Lancashire 1877-89, England 1881-88
Matches: 8 (Won 3, Drew 3, Lost 2)
Right-hand lower order batsman – Wicket-keeper

No	Date	Opposition	Venue	R	Bat	C	St	B
1+	31/12/1881	Australia	Melbourne	D	5	1	2	4
					3			9
2+	17/02/1882	Australia	Sydney	L	3			1
					9			3
3+	03/03/1882	Australia	Sydney	L	12	2		6
					23	1		2
4+	10/03/1882	Australia	Melbourne	D	6*	1		2

No	Date	Opposition	Venue	R	Bat	C	St	B
5+	10/07/1884	Australia	Old Trafford	D	0	1		0
					3			
6+	05/07/1886	Australia	Old Trafford	W	2	1		0
						1		3
7+	10/02/1888	Australia	Sydney	W	3	1	1	6
					5	1		2
8+	30/08/1888	Australia	Old Trafford	W	17		1	2
								2

Batting & Fielding

Mat	Inns	N/O	Runs	H/S	Avg	100s	50s	Cat	St	Byes
8	13	1	91	23	7.58	0	0	10	4	42

W.PLACE

Full Name: Winston Place
Born: 07/12/1914, Rawtenstall, Lancashire
Teams: Lancashire 1937-55, England 1948
Matches: 3 (Won 0, Drew 1, Lost 2)
Right-hand opening/middle order batsman – Right-arm slow bowler

No	Date	Opposition	Venue	R	Bat	C
1	21/01/1948	West Indies	Bridgetown	D	12	
					1*	
2	03/03/1948	West Indies	Georgetown	L	1	
					15	
3	27/03/1948	West Indies	Kingston	L	8	
					107	

Batting & Fielding

Mat	Inns	N/O	Runs	H/S	Avg	100s	50s	Cat
3	6	1	144	107	28.80	1	0	0

P.I.POCOCK

Full Name: Patrick Ian Pocock (known as Pat)
Born: 24/09/1946, Bangor, Caernarvonshire
Teams: Surrey 1964-86, Northern Transvaal 1971/72, England 1968-85
Matches: 25 (Won 4, Drew 13, Lost 8)
Right-hand lower order batsman – Off break bowler

No	Date	Opposition	Venue	R	Bat	C	Bowling			
1	29/02/1968	West Indies	Bridgetown	D	6	1	28	11	55	1
							13	0	78	1
2	28/03/1968	West Indies	Georgetown	D	13		38	11	78	1
					0		17	1	66	2
3	06/06/1968	Australia	Old Trafford	L	6		25	5	77	0
					10	2	33	10	79	6
4	21/02/1969	Pakistan	Lahore (2)	D	12	1	10	3	39	1
					1	2	16	4	41	0
5	20/12/1972	India	Delhi	W	0	1	6	1	13	0
							33	7	72	3
6	30/12/1972	India	Calcutta	L	3		19	10	26	0
					5		8	1	19	0
7	12/01/1973	India	Madras (1)	L	2		46	15	114	4
					0		13	3	28	4
8	06/02/1973	India	Bombay (2)	D	0*		25	7	63	1
							27	5	75	2
9	02/03/1973	Pakistan	Lahore (2)	D	5		24	6	73	0
						1	15	3	42	1
10	16/03/1973	Pakistan	Hyderabad	D	33	1	52	9	169	5
11	24/03/1973	Pakistan	Karachi (1)	D	4	1	38	7	93	2
12	02/02/1974	West Indies	Port-of-Spain	L	2		43	12	110	5
					0		16	6	49	1
13	16/02/1974	West Indies	Kingston	D	23		57	14	152	0
					4					
14	06/03/1974	West Indies	Bridgetown	D	18		28	4	93	0
15	30/03/1974	West Indies	Port-of-Spain	W	0	3	31	7	86	2
					5		25	7	60	1

No	Date	Opposition	Venue	R	Bat	C		Bowling		
16	17/06/1976	West Indies	Lord's	D	0*		3	0	13	0
					3		27	9	52	1
17	08/07/1976	West Indies	Old Trafford	L	7		4	2	10	1
					3		27	4	98	2
18	26/07/1984	West Indies	Old Trafford	L	0		45.3	14	121	4
					0					
19	09/08/1984	West Indies	The Oval	L	0					
					0		8	3	24	0
20	23/08/1984	Sri Lanka	Lord's	D	2		41	17	75	2
							29	10	78	1
21	28/11/1984	India	Bombay (3)	L	8		46	10	133	3
					22*		2.1	0	10	0
22	12/12/1984	India	Delhi	W	0	1	33	8	70	3
						1	38.4	9	93	4
23	31/12/1984	India	Calcutta	D	5		52	14	108	1
							2	1	4	0
24	13/01/1985	India	Madras (1)	W			7	1	28	0
							33	8	130	1
25	31/01/1985	India	Kanpur	D	4*		24	2	79	1

Batting & Fielding

Mat	Inns	N/O	Runs	H/S	Avg	100s	50s	Cat
25	37	4	206	33	6.24	0	0	15

Bowling

Balls	Runs	Wkts	Avg	Best	5WI	10WM	S/R
6650	2976	67	44.41	6-79	3	0	99.25

R.POLLARD

Full Name: Richard Pollard (known as Dick)
Born: 19/06/1912, Westhoughton, Lancashire
Died: 16/12/1985, Westhoughton, Lancashire
Teams: Lancashire 1933-50, England 1946-48
Matches: 4 (Won 0, Drew 3, Lost 1)
Right-hand lower order batsman – Right-arm fast medium bowler

No	Date	Opposition	Venue	R	Bat	C		Bowling		
1	20/07/1946	India	Old Trafford	D	10*	1	27	16	24	5
						1	25	10	63	2
2	21/03/1947	New Zealand	Christchurch	D			29.4	8	73	3
3	08/07/1948	Australia	Old Trafford	D	3		32	9	53	3
							10	8	6	0
4	22/07/1948	Australia	Headingley	L	0*		38	6	104	2
						1	22	6	55	0

Batting & Fielding

Mat	Inns	N/O	Runs	H/S	Avg	100s	50s	Cat
4	3	2	13	10*	13.00	0	0	3

Bowling

Balls	Runs	Wkts	Avg	Best	5WI	10WM	S/R
1102	378	15	25.20	5-24	1	0	73.46

C.J.POOLE

Full Name: Cyril John Poole
Born: 13/03/1921, Forest Town, Mansfield, Nottinghamshire
Died: 11/02/1996, Balderton, Nottinghamshire
Teams: Nottinghamshire 1948-62, England 1951-52
Matches: 3 (Won 1, Drew 1, Lost 1)
Left-hand middle order batsman – Left-arm medium bowler – Occasional wicket-keeper

No	Date	Opposition	Venue	R	Bat	C		Bowling		
1	30/12/1951	India	Calcutta	D	55					
					69*		5	1	9	0
2	12/01/1952	India	Kanpur	W	19	1				
3	06/02/1952	India	Madras (1)	L	15					
					3					

Batting & Fielding

Mat	Inns	N/O	Runs	H/S	Avg	100s	50s	Cat
3	5	1	161	69*	40.25	0	2	1

Bowling

Balls	Runs	Wkts	Avg	Best	5WI	10WM	S/R
30	9	0	–	0-9	0	0	–

G.H.POPE

Full Name: George Henry Pope
Born: 27/01/1911, Tibshelf, Derbyshire
Died: 29/10/1993, Spital, Chesterfield, Derbyshire
Teams: Derbyshire 1933-48, England 1947
Matches: 1 (Won 1, Drew 0, Lost 0)
Right-hand middle order batsman – Right-arm fast medium bowler

No	Date	Opposition	Venue	R	Bat	C		Bowling		
1	21/06/1947	South Africa	Lord's	W	8*		19.2	5	49	1
							17	7	36	0

Batting & Fielding

Mat	Inns	N/O	Runs	H/S	Avg	100s	50s	Cat
1	1	1	8	8*	–	0	0	0

Bowling

Balls	Runs	Wkts	Avg	Best	5WI	10WM	S/R
218	85	1	85.00	1-49	0	0	218.00

A.D.POUGHER

Full Name: Arthur Dick Pougher (known as Dick)
Born: 19/04/1865, Leicester
Died: 20/05/1926, Aylestone Park, Leicester
Teams: Leicestershire 1894-1901, England 1892
Matches: 1 (Won 1, Drew 0, Lost 0)
Right-hand middle order batsman – Right-arm fast medium bowler

No	Date	Opposition	Venue	R	Bat	C		Bowling		
1	19/03/1892	South Africa	Cape Town	W	17	1	21	8	26	3
						1				

Batting & Fielding

Mat	Inns	N/O	Runs	H/S	Avg	100s	50s	Cat
1	1	0	17	17	17.00	0	0	2

Bowling

Balls	Runs	Wkts	Avg	Best	5WI	10WM	S/R
105	26	3	8.66	3-26	0	0	35.00

J.S.E.PRICE

Full Name: John Sidney Ernest Price
Born: 22/07/1937, Harrow, Middlesex
Teams: Middlesex 1961-75, England 1964-72
Matches: 15 (Won 1, Drew 12, Lost 2)
Left-hand lower order batsman – Right-arm fast medium bowler

No	Date	Opposition	Venue	R	Bat	C		Bowling		
1	21/01/1964	India	Bombay (2)	D	32	1	19	2	66	3
							17	1	47	2
2	29/01/1964	India	Calcutta	D	1*	1	23	4	73	5
							7	0	31	0
3	08/02/1964	India	Delhi	D	0		23	3	71	1
							9	1	36	1
4	15/02/1964	India	Kanpur	D			16.1	5	32	2
							10	2	27	0
5	23/07/1964	Australia	Old Trafford	D	1	2	45	4	183	3
6	13/08/1964	Australia	The Oval	D	0*		21	2	67	1

No	Date	Opposition	Venue	R	Bat	C	Bowling			
7	04/12/1964	South Africa	Durban (2)	W		1	6	2	19	1
							9	7	7	1
8	23/12/1964	South Africa	Johannesburg (3)	D	0	1	32	11	66	2
							15	3	49	0
9	01/01/1965	South Africa	Cape Town	D	0*		34	6	133	0
							11	4	19	1
10	22/01/1965	South Africa	Johannesburg (3)	D	0		17	1	68	2
							14	1	56	1
11	17/06/1971	Pakistan	Lord's	D			11.4	5	29	3
12	22/07/1971	India	Lord's	D	5*	1	25	9	46	2
					0		4	0	26	1
13	05/08/1971	India	Old Trafford	D	0		22	7	44	2
							10	3	30	2
14	19/08/1971	India	The Oval	L	1*		15	2	51	1
					3		5	0	10	0
15	22/06/1972	Australia	Lord's	L	4*		26.1	5	87	2
					19		7	0	28	1

Batting & Fielding

Mat	Inns	N/O	Runs	H/S	Avg	100s	50s	Cat
15	15	6	66	32	7.33	0	0	7

Bowling

Balls	Runs	Wkts	Avg	Best	5WI	10WM	S/R
2724	1401	40	35.02	5-73	1	0	68.10

W.F.F.PRICE

Full Name: Wilfred Frederick Frank Price (known as Fred)
Born: 25/04/1902, Westminster, London
Died: 13/01/1969, Hendon, Middlesex
Teams: Middlesex 1926-47, England 1938
Matches: 1 (Won 0, Drew 0, Lost 1)
Right-hand opening/middle order batsman – Wicket-keeper

No	Date	Opposition	Venue	R	Bat	C	St	B
1+	22/07/1938	Australia	Headingley	L	0	2		2
					6			4

Batting & Fielding

Mat	Inns	N/O	Runs	H/S	Avg	100s	50s	Cat	St	Byes
1	2	0	6	6	3.00	0	0	2	0	6

R.M.PRIDEAUX

Full Name: Roger Malcolm Prideaux
Born: 31/07/1939, Chelsea, London
Teams: Cambridge University 1958-60, Kent 1960-61, Northamptonshire 1962-70, Sussex 1971-73, Orange Free State 1971/72-74/75, England 1968-69
Matches: 3 (Won 0, Drew 3, Lost 0)
Right-hand opening batsman – Right-arm medium bowler

No	Date	Opposition	Venue	R	Bat	C	Bowling			
1	25/07/1968	Australia	Headingley	D	64					
					2					
2	21/02/1969	Pakistan	Lahore (2)	D	9					
					5		2	2	0	0
3	28/02/1969	Pakistan	Dacca	D	4					
					18*					

Batting & Fielding

Mat	Inns	N/O	Runs	H/S	Avg	100s	50s	Cat
3	6	1	102	64	20.40	0	1	0

Bowling

Balls	Runs	Wkts	Avg	Best	5WI	10WM	S/R
12	0	0	–	0-0	0	0	–

D.R.PRINGLE

Full Name: Derek Raymond Pringle
Born: 18/09/1958, Nairobi, Kenya
Teams: Cambridge University 1979-82, Essex 1978-93, England 1982-92
Matches: 30 (Won 7, Drew 8, Lost 15)
Right-hand middle order batsman – Right-arm medium bowler

No	Date	Opposition	Venue	R	Bat	C	Bowling			
1	10/06/1982	India	Lord's	W	7		9	4	16	2
							19	4	58	2
2	24/06/1982	India	Old Trafford	D	23		15	4	33	1
3	08/07/1982	India	The Oval	D	9		28	5	80	0
							11	5	32	2
4	12/08/1982	Pakistan	Lord's	L	5		26	9	62	0
					14					
5	12/11/1982	Australia	Perth	D	0		10	1	37	0
					47*		2	0	3	0
6	10/12/1982	Australia	Adelaide	L	1*		33	5	97	2
					9		1.5	0	11	0
7	26/12/1982	Australia	Melbourne	W	9		15	2	40	1
					42		12	4	26	1
8	14/06/1984	West Indies	Edgbaston	L	4	1	31	5	108	5
					46*					
9	28/06/1984	West Indies	Lord's	L	2	1	11	0	54	0
					8		8	0	44	0
10	12/07/1984	West Indies	Headingley	L	19	1	13	3	26	0
					2		8.3	2	25	0
11	05/06/1986	India	Lord's	L	63	1	25	7	58	3
					6		15	5	30	1
12	19/06/1986	India	Headingley	L	8	1	27	6	47	3
					8		22.3	6	73	4
13	03/07/1986	India	Edgbaston	D	44	1	21	2	61	2
					7	1	16	5	33	0
14	07/08/1986	New Zealand	Trent Bridge	L	21		20	1	58	0
					9		2	0	16	0
15	02/06/1988	West Indies	Trent Bridge	D	39		34	11	82	1
16	16/06/1988	West Indies	Lord's	L	1		7	3	20	0
					0		21	4	60	2
17	21/07/1988	West Indies	Headingley	L	0		27	7	95	5
					3					
18	04/08/1988	West Indies	The Oval	L	1		17	4	45	3
					8		13	4	24	0
19	25/08/1988	Sri Lanka	Lord's	W	14		6.5	1	17	2
							11	2	30	1
20	08/06/1989	Australia	Headingley	L	6		33	5	123	0
					0		12.5	1	60	1
21	24/08/1989	Australia	The Oval	D	27		24.3	6	70	4
							16	0	53	0
22	06/06/1991	West Indies	Headingley	W	16		9	3	14	2
					27	1	22	6	38	2
23	20/06/1991	West Indies	Lord's	D	35		35.1	6	100	5
24	04/07/1991	West Indies	Trent Bridge	L	0		25	6	71	2
					3		7	2	20	0
25	25/07/1991	West Indies	Edgbaston	L	2		23	9	48	1
					45		7	1	31	0
26	18/01/1992	New Zealand	Christchurch	W	10		15	2	54	1
						2	21	5	64	1
27	30/01/1992	New Zealand	Auckland	W	41		15	7	21	2
					2		7	2	23	1
28	04/06/1992	Pakistan	Edgbaston	D	0*		28	2	92	0
29	23/07/1992	Pakistan	Headingley	W	0		17	6	41	2
							19	2	66	3
30	06/08/1992	Pakistan	The Oval	L	1		6	0	28	0
					1					

Batting & Fielding

Mat	Inns	N/O	Runs	H/S	Avg	100s	50s	Cat
30	50	4	695	63	15.10	0	1	10

Bowling

Balls	Runs	Wkts	Avg	Best	5WI	10WM	S/R
5287	2518	70	35.97	5-95	3	0	75.52

G.PULLAR

Full Name: Geoffrey Pullar (known as Geoff)
Born: 01/08/1935, Swinton, Lancashire
Teams: Lancashire 1954-68, Gloucestershire 1969-70, England 1959-63
Matches: 28 (Won 9, Drew 16, Lost 3)
Left-hand opening batsman – Leg break bowler

No	Date	Opposition	Venue	R	Bat	C		Bowling		
1	02/07/1959	India	Headingley	W	75					
2	23/07/1959	India	Old Trafford	W	131					
					14					
3	20/08/1959	India	The Oval	W	22					
4	06/01/1960	West Indies	Bridgetown	D	65					
					46*					
5	28/01/1960	West Indies	Port-of-Spain	W	17					
					28					
6	17/02/1960	West Indies	Kingston	D	19					
					66					
7	09/03/1960	West Indies	Georgetown	D	33					
					47					
8	25/03/1960	West Indies	Port-of-Spain	D	10					
					54		1	0	1	1
9	09/06/1960	South Africa	Edgbaston	W	37					
					1*					
10	21/07/1960	South Africa	Old Trafford	D	12					
					9		1	0	6	0
11	18/08/1960	South Africa	The Oval	D	59					
					175					
12	08/06/1961	Australia	Edgbaston	D	17					
					28					
13	22/06/1961	Australia	Lord's	L	11					
					42					
14	06/07/1961	Australia	Headingley	W	53					
					26*					
15	27/07/1961	Australia	Old Trafford	L	63					
					26					
16	17/08/1961	Australia	The Oval	D	8					
					13					
17	21/10/1961	Pakistan	Lahore (2)	W	0					
					0	1				
18	11/11/1961	India	Bombay (2)	D	83					
19	01/12/1961	India	Kanpur	D	46					
					119					
20	13/12/1961	India	Delhi	D	89	1				
21	19/01/1962	Pakistan	Dacca	D	165					
					8*		9	3	30	0
22	02/02/1962	Pakistan	Karachi (1)	D	60					
23	31/05/1962	Pakistan	Edgbaston	W	22					
24	26/07/1962	Pakistan	Trent Bridge	D	5					
25	30/11/1962	Australia	Brisbane (2)	D	33					
					56					
26	29/12/1962	Australia	Melbourne	W	11					
					5					
27	11/01/1963	Australia	Sydney	L	53					
					0					
28	25/01/1963	Australia	Adelaide	D	9					
					3					

Batting & Fielding

Mat	Inns	N/O	Runs	H/S	Avg	100s	50s	Cat
28	49	4	1974	175	43.86	4	12	2

Bowling

Balls	Runs	Wkts	Avg	Best	5WI	10WM	S/R
66	37	1	37.00	1-1	0	0	66.00

W.G.QUAIFE

Full Name: William Quaife (known as Willie) (initial G added to differentiate him from brother Walter)
Born: 17/03/1872, Newhaven, Sussex
Died: 13/10/1951, Edgbaston, Birmingham
Teams: Warwickshire 1894-1928, London County 1900-03, Griqualand West 1912/13, England 1899-1902
Matches: 7 (Won 1, Drew 2, Lost 4)
Right-hand middle order batsman – Right-arm medium or leg break bowler

No	Date	Opposition	Venue	R	Bat	C		Bowling		
1	29/06/1899	Australia	Headingley	D	20					
					1*					
2	17/07/1899	Australia	Old Trafford	D	8					
					15			3	1	6	0
3	13/12/1901	Australia	Sydney	W	21	2				
4	01/01/1902	Australia	Melbourne	L	0	1				
					25					
5	17/01/1902	Australia	Adelaide	L	68					
					44					
6	14/02/1902	Australia	Sydney	L	4					
					15					
7	28/02/1902	Australia	Melbourne	L	3	1				
					4					

Batting & Fielding

Mat	Inns	N/O	Runs	H/S	Avg	100s	50s	Cat
7	13	1	228	68	19.00	0	1	4

Bowling

Balls	Runs	Wkts	Avg	Best	5WI	10WM	S/R
15	6	0	–	0-6	0	0	–

N.V.RADFORD

Full Name: Neal Victor Radford
Born: 07/06/1957, Luanshya, Northern Rhodesia
Teams: Lancashire 1980-84, Worcestershire 1985-95, Transvaal 1978/79-88/89, England 1986-88
Matches: 3 (Won 0, Drew 3, Lost 0)
Right-hand lower order batsman – Right-arm fast medium bowler

No	Date	Opposition	Venue	R	Bat	C		Bowling		
1	03/07/1986	India	Edgbaston	D	0		35	3	131	2
					1		3	0	17	0
2	24/07/1986	New Zealand	Lord's	D	12*		25	4	71	1
3	25/02/1988	New Zealand	Auckland	D	8		30	4	79	0
							20	4	53	1

Batting & Fielding

Mat	Inns	N/O	Runs	H/S	Avg	100s	50s	Cat
3	4	1	21	12*	7.00	0	0	0

Bowling

Balls	Runs	Wkts	Avg	Best	5WI	10WM	S/R
678	351	4	87.75	2-131	0	0	169.50

C.T.RADLEY

Full Name: Clive Thornton Radley
Born: 13/05/1944, Hertford
Teams: Middlesex 1964-87, England 1978
Matches: 8 (Won 6, Drew 2, Lost 0)
Right-hand middle order batsman – Leg break bowler

No	Date	Opposition	Venue	R	Bat	C
1	24/02/1978	New Zealand	Christchurch	W	15	
2	04/03/1978	New Zealand	Auckland	D	158	
3	01/06/1978	Pakistan	Edgbaston	W	106	1
4	15/06/1978	Pakistan	Lord's	W	8	1
5	29/06/1978	Pakistan	Headingley	D	7	
6	27/07/1978	New Zealand	The Oval	W	49 2	1
7	10/08/1978	New Zealand	Trent Bridge	W	59	
8	24/08/1978	New Zealand	Lord's	W	77 0	1

Batting & Fielding

Mat	Inns	N/O	Runs	H/S	Avg	100s	50s	Cat
8	10	0	481	158	48.10	2	2	4

M.R.RAMPRAKASH

Full Name: Mark Ravin Ramprakash
Born: 05/09/1969, Bushey, Hertfordshire
Teams: Middlesex 1987-96, England 1991-95
Matches: 19 (Won 7, Drew 5, Lost 7)
Right-hand middle order batsman – Off break bowler

No	Date	Opposition	Venue	R	Bat	C	Bowling			
1	06/06/1991	West Indies	Headingley	W	27 27	2				
2	20/06/1991	West Indies	Lord's	D	24					
3	04/07/1991	West Indies	Trent Bridge	L	13 21	1				
4	25/07/1991	West Indies	Edgbaston	L	29 25					
5	08/08/1991	West Indies	The Oval	W	25 19	1				
6	22/08/1991	Sri Lanka	Lord's	W	0					
7	04/06/1992	Pakistan	Edgbaston	D	0		1	0	3	0
8	23/07/1992	Pakistan	Headingley	W	0 12*	1				
9	06/08/1992	Pakistan	The Oval	L	2 17		0.1	0	5	0
10	19/08/1993	Australia	The Oval	W	6 64	1 1				
11	17/03/1994	West Indies	Georgetown	L	2 5		15	1	35	0
12	25/03/1994	West Indies	Port-of-Spain	L	23 1		2	1	8	0
13	08/04/1994	West Indies	Bridgetown	W	20	1 1				
14	16/04/1994	West Indies	St John's	D	19		3	1	5	0
15	03/02/1995	Australia	Perth	L	72 42	1 1	11 8	0 1	43 31	0 0
16	08/06/1995	West Indies	Headingley	L	4 18					
17	22/06/1995	West Indies	Lord's	W	0 0	1				
18	16/11/1995	South Africa	Centurion	D	9					
19	30/11/1995	South Africa	Johannesburg (3)	D	4 0	1	4	0	19	0

Batting & Fielding

Mat	Inns	N/O	Runs	H/S	Avg	100s	50s	Cat
19	33	1	533	72	16.65	0	2	13

Bowling

Balls	Runs	Wkts	Avg	Best	5WI	10WM	S/R
265	149	0	–	0-3	0	0	–

D.W.RANDALL

Full Name: Derek William Randall
Born: 24/02/1951, Retford, Nottinghamshire
Teams: Nottinghamshire 1972-92, England 1977-84
Matches: 47 (Won 17, Drew 17, Lost 13)
Right-hand middle order batsman – Right-arm medium bowler

No	Date	Opposition	Venue	R	Bat	C	Bowling
1	01/01/1977	India	Calcutta	W	37		
2	14/01/1977	India	Madras (1)	W	2	1	
					0		
3	28/01/1977	India	Bangalore	L	10	1	
					0	1	
4	11/02/1977	India	Bombay (3)	D	22		
					15		
5	12/03/1977	Australia	Melbourne	L	4		
					174		
6	16/06/1977	Australia	Lord's	D	53		
					0		
7	07/07/1977	Australia	Old Trafford	W	79		
						2	
8	28/07/1977	Australia	Trent Bridge	W	13		
					19*	1	
9	11/08/1977	Australia	Headingley	W	20		
						1	
10	25/08/1977	Australia	The Oval	D	3		
					20*		
11	14/12/1977	Pakistan	Lahore (2)	D	19		1 0 2 0
12	02/01/1978	Pakistan	Hyderabad	D	7		
13	18/01/1978	Pakistan	Karachi (1)	D	23		
					55		
14	10/02/1978	New Zealand	Wellington	L	4		
					9		
15	24/02/1978	New Zealand	Christchurch	W	0		
					13		
16	04/03/1978	New Zealand	Auckland	D	30	1	1 0 1 0
						1	
17	01/12/1978	Australia	Brisbane (2)	W	75		
					74*		
18	15/12/1978	Australia	Perth	W	0		
					45		
19	29/12/1978	Australia	Melbourne	L	13	2	
					2	1	
20	06/01/1979	Australia	Sydney	W	0		
					150		
21	27/01/1979	Australia	Adelaide	W	4	1	
					15		
22	10/02/1979	Australia	Sydney	W	7		
					0*		
23	12/07/1979	India	Edgbaston	W	15		
						2	
24	02/08/1979	India	Lord's	D	57	1	
						1	
25	16/08/1979	India	Headingley	D	11		
26	14/12/1979	Australia	Perth	L	0		
					1	1	
27	04/01/1980	Australia	Sydney	L	0		
					25		
28	10/06/1982	India	Lord's	W	126		
29	24/06/1982	India	Old Trafford	D	0	1	
30	08/07/1982	India	The Oval	D	95		
31	29/07/1982	Pakistan	Edgbaston	W	17		
					105	1	

No	Date	Opposition	Venue	R	Bat	C		Bowling			
32	12/08/1982	Pakistan	Lord's	L	29						
					9						
33	26/08/1982	Pakistan	Headingley	W	8						
					0	2					
34	12/11/1982	Australia	Perth	D	78						
					115						
35	26/11/1982	Australia	Brisbane (2)	L	37	1					
					4						
36	10/12/1982	Australia	Adelaide	L	0						
					17	1					
37	02/01/1983	Australia	Sydney	D	70						
					44	1					
38	14/07/1983	New Zealand	The Oval	W	75*	1					
					3						
39	28/07/1983	New Zealand	Headingley	L	4						
					16	2					
40	25/08/1983	New Zealand	Trent Bridge	W	83						
					13						
41	20/01/1984	New Zealand	Wellington	D	164						
42	03/02/1984	New Zealand	Christchurch	L	0	1					
					25						
43	10/02/1984	New Zealand	Auckland	D	104	1					
44	02/03/1984	Pakistan	Karachi (1)	L	8						
					16						
45	12/03/1984	Pakistan	Faisalabad	D	65						
46	19/03/1984	Pakistan	Lahore (2)	D	14						
					0						
47	14/06/1984	West Indies	Edgbaston	L	0	1					
					1						

Batting & Fielding

Mat	Inns	N/O	Runs	H/S	Avg	100s	50s	Cat
47	79	5	2470	174	33.37	7	12	31

Bowling

Balls	Runs	Wkts	Avg	Best	5WI	10WM	S/R
16	3	0	–	0-1	0	0	–

K.S.RANJITSINHJI

Full Name: Kumar Shri Ranjitsinhji (Prince Ranjitsinhji, known as Ranji)
Born: 10/09/1872, Sarodar, Kathiawar, India
Died: 02/04/1933, Jamnagar, India
Teams: Cambridge University 1893-94, Sussex 1895-1920, London County 1901-04,
England 1896-1902
Matches: 15 (Won 2, Drew 6, Lost 7)
Right-hand middle order batsman – Right-arm slow bowler

No	Date	Opposition	Venue	R	Bat	C		Bowling			
1	16/07/1896	Australia	Old Trafford	L	62						
					154*	2					
2	10/08/1896	Australia	The Oval	W	8						
					11						
3	13/12/1897	Australia	Sydney	W	175						
					8*						
4	01/01/1898	Australia	Melbourne	L	71	1					
					27						
5	14/01/1898	Australia	Adelaide	L	6						
					77						
6	29/01/1898	Australia	Melbourne	L	24						
					55		3.4	1	9	0	
7	26/02/1898	Australia	Sydney	L	2	2					
					12						
8	01/06/1899	Australia	Trent Bridge	D	42						
					93*	2					
9	15/06/1899	Australia	Lord's	L	8	1		2	0	6	0
					0						
10	29/06/1899	Australia	Headingley	D	11	1					
						2					
11	17/07/1899	Australia	Old Trafford	D	21			1	0	1	0
					49*	2		12	5	23	1

No	Date	Opposition	Venue	R	Bat	C	Bowling
12	14/08/1899	Australia	The Oval	D	54		
13	29/05/1902	Australia	Edgbaston	D	13		
14	12/06/1902	Australia	Lord's	D	0		
15	24/07/1902	Australia	Old Trafford	L	2		
					4		

Batting & Fielding

Mat	Inns	N/O	Runs	H/S	Avg	100s	50s	Cat
15	26	4	989	175	44.95	2	6	13

Bowling

Balls	Runs	Wkts	Avg	Best	5WI	10WM	S/R
97	39	1	39.00	1-23	0	0	97.00

H.D.READ

Full Name: Holcombe Douglas Read (known as Hopper)
Born: 28/01/1910, Woodford Green, Essex
Teams: Surrey 1933, Essex 1933-35, England 1935
Matches: 1 (Won 0, Drew 1, Lost 0)
Right-hand lower order batsman – Right-arm fast bowler

No	Date	Opposition	Venue	R	Bat	C		Bowling		
1	17/08/1935	South Africa	The Oval	D			35	13	136	4
							10	1	64	2

Batting & Fielding

Mat	Inns	N/O	Runs	H/S	Avg	100s	50s	Cat
1	0	–	–	–	–	–	–	0

Bowling

Balls	Runs	Wkts	Avg	Best	5WI	10WM	S/R
270	200	6	33.33	4-136	0	0	45.00

J.M.READ

Full Name: John Maurice Read (known as Maurice)
Born: 09/02/1859, Thames Ditton, Surrey
Died: 17/02/1929, Winchester, Hampshire
Teams: Surrey 1880-95, England 1882-93
Matches: 17 (Won 11, Drew 1, Lost 5)
Right-hand middle order batsman – Right-arm fast medium bowler

No	Date	Opposition	Venue	R	Bat	C
1	28/08/1882	Australia	The Oval	L	19*	1
					0	
2	12/12/1884	Australia	Adelaide	W	14	1
3	01/01/1885	Australia	Melbourne	W	3	1
4	20/02/1885	Australia	Sydney	L	4	1
					56	
5	14/03/1885	Australia	Sydney	L	47	1
					6	
6	21/03/1885	Australia	Melbourne	W	13	
7	28/01/1887	Australia	Sydney	W	5	
					0	1
8	25/02/1887	Australia	Sydney	W	11	
					2	
9	10/02/1888	Australia	Sydney	W	0	
					39	
10	12/03/1889	South Africa	Port Elizabeth	W	1	
					3	
11	25/03/1889	South Africa	Cape Town	W	12	
12	21/07/1890	Australia	Lord's	W	34	
					2*	

No	Date	Opposition	Venue	R	Bat	C
13	11/08/1890	Australia	The Oval	W	19	
					35	
14	01/01/1892	Australia	Melbourne	L	38	1
					11	
15	29/01/1892	Australia	Sydney	L	3	
					22	1
16	24/03/1892	Australia	Adelaide	W	57	
17	17/07/1893	Australia	Lord's	D	6	
					1	

Batting & Fielding

Mat	Inns	N/O	Runs	H/S	Avg	100s	50s	Cat
17	29	2	463	57	17.14	0	2	8

W.W.READ

Full Name: Walter William Read (also known as W.W.)
Born: 23/11/1855, Reigate, Surrey
Died: 06/01/1907, Bingham Road, Addiscombe Park, Surrey
Teams: Surrey 1873-97, England 1882-93
Matches: 18 (Won 13, Drew 2, Lost 3)
England Captain: 2 times 1888-92 (Won 2, Drew 0, Lost 0) **Toss:** 0-2
Right-hand middle order batsman – Right-arm lob bowler (previously right-hand fast round-arm)

No	Date	Opposition	Venue	R	Bat	C	Bowling			
1	30/12/1882	Australia	Melbourne	L	19		8	2	27	0
					29					
2	19/01/1883	Australia	Melbourne	W	75	1				
3	26/01/1883	Australia	Sydney	W	66					
					21					
4	17/02/1883	Australia	Sydney	L	11					
					7					
5	21/07/1884	Australia	Lord's	W	12					
6	11/08/1884	Australia	The Oval	D	117	2	7	0	36	0
7	05/07/1886	Australia	Old Trafford	W	51					
					9					
8	19/07/1886	Australia	Lord's	W	22					
9	12/08/1886	Australia	The Oval	W	94	1				
						2				
10*	10/02/1888	Australia	Sydney	W	10	2				
					8					
11	16/07/1888	Australia	Lord's	L	4					
					3					
12	13/08/1888	Australia	The Oval	W	18					
						1				
13	30/08/1888	Australia	Old Trafford	W	19	2				
14	21/07/1890	Australia	Lord's	W	1					
					13					
15	11/08/1890	Australia	The Oval	W	1	1				
					6					
16*	19/03/1892	South Africa	Cape Town	W	40					
17	14/08/1893	Australia	The Oval	W	52					
						2				
18	24/08/1893	Australia	Old Trafford	D	12	1				
					0*	1				

Batting & Fielding

Mat	Inns	N/O	Runs	H/S	Avg	100s	50s	Cat
18	27	1	720	117	27.69	1	5	16

Bowling

Balls	Runs	Wkts	Avg	Best	5WI	10WM	S/R
60	63	0	–	0-27	0	0	–

D.A.REEVE

Full Name: Dermot Alexander Reeve
Born: 02/04/1963, Kowloon, Hong Kong
Teams: Sussex 1983-87, Warwickshire 1988-96, England 1992
Matches: 3 (Won 2, Drew 1, Lost 0)
Right-hand middle order batsman – Right-arm medium bowler

No	Date	Opposition	Venue	R	Bat	C	Bowling			
1	18/01/1992	New Zealand	Christchurch	W	59		8	4	16	1
							2	0	8	0
2	30/01/1992	New Zealand	Auckland	W	22		7	1	21	0
					25					
3	06/02/1992	New Zealand	Wellington	D	18	1	3	1	11	0
					0		4.5	2	4	1

Batting & Fielding

Mat	Inns	N/O	Runs	H/S	Avg	100s	50s	Cat
3	5	0	124	59	24.80	0	1	1

Bowling

Balls	Runs	Wkts	Avg	Best	5WI	10WM	S/R
149	60	2	30.00	1-4	0	0	74.50

A.E.RELF

Full Name: Albert Edward Relf
Born: 26/06/1874, Burwash, Sussex
Died: 26/03/1937, Wellington College, Crowthorne, Berkshire
Teams: Sussex 1900-21, London County 1904, Auckland 1907/08-09/10, England 1903-14
Matches: 13 (Won 7, Drew 1, Lost 5)
Right-hand middle order batsman – Right-arm medium off break bowler

No	Date	Opposition	Venue	R	Bat	C	Bowling			
1	11/12/1903	Australia	Sydney	W	31	1	6	1	27	0
						2	13	5	35	0
2	01/01/1904	Australia	Melbourne	W	3*		2	0	12	1
					10*	2	1	0	5	0
3	02/01/1906	South Africa	Johannesburg (1)	L	8	1				
					17	1	21.5	7	47	2
4	06/03/1906	South Africa	Johannesburg (1)	L	24		18	4	36	1
					37					
5	10/03/1906	South Africa	Johannesburg (1)	L	33	1	14	1	47	1
					18		9	0	37	0
6	24/03/1906	South Africa	Cape Town	W	28		6	2	17	1
					18					
7	30/03/1906	South Africa	Cape Town	L	25	1	21	6	40	3
					21					
8	14/06/1909	Australia	Lord's	L	17		45	14	85	5
					3		7.4	4	9	1
9	13/12/1913	South Africa	Durban (1)	W	1		5	2	9	0
						2	16.2	3	31	3
10	26/12/1913	South Africa	Johannesburg (1)	W	63		14	1	34	0
						1	9	3	19	1
11	01/01/1914	South Africa	Johannesburg (1)	W	0		14	7	24	1
					25	1	29	12	40	2
12	14/02/1914	South Africa	Durban (1)	D	11		8	3	15	0
13	27/02/1914	South Africa	Port Elizabeth	W	23*		11	5	26	1
						1	23.1	11	29	2

Batting & Fielding

Mat	Inns	N/O	Runs	H/S	Avg	100s	50s	Cat
13	21	3	416	63	23.11	0	1	14

Bowling

Balls	Runs	Wkts	Avg	Best	5WI	10WM	S/R
1764	624	25	24.96	5-85	1	0	70.56

H.J.RHODES

Full Name: Harold James Rhodes (also known as Dusty)
Born: 22/07/1936, Hadfield, Glossop, Derbyshire
Teams: Derbyshire 1953-75, England 1959
Matches: 2 (Won 2, Drew 0, Lost 0)
Right-hand lower order batsman – Right-arm fast bowler

No	Date	Opposition	Venue	R	Bat	C		Bowling		
1	02/07/1959	India	Headingley	W			18.5	3	50	4
							10	2	35	0
2	23/07/1959	India	Old Trafford	W	0*		18	3	72	3
							28	2	87	2

Batting & Fielding

Mat	Inns	N/O	Runs	H/S	Avg	100s	50s	Cat
2	1	1	0	0*	–	0	0	0

Bowling

Balls	Runs	Wkts	Avg	Best	5WI	10WM	S/R
449	244	9	27.11	4-50	0	0	49.88

S.J.RHODES

Full Name: Steven John Rhodes (known as Steve)
Born: 17/06/1964, Dirk Hill, Bradford, Yorkshire
Teams: Yorkshire 1981-84, Worcestershire 1985-96, England 1994-95
Matches: 11 (Won 3, Drew 4, Lost 4)
Right-hand middle order batsman – Wicket-keeper

No	Date	Opposition	Venue	R	Bat	C	St	B
1+	02/06/1994	New Zealand	Trent Bridge	W	49	3		0
						3		0
2+	16/06/1994	New Zealand	Lord's	D	32*	1		3
					24*			0
3+	30/06/1994	New Zealand	Old Trafford	D	12	4		0
						1		8
4+	21/07/1994	South Africa	Lord's	L	15	4		0
					14*	1	1	8
5+	04/08/1994	South Africa	Headingley	D	65*	2	1	8
						1		2
6+	18/08/1994	South Africa	The Oval	W	11	3		8
						3		0
7+	25/11/1994	Australia	Brisbane (2)	L	4	1		5
					2	2		2
8+	24/12/1994	Australia	Melbourne	L	0	1		0
					16		1	1
9+	01/01/1995	Australia	Sydney	D	1	1		6
						3		12
10+	26/01/1995	Australia	Adelaide	W	6	4		2
					2	3		3
11+	03/02/1995	Australia	Perth	L	2	3		14
					39*	2		1

Batting & Fielding

Mat	Inns	N/O	Runs	H/S	Avg	100s	50s	Cat	St	Byes
11	17	5	294	65*	24.50	0	1	46	3	83

W.RHODES

Full Name: Wilfred Rhodes
Born: 29/10/1877, Kirkheaton, Yorkshire
Died: 08/07/1973, Branksome Park, Dorset
Teams: Yorkshire 1898-1930, Patiala 1926/27, Europeans 1921/22-22/23, England 1899-1930
Matches: 58 (Won 24, Drew 13, Lost 21)
Right-hand middle order batsman – Left-arm slow bowler

No	Date	Opposition	Venue	R	Bat	C		Bowling		
1	01/06/1899	Australia	Trent Bridge	D	6		35.2	13	58	4
							20	3	60	3
2	15/06/1899	Australia	Lord's	L	2		39	10	108	3
					2		5	1	9	0
3	14/08/1899	Australia	The Oval	D	8*		25	2	79	0
						1	22	8	27	3
4	29/05/1902	Australia	Edgbaston	D	38*		11	3	17	7
							10	5	9	1
5	12/06/1902	Australia	Lord's	D						
6	03/07/1902	Australia	Bramall Lane	L	7*	1	13	3	33	1
					7*		17.1	3	63	5
7	24/07/1902	Australia	Old Trafford	L	5	2	25	3	104	4
					4*		14.4	5	26	3

No	Date	Opposition	Venue	R	Bat	C		Bowling		
8	11/08/1902	Australia	The Oval	W	0*	1	28	9	46	0
					6*		22	7	38	1
9	11/12/1903	Australia	Sydney	W	40*		17.2	3	41	2
							40.2	10	94	5
10	01/01/1904	Australia	Melbourne	W	2	1	15.2	3	56	7
					9	2	15	0	68	8
11	15/01/1904	Australia	Adelaide	L	9		14	3	45	1
					8	1	21	4	46	1
12	26/02/1904	Australia	Sydney	W	10		11	3	33	4
					29		11	7	12	0
13	05/03/1904	Australia	Melbourne	L	3	1	12	1	41	1
					16*		15	2	52	2
14	29/05/1905	Australia	Trent Bridge	W	29		18	6	37	1
					39*		30	8	58	1
15	15/06/1905	Australia	Lord's	D	15		16.1	1	70	3
16	24/07/1905	Australia	Old Trafford	W	27*	1	5.5	1	25	2
						4	11.3	3	36	3
17	14/08/1905	Australia	The Oval	D	36	1	21	2	59	0
							8	0	29	0
18	13/12/1907	Australia	Sydney	L	1		5	2	13	1
					29		7	3	13	0
19	01/01/1908	Australia	Melbourne	W	32		11	0	37	1
					15		16	6	38	0
20	10/01/1908	Australia	Adelaide	L	38		15	5	35	0
					9	1	27	9	81	0
21	07/02/1908	Australia	Melbourne	L	0		5	0	21	0
					2		24	5	66	1
22	21/02/1908	Australia	Sydney	L	10		10	5	15	0
					69		37.4	7	102	4
23	27/05/1909	Australia	Edgbaston	W	15*	1				
						1	1	0	8	0
24	01/07/1909	Australia	Headingley	L	12		8	2	38	4
					16	1	19	3	44	2
25	26/07/1909	Australia	Old Trafford	D	5					
					0*		25	0	83	5
26	09/08/1909	Australia	The Oval	D	66	3	12	3	34	0
					54		14	1	35	0
27	01/01/1910	South Africa	Johannesburg (1)	L	66		9	1	34	1
					2	2	9	3	25	0
28	21/01/1910	South Africa	Durban (1)	L	44		5	1	11	0
					17	2	19	6	43	0
29	26/02/1910	South Africa	Johannesburg (1)	W	14	2	1	0	4	1
					1		4	1	6	0
30	07/03/1910	South Africa	Cape Town	L	0	1				
					5	1	3	2	2	0
31	11/03/1910	South Africa	Cape Town	W	77	2				
					0*		7	0	22	0
32	15/12/1911	Australia	Sydney	L	41		8	0	26	0
					0	1	3	1	4	0
33	30/12/1911	Australia	Melbourne	W	61					
					28		3	1	3	0
34	12/01/1912	Australia	Adelaide	W	59	1				
					57*		1	0	6	0
35	09/02/1912	Australia	Melbourne	W	179	2	2	1	1	0
36	23/02/1912	Australia	Sydney	W	8					
					30	1	2	0	17	0
37	10/06/1912	South Africa	Lord's	W	36					
38	24/06/1912	Australia	Lord's	D	59		19.2	5	59	3
39	08/07/1912	South Africa	Headingley	W	7					
					10		4	1	14	0
40	29/07/1912	Australia	Old Trafford	D	92					
41	12/08/1912	South Africa	The Oval	W	0	1				
42	19/08/1912	Australia	The Oval	W	49	2				
					4		2	1	1	0
43	13/12/1913	South Africa	Durban (1)	W	18		7	0	26	0
						1				
44	26/12/1913	South Africa	Johannesburg (1)	W	152	1	13	5	23	1
						2	9	2	20	0

No	Date	Opposition	Venue	R	Bat	C	Bowling			
45	01/01/1914	South Africa	Johannesburg (1)	W	35	2	3.5	1	9	1
					0		6	1	17	0
46	14/02/1914	South Africa	Durban (1)	D	22	1	14	5	33	3
					35	1	26	6	53	1
47	27/02/1914	South Africa	Port Elizabeth	W	27					
					0*	2	10	4	14	0
48	17/12/1920	Australia	Sydney	L	3					
					45		22	2	67	0
49	31/12/1920	Australia	Melbourne	L	7	1	8.3	1	26	1
					28					
50	14/01/1921	Australia	Adelaide	L	16	1	5	1	23	0
					4		25.5	8	61	3
51	11/02/1921	Australia	Melbourne	L	11	1				
					73	1	10	2	25	0
52	25/02/1921	Australia	Sydney	L	26		7	0	23	0
					25		7.2	1	20	0
53	28/05/1921	Australia	Trent Bridge	L	19	2	13	3	33	2
					10					
54	14/08/1926	Australia	The Oval	W	28		25	15	35	2
					14		20	9	44	4
55	11/01/1930	West Indies	Bridgetown	D	14*	1	27.1	9	44	0
						1	51	10	110	3
56	01/02/1930	West Indies	Port-of-Spain	W	2		20	5	40	1
					6*		22	12	31	0
57	21/02/1930	West Indies	Georgetown	L	0	1	40	8	96	2
					10*		51	23	93	2
58	03/04/1930	West Indies	Kingston	D	8*		20.5	12	17	1
					11*		24	13	22	1

Batting & Fielding

Mat	Inns	N/O	Runs	H/S	Avg	100s	50s	Cat
58	98	21	2325	179	30.19	2	11	60

Bowling

Balls	Runs	Wkts	Avg	Best	5WI	10WM	S/R
8231	3425	127	26.96	8-68	6	1	64.81

C.J.RICHARDS

Full Name: Clifton James Richards (known as Jack)
Born: 10/08/1958, Penzance, Cornwall
Teams: Surrey 1976-88, Orange Free State 1983/84, England 1986-88
Matches: 8 (Won 2, Drew 2, Lost 4)
Right-hand middle order batsman – Wicket-keeper – Occasional right-arm medium bowler

No	Date	Opposition	Venue	R	Bat	C	St	B
1+	14/11/1986	Australia	Brisbane (2)	W	0	3		2
							1	5
2+	28/11/1986	Australia	Perth	D	133	1		9
					15			9
3+	12/12/1986	Australia	Adelaide	D	29	2		0
								4
4+	26/12/1986	Australia	Melbourne	W	3	5		1
								0
5+	10/01/1987	Australia	Sydney	L	46	3		12
					38	1		5
6+	02/07/1987	Pakistan	Headingley	L	6	2		5
					2			
7+	21/07/1988	West Indies	Headingley	L	2	1		0
					8			0
8+	04/08/1988	West Indies	The Oval	L	0	1		0
					3	1		2

Batting & Fielding

Mat	Inns	N/O	Runs	H/S	Avg	100s	50s	Cat	St	Byes
8	13	0	285	133	21.92	1	0	20	1	54

D.W.RICHARDSON

Full Name: Derek Walter Richardson (known as Dick)
Born: 03/11/1934, Hereford
Teams: Worcestershire 1952-67, England 1957
Matches: 1 (Won 0, Drew 1, Lost 0)
Left-hand middle order batsman – Left-arm medium bowler

No	Date	Opposition	Venue	R	Bat	C
1	04/07/1957	West Indies	Trent Bridge	D	33	1

Batting & Fielding

Mat	Inns	N/O	Runs	H/S	Avg	100s	50s	Cat
1	1	0	33	33	33.00	0	0	1

P.E.RICHARDSON

Full Name: Peter Edward Richardson
Born: 04/07/1931, Hereford
Teams: Worcestershire 1949-58, Kent 1959-65, England 1956-63
Matches: 34 (Won 13, Drew 12, Lost 9)
Left-hand opening batsman

No	Date	Opposition	Venue	R	Bat	C	Bowling
1	07/06/1956	Australia	Trent Bridge	D	81		
					73		
2	21/06/1956	Australia	Lord's	L	9		
					21		
3	12/07/1956	Australia	Headingley	W	5	1	
4	26/07/1956	Australia	Old Trafford	W	104		
5	23/08/1956	Australia	The Oval	D	37		
					34		
6	24/12/1956	South Africa	Johannesburg (3)	W	117		
					10		
7	01/01/1957	South Africa	Cape Town	W	45		
					44		
8	25/01/1957	South Africa	Durban (2)	D	68		
					32		
9	15/02/1957	South Africa	Johannesburg (3)	L	11		
					39		
10	01/03/1957	South Africa	Port Elizabeth	L	0		
					3		
11	30/05/1957	West Indies	Edgbaston	D	47		
					34		
12	20/06/1957	West Indies	Lord's	W	76		
13	04/07/1957	West Indies	Trent Bridge	D	126		
					11		
14	25/07/1957	West Indies	Headingley	W	10		
15	22/08/1957	West Indies	The Oval	W	107		
16	05/06/1958	New Zealand	Edgbaston	W	4		
					100		
17	19/06/1958	New Zealand	Lord's	W	36		
18	24/07/1958	New Zealand	Old Trafford	W	74		
19	21/08/1958	New Zealand	The Oval	D	28		
20	05/12/1958	Australia	Brisbane (2)	L	11		
					8		
21	31/12/1958	Australia	Melbourne	L	3		
					2		
22	30/01/1959	Australia	Adelaide	L	4		
					43		
23	13/02/1959	Australia	Melbourne	L	68		
					23		
24	27/02/1959	New Zealand	Christchurch	W	8		
25	14/03/1959	New Zealand	Auckland	D	67		
26	21/10/1961	Pakistan	Lahore (2)	W	4		
					48		
27	11/11/1961	India	Bombay (2)	D	71	1	
					43	1	6 3 10 2
28	01/12/1961	India	Kanpur	D	22	1	
					48		
29	13/12/1961	India	Delhi	D	1	1	

No	Date	Opposition	Venue	R	Bat	C		Bowling			
30	30/12/1961	India	Calcutta	L	62						
					42						
31	10/01/1962	India	Madras (2)	L	13						
					2						
32	19/01/1962	Pakistan	Dacca	D	19						
					21*	1		12	5	28	1
33	02/02/1962	Pakistan	Karachi (1)	D	26						
								2	1	10	0
34	04/07/1963	West Indies	Edgbaston	W	2						
					14						

Batting & Fielding

Mat	Inns	N/O	Runs	H/S	Avg	100s	50s	Cat
34	56	1	2061	126	37.47	5	9	6

Bowling

Balls	Runs	Wkts	Avg	Best	5WI	10WM	S/R
120	48	3	16.00	2-10	0	0	40.00

T.RICHARDSON

Full Name: Thomas Richardson (known as Tom)
Born: 11/08/1870, Byfleet, Surrey
Died: 02/07/1912, St Jean d'Arvey, Savoie, France
Teams: Surrey 1892-1904, Somerset 1905, London County 1904, England 1893-98
Matches: 14 (Won 6, Drew 1, Lost 7)
Right-hand lower order batsman – Right-arm fast bowler

No	Date	Opposition	Venue	R	Bat	C		Bowling		
1	24/08/1893	Australia	Old Trafford	D	16		23.4	5	49	5
							44	15	107	5
2	14/12/1894	Australia	Sydney	W	0*		55.3	13	181	5
					12*		11	3	27	1
3	29/12/1894	Australia	Melbourne	W	0		23	6	57	5
					11		40	10	100	2
4	11/01/1895	Australia	Adelaide	L	0		21	4	75	5
					12		31.2	8	89	3
5	01/02/1895	Australia	Sydney	L	2	1	22	5	78	2
					10*					
6	01/03/1895	Australia	Melbourne	W	11		42	7	138	3
							45.2	7	104	6
7	22/06/1896	Australia	Lord's	W	6		11.3	3	39	6
							47	15	134	5
8	16/07/1896	Australia	Old Trafford	L	2	1	68	23	168	7
					1		42.3	16	76	6
9	10/08/1896	Australia	The Oval	W	1*		5	0	22	0
					10*	1	1	1	0	0
10	13/12/1897	Australia	Sydney	W	24*	1	27	8	71	3
							41	9	121	2
11	01/01/1898	Australia	Melbourne	L	3	1	48	12	114	1
					2*					
12	14/01/1898	Australia	Adelaide	L	25*		56	11	164	4
					0					
13	29/01/1898	Australia	Melbourne	L	20		26	2	102	2
					2					
14	26/02/1898	Australia	Sydney	L	1		36.1	7	94	8
					6		21.4	1	110	2

Batting & Fielding

Mat	Inns	N/O	Runs	H/S	Avg	100s	50s	Cat
14	24	8	177	25*	11.06	0	0	5

Bowling

Balls	Runs	Wkts	Avg	Best	5WI	10WM	S/R
4497	2220	88	25.22	8-94	11	4	51.10

T.L.RICHMOND

Full Name: Thomas Leonard Richmond (known as Tom)
Born: 23/06/1890, Radcliffe-on-Trent, Nottinghamshire
Died: 29/12/1957, Saxondale, Nottinghamshire
Teams: Nottinghamshire 1912-28, England 1921
Matches: 1 (Won 0, Drew 0, Lost 1)
Right-hand lower order batsman – Leg break & googly bowler

No	Date	Opposition	Venue	R	Bat	C		Bowling		
1	28/05/1921	Australia	Trent Bridge	L	4		16	3	69	2
					2		3	0	17	0

Batting & Fielding

Mat	Inns	N/O	Runs	H/S	Avg	100s	50s	Cat
1	2	0	6	4	3.00	0	0	0

Bowling

Balls	Runs	Wkts	Avg	Best	5WI	10WM	S/R
114	86	2	43.00	2-69	0	0	57.00

F.RIDGWAY

Full Name: Frederick Ridgway (known as Fred)
Born: 10/08/1923, Stockport, Cheshire
Teams: Kent 1946-61, England 1951-52
Matches: 5 (Won 1, Drew 3, Lost 1)
Right-hand lower order batsman – Right-arm fast medium bowler

No	Date	Opposition	Venue	R	Bat	C		Bowling		
1	02/11/1951	India	Delhi	D	15		20	1	55	0
2	14/12/1951	India	Bombay (2)	D	5		32	5	137	0
							16	3	33	2
3	30/12/1951	India	Calcutta	D	24		38.1	10	83	4
							2	1	8	0
4	12/01/1952	India	Kanpur	W	5	1	7	1	16	0
						2				
5	06/02/1952	India	Madras (1)	L	0		17	2	47	1
					0					

Batting & Fielding

Mat	Inns	N/O	Runs	H/S	Avg	100s	50s	Cat
5	6	0	49	24	8.16	0	0	3

Bowling

Balls	Runs	Wkts	Avg	Best	5WI	10WM	S/R
793	379	7	54.14	4-83	0	0	113.28

J.D.B.ROBERTSON

Full Name: John David Benbow Robertson (known as Jack)
Born: 22/02/1917, Chiswick, Middlesex
Teams: Middlesex 1937-59, England 1947-52
Matches: 11 (Won 1, Drew 7, Lost 3)
Right-hand opening batsman – Off break bowler

No	Date	Opposition	Venue	R	Bat	C		Bowling		
1	16/08/1947	South Africa	The Oval	D	4					
					30					
2	21/01/1948	West Indies	Bridgetown	D	80	1				
					51*	1				
3	11/02/1948	West Indies	Port-of-Spain	D	2	1				
					133					
4	03/03/1948	West Indies	Georgetown	L	23					
					9					
5	27/03/1948	West Indies	Kingston	L	64					
					28					
6	25/06/1949	New Zealand	Lord's	D	26	1				
					121					
7	02/11/1951	India	Delhi	D	50		5	1	12	0
					22					
8	14/12/1951	India	Bombay (2)	D	44	1	1	0	1	0
9	30/12/1951	India	Calcutta	D	13	1				
					22		5	1	10	0
10	12/01/1952	India	Kanpur	W	21					
					5*		7	1	17	2
11	06/02/1952	India	Madras (1)	L	77		5	1	18	0
					56					

Batting & Fielding

Mat	Inns	N/O	Runs	H/S	Avg	100s	50s	Cat
11	21	2	881	133	46.36	2	6	6

Bowling

Balls	Runs	Wkts	Avg	Best	5WI	10WM	S/R
138	58	2	29.00	2-17	0	0	69.00

R.W.V.ROBINS

Full Name: Robert Walter Vivian Robins (known as Walter)
Born: 03/06/1906, Stafford
Died: 12/12/1968, Marylebone, London
Teams: Cambridge University 1926-28, Middlesex 1925-51, England 1929-37
Matches: 19 (Won 7, Drew 9, Lost 3)
England Captain: 3 times 1937 (Won 1, Drew 2, Lost 0) **Toss:** 2-1
Right-hand middle order batsman – Leg break bowler

No	Date	Opposition	Venue	R	Bat	C		Bowling	
1	29/06/1929	South Africa	Lord's	D	4		24	5 47	2
					0		19	4 32	3
2	13/06/1930	Australia	Trent Bridge	W	50*		17	4 51	4
					4	1	17.2	1 81	3
3	27/06/1930	Australia	Lord's	L	5		42	1 172	1
					11*		9	1 34	2
4	27/06/1931	New Zealand	Lord's	D	12		13	3 38	3
							37	5 126	2
5	25/06/1932	India	Lord's	W	21	3	17	4 39	2
					30		14	5 57	1
6	24/06/1933	West Indies	Lord's	W	8		11.5	1 32	6
							12	2 36	1
7	22/07/1933	West Indies	Old Trafford	D	55	1	28.4	2 111	3
							11.1	0 41	1
8	15/06/1935	South Africa	Trent Bridge	D		1	19	4 65	1
9	27/07/1935	South Africa	Old Trafford	D	108		10	0 34	1
					14		19	8 31	2
10	17/08/1935	South Africa	The Oval	D	10*	1	22	3 73	3
							17	1 61	2
11	27/06/1936	India	Lord's	W	0		13	4 50	3
						1	5	1 17	1
12	25/07/1936	India	Old Trafford	D	76		9.1	1 34	2
						1	29	2 103	3
13	04/12/1936	Australia	Brisbane (2)	W	38		17	0 48	0
					0				
14	18/12/1936	Australia	Sydney	W			1	0 5	0
							7	0 26	0
15	01/01/1937	Australia	Melbourne	L	0	1	7	0 31	2
					61		11	2 46	0
16	29/01/1937	Australia	Adelaide	L	10		7	1 26	1
					4		6	0 38	1
17*	26/06/1937	New Zealand	Lord's	D	18		21	5 58	3
					38*	1	16	3 51	1
18*	24/07/1937	New Zealand	Old Trafford	W	14				
					12				
19*	14/08/1937	New Zealand	The Oval	D	9		14.1	2 40	4
						1	11	2 24	0

Batting & Fielding

Mat	Inns	N/O	Runs	H/S	Avg	100s	50s	Cat
19	27	4	612	108	26.60	1	4	12

Bowling

Balls	Runs	Wkts	Avg	Best	5WI	10WM	S/R
3318	1758	64	27.46	6-32	1	0	51.84

R.T.ROBINSON

Full Name: Robert Timothy Robinson (known as Tim)
Born: 21/11/1958, Skegby, Sutton-in-Ashfield, Nottinghamshire
Teams: Nottinghamshire 1978-96, England 1984-89
Matches: 29 (Won 6, Drew 13, Lost 10)
Right-hand opening/middle order batsman – Right-arm medium bowler

No	Date	Opposition	Venue	R	Bat	C	Bowling
1	28/11/1984	India	Bombay (3)	L	22		
					1		
2	12/12/1984	India	Delhi	W	160		
					18		
3	31/12/1984	India	Calcutta	D	36		1 1 0 0
4	13/01/1985	India	Madras (1)	W	74		
					21*		
5	31/01/1985	India	Kanpur	D	96		
					16*		
6	13/06/1985	Australia	Headingley	W	175		
					21	1	
7	27/06/1985	Australia	Lord's	L	6		
					12		
8	11/07/1985	Australia	Trent Bridge	D	38	1	
					77*		
9	01/08/1985	Australia	Old Trafford	D	10		
10	15/08/1985	Australia	Edgbaston	W	148	1	
						1	
11	29/08/1985	Australia	The Oval	W	3	1	
12	21/02/1986	West Indies	Kingston	L	6		
					0		
13	21/03/1986	West Indies	Bridgetown	L	3		
					43		
14	03/04/1986	West Indies	Port-of-Spain	L	0		
					5		
15	11/04/1986	West Indies	St John's	L	12		
					3	1	
16	05/06/1986	India	Lord's	L	35		
					11		
17	04/06/1987	Pakistan	Old Trafford	D	166		
18	18/06/1987	Pakistan	Lord's	D	7		
19	02/07/1987	Pakistan	Headingley	L	0		
					2		
20	23/07/1987	Pakistan	Edgbaston	D	80		
					4		
21	06/08/1987	Pakistan	The Oval	D	30		
					10		
22	25/11/1987	Pakistan	Lahore (2)	L	6		
					1		
23	07/12/1987	Pakistan	Faisalabad	D	2	1	
					7*		
24	29/01/1988	Australia	Sydney	D	43		
25	12/02/1988	New Zealand	Christchurch	D	70		
					2		
26	25/02/1988	New Zealand	Auckland	D	54		
27	03/03/1988	New Zealand	Wellington	D	0		
28	25/08/1988	Sri Lanka	Lord's	W	19		
					34*		
29	27/07/1989	Australia	Old Trafford	L	0		
					12	1	

Batting & Fielding

Mat	Inns	N/O	Runs	H/S	Avg	100s	50s	Cat
29	49	5	1601	175	36.38	4	6	8

Bowling

Balls	Runs	Wkts	Avg	Best	5WI	10WM	S/R
6	0	0	–	0-0	0	0	–

G.R.J.ROOPE

Full Name: Graham Richard James Roope
Born: 12/07/1946, Fareham, Hampshire
Teams: Surrey 1964-82, Griqualand West 1973/74, England 1973-78
Matches: 21 (Won 7, Drew 12, Lost 2)
Right-hand middle order batsman – Right-arm medium bowler

No	Date	Opposition	Venue	R	Bat	C		Bowling		
1	25/01/1973	India	Kanpur	D	11					
						1	5	1	14	0
2	06/02/1973	India	Bombay (2)	D	10	2				
					26*					
3	02/03/1973	Pakistan	Lahore (2)	D	15	2				
					0	1				
4	16/03/1973	Pakistan	Hyderabad	D	27	2				
					18					
5	07/06/1973	New Zealand	Trent Bridge	W	28	2				
					2	2	9	2	17	0
6	21/06/1973	New Zealand	Lord's	D	56		6	1	15	0
					51					
7	05/07/1973	New Zealand	Headingley	W	18	1				
						2				
8	26/07/1973	West Indies	The Oval	L	9	1	6	1	26	0
					31	1				
9	28/08/1975	Australia	The Oval	D	0	1				
					77					
10	11/08/1977	Australia	Headingley	W	34					
11	25/08/1977	Australia	The Oval	D	38					
12	14/12/1977	Pakistan	Lahore (2)	D	19					
13	02/01/1978	Pakistan	Hyderabad	D	1	1	1	0	2	0
14	18/01/1978	Pakistan	Karachi (1)	D	56	2				
					33*					
15	10/02/1978	New Zealand	Wellington	L	37					
					0	3				
16	24/02/1978	New Zealand	Christchurch	W	50	1				
					9*	2				
17	04/03/1978	New Zealand	Auckland	D	68	2				
						1	1	0	2	0
18	01/06/1978	Pakistan	Edgbaston	W	32	2				
						1				
19	15/06/1978	Pakistan	Lord's	W	69					
						3				
20	29/06/1978	Pakistan	Headingley	D	11					
21	27/07/1978	New Zealand	The Oval	W	14					
					10*					

Batting & Fielding

Mat	Inns	N/O	Runs	H/S	Avg	100s	50s	Cat
21	32	4	860	77	30.71	0	7	35

Bowling

Balls	Runs	Wkts	Avg	Best	5WI	10WM	S/R
172	76	0	–	0-2	0	0	–

C.F.ROOT

Full Name: Charles Frederick Root (known as Fred)
Born: 16/04/1890, Somercotes, Derbyshire
Died: 20/01/1954, Wolverhampton, Staffordshire
Teams: Derbyshire 1910-20, Worcestershire 1921-32, England 1926
Matches: 3 (Won 0, Drew 3, Lost 0)
Right-hand lower order batsman – Right-arm fast medium bowler

No	Date	Opposition	Venue	R	Bat	C		Bowling		
1	12/06/1926	Australia	Trent Bridge	D						
2	26/06/1926	Australia	Lord's	D			36	11	70	2
						1	19	9	40	2
3	24/07/1926	Australia	Old Trafford	D			52	27	84	4

Batting & Fielding

Mat	Inns	N/O	Runs	H/S	Avg	100s	50s	Cat
3	0	–	–	–	–	–	–	1

Bowling

Balls	Runs	Wkts	Avg	Best	5WI	10WM	S/R
642	194	8	24.25	4-84	0	0	80.25

B.C.ROSE

Full Name: Brian Charles Rose
Born: 04/06/1950, Dartford, Kent
Teams: Somerset 1969-87, England 1977-81
Matches: 9 (Won 1, Drew 6, Lost 2)
Left-hand opening batsman – Left-arm medium bowler

No	Date	Opposition	Venue	R	Bat	C
1	14/12/1977	Pakistan	Lahore (2)	D	1	1
2	02/01/1978	Pakistan	Hyderabad	D	27	
3	18/01/1978	Pakistan	Karachi (1)	D	10	
					18	
4	10/02/1978	New Zealand	Wellington	L	21	1
					5*	
5	24/02/1978	New Zealand	Christchurch	W	11	
					7	
6	10/07/1980	West Indies	Old Trafford	D	70	
					32	
7	24/07/1980	West Indies	The Oval	D	50	2
					41	
8	07/08/1980	West Indies	Headingley	D	7	
					43*	
9	13/02/1981	West Indies	Port-of-Spain	L	10	
					5	

Batting & Fielding

Mat	Inns	N/O	Runs	H/S	Avg	100s	50s	Cat
9	16	2	358	70	25.57	0	2	4

V.P.F.A.ROYLE

Full Name: Rev Vernon Peter Fanshawe Archer Royle
Born: 29/01/1854, Brooklands, Cheshire
Died: 21/05/1929, Stanmore Park, Middlesex
Teams: Oxford University 1875-76, Lancashire 1873-91, England 1879
Matches: 1 (Won 0, Drew 0, Lost 1)
Right-hand middle order batsman – Right-hand round-arm slow bowler

No	Date	Opposition	Venue	R	Bat	C		Bowling		
1	02/01/1879	Australia	Melbourne	L	3	2	4	1	6	0
					18					

Batting & Fielding

Mat	Inns	N/O	Runs	H/S	Avg	100s	50s	Cat
1	2	0	21	18	10.50	0	0	2

Bowling

Balls	Runs	Wkts	Avg	Best	5WI	10WM	S/R
16	6	0	–	0-6	0	0	–

F.E.RUMSEY

Full Name: Frederick Edward Rumsey (known as Fred)
Born: 04/12/1935, Stepney, London
Teams: Worcestershire 1960-62, Somerset 1963-68, Derbyshire 1970, England 1964-65
Matches: 5 (Won 3, Drew 2, Lost 0)
Right-hand lower order batsman – Left-arm fast medium bowler

No	Date	Opposition	Venue	R	Bat	C		Bowling	
1	23/07/1964	Australia	Old Trafford	D	3*		35.5	4	99	2

No	Date	Opposition	Venue	R	Bat	C	Bowling			
2	27/05/1965	New Zealand	Edgbaston	W	21*		9	2	22	0
							17	5	32	0
3	17/06/1965	New Zealand	Lord's	W	3		13	4	25	4
							26	10	42	1
4	08/07/1965	New Zealand	Headingley	W			24	6	59	1
							15	5	49	3
5	22/07/1965	South Africa	Lord's	D	3		30	9	84	3
					0*		21	8	49	3

Batting & Fielding

Mat	Inns	N/O	Runs	H/S	Avg	100s	50s	Cat
5	5	3	30	21*	15.00	0	0	0

Bowling

Balls	Runs	Wkts	Avg	Best	5WI	10WM	S/R
1145	461	17	27.11	4-25	0	0	67.35

C.A.G.RUSSELL

Full Name: Charles Albert George Russell (known as Albert Charles or Jack)
Born: 07/10/1887, Leyton, Essex
Died: 23/03/1961, Whipps Cross, Leytonstone, Essex
Teams: Essex 1908-30, England 1920-23
Matches: 10 (Won 2, Drew 4, Lost 4)
Right-hand opening batsman – Right-arm slow medium bowler

No	Date	Opposition	Venue	R	Bat	C
1	17/12/1920	Australia	Sydney	L	0	
					5	1
2	31/12/1920	Australia	Melbourne	L	0	1
					5	
3	14/01/1921	Australia	Adelaide	L	135*	
					59	
4	25/02/1921	Australia	Sydney	L	19	
					35	
5	23/07/1921	Australia	Old Trafford	D	101	1
6	13/08/1921	Australia	The Oval	D	13	
					102*	
7	01/01/1923	South Africa	Cape Town	W	39	
					8	
8	18/01/1923	South Africa	Durban (2)	D	34	
9	09/02/1923	South Africa	Johannesburg (1)	D	8	3
					96	1
10	16/02/1923	South Africa	Durban (2)	W	140	1
					111	

Batting & Fielding

Mat	Inns	N/O	Runs	H/S	Avg	100s	50s	Cat
10	18	2	910	140	56.87	5	2	8

R.C.RUSSELL

Full Name: Robert Charles Russell (known as Jack)
Born: 15/08/1963, Stroud, Gloucestershire
Teams: Gloucestershire 1981-96, England 1988-96
Matches: 49 (Won 11, Drew 22, Lost 16)
Left-hand middle order batsman – Wicket-keeper

No	Date	Opposition	Venue	R	Bat	C	St	B
1+	25/08/1988	Sri Lanka	Lord's	W	94	2		1
						1		0
2+	08/06/1989	Australia	Headingley	L	15	3		0
					2	1		2
3+	22/06/1989	Australia	Lord's	L	64*	2		0
					29	1		3
4+	06/07/1989	Australia	Edgbaston	D	42		1	0
								4
5+	27/07/1989	Australia	Old Trafford	L	1	2	1	5
					128*			0
6+	10/08/1989	Australia	Trent Bridge	L	20		2	6
					1			

No	Date	Opposition	Venue	R	Bat	C	St	B
7+	24/08/1989	Australia	The Oval	D	12 0*	4 1		1 2
8+	24/02/1990	West Indies	Kingston	W	26	1		9 14
9+	23/03/1990	West Indies	Port-of-Spain	D	15 5*	4 1		0 2
10+	05/04/1990	West Indies	Bridgetown	L	7 55	5		0 0
11+	12/04/1990	West Indies	St John's	L	7 24	3		0
12+	07/06/1990	New Zealand	Trent Bridge	D	28	1 2		1 0
13+	21/06/1990	New Zealand	Lord's	D	13	2		12
14+	05/07/1990	New Zealand	Edgbaston	W	43 0	2		9 0
15+	26/07/1990	India	Lord's	W		3 3		0 3
16+	09/08/1990	India	Old Trafford	D	8 16*	2		5 17
17+	23/08/1990	India	The Oval	D	35	3	1	7
18+	23/11/1990	Australia	Brisbane (2)	L	16 15	1		1 3
19+	26/12/1990	Australia	Melbourne	L	15 1	6		4 4
20+	04/01/1991	Australia	Sydney	D	30* 1	1 1	1	5 0
21+	06/06/1991	West Indies	Headingley	W	5 4	1		0 0
22+	20/06/1991	West Indies	Lord's	D	46	1		3 0
23+	04/07/1991	West Indies	Trent Bridge	L	3 3	1		2 0
24+	25/07/1991	West Indies	Edgbaston	L	12 0			0 0
25+	22/08/1991	Sri Lanka	Lord's	W	17 12*	1 2		0 1
26+	18/01/1992	New Zealand	Christchurch	W	36	3	1	1 1
27+	30/01/1992	New Zealand	Auckland	W	33 24	1 2		0 0
28+	06/02/1992	New Zealand	Wellington	D	18 24*	1 1		1 0
29+	04/06/1992	Pakistan	Edgbaston	D	29*	1		2
30+	18/06/1992	Pakistan	Lord's	L	22* 1	2 2		4 2
31+	02/07/1992	Pakistan	Old Trafford	D	4	1	1	9 8
32+	19/02/1994	West Indies	Kingston	L	0 32	1		0 5
33+	17/03/1994	West Indies	Georgetown	L	13 6	3		2
34+	25/03/1994	West Indies	Port-of-Spain	L	23 4	2		1 8
35+	08/04/1994	West Indies	Bridgetown	W	38 17*	1 1		0 1
36+	16/04/1994	West Indies	St John's	D	62	2		0 0
37+	27/07/1995	West Indies	Old Trafford	W	35 31*	2 1		0 5
38+	10/08/1995	West Indies	Trent Bridge	D	35 7	1 2	1	2 0
39+	24/08/1995	West Indies	The Oval	D	91	3		5
40+	16/11/1995	South Africa	Centurion	D	50*			
41+	30/11/1995	South Africa	Johannesburg (3)	D	12 29*	6 5		1 5
42+	14/12/1995	South Africa	Durban (2)	D	8	3		0
43+	26/12/1995	South Africa	Port Elizabeth	D	30	4 3	1 1	0 8

No	Date	Opposition	Venue	R	Bat	C	St	B
44+	02/01/1996	South Africa	Cape Town	L	9	4		0
					2			0
45+	06/06/1996	India	Edgbaston	W	0	1		3
						2		4
46+	20/06/1996	India	Lord's	D	124	2		11
					38			
47+	04/07/1996	India	Trent Bridge	D	0	3		6
								1
48+	25/07/1996	Pakistan	Lord's	L	41*	2		3
					1	2		4
49+	08/08/1996	Pakistan	Headingley	D	9	3		4
						2		4

Batting & Fielding

Mat	Inns	N/O	Runs	H/S	Avg	100s	50s	Cat	St	Byes
49	77	15	1807	128*	29.14	2	6	141	11	237

W.E.RUSSELL

Full Name: William Eric Russell (known as Eric)
Born: 03/07/1936, Dumbarton, Scotland
Teams: Middlesex 1956-72, England 1961-67
Matches: 10 (Won 1, Drew 6, Lost 3)
Right-hand opening batsman – Right-arm medium bowler

No	Date	Opposition	Venue	R	Bat	C		Bowling		
1	21/10/1961	Pakistan	Lahore (2)	W	34		19	9	25	0
					0					
2	30/12/1961	India	Calcutta	L	10		5	0	19	0
					9					
3	26/08/1965	South Africa	The Oval	D	0					
					70					
4	10/12/1965	Australia	Brisbane (2)	D	0*					
5	25/02/1966	New Zealand	Christchurch	D	30					
					25	1				
6	04/03/1966	New Zealand	Dunedin	D	11					
7	11/03/1966	New Zealand	Auckland	D	56	2				
					1					
8	02/06/1966	West Indies	Old Trafford	L	26	1				
					20					
9	30/06/1966	West Indies	Trent Bridge	L	4					
					11					
10	27/07/1967	Pakistan	Lord's	D	43					
					12					

Batting & Fielding

Mat	Inns	N/O	Runs	H/S	Avg	100s	50s	Cat
10	18	1	362	70	21.29	0	2	4

Bowling

Balls	Runs	Wkts	Avg	Best	5WI	10WM	S/R
144	44	0	–	0-19	0	0	–

I.D.K.SALISBURY

Full Name: Ian David Kenneth Salisbury
Born: 21/01/1970, Northampton
Teams: Sussex 1989-96, England 1992-96
Matches: 9 (Won 0, Drew 1, Lost 8)
Right-hand middle/lower order batsman – Leg break & googly bowler

No	Date	Opposition	Venue	R	Bat	C		Bowling		
1	18/06/1992	Pakistan	Lord's	L	4		23	3	73	2
					12		14.1	0	49	3
2	02/07/1992	Pakistan	Old Trafford	D	50		20	0	117	0
							13	0	67	0
3	29/01/1993	India	Calcutta	L	28	1	17	2	72	1
					26		6	3	16	0
4	11/02/1993	India	Madras (1)	L	4	1	29	1	142	2
					12					

No	Date	Opposition	Venue	R	Bat	C		Bowling		
5	17/03/1994	West Indies	Georgetown	L	8		37	4	163	4
					19					
6	25/03/1994	West Indies	Port-of-Spain	L	36		22	4	72	2
					0	1	9	1	41	1
7	21/07/1994	South Africa	Lord's	L	6*		25	2	68	0
					0		19	4	53	1
8	25/07/1996	Pakistan	Lord's	L	5		12.2	1	42	1
					40		20	4	63	0
9	22/08/1996	Pakistan	The Oval	L	5		29	3	116	1
					0*					

Batting & Fielding

Mat	Inns	N/O	Runs	H/S	Avg	100s	50s	Cat
9	17	2	255	50	17.00	0	1	3

Bowling

Balls	Runs	Wkts	Avg	Best	5WI	10WM	S/R
1773	1154	18	64.11	4-163	0	0	98.50

A.SANDHAM

Full Name: Andrew Sandham (known as Andy)
Born: 06/07/1890, Streatham, London
Died: 20/04/1982, Westminster, London
Teams: Surrey 1911-37, England 1921-30
Matches: 14 (Won 3, Drew 7, Lost 4)
Right-hand opening batsman

No	Date	Opposition	Venue	R	Bat	C
1	13/08/1921	Australia	The Oval	D	21	
2	23/12/1922	South Africa	Johannesburg (1)	L	26	
					25	
3	01/01/1923	South Africa	Cape Town	W	19	
					17	
4	18/01/1923	South Africa	Durban (2)	D	0	
5	09/02/1923	South Africa	Johannesburg (1)	D	6	
					58	
6	16/02/1923	South Africa	Durban (2)	W	1	
					40	
7	26/07/1924	South Africa	Old Trafford	D		
8	16/08/1924	South Africa	The Oval	D	46	1
9	19/12/1924	Australia	Sydney	L	7	
					2	
10	27/02/1925	Australia	Sydney	L	4	
					15	
11	11/01/1930	West Indies	Bridgetown	D	152	1
					51	
12	01/02/1930	West Indies	Port-of-Spain	W	0	
					5	1
13	21/02/1930	West Indies	Georgetown	L	9	
					0	
14	03/04/1930	West Indies	Kingston	D	325	
					50	1

Batting & Fielding

Mat	Inns	N/O	Runs	H/S	Avg	100s	50s	Cat
14	23	0	879	325	38.21	2	3	4

S.S.SCHULTZ

Full Name: Sandford Spence Schultz (later Storey)
Born: 29/08/1857, Birkenhead, Cheshire
Died: 18/12/1937, South Kensington, London
Teams: Cambridge University 1876-77, Lancashire 1877-82, England 1879
Matches: 1 (Won 0, Drew 0, Lost 1)
Right-hand lower order batsman – Right-hand round-arm fast bowler

No	Date	Opposition	Venue	R	Bat	C		Bowling		
1	02/01/1879	Australia	Melbourne	L	0*		6.3	3	16	1
					20		2	0	10	0

Batting & Fielding

Mat	Inns	N/O	Runs	H/S	Avg	100s	50s	Cat
1	2	1	20	20	20.00	0	0	0

Bowling

Balls	Runs	Wkts	Avg	Best	5WI	10WM	S/R
35	26	1	26.00	1-16	0	0	35.00

W.H.SCOTTON

Full Name: William Henry Scotton
Born: 15/01/1856, Nottingham
Died: 09/07/1893, St John's Wood, London
Teams: Nottinghamshire 1875-90, England 1881-87
Matches: 15 (Won 8, Drew 3, Lost 4)
Left-hand opening batsman – Left-arm fast medium bowler

No	Date	Opposition	Venue	R	Bat	C		Bowling		
1	31/12/1881	Australia	Melbourne	D	21					
					50*					
2	17/02/1882	Australia	Sydney	L	30					
					12					
3	03/03/1882	Australia	Sydney	L	18					
					1					
4	10/03/1882	Australia	Melbourne	D	26	1				
5	11/08/1884	Australia	The Oval	D	90		5	1	20	0
6	12/12/1884	Australia	Adelaide	W	82					
					2					
7	01/01/1885	Australia	Melbourne	W	13					
					7*					
8	20/02/1885	Australia	Sydney	L	22	1				
					2					
9	14/03/1885	Australia	Sydney	L	4					
					0					
10	21/03/1885	Australia	Melbourne	W	27					
11	05/07/1886	Australia	Old Trafford	W	21	2				
					20					
12	19/07/1886	Australia	Lord's	W	19					
13	12/08/1886	Australia	The Oval	W	34					
14	28/01/1887	Australia	Sydney	W	1					
					6					
15	25/02/1887	Australia	Sydney	W	0					
					2					

Batting & Fielding

Mat	Inns	N/O	Runs	H/S	Avg	100s	50s	Cat
15	25	2	510	90	22.17	0	3	4

Bowling

Balls	Runs	Wkts	Avg	Best	5WI	10WM	S/R
20	20	0	–	0-20	0	0	–

J.SELBY

Full Name: John Selby (birth registered as John Burrows)
Born: 01/07/1849, Nottingham
Died: 11/03/1894, Standard Hill, Nottingham
Teams: Nottinghamshire 1870-87, England 1877-82
Matches: 6 (Won 1, Drew 2, Lost 3)
Right-hand opening/middle order batsman – Wicket-keeper – Right-arm medium bowler

No	Date	Opposition	Venue	R	Bat	C	St	B
1+	15/03/1877	Australia	Melbourne	L	7			4
					38	1		5
2+	31/03/1877	Australia	Melbourne	W	7			0
					2			
3	31/12/1881	Australia	Melbourne	D	55			
					70			

No	Date	Opposition	Venue	R	Bat	C	St	B
4	17/02/1882	Australia	Sydney	L	6			
					2			
5	03/03/1882	Australia	Sydney	L	13			
					1			
6	10/03/1882	Australia	Melbourne	D	7			
					48*			

Batting & Fielding

Mat	Inns	N/O	Runs	H/S	Avg	100s	50s	Cat	St	Byes
6	12	1	256	70	23.27	0	2	1	0	9

M.W.W.SELVEY

Full Name: Michael Walter William Selvey (known as Mike)
Born: 25/04/1948, Chiswick, Middlesex
Teams: Cambridge University 1971, Surrey 1968-71, Middlesex 1972-82, Glamorgan 1983-84, Orange Free State 1973/74, England 1976-77
Matches: 3 (Won 0, Drew 1, Lost 2)
Right-hand lower order batsman – Right-arm fast medium bowler

No	Date	Opposition	Venue	R	Bat	C		Bowling		
1	08/07/1976	West Indies	Old Trafford	L	2*		17	4	41	4
					4		26	3	111	2
2	12/08/1976	West Indies	The Oval	L	0	1	15	0	67	0
					4*		9	1	44	0
3	11/02/1977	India	Bombay (3)	D	5*		15	1	80	0

Batting & Fielding

Mat	Inns	N/O	Runs	H/S	Avg	100s	50s	Cat
3	5	3	15	5*	7.50	0	0	1

Bowling

Balls	Runs	Wkts	Avg	Best	5WI	10WM	S/R
492	343	6	57.16	4-41	0	0	82.00

D.SHACKLETON

Full Name: Derek Shackleton
Born: 12/08/1924, Todmorden, Yorkshire
Teams: Hampshire 1948-69, England 1950-63
Matches: 7 (Won 2, Drew 2, Lost 3)
Right-hand lower order batsman – Right-arm medium bowler

No	Date	Opposition	Venue	R	Bat	C		Bowling		
1	20/07/1950	West Indies	Trent Bridge	L	42		43	7	128	1
					1		6	2	7	0
2	16/08/1951	South Africa	The Oval	W	14		15	5	20	1
					5*		10	2	19	0
3	02/11/1951	India	Delhi	D	10		29	7	76	1
					21*					
4	20/06/1963	West Indies	Lord's	D	8		50.2	22	93	3
					4		34	14	72	4
5	04/07/1963	West Indies	Edgbaston	W	6*		21	9	60	1
							17	4	37	2
6	25/07/1963	West Indies	Headingley	L	1*	1	42	10	88	1
					1*		26	2	63	3
7	22/08/1963	West Indies	The Oval	L	0*		21	5	37	1
					0*		32	7	68	0

Batting & Fielding

Mat	Inns	N/O	Runs	H/S	Avg	100s	50s	Cat
7	13	7	113	42	18.83	0	0	1

Bowling

Balls	Runs	Wkts	Avg	Best	5WI	10WM	S/R
2078	768	18	42.66	4-72	0	0	115.44

J.SHARP

Full Name: John Sharp
Born: 15/02/1878, Hereford
Died: 28/01/1938, Wavertree, Liverpool, Lancashire
Teams: Lancashire 1899-1925, England 1909
Matches: 3 (Won 0, Drew 2, Lost 1)
Right-hand middle order batsman – Left-arm fast medium bowler

No	Date	Opposition	Venue	R	Bat	C		Bowling	
1	01/07/1909	Australia	Headingley	L	61				
					11	1	1	0 7 0	
2	26/07/1909	Australia	Old Trafford	D	3				
					8*		1	0 3 0	
3	09/08/1909	Australia	The Oval	D	105		16.3	3 67 3	
					0*		12	0 34 0	

Batting & Fielding

Mat	Inns	N/O	Runs	H/S	Avg	100s	50s	Cat
3	6	2	188	105	47.00	1	1	1

Bowling

Balls	Runs	Wkts	Avg	Best	5WI	10WM	S/R
183	111	3	37.00	3-67	0	0	61.00

J.W.SHARPE

Full Name: John William Sharpe
Born: 09/12/1866, Ruddington, Nottinghamshire
Died: 19/06/1936, Ruddington, Nottinghamshire
Teams: Surrey 1889-93, Nottinghamshire 1894, England 1890-92
Matches: 3 (Won 1, Drew 0, Lost 2)
Right-hand lower order batsman – Right-arm fast medium bowler

No	Date	Opposition	Venue	R	Bat	C		Bowling	
1	11/08/1890	Australia	The Oval	W	5*	1	6	3 8 1	
					2*		9	5 10 1	
2	01/01/1892	Australia	Melbourne	L	2		51	20 84 6	
					5*		54	25 81 2	
3	29/01/1892	Australia	Sydney	L	26		10	1 31 0	
					4*	1	35	7 91 1	

Batting & Fielding

Mat	Inns	N/O	Runs	H/S	Avg	100s	50s	Cat
3	6	4	44	26	22.00	0	0	2

Bowling

Balls	Runs	Wkts	Avg	Best	5WI	10WM	S/R
975	305	11	27.72	6-84	1	0	88.63

P.J.SHARPE

Full Name: Philip John Sharpe
Born: 27/12/1936, Shipley, Yorkshire
Teams: Yorkshire 1958-74, Derbyshire 1975-76, England 1963-69
Matches: 12 (Won 5, Drew 5, Lost 2)
Right-hand opening batsman – Off break bowler

No	Date	Opposition	Venue	R	Bat	C
1	04/07/1963	West Indies	Edgbaston	W	23	1
					85*	1
2	25/07/1963	West Indies	Headingley	L	0	
					13	2
3	22/08/1963	West Indies	The Oval	L	63	
					83	
4	10/01/1964	India	Madras (2)	D	27	
					31*	
5	04/06/1964	Australia	Trent Bridge	D	35*	
					1	
6	18/06/1964	Australia	Lord's	D	35	
7	12/06/1969	West Indies	Old Trafford	W	2	
						2

No	Date	Opposition	Venue	R	Bat	C
8	26/06/1969	West Indies	Lord's	D	11	1
					86	2
9	10/07/1969	West Indies	Headingley	W	6	1
					15	2
10	24/07/1969	New Zealand	Lord's	W	20	1
					46	1
11	07/08/1969	New Zealand	Trent Bridge	D	111	1
12	21/08/1969	New Zealand	The Oval	W	48	2
					45*	

Batting & Fielding

Mat	Inns	N/O	Runs	H/S	Avg	100s	50s	Cat
12	21	4	786	111	46.23	1	4	17

A.SHAW

Full Name: Alfred Shaw
Born: 29/08/1842, Burton Joyce, Nottinghamshire
Died: 16/01/1907, Gedling, Nottinghamshire
Teams: Nottinghamshire 1864-97, Sussex 1894-95, England 1877-82
Matches: 7 (Won 2, Drew 2, Lost 3)
England Captain: 4 times 1881-82 (Won 0, Drew 2, Lost 2) **Toss:** 4-0
Right-hand lower order batsman – Right-arm slow medium bowler (previously right-arm medium)

No	Date	Opposition	Venue	R	Bat	C	Bowling			
1	15/03/1877	Australia	Melbourne	L	10		55.3	34	51	3
					2		34	16	38	5
2	31/03/1877	Australia	Melbourne	W	1		42	27	30	0
					0*	1	32	19	27	0
3	06/09/1880	Australia	The Oval	W	0		13	5	21	1
						2	33	18	42	1
4*	31/12/1881	Australia	Melbourne	D	5		20	11	21	0
					40					
5*	17/02/1882	Australia	Sydney	L	11	1				
					30		21	15	12	1
6*	03/03/1882	Australia	Sydney	L	3		8	4	14	0
					6					
7*	10/03/1882	Australia	Melbourne	D	3		16	6	29	1

Batting & Fielding

Mat	Inns	N/O	Runs	H/S	Avg	100s	50s	Cat
7	12	1	111	40	10.09	0	0	4

Bowling

Balls	Runs	Wkts	Avg	Best	5WI	10WM	S/R
1099	285	12	23.75	5-38	1	0	91.58

Rev.D.S.SHEPPARD

Full Name: Rt Rev David Stuart Sheppard
Born: 06/03/1929, Reigate, Surrey
Teams: Cambridge United 1950-52, Sussex 1947-62, England 1950-63
Matches: 22 (Won 12, Drew 7, Lost 3)
England Captain: 2 times 1954 (Won 1, Drew 1, Lost 0) **Toss:** 1-1
Right-hand opening batsman – Left-arm slow bowler

No	Date	Opposition	Venue	R	Bat	C
1	12/08/1950	West Indies	The Oval	L	11	
					29	
2	02/02/1951	Australia	Adelaide	L	9	
					41	
3	23/02/1951	Australia	Melbourne	W	1	
4	24/03/1951	New Zealand	Wellington	W	3	
					4*	1
5	17/07/1952	India	Old Trafford	W	34	1
6	14/08/1952	India	The Oval	D	119	
7*	01/07/1954	Pakistan	Trent Bridge	W	37	1
						1
8*	22/07/1954	Pakistan	Old Trafford	D	13	1
						1

No	Date	Opposition	Venue	R	Bat	C
9	26/07/1956	Australia	Old Trafford	W	113	
10	23/08/1956	Australia	The Oval	D	24	
					62	
11	25/07/1957	West Indies	Headingley	W	68	
						1
12	22/08/1957	West Indies	The Oval	W	40	
						1
13	26/07/1962	Pakistan	Trent Bridge	D	83	
14	16/08/1962	Pakistan	The Oval	W	57	
					9*	
15	30/11/1962	Australia	Brisbane (2)	D	31	
					53	1
16	29/12/1962	Australia	Melbourne	W	0	
					113	
17	11/01/1963	Australia	Sydney	L	3	
					12	
18	25/01/1963	Australia	Adelaide	D	30	1
					1	
19	15/02/1963	Australia	Sydney	D	19	
					68	
20	23/02/1963	New Zealand	Auckland	W	12	1
21	01/03/1963	New Zealand	Wellington	W	0	1
22	15/03/1963	New Zealand	Christchurch	W	42	
					31	

Batting & Fielding

Mat	Inns	N/O	Runs	H/S	Avg	100s	50s	Cat
22	33	2	1172	119	37.80	3	6	12

M.SHERWIN

Full Name: Mordecai Sherwin
Born: 26/02/1851, Greasley, Nottinghamshire
Died: 03/07/1910, Nottingham
Teams: Nottinghamshire 1876-96, England 1887-88
Matches: 3 (Won 2, Drew 0, Lost 1)
Right-hand lower order batsman – Wicket-keeper – Occasional right-arm fast bowler

No	Date	Opposition	Venue	R	Bat	C	St	B
1+	28/01/1887	Australia	Sydney	W	0*	1		1
					21*			12
2+	25/02/1887	Australia	Sydney	W	4*			5
					5	2	2	9
3+	16/07/1888	Australia	Lord's	L	0*	1		5
					0	1		3

Batting & Fielding

Mat	Inns	N/O	Runs	H/S	Avg	100s	50s	Cat	St	Byes
3	6	4	30	21*	15.00	0	0	5	2	35

A.SHREWSBURY

Full Name: Arthur Shrewsbury
Born: 11/04/1856, New Lenton, Nottinghamshire
Died: 19/05/1903, Gedling, Nottinghamshire
Teams: Nottinghamshire 1875-1902, England 1881-93
Matches: 23 (Won 13, Drew 6, Lost 4)
England Captain: 7 times 1884-87 (Won 5, Drew 0, Lost 2) **Toss:** 3-4
Right-hand opening batsman

No	Date	Opposition	Venue	R	Bat	C	Bowling
1	31/12/1881	Australia	Melbourne	D	11		
					16		
2	17/02/1882	Australia	Sydney	L	7	3	
					22		
3	03/03/1882	Australia	Sydney	L	82		
					47		
4	10/03/1882	Australia	Melbourne	D	1	1	

No	Date	Opposition	Venue	R	Bat	C	Bowling
5	10/07/1884	Australia	Old Trafford	D	43	1	
					25		
6	21/07/1884	Australia	Lord's	W	27		
						2	
7	11/08/1884	Australia	The Oval	D	10		3 2 2 0
					37		
8*	12/12/1884	Australia	Adelaide	W	0	1	
					26*	2	
9*	01/01/1885	Australia	Melbourne	W	72	1	
					0*		
10*	20/02/1885	Australia	Sydney	L	18		
					24	1	
11*	14/03/1885	Australia	Sydney	L	40	1	
					16		
12*	21/03/1885	Australia	Melbourne	W	105*		
13	05/07/1886	Australia	Old Trafford	W	31		
					4	1	
14	19/07/1886	Australia	Lord's	W	164	1	
15	12/08/1886	Australia	The Oval	W	44	1	
						1	
16*	28/01/1887	Australia	Sydney	W	2	2	
					29	1	
17*	25/02/1887	Australia	Sydney	W	9		
					6		
18	10/02/1888	Australia	Sydney	W	44	3	
					1	3	
19	21/07/1890	Australia	Lord's	W	4		
					13		
20	11/08/1890	Australia	The Oval	W	4		
					9		
21	17/07/1893	Australia	Lord's	D	106	1	
					81		
22	14/08/1893	Australia	The Oval	W	66		
						1	
23	24/08/1893	Australia	Old Trafford	D	12		
					19*	1	

Batting & Fielding

Mat	Inns	N/O	Runs	H/S	Avg	100s	50s	Cat
23	40	4	1277	164	35.47	3	4	29

Bowling

Balls	Runs	Wkts	Avg	Best	5WI	10WM	S/R
12	2	0	–	0-2	0	0	–

J.SHUTER

Full Name: John Shuter
Born: 09/02/1855, Thornton Heath, Surrey
Died: 05/07/1920, Blackheath, London
Teams: Kent 1874, Surrey 1877-1909, England 1888
Matches: 1 (Won 1, Drew 0, Lost 0)
Right-hand opening batsman

No	Date	Opposition	Venue	R	Bat	C
1	13/08/1888	Australia	The Oval	W	28	

Batting & Fielding

Mat	Inns	N/O	Runs	H/S	Avg	100s	50s	Cat
1	1	0	28	28	28.00	0	0	0

K.SHUTTLEWORTH

Full Name: Kenneth Shuttleworth (known as Ken)
Born: 13/11/1944, St Helens, Lancashire
Teams: Lancashire 1964-75, Leicestershire 1977-80, England 1970-71
Matches: 5 (Won 1, Drew 4, Lost 0)
Right-hand lower order batsman – Right-arm fast bowler

No	Date	Opposition	Venue	R	Bat	C	Bowling
1	27/11/1970	Australia	Brisbane (2)	D	7		27 6 81 0
						1	17.5 2 47 5

No	Date	Opposition	Venue	R	Bat	C		Bowling		
2	11/12/1970	Australia	Perth	D	2		28	4	105	2
							3	1	9	0
3	25/02/1971	New Zealand	Christchurch	W	5		8	1	14	3
							12	1	27	2
4	05/03/1971	New Zealand	Auckland	D	0		17	3	49	0
							11	4	0	12	0
5	03/06/1971	Pakistan	Edgbaston	D	21		23	2	83	0

Batting & Fielding

Mat	Inns	N/O	Runs	H/S	Avg	100s	50s	Cat
5	6	0	46	21	7.66	0	0	1

Bowling

Balls	Runs	Wkts	Avg	Best	5WI	10WM	S/R
1071	427	12	35.58	5-47	1	0	89.25

A.SIDEBOTTOM

Full Name: Arnold Sidebottom (known as Arnie)
Born: 01/04/1954, Shawlands, Barnsley, Yorkshire
Teams: Yorkshire 1973-91, Orange Free state 1981/82-83/84, England 1985
Matches: 1 (Won 0, Drew 1, Lost 0)
Right-hand lower order batsman – Right-arm fast medium bowler

No	Date	Opposition	Venue	R	Bat	C		Bowling		
1	11/07/1985	Australia	Trent Bridge	D	2		18.4	3	65	1

Batting & Fielding

Mat	Inns	N/O	Runs	H/S	Avg	100s	50s	Cat
1	1	0	2	2	2.00	0	0	0

Bowling

Balls	Runs	Wkts	Avg	Best	5WI	10WM	S/R
112	65	1	65.00	1-65	0	0	112.00

R.T.SIMPSON

Full Name: Reginald Thomas Simpson (known as Reg)
Born: 27/02/1920, Sherwood Rise, Nottingham
Teams: Nottinghamshire 1946-63, Sind 1944/45-45/46, Europeans 1944/45-45/46, England 1948-55
Matches: 27 (Won 11, Drew 7, Lost 9)
Right-hand opening batsman – Off break bowler

No	Date	Opposition	Venue	R	Bat	C		Bowling		
1	16/12/1948	South Africa	Durban (2)	W	5					
					0					
2	23/07/1949	New Zealand	Old Trafford	D	103					
							2	1	9	0
3	13/08/1949	New Zealand	The Oval	D	68					
4	08/06/1950	West Indies	Old Trafford	W	27					
					0					
5	20/07/1950	West Indies	Trent Bridge	L	4					
					94		1.3	0	9	0
6	12/08/1950	West Indies	The Oval	L	30					
					16					
7	01/12/1950	Australia	Brisbane (2)	L	12	2				
					0	2				
8	22/12/1950	Australia	Melbourne	L	4					
					23					
9	05/01/1951	Australia	Sydney	L	49					
					0					
10	02/02/1951	Australia	Adelaide	L	29					
					61					
11	23/02/1951	Australia	Melbourne	W	156*					
					15					
12	17/03/1951	New Zealand	Christchurch	D	81					
							4	1	4	2
13	24/03/1951	New Zealand	Wellington	W	6					
					5					
14	07/06/1951	South Africa	Trent Bridge	L	137					
					7					
15	21/06/1951	South Africa	Lord's	W	26					

No	Date	Opposition	Venue	R	Bat	C	Bowling
16	05/07/1951	South Africa	Old Trafford	W	11		
					4*		
17	05/06/1952	India	Headingley	W	23		
					51		
18	19/06/1952	India	Lord's	W	53		
					2		
19	11/06/1953	Australia	Trent Bridge	D	0		
					28*	1	
20	09/07/1953	Australia	Old Trafford	D	31		
21	23/07/1953	Australia	Headingley	D	15		
					0		
22	10/06/1954	Pakistan	Lord's	D	40		
23	01/07/1954	Pakistan	Trent Bridge	W	101		
24	12/08/1954	Pakistan	The Oval	L	2		
					27		
25	26/11/1954	Australia	Brisbane (2)	L	2		
					9		
26	11/03/1955	New Zealand	Dunedin	W	21		
27	25/03/1955	New Zealand	Auckland	W	23		

Batting & Fielding

Mat	Inns	N/O	Runs	H/S	Avg	100s	50s	Cat
27	45	3	1401	156*	33.35	4	6	5

Bowling

Balls	Runs	Wkts	Avg	Best	5WI	10WM	S/R
45	22	2	11.00	2-4	0	0	22.50

G.H.T.SIMPSON-HAYWARD

Full Name: George Hayward Thomas Simpson (Simpson-Hayward from 1898)
Born: 07/06/1875, Stoneleigh, Kenilworth, Warwickshire
Died: 02/10/1936, Icomb Place, Gloucestershire
Teams: Cambridge University 1895-97, Worcestershire 1899-1914, England 1910
Matches: 5 (Won 2, Drew 0, Lost 3)
Right-hand middle order batsman – Right-hand slow under-arm bowler

No	Date	Opposition	Venue	R	Bat	C	Bowling			
1	01/01/1910	South Africa	Johannesburg (1)	L	29*		16	3	43	6
					14		24	3	59	2
2	21/01/1910	South Africa	Durban (1)	L	0		23.5	3	42	4
					16		23	4	66	3
3	26/02/1910	South Africa	Johannesburg (1)	W	5		14	1	46	1
							22	2	69	5
4	07/03/1910	South Africa	Cape Town	L	13		9	1	33	1
					9		5	0	12	0
5	11/03/1910	South Africa	Cape Town	W	19		4.5	0	15	1
						1	8	1	35	0

Batting & Fielding

Mat	Inns	N/O	Runs	H/S	Avg	100s	50s	Cat
5	8	1	105	29*	15.00	0	0	1

Bowling

Balls	Runs	Wkts	Avg	Best	5WI	10WM	S/R
898	420	23	18.26	6-43	2	0	39.04

J.M.SIMS

Full Name: James Morton Sims (known as Jim)
Born: 13/05/1903, Leyton, Essex
Died: 27/04/1973, Canterbury, Kent
Teams: Middlesex 1929-52, England 1935-37
Matches: 4 (Won 2, Drew 1, Lost 1)
Right-hand lower order batsman – Leg break bowler

No	Date	Opposition	Venue	R	Bat	C	Bowling			
1	13/07/1935	South Africa	Headingley	D	12		9	4	20	0
					27		13	48	1	

No	Date	Opposition	Venue	R	Bat	C		Bowling		
2	15/08/1936	India	The Oval	W	1		18.5	1	73	5
						1	25	1	95	2
3	18/12/1936	Australia	Sydney	W		3	2	0	20	0
							17	0	80	1
4	01/01/1937	Australia	Melbourne	L	3	2	9	1	35	0
					0		23	1	109	2

Batting & Fielding

Mat	Inns	N/O	Runs	H/S	Avg	100s	50s	Cat
4	4	0	16	12	4.00	0	0	6

Bowling

Balls	Runs	Wkts	Avg	Best	5WI	10WM	S/R
887	480	11	43.63	5-73	1	0	80.63

R.A.SINFIELD

Full Name: Reginald Albert Sinfield (known as Reg)
Born: 24/12/1900, Benington, Stevenage, Hertfordshire
Died: 17/03/1988, Ham Green, Bristol
Teams: Gloucestershire 1924-39, England 1938
Matches: 1 (Won 0, Drew 1, Lost 0)
Right-hand middle order batsman – Off break bowler (previously right-arm fast medium)

No	Date	Opposition	Venue	R	Bat	C		Bowling		
1	10/06/1938	Australia	Trent Bridge	D	6		28	8	51	1
							35	8	72	1

Batting & Fielding

Mat	Inns	N/O	Runs	H/S	Avg	100s	50s	Cat
1	1	0	6	6	6.00	0	0	0

Bowling

Balls	Runs	Wkts	Avg	Best	5WI	10WM	S/R
378	123	2	61.50	1-51	0	0	189.00

W.N.SLACK

Full Name: Wilfred Norris Slack (known as Wilf)
Born: 12/12/1954, Troumaca, St Vincent
Died: 15/01/1989, Banjul, The Gambia
Teams: Middlesex 1977-88, Winward Islands 1981/82-82/83, England 1986
Matches: 3 (Won 0, Drew 0, Lost 3)
Left-hand opening batsman – Right-arm medium bowler

No	Date	Opposition	Venue	R	Bat	C
1	07/03/1986	West Indies	Port-of-Spain	L	2	
					0	
2	11/04/1986	West Indies	St John's	L	52	1
					8	
3	19/06/1986	India	Headingley	L	0	1
					19	1

Batting & Fielding

Mat	Inns	N/O	Runs	H/S	Avg	100s	50s	Cat
3	6	0	81	52	13.50	0	1	3

T.F.SMAILES

Full Name: Thomas Francis Smailes (known as Frank)
Born: 27/03/1910, Ripley, Yorkshire
Died: 01/12/1970, Starbeck, Harrogate, Yorkshire
Teams: Yorkshire 1932-48, England 1946
Matches: 1 (Won 1, Drew 0, Lost 0)
Left-hand lower order batsman – Right-arm medium bowler

No	Date	Opposition	Venue	R	Bat	C		Bowling		
1	22/06/1946	India	Lord's	W	25		5	1	18	0
							15	2	44	3

Batting & Fielding

Mat	Inns	N/O	Runs	H/S	Avg	100s	50s	Cat
1	1	0	25	25	25.00	0	0	0

Bowling

Balls	Runs	Wkts	Avg	Best	5WI	10WM	S/R
120	62	3	20.66	3-44	0	0	40.00

G.C.SMALL

Full Name: Gladstone Cleophas Small
Born: 18/10/1961, Brighton, St George, Barbados
Teams: Warwickshire 1980-96, South Australia 1985/86, England 1986-91
Matches: 17 (Won 3, Drew 7, Lost 7)
Right-hand lower order batsman – Right-arm fast medium bowler

No	Date	Opposition	Venue	R	Bat	C		Bowling		
1	07/08/1986	New Zealand	Trent Bridge	L	2*		38	12	88	3
					12		8	3	10	1
2	21/08/1986	New Zealand	The Oval	D	18		5	36	0	
3	26/12/1986	Australia	Melbourne	W	21*		22.4	7	48	5
						1	15	3	40	2
4	10/01/1987	Australia	Sydney	L	14		33	11	75	5
					0		8	2	17	0
5	16/06/1988	West Indies	Lord's	L	5*		18.5	5	64	4
					7		19	1	76	0
6	24/08/1989	Australia	The Oval	D	59		40	8	141	3
							20	4	57	1
7	24/02/1990	West Indies	Kingston	W	4	2	15	6	44	1
							22	6	58	4
8	23/03/1990	West Indies	Port-of-Spain	D	0		17	4	41	2
							21	8	56	1
9	05/04/1990	West Indies	Bridgetown	L	1*		35	5	109	4
					0	1	20	1	74	4
10	12/04/1990	West Indies	St John's	L	8		31	3	123	1
					4					
11	07/06/1990	New Zealand	Trent Bridge	D	26		29	9	49	2
							6	2	14	1
12	21/06/1990	New Zealand	Lord's	D	3	1	35	4	127	1
13	05/07/1990	New Zealand	Edgbaston	W	44*		18	7	44	0
					11*		16	5	56	1
14	23/11/1990	Australia	Brisbane (2)	L	12*	2	16	4	34	3
					15		15	2	36	0
15	04/01/1991	Australia	Sydney	D	10	1	31	5	103	1
							2	1	6	0
16	25/01/1991	Australia	Adelaide	D	1		34	10	92	2
							18	3	64	1
17	01/02/1991	Australia	Perth	L	0	1	23	3	65	2
					4		10	5	24	0

Batting & Fielding

Mat	Inns	N/O	Runs	H/S	Avg	100s	50s	Cat
17	24	7	263	59	15.47	0	1	9

Bowling

Balls	Runs	Wkts	Avg	Best	5WI	10WM	S/R
3927	1871	55	34.01	5-48	2	0	71.40

A.C.SMITH

Full Name: Alan Christopher Smith (also known as A.C.)
Born: 25/10/1936, Hall Green, Birmingham
Teams: Oxford University 1958-60, Warwickshire 1958-74, England 1962-63
Matches: 6 (Won 3, Drew 3, Lost 0)
Right-hand middle order batsman – Wicket-keeper – Occasional right-arm fast medium bowler

No	Date	Opposition	Venue	R	Bat	C	St	B
1+	30/11/1962	Australia	Brisbane (2)	D	21	2		5
						1		4
2+	29/12/1962	Australia	Melbourne	W	6*	2		2
						1		4
3+	25/01/1963	Australia	Adelaide	D	13	2		0
						3		1

No	Date	Opposition	Venue	R	Bat	C	St	B
4+	15/02/1963	Australia	Sydney	D	6	1		6
					1	1		4
5+	01/03/1963	New Zealand	Wellington	W	69*	3		13
								13
6+	15/03/1963	New Zealand	Christchurch	W	2*	2		1
						2		0

Batting & Fielding

Mat	Inns	N/O	Runs	H/S	Avg	100s	50s	Cat	St	Byes
6	7	3	118	69*	29.50	0	1	20	0	53

C.A.SMITH

Full Name: Sir Charles Aubrey Smith (known as Aubrey)
Born: 21/07/1863, City of London
Died: 20/12/1948, Beverly Hills, California, USA
Teams: Cambridge University 1882-85, Sussex 1882-96, Transvaal 1889/90, England 1889
Matches: 1 (Won 1, Drew 0, Lost 0)
England Captain: Once 1889 (Won 1, Drew 0, Lost 0) **Toss:** 0-1
Right-hand lower order batsman – Right-arm fast bowler

No	Date	Opposition	Venue	R	Bat	C		Bowling		
1*	12/03/1889	South Africa	Port Elizabeth	W	3		13.2	6	19	5
							25	10	42	2

Batting & Fielding

Mat	Inns	N/O	Runs	H/S	Avg	100s	50s	Cat
1	1	0	3	3	3.00	0	0	0

Bowling

Balls	Runs	Wkts	Avg	Best	5WI	10WM	S/R
154	61	7	8.71	5-19	1	0	22.00

C.I.J.SMITH

Full Name: Cedric Ivan James Smith (known as Big Jim)
Born: 25/08/1906, Corsham, Wiltshire
Died: 09/02/1979, Mellor, Lancashire
Teams: Middlesex 1934-39, England 1935-37
Matches: 5 (Won 2, Drew 1, Lost 2)
Right-hand lower order batsman – Right-arm fast bowler

No	Date	Opposition	Venue	R	Bat	C		Bowling		
1	08/01/1935	West Indies	Bridgetown	W	0		7	3	8	0
					0		8	4	16	5
2	24/01/1935	West Indies	Port-of-Spain	L	8		26	3	100	4
					3		30	9	73	2
3	14/02/1935	West Indies	Georgetown	D	25		22	8	37	0
					4		4	2	13	0
4	14/03/1935	West Indies	Kingston	L	10		22	2	83	0
					4					
5	24/07/1937	New Zealand	Old Trafford	W	21	1	22	7	29	2
					27		14	2	34	2

Batting & Fielding

Mat	Inns	N/O	Runs	H/S	Avg	100s	50s	Cat
5	10	0	102	27	10.20	0	0	1

Bowling

Balls	Runs	Wkts	Avg	Best	5WI	10WM	S/R
930	393	15	26.20	5-16	1	0	62.00

C.L.SMITH

Full Name: Christopher Lyall Smith (known as Chris)
Born: 15/10/1958, Durban, South Africa
Teams: Glamorgan 1979, Hampshire 1980-91, Natal 1977/78-82/83, England 1983-86
Matches: 8 (Won 2, Drew 4, Lost 2)
Right-hand opening batsman – Off break bowler

No	Date	Opposition	Venue	R	Bat	C		Bowling		
1	11/08/1983	New Zealand	Lord's	W	0					
					43					
2	25/08/1983	New Zealand	Trent Bridge	W	31	2				
					4		12	2	31	2
3	20/01/1984	New Zealand	Wellington	D	27					
					30*		3	1	6	0
4	10/02/1984	New Zealand	Auckland	D	91					
5	02/03/1984	Pakistan	Karachi (1)	L	28	1				
					5					
6	12/03/1984	Pakistan	Faisalabad	D	66					
7	19/03/1984	Pakistan	Lahore (2)	D	18	1	1	0	2	1
					15	1	1	1	0	0
8	19/06/1986	India	Headingley	L	6					
					28					

Batting & Fielding

Mat	Inns	N/O	Runs	H/S	Avg	100s	50s	Cat
8	14	1	392	91	30.15	0	2	5

Bowling

Balls	Runs	Wkts	Avg	Best	5WI	10WM	S/R
102	39	3	13.00	2-31	0	0	34.00

D.SMITH

Full Name: Denis Smith
Born: 24/01/1907, Somercotes, Derbyshire
Died: 12/09/1979, Derby
Teams: Derbyshire 1927-52, England 1935
Matches: 2 (Won 0, Drew 2, Lost 0)
Left-hand opening batsman – Right-arm medium bowler – Occasional wicket-keeper

No	Date	Opposition	Venue	R	Bat	C
1	13/07/1935	South Africa	Headingley	D	36	1
					57	
2	27/07/1935	South Africa	Old Trafford	D	35	
					0	

Batting & Fielding

Mat	Inns	N/O	Runs	H/S	Avg	100s	50s	Cat
2	4	0	128	57	32.00	0	1	1

D.M.SMITH

Full Name: David Mark Smith
Born: 09/01/1956, Balham, London
Teams: Surrey 1973-88, Worcestershire 1984-86, Sussex 1989-92, England 1986
Matches: 2 (Won 0, Drew 0, Lost 2)
Left-hand middle order batsman – Right-arm medium bowler

No	Date	Opposition	Venue	R	Bat	C
1	21/02/1986	West Indies	Kingston	L	1	
					0	
2	03/04/1986	West Indies	Port-of-Spain	L	47	
					32	

Batting & Fielding

Mat	Inns	N/O	Runs	H/S	Avg	100s	50s	Cat
2	4	0	80	47	20.00	0	0	0

D.R.SMITH

Full Name: David Robert Smith
Born: 05/10/1934, Fishponds, Bristol, Gloucestershire
Teams: Gloucestershire 1956-70, England 1961-62
Matches: 5 (Won 0, Drew 3, Lost 2)
Right-hand lower order batsman – Right-arm medium bowler

No	Date	Opposition	Venue	R	Bat	C		Bowling		
1	11/11/1961	India	Bombay (2)	D			31	12	54	1
							7	2	18	1
2	01/12/1961	India	Kanpur	D	0		44	11	111	0
3	13/12/1961	India	Delhi	D		1	30	11	66	1
4	30/12/1961	India	Calcutta	L	0	1	31	10	60	2
					2		3	0	15	0
5	10/01/1962	India	Madras (2)	L	34		9	1	20	0
					2*		7	0	15	1

Batting & Fielding

Mat	Inns	N/O	Runs	H/S	Avg	100s	50s	Cat
5	5	1	38	34	9.50	0	0	2

Bowling

Balls	Runs	Wkts	Avg	Best	5WI	10WM	S/R
972	359	6	59.83	2-60	0	0	162.00

D.V.SMITH

Full Name: Donald Victor Smith (also known as Don)
Born: 14/06/1923, Broadwater, Sussex
Teams: Sussex 1946-62, England 1957
Matches: 3 (Won 2, Drew 1, Lost 0)
Left-hand opening batsman – Left-arm medium bowler

No	Date	Opposition	Venue	R	Bat	C		Bowling		
1	20/06/1957	West Indies	Lord's	W	8					
2	04/07/1957	West Indies	Trent Bridge	D	1		12	1	38	0
					16*		12	5	23	0
3	25/07/1957	West Indies	Headingley	W	0		17	6	24	0
							4	1	12	1

Batting & Fielding

Mat	Inns	N/O	Runs	H/S	Avg	100s	50s	Cat
3	4	1	25	16*	8.33	0	0	0

Bowling

Balls	Runs	Wkts	Avg	Best	5WI	10WM	S/R
270	97	1	97.00	1-12	0	0	270.00

E.J.SMITH

Full Name: Ernest James Smith (known as Jim or Tiger)
Born: 06/02/1886, Highgate, Birmingham
Died: 31/08/1979, Northfield, Birmingham
Teams: Warwickshire 1904-30, England 1911-13
Matches: 11 (Won 9, Drew 2, Lost 0)
Right-hand opening batsman – Wicket-keeper

No	Date	Opposition	Venue	R	Bat	C	St	B
1+	30/12/1911	Australia	Melbourne	W	5	3		5
						1		14
2+	12/01/1912	Australia	Adelaide	W	22	1	1	3
						1		26
3+	09/02/1912	Australia	Melbourne	W	7			1
						1		9
4+	23/02/1912	Australia	Sydney	W	0	1		14
					13	1		22
5+	10/06/1912	South Africa	Lord's	W	2			12
						1		17
6+	24/06/1912	Australia	Lord's	D	14*	2		17
7+	08/07/1912	South Africa	Headingley	W	13	1		4
					11	1	1	5
8+	29/07/1912	Australia	Old Trafford	D	4			2
9+	12/08/1912	South Africa	The Oval	W	9			8
						1	1	18

No	Date	Opposition	Venue	R	Bat	C	St	B
10+	19/08/1912	Australia	The Oval	W	4	1		12
					0			1
11	26/12/1913	South Africa	Johannesburg (1)	W	9	1		

Batting & Fielding

Mat	Inns	N/O	Runs	H/S	Avg	100s	50s	Cat	St	Byes
11	14	1	113	22	8.69	0	0	17	3	190

H.SMITH

Full Name: Harry Smith
Born: 21/05/1891, Fishponds, Bristol
Died: 12/11/1937, Downend, Bristol
Teams: Gloucestershire 1912-35, England 1928
Matches: 1 (Won 1, Drew 0, Lost 0)
Right-hand middle order batsman – Wicket-keeper

No	Date	Opposition	Venue	R	Bat	C	St	B
1+	23/06/1928	West Indies	Lord's	W	7	1		13
								10

Batting & Fielding

Mat	Inns	N/O	Runs	H/S	Avg	100s	50s	Cat	St	Byes
1	1	0	7	7	7.00	0	0	1	0	23

M.J.K.SMITH

Full Name: Michael John Knight Smith, OBE (known as Mike or M.J.K.)
Born: 30/06/1933, Westcotes, Leicester
Teams: Oxford University 1954-56, Leicestershire 1951-55, Warwickshire 1956-75, England 1958-72
Matches: 50 (Won 16, Drew 29, Lost 5)
England Captain: 25 times 1964-66 (Won 5, Drew 17, Lost 3) **Toss:** 10-15
Right-hand middle order batsman – Right-arm slow medium bowler

No	Date	Opposition	Venue	R	Bat	C		Bowling		
1	05/06/1958	New Zealand	Edgbaston	W	0					
					7	1				
2	19/06/1958	New Zealand	Lord's	W	47					
3	03/07/1958	New Zealand	Headingley	W	3	2				
4	23/07/1959	India	Old Trafford	W	100	1				
					9					
5	20/08/1959	India	The Oval	W	98					
6	06/01/1960	West Indies	Bridgetown	D	39	1				
7	28/01/1960	West Indies	Port-of-Spain	W	108					
					12	1				
8	17/02/1960	West Indies	Kingston	D	0	1				
					10					
9	09/03/1960	West Indies	Georgetown	D	0					
					23					
10	25/03/1960	West Indies	Port-of-Spain	D	20					
					96		1	0	15	0
11	09/06/1960	South Africa	Edgbaston	W	54	1				
					28					
12	23/06/1960	South Africa	Lord's	W	99	1				
13	07/07/1960	South Africa	Trent Bridge	W	0					
14	18/08/1960	South Africa	The Oval	D	0	2				
					11					
15	08/06/1961	Australia	Edgbaston	D	0					
					1*					
16	21/10/1961	Pakistan	Lahore (2)	W	99	1				
					34	1				
17	11/11/1961	India	Bombay (2)	D	36					
					0		8	3	10	1
18	01/12/1961	India	Kanpur	D	0					
					0					
19	13/12/1961	India	Delhi	D	2					

No	Date	Opposition	Venue	R	Bat	C	Bowling			
20	10/01/1962	India	Madras (2)	L	73					
					15	1				
21	19/01/1962	Pakistan	Dacca	D	10	1				
22	02/02/1962	Pakistan	Karachi (1)	D	56					
						1				
23*	10/01/1964	India	Madras (2)	D	3	1				
					57					
24*	21/01/1964	India	Bombay (2)	D	46					
					31*	1				
25*	29/01/1964	India	Calcutta	D	19					
					75*	1				
26*	08/02/1964	India	Delhi	D	37	1				
							13	0	52	0
27*	15/02/1964	India	Kanpur	D	38					
28*	04/12/1964	South Africa	Durban (2)	W	35	2				
						2				
29*	23/12/1964	South Africa	Johannesburg (3)	D	25	2				
						2				
30*	01/01/1965	South Africa	Cape Town	D	121	1				
						1	11	1	43	0
31*	22/01/1965	South Africa	Johannesburg (3)	D	42					
					8					
32*	12/02/1965	South Africa	Port Elizabeth	D	26					
33*	27/05/1965	New Zealand	Edgbaston	W	0	1				
34*	17/06/1965	New Zealand	Lord's	W	44					
						1				
35*	08/07/1965	New Zealand	Headingley	W	2*	1				
36*	22/07/1965	South Africa	Lord's	D	26					
					13					
37*	05/08/1965	South Africa	Trent Bridge	L	32					
					24					
38*	26/08/1965	South Africa	The Oval	D	7	1				
					10*	1				
39*	10/12/1965	Australia	Brisbane (2)	D	16					
					10*					
40*	30/12/1965	Australia	Melbourne	D	41					
						1	2	0	8	0
41*	07/01/1966	Australia	Sydney	W	6					
						3				
42*	28/01/1966	Australia	Adelaide	L	29					
					5					
43*	11/02/1966	Australia	Melbourne	D	0					
44*	25/02/1966	New Zealand	Christchurch	D	54	2				
					87	1				
45*	04/03/1966	New Zealand	Dunedin	D	20	1				
						1				
46*	11/03/1966	New Zealand	Auckland	D	18	2				
					30	1				
47*	02/06/1966	West Indies	Old Trafford	L	5	2				
					6					
48	08/06/1972	Australia	Old Trafford	W	10	1				
					34					
49	22/06/1972	Australia	Lord's	L	34	2				
					30					
50	13/07/1972	Australia	Trent Bridge	D	17	1				
					15					

Batting & Fielding

Mat	Inns	N/O	Runs	H/S	Avg	100s	50s	Cat
50	78	6	2278	121	31.63	3	11	53

Bowling

Balls	Runs	Wkts	Avg	Best	5WI	10WM	S/R
214	128	1	128.00	1-10	0	0	214.00

R.A.SMITH

Full Name: Robin Arnold Smith
Born: 13/09/1963, Durban, South Africa
Teams: Hampshire 1982-96, Natal 1980/81-84/85, England 1988-96
Matches: 62 (Won 14, Drew 20, Lost 28)
Right-hand middle order batsman – Off break bowler

No	Date	Opposition	Venue	R	Bat	C	Bowling
1	21/07/1988	West Indies	Headingley	L	38	1	
					11		
2	04/08/1988	West Indies	The Oval	L	57		
					0		
3	25/08/1988	Sri Lanka	Lord's	W	31	1	
					8*		
4	08/06/1989	Australia	Headingley	L	66		
					0		
5	22/06/1989	Australia	Lord's	L	32	1	
					96		
6	27/07/1989	Australia	Old Trafford	L	143		
					1		
7	10/08/1989	Australia	Trent Bridge	L	101		
					26		
8	24/08/1989	Australia	The Oval	D	11		
					77*		
9	24/02/1990	West Indies	Kingston	W	57		
10	23/03/1990	West Indies	Port-of-Spain	D	5		
					2		
11	05/04/1990	West Indies	Bridgetown	L	62		
					40*	1	
12	12/04/1990	West Indies	St John's	L	12	1	
					8*		
13	07/06/1990	New Zealand	Trent Bridge	D	55		
14	21/06/1990	New Zealand	Lord's	D	64		
					0		
15	05/07/1990	New Zealand	Edgbaston	W	19	1	
					14	1	
16	26/07/1990	India	Lord's	W	100*		
					15		
17	09/08/1990	India	Old Trafford	D	121*	1	
					61*		
18	23/08/1990	India	The Oval	D	57		
					7*		
19	23/11/1990	Australia	Brisbane (2)	L	7	1	
					1		
20	26/12/1990	Australia	Melbourne	L	30		
					8		
21	04/01/1991	Australia	Sydney	D	18	1	
					10*	1	
22	25/01/1991	Australia	Adelaide	D	53		
					10*		
23	01/02/1991	Australia	Perth	L	58		
					43		
24	06/06/1991	West Indies	Headingley	W	54		
					0	1	
25	20/06/1991	West Indies	Lord's	D	148*		
26	04/07/1991	West Indies	Trent Bridge	L	64*	1	
					15		
27	08/08/1991	West Indies	The Oval	W	109		
					26		
28	22/08/1991	Sri Lanka	Lord's	W	4	1	
					63*		
29	18/01/1992	New Zealand	Christchurch	W	96	1	
						3	4 2 6 0
30	30/01/1992	New Zealand	Auckland	W	0	1	
					35		
31	06/02/1992	New Zealand	Wellington	D	6		
					76		
32	04/06/1992	Pakistan	Edgbaston	D	127		
33	18/06/1992	Pakistan	Lord's	L	9	2	
					8	1	

No	Date	Opposition	Venue	R	Bat	C	Bowling
34	02/07/1992	Pakistan	Old Trafford	D	11		
						1	
35	23/07/1992	Pakistan	Headingley	W	42	1	
					0	1	
36	06/08/1992	Pakistan	The Oval	L	33	1	
					84*		
37	29/01/1993	India	Calcutta	L	1		
					8		
38	11/02/1993	India	Madras (1)	L	17	1	
					56		
39	19/02/1993	India	Bombay (3)	L	2	1	
					62		
40	13/03/1993	Sri Lanka	Colombo (2)	L	128	1	
					35		
41	03/06/1993	Australia	Old Trafford	L	4		
					18		
42	17/06/1993	Australia	Lord's	L	22		
					5		
43	01/07/1993	Australia	Trent Bridge	D	86	1	
					50		
44	22/07/1993	Australia	Headingley	L	23		
					35		
45	05/08/1993	Australia	Edgbaston	L	21	1	
					19		
46	19/02/1994	West Indies	Kingston	L	0		
					2		
47	17/03/1994	West Indies	Georgetown	L	84		
					24		
48	25/03/1994	West Indies	Port-of-Spain	L	12	1	
					0		
49	08/04/1994	West Indies	Bridgetown	W	10		
					13		
50	16/04/1994	West Indies	St John's	D	175		
51	02/06/1994	New Zealand	Trent Bridge	W	78		
52	16/06/1994	New Zealand	Lord's	D	6	2	
					23		
53	30/06/1994	New Zealand	Old Trafford	D	13		
						1	
54	08/06/1995	West Indies	Headingley	L	16		
					6		
55	22/06/1995	West Indies	Lord's	W	61		
					90		
56	06/07/1995	West Indies	Edgbaston	L	46		
					41		
57	27/07/1995	West Indies	Old Trafford	W	44		
					1*		
58	16/11/1995	South Africa	Centurion	D	43		
59	30/11/1995	South Africa	Johannesburg (3)	D	52	1	
					44		
60	14/12/1995	South Africa	Durban (2)	D	34	1	
61	26/12/1995	South Africa	Port Elizabeth	D	2	1	
62	02/01/1996	South Africa	Cape Town	L	66	1	
					13		

Batting & Fielding

Mat	Inns	N/O	Runs	H/S	Avg	100s	50s	Cat
62	112	15	4236	175	43.67	9	28	39

Bowling

Balls	Runs	Wkts	Avg	Best	5WI	10WM	S/R
24	6	0	–	0-6	0	0	–

T.P.B.SMITH

Full Name: Thomas Peter Bromly Smith (known as Peter)
Born: 30/10/1908, Ipswich, Suffolk
Died: 04/08/1967, Hyeres, France
Teams: Essex 1929-51, England 1946-47
Matches: 4 (Won 0, Drew 2, Lost 2)
Right-hand lower order batsman – Leg break & googly bowler

No	Date	Opposition	Venue	R	Bat	C	Bowling			
1	17/08/1946	India	The Oval	D			21	4	58	1
2	13/12/1946	Australia	Sydney	L	4		37	1	172	2
					2					
3	28/02/1947	Australia	Sydney	L	2	1	8	0	38	0
					24		2	0	8	0
4	21/03/1947	New Zealand	Christchurch	D	1		6	0	43	0

Batting & Fielding

Mat	Inns	N/O	Runs	H/S	Avg	100s	50s	Cat
4	5	0	33	24	6.60	0	0	1

Bowling

Balls	Runs	Wkts	Avg	Best	5WI	10WM	S/R
538	319	3	106.33	2-172	0	0	179.33

G.A.SMITHSON

Full Name: Gerald Arthur Smithson
Born: 01/11/1926, Spofforth, Yorkshire
Died: 06/09/1970, Abingdon, Berkshire
Teams: Yorkshire 1946-50, Leicestershire 1951-56, England 1948
Matches: 2 (Won 0, Drew 2, Lost 0)
Left-hand middle order batsman – Right-arm medium bowler

No	Date	Opposition	Venue	R	Bat	C
1	21/01/1948	West Indies	Bridgetown	D	0	
2	11/02/1948	West Indies	Port-of-Spain	D	35	
					35	

Batting & Fielding

Mat	Inns	N/O	Runs	H/S	Avg	100s	50s	Cat
2	3	0	70	35	23.33	0	0	0

J.A.SNOW

Full Name: John Augustine Snow
Born: 13/10/1941, Peopleton, Worcestershire
Teams: Sussex 1961-77, England 1965-76
Matches: 49 (Won 16, Drew 23, Lost 10)
Right-hand lower order batsman – Right-arm fast medium bowler

No	Date	Opposition	Venue	R	Bat	C	Bowling			
1	17/06/1965	New Zealand	Lord's	W	2*		11	2	27	2
						1	24	4	53	2
2	05/08/1965	South Africa	Trent Bridge	L	3		22	6	63	1
					0		33	6	83	3
3	30/06/1966	West Indies	Trent Bridge	L	0		25	7	82	4
					3		38	10	117	0
4	04/08/1966	West Indies	Headingley	L	0		42	6	146	3
					0*					
5	18/08/1966	West Indies	The Oval	W	59*		20.5	1	66	2
							13	5	40	3
6	08/06/1967	India	Headingley	W			17	7	34	2
						1	41	11	108	2
7	22/06/1967	India	Lord's	W	8*		20.4	5	49	3
						1	8	4	12	1
8	13/07/1967	India	Edgbaston	W	10		12	3	28	2
					9		14	0	33	0
9	27/07/1967	Pakistan	Lord's	D	0		45.1	11	120	3
					7		4	2	6	0
10	08/02/1968	West Indies	Kingston	D	10		21	7	49	7
							27	4	91	1

No	Date	Opposition	Venue	R	Bat	C	Bowling			
11	29/02/1968	West Indies	Bridgetown	D	37		35	11	86	5
						1	10	2	39	3
12	14/03/1968	West Indies	Port-of-Spain	W	0		20	3	68	0
							9	0	29	1
13	28/03/1968	West Indies	Georgetown	D	0		27.4	2	82	4
					1		15.2	0	60	6
14	06/06/1968	Australia	Old Trafford	L	18*		34	5	97	4
					2	1	17	2	51	1
15	20/06/1968	Australia	Lord's	D	0*		9	5	14	1
							12	5	30	1
16	11/07/1968	Australia	Edgbaston	D	19		17	3	46	1
							9	1	32	1
17	25/07/1968	Australia	Headingley	D	0		35	3	98	3
						1	24	3	51	2
18	22/08/1968	Australia	The Oval	W	4		35	12	67	3
					13	1	11	5	22	0
19	28/02/1969	Pakistan	Dacca	D	9		25	5	70	4
						1	12	7	15	0
20	06/03/1969	Pakistan	Karachi (1)	D	9					
21	12/06/1969	West Indies	Old Trafford	W	0		15	2	54	4
							22.3	4	76	2
22	26/06/1969	West Indies	Lord's	D	9*		39	5	114	5
							22	4	69	1
23	10/07/1969	West Indies	Headingley	W	1*	1	20	4	50	2
					15*		21	7	43	1
24	07/08/1969	New Zealand	Trent Bridge	D	4*		24	4	61	0
							6	2	19	0
25	21/08/1969	New Zealand	The Oval	W	21*		10	4	22	1
							21	4	52	2
26	27/11/1970	Australia	Brisbane (2)	D	34		32.3	6	114	6
						1	20	3	48	2
27	11/12/1970	Australia	Perth	D	4*		33.5	3	143	4
							9	4	17	2
28	09/01/1971	Australia	Sydney	W	37		14	6	23	1
							17.5	5	40	7
29	21/01/1971	Australia	Melbourne	D	1	1	29	4	94	2
							12	4	21	2
30	29/01/1971	Australia	Adelaide	D	38		21	4	73	2
							17	3	60	1
31	12/02/1971	Australia	Sydney	W	7		18	2	68	1
					20		2	1	7	1
32	22/07/1971	India	Lord's	D	73		31	9	64	2
					9	1	8	0	23	1
33	19/08/1971	India	The Oval	L	3		24	5	68	2
					0		11	7	14	1
34	08/06/1972	Australia	Old Trafford	W	3		20	7	41	4
					0	1	27	2	87	4
35	22/06/1972	Australia	Lord's	L	37		32	13	57	5
					0		8	2	15	0
36	13/07/1972	Australia	Trent Bridge	D	6		31	8	92	5
							24	1	94	3
37	27/07/1972	Australia	Headingley	W	48		13	5	11	2
							10	2	26	0
38	10/08/1972	Australia	The Oval	L	3	1	34.5	5	111	1
					14		6	1	21	0
39	07/06/1973	New Zealand	Trent Bridge	W	8		13	5	21	0
					7		43	10	104	2
40	21/06/1973	New Zealand	Lord's	D	2		38	4	109	3
					0					
41	05/07/1973	New Zealand	Headingley	W	6		21.4	4	52	2
							19.3	4	34	3
42	26/07/1973	West Indies	The Oval	L	0		31	8	71	0
					1		18	4	62	3
43	10/07/1975	Australia	Edgbaston	L	0		33	6	86	3
					34					
44	31/07/1975	Australia	Lord's	D	11		21	4	66	4
							19	3	82	0
45	14/08/1975	Australia	Headingley	D	0		18.5	7	22	3
					9		15	6	21	0
46	28/08/1975	Australia	The Oval	D	30		27	4	74	1
					0		2	1	4	0
47	03/06/1976	West Indies	Trent Bridge	D	20*		31	5	123	1
							11	2	53	4

No	Date	Opposition	Venue		R	Bat	C			Bowling		
48	17/06/1976	West Indies	Lord's		D	0	2	19	3	68	4
						6*		7	2	22	0
49	22/07/1976	West Indies	Headingley		L	20		18.4	3	77	4
						8		20	1	80	2

Batting & Fielding

Mat	Inns	N/O	Runs	H/S	Avg	100s	50s	Cat
49	71	14	772	73	13.54	0	2	16

Bowling

Balls	Runs	Wkts	Avg	Best	5WI	10WM	S/R
12021	5387	202	26.66	7-40	8	1	59.50

J.SOUTHERTON

Full Name: James Southerton
Born: 16/11/1827, Petworth, Sussex
Died: 16/06/1880, Mitcham, Surrey
Teams: Surrey 1854-79, Sussex 1858-72, Hampshire 1861-67, England 1877
Matches: 2 (Won 1, Drew 0, Lost 1)
Right-hand lower order batsman – Right-hand round-arm slow bowler

No	Date	Opposition	Venue		R	Bat	C			Bowling		
1	15/03/1877	Australia	Melbourne		L	6	1	37	17	61	3
						1*	1				
2	31/03/1877	Australia	Melbourne		W	0					
								28.3	13	46	4

Batting & Fielding

Mat	Inns	N/O	Runs	H/S	Avg	100s	50s	Cat
2	3	1	7	6	3.50	0	0	2

Bowling

Balls	Runs	Wkts	Avg	Best	5WI	10WM	S/R
263	107	7	15.28	4-46	0	0	37.57

R.H.SPOONER

Full Name: Reginald Herbert Spooner
Born: 21/10/1880, Litherland, Lancashire
Died: 02/10/1961, Lincoln
Teams: Lancashire 1899-1921, England 1905-12
Matches: 10 (Won 5, Drew 5, Lost 0)
Right-hand opening batsman – Right-arm slow bowler

No	Date	Opposition	Venue	R	Bat	C
1	24/07/1905	Australia	Old Trafford	W	52	
						1
2	14/08/1905	Australia	The Oval	D	0	
					79	1
3	26/07/1909	Australia	Old Trafford	D	25	
					58	
4	09/08/1909	Australia	The Oval	D	13	
					3	
5	10/06/1912	South Africa	Lord's	W	119	
6	24/06/1912	Australia	Lord's	D	1	
7	08/07/1912	South Africa	Headingley	W	21	1
					82	
8	29/07/1912	Australia	Old Trafford	D	1	
9	12/08/1912	South Africa	The Oval	W	26	
						1
10	19/08/1912	Australia	The Oval	W	1	
					0	

Batting & Fielding

Mat	Inns	N/O	Runs	H/S	Avg	100s	50s	Cat
10	15	0	481	119	32.06	1	4	4

R.T.SPOONER

Full Name: Richard Thompson Spooner (known as Dick)
Born: 30/12/1919, Stockton-on-Tees, Co Durham
Teams: Warwickshire 1948-59, England 1951-55
Matches: 7 (Won 2, Drew 4, Lost 1)
Left-hand opening batsman – Wicket-keeper

No	Date	Opposition	Venue	R	Bat	C	St	B
1+	02/11/1951	India	Delhi	D	11	1		12
					1			
2+	14/12/1951	India	Bombay (2)	D	46	2		0
					5*	1		6
3+	30/12/1951	India	Calcutta	D	71	1		3
					92			1
4+	12/01/1952	India	Kanpur	W	21		1	8
					0	1		2
5+	06/02/1952	India	Madras (1)	L	66	2	1	8
					6			
6+	17/03/1954	West Indies	Port-of-Spain	D	19			6
					16			0
7+	13/08/1955	South Africa	The Oval	W	0	2		0
					0			0

Batting & Fielding

Mat	Inns	N/O	Runs	H/S	Avg	100s	50s	Cat	St	Byes
7	14	1	354	92	27.23	0	3	10	2	46

R.T.STANYFORTH

Full Name: Ronald Thomas Stanyforth
Born: 30/05/1892, Chelsea, London
Died: 20/02/1964, Kirk Hammerton Hall, Yorkshire
Teams: Oxford University 1914, Yorkshire 1928, England 1927-28
Matches: 4 (Won 2, Drew 1, Lost 1)
England Captain: 4 times 1927-28 (Won 2, Drew 1, Lost 1) **Toss:** 4-0
Right-hand lower order batsman – Wicket-keeper

No	Date	Opposition	Venue	R	Bat	C	St	B
1*+	24/12/1927	South Africa	Johannesburg (1)	W	1			0
						1		5
2*+	31/12/1927	South Africa	Cape Town	W	4	1		2
					1			6
3*+	21/01/1928	South Africa	Durban (2)	D	0		1	1
						1	1	22
4*+	28/01/1928	South Africa	Johannesburg (1)	L	1	3		8
					6*	1		16

Batting & Fielding

Mat	Inns	N/O	Runs	H/S	Avg	100s	50s	Cat	St	Byes
4	6	1	13	6*	2.60	0	0	7	2	60

S.J.STAPLES

Full Name: Samuel James Staples (known as Sam)
Born: 18/09/1892, Newstead Colliery, Nottinghamshire
Died: 04/06/1950, Standard Hill, Nottingham
Teams: Nottinghamshire 1920-34, England 1928
Matches: 3 (Won 0, Drew 1, Lost 2)
Right-hand lower order batsman – Off break bowler

No	Date	Opposition	Venue	R	Bat	C	Bowling			
1	21/01/1928	South Africa	Durban (2)	D	11		36	17	50	3
							47	9	111	2
2	28/01/1928	South Africa	Johannesburg (1)	L	39		32.3	7	81	3
					6		21	1	67	3
3	04/02/1928	South Africa	Durban (2)	L	2		44	13	96	3
					7		11	3	30	1

Batting & Fielding

Mat	Inns	N/O	Runs	H/S	Avg	100s	50s	Cat
3	5	0	65	39	13.00	0	0	0

Bowling

Balls	Runs	Wkts	Avg	Best	5WI	10WM	S/R
1149	435	15	29.00	3-50	0	0	76.60

J.B.STATHAM

Full Name: John Brian Statham, CBE (known as Brian)
Born: 17/06/1930, Gorton, Manchester, Lancashire
Teams: Lancashire 1950-68, England 1951-65
Matches: 70 (Won 28, Drew 26, Lost 16)
Left-hand lower order batsman – Right-arm fast medium bowler

No	Date	Opposition	Venue	R	Bat	C		Bowling		
1	17/03/1951	New Zealand	Christchurch	D	9		24	6	47	1
2	21/06/1951	South Africa	Lord's	W	1		6	3	7	0
							18	6	33	2
3	05/07/1951	South Africa	Old Trafford	W	1		7	2	8	1
							17	3	30	1
4	02/11/1951	India	Delhi	D	4		21	4	49	1
5	14/12/1951	India	Bombay (2)	D	27		29	5	96	4
							20	11	30	1
6	30/12/1951	India	Calcutta	D	1		27	10	46	1
							4	0	8	0
7	12/01/1952	India	Kanpur	W	12*	1	6	3	10	0
8	06/02/1952	India	Madras (1)	L	6		19	3	54	1
					9					
9	25/06/1953	Australia	Lord's	D	17*	1	28	7	48	1
						1	15	3	40	1
10	15/01/1954	West Indies	Kingston	L	8		36	6	90	4
					1		17	2	50	2
11	06/02/1954	West Indies	Bridgetown	L	3		27	6	90	3
					0	1	15	1	49	1
12	24/02/1954	West Indies	Georgetown	W	10*		27	6	64	4
							22	3	86	2
13	17/03/1954	West Indies	Port-of-Spain	D	6*		9	0	31	0
14	10/06/1954	Pakistan	Lord's	D	0		13	6	18	4
						1	5	2	17	0
15	01/07/1954	Pakistan	Trent Bridge	W			18	3	38	2
						2	20	3	66	3
16	22/07/1954	Pakistan	Old Trafford	D			4	0	11	0
17	12/08/1954	Pakistan	The Oval	L	1		11	5	26	2
					2*	1	18	7	37	0
18	26/11/1954	Australia	Brisbane (2)	L	11		34	2	123	2
					14					
19	17/12/1954	Australia	Sydney	W	14*		18	1	83	2
					25		19	6	45	3
20	31/12/1954	Australia	Melbourne	W	3		16.3	0	60	5
					0		11	1	38	2
21	28/01/1955	Australia	Adelaide	W	0	1	19	4	70	0
							12	1	38	3
22	25/02/1955	Australia	Sydney	D			9	1	31	0
							5	0	11	1
23	11/03/1955	New Zealand	Dunedin	W		1	17	9	24	4
							15	5	30	1
24	25/03/1955	New Zealand	Auckland	W	13	1	17.4	7	28	4
							9	3	9	3
25	09/06/1955	South Africa	Trent Bridge	W	20		25	5	47	1
							10	4	16	0
26	23/06/1955	South Africa	Lord's	W	0		27	9	49	7
					11		29	12	39	7
27	21/07/1955	South Africa	Headingley	L	4		20.2	7	35	3
					3		40	10	129	2
28	13/08/1955	South Africa	The Oval	W	4*		15	3	31	2
					0		11	4	17	0
29	21/06/1956	Australia	Lord's	L	0*		35	9	70	2
					0*		26	5	59	1
30	26/07/1956	Australia	Old Trafford	W	0	1	6	3	48	0
							16	10	15	0
31	23/08/1956	Australia	The Oval	D	0	1	21	8	33	3
							2	1	1	1

No	Date	Opposition	Venue	R	Bat	C		Bowling		
32	24/12/1956	South Africa	Johannesburg (3)	W	0		24.1	4	71	3
					2		13	4	22	2
33	01/01/1957	South Africa	Cape Town	W	2*		16	0	38	1
							8	2	12	0
34	25/01/1957	South Africa	Durban (2)	D	6		22	4	56	2
					9		11	0	32	1
35	15/02/1957	South Africa	Johannesburg (3)	L	12*		23	5	81	2
					4*	1	13	1	37	3
36	30/05/1957	West Indies	Edgbaston	D	13	1	39	4	114	3
							2	0	6	0
37	20/06/1957	West Indies	Lord's	W	7		18	3	46	1
						1	29.1	9	71	3
38	04/07/1957	West Indies	Trent Bridge	D			28.4	9	78	1
							41.2	12	118	5
39	24/07/1958	New Zealand	Old Trafford	W			33	10	71	4
						1	9	4	12	1
40	21/08/1958	New Zealand	The Oval	D			18	6	21	1
							7	0	26	1
41	05/12/1958	Australia	Brisbane (2)	L	2		20	2	57	1
					3	1	6	1	13	0
42	31/12/1958	Australia	Melbourne	L	13		28	6	57	7
					8*		5	1	11	1
43	09/01/1959	Australia	Sydney	D	0*	1	16	2	48	0
							2	0	6	0
44	30/01/1959	Australia	Adelaide	L	36*		23	0	83	3
					2		4	0	11	0
45	04/06/1959	India	Trent Bridge	W	29*		23.5	11	46	2
							21	10	31	5
46	18/06/1959	India	Lord's	W	38		16	6	27	2
							17	7	45	3
47	20/08/1959	India	The Oval	W	3*		16.3	6	24	2
							18	4	50	3
48	28/01/1960	West Indies	Port-of-Spain	W	1		19.3	8	42	3
							25	12	44	2
49	17/02/1960	West Indies	Kingston	D	13	1	32.1	8	76	3
					12		18	6	45	1
50	09/03/1960	West Indies	Georgetown	D	20*		36	8	79	1
51	09/06/1960	South Africa	Edgbaston	W	14*	1	28	8	67	2
					22		18	5	41	3
52	23/06/1960	South Africa	Lord's	W	2*		20	5	63	6
							21	6	34	5
53	07/07/1960	South Africa	Trent Bridge	W	2		14	5	27	3
							26	3	71	2
54	21/07/1960	South Africa	Old Trafford	D	0		22	11	32	3
							4	2	3	0
55	18/08/1960	South Africa	The Oval	D	13*		38	8	96	1
					4		12	1	57	2
56	08/06/1961	Australia	Edgbaston	D	7*		43	6	147	3
57	22/06/1961	Australia	Lord's	L	11*		44	10	89	2
					2*		10.5	3	31	3
58	27/07/1961	Australia	Old Trafford	L	4		21	3	53	5
					8	1	44	9	106	1
59	17/08/1961	Australia	The Oval	D	18		38.5	10	75	3
					9*					
60	31/05/1962	Pakistan	Edgbaston	W			21	9	54	4
							19	6	32	2
61	05/07/1962	Pakistan	Headingley	W	26*	1	20	9	40	2
						1	20	3	50	4
62	26/07/1962	Pakistan	Trent Bridge	D			18.1	5	55	2
						1	22	8	47	2
63	30/11/1962	Australia	Brisbane (2)	D	8*	1	16	1	75	1
						1	16	1	67	1
64	29/12/1962	Australia	Melbourne	W	1		22	2	83	1
							23	1	52	2
65	11/01/1963	Australia	Sydney	L	0		21.2	2	67	1
					2		3	0	15	0
66	25/01/1963	Australia	Adelaide	D	1	1	21	5	66	3
							21	2	71	3
67	15/02/1963	Australia	Sydney	D	17*		18	1	76	1
							4	1	8	0
68	06/06/1963	West Indies	Old Trafford	L	0		37	6	121	0
					7					

No	Date	Opposition	Venue	R	Bat	C		Bowling		
69	22/08/1963	West Indies	The Oval	L	8		22	3	68	3
					14		22	2	54	0
70	26/08/1965	South Africa	The Oval	D	0		24.2	11	40	5
							29	1	105	2

Batting & Fielding

Mat	Inns	N/O	Runs	H/S	Avg	100s	50s	Cat
70	87	28	675	38	11.44	0	0	28

Bowling

Balls	Runs	Wkts	Avg	Best	5WI	10WM	S/R
16056	6261	252	24.84	7-39	9	1	63.71

A.G.STEEL

Full Name: Allan Gibson Steel (birth registered as Alan)
Born: 24/09/1858, West Derby, Liverpool, Lancashire
Died: 15/06/1914, Hyde Park, London
Teams: Cambridge University 1878-81, Lancashire 1877-93, England 1880-88
Matches: 13 (Won 7, Drew 2, Lost 4)
England Captain: 4 times 1886-88 (Won 3, Drew 0, Lost 1) **Toss:** 2-2
Right-hand middle order batsman – Right-arm slow medium or fast medium bowler

No	Date	Opposition	Venue	R	Bat	C		Bowling		
1	06/09/1880	Australia	The Oval	W	42		29	9	58	3
						1	31	6	73	2
2	28/08/1882	Australia	The Oval	L	14		2	1	1	0
					0		7	0	15	2
3	30/12/1882	Australia	Melbourne	L	27	1	33	16	68	2
					29		9	4	17	0
4	19/01/1883	Australia	Melbourne	W	39					
5	26/01/1883	Australia	Sydney	W	17	1	26	14	27	3
					6	1				
6	17/02/1883	Australia	Sydney	L	135*		19	6	34	3
					21		43	9	49	3
7	10/07/1884	Australia	Old Trafford	D	15		13	5	32	2
					18					
8	21/07/1884	Australia	Lord's	W	148		1.2	0	6	1
							10	2	26	1
9	11/08/1884	Australia	The Oval	D	31	1	34	7	71	0
10*	05/07/1886	Australia	Old Trafford	W	12		27	5	47	2
					19*		8	3	9	1
11*	19/07/1886	Australia	Lord's	W	5		21	8	34	2
							16	9	14	0
12*	12/08/1886	Australia	The Oval	W	9					
							7	1	20	1
13*	16/07/1888	Australia	Lord's	L	3		3.2	2	4	1
					10*		1	1	0	0

Batting & Fielding

Mat	Inns	N/O	Runs	H/S	Avg	100s	50s	Cat
13	20	3	600	148	35.29	2	0	5

Bowling

Balls	Runs	Wkts	Avg	Best	5WI	10WM	S/R
1364	605	29	20.86	3-27	0	0	47.03

D.S.STEELE

Full Name: David Stanley Steele
Born: 29/09/1941, Bradeley, Staffordshire
Teams: Northamptonshire 1963-84, Derbyshire 1979-81, Leicestershire 1980/81, England 1975-76
Matches: 8 (Won 0, Drew 5, Lost 3)
Right-hand middle order batsman – Left-arm slow bowler

No	Date	Opposition	Venue	R	Bat	C		Bowling		
1	31/07/1975	Australia	Lord's	D	50		0.4	0	1	1
					45		9	4	19	1
2	14/08/1975	Australia	Headingley	D	73	1				
					92	1				

No	Date	Opposition	Venue	R	Bat	C	O	M	R	W
3	28/08/1975	Australia	The Oval	D	39	2	2	1	1	0
					66					
4	03/06/1976	West Indies	Trent Bridge	D	106	1				
					6					
5	17/06/1976	West Indies	Lord's	D	7					
					64					
6	08/07/1976	West Indies	Old Trafford	L	20	1				
					15					
7	22/07/1976	West Indies	Headingley	L	4	1				
					0					
8	12/08/1976	West Indies	The Oval	L	44		3	0	18	0
					42					

Batting & Fielding

Mat	Inns	N/O	Runs	H/S	Avg	100s	50s	Cat
8	16	0	673	106	42.06	1	5	7

Bowling

Balls	Runs	Wkts	Avg	Best	5WI	10WM	S/R
88	39	2	19.50	1-1	0	0	44.00

J.P.STEPHENSON

Full Name: John Patrick Stephenson
Born: 14/03/1965, Stebbing, Essex
Teams: Essex 1985-94, Hampshire 1995-96, Boland 1988/89, England 1989
Matches: 1 (Won 0, Drew 1, Lost 0)
Right-hand opening batsman – Right-arm fast medium bowler

No	Date	Opposition	Venue	R	Bat	C
1	24/08/1989	Australia	The Oval	D	25	
					11	

Batting & Fielding

Mat	Inns	N/O	Runs	H/S	Avg	100s	50s	Cat
1	2	0	36	25	18.00	0	0	0

G.T.S.STEVENS

Full Name: Greville Thomas Scott Stevens
Born: 07/01/1901, Hampstead, London
Died: 19/09/1970, Islington, London
Teams: Oxford University 1920-23, Middlesex 1919-32, England 1922-30
Matches: 10 (Won 4, Drew 3, Lost 3)
England Captain: Once 1928 (Won 0, Drew 0, Lost 1) **Toss:** 0-1
Right-hand middle order batsman – Leg break bowler

No	Date	Opposition	Venue	R	Bat	C	O	M	R	W
1	23/12/1922	South Africa	Johannesburg (1)	L	11					
					2		4	0	19	0
2	24/07/1926	Australia	Old Trafford	D	24	1	32	3	86	3
3	14/08/1926	Australia	The Oval	W	17	2	29	3	85	1
					22		3	1	13	1
4	24/12/1927	South Africa	Johannesburg (1)	W	0	1	19	3	58	3
					8		3	3	13	0
5	31/12/1927	South Africa	Cape Town	W	0	1	10	1	26	1
					2		5	0	17	0
6	21/01/1928	South Africa	Durban (2)	D	69	1	4	0	12	0
							11	0	58	0
7	28/01/1928	South Africa	Johannesburg (1)	L	14	2	1	0	9	0
					20		1	1	0	0
8*	04/02/1928	South Africa	Durban (2)	L	13		2	0	11	0
					18					
9	11/01/1930	West Indies	Bridgetown	D	9		27	5	105	5
					5	1	26.4	1	90	5
10	01/02/1930	West Indies	Port-of-Spain	W	8		7	1	25	0
					29		8	2	21	1

Batting & Fielding

Mat	Inns	N/O	Runs	H/S	Avg	100s	50s	Cat
10	17	0	263	69	15.47	0	1	9

Bowling

Balls	Runs	Wkts	Avg	Best	5WI	10WM	S/R
1186	648	20	32.40	5-90	2	1	59.30

G.B.STEVENSON

Full Name: Graham Barry Stevenson (also known as Stevo)
Born: 16/12/1955, Ackworth, Yorkshire
Teams: Yorkshire 1973-86, Northamptonshire 1987, England 1980-81
Matches: 2 (Won 1, Drew 1, Lost 0)
Right-hand lower order batsman – Right-arm medium bowler

No	Date	Opposition	Venue	R	Bat	C		Bowling		
1	15/02/1980	India	Bombay (3)	W	27*		14	1	59	2
							5	1	13	0
2	27/03/1981	West Indies	St John's	D	1		33	5	111	3

Batting & Fielding

Mat	Inns	N/O	Runs	H/S	Avg	100s	50s	Cat
2	2	1	28	27*	28.00	0	0	0

Bowling

Balls	Runs	Wkts	Avg	Best	5WI	10WM	S/R
312	183	5	36.60	3-111	0	0	62.40

A.J.STEWART

Full Name: Alec James Stewart
Born: 08/04/1963, Merton, Surrey
Teams: Surrey 1981-96, England 1990-96
Matches: 58 (Won 12, Drew 20, Lost 26)
England Captain: 2 times 1993 (Won 0, Drew 0, Lost 2) **Toss:** 1-1
Right-hand opening/middle order batsman – Wicket-keeper – Occasional right-arm medium bowler

No	Date	Opposition	Venue	R	Bat	C	St	B	Bowling
1	24/02/1990	West Indies	Kingston	W	13				
					0*				
2	23/03/1990	West Indies	Port-of-Spain	D	9	1			
					31				
3	05/04/1990	West Indies	Bridgetown	L	45	1			
					37				
4	12/04/1990	West Indies	St John's	L	27				
					8				
5	07/06/1990	New Zealand	Trent Bridge	D	27	2			
6	21/06/1990	New Zealand	Lord's	D	54	2			
					42				
7	05/07/1990	New Zealand	Edgbaston	W	9	1			
					15				
8	23/11/1990	Australia	Brisbane (2)	L	4				
					6				
9	26/12/1990	Australia	Melbourne	L	79				
					8				
10	04/01/1991	Australia	Sydney	D	91	1			
					7	1			
11+	25/01/1991	Australia	Adelaide	D	11	2			2
					9				1
12+	01/02/1991	Australia	Perth	L	2	3			2
					7	1			0
13+	08/08/1991	West Indies	The Oval	W	31	3			0
					38*	1			7
14	22/08/1991	Sri Lanka	Lord's	W	113*				
					43				
15	18/01/1992	New Zealand	Christchurch	W	148	2			
16	30/01/1992	New Zealand	Auckland	W	4				
					8	1			
17	06/02/1992	New Zealand	Wellington	D	107				
					63				
18	04/06/1992	Pakistan	Edgbaston	D	190	1			
19	18/06/1992	Pakistan	Lord's	L	74				
					69*				
20	02/07/1992	Pakistan	Old Trafford	D	15				

No	Date	Opposition	Venue	R	Bat	C	St	B	Bowling
21+	23/07/1992	Pakistan	Headingley	W	8			1	
					2	2		4	
22+	06/08/1992	Pakistan	The Oval	L	31	2		2	
					8	0		6	
23+	29/01/1993	India	Calcutta	L	0	0		6	
					49		1	0	
24*	11/02/1993	India	Madras (1)	L	74				
					0				
25	19/02/1993	India	Bombay (3)	L	13				
					10				
26*+	13/03/1993	Sri Lanka	Colombo (2)	L	63	3	1	2	
					3	2		1	
27+	03/06/1993	Australia	Old Trafford	L	27	1	1	8	
					11			6	
28+	17/06/1993	Australia	Lord's	L	3		1	0	
					62				
29+	01/07/1993	Australia	Trent Bridge	D	25	3		4	
					6	1		5	
30+	22/07/1993	Australia	Headingley	L	5			8	
					78				
31+	05/08/1993	Australia	Edgbaston	L	45	3		7	
					5			3	
32+	19/08/1993	Australia	The Oval	W	76	4		5	
					35	2		2	
33	19/02/1994	West Indies	Kingston	L	70				2.2 0 5 0
					19				
34	17/03/1994	West Indies	Georgetown	L	0				
					79				
35	25/03/1994	West Indies	Port-of-Spain	L	6				
					18	1			
36	08/04/1994	West Indies	Bridgetown	W	118				
					143	1			
37	16/04/1994	West Indies	St John's	D	24				1 0 8 0
38	02/06/1994	New Zealand	Trent Bridge	W	8	1			
39	16/06/1994	New Zealand	Lord's	D	45	1			
					119				
40	30/06/1994	New Zealand	Old Trafford	D	24	1			
41	21/07/1994	South Africa	Lord's	L	12				
					27				
42	04/08/1994	South Africa	Headingley	D	89	1			
					36*				
43	18/08/1994	South Africa	The Oval	W	62	1			
44	25/11/1994	Australia	Brisbane (2)	L	16	1			
					33	1			
45	24/12/1994	Australia	Melbourne	L	16				
					8*				
46+	08/06/1995	West Indies	Headingley	L	2	2		4	
					4			1	
47+	22/06/1995	West Indies	Lord's	W	34	2		8	
					36	3		0	
48+	06/07/1995	West Indies	Edgbaston	L	37	2		5	
49	16/11/1995	South Africa	Centurion	D	6				
50	30/11/1995	South Africa	Johannesburg (3)	D	45	1			
					38				
51	14/12/1995	South Africa	Durban (2)	D	41				
52	26/12/1995	South Africa	Port Elizabeth	D	4				
					81				
53	02/01/1996	South Africa	Cape Town	L	13				
					7				
54	20/06/1996	India	Lord's	D	20	1			
					66				
55	04/07/1996	India	Trent Bridge	D	50	2			
56	25/07/1996	Pakistan	Lord's	L	39				
					89				
57	08/08/1996	Pakistan	Headingley	D	170	1			

No	Date	Opposition	Venue	R	Bat	C	St	B	Bowling
58+	22/08/1996	Pakistan	The Oval	L	44	1	1	4	
					54			0	

Batting & Fielding

Mat	Inns	N/O	Runs	H/S	Avg	100s	50s	Cat	St	Byes
58	103	6	3935	190	40.56	8	20	70	5	98

Bowling

Balls	Runs	Wkts	Avg	Best	5WI	10WM	S/R
20	13	0	–	0-5	0	0	–

M.J.STEWART

Full Name: Michael James Stewart, OBE (known as Micky)
Born: 16/09/1932, Herne Hill, London
Teams: Surrey 1954-72, England 1962-64
Matches: 8 (Won 3, Drew 3, Lost 2)
Right-hand opening batsman – Right-arm medium bowler

No	Date	Opposition	Venue	R	Bat	C
1	21/06/1962	Pakistan	Lord's	W	39	1
					34*	
2	05/07/1962	Pakistan	Headingley	W	86	
3	06/06/1963	West Indies	Old Trafford	L	37	
					87	
4	20/06/1963	West Indies	Lord's	D	2	1
					17	2
5	04/07/1963	West Indies	Edgbaston	W	39	
					27	
6	25/07/1963	West Indies	Headingley	L	2	2
					0	
7	10/01/1964	India	Madras (2)	D	15	
8	21/01/1964	India	Bombay (2)	D		

Batting & Fielding

Mat	Inns	N/O	Runs	H/S	Avg	100s	50s	Cat
8	12	1	385	87	35.00	0	2	6

A.E.STODDART

Full Name: Andrew Ernest Stoddart
Born: 11/03/1863, Westoe, South Shields, Co Durham
Died: 04/04/1915, St John's Wood, London
Teams: Middlesex 1885-1900, England 1888-98
Matches: 16 (Won 7, Drew 2, Lost 7)
England Captain: 8 times 1893-98 (Won 3, Drew 1, Lost 4) **Toss:** 2-6
Right-hand opening batsman – Right-arm medium bowler

No	Date	Opposition	Venue	R	Bat	C		Bow	ling	
1	10/02/1888	Australia	Sydney	W	16	1				
					17					
2	01/01/1892	Australia	Melbourne	L	0		5	2	10	0
					35					
3	29/01/1892	Australia	Sydney	L	27					
					69		4	1	12	0
4	24/03/1892	Australia	Adelaide	W	134					
						1				
5*	17/07/1893	Australia	Lord's	D	24					
					13					
6	14/08/1893	Australia	The Oval	W	83					
7	24/08/1893	Australia	Old Trafford	D	0					
					42					
8*	14/12/1894	Australia	Sydney	W	12	1	3	0	31	1
					36					
9*	29/12/1894	Australia	Melbourne	W	10					
					173	1				
10*	11/01/1895	Australia	Adelaide	L	1					
					34*					

No	Date	Opposition	Venue	R	Bat	C			Bowling		
11*	01/02/1895	Australia	Sydney	L	7						
					0						
12*	01/03/1895	Australia	Melbourne	W	68						
					11						
13	22/06/1896	Australia	Lord's	W	17						
					30*						
14	16/07/1896	Australia	Old Trafford	L	15	1		6	2	9	0
					41						
15*	14/01/1898	Australia	Adelaide	L	15			4	1	10	1
					24						
16*	29/01/1898	Australia	Melbourne	L	17	1		6	1	22	0
					25						

Batting & Fielding

Mat	Inns	N/O	Runs	H/S	Avg	100s	50s	Cat
16	30	2	996	173	35.57	2	3	6

Bowling

Balls	Runs	Wkts	Avg	Best	5WI	10WM	S/R
162	94	2	47.00	1-10	0	0	81.00

W.STORER

Full Name: William Storer (known as Bill)
Born: 25/01/1867, Butterley, Derbyshire
Died: 28/02/1912, Derby
Teams: Derbyshire 1887-1905, London County 1900, England 1897-99
Matches: 6 (Won 1, Drew 1, Lost 4)
Right-hand middle order batsman – Wicket-keeper – Leg break bowler

No	Date	Opposition	Venue	R	Bat	C	St	B	Bowling			
1+	13/12/1897	Australia	Sydney	W	43	1		1				
								12				
2+	01/01/1898	Australia	Melbourne	L	51	1		14	16	4	55	1
					1							
3+	14/01/1898	Australia	Adelaide	L	4	3		16	3	0	16	0
					6							
4+	29/01/1898	Australia	Melbourne	L	2	3		3	4	0	24	1
					26			0				
5+	26/02/1898	Australia	Sydney	L	44	3		5	5	1	13	0
					31			6				
6+	01/06/1899	Australia	Trent Bridge	D	4			8				
					3			0				

Batting & Fielding

Mat	Inns	N/O	Runs	H/S	Avg	100s	50s	Cat	St	Byes
6	11	0	215	51	19.54	0	1	11	0	65

Bowling

Balls	Runs	Wkts	Avg	Best	5WI	10WM	S/R
168	108	2	54.00	1-24	0	0	84.00

G.B.STREET

Full Name: George Benjamin Street
Born: 06/12/1889, Charlwood, Surrey
Died: 24/04/1924, Portslade, Sussex
Teams: Sussex 1909-23, England 1923
Matches: 1 (Won 0, Drew 1, Lost 0)
Right-hand middle order batsman – Wicket-keeper

No	Date	Opposition	Venue	R	Bat	C	St	B
1+	18/01/1923	South Africa	Durban (2)	D	4		1	15
					7*			

Batting & Fielding

Mat	Inns	N/O	Runs	H/S	Avg	100s	50s	Cat	St	Byes
1	2	1	11	7*	11.00	0	0	0	1	15

H.STRUDWICK

Full Name: Herbert Strudwick (known as Bert)
Born: 28/01/1880, Mitcham, Surrey
Died: 14/02/1970, Shoreham, Sussex
Teams: Surrey 1902-27, England 1910-26
Matches: 28 (Won 8, Drew 6, Lost 14)
Right-hand lower order batsman – Wicket-keeper

No	Date	Opposition	Venue	R	Bat	C	St	B
1+	01/01/1910	South Africa	Johannesburg (1)	L	7	1	1	1
					1*	1		2
2+	21/01/1910	South Africa	Durban (1)	L	1	1		7
					7	1		12
3+	26/02/1910	South Africa	Johannesburg (1)	W	18	2		9
					5			1
4+	07/03/1910	South Africa	Cape Town	L	7			10
					3	1		15
5	11/03/1910	South Africa	Cape Town	W	2			
6+	15/12/1911	Australia	Sydney	L	0*	1	1	9
					12*			16
7+	13/12/1913	South Africa	Durban (1)	W	2*	2		6
						1		6
8+	26/12/1913	South Africa	Johannesburg (1)	W	14	2	2	10
						2	1	9
9+	01/01/1914	South Africa	Johannesburg (1)	W	9*			4
					0	2		17
10+	14/02/1914	South Africa	Durban (1)	D	0	2	1	6
						1		12
11+	27/02/1914	South Africa	Port Elizabeth	W	3	2	1	2
						1	1	6
12+	17/12/1920	Australia	Sydney	L	2	1	1	4
					1*	1		17
13+	31/12/1920	Australia	Melbourne	L	21*	2		1
					24			
14+	14/01/1921	Australia	Adelaide	L	9	2	1	6
					1	2		5
15+	25/02/1921	Australia	Sydney	L	2	2		18
					5*	1		3
16+	28/05/1921	Australia	Trent Bridge	L	0			8
					0			0
17+	11/06/1921	Australia	Lord's	L	8	2		2
					12			3
18+	16/08/1924	South Africa	The Oval	D	2*	1		4
19+	19/12/1924	Australia	Sydney	L	6	3		10
					2	2		2
20+	01/01/1925	Australia	Melbourne	L	4	3		18
					22	1		11
21+	16/01/1925	Australia	Adelaide	L	1	2	1	0
					2*			4
22+	13/02/1925	Australia	Melbourne	W	7*	1		13
						2		15
23+	27/02/1925	Australia	Sydney	L	1*	2		2
					0		1	6
24+	12/06/1926	Australia	Trent Bridge	D				
25+	26/06/1926	Australia	Lord's	D		2		12
								5
26+	10/07/1926	Australia	Headingley	D	1	1		2
27+	24/07/1926	Australia	Old Trafford	D		1		2
28+	14/08/1926	Australia	The Oval	W	4*	2		5
					2			0

Batting & Fielding

Mat	Inns	N/O	Runs	H/S	Avg	100s	50s	Cat	St	Byes
28	42	13	230	24	7.93	0	0	60	12	338

C.T.STUDD

Full Name: Charles Thomas Studd (also known as C.T.)
Born: 02/12/1860, Spratton, Northamptonshire
Died: 16/07/1931, Ibambi, Belgian Congo
Teams: Cambridge University 1880-83, Middlesex 1879-84, England 1882-83
Matches: 5 (Won 2, Drew 0, Lost 3)
Right-hand middle order batsman – Right-arm fast medium bowler

No	Date	Opposition	Venue	R	Bat	C		Bowling			
1	28/08/1882	Australia	The Oval	L	0						
					0*	1		4	1	9	0

No	Date	Opposition	Venue	R	Bat	C		Bowling		
2	30/12/1882	Australia	Melbourne	L	0	2	46	30	35	2
					21		14	11	7	0
3	19/01/1883	Australia	Melbourne	W	14		4	1	22	0
						1				
4	26/01/1883	Australia	Sydney	W	21		14	11	5	0
					25	1				
5	17/02/1883	Australia	Sydney	L	48		6	2	12	0
					31		8	4	8	1

Batting & Fielding

Mat	Inns	N/O	Runs	H/S	Avg	100s	50s	Cat
5	9	1	160	48	20.00	0	0	5

Bowling

Balls	Runs	Wkts	Avg	Best	5WI	10WM	S/R
384	98	3	32.66	2-35	0	0	128.00

G.B.STUDD

Full Name: George Brown Studd
Born: 20/10/1859, Netheravon, Wiltshire
Died: 13/02/1945, Pasadena, California, USA
Teams: Cambridge University 1879-82, Middlesex 1879-86, England 1882-83
Matches: 4 (Won 2, Drew 0, Lost 2)
Right-hand middle order batsman

No	Date	Opposition	Venue	R	Bat	C
1	30/12/1882	Australia	Melbourne	L	7	
					0	
2	19/01/1883	Australia	Melbourne	W	1	
						1
3	26/01/1883	Australia	Sydney	W	3	2
					8	1
4	17/02/1883	Australia	Sydney	L	3	3
					9	1

Batting & Fielding

Mat	Inns	N/O	Runs	H/S	Avg	100s	50s	Cat
4	7	0	31	9	4.42	0	0	8

R.SUBBA ROW

Full Name: Raman Subba Row, CBE
Born: 29/01/1932, Streatham, London
Teams: Cambridge University 1951-53, Surrey 1953-54, Northamptonshire 1955-61, England 1958-61
Matches: 13 (Won 6, Drew 5, Lost 2)
Left-hand opening/middle order batsman – Leg break & googly bowler

No	Date	Opposition	Venue	R	Bat	C		Bowling		
1	24/07/1958	New Zealand	Old Trafford	W	9					
						1				
2	20/08/1959	India	The Oval	W	94					
3	09/03/1960	West Indies	Georgetown	D	27					
					100					
4	25/03/1960	West Indies	Port-of-Spain	D	22					
					13		1	0	2	0
5	09/06/1960	South Africa	Edgbaston	W	56					
					32					
6	23/06/1960	South Africa	Lord's	W	90					
7	07/07/1960	South Africa	Trent Bridge	W	30	1				
					16*					
8	21/07/1960	South Africa	Old Trafford	D	27	1				
9	08/06/1961	Australia	Edgbaston	D	59					
					112					
10	22/06/1961	Australia	Lord's	L	48					
					8					
11	06/07/1961	Australia	Headingley	W	35					
					6					

No	Date	Opposition	Venue	R	Bat	C	Bowling
-12	27/07/1961	Australia	Old Trafford	L	2	1	
					49		
13	17/08/1961	Australia	The Oval	D	12	1	
					137		

Batting & Fielding

Mat	Inns	N/O	Runs	H/S	Avg	100s	50s	Cat
13	22	1	984	137	46.85	3	4	5

Bowling

Balls	Runs	Wkts	Avg	Best	5WI	10WM	S/R
6	2	0	–	0-2	0	0	–

P.M.SUCH

Full Name: Peter Mark Such
Born: 12/06/1964, Helensburgh, Dumbartonshire, Scotland
Teams: Nottinghamshire 1982-86, Leicestershire 1987-89, Essex 1990-96, England 1993-94
Matches: 8 (Won 2, Drew 3, Lost 3)
Right-hand lower order batsman – Off break bowler

No	Date	Opposition	Venue	R	Bat	C	Bowling			
1	03/06/1993	Australia	Old Trafford	L	14*	2	33.3	9	67	6
					9		31	6	78	2
2	17/06/1993	Australia	Lord's	L	7		36	6	90	0
					4					
3	01/07/1993	Australia	Trent Bridge	D	0*		20	7	51	2
							23	6	58	2
4	05/08/1993	Australia	Edgbaston	L	1		52.5	18	90	3
					7*		20.3	4	58	1
5	19/08/1993	Australia	The Oval	W	4		14	4	32	0
					10		9	4	17	0
6	02/06/1994	New Zealand	Trent Bridge	W			19	7	28	1
							34	12	50	2
7	16/06/1994	New Zealand	Lord's	D	4		30	8	84	2
							25	5	55	1
8	30/06/1994	New Zealand	Old Trafford	D	5*		5	2	8	0
							10	2	39	0

Batting & Fielding

Mat	Inns	N/O	Runs	H/S	Avg	100s	50s	Cat
8	11	4	65	14*	9.28	0	0	2

Bowling

Balls	Runs	Wkts	Avg	Best	5WI	10WM	S/R
2177	805	22	36.59	6-67	1	0	98.95

F.H.SUGG

Full Name: Frank Howe Sugg
Born: 11/01/1862, Ilkeston, Derbyshire
Died: 29/05/1933, Waterloo, Liverpool, Lancashire
Teams: Yorkshire 1883, Derbyshire 1884-86, Lancashire 1887-99, England 1888
Matches: 2 (Won 2, Drew 0, Lost 0)
Right-hand middle order batsman

No	Date	Opposition	Venue	R	Bat	C
1	13/08/1888	Australia	The Oval	W	31	
2	30/08/1888	Australia	Old Trafford	W	24	

Batting & Fielding

Mat	Inns	N/O	Runs	H/S	Avg	100s	50s	Cat
2	2	0	55	31	27.50	0	0	0

H.SUTCLIFFE

Full Name: Herbert Sutcliffe
Born: 24/11/1894, Summerbridge, Harrogate, Yorkshire
Died: 22/01/1978, Cross Hills, Yorkshire
Teams: Yorkshire 1919-45, England 1924-35
Matches: 54 (Won 25, Drew 18, Lost 11)
Right-hand opening batsman – Right-arm medium bowler

No	Date	Opposition	Venue	R	Bat	C
1	14/06/1924	South Africa	Edgbaston	W	64	
2	28/06/1924	South Africa	Lord's	W	122	
						1
3	12/07/1924	South Africa	Headingley	W	83	
					29*	
4	26/07/1924	South Africa	Old Trafford	D		
5	16/08/1924	South Africa	The Oval	D	5	1
6	19/12/1924	Australia	Sydney	L	59	
					115	
7	01/01/1925	Australia	Melbourne	L	176	
					127	
8	16/01/1925	Australia	Adelaide	L	33	
					59	1
9	13/02/1925	Australia	Melbourne	W	143	
						1
10	27/02/1925	Australia	Sydney	L	22	
					0	
11	12/06/1926	Australia	Trent Bridge	D	13*	
12	26/06/1926	Australia	Lord's	D	82	2
						3
13	10/07/1926	Australia	Headingley	D	26	2
					94	
14	24/07/1926	Australia	Old Trafford	D	20	
15	14/08/1926	Australia	The Oval	W	76	
					161	1
16	24/12/1927	South Africa	Johannesburg (1)	W	102	
					41*	
17	31/12/1927	South Africa	Cape Town	W	29	
					99	
18	21/01/1928	South Africa	Durban (2)	D	25	
					8	
19	28/01/1928	South Africa	Johannesburg (1)	L	37	
					3	
20	04/02/1928	South Africa	Durban (2)	L	51	
					23	
21	23/06/1928	West Indies	Lord's	W	48	1
22	21/07/1928	West Indies	Old Trafford	W	54	
						1
23	11/08/1928	West Indies	The Oval	W	63	
24	30/11/1928	Australia	Brisbane (1)	W	38	
					32	
25	14/12/1928	Australia	Sydney	W	11	
26	29/12/1928	Australia	Melbourne	W	58	
					135	
27	01/02/1929	Australia	Adelaide	W	64	
					17	
28	15/06/1929	South Africa	Edgbaston	D	26	
					114	
29	29/06/1929	South Africa	Lord's	D	100	
					10	
30	13/07/1929	South Africa	Headingley	W	37	
					4	1
31	27/07/1929	South Africa	Old Trafford	W	9	1
32	17/08/1929	South Africa	The Oval	D	104	
					109*	
33	13/06/1930	Australia	Trent Bridge	W	29	
					58*	
34	11/07/1930	Australia	Headingley	D	32	
					28*	
35	25/07/1930	Australia	Old Trafford	D	74	1
36	16/08/1930	Australia	The Oval	L	161	1
					54	
37	29/07/1931	New Zealand	The Oval	W	117	

No	Date	Opposition	Venue	R	Bat	C
38	15/08/1931	New Zealand	Old Trafford	D	109*	
39	25/06/1932	India	Lord's	W	3	
					19	
40	02/12/1932	Australia	Sydney	W	194	
					1*	
41	30/12/1932	Australia	Melbourne	L	52	1
					33	
42	13/01/1933	Australia	Adelaide	W	9	
					7	
43	10/02/1933	Australia	Brisbane (2)	W	86	
					2	
44	23/02/1933	Australia	Sydney	W	56	
45	24/03/1933	New Zealand	Christchurch	D	0	
46	31/03/1933	New Zealand	Auckland	D	24	
47	24/06/1933	West Indies	Lord's	W	21	
						1
48	22/07/1933	West Indies	Old Trafford	D	20	
						1
49	08/06/1934	Australia	Trent Bridge	L	62	
					24	
50	22/06/1934	Australia	Lord's	W	20	2
51	06/07/1934	Australia	Old Trafford	D	63	
					69*	
52	18/08/1934	Australia	The Oval	L	38	
					28	
53	15/06/1935	South Africa	Trent Bridge	D	61	
54	29/06/1935	South Africa	Lord's	L	3	
					38	

Batting & Fielding

Mat	Inns	N/O	Runs	H/S	Avg	100s	50s	Cat
54	84	9	4555	194	60.73	16	23	23

R.SWETMAN

Full Name: Roy Swetman
Born: 25/10/1933, Westminster, London
Teams: Surrey 1954-61, Nottinghamshire 1966-67, Gloucestershire 1972-74, England 1959-60
Matches: 11 (Won 5, Drew 5, Lost 1)
Right-hand lower order batsman – Wicket-keeper – Occasional off break bowler

No	Date	Opposition	Venue	R	Bat	C	St	B
1+	09/01/1959	Australia	Sydney	D	41	1		5
					5			6
2+	13/02/1959	Australia	Melbourne	L	1	2		5
					9			0
3+	27/02/1959	New Zealand	Christchurch	W	9	1	1	5
						1		1
4+	14/03/1959	New Zealand	Auckland	D	17	2		7
5+	02/07/1959	India	Headingley	W	19*	4		0
						1		0
6+	23/07/1959	India	Old Trafford	W	9	1		0
					21*	1		8
7+	20/08/1959	India	The Oval	W	65	2		1
						2		4
8+	06/01/1960	West Indies	Bridgetown	D	45	1		8
9+	28/01/1960	West Indies	Port-of-Spain	W	1	1		0
					0	2		11
10+	17/02/1960	West Indies	Kingston	D	0	1		6
					5			9
11+	09/03/1960	West Indies	Georgetown	D	4	1	1	4
					3			

Batting & Fielding

Mat	Inns	N/O	Runs	H/S	Avg	100s	50s	Cat	St	Byes
11	17	2	254	65	16.93	0	1	24	2	80

F.W.TATE

Full Name: Frederick William Tate (known as Fred)
Born: 24/07/1867, Brighton, Sussex
Died: 24/02/1943, Burgess Hill, Sussex
Teams: Sussex 1887-1905, England 1902
Matches: 1 (Won 0, Drew 0, Lost 1)
Right-hand lower order batsman – Right-arm medium bowler

No	Date	Opposition	Venue	R	Bat	C	Bowling			
1	24/07/1902	Australia	Old Trafford	L	5*	1	11	1	44	0
					4	1	5	3	7	2

Batting & Fielding

Mat	Inns	N/O	Runs	H/S	Avg	100s	50s	Cat
1	2	1	9	5*	9.00	0	0	2

Bowling

Balls	Runs	Wkts	Avg	Best	5WI	10WM	S/R
96	51	2	25.50	2-7	0	0	48.00

M.W.TATE

Full Name: Maurice William Tate
Born: 30/05/1895, Brighton, Sussex
Died: 18/05/1956, Wadhurst, Sussex
Teams: Sussex 1912-37, England 1924-35
Matches: 39 (Won 15, Drew 16, Lost 8)
Right-hand middle order batsman – Right-arm fast medium bowler (previously off break bowler)

No	Date	Opposition	Venue	R	Bat	C	Bowling			
1	14/06/1924	South Africa	Edgbaston	W	19		6	1	12	4
						1	50.4	19	103	4
2	28/06/1924	South Africa	Lord's	W	34	1				
							26.4	8	43	2
3	12/07/1924	South Africa	Headingley	W	29	1	17	4	42	6
							30	6	64	3
4	26/07/1924	South Africa	Old Trafford	D	24			8	34	3
5	16/08/1924	South Africa	The Oval	D	50		29	10	64	3
6	19/12/1924	Australia	Sydney	L	7		55.1	11	130	6
					0		33.7	8	98	5
7	01/01/1925	Australia	Melbourne	L	34		45	10	142	3
					0		33.3	8	99	6
8	16/01/1925	Australia	Adelaide	L	27		18	1	43	2
					21	1	10	4	17	0
9	13/02/1925	Australia	Melbourne	W	8		16	2	70	2
							25.5	6	75	5
10	27/02/1925	Australia	Sydney	L	25		39.5	6	92	4
					33		39.3	6	115	5
11	12/06/1926	Australia	Trent Bridge	D						
12	26/06/1926	Australia	Lord's	D			50	12	111	2
							25	11	38	1
13	10/07/1926	Australia	Headingley	D	5		51	13	99	4
14	24/07/1926	Australia	Old Trafford	D			36.2	7	88	2
15	14/08/1926	Australia	The Oval	W	23		37.1	17	40	3
					33*	1	9	4	12	1
16	23/06/1928	West Indies	Lord's	W	22		27	8	54	2
							22	10	28	2
17	21/07/1928	West Indies	Old Trafford	W	28		35	13	68	1
						1	9	4	10	1
18	11/08/1928	West Indies	The Oval	W	54		21	4	59	4
							13	4	27	3
19	30/11/1928	Australia	Brisbane (1)	W	26	1	21	6	50	3
					20		11	3	26	2

No	Date	Opposition	Venue	R	Bat	C		Bowling	
20	14/12/1928	Australia	Sydney	W	25		21	9	29	0
					4		46	14	99	4
21	29/12/1928	Australia	Melbourne	W	21		46	17	87	2
					0		47	15	70	2
22	01/02/1929	Australia	Adelaide	W	2		42	10	77	4
					47	2	37	9	75	0
23	08/03/1929	Australia	Melbourne	L	15	2	62	26	108	0
					54		38	13	76	0
24	15/06/1929	South Africa	Edgbaston	D	40		44	14	65	3
							16	4	43	0
25	29/06/1929	South Africa	Lord's	D	15		39	9	108	3
					100*		11	3	27	1
26	13/07/1929	South Africa	Headingley	W	3		26	8	40	2
					24*		26	5	50	1
27	13/06/1930	Australia	Trent Bridge	W	13		19	8	20	3
					24		50	20	69	3
28	27/06/1930	Australia	Lord's	L	54		64	16	148	1
					10		13	6	21	1
29	11/07/1930	Australia	Headingley	D	22		39	9	124	5
30	25/07/1930	Australia	Old Trafford	D	15		30	11	39	1
31	16/08/1930	Australia	The Oval	L	10		65.1	12	153	1
					0					
32	24/12/1930	South Africa	Johannesburg (1)	L	8		12.2	4	20	2
					28		18	2	47	1
33	01/01/1931	South Africa	Cape Town	D	15		43	13	79	3
					3					
34	16/01/1931	South Africa	Durban (2)	D			27	13	33	2
							9	3	12	1
35	13/02/1931	South Africa	Johannesburg (1)	D	26		27	9	46	2
					38		22	6	52	2
36	21/02/1931	South Africa	Durban (2)	D	50		22	6	35	1
					24*		9	2	17	0
37	29/07/1931	New Zealand	The Oval	W			18	9	15	1
							21	6	22	3
38	24/03/1933	New Zealand	Christchurch	D	10*		37	16	42	2
							3	1	5	0
39	27/07/1935	South Africa	Old Trafford	D	34		22.3	5	67	2
					0		9	2	20	0

Batting & Fielding

Mat	Inns	N/O	Runs	H/S	Avg	100s	50s	Cat
39	52	5	1198	100*	25.48	1	5	11

Bowling

Balls	Runs	Wkts	Avg	Best	5WI	10WM	S/R
12523	4055	155	26.16	6-42	7	1	80.79

R.TATTERSALL

Full Name: Roy Tattersall
Born: 17/08/1922, Tonge Moor, Bolton, Lancashire
Teams: Lancashire 1948-60, England 1951-54
Matches: 16 (Won 6, Drew 7, Lost 3)
Left-hand lower order batsman – Off break bowler

No	Date	Opposition	Venue	R	Bat	C		Bowling	
1	02/02/1951	Australia	Adelaide	L	0		25.5	5	95	3
					6		27	2	116	1
2	23/02/1951	Australia	Melbourne	W	10	1	11	3	40	0
							5	2	6	0
3	17/03/1951	New Zealand	Christchurch	D	2		16	3	48	1
4	24/03/1951	New Zealand	Wellington	W	1		15	9	16	1
							21	6	44	6
5	07/06/1951	South Africa	Trent Bridge	L		1	47	20	80	1
					0*		23	6	56	3
6	21/06/1951	South Africa	Lord's	W	1	1	28	10	52	7
							32.2	14	49	5
7	05/07/1951	South Africa	Old Trafford	W	1		18	6	29	1
						1	18	3	41	1
8	26/07/1951	South Africa	Headingley	D	4	1	60	23	83	1
							16	9	13	0
9	16/08/1951	South Africa	The Oval	W	0*		14	7	26	1
							5	1	10	1

No	Date	Opposition	Venue	R	Bat	C		Bowling		
10	02/11/1951	India	Delhi	D	4*		53	17	95	2
11	14/12/1951	India	Bombay (2)	D	10*		34	8	112	3
							20	6	55	2
12	30/12/1951	India	Calcutta	D	5*	1	48	13	104	4
							4	2	4	0
13	12/01/1952	India	Kanpur	W	2		21	3	48	6
							27.5	7	77	2
14	06/02/1952	India	Madras (1)	L	2*		39	13	94	2
					0*					
15	11/06/1953	Australia	Trent Bridge	D	2		23	5	59	0
						2	5	0	22	3
16	10/06/1954	Pakistan	Lord's	D			15	8	12	1
							10	1	27	0

Batting & Fielding

Mat	Inns	N/O	Runs	H/S	Avg	100s	50s	Cat
16	17	7	50	10*	5.00	0	0	8

Bowling

Balls	Runs	Wkts	Avg	Best	5WI	10WM	S/R
4228	1513	58	26.08	7-52	4	1	72.89

C.J.TAVARE

Full Name: Christopher James Tavare (known as Chris)
Born: 27/10/1954, Orpington, Kent
Teams: Oxford University 1975-77, Kent 1974-88, Somerset 1989-92, England 1980-89
Matches: 31 (Won 9, Drew 14, Lost 8)
Right-hand opening/middle order batsman – Off break bowler

No	Date	Opposition	Venue	R	Bat	C		Bowling	
1	05/06/1980	West Indies	Trent Bridge	L	13	1			
					4				
2	19/06/1980	West Indies	Lord's	D	42	1			
					6				
3	13/08/1981	Australia	Old Trafford	W	69				
					78				
4	27/08/1981	Australia	The Oval	D	24				
					8	1			
5	27/11/1981	India	Bombay (3)	L	56	1			
					0	1			
6	09/12/1981	India	Bangalore	D	22				
					31				
7	23/12/1981	India	Delhi	D	149				
8	01/01/1982	India	Calcutta	D	7	1			
					25	1			
9	13/01/1982	India	Madras (1)	D	35	1			
							2	0	11	0
10	30/01/1982	India	Kanpur	D	24				
11	17/02/1982	Sri Lanka	Colombo (1)	W	0				
					85				
12	10/06/1982	India	Lord's	W	4	1			
					3				
13	24/06/1982	India	Old Trafford	D	57				
14	08/07/1982	India	The Oval	D	39				
					75*				
15	29/07/1982	Pakistan	Edgbaston	W	54	1			
					17				
16	12/08/1982	Pakistan	Lord's	L	8	1			
					82				
17	26/08/1982	Pakistan	Headingley	W	22	1			
					33				
18	12/11/1982	Australia	Perth	D	89				
					9				
19	26/11/1982	Australia	Brisbane (2)	L	1	1			
					13				
20	10/12/1982	Australia	Adelaide	L	1				
					0				
21	26/12/1982	Australia	Melbourne	W	89				
					0	1			

No	Date	Opposition	Venue	R	Bat	C		Bowling		
22	02/01/1983	Australia	Sydney	D	0					
					16					
23	14/07/1983	New Zealand	The Oval	W	45					
					109					
24	28/07/1983	New Zealand	Headingley	L	69	1				
					23					
25	11/08/1983	New Zealand	Lord's	W	51					
					16					
26	25/08/1983	New Zealand	Trent Bridge	W	4					
					13	1				
27	20/01/1984	New Zealand	Wellington	D	9					
					36*					
28	03/02/1984	New Zealand	Christchurch	L	3	1				
					6					
29	09/08/1984	West Indies	The Oval	L	16	1				
					49	1				
30	23/08/1984	Sri Lanka	Lord's	D	14					
								3 3 0 0		
31	06/07/1989	Australia	Edgbaston	D	2					

Batting & Fielding

Mat	Inns	N/O	Runs	H/S	Avg	100s	50s	Cat
31	56	2	1755	149	32.50	2	12	20

Bowling

Balls	Runs	Wkts	Avg	Best	5WI	10WM	S/R
30	11	0	–	0-0	0	0	–

J.P.TAYLOR

Full Name: Jonathan Paul Taylor (known as Paul)
Born: 08/08/1964, Ashby-de-la-Zouch, Leicestershire
Teams: Derbyshire 1984-87, Northamptonshire 1991-96, England 1993-94
Matches: 2 (Won 0, Drew 1, Lost 1)
Left-hand lower order batsman – Left-arm fast medium bowler

No	Date	Opposition	Venue	R	Bat	C	Bowling			
1	29/01/1993	India	Calcutta	L	17		19	2	65	1
					17*		3	1	9	0
2	16/06/1994	New Zealand	Lord's	D	0		20	4	64	1
					0*		6	2	18	1

Batting & Fielding

Mat	Inns	N/O	Runs	H/S	Avg	100s	50s	Cat
2	4	2	34	17*	17.00	0	0	0

Bowling

Balls	Runs	Wkts	Avg	Best	5WI	10WM	S/R
288	156	3	52.00	1-18	0	0	96.00

K.TAYLOR

Full Name: Kenneth Taylor (known as Ken)
Born: 21/08/1935, Primrose Hill, Huddersfield, Yorkshire
Teams: Yorkshire 1953-68, Auckland 1963/64, England 1959-64
Matches: 3 (Won 2, Drew 0, Lost 1)
Right-hand opening/middle order batsman – Right-arm medium or leg break bowler

No	Date	Opposition	Venue	R	Bat	C		Bowling		
1	04/06/1959	India	Trent Bridge	W	24	1				
2	18/06/1959	India	Lord's	W	6					
					3					
3	02/07/1964	Australia	Headingley	L	9			2 0 6 0		
					15					

Batting & Fielding

Mat	Inns	N/O	Runs	H/S	Avg	100s	50s	Cat
3	5	0	57	24	11.40	0	0	1

Bowling

Balls	Runs	Wkts	Avg	Best	5WI	10WM	S/R
12	6	0	–	0-6	0	0	–

L.B.TAYLOR

Full Name: Leslie Brian Taylor (known as Les)
Born: 25/10/1953, Earl Shilton, Leicestershire
Teams: Leicestershire 1977-90, Natal 1981/82-83/84, England 1985
Matches: 2 (Won 2, Drew 0, Lost 0)
Right-hand lower order batsman – Right-arm fast medium bowler

No	Date	Opposition	Venue	R	Bat	C		Bowling		
1	15/08/1985	Australia	Edgbaston	W			26	5	78	1
							13	4	27	0
2	29/08/1985	Australia	The Oval	W	1*		13	1	39	1
						1	11.3	1	34	2

Batting & Fielding

Mat	Inns	N/O	Runs	H/S	Avg	100s	50s	Cat
2	1	1	1	1*	–	0	0	1

Bowling

Balls	Runs	Wkts	Avg	Best	5WI	10WM	S/R
381	178	4	44.50	2-34	0	0	95.25

R.W.TAYLOR

Full Name: Robert William Taylor, MBE (known as Bob)
Born: 17/07/1941, Stoke-on-Trent, Staffordshire
Teams: Derbyshire 1961-84, England 1971-84
Matches: 57 (Won 24, Drew 21, Lost 12)
Right-hand lower order batsman – Wicket-keeper – Occasional right-arm medium bowler

No	Date	Opposition	Venue	R	Bat	C	St	B	Bowling
1+	25/02/1971	New Zealand	Christchurch	W	4	2	1	9	
					6				
2+	14/12/1977	Pakistan	Lahore (2)	D	32	1	1	1	
						1		0	
3+	02/01/1978	Pakistan	Hyderabad	D	0	1		4	
						1		13	
4+	18/01/1978	Pakistan	Karachi (1)	D	36	1		2	
					18*				
5+	10/02/1978	New Zealand	Wellington	L	8	4		12	
					0			2	
6+	24/02/1978	New Zealand	Christchurch	W	45	1		4	
						1		0	
7+	04/03/1978	New Zealand	Auckland	D	16	1		5	
						2		6	
8+	01/06/1978	Pakistan	Edgbaston	W		3		0	
								4	
9+	15/06/1978	Pakistan	Lord's	W	10	1		0	
						3		1	
10+	29/06/1978	Pakistan	Headingley	D	2	1		0	
11+	27/07/1978	New Zealand	The Oval	W	8	1		1	
						1		8	
12+	10/08/1978	New Zealand	Trent Bridge	W	22	5		0	
						1		0	
13+	24/08/1978	New Zealand	Lord's	W	1	1	1	4	
						3		0	
14+	01/12/1978	Australia	Brisbane (2)	W	20	5		0	
								9	
15+	15/12/1978	Australia	Perth	W	12	3		0	
					2	3		0	
16+	29/12/1978	Australia	Melbourne	L	1	1		0	
					5	1	1	4	
17+	06/01/1979	Australia	Sydney	W	10			2	
					21*			0	
18+	27/01/1979	Australia	Adelaide	W	4	2		1	
					97			0	
19+	10/02/1979	Australia	Sydney	W	36*	1	1	0	
						2		3	

No	Date	Opposition	Venue	R	Bat	C	St	B	Bowling
20+	12/07/1979	India	Edgbaston	W		1		1	
								7	
								0	
21+	02/08/1979	India	Lord's	D	64	3		2	
22+	16/08/1979	India	Headingley	D	1	1		11	
23+	14/12/1979	Australia	Perth	L	14	3		4	
					15	3	1	4	
					8	1		2	
24+	04/01/1980	Australia	Sydney	L	10	3		0	
					8	1		13	
25+	01/02/1980	Australia	Melbourne	L	23			0	
					32			5	
26+	15/02/1980	India	Bombay (3)	W	43	7		4	
						3		6	
27+	02/07/1981	Australia	Lord's	D	0	3		0	
					9	1		4	
28+	16/07/1981	Australia	Headingley	W	5	3		2	
					1	4		4	
29+	30/07/1981	Australia	Edgbaston	W	0	1		1	
					8	1		0	
30+	27/11/1981	India	Bombay (3)	L	9*	4		8	
					1	3		2	
31+	09/12/1981	India	Bangalore	D	33	2		0	
32+	23/12/1981	India	Delhi	D	0	1	1	20	
33+	01/01/1982	India	Calcutta	D	6	2		2	
								0	
34+	13/01/1982	India	Madras (1)	D	8	2		0	2 0 60
								12	
35+	30/01/1982	India	Kanpur	D	0	1		1	
36+	17/02/1982	Sri Lanka	Colombo (1)	W	31*	1		2	
					2	2		0	
37+	10/06/1982	India	Lord's	W	31	1		0	
					1	2		0	
38+	24/06/1982	India	Old Trafford	D	1*	2		6	
39+	08/07/1982	India	The Oval	D	3	1		3	
						3		0	
40+	29/07/1982	Pakistan	Edgbaston	W	1	2		5	
					54	3		0	
41+	12/08/1982	Pakistan	Lord's	L	5	2		3	
					24*			1	
42+	26/08/1982	Pakistan	Headingley	W	18	2		1	
					6*	3		0	
43+	12/11/1982	Australia	Perth	D	29*	1		4	
					31	1		0	
44+	26/11/1982	Australia	Brisbane (2)	L	1	3		2	
					3			2	
45+	10/12/1982	Australia	Adelaide	L	2	3		0	
					3*	1		0	
46+	26/12/1982	Australia	Melbourne	W	1	1		0	
					37	1		5	
47+	02/01/1983	Australia	Sydney	D	0	1		3	
					28*	1		0	
48+	14/07/1983	New Zealand	The Oval	W	0	1		0	
						4		3	
49+	28/07/1983	New Zealand	Headingley	L	10*	1		1	
					9			8	
50+	11/08/1983	New Zealand	Lord's	W	16			0	
					7	2		3	
51+	25/08/1983	New Zealand	Trent Bridge	W	21			0	
					0	4		2	
52+	20/01/1984	New Zealand	Wellington	D	14	3		4	
						2		4	
53+	03/02/1984	New Zealand	Christchurch	L	2	4		8	
					15				
54+	10/02/1984	New Zealand	Auckland	D	23			0	
								0	
55+	02/03/1984	Pakistan	Karachi (1)	L	4	1		0	
					19			1	
56+	12/03/1984	Pakistan	Faisalabad	D	0			0	
						1		0	

No	Date	Opposition	Venue	R	Bat	C	St	B	Bowling
57+	19/03/1984	Pakistan	Lahore (2)	D	1	1		0	
					5			0	

Batting & Fielding

Mat	Inns	N/O	Runs	H/S	Avg	100s	50s	Cat	St	Byes
57	83	12	1156	97	16.28	0	3	167	7	285

Bowling

Balls	Runs	Wkts	Avg	Best	5WI	10WM	S/R
12	6	0	–	0-6	0	0	–

Hon.L.H.TENNYSON

Full Name: Hon.Lionel Hallam Tennyson (3rd Baron Tennyson from 1928)
Born: 07/11/1889, Westminster, London
Died: 06/06/1951, Bexhill-on-Sea, Sussex
Teams: Hampshire 1913-35, England 1913-21
Matches: 9 (Won 4, Drew 3, Lost 2)
England Captain: 3 times 1921 (Won 0, Drew 2, Lost 1) **Toss:** 2-1
Right-hand middle order batsman – Right-arm fast bowler

No	Date	Opposition	Venue	R	Bat	C		Bowling			
1	13/12/1913	South Africa	Durban (1)	W	52						
2	26/12/1913	South Africa	Johannesburg (1)	W	13						
3	01/01/1914	South Africa	Johannesburg (1)	W	21						
					6	2					
4	14/02/1914	South Africa	Durban (1)	D	1						
					0	2					
5	27/02/1914	South Africa	Port Elizabeth	W	23						
								1	0	1	0
6	11/06/1921	Australia	Lord's	L	5						
					74*						
7*	02/07/1921	Australia	Headingley	L	63						
					36	1					
8*	23/07/1921	Australia	Old Trafford	D		1					
9*	13/08/1921	Australia	The Oval	D	51						

Batting & Fielding

Mat	Inns	N/O	Runs	H/S	Avg	100s	50s	Cat
9	12	1	345	74*	31.36	0	4	6

Bowling

Balls	Runs	Wkts	Avg	Best	5WI	10WM	S/R
6	1	0	–	0-1	0	0	–

V.P.TERRY

Full Name: Vivian Paul Terry (known as Paul)
Born: 14/01/1959, Osnabruck, West Germany
Teams: Hampshire 1978-96, England 1984
Matches: 2 (Won 0, Drew 0, Lost 2)
Right-hand opening/middle order batsman – Right-arm medium bowler

No	Date	Opposition	Venue	R	Bat	C
1	12/07/1984	West Indies	Headingley	L	8	
					1	1
2	26/07/1984	West Indies	Old Trafford	L	7	1

Batting & Fielding

Mat	Inns	N/O	Runs	H/S	Avg	100s	50s	Cat
2	3	0	16	8	5.33	0	0	2

J.G.THOMAS

Full Name: John Gregory Thomas (known as Greg)
Born: 12/08/1960, Trebanos, Glamorgan
Teams: Glamorgan 1979-88, Northamptonshire 1989-91, Border 1983/84-86/87, Eastern Province 1987/88, England 1986
Matches: 5 (Won 0, Drew 0, Lost 5)
Right-hand lower order batsman – Right-arm fast bowler

No	Date	Opposition	Venue	R	Bat	C	Bowling			
1	21/02/1986	West Indies	Kingston	L	0		28.5	6	82	2
					1*		1	0	4	0
2	07/03/1986	West Indies	Port-of-Spain	L	4		20	4	86	2
					31*		5	1	21	0
3	21/03/1986	West Indies	Bridgetown	L	4*		16.1	2	70	4
					0					
4	03/04/1986	West Indies	Port-of-Spain	L	5*		15	0	101	0
					0					
5	07/08/1986	New Zealand	Trent Bridge	L	28		39	5	124	2
					10		4	0	16	0

Batting & Fielding

Mat	Inns	N/O	Runs	H/S	Avg	100s	50s	Cat
5	10	4	83	31*	13.83	0	0	0

Bowling

Balls	Runs	Wkts	Avg	Best	5WI	10WM	S/R
774	504	10	50.40	4-70	0	0	77.40

G.J.THOMPSON

Full Name: George Joseph Thompson
Born: 27/10/1877, Cogenhoe, Northampton
Died: 03/03/1943, Clifton, Bristol
Teams: Northamptonshire 1905-22, Auckland 1911/12, England 1909-10
Matches: 6 (Won 3, Drew 0, Lost 3)
Right-hand middle order batsman – Right-arm fast medium bowler

No	Date	Opposition	Venue	R	Bat	C	Bowling			
1	27/05/1909	Australia	Edgbaston	W	6					
						2	4	0	19	0
2	01/01/1910	South Africa	Johannesburg (1)	L	16		11	3	25	0
					63		28	6	100	1
3	21/01/1910	South Africa	Durban (1)	L	38	1	28	13	52	3
					46*		38.2	13	78	2
4	26/02/1910	South Africa	Johannesburg (1)	W	21		17	6	74	2
					10	2	23	9	54	3
5	07/03/1910	South Africa	Cape Town	L	16		16	3	50	4
					6		20.3	2	62	3
6	11/03/1910	South Africa	Cape Town	W	51		12	6	28	2
							30	5	96	3

Batting & Fielding

Mat	Inns	N/O	Runs	H/S	Avg	100s	50s	Cat
6	10	1	273	63	30.33	0	2	5

Bowling

Balls	Runs	Wkts	Avg	Best	5WI	10WM	S/R
1367	638	23	27.73	4-50	0	0	59.43

N.I.THOMSON

Full Name: Norman Ian Thomson (known as Ian)
Born: 23/01/1929, Walsall, Staffordshire
Teams: Sussex 1952-72, England 1964-65
Matches: 5 (Won 1, Drew 4, Lost 0)
Right-hand lower order batsman – Right-arm medium bowler

No	Date	Opposition	Venue	R	Bat	C	Bowling		
1	04/12/1964	South Africa	Durban (2)	W		1	15	5	23	1
							13	6	25	1
2	23/12/1964	South Africa	Johannesburg (3)	D	27*	1	23	8	47	1
							16	5	36	0
3	01/01/1965	South Africa	Cape Town	D	0		45	19	89	2
							14	4	31	1
4	22/01/1965	South Africa	Johannesburg (3)	D	3		31	3	91	0
							19	4	43	0
5	12/02/1965	South Africa	Port Elizabeth	D	39		47	7	128	1
						1	25	7	55	2

Batting & Fielding

Mat	Inns	N/O	Runs	H/S	Avg	100s	50s	Cat
5	4	1	69	39	23.00	0	0	3

Bowling

Balls	Runs	Wkts	Avg	Best	5WI	10WM	S/R
1488	568	9	63.11	2-55	0	0	165.33

G.P.THORPE

Full Name: Graham Paul Thorpe
Born: 01/08/1969, Farnham, Surrey
Teams: Surrey 1988-96, England 1993-96
Matches: 32 (Won 6, Drew 13, Lost 13)
Left-hand middle order batsman – Right-arm medium bowler

No	Date	Opposition	Venue	R	Bat	C		Bowling		
1	01/07/1993	Australia	Trent Bridge	D	6	1				
					114*	1				
2	22/07/1993	Australia	Headingley	L	0		6	1	14	0
					13					
3	05/08/1993	Australia	Edgbaston	L	37	1				
					60	2				
4	19/02/1994	West Indies	Kingston	L	16	1				
					14					
5	17/03/1994	West Indies	Georgetown	L	0	1				
					20					
6	25/03/1994	West Indies	Port-of-Spain	L	86	1				
					3					
7	08/04/1994	West Indies	Bridgetown	W	7	2				
					84	2				
8	16/04/1994	West Indies	St John's	D	9					
							2	1	1	0
9	04/08/1994	South Africa	Headingley	D	72					
					73					
10	18/08/1994	South Africa	The Oval	W	79					
					15*	2				
11	25/11/1994	Australia	Brisbane (2)	L	28					
					67					
12	24/12/1994	Australia	Melbourne	L	51	1				
					9	1				
13	01/01/1995	Australia	Sydney	D	10	1				
					47*					
14	26/01/1995	Australia	Adelaide	W	26	1				
					83	1				
15	03/02/1995	Australia	Perth	L	123					
					0					
16	08/06/1995	West Indies	Headingley	L	20	1				
					61					
17	22/06/1995	West Indies	Lord's	W	52					
					42					
18	06/07/1995	West Indies	Edgbaston	L	30					
					0					
19	27/07/1995	West Indies	Old Trafford	W	94	1				
					0					
20	10/08/1995	West Indies	Trent Bridge	D	19					
					76					
21	24/08/1995	West Indies	The Oval	D	74					
					38					
22	16/11/1995	South Africa	Centurion	D	13					
23	30/11/1995	South Africa	Johannesburg (3)	D	34					
					17					
24	14/12/1995	South Africa	Durban (2)	D	2					
25	26/12/1995	South Africa	Port Elizabeth	D	27	1				
					12*					
26	02/01/1996	South Africa	Cape Town	L	20					
					59					
27	06/06/1996	India	Edgbaston	W	21	2				
					17*	1				
28	20/06/1996	India	Lord's	D	89					
					21					

No	Date	Opposition	Venue	R	Bat	C	Bowling			
29	04/07/1996	India	Trent Bridge	D	45		1	0	3	0
						2				
30	25/07/1996	Pakistan	Lord's	L	77	1				
					3					
31	08/08/1996	Pakistan	Headingley	D	16	1	3	1	9	0
							10	3	10	0
32	22/08/1996	Pakistan	The Oval	L	54					
					9					

Batting & Fielding

Mat	Inns	N/O	Runs	H/S	Avg	100s	50s	Cat
32	59	5	2194	123	40.62	2	18	29

Bowling

Balls	Runs	Wkts	Avg	Best	5WI	10WM	S/R
132	37	0	–	0-1	0	0	–

F.J.TITMUS

Full Name: Frederick John Titmus, MBE (known as Fred)
Born: 24/11/1932, Kentish Town, London
Teams: Middlesex 1949-82, Surrey 1978, Orange Free State 1975/76, England 1955-75
Matches: 53 (Won 14, Drew 27, Lost 12)
Right-hand middle order batsman – Off break bowler

No	Date	Opposition	Venue	R	Bat	C	Bowling			
1	23/06/1955	South Africa	Lord's	W	4	1	14	3	50	1
					16					
2	07/07/1955	South Africa	Old Trafford	L	0		19	7	51	0
					19	1				
3	05/07/1962	Pakistan	Headingley	W	2		4	1	3	2
						1	11	2	20	0
4	26/07/1962	Pakistan	Trent Bridge	D	11*	1	13	2	22	0
					16		7	29	1	
5	30/11/1962	Australia	Brisbane (2)	D	21		33	8	91	1
					3*		26	3	81	1
6	29/12/1962	Australia	Melbourne	W	15		15	2	43	4
							14	4	25	1
7	11/01/1963	Australia	Sydney	L	32	1	37	14	79	7
					6					
8	25/01/1963	Australia	Adelaide	D	59*		20.1	2	88	2
						1	24	5	69	0
9	15/02/1963	Australia	Sydney	D	34	1	47.2	9	103	5
					12*		20	7	37	0
10	23/02/1963	New Zealand	Auckland	W	26		25	9	44	2
						1	6	5	2	1
11	01/03/1963	New Zealand	Wellington	W	33		18	3	40	1
							31	15	50	4
12	15/03/1963	New Zealand	Christchurch	W	4		30	13	45	1
							21	8	46	4
13	06/06/1963	West Indies	Old Trafford	L	0	1	40	13	105	1
					17					
14	20/06/1963	West Indies	Lord's	D	52*					
					11		17	3	47	0
15	04/07/1963	West Indies	Edgbaston	W	27					
					0					
16	25/07/1963	West Indies	Headingley	L	33		25	5	60	1
					5	1	19	2	44	4
17	10/01/1964	India	Madras (2)	D	14		50	14	116	5
					10		19.5	4	46	4
18	21/01/1964	India	Bombay (2)	D	84*	1	36	17	56	2
						1	46	18	79	3
19	29/01/1964	India	Calcutta	D	26		15	4	46	1
							46	23	67	2
20	08/02/1964	India	Delhi	D	4*		49	15	100	3
							43	12	105	0
21	15/02/1964	India	Kanpur	D	5	2	60	37	73	6
							34	12	59	1
22	04/06/1964	Australia	Trent Bridge	D	16		4	1	6	1
					17					
23	18/06/1964	Australia	Lord's	D	15	1	17	6	29	0
							17	7	21	2
24	02/07/1964	Australia	Headingley	L	3		50	24	69	4
					14		27	19	25	2

No	Date	Opposition	Venue	R	Bat	C	O	M	R	W
25	23/07/1964	Australia	Old Trafford	D	9		44	14	100	0
							1	1	0	0
26	13/08/1964	Australia	The Oval	D	8		42	20	51	1
					56					
27	04/12/1964	South Africa	Durban (2)	W			20	9	20	1
							45.5	19	66	5
28	23/12/1964	South Africa	Johannesburg (3)	D	2		39.5	15	73	4
							45	18	101	1
29	01/01/1965	South Africa	Cape Town	D	4		50.2	11	133	2
							6	2	21	0
30	22/01/1965	South Africa	Johannesburg (3)	D	1		29	2	68	1
					13		31	4	98	1
31	12/02/1965	South Africa	Port Elizabeth	D	12	1	37.1	7	87	2
						1	5	0	27	1
32	27/05/1965	New Zealand	Edgbaston	W	13	1	26	17	18	4
						1	59	30	85	2
33	17/06/1965	New Zealand	Lord's	W	13	1	15	7	25	2
					1		39	12	71	2
34	08/07/1965	New Zealand	Headingley	W	6		6	2	16	0
						1	26	17	19	5
35	22/07/1965	South Africa	Lord's	D	59	1	29	10	59	2
					9*	1	26	13	36	1
36	05/08/1965	South Africa	Trent Bridge	L	20		22	8	44	1
					4	1	19.4	5	46	2
37	26/08/1965	South Africa	The Oval	D	2*		26	12	57	1
						1	27	3	74	1
38	10/12/1965	Australia	Brisbane (2)	D	60	1	38	9	99	1
39	30/12/1965	Australia	Melbourne	D	56*	1	31	7	93	0
							22	6	43	0
40	07/01/1966	Australia	Sydney	W	14	1	23	8	40	0
							17.3	4	40	4
41	28/01/1966	Australia	Adelaide	L	33	1	37	6	116	3
					53					
42	11/02/1966	Australia	Melbourne	D	42*	1	42	12	86	1
43	02/06/1966	West Indies	Old Trafford	L	15		35	10	83	5
					12					
44	16/06/1966	West Indies	Lord's	D	6	2	5	0	18	0
							19	3	30	0
45	04/08/1966	West Indies	Headingley	L	6	1	22	7	59	0
					22					
46	10/08/1967	Pakistan	Trent Bridge	W	13	1	7	3	12	0
							23	11	36	2
47	24/08/1967	Pakistan	The Oval	W	65		13	6	21	2
							29.1	8	64	2
48	19/01/1968	West Indies	Port-of-Spain	D	15		34	9	91	1
						1	27	13	42	2
49	08/02/1968	West Indies	Kingston	D	19					
					4		7	2	32	1
50	13/12/1974	Australia	Perth	L	10		28	3	84	2
					61		22	11	43	2
51	26/12/1974	Australia	Melbourne	D	10		29	10	64	2
					0		16	2	65	1
52	04/01/1975	Australia	Sydney	L	22		7.3	2	24	0
					4		7	1	27	0
53	25/01/1975	Australia	Adelaide	L	11		13	1	53	0
					20					

Batting & Fielding

Mat	Inns	N/O	Runs	H/S	Avg	100s	50s	Cat
53	76	11	1449	84*	22.29	0	10	35

Bowling

Balls	Runs	Wkts	Avg	Best	5WI	10WM	S/R
15118	4931	153	32.22	7-79	7	0	98.81

R.W.TOLCHARD

Full Name: Roger William Tolchard
Born: 15/06/1946, Torquay, Devon
Teams: Leicestershire 1965-83, England 1977
Matches: 4 (Won 2, Drew 1, Lost 1)
Right-hand middle order batsman – Wicket-keeper – Occasional off break bowler

No	Date	Opposition	Venue	R	Bat	C
1	01/01/1977	India	Calcutta	W	67	1
						1
2	14/01/1977	India	Madras (1)	W	8*	
					10*	
3	28/01/1977	India	Bangalore	L	0	1
					14	1
4	11/02/1977	India	Bombay (3)	D	4	1
					26	

Batting & Fielding

Mat	Inns	N/O	Runs	H/S	Avg	100s	50s	Cat
4	7	2	129	67	25.80	0	1	5

C.L.TOWNSEND

Full Name: Charles Lucas Townsend (known as Charlie)
Born: 07/11/1876, Clifton, Bristol
Died: 17/10/1958, Elton Manor, Stockton-on-Tees, Co Durham
Teams: Gloucestershire 1893-1922, London County 1900, England 1899
Matches: 2 (Won 0, Drew 1, Lost 1)
Left-hand middle order batsman – Leg break bowler

No	Date	Opposition	Venue	R	Bat	C		Bowling		
1	15/06/1899	Australia	Lord's	L	5		15	1	50	3
					8					
2	14/08/1899	Australia	The Oval	D	38		5	0	16	0
							8	4	9	0

Batting & Fielding

Mat	Inns	N/O	Runs	H/S	Avg	100s	50s	Cat
2	3	0	51	38	17.00	0	0	0

Bowling

Balls	Runs	Wkts	Avg	Best	5WI	10WM	S/R
140	75	3	25.00	3-50	0	0	46.66

D.C.H.TOWNSEND

Full Name: David Charles Humphery Townsend
Born: 20/04/1912, Norton-on-Tees, Co Durham
Teams: Oxford University 1933-34, England 1935
Matches: 3 (Won 0, Drew 1, Lost 2)
Right-hand opening batsman – Right-arm medium bowler

No	Date	Opposition	Venue	R	Bat	C		Bowling		
1	24/01/1935	West Indies	Port-of-Spain	L	5					
					36					
2	14/02/1935	West Indies	Georgetown	D	16		1	0	9	0
					1					
3	14/03/1935	West Indies	Kingston	L	8	1				
					11					

Batting & Fielding

Mat	Inns	N/O	Runs	H/S	Avg	100s	50s	Cat
3	6	0	77	36	12.83	0	0	1

Bowling

Balls	Runs	Wkts	Avg	Best	5WI	10WM	S/R
6	9	0	–	0-9	0	0	–

L.F.TOWNSEND

Full Name: Leslie Fletcher Townsend
Born: 08/06/1903, Long Eaton, Derbyshire
Died: 17/02/1993, Richmond, Nelson, New Zealand
Teams: Derbyshire 1922-39, Auckland 1934/35-35/36, England 1930-34
Matches: 4 (Won 2, Drew 1, Lost 1)
Right-hand middle order batsman – Right-arm medium off break bowler

No	Date	Opposition	Venue	R	Bat	C		Bowling		
1	21/02/1930	West Indies	Georgetown	L	3	1	16	6	48	2
					21	1	7.3	2	25	2
2	15/12/1933	India	Bombay (1)	W	15		9	2	25	0
							12	5	33	0
3	05/01/1934	India	Calcutta	D	40		8	4	19	0
							8	3	22	2
4	10/02/1934	India	Madras (1)	W	10		3	0	14	0
					8		3	0	19	0

Batting & Fielding

Mat	Inns	N/O	Runs	H/S	Avg	100s	50s	Cat
4	6	0	97	40	16.16	0	0	2

Bowling

Balls	Runs	Wkts	Avg	Best	5WI	10WM	S/R
399	205	6	34.16	2-22	0	0	66.50

M.F.TREMLETT

Full Name: Maurice Fletcher Tremlett
Born: 05/07/1923, Stockport, Cheshire
Died: 30/07/1984, Southampton, Hampshire
Teams: Somerset 1947-60, Central Districts 1951/52, England 1948
Matches: 3 (Won 0, Drew 1, Lost 2)
Right-hand middle order batsman – Right-arm fast medium bowler

No	Date	Opposition	Venue	R	Bat	C		Bowling		
1	21/01/1948	West Indies	Bridgetown	D	0*		26	8	49	1
							10	0	40	0
2	03/03/1948	West Indies	Georgetown	L	0		14	4	35	1
					18*					
3	27/03/1948	West Indies	Kingston	L	0		31	1	98	2
					2		1	0	4	0

Batting & Fielding

Mat	Inns	N/O	Runs	H/S	Avg	100s	50s	Cat
3	5	2	20	18*	6.66	0	0	0

Bowling

Balls	Runs	Wkts	Avg	Best	5WI	10WM	S/R
492	226	4	56.50	2-98	0	0	123.00

A.E.TROTT

Full Name: Albert Edwin Trott
Born: 06/02/1873, Abbotsford, Melbourne, Victoria, Australia
Died: 30/07/1914, Harlesden, Willesden, Middlesex
Teams: Middlesex 1898-1910, London County 1900-04, Victoria 1892/93-95/96,
Hawke's Bay 1901/02, Australia 1895, England 1899,
Matches: 2 (Won 2, Drew 0, Lost 0), 3 (Won 2, Drew 0, Lost 1)
Right-hand middle order batsman – Right-arm fast medium or medium off break bowler

No	Date	Opposition	Venue	R	Bat	C		Bowling		
1	14/02/1899	South Africa	Johannesburg (1)	W	0		30.1	13	61	4
					6		33.1	14	49	5
2	01/04/1899	South Africa	Cape Town	W	1		20.2	5	69	4
					16		11	5	19	4

For Australia

No	Date	Opposition	Venue	R	Bat	C		Bowling		
1	11/01/1895	England	Adelaide	W	38*		3	1	9	0
					72*	3	27	10	43	8
2	01/02/1895	England	Sydney	W	85*					
3	01/03/1895	England	Melbourne	L	10	1	30	4	84	1
					0		19	2	56	0

Batting & Fielding

Mat	Inns	N/O	Runs	H/S	Avg	100s	50s	Cat	
2	4	0	23	16	5.75	0	0	0	(England)
3	5	3	205	85*	102.50	0	2	4	(Australia)
5	9	3	228	85*	38.00	0	2	4	(Total)

Bowling

Balls	Runs	Wkts	Avg	Best	5WI	10WM	S/R	
474	198	17	11.64	5-49	1	0	27.88	(England)
474	192	9	21.33	8-43	1	0	52.66	(Australia)
948	390	26	15.00	8-43	2	0	36.46	(Total)

F.S.TRUEMAN

Full Name: Frederick Sewards Trueman, OBE (known as Fred)
Born: 06/02/1931, Stainton, Yorkshire
Teams: Yorkshire 1949-68, England 1952-65
Matches: 67 (Won 33, Drew 23, Lost 11)
Right-hand lower order batsman – Right-arm fast bowler

No	Date	Opposition	Venue	R	Bat	C		Bowling		
1	05/06/1952	India	Headingley	W	0*		26	6	89	3
							9	1	27	4
2	19/06/1952	India	Lord's	W	17		25	3	72	4
							27	4	110	4
3	17/07/1952	India	Old Trafford	W			8.4	2	31	8
							8	5	9	1
4	14/08/1952	India	The Oval	D		1	16	4	48	5
5	15/08/1953	Australia	The Oval	W	10		24.3	3	86	4
						2	2	1	4	0
6	15/01/1954	West Indies	Kingston	L	18		34.4	8	107	2
					1		6	0	32	0
7	17/03/1954	West Indies	Port-of-Spain	D	19		33	3	131	1
							15	5	23	1
8	30/03/1954	West Indies	Kingston	W	0*		15.4	4	39	2
							29	7	88	3
9	23/06/1955	South Africa	Lord's	W	2*		16	2	73	2
					6*		19	2	39	0
10	21/06/1956	Australia	Lord's	L	7	1	28	6	54	2
					2		28	2	90	5
11	12/07/1956	Australia	Headingley	W	0	2	8	2	19	1
						1	11	3	21	1
12	30/05/1957	West Indies	Edgbaston	D	29*		30	4	99	2
						1	5	3	7	2
13	20/06/1957	West Indies	Lord's	W	36*		12.3	2	30	2
						2	23	5	73	2
14	04/07/1957	West Indies	Trent Bridge	D			30	8	63	5
							35	5	80	4
15	25/07/1957	West Indies	Headingley	W	2*		17	4	33	2
						1	11	0	42	2
16	22/08/1957	West Indies	The Oval	W	22	2	5	1	9	0
							5	2	19	1
17	05/06/1958	New Zealand	Edgbaston	W	0		21	8	31	5
						1	17	5	33	1
18	19/06/1958	New Zealand	Lord's	W	8	2	4	1	6	1
						1	11	6	24	2
19	03/07/1958	New Zealand	Headingley	W			11	5	18	1
						1	14	6	22	0
20	24/07/1958	New Zealand	Old Trafford	W	5	1	29.5	4	67	3
							2	1	11	0
21	21/08/1958	New Zealand	The Oval	D	39*		16	3	41	2
							6	5	3	0
22	09/01/1959	Australia	Sydney	D	18		18	3	37	1
					0		4	1	9	0
23	30/01/1959	Australia	Adelaide	L	0		30.1	6	90	4
					0		3	1	3	0
24	13/02/1959	Australia	Melbourne	L	21	3	25	0	92	4
					36		6.7	0	45	0
25	27/02/1959	New Zealand	Christchurch	W	21	1	10.5	3	39	1
						2	8	2	20	1
26	14/03/1959	New Zealand	Auckland	D	21*	1	26	12	46	3
27	04/06/1959	India	Trent Bridge	W	28		24	9	45	4
						1	22.3	10	44	2
28	18/06/1959	India	Lord's	W	7		16	4	40	1
							21	3	55	2
29	02/07/1959	India	Headingley	W	17	1	15	6	30	3
						1	10	1	29	2

No	Date	Opposition	Venue	R	Bat	C	O	M	R	W
30	23/07/1959	India	Old Trafford	W	0		15	4	29	1
					8	1	23.1	6	75	2
31	20/08/1959	India	The Oval	W	1		17	6	24	4
						1	14	4	30	3
32	06/01/1960	West Indies	Bridgetown	D	3	1	47	15	93	4
33	28/01/1960	West Indies	Port-of-Spain	W	7	1	21	11	35	5
					37	1	19	9	44	1
34	17/02/1960	West Indies	Kingston	D	17		33	10	82	2
					4		18	4	54	4
35	09/03/1960	West Indies	Georgetown	D	6	1	40	6	116	3
36	25/03/1960	West Indies	Port-of-Spain	D	10*		37.3	6	103	2
					2*	2	5	1	22	0
37	09/06/1960	South Africa	Edgbaston	W	11		24.5	4	58	4
					25		22	4	58	3
38	23/06/1960	South Africa	Lord's	W	0		13	2	49	0
							17	5	44	2
39	07/07/1960	South Africa	Trent Bridge	W	15	1	14.3	6	27	5
							22	3	77	4
40	21/07/1960	South Africa	Old Trafford	D	10	2	20	2	58	3
					14*		6	1	10	0
41	18/08/1960	South Africa	The Oval	D	0	1	31.1	4	93	2
					24		10	0	34	2
42	08/06/1961	Australia	Edgbaston	D	20	1	36.5	1	136	2
43	22/06/1961	Australia	Lord's	L	25		34	3	118	4
					0		10	0	40	2
44	06/07/1961	Australia	Headingley	W	4		22	5	58	5
							15.5	5	30	6
45	27/07/1961	Australia	Old Trafford	L	3		14	1	55	1
					8	1	32	6	92	0
46	31/05/1962	Pakistan	Edgbaston	D			13	3	59	2
						1	24	5	70	2
47	21/06/1962	Pakistan	Lord's	W	29		17.4	6	31	6
						1	33.3	6	85	3
48	05/07/1962	Pakistan	Headingley	W	20	1	23	6	55	2
						1	10.4	3	33	2
49	26/07/1962	Pakistan	Trent Bridge	D			24	3	71	4
						2	19	5	35	1
50	30/11/1962	Australia	Brisbane (2)	D	19	2	18	0	76	3
							15	0	59	0
51	29/12/1962	Australia	Melbourne	W	6		23	1	83	3
						1	20	1	62	5
52	11/01/1963	Australia	Sydney	L	32	2	20	2	68	0
					9		6	1	20	2
53	25/01/1963	Australia	Adelaide	D	38	1	19	1	54	1
							23.3	3	60	4
54	15/02/1963	Australia	Sydney	D	30	1	11	0	33	1
					8		3	0	6	1
55	01/03/1963	New Zealand	Wellington	W	3		20	5	46	4
							18	7	27	1
56	15/03/1963	New Zealand	Christchurch	W	11		30.2	9	75	7
							19.4	8	16	2
57	06/06/1963	West Indies	Old Trafford	L	5		40	7	95	2
					29*					
58	20/06/1963	West Indies	Lord's	D	10		44	16	100	6
					0		26	9	52	5
59	04/07/1963	West Indies	Edgbaston	W	4	1	26	5	75	5
					1		14.3	2	44	7
60	25/07/1963	West Indies	Headingley	L	4		46	10	117	4
					5	1	13	1	46	2
61	22/08/1963	West Indies	The Oval	L	19	1	26.1	2	65	3
					5		1	1	0	0
62	04/06/1964	Australia	Trent Bridge	D	0	1	20.3	3	58	3
					4		5	0	28	0
63	18/06/1964	Australia	Lord's	D	8		25	8	48	5
							18	6	52	1
64	02/07/1964	Australia	Headingley	L	4		24.3	2	98	3
					12*		7	0	28	1
65	13/08/1964	Australia	The Oval	D	14	2	33.3	6	87	4
66	27/05/1965	New Zealand	Edgbaston	W	3	1	18	3	49	1
							32.4	8	79	3
67	17/06/1965	New Zealand	Lord's	W	3		19.5	8	40	2
							26	4	69	0

Batting & Fielding

Mat	Inns	N/O	Runs	H/S	Avg	100s	50s	Cat
67	85	14	981	39*	13.81	0	0	64

Bowling

Balls	Runs	Wkts	Avg	Best	5WI	10WM	S/R
15178	6625	307	21.57	8-31	17	3	49.43

N.C.TUFNELL

Full Name: Neville Charsley Tufnell
Born: 13/06/1887, Simla, India
Died: 03/08/1951, Whitechapel, London
Teams: Cambridge University 1908-10, Surrey 1922, England 1910
Matches: 1 (Won 1, Drew 0, Lost 0)
Right-hand lower order batsman – Wicket-keeper – Occasional right-arm slow bowler

No	Date	Opposition	Venue	R	Bat	C	St	B
1+	11/03/1910	South Africa	Cape Town	W	14			0
							1	25

Batting & Fielding

Mat	Inns	N/O	Runs	H/S	Avg	100s	50s	Cat	St	Byes
1	1	0	14	14	14.00	0	0	0	1	25

P.C.R.TUFNELL

Full Name: Philip Clive Roderick Tufnell (known as Phil)
Born: 29/04/1966, Barnet, Hertfordshire
Teams: Middlesex 1986-96, England 1990-95
Matches: 22 (Won 6, Drew 6, Lost 10)
Right-hand lower order batsman – Left-arm slow bowler

No	Date	Opposition	Venue	R	Bat	C	Bowling			
1	26/12/1990	Australia	Melbourne	L	0*		21	5	62	0
					0*		24	12	36	0
2	04/01/1991	Australia	Sydney	D	5*		30	6	95	1
						1	37	18	61	5
3	25/01/1991	Australia	Adelaide	D	0*		5	0	38	0
							16	3	28	1
4	01/02/1991	Australia	Perth	L	0		7	1	25	2
					8					
5	08/08/1991	West Indies	The Oval	W	2		14.3	3	25	6
							46	6	150	1
6	22/08/1991	Sri Lanka	Lord's	W	0	1	7	2	23	0
							34.3	14	94	5
7	18/01/1992	New Zealand	Christchurch	W			39	10	100	4
							46.1	25	47	7
8	30/01/1992	New Zealand	Auckland	W	6*		4	2	16	1
					0*	1	17	5	45	2
9	06/02/1992	New Zealand	Wellington	D	2*		71	22	147	2
							9	5	12	0
10	06/08/1992	Pakistan	The Oval	L	0*	1	34	9	87	1
					0					
11	11/02/1993	India	Madras (1)	L	2		41	3	132	0
					22*					
12	19/02/1993	India	Bombay (3)	L	2*		39.3	6	142	4
					2*					
13	13/03/1993	Sri Lanka	Colombo (2)	L	1		33	5	108	1
					1		7.4	1	34	2
14	03/06/1993	Australia	Old Trafford	L	1	1	28	5	78	2
					0*		37	4	112	1
15	17/06/1993	Australia	Lord's	L	2*		39	3	129	2
					0					
16	08/04/1994	West Indies	Bridgetown	W	0*	1	32	12	76	1
						1	36	12	100	3
17	16/04/1994	West Indies	St John's	D	0		39	8	110	0
							6	4	5	0
18	04/08/1994	South Africa	Headingley	D			32	13	81	2
						1	23	8	31	2
19	25/11/1994	Australia	Brisbane (2)	L	0		25	3	72	0
					2*		38	10	79	4

No	Date	Opposition	Venue	R	Bat	C		Bowling		
20	24/12/1994	Australia	Melbourne	L	0		28	7	59	2
					0		48	8	90	3
21	01/01/1995	Australia	Sydney	D	4*					
						1	35.4	9	61	0
22	26/01/1995	Australia	Adelaide	W	0*		24	5	64	0
					0	1	9	3	17	1

Batting & Fielding

Mat	Inns	N/O	Runs	H/S	Avg	100s	50s	Cat
22	32	17	62	22*	4.13	0	0	10

Bowling

Balls	Runs	Wkts	Avg	Best	5WI	10WM	S/R
6378	2671	68	39.27	7-47	4	1	93.79

M.J.L.TURNBULL

Full Name: Maurice Joseph Lawson Turnbull
Born: 16/03/1906, Cardiff, Glamorgan
Died: 05/08/1944, near Montchamp, France
Teams: Cambridge University 1926-29, Glamorgan 1924-39, Wales 1928, England 1930-36
Matches: 9 (Won 3, Drew 5, Lost 1)
Right-hand middle order batsman

No	Date	Opposition	Venue	R	Bat	C
1	10/01/1930	New Zealand	Christchurch	W	7	
2	24/12/1930	South Africa	Johannesburg (1)	L	28	
					61	
3	01/01/1931	South Africa	Cape Town	D	7	1
					14	
4	16/01/1931	South Africa	Durban (2)	D		
5	13/02/1931	South Africa	Johannesburg (1)	D	25	
					0*	
6	21/02/1931	South Africa	Durban (2)	D	6	
					7	
7	24/06/1933	West Indies	Lord's	D	28	
8	12/08/1933	West Indies	The Oval	W	4	
9	27/06/1936	India	Lord's	W	0	
					37*	

Batting & Fielding

Mat	Inns	N/O	Runs	H/S	Avg	100s	50s	Cat
9	13	2	224	61	20.36	0	1	1

G.E.TYLDESLEY

Full Name: George Ernest Tyldesley (known as Ernest)
Born: 05/02/1889, Roe Green, Worsley, Lancashire
Died: 05/05/1962, Rhos-on-Sea, Denbighshire
Teams: Lancashire 1909-36, England 1921-29
Matches: 14 (Won 6, Drew 4, Lost 4)
Right-hand middle order batsman – Right-arm slow medium bowler

No	Date	Opposition	Venue	R	Bat	C	Bowling
1	28/05/1921	Australia	Trent Bridge	L	0		
					7		
2	23/07/1921	Australia	Old Trafford	D	78*	1	
3	13/08/1921	Australia	The Oval	D	39		
4	12/07/1924	South Africa	Headingley	W	15		
5	24/07/1926	Australia	Old Trafford	D	81	1	
6	24/12/1927	South Africa	Johannesburg (1)	W	122		
7	31/12/1927	South Africa	Cape Town	W	0		
					87		

No	Date	Opposition	Venue	R	Bat	C	Bowling
8	21/01/1928	South Africa	Durban (2)	D	78		
					62*		
9	28/01/1928	South Africa	Johannesburg (1)	L	42		
					8		
10	04/02/1928	South Africa	Durban (2)	L	100		0.3　0　2　0
					21		
11	23/06/1928	West Indies	Lord's	W	122		
12	21/07/1928	West Indies	Old Trafford	W	3		
13	11/08/1928	West Indies	The Oval	W	73		
14	08/03/1929	Australia	Melbourne	L	31		
					21		

Batting & Fielding

Mat	Inns	N/O	Runs	H/S	Avg	100s	50s	Cat
14	20	2	990	122	55.00	3	6	2

Bowling

Balls	Runs	Wkts	Avg	Best	5WI	10WM	S/R
3	2	0	–	0-2	0	0	–

J.T.TYLDESLEY

Full Name: John Thomas Tyldesley (known as Johnny or J.T.)
Born: 22/11/1873, Roe Green, Worsley, Lancashire
Died: 27/11/1930, Monton, Salford, Lancashire
Teams: Lancashire 1895-1923, England 1899-1909
Matches: 31 (Won 11, Drew 9, Lost 11)
Right-hand middle order batsman

No	Date	Opposition	Venue	R	Bat	C
1	14/02/1899	South Africa	Johannesburg (1)	W	17	1
					17	1
2	01/04/1899	South Africa	Cape Town	W	13	1
					112	
3	01/06/1899	Australia	Trent Bridge	D	22	
					10	
4	15/06/1899	Australia	Lord's	L	14	
					4	
5	13/12/1901	Australia	Sydney	W	1	
6	01/01/1902	Australia	Melbourne	L	2	1
					66	1
7	17/01/1902	Australia	Adelaide	L	0	1
					25	
8	14/02/1902	Australia	Sydney	L	79	
					10	
9	28/02/1902	Australia	Melbourne	L	13	
					36	
10	29/05/1902	Australia	Edgbaston	D	138	
11	12/06/1902	Australia	Lord's	D		
12	03/07/1902	Australia	Bramall Lane	L	22	
					14	
13	24/07/1902	Australia	Old Trafford	L	22	
					16	1
14	11/08/1902	Australia	The Oval	W	33	
					0	1
15	11/12/1903	Australia	Sydney	W	53	
					9	
16	01/01/1904	Australia	Melbourne	W	97	1
					62	
17	15/01/1904	Australia	Adelaide	L	0	1
					10	
18	26/02/1904	Australia	Sydney	W	16	1
					5	
19	05/03/1904	Australia	Melbourne	L	10	
					15	
20	29/05/1905	Australia	Trent Bridge	W	56	
					61	

No	Date	Opposition	Venue	R	Bat	C
21	15/06/1905	Australia	Lord's	D	43	
					12	
22	03/07/1905	Australia	Headingley	D	0	
					100	
23	24/07/1905	Australia	Old Trafford	W	24	1
24	14/08/1905	Australia	The Oval	D	16	
					112*	
25	01/07/1907	South Africa	Lord's	D	52	
26	29/07/1907	South Africa	Headingley	W	12	
					30	1
27	19/08/1907	South Africa	The Oval	D	8	
					11	
28	27/05/1909	Australia	Edgbaston	W	24	
						1
29	14/06/1909	Australia	Lord's	L	46	
					3	
30	01/07/1909	Australia	Headingley	L	55	
					7	
31	26/07/1909	Australia	Old Trafford	D	15	1
					11	1

Batting & Fielding

Mat	Inns	N/O	Runs	H/S	Avg	100s	50s	Cat
31	55	1	1661	138	30.75	4	9	16

R.K.TYLDESLEY

Full Name: Richard Knowles Tyldesley (known as Dick)
Born: 11/03/1897, Westhoughton, Lancashire
Died: 17/09/1943, Over Hulton, Bolton, Lancashire
Teams: Lancashire 1919-31, England 1924-30
Matches: 7 (Won 3, Drew 3, Lost 1)
Right-hand lower order batsman – Right-arm slow bowler

No	Date	Opposition	Venue	R	Bat	C		Bowling		
1	28/06/1924	South Africa	Lord's	W			24	10	52	3
							36	18	50	3
2	12/07/1924	South Africa	Headingley	W	29		13	4	37	0
							24	8	63	3
3	26/07/1924	South Africa	Old Trafford	D			11.5	4	11	1
4	16/08/1924	South Africa	The Oval	D	1*	1	22	6	36	2
5	01/01/1925	Australia	Melbourne	L	5		35	3	130	0
					0		2	0	6	0
6	13/06/1930	Australia	Trent Bridge	W	1		21	8	53	2
					5		35	10	77	3
7	11/07/1930	Australia	Headingley	D	6		33	5	104	2

Batting & Fielding

Mat	Inns	N/O	Runs	H/S	Avg	100s	50s	Cat
7	7	1	47	29	7.83	0	0	1

Bowling

Balls	Runs	Wkts	Avg	Best	5WI	10WM	S/R
1615	619	19	32.57	3-50	0	0	85.00

E.F.S.TYLECOTE

Full Name: Edward Ferdinando Sutton Tylecote
Born: 23/06/1849, Marston Moretaine, Bedfordshire
Died: 15/03/1938, New Hunstanton, Norfolk
Teams: Oxford University 1869-72, Kent 1875-83, England 1882-86
Matches: 6 (Won 4, Drew 0, Lost 2)
Right-hand middle order batsman – Wicket-keeper

No	Date	Opposition	Venue	R	Bat	C	St	B
1+	30/12/1882	Australia	Melbourne	L	33	1	2	4
					38			0
2+	19/01/1883	Australia	Melbourne	W	0			6
								1

No	Date	Opposition	Venue	R	Bat	C	St	B
3+	26/01/1883	Australia	Sydney	W	66		1	6
					0			6
4+	17/02/1883	Australia	Sydney	L	5			10
					0		1	10
5+	19/07/1886	Australia	Lord's	W	0	1		4
						1		13
6+	12/08/1886	Australia	The Oval	W	10*	1		4
						1	1	7

Batting & Fielding

Mat	Inns	N/O	Runs	H/S	Avg	100s	50s	Cat	St	Byes
6	9	1	152	66	19.00	0	1	5	5	71

E.J.TYLER

Full Name: Edwin James Tyler
Born: 13/10/1864, Kidderminster, Worcestershire
Died: 25/01/1917, North Town, Taunton, Somerset
Teams: Somerset 1891-1907, England 1896
Matches: 1 (Won 1, Drew 0, Lost 0)
Left-hand lower order batsman – Left-arm slow bowler

No	Date	Opposition	Venue	R	Bat	C		Bowling	
1	21/03/1896	South Africa	Cape Town	W	0		18	3 49	3
							11	3 16	1

Batting & Fielding

Mat	Inns	N/O	Runs	H/S	Avg	100s	50s	Cat
1	1	0	0	0	0.00	0	0	0

Bowling

Balls	Runs	Wkts	Avg	Best	5WI	10WM	S/R
145	65	4	16.25	3-49	0	0	36.25

F.H.TYSON

Full Name: Frank Holmes Tyson
Born: 06/06/1930, Farnworth, Lancashire
Teams: Northamptonshire 1952-60, England 1954-59
Matches: 17 (Won 8, Drew 3, Lost 6)
Right-hand lower order batsman – Right-arm fast bowler

No	Date	Opposition	Venue	R	Bat	C		Bowling	
1	12/08/1954	Pakistan	The Oval	L	3		13.4	3 35	4
					3		9	2 22	1
2	26/11/1954	Australia	Brisbane (2)	L	7		29	1 160	1
					37*				
3	17/12/1954	Australia	Sydney	W	0		13	2 45	4
					9	1	18.4	1 85	6
4	31/12/1954	Australia	Melbourne	W	6		21	2 68	2
					6		12.3	1 27	7
5	28/01/1955	Australia	Adelaide	W	1		26.1	4 85	3
							15	2 47	3
6	25/02/1955	Australia	Sydney	D		1	11	1 46	2
							5	2 20	0
7	11/03/1955	New Zealand	Dunedin	W	16		19	7 23	3
							12	6 16	4
8	25/03/1955	New Zealand	Auckland	W	27*		11	2 41	2
							7	2 10	2
9	09/06/1955	South Africa	Trent Bridge	W	0		24	5 51	2
							21.3	7 28	6
10	07/07/1955	South Africa	Old Trafford	L	2		44	5 124	3
					8		13.3	2 55	3
11	23/08/1956	Australia	The Oval	D	3	1	14	5 34	1
12	24/12/1956	South Africa	Johannesburg (3)	W	22		9	1 22	0
					2				
13	01/03/1957	South Africa	Port Elizabeth	L	1	1	17	6 38	2
					23		23	7 40	6
14	30/01/1959	Australia	Adelaide	L	0		28	1 100	1
					33				
15	13/02/1959	Australia	Melbourne	L	9		20	1 73	1
					6		6	0 20	1

No	Date	Opposition	Venue	R	Bat	C		Bowling		
16	27/02/1959	New Zealand	Christchurch	W	6*		14	4	23	3
							14	6	23	2
17	14/03/1959	New Zealand	Auckland	D			20	9	50	1

Batting & Fielding

Mat	Inns	N/O	Runs	H/S	Avg	100s	50s	Cat
17	24	3	230	37*	10.95	0	0	4

Bowling

Balls	Runs	Wkts	Avg	Best	5WI	10WM	S/R
3452	1411	76	18.56	7-27	4	1	45.42

G.ULYETT

Full Name: George Ulyett
Born: 21/10/1851, Crabtree, Pitsmoor, Sheffield, Yorkshire
Died: 18/06/1898, Pitsmoor, Sheffield, Yorkshire
Teams: Yorkshire 1873-93, England 1877-90
Matches: 25 (Won 14, Drew 4, Lost 7)
Right-hand opening batsman – Right-hand round-arm fast bowler

No	Date	Opposition	Venue	R	Bat	C		Bowling		
1	15/03/1877	Australia	Melbourne	L	10	1	25	12	36	0
					24		19	7	39	3
2	31/03/1877	Australia	Melbourne	W	52		14.1	6	15	2
					63	1	19	9	33	1
3	02/01/1879	Australia	Melbourne	L	0		62	24	93	1
					14		1	0	9	0
4	31/12/1881	Australia	Melbourne	D	87		20	5	41	2
					23		15	3	30	1
5	17/02/1882	Australia	Sydney	L	25		22.2	16	11	2
					67		15	4	48	2
6	03/03/1882	Australia	Sydney	L	0	1	3	1	10	0
					23					
7	10/03/1882	Australia	Melbourne	D	149	2	24	8	40	1
					64					
8	28/08/1882	Australia	The Oval	L	26		9	5	11	1
					11		6	2	10	1
9	10/07/1884	Australia	Old Trafford	D	5		30	17	41	3
					1					
10	21/07/1884	Australia	Lord's	W	32		11	3	21	0
						2	39.1	23	36	7
11	11/08/1884	Australia	The Oval	D	10	1	56	24	96	1
12	12/12/1884	Australia	Adelaide	W	68		10	3	23	0
							2	1	3	0
13	01/01/1885	Australia	Melbourne	W	0		15	7	23	0
							8	3	19	1
14	20/02/1885	Australia	Sydney	L	2	1	12.2	8	17	1
					4	1	39	25	42	2
15	14/03/1885	Australia	Sydney	L	10		54	25	91	3
					2	1				
16	21/03/1885	Australia	Melbourne	W	1		23	7	52	4
							15	7	25	3
17	05/07/1886	Australia	Old Trafford	W	17		36.1	20	46	4
					8	2	6.3	3	7	1
18	19/07/1886	Australia	Lord's	W	19	1				
							8	3	13	0
19	12/08/1886	Australia	The Oval	W	0	1				
20	10/02/1888	Australia	Sydney	W	5	1				
					5					
21	13/08/1888	Australia	The Oval	W	0					
22	30/08/1888	Australia	Old Trafford	W	0					
23	12/03/1889	South Africa	Port Elizabeth	W	4		1	0	1	0
					22	3	20	9	27	2
24	25/03/1889	South Africa	Cape Town	W	22		4	4	0	0
25	21/07/1890	Australia	Lord's	W	74		3	3	0	1
							6	2	11	0

Batting & Fielding

Mat	Inns	N/O	Runs	H/S	Avg	100s	50s	Cat
25	39	0	949	149	24.33	1	7	19

Bowling

Balls	Runs	Wkts	Avg	Best	5WI	10WM	S/R
2627	1020	50	20.40	7-36	1	0	52.54

D.L.UNDERWOOD

Full Name: Derek Leslie Underwood, MBE
Born: 08/06/1945, Bromley, Kent
Teams: Kent 1963-87, England 1966-82
Matches: 86 (Won 27, Drew 38, Lost 21)
Right-hand lower order batsman – Left-arm medium or slow medium bowler

No	Date	Opposition	Venue	R	Bat	C	Bowling			
1	30/06/1966	West Indies	Trent Bridge	L	12*	1	2	1	5	0
					10*	1	43	15	86	0
2	04/08/1966	West Indies	Headingley	L	0		24	9	81	1
					0					
3	10/08/1967	Pakistan	Trent Bridge	W			5	2	17	1
							26	8	52	5
4	24/08/1967	Pakistan	The Oval	W	2*	1	9	5	12	0
							26	12	48	2
5	20/06/1968	Australia	Lord's	D		1	18	15	8	2
6	11/07/1968	Australia	Edgbaston	D	14*	1	25	9	48	3
							8	4	14	0
7	25/07/1968	Australia	Headingley	D	45*		27.4	13	41	4
							45.1	22	52	2
8	22/08/1968	Australia	The Oval	W	9*		54.3	21	89	2
					1*		31.3	19	50	7
9	21/02/1969	Pakistan	Lahore (2)	D	0		16	4	36	1
					6		19	8	29	1
10	28/02/1969	Pakistan	Dacca	D	22		27	13	45	1
							44	15	94	5
11	06/03/1969	Pakistan	Karachi (1)	D						
12	12/06/1969	West Indies	Old Trafford	W	11*		12	6	15	1
						1	19	11	31	1
13	10/07/1969	West Indies	Headingley	W	4	1				
					16	1	22	12	55	4
14	24/07/1969	New Zealand	Lord's	W	1		29.3	16	38	4
					4		31	18	32	7
15	07/08/1969	New Zealand	Trent Bridge	D	16		22	8	44	1
							3	1	5	0
16	21/08/1969	New Zealand	The Oval	W	3		26	12	41	6
						1	38.3	15	60	6
17	27/11/1970	Australia	Brisbane (2)	D	2*		28	6	101	3
						1	20	10	23	1
18	09/01/1971	Australia	Sydney	W	0	2	22	7	66	4
							8	2	17	0
19	21/01/1971	Australia	Melbourne	D	5		19	4	78	1
							12	0	38	1
20	29/01/1971	Australia	Adelaide	D	1*		21	6	45	1
							35	7	85	1
21	12/02/1971	Australia	Sydney	W	8*	1	16	3	39	2
					0		13.6	5	28	2
22	25/02/1971	New Zealand	Christchurch	W	0*		11.6	7	12	6
							32.3	7	85	6
23	05/03/1971	New Zealand	Auckland	D	1*	3	38	12	108	5
					8*		2	2	0	0
24	03/06/1971	Pakistan	Edgbaston	D	9*	1	41	13	102	0
25	19/08/1971	India	The Oval	L	22		25	6	49	1
					11	1	38	14	72	3
26	27/07/1972	Australia	Headingley	W	5		31	16	37	4
							21	6	45	6
27	10/08/1972	Australia	The Oval	L	3*		38	16	90	4
					0*		35	11	94	2
28	20/12/1972	India	Delhi	W	6		9	1	16	0
							30	13	56	4

No	Date	Opposition	Venue	R	Bat	C	Bowling			
29	30/12/1972	India	Calcutta	L	0		20.4	11	43	2
					4		14	4	36	1
30	25/01/1973	India	Kanpur	D	0*		51	20	90	3
						1	26	11	46	2
31	06/02/1973	India	Bombay (2)	D	9	1	26	6	100	1
						1	38	16	70	2
32	02/03/1973	Pakistan	Lahore (2)	D	5*		35	15	58	3
							13	5	38	0
33	16/03/1973	Pakistan	Hyderabad	D	20*		48	15	119	0
34	05/07/1973	New Zealand	Headingley	W	20*		11	4	27	0
							7	2	14	0
35	26/07/1973	West Indies	The Oval	L	0		23.3	8	68	2
					7	1	19	5	51	1
36	09/08/1973	West Indies	Edgbaston	D	2		24.3	10	40	3
							32	9	66	2
37	23/08/1973	West Indies	Lord's	L	12	1	34	6	105	0
					14					
38	02/02/1974	West Indies	Port-of-Spain	L	10*	1	23	8	56	1
					9		12	2	48	2
39	16/02/1974	West Indies	Kingston	D	24		36	12	98	0
					12					
40	22/03/1974	West Indies	Georgetown	D	7*		17.5	4	36	1
41	30/03/1974	West Indies	Port-of-Spain	W	4		34	12	57	0
					1*	1	15	7	19	1
42	06/06/1974	India	Old Trafford	W	7		19	7	50	1
					9		15	4	45	1
43	20/06/1974	India	Lord's	W	9	2	15	10	18	1
44	04/07/1974	India	Edgbaston	W			15	3	30	1
							3	1	3	0
45	25/07/1974	Pakistan	Headingley	D	9		12	6	26	1
							1	1	0	0
46	08/08/1974	Pakistan	Lord's	D	12*		14	8	20	5
							34.5	17	51	8
47	22/08/1974	Pakistan	The Oval	D	43		44	14	106	2
							8	2	15	1
48	29/11/1974	Australia	Brisbane (2)	L	25		20	6	54	2
					30		26	6	63	2
49	26/12/1974	Australia	Melbourne	D	9		22	6	62	0
					4		19	7	43	0
50	04/01/1975	Australia	Sydney	L	27		13	3	54	0
					5		12	1	65	2
51	25/01/1975	Australia	Adelaide	L	0		29	3	113	7
					0		26	5	102	4
52	08/02/1975	Australia	Melbourne	W	11					
							18	5	39	0
53	20/02/1975	New Zealand	Auckland	W			16	6	38	3
							25	9	47	2
54	28/02/1975	New Zealand	Christchurch	D			13.5	3	35	2
55	10/07/1975	Australia	Edgbaston	L	10		7	3	10	1
					3					
56	31/07/1975	Australia	Lord's	D	0*		13	5	29	1
							31	14	64	0
57	14/08/1975	Australia	Headingley	D	0	1	19	12	22	1
					0*		15	4	40	1
58	28/08/1975	Australia	The Oval	D	3*		44	13	96	1
							2	0	5	1
59	03/06/1976	West Indies	Trent Bridge	D	0		27	8	82	4
							7	3	9	0
60	17/06/1976	West Indies	Lord's	D	31		18.4	7	39	5
					2		24.3	8	73	2
61	08/07/1976	West Indies	Old Trafford	L	0	1	24	5	55	3
					0	1	35	9	90	0
62	22/07/1976	West Indies	Headingley	L	1		18	2	80	0
					0					
63	12/08/1976	West Indies	The Oval	L	4	1	60.5	15	165	3
					2		9	2	38	0
64	17/12/1976	India	Delhi	W	7*		9	3	19	1
						1	44	15	78	4
65	01/01/1977	India	Calcutta	W	4		13	5	24	1
							32.5	18	50	3

No	Date	Opposition	Venue	R	Bat	C	Bowling			
66	14/01/1977	India	Madras (1)	W	23	2	17	9	16	2
					8		14	7	28	4
67	28/01/1977	India	Bangalore	L	12	1	21	7	45	1
					10		31	8	76	4
68	11/02/1977	India	Bombay (3)	D	7	1	38	13	89	4
							33	10	84	5
69	12/03/1977	Australia	Melbourne	L	7		11.6	2	16	3
					7		12	2	38	1
70	16/06/1977	Australia	Lord's	D	11*		25	6	42	0
					12*		10	3	16	2
71	07/07/1977	Australia	Old Trafford	W	10		20.2	7	53	1
						2	32.5	13	66	6
72	28/07/1977	Australia	Trent Bridge	W	7		11	5	18	1
							27	15	49	2
73	11/08/1977	Australia	Headingley	W	6					
							8	3	16	0
74	25/08/1977	Australia	The Oval	D	20	1	35	9	102	1
75	14/12/1979	Australia	Perth	L	13	1	13	4	33	1
					0		41	14	82	3
76	04/01/1980	Australia	Sydney	L	12	1	13.2	3	39	2
					43		26	6	71	3
77	01/02/1980	Australia	Melbourne	L	3	2	53	19	131	3
					0		14	2	49	1
78	15/02/1980	India	Bombay (3)	W	1		6	1	23	0
							1	0	5	0
79	19/06/1980	West Indies	Lord's	D	3		29.2	7	108	1
80	27/11/1981	India	Bombay (3)	L	8		4	2	12	1
					13*		11	4	14	0
81	09/12/1981	India	Bangalore	D	2*	1	43	21	88	3
82	23/12/1981	India	Delhi	D	2*		48	18	97	2
83	01/01/1982	India	Calcutta	D	13		29	13	45	3
							31	18	38	0
84	13/01/1982	India	Madras (1)	D	0		22	7	59	0
							15	8	30	1
85	30/01/1982	India	Kanpur	D	0*		25	8	55	0
86	17/02/1982	Sri Lanka	Colombo (1)	W	0		18	6	28	5
							37.5	15	67	3

Batting & Fielding

Mat	Inns	N/O	Runs	H/S	Avg	100s	50s	Cat
86	116	35	937	45*	11.56	0	0	44

Bowling

Balls	Runs	Wkts	Avg	Best	5WI	10WM	S/R
21862	7674	297	25.83	8-51	17	6	73.60

B.H.VALENTINE

Full Name: Bryan Herbert Valentine
Born: 17/01/1908, Blackheath, Kent
Died: 02/02/1983, Otford, Kent
Teams: Cambridge University 1928-29, Kent 1927-48, England 1933-39
Matches: 7 (Won 2, Drew 5, Lost 0)
Right-hand middle order batsman – Right-arm medium bowler

No	Date	Opposition	Venue	R	Bat	C
1	15/12/1933	India	Bombay (1)	W	136	
						1
2	05/01/1934	India	Calcutta	D	40	
					3	
3	24/12/1938	South Africa	Johannesburg (1)	D	97	
4	31/12/1938	South Africa	Cape Town	D	112	1
5	20/01/1939	South Africa	Durban (2)	W		
6	18/02/1939	South Africa	Johannesburg (1)	D	11	
					25*	
7	03/03/1939	South Africa	Durban (2)	D	26	
					4*	

Batting & Fielding

Mat	Inns	N/O	Runs	H/S	Avg	100s	50s	Cat
7	9	2	454	136	64.85	2	1	2

H.VERITY

Full Name: Hedley Verity
Born: 18/05/1905, Headingley, Leeds, Yorkshire
Died: 31/07/1943, Caserta, Italy
Teams: Yorkshire 1930-39, England 1931-39
Matches: 40 (Won 16, Drew 17, Lost 7)
Right-hand lower order batsman – Left-arm slow bowler

No	Date	Opposition	Venue	R	Bat	C		Bowling		
1	29/07/1931	New Zealand	The Oval	W			22.1	8	52	2
							12.3	4	33	2
2	15/08/1931	New Zealand	Old Trafford	D						
3	02/12/1932	Australia	Sydney	W	2		13	4	35	0
							4	1	15	0
4	13/01/1933	Australia	Adelaide	W	45		16	7	31	0
					40	1	20	12	26	1
5	10/02/1933	Australia	Brisbane (2)	W	23*	1	27	12	39	0
							19	6	30	2
6	23/02/1933	Australia	Sydney	W	4		17	3	62	3
						1	19	9	33	5
7	24/03/1933	New Zealand	Christchurch	D			23	7	58	1
							3	1	6	0
8	24/06/1933	West Indies	Lord's	W	21	1	16	8	21	1
						1	18.1	4	45	4
9	22/07/1933	West Indies	Old Trafford	D	0*		32	14	47	2
						1	13	2	40	0
10	15/12/1933	India	Bombay (1)	W	24		27	11	44	3
							20	9	50	1
11	05/01/1934	India	Calcutta	D	55*	1	28.4	13	64	4
							31	12	76	4
12	10/02/1934	India	Madras (1)	W	42		23.5	10	49	7
						1	27.2	6	104	4
13	08/06/1934	Australia	Trent Bridge	L	0	1	34	9	65	1
					0*	1	17	8	48	1
14	22/06/1934	Australia	Lord's	W	29	1	36	15	61	7
						1	22.3	8	43	8
15	06/07/1934	Australia	Old Trafford	D	60*	1	53	24	78	4
							5	4	2	0
16	20/07/1934	Australia	Headingley	D	2*		46.5	15	113	3
17	18/08/1934	Australia	The Oval	L	11		43	7	123	0
					1		14	3	43	0
18	15/06/1935	South Africa	Trent Bridge	D			41	18	52	3
						1				
19	29/06/1935	South Africa	Lord's	L	17		28	10	61	3
					8		38	16	56	3
20	13/07/1935	South Africa	Headingley	D	1		12	9	5	2
							13	11	4	0
21	27/07/1935	South Africa	Old Trafford	D	16	2	20	4	48	1
							20	10	24	0
22	27/06/1936	India	Lord's	W	2*		18.1	5	42	2
						1	16	8	17	4
23	25/07/1936	India	Old Trafford	D	66*		17	5	41	4
							22	8	66	1
24	15/08/1936	India	The Oval	W	4		25	12	30	3
							16	6	32	1
25	04/12/1936	Australia	Brisbane (2)	W	7		28	11	52	1
					19					
26	18/12/1936	Australia	Sydney	W	0*	1	3	0	17	2
							19	7	55	1
27	01/01/1937	Australia	Melbourne	L	0	1	14	4	24	2
					11	1	37.7	9	79	3
28	29/01/1937	Australia	Adelaide	L	19		16	4	47	0
					17		37	17	54	0
29	26/02/1937	Australia	Melbourne	L	0	1	41	5	127	1
					2*					
30	26/06/1937	New Zealand	Lord's	D	3	2	25	13	48	1
						1	14	7	33	1

No	Date	Opposition	Venue	R	Bat	C	Bowling			
31	10/06/1938	Australia	Trent Bridge	D	3		7.3	0	36	1
							62	27	102	3
32	24/06/1938	Australia	Lord's	D	5	1	35.4	9	103	4
					11		13	5	29	2
33	22/07/1938	Australia	Headingley	L	25*		19	6	30	1
					0	1	5	2	24	1
34	20/08/1938	Australia	The Oval	W	8*		5	1	15	0
							7	3	15	2
35	24/12/1938	South Africa	Johannesburg (1)	D	26	1	44.1	16	61	4
							16	8	17	0
36	31/12/1938	South Africa	Cape Town	D	29		36.6	13	70	5
							10	5	13	0
37	20/01/1939	South Africa	Durban (2)	W			8	4	9	0
							35	10	71	3
38	18/02/1939	South Africa	Johannesburg (1)	D	8	1	37.5	10	127	3
39	03/03/1939	South Africa	Durban (2)	D	3	1	55.6	14	97	2
							40	9	87	2
40	24/06/1939	West Indies	Lord's	W			16	3	34	0
						1	14	4	20	2

Batting & Fielding

Mat	Inns	N/O	Runs	H/S	Avg	100s	50s	Cat
40	44	12	669	66*	20.90	0	3	30

Bowling

Balls	Runs	Wkts	Avg	Best	5WI	10WM	S/R
11173	3510	144	24.37	8-43	5	2	77.59

G.F.VERNON

Full Name: George Frederick Vernon
Born: 20/06/1856, Marylebone, London
Died: 10/08/1902, Elmina, Gold Coast
Teams: Middlesex 1878-95, England 1882
Matches: 1 (Won 0, Drew 0, Lost 1)
Right-hand middle order batsman – Occasional under-arm slow bowler

No	Date	Opposition	Venue	R	Bat	C
1	30/12/1882	Australia	Melbourne	L	11*	
					3	

Batting & Fielding

Mat	Inns	N/O	Runs	H/S	Avg	100s	50s	Cat
1	2	1	14	11*	14.00	0	0	0

J.VINE

Full Name: Joseph Vine (also known as Joe)
Born: 15/05/1875, Willingdon, Sussex
Died: 25/04/1946, Aldrington, Hove, Sussex
Teams: Sussex 1896-1922, London County 1901-04, England 1912
Matches: 2 (Won 2, Drew 0, Lost 0)
Right-hand opening batsman – Leg break bowler

No	Date	Opposition	Venue	R	Bat	C
1	09/02/1912	Australia	Melbourne	W	4*	
2	23/02/1912	Australia	Sydney	W	36	
					6*	

Batting & Fielding

Mat	Inns	N/O	Runs	H/S	Avg	100s	50s	Cat
2	3	2	46	36	46.00	0	0	0

W.VOCE

Full Name: William Voce (known as Bill)
Born: 08/08/1909, Annesley, Woodhouse, Nottinghamshire
Died: 06/06/1984, Nottingham
Teams: Nottinghamshire 1927-52, England 1930-47
Matches: 27 (Won 8, Drew 12, Lost 7)
Right-hand lower order batsman – Left-arm fast medium or slow bowler

No	Date	Opposition	Venue	R	Bat	C		Bowling		
1	11/01/1930	West Indies	Bridgetown	D	10		27	1	120	2
							3	0	15	0
2	01/02/1930	West Indies	Port-of-Spain	W	2*	2	28	5	79	4
							37.2	15	70	7
3	21/02/1930	West Indies	Georgetown	L	1*		26	4	81	2
					2		16	4	44	0
4	03/04/1930	West Indies	Kingston	D	20		22	3	81	2
					6*		29	3	94	0
5	24/12/1930	South Africa	Johannesburg (1)	L	8		26	11	45	4
					0		27.2	8	59	4
6	01/01/1931	South Africa	Cape Town	D	30		33	11	95	0
					1*					
7	16/01/1931	South Africa	Durban (2)	D		1	29.2	3	58	5
							12	3	14	1
8	13/02/1931	South Africa	Johannesburg (1)	D	41*		42	11	106	1
					5		32	7	87	4
9	21/02/1931	South Africa	Durban (2)	D	0		27	10	51	2
							22	1	46	2
10	27/06/1931	New Zealand	Lord's	D	1*		10	1	40	0
						1	32	11	60	0
11	25/06/1932	India	Lord's	W	4*		17	6	23	3
					0*		12	3	28	2
12	02/12/1932	Australia	Sydney	W	0*		29	4	110	4
						2	17.3	5	54	2
13	30/12/1932	Australia	Melbourne	L	6		20	3	54	3
					0		15	2	47	2
14	13/01/1933	Australia	Adelaide	W	8	1	14	5	21	1
					8		4	1	7	0
15	23/02/1933	Australia	Sydney	W	7*		24	4	80	1
							10	0	34	2
16	24/03/1933	New Zealand	Christchurch	D	66	1	17.1	3	27	3
							4	0	13	0
17	31/03/1933	New Zealand	Auckland	D	16		9.5	3	20	2
							1.3	0	2	0
18	15/08/1936	India	The Oval	W	1*		20	5	46	1
						2	20	5	40	0
19	04/12/1936	Australia	Brisbane (2)	W	4*		20.6	5	41	6
					2*	1	6.3	0	16	4
20	18/12/1936	Australia	Sydney	W		1	8	1	10	4
							19	4	66	3
21	01/01/1937	Australia	Melbourne	L	0*		18	3	49	2
					0	1	29	2	120	3
22	29/01/1937	Australia	Adelaide	L	8		12	0	49	0
					1		20	2	86	1
23	26/02/1937	Australia	Melbourne	L	3	1	29	3	123	3
					1					
24	26/06/1937	New Zealand	Lord's	D	27		24.2	2	74	2
							18.5	8	41	3
25	20/07/1946	India	Old Trafford	D	0		20	3	44	1
							6	5	2	0
26	29/11/1946	Australia	Brisbane (2)	L	1*	1	28	9	92	0
					18					
27	01/01/1947	Australia	Melbourne	D	0		10	2	40	0
							6	1	29	0

Batting & Fielding

Mat	Inns	N/O	Runs	H/S	Avg	100s	50s	Cat
27	38	15	308	66	13.39	0	1	15

Bowling

Balls	Runs	Wkts	Avg	Best	5WI	10WM	S/R
6360	2733	98	27.88	7-70	3	2	64.89

A.WADDINGTON

Full Name: Abraham Waddington (known as Abram or Abe)
Born: 04/02/1893, Clayton, Thornton, Yorkshire
Died: 28/10/1959, Throxenby, Scarborough, Yorkshire
Teams: Yorkshire 1919-27, England 1920-21
Matches: 2 (Won 0, Drew 0, Lost 2)
Right-hand lower order batsman – Left-arm fast medium bowler

No	Date	Opposition	Venue	R	Bat	C	Bowling			
1	17/12/1920	Australia	Sydney	L	7		18	3	35	1
					3	1	23	4	53	0
2	11/02/1921	Australia	Melbourne	L	0		5	0	31	0
					6					

Batting & Fielding

Mat	Inns	N/O	Runs	H/S	Avg	100s	50s	Cat
2	4	0	16	7	4.00	0	0	1

Bowling

Balls	Runs	Wkts	Avg	Best	5WI	10WM	S/R
276	119	1	119.00	1-35	0	0	276.00

E.WAINWRIGHT

Full Name: Edward Wainwright (known as Ted)
Born: 08/04/1865, Tinsley, Sheffield, Yorkshire
Died: 28/10/1919, Sheffield, Yorkshire
Teams: Yorkshire 1888-1902, England 1893-98
Matches: 5 (Won 1, Drew 1, Lost 3)
Right-hand middle order batsman – Right-arm medium off break bowler

No	Date	Opposition	Venue	R	Bat	C	Bowling			
1	17/07/1893	Australia	Lord's	D	1		11	3	41	0
					26					
2	13/12/1897	Australia	Sydney	W	10					
3	01/01/1898	Australia	Melbourne	L	21	1				
					11					
4	29/01/1898	Australia	Melbourne	L	6		3	1	11	0
					2		9	2	21	0
5	26/02/1898	Australia	Sydney	L	49					
					6	1				

Batting & Fielding

Mat	Inns	N/O	Runs	H/S	Avg	100s	50s	Cat
5	9	0	132	49	14.66	0	0	2

Bowling

Balls	Runs	Wkts	Avg	Best	5WI	10WM	S/R
127	73	0	–	0-11	0	0	–

P.M.WALKER

Full Name: Peter Michael Walker
Born: 17/02/1936, Clifton, Bristol
Teams: Glamorgan 1956-72, Transvaal 1956/57-57/58, Western Province 1962/63, England 1960
Matches: 3 (Won 3, Drew 0, Lost 0)
Right-hand middle order batsman – Left-arm slow bowler (previously left-arm medium)

No	Date	Opposition	Venue	R	Bat	C	Bowling			
1	09/06/1960	South Africa	Edgbaston	W	9		6	1	13	0
					37	2	4	2	8	0
2	23/06/1960	South Africa	Lord's	W	52	1				
3	07/07/1960	South Africa	Trent Bridge	W	30	2				
							3	0	13	0

Batting & Fielding

Mat	Inns	N/O	Runs	H/S	Avg	100s	50s	Cat
3	4	0	128	52	32.00	0	1	5

Bowling

Balls	Runs	Wkts	Avg	Best	5WI	10WM	S/R
78	34	0	–	0-8	0	0	–

C.F.WALTERS

Full Name: Cyril Frederick Walters
Born: 28/08/1905, Bedlinog, Glamorgan
Died: 23/12/1992, Neath, Glamorgan
Teams: Glamorgan 1923-28, Worcestershire 1928-35, Wales 1927-29, England 1933-34
Matches: 11 (Won 5, Drew 4, Lost 2)
England Captain: Once 1934 (Won 0, Drew 0, Lost 1) **Toss:** 0-1
Right-hand opening batsman

No	Date	Opposition	Venue	R	Bat	C
1	24/06/1933	West Indies	Lord's	W	51	
2	22/07/1933	West Indies	Old Trafford	D	46	
3	12/08/1933	West Indies	The Oval	W	2	
4	15/12/1933	India	Bombay (1)	W	78	
					14*	
5	05/01/1934	India	Calcutta	D	29	1
					2*	
6	10/02/1934	India	Madras (1)	W	59	
					102	
7*	08/06/1934	Australia	Trent Bridge	L	17	
					46	
8	22/06/1934	Australia	Lord's	W	82	
						1
9	06/07/1934	Australia	Old Trafford	D	52	2
					50*	
10	20/07/1934	Australia	Headingley	D	44	
					45	
11	18/08/1934	Australia	The Oval	L	64	
					1	2

Batting & Fielding

Mat	Inns	N/O	Runs	H/S	Avg	100s	50s	Cat
11	18	3	784	102	52.26	1	7	6

ALAN WARD

Full Name: Alan Ward
Born: 10/08/1947, Dronfield, Derbyshire
Teams: Derbyshire 1966-76, Leicestershire 1977-78, Border 1971/72, England 1969-76
Matches: 5 (Won 2, Drew 2, Lost 1)
Right-hand lower order batsman – Right-arm fast bowler

No	Date	Opposition	Venue	R	Bat	C		Bowling		
1	24/07/1969	New Zealand	Lord's	W	0	2	14	2	49	2
					19*		10.5	0	48	5
2	07/08/1969	New Zealand	Trent Bridge	D			23	3	61	4
							3	0	14	0
3	21/08/1969	New Zealand	The Oval	W	21		5	0	10	0
							18	10	28	2
4	03/06/1971	Pakistan	Edgbaston	D	0		29	3	115	0
5	22/07/1976	West Indies	Headingley	L	0	1	15	0	103	2
					0		9	2	25	2

Batting & Fielding

Mat	Inns	N/O	Runs	H/S	Avg	100s	50s	Cat
5	6	1	40	21	8.00	0	0	3

Bowling

Balls	Runs	Wkts	Avg	Best	5WI	10WM	S/R
761	453	14	32.35	4-61	0	0	54.35

ALBERT WARD

Full Name: Albert Ward
Born: 21/11/1865, Waterloo, Leeds, Yorkshire
Died: 06/01/1939, Heaton, Bolton, Lancashire
Teams: Yorkshire 1886, Lancashire 1889-1904, England 1893-95
Matches: 7 (Won 4, Drew 1, Lost 2)
Right-hand opening batsman – Right-arm slow bowler

No	Date	Opposition	Venue	R	Bat	C
1	14/08/1893	Australia	The Oval	W	55	
2	24/08/1893	Australia	Old Trafford	D	13 0	
3	14/12/1894	Australia	Sydney	W	75 117	
4	29/12/1894	Australia	Melbourne	W	30 41	1
5	11/01/1895	Australia	Adelaide	L	5 13	
6	01/02/1895	Australia	Sydney	L	7 6	
7	01/03/1895	Australia	Melbourne	W	32 93	

Batting & Fielding

Mat	Inns	N/O	Runs	H/S	Avg	100s	50s	Cat
7	13	0	487	117	37.46	1	3	1

J.H.WARDLE

Full Name: John Henry Wardle (known as Johnny)
Born: 08/01/1923, Ardsley, Yorkshire
Died: 23/07/1985, Hatfield, Doncaster, Yorkshire
Teams: Yorkshire 1946-58, England 1948-57
Matches: 28 (Won 14, Drew 8, Lost 6)
Left-hand lower order batsman – Left-arm leg break, googly & chinaman bowler

No	Date	Opposition	Venue	R	Bat	C		Bowling		
1	11/02/1948	West Indies	Port-of-Spain	D	4 2*		3	0	9	0
2	24/06/1950	West Indies	Lord's	L	33* 21		17 30	6 10	46 58	2 0
3	07/06/1951	South Africa	Trent Bridge	L	5 30		49 4	21 3	77 4	1 0
4	21/06/1951	South Africa	Lord's	W	18		22.5 20	10 5	46 44	3 1
5	11/06/1953	Australia	Trent Bridge	D	29*		35 12	16 3	55 24	1 0
6	25/06/1953	Australia	Lord's	D	23 0*		29 46	8 18	77 111	4 1
7	09/07/1953	Australia	Old Trafford	D	5		28.3 5	10 2	70 7	3 4
8	24/02/1954	West Indies	Georgetown	W	38		22 12.3	4 4	60 24	0 3
9	30/03/1954	West Indies	Kingston	W	66	1 1	10 39	1 14	20 83	0 1
10	10/06/1954	Pakistan	Lord's	D	3		30.5 8	22 6	33 6	4 0
11	01/07/1954	Pakistan	Trent Bridge	W	14*		6 32	3 17	9 44	1 3
12	22/07/1954	Pakistan	Old Trafford	D	54	2 1	24 7	16 2	19 9	4 1
13	12/08/1954	Pakistan	The Oval	L	8 9	3	35	16	56	7
14	17/12/1954	Australia	Sydney	W	35 8		4 6	2 0	11 20	0 1
15	31/12/1954	Australia	Melbourne	W	0 38		1	0	1	0
16	28/01/1955	Australia	Adelaide	W	23		19 4.2	5 1	59 8	0 1
17	25/02/1955	Australia	Sydney	D	5*	1	24.4 12	6 1	79 51	5 3
18	11/03/1955	New Zealand	Dunedin	W	32*		26 14.3	15 4	31 41	1 2
19	25/03/1955	New Zealand	Auckland	W	0		31 5	19 5	44 0	1 1
20	09/06/1955	South Africa	Trent Bridge	W	2		32 29	23 17	24 33	4 1
21	23/06/1955	South Africa	Lord's	W	20 4		29 9.4	10 4	65 18	4 2
22	21/07/1955	South Africa	Headingley	L	24 21		9 57	1 22	33 100	0 4

No	Date	Opposition	Venue	R	Bat	C	Bowling		
23	21/06/1956	Australia	Lord's	L	0		20	7 40	1
					0		7	2 19	0
24	24/12/1956	South Africa	Johannesburg (3)	W	6*		20	4 52	3
					0		3	0 18	0
25	01/01/1957	South Africa	Cape Town	W	3		23.6	9 53	5
						1	19	3 36	7
26	25/01/1957	South Africa	Durban (2)	D	13		20.2	6 61	5
					8		20	7 42	2
27	15/02/1957	South Africa	Johannesburg (3)	L	16	2	19.6	4 68	2
					22		14	4 29	2
28	20/06/1957	West Indies	Lord's	W	11				
							22	5 53	1

Batting & Fielding

Mat	Inns	N/O	Runs	H/S	Avg	100s	50s	Cat
28	41	8	653	66	19.78	0	2	12

Bowling

Balls	Runs	Wkts	Avg	Best	5WI	10WM	S/R
6597	2080	102	20.39	7-36	5	1	64.67

P.F.WARNER

Full Name: Sir Pelham Francis Warner (known as Plum)
Born: 02/10/1873, The Hall, Port-of-Spain, Trinidad
Died: 30/01/1963, West Lavington, Sussex
Teams: Oxford University 1894-96, Middlesex 1894-1920, England 1899-1912
Matches: 15 (Won 7, Drew 2, Lost 6)
England Captain: 10 times 1903-06 (Won 4, Drew 0, Lost 6) **Toss:** 5-5
Right-hand opening batsman – Right-arm slow bowler

No	Date	Opposition	Venue	R	Bat	C
1	14/02/1899	South Africa	Johannesburg (1)	W	21	
					132*	
2	01/04/1899	South Africa	Cape Town	W	31	
					23	
3*	11/12/1903	Australia	Sydney	W	0	
					8	
4*	01/01/1904	Australia	Melbourne	W	68	
					3	
5*	15/01/1904	Australia	Adelaide	L	48	
					79	
6*	26/02/1904	Australia	Sydney	W	0	
					31*	
7*	05/03/1904	Australia	Melbourne	L	1	
					11	2
8*	02/01/1906	South Africa	Johannesburg (1)	L	6	
					51	1
9*	06/03/1906	South Africa	Johannesburg (1)	L	2	
					0	
10*	10/03/1906	South Africa	Johannesburg (1)	L	19	
					2	
11*	24/03/1906	South Africa	Cape Town	W	1	
					4	
12*	30/03/1906	South Africa	Cape Town	L	0	
					4	
13	26/07/1909	Australia	Old Trafford	D	9	
					25	
14	10/06/1912	South Africa	Lord's	W	39	
15	24/06/1912	Australia	Lord's	D	4	

Batting & Fielding

Mat	Inns	N/O	Runs	H/S	Avg	100s	50s	Cat
15	28	2	622	132*	23.92	1	3	3

J.J.WARR

Full Name: John James Warr
Born: 16/07/1927, Ealing, Middlesex
Teams: Cambridge University 1949-52, Middlesex 1949-60, England 1951
Matches: 2 (Won 0, Drew 0, Lost 2)
Right-hand lower order batsman – Right-arm fast medium bowler

No	Date	Opposition	Venue	R	Bat	C		Bowling	
1	05/01/1951	Australia	Sydney	L	4		36	4 142	0
					0				
2	02/02/1951	Australia	Adelaide	L	0		16	2 63	0
					0		21	0 76	1

Batting & Fielding

Mat	Inns	N/O	Runs	H/S	Avg	100s	50s	Cat
2	4	0	4	4	1.00	0	0	0

Bowling

Balls	Runs	Wkts	Avg	Best	5WI	10WM	S/R
584	281	1	281.00	1-76	0	0	584.00

A.WARREN

Full Name: Arnold Warren
Born: 02/04/1875, Codnor Park, Derbyshire
Died: 03/09/1951, Codnor, Derbyshire
Teams: Derbyshire 1897-1920, England 1905
Matches: 1 (Won 0, Drew 1, Lost 0)
Right-hand lower order batsman – Right-arm fast bowler

No	Date	Opposition	Venue	R	Bat	C		Bowling	
1	03/07/1905	Australia	Headingley	D	7		19.2	5 57	5
						1	20	4 56	1

Batting & Fielding

Mat	Inns	N/O	Runs	H/S	Avg	100s	50s	Cat
1	1	0	7	7	7.00	0	0	1

Bowling

Balls	Runs	Wkts	Avg	Best	5WI	10WM	S/R
236	113	6	18.83	5-57	1	0	39.33

C.WASHBROOK

Full Name: Cyril Washbrook, CBE
Born: 06/12/1914, Barrow, Clitheroe, Lancashire
Teams: Lancashire 1933-59, England 1937-56
Matches: 37 (Won 9, Drew 16, Lost 12)
Right-hand opening batsman – Right-arm medium bowler

No	Date	Opposition	Venue	R	Bat	C	Bowling
1	14/08/1937	New Zealand	The Oval	D	9	1	
					8*		
2	22/06/1946	India	Lord's	W	27		
					24*		
3	20/07/1946	India	Old Trafford	D	52		
					26		
4	17/08/1946	India	The Oval	D	17	1	
5	29/11/1946	Australia	Brisbane (2)	L	6		
					13		
6	13/12/1946	Australia	Sydney	L	1	1	
					41		
7	01/01/1947	Australia	Melbourne	D	62		
					112	1	
8	31/01/1947	Australia	Adelaide	D	65		
					39		
9	28/02/1947	Australia	Sydney	L	0		
					24		
10	21/03/1947	New Zealand	Christchurch	D	2		

No	Date	Opposition	Venue	R	Bat	C		Bowling		
11	07/06/1947	South Africa	Trent Bridge	D	25					
					59					
12	21/06/1947	South Africa	Lord's	W	65					
					13*					
13	05/07/1947	South Africa	Old Trafford	W	29					
					40					
14	26/07/1947	South Africa	Headingley	W	75					
					15*					
15	16/08/1947	South Africa	The Oval	D	32					
					43					
16	10/06/1948	Australia	Trent Bridge	L	6					
					1					
17	24/06/1948	Australia	Lord's	L	8					
					37	1				
18	08/07/1948	Australia	Old Trafford	D	11	2				
					85*					
19	22/07/1948	Australia	Headingley	L	143					
					65					
20	16/12/1948	South Africa	Durban (2)	W	35					
					25					
21	27/12/1948	South Africa	Johannesburg (2)	D	195					
22	01/01/1949	South Africa	Cape Town	D	74					
					9					
23	12/02/1949	South Africa	Johannesburg (2)	D	97					
					31					
24	05/03/1949	South Africa	Port Elizabeth	W	36					
					40					
25	11/06/1949	New Zealand	Headingley	D	10	1				
					103*					
26	23/07/1949	New Zealand	Old Trafford	D	44	1				
							2	0	8	0
27	24/06/1950	West Indies	Lord's	L	36					
					114					
28	20/07/1950	West Indies	Trent Bridge	L	3					
					102					
29	01/12/1950	Australia	Brisbane (2)	L	19					
					6					
30	22/12/1950	Australia	Melbourne	L	21					
					8					
31	05/01/1951	Australia	Sydney	L	18					
					34					
32	02/02/1951	Australia	Adelaide	L	2					
					31					
33	23/02/1951	Australia	Melbourne	W	27	1				
					7					
34	17/03/1951	New Zealand	Christchurch	D	58					
							4	0	25	1
35	12/07/1956	Australia	Headingley	W	98					
						1				
36	26/07/1956	Australia	Old Trafford	W	6					
37	23/08/1956	Australia	The Oval	D	0	1				

Batting & Fielding

Mat	Inns	N/O	Runs	H/S	Avg	100s	50s	Cat
37	66	6	2569	195	42.81	6	12	12

Bowling

Balls	Runs	Wkts	Avg	Best	5WI	10WM	S/R
36	33	1	33.00	1-25	0	0	36.00

S.L.WATKIN

Full Name: Steven Llewellyn Watkin (known as Steve)
Born: 15/09/1964, Duffryn Rhondda, Maesteg, Glamorgan
Teams: Glamorgan 1986-96, England 1991-93
Matches: 3 (Won 2, Drew 1, Lost 0)
Right-hand lower order batsman – Right-arm fast medium bowler

No	Date	Opposition	Venue	R	Bat	C		Bowling		
1	06/06/1991	West Indies	Headingley	W	2		14	2	55	2
					0		7	0	38	3

No	Date	Opposition	Venue		R	Bat	C		Bowling		
2	20/06/1991	West Indies	Lord's		D	6		15	2	60	0
3	19/08/1993	Australia	The Oval		W	13		28	4	87	2
						4	1	25	9	65	4

Batting & Fielding

Mat	Inns	N/O	Runs	H/S	Avg	100s	50s	Cat
3	5	0	25	13	5.00	0	0	1

Bowling

Balls	Runs	Wkts	Avg	Best	5WI	10WM	S/R
534	305	11	27.72	4-65	0	0	48.54

A.J.WATKINS

Full Name: Albert John Watkins (known as Allan)
Born: 21/04/1922, Usk, Monmouthshire
Teams: Glamorgan 1939-62, England 1948-52
Matches: 15 (Won 6, Drew 7, Lost 2)
Left-hand middle order batsman – Left-arm fast medium bowler

No	Date	Opposition	Venue	R	Bat	C		Bowling		
1	14/08/1948	Australia	The Oval	L	0		4	1	19	0
					2					
2	16/12/1948	South Africa	Durban (2)	W	9	1	3	0	11	0
					4	1				
3	27/12/1948	South Africa	Johannesburg (2)	D	7	2	5	2	5	1
							12	2	48	0
4	01/01/1949	South Africa	Cape Town	D	27	1	10	0	36	1
					64*					
5	12/02/1949	South Africa	Johannesburg (2)	D	111		2	0	9	0
					10		3	0	16	2
6	05/03/1949	South Africa	Port Elizabeth	W	14	1	5	0	24	0
					5*					
7	25/06/1949	New Zealand	Lord's	D	6	1	3	1	11	0
					49*					
8	02/11/1951	India	Delhi	D	40		31	7	60	0
					137*					
9	14/12/1951	India	Bombay (2)	D	80		32	2	97	0
						1	13	4	20	3
10	30/12/1951	India	Calcutta	D	68	1	21	9	31	0
					2					
11	12/01/1952	India	Kanpur	W	66		5	3	6	0
12	06/02/1952	India	Madras (1)	L	9	2	14	1	50	1
					48					
13	05/06/1952	India	Headingley	W	48	3	11	1	21	0
							11	2	32	0
14	19/06/1952	India	Lord's	W	0	1	17	7	37	3
							8	0	20	0
15	17/07/1952	India	Old Trafford	W	4					
						2	4	3	1	0

Batting & Fielding

Mat	Inns	N/O	Runs	H/S	Avg	100s	50s	Cat
15	24	4	810	137*	40.50	2	4	17

Bowling

Balls	Runs	Wkts	Avg	Best	5WI	10WM	S/R
1364	554	11	50.36	3-20	0	0	124.00

M.WATKINSON

Full Name: Michael Watkinson (known as Mike)
Born: 01/08/1961, Westhoughton, Lancashire
Teams: Lancashire 1982-96, England 1995-96
Matches: 4 (Won 1, Drew 2, Lost 1)
Right-hand middle order batsman – Right-arm medium or off break bowler

No	Date	Opposition	Venue	R	Bat	C		Bowling		
1	27/07/1995	West Indies	Old Trafford	W	37		9	2	28	2
						1	23	4	64	3
2	10/08/1995	West Indies	Trent Bridge	D	24		35	12	84	3
					82*					

No	Date	Opposition	Venue	R	Bat	C		Bowling		
3	24/08/1995	West Indies	The Oval	D	13		26	3	113	0
4	02/01/1996	South Africa	Cape Town	L	11		15	3	35	2
					0		4	0	24	0

Batting & Fielding

Mat	Inns	N/O	Runs	H/S	Avg	100s	50s	Cat
4	6	1	167	82*	33.40	0	1	1

Bowling

Balls	Runs	Wkts	Avg	Best	5WI	10WM	S/R
672	348	10	34.80	3-64	0	0	67.20

W.WATSON

Full Name: William Watson (known as Willie)
Born: 07/03/1920, Bolton-on-Dearne, Yorkshire
Teams: Yorkshire 1939-57, Leicestershire 1958-64, England 1951-59
Matches: 23 (Won 8, Drew 9, Lost 6)
Left-hand middle order batsman

No	Date	Opposition	Venue	R	Bat	C
1	07/06/1951	South Africa	Trent Bridge	L	57	
					5	
2	21/06/1951	South Africa	Lord's	W	79	1
3	05/07/1951	South Africa	Old Trafford	W	21	
4	26/07/1951	South Africa	Headingley	D	32	
5	16/08/1951	South Africa	The Oval	W	31	
					15	
6	14/08/1952	India	The Oval	D	18*	
7	25/06/1953	Australia	Lord's	D	4	1
					109	
8	09/07/1953	Australia	Old Trafford	D	16	
9	23/07/1953	Australia	Headingley	D	24	
					15	
10	15/01/1954	West Indies	Kingston	L	3	
					116	
11	06/02/1954	West Indies	Bridgetown	L	6	
					0	
12	24/02/1954	West Indies	Georgetown	W	12	1
					27*	
13	17/03/1954	West Indies	Port-of-Spain	D	4	
					32	
14	30/03/1954	West Indies	Kingston	W	4	1
					20*	1
15	13/08/1955	South Africa	The Oval	W	25	
					3	1
16	07/06/1956	Australia	Trent Bridge	D	0	
					8	
17	21/06/1956	Australia	Lord's	L	6	
					18	
18	24/07/1958	New Zealand	Old Trafford	W	66	
						1
19	21/08/1958	New Zealand	The Oval	D	10	1
20	31/12/1958	Australia	Melbourne	L	0	
					7	
21	30/01/1959	Australia	Adelaide	L	25	
					40	
22	27/02/1959	New Zealand	Christchurch	W	10	
23	14/03/1959	New Zealand	Auckland	D	11	

Batting & Fielding

Mat	Inns	N/O	Runs	H/S	Avg	100s	50s	Cat
23	37	3	879	116	25.85	2	3	8

A.J.WEBBE

Full Name: Alexander Josiah Webbe
Born: 16/01/1855, Bethnal Green, London
Died: 19/02/1941, Fulvens, Hoe, Abinger Hammer, Surrey
Teams: Oxford University 1875-78, Middlesex 1875-1900, England 1879
Matches: 1 (Won 0, Drew 0, Lost 1)
Right-hand opening batsman – Right-arm fast bowler

No	Date	Opposition	Venue	R	Bat	C
1	02/01/1879	Australia	Melbourne	L	4	2
					0	

Batting & Fielding

Mat	Inns	N/O	Runs	H/S	Avg	100s	50s	Cat
1	2	0	4	4	2.00	0	0	2

A.W.WELLARD

Full Name: Arthur William Wellard
Born: 08/04/1902, Southfleet, Kent
Died: 31/12/1980, Eastbourne, Sussex
Teams: Somerset 1927-50, England 1937-38
Matches: 2 (Won 1, Drew 1, Lost 0)
Right-hand lower order batsman – Right-arm fast medium or off break bowler

No	Date	Opposition	Venue	R	Bat	C	Bowling			
1	24/07/1937	New Zealand	Old Trafford	W	5		30	4	81	4
					0	2	14	2	30	0
2	24/06/1938	Australia	Lord's	D	4		23	2	96	2
					38		9	1	30	1

Batting & Fielding

Mat	Inns	N/O	Runs	H/S	Avg	100s	50s	Cat
2	4	0	47	38	11.75	0	0	2

Bowling

Balls	Runs	Wkts	Avg	Best	5WI	10WM	S/R
456	237	7	33.85	4-81	0	0	65.14

A.P.WELLS

Full Name: Alan Peter Wells
Born: 02/10/1961, Newhaven, Sussex
Teams: Sussex 1981-96, England 1995
Matches: 1 (Won 0, Drew 1, Lost 0)
Right-hand middle order batsman – Right-arm medium bowler

No	Date	Opposition	Venue	R	Bat	C
1	24/08/1995	West Indies	The Oval	D	0	
					3*	

Batting & Fielding

Mat	Inns	N/O	Runs	H/S	Avg	100s	50s	Cat
1	2	1	3	3*	3.00	0	0	0

A.WHARTON

Full Name: Alan Wharton
Born: 30/04/1923, Heywood, Lancashire
Died: 26/08/1993, Colne, Lancashire
Teams: Lancashire 1946-60, Leicestershire 1961-63, England 1949
Matches: 1 (Won 0, Drew 1, Lost 0)
Left-hand opening/middle order batsman – Right-arm medium bowler

No	Date	Opposition	Venue	R	Bat	C
1	11/06/1949	New Zealand	Headingley	D	7	
					13	

Batting & Fielding

Mat	Inns	N/O	Runs	H/S	Avg	100s	50s	Cat
1	2	0	20	13	10.00	0	0	0

J.J.WHITAKER

Full Name: John James Whitaker (known as James)
Born: 05/05/1962, Skipton, Yorkshire
Teams: Leicestershire 1983-96, England 1986
Matches: 1 (Won 0, Drew 1, Lost 0)
Right-hand middle order batsman – Off break bowler

No	Date	Opposition	Venue	R	Bat	C
1	12/12/1986	Australia	Adelaide	D	11	1

Batting & Fielding

Mat	Inns	N/O	Runs	H/S	Avg	100s	50s	Cat
1	1	0	11	11	11.00	0	0	1

C.WHITE

Full Name: Craig White
Born: 16/12/1969, Morley, Yorkshire
Teams: Yorkshire 1990-96, Victoria 1990/91, England 1994-95
Matches: 6 (Won 2, Drew 3, Lost 1)
Right-hand middle order batsman – Right-arm medium bowler (previously off break)

No	Date	Opposition	Venue	R	Bat	C		Bowling		
1	02/06/1994	New Zealand	Trent Bridge	W	19	1	13	3	38	1
						2	3	3	0	0
2	16/06/1994	New Zealand	Lord's	D	51		21.1	4	84	1
					9		4	1	21	0
3	30/06/1994	New Zealand	Old Trafford	D	42		7	1	18	3
							14	3	36	1
4	21/07/1994	South Africa	Lord's	L	10		13	2	43	2
					0		3	0	18	0
5	27/07/1995	West Indies	Old Trafford	W	23		5	0	23	0
					1		6	0	23	0
6	10/08/1995	West Indies	Trent Bridge	D	1		5	0	30	0
					1					

Batting & Fielding

Mat	Inns	N/O	Runs	H/S	Avg	100s	50s	Cat
6	10	0	157	51	15.70	0	1	3

Bowling

Balls	Runs	Wkts	Avg	Best	5WI	10WM	S/R
565	334	8	41.75	3-18	0	0	70.62

D.W.WHITE

Full Name: David William White (also known as Butch)
Born: 14/12/1935, Sutton Coldfield, Warwickshire
Teams: Hampshire 1957-71, Glamorgan 1972, England 1961-62
Matches: 2 (Won 1, Drew 1, Lost 0)
Left-hand lower order batsman – Right-arm fast bowler

No	Date	Opposition	Venue	R	Bat	C		Bowling		
1	21/10/1961	Pakistan	Lahore (2)	W	0		22	3	65	3
							12	2	42	0
2	02/02/1962	Pakistan	Karachi (1)	D	0		2.4	0	12	1

Batting & Fielding

Mat	Inns	N/O	Runs	H/S	Avg	100s	50s	Cat
2	2	0	0	0	0.00	0	0	0

Bowling

Balls	Runs	Wkts	Avg	Best	5WI	10WM	S/R
220	119	4	29.75	3-65	0	0	55.00

J.C.WHITE

Full Name: John Cornish White (known as Jack or farmer)
Born: 19/02/1891, Holford, Somerset
Died: 02/05/1961, Yarde Farm, Combe-Florey, Somerset
Teams: Somerset 1909-37, England 1921-31
Matches: 15 (Won 6, Drew 5, Lost 4)
England Captain: 4 times 1929 (Won 1, Drew 2, Lost 1) **Toss:** 3-1
Right-hand lower order batsman – Left-arm slow bowler

No	Date	Opposition	Venue	R	Bat	C		Bowling	
1	02/07/1921	Australia	Headingley	L	1		25	4 70	0
					6*		11	3 37	3
2	21/07/1928	West Indies	Old Trafford	W	21*	1	13	6 12	0
							14.3	4 41	3
3	30/11/1928	Australia	Brisbane (1)	W	14				
							6.3	2 7	4
4	14/12/1928	Australia	Sydney	W	29		38	10 79	0
					2*		30	5 83	0
5	29/12/1928	Australia	Melbourne	W	8*		57	30 64	1
							56.5	20 107	5
6	01/02/1929	Australia	Adelaide	W	0		60	16 130	5
					4*	1	64.5	21 126	8
7*	08/03/1929	Australia	Melbourne	L	9*		75.3	22 136	2
					4		18	8 28	0
8*	15/06/1929	South Africa	Edgbaston	D	5		32	19 28	0
						1	13	5 23	0
9*	29/06/1929	South Africa	Lord's	D	8		35	12 61	2
					18*		9	3 11	0
10*	13/07/1929	South Africa	Headingley	W	20*		17	6 24	0
						1	23	7 40	3
11	27/06/1930	Australia	Lord's	L	23*		51	7 158	3
					10		2	0 8	0
12	24/12/1930	South Africa	Johannesburg (1)	L	14				
					2		16	3 53	0
13	01/01/1931	South Africa	Cape Town	D	23	1	46	15 101	2
					8				
14	16/01/1931	South Africa	Durban (2)	D			16	6 21	3
							18	4 33	3
15	21/02/1931	South Africa	Durban (2)	D	10	1	35	9 63	1
							17	6 37	1

Batting & Fielding

Mat	Inns	N/O	Runs	H/S	Avg	100s	50s	Cat
15	22	9	239	29	18.38	0	0	6

Bowling

Balls	Runs	Wkts	Avg	Best	5WI	10WM	S/R
4801	1581	49	32.26	8-126	3	1	97.97

W.W.WHYSALL

Full Name: William Wilfrid Whysall (known as Dodger)
Born: 31/10/1887, Woodborough, Nottinghamshire
Died: 11/11/1930, Nottingham
Teams: Nottinghamshire 1910-30, England 1925-30
Matches: 4 (Won 1, Drew 0, Lost 3)
Right-hand opening batsman – Right-arm medium bowler – Wicket-keeper

No	Date	Opposition	Venue	R	Bat	C		Bowling	
1	16/01/1925	Australia	Adelaide	L	9	1	2	0 9	0
					75	1			
2	13/02/1925	Australia	Melbourne	W	76				
						1			
3	27/02/1925	Australia	Sydney	L	8	2			
					18	2			
4	16/08/1930	Australia	The Oval	L	13				
					10				

Batting & Fielding

Mat	Inns	N/O	Runs	H/S	Avg	100s	50s	Cat
4	7	0	209	76	29.85	0	2	7

Bowling

Balls	Runs	Wkts	Avg	Best	5WI	10WM	S/R
16	9	0	–	0-9	0	0	–

L.L.WILKINSON

Full Name: Leonard Litton Wilkinson (known as Len)
Born: 05/11/1916, Northwich, Cheshire
Teams: Lancashire 1937-47, England 1938-39
Matches: 3 (Won 1, Drew 2, Lost 0)
Right-hand lower order batsman – Leg break bowler

No	Date	Opposition	Venue	R	Bat	C		Bowling		
1	24/12/1938	South Africa	Johannesburg (1)	D	2		22	0	93	2
							8	3	18	0
2	20/01/1939	South Africa	Durban (2)	W			6.5	2	12	2
							26	4	103	2
3	18/02/1939	South Africa	Johannesburg (1)	D	1*		9	0	45	1

Batting & Fielding

Mat	Inns	N/O	Runs	H/S	Avg	100s	50s	Cat
3	2	1	3	2	3.00	0	0	0

Bowling

Balls	Runs	Wkts	Avg	Best	5WI	10WM	S/R
573	271	7	38.71	2-12	0	0	81.85

P.WILLEY

Full Name: Peter Willey
Born: 06/12/1949, Sedgefield, Co Durham
Teams: Northamptonshire 1966-83, Leicestershire 1984-91, Eastern Province 1982/83-84/85, England 1976-86
Matches: 26 (Won 3, Drew 10, Lost 13)
Right-hand middle order batsman – Off break bowler

No	Date	Opposition	Venue	R	Bat	C		Bowling		
1	22/07/1976	West Indies	Headingley	L	36		1	0	4	0
					45					
2	12/08/1976	West Indies	The Oval	L	33		3	0	11	0
					1					
3	30/08/1979	India	The Oval	D	52		4	1	10	0
					31		43.5	15	96	2
4	14/12/1979	Australia	Perth	L	9		1	0	1	0
					12	1	1	0	1	0
5	04/01/1980	Australia	Sydney	L	8		1	0	2	0
					3		4	0	17	0
6	01/02/1980	Australia	Melbourne	L	1	1	13	2	36	0
					2					
7	05/06/1980	West Indies	Trent Bridge	L	13		5	3	4	0
					38		2	0	12	0
8	19/06/1980	West Indies	Lord's	D	4		25	8	73	2
9	10/07/1980	West Indies	Old Trafford	D	0					
					62*					
10	24/07/1980	West Indies	The Oval	D	34	1	11	5	22	0
					100*					
11	07/08/1980	West Indies	Headingley	D	1					
					10					
12	28/08/1980	Australia	Lord's	D	5		1	0	7	0
13	13/02/1981	West Indies	Port-of-Spain	L	13		3	1	4	0
					21					
14	13/03/1981	West Indies	Bridgetown	L	19*					
					17		6	0	23	0
15	27/03/1981	West Indies	St John's	D	102*		20	8	30	0
					1*					
16	10/04/1981	West Indies	Kingston	D	4		18	3	54	1
					67					
17	18/06/1981	Australia	Trent Bridge	L	10					
					13					
18	02/07/1981	Australia	Lord's	D	82					
					12					
19	16/07/1981	Australia	Headingley	W	8		13	2	31	1
					33		3	1	4	0
20	30/07/1981	Australia	Edgbaston	W	16					
					5					
21	13/06/1985	Australia	Headingley	W	36					
					3*					
22	21/02/1986	West Indies	Kingston	L	0		4	0	15	1
					71					
23	07/03/1986	West Indies	Port-of-Spain	L	5					
					26					
24	21/03/1986	West Indies	Bridgetown	L	5					
					17					
25	03/04/1986	West Indies	Port-of-Spain	L	10					
					2					
26	24/07/1986	New Zealand	Lord's	D	44					
					42					

Batting & Fielding

Mat	Inns	N/O	Runs	H/S	Avg	100s	50s	Cat
26	50	6	1184	102*	26.90	2	5	3

Bowling

Balls	Runs	Wkts	Avg	Best	5WI	10WM	S/R
1091	456	7	65.14	2-73	0	0	155.85

N.F.WILLIAMS

Full Name: Neil Fitzgerald Williams
Born: 02/07/1962, Hopewell, St Vincent
Teams: Middlesex 1982-94, Essex 1995-96, Winward Islands 1982/83-91/92, Tasmania 1983/84, England 1990
Matches: 1 (Won 0, Drew 1, Lost 0)
Right-hand lower order batsman – Right-arm fast medium bowler

No	Date	Opposition	Venue	R	Bat	C		Bowling		
1	23/08/1990	India	The Oval	D	38		41	5	148	2

Batting & Fielding

Mat	Inns	N/O	Runs	H/S	Avg	100s	50s	Cat
1	1	0	38	38	38.00	0	0	0

Bowling

Balls	Runs	Wkts	Avg	Best	5WI	10WM	S/R
246	148	2	74.00	2-148	0	0	123.00

R.G.D.WILLIS

Full Name: Robert George Dylan Willis, MBE (known as Bob)
Born: 30/05/1949, Sunderland, Co Durham
Teams: Surrey 1969-71, Warwickshire 1972-84, Northern Transvaal 1972/73, England 1971-84
Matches: 90 (Won 32, Drew 32, Lost 26)
England Captain: 18 times 1982-84 (Won 7, Drew 6, Lost 5) **Toss:** 8-10
Right-hand lower order batsman – Right-arm fast bowler

No	Date	Opposition	Venue	R	Bat	C		Bowling		
1	09/01/1971	Australia	Sydney	W	15*		9	2	26	0
						1	3	2	1	1
2	21/01/1971	Australia	Melbourne	D	5*		20	5	73	3
							10	1	42	1
3	29/01/1971	Australia	Adelaide	D	4		12	3	49	2
						1	13	1	48	1
4	12/02/1971	Australia	Sydney	W	11	1	12	1	58	3
					2*		9	1	32	1
5	05/03/1971	New Zealand	Auckland	D	7		14	2	54	2
					3		6	1	15	0
6	23/08/1973	West Indies	Lord's	L	5*	2	35	3	118	4
					0					
7	02/02/1974	West Indies	Port-of-Spain	L	6		19	5	52	1
					0*		4	1	6	0
8	16/02/1974	West Indies	Kingston	D	6*	2	24	5	97	3
					3*					
9	06/03/1974	West Indies	Bridgetown	D	10*	1	26	4	100	1
10	06/06/1974	India	Old Trafford	W	24	1	24	3	64	4
							12	5	33	1
11	22/08/1974	Pakistan	The Oval	D	1*		28	3	102	2
							7	1	27	0
12	29/11/1974	Australia	Brisbane (2)	L	13*		21.5	3	56	4
					3*		15	3	45	3
13	13/12/1974	Australia	Perth	L	4*		22	0	91	2
					0*		2	0	8	0
14	26/12/1974	Australia	Melbourne	D	13		21.7	4	61	5
					15		14	2	56	1
15	04/01/1975	Australia	Sydney	L	2		18	2	80	0
					12		11	1	52	1
16	25/01/1975	Australia	Adelaide	L	11*	1	10	0	46	1
					3		5	0	27	0
17	22/07/1976	West Indies	Headingley	L	0*	1	20	2	71	3
					0		15.3	6	42	5

No	Date	Opposition	Venue	R	Bat	C	O	M	R	W
18	12/08/1976	West Indies	The Oval	L	5*		15	3	73	1
					0		7	0	48	0
19	17/12/1976	India	Delhi	W	1	2	7	3	21	0
							9	3	24	1
20	01/01/1977	India	Calcutta	W	0*		20	3	27	5
							13	1	32	2
21	14/01/1977	India	Madras (1)	W	7		19	5	46	1
					4*		13	4	18	3
22	28/01/1977	India	Bangalore	L	7		17	2	53	6
					0		18	2	47	2
23	11/02/1977	India	Bombay (3)	D	0		13	1	52	0
						1	6	1	15	0
24	12/03/1977	Australia	Melbourne	L	1*		8	0	33	2
					5*	1	22	0	91	0
25	16/06/1977	Australia	Lord's	D	17		30.1	7	78	7
					0	1	10	1	40	2
26	07/07/1977	Australia	Old Trafford	W	1*		21	8	45	2
							16	2	56	2
27	28/07/1977	Australia	Trent Bridge	W	2*		15	0	58	1
							26	6	88	5
28	11/08/1977	Australia	Headingley	W	5*		5	0	35	0
							14	7	32	3
29	25/08/1977	Australia	The Oval	D	24*	1	29.3	5	102	5
30	14/12/1977	Pakistan	Lahore (2)	D	14		17	3	67	0
							7	0	34	2
31	02/01/1978	Pakistan	Hyderabad	D	8*		16	2	40	2
							11	2	26	2
32	18/01/1978	Pakistan	Karachi (1)	D	5	1	8	1	23	1
33	10/02/1978	New Zealand	Wellington	L	6*		25	7	65	2
					3		15	2	32	5
34	24/02/1978	New Zealand	Christchurch	W	6*		20	5	45	1
							7	2	14	4
35	04/03/1978	New Zealand	Auckland	D	0*		26.6	8	57	2
							10	3	42	0
36	01/06/1978	Pakistan	Edgbaston	W			16	2	42	2
							23.4	3	70	2
37	15/06/1978	Pakistan	Lord's	W	18	1	13	1	47	5
							10	2	26	2
38	29/06/1978	Pakistan	Headingley	D			26	8	48	2
39	27/07/1978	New Zealand	The Oval	W	3*		20.2	9	42	5
							13	2	39	1
40	10/08/1978	New Zealand	Trent Bridge	W	1*		12	5	22	1
							9	0	31	0
41	24/08/1978	New Zealand	Lord's	W	7*		29	9	79	1
							16	8	16	4
42	01/12/1978	Australia	Brisbane (2)	W	8		14	2	44	4
						1	27.6	3	69	3
43	15/12/1978	Australia	Perth	W	2		18.5	5	44	5
					3*		12	1	36	1
44	29/12/1978	Australia	Melbourne	L	19		13	2	47	0
					3		7	0	21	0
45	06/01/1979	Australia	Sydney	W	7*		9	2	33	2
					0		2	0	8	0
46	27/01/1979	Australia	Adelaide	W	24	1	11	1	55	1
					12		12	3	41	3
47	10/02/1979	Australia	Sydney	W	10		11	4	48	1
						1	3	0	15	0
48	12/07/1979	India	Edgbaston	W			24	9	69	3
							14	3	45	1
49	16/08/1979	India	Headingley	D	4*		18	5	42	2
50	30/08/1979	India	The Oval	D	10*		18	2	53	3
							28	4	89	1
51	14/12/1979	Australia	Perth	L	11		23	7	47	0
					0		26	7	52	1
52	04/01/1980	Australia	Sydney	L	3		11	3	30	1
					1		12	2	26	1
53	01/02/1980	Australia	Melbourne	L	4		21	4	61	0
					2		5	3	8	0
54	05/06/1980	West Indies	Trent Bridge	L	8		20.1	5	82	4
					9		26	4	65	5

No	Date	Opposition	Venue	R	Bat	C	Bowling			
55	19/06/1980	West Indies	Lord's	D	14		31	12	103	3
56	10/07/1980	West Indies	Old Trafford	D	5*		14	1	99	1
57	24/07/1980	West Indies	The Oval	D	1*		19	5	58	1
					24*					
58	18/06/1981	Australia	Trent Bridge	L	0		30	14	47	3
					1		13	2	28	1
59	02/07/1981	Australia	Lord's	D	5	1	27.4	9	50	3
							12	3	35	1
60	16/07/1981	Australia	Headingley	W	1*		30	8	72	0
					2		15.1	3	43	8
61	30/07/1981	Australia	Edgbaston	W	13	1	19	3	63	0
					2		20	6	37	2
62	13/08/1981	Australia	Old Trafford	W	11		14	0	63	4
					5*		30.5	2	96	3
63	27/08/1981	Australia	The Oval	D	3		31	6	91	4
							10	0	41	0
64	27/11/1981	India	Bombay (3)	L	1		12	5	33	1
					13		13	4	31	1
65	23/12/1981	India	Delhi	D			26	3	99	2
66	01/01/1982	India	Calcutta	D	11*		14	3	28	2
							6	0	21	0
67	13/01/1982	India	Madras (1)	D	1*		28.1	7	79	2
							7	2	15	1
68	30/01/1982	India	Kanpur	D			23	5	75	3
69	17/02/1982	Sri Lanka	Colombo (1)	W	0		19	7	46	2
						2	9	3	24	1
70*	10/06/1982	India	Lord's	W	28		16	2	41	3
							28	3	101	6
71*	24/06/1982	India	Old Trafford	D	6		17	2	94	2
72*	08/07/1982	India	The Oval	D	1*		23	4	78	3
							4	0	16	1
73*	29/07/1982	Pakistan	Edgbaston	W	0*	2	15	3	42	2
					28*		14	2	49	2
74*	26/08/1982	Pakistan	Headingley	W	1*	1	26	6	76	3
							19	3	55	3
75*	12/11/1982	Australia	Perth	D	26	2	31.5	4	95	3
					0		6	1	23	2
76*	26/11/1982	Australia	Brisbane (2)	L	1		29.4	3	66	5
					10*		4	1	24	0
77*	10/12/1982	Australia	Adelaide	L	1		25	8	76	2
					10		8	1	17	1
78*	26/12/1982	Australia	Melbourne	W	6*		15	2	38	3
					8*	1	17	0	57	0
79*	02/01/1983	Australia	Sydney	D	1	1	20	6	57	1
							10	2	33	1
80*	14/07/1983	New Zealand	The Oval	W	4	1	20	8	43	4
						1	12	3	26	2
81*	28/07/1983	New Zealand	Headingley	L	9	1	23.3	6	57	4
					4		14	5	35	5
82*	11/08/1983	New Zealand	Lord's	W	7	1	13	6	28	1
					2*		12	5	24	1
83*	25/08/1983	New Zealand	Trent Bridge	W	25*		10	2	23	0
					16		19	3	37	1
84*	20/01/1984	New Zealand	Wellington	D	5*		19	7	37	1
							37	8	102	2
85*	03/02/1984	New Zealand	Christchurch	L	6		22.1	5	51	4
					0					
86*	10/02/1984	New Zealand	Auckland	D	3		34	7	109	3
							3	1	7	0
87*	02/03/1984	Pakistan	Karachi (1)	L	6	1	17	6	33	2
					2		2	0	13	0
88	14/06/1984	West Indies	Edgbaston	L	10*	1	25	3	108	2
					22					
89	28/06/1984	West Indies	Lord's	L	2		19	5	48	2
							15	5	48	0
90	12/07/1984	West Indies	Headingley	L	4*		18	1	123	2
					5*		8	1	40	0

Batting & Fielding

Mat	Inns	N/O	Runs	H/S	Avg	100s	50s	Cat
90	128	55	840	28*	11.50	0	0	39

Bowling

Balls	Runs	Wkts	Avg	Best	5WI	10WM	S/R
17357	8190	325	25.20	8-43	16	0	53.40

C.E.M.WILSON

Full Name: Rev Clement Eustace Macro Wilson (known as Clem)
Born: 15/05/1875, Bolsterstone, Yorkshire
Died: 08/02/1944, Calverhall, Shropshire
Teams: Cambridge University 1895-98, Yorkshire 1896-99, England 1899
Matches: 2 (Won 2, Drew 0, Lost 0)
Right-hand middle order batsman – Right-arm fast medium bowler

No	Date	Opposition	Venue	R	Bat	C
1	14/02/1899	South Africa	Johannesburg (1)	W	8	
					18	
2	01/04/1899	South Africa	Cape Town	W	10*	
					6	

Batting & Fielding

Mat	Inns	N/O	Runs	H/S	Avg	100s	50s	Cat
2	4	1	42	18	14.00	0	0	0

D.WILSON

Full Name: Donald Wilson (known as Don)
Born: 07/08/1937, Settle, Yorkshire
Teams: Yorkshire 1957-74, England 1964-71
Matches: 6 (Won 1, Drew 5, Lost 0)
Left-hand lower order batsman – Left-arm slow bowler

No	Date	Opposition	Venue	R	Bat	C		Bowling		
1	10/01/1964	India	Madras (2)	D	42		24	6	67	1
							4	2	2	1
2	21/01/1964	India	Bombay (2)	D	1	1	15	5	28	1
					2		23	10	41	0
3	29/01/1964	India	Calcutta	D	1		16	10	17	2
							21	7	55	1
4	08/02/1964	India	Delhi	D	6		22	9	41	1
							41	17	74	2
5	15/02/1964	India	Kanpur	D	18*		27	9	47	0
							19	10	26	0
6	25/02/1971	New Zealand	Christchurch	W	5		4	2	12	1
							21	6	56	1

Batting & Fielding

Mat	Inns	N/O	Runs	H/S	Avg	100s	50s	Cat
6	7	1	75	42	12.50	0	0	1

Bowling

Balls	Runs	Wkts	Avg	Best	5WI	10WM	S/R
1472	466	11	42.36	2-17	0	0	133.81

E.R.WILSON

Full Name: Evelyn Rockley Wilson (known as Rockley)
Born: 25/03/1879, Bolsterstone, Yorkshire
Died: 21/07/1957, Winchester, Hampshire
Teams: Cambridge University 1899-1902, Yorkshire 1899-1923, England 1921
Matches: 1 (Won 0, Drew 0, Lost 1)
Right-hand middle/lower order batsman – Right-arm slow bowler

No	Date	Opposition	Venue	R	Bat	C		Bowling		
1	25/02/1921	Australia	Sydney	L	5		14.3	4	28	2
					5		6	1	8	1

Batting & Fielding

Mat	Inns	N/O	Runs	H/S	Avg	100s	50s	Cat
1	2	0	10	5	5.00	0	0	0

Bowling

Balls	Runs	Wkts	Avg	Best	5WI	10WM	S/R
123	36	3	12.00	2-28	0	0	41.00

A.WOOD

Full Name: Arthur Wood
Born: 25/08/1898, Fagley, Bradford, Yorkshire
Died: 01/04/1973, Middleton, Ilkley, Yorkshire
Teams: Yorkshire 1927-46, England 1938-39
Matches: 4 (Won 2, Drew 2, Lost 0)
Right-hand lower order batsman – Wicket-keeper

No	Date	Opposition	Venue	R	Bat	C	St	B
1+	20/08/1938	Australia	The Oval	W	53	2		4
						1		1
2+	24/06/1939	West Indies	Lord's	W	0*	2		3
						2		6
3+	22/07/1939	West Indies	Old Trafford	D	26	2		0
						1		0
4+	19/08/1939	West Indies	The Oval	D	0	1	1	0

Batting & Fielding

Mat	Inns	N/O	Runs	H/S	Avg	100s	50s	Cat	St	Byes
4	5	1	80	53	20.00	0	1	10	1	14

B.WOOD

Full Name: Barry Wood
Born: 26/12/1942, Ossett, Yorkshire
Teams: Yorkshire 1964, Lancashire 1966-79, Derbyshire 1980-83, Eastern Province 1971/72-73/74, England 1972-78
Matches: 12 (Won 3, Drew 6, Lost 3)
Right-hand opening batsman – Right-arm medium bowler

No	Date	Opposition	Venue	R	Bat	C		Bowling		
1	10/08/1972	Australia	The Oval	L	26					
					90					
2	20/12/1972	India	Delhi	W	19					
					45		2	0	13	0
3	30/12/1972	India	Calcutta	L	11	1				
					1					
4	12/01/1973	India	Madras (1)	L	20	2				
					5					
5	24/03/1973	Pakistan	Karachi (1)	D	3					
					5					
6	20/02/1975	New Zealand	Auckland	W	0	1				
7	28/02/1975	New Zealand	Christchurch	D	33	2		4	0	19	0
8	31/07/1975	Australia	Lord's	D	6					
					52			1	0	6	0
9	14/08/1975	Australia	Headingley	D	9			5	2	10	0
					25					
10	28/08/1975	Australia	The Oval	D	32					
					22					
11	17/06/1976	West Indies	Lord's	D	6					
					30					
12	01/06/1978	Pakistan	Edgbaston	W	14			3	2	2	0

Batting & Fielding

Mat	Inns	N/O	Runs	H/S	Avg	100s	50s	Cat
12	21	0	454	90	21.61	0	2	6

Bowling

Balls	Runs	Wkts	Avg	Best	5WI	10WM	S/R
98	50	0	–	0-2	0	0	–

G.E.C.WOOD

Full Name: George Edward Charles Wood
Born: 22/08/1893, Blackheath, Kent
Died: 18/03/1971, Christchurch, Hampshire
Teams: Cambridge University 1913-20, Kent 1919-27, England 1924
Matches: 3 (Won 3, Drew 0, Lost 0)
Right-hand opening/middle order batsman – Wicket-keeper – Occasional right-arm medium bowler

No	Date	Opposition	Venue	R	Bat	C	St	B
1+	14/06/1924	South Africa	Edgbaston	W	1			1
						1		4
2+	28/06/1924	South Africa	Lord's	W		1		3
								13
3+	12/07/1924	South Africa	Headingley	W	6	2		0
						1	1	14

Batting & Fielding

Mat	Inns	N/O	Runs	H/S	Avg	100s	50s	Cat	St	Byes
3	2	0	7	6	3.50	0	0	5	1	35

H.WOOD

Full Name: Henry Wood (known as Harry)
Born: 14/12/1853, Dartford, Kent
Died: 30/04/1919, Waddon, Surrey
Teams: Kent 1876-82, Surrey 1884-1900, England 1888-92
Matches: 4 (Won 4, Drew 0, Lost 0)
Right-hand middle order batsman – Wicket-keeper – Right-hand round-arm fast bowler

No	Date	Opposition	Venue	R	Bat	C	St	B
1+	13/08/1888	Australia	The Oval	W	8			1
						1	1	0
2+	12/03/1889	South Africa	Port Elizabeth	W	3			8
								7
3+	25/03/1889	South Africa	Cape Town	W	59			2
								2
4+	19/03/1892	South Africa	Cape Town	W	134*	1		5

Batting & Fielding

Mat	Inns	N/O	Runs	H/S	Avg	100s	50s	Cat	St	Byes
4	4	1	204	134*	68.00	1	1	2	1	25

R.WOOD

Full Name: Reginald Wood
Born: 07/03/1860, Woodchurch, Cheshire
Died: 06/01/1915, Manly, Sydney, New South Wales, Australia
Teams: Lancashire 1880-84, Victoria 1886/87, England 1887
Matches: 1 (Won 1, Drew 0, Lost 0)
Left-hand middle order batsman – Left-arm medium bowler

No	Date	Opposition	Venue	R	Bat	C
1	25/02/1887	Australia	Sydney	W	6	
					0	

Batting & Fielding

Mat	Inns	N/O	Runs	H/S	Avg	100s	50s	Cat
1	2	0	6	6	3.00	0	0	0

S.M.J.WOODS

Full Name: Samuel Moses James Woods (known as Sammy)
Born: 13/04/1867, Ashfield, Sydney, New South Wales, Australia
Died: 30/04/1931, Taunton, Somerset
Teams: Cambridge University 1888-91, Somerset 1891-1910, Australia 1888, England 1896
Matches: 3 (Won 3, Drew 0, Lost 0), 3 (Won 1, Drew 0, Lost 2)
Right-hand middle order batsman – Right-arm fast medium bowler

No	Date	Opposition	Venue	R	Bat	C	Bowling
1	13/02/1896	South Africa	Port Elizabeth	W	7		
					53		

No	Date	Opposition	Venue	R	Bat	C		Bowling		
2	02/03/1896	South Africa	Johannesburg (1)	W	32		20	2	74	1
							6	1	27	1
3	21/03/1896	South Africa	Cape Town	W	30	3				
						1	13	5	28	3

For Australia

No	Date	Opposition	Venue	R	Bat	C		Bowling		
1	16/07/1888	England	Lord's	W	18	1	4	2	6	1
					3					
2	13/08/1888	England	The Oval	L	0		32	10	80	2
					7					
3	30/08/1888	England	Old Trafford	L	4		18.1	6	35	2
					0					

Batting & Fielding

Mat	Inns	N/O	Runs	H/S	Avg	100s	50s	Cat	
3	4	0	122	53	30.50	0	1	4	(England)
3	6	0	32	18	5.33	0	0	1	(Australia)
6	10	0	154	53	15.40	0	1	5	(Total)

Bowling

Balls	Runs	Wkts	Avg	Best	5WI	10WM	S/R	
195	129	5	25.80	3-28	0	0	39.00	(England)
217	121	5	24.20	2-35	0	0	43.40	(Australia)
412	250	10	25.00	3-28	0	0	41.20	(Total)

F.E.WOOLLEY

Full Name: Frank Edward Woolley
Born: 27/05/1887, Tonbridge, Kent
Died: 18/10/1978, Halifax, Nova Scotia, Canada
Teams: Kent 1906-38, England 1909-34
Matches: 64 (Won 26, Drew 19, Lost 19)
Left-hand middle order batsman – Left-arm slow bowler (previously left-arm medium)

No	Date	Opposition	Venue	R	Bat	C		Bowling		
1	09/08/1909	Australia	The Oval	D	8		4	1	6	0
						1	6	0	31	0
2	01/01/1910	South Africa	Johannesburg (1)	L	14	1	1	0	4	0
					25	1	4	1	13	0
3	21/01/1910	South Africa	Durban (1)	L	22	1	15	5	23	1
					4	1	10	3	34	1
4	26/02/1910	South Africa	Johannesburg (1)	W	58*	3	21	4	54	1
					0	1	18	6	29	0
5	07/03/1910	South Africa	Cape Town	L	69		6	2	23	1
					64	1	3	0	24	0
6	11/03/1910	South Africa	Cape Town	W	0					
						1	13	3	47	3
7	15/12/1911	Australia	Sydney	L	39	1	21	2	77	2
					7		6	1	15	0
8	30/12/1911	Australia	Melbourne	W	23		0.1	0	0	1
							3	0	21	0
9	12/01/1912	Australia	Adelaide	W	20					
							7	1	30	1
10	09/02/1912	Australia	Melbourne	W	56		11	3	22	1
							2	0	7	0
11	23/02/1912	Australia	Sydney	W	133*	2	2	1	1	2
					11	4	16	5	36	1
12	10/06/1912	South Africa	Lord's	W	73					
							4	0	19	0
13	24/06/1912	Australia	Lord's	D	20					
14	08/07/1912	South Africa	Headingley	W	57		6	2	13	1
					4					
15	29/07/1912	Australia	Old Trafford	D	13		6	3	6	0
16	12/08/1912	South Africa	The Oval	W	13		15.3	1	41	5
							9	2	24	1
17	19/08/1912	Australia	The Oval	W	62	1	9.4	3	29	5
					4	1	7.4	1	20	5
18	13/12/1913	South Africa	Durban (1)	W	31	2	7	0	24	1
						1	9	3	16	2
19	26/12/1913	South Africa	Johannesburg (1)	W	0	1	3	1	5	1
							21	5	45	0

No	Date	Opposition	Venue	R	Bat	C	Bowling			
20	01/01/1914	South Africa	Johannesburg (1)	W	7	1	5	1	13	0
					37		7	0	24	0
21	14/02/1914	South Africa	Durban (1)	D	9		10	3	27	0
					0*		13	2	26	0
22	27/02/1914	South Africa	Port Elizabeth	W	54		22	4	71	3
						2	5	2	23	0
23	17/12/1920	Australia	Sydney	L	52		23	7	35	2
					16	1	36	10	90	2
24	31/12/1920	Australia	Melbourne	L	5	2	27	8	87	2
					50					
25	14/01/1921	Australia	Adelaide	L	79		21	6	47	0
					0	1	38	4	91	0
26	11/02/1921	Australia	Melbourne	L	29		32.1	14	56	3
					0		14	4	39	0
27	25/02/1921	Australia	Sydney	L	53	2	15	1	58	0
					1		11	3	27	0
28	28/05/1921	Australia	Trent Bridge	L	20		22	8	46	3
					34					
29	11/06/1921	Australia	Lord's	L	95	1	11	2	44	0
					93		3	0	10	0
30	02/07/1921	Australia	Headingley	L	0	2	5	0	34	1
					37	1	18	4	45	1
31	23/07/1921	Australia	Old Trafford	D	41		39	22	38	0
32	13/08/1921	Australia	The Oval	D	23	2	11	2	31	2
33	23/12/1922	South Africa	Johannesburg (1)	L	26					
					15	1	16	4	33	0
34	01/01/1923	South Africa	Cape Town	W	0		2	1	1	0
					5		11	3	22	0
35	18/01/1923	South Africa	Durban (2)	D	0	3	15	3	47	0
36	09/02/1923	South Africa	Johannesburg (1)	D	15	1	6	3	10	0
					115*		6	2	26	0
37	16/02/1923	South Africa	Durban (2)	W	2	1	6	3	9	0
					8	1	3	2	3	0
38	14/06/1924	South Africa	Edgbaston	W	64					
							10	2	41	0
39	28/06/1924	South Africa	Lord's	W	134*	1				
							4	1	9	0
40	12/07/1924	South Africa	Headingley	W	0					
							9	2	21	0
41	26/07/1924	South Africa	Old Trafford	D						
42	16/08/1924	South Africa	The Oval	D	51	1	14	4	22	1
43	19/12/1924	Australia	Sydney	L	0	2	9	0	35	0
					123	2				
44	01/01/1925	Australia	Melbourne	L	0		11	3	26	0
					50					
45	16/01/1925	Australia	Adelaide	L	16		43	5	135	1
					21	1	19	1	77	4
46	13/02/1925	Australia	Melbourne	W	40	1	9	1	53	1
						1	6	0	17	1
47	27/02/1925	Australia	Sydney	L	47	1	5	0	18	0
					28	1	8	1	14	1
48	12/06/1926	Australia	Trent Bridge	D						
49	26/06/1926	Australia	Lord's	D	87		2	0	5	0
							7	1	13	1
50	10/07/1926	Australia	Headingley	D	27		4	0	26	0
					20					
51	24/07/1926	Australia	Old Trafford	D	58	1	2	0	19	0
52	14/08/1926	Australia	The Oval	W	18					
					27	2				
53	13/07/1929	South Africa	Headingley	W	83					
					95*		13.1	3	35	3
54	27/07/1929	South Africa	Old Trafford	W	154		9	3	22	0
						1	18	5	51	1
55	17/08/1929	South Africa	The Oval	D	46	1	13	4	25	1
56	10/01/1930	New Zealand	Christchurch	W	31					
					17*		9	2	37	2

No	Date	Opposition	Venue	R	Bat	C		Bowling		
57	24/01/1930	New Zealand	Wellington	D	6		28.3	5	76	7
					23		23	9	48	2
58	14/02/1930	New Zealand	Auckland	D	59					
59	21/02/1930	New Zealand	Auckland	D	10		41	10	100	2
60	13/06/1930	Australia	Trent Bridge	W	0					
					5		3	1	3	0
61	27/06/1930	Australia	Lord's	L	41	1	6	0	35	0
					28					
62	27/06/1931	New Zealand	Lord's	D	80					
					9					
63	25/06/1932	India	Lord's	W	9					
					21					
64	18/08/1934	Australia	The Oval	L	4					
					0	1				

Batting & Fielding

Mat	Inns	N/O	Runs	H/S	Avg	100s	50s	Cat
64	98	7	3283	154	36.07	5	23	64

Bowling

Balls	Runs	Wkts	Avg	Best	5WI	10WM	S/R
6495	2815	83	33.91	7-76	4	1	78.25

R.A.WOOLMER

Full Name: Robert Andrew Woolmer (known as Bob)
Born: 14/05/1948, Kanpur, India
Teams: Kent 1968-84, Natal 1973/74-75/76, Western Province 1980/81, England 1975-81
Matches: 19 (Won 5, Drew 8, Lost 6)
Right-hand opening/middle order batsman – Right-arm medium bowler

No	Date	Opposition	Venue	R	Bat	C		Bowling		
1	31/07/1975	Australia	Lord's	D	33		13	5	31	1
					31		3	1	3	0
2	28/08/1975	Australia	The Oval	D	5		18	3	38	1
					149	1				
3	03/06/1976	West Indies	Trent Bridge	D	82		10	2	47	0
4	17/06/1976	West Indies	Lord's	D	38	2				
					29					
5	08/07/1976	West Indies	Old Trafford	L	3	.	3	0	22	0
					0					
6	22/07/1976	West Indies	Headingley	L	18		6	0	25	1
					37		7	0	26	0
7	12/08/1976	West Indies	The Oval	L	8		9	0	44	0
					30		5	0	30	0
8	17/12/1976	India	Delhi	W	4					
						1				
9	14/01/1977	India	Madras (1)	W	22		1	0	2	0
					16	2				
10	12/03/1977	Australia	Melbourne	L	9					
					12					
11	16/06/1977	Australia	Lord's	D	79		5	1	20	0
					120	1				
12	07/07/1977	Australia	Old Trafford	W	137					
					0*	1				
13	28/07/1977	Australia	Trent Bridge	W	0					
							3	0	3	0
14	11/08/1977	Australia	Headingley	W	37					
							8	4	8	1
15	25/08/1977	Australia	The Oval	D	15					
					6					
16	05/06/1980	West Indies	Trent Bridge	L	46					
					29					
17	19/06/1980	West Indies	Lord's	D	15					
					19*					
18	18/06/1981	Australia	Trent Bridge	L	0	1				
					0	1				
19	02/07/1981	Australia	Lord's	D	21					
					9					

Batting & Fielding

Mat	Inns	N/O	Runs	H/S	Avg	100s	50s	Cat
19	34	2	1059	149	33.09	3	2	10

Bowling

Balls	Runs	Wkts	Avg	Best	5WI	10WM	S/R
546	299	4	74.75	1-8	0	0	136.50

T.S.WORTHINGTON

Full Name: Thomas Stanley Worthington (known as Stan)
Born: 21/08/1905, Bolsover, Derbyshire
Died: 31/08/1973, Kings Lynn, Norfolk
Teams: Derbyshire 1924-47, England 1930-37
Matches: 9 (Won 3, Drew 4, Lost 2)
Right-hand middle order batsman – Right-arm fast medium bowler

No	Date	Opposition	Venue	R	Bat	C	Bowling			
1	10/01/1930	New Zealand	Christchurch	W	0		7.1	1	24	1
						1	13	4	19	2
2	24/01/1930	New Zealand	Wellington	D	32	1	22	3	63	2
							10	0	44	1
3	14/02/1930	New Zealand	Auckland	D			6	1	11	0
4	21/02/1930	New Zealand	Auckland	D	0		15	5	25	1
5	25/07/1936	India	Old Trafford	D	87	1	4	0	15	1
							13	4	27	0
6	15/08/1936	India	The Oval	W	128	1				
						1	2	0	10	0
7	04/12/1936	Australia	Brisbane (2)	W	0	1				
					8					
8	01/01/1937	Australia	Melbourne	L	0	1				
					16		4	0	18	0
9	26/02/1937	Australia	Melbourne	L	44	1	6	0	60	0
					6					

Batting & Fielding

Mat	Inns	N/O	Runs	H/S	Avg	100s	50s	Cat
9	11	0	321	128	29.18	1	1	8

Bowling

Balls	Runs	Wkts	Avg	Best	5WI	10WM	S/R
633	316	8	39.50	2-19	0	0	79.12

C.W.WRIGHT

Full Name: Charles William Wright
Born: 27/05/1863, Harewood, Yorkshire
Died: 10/01/1936, Saxelby Park, Melton Mowbray, Leicestershire
Teams: Cambridge University 1882-85, Nottinghamshire 1882-99, England 1896
Matches: 3 (Won 3, Drew 0, Lost 0)
Right-hand opening batsman – Wicket-keeper

No	Date	Opposition	Venue	R	Bat	C
1	13/02/1896	South Africa	Port Elizabeth	W	19	
					33	
2	02/03/1896	South Africa	Johannesburg (1)	W	71	
3	21/03/1896	South Africa	Cape Town	W	2	

Batting & Fielding

Mat	Inns	N/O	Runs	H/S	Avg	100s	50s	Cat
3	4	0	125	71	31.25	0	1	0

D.V.P.WRIGHT

Full Name: Douglas Vivian Parson Wright (known as Doug)
Born: 21/08/1914, Sidcup, Kent
Teams: Kent 1932-57, England 1938-51
Matches: 34 (Won 9, Drew 15, Lost 10)
Right-hand lower order batsman – Right-arm medium leg break & googly bowler

No	Date	Opposition	Venue	R	Bat	C		Bowl	ing	
1	10/06/1938	Australia	Trent Bridge	D	1*	1	39	6	153	4
							37	8	85	1
2	24/06/1938	Australia	Lord's	D	6		16	2	68	1
					10*	1	8	0	56	1
3	22/07/1938	Australia	Headingley	L	22		15	4	38	2
					0		5	0	26	3
4	31/12/1938	South Africa	Cape Town	D	33		26	3	83	2
							12	0	62	0
5	20/01/1939	South Africa	Durban (2)	W			12	1	37	2
							15	2	56	0
6	03/03/1939	South Africa	Durban (2)	D	26		37	6	142	2
						1	32	7	146	3
7	24/06/1939	West Indies	Lord's	W			13	1	57	2
						1	17	0	75	3
8	22/07/1939	West Indies	Old Trafford	D	1*		5	1	20	0
					0*		3	0	9	1
9	19/08/1939	West Indies	The Oval	L	6	1	13	2	53	0
10	22/06/1946	India	Lord's	W	3		17	4	53	2
							20	3	68	2
11	20/07/1946	India	Old Trafford	D	0		2	0	12	0
							2	0	17	0
12	29/11/1946	Australia	Brisbane (2)	L	4		43.6	4	167	5
					10*					
13	13/12/1946	Australia	Sydney	L	15*	1	46	8	169	1
					0					
14	01/01/1947	Australia	Melbourne	D	10		26	2	124	2
						1	32	3	131	3
15	31/01/1947	Australia	Adelaide	D	0		32.4	1	152	3
							9	0	49	0
16	28/02/1947	Australia	Sydney	L	7		29	4	105	7
					1*		22	1	93	2
17	21/03/1947	New Zealand	Christchurch	D			13	1	61	0
18	21/06/1947	South Africa	Lord's	W			39	10	95	5
							32.2	6	80	5
19	05/07/1947	South Africa	Old Trafford	W	4*		9	1	30	0
							10	2	32	3
20	26/07/1947	South Africa	Headingley	W			20	9	24	2
							14	7	31	0
21	16/08/1947	South Africa	The Oval	D	14		29	7	89	2
							30	8	103	2
22	24/06/1948	Australia	Lord's	L	13*		21.3	8	54	1
					4		19	4	69	1
23	16/12/1948	South Africa	Durban (2)	W	0		9	3	29	1
							26	3	72	0
24	27/12/1948	South Africa	Johannesburg (2)	D	1*		26	2	104	3
							14	3	35	1
25	01/01/1949	South Africa	Cape Town	D	11		9	0	58	0
							2	0	18	0
26	13/08/1949	New Zealand	The Oval	D	0		22	1	93	1
						2	6	0	21	0
27	12/08/1950	West Indies	The Oval	L	4		53	16	141	5
					6*					
28	01/12/1950	Australia	Brisbane (2)	L	2		16	0	81	1
29	22/12/1950	Australia	Melbourne	L	2		8	0	63	0
					2		9	0	42	1
30	05/01/1951	Australia	Sydney	L	0					
31	02/02/1951	Australia	Adelaide	L	14		25	1	99	4
					0*		21	2	109	2
32	23/02/1951	Australia	Melbourne	W	3		9	1	50	0
							15	2	56	3
33	17/03/1951	New Zealand	Christchurch	D	45		27	2	99	2
34	24/03/1951	New Zealand	Wellington	W	9*	1	19	3	48	5
							12	2	32	0

Batting & Fielding

Mat	Inns	N/O	Runs	H/S	Avg	100s	50s	Cat
34	39	13	289	45	11.11	0	0	10

Bowling

Balls	Runs	Wkts	Avg	Best	5WI	10WM	S/R
8135	4224	108	39.11	7-105	6	1	75.32

R.E.S.WYATT

Full Name: Robert Elliott Storey Wyatt (known as Bob)
Born: 02/05/1901, Milford, Surrey
Died: 20/04/1995, Truro, Cornwall
Teams: Warwickshire 1923-39, Worcestershire 1946-51, England 1927-37
Matches: 40 (Won 11, Drew 17, Lost 12)
England Captain: 16 times 1930-35 (Won 3, Drew 8, Lost 5) **Toss:** 12-4
Right-hand middle order batsman – Right-arm fast medium bowler

No	Date	Opposition	Venue	R	Bat	C		Bowling		
1	24/12/1927	South Africa	Johannesburg (1)	W	0		4	1	6	0
2	31/12/1927	South Africa	Cape Town	W	2					
					91		3	0	5	0
3	21/01/1928	South Africa	Durban (2)	D	0		13	10	4	3
							15	6	31	0
4	28/01/1928	South Africa	Johannesburg (1)	L	58	1	11	0	44	1
					39	1	2	0	6	0
5	04/02/1928	South Africa	Durban (2)	L	22		3	0	16	0
					20*	1				
6	27/07/1929	South Africa	Old Trafford	W	113		2	1	8	0
							4	0	13	1
7	17/08/1929	South Africa	The Oval	D	6		16	4	54	1
8	21/02/1930	West Indies	Georgetown	L	0		9	0	56	2
					28					
9	03/04/1930	West Indies	Kingston	D	58		4	0	11	0
					10		24.3	7	58	2
10*	16/08/1930	Australia	The Oval	L	64	1	14	1	58	1
					7					
11	24/12/1930	South Africa	Johannesburg (1)	L	8					
					5		2	0	20	0
12	01/01/1931	South Africa	Cape Town	D	40		2	0	4	0
					29					
13	16/01/1931	South Africa	Durban (2)	D	54	1				
14	13/02/1931	South Africa	Johannesburg (1)	D	37		2	0	10	0
					7					
15	21/02/1931	South Africa	Durban (2)	D	24					
					1		4	2	6	1
16	02/12/1932	Australia	Sydney	W	38					
					0*					
17	30/12/1932	Australia	Melbourne	L	13					
					25					
18	13/01/1933	Australia	Adelaide	W	78					
					49					
19	10/02/1933	Australia	Brisbane (2)	W	12					
20	23/02/1933	Australia	Sydney	W	51*		2	0	12	0
					61*	2				
21	24/03/1933	New Zealand	Christchurch	D	20	1				
22*	31/03/1933	New Zealand	Auckland	D	60					
23	22/07/1933	West Indies	Old Trafford	D	18		7	1	14	1
							4	1	11	0
24*	12/08/1933	West Indies	The Oval	W	15					
25*	22/06/1934	Australia	Lord's	W	33					
26*	06/07/1934	Australia	Old Trafford	D	0	1				
27*	20/07/1934	Australia	Headingley	D	19	1				
					44					
28*	18/08/1934	Australia	The Oval	L	17		4	0	28	0
					22					
29*	08/01/1935	West Indies	Bridgetown	W	8					
					6*					

No	Date	Opposition	Venue	R	Bat	C		Bowling		
30*	24/01/1935	West Indies	Port-of-Spain	L	15		17	7	33	3
					2	1	8	2	26	0
31*	14/02/1935	West Indies	Georgetown	D	21		10	5	10	0
					71		4	2	7	1
32*	14/03/1935	West Indies	Kingston	L	1*	1	5	1	12	0
33*	15/06/1935	South Africa	Trent Bridge	D	149					
34*	29/06/1935	South Africa	Lord's	L	53		4	2	9	0
					16	1	4	2	2	0
35*	13/07/1935	South Africa	Headingley	D	0		4	3	1	1
					44		6	2	12	0
36*	27/07/1935	South Africa	Old Trafford	D	3		4	1	12	0
					15*					
37*	17/08/1935	South Africa	The Oval	D	37	1	2	0	3	0
							3	0	25	0
38	27/06/1936	India	Lord's	W	0	1	3	2	7	0
							7	4	8	0
39	29/01/1937	Australia	Adelaide	L	3					
					50	1				
40	26/02/1937	Australia	Melbourne	L	38					
					9					

Batting & Fielding

Mat	Inns	N/O	Runs	H/S	Avg	100s	50s	Cat
40	64	6	1839	149	31.70	2	12	16

Bowling

Balls	Runs	Wkts	Avg	Best	5WI	10WM	S/R
1395	642	18	35.66	3-4	0	0	77.50

E.G.WYNYARD

Full Name: Edward George Wynyard (known as Teddy)
Born: 01/04/1861, Saharanpur, India
Died: 30/10/1936, Knotty Green, Beaconsfield, Buckinghamshire
Teams: Hampshire 1878-1908, England 1896-1906
Matches: 3 (Won 1, Drew 0, Lost 2)
Right-hand opening/middle order batsman – Under-arm slow bowler

No	Date	Opposition	Venue	R	Bat	C		Bowling		
1	10/08/1896	Australia	The Oval	W	10					
					3					
2	02/01/1906	South Africa	Johannesburg (1)	L	29					
					0		3	0	15	0
3	06/03/1906	South Africa	Johannesburg (1)	L	0		1	0	2	0
					30					

Batting & Fielding

Mat	Inns	N/O	Runs	H/S	Avg	100s	50s	Cat
3	6	0	72	30	12.00	0	0	0

Bowling

Balls	Runs	Wkts	Avg	Best	5WI	10WM	S/R
24	17	0	–	0-2	0	0	–

N.W.D.YARDLEY

Full Name: Norman Walter Dransfield Yardley
Born: 19/03/1915, Gawber, Barnsley, Yorkshire
Died: 03/10/1989, Lodge Moor, Sheffield, Yorkshire
Teams: Cambridge University 1935-38, Yorkshire 1936-55, England 1938-50
Matches: 20 (Won 4, Drew 7, Lost 9)
England Captain: 14 times 1947-50 (Won 4, Drew 3, Lost 7) **Toss:** 9-5
Right-hand middle order batsman – Right-arm medium bowler

No	Date	Opposition	Venue	R	Bat	C		Bowling		
1	24/12/1938	South Africa	Johannesburg (1)	D	7					
2	29/11/1946	Australia	Brisbane (2)	L	29	1	13	1	47	0
					0					
3	13/12/1946	Australia	Sydney	L	25		9	0	23	1
					35					
4	01/01/1947	Australia	Melbourne	D	61		20	4	50	2
					53*	1	20	0	67	3

No	Date	Opposition	Venue	R	Bat	C		Bowling		
5	31/01/1947	Australia	Adelaide	D	18*		31	7	101	3
					18			13	0	69	1
6*	28/02/1947	Australia	Sydney	L	2	1	5	2	8	0
					11		3	1	7	0
7	21/03/1947	New Zealand	Christchurch	D	22		4	0	12	1
8*	07/06/1947	South Africa	Trent Bridge	D	22	1	5	0	24	0
					99					
9*	21/06/1947	South Africa	Lord's	W	5					
						2				
10*	05/07/1947	South Africa	Old Trafford	W	41	1				
11*	26/07/1947	South Africa	Headingley	W	36	1				
						1				
12*	16/08/1947	South Africa	The Oval	D	59	1				
					11		1	0	1	0
13*	10/06/1948	Australia	Trent Bridge	L	3		17	6	32	2
					22					
14*	24/06/1948	Australia	Lord's	L	44	1	15	4	35	2
					11		13	4	36	2
15*	08/07/1948	Australia	Old Trafford	D	22		4	0	12	0
16*	22/07/1948	Australia	Headingley	L	25		17	6	38	2
					7		13	1	44	1
17*	14/08/1948	Australia	The Oval	L	7		5	1	7	0
					9					
18*	08/06/1950	West Indies	Old Trafford	W	0					
					25	1				
19*	24/06/1950	West Indies	Lord's	L	16		4	1	12	0
					19					
20*	20/07/1950	West Indies	Trent Bridge	L	41	2	27	3	82	1
					7					

Batting & Fielding

Mat	Inns	N/O	Runs	H/S	Avg	100s	50s	Cat
20	34	2	812	99	25.37	0	4	14

Bowling

Balls	Runs	Wkts	Avg	Best	5WI	10WM	S/R
1662	707	21	33.66	3-67	0	0	79.14

H.I.YOUNG

Full Name: Harding Isaac Young (known as sailor)
Born: 05/02/1876, Leyton, Essex
Died: 12/12/1964, Rochford, Essex
Teams: Essex 1898-1912, England 1899
Matches: 2 (Won 0, Drew 2, Lost 0)
Right-hand lower order batsman – Left-arm medium bowler

No	Date	Opposition	Venue	R	Bat	C		Bowling		
1	29/06/1899	Australia	Headingley	D	0	1	19.1	11	30	4
							26	5	72	2
2	17/07/1899	Australia	Old Trafford	D	43		29	10	79	4
							37	12	81	2

Batting & Fielding

Mat	Inns	N/O	Runs	H/S	Avg	100s	50s	Cat
2	2	0	43	43	21.50	0	0	1

Bowling

Balls	Runs	Wkts	Avg	Best	5WI	10WM	S/R
556	262	12	21.83	4-30	0	0	46.33

J.A.YOUNG

Full Name: John Albert Young (known as Jack)
Born: 14/10/1912, Paddington, London
Died: 05/02/1993, St John's Wood, London
Teams: Middlesex 1933-56, England 1947-49
Matches: 8 (Won 2, Drew 4, Lost 2)
Right-hand lower order batsman – Left-arm slow bowler

No	Date	Opposition	Venue	R	Bat	C		Bowling	
1	26/07/1947	South Africa	Headingley	W	0*	1	17	5	31	0
							19	7	54	2
2	10/06/1948	Australia	Trent Bridge	L	1*	1	60	28	79	1
					9		10	3	28	0
3	08/07/1948	Australia	Old Trafford	D	4		14	5	36	1
							21	12	31	1
4	14/08/1948	Australia	The Oval	L	0	1	51	16	118	2
					3*					
5	12/02/1949	South Africa	Johannesburg (2)	D	10*		23	6	52	2
							11	6	14	0
6	05/03/1949	South Africa	Port Elizabeth	W	0		48	9	122	0
							23	9	34	2
7	11/06/1949	New Zealand	Headingley	D	0	1	22	6	52	1
							14	3	41	2
8	25/06/1949	New Zealand	Lord's	D	1*	1	26.4	4	65	3

Batting & Fielding

Mat	Inns	N/O	Runs	H/S	Avg	100s	50s	Cat
8	10	5	28	10*	5.60	0	0	5

Bowling

Balls	Runs	Wkts	Avg	Best	5WI	10WM	S/R
2368	757	17	44.52	3-65	0	0	139.29

R.A.YOUNG

Full Name: Richard Alfred Young (known as Dick)
Born: 16/09/1885, Dharwar, India
Died: 01/07/1968, Hastings, Sussex
Teams: Cambridge University 1905-08, Sussex 1905-25, England 1907-08
Matches: 2 (Won 0, Drew 0, Lost 2)
Right-hand middle order batsman – Wicket-keeper

No	Date	Opposition	Venue	R	Bat	C	St	B
1+	13/12/1907	Australia	Sydney	L	13	1		4
					3	1		6
2+	21/02/1908	Australia	Sydney	L	0	2		9
					11	2		21

Batting & Fielding

Mat	Inns	N/O	Runs	H/S	Avg	100s	50s	Cat	St	Byes
2	4	0	27	13	6.75	0	0	6	0	40

England's Test Match Records

Venues

TEST MATCH VENUES 1877–1996

England			First Test	No	First England Test	No
The Oval	2nd	London	06/09/1880	79	06/09/1880	79
Old Trafford	4th	Manchester	10/07/1884	62	10/07/1884	61
Lord's	5th	London	21/07/1884	95	21/07/1884	94
Trent Bridge	10th	Nottingham	01/06/1899	44	01/06/1899	43
Headingley	11th	Leeds	29/06/1899	58	29/06/1899	58
Edgbaston	12th	Birmingham	29/05/1902	32	29/05/1902	32
Bramall lane	13th	Sheffield	03/07/1902	1	03/07/1902	1
				371		368

Australia						
Melbourne Cricket Ground	1st	Melbourne	15/03/1877	88	15/03/1877	50
Sydney Cricket Ground	3rd	Sydney	17/02/1882	82	17/02/1882	50
Adelaide Oval	6th	Adelaide	12/12/1884	54	12/12/1884	26
Exhibition Ground	16th	Brisbane (1)	30/11/1928	2	30/11/1928	1
Woolloongabba	24th	Brisbane (2)	27/11/1931	38	10/02/1933	15
Western Australia C.A. Ground	45th	Perth	11/12/1970	23	11/12/1970	8
Bellerive Oval	62nd	Hobart	16/12/1989	3	No matches	–
				290		150

South Africa						
St George's Park	7th	Port Elizabeth	12/03/1889	14	12/03/1889	7
Newlands	8th	Cape Town	25/03/1889	28	25/03/1889	16
Old Wanderers	9th	Johannesburg (1)	02/03/1896	22	02/03/1896	17
Lord's	14th	Durban (1)	21/01/1910	4	21/01/1910	3
Kingsmead	15th	Durban (2)	18/01/1923	23	18/01/1923	12
Ellis Park	30th	Johannesburg (2)	27/12/1948	6	27/12/1948	2
Wanderers Stadium	41st	Johannesburg (3)	24/12/1956	16	24/12/1956	5
Centurion	76th	Centurion	16/11/1995	1	16/11/1995	1
				114		63

West Indies						
Kensington Oval	18th	Bridgetown	11/01/1930	32	11/01/1930	11
Queen's Park Oval	20th	Port-of-Spain	01/02/1930	44	01/02/1930	15
Bourda	22nd	Georgetown	21/02/1930	23	21/02/1930	8
Sabina Park	23rd	Kingston	03/04/1930	31	03/04/1930	12
Recreation Ground	52nd	St John's	27/03/1981	10	27/03/1981	4
				140		50

New Zealand						
Lancaster Park	17th	Christchurch	10/01/1930	34	10/01/1930	13
Basin Reserve	19th	Wellington	24/01/1930	30	24/01/1930	7
Eden Park	21st	Auckland	17/02/1930	38	14/02/1930	13
Carisbrook	38th	Dunedin	11/03/1955	9	11/03/1955	2
McLean Park	50th	Napier	16/02/1979	3	No matches	–
Trust Bank (Seddon) Park	64th	Hamilton	22/02/1991	4	No matches	–
				118		35

India						
Gymkhana Ground	25th	Bombay (1)	15/12/1933	1	15/12/1933	1
Eden Gardens	26th	Calcutta	05/01/1934	27	05/01/1934	9
Chepauk (Chidambaram Stadium)	27th	Madras (1)	10/02/1934	22	10/02/1934	7
Feroz Shah Kotla	28th	Delhi	10/11/1948	23	02/11/1951	7
Brabourne Stadium	29th	Bombay (2)	09/12/1948	17	14/12/1951	4
Green Park (Modi Stadium)	31st	Kanpur	12/01/1952	16	12/01/1952	6
University Ground	32nd	Lucknow	23/10/1952	1	No matches	–
Fateh Maidan (Lal Bahadur Stadium)	39th	Hyderabad (Deccan)	19/11/1955	3	No matches	–
Corporation (Nehru) Stadium	40th	Madras (2)	06/01/1956	9	10/01/1962	2
Vidarbha C.A. Ground	44th	Nagpur	03/10/1969	4	No matches	–
Karnataka State C.A. Ground (Chinnaswamy Stadium)	47th	Bangalore	22/11/1974	11	28/01/1977	2
Wankhede Stadium	48th	Bombay (3)	23/01/1975	15	11/02/1977	5
Burlton Park	55th	Jullundur	24/09/1983	1	No matches	–
Gujarat Stadium	56th	Ahmedabad	12/11/1983	3	No matches	–
Barabati Stadium	60th	Cuttack	04/01/1987	2	No matches	–
Sawai Mansingh Stadium	61st	Jaipur	21/02/1987	1	No matches	–
Sector 16 Stadium	63rd	Chandigarh	23/11/1990	1	No matches	–
K.D. Singh "Babu" Stadium	72nd	Lucknow	18/01/1994	1	No matches	–

Punjab C.A. Stadium	74th	Mohali	10/12/1994	1	No matches	–
				159		**43**

Pakistan

Dacca Stadium	33rd	Dacca	01/01/1955	7	19/01/1962	2
Dring Stadium	34th	Bahawalpur	15/01/1955	1	No matches	–
Lawrence Gardens	35th	Lahore (1)	29/01/1955	3	No matches	–
Services Club Ground	36th	Peshawar (1)	13/02/1955	1	No matches	–
National Stadium	37th	Karachi (1)	26/02/1955	31	02/02/1962	6
Gaddafi Stadium	42nd	Lahore (2)	21/11/1959	27	21/10/1961	6
Pindi Club Ground	43rd	Rawalpindi (1)	27/03/1965	1	No matches	–
Niaz Stadium	46th	Hyderabad (Sind)	16/03/1973	5	16/03/1973	2
Iqbal Stadium	49th	Faisalabad	16/10/1978	17	12/03/1984	2
Ibn–e–Qasim Bagh Stadium	51st	Multan	30/12/1980	1	No matches	–
Jinnah Stadium	59th	Sialkot	27/10/1985	4	No matches	–
Municipal Stadium	65th	Gujranwala	20/12/1991	1	No matches	–
Defence Stadium	70th	Karachi (2)	01/12/1993	1	No matches	–
Rawalpindi Cricket Stadium	71st	Rawalpindi (2)	09/12/1993	2	No matches	–
Arbab Niaz Stadium	75th	Peshawar (2)	08/09/1995	1	No matches	–
				103		**18**

Sri Lanka

P.Saravanamuttu Stadium	53rd	Colombo (1)	17/02/1982	6	17/02/1982	1
Asgiriya Stadium	54th	Kandy	22/04/1983	6	No matches	–
Sinhalese Sports Club Ground	57th	Colombo (2)	16/03/1984	7	13/03/1993	1
Colombo Cricket Club Ground	58th	Colombo (3)	24/03/1984	3	No matches	–
Khettarama Stadium	66th	Colombo (4)	28/08/1992	1	No matches	–
Tyronne Fernando Stadium	67th	Moratuwa	08/09/1992	4	No matches	–
				27		**2**

Zimbabwe

Harare Sports Club	68th	Harare	18/10/1992	7	No matches	–
Bulawayo Athletic Club	69th	Bulawayo (1)	01/11/1992	1	No matches	–
Queens Sports Club	73rd	Bulawayo (2)	20/10/1994	2	No matches	–
				10		**0**
				1332		**729**

England have played Test matches at 46 of the 76 Test match venues.

Results

TEST MATCH RESULTS 1877–1996

No	First Day	Opposition	Venue	Result
1–1	15/03/1877	Australia	Melbourne	Australia won by 45 runs
2–2	31/03/1877	Australia	Melbourne	England won by 4 wkts
3–3	02/01/1879	Australia	Melbourne	Australia won by 10 wkts
4–4	06/09/1880	Australia	The Oval	England won by 5 wkts
5–5	31/12/1881	Australia	Melbourne	Match drawn
6–6	17/02/1882	Australia	Sydney	Australia won by 5 wkts
7–7	03/03/1882	Australia	Sydney	Australia won by 6 wkts
8–8	10/03/1882	Australia	Melbourne	Match drawn
9–9	28/08/1882	Australia	The Oval	Australia won by 7 runs
10–10	30/12/1882	Australia	Melbourne	Australia won by 9 wkts
11–11	19/01/1883	Australia	Melbourne	England won by inns & 27 runs
12–12	26/01/1883	Australia	Sydney	England won by 69 runs
13–13	17/02/1883	Australia	Sydney	Australia won by 4 wkts
14–14	10/07/1884	Australia	Old Trafford	Match drawn
15–15	21/07/1884	Australia	Lord's	England won by inns & 5 runs
16–16	11/08/1884	Australia	The Oval	Match drawn
17–17	12/12/1884	Australia	Adelaide	England won by 8 wkts
18–18	01/01/1885	Australia	Melbourne	England won by 10 wkts

No	First Day	Opposition	Venue	Result
19–19	20/02/1885	Australia	Sydney	Australia won by 6 runs
20–20	14/03/1885	Australia	Sydney	Australia won by 8 wkts
21–21	21/03/1885	Australia	Melbourne	England won by inns & 98 runs
22–22	05/07/1886	Australia	Old Trafford	England won by 4 wkts
23–23	19/07/1886	Australia	Lord's	England won by inns & 106 runs
24–24	12/08/1886	Australia	The Oval	England won by inns & 217 runs
25–25	28/01/1887	Australia	Sydney	England won by 13 runs
26–26	25/02/1887	Australia	Sydney	England won by 71 runs
27–27	10/02/1888	Australia	Sydney	England won by 126 runs
28–28	16/07/1888	Australia	Lord's	Australia won by 61 runs
29–29	13/08/1888	Australia	The Oval	England won by inns & 137 runs
30–30	30/08/1888	Australia	Old Trafford	England won by inns & 21 runs
31–1	12/03/1889	South Africa	Port Elizabeth	England won by 8 wkts
32–2	25/03/1889	South Africa	Cape Town	England won by inns & 202 runs
33–31	21/07/1890	Australia	Lord's	England won by 7 wkts
34–32	11/08/1890	Australia	The Oval	England won by 2 wkts
35–33	01/01/1892	Australia	Melbourne	Australia won by 54 runs
36–34	29/01/1892	Australia	Sydney	Australia won by 72 runs
37–35	24/03/1892	Australia	Adelaide	England won by inns & 230 runs
38–3	19/03/1892	South Africa	Cape Town	England won by inns & 189 runs
39–36	17/07/1893	Australia	Lord's	Match drawn
40–37	14/08/1893	Australia	The Oval	England won by inns & 43 runs
41–38	24/08/1893	Australia	Old Trafford	Match drawn
42–39	14/12/1894	Australia	Sydney	England won by 10 runs
43–40	29/12/1894	Australia	Melbourne	England won by 94 runs
44–41	11/01/1895	Australia	Adelaide	Australia won by 382 runs
45–42	01/02/1895	Australia	Sydney	Australia won by inns & 147 runs
46–43	01/03/1895	Australia	Melbourne	England won by 6 wkts
47–4	13/02/1896	South Africa	Port Elizabeth	England won by 288 runs
48–5	02/03/1896	South Africa	Johannesburg (1)	England won by inns & 197 runs
49–6	21/03/1896	South Africa	Cape Town	England won by inns & 33 runs
50–44	22/06/1896	Australia	Lord's	England won by 6 wkts
51–45	16/07/1896	Australia	Old Trafford	Australia won by 3 wkts
52–46	10/08/1896	Australia	The Oval	England won by 66 runs
53–47	13/12/1897	Australia	Sydney	England won by 9 wkts
54–48	01/01/1898	Australia	Melbourne	Australia won by inns & 55 runs
55–49	14/01/1898	Australia	Adelaide	Australia won by inns & 13 runs
56–50	29/01/1898	Australia	Melbourne	Australia won by 8 wkts
57–51	26/02/1898	Australia	Sydney	Australia won by 6 wkts
58–7	14/02/1899	South Africa	Johannesburg (1)	England won by 32 runs
59–8	01/04/1899	South Africa	Cape Town	England won by 210 runs
60–52	01/06/1899	Australia	Trent Bridge	Match drawn
61–53	15/06/1899	Australia	Lord's	Australia won by 10 wkts
62–54	29/06/1899	Australia	Headingley	Match drawn
63–55	17/07/1899	Australia	Old Trafford	Match drawn
64–56	14/08/1899	Australia	The Oval	Match drawn
65–57	13/12/1901	Australia	Sydney	England won by inns & 124 runs
66–58	01/01/1902	Australia	Melbourne	Australia won by 229 runs
67–59	17/01/1902	Australia	Adelaide	Australia won by 4 wkts
68–60	14/02/1902	Australia	Sydney	Australia won by 7 wkts
69–61	28/02/1902	Australia	Melbourne	Australia won by 32 runs
70–62	29/05/1902	Australia	Edgbaston	Match drawn
71–63	12/06/1902	Australia	Lord's	Match drawn
72–64	03/07/1902	Australia	Bramall Lane	Australia won by 143 runs
73–65	24/07/1902	Australia	Old Trafford	Australia won by 3 runs
74–66	11/08/1902	Australia	The Oval	England won by 1 wkt

No	First Day	Opposition	Venue	Result
75–67	11/12/1903	Australia	Sydney	England won by 5 wkts
76–68	01/01/1904	Australia	Melbourne	England won by 185 runs
77–69	15/01/1904	Australia	Adelaide	Australia won by 216 runs
78–70	26/02/1904	Australia	Sydney	England won by 157 runs
79–71	05/03/1904	Australia	Melbourne	Australia won by 218 runs
80–72	29/05/1905	Australia	Trent Bridge	England won by 213 runs
81–73	15/06/1905	Australia	Lord's	Match drawn
82–74	03/07/1905	Australia	Headingley	Match drawn
83–75	24/07/1905	Australia	Old Trafford	England won by inns & 80 runs
84–76	14/08/1905	Australia	The Oval	Match drawn
85–9	02/01/1906	South Africa	Johannesburg (1)	South Africa won by 1 wkt
86–10	06/03/1906	South Africa	Johannesburg (1)	South Africa won by 9 wkts
87–11	10/03/1906	South Africa	Johannesburg (1)	South Africa won by 243 runs
88–12	24/03/1906	South Africa	Cape Town	England won by 4 wkts
89–13	30/03/1906	South Africa	Cape Town	South Africa won by inns & 16 runs
90–14	01/07/1907	South Africa	Lord's	Match drawn
91–15	29/07/1907	South Africa	Headingley	England won by 53 runs
92–16	19/08/1907	South Africa	The Oval	Match drawn
93–77	13/12/1907	Australia	Sydney	Australia won by 2 wkts
94–78	01/01/1908	Australia	Melbourne	England won by 1 wkt
95–79	10/01/1908	Australia	Adelaide	Australia won by 245 runs
96–80	07/02/1908	Australia	Melbourne	Australia won by 308 runs
97–81	21/02/1908	Australia	Sydney	Australia won by 49 runs
98–82	27/05/1909	Australia	Edgbaston	England won by 10 wkts
99–83	14/06/1909	Australia	Lord's	Australia won by 9 wkts
100–84	01/07/1909	Australia	Headingley	Australia won by 126 runs
101–85	26/07/1909	Australia	Old Trafford	Match drawn
102–86	09/08/1909	Australia	The Oval	Match drawn
103–17	01/01/1910	South Africa	Johannesburg (1)	South Africa won by 19 runs
104–18	21/01/1910	South Africa	Durban (1)	South Africa won by 95 runs
105–19	26/02/1910	South Africa	Johannesburg (1)	England won by 3 wkts
106–20	07/03/1910	South Africa	Cape Town	South Africa won by 4 wkts
107–21	11/03/1910	South Africa	Cape Town	England won by 9 wkts
108–87	15/12/1911	Australia	Sydney	Australia won by 146 runs
109–88	30/12/1911	Australia	Melbourne	England won by 8 wkts
110–89	12/01/1912	Australia	Adelaide	England won by 7 wkts
111–90	09/02/1912	Australia	Melbourne	England won by inns & 225 runs
112–91	23/02/1912	Australia	Sydney	England won by 70 runs
113–22	10/06/1912	South Africa	Lord's	England won by inns & 62 runs
114–92	24/06/1912	Australia	Lord's	Match drawn
115–23	08/07/1912	South Africa	Headingley	England won by 174 runs
116–93	29/07/1912	Australia	Old Trafford	Match drawn
117–24	12/08/1912	South Africa	The Oval	England won by 10 wkts
118–94	19/08/1912	Australia	The Oval	England won by 244 runs
119–25	13/12/1913	South Africa	Durban (1)	England won by inns & 157 runs
120–26	26/12/1913	South Africa	Johannesburg (1)	England won by inns & 12 runs
121–27	01/01/1914	South Africa	Johannesburg (1)	England won by 91 runs
122–28	14/02/1914	South Africa	Durban (1)	Match drawn
123–29	27/02/1914	South Africa	Port Elizabeth	England won by 10 wkts
124–95	17/12/1920	Australia	Sydney	Australia won by 377 runs
125–96	31/12/1920	Australia	Melbourne	Australia won by inns & 91 runs
126–97	14/01/1921	Australia	Adelaide	Australia won by 119 runs
127–98	11/02/1921	Australia	Melbourne	Australia won by 8 wkts
128–99	25/02/1921	Australia	Sydney	Australia won by 9 wkts
129–100	28/05/1921	Australia	Trent Bridge	Australia won by 10 wkts
130–101	11/06/1921	Australia	Lord's	Australia won by 8 wkts
131–102	02/07/1921	Australia	Headingley	Australia won by 219 runs
132–103	23/07/1921	Australia	Old Trafford	Match drawn
133–104	13/08/1921	Australia	The Oval	Match drawn
134–30	23/12/1922	South Africa	Johannesburg (1)	South Africa won by 168 runs
135–31	01/01/1923	South Africa	Cape Town	England won by 1 wkt
136–32	18/01/1923	South Africa	Durban (2)	Match drawn

No	First Day	Opposition	Venue	Result
137–33	09/02/1923	South Africa	Johannesburg (1)	Match drawn
138–34	16/02/1923	South Africa	Durban (2)	England won by 109 runs
139–35	14/06/1924	South Africa	Edgbaston	England won by inns & 18 runs
140–36	28/06/1924	South Africa	Lord's	England won by inns & 18 runs
141–37	12/07/1924	South Africa	Headingley	England won by 9 wkts
142–38	26/07/1924	South Africa	Old Trafford	Match drawn
143–39	16/08/1924	South Africa	The Oval	Match drawn
144–105	19/12/1924	Australia	Sydney	Australia won by 193 runs
145–106	01/01/1925	Australia	Melbourne	Australia won by 81 runs
146–107	16/01/1925	Australia	Adelaide	Australia won by 11 runs
147–108	13/02/1925	Australia	Melbourne	England won by inns & 29 runs
148–109	27/02/1925	Australia	Sydney	Australia won by 307 runs
149–110	12/06/1926	Australia	Trent Bridge	Match drawn
150–111	26/06/1926	Australia	Lord's	Match drawn
151–112	10/07/1926	Australia	Headingley	Match drawn
152–113	24/07/1926	Australia	Old Trafford	Match drawn
153–114	14/08/1926	Australia	The Oval	England won by 289 runs
154–40	24/12/1927	South Africa	Johannesburg (1)	England won by 10 wkts
155–41	31/12/1927	South Africa	Cape Town	England won by 87 runs
156–42	21/01/1928	South Africa	Durban (2)	Match drawn
157–43	28/01/1928	South Africa	Johannesburg (1)	South Africa won by 4 wkts
158–44	04/02/1928	South Africa	Durban (2)	South Africa won by 8 wkts
159–1	23/06/1928	West Indies	Lord's	England won by inns & 58 runs
160–2	21/07/1928	West Indies	Old Trafford	England won by inns & 30 runs
161–3	11/08/1928	West Indies	The Oval	England won by inns & 71 runs
162–115	30/11/1928	Australia	Brisbane (1)	England won by 675 runs
163–116	14/12/1928	Australia	Sydney	England won by 8 wkts
164–117	29/12/1928	Australia	Melbourne	England won by 3 wkts
165–118	01/02/1929	Australia	Adelaide	England won by 12 runs
166–119	08/03/1929	Australia	Melbourne	Australia won by 5 wkts
167–45	15/06/1929	South Africa	Edgbaston	Match drawn
168–46	29/06/1929	South Africa	Lord's	Match drawn
169–47	13/07/1929	South Africa	Headingley	England won by 5 wkts
170–48	27/07/1929	South Africa	Old Trafford	England won by inns & 32 runs
171–49	17/08/1929	South Africa	The Oval	Match drawn
172–1	10/01/1930	New Zealand	Christchurch	England won by 8 wkts
173–2	24/01/1930	New Zealand	Wellington	Match drawn
174–3	14/02/1930	New Zealand	Auckland	Match drawn
175–4	21/02/1930	New Zealand	Auckland	Match drawn
176–4	11/01/1930	West Indies	Bridgetown	Match drawn
177–5	01/02/1930	West Indies	Port-of-Spain	England won by 167 runs
178–6	21/02/1930	West Indies	Georgetown	West Indies won by 289 runs
179–7	03/04/1930	West Indies	Kingston	Match drawn
180–120	13/06/1930	Australia	Trent Bridge	England won by 93 runs
181–121	27/06/1930	Australia	Lord's	Australia won by 7 wkts
182–122	11/07/1930	Australia	Headingley	Match drawn
183–123	25/07/1930	Australia	Old Trafford	Match drawn
184–124	16/08/1930	Australia	The Oval	Australia won by inns & 39 runs
185–50	24/12/1930	South Africa	Johannesburg (1)	South Africa won by 28 runs
186–51	01/01/1931	South Africa	Cape Town	Match drawn
187–52	16/01/1931	South Africa	Durban (2)	Match drawn
188–53	13/02/1931	South Africa	Johannesburg (1)	Match drawn
189–54	21/02/1931	South Africa	Durban (2)	Match drawn
190–5	27/06/1931	New Zealand	Lord's	Match drawn
191–6	29/07/1931	New Zealand	The Oval	England won by inns & 26 runs
192–7	15/08/1931	New Zealand	Old Trafford	Match drawn
193–1	25/06/1932	India	Lord's	England won by 158 runs
194–125	02/12/1932	Australia	Sydney	England won by 10 wkts
195–126	30/12/1932	Australia	Melbourne	Australia won by 111 runs
196–127	13/01/1933	Australia	Adelaide	England won by 338 runs

No	First Day	Opposition	Venue	Result
197–128	10/02/1933	Australia	Brisbane (2)	England won by 6 wkts
198–129	23/02/1933	Australia	Sydney	England won by 8 wkts
199–8	24/03/1933	New Zealand	Christchurch	Match drawn
200–9	31/03/1933	New Zealand	Auckland	Match drawn
201–8	24/06/1933	West Indies	Lord's	England won by inns & 27 runs
202–9	22/07/1933	West Indies	Old Trafford	Match drawn
203–10	12/08/1933	West Indies	The Oval	England won by inns & 17 runs
204–2	15/12/1933	India	Bombay (1)	England won by 9 wkts
205–3	05/01/1934	India	Calcutta	Match drawn
206–4	10/02/1934	India	Madras (1)	England won by 202 runs
207–130	08/06/1934	Australia	Trent Bridge	Australia won by 238 runs
208–131	22/06/1934	Australia	Lord's	England won by inns & 38 runs
209–132	06/07/1934	Australia	Old Trafford	Match drawn
210–133	20/07/1934	Australia	Headingley	Match drawn
211–134	18/08/1934	Australia	The Oval	Australia won by 562 runs
212–11	08/01/1935	West Indies	Bridgetown	England won by 4 wkts
213–12	24/01/1935	West Indies	Port-of-Spain	West Indies won by 217 runs
214–13	14/02/1935	West Indies	Georgetown	Match drawn
215–14	14/03/1935	West Indies	Kingston	West Indies won by inns & 161 runs
216–55	15/06/1935	South Africa	Trent Bridge	Match drawn
217–56	29/06/1935	South Africa	Lord's	South Africa won by 157 runs
218–57	13/07/1935	South Africa	Headingley	Match drawn
219–58	27/07/1935	South Africa	Old Trafford	Match drawn
220–59	17/08/1935	South Africa	The Oval	Match drawn
221–5	27/06/1936	India	Lord's	England won by 9 wkts
222–6	25/07/1936	India	Old Trafford	Match drawn
223–7	15/08/1936	India	The Oval	England won by 9 wkts
224–135	04/12/1936	Australia	Brisbane (2)	England won by 322 runs
225–136	18/12/1936	Australia	Sydney	England won by inns & 22 runs
226–137	01/01/1937	Australia	Melbourne	Australia won by 365 runs
227–138	29/01/1937	Australia	Adelaide	Australia won by 148 runs
228–139	26/02/1937	Australia	Melbourne	Australia won by inns & 200 runs
229–10	26/06/1937	New Zealand	Lord's	Match drawn
230–11	24/07/1937	New Zealand	Old Trafford	England won by 130 runs
231–12	14/08/1937	New Zealand	The Oval	Match drawn
232–140	10/06/1938	Australia	Trent Bridge	Match drawn
233–141	24/06/1938	Australia	Lord's	Match drawn
234–142	22/07/1938	Australia	Headingley	Australia won by 5 wkts
235–143	20/08/1938	Australia	The Oval	England won by inns & 579 runs
236–60	24/12/1938	South Africa	Johannesburg (1)	Match drawn
237–61	31/12/1938	South Africa	Cape Town	Match drawn
238–62	20/01/1939	South Africa	Durban (2)	England won by inns & 13 runs
239–63	18/02/1939	South Africa	Johannesburg (1)	Match drawn
240–64	03/03/1939	South Africa	Durban (2)	Match drawn
241–15	24/06/1939	West Indies	Lord's	England won by 8 wkts
242–16	22/07/1939	West Indies	Old Trafford	Match drawn
243–17	19/08/1939	West Indies	The Oval	Match drawn
244–8	22/06/1946	India	Lord's	England won by 10 wkts
245–9	20/07/1946	India	Old Trafford	Match drawn
246–10	17/08/1946	India	The Oval	Match drawn
247–144	29/11/1946	Australia	Brisbane (2)	Australia won by inns & 332 runs
248–145	13/12/1946	Australia	Sydney	Australia won by inns & 33 runs
249–146	01/01/1947	Australia	Melbourne	Match drawn
250–147	31/01/1947	Australia	Adelaide	Match drawn
251–148	28/02/1947	Australia	Sydney	Australia won by 5 wkts
252–13	21/03/1947	New Zealand	Christchurch	Match drawn
253–65	07/06/1947	South Africa	Trent Bridge	Match drawn
254–66	21/06/1947	South Africa	Lord's	England won by 10 wkts

No	First Day	Opposition	Venue	Result
255–67	05/07/1947	South Africa	Old Trafford	England won by 7 wkts
256–68	26/07/1947	South Africa	Headingley	England won by 10 wkts
257–69	16/08/1947	South Africa	The Oval	Match drawn
258–18	21/01/1948	West Indies	Bridgetown	Match drawn
259–19	11/02/1948	West Indies	Port-of-Spain	Match drawn
260–20	03/03/1948	West Indies	Georgetown	West Indies won by 7 wkts
261–21	27/03/1948	West Indies	Kingston	West Indies won by 10 wkts
262–149	10/06/1948	Australia	Trent Bridge	Australia won by 8 wkts
263–150	24/06/1948	Australia	Lord's	Australia won by 409 runs
264–151	08/07/1948	Australia	Old Trafford	Match drawn
265–152	22/07/1948	Australia	Headingley	Australia won by 7 wkts
266–153	14/08/1948	Australia	The Oval	Australia won by inns & 149 runs
267–70	16/12/1948	South Africa	Durban (2)	England won by 2 wkts
268–71	27/12/1948	South Africa	Johannesburg (2)	Match drawn
269–72	01/01/1949	South Africa	Cape Town	Match drawn
270–73	12/02/1949	South Africa	Johannesburg (2)	Match drawn
271–74	05/03/1949	South Africa	Port Elizabeth	England won by 3 wkts
272–14	11/06/1949	New Zealand	Headingley	Match drawn
273–15	25/06/1949	New Zealand	Lord's	Match drawn
274–16	23/07/1949	New Zealand	Old Trafford	Match drawn
275–17	13/08/1949	New Zealand	The Oval	Match drawn
276–22	08/06/1950	West Indies	Old Trafford	England won by 202 runs
277–23	24/06/1950	West Indies	Lord's	West Indies won by 326 runs
278–24	20/07/1950	West Indies	Trent Bridge	West Indies won by 10 wkts
279–25	12/08/1950	West Indies	The Oval	West Indies won by inns & 56 runs
280–154	01/12/1950	Australia	Brisbane (2)	Australia won by 70 runs
281–155	22/12/1950	Australia	Melbourne	Australia won by 28 runs
282–156	05/01/1951	Australia	Sydney	Australia won by inns & 13 runs
283–157	02/02/1951	Australia	Adelaide	Australia won by 274 runs
284–158	23/02/1951	Australia	Melbourne	England won by 8 wkts
285–18	17/03/1951	New Zealand	Christchurch	Match drawn
286–19	24/03/1951	New Zealand	Wellington	England won by 6 wkts
287–75	07/06/1951	South Africa	Trent Bridge	South Africa won by 71 runs
288–76	21/06/1951	South Africa	Lord's	England won by 10 wkts
289–77	05/07/1951	South Africa	Old Trafford	England won by 9 wkts
290–78	26/07/1951	South Africa	Headingley	Match drawn
291–79	16/08/1951	South Africa	The Oval	England won by 4 wkts
292–11	02/11/1951	India	Delhi	Match drawn
293–12	14/12/1951	India	Bombay (2)	Match drawn
294–13	30/12/1951	India	Calcutta	Match drawn
295–14	12/01/1952	India	Kanpur	England won by 8 wkts
296–15	06/02/1952	India	Madras (1)	India won by inns & 8 runs
297–16	05/06/1952	India	Headingley	England won by 7 wkts
298–17	19/06/1952	India	Lord's	England won by 8 wkts
299–18	17/07/1952	India	Old Trafford	England won by inns & 207 runs
300–19	14/08/1952	India	The Oval	Match drawn
301–159	11/06/1953	Australia	Trent Bridge	Match drawn
302–160	25/06/1953	Australia	Lord's	Match drawn
303–161	09/07/1953	Australia	Old Trafford	Match drawn
304–162	23/07/1953	Australia	Headingley	Match drawn
305–163	15/08/1953	Australia	The Oval	England won by 8 wkts
306–26	15/01/1954	West Indies	Kingston	West Indies won by 140 runs
307–27	06/02/1954	West Indies	Bridgetown	West Indies won by 181 runs
308–28	24/02/1954	West Indies	Georgetown	England won by 9 wkts
309–29	17/03/1954	West Indies	Port-of-Spain	Match drawn
310–30	30/03/1954	West Indies	Kingston	England won by 9 wkts
311–1	10/06/1954	Pakistan	Lord's	Match drawn
312–2	01/07/1954	Pakistan	Trent Bridge	England won by inns & 129 runs
313–3	22/07/1954	Pakistan	Old Trafford	Match drawn
314–4	12/08/1954	Pakistan	The Oval	Pakistan won by 24 runs

No	First Day	Opposition	Venue	Result
315–164	26/11/1954	Australia	Brisbane (2)	Australia won by inns & 154 runs
316–165	17/12/1954	Australia	Sydney	England won by 38 runs
317–166	31/12/1954	Australia	Melbourne	England won by 128 runs
318–167	28/01/1955	Australia	Adelaide	England won by 5 wkts
319–168	25/02/1955	Australia	Sydney	Match drawn
320–20	11/03/1955	New Zealand	Dunedin	England won by 8 wkts
321–21	25/03/1955	New Zealand	Auckland	England won by inns & 20 runs
322–80	09/06/1955	South Africa	Trent Bridge	England won by inns & 5 runs
323–81	23/06/1955	South Africa	Lord's	England won by 71 runs
324–82	07/07/1955	South Africa	Old Trafford	South Africa won by 3 wkts
325–83	21/07/1955	South Africa	Headingley	South Africa won by 224 runs
326–84	13/08/1955	South Africa	The Oval	England won by 92 runs
327–169	07/06/1956	Australia	Trent Bridge	Match drawn
328–170	21/06/1956	Australia	Lord's	Australia won by 185 runs
329–171	12/07/1956	Australia	Headingley	England won by inns & 42 runs
330–172	26/07/1956	Australia	Old Trafford	England won by inns & 170 runs
331–173	23/08/1956	Australia	The Oval	Match drawn
332–85	24/12/1956	South Africa	Johannesburg (3)	England won by 131 runs
333–86	01/01/1957	South Africa	Cape Town	England won by 312 runs
334–87	25/01/1957	South Africa	Durban (2)	Match drawn
335–88	15/02/1957	South Africa	Johannesburg (3)	South Africa won by 17 runs
336–89	01/03/1957	South Africa	Port Elizabeth	South Africa won by 58 runs
337–31	30/05/1957	West Indies	Edgbaston	Match drawn
338–32	20/06/1957	West Indies	Lord's	England won by inns & 36 runs
339–33	04/07/1957	West Indies	Trent Bridge	Match drawn
340–34	25/07/1957	West Indies	Headingley	England won by inns & 5 runs
341–35	22/08/1957	West Indies	The Oval	England won by inns & 237 runs
342–22	05/06/1958	New Zealand	Edgbaston	England won by 205 runs
343–23	19/06/1958	New Zealand	Lord's	England won by inns & 148 runs
344–24	03/07/1958	New Zealand	Headingley	England won by inns & 71 runs
345–25	24/07/1958	New Zealand	Old Trafford	England won by inns & 13 runs
346–26	21/08/1958	New Zealand	The Oval	Match drawn
347–174	05/12/1958	Australia	Brisbane (2)	Australia won by 8 wkts
348–175	31/12/1958	Australia	Melbourne	Australia won by 8 wkts
349–176	09/01/1959	Australia	Sydney	Match drawn
350–177	30/01/1959	Australia	Adelaide	Australia won by 10 wkts
351–178	13/02/1959	Australia	Melbourne	Australia won by 9 wkts
352–27	27/02/1959	New Zealand	Christchurch	England won by inns & 99 runs
353–28	14/03/1959	New Zealand	Auckland	Match drawn
354–20	04/06/1959	India	Trent Bridge	England won by inns & 59 runs
355–21	18/06/1959	India	Lord's	England won by 8 wkts
356–22	02/07/1959	India	Headingley	England won by inns & 173 runs
357–23	23/07/1959	India	Old Trafford	England won by 171 runs
358–24	20/08/1959	India	The Oval	England won by inns & 27 runs
359–36	06/01/1960	West Indies	Bridgetown	Match drawn
360–37	28/01/1960	West Indies	Port-of-Spain	England won by 256 runs
361–38	17/02/1960	West Indies	Kingston	Match drawn
362–39	09/03/1960	West Indies	Georgetown	Match drawn
363–40	25/03/1960	West Indies	Port-of-Spain	Match drawn
364–90	09/06/1960	South Africa	Edgbaston	England won by 100 runs
365–91	23/06/1960	South Africa	Lord's	England won by inns & 73 runs
366–92	07/07/1960	South Africa	Trent Bridge	England won by 8 wkts
367–93	21/07/1960	South Africa	Old Trafford	Match drawn
368–94	18/08/1960	South Africa	The Oval	Match drawn
369–179	08/06/1961	Australia	Edgbaston	Match drawn
370–180	22/06/1961	Australia	Lord's	Australia won by 5 wkts
371–181	06/07/1961	Australia	Headingley	England won by 8 wkts
372–182	27/07/1961	Australia	Old Trafford	Australia won by 54 runs
373–183	17/08/1961	Australia	The Oval	Match drawn
374–5	21/10/1961	Pakistan	Lahore (2)	England won by 5 wkts

No	First Day	Opposition	Venue	Result
375–25	11/11/1961	India	Bombay (2)	Match drawn
376–26	01/12/1961	India	Kanpur	Match drawn
377–27	13/12/1961	India	Delhi	Match drawn
378–28	30/12/1961	India	Calcutta	India won by 187 runs
379–29	10/01/1962	India	Madras (2)	India won by 128 runs
380–6	19/01/1962	Pakistan	Dacca	Match drawn
381–7	02/02/1962	Pakistan	Karachi (1)	Match drawn
382–8	31/05/1962	Pakistan	Edgbaston	England won by inns & 24 runs
383–9	21/06/1962	Pakistan	Lord's	England won by 9 wkts
384–10	05/07/1962	Pakistan	Headingley	England won by inns & 117 runs
385–11	26/07/1962	Pakistan	Trent Bridge	Match drawn
386–12	16/08/1962	Pakistan	The Oval	England won by 10 wkts
387–184	30/11/1962	Australia	Brisbane (2)	Match drawn
388–185	29/12/1962	Australia	Melbourne	England won by 7 wkts
389–186	11/01/1963	Australia	Sydney	Australia won by 8 wkts
390–187	25/01/1963	Australia	Adelaide	Match drawn
391–188	15/02/1963	Australia	Sydney	Match drawn
392–29	23/02/1963	New Zealand	Auckland	England won by inns & 215 runs
393–30	01/03/1963	New Zealand	Wellington	England won by inns & 47 runs
394–31	15/03/1963	New Zealand	Christchurch	England won by 7 wkts
395–41	06/06/1963	West Indies	Old Trafford	West Indies won by 10 wkts
396–42	20/06/1963	West Indies	Lord's	Match drawn
397–43	04/07/1963	West Indies	Edgbaston	England won by 217 runs
398–44	25/07/1963	West Indies	Headingley	West Indies won by 221 runs
399–45	22/08/1963	West Indies	The Oval	West Indies won by 8 wkts
400–30	10/01/1964	India	Madras (2)	Match drawn
401–31	21/01/1964	India	Bombay (2)	Match drawn
402–32	29/01/1964	India	Calcutta	Match drawn
403–33	08/02/1964	India	Delhi	Match drawn
404–34	15/02/1964	India	Kanpur	Match drawn
405–189	04/06/1964	Australia	Trent Bridge	Match drawn
406–190	18/06/1964	Australia	Lord's	Match drawn
407–191	02/07/1964	Australia	Headingley	Australia won by 7 wkts
408–192	23/07/1964	Australia	Old Trafford	Match drawn
409–193	13/08/1964	Australia	The Oval	Match drawn
410–95	04/12/1964	South Africa	Durban (2)	England won by inns & 104 runs
411–96	23/12/1964	South Africa	Johannesburg (3)	Match drawn
412–97	01/01/1965	South Africa	Cape Town	Match drawn
413–98	22/01/1965	South Africa	Johannesburg (3)	Match drawn
414–99	12/02/1965	South Africa	Port Elizabeth	Match drawn
415–32	27/05/1965	New Zealand	Edgbaston	England won by 9 wkts
416–33	17/06/1965	New Zealand	Lord's	England won by 7 wkts
417–34	08/07/1965	New Zealand	Headingley	England won by inns & 187 runs
418–100	22/07/1965	South Africa	Lord's	Match drawn
419–101	05/08/1965	South Africa	Trent Bridge	South Africa won by 94 runs
420–102	26/08/1965	South Africa	The Oval	Match drawn
421–194	10/12/1965	Australia	Brisbane (2)	Match drawn
422–195	30/12/1965	Australia	Melbourne	Match drawn
423–196	07/01/1966	Australia	Sydney	England won by inns & 93 runs
424–197	28/01/1966	Australia	Adelaide	Australia won by inns & 9 runs
425–198	11/02/1966	Australia	Melbourne	Match drawn
426–35	25/02/1966	New Zealand	Christchurch	Match drawn
427–36	04/03/1966	New Zealand	Dunedin	Match drawn
428–37	11/03/1966	New Zealand	Auckland	Match drawn
429–46	02/06/1966	West Indies	Old Trafford	West Indies won by inns & 40 runs
430–47	16/06/1966	West Indies	Lord's	Match drawn
431–48	30/06/1966	West Indies	Trent Bridge	West Indies won by 139 runs
432–49	04/08/1966	West Indies	Headingley	West Indies won by inns & 55 runs
433–50	18/08/1966	West Indies	The Oval	England won by inns & 34 runs
434–35	08/06/1967	India	Headingley	England won by 6 wkts

No	First Day	Opposition	Venue	Result
435–36	22/06/1967	India	Lord's	England won by inns & 124 runs
436–37	13/07/1967	India	Edgbaston	England won by 132 runs
437–13	27/07/1967	Pakistan	Lord's	Match drawn
438–14	10/08/1967	Pakistan	Trent Bridge	England won by 10 wkts
439–15	24/08/1967	Pakistan	The Oval	England won by 8 wkts
440–51	19/01/1968	West Indies	Port-of-Spain	Match drawn
441–52	08/02/1968	West Indies	Kingston	Match drawn
442–53	29/02/1968	West Indies	Bridgetown	Match drawn
443–54	14/03/1968	West Indies	Port-of-Spain	England won by 7 wkts
444–55	28/03/1968	West Indies	Georgetown	Match drawn
445–199	06/06/1968	Australia	Old Trafford	Australia won by 159 runs
446–200	20/06/1968	Australia	Lord's	Match drawn
447–201	11/07/1968	Australia	Edgbaston	Match drawn
448–202	25/07/1968	Australia	Headingley	Match drawn
449–203	22/08/1968	Australia	The Oval	England won by 226 runs
450–16	21/02/1969	Pakistan	Lahore (2)	Match drawn
451–17	28/02/1969	Pakistan	Dacca	Match drawn
452–18	06/03/1969	Pakistan	Karachi (1)	Match drawn
453–56	12/06/1969	West Indies	Old Trafford	England won by 10 wkts
454–57	26/06/1969	West Indies	Lord's	Match drawn
455–58	10/07/1969	West Indies	Headingley	England won by 30 runs
456–38	24/07/1969	New Zealand	Lord's	England won by 230 runs
457–39	07/08/1969	New Zealand	Trent Bridge	Match drawn
458–40	21/08/1969	New Zealand	The Oval	England won by 8 wkts
459–204	27/11/1970	Australia	Brisbane (2)	Match drawn
460–205	11/12/1970	Australia	Perth	Match drawn
461–206	09/01/1971	Australia	Sydney	England won by 299 runs
462–207	21/01/1971	Australia	Melbourne	Match drawn
463–208	29/01/1971	Australia	Adelaide	Match drawn
464–209	12/02/1971	Australia	Sydney	England won by 62 runs
465–41	25/02/1971	New Zealand	Christchurch	England won by 8 wkts
466–42	05/03/1971	New Zealand	Auckland	Match drawn
467–19	03/06/1971	Pakistan	Edgbaston	Match drawn
468–20	17/06/1971	Pakistan	Lord's	Match drawn
469–21	08/07/1971	Pakistan	Headingley	England won by 25 runs
470–38	22/07/1971	India	Lord's	Match drawn
471–39	05/08/1971	India	Old Trafford	Match drawn
472–40	19/08/1971	India	The Oval	India won by 4 wkts
473–210	08/06/1972	Australia	Old Trafford	England won by 89 runs
474–211	22/06/1972	Australia	Lord's	Australia won by 8 wkts
475–212	13/07/1972	Australia	Trent Bridge	Match drawn
476–213	27/07/1972	Australia	Headingley	England won by 9 wkts
477–214	10/08/1972	Australia	The Oval	Australia won by 5 wkts
478–41	20/12/1972	India	Delhi	England won by 6 wkts
479–42	30/12/1972	India	Calcutta	India won by 28 runs
480–43	12/01/1973	India	Madras (1)	India won by 4 wkts
481–44	25/01/1973	India	Kanpur	Match drawn
482–45	06/02/1973	India	Bombay (2)	Match drawn
483–22	02/03/1973	Pakistan	Lahore (2)	Match drawn
484–23	16/03/1973	Pakistan	Hyderabad	Match drawn
485–24	24/03/1973	Pakistan	Karachi (1)	Match drawn
486–43	07/06/1973	New Zealand	Trent Bridge	England won by 38 runs
487–44	21/06/1973	New Zealand	Lord's	Match drawn
488–45	05/07/1973	New Zealand	Headingley	England won by inns & 1 run
489–59	26/07/1973	West Indies	The Oval	West Indies won by 158 runs
490–60	09/08/1973	West Indies	Edgbaston	Match drawn
491–61	23/08/1973	West Indies	Lord's	West Indies won by inns & 226 runs
492–62	02/02/1974	West Indies	Port-of-Spain	West Indies won by 7 wkts

No	First Day	Opposition	Venue	Result
493–63	16/02/1974	West Indies	Kingston	Match drawn
494–64	06/03/1974	West Indies	Bridgetown	Match drawn
495–65	22/03/1974	West Indies	Georgetown	Match drawn
496–66	30/03/1974	West Indies	Port-of-Spain	England won by 26 runs
497–46	06/06/1974	India	Old Trafford	England won by 113 runs
498–47	20/06/1974	India	Lord's	England won by inns & 285 runs
499–48	04/07/1974	India	Edgbaston	England won by inns & 78 runs
500–25	25/07/1974	Pakistan	Headingley	Match drawn
501–26	08/08/1974	Pakistan	Lord's	Match drawn
502–27	22/08/1974	Pakistan	The Oval	Match drawn
503–215	29/11/1974	Australia	Brisbane (2)	Australia won by 166 runs
504–216	13/12/1974	Australia	Perth	Australia won by 9 wkts
505–217	26/12/1974	Australia	Melbourne	Match drawn
506–218	04/01/1975	Australia	Sydney	Australia won by 171 runs
507–219	25/01/1975	Australia	Adelaide	Australia won by 163 runs
508–220	08/02/1975	Australia	Melbourne	England won by inns & 4 runs
509–46	20/02/1975	New Zealand	Auckland	England won by inns & 83 runs
510–47	28/02/1975	New Zealand	Christchurch	Match drawn
511–221	10/07/1975	Australia	Edgbaston	Australia won by inns & 85 runs
512–222	31/07/1975	Australia	Lord's	Match drawn
513–223	14/08/1975	Australia	Headingley	Match drawn
514–224	28/08/1975	Australia	The Oval	Match drawn
515–67	03/06/1976	West Indies	Trent Bridge	Match drawn
516–68	17/06/1976	West Indies	Lord's	Match drawn
517–69	08/07/1976	West Indies	Old Trafford	West Indies won by 425 runs
518–70	22/07/1976	West Indies	Headingley	West Indies won by 55 runs
519–71	12/08/1976	West Indies	The Oval	West Indies won by 231 runs
520–49	17/12/1976	India	Delhi	England won by inns & 25 runs
521–50	01/01/1977	India	Calcutta	England won by 10 wkts
522–51	14/01/1977	India	Madras (1)	England won by 200 runs
523–52	28/01/1977	India	Bangalore	India won by 140 runs
524–53	11/02/1977	India	Bombay (3)	Match drawn
525–225	12/03/1977	Australia	Melbourne	Australia won by 45 runs
526–226	16/06/1977	Australia	Lord's	Match drawn
527–227	07/07/1977	Australia	Old Trafford	England won by 9 wkts
528–228	28/07/1977	Australia	Trent Bridge	England won by 7 wkts
529–229	11/08/1977	Australia	Headingley	England won by inns & 85 runs
530–230	25/08/1977	Australia	The Oval	Match drawn
531–28	14/12/1977	Pakistan	Lahore (2)	Match drawn
532–29	02/01/1978	Pakistan	Hyderabad	Match drawn
533–30	18/01/1978	Pakistan	Karachi (1)	Match drawn
534–48	10/02/1978	New Zealand	Wellington	New Zealand won by 72 runs
535–49	24/02/1978	New Zealand	Christchurch	England won by 174 runs
536–50	04/03/1978	New Zealand	Auckland	Match drawn
537–31	01/06/1978	Pakistan	Edgbaston	England won by inns & 57 runs
538–32	15/06/1978	Pakistan	Lord's	England won by inns & 120 runs
539–33	29/06/1978	Pakistan	Headingley	Match drawn
540–51	27/07/1978	New Zealand	The Oval	England won by 7 wkts
541–52	10/08/1978	New Zealand	Trent Bridge	England won by inns & 119 runs
542–53	24/08/1978	New Zealand	Lord's	England won by 7 wkts
543–231	01/12/1978	Australia	Brisbane (2)	England won by 7 wkts
544–232	15/12/1978	Australia	Perth	England won by 166 runs
545–233	29/12/1978	Australia	Melbourne	Australia won by 103 runs
546–234	06/01/1979	Australia	Sydney	England won by 93 runs
547–235	27/01/1979	Australia	Adelaide	England won by 205 runs
548–236	10/02/1979	Australia	Sydney	England won by 9 wkts
549–54	12/07/1979	India	Edgbaston	England won by inns & 83 runs
550–55	02/08/1979	India	Lord's	Match drawn
551–56	16/08/1979	India	Headingley	Match drawn
552–57	30/08/1979	India	The Oval	Match drawn

No	First Day	Opposition	Venue	Result
553–237	14/12/1979	Australia	Perth	Australia won by 138 runs
554–238	04/01/1980	Australia	Sydney	Australia won by 6 wkts
555–239	01/02/1980	Australia	Melbourne	Australia won by 8 wkts
556–58	15/02/1980	India	Bombay (3)	England won by 10 wkts
557–72	05/06/1980	West Indies	Trent Bridge	West Indies won by 2 wkts
558–73	19/06/1980	West Indies	Lord's	Match drawn
559–74	10/07/1980	West Indies	Old Trafford	Match drawn
560–75	24/07/1980	West Indies	The Oval	Match drawn
561–76	07/08/1980	West Indies	Headingley	Match drawn
562–240	28/08/1980	Australia	Lord's	Match drawn
563–77	13/02/1981	West Indies	Port-of-Spain	West Indies won by inns & 79 runs
564–78	13/03/1981	West Indies	Bridgetown	West Indies won by 298 runs
565–79	27/03/1981	West Indies	St John's	Match drawn
566–80	10/04/1981	West Indies	Kingston	Match drawn
567–241	18/06/1981	Australia	Trent Bridge	Australia won by 4 wkts
568–242	02/07/1981	Australia	Lord's	Match drawn
569–243	16/07/1981	Australia	Headingley	England won by 18 runs
570–244	30/07/1981	Australia	Edgbaston	England won by 29 runs
571–245	13/08/1981	Australia	Old Trafford	England won by 103 runs
572–246	27/08/1981	Australia	The Oval	Match drawn
573–59	27/11/1981	India	Bombay (3)	India won by 138 runs
574–60	09/12/1981	India	Bangalore	Match drawn
575–61	23/12/1981	India	Delhi	Match drawn
576–62	01/01/1982	India	Calcutta	Match drawn
577–63	13/01/1982	India	Madras (1)	Match drawn
578–64	30/01/1982	India	Kanpur	Match drawn
579–1	17/02/1982	Sri Lanka	Colombo (1)	England won by 7 wkts
580–65	10/06/1982	India	Lord's	England won by 7 wkts
581–66	24/06/1982	India	Old Trafford	Match drawn
582–67	08/07/1982	India	The Oval	Match drawn
583–34	29/07/1982	Pakistan	Edgbaston	England won by 113 runs
584–35	12/08/1982	Pakistan	Lord's	Pakistan won by 10 wkts
585–36	26/08/1982	Pakistan	Headingley	England won by 3 wkts
586–247	12/11/1982	Australia	Perth	Match drawn
587–248	26/11/1982	Australia	Brisbane (2)	Australia won by 7 wkts
588–249	10/12/1982	Australia	Adelaide	Australia won by 8 wkts
589–250	26/12/1982	Australia	Melbourne	England won by 3 runs
590–251	02/01/1983	Australia	Sydney	Match drawn
591–54	14/07/1983	New Zealand	The Oval	England won by 189 runs
592–55	28/07/1983	New Zealand	Headingley	New Zealand won by 5 wkts
593–56	11/08/1983	New Zealand	Lord's	England won by 127 runs
594–57	25/08/1983	New Zealand	Trent Bridge	England won by 165 runs
595–58	20/01/1984	New Zealand	Wellington	Match drawn
596–59	03/02/1984	New Zealand	Christchurch	New Zealand won by inns & 132 runs
597–60	10/02/1984	New Zealand	Auckland	Match drawn
598–37	02/03/1984	Pakistan	Karachi (1)	Pakistan won by 3 wkts
599–38	12/03/1984	Pakistan	Faisalabad	Match drawn
600–39	19/03/1984	Pakistan	Lahore (2)	Match drawn
601–81	14/06/1984	West Indies	Edgbaston	West Indies won by inns & 180 runs
602–82	28/06/1984	West Indies	Lord's	West Indies won by 9 wkts
603–83	12/07/1984	West Indies	Headingley	West Indies won by 8 wkts
604–84	26/07/1984	West Indies	Old Trafford	West Indies won by inns & 64 runs
605–85	09/08/1984	West Indies	The Oval	West Indies won by 172 runs
606–2	23/08/1984	Sri Lanka	Lord's	Match drawn
607–68	28/11/1984	India	Bombay (3)	India won by 8 wkts
608–69	12/12/1984	India	Delhi	England won by 8 wkts
609–70	31/12/1984	India	Calcutta	Match drawn
610–71	13/01/1985	India	Madras (1)	England won by 9 wkts

No	First Day	Opposition	Venue	Result
611–72	31/01/1985	India	Kanpur	Match drawn
612–252	13/06/1985	Australia	Headingley	England won by 5 wkts
613–253	27/06/1985	Australia	Lord's	Australia won by 4 wkts
614–254	11/07/1985	Australia	Trent Bridge	Match drawn
615–255	01/08/1985	Australia	Old Trafford	Match drawn
616–256	15/08/1985	Australia	Edgbaston	England won by inns & 118 runs
617–257	29/08/1985	Australia	The Oval	England won by inns & 94 runs
618–86	21/02/1986	West Indies	Kingston	West Indies won by 10 wkts
619–87	07/03/1986	West Indies	Port-of-Spain	West Indies won by 7 wkts
620–88	21/03/1986	West Indies	Bridgetown	West Indies won by inns & 30 runs
621–89	03/04/1986	West Indies	Port-of-Spain	West Indies won by 10 wkts
622–90	11/04/1986	West Indies	St John's	West Indies won by 240 runs
623–73	05/06/1986	India	Lord's	India won by 5 wkts
624–74	19/06/1986	India	Headingley	India won by 279 runs
625–75	03/07/1986	India	Edgbaston	Match drawn
626–61	24/07/1986	New Zealand	Lord's	Match drawn
627–62	07/08/1986	New Zealand	Trent Bridge	New Zealand won by 8 wkts
628–63	21/08/1986	New Zealand	The Oval	Match drawn
629–258	14/11/1986	Australia	Brisbane (2)	England won by 7 wkts
630–259	28/11/1986	Australia	Perth	Match drawn
631–260	12/12/1986	Australia	Adelaide	Match drawn
632–261	26/12/1986	Australia	Melbourne	England won by inns & 14 runs
633–262	10/01/1987	Australia	Sydney	Australia won by 55 runs
634–40	04/06/1987	Pakistan	Old Trafford	Match drawn
635–41	18/06/1987	Pakistan	Lord's	Match drawn
636–42	02/07/1987	Pakistan	Headingley	Pakistan won by inns & 18 runs
637–43	23/07/1987	Pakistan	Edgbaston	Match drawn
638–44	06/08/1987	Pakistan	The Oval	Match drawn
639–45	25/11/1987	Pakistan	Lahore (2)	Pakistan won by inns & 87 runs
640–46	07/12/1987	Pakistan	Faisalabad	Match drawn
641–47	16/12/1987	Pakistan	Karachi (1)	Match drawn
642–263	29/01/1988	Australia	Sydney	Match drawn
643–64	12/02/1988	New Zealand	Christchurch	Match drawn
644–65	25/02/1988	New Zealand	Auckland	Match drawn
645–66	03/03/1988	New Zealand	Wellington	Match drawn
646–91	02/06/1988	West Indies	Trent Bridge	Match drawn
647–92	16/06/1988	West Indies	Lord's	West Indies won by 134 runs
648–93	30/06/1988	West Indies	Old Trafford	West Indies won by inns & 156 runs
649–94	21/07/1988	West Indies	Headingley	West Indies won by 10 wkts
650–95	04/08/1988	West Indies	The Oval	West Indies won by 8 wkts
651–3	25/08/1988	Sri Lanka	Lord's	England won by 7 wkts
652–264	08/06/1989	Australia	Headingley	Australia won by 210 runs
653–265	22/06/1989	Australia	Lord's	Australia won by 6 wkts
654–266	06/07/1989	Australia	Edgbaston	Match drawn
655–267	27/07/1989	Australia	Old Trafford	Australia won by 9 wkts
656–268	10/08/1989	Australia	Trent Bridge	Australia won by inns & 180 runs
657–269	24/08/1989	Australia	The Oval	Match drawn
658–96	24/02/1990	West Indies	Kingston	England won by 9 wkts
659–97	23/03/1990	West Indies	Port-of-Spain	Match drawn
660–98	05/04/1990	West Indies	Bridgetown	West Indies won by 164 runs
661–99	12/04/1990	West Indies	St John's	West Indies won by inns & 32 runs
662–67	07/06/1990	New Zealand	Trent Bridge	Match drawn
663–68	21/06/1990	New Zealand	Lord's	Match drawn
664–69	05/07/1990	New Zealand	Edgbaston	England won by 114 runs
665–76	26/07/1990	India	Lord's	England won by 247 runs
666–77	09/08/1990	India	Old Trafford	Match drawn
667–78	23/08/1990	India	The Oval	Match drawn
668–270	23/11/1990	Australia	Brisbane (2)	Australia won by 10 wkts

No	First Day	Opposition	Venue	Result
669–271	26/12/1990	Australia	Melbourne	Australia won by 8 wkts
670–272	04/01/1991	Australia	Sydney	Match drawn
671–273	25/01/1991	Australia	Adelaide	Match drawn
672–274	01/02/1991	Australia	Perth	Australia won by 9 wkts
673–100	06/06/1991	West Indies	Headingley	England won by 115 runs
674–101	20/06/1991	West Indies	Lord's	Match drawn
675–102	04/07/1991	West Indies	Trent Bridge	West Indies won by 9 wkts
676–103	25/07/1991	West Indies	Edgbaston	West Indies won by 7 wkts
677–104	08/08/1991	West Indies	The Oval	England won by 5 wkts
678–4	22/08/1991	Sri Lanka	Lord's	England won by 137 runs
679–70	18/01/1992	New Zealand	Christchurch	England won by inns & 4 runs
680–71	30/01/1992	New Zealand	Auckland	England won by 168 runs
681–72	06/02/1992	New Zealand	Wellington	Match drawn
682–48	04/06/1992	Pakistan	Edgbaston	Match drawn
683–49	18/06/1992	Pakistan	Lord's	Pakistan won by 2 wkts
684–50	02/07/1992	Pakistan	Old Trafford	Match drawn
685–51	23/07/1992	Pakistan	Headingley	England won by 6 wkts
686–52	06/08/1992	Pakistan	The Oval	Pakistan won by 10 wkts
687–79	29/01/1993	India	Calcutta	India won by 8 wkts
688–80	11/02/1993	India	Madras (1)	India won by inns & 22 runs
689–81	19/02/1993	India	Bombay (3)	India won by inns & 15 runs
690–5	13/03/1993	Sri Lanka	Colombo (2)	Sri Lanka won by 5 wkts
691–275	03/06/1993	Australia	Old Trafford	Australia won by 179 runs
692–276	17/06/1993	Australia	Lord's	Australia won by inns & 62 runs
693–277	01/07/1993	Australia	Trent Bridge	Match drawn
694–278	22/07/1993	Australia	Headingley	Australia won by inns & 148 runs
695–279	05/08/1993	Australia	Edgbaston	Australia won by 8 Wkts
696–280	19/08/1993	Australia	The Oval	England won by 161 runs
697–105	19/02/1994	West Indies	Kingston	West Indies won by 8 wkts
698–106	17/03/1994	West Indies	Georgetown	West Indies won by inns & 44 runs
699–107	25/03/1994	West Indies	Port-of-Spain	West Indies won by 147 runs
700–108	08/04/1994	West Indies	Bridgetown	England won by 208 runs
701–109	16/04/1994	West Indies	St John's	Match drawn
702–73	02/06/1994	New Zealand	Trent Bridge	England won by inns & 90 runs
703–74	16/06/1994	New Zealand	Lord's	Match drawn
704–75	30/06/1994	New Zealand	Old Trafford	Match drawn
705–103	21/07/1994	South Africa	Lord's	South Africa won by 356 runs
706–104	04/08/1994	South Africa	Headingley	Match drawn
707–105	18/08/1994	South Africa	The Oval	England won by 8 wkts
708–281	25/11/1994	Australia	Brisbane (2)	Australia won by 184 runs
709–282	24/12/1994	Australia	Melbourne	Australia won by 295 runs
710–283	01/01/1995	Australia	Sydney	Match drawn
711–284	26/01/1995	Australia	Adelaide	England won by 106 runs
712–285	03/02/1995	Australia	Perth	Australia won by 329 runs
713–110	08/06/1995	West Indies	Headingley	West Indies won by 9 wkts
714–111	22/06/1995	West Indies	Lord's	England won by 72 runs
715–112	06/07/1995	West Indies	Edgbaston	West Indies won by inns & 64 runs
716–113	27/07/1995	West Indies	Old Trafford	England won by 6 wkts
717–114	10/08/1995	West Indies	Trent Bridge	Match drawn
718–115	24/08/1995	West Indies	The Oval	Match drawn
719–106	16/11/1995	South Africa	Centurion	Match drawn
720–107	30/11/1995	South Africa	Johannesburg (3)	Match drawn
721–108	14/12/1995	South Africa	Durban (2)	Match drawn
722–109	26/12/1995	South Africa	Port Elizabeth	Match drawn
723–110	02/01/1996	South Africa	Cape Town	South Africa won by 10 wkts
724–82	06/06/1996	India	Edgbaston	England won by 8 wkts
725–83	20/06/1996	India	Lord's	Match drawn
726–84	04/07/1996	India	Trent Bridge	Match drawn
727–53	25/07/1996	Pakistan	Lord's	Pakistan won by 164 runs

No	First Day	Opposition	Venue	Result
728–54	08/08/1996	Pakistan	Headingley	Match drawn
729–55	22/08/1996	Pakistan	The Oval	Pakistan won by 9 wkts

SUMMARY OF TEST MATCH RESULTS

	Tests	Won	Drawn	Lost	% Won	% Drawn	% Lost
Australia	285	90	84	111	31.57	29.47	38.94
South Africa	110	47	43	20	42.72	39.09	18.18
West Indies	115	27	40	48	23.47	34.78	41.73
New Zealand	75	34	37	4	45.33	49.33	5.33
India	84	32	38	14	38.09	45.23	16.66
Pakistan	55	14	32	9	25.45	58.18	16.36
Sri Lanka	5	3	1	1	60.00	20.00	20.00
TOTAL	**729**	**247**	**275**	**207**	**33.88**	**37.72**	**28.39**

GREATEST VICTORIES

Victory by an innings

Margin of victory	Opposition	Venue	Date
Innings & 579 runs	Australia	The Oval	1938
Innings & 285 runs	India	Lord's	1974
Innings & 237 runs	West Indies	The Oval	1957
Innings & 230 runs	Australia	Adelaide	1891/92
Innings & 225 runs	Australia	Melbourne	1911/12
Innings & 217 runs	Australia	The Oval	1886
Innings & 215 runs	New Zealand	Auckland	1962/63
Innings & 207 runs	India	Old Trafford	1952
Innings & 202 runs	South Africa	Cape Town	1888/89
Innings & 197 runs	South Africa	Johannesburg (1)	1895/96
Innings & 189 runs	South Africa	Cape Town	1891/92
Innings & 187 runs	New Zealand	Headingley	1965
Innings & 173 runs	India	Headingley	1959
Innings & 170 runs	Australia	Old Trafford	1956
Innings & 157 runs	South Africa	Durban (1)	1913/14
Innings & 148 runs	New Zealand	Lord's	1958
Innings & 137 runs	Australia	The Oval	1888
Innings & 129 runs	Pakistan	Trent Bridge	1954
Innings & 124 runs	Australia	Sydney	1901/02
Innings & 124 runs	India	Lord's	1967
Innings & 120 runs	Pakistan	Lord's	1978
Innings & 119 runs	New Zealand	Trent Bridge	1978
Innings & 118 runs	Australia	Edgbaston	1985
Innings & 117 runs	Pakistan	Headingley	1962
Innings & 106 runs	Australia	Lord's	1886
Innings & 104 runs	South Africa	Durban (2)	1964/65
Innings & 99 runs	New Zealand	Christchurch	1958/59
Innings & 98 runs	Australia	Melbourne	1884/85
Innings & 94 runs	Australia	The Oval	1985
Innings & 93 runs	Australia	Sydney	1965/66
Innings & 90 runs	New Zealand	Trent Bridge	1994
Innings & 85 runs	Australia	Headingley	1977
Innings & 83 runs	New Zealand	Auckland	1974/75
Innings & 83 runs	India	Edgbaston	1979
Innings & 80 runs	Australia	Old Trafford	1905
Innings & 80 runs	Australia	Old Trafford	1905
Innings & 78 runs	India	Edgbaston	1974
Innings & 73 runs	South Africa	Lord's	1960
Innings & 71 runs	West Indies	The Oval	1928
Innings & 71 runs	New Zealand	Headingley	1958
Innings & 62 runs	South Africa	Lord's	1912
Innings & 59 runs	India	Trent Bridge	1959
Innings & 58 runs	West Indies	Lord's	1928
Innings & 57 runs	Pakistan	Edgbaston	1978
Innings & 47 runs	New Zealand	Wellington	1962/63
Innings & 43 runs	Australia	The Oval	1893
Innings & 42 runs	Australia	Headingley	1956
Innings & 38 runs	Australia	Lord's	1934
Innings & 36 runs	West Indies	Lord's	1957
Innings & 34 runs	West Indies	The Oval	1966
Innings & 33 runs	South Africa	Cape Town	1895/96
Innings & 32 runs	South Africa	Old Trafford	1929
Innings & 30 runs	West Indies	Old Trafford	1928

Margin of victory

Margin of victory	Opposition	Venue	Date
Innings & 29 runs	Australia	Melbourne	1924/25
Innings & 27 runs	Australia	Melbourne	1882/83
Innings & 27 runs	West Indies	Lord's	1933
Innings & 27 runs	India	The Oval	1959
Innings & 26 runs	New Zealand	The Oval	1931
Innings & 25 runs	India	Delhi	1976/77
Innings & 24 runs	Pakistan	Edgbaston	1962
Innings & 22 runs	Australia	Sydney	1936/37
Innings & 21 runs	Australia	Old Trafford	1888
Innings & 20 runs	New Zealand	Auckland	1954/55
Innings & 18 runs	South Africa	Edgbaston	1924
Innings & 18 runs	South Africa	Lord's	1924
Innings & 17 runs	West Indies	The Oval	1933
Innings & 14 runs	Australia	Melbourne	1986/87
Innings & 13 runs	South Africa	Durban (2)	1938/39
Innings & 13 runs	New Zealand	Old Trafford	1958
Innings & 12 runs	South Africa	Johannesburg (1)	1913/14
Innings & 5 runs	Australia	Lord's	1884
Innings & 5 runs	South Africa	Trent Bridge	1955
Innings & 5 runs	West Indies	Headingley	1957
Innings & 4 runs	Australia	Melbourne	1974/75
Innings & 4 runs	New Zealand	Christchurch	1991/92
Innings & 1 run	New Zealand	Headingley	1973

Ten Wicket Victories

Opposition	Venue	Date		1st wicket partnership
Australia	Melbourne	1884/85	7*	A.Shrewsbury & W.H.Scotton
Australia	Edgbaston	1909	105*	J.B.Hobbs & C.B.Fry
South Africa	The Oval	1912	14*	J.B.Hobbs & J.W.Hearne
South Africa	Port Elizabeth	1913/14	11*	J.B.Hobbs & W.Rhodes
South Africa	Johannesburg (1)	1927/28	57*	P.Holmes & H.Sutcliffe
Australia	Sydney	1932/33	1*	H.Sutcliffe & R.E.S.Wyatt
India	Lord's	1946	48*	L.Hutton & C.Washbrook
South Africa	Lord's	1947	26*	L.Hutton & C.Washbrook
South Africa	Headingley	1947	47*	L.Hutton & C.Washbrook
South Africa	Lord's	1951	16*	L.Hutton & J.T.Ikin
Pakistan	The Oval	1962	27*	Rev.D.S.Sheppard & J.T.Murray
Pakistan	Trent Bridge	1967	3*	G.Boycott & M.C.Cowdrey
West Indies	Old Trafford	1969	12*	G.Boycott & J.H.Edrich
India	Calcutta	1976/77	16*	D.L.Amiss & G.D.Barlow
India	Bombay (3)	1979/80	98*	G.A.Gooch & G.Boycott

Nine Wicket Victories

Opposition	Venue	Date		2nd wicket partnership
Australia	Sydney	1897/98	16*	A.C.MacLaren & K.S.Ranjitsinhji
South Africa	Cape Town	1909/10	16*	W.Rhodes & D.Denton
South Africa	Headingley	1924	43*	H.Sutcliffe & J.W.Hearne
India	Bombay (1)	1933/34	25*	C.F.Walters & C.J.Barnett
India	Lord's	1936	108*	H.Gimblett & M.J.L.Turnbull
India	The Oval	1936	16*	C.J.Barnett & W.R.Hammond
South Africa	Old Trafford	1951	21*	L.Hutton & R.T.Simpson
West Indies	Georgetown	1953/54	57*	W.Watson & T.W.Graveney
West Indies	Kingston	1953/54	72*	P.B.H.May & W.Watson
Pakistan	Lord's	1962	50*	M.J.Stewart & E.R.Dexter
New Zealand	Edgbaston	1965	4*	G.Boycott & E.R.Dexter
Australia	Headingley	1972	14*	B.W.Luckhurst & P.H.Parfitt
Australia	Old Trafford	1977	7*	D.L.Amiss & R.A.Woolmer
Australia	Sydney	1978/79	4*	J.M.Brearley & D.W.Randall
India	Madras (1)	1984/85	28*	R.T.Robinson & M.W.Gatting
West Indies	Kingston	1989/90	6*	W.Larkins & A.J.Stewart

Victory by 200 or more runs

Margin	Opposition	Venue	Date
675 runs	Australia	Brisbane (1)	1928/29
338 runs	Australia	Adelaide	1932/33
322 runs	Australia	Brisbane (2)	1936/37
312 runs	South Africa	Cape Town	1956/57
299 runs	Australia	Sydney	1970/71
289 runs	Australia	The Oval	1926
288 runs	South Africa	Port Elizabeth	1895/96
256 runs	West Indies	Port-of-Spain	1959/60

Margin	Opposition	Venue	Date
247 runs	India	Lord's	1990
244 runs	Australia	The Oval	1912
230 runs	New Zealand	Lord's	1969
226 runs	Australia	The Oval	1968
217 runs	West Indies	Edgbaston	1963
213 runs	Australia	Trent Bridge	1905
210 runs	South Africa	Cape Town	1898/99
208 runs	West Indies	Bridgetown	1993/94
205 runs	New Zealand	Edgbaston	1958
205 runs	Australia	Adelaide	1978/79
202 runs	India	Madras (1)	1933/34
202 runs	West Indies	Old Trafford	1950
200 runs	India	Madras (1)	1976/77

GREATEST VICTORIES AGAINST EACH OPPOSITION

Australia
Innings & 579 runs	The Oval	1938
Innings & 230 runs	Adelaide	1891/92
Innings & 225 runs	Melbourne	1911/12
Innings & 217 runs	The Oval	1886
Innings & 170 runs	Old Trafford	1956

South Africa
Innings & 202 runs	Cape Town	1888/89
Innings & 197 runs	Johannesburg (1)	1895/96
Innings & 189 runs	Cape Town	1891/92
Innings & 157 runs	Durban (1)	1913/14
Innings & 104 runs	Durban (2)	1964/65

West Indies
Innings & 237 runs	The Oval	1957
Innings & 71 runs	The Oval	1928
Innings & 58 runs	Lord's	1928
Innings & 36 runs	Lord's	1957
Innings & 34 runs	The Oval	1966

New Zealand
Innings & 215 runs	Auckland	1962/63
Innings & 187 runs	Headingley	1965
Innings & 148 runs	Lord's	1958
Innings & 119 runs	Trent Bridge	1978
Innings & 99 runs	Christchurch	1958/59

India
Innings & 285 runs	Lord's	1974
Innings & 207 runs	Old Trafford	1952
Innings & 173 runs	Headingley	1959
Innings & 124 runs	Lord's	1967
Innings & 83 runs	Edgbaston	1979

Pakistan
Innings & 129 runs	Trent Bridge	1954
Innings & 120 runs	Lord's	1978
Innings & 117 runs	Headingley	1962
Innings & 57 runs	Edgbaston	1978
Innings & 24 runs	Edgbaston	1962

Sri Lanka
7 wickets	Colombo (1)	1981/82
7 wickets	Lord's	1988
137 runs	Lord's	1991

GREATEST VICTORIES PER VENUE

ENGLAND (Victory by an innings or the single greatest victory at each venue)

The Oval
Innings & 579 runs	Australia	1938
Innings & 237 runs	West Indies	1957
Innings & 217 runs	Australia	1886
Innings & 137 runs	Australia	1888

Innings & 94 runs	Australia	1985
Innings & 71 runs	West Indies	1928
Innings & 43 runs	Australia	1893
Innings & 34 runs	West Indies	1966
Innings & 27 runs	India	1959
Innings & 26 runs	New Zealand	1931
Innings & 17 runs	West Indies	1933

Old Trafford

Innings & 207 runs	India	1952
Innings & 170 runs	Australia	1956
Innings & 80 runs	Australia	1905
Innings & 32 runs	South Africa	1929
Innings & 30 runs	West Indies	1928
Innings & 21 runs	Australia	1888
Innings & 13 runs	New Zealand	1958

Lord's

Innings & 285 runs	India	1974
Innings & 148 runs	New Zealand	1958
Innings & 124 runs	India	1967
Innings & 120 runs	Pakistan	1978
Innings & 106 runs	Australia	1886
Innings & 73 runs	South Africa	1960
Innings & 62 runs	South Africa	1912
Innings & 58 runs	West Indies	1928
Innings & 38 runs	Australia	1934
Innings & 36 runs	West Indies	1957
Innings & 27 runs	West Indies	1933
Innings & 18 runs	South Africa	1924
Innings & 5 runs	Australia	1884

Trent Bridge

Innings & 129 runs	Pakistan	1954
Innings & 119 runs	New Zealand	1978
Innings & 90 runs	New Zealand	1994
Innings & 59 runs	India	1959
Innings & 5 runs	South Africa	1955

Headingley

Innings & 187 runs	New Zealand	1965
Innings & 173 runs	India	1959
Innings & 117 runs	Pakistan	1962
Innings & 85 runs	Australia	1977
Innings & 71 runs	New Zealand	1958
Innings & 42 runs	Australia	1956
Innings & 5 runs	West Indies	1957
Innings & 1 run	New Zealand	1973

Edgbaston

Innings & 118 runs	Australia	1985
Innings & 83 runs	India	1979
Innings & 78 runs	India	1974
Innings & 57 runs	Pakistan	1978
Innings & 24 runs	Pakistan	1962
Innings & 18 runs	South Africa	1924

Bramall Lane
England have not won at Bramall Lane

AUSTRALIA

Melbourne

Innings & 225 runs	Australia	1911/12
Innings & 98 runs	Australia	1884/85
Innings & 29 runs	Australia	1924/25
Innings & 27 runs	Australia	1882/83
Innings & 14 runs	Australia	1987/88
Innings & 4 runs	Australia	1974/75

Sydney

Innings & 124 runs	Australia	1901/02
Innings & 93 runs	Australia	1965/66
Innings & 22 runs	Australia	1936/37

Adelaide
Innings & 230 runs   Australia   1891/92

Brisbane (1)
675 runs   Australia   1928/29

Brisbane (2)
322 runs   Australia   1936/37

Perth
166 runs   Australia   1978/79

SOUTH AFRICA

Port Elizabeth
10 wickets   South Africa   1913/14

Cape Town
Innings & 202 runs   South Africa   1888/89
Innings & 189 runs   South Africa   1891/92
Innings & 33 runs   South Africa   1895/96

Johannesburg (1)
Innings & 197 runs   South Africa   1895/96
Innings & 12 runs   South Africa   1913/14

Durban (1)
Innings & 157 runs   South Africa   1913/14

Durban (2)
Innings & 104 runs   South Africa   1964/65
Innings & 13 runs   South Africa   1938/39

Johannesburg (2)
England have not won at Johannesburg (2)

Johannesburg (3)
131 runs   South Africa   1956/57

Centurion
England have not won at Centurion

WEST INDIES

Bridgetown
208 runs   West Indies   1993/94

Port-of-Spain
256 runs   West Indies   1959/60

Georgetown
9 wickets   West Indies   1953/54

Kingston
9 wickets   West Indies   1953/54

St John's
England have not won at St John's

NEW ZEALAND

Christchurch
Innings & 99 runs   New Zealand   1958/59
Innings & 4 runs   New Zealand   1991/92

Wellington
Innings & 47 runs   New Zealand   1962/63

Auckland
Innings & 215 runs   New Zealand   1962/63
Innings & 83 runs   New Zealand   1974/75
Innings & 20 runs   New Zealand   1954/55

Dunedin
8 wickets   New Zealand   1954/55

INDIA

Bombay (1)
| 9 wickets | India | 1933/34 |

Calcutta
| 10 wickets | India | 1976/77 |

Madras (1)
| 9 wickets | India | 1984/85 |

Delhi
| Innings & 25 runs | India | 1976/77 |

Bombay (2)
England have not won at Bombay (2)

Kanpur
| 8 wickets | India | 1951/52 |

Madras (2)
England have not won at Madras (2)

Bangalore
England have not won at Bangalore

Bombay (3)
| 10 wickets | India | 1979/80 |

PAKISTAN

Dacca
England have not won at Dacca

Karachi (1)
England have not won at Karachi (1)

Lahore (2)
| 5 wickets | Pakistan | 1961/62 |

Hyderabad
England have not won at Hyderabad

Faisalabad
England have not won at Faisalabad

SRI LANKA

Colombo (1)
| 7 wickets | Sri Lanka | 1981/82 |

Colombo (2)
England have not won at Colombo (2)

NARROWEST VICTORIES

Victory by 30 or less runs

Margin	Opposition	Venue	Date
3 runs	Australia	Melbourne	1982/83
10 runs	Australia	Sydney	1894/95
12 runs	Australia	Adelaide	1928/29
13 runs	Australia	Sydney	1886/87
18 runs	Australia	Headingley	1981
25 runs	Pakistan	Headingley	1971
26 runs	West Indies	Port-of-Spain	1973/74
29 runs	Australia	Edgbaston	1981
30 runs	West Indies	Headingley	1969

One wicket victories

Opposition	Venue	Date		10th wicket partnership
Australia	The Oval	1902	15*	G.H.Hirst & W.Rhodes
Australia	Melbourne	1907/08	39*	S.F.Barnes & A.Fielder
South Africa	Cape Town	1922/23	5*	A.S.Kennedy & G.G.Macaulay

Two wicket victories

Opposition	Venue	Date		9th wicket partnership
Australia	The Oval	1890	2*	G.MacGregor & J.W.Sharpe
South Africa	Durban (2)	1948/49	12*	A.V.Bedser & C.Gladwin

HEAVIEST DEFEATS

Defeat by an innings

Margin of defeat	Opposition	Venue	Date
Innings & 332 runs	Australia	Brisbane (2)	1946/47
Innings & 226 runs	West Indies	Lord's	1973
Innings & 200 runs	Australia	Melbourne	1936/37
Innings & 180 runs	West Indies	Edgbaston	1984
Innings & 180 runs	Australia	Trent Bridge	1989
Innings & 161 runs	West Indies	Kingston	1934/35
Innings & 156 runs	West Indies	Old Trafford	1988
Innings & 154 runs	Australia	Brisbane (2)	1954/55
Innings & 149 runs	Australia	The Oval	1948
Innings & 148 runs	Australia	Headingley	1993
Innings & 147 runs	Australia	Sydney	1894/95
Innings & 132 runs	New Zealand	Christchurch	1983/84
Innings & 91 runs	Australia	Melbourne	1920/21
Innings & 87 runs	Pakistan	Lahore (2)	1987/88
Innings & 85 runs	Australia	Edgbaston	1975
Innings & 79 runs	West Indies	Port-of-Spain	1980/81
Innings & 64 runs	West Indies	Old Trafford	1984
Innings & 64 runs	West Indies	Edgbaston	1995
Innings & 62 runs	Australia	Lord's	1993
Innings & 56 runs	West Indies	The Oval	1950
Innings & 55 runs	Australia	Melbourne	1897/98
Innings & 55 runs	West Indies	Headingley	1966
Innings & 44 runs	West Indies	Georgetown	1993/94
Innings & 40 runs	West Indies	Old Trafford	1966
Innings & 39 runs	Australia	The Oval	1930
Innings & 33 runs	Australia	Sydney	1946/47
Innings & 32 runs	West Indies	St John's	1989/90
Innings & 30 runs	West Indies	Bridgetown	1985/86
Innings & 22 runs	India	Madras (1)	1992/93
Innings & 18 runs	Pakistan	Headingley	1987
Innings & 16 runs	South Africa	Cape Town	1905/06
Innings & 15 runs	India	Bombay (3)	1992/93
Innings & 13 runs	Australia	Adelaide	1897/98
Innings & 13 runs	Australia	Sydney	1950/51
Innings & 9 runs	Australia	Adelaide	1965/66
Innings & 8 runs	India	Madras (1)	1951/52

Ten wicket defeats

Opposition	Venue	Date		1st wicket partnership
Australia	Melbourne	1878/79	19*	C.Bannerman & W.L.Murdoch
Australia	Lord's	1899	28*	J.Worrall & J.Darling
Australia	Trent Bridge	1921	30*	W.Bardsley & C.G.Macartney
West Indies	Kingston	1947/48	76	J.D.C.Goddard & J.B.Stollmeyer
West Indies	Trent Bridge	1950	103*	A.F.Rae & J.B.Stollmeyer
Australia	Adelaide	1958/59	36*	J.W.Burke & L.E.Favell
West Indies	Old Trafford	1963	1*	C.C.Hunte & M.C.Carew
Pakistan	Lord's	1982	77*	Mohsin Khan & Javed Miandad
West Indies	Kingston	1985/86	5*	D.L.Haynes & R.B.Richardson
West Indies	Port-of-Spain	1985/86	39*	D.L.Haynes & R.B.Richardson
West Indies	Headingley	1988	67*	D.L.Haynes & P.J.L.Dujon
Australia	Brisbane (2)	1990/91	157*	G.R.Marsh & M.A.Taylor
Pakistan	The Oval	1992	5*	Aamir Sohail & Ramiz Raja
South Africa	Cape Town	1995/96	70*	G.Kirsten & A.C.Hudson

Nine wicket defeats

Opposition	Venue	Date		2nd wicket partnership
Australia	Melbourne	1882/83	58*	A.C.Bannerman & W.L.Murdoch
South Africa	Johannesburg (1)	1905/06	34*	L.J.Tancred & G.C.White
Australia	Lord's	1909	37*	P.A.McAlister & S.E.Gregory
Australia	Sydney	1920/21	2*	W.Bardsley & C.G.Macartney
Australia	Melbourne	1958/59	3*	C.C.McDonald & R.N.Harvey
Australia	Perth	1974/75	19*	I.R.Redpath & I.M.Chappell

Opposition	Venue	Date		2nd wicket partnership
West Indies	Lord's	1984	287*	C.G.Greenidge & H.A.Gomes
Australia	Old Trafford	1989	19*	M.A.Taylor & D.C.Boon
Australia	Perth	1990/91	81*	G.R.Marsh & D.C.Boon
West Indies	Trent Bridge	1991	114*	D.L.Haynes & R.B.Richardson
West Indies	Headingley	1995	118*	C.L.Hooper & B.C.Lara
Pakistan	The Oval	1996	41*	Aamir Sohail & Ijaz Ahmed

Defeat by 200 or more runs

Margin	Opposition	Venue	Date
562 runs	Australia	The Oval	1934
425 runs	West Indies	Old Trafford	1976
409 runs	Australia	Lord's	1948
382 runs	Australia	Adelaide	1894/95
377 runs	Australia	Sydney	1920/21
365 runs	Australia	Melbourne	1936/37
356 runs	South Africa	Lord's	1994
329 runs	Australia	Perth	1994/95
326 runs	West Indies	Lord's	1950
308 runs	Australia	Melbourne	1907/08
307 runs	Australia	Sydney	1924/25
298 runs	West Indies	Bridgetown	1980/81
295 runs	Australia	Melbourne	1994/95
289 runs	West Indies	Georgetown	1929/30
274 runs	Australia	Adelaide	1950/51
279 runs	India	Headingley	1986
245 runs	Australia	Adelaide	1907/08
243 runs	South Africa	Johannesburg (1)	1905/06
240 runs	West Indies	St John's	1985/86
238 runs	Australia	Trent Bridge	1934
231 runs	West Indies	The Oval	1976
229 runs	Australia	Melbourne	1901/02
224 runs	South Africa	Headingley	1955
221 runs	West Indies	Headingley	1963
219 runs	Australia	Headingley	1921
218 runs	Australia	Melbourne	1903/04
217 runs	West Indies	Port-of-Spain	1934/35
216 runs	Australia	Adelaide	1903/04
210 runs	Australia	Headingley	1989

HEAVIEST DEFEATS AGAINST EACH OPPOSITION

Australia

Innings & 332 runs	Brisbane (2)	1946/47
Innings & 200 runs	Melbourne	1936/37
Innings & 180 runs	Trent Bridge	1989
Innings & 154 runs	Brisbane (2)	1954/55
Innings & 149 runs	The Oval	1948

South Africa

Innings & 16 runs	Cape Town	1905/06
10 wickets	Cape Town	1995/96
9 wickets	Johannesburg (1)	1905/06
356 runs	Lord's	1994
243 runs	Johannesburg (1)	1905/06

West Indies

Innings & 226 runs	Lord's	1973
Innings & 180 runs	Edgbaston	1984
Innings & 161 runs	Kingston	1934/35
Innings & 156 runs	Old Trafford	1988
Innings & 79 runs	Port-of-Spain	1980/81

New Zealand

Innings & 132 runs	Christchurch	1983/84
8 wickets	Trent Bridge	1986
5 wickets	Headingley	1983
72 runs	Wellington	1977/78

India

Innings & 22 runs	Madras (1)	1992/93
Innings & 15 runs	Bombay (3)	1992/93
Innings & 8 runs	Madras (1)	1951/52
279 runs	Headingley	1986

| 8 wickets | Bombay (3) | 1984/85 |

Pakistan

Innings & 87 runs	Lahore (2)	1987/88
Innings & 18 runs	Headingley	1987
10 wickets	Lord's	1982
10 wickets	The Oval	1992
9 wickets	The Oval	1996

Sri Lanka

| 5 wickets | Colombo (2) | 1992/93 |

HEAVIEST DEFEATS PER VENUE

ENGLAND (Defeats by an innings or the single heaviest defeat at each venue)

The Oval

Innings & 149 runs	Australia	1948
Innings & 56 runs	West Indies	1950
Innings & 39 runs	Australia	1930

Old Trafford

Innings & 156 runs	West Indies	1988
Innings & 64 runs	West Indies	1984
Innings & 40 runs	West Indies	1966

Lord's

| Innings & 226 runs | West Indies | 1973 |
| Innings & 62 runs | Australia | 1993 |

Trent Bridge

| Innings & 180 runs | Australia | 1989 |

Headingley

Innings & 148 runs	Australia	1993
Innings & 55 runs	West Indies	1966
Innings & 18 runs	Pakistan	1987

Edgbaston

Innings & 180 runs	West Indies	1984
Innings & 85 runs	Australia	1975
Innings & 64 runs	West Indies	1995

Bramall Lane

| 143 runs | Australia | 1902 |

AUSTRALIA

Melbourne

Innings & 200 runs	Australia	1936/37
Innings & 91 runs	Australia	1920/21
Innings & 55 runs	Australia	1897/98

Sydney

Innings & 147 runs	Australia	1894/95
Innings & 33 runs	Australia	1946/47
Innings & 13 runs	Australia	1950/51

Adelaide

| Innings & 13 runs | Australia | 1897/98 |
| Innings & 9 runs | Australia | 1965/66 |

Brisbane (1)

England have not lost at Brisbane (1)

Brisbane (2)

| Innings & 332 runs | Australia | 1946/47 |
| Innings & 154 runs | Australia | 1954/55 |

Perth

| 9 wickets | Australia | 1990/91 |

SOUTH AFRICA

Port Elizabeth
58 runs | South Africa | 1956/57

Cape Town
Innings & 16 runs | South Africa | 1905/06

Johannesburg (1)
9 wickets | South Africa | 1905/06

Durban (1)
95 runs | South Africa | 1909/10

Durban (2)
8 wickets | South Africa | 1927/28

Johannesburg (2)
England have not lost at Johannesburg (2)

Johannesburg (3)
17 runs | South Africa | 1956/57

Centurion
England have not lost at Centurion

WEST INDIES

Bridgetown
Innings & 30 runs | West Indies | 1984/85

Port-of-Spain
Innings & 79 runs | West Indies | 1980/81

Georgetown
Innings & 44 runs | West Indies | 1993/94

Kingston
Innings & 161 runs | West Indies | 1934/35

St John's
Innings & 32 runs | West Indies | 1989/90

NEW ZEALAND

Christchurch
Innings & 132 runs | New Zealand | 1983/84

Wellington
72 runs | New Zealand | 1977/78

Auckland
England have not lost at Auckland

Dunedin
England have not lost at Dunedin

INDIA

Bombay (1)
England have not lost at Bombay (1)

Calcutta
8 wickets | India | 1992/93

Madras (1)
Innings & 22 runs | India | 1992/93
Innings & 8 runs | India | 1951/52

Delhi
England have not lost at Delhi

Bombay (2)
England have not lost at Bombay (2)

Kanpur
England have not lost at Kanpur

Madras (2)		
128 runs	India	1961/62

Bangalore		
140 runs	India	1976/77

Bombay (3)		
Innings & 15 runs	India	1992/93

PAKISTAN

Dacca
England have not lost at Dacca

Karachi (1)		
3 wickets	Pakistan	1983/84

Lahore (2)		
Innings & 87 runs	Pakistan	1987/88

Hyderabad
England have not lost at Hyderabad

Faisalabad
England have not lost at Faisalabad

SRI LANKA

Colombo (1)
England have not lost at Colombo (1)

Colombo (2)		
5 wickets	Sri Lanka	1992/93

NARROWEST DEFEATS

Defeat by 30 or less runs

Margin	Opposition	Venue	Date
3 runs	Australia	Old Trafford	1902
6 runs	Australia	Sydney	1884/85
7 runs	Australia	The Oval	1882
11 runs	Australia	Adelaide	1924/25
17 runs	South Africa	Johannesburg (3)	1956/57
19 runs	South Africa	Johannesburg (1)	1909/10
24 runs	Pakistan	The Oval	1954
28 runs	South Africa	Johannesburg (1)	1930/31
28 runs	Australia	Melbourne	1950/51
28 runs	India	Calcutta	1972/73

One wicket defeats

Opposition	Venue	Date		10th wicket partnership
South Africa	Johannesburg (1)	1905/06	48*	A.W.Nourse & P.W.Sherwell

Two wicket defeats

Opposition	Venue	Date		9th wicket partnership
Australia	Sydney	1907/08	56*	G.R.Hazlitt & A.Cotter
West Indies	Trent Bridge	1980	4*	A.M.E.Roberts & M.A.Holding
Pakistan	Lord's	1992	46*	Wasim Akram & Waqar Younis

MOST CONSECUTIVE VICTORIES

7 – 21/03/1885 – 10/02/1888

Australia	1884/85	1
Australia	1886	3
Australia	1886/87	2
Australia	1887/88	1

7 – 23/06/1928 – 01/02/1929

West Indies	1928	3
Australia	1928/29	4

MOST CONSECUTIVE DRAWS

7 – 10/01/1964 – 18/06/1964

India	1963/64	5
Australia	1964	2

7 – 07/12/1987 – 02/06/1988

Pakistan	1987/88	2
Australia	1987/88	1
New Zealand	1987/88	3
West Indies	1988	1

MOST CONSECUTIVE DEFEATS

8 – 17/12/1920 – 02/07/1921

Australia	1920/21	5
Australia	1921	3

7 – 24/06/1950 – 02/02/1951

West Indies	1950	3
Australia	1950/51	4

7 – 21/02/1986 – 19/06/1986

West Indies	1985/86	5
India	1986	2

7 – 06/08/1992 – 17/06/1993

Pakistan	1992	1
India	1992/93	3
Sri Lanka	1992/93	1
Australia	1993	2

MOST CONSECUTIVE MATCHES WITHOUT DEFEAT

26 matches 20/06/1968 – 05/08/1971

Australia	1968	4	Drew, Drew, Drew, Won
Pakistan	1968/69	3	Drew, Drew, Drew
West Indies	1969	3	Won, Drew, Won
New Zealand	1969	3	Won, Drew, Won
Australia	1970/71	6	Drew, Drew, Won, Drew, Drew, Won
New Zealand	1970/71	2	Won, Drew
Pakistan	1971	3	Drew, Drew, Won
India	1971	2	Drew, Drew

18 matches 27/02/1959 – 08/06/1961

New Zealand	1958/59	2	Won, Drew
India	1959	5	Won, Won, Won, Won, Won
West Indies	1959/60	5	Drew, Won, Drew, Drew, Drew
South Africa	1960	5	Won, Won, Won, Drew, Drew
Australia	1961	1	Drew

15 matches 30/12/1911 – 27/02/1914

Australia	1911/12	4	Won, Won, Won, Won
South Africa	1912	3	Won, Won, Won
Australia	1912	3	Drew, Drew, Won
South Africa	1913/14	5	Won, Won, Won, Drew, Won

12 matches 20/08/1938 – 17/08/1946

Australia	1938	1	Won
South Africa	1938/39	5	Drew, Drew, Won, Drew, Drew
West Indies	1939	3	Won, Drew, Drew
India	1946	3	Won, Drew, Drew

12 matches 18/08/1966 – 28/03/1968

West Indies	1966	1	Won
India	1967	3	Won, Won, Won
Pakistan	1967	3	Drew, Won, Won
West Indies	1967/68	5	Drew, Drew, Drew, Won, Drew

MOST CONSECUTIVE MATCHES WITHOUT A DRAW

22 – 12/12/1884 – 19/03/1892

Australia	1884/85	5	Won, Won, Lost, Lost, Won

Australia	1886	3	Won, Won, Won
Australia	1886/87	2	Won, Won
Australia	1887/88	1	Won
Australia	1888	3	Lost, Won, Won
South Africa	1888/89	2	Won, Won
Australia	1890	2	Won, Won
Australia	1891/92	3	Lost, Lost, Won
South Africa	1891/92	1	Won

18 – 14/12/1894 – 01/04/1899

Australia	1894/95	5	Won, Won, Lost, Lost, Won
South Africa	1895/96	3	Won, Won, Won
Australia	1896	3	Won, Lost, Won
Australia	1897/98	5	Won, Lost, Lost, Lost, Lost
South Africa	1898/99	2	Won, Won

MOST CONSECUTIVE MATCHES WITHOUT VICTORY

18 matches 10/01/1987 – 04/08/1988

Australia	1986/87	1	Lost
Pakistan	1987	5	Drew, Drew, Lost, Drew, Drew
Pakistan	1987/88	3	Lost, Drew, Drew
Australia	1987/88	1	Drew
New Zealand	1987/88	3	Drew, Drew, Drew
West Indies	1988	5	Drew, Lost, Lost, Lost, Lost

13 matches 20/01/1984 – 28/11/1984

New Zealand	1983/84	3	Drew, Lost, Drew
Pakistan	1983/84	3	Lost, Drew, Drew
West Indies	1984	5	Lost, Lost, Lost, Lost, Lost
Sri Lanka	1984	1	Drew
India	1984/85	1	Lost

12 matches 25/07/1963 – 13/08/1964

West Indies	1963	2	Lost, Lost
India	1963/64	5	Drew, Drew, Drew, Drew, Drew
Australia	1964	5	Drew, Drew, Lost, Drew, Drew

12 matches 05/06/1980 – 02/07/1981

West Indies	1980	5	Lost, Drew, Drew, Drew, Drew
Australia	1980	1	Drew
West Indies	1980/81	4	Lost, Lost, Drew, Drew
Australia	1981	2	Lost, Drew

MOST CONSECUTIVE VICTORIES AGAINST EACH OPPOSITION

Australia – 7 matches 21/03/1885 – 10/02/1888

1884/85	1
1886	3
1886/87	2
1887/88	1

South Africa – 8 matches 12/03/1889 – 01/04/1899

1888/89	2
1891/92	1
1895/96	3
1898/99	2

West Indies – 3 matches 23/06/1928 – 11/08/1928

1928	3

New Zealand – 7 matches 24/03/1951 – 24/07/1958

1950/51	1
1954/55	2
1958	4

India – 6 matches 06/06/1974 – 14/01/1977

1974	3
1976/77	3

Pakistan – 3 matches 31/05/1962 – 05/07/1962

1962	3

Sri Lanka – 2 matches 25/08/1988 – 22/08/1991

1988	1
1991	1

MOST CONSECUTIVE DEFEATS AGAINST EACH OPPOSITION

Australia – 8 matches 17/12/1920 – 02/07/1921
1920/21 5
1921 3

South Africa – 3 matches 02/01/1906 – 10/03/1906
1905/06 3

West Indies – 10 matches 14/06/1984 – 11/04/1986
1984 5
1985/86 5

New Zealand – 1 match on four separate occasions 10/02/1978, 28/07/1983, 03/02/1984, 07/08/1986
1977/78 1
1983 1
1983/84 1
1986 1

India – 3 matches 29/01/1993 – 19/02/1993
1992/93 3

Pakistan – 2 matches 06/08/1992 – 25/07/1996
1992 1
1996 1

Sri Lanka – 1 match – 13/03/1993
1992/93 1

MOST CONSECUTIVE MATCHES WITHOUT DEFEAT AGAINST EACH OPPOSITION

Australia – 11 matches 20/06/1968 – 08/06/1972
1968	4	Drew, Drew, Drew, Won
1970/71	6	Drew, Drew, Won, Drew, Drew, Won
1972	1	Won

South Africa – 18 matches 13/07/1935 – 05/03/1949
1935	3	Drew, Drew, Drew
1938/39	5	Drew, Drew, Won, Drew, Drew
1947	5	Drew, Won, Won, Won, Drew
1948/49	5	Won, Drew, Drew, Drew, Won

West Indies – 13 matches 24/02/1954 – 25/03/1960
1953/54	3	Won, Drew, Won
1957	5	Drew, Won, Drew, Won, Won
1959/60	5	Drew, Won, Drew, Drew, Drew

New Zealand – 47 matches 10/01/1930 – 28/02/1975
1929/30	4	Won, Drew, Drew, Drew
1931	3	Drew, Won, Drew
1932/33	2	Drew, Drew
1937	3	Drew, Won, Drew
1946/47	1	Drew
1949	4	Drew, Drew, Drew, Drew
1950/51	2	Drew, Won
1954/55	2	Won, Won
1958	5	Won, Won, Won, Won, Drew
1958/59	2	Won, Drew
1962/63	3	Won, Won, Won
1965	3	Won, Won, Won
1965/66	3	Drew, Drew, Drew
1969	3	Won, Drew, Won
1970/71	2	Won, Drew
1973	3	Won, Drew, Won
1974/75	2	Won, Drew

India – 14 matches 25/06/1932 – 12/01/1952
1932	1	Won
1933/34	3	Won, Drew, Won
1936	3	Won, Drew, Won
1946	3	Won, Drew, Drew
1951/52	4	Drew, Drew, Drew, Won

Pakistan – 30 matches 21/10/1961 – 29/07/1982

1961/62	3	Won, Drew, Drew
1962	5	Won, Won, Won, Drew, Won
1967	3	Drew, Won, Won
1968/69	3	Drew, Drew, Drew
1971	3	Drew, Drew, Won
1972/73	3	Drew, Drew, Drew
1974	3	Drew, Drew, Drew
1977/78	3	Drew, Drew, Drew
1978	3	Won, Won, Drew
1982	1	Won

Sri Lanka – 4 matches 17/02/1982 – 22/08/1991

1981/82	1	Won
1984	1	Drew
1988	1	Won
1991	1	Won

MOST CONSECUTIVE MATCHES WITHOUT VICTORY AGAINST EACH OPPOSITION

Australia – 18 matches 10/01/1987 – 05/08/1993

1986/87	1	Lost
1987/88	1	Drew
1989	6	Lost, Lost, Drew, Lost, Lost, Drew
1990/91	5	Lost, Lost, Drew, Drew, Lost
1993	5	Lost, Lost, Drew, Lost, Lost

South Africa – 13 matches 17/08/1929 – 31/12/1938

1929	1	Drew
1930/31	5	Lost, Drew, Drew, Drew, Drew
1935	5	Drew, Lost, Drew, Drew, Drew
1938/39	2	Drew, Drew

West Indies – 29 matches 03/06/1976 – 04/08/1988

1976	5	Drew, Drew, Lost, Lost, Lost
1980	5	Lost, Drew, Drew, Drew, Drew
1980/81	4	Lost, Lost, Drew, Drew
1984	5	Lost, Lost, Lost, Lost, Lost
1985/86	5	Lost, Lost, Lost, Lost, Lost
1988	5	Drew, Lost, Lost, Lost, Lost

New Zealand – 11 matches 20/01/1984 – 21/06/1990

1983/84	3	Drew, Lost, Drew
1986	3	Drew, Lost, Drew
1987/88	3	Drew, Drew, Drew
1990	2	Drew, Drew

India – 10 matches 11/11/1961 – 15/02/1964

1961/62	5	Drew, Drew, Drew, Lost, Lost
1963/64	5	Drew, Drew, Drew, Drew, Drew

Pakistan – 14 matches 02/03/1984 – 02/07/1992

1983/84	3	Lost, Drew, Drew
1987	5	Drew, Drew, Lost, Drew, Drew
1987/88	3	Lost, Drew, Drew
1992	3	Drew, Lost, Drew

Sri Lanka – 1 match (twice) 23/08/1984 & 13/03/1993

1984	1	Drew
1993	1	Lost

SERIES RESULTS 1877–1996

No	Date	Opposition	Tests	Won	Drawn	Lost	Series
1	1876/77	Australia	2	1	0	1	Drew 1–1
2	1878/79	Australia	1	0	0	1	Lost 0–1
3	1880	Australia	1	1	0	0	Won 1–0
4	1881/82	Australia	4	0	2	2	Lost 0–2
5	1882	Australia	1	0	0	1	Lost 0–1
6	1882/83	Australia	4	2	0	2	Drew 2–2
7	1884	Australia	3	1	2	0	Won 1–0
8	1884/85	Australia	5	3	0	2	Won 3–2
9	1886	Australia	3	3	0	0	Won 3–0
10	1886/87	Australia	2	2	0	0	Won 2–0
11	1887/88	Australia	1	1	0	0	Won 1–0
12	1888	Australia	3	2	0	1	Won 2–1

No	Date	Opposition	Tests	Won	Drawn	Lost	Series
13	1888/89	South Africa	2	2	0	0	Won 2–0
14	1890	Australia	2	2	0	0	Won 2–0
15	1891/92	Australia	3	1	0	2	Lost 1–2
16	1891/92	South Africa	1	1	0	0	Won 1–0
17	1893	Australia	3	1	2	0	Won 1–0
18	1894/95	Australia	5	3	0	2	Won 3–2
19	1895/96	South Africa	3	3	0	0	Won 3–0
20	1896	Australia	3	2	0	1	Won 2–1
21	1897/98	Australia	5	1	0	4	Lost 1–4
22	1898/99	South Africa	2	2	0	0	Won 2–0
23	1899	Australia	5	0	4	1	Lost 0–1
24	1901/02	Australia	5	1	0	4	Lost 1–4
25	1902	Australia	5	1	2	2	Lost 1–2
26	1903/04	Australia	5	3	0	2	Won 3–2
27	1905	Australia	5	2	3	0	Won 2–0
28	1905/06	South Africa	5	1	0	4	Lost 1–4
29	1907	South Africa	3	1	2	0	Won 1–0
30	1907/08	Australia	5	1	0	4	Lost 1–4
31	1909	Australia	5	1	2	2	Lost 1–2
32	1909/10	South Africa	5	2	0	3	Lost 2–3
33	1911/12	Australia	5	4	0	1	Won 4–1
34	1912	South Africa	3	3	0	0	Won 3–0
35	1912	Australia	3	1	2	0	Won 1–0
36	1913/14	South Africa	5	4	1	0	Won 4–0
37	1920/21	Australia	5	0	0	5	Lost 0–5
38	1921	Australia	5	0	2	3	Lost 0–3
39	1922/23	South Africa	5	2	2	1	Won 2–1
40	1924	South Africa	5	3	2	0	Won 3–0
41	1924/25	Australia	5	1	0	4	Lost 1–4
42	1926	Australia	5	1	4	0	Won 1–0
43	1927/28	South Africa	5	2	1	2	Drew 2–2
44	1928	West Indies	3	3	0	0	Won 3–0
45	1928/29	Australia	5	4	0	1	Won 4–1
46	1929	South Africa	5	2	3	0	Won 2–0
47	1929/30	New Zealand	4	1	3	0	Won 1–0
48	1929/30	West Indies	4	1	2	1	Drew 1–1
49	1930	Australia	5	1	2	2	Lost 1–2
50	1930/31	South Africa	5	0	4	1	Lost 0–1
51	1931	New Zealand	3	1	2	0	Won 1–0
52	1932	India	1	1	0	0	Won 1–0
53	1932/33	Australia	5	4	0	1	Won 4–1
54	1932/33	New Zealand	2	0	2	0	Drew 0–0
55	1933	West Indies	3	2	1	0	Won 2–0
56	1933/34	India	3	2	1	0	Won 2–0
57	1934	Australia	5	1	2	2	Lost 1–2
58	1934/35	West Indies	4	1	1	2	Lost 1–2
59	1935	South Africa	5	0	4	1	Lost 0–1
60	1936	India	3	2	1	0	Won 2–0
61	1936/37	Australia	5	2	0	3	Lost 2–3
62	1937	New Zealand	3	1	2	0	Won 1–0
63	1938	Australia	4	1	2	1	Drew 1–1
64	1938/39	South Africa	5	1	4	0	Won 1–0
65	1939	West Indies	3	1	2	0	Won 1–0
66	1946	India	3	1	2	0	Won 1–0
67	1946/47	Australia	5	0	2	3	Lost 0–3
68	1946/47	New Zealand	1	0	1	0	Drew 0–0
69	1947	South Africa	5	3	2	0	Won 3–0
70	1947/48	West Indies	4	0	2	2	Lost 0–2
71	1948	Australia	5	0	1	4	Lost 0–4
72	1948/49	South Africa	5	2	3	0	Won 2–0
73	1949	New Zealand	4	0	4	0	Drew 0–0
74	1950	West Indies	4	1	0	3	Lost 1–3
75	1950/51	Australia	5	1	0	4	Lost 1–4
76	1950/51	New Zealand	2	1	1	0	Won 1–0
77	1951	South Africa	5	3	1	1	Won 3–1
78	1951/52	India	5	1	3	1	Drew 1–1
79	1952	India	4	3	1	0	Won 3–0
80	1953	Australia	5	1	4	0	Won 1–0
81	1953/54	West Indies	5	2	1	2	Drew 2–2
82	1954	Pakistan	4	1	2	1	Drew 1–1
83	1954/55	Australia	5	3	1	1	Won 3–1
84	1954/55	New Zealand	2	2	0	0	Won 2–0
85	1955	South Africa	5	3	0	2	Won 3–2
86	1956	Australia	5	2	2	1	Won 2–1

No	Date	Opposition	Tests	Won	Drawn	Lost	Series
87	1956/57	South Africa	5	2	1	2	Drew 2–2
88	1957	West Indies	5	3	2	0	Won 3–0
89	1958	New Zealand	5	4	1	0	Won 4–0
90	1958/59	Australia	5	0	1	4	Lost 0–4
91	1958/59	New Zealand	2	1	1	0	Won 1–0
92	1959	India	5	5	0	0	Won 5–0
93	1959/60	West Indies	5	1	4	0	Won 1–0
94	1960	South Africa	5	3	2	0	Won 3–0
95	1961	Australia	5	1	2	2	Lost 1–2
96	1961/62	Pakistan	3	1	2	0	Won 1–0
97	1961/62	India	5	0	3	2	Lost 0–2
98	1962	Pakistan	5	4	1	0	Won 4–0
99	1962/63	Australia	5	1	3	1	Drew 1–1
100	1962/63	New Zealand	3	3	0	0	Won 3–0
101	1963	West Indies	5	1	1	3	Lost 1–3
102	1963/64	India	5	0	5	0	Drew 0–0
103	1964	Australia	5	0	4	1	Lost 0–1
104	1964/65	South Africa	5	1	4	0	Won 1–0
105	1965	New Zealand	3	3	0	0	Won 3–0
106	1965	South Africa	3	0	2	1	Lost 0–1
107	1965/66	Australia	5	1	3	1	Drew 1–1
108	1965/66	New Zealand	3	0	3	0	Drew 0–0
109	1966	West Indies	5	1	1	3	Lost 1–3
110	1967	India	3	3	0	0	Won 3–0
111	1967	Pakistan	3	2	1	0	Won 2–0
112	1967/68	West Indies	5	1	4	0	Won 1–0
113	1968	Australia	5	1	3	1	Drew 1–1
114	1968/69	Pakistan	3	0	3	0	Drew 0–0
115	1969	West Indies	3	2	1	0	Won 2–0
116	1969	New Zealand	3	2	1	0	Won 2–0
117	1970/71	Australia	6	2	4	0	Won 2–0
118	1970/71	New Zealand	2	1	1	0	Won 1–0
119	1971	Pakistan	3	1	2	0	Won 1–0
120	1971	India	3	0	2	1	Lost 0–1
121	1972	Australia	5	2	1	2	Drew 2–2
122	1972/73	India	5	1	2	2	Lost 1–2
123	1972/73	Pakistan	3	0	3	0	Drew 0–0
124	1973	New Zealand	3	2	1	0	Won 2–0
125	1973	West Indies	3	0	1	2	Lost 0–2
126	1973/74	West Indies	5	1	3	1	Drew 1–1
127	1974	India	3	3	0	0	Won 3–0
128	1974	Pakistan	3	0	3	0	Drew 0–0
129	1974/75	Australia	6	1	1	4	Lost 1–4
130	1974/75	New Zealand	2	1	1	0	Won 1–0
131	1975	Australia	4	0	3	1	Lost 0–1
132	1976	West Indies	5	0	2	3	Lost 0–3
133	1976/77	India	5	3	1	1	Won 3–1
134	1976/77	Australia	1	0	0	1	Lost 0–1
135	1977	Australia	5	3	2	0	Won 3–0
136	1977/78	Pakistan	3	0	3	0	Drew 0–0
137	1977/78	New Zealand	3	1	1	1	Drew 1–1
138	1978	Pakistan	3	2	1	0	Won 2–0
139	1978	New Zealand	3	3	0	0	Won 3–0
140	1978/79	Australia	6	5	0	1	Won 5–1
141	1979	India	4	1	3	0	Won 1–0
142	1979/80	Australia	3	0	0	3	Lost 0–3
143	1979/80	India	1	1	0	0	Won 1–0
144	1980	West Indies	5	0	4	1	Lost 0–1
145	1980	Australia	1	0	1	0	Drew 0–0
146	1980/81	West Indies	4	0	2	2	Lost 0–2
147	1981	Australia	6	3	2	1	Won 3–1
148	1981/82	India	6	0	5	1	Lost 0–1
149	1981/82	Sri Lanka	1	1	0	0	Won 1–0
150	1982	India	3	1	2	0	Won 1–0
151	1982	Pakistan	3	2	0	1	Won 2–1
152	1982/83	Australia	5	1	2	2	Lost 1–2
153	1983	New Zealand	4	3	0	1	Won 3–1
154	1983/84	New Zealand	3	0	2	1	Lost 0–1
155	1983/84	Pakistan	3	0	2	1	Lost 0–1
156	1984	West Indies	5	0	0	5	Lost 0–5
157	1984	Sri Lanka	1	0	1	0	Drew 0–0
158	1984/85	India	5	2	2	1	Won 2–1
159	1985	Australia	6	3	2	1	Won 3–1
160	1985/86	West Indies	5	0	0	5	Lost 0–5

No	Date	Opposition	Tests	Won	Drawn	Lost	Series
161	1986	India	3	0	1	2	Lost 0–2
162	1986	New Zealand	3	0	2	1	Lost 0–1
163	1986/87	Australia	5	2	2	1	Won 2–1
164	1987	Pakistan	5	0	4	1	Lost 0–1
165	1987/88	Pakistan	3	0	2	1	Lost 0–1
166	1987/88	Australia	1	0	1	0	Drew0–0
167	1987/88	New Zealand	3	0	3	0	Drew0–0
168	1988	West Indies	5	0	1	4	Lost 0–4
169	1988	Sri Lanka	1	1	0	0	Won 1–0
170	1989	Australia	6	0	2	4	Lost 0–4
171	1989/90	West Indies	4	1	1	2	Lost 1–2
172	1990	New Zealand	3	1	2	0	Won 1–0
173	1990	India	3	1	2	0	Won 1–0
174	1990/91	Australia	5	0	2	3	Lost 0–3
175	1991	West Indies	5	2	1	2	Drew2–2
176	1991	Sri Lanka	1	1	0	0	Won 1–0
177	1991/92	New Zealand	3	2	1	0	Won 2–0
178	1992	Pakistan	5	1	2	2	Lost 1–2
179	1992/93	India	3	0	0	3	Lost 0–3
180	1992/93	Sri Lanka	1	0	0	1	Lost 0–1
181	1993	Australia	6	1	1	4	Lost 1–4
182	1993/94	West Indies	5	1	1	3	Lost 1–3
183	1994	New Zealand	3	1	2	0	Won 1–0
184	1994	South Africa	3	1	1	1	Drew1–1
185	1994/95	Australia	5	1	1	3	Lost 1–3
186	1995	West Indies	6	2	2	2	Drew2–2
187	1995/96	South Africa	5	0	4	1	Lost 0–1
188	1996	India	3	1	2	0	Won 1–0
189	1996	Pakistan	3	0	1	2	Lost 0–2
	TOTAL		**729**	**247**	**275**	**207**	**93–31–65**

SERIES RESULTS AGAINST AUSTRALIA 1877–1995

No	Date	Tests	Won	Drawn	Lost	Series	
1	1876/77	2	1	0	1	Drew	1–1
2	1878/79	1	0	0	1	Lost	0–1
3	1880	1	1	0	0	Won	1–0
4	1881/82	4	0	2	2	Lost	0–2
5	1882	1	0	0	1	Lost	0–1
6	1882/83	4	2	0	2	Drew	2–2
7	1884	3	1	2	0	Won	1–0
8	1884/85	5	3	0	2	Won	3–2
9	1886	3	3	0	0	Won	3–0
10	1886/87	2	2	0	0	Won	2–0
11	1887/88	1	1	0	0	Won	1–0
12	1888	3	2	0	1	Won	2–1
13	1890	2	2	0	0	Won	2–0
14	1891/92	3	1	0	2	Lost	1–2
15	1893	3	1	2	0	Won	1–0
16	1894/95	5	3	0	2	Won	3–2
17	1896	3	2	0	1	Won	2–1
18	1897/98	5	1	0	4	Lost	1–4
19	1899	5	0	4	1	Lost	0–1
20	1901/02	5	1	0	4	Lost	1–4
21	1902	5	1	2	2	Lost	1–2
22	1903/04	5	3	0	2	Won	3–2
23	1905	5	2	3	0	Won	2–0
24	1907/08	5	1	0	4	Lost	1–4
25	1909	5	1	2	2	Lost	1–2
26	1911/12	5	4	0	1	Won	4–1
27	1912	3	1	2	0	Won	1–0
28	1920/21	5	0	0	5	Lost	0–5
29	1921	5	0	2	3	Lost	0–3
30	1924/25	5	1	0	4	Lost	1–4
31	1926	5	1	4	0	Won	1–0
32	1928/29	5	4	0	1	Won	4–1
33	1930	5	1	2	2	Lost	1–2
34	1932/33	5	4	0	1	Won	4–1
35	1934	5	1	2	2	Lost	1–2
36	1936/37	5	2	0	3	Lost	2–3
37	1938	4	1	2	1	Drew	1–1
38	1946/47	5	0	2	3	Lost	0–3
39	1948	5	0	1	4	Lost	0–4
40	1950/51	5	1	0	4	Lost	1–4

No	Date	Tests	Won	Drawn	Lost	Series	
41	1953	5	1	4	0	Won	1–0
42	1954/55	5	3	1	1	Won	3–1
43	1956	5	2	2	1	Won	2–1
44	1958/59	5	0	1	4	Lost	0–4
45	1961	5	1	2	2	Lost	1–2
46	1962/63	5	1	3	1	Drew	1–1
47	1964	5	0	4	1	Lost	0–1
48	1965/66	5	1	3	1	Drew	1–1
49	1968	5	1	3	1	Drew	1–1
50	1970/71	6	2	4	0	Won	2–0
51	1972	5	2	1	2	Drew	2–2
52	1974/75	6	1	1	4	Lost	1–4
53	1975	4	0	3	1	Lost	0–1
54	1976/77	1	0	0	1	Lost	0–1
55	1977	5	3	2	0	Won	3–0
56	1978/79	6	5	0	1	Won	5–1
57	1979/80	3	0	0	3	Lost	0–3
58	1980	1	0	1	0	Drew	0–0
59	1981	6	3	2	1	Won	3–1
60	1982/83	5	1	2	2	Lost	1–2
61	1985	6	3	2	1	Won	3–1
62	1986/87	5	2	2	1	Won	2–1
63	1987/88	1	0	1	0	Drew	0–0
64	1989	6	0	2	4	Lost	0–4
65	1990/91	5	0	2	3	Lost	0–3
66	1993	6	1	1	4	Lost	1–4
67	1994/95	5	1	1	3	Lost	1–3
	TOTAL	285	90	84	111	27–9–31	

SERIES RESULTS AGAINST SOUTH AFRICA 1889–1996

No	Date	Tests	Won	Drawn	Lost	Series	
1	1888/89	2	2	0	0	Won	2–0
2	1891/92	1	1	0	0	Won	1–0
3	1895/96	3	3	0	0	Won	3–0
4	1898/99	2	2	0	0	Won	2–0
5	1905/06	5	1	0	4	Lost	1–4
6	1907	3	1	2	0	Won	1–0
7	1909/10	5	2	0	3	Lost	2–3
8	1912	3	3	0	0	Won	3–0
9	1913/14	5	4	1	0	Won	4–0
10	1922/23	5	2	2	1	Won	2–1
11	1924	5	3	2	0	Won	3–0
12	1927/28	5	2	1	2	Drew	2–2
13	1929	5	2	3	0	Won	2–0
14	1930/31	5	0	4	1	Lost	0–1
15	1935	5	0	4	1	Lost	0–1
16	1938/39	5	1	4	0	Won	1–0
17	1947	5	3	2	0	Won	3–0
18	1948/49	5	2	3	0	Won	2–0
19	1951	5	3	1	1	Won	3–1
20	1955	5	3	0	2	Won	3–2
21	1956/57	5	2	1	2	Drew	2–2
22	1960	5	3	2	0	Won	3–0
23	1964/65	5	1	4	0	Won	1–0
24	1965	3	0	2	1	Lost	0–1
25	1994	3	1	1	1	Drew	1–1
26	1995/95	5	0	4	1	Lost	0–1
	TOTAL	110	47	43	20	17–3–6	

SERIES RESULTS AGAINST THE WEST INDIES 1928–1995

No	Date	Tests	Won	Drawn	Lost	Series	
1	1928	3	3	0	0	Won	3–0
2	1929/30	4	1	2	1	Drew	1–1
3	1933	3	2	1	0	Won	2–0
4	1934/35	4	1	1	2	Lost	1–2
5	1939	3	1	2	0	Won	1–0
6	1947/48	4	0	2	2	Lost	0–2
7	1950	4	1	0	3	Lost	1–3
8	1953/54	5	2	1	2	Drew	2–2
9	1957	5	3	2	0	Won	3–0
10	1959/60	5	1	4	0	Won	1–0
11	1963	5	1	1	3	Lost	1–3
12	1966	5	1	1	3	Lost	1–3

13	1967/68	5	1	4	0	Won	1–0
14	1969	3	2	1	0	Won	2–0
15	1973	3	0	1	2	Lost	0–2
16	1973/74	5	1	3	1	Drew	1–1
17	1976	5	0	2	3	Lost	0–3
18	1980	5	0	4	1	Lost	0–1
19	1980/81	4	0	2	2	Lost	0–2
20	1984	5	0	0	5	Lost	0–5
21	1985/86	5	0	0	5	Lost	0–5
22	1988	5	0	1	4	Lost	0–4
23	1989/90	4	1	1	2	Lost	1–2
24	1991	5	2	1	2	Drew	2–2
25	1993/94	5	1	1	3	Lost	1–3
26	1995	6	2	2	2	Drew	2–2
	TOTAL	**115**	**27**	**40**	**48**	**7-5-14**	

SERIES RESULTS AGAINST NEW ZEALAND 1930–1994

No	Date	Tests	Won	Drawn	Lost	Series	
1	1929/30	4	1	3	0	Won	1–0
2	1931	3	1	2	0	Won	1–0
3	1932/33	2	0	2	0	Drew	0–0
4	1937	3	1	2	0	Won	1–0
5	1946/47	1	0	1	0	Drew	0–0
6	1949	4	0	4	0	Drew	0–0
7	1950/51	2	1	1	0	Won	1–0
8	1954/55	2	2	0	0	Won	2–0
9	1958	5	4	1	0	Won	4–0
10	1958/59	2	1	1	0	Won	1–0
11	1962/63	3	3	0	0	Won	3–0
12	1965	3	3	0	0	Won	3–0
13	1965/66	3	0	3	0	Drew	0–0
14	1969	3	2	1	0	Won	2–0
15	1970/71	2	1	1	0	Won	1–0
16	1973	3	2	1	0	Won	2–0
17	1974/75	2	1	1	0	Won	1–0
18	1977/78	3	1	1	1	Drew	1–1
19	1978	3	3	0	0	Won	3–0
20	1983	4	3	0	1	Won	3–1
21	1983/84	3	0	2	1	Lost	0–1
22	1986	3	0	2	1	Lost	0–1
23	1987/88	3	0	3	0	Drew	0–0
24	1990	3	1	2	0	Won	1–0
25	1991/92	3	2	1	0	Won	2–0
26	1994	3	1	2	0	Won	1–0
	TOTAL	**75**	**34**	**37**	**4**	**18–6–2**	

SERIES RESULTS AGAINST INDIA 1932–1996

No	Date	Tests	Won	Drawn	Lost	Series	
1	1932	1	1	0	0	Won	1–0
2	1933/34	3	2	1	0	Won	2–0
3	1936	3	2	1	0	Won	2–0
4	1946	3	1	2	0	Won	1–0
5	1951/52	5	1	3	1	Drew	1–1
6	1952	4	3	1	0	Won	3–0
7	1959	5	5	0	0	Won	5–0
8	1961/62	5	0	3	2	Lost	0–2
9	1963/64	5	0	5	0	Drew	0–0
10	1967	3	3	0	0	Won	3–0
11	1971	3	0	2	1	Lost	0–1
12	1972/73	5	1	2	2	Lost	1–2
13	1974	3	3	0	0	Won	3–0
14	1976/77	5	3	1	1	Won	3–1
15	1979	4	1	3	0	Won	1–0
16	1979/80	1	1	0	0	Won	1–0
17	1981/82	6	0	5	1	Lost	0–1
18	1982	3	1	2	0	Won	1–0
19	1984/85	5	2	2	1	Won	2–1
20	1986	3	0	1	2	Lost	0–2
21	1990	3	1	2	0	Won	1–0
22	1992/93	3	0	0	3	Lost	0–3
23	1996	3	1	2	0	Won	1–0
	TOTAL	**84**	**32**	**38**	**14**	**15–2–6**	

SERIES RESULTS AGAINST PAKISTAN 1954–1996

No	Date	Tests	Won	Drawn	Lost	Series	
1	1954	4	1	2	1	Drew	1–1
2	1961/62	3	1	2	0	Won	1–0
3	1962	5	4	1	0	Won	4–0
4	1967	3	2	1	0	Won	2–0
5	1968/69	3	0	3	0	Drew	0–0
6	1971	3	1	2	0	Won	1–0
7	1972/73	3	0	3	0	Drew	0–0
8	1974	3	0	3	0	Drew	0–0
9	1977/78	3	0	3	0	Drew	0–0
10	1978	3	2	1	0	Won	2–0
11	1982	3	2	0	1	Won	2–1
12	1983/84	3	0	2	1	Lost	0–1
13	1987	5	0	4	1	Lost	0–1
14	1987/88	3	0	2	1	Lost	0–1
15	1992	5	1	2	2	Lost	1–2
16	1996	3	0	1	2	Lost	0–2
	TOTAL	55	14	32	9	6–5–5	

SERIES RESULTS AGAINST SRI LANKA 1982–1993

No	Date	Tests	Won	Drawn	Lost	Series	
1	1981/82	1	1	0	0	Won	1–0
2	1984	1	0	1	0	Drew	0–0
3	1988	1	1	0	0	Won	1–0
4	1991	1	1	0	0	Won	1–0
5	1992/93	1	0	0	1	Lost	0–1
	TOTAL	5	3	1	1	3–1–1	

SUMMARY OF SERIES RESULTS (Including Single Tests)

Opponents	Series	Won	Drew	Lost	% Won	% Drawn	% Lost
Australia	67	27	9	31	40.29	13.43	46.26
South Africa	26	17	3	6	65.38	11.53	23.07
West Indies	26	7	5	14	26.92	19.23	53.84
New Zealand	26	18	6	2	69.23	23.07	7.69
India	23	15	2	6	65.21	8.69	26.08
Pakistan	16	6	5	5	37.50	31.25	31.25
Sri Lanka	5	3	1	1	60.00	20.00	20.00
TOTAL	189	93	31	65	49.20	16.40	34.39

TEST MATCH RESULTS PER VENUE

England	Tests	Won	Drawn	Lost	% Won	% Drawn	% Lost
The Oval	79	31	33	15	39.24	41.77	18.98
Old Trafford	61	19	30	12	31.14	49.18	19.67
Lord's	94	34	38	22	36.17	40.42	23.40
Trent Bridge	43	12	19	12	27.90	44.18	27.90
Headingley	58	24	17	17	41.37	29.31	29.31
Edgbaston	32	16	11	5	50.00	34.37	15.62
Bramall Lane	1	0	0	1	0.00	0.00	100.00
Total	368	136	148	84	36.95	40.21	22.82

Australia	Tests	Won	Drawn	Lost	% Won	% Drawn	% Lost
Melbourne	50	18	7	25	36.00	14.00	50.00
Sydney	50	20	7	23	40.00	14.00	46.00
Adelaide	26	8	5	13	30.76	19.23	50.00
Brisbane (1)	1	1	0	0	100.00	0.00	0.00
Brisbane (2)	15	4	3	8	26.66	20.00	53.33
Perth	8	1	3	4	12.50	37.50	50.00
Total	150	52	25	73	34.66	16.66	48.66

South Africa	Tests	Won	Drawn	Lost	% Won	% Drawn	% Lost
Port Elizabeth	7	4	2	1	57.14	28.57	14.28
Cape Town	16	9	4	3	56.25	25.00	18.75
Johannesburg (1)	17	6	4	7	35.29	23.52	41.17
Durban (1)	3	1	1	1	33.33	33.33	33.33
Durban (2)	12	4	7	1	33.33	58.33	8.33
Johannesburg (2)	2	0	2	0	0.00	100.00	0.00
Johannesburg (3)	5	1	3	1	20.00	60.00	20.00
Centurion	1	0	1	0	0.00	100.00	0.00
Total	63	25	24	14	39.68	38.09	22.22

West Indies	Tests	Won	Drew	Lost	% Won	% Drawn	% Lost
Bridgetown	11	2	5	4	18.18	45.45	36.36
Port-of-Spain	15	4	5	6	26.66	33.33	40.00
Georgetown	8	1	4	3	12.50	50.00	37.50
Kingston	12	2	5	5	16.66	41.66	41.66
St Johns	4	0	2	2	0.00	50.00	50.00
Total	**50**	**9**	**21**	**20**	**18.00**	**42.00**	**40.00**

New Zealand	Tests	Won	Drew	Lost	% Won	% Drawn	% Lost
Christchurch	13	6	6	1	46.15	46.15	7.69
Wellington	7	2	4	1	28.57	57.14	14.28
Auckland	13	4	9	0	30.76	69.23	0.00
Dunedin	2	1	1	0	50.00	50.00	0.00
Total	**35**	**13**	**20**	**2**	**37.14**	**57.14**	**5.71**

India	Tests	Won	Drew	Lost	% Won	% Drawn	% Lost
Bombay (1)	1	1	0	0	100.00	0.00	0.00
Calcutta	9	1	5	3	11.11	55.55	33.33
Madras (1)	7	3	1	3	42.85	14.28	42.85
Delhi	7	3	4	0	42.85	57.14	0.00
Bombay (2)	4	0	4	0	0.00	100.00	0.00
Kanpur	6	1	5	0	16.66	83.33	0.00
Madras (2)	2	0	1	1	0.00	50.00	50.00
Bangalore	2	0	1	1	0.00	50.00	50.00
Bombay (3)	5	1	1	3	20.00	20.00	60.00
Total	**43**	**10**	**22**	**11**	**23.25**	**51.16**	**25.58**

Pakistan	Tests	Won	Drew	Lost	% Won	% Drawn	% Lost
Dacca	2	0	2	0	0.00	100.00	0.00
Karachi (1)	6	0	5	1	0.00	83.33	16.66
Lahore (2)	6	1	4	1	16.66	66.66	16.66
Hyderabad	2	0	2	0	0.00	100.00	0.00
Faisalabad	2	0	2	0	0.00	100.00	0.00
Total	**18**	**1**	**15**	**2**	**5.55**	**83.33**	**11.11**

Sri Lanka	Tests	Won	Drew	Lost	% Won	% Drawn	% Lost
Colombo (1)	1	1	0	0	100.00	0.00	0.00
Colombo (2)	1	0	0	1	0.00	0.00	100.00
Total	**2**	**1**	**0**	**1**	**50.00**	**0.00**	**50.00**

	Tests	Won	Drew	Lost	% Won	% Drawn	% Lost
Home	368	136	148	84	36.95	40.21	22.82
Abroad	361	111	127	123	30.74	35.18	34.07
Total	**729**	**247**	**275**	**207**	**33.88**	**37.72**	**28.39**

Totals

HIGHEST TOTALS

Total	Inns	Opposition	Venue	Date
903 for 7 declared	1st	Australia	The Oval	1938
849	1st	West Indies	Kingston	1929/30
658 for 8 declared	1st	Australia	Trent Bridge	1938
654 for 5	4th	South Africa	Durban (2)	1938/39
653 for 4 declared	1st	India	Lord's	1990
652 for 7 declared	2nd	India	Madras (1)	1984/85
636	2nd	Australia	Sydney	1928/29
633 for 5 declared	1st	India	Edgbaston	1979
629	1st	India	Lord's	1974
627 for 9 declared	1st	Australia	Old Trafford	1934
619 for 6 declared	1st	West Indies	Trent Bridge	1957
611	2nd	Australia	Old Trafford	1964
608	1st	South Africa	Johannesburg (2)	1948/49
595 for 5 declared	2nd	Australia	Edgbaston	1985
594	1st	India	The Oval	1982
593 for 6 declared	1st	New Zealand	Auckland	1974/75
593	2nd	West Indies	St John's	1993/94
592 for 8 declared	1st	Australia	Perth	1986/87
589	2nd	Australia	Melbourne	1911/12
583 for 4 declared	3rd	West Indies	Edgbaston	1957
580 for 9 declared	1st	New Zealand	Christchurch	1991/92

Total	Inns	Opposition	Venue	Date
577	2nd	Australia	Sydney	1903/04
576	1st	Australia	The Oval	1899
571 for 8 declared	2nd	India	Old Trafford	1936
568	1st	West Indies	Port-of-Spain	1967/68
567 for 8 declared	2nd	New Zealand	Trent Bridge	1994
564 for 9 declared	2nd	India	Trent Bridge	1996
562 for 7 declared	1st	New Zealand	Auckland	1962/63
560 for 8 declared	1st	New Zealand	Christchurch	1932/33
559 for 8 declared	1st	India	Kanpur	1963/64
559 for 9 declared	1st	South Africa	Cape Town	1938/39
558 for 6 declared	2nd	Pakistan	Trent Bridge	1954
558	2nd	Australia	Melbourne	1965/66
554 for 8 declared	1st	South Africa	Lord's	1947
551	1st	Australia	Sydney	1897/98
551	3rd	South Africa	Trent Bridge	1947
550 for 4 declared	1st	India	Headingley	1967
550	2nd	New Zealand	Christchurch	1950/51
548 for 7 declared	2nd	New Zealand	Auckland	1932/33
548	1st	Australia	Melbourne	1924/25
546 for 4 declared	1st	New Zealand	Headingley	1965
546 for 8 declared	2nd	Pakistan	Faisalabad	1983/84
545	2nd	Pakistan	The Oval	1974
544 for 5 declared	1st	Pakistan	Edgbaston	1962
540	1st	New Zealand	Auckland	1929/30
538	3rd	Australia	The Oval	1975
537	2nd	India	Lord's	1952
537	2nd	West Indies	Port-of-Spain	1953/54
534 for 6 declared	2nd	South Africa	The Oval	1935
533	2nd	Australia	Headingley	1985
531 for 2 declared	2nd	South Africa	Lord's	1924
531	1st	South Africa	Johannesburg (3)	1964/65
529	2nd	Australia	Melbourne	1974/75
527	2nd	West Indies	The Oval	1966
524	2nd	Australia	Sydney	1932/33
521	2nd	Australia	Brisbane (1)	1928/29
521	1st	Pakistan	Edgbaston	1987
519	1st	Australia	Melbourne	1928/29
519	1st	India	Old Trafford	1990
507	2nd	Pakistan	Karachi (1)	1961/62
505	2nd	South Africa	Headingley	1951
502 for 7 declared	1st	Pakistan	Karachi (1)	1968/69
501	2nd	Australia	Adelaide	1911/12
501	2nd	Pakistan	Headingley	1996
500 for 8 declared	1st	India	Bombay (2)	1961/62
499	1st	Australia	Adelaide	1891/92
497 for 5 declared	3rd	India	Kanpur	1961/62
496	1st	Australia	Headingley	1948
494	1st	Australia	Lord's	1938
494	1st	Australia	The Oval	1968
490	1st	India	Old Trafford	1959
488	1st	Australia	Sydney	1965/66
487	1st	Pakistan	Hyderabad	1972/73
485 for 5 declared	1st	South Africa	Durban (2)	1964/65
485 for 9 declared	1st	Australia	Melbourne	1965/66
483 for 8 declared	2nd	India	Headingley	1959
483	1st	Australia	The Oval	1893
482 for 9 declared	2nd	Australia	Old Trafford	1985
482	1st	South Africa	Johannesburg (1)	1895/96
482	2nd	New Zealand	The Oval	1949
482	1st	West Indies	Bridgetown	1959/60
480 for 5 declared	1st	Pakistan	The Oval	1962
480	2nd	India	Bombay (2)	1972/73
479 for 9 declared	3rd	South Africa	The Oval	1960
479	2nd	Australia	Melbourne	1924/25
478	2nd	South Africa	Old Trafford	1947
477 for 4 declared	3rd	India	The Oval	1990
477 for 9 declared	1st	South Africa	Headingley	1994
476 for 9 declared	1st	India	Delhi	1981/82
475 for 3 declared	2nd	Australia	Lord's	1926
475	3rd	Australia	Melbourne	1894/95
471 for 8 declared	1st	India	The Oval	1936
470	1st	Australia	Adelaide	1970/71
469 for 4 declared	1st	South Africa	Durban (2)	1938/39
469 for 8 declared	2nd	Australia	Sydney	1990/91

Total	Inns	Opposition	Venue	Date
467	2nd	West Indies	Bridgetown	1929/30
464	1st	Australia	Sydney	1901/02
464	2nd	Australia	Brisbane (2)	1970/71
464	1st	Australia	The Oval	1985
463 for 9 declared	3rd	New Zealand	Lord's	1973
463	2nd	New Zealand	Wellington	1983/84
460	1st	Australia	Adelaide	1946/47
459 for 2 declared	2nd	India	Edgbaston	1974
459 for 7 declared	2nd	Pakistan	Edgbaston	1992
459	1st	Australia	Old Trafford	1956
456	2nd	India	Bombay (2)	1951/52
456	1st	Australia	Trent Bridge	1985
456	1st	Australia	Brisbane (2)	1986/87
455	2nd	Australia	Adelaide	1986/87
454	2nd	New Zealand	Lord's	1931
454	2nd	Australia	Sydney	1932/33
454	1st	West Indies	The Oval	1995
452 for 8 declared	2nd	Pakistan	Edgbaston	1978
451 for 8 declared	2nd	New Zealand	Trent Bridge	1969
451	2nd	India	Delhi	1963/64
450	2nd	South Africa	Durban (1)	1913/14

HIGHEST TOTALS PER INNINGS

First innings

903 for 7 declared	Australia	The Oval	1938
849	West Indies	Kingston	1929/30
658 for 8 declared	Australia	Trent Bridge	1938
653 for 4 declared	India	Lord's	1990
633 for 5 declared	India	Edgbaston	1979
629	India	Lord's	1974
627 for 9 declared	Australia	Old Trafford	1934
619 for 6 declared	West Indies	Trent Bridge	1957
608	South Africa	Johannesburg (2)	1948/49
594	India	The Oval	1982

Second innings

652 for 7 declared	India	Madras (1)	1984/85
636	Australia	Sydney	1928/29
611	Australia	Old Trafford	1964
595 for 5 declared	Australia	Edgbaston	1985
593	West Indies	St John's	1993/94
589	Australia	Melbourne	1911/12
577	Australia	Sydney	1903/04
571 for 8 declared	India	Old Trafford	1936
567 for 8 declared	New Zealand	Trent Bridge	1994
564 for 9 declared	India	Trent Bridge	1996

Third innings

583 for 4 declared	West Indies	Edgbaston	1957
551	South Africa	Trent Bridge	1947
538	Australia	The Oval	1975
497 for 5 declared	India	Kanpur	1961/62
479 for 9 declared	South Africa	The Oval	1960
477 for 4 declared	India	The Oval	1990
475	Australia	Melbourne	1894/95
463 for 9 declared	New Zealand	Lord's	1973
446 for 6 declared	New Zealand	The Oval	1983
441	Australia	Trent Bridge	1948

Fourth innings

654 for 5	South Africa	Durban (2)	1938/39
417	Australia	Melbourne	1976/77
411	Australia	Sydney	1924/25
370	Australia	Adelaide	1920/21
363	Australia	Adelaide	1924/25
351 for 5	South Africa	Johannesburg (3)	1995/96
335 for 5	Australia	Adelaide	1990/91
332 for 7	Australia	Melbourne	1928/29
332	Australia	Old Trafford	1993
327	West Indies	Georgetown	1929/30

HIGHEST TOTALS AGAINST EACH OPPOSITION

(All totals above 500 or the single highest total against each country)

Australia

903 for 7 declared	1st	The Oval	1938
658 for 8 declared	1st	Trent Bridge	1938
636	2nd	Sydney	1928/29
627 for 9 declared	1st	Old Trafford	1934
611	2nd	Old Trafford	1964
595 for 5 declared	2nd	Edgbaston	1985
592 for 8 declared	1st	Perth	1986/87
589	2nd	Melbourne	1911/12
577	2nd	Sydney	1903/04
576	1st	The Oval	1899
558	2nd	Melbourne	1965/66
551	1st	Sydney	1897/98
548	1st	Melbourne	1924/25
538	3rd	The Oval	1975
533	2nd	Headingley	1985
529	2nd	Melbourne	1974/75
524	2nd	Sydney	1932/33
521	2nd	Brisbane (1)	1928/29
519	1st	Melbourne	1928/29
501	2nd	Adelaide	1911/12

South Africa

654 for 5	4th	Durban (2)	1938/39
608	1st	Johannesburg (2)	1948/49
559 for 9 declared	1st	Cape Town	1938/39
554 for 8 declared	1st	Lord's	1947
551	3rd	Trent Bridge	1947
534 for 6 declared	2nd	The Oval	1935
531 for 2 declared	2nd	Lord's	1924
531	1st	Johannesburg (3)	1964/65
505	2nd	Headingley	1951

West Indies

849	1st	Kingston	1929/30
619 for 6 declared	1st	Trent Bridge	1957
593	2nd	St John's	1993/94
583 for 4 declared	3rd	Edgbaston	1957
568	1st	Port-of-Spain	1967/68
537	2nd	Port-of-Spain	1953/54
527	2nd	The Oval	1966

New Zealand

593 for 6 declared	1st	Auckland	1974/75
580 for 9 declared	1st	Christchurch	1991/92
567 for 8 declared	2nd	Trent Bridge	1994
562 for 7 declared	1st	Auckland	1962/63
560 for 8 declared	1st	Christchurch	1932/33
550	2nd	Christchurch	1950/51
548 for 7 declared	2nd	Auckland	1932/33
546 for 4 declared	1st	Headingley	1965
540	1st	Auckland	1929/30

India

653 for 4 declared	1st	Lord's	1990
652 for 7 declared	2nd	Madras (1)	1984/85
633 for 5 declared	1st	Edgbaston	1979
629	1st	Lord's	1974
594	1st	The Oval	1982
571 for 8 declared	2nd	Old Trafford	1936
564 for 9 declared	2nd	Trent Bridge	1996
559 for 8 declared	1st	Kanpur	1963/64
550 for 4 declared	1st	Headingley	1967
537	2nd	Lord's	1952
519	1st	Old Trafford	1990
500 for 8 declared	1st	Bombay (2)	1961/62

Pakistan

558 for 6 declared	2nd	Trent Bridge	1954
546 for 8 declared	2nd	Faisalabad	1983/84
545	2nd	The Oval	1974

544 for 5 declared	1st	Edgbaston	1962
521	1st	Edgbaston	1987
507	2nd	Karachi (1)	1961/62
502 for 7 declared	1st	Karachi (1)	1968/69
501	2nd	Headingley	1996

Sri Lanka

429	2nd	Lord's	1988

HIGHEST TOTALS PER VENUE

ENGLAND (Totals above 500 or the highest single total for each venue)

The Oval

903 for 7 declared	1st	Australia	1938
594	1st	India	1982
576	1st	Australia	1899
545	2nd	Pakistan	1974
538	3rd	Australia	1975
534 for 6 declared	2nd	South Africa	1935
527	2nd	West Indies	1966

Old Trafford

627 for 9 declared	1st	Australia	1934
611	2nd	Australia	1964
571 for 8 declared	2nd	India	1936
519	1st	India	1990

Lord's

653 for 4 declared	1st	India	1990
629	1st	India	1974
554 for 8 declared	1st	South Africa	1947
537	2nd	India	1952
531 for 2 declared	2nd	South Africa	1924

Trent Bridge

658 for 8 declared	1st	Australia	1938
619 for 6 declared	1st	West Indies	1957
567 for 8 declared	2nd	New Zealand	1994
564 for 9 declared	2nd	India	1996
558 for 6 declared	2nd	Pakistan	1954
551	3rd	South Africa	1947

Headingley

550 for 4 declared	1st	India	1967
546 for 4 declared	1st	New Zealand	1965
533	2nd	Australia	1985
505	2nd	South Africa	1951
501	2nd	Pakistan	1996

Edgbaston

633 for 5 declared	1st	India	1979
595 for 5 declared	2nd	Australia	1985
583 for 4 declared	3rd	West Indies	1957
544 for 5 declared	1st	Pakistan	1962
521	1st	Pakistan	1987

Bramall Lane

195	4th	Australia	1902

AUSTRALIA

Melbourne

589	2nd	Australia	1911/12
558	2nd	Australia	1965/66
548	1st	Australia	1924/25
529	2nd	Australia	1974/75
519	1st	Australia	1928/29

Sydney

636	2nd	Australia	1928/29
577	2nd	Australia	1903/04
551	1st	Australia	1897/98
524	2nd	Australia	1932/33

Adelaide
| 501 | 2nd | Australia | 1911/12 |

Brisbane (1)
| 521 | 2nd | Australia | 1928/29 |

Brisbane (2)
| 464 | 2nd | Australia | 1970/71 |

Perth
| 592 for 8 declared | 1st | Australia | 1986/87 |

SOUTH AFRICA

Port Elizabeth
| 435 | 2nd | South Africa | 1964/65 |

Cape Town
| 559 for 9 declared | 1st | South Africa | 1938/39 |

Johannesburg (1)
| 482 | 1st | South Africa | 1895/96 |

Durban (1)
| 450 | 2nd | South Africa | 1913/14 |

Durban (2)
| 654 for 5 | 4th | South Africa | 1938/39 |

Johannesburg (2)
| 608 | 1st | South Africa | 1948/49 |

Johannesburg (3)
| 531 | 1st | South Africa | 1964/65 |

Centurion
| 381 for 9 declared | 1st | South Africa | 1995/96 |

WEST INDIES

Bridgetown
| 482 | 1st | West Indies | 1959/60 |

Port-of-Spain
| 568 | 1st | West Indies | 1967/68 |
| 537 | 2nd | West Indies | 1953/54 |

Georgetown
| 448 | 1st | West Indies | 1973/74 |

Kingston
| 849 | 1st | West Indies | 1929/30 |

St John's
| 593 | 2nd | West Indies | 1993/94 |

NEW ZEALAND

Christchurch
580 for 9 declared	1st	New Zealand	1991/92
560 for 8 declared	1st	New Zealand	1932/33
550	2nd	New Zealand	1950/51

Wellington
| 463 | 2nd | New Zealand | 1983/84 |

Auckland
593 for 6 declared	1st	New Zealand	1974/75
562 for 7 declared	1st	New Zealand	1962/63
548 for 7 declared	2nd	New Zealand	1932/33
540	1st	New Zealand	1929/30

Dunedin
| 254 for 8 declared | 2nd | New Zealand | 1965/66 |

INDIA

Bombay (1)

438	2nd	India	1933/34

Calcutta

403	1st	India	1933/34

Madras (1)

652 for 7 declared	2nd	India	1984/85

Delhi

476 for 9 declared	1st	India	1981/82

Bombay (2)

500 for 8 declared	1st	India	1961/62

Kanpur

559 for 8 declared	1st	India	1963/64

Madras (2)

317	2nd	India	1963/64

Bangalore

400	1st	India	1981/82

Bombay (3)

347	1st	India	1992/93

PAKISTAN

Dacca

439	2nd	Pakistan	1961/62

Karachi (1)

507	2nd	Pakistan	1961/62
502 for 7 declared	1st	Pakistan	1968/69

Lahore (2)

380	2nd	Pakistan	1961/62

Hyderabad

487	1st	Pakistan	1972/73

Faisalabad

546 for 8 declared	2nd	Pakistan	1983/84

SRI LANKA

Colombo (1)

223	2nd	Sri Lanka	1981/82

Colombo (2)

380	1st	Sri Lanka	1992/93

HIGHEST TOTALS CONCEDED

729 for 6 declared	2nd	Australia	Lord's	1930
708	1st	Pakistan	The Oval	1987
701	1st	Australia	The Oval	1934
695	2nd	Australia	The Oval	1930
692 for 8 declared	2nd	West Indies	The Oval	1995
687 for 8 declared	1st	West Indies	The Oval	1976
681 for 8 declared	1st	West Indies	Port-of-Spain	1953/54
659 for 8 declared	2nd	Australia	Sydney	1946/47
656 for 8 declared	1st	Australia	Old Trafford	1964
653 for 4 declared	1st	Australia	Headingley	1993
652 for 8 declared	1st	West Indies	Lord's	1973
645	1st	Australia	Brisbane (2)	1946/47
632 for 4 declared	1st	Australia	Lord's	1993
608 for 7 declared	1st	Pakistan	Edgbaston	1971
606 for 9 declared	1st	India	The Oval	1990
606	2nd	West Indies	Edgbaston	1984
604	1st	Australia	Melbourne	1936/37
602 for 6 declared	1st	Australia	Trent Bridge	1989

601 for 7 declared	1st	Australia	Headingley	1989
601 for 8 declared	1st	Australia	Brisbane (2)	1954/55
600 for 7 declared	1st	Pakistan	The Oval	1974
600	1st	Australia	Melbourne	1924/25
596 for 8 declared	2nd	West Indies	Bridgetown	1973/74
593 for 5 declared	1st	West Indies	St John's	1993/94
591	2nd	India	Bombay (3)	1992/93
586	1st	Australia	Sydney	1894/95
584	2nd	Australia	Headingley	1934
583 for 9 declared	2nd	West Indies	Kingston	1973/74
582	3rd	Australia	Adelaide	1920/21
581	3rd	Australia	Sydney	1920/21
573	1st	Australia	Adelaide	1897/98
569 for 9 declared	2nd	Pakistan	Hyderabad	1972/73
566	1st	Australia	Headingley	1930
564	3rd	Australia	Melbourne	1936/37
563 for 8 declared	2nd	West Indies	Bridgetown	1959/60
560 for 6 declared	1st	India	Madras (1)	1992/93
558	2nd	West Indies	Trent Bridge	1950
556	2nd	West Indies	Georgetown	1993/94
553 for 8 declared	1st	India	Kanpur	1984/85
551 for 9 declared	2nd	New Zealand	Lord's	1973
551	1st	Australia	The Oval	1884
543 for 8 declared	2nd	Australia	Melbourne	1965/66
539	2nd	Australia	Trent Bridge	1985
538	1st	South Africa	Headingley	1951
537	3rd	New Zealand	Wellington	1983/84
536	3rd	Australia	Melbourne	1946/47
535 for 7 declared	1st	West Indies	Kingston	1934/35
533	1st	South Africa	Trent Bridge	1947
532 for 9 declared	1st	Australia	The Oval	1975
530	1st	South Africa	Durban (2)	1938/39
528	2nd	Australia	Lord's	1989
526 for 7 declared	1st	West Indies	Port-of-Spain	1967/68
521 for 8 declared	2nd	South Africa	Old Trafford	1955
521 for 8 declared	2nd	Pakistan	The Oval	1996
521	1st	India	Trent Bridge	1996
520	1st	Australia	Melbourne	1897/98
518	2nd	West Indies	Lord's	1980
518	1st	Australia	Sydney	1990/91
516 for 9 declared	2nd	Australia	Edgbaston	1961
516	2nd	Australia	Adelaide	1965/66
514 for 5 declared	1st	Australia	Adelaide	1986/87
513 for 8 declared	1st	South Africa	Cape Town	1930/31
512 for 6 declared	1st	New Zealand	Wellington	1987/88
510	3rd	India	Headingley	1967
509	2nd	Australia	Trent Bridge	1948
506	3rd	Australia	Adelaide	1907/08
505 for 9 declared	1st	Pakistan	Old Trafford	1992
503	1st	West Indies	The Oval	1950
502	1st	South Africa	Port Elizabeth	1964/65
501 for 6 declared	1st	West Indies	Old Trafford	1963
501 for 7 declared	1st	South Africa	Cape Town	1964/65
500 for 9 declared	1st	West Indies	Headingley	1966
500	3rd	South Africa	Headingley	1955
500	1st	West Indies	Old Trafford	1984
499	1st	Australia	Melbourne	1920/21
498	2nd	West Indies	The Oval	1939
497	2nd	West Indies	Port-of-Spain	1947/48
496 for 9 declared	1st	New Zealand	Auckland	1983/84
494	1st	Australia	Headingley	1926
494	2nd	Australia	The Oval	1961
494	1st	West Indies	Trent Bridge	1976
493 for 9 declared	1st	Australia	Melbourne	1970/71
492 for 8 declared	2nd	South Africa	The Oval	1929
491 for 7 declared	1st	Sri Lanka	Lord's	1984
491	2nd	Australia	Melbourne	1928/29
491	2nd	Australia	Old Trafford	1934
490	2nd	West Indies	Kingston	1947/48
489	1st	Australia	Adelaide	1924/25
487	2nd	Australia	Adelaide	1946/47
487	2nd	India	Delhi	1981/82
485 for 9 declared	1st	India	Bombay (2)	1951/52
485	3rd	Australia	Sydney	1903/04
484	2nd	New Zealand	Lord's	1949

484	1st	West Indies	Old Trafford	1966
483 for 9 declared	1st	South Africa	Trent Bridge	1951
482 for 5 declared	3rd	West Indies	Trent Bridge	1966
481 for 4 declared	1st	India	Madras (1)	1981/82
481	3rd	South Africa	Durban (2)	1938/39
481	2nd	Australia	Perth	1974/75
477	2nd	Australia	Melbourne	1979/80
476	3rd	Australia	Adelaide	1911/12
476	1st	South Africa	The Oval	1935
476	1st	Australia	Adelaide	1958/59
476	1st	New Zealand	Lord's	1994
474	2nd	West Indies	Edgbaston	1957
474	1st	West Indies	St John's	1985/86
471	1st	West Indies	Georgetown	1929/30
469 for 9 declared	3rd	New Zealand	Lord's	1931
469	2nd	Sri Lanka	Colombo (2)	1992/93
468 for 9 declared	2nd	West Indies	St John's	1980/81
468	1st	Australia	The Oval	1989
467 for 8 declared	1st	India	Kanpur	1961/62
466	1st	India	Delhi	1961/62
465 for 8 declared	2nd	India	Bombay (3)	1984/85
464 for 8 declared	3rd	South Africa	Durban (2)	1927/28
463 for 4 declared	3rd	India	Delhi	1963/64
462 for 9 declared	2nd	New Zealand	Lord's	1990
460 for 7 declared	3rd	Australia	Lord's	1948
458	2nd	Australia	Headingley	1948
457 for 7 declared	1st	India	Madras (2)	1963/64
457 for 9 declared	2nd	India	Madras (1)	1951/52
454	2nd	India	Lord's	1990
452	3rd	Australia	Sydney	1924/25
450	1st	Australia	Sydney	1924/25
450	1st	West Indies	Headingley	1976

HIGHEST TOTALS CONCEDED PER INNINGS

First innings

708	Pakistan	The Oval	1987
701	Australia	The Oval	1934
687 for 8 declared	West Indies	The Oval	1976
681 for 8 declared	West Indies	Port-of-Spain	1953/54
656 for 8 declared	Australia	Old Trafford	1964
653 for 4 declared	Australia	Headingley	1993
652 for 8 declared	West Indies	Lord's	1973
645	Australia	Brisbane (2)	1946/47
632 for 4 declared	Australia	Lord's	1993
608 for 7 declared	Pakistan	Edgbaston	1971

Second innings

729 for 6 declared	Australia	Lord's	1930
695	Australia	The Oval	1930
692 for 8 declared	West Indies	The Oval	1995
659 for 8 declared	Australia	Sydney	1946/47
606	West Indies	Edgbaston	1984
596 for 8 declared	West Indies	Bridgetown	1973/74
591	India	Bombay (3)	1992/93
584	Australia	Headingley	1934
583 for 9 declared	West Indies	Kingston	1973/74
569 for 9 declared	Pakistan	Hyderabad	1972/73

Third innings

582	Australia	Adelaide	1920/21
581	Australia	Sydney	1920/21
564	Australia	Melbourne	1936/37
537	New Zealand	Wellington	1983/84
536	Australia	Melbourne	1946/47
510	India	Headingley	1967
506	Australia	Adelaide	1907/08
500	South Africa	Headingley	1955
485	Australia	Sydney	1903/04
482 for 5 declared	West Indies	Trent Bridge	1966

Fourth innings

440	New Zealand	Trent Bridge	1973
429 for 8	India	The Oval	1979
423 for 7	South Africa	The Oval	1947

408 for 5	West Indies	Kingston	1929/30
404 for 3	Australia	Headingley	1948
402	Australia	Old Trafford	1981
376	India	Old Trafford	1959
345	New Zealand	Trent Bridge	1983
344 for 1	West Indies	Lord's	1984
344 for 7	Australia	Sydney	1994/95

HIGHEST TOTALS CONCEDED AGAINST EACH OPPOSITION

(All totals above 500 or the single highest total conceded against each country)

Australia

729 for 6 declared	2nd	Lord's	1930
701	1st	The Oval	1934
695	2nd	The Oval	1930
659 for 8 declared	2nd	Sydney	1946/47
656 for 8 declared	1st	Old Trafford	1964
653 for 4 declared	1st	Headingley	1993
645	1st	Brisbane (2)	1946/47
632 for 4 declared	1st	Lord's	1993
604	1st	Melbourne	1936/37
602 for 6 declared	1st	Trent Bridge	1989
601 for 7 declared	1st	Headingley	1989
601 for 8 declared	1st	Brisbane (2)	1954/55
600	1st	Melbourne	1924/25
586	1st	Sydney	1894/95
584	2nd	Headingley	1934
582	3rd	Adelaide	1920/21
581	3rd	Sydney	1920/21
573	1st	Adelaide	1897/98
566	1st	Headingley	1930
564	3rd	Melbourne	1936/37
551	1st	The Oval	1884
543 for 8 declared	2nd	Melbourne	1965/66
539	2nd	Trent Bridge	1985
536	3rd	Melbourne	1946/47
532 for 9 declared	1st	The Oval	1975
528	2nd	Lord's	1989
520	1st	Melbourne	1897/98
518	1st	Sydney	1990/91
516 for 9 declared	2nd	Edgbaston	1961
516	2nd	Adelaide	1965/66
514 for 5 declared	1st	Adelaide	1986/87
509	2nd	Trent Bridge	1948
506	3rd	Adelaide	1907/08

South Africa

538	1st	Headingley	1951
533	1st	Trent Bridge	1947
530	1st	Durban (2)	1938/39
521 for 8 declared	2nd	Old Trafford	1955
513 for 8 declared	1st	Cape Town	1930/31
502	1st	Port Elizabeth	1964/65
501 for 7 declared	1st	Cape Town	1964/65
500	3rd	Headingley	1955

West Indies

692 for 8 declared	2nd	The Oval	1995
687 for 8 declared	1st	The Oval	1976
681 for 8 declared	1st	Port-of-Spain	1953/54
652 for 8 declared	1st	Lord's	1973
606	2nd	Edgbaston	1984
596 for 8 declared	2nd	Bridgetown	1973/74
593 for 5 declared	1st	St John's	1993/94
583 for 9 declared	2nd	Kingston	1973/74
563 for 8 declared	2nd	Bridgetown	1959/60
558	2nd	Trent Bridge	1950
556	2nd	Georgetown	1993/94
535 for 7 declared	1st	Kingston	1934/35
526 for 7 declared	1st	Port-of-Spain	1967/68
518	2nd	Lord's	1980
503	1st	The Oval	1950
501 for 6 declared	1st	Old Trafford	1963
500 for 9 declared	1st	Headingley	1966
500	1st	Old Trafford	1984

New Zealand

551 for 9 declared	2nd	Lord's	1973
537	3rd	Wellington	1983/84
512 for 6 declared	1st	Wellington	1987/88

India

606 for 9 declared	1st	The Oval	1990
591	2nd	Bombay (3)	1992/93
560 for 6 declared	1st	Madras (1)	1992/93
553 for 8 declared	1st	Kanpur	1984/85
521	1st	Trent Bridge	1996
510	3rd	Headingley	1967

Pakistan

708	1st	The Oval	1987
608 for 7 declared	1st	Edgbaston	1971
600 for 7 declared	1st	The Oval	1974
569 for 9 declared	2nd	Hyderabad	1972/73
521 for 8 declared	2nd	The Oval	1996
505 for 9 declared	1st	Old Trafford	1992

Sri Lanka

491 for 7 declared	1st	Lord's	1984

HIGHEST TOTALS CONCEDED PER VENUE

ENGLAND (Totals above 500 or the highest single total conceded for each venue)

The Oval

708	1st	Pakistan	1987
701	1st	Australia	1934
695	2nd	Australia	1930
692 for 8 declared	2nd	West Indies	1995
687 for 8 declared	1st	West Indies	1976
606 for 9 declared	1st	India	1990
600 for 7 declared	1st	Pakistan	1974
551	1st	Australia	1884
532 for 9 declared	1st	Australia	1975
521 for 8 declared	2nd	Pakistan	1996
503	1st	West Indies	1950

Old Trafford

656 for 8 declared	1st	Australia	1964
521 for 8 declared	2nd	South Africa	1955
505 for 9 declared	1st	Pakistan	1992
501 for 6 declared	1st	West Indies	1963
500	1st	West Indies	1984

Lord's

729 for 6 declared	2nd	Australia	1930
652 for 8 declared	1st	West Indies	1973
632 for 4 declared	1st	Australia	1993
551 for 9 declared	2nd	New Zealand	1973
528	2nd	Australia	1989
518	2nd	West Indies	1980

Trent Bridge

602 for 6 declared	1st	Australia	1989
558	2nd	West Indies	1950
539	2nd	Australia	1985
533	1st	South Africa	1947
521	1st	India	1996
509	2nd	Australia	1948

Headingley

653 for 4 declared	1st	Australia	1993
601 for 7 declared	1st	Australia	1989
584	2nd	Australia	1934
566	1st	Australia	1930
538	1st	South Africa	1951
510	3rd	India	1967
500 for 9 declared	1st	West Indies	1966
500	3rd	South Africa	1955

Edgbaston

608 for 7 declared	1st	Pakistan	1971
606	2nd	West Indies	1984
516 for 9 declared	2nd	Australia	1961

Bramall Lane

289	3rd	Australia	1902

AUSTRALIA

Melbourne

604	1st	Australia	1936/37
600	1st	Australia	1924/25
564	3rd	Australia	1936/37
543 for 8 declared	2nd	Australia	1965/66
536	3rd	Australia	1946/47
520	1st	Australia	1897/98

Sydney

659 for 8 declared	2nd	Australia	1946/47
586	1st	Australia	1894/95
581	3rd	Australia	1920/21
518	1st	Australia	1990/91

Adelaide

582	3rd	Australia	1920/21
573	1st	Australia	1897/98
516	2nd	Australia	1965/66
514 for 5 declared	1st	Australia	1986/87
506	3rd	Australia	1907/08

Brisbane (1)

122	2nd	Australia	1928/29

Brisbane (2)

645	1st	Australia	1946/47
601 for 8 declared	1st	Australia	1954/55

Perth

481	2nd	Australia	1974/75

SOUTH AFRICA

Port Elizabeth

502	1st	South Africa	1964/65

Cape Town

513 for 8 declared	1st	South Africa	1930/31
501 for 7 declared	1st	South Africa	1964/65

Johannesburg (1)

420	3rd	South Africa	1922/23

Durban (1)

347	3rd	South Africa	1909/10

Durban (2)

530	1st	South Africa	1938/39

Johannesburg (2)

315	2nd	South Africa	1948/49

Johannesburg (3)

390 for 6 declared	1st	South Africa	1964/65

Centurion
South Africa have not batted against England at Centurion

WEST INDIES

Bridgetown

596 for 8 declared	2nd	West Indies	1973/74
563 for 8 declared	2nd	West Indies	1959/60

Port-of-Spain

681 for 8 declared	1st	West Indies	1953/54
526 for 7 declared	1st	West Indies	1967/68

Georgetown

556	2nd	West Indies	1993/94

Kingston

583 for 9 declared	2nd	West Indies	1973/74
535 for 7 declared	1st	West Indies	1934/35

St John's

593 for 5 declared	1st	West Indies	1993/94

NEW ZEALAND

Christchurch

417 for 8 declared	1st	New Zealand	1950/51

Wellington

537	3rd	New Zealand	1983/84
512 for 6 declared	1st	New Zealand	1987/88

Auckland

496 for 9 declared	1st	New Zealand	1983/84

Dunedin

192	1st	New Zealand	1965/66

INDIA

Bombay (1)

258	3rd	India	1933/34

Calcutta

437 for 7 declared	1st	India	1984/85

Madras (1)

560 for 6 declared	1st	India	1992/93

Delhi

487	2nd	India	1981/82

Bombay (2)

485 for 9 declared	1st	India	1951/52

Kanpur

553 for 8 declared	1st	India	1984/85

Madras (2)

457 for 7 declared	1st	India	1963/64

Bangalore

428	2nd	India	1981/82

Bombay (3)

591	2nd	India	1992/93

PAKISTAN

Dacca

393 for 7 declared	1st	Pakistan	1961/62

Karachi (1)

445 for 6 declared	1st	Pakistan	1972/73

Lahore (2)

422	2nd	Pakistan	1972/73

Hyderabad

569 for 9 declared	2nd	Pakistan	1972/73

Faisalabad

449 for 8 declared	1st	Pakistan	1983/84

SRI LANKA

Colombo (1)

218	1st	Sri Lanka	1981/82

Colombo (2)

469	2nd	Sri Lanka	1992/93

LOWEST COMPLETED TOTALS

Total	Inns	Opposition	Venue	Date
45	1st	Australia	Sydney	1886/87
46	4th	West Indies	Port-of-Spain	1993/94
52	1st	Australia	The Oval	1948
53	2nd	Australia	Lord's	1888
61	2nd	Australia	Melbourne	1901/02
61	2nd	Australia	Melbourne	1903/04
62	4th	Australia	Lord's	1888
64	4th	New Zealand	Wellington	1977/78
65+	2nd	Australia	Sydney	1894/95
71	2nd	West Indies	Old Trafford	1976
72+	3rd	Australia	Sydney	1894/95
75	1st	Australia	Melbourne	1894/95
76	1st	South Africa	Headingley	1907
77	4th	Australia	The Oval	1882
77	3rd	Australia	Sydney	1884/85
82	2nd	New Zealand	Christchurch	1983/84
84	3rd	Australia	The Oval	1896
87+	4th	Australia	Headingley	1909
87	3rd	Australia	Melbourne	1958/59
89+	3rd	West Indies	Edgbaston	1995
92	1st	South Africa	Cape Town	1898/99
92	4th	Australia	Melbourne	1994/95
93	3rd	New Zealand	Christchurch	1983/84
93	3rd	West Indies	Old Trafford	1988
95	1st	Australia	Old Trafford	1884
95	2nd	Australia	Melbourne	1976/77
99	3rd	Australia	Sydney	1901/02
99	4th	South Africa	Lord's	1994

LOWEST COMPLETED TOTALS AGAINST EACH OPPOSITION

(All totals below 100 or the single lowest total against each country)

Australia

45	1st	Sydney	1886/87
52	1st	The Oval	1948
53	2nd	Lord's	1888
61	2nd	Melbourne	1901/02
61	2nd	Melbourne	1903/04
62	4th	Lord's	1888
65+	2nd	Sydney	1894/95
72+	3rd	Sydney	1894/95
75	1st	Melbourne	1894/95
77	4th	The Oval	1882
77	3rd	Sydney	1884/85
84	3rd	The Oval	1896
87	3rd	Melbourne	1958/59
87+	4th	Headingley	1909
92	4th	Melbourne	1994/95
95	1st	Old Trafford	1884
95	2nd	Melbourne	1976/77
99	3rd	Sydney	1901/02

South Africa

76	1st	Headingley	1907
92	1st	Cape Town	1898/99
99	4th	Lord's	1994

West Indies

46	4th	Port-of-Spain	1993/94
71	2nd	Old Trafford	1976
89+	3rd	Edgbaston	1995
93	3rd	Old Trafford	1988

New Zealand

64	4th	Wellington	1977/78
82	2nd	Christchurch	1983/84
93	3rd	Christchurch	1983/84

India

101	3rd	The Oval	1971

Pakistan

130	2nd	The Oval	1954
130	3rd	Lahore (2)	1987/88

Sri Lanka

223	2nd	Colombo (1)	1981/82

LOWEST COMPLETED TOTALS PER VENUE

ENGLAND

The Oval

52	1st	Australia	1948

Old Trafford

71	2nd	West Indies	1976

Lord's

53	2nd	Australia	1888

Trent Bridge

112	1st	Australia	1921

Headingley

76	1st	South Africa	1907

Edgbaston

89+	3rd	West Indies	1995

Bramall Lane

145	2nd	Australia	1902

AUSTRALIA

Melbourne

61	2nd	Australia	1901/02
61	2nd	Australia	1903/04

Sydney

45	1st	Australia	1886/87

Adelaide

124	2nd	Australia	1894/95

Brisbane (1)

521	1st	Australia	1928/29

Brisbane (2)

114	3rd	Australia	1990/91

Perth

123	4th	Australia	1994/95

SOUTH AFRICA

Port Elizabeth

110	2nd	South Africa	1956/57

Cape Town

92	1st	South Africa	1898/99

Johannesburg (1)

145	1st	South Africa	1898/99

Durban (1)
163   2nd   South Africa   1913/14

Durban (2)
118   3rd   South Africa   1927/28

Johannesburg (2)
379   1st   South Africa   1948/49

Johannesburg (3)
150   3rd   South Africa   1956/57

Centurion
England have not been dismissed at Centurion

WEST INDIES

Bridgetown
122   2nd   West Indies   1980/81

Port-of-Spain
46   4th   West Indies   1993/94

Georgetown
111   2nd   West Indies   1947/48

Kingston
103+   3rd   West Indies   1934/35

St John's
154+   3rd   West Indies   1989/90

NEW ZEALAND

Christchurch
82   2nd   New Zealand   1983/84

Wellington
64   4th   New Zealand   1977/78

Auckland
203   1st   New Zealand   1991/92

Dunedin
England have not been dismissed at Dunedin

INDIA

Bombay (1)
438   2nd   India   1933/34

Calcutta
163   2nd   India   1992/93

Madras (1)
159   3rd   India   1972/73

Delhi
200   2nd   India   1972/73

Bombay (2)
233+   2nd   India   1963/64

Kanpur
203   2nd   India   1951/52

Madras (2)
209   4th   India   1961/62

Bangalore
177   4th   India   1976/77

Bombay (3)
102   4th   India   1981/82

PAKISTAN

Dacca

274	2nd	Pakistan	1968/69

Karachi (1)

159	3rd	Pakistan	1983/84

Lahore (2)

130	3rd	Pakistan	1987/88

Hyderabad

191	2nd	Pakistan	1977/78

Faisalabad

292	1st	Pakistan	1987/88

SRI LANKA

Colombo (1)

223	2nd	Sri Lanka	1981/82

Colombo (2)

228	3rd	Sri Lanka	1992/93

+ One batsman absent or retired hurt/ill

LOWEST COMPLETED TOTALS AGAINST ENGLAND

Total	Inns	Opposition	Venue	Date
26	3rd	New Zealand	Auckland	1954/55
30	4th	South Africa	Port Elizabeth	1895/96
30	2nd	South Africa	Edgbaston	1924
35	4th	South Africa	Cape Town	1898/99
36	2nd	Australia	Edgbaston	1902
42	2nd	Australia	Sydney	1887/88
42+	3rd	India	Lord's	1974
43	3rd	South Africa	Cape Town	1888/89
44	4th	Australia	The Oval	1896
47	2nd	South Africa	Cape Town	1888/89
47	2nd	New Zealand	Lord's	1958
53	1st	Australia	Lord's	1896
58	2nd	India	Old Trafford	1952
58	1st	South Africa	Lord's	1912
58+	4th	Australia	Brisbane (2)	1936/37
60	3rd	Australia	Lord's	1888
63	1st	Australia	The Oval	1882
65	4th	Australia	The Oval	1912
65	1st	New Zealand	Christchurch	1970/71
66#	4th	Australia	Brisbane (1)	1928/29
67	1st	New Zealand	Headingley	1958
67	3rd	New Zealand	Lord's	1978
68	2nd	Australia	The Oval	1886
70	3rd	Australia	Old Trafford	1888
72	4th	South Africa	Johannesburg (3)	1956/57
72	4th	South Africa	Cape Town	1956/57
74	1st	Australia	Edgbaston	1909
74	3rd	New Zealand	Lord's	1958
75	4th	South Africa	Headingley	1907
78+	2nd	Australia	Lord's	1968
80	1st	Australia	The Oval	1888
80+	2nd	Australia	Sydney	1936/37
81	2nd	Australia	Old Trafford	1888
82	4th	Australia	Sydney	1887/88
82	3rd	India	Old Trafford	1952
83	4th	Australia	Sydney	1882/83
83	3rd	South Africa	Cape Town	1891/92
83+	4th	India	Madras (1)	1976/77
84	2nd	Australia	Sydney	1886/87
84	1st	South Africa	Port Elizabeth	1888/89
84	2nd	Australia	Old Trafford	1956
85	3rd	New Zealand	Old Trafford	1958
86+	3rd	West Indies	The Oval	1957
86	3rd	Australia	Old Trafford	1902
87	1st	Pakistan	Lord's	1954

Total	Inns	Opposition	Venue	Date
88	2nd	South Africa	Trent Bridge	1960
89+	2nd	West Indies	The Oval	1957
89	3rd	New Zealand	Auckland	1962/63
90	2nd	Pakistan	Old Trafford	1954
91	2nd	Australia	The Oval	1893
91	2nd	South Africa	Johannesburg (1)	1905/06
91	4th	West Indies	Edgbaston	1963
92	1st	Australia	The Oval	1890
92	2nd	India	Edgbaston	1967
93	2nd	South Africa	Port Elizabeth	1895/96
93	3rd	South Africa	The Oval	1912
93	3rd	India	Lord's	1936
94	2nd	New Zealand	Edgbaston	1958
95	1st	South Africa	The Oval	1912
96	1st	India	Lord's	1979
97	4th	Australia	Sydney	1886/87
97	1st	South Africa	Cape Town	1891/92
97	2nd	West Indies	Lord's	1933
97	2nd	New Zealand	Trent Bridge	1973
98	2nd	India	The Oval	1952
99	4th	South Africa	Johannesburg (1)	1898/99

LOWEST COMPLETED TOTALS AGAINST ENGLAND PER OPPOSITION

(All totals below 100 or the single lowest total by each country)

Australia

36	2nd	Edgbaston	1902
42	2nd	Sydney	1887/88
44	4th	The Oval	1896
53	1st	Lord's	1896
58+	4th	Brisbane (2)	1936/37
60	3rd	Lord's	1888
63	1st	The Oval	1882
65	4th	The Oval	1912
66#	4th	Brisbane (1)	1928/29
68	2nd	The Oval	1886
70	3rd	Old Trafford	1888
74	1st	Edgbaston	1909
78+	2nd	Lord's	1968
80	1st	The Oval	1888
80+	2nd	Sydney	1936/37
81	2nd	Old Trafford	1888
82	4th	Sydney	1887/88
83	4th	Sydney	1882/83
84	2nd	Sydney	1886/87
84	2nd	Old Trafford	1956
86	3rd	Old Trafford	1902
91	2nd	The Oval	1893
92	1st	The Oval	1890
97	4th	Sydney	1886/87

South Africa

30	4th	Port Elizabeth	1895/96
30	2nd	Edgbaston	1924
35	4th	Cape Town	1898/99
43	3rd	Cape Town	1888/89
47	2nd	Cape Town	1888/89
58	1st	Lord's	1912
72	4th	Johannesburg (3)	1956/57
72	4th	Cape Town	1956/57
75	4th	Headingley	1907
83	3rd	Cape Town	1891/92
84	1st	Port Elizabeth	1888/89
88	2nd	Trent Bridge	1960
91	2nd	Johannesburg (1)	1905/06
93	2nd	Port Elizabeth	1895/96
93	3rd	The Oval	1912
95	1st	The Oval	1912
97	1st	Cape Town	1891/92
99	4th	Johannesburg (1)	1898/99

West Indies

86+	3rd	The Oval	1957
89+	2nd	The Oval	1957
91	4th	Edgbaston	1963
97	2nd	Lord's	1933

New Zealand

26	3rd	Auckland	1954/55
47	2nd	Lord's	1958
65	1st	Christchurch	1970/71
67	1st	Headingley	1958
67	3rd	Lord's	1978
74	3rd	Lord's	1958
85	3rd	Old Trafford	1958
89	3rd	Auckland	1962/63
94	2nd	Edgbaston	1958
97	2nd	Trent Bridge	1973

India

42+	3rd	Lord's	1974
58	2nd	Old Trafford	1952
82	3rd	Old Trafford	1952
83+	4th	Madras (1)	1976/77
92	2nd	Edgbaston	1967
93	3rd	Lord's	1936
96	1st	Lord's	1979
98	2nd	The Oval	1952

Pakistan

87	1st	Lord's	1954
90	2nd	Old Trafford	1954

Sri Lanka

175	3rd	Colombo (1)	1981/82

LOWEST TOTALS AGAINST ENGLAND PER VENUE

ENGLAND

The Oval

44	4th	Australia	1896

Old Trafford

58	2nd	India	1952

Lord's

42+	3rd	India	1974

Trent Bridge

88	2nd	South Africa	1960

Headingley

67	1st	New Zealand	1958

Edgbaston

30	2nd	South Africa	1924

Bramall Lane

194	1st	Australia	1902

AUSTRALIA

Melbourne

104	3rd	Australia	1876/77

Sydney

42	2nd	Australia	1887/88

Adelaide

100	2nd	Australia	1891/92

Brisbane (1)

66#	4th	Australia	1928/29

Brisbane (2)
58+   4th   Australia   1936/37

Perth
161   4th   Australia   1978/79

SOUTH AFRICA

Port Elizabeth
30   4th   South Africa   1895/96

Cape Town
35   4th   South Africa   1898/99

Johannesburg (1)
91   2nd   South Africa   1905/06

Durban (1)
111   3rd   South Africa   1913/14

Durban (2)
103   2nd   South Africa   1938/39

Johannesburg (2)
315   2nd   South Africa   1948/49

Johannesburg (3)
72   4th   South Africa   1956/57

Centurion
South Africa have not batted against England at Centurion

WEST INDIES

Bridgetown
102   1st   West Indies   1934/35

Port-of-Spain
112   2nd   West Indies   1959/60

Georgetown
184   2nd   West Indies   1934/35

Kingston
139   1st   West Indies   1953/54

St John's
446   2nd   West Indies   1989/90

NEW ZEALAND

Christchurch
65   1st   New Zealand   1970/71

Wellington
123   3rd   New Zealand   1977/78

Auckland
26   3rd   New Zealand   1954/55

Dunedin
125   1st   New Zealand   1954/55

INDIA

Bombay (1)
219   1st   India   1933/34

Calcutta
155   3rd   India   1972/73
155   1st   India   1976/77

Madras (1)
| 83+ | 4th | India | 1976/77 |

Delhi
| 122 | 2nd | India | 1976/77 |

Bombay (2)
| 208 | 3rd | India | 1951/52 |

Kanpur
| 121 | 1st | India | 1951/52 |

Madras (2)
| 190 | 3rd | India | 1961/62 |

Bangalore
| 253 | 1st | India | 1976/77 |

Bombay (3)
| 149 | 3rd | India | 1979/80 |

PAKISTAN

Dacca
| 216 | 3rd | Pakistan | 1961/62 |

Karachi (1)
| 199 | 3rd | Pakistan | 1972/73 |

Lahore (2)
| 200 | 3rd | Pakistan | 1961/62 |

Hyderabad
| 275 | 1st | Pakistan | 1977/78 |

Faisalabad
| 191 | 2nd | Pakistan | 1987/88 |

SRI LANKA

Colombo (1)
| 175 | 3rd | Sri Lanka | 1981/82 |

Colombo (2)
| 469 | 2nd | Sri Lanka | 1992/93 |

+ One batsman absent or retired hurt/ill
# Two batsmen absent or retired hurt/ill

Appearance Records

TOTAL APPEARANCES

Players	First Test	Tests	Aus	SA	WI	NZ	Ind	Pak	SL
G.A.Gooch	10/07/1975	118	42	3	26	15	19	10	3
D.I.Gower	01/06/1978	117	42	–	19	13	24	17	2
M.C.Cowdrey	26/11/1954	114	43	14	21	18	8	10	–
G.Boycott	04/06/1964	108	38	7	29	15	13	6	–
I.T.Botham	28/07/1977	102	36	–	20	15	14	14	3
A.P.E.Knott	10/08/1967	95	34	–	22	9	16	14	–
T.G.Evans	17/08/1946	91	31	19	16	14	7	4	–
R.G.D.Willis	09/01/1971	90	35	–	13	14	17	10	1
D.L.Underwood	30/06/1966	86	29	–	17	8	20	11	1
W.R.Hammond	24/12/1927	85	33	24	13	9	6	–	–
K.F.Barrington	09/06/1955	82	23	14	17	5	14	9	–
L.Hutton	26/06/1937	79	27	19	13	11	7	2	–
T.W.Graveney	05/07/1951	79	22	6	19	8	11	13	–
M.W.Gatting	18/01/1978	79	27	–	9	11	16	15	1
A.J.Lamb	10/06/1982	79	20	–	22	14	13	8	2
D.C.S.Compton	14/08/1937	78	28	24	9	8	5	4	–
J.H.Edrich	06/06/1963	77	32	1	14	11	10	9	–

Players	First Test	Tests	Aus	SA	WI	NZ	Ind	Pak	SL
J.B.Statham	17/03/1951	70	22	16	12	5	8	7	–
F.S.Trueman	05/06/1952	67	19	6	18	11	9	4	–
P.B.H.May	26/07/1951	66	21	12	13	9	7	4	–
F.E.Woolley	09/08/1909	64	32	26	–	5	1	–	–
J.E.Emburey	24/08/1978	64	25	–	15	6	8	7	3
E.R.Dexter	24/07/1958	62	19	10	10	8	7	8	–
R.A.Smith	21/07/1988	62	15	5	19	9	6	5	3
M.A.Atherton	10/08/1989	62	18	8	16	6	7	6	1
J.B.Hobbs	01/01/1908	61	41	18	2	–	–	–	–
T.E.Bailey	11/06/1949	61	23	12	11	12	0	3	–
R.Illingworth	24/07/1958	61	18	4	13	13	8	5	–
K.W.R.Fletcher	25/07/1968	59	15	–	7	8	19	9	1
W.Rhodes	01/06/1899	58	41	13	4	–	–	–	–
A.W.Greig	08/06/1972	58	21	–	13	5	13	6	–
A.J.Stewart	24/02/1990	58	13	8	13	9	5	8	2
R.W.Taylor	25/02/1971	57	17	–	–	14	13	12	1
H.Sutcliffe	14/06/1924	54	27	17	5	4	1	–	–
F.J.Titmus	23/06/1955	53	19	10	9	6	5	4	–
E.H.Hendren	17/12/1920	51	28	14	9	–	–	–	–
A.V.Bedser	22/06/1946	51	21	13	3	5	7	2	–
P.H.Edmonds	14/08/1975	51	13	–	3	11	14	10	–
M.J.K.Smith	05/06/1958	50	9	12	6	9	11	3	–
D.L.Amiss	18/08/1966	50	11	–	10	5	14	10	–
G.A.R.Lock	17/07/1952	49	13	4	13	7	7	5	–
J.A.Snow	17/06/1965	49	20	1	14	6	5	3	–
R.C.Russell	25/08/1988	49	9	5	16	6	6	5	2
L.E.G.Ames	17/08/1929	47	17	10	11	8	1	–	–
D.W.Randall	01/01/1977	47	18	–	1	9	10	9	–
J.C.Laker	21/01/1948	46	15	8	13	5	4	1	–
J.M.Parks	22/07/1954	46	10	13	12	5	5	1	–
C.M.Old	30/12/1972	46	12	–	9	6	11	8	–
G.A.Hick	06/06/1991	46	6	8	14	6	6	5	1
B.L.D'Oliveira	16/06/1966	44	13	–	12	5	5	9	–
P.A.J.DeFreitas	14/11/1986	44	13	3	11	10	1	5	1
M.Leyland	11/08/1928	41	20	14	5	–	2	–	–
G.R.Dilley	14/12/1979	41	12	–	11	6	6	6	–
R.E.S.Wyatt	24/12/1927	40	12	17	8	2	1	–	–
H.Verity	29/07/1931	40	18	9	3	4	6	–	–
M.W.Tate	14/06/1924	39	20	14	3	2	–	–	–
W.J.Edrich	10/06/1938	39	21	9	2	5	1	1	–
D.A.Allen	06/01/1960	39	10	6	8	3	5	7	–
J.M.Brearley	03/06/1976	39	19	–	2	3	10	5	–
C.Washbrook	14/08/1937	37	17	10	2	5	3	–	–
P.H.Parfitt	30/12/1961	37	9	7	1	8	5	7	–
D.E.Malcolm	10/08/1989	36	11	3	9	4	5	3	1
A.C.MacLaren	14/12/1894	35	35	–	–	–	–	–	–
T.W.Hayward	13/02/1896	35	29	6	–	–	–	–	–
A.F.A.Lilley	22/06/1896	35	32	3	–	–	–	–	–
D.V.P.Wright	10/06/1938	34	14	10	4	4	2	–	–
P.E.Richardson	07/06/1956	34	9	5	6	6	5	3	–
G.G.Arnold	10/08/1967	34	8	–	6	6	6	8	–
G.Miller	12/08/1976	34	14	–	4	5	4	7	–
J.Briggs	12/12/1884	33	31	2	–	–	–	–	–
A.R.C.Fraser	06/07/1989	32	10	5	11	3	3	–	–
C.C.Lewis	05/07/1990	32	5	–	7	3	8	7	2
G.P.Thorpe	01/07/1993	32	8	7	11	–	3	3	–
J.T.Tyldesley	14/02/1899	31	26	5	–	–	–	–	–
C.J.Tavare	05/06/1980	31	8	–	3	6	9	3	2
M.Hendrick	06/06/1974	30	13	–	4	4	7	2	–
P.R.Downton	13/02/1981	30	7	–	16	–	6	–	1
D.R.Pringle	10/06/1982	30	5	–	11	3	6	4	1
B.R.Knight	01/12/1961	29	5	–	4	7	9	4	–
N.A.Foster	11/08/1983	29	6	–	6	4	3	9	1
R.T.Robinson	28/11/1984	29	8	–	4	3	6	7	1
H.Strudwick	01/01/1910	28	17	11	–	–	–	–	–
J.H.Wardle	11/02/1948	28	8	9	5	2	–	4	–
G.Pullar	02/07/1959	28	9	3	5	–	6	5	–
R.W.Barber	09/06/1960	28	7	8	2	3	5	3	–
M.H.Denness	21/08/1969	28	6	–	5	3	8	6	–
S.F.Barnes	13/12/1901	27	20	7	–	–	–	–	–
W.Voce	11/01/1930	27	11	5	4	4	3	–	–
R.T.Simpson	16/12/1948	27	9	4	3	6	2	3	–
C.B.Fry	13/02/1896	26	18	8	–	–	–	–	–
A.P.F.Chapman	14/06/1924	26	16	7	3	–	–	–	–

Players	First Test	Tests	Aus	SA	WI	NZ	Ind	Pak	SL
D.J.Brown	22/07/1965	26	8	2	8	3	2	3	–
P.Willey	22/07/1976	26	9	–	15	1	1	–	–
G.Ulyett	15/03/1877	25	23	2	–	–	–	–	–
G.O.B.Allen	27/06/1930	25	13	–	4	5	3	–	–
P.I.Pocock	29/02/1968	25	1	–	10	–	9	4	1
B.C.Broad	28/06/1984	25	8	–	6	3	–	7	1
G.H.Hirst	13/12/1897	24	21	3	–	–	–	–	–
G.Duckworth	26/07/1924	24	10	9	1	1	3	–	–
J.W.Hearne	15/12/1911	24	16	8	–	–	–	–	–
A.Shrewsbury	31/12/1881	23	23	–	–	–	–	–	–
L.C.Braund	13/12/1901	23	20	3	–	–	–	–	–
J.W.H.T.Douglas	01/01/1925	23	17	6	–	–	–	–	–
J.Hardstaff jnr	13/07/1935	23	9	1	6	3	4	–	–
W.Watson	07/06/1951	23	7	6	5	4	1	–	–
C.W.J.Athey	28/08/1980	23	7	–	3	4	2	7	–
W.G.Grace	06/09/1880	22	22	–	–	–	–	–	–
D.R.Jardine	23/06/1928	22	10	–	4	4	4	–	–
F.R.Brown	29/07/1931	22	6	5	1	9	1	–	–
D.B.Close	23/07/1949	22	2	1	11	1	4	3	–
Rev.D.S.Sheppard	12/08/1950	22	9	–	3	4	2	4	–
P.C.R.Tufnell	26/12/1990	22	10	1	3	3	2	1	2
W.Barnes	06/09/1880	21	21	–	–	–	–	–	–
H.Larwood	26/06/1926	21	15	3	2	1	–	–	–
J.T.Murray	08/06/1961	21	6	1	1	2	6	5	–
B.W.Luckhurst	27/11/1970	21	11	–	2	2	3	3	–
G.R.J.Roope	25/01/1973	21	3	–	1	7	2	8	–
J.K.Lever	17/12/1976	21	6	–	1	1	10	3	–
G.Fowler	26/08/1982	21	3	–	5	4	5	3	1
R.Peel	12/12/1884	20	20	–	–	–	–	–	–
Hon.F.S.Jackson	17/07/1893	20	20	–	–	–	–	–	–
E.Paynter	15/08/1931	20	7	5	2	5	1	–	–
C.J.Barnett	12/08/1933	20	9	3	1	3	4	–	–
N.W.D.Yardley	24/12/1938	20	10	6	3	1	–	–	–
C.Blythe	13/12/1901	19	9	10	–	–	–	–	–
R.W.V.Robins	29/06/1929	19	6	4	2	4	3	–	–
R.A.Woolmer	31/07/1975	19	10	–	7	–	2	–	–
N.G.Cowans	12/11/1982	19	5	–	1	6	5	2	–
M.R.Ramprakash	06/06/1991	19	2	2	11	–	–	3	1
W.W.Read	30/12/1882	18	17	1	–	–	–	–	–
G.A.Lohmann	05/07/1886	18	15	3	–	–	–	–	–
G.L.Jessop	15/06/1899	18	13	5	–	–	–	–	–
J.T.Ikin	22/06/1946	18	5	4	4	1	4	–	–
R.G.Barlow	31/12/1881	17	17	–	–	–	–	–	–
J.M.Read	28/08/1882	17	15	2	–	–	–	–	–
C.P.Mead	15/12/1911	17	7	10	–	–	–	–	–
F.H.Tyson	12/08/1954	17	8	4	–	4	–	1	–
P.Lever	11/12/1970	17	9	–	–	4	1	3	–
G.C.Small	07/08/1986	17	7	–	5	5	–	–	–
A.E.Stoddart	10/02/1888	16	16	–	–	–	–	–	–
R.Tattersall	02/02/1951	16	3	5	–	2	5	1	–
E.E.Hemmings	29/07/1982	16	6	–	–	4	3	3	–
B.N.French	19/06/1986	16	1	–	–	6	2	7	–
D.G.Cork	22/06/1995	16	–	5	5	–	3	3	–
W.Bates	31/12/1881	15	15	–	–	–	–	–	–
W.H.Scotton	31/12/1881	15	15	–	–	–	–	–	–
K.S.Ranjitsinhji	16/07/1896	15	15	–	–	–	–	–	–
P.F.Warner	14/02/1899	15	7	8	–	–	–	–	–
G.Gunn	13/12/1907	15	11	–	4	–	–	–	–
J.C.White	02/07/1921	15	7	7	1	–	–	–	–
W.E.Bowes	25/06/1932	15	6	4	2	1	2	–	–
K.Farnes	08/06/1934	15	8	5	2	–	–	–	–
A.J.Watkins	14/08/1948	15	1	5	–	1	8	–	–
I.J.Jones	21/01/1964	15	4	–	7	3	1	–	–
J.S.E.Price	21/01/1964	15	3	4	–	–	7	1	–
K.Higgs	26/08/1965	15	2	1	5	3	1	3	–
N.Gifford	21/06/1973	15	5	–	–	2	4	4	–
N.G.B.Cook	11/08/1983	15	3	–	3	3	–	6	–
D.J.Capel	02/07/1987	15	2	–	6	3	–	4	–
T.Richardson	24/08/1893	14	14	–	–	–	–	–	–
F.L.Fane	02/01/1906	14	4	10	–	–	–	–	–
G.E.Tyldesley	28/05/1921	14	5	6	3	–	–	–	–
A.Sandham	13/08/1921	14	3	7	4	–	–	–	–
G.Geary	26/07/1924	14	9	5	–	–	–	–	–
M.S.Nichols	10/01/1930	14	1	4	2	4	3	–	–

Players	First Test	Tests	Aus	SA	WI	NZ	Ind	Pak	SL
A.G.Steel	06/09/1880	13	13	–	–	–	–	–	–
R.Abel	16/07/1888	13	11	2	–	–	–	–	–
A.E.Relf	27/02/1914	13	3	10	–	–	–	–	–
P.G.H.Fender	14/01/1921	13	5	8	–	–	–	–	–
I.A.R.Peebles	24/12/1927	13	2	8	–	3	–	–	–
W.E.Hollies	08/01/1935	13	1	3	5	4	–	–	–
P.J.Loader	12/08/1954	13	2	5	2	3	–	1	–
R.Subba Row	24/07/1958	13	5	4	2	1	1	–	–
W.Larkins	01/02/1980	13	5	–	7	–	1	–	–
P.J.W.Allott	01/08/1985	13	5	–	3	–	3	–	2
J.T.Hearne	19/03/1892	12	11	1	–	–	–	–	–
W.H.Lockwood	17/07/1893	12	12	–	–	–	–	–	–
A.O.Jones	14/08/1899	12	12	–	–	–	–	–	–
J.N.Crawford	02/01/1906	12	5	7	–	–	–	–	–
A.P.Freeman	19/12/1924	12	2	7	3	–	–	–	–
K.S.Duleepsinhji	15/06/1929	12	4	1	–	7	–	–	–
P.J.Sharpe	04/07/1963	12	2	–	6	3	1	–	–
B.Wood	10/08/1972	12	4	–	1	2	3	2	–
N.Hussain	24/02/1990	12	4	–	3	–	3	2	–
D.Gough	30/06/1994	12	3	5	3	1	–	–	–
J.P.Crawley	21/07/1994	12	3	4	3	–	–	2	–
W.Gunn	28/01/1887	11	11	–	–	–	–	–	–
S.Haigh	14/02/1899	11	4	7	–	–	–	–	–
D.Denton	03/07/1905	11	1	10	–	–	–	–	–
F.R.Foster	15/12/1911	11	8	3	–	–	–	–	–
E.J.Smith	30/12/1911	11	7	4	–	–	–	–	–
A.W.Carr	23/12/1922	11	4	7	–	–	–	–	–
A.E.R.Gilligan	23/12/1922	11	5	6	–	–	–	–	–
C.F.Walters	24/06/1933	11	5	–	3	–	3	–	–
J.D.B.Robertson	16/08/1947	11	–	1	4	1	5	–	–
R.Swetman	09/01/1959	11	2	–	4	2	3	–	–
R.M.Ellison	09/08/1984	11	2	–	4	–	4	–	1
S.J.Rhodes	02/06/1994	11	5	3	–	3	–	–	–
W.Attewell	12/12/1884	10	10	–	–	–	–	–	–
E.G.Arnold	11/12/1903	10	8	2	–	–	–	–	–
R.H.Spooner	24/07/1905	10	7	3	–	–	–	–	–
M.C.Bird	01/01/1910	10	–	10	–	–	–	–	–
C.H.Parkin	17/12/1920	10	9	1	–	–	–	–	–
C.A.G.Russell	17/12/1920	10	6	4	–	–	–	–	–
G.T.S.Stevens	23/12/1922	10	2	6	2	–	–	–	–
W.E.Russell	21/10/1961	10	1	1	2	3	1	2	–
J.D.F.Larter	16/08/1962	10	–	2	–	4	3	1	–
M.D.Moxon	24/07/1986	10	2	–	2	5	–	1	–
N.H.Fairbrother	13/03/1993	10	–	–	–	5	2	2	1
E.Peate	31/12/1881	9	9	–	–	–	–	–	–
Hon.L.H.Tennyson	13/12/1913	9	4	5	–	–	–	–	–
R.Kilner	14/06/1924	9	7	2	–	–	–	–	–
W.E.Astill	24/12/1927	9	–	5	4	–	–	–	–
M.J.L.Turnbull	10/01/1930	9	–	5	2	1	1	–	–
T.S.Worthington	10/01/1930	9	3	–	–	4	2	–	–
R.O.Jenkins	16/12/1948	9	–	5	2	–	2	–	–
D.J.Insole	20/07/1950	9	1	6	2	–	–	–	–
A.E.Moss	15/01/1954	9	1	2	3	–	3	–	–
R.Appleyard	01/07/1954	9	5	1	–	2	–	1	–
J.B.Mortimore	13/02/1959	9	2	–	–	2	5	–	–
C.Milburn	02/06/1966	9	2	–	4	–	1	2	–
A.R.Lewis	20/12/1972	9	–	–	–	1	5	3	–
F.C.Hayes	26/07/1973	9	–	–	9	–	–	–	–
D.Lloyd	20/06/1974	9	4	–	–	–	2	3	–
B.C.Rose	14/12/1977	9	–	–	4	2	–	3	–
P.W.Jarvis	12/02/1988	9	2	–	2	2	2	–	1
R.K.Illingworth	04/07/1991	9	–	3	6	–	–	–	–
I.D.K.Salisbury	18/06/1992	9	–	1	2	–	2	4	–
A.R.Caddick	03/06/1993	9	4	–	4	–	–	1	–
R.Pilling	31/12/1881	8	8	–	–	–	–	–	–
W.Flowers	12/12/1884	8	8	–	–	–	–	–	–
G.MacGregor	21/07/1890	8	8	–	–	–	–	–	–
J.T.Brown	14/12/1894	8	8	–	–	–	–	–	–
R.E.Foster	11/12/1903	8	5	3	–	–	–	–	–
V.W.C.Jupp	28/05/1921	8	2	4	2	–	–	–	–
G.G.Macaulay	01/01/1923	8	1	5	2	–	–	–	–
E.W.Clark	17/08/1929	8	2	1	2	–	3	–	–
T.W.J.Goddard	25/07/1930	8	1	3	2	2	–	–	–
James Langridge	22/07/1933	8	–	1	2	–	5	–	–

Players	First Test	Tests	Aus	SA	WI	NZ	Ind	Pak	SL
P.A.Gibb	24/12/1938	8	1	5	–	–	2	–	–
K.Cranston	05/07/1947	8	1	3	4	–	–	–	–
C.Gladwin	05/07/1947	8	–	7	–	1	–	–	–
J.A.Young	26/07/1947	8	3	3	–	2	–	–	–
D.Kenyon	02/11/1951	8	2	3	–	–	3	–	–
M.J.Stewart	21/06/1962	8	–	–	4	–	2	2	–
J.H.Hampshire	26/06/1969	8	4	–	2	2	–	–	–
D.S.Steele	31/07/1975	8	3	–	5	–	–	–	–
C.T.Radley	24/02/1978	8	–	–	–	5	–	3	–
C.L.Smith	11/08/1983	8	–	–	–	4	1	3	–
C.J.Richards	14/11/1986	8	5	–	2	–	–	1	–
P.M.Such	03/06/1993	8	5	–	–	3	–	–	–
T.Emmett	15/03/1877	7	7	–	–	–	–	–	–
A.Shaw	15/03/1877	7	7	–	–	–	–	–	–
Albert Ward	14/08/1893	7	7	–	–	–	–	–	–
W.Brockwell	24/08/1893	7	7	–	–	–	–	–	–
W.G.Quaife	29/06/1899	7	7	–	–	–	–	–	–
B.J.T.Bosanquet	11/12/1903	7	7	–	–	–	–	–	–
K.L.Hutchings	13/12/1907	7	7	–	–	–	–	–	–
J.W.Hitch	30/12/1911	7	6	1	–	–	–	–	–
P.Holmes	28/05/1921	7	1	5	–	–	1	–	–
G.Brown	02/07/1921	7	3	4	–	–	–	–	–
R.K.Tyldesley	28/06/1924	7	3	4	–	–	–	–	–
B.H.Valentine	15/12/1933	7	–	5	–	–	2	–	–
J.F.Crapp	08/07/1948	7	3	4	–	–	–	–	–
F.G.Mann	16/12/1948	7	–	5	–	2	–	–	–
W.G.A.Parkhouse	24/06/1950	7	2	–	2	1	2	–	–
D.Shackleton	20/07/1950	7	–	1	5	–	1	–	–
F.A.Lowson	26/07/1951	7	–	3	–	–	4	–	–
R.T.Spooner	02/11/1951	7	–	1	1	–	5	–	–
L.J.Coldwell	21/06/1962	7	4	–	–	1	–	2	–
J.B.Bolus	25/07/1963	7	–	–	2	–	5	–	–
R.N.S.Hobbs	08/06/1967	7	–	–	1	–	3	3	–
G.Cook	17/02/1982	7	3	–	–	–	3	–	1
P.J.Martin	08/06/1995	7	–	3	3	–	1	–	–
J.Selby	15/03/1877	6	6	–	–	–	–	–	–
E.F.S.Tylecote	30/12/1882	6	6	–	–	–	–	–	–
W.Storer	13/12/1897	6	6	–	–	–	–	–	–
J.H.Board	14/02/1899	6	–	6	–	–	–	–	–
J.R.Gunn	13/12/1901	6	6	–	–	–	–	–	–
A.Fielder	01/01/1904	6	6	–	–	–	–	–	–
G.J.Thompson	27/05/1909	6	1	5	–	–	–	–	–
A.H.Bakewell	27/06/1931	6	–	2	1	2	1	–	–
A.Mitchell	15/12/1933	6	–	2	–	–	4	–	–
C.A.Milton	03/07/1958	6	2	–	–	2	2	–	–
G.Millman	30/12/1961	6	–	–	–	–	2	4	–
A.C.Smith	30/11/1962	6	4	–	–	2	–	–	–
D.Wilson	10/01/1964	6	–	–	–	1	5	–	–
V.J.Marks	26/08/1982	6	–	–	–	2	–	4	–
C.S.Cowdrey	28/11/1984	6	–	–	1	–	5	–	–
C.White	02/06/1994	6	–	1	2	3	–	–	–
N.V.Knight	27/07/1995	6	–	–	2	–	1	3	–
A.D.Mullally	06/06/1996	6	–	–	–	–	3	3	–
A.P.Lucas	02/01/1879	5	5	–	–	–	–	–	–
C.T.Studd	28/08/1882	5	5	–	–	–	–	–	–
T.C.O'Brien	10/07/1884	5	2	3	–	–	–	–	–
J.Hunter	12/12/1884	5	5	–	–	–	–	–	–
H.Philipson	24/03/1892	5	5	–	–	–	–	–	–
E.Wainwright	17/07/1893	5	5	–	–	–	–	–	–
F.G.J.Ford	14/12/1894	5	5	–	–	–	–	–	–
Lord Hawke	13/02/1896	5	–	5	–	–	–	–	–
N.F.Druce	13/12/1897	5	5	–	–	–	–	–	–
J.R.Mason	13/12/1897	5	5	–	–	–	–	–	–
E.G.Hayes	02/01/1906	5	1	4	–	–	–	–	–
W.S.Lees	02/01/1906	5	–	5	–	–	–	–	–
J.Hardstaff snr	13/12/1907	5	5	–	–	–	–	–	–
G.H.T.Simpson-Hayward	01/01/1910	5	–	5	–	–	–	–	–
H.Howell	31/12/1920	5	4	1	–	–	–	–	–
N.E.Haig	11/06/1921	5	1	–	4	–	–	–	–
A.S.Kennedy	23/12/1922	5	–	5	–	–	–	–	–
F.T.Mann	23/12/1922	5	–	5	–	–	–	–	–
G.B.Legge	24/12/1927	5	–	1	–	4	–	–	–
E.W.Dawson	04/02/1928	5	–	1	–	4	–	–	–
E.H.Bowley	13/07/1929	5	–	2	–	3	–	–	–

Players	First Test	Tests	Aus	SA	WI	NZ	Ind	Pak	SL
F.Barratt	27/07/1929	5	–	1	–	4	–	–	–
M.J.C.Allom	10/01/1930	5	–	1	–	4	–	–	–
T.B.Mitchell	10/02/1933	5	3	1	–	1	–	–	–
E.R.T.Holmes	08/01/1935	5	–	1	4	–	–	–	–
J.Iddon	08/01/1935	5	–	1	4	–	–	–	–
C.I.J.Smith	08/01/1935	5	–	–	4	1	–	–	–
A.E.Fagg	25/07/1936	5	2	–	1	–	2	–	–
R.Howorth	16/08/1947	5	–	1	4	–	–	–	–
J.G.Dewes	14/08/1948	5	3	–	2	–	–	–	–
F.Ridgway	02/11/1951	5	–	–	–	–	5	–	–
D.R.Smith	11/11/1961	5	–	–	–	–	5	–	–
T.W.Cartwright	23/07/1964	5	2	2	–	1	–	–	–
F.E.Rumsey	23/07/1964	5	1	1	–	3	–	–	–
N.I.Thomson	04/12/1964	5	–	5	–	–	–	–	–
Alan Ward	24/07/1969	5	–	–	1	3	–	1	–
K.Shuttleworth	27/11/1970	5	2	–	2	–	1	–	–
R.A.Hutton	17/06/1971	5	–	–	–	–	3	2	–
J.Birkenshaw	25/01/1973	5	–	–	2	–	2	1	–
J.G.Thomas	21/02/1986	5	–	–	4	1	–	–	–
T.S.Curtis	21/07/1988	5	3	–	2	–	–	–	–
D.V.Lawrence	25/08/1988	5	–	–	2	1	–	–	2
M.C.Ilott	01/07/1993	5	3	2	–	–	–	–	–
Hon.A.Lyttelton	06/09/1880	4	4	–	–	–	–	–	–
F.Morley	06/09/1880	4	4	–	–	–	–	–	–
W.E.Midwinter	31/12/1881	4	4	–	–	–	–	–	–
Hon.I.F.W.Bligh	30/12/1882	4	4	–	–	–	–	–	–
C.F.H.Leslie	30/12/1882	4	4	–	–	–	–	–	–
G.B.Studd	30/12/1882	4	4	–	–	–	–	–	–
Lord Harris	11/08/1884	4	4	–	–	–	–	–	–
H.Wood	13/08/1888	4	1	3	–	–	–	–	–
H.R.Bromley-Davenport	13/02/1896	4	–	4	–	–	–	–	–
W.Brearley	24/07/1905	4	3	1	–	–	–	–	–
L.J.Moon	06/03/1906	4	–	4	–	–	–	–	–
C.P.Buckenham	01/01/1910	4	–	4	–	–	–	–	–
J.W.H.Makepeace	31/12/1920	4	4	–	–	–	–	–	–
W.W.Whysall	16/01/1925	4	4	–	–	–	–	–	–
R.T.Stanyforth	24/12/1927	4	–	4	–	–	–	–	–
H.Elliott	04/02/1928	4	–	1	1	–	2	–	–
J.O'Connor	29/06/1929	4	–	1	3	–	–	–	–
W.L.Cornford	10/01/1930	4	–	–	–	4	–	–	–
A.H.H.Gilligan	10/01/1930	4	–	–	–	4	–	–	–
Hon.F.S.G.Calthorpe	11/01/1930	4	–	–	4	–	–	–	–
L.F.Townsend	21/02/1930	4	–	–	1	–	3	–	–
W.Farrimond	13/02/1931	4	–	3	1	–	–	–	–
G.A.E.Paine	08/01/1935	4	–	–	4	–	–	–	–
J.M.Sims	13/07/1935	4	2	1	–	–	1	–	–
L.B.Fishlock	25/07/1936	4	1	–	–	–	3	–	–
A.R.Gover	25/07/1936	4	–	–	–	2	2	–	–
A.Wood	20/08/1938	4	1	–	3	–	–	–	–
R.Pollard	20/07/1946	4	2	–	–	1	1	–	–
T.P.B.Smith	17/08/1946	4	2	–	–	1	1	–	–
H.E.Dollery	07/06/1947	4	2	1	1	–	–	–	–
M.J.Hilton	12/08/1950	4	–	1	1	–	2	–	–
N.D.Howard	02/11/1951	4	–	–	–	–	4	–	–
T.Greenhough	04/06/1959	4	–	1	–	–	3	–	–
J.A.Flavell	27/07/1961	4	4	–	–	–	–	–	–
R.M.H.Cottam	21/02/1969	4	–	–	–	–	2	2	–
J.A.Jameson	05/08/1971	4	–	–	2	–	2	–	–
R.W.Tolchard	01/01/1977	4	–	–	–	–	4	–	–
D.L.Bairstow	30/08/1979	4	1	–	2	–	1	–	–
R.D.Jackman	13/03/1981	4	–	–	2	–	–	2	–
R.J.Bailey	04/08/1988	4	–	–	4	–	–	–	–
M.P.Maynard	04/08/1988	4	2	–	2	–	–	–	–
K.J.Barnett	25/08/1988	4	3	–	–	–	–	–	1
M.Watkinson	27/07/1995	4	–	1	3	–	–	–	–
A.N.Hornby	02/01/1879	3	3	–	–	–	–	–	–
M.Sherwin	28/01/1887	3	3	–	–	–	–	–	–
J.W.Sharpe	11/08/1890	3	3	–	–	–	–	–	–
G.Bean	01/01/1892	3	3	–	–	–	–	–	–
A.W.Mold	17/07/1893	3	3	–	–	–	–	–	–
H.R.Butt	13/02/1896	3	–	3	–	–	–	–	–
A.J.L.Hill	13/02/1896	3	–	3	–	–	–	–	–
S.M.J.Woods	13/02/1896	3	–	3	–	–	–	–	–
C.W.Wright	13/02/1896	3	–	3	–	–	–	–	–

Players	First Test	Tests	Aus	SA	WI	NZ	Ind	Pak	SL
E.G.Wynyard	10/08/1896	3	1	2	–	–	–	–	–
A.E.Knight	01/01/1904	3	3	–	–	–	–	–	–
J.Humphries	01/01/1908	3	3	–	–	–	–	–	–
J.Sharp	01/07/1909	3	3	–	–	–	–	–	–
H.D.G.Leveson Gower	01/01/1910	3	–	3	–	–	–	–	–
H.Dean	24/06/1912	3	2	1	–	–	–	–	–
G.E.C.Wood	14/06/1924	3	–	3	–	–	–	–	–
C.F.Root	12/06/1926	3	3	–	–	–	–	–	–
S.J.Staples	21/01/1928	3	–	3	–	–	–	–	–
Nawab of Pataudi snr	02/12/1932	3	3	–	–	–	–	–	–
D.C.H.Townsend	24/01/1935	3	–	–	3	–	–	–	–
H.Gimblett	27/06/1936	3	–	–	1	–	2	–	–
L.L.Wilkinson	24/12/1938	3	–	3	–	–	–	–	–
W.H.Copson	24/06/1939	3	–	1	2	–	–	–	–
W.Place	21/01/1948	3	–	–	3	–	–	–	–
M.F.Tremlett	21/01/1948	3	–	–	3	–	–	–	–
S.C.Griffith	11/02/1948	3	–	2	1	–	–	–	–
A.J.W.McIntyre	12/08/1950	3	1	1	1	–	–	–	–
C.J.Poole	30/12/1951	3	–	–	–	–	3	–	–
D.V.Smith	20/06/1957	3	–	–	3	–	–	–	–
K.Taylor	04/06/1959	3	1	–	–	–	2	–	–
P.M.Walker	09/06/1960	3	–	3	–	–	–	–	–
R.M.Prideaux	25/07/1968	3	1	–	–	–	–	2	–
M.W.W.Selvey	08/07/1976	3	–	–	2	–	1	–	–
G.D.Barlow	17/12/1976	3	1	–	–	–	2	–	–
G.A.Cope	14/12/1977	3	–	–	–	–	–	3	–
R.O.Butcher	13/03/1981	3	–	–	3	–	–	–	–
J.P.Agnew	09/08/1984	3	1	–	1	–	–	–	1
W.N.Slack	07/03/1986	3	–	–	2	–	1	–	–
N.V.Radford	03/07/1986	3	–	–	–	2	1	–	–
P.J.Newport	25/08/1988	3	2	–	–	–	–	–	1
A.P.Igglesden	24/08/1989	3	1	–	2	–	–	–	–
J.E.Morris	26/07/1990	3	–	–	–	–	3	–	–
S.L.Watkin	06/06/1991	3	1	–	2	–	–	–	–
H.Morris	25/07/1991	3	–	–	2	–	–	–	1
D.A.Reeve	18/01/1992	3	–	–	–	3	–	–	–
M.J.McCague	01/07/1993	3	3	–	–	–	–	–	–
J.E.R.Gallian	06/07/1995	3	–	1	2	–	–	–	–
T.Armitage	15/03/1877	2	2	–	–	–	–	–	–
H.R.J.Charlwood	15/03/1877	2	2	–	–	–	–	–	–
A.Greenwood	15/03/1877	2	2	–	–	–	–	–	–
A.Hill	15/03/1877	2	2	–	–	–	–	–	–
H.Jupp	15/03/1877	2	2	–	–	–	–	–	–
James Lillywhite	15/03/1877	2	2	–	–	–	–	–	–
J.Southerton	15/03/1877	2	2	–	–	–	–	–	–
F.H.Sugg	13/08/1888	2	2	–	–	–	–	–	–
M.P.Bowden	12/03/1889	2	–	2	–	–	–	–	–
Hon.C.J.Coventry	12/03/1889	2	–	2	–	–	–	–	–
A.J.Fothergill	12/03/1889	2	–	2	–	–	–	–	–
B.A.F.Grieve	12/03/1889	2	–	2	–	–	–	–	–
F.Hearne	12/03/1889	2	–	2	–	–	–	–	–
F.Martin	11/08/1890	2	1	1	–	–	–	–	–
C.Heseltine	02/03/1896	2	–	2	–	–	–	–	–
W.R.Cuttell	14/02/1899	2	–	2	–	–	–	–	–
F.W.Milligan	14/02/1899	2	–	2	–	–	–	–	–
F.Mitchell	14/02/1899	2	–	2	–	–	–	–	–
A.E.Trott	14/02/1899	2	–	2	–	–	–	–	–
C.E.M.Wilson	14/02/1899	2	–	2	–	–	–	–	–
C.L.Townsend	15/06/1899	2	2	–	–	–	–	–	–
H.I.Young	29/06/1899	2	2	–	–	–	–	–	–
W.M.Bradley	17/07/1899	2	2	–	–	–	–	–	–
C.P.McGahey	14/02/1902	2	2	–	–	–	–	–	–
L.C.H.Palairet	24/07/1902	2	2	–	–	–	–	–	–
J.C.Hartley	10/03/1906	2	–	2	–	–	–	–	–
N.A.Knox	29/07/1907	2	–	2	–	–	–	–	–
R.A.Young	13/12/1907	2	2	–	–	–	–	–	–
J.Vine	09/02/1912	2	2	–	–	–	–	–	–
M.W.Booth	13/12/1913	2	–	2	–	–	–	–	–
A.Waddington	17/12/1920	2	2	–	–	–	–	–	–
D.J.Knight	28/05/1921	2	2	–	–	–	–	–	–
C.Hallows	23/07/1921	2	1	–	1	–	–	–	–
E.T.Killick	15/06/1929	2	–	2	–	–	–	–	–
J.L.Hopwood	06/07/1934	2	2	–	–	–	–	–	–
W.W.Keeton	20/07/1934	2	1	–	1	–	–	–	–

Players	First Test	Tests	Aus	SA	WI	NZ	Ind	Pak	SL
W.Barber	13/07/1935	2	–	2	–	–	–	–	–
D.Smith	13/07/1935	2	–	2	–	–	–	–	–
A.W.Wellard	24/07/1937	2	1	–	–	1	–	–	–
R.T.D.Perks	03/03/1939	2	–	1	1	–	–	–	–
H.J.Butler	26/07/1947	2	–	1	1	–	–	–	–
G.A.Smithson	21/01/1948	2	–	–	2	–	–	–	–
H.L.Jackson	23/07/1949	2	1	–	–	1	–	–	–
R.Berry	08/06/1950	2	–	–	2	–	–	–	–
G.H.G.Doggart	08/06/1950	2	–	–	2	–	–	–	–
J.J.Warr	05/01/1951	2	2	–	–	–	–	–	–
D.V.Brennan	26/07/1951	2	–	2	–	–	–	–	–
D.B.Carr	02/11/1951	2	–	–	–	–	2	–	–
E.Leadbeater	14/12/1951	2	–	–	–	–	2	–	–
J.E.McConnon	22/07/1954	2	–	–	–	–	–	2	–
K.V.Andrew	26/11/1954	2	1	–	1	–	–	–	–
A.S.M.Oakman	12/07/1956	2	2	–	–	–	–	–	–
M.J.Horton	04/06/1959	2	–	–	–	–	2	–	–
H.J.Rhodes	02/07/1959	2	–	–	–	–	2	–	–
D.E.V.Padgett	21/07/1960	2	–	2	–	–	–	–	–
A.Brown	21/10/1961	2	–	–	–	–	1	1	–
D.W.White	21/10/1961	2	–	–	–	–	–	2	–
J.G.Binks	21/01/1964	2	–	–	–	–	2	–	–
J.C.Balderstone	22/07/1976	2	–	–	2	–	–	–	–
G.B.Stevenson	15/02/1980	2	–	–	1	–	1	–	–
I.A.Greig	29/07/1982	2	–	–	–	–	–	2	–
V.P.Terry	12/07/1984	2	–	–	2	–	–	–	–
L.B.Taylor	15/08/1985	2	2	–	–	–	–	–	–
D.M.Smith	21/02/1986	2	–	–	2	–	–	–	–
J.H.Childs	30/06/1988	2	–	–	2	–	–	–	–
T.A.Munton	02/07/1992	2	–	–	–	–	–	2	–
N.A.Mallender	23/07/1992	2	–	–	–	–	–	2	–
J.P.Taylor	29/01/1993	2	–	–	–	1	1	–	–
R.J.Blakey	11/02/1993	2	–	–	–	–	2	–	–
M.N.Lathwell	01/07/1993	2	2	–	–	–	–	–	–
M.P.Bicknell	22/07/1993	2	2	–	–	–	–	–	–
R.C.Irani	06/06/1996	2	–	–	–	–	2	–	–
M.M.Patel	06/06/1996	2	–	–	–	–	2	–	–
M.A.Ealham	04/07/1996	2	–	–	–	–	1	1	–
C.A.Absolom	02/01/1879	1	1	–	–	–	–	–	–
L.Hone	02/01/1879	1	1	–	–	–	–	–	–
F.A.MacKinnon	02/01/1879	1	1	–	–	–	–	–	–
V.P.F.A.Royle	02/01/1879	1	1	–	–	–	–	–	–
S.S.Schultz	02/01/1879	1	1	–	–	–	–	–	–
A.J.Webbe	02/01/1879	1	1	–	–	–	–	–	–
E.M.Grace	06/09/1880	1	1	–	–	–	–	–	–
G.F.Grace	06/09/1880	1	1	–	–	–	–	–	–
F.Penn	06/09/1880	1	1	–	–	–	–	–	–
G.F.Vernon	30/12/1882	1	1	–	–	–	–	–	–
S.Christopherson	21/07/1884	1	1	–	–	–	–	–	–
R.Wood	25/02/1887	1	1	–	–	–	–	–	–
W.Newham	10/02/1888	1	1	–	–	–	–	–	–
J.Shuter	13/08/1888	1	1	–	–	–	–	–	–
C.A.Smith	12/03/1889	1	–	1	–	–	–	–	–
J.E.P.McMaster	25/03/1889	1	–	1	–	–	–	–	–
J.Cranston	11/08/1890	1	1	–	–	–	–	–	–
V.A.Barton	19/03/1892	1	–	1	–	–	–	–	–
W.Chatterton	19/03/1892	1	–	1	–	–	–	–	–
J.J.Ferris	19/03/1892	1	–	1	–	–	–	–	–
A.Hearne	19/03/1892	1	–	1	–	–	–	–	–
G.G.Hearne	19/03/1892	1	–	1	–	–	–	–	–
W.L.Murdoch	19/03/1892	1	–	1	–	–	–	–	–
A.D.Pougher	19/03/1892	1	–	1	–	–	–	–	–
L.H.Gay	14/12/1894	1	1	–	–	–	–	–	–
A.M.Miller	13/02/1896	1	–	1	–	–	–	–	–
E.J.Tyler	21/03/1896	1	–	1	–	–	–	–	–
A.G.Archer	01/04/1899	1	–	1	–	–	–	–	–
W.Mead	15/06/1899	1	1	–	–	–	–	–	–
F.W.Tate	24/07/1902	1	1	–	–	–	–	–	–
A.Warren	03/07/1905	1	1	–	–	–	–	–	–
J.H.King	14/06/1909	1	1	–	–	–	–	–	–
D.W.Carr	09/08/1909	1	1	–	–	–	–	–	–
N.C.Tufnell	11/03/1910	1	–	1	–	–	–	–	–
S.P.Kinneir	15/12/1911	1	1	–	–	–	–	–	–
A.Dolphin	11/02/1921	1	1	–	–	–	–	–	–

Players	First Test	Tests	Aus	SA	WI	NZ	Ind	Pak	SL
E.R.Wilson	25/02/1921	1	1	–	–	–	–	–	–
T.L.Richmond	28/05/1921	1	1	–	–	–	–	–	–
A.E.Dipper	11/06/1921	1	1	–	–	–	–	–	–
F.J.Durston	11/06/1921	1	1	–	–	–	–	–	–
A.J.Evans	11/06/1921	1	1	–	–	–	–	–	–
A.Ducat	02/07/1921	1	1	–	–	–	–	–	–
H.T.W.Hardinge	02/07/1921	1	1	–	–	–	–	–	–
C.W.L.Parker	23/07/1921	1	1	–	–	–	–	–	–
G.B.Street	18/01/1923	1	–	1	–	–	–	–	–
J.C.W.MacBryan	26/07/1924	1	–	1	–	–	–	–	–
H.Smith	23/06/1928	1	–	–	1	–	–	–	–
H.W.Lee	13/02/1931	1	–	1	–	–	–	–	–
J.Arnold	27/06/1931	1	–	–	–	1	–	–	–
C.S.Marriott	12/08/1933	1	–	–	1	–	–	–	–
W.H.V.Levett	05/01/1934	1	–	–	–	–	1	–	–
N.S.Mitchell-Innes	15/06/1935	1	–	1	–	–	–	–	–
J.C.Clay	17/08/1935	1	–	1	–	–	–	–	–
H.D.Read	17/08/1935	1	–	1	–	–	–	–	–
J.H.Parks	26/06/1937	1	–	–	–	1	–	–	–
A.D.G.Matthews	14/08/1937	1	–	–	–	1	–	–	–
R.A.Sinfield	10/06/1938	1	1	–	–	–	–	–	–
W.F.F.Price	22/07/1938	1	1	–	–	–	–	–	–
N.Oldfield	19/08/1939	1	–	–	1	–	–	–	–
T.F.Smailes	22/06/1946	1	–	–	–	–	1	–	–
C.Cook	07/06/1947	1	–	1	–	–	–	–	–
J.W.Martin	07/06/1947	1	–	1	–	–	–	–	–
G.H.Pope	21/06/1947	1	–	1	–	–	–	–	–
D.Brookes	21/01/1948	1	–	–	1	–	–	–	–
A.Coxon	24/06/1948	1	1	–	–	–	–	–	–
G.M.Emmett	08/07/1948	1	1	–	–	–	–	–	–
A.Wharton	11/06/1949	1	–	–	–	1	–	–	–
C.H.Palmer	06/02/1954	1	–	–	1	–	–	–	–
D.W.Richardson	04/07/1957	1	–	–	1	–	–	–	–
K.E.Palmer	12/02/1965	1	–	1	–	–	–	–	–
A.R.Butcher	30/08/1979	1	–	–	–	–	1	–	–
P.W.G.Parker	27/08/1981	1	1	–	–	–	–	–	–
A.C.S.Pigott	03/02/1984	1	–	–	–	1	–	–	–
T.A.Lloyd	14/06/1984	1	–	–	1	–	–	–	–
A.Sidebottom	11/07/1985	1	1	–	–	–	–	–	–
M.R.Benson	03/07/1986	1	–	–	–	–	1	–	–
J.J.Whitaker	12/12/1986	1	1	–	–	–	–	–	–
J.P.Stephenson	24/08/1989	1	1	–	–	–	–	–	–
N.F.Williams	23/08/1990	1	–	–	–	–	1	–	–
J.E.Benjamin	18/08/1994	1	–	1	–	–	–	–	–
A.P.Wells	24/08/1995	1	–	–	1	–	–	–	–
S.J.E.Brown	25/07/1996	1	–	–	–	–	–	1	–
R.D.B.Croft	22/08/1996	1	–	–	–	–	–	1	–
		8019	3135	1210	1265	825	924	605	55

MOST APPEARANCES AGAINST EACH OPPOSITION

Australia
M.C.Cowdrey	43
G.A.Gooch	42
D.I.Gower	42
W.Rhodes	41
J.B.Hobbs	41

South Africa
F.E.Woolley	26
W.R.Hammond	24
D.C.S.Compton	24
T.G.Evans	19
L.Hutton	19

West Indies
G.Boycott	29
G.A.Gooch	26
A.P.E.Knott	22
A.J.Lamb	22
M.C.Cowdrey	21

New Zealand
M.C.Cowdrey	18

G.Boycott	15
G.A.Gooch	15
I.T.Botham	15
T.G.Evans	14
R.G.D.Willis	14
R.W.Taylor	14
A.J.Lamb	14

India

D.I.Gower	24
D.L.Underwood	20
K.W.R.Fletcher	19
G.A.Gooch	19
R.G.D.Willis	17

Pakistan

D.I.Gower	17
M.W.Gatting	15
A.P.E.Knott	14
I.T.Botham	14
T.W.Graveney	13

Sri Lanka

I.T.Botham	3
J.E.Emburey	3
G.A.Gooch	3
R.A.Smith	3

NUMBER OF APPEARANCES PER PLAYER

Matches	No of players
More than 100	5
90-99	3
80-89	3
70-79	7
60-69	10
50-59	12
40-49	15
30-39	23
20-29	46
10-19	85
6-9	83
5	43
4	43
3	47
2	74
1	83

Batting Records

LEADING RUN SCORERS

Batsman	Mat	Inn	NO	Runs	H/S	Avg	100	50
G.A.Gooch	118	215	6	8900	333	42.58	20	46
D.I.Gower	117	204	18	8231	215	44.25	18	39
G.Boycott	108	193	23	8114	246*	47.72	22	42
M.C.Cowdrey	114	188	15	7624	182	44.06	22	38
W.R.Hammond	85	140	16	7249	336*	58.45	22	24
L.Hutton	79	138	15	6971	364	56.67	19	33
K.F.Barrington	82	131	15	6806	256	58.67	20	35
D.C.S.Compton	78	131	15	5807	278	50.06	17	28
J.B.Hobbs	61	102	7	5410	211	56.94	15	28
I.T.Botham	102	161	6	5200	208	33.54	14	22
J.H.Edrich	77	127	9	5138	310*	43.54	12	24
T.W.Graveney	79	123	13	4882	258	44.38	11	20
A.J.Lamb	79	139	10	4656	142	36.09	14	18
M.A.Atherton	62	114	3	4627	185*	41.68	10	29
H.Sutcliffe	54	84	9	4555	194	60.73	16	23
P.B.H.May	66	106	9	4537	285*	46.77	13	22
E.R.Dexter	62	102	8	4502	205	47.89	9	27
M.W.Gatting	79	138	14	4409	207	35.55	10	21

Batsman	Mat	Inn	NO	Runs	H/S	Avg	100	50
A.P.E.Knott	95	149	15	4389	135	32.75	5	30
R.A.Smith	62	112	15	4236	175	43.67	9	28
A.J.Stewart	58	103	6	3935	190	40.56	8	20
D.L.Amiss	50	88	10	3612	262*	46.30	11	11
A.W.Greig	58	93	4	3599	148	40.43	8	20
E.H.Hendren	51	83	9	3525	205*	47.63	7	21
F.E.Woolley	64	98	7	3283	154	36.07	5	23
K.W.R.Fletcher	59	96	14	3272	216	39.90	7	19
M.Leyland	41	65	5	2764	187	46.06	9	10
G.A.Hick	46	80	6	2672	178	36.10	4	15
C.Washbrook	37	66	6	2569	195	42.81	6	12
B.L.D'Oliveira	44	70	8	2484	158	40.06	5	15
D.W.Randall	47	79	5	2470	174	33.37	7	12
W.J.Edrich	39	63	2	2440	219	40.00	6	13
T.G.Evans	91	133	14	2439	104	20.49	2	8
L.E.G.Ames	47	72	12	2434	149	40.56	8	7
W.Rhodes	58	98	21	2325	179	30.19	2	11
T.E.Bailey	61	91	14	2290	134*	29.74	1	10
M.J.K.Smith	50	78	6	2278	121	31.63	3	11
G.P.Thorpe	32	59	5	2194	123	40.62	2	18
P.E.Richardson	34	56	1	2061	126	37.47	5	9
T.W.Hayward	35	60	2	1999	137	34.46	3	12
G.Pullar	28	49	4	1974	175	43.86	4	12
J.M.Parks	46	68	7	1962	108*	32.16	2	9
A.C.MacLaren	35	61	4	1931	140	33.87	5	8
P.H.Parfitt	37	52	6	1882	131*	40.91	7	6
R.E.S.Wyatt	40	64	6	1839	149	31.70	2	12
R.Illingworth	61	90	11	1836	113	23.24	2	5
R.C.Russell	49	77	15	1807	128*	29.14	2	6
C.J.Tavare	31	56	2	1755	149	32.50	2	12
J.E.Emburey	64	96	20	1703	75	22.53	0	10
M.H.Denness	28	45	3	1667	188	39.69	4	7
B.C.Broad	25	44	2	1661	162	39.54	6	6
J.T.Tyldesley	31	55	1	1661	138	30.75	4	9
J.Hardstaff jnr	23	38	3	1636	205*	46.74	4	10
R.T.Robinson	29	49	5	1601	175	36.38	4	6
E.Paynter	20	31	5	1540	243	59.23	4	7
R.W.Barber	28	45	3	1495	185	35.59	1	9
F.J.Titmus	53	76	11	1449	84*	22.29	0	10
J.M.Brearley	39	66	3	1442	91	22.88	0	9
Hon.F.S.Jackson	20	33	4	1415	144*	48.79	5	6
R.T.Simpson	27	45	3	1401	156*	33.35	4	6
G.Fowler	21	37	0	1307	201	35.32	3	8
B.W.Luckhurst	21	41	5	1298	131	36.05	4	5
D.R.Jardine	22	33	6	1296	127	48.00	1	10
A.Shrewsbury	23	40	4	1277	164	35.47	3	4
C.B.Fry	26	41	3	1223	144	32.18	2	7
G.Miller	34	51	4	1213	98*	25.80	0	7
M.W.Tate	39	52	5	1198	100*	25.48	1	5
C.P.Mead	17	26	2	1185	182*	49.37	4	3
P.Willey	26	50	6	1184	102*	26.90	2	5
Rev.D.S.Sheppard	22	33	2	1172	119	37.80	3	6
R.W.Taylor	57	83	12	1156	97	16.28	0	3
G.Gunn	15	29	1	1120	122*	40.00	2	7
C.C.Lewis	32	51	3	1105	117	23.02	1	4
C.J.Barnett	20	35	4	1098	129	35.41	2	5
W.G.Grace	22	36	2	1098	170	32.29	2	5
R.A.Woolmer	19	34	2	1059	149	33.09	3	2

HIGHEST AVERAGES

(Minimum qualification: five completed innings)

Batsman	Avg	Runs	Tests	Inn	NO
B.H.Valentine	64.85	454	7	9	2
H.Sutcliffe	60.73	4555	54	84	9
E.Paynter	59.23	1540	20	31	5
K.F.Barrington	58.67	6806	82	131	15
K.S.Duleepsinhji	58.52	995	12	19	2
W.R.Hammond	58.45	7249	85	140	16
J.B.Hobbs	56.94	5410	61	102	7
C.A.G.Russell	56.87	910	10	18	2
L.Hutton	56.67	6971	79	138	15
G.E.Tyldesley	55.00	990	14	20	2

Batsman	Avg	Runs	Tests	Inn	NO
C.F.Walters	52.26	784	11	18	3
D.C.S.Compton	50.06	5807	78	131	15
G.B.Legge	49.83	299	5	7	1
C.P.Mead	49.37	1185	17	26	2
Hon.F.S.Jackson	48.79	1415	20	33	4
C.T.Radley	48.10	481	8	10	0
D.R.Jardine	48.00	1296	22	33	6
E.R.Dexter	47.89	4502	62	102	8
G.Boycott	47.72	8114	108	193	23
E.H.Hendren	47.63	3525	51	83	9
R.Subba Row	46.85	984	13	22	1
P.B.H.May	46.77	4537	66	106	9
J.Hardstaff jnr	46.74	1636	23	38	3
C.Milburn	46.71	654	9	16	2
J.D.B.Robertson	46.36	881	11	21	2
D.L.Amiss	46.30	3612	50	88	10
R.E.Foster	46.30	602	8	14	0
P.J.Sharpe	46.23	786	12	21	4
M.Leyland	46.06	2764	41	65	5
A.H.Bakewell	45.44	409	6	9	0
K.S.Ranjitsinhji	44.95	989	15	26	4
P.A.Gibb	44.69	581	8	13	0
T.W.Graveney	44.38	4882	79	123	13
D.I.Gower	44.25	8231	117	204	18
M.C.Cowdrey	44.06	7624	114	188	15
G.Pullar	43.86	1974	28	49	4
R.A.Smith	43.67	4236	62	112	15
J.H.Edrich	43.54	5138	77	127	9
C.Washbrook	42.81	2569	37	66	6
G.A.Gooch	42.58	8900	118	215	6
D.Lloyd	42.46	552	9	15	2
D.S.Steele	42.06	673	8	16	0
M.A.Atherton	41.68	4627	62	114	3
J.B.Bolus	41.33	496	7	12	0
P.H.Parfitt	40.91	1882	37	52	6
G.P.Thorpe	40.62	2194	32	59	5
L.E.G.Ames	40.56	2434	47	72	12
A.J.Stewart	40.56	3935	58	103	6
A.J.Watkins	40.50	810	15	24	4
A.W.Greig	40.43	3599	58	93	4
B.L.D'Oliveira	40.06	2484	44	70	8
W.J.Edrich	40.00	2440	39	63	2
G.Gunn	40.00	1120	15	29	1

HIGHEST INDIVIDUAL SCORES

Score	Batsman	Opposition	Venue	Date	No
364	L.Hutton	Australia	The Oval	1938	175
336*	W.R.Hammond	New Zealand	Auckland	1932/33	144
333	G.A.Gooch	India	Lord's	1990	539
325	A.Sandham	West Indies	Kingston	1929/30	125
310*	J.H.Edrich	New Zealand	Headingley	1965	341
287	R.E.Foster	Australia	Sydney	1903/04	38
285*	P.B.H.May	West Indies	Edgbaston	1957	265
278	D.C.S.Compton	Pakistan	Trent Bridge	1954	252
262*	D.L.Amiss	West Indies	Kingston	1973/74	406
258	T.W.Graveney	West Indies	Trent Bridge	1957	269
256	K.F.Barrington	Australia	Old Trafford	1964	330
251	W.R.Hammond	Australia	Sydney	1928/29	101
246*	G.Boycott	India	Headingley	1967	354
243	E.Paynter	South Africa	Durban (2)	1938/39	184
240	W.R.Hammond	Australia	Lord's	1938	174
231*	W.R.Hammond	Australia	Sydney	1936/37	163
227	W.R.Hammond	New Zealand	Christchurch	1932/33	142
219	W.J.Edrich	South Africa	Durban (2)	1938/39	188
217	W.R.Hammond	India	The Oval	1936	160
216*	E.Paynter	Australia	Trent Bridge	1938	172
216	K.W.R.Fletcher	New Zealand	Auckland	1974/75	426
215	D.I.Gower	Australia	Edgbaston	1985	505
214*	D.Lloyd	India	Edgbaston	1974	417
211	J.B.Hobbs	South Africa	Lord's	1924	78
210	G.A.Gooch	New Zealand	Trent Bridge	1994	576
208	D.C.S.Compton	South Africa	Lord's	1947	201
208	I.T.Botham	India	The Oval	1982	476

Score	Batsman	Opposition	Venue	Date	No
207	M.W.Gatting	India	Madras (1)	1984/85	500
206	L.Hutton	New Zealand	The Oval	1949	225
205*	E.H.Hendren	West Indies	Port-of-Spain	1929/30	122
205*	J.Hardstaff jnr	India	Lord's	1946	193
205	L.Hutton	West Indies	Kingston	1953/54	250
205	E.R.Dexter	Pakistan	Karachi (1)	1961/62	306
203	D.L.Amiss	West Indies	The Oval	1976	433
202*	L.Hutton	West Indies	The Oval	1950	230
201	G.Fowler	India	Madras (1)	1984/85	499
200*	D.I.Gower	India	Edgbaston	1979	453
200	W.R.Hammond	Australia	Melbourne	1928/29	103
196	G.B.Legge	New Zealand	Auckland	1929/30	120
196	L.Hutton	West Indies	Lord's	1939	189
196	G.A.Gooch	Australia	The Oval	1985	507
195	C.Washbrook	South Africa	Johannesburg (2)	1948/49	214
194	H.Sutcliffe	Australia	Sydney	1932/33	138
191	W.J.Edrich	South Africa	Old Trafford	1947	202
191	G.Boycott	Australia	Headingley	1977	441
190	A.J.Stewart	Pakistan	Edgbaston	1992	561
189	W.J.Edrich	South Africa	Lord's	1947	200
188	D.L.Amiss	India	Lord's	1974	414
188	M.H.Denness	Australia	Melbourne	1974/75	423
187	J.B.Hobbs	South Africa	Cape Town	1909/10	54
187	J.B.Hobbs	Australia	Adelaide	1911/12	57
187	M.Leyland	Australia	The Oval	1938	176
185*	M.A.Atherton	South Africa	Johannesburg (3)	1995/96	585
185	R.W.Barber	Australia	Sydney	1965/66	346
184	D.C.S.Compton	Australia	Trent Bridge	1948	209
183*	M.W.Gatting	India	Edgbaston	1986	510
183	D.L.Amiss	Pakistan	The Oval	1974	419
183	G.A.Gooch	New Zealand	Lord's	1986	511
182*	C.P.Mead	Australia	The Oval	1921	73
182	M.C.Cowdrey	Pakistan	The Oval	1962	314
181	C.P.Mead	South Africa	Durban (2)	1922/23	74
181	W.R.Hammond	South Africa	Cape Town	1938/39	181
181	M.H.Denness	New Zealand	Auckland	1974/75	425
180	E.R.Dexter	Australia	Edgbaston	1961	297
179	W.Rhodes	Australia	Melbourne	1911/12	59
179	D.L.Amiss	India	Delhi	1976/77	434
178	J.B.Hobbs	Australia	Melbourne	1911/12	58
178	K.W.R.Fletcher	New Zealand	Lord's	1973	402
178	G.A.Hick	India	Bombay (3)	1992/93	565
177	W.R.Hammond	Australia	Adelaide	1928/29	105
176	H.Sutcliffe	Australia	Melbourne	1924/25	87
175	K.S.Ranjitsinhji	Australia	Sydney	1897/98	26
175	T.W.Graveney	India	Bombay (2)	1951/52	239
175	G.Pullar	South Africa	The Oval	1960	294
175	J.H.Edrich	Australia	Lord's	1975	428
175	R.T.Robinson	Australia	Headingley	1985	501
175	R.A.Smith	West Indies	St John's	1993/94	574
174	E.R.Dexter	Australia	Old Trafford	1964	329
174	D.L.Amiss	West Indies	Port-of-Spain	1973/74	405
174	D.W.Randall	Australia	Melbourne	1976/77	436
174	G.A.Gooch	Sri Lanka	Lord's	1991	555
173*	D.I.Gower	Pakistan	Lahore (2)	1983/84	491
173	A.E.Stoddart	Australia	Melbourne	1894/95	19
173	K.S.Duleepsinhji	Australia	Lord's	1930	127
172	K.F.Barrington	India	Kanpur	1961/62	302
172	E.R.Dexter	Pakistan	The Oval	1962	315
172	E.R.Dexter	South Africa	Johannesburg (3)	1964/65	334
170	W.G.Grace	Australia	The Oval	1886	10
170	A.J.Stewart	Pakistan	Headingley	1996	590
169*	J.Hardstaff jnr	Australia	The Oval	1938	177
169	E.H.Hendren	Australia	Brisbane (1)	1928/29	100
169	L.Hutton	West Indies	Georgetown	1953/54	247
167	W.R.Hammond	India	Old Trafford	1936	159
166	D.I.Gower	Australia	Trent Bridge	1985	502
166	R.T.Robinson	Pakistan	Old Trafford	1987	521
165*	L.Hutton	West Indies	The Oval	1939	191
165	G.Pullar	Pakistan	Dacca	1961/62	305
165	T.W.Graveney	West Indies	The Oval	1966	352
164*	D.L.Amiss	New Zealand	Christchurch	1974/75	427
164	A.Shrewsbury	Australia	Lord's	1886	9
164	T.W.Graveney	West Indies	The Oval	1957	272

Score	Batsman	Opposition	Venue	Date	No
164	J.H.Edrich	Australia	The Oval	1968	367
164	D.W.Randall	New Zealand	Wellington	1983/84	488
163	D.C.S.Compton	South Africa	Trent Bridge	1947	199
163	K.F.Barrington	New Zealand	Headingley	1965	342
162	B.C.Broad	Australia	Perth	1986/87	515
161	H.Sutcliffe	Australia	The Oval	1926	94
161	H.Sutcliffe	Australia	The Oval	1930	130
161	M.Leyland	South Africa	The Oval	1935	157
160	M.C.Cowdrey	India	Headingley	1959	282
160	R.T.Robinson	India	Delhi	1984/85	498
160	M.W.Gatting	Australia	Old Trafford	1985	503
160	M.A.Atherton	India	Trent Bridge	1996	588
159	J.B.Hobbs	West Indies	The Oval	1928	99
159	M.C.Cowdrey	Pakistan	Edgbaston	1962	308
158	L.Hutton	South Africa	Johannesburg (2)	1948/49	213
158	D.C.S.Compton	South Africa	Old Trafford	1955	258
158	B.L.D'Oliveira	Australia	The Oval	1968	368
158	D.L.Amiss	Pakistan	Hyderabad	1972/73	399
158	C.T.Radley	New Zealand	Auckland	1977/78	444
157*	D.I.Gower	India	The Oval	1990	547
157	D.I.Gower	Australia	The Oval	1985	508
156*	L.Hutton	Australia	Adelaide	1950/51	231
156*	R.T.Simpson	Australia	Melbourne	1950/51	232
155	M.C.Cowdrey	South Africa	The Oval	1960	295
155	J.H.Edrich	New Zealand	Trent Bridge	1969	378
155	G.Boycott	India	Edgbaston	1979	452
154*	K.S.Ranjitsinhji	Australia	Old Trafford	1896	24
154*	D.I.Gower	West Indies	Kingston	1980/81	465
154*	G.A.Gooch	West Indies	Headingley	1991	552
154	J.B.Hobbs	Australia	Melbourne	1924/25	86
154	F.E.Woolley	South Africa	Old Trafford	1929	114
154	M.C.Cowdrey	West Indies	Edgbaston	1957	266
154	G.A.Gooch	New Zealand	Edgbaston	1990	538
153	M.Leyland	Australia	Old Trafford	1934	152
153	T.W.Graveney	Pakistan	Lord's	1962	310
153	G.A.Gooch	West Indies	Kingston	1980/81	464
152	W.G.Grace	Australia	The Oval	1880	1
152	W.Rhodes	South Africa	Johannesburg (1)	1913/14	64
152	A.Sandham	West Indies	Bridgetown	1929/30	121
152	M.C.Cowdrey	West Indies	Lord's	1957	267
152	D.I.Gower	Pakistan	Faisalabad	1983/84	490
151*	K.F.Barrington	India	Bombay (2)	1961/62	300
151	M.C.Cowdrey	India	Delhi	1963/64	325
151	T.W.Graveney	India	Lord's	1967	356
151	M.A.Atherton	New Zealand	Trent Bridge	1990	537
150*	M.W.Gatting	Pakistan	The Oval	1987	524
150	L.Hutton	India	Lord's	1952	240
150	D.W.Randall	Australia	Sydney	1978/79	451
149*	I.T.Botham	Australia	Headingley	1981	466
149	G.Ulyett	Australia	Melbourne	1881/82	2
149	L.E.G.Ames	West Indies	Kingston	1929/30	126
149	R.E.S.Wyatt	South Africa	Trent Bridge	1935	155
149	R.A.Woolmer	Australia	The Oval	1975	429
149	C.J.Tavare	India	Delhi	1981/82	470
148*	L.E.G.Ames	South Africa	The Oval	1935	158
148*	K.F.Barrington	South Africa	Durban (2)	1964/65	332
148*	R.A.Smith	West Indies	Lord's	1991	553
148	A.G.Steel	Australia	Lord's	1884	4
148	K.F.Barrington	Pakistan	Lord's	1967	357
148	M.C.Cowdrey	West Indies	Port-of-Spain	1967/68	364
148	A.W.Greig	India	Bombay (2)	1972/73	397
148	A.W.Greig	West Indies	Bridgetown	1973/74	408
148	R.T.Robinson	Australia	Edgbaston	1985	504
148	A.J.Stewart	New Zealand	Christchurch	1991/92	557
147	D.C.S.Compton	Australia	Adelaide	1946/47	196
146	J.H.Edrich	West Indies	Bridgetown	1967/68	363
146	K.W.R.Fletcher	Australia	Melbourne	1974/75	424
146	G.A.Gooch	West Indies	Trent Bridge	1988	528
145*	D.C.S.Compton	Australia	Old Trafford	1948	210
145	L.Hutton	Australia	Lord's	1953	244
144*	Hon.F.S.Jackson	Australia	Headingley	1905	42
144	C.B.Fry	Australia	The Oval	1905	45
144	M.A.Atherton	West Indies	Georgetown	1993/94	570
143	F.L.Fane	South Africa	Johannesburg (1)	1905/06	46

Score	Batsman	Opposition	Venue	Date	No
143	H.Sutcliffe	Australia	Melbourne	1924/25	90
143	C.Washbrook	Australia	Headingley	1948	211
143	K.F.Barrington	West Indies	Port-of-Spain	1967/68	360
143	R.A.Smith	Australia	Old Trafford	1989	532
143	A.J.Stewart	West Indies	Bridgetown	1993/94	572
142*	G.Boycott	Australia	Sydney	1970/71	382
142	E.H.Hendren	South Africa	The Oval	1924	82
142	J.B.Hobbs	Australia	Melbourne	1928/29	106
142	K.F.Barrington	Pakistan	The Oval	1967	359
142	I.T.Botham	India	Kanpur	1981/82	472
142	A.J.Lamb	New Zealand	Wellington	1991/92	560
141	E.R.Dexter	New Zealand	Christchurch	1958/59	279
141	G.A.Hick	South Africa	Centurion	1995/96	584
140	J.T.Brown	Australia	Melbourne	1894/95	20
140	A.C.MacLaren	Australia	Trent Bridge	1905	40
140	C.A.G.Russell	South Africa	Durban (2)	1922/23	76
140	W.R.Hammond	New Zealand	Lord's	1937	167
140	W.R.Hammond	South Africa	Durban (2)	1938/39	187
140	S.C.Griffith	West Indies	Port-of-Spain	1947/48	207
139	K.F.Barrington	Pakistan	Lahore (2)	1961/62	299
139	C.Milburn	Pakistan	Karachi (1)	1968/69	371
139	A.W.Greig	New Zealand	Trent Bridge	1973	401
139	B.C.Broad	Australia	Sydney	1987/88	526
139	A.J.Lamb	India	Lord's	1990	541
138*	W.R.Hammond	South Africa	Edgbaston	1929	109
138*	D.L.Amiss	New Zealand	Trent Bridge	1973	400
138	J.T.Tyldesley	Australia	Edgbaston	1902	35
138	W.R.Hammond	West Indies	The Oval	1939	192
138	P.B.H.May	South Africa	Headingley	1951	237
138	I.T.Botham	New Zealand	Wellington	1983/84	487
138	I.T.Botham	Australia	Brisbane (2)	1986/87	514
137*	A.J.Watkins	India	Delhi	1951/52	238
137*	A.J.Lamb	New Zealand	Trent Bridge	1983	485
137	T.W.Hayward	Australia	The Oval	1899	32
137	M.Leyland	Australia	Melbourne	1928/29	107
137	L.E.G.Ames	New Zealand	Lord's	1931	132
137	R.T.Simpson	South Africa	Trent Bridge	1951	234
137	R.Subba Row	Australia	The Oval	1961	298
137	K.F.Barrington	New Zealand	Edgbaston	1965	339
137	R.A.Woolmer	Australia	Old Trafford	1977	438
137	I.T.Botham	India	Headingley	1979	454
137	G.Boycott	Australia	The Oval	1981	468
136*	W.R.Hammond	South Africa	Durban (2)	1930/31	131
136*	F.G.Mann	South Africa	Port Elizabeth	1948/49	218
136*	E.R.Dexter	West Indies	Bridgetown	1959/60	286
136	B.H.Valentine	India	Bombay (1)	1933/34	147
136	M.W.Gatting	India	Bombay (3)	1984/85	497
136	D.I.Gower	Australia	Perth	1986/87	516
135*	A.G.Steel	Australia	Sydney	1882/83	3
135*	C.A.G.Russell	Australia	Adelaide	1920/21	69
135	H.Sutcliffe	Australia	Melbourne	1928/29	102
135	P.B.H.May	West Indies	Port-of-Spain	1953/54	248
135	A.P.E.Knott	Australia	Trent Bridge	1977	440
135	G.A.Gooch	Pakistan	Headingley	1992	563
135	M.A.Atherton	West Indies	St John's	1993/94	573
134*	H.Wood	South Africa	Cape Town	1891/92	14
134*	F.E.Woolley	South Africa	Lord's	1924	80
134*	T.E.Bailey	New Zealand	Christchurch	1950/51	233
134	W.Barnes	Australia	Adelaide	1884/85	6
134	A.E.Stoddart	Australia	Adelaide	1891/92	13
133*	F.E.Woolley	Australia	Sydney	1911/12	60
133	J.D.B.Robertson	West Indies	Port-of-Spain	1947/48	206
133	D.C.S.Compton	West Indies	Port-of-Spain	1953/54	249
133	C.J.Richards	Australia	Perth	1986/87	517
133	G.A.Gooch	Australia	Old Trafford	1993	567
132*	R.Abel	Australia	Sydney	1891/92	12
132*	P.F.Warner	South Africa	Johannesburg (1)	1898/99	28
132*	K.F.Barrington	Australia	Adelaide	1962/63	318
132	E.H.Hendren	South Africa	Headingley	1924	81
132	E.H.Hendren	Australia	Old Trafford	1934	151
132	A.J.Lamb	West Indies	Kingston	1989/90	535
131*	P.H.Parfitt	New Zealand	Auckland	1962/63	321
131	G.Pullar	India	Old Trafford	1959	283
131	B.W.Luckhurst	Australia	Perth	1970/71	380

Score	Batsman	Opposition	Venue	Date	No
131	G.Boycott	New Zealand	Trent Bridge	1978	449
131	D.I.Gower	New Zealand	The Oval	1986	512
131	M.A.Atherton	India	Old Trafford	1990	544
130	T.W.Hayward	Australia	Old Trafford	1899	30
130	J.H.Edrich	Australia	Adelaide	1970/71	386
129*	K.W.R.Fletcher	West Indies	Bridgetown	1973/74	407
129	C.B.Fry	South Africa	The Oval	1907	48
129	C.J.Barnett	Australia	Adelaide	1936/37	165
128*	M.C.Cowdrey	New Zealand	Wellington	1962/63	323
128*	G.Boycott	Australia	Lord's	1980	460
128*	R.C.Russell	Australia	Old Trafford	1989	533
128	Hon.F.S.Jackson	Australia	Old Trafford	1902	36
128	T.S.Worthington	India	The Oval	1936	161
128	K.F.Barrington	West Indies	Bridgetown	1959/60	285
128	G.Boycott	West Indies	Old Trafford	1969	373
128	I.T.Botham	India	Old Trafford	1982	474
128	R.A.Smith	Sri Lanka	Colombo (2)	1992/93	566
128	N.Hussain	India	Edgbaston	1996	586
127*	E.H.Hendren	Australia	Lord's	1926	92
127	H.Sutcliffe	Australia	Melbourne	1924/25	88
127	D.R.Jardine	West Indies	Old Trafford	1933	145
127	B.R.Knight	India	Kanpur	1963/64	326
127	G.A.Gooch	India	Madras (1)	1981/82	471
127	R.A.Smith	Pakistan	Edgbaston	1992	562
126*	J.B.Hobbs	Australia	Melbourne	1911/12	55
126*	E.R.Dexter	India	Kanpur	1961/62	303
126*	C.Milburn	West Indies	Lord's	1966	350
126	K.L.Hutchings	Australia	Melbourne	1907/08	50
126	L.E.G.Ames	West Indies	Kingston	1934/35	154
126	M.Leyland	Australia	Brisbane (2)	1936/37	162
126	C.J.Barnett	Australia	Trent Bridge	1938	170
126	P.E.Richardson	West Indies	Trent Bridge	1957	268
126	K.F.Barrington	New Zealand	Auckland	1962/63	320
126	D.W.Randall	India	Lord's	1982	473
125	B.R.Knight	New Zealand	Auckland	1962/63	322
125	A.R.Lewis	India	Kanpur	1972/73	395
125	G.Boycott	India	The Oval	1979	455
125	A.J.Lamb	Australia	Headingley	1989	530
124*	P.B.H.May	New Zealand	Auckland	1958/59	280
124	A.J.L.Hill	South Africa	Cape Town	1895/96	23
124	A.C.MacLaren	Australia	Adelaide	1897/98	27
124	M.W.Gatting	Pakistan	Edgbaston	1987	523
124	R.C.Russell	India	Lord's	1996	587
123*	K.W.R.Fletcher	India	Old Trafford	1974	413
123	J.B.Hobbs	Australia	Adelaide	1920/21	68
123	F.E.Woolley	Australia	Sydney	1924/25	85
123	E.H.Hendren	West Indies	Georgetown	1929/30	124
123	L.Hutton	South Africa	Johannesburg (2)	1948/49	216
123	G.A.Gooch	West Indies	Lord's	1980	458
123	C.W.J.Athey	Pakistan	Lord's	1987	522
123	G.A.Gooch	India	Lord's	1990	540
123	D.I.Gower	Australia	Sydney	1990/91	550
123	G.P.Thorpe	Australia	Perth	1994/95	581
122*	G.Gunn	Australia	Sydney	1907/08	51
122*	L.Hutton	Australia	Sydney	1946/47	198
122*	P.H.Parfitt	South Africa	Johannesburg (3)	1964/65	337
122	T.W.Hayward	South Africa	Johannesburg (1)	1895/96	22
122	J.B.Hobbs	Australia	Melbourne	1920/21	67
122	H.Sutcliffe	South Africa	Lord's	1924	79
122	G.E.Tyldesley	South Africa	Johannesburg (1)	1927/28	96
122	G.E.Tyldesley	West Indies	Lord's	1928	98
122	G.O.B.Allen	New Zealand	Lord's	1931	133
122	K.W.R.Fletcher	Pakistan	The Oval	1974	420
121*	G.Boycott	Pakistan	Lord's	1971	391
121*	R.A.Smith	India	Old Trafford	1990	546
121	J.Briggs	Australia	Melbourne	1884/85	7
121	A.P.F.Chapman	Australia	Lord's	1930	128
121	J.D.B.Robertson	New Zealand	Lord's	1949	222
121	K.F.Barrington	West Indies	Port-of-Spain	1959/60	287
121	P.H.Parfitt	India	Kanpur	1963/64	327
121	K.F.Barrington	South Africa	Johannesburg (3)	1964/65	335
121	M.J.K.Smith	South Africa	Cape Town	1964/65	336
121	A.W.Greig	West Indies	Georgetown	1973/74	410
121	M.W.Gatting	New Zealand	The Oval	1986	513

Score	Batsman	Opposition	Venue	Date	No
120	R.Abel	South Africa	Cape Town	1888/89	11
120	A.C.MacLaren	Australia	Melbourne	1894/95	21
120	L.E.G.Ames	Australia	Lord's	1934	150
120	W.R.Hammond	South Africa	Durban (2)	1938/39	185
120	P.A.Gibb	South Africa	Durban (2)	1938/39	186
120	D.C.S.Compton	West Indies	Lord's	1939	190
120	J.H.Edrich	Australia	Lord's	1964	328
120	R.A.Woolmer	Australia	Lord's	1977	437
120	G.A.Gooch	Australia	Trent Bridge	1993	568
119*	W.R.Hammond	Australia	Adelaide	1928/29	104
119*	G.Boycott	Australia	Adelaide	1970/71	385
119*	I.T.Botham	Australia	Melbourne	1979/80	456
119	G.Gunn	Australia	Sydney	1907/08	49
119	R.H.Spooner	South Africa	Lord's	1912	61
119	J.W.H.T.Douglas	South Africa	Durban (1)	1913/14	63
119	J.B.Hobbs	Australia	Adelaide	1924/25	89
119	J.B.Hobbs	Australia	Lord's	1926	91
119	W.J.Edrich	Australia	Sydney	1946/47	194
119	Rev.D.S.Sheppard	India	The Oval	1952	243
119	M.C.Cowdrey	West Indies	Port-of-Spain	1959/60	292
119	G.Pullar	India	Kanpur	1961/62	301
119	P.H.Parfitt	Pakistan	Headingley	1962	311
119	M.C.Cowdrey	New Zealand	Lord's	1965	340
119	A.J.Lamb	West Indies	Bridgetown	1989/90	536
119	A.J.Stewart	New Zealand	Lord's	1994	577
118*	G.A.Hick	West Indies	Trent Bridge	1995	583
118	Hon.F.S.Jackson	Australia	The Oval	1899	31
118	T.W.Graveney	West Indies	Port-of-Spain	1967/68	361
118	D.L.Amiss	West Indies	Georgetown	1973/74	409
118	M.H.Denness	India	Lord's	1974	415
118	I.T.Botham	Australia	Old Trafford	1981	467
118	A.J.Stewart	West Indies	Bridgetown	1993/94	571
117	W.W.Read	Australia	The Oval	1884	5
117	Albert Ward	Australia	Sydney	1894/95	18
117	C.P.Mead	South Africa	Port Elizabeth	1913/14	66
117	J.W.H.Makepeace	Australia	Melbourne	1920/21	70
117	K.S.Duleepsinhji	New Zealand	Auckland	1929/30	119
117	H.Sutcliffe	New Zealand	The Oval	1931	134
117	E.Paynter	South Africa	Johannesburg (1)	1938/39	179
117	P.B.H.May	South Africa	Old Trafford	1955	257
117	P.E.Richardson	South Africa	Johannesburg (3)	1956/57	262
117	G.Boycott	South Africa	Port Elizabeth	1964/65	338
117	B.L.D'Oliveira	Australia	Melbourne	1970/71	384
117	G.A.Gooch	Australia	Adelaide	1990/91	551
117	C.C.Lewis	India	Madras (1)	1992/93	564
117	M.W.Gatting	Australia	Adelaide	1994/95	580
116	A.C.MacLaren	Australia	Sydney	1901/02	33
116	D.C.S.Compton	New Zealand	Lord's	1949	223
116	W.Watson	West Indies	Kingston	1953/54	246
116	G.Boycott	West Indies	Georgetown	1967/68	365
116	A.P.E.Knott	Pakistan	Edgbaston	1971	390
116	A.W.Greig	West Indies	Headingley	1976	431
116	A.P.E.Knott	West Indies	Headingley	1976	432
116	G.A.Gooch	West Indies	Bridgetown	1980/81	461
116	B.C.Broad	Australia	Adelaide	1986/87	518
116	B.C.Broad	Pakistan	Faisalabad	1987/88	525
116	G.A.Gooch	India	Old Trafford	1990	543
115*	F.E.Woolley	South Africa	Johannesburg (1)	1922/23	75
115*	J.H.Edrich	Australia	Perth	1970/71	381
115	J.B.Hobbs	Australia	Sydney	1924/25	83
115	H.Sutcliffe	Australia	Sydney	1924/25	84
115	L.E.G.Ames	South Africa	Cape Town	1938/39	182
115	D.C.S.Compton	South Africa	Old Trafford	1947	203
115	K.F.Barrington	Australia	Melbourne	1965/66	349
115	J.H.Edrich	New Zealand	Lord's	1969	377
115	G.Boycott	New Zealand	Headingley	1973	403
115	D.W.Randall	Australia	Perth	1982/83	478
114*	B.L.D'Oliveira	Pakistan	Dacca	1968/69	370
114*	G.P.Thorpe	Australia	Trent Bridge	1993	569
114	J.W.Hearne	Australia	Melbourne	1911/12	56
114	H.Sutcliffe	South Africa	Edgbaston	1929	108
114	J.Hardstaff jnr	New Zealand	Lord's	1937	166
114	D.C.S.Compton	South Africa	Johannesburg (2)	1948/49	215
114	D.C.S.Compton	New Zealand	Headingley	1949	221

Score	Batsman	Opposition	Venue	Date	No
114	C.Washbrook	West Indies	Lord's	1950	228
114	M.C.Cowdrey	West Indies	Kingston	1959/60	289
114	T.W.Graveney	Pakistan	Trent Bridge	1962	312
114	I.T.Botham	India	Bombay (3)	1979/80	457
114	D.I.Gower	Australia	Adelaide	1982/83	479
114	G.A.Gooch	India	Lord's	1986	509
114	B.C.Broad	New Zealand	Christchurch	1987/88	527
114	G.A.Gooch	New Zealand	Auckland	1991/92	558
113*	P.B.H.May	New Zealand	Headingley	1958	275
113*	K.F.Barrington	India	Delhi	1961/62	304
113*	A.J.Stewart	Sri Lanka	Lord's	1991	556
113	Hon.F.S.Jackson	Australia	Old Trafford	1905	43
113	R.E.S.Wyatt	South Africa	Old Trafford	1929	113
113	W.R.Hammond	Australia	Headingley	1930	129
113	D.C.S.Compton	South Africa	The Oval	1947	205
113	Rev.D.S.Sheppard	Australia	Old Trafford	1956	261
113	P.B.H.May	Australia	Melbourne	1958/59	277
113	Rev.D.S.Sheppard	Australia	Melbourne	1962/63	316
113	M.C.Cowdrey	Australia	Melbourne	1962/63	317
113	G.Boycott	Australia	The Oval	1964	331
113	R.Illingworth	West Indies	Lord's	1969	376
113	K.W.R.Fletcher	India	Bombay (2)	1972/73	396
113	A.J.Lamb	West Indies	Lord's	1988	529
113	M.A.Atherton	West Indies	Trent Bridge	1995	582
113	N.V.Knight	Pakistan	Headingley	1996	591
112*	J.T.Tyldesley	Australia	The Oval	1905	44
112*	D.I.Gower	New Zealand	Headingley	1983	483
112	J.T.Tyldesley	South Africa	Cape Town	1898/99	29
112	W.R.Hammond	Australia	Sydney	1932/33	139
112	B.H.Valentine	South Africa	Cape Town	1938/39	183
112	C.Washbrook	Australia	Melbourne	1946/47	195
112	D.C.S.Compton	South Africa	Trent Bridge	1951	235
112	P.B.H.May	South Africa	Lord's	1955	256
112	R.Subba Row	Australia	Edgbaston	1961	296
112	J.T.Murray	West Indies	The Oval	1966	353
112	G.Boycott	Pakistan	Headingley	1971	392
112	D.L.Amiss	Pakistan	Lahore (2)	1972/73	398
112	G.Boycott	West Indies	Port-of-Spain	1973/74	411
112	B.C.Broad	Australia	Melbourne	1986/87	520
111*	M.Leyland	Australia	Melbourne	1936/37	164
111	C.A.G.Russell	South Africa	Durban (2)	1922/23	77
111	W.J.Edrich	Australia	Headingley	1948	212
111	A.J.Watkins	South Africa	Johannesburg (2)	1948/49	217
111	T.W.Graveney	Australia	Sydney	1954/55	255
111	P.H.Parfitt	Pakistan	Karachi (1)	1961/62	307
111	P.J.Sharpe	New Zealand	Trent Bridge	1969	379
111	D.I.Gower	New Zealand	The Oval	1978	448
111	M.A.Atherton	New Zealand	Old Trafford	1994	578
110*	D.J.Insole	South Africa	Durban (2)	1956/57	264
110	M.Leyland	Australia	The Oval	1934	153
110	E.R.Dexter	West Indies	Georgetown	1959/60	291
110	A.W.Greig	Australia	Brisbane (2)	1974/75	421
110	A.J.Lamb	West Indies	Lord's	1984	493
110	G.A.Hick	South Africa	Headingley	1994	579
109*	H.Sutcliffe	South Africa	The Oval	1929	116
109*	H.Sutcliffe	New Zealand	Old Trafford	1931	137
109*	K.F.Barrington	Pakistan	Trent Bridge	1967	358
109	A.C.MacLaren	Australia	Sydney	1897/98	25
109	E.H.Bowley	New Zealand	Auckland	1929/30	118
109	K.S.Duleepsinhji	New Zealand	The Oval	1931	135
109	M.Leyland	Australia	Lord's	1934	149
109	W.Watson	Australia	Lord's	1953	245
109	J.H.Edrich	Australia	Melbourne	1965/66	344
109	T.W.Graveney	West Indies	Trent Bridge	1966	351
109	B.L.D'Oliveira	India	Headingley	1967	355
109	B.W.Luckhurst	Australia	Melbourne	1970/71	383
109	C.J.Tavare	New Zealand	The Oval	1983	481
109	A.J.Lamb	India	Old Trafford	1990	545
109	R.A.Smith	West Indies	The Oval	1991	554
108*	J.M.Parks	South Africa	Durban (2)	1964/65	333
108*	B.W.Luckhurst	Pakistan	Edgbaston	1971	389
108	R.W.V.Robins	South Africa	Old Trafford	1935	156
108	M.J.K.Smith	West Indies	Port-of-Spain	1959/60	288
108	I.T.Botham	Pakistan	Lord's	1978	447

Score	Batsman	Opposition	Venue	Date	No
108	D.I.Gower	New Zealand	Lord's	1983	484
107*	N.Hussain	India	Trent Bridge	1996	589
107	J.B.Hobbs	Australia	Lord's	1912	62
107	A.H.Bakewell	West Indies	The Oval	1933	146
107	W.Place	West Indies	Kingston	1947/48	208
107	P.E.Richardson	West Indies	The Oval	1957	271
107	M.C.Cowdrey	India	Calcutta	1963/64	324
107	J.H.Hampshire	West Indies	Lord's	1969	375
107	R.Illingworth	India	Old Trafford	1971	394
107	G.Boycott	Australia	Trent Bridge	1977	439
107	A.J.Lamb	India	The Oval	1982	475
107	A.J.Lamb	Sri Lanka	Lord's	1984	496
107	A.J.Stewart	New Zealand	Wellington	1991/92	559
106*	F.C.Hayes	West Indies	The Oval	1973	404
106*	A.P.E.Knott	Australia	Adelaide	1974/75	422
106	A.Shrewsbury	Australia	Lord's	1893	15
106	P.A.Gibb	South Africa	Johannesburg (1)	1938/39	178
106	P.B.H.May	India	Trent Bridge	1959	281
106	G.Boycott	West Indies	Lord's	1969	374
106	A.W.Greig	India	Lord's	1974	416
106	D.S.Steele	West Indies	Trent Bridge	1976	430
106	C.T.Radley	Pakistan	Edgbaston	1978	445
106	G.Fowler	West Indies	Lord's	1984	492
106	D.I.Gower	Australia	Lord's	1989	531
106	J.P.Crawley	Pakistan	The Oval	1996	592
105*	A.Shrewsbury	Australia	Melbourne	1884/85	8
105	J.Sharp	Australia	The Oval	1909	52
105	L.E.G.Ames	West Indies	Port-of-Spain	1929/30	123
105	M.C.Cowdrey	South Africa	Trent Bridge	1965	343
105	T.W.Graveney	Pakistan	Karachi (1)	1968/69	372
105	G.Boycott	India	Delhi	1981/82	469
105	D.W.Randall	Pakistan	Edgbaston	1982	477
105	G.Fowler	New Zealand	The Oval	1983	480
105	M.A.Atherton	Australia	Sydney	1990/91	549
104*	C.A.Milton	New Zealand	Headingley	1958	274
104*	G.Boycott	West Indies	St John's	1980/81	462
104	G.L.Jessop	Australia	The Oval	1902	37
104	L.C.Braund	South Africa	Lord's	1907	47
104	D.Denton	South Africa	Johannesburg (1)	1909/10	53
104	H.Sutcliffe	South Africa	The Oval	1929	115
104	T.G.Evans	West Indies	Old Trafford	1950	227
104	T.G.Evans	India	Lord's	1952	241
104	L.Hutton	India	Old Trafford	1952	242
104	P.B.H.May	Australia	Sydney	1954/55	253
104	P.E.Richardson	Australia	Old Trafford	1956	260
104	P.B.H.May	West Indies	Trent Bridge	1957	270
104	M.C.Cowdrey	Australia	Melbourne	1965/66	345
104	M.C.Cowdrey	Australia	Edgbaston	1968	366
104	D.W.Randall	New Zealand	Auckland	1983/84	489
103*	L.C.Braund	Australia	Adelaide	1901/02	34
103*	D.C.S.Compton	Australia	Adelaide	1946/47	197
103*	C.Washbrook	New Zealand	Headingley	1949	220
103	Hon.F.S.Jackson	Australia	The Oval	1893	16
103	L.E.G.Ames	New Zealand	Christchurch	1932/33	143
103	J.Hardstaff jnr	New Zealand	The Oval	1937	169
103	R.T.Simpson	New Zealand	Old Trafford	1949	224
103	J.H.Edrich	Australia	Sydney	1965/66	347
103	A.W.Greig	India	Calcutta	1976/77	435
103	I.T.Botham	New Zealand	Christchurch	1977/78	443
103	I.T.Botham	New Zealand	Trent Bridge	1983	486
102*	W.Gunn	Australia	Old Trafford	1893	17
102*	C.A.G.Russell	Australia	The Oval	1921	72
102*	P.Willey	West Indies	St John's	1980/81	463
102*	A.J.Lamb	New Zealand	The Oval	1983	482
102	L.C.Braund	Australia	Sydney	1903/04	39
102	C.P.Mead	South Africa	Johannesburg (1)	1913/14	65
102	H.Sutcliffe	South Africa	Johannesburg (1)	1927/28	95
102	M.Leyland	South Africa	Lord's	1929	111
102	Nawab of Pataudi snr	Australia	Sydney	1932/33	140
102	C.F.Walters	India	Madras (1)	1933/34	148
102	D.C.S.Compton	Australia	Trent Bridge	1938	173
102	C.Washbrook	West Indies	Trent Bridge	1950	229
102	M.C.Cowdrey	Australia	Melbourne	1954/55	254
102	K.F.Barrington	Australia	Adelaide	1965/66	348

Score	Batsman	Opposition	Venue	Date	No
102	D.I.Gower	Australia	Perth	1978/79	450
101*	W.R.Hammond	South Africa	The Oval	1929	117
101*	J.M.Parks	West Indies	Port-of-Spain	1959/60	293
101*	P.H.Parfitt	Pakistan	Edgbaston	1962	309
101*	P.H.Parfitt	Pakistan	Trent Bridge	1962	313
101	C.A.G.Russell	Australia	Old Trafford	1921	71
101	W.R.Hammond	Australia	Sydney	1932/33	141
101	L.Hutton	New Zealand	Headingley	1949	219
101	R.T.Simpson	Pakistan	Trent Bridge	1954	251
101	P.B.H.May	Australia	Headingley	1956	259
101	M.C.Cowdrey	South Africa	Cape Town	1956/57	263
101	P.B.H.May	New Zealand	Old Trafford	1958	276
101	K.F.Barrington	Australia	Sydney	1962/63	319
101	M.C.Cowdrey	West Indies	Kingston	1967/68	362
101	A.P.E.Knott	New Zealand	Auckland	1970/71	388
101	B.W.Luckhurst	India	Old Trafford	1971	393
101	R.A.Smith	Australia	Trent Bridge	1989	534
101	M.A.Atherton	New Zealand	Trent Bridge	1994	575
100*	M.W.Tate	South Africa	Lord's	1929	112
100*	W.R.Hammond	New Zealand	The Oval	1931	136
100*	M.C.Cowdrey	Australia	Sydney	1958/59	278
100*	J.H.Edrich	India	Old Trafford	1974	412
100*	G.Boycott	Pakistan	Hyderabad	1977/78	442
100*	P.Willey	West Indies	The Oval	1980	459
100*	A.J.Lamb	West Indies	Old Trafford	1984	495
100*	M.W.Gatting	Australia	Edgbaston	1985	506
100*	R.A.Smith	India	Lord's	1990	542
100	J.T.Tyldesley	Australia	Headingley	1905	41
100	J.B.Hobbs	Australia	The Oval	1926	93
100	G.E.Tyldesley	South Africa	Durban (2)	1927/28	97
100	H.Sutcliffe	South Africa	Lord's	1929	110
100	L.Hutton	New Zealand	Old Trafford	1937	168
100	L.Hutton	Australia	Trent Bridge	1938	171
100	E.Paynter	South Africa	Johannesburg (1)	1938/39	180
100	L.Hutton	South Africa	Headingley	1947	204
100	W.J.Edrich	New Zealand	The Oval	1949	226
100	L.Hutton	South Africa	Headingley	1951	236
100	P.E.Richardson	New Zealand	Edgbaston	1958	273
100	M.J.K.Smith	India	Old Trafford	1959	284
100	R.Subba Row	West Indies	Georgetown	1959/60	290
100	M.C.Cowdrey	Pakistan	Lahore (2)	1968/69	369
100	B.L.D'Oliveira	New Zealand	Christchurch	1970/71	387
100	M.H.Denness	India	Edgbaston	1974	418
100	I.T.Botham	Pakistan	Edgbaston	1978	446
100	A.J.Lamb	West Indies	Headingley	1984	494
100	M.W.Gatting	Australia	Adelaide	1986/87	519
100	D.I.Gower	Australia	Melbourne	1990/91	548

HIGHEST INDIVIDUAL SCORES AGAINST EACH OPPOSITION

Australia

364	L.Hutton	The Oval	1938
287	R.E.Foster	Sydney	1903/04
256	K.F.Barrington	Old Trafford	1964
251	W.R.Hammond	Sydney	1928/29
240	W.R.Hammond	Lord's	1938

South Africa

243	E.Paynter	Durban (2)	1938/39
219	W.J.Edrich	Durban (2)	1938/39
211	J.B.Hobbs	Lord's	1924
208	D.C.S.Compton	Lord's	1947
195	C.Washbrook	Johannesburg (2)	1948/49

West Indies

325	A.Sandham	Kingston	1929/30
285*	P.B.H.May	Edgbaston	1957
262*	D.L.Amiss	Kingston	1973/74
258	T.W.Graveney	Trent Bridge	1957
205*	E.H.Hendren	Port-of-Spain	1929/30

New Zealand

336*	W.R.Hammond	Auckland	1932/33
310*	J.H.Edrich	Headingley	1965

227	W.R.Hammond	Christchurch	1932/33
216	K.W.R.Fletcher	Auckland	1974/75
210	G.A.Gooch	Trent Bridge	1994

India

333	G.A.Gooch	Lord's	1990
246*	G.Boycott	Headingley	1967
217	W.R.Hammond	The Oval	1936
214*	D.Lloyd	Edgbaston	1974
208	I.T.Botham	The Oval	1982

Pakistan

278	D.C.S.Compton	Trent Bridge	1954
205	E.R.Dexter	Karachi (1)	1961/62
190	A.J.Stewart	Edgbaston	1992
183	D.L.Amiss	The Oval	1974
182	M.C.Cowdrey	The Oval	1962

Sri Lanka

174	G.A.Gooch	Lord's	1991
128	R.A.Smith	Colombo (2)	1992/93
113*	A.J.Stewart	Lord's	1991
107	A.J.Lamb	Lord's	1984
94	R.C.Russell	Lord's	1988

HIGHEST INDIVIDUAL SCORES PER VENUE

(Five highest scores above 100 or the single highest score for each venue)

ENGLAND

The Oval

364	L.Hutton	Australia	1938
217	W.R.Hammond	India	1936
208	I.T.Botham	India	1982
206	L.Hutton	New Zealand	1949
203	D.L.Amiss	West Indies	1976

Old Trafford

256	K.F.Barrington	Australia	1964
191	W.J.Edrich	South Africa	1947
174	E.R.Dexter	Australia	1964
167	W.R.Hammond	India	1936
166	R.T.Robinson	Pakistan	1987

Lord's

333	G.A.Gooch	India	1990
240	W.R.Hammond	Australia	1938
211	J.B.Hobbs	South Africa	1924
208	D.C.S.Compton	South Africa	1947
205*	J.Hardstaff jnr	India	1946

Trent Bridge

278	D.C.S.Compton	Pakistan	1954
258	T.W.Graveney	West Indies	1957
216*	E.Paynter	Australia	1938
210	G.A.Gooch	New Zealand	1994
184	D.C.S.Compton	Australia	1948

Headingley

310*	J.H.Edrich	New Zealand	1965
246*	G.Boycott	India	1967
191	G.Boycott	Australia	1977
175	R.T.Robinson	Australia	1985
170	A.J.Stewart	Pakistan	1996

Edgbaston

285*	P.B.H.May	West Indies	1957
215	D.I.Gower	Australia	1985
214*	D.Lloyd	India	1974
200*	D.I.Gower	India	1979
190	A.J.Stewart	Pakistan	1992

Bramall Lane

63	A.C.MacLaren	Australia	1902

AUSTRALIA

Melbourne
200	W.R.Hammond	Australia	1928/29
188	M.H.Denness	Australia	1974/75
179	W.Rhodes	Australia	1911/12
178	J.B.Hobbs	Australia	1911/12
176	H.Sutcliffe	Australia	1924/25

Sydney
287	R.E.Foster	Australia	1903/04
251	W.R.Hammond	Australia	1928/29
231*	W.R.Hammond	Australia	1936/37
194	H.Sutcliffe	Australia	1932/33
185	R.W.Barber	Australia	1965/66

Adelaide
187	J.B.Hobbs	Australia	1911/12
177	W.R.Hammond	Australia	1928/29
156*	L.Hutton	Australia	1950/51
147	D.C.S.Compton	Australia	1946/47
135*	C.A.G.Russell	Australia	1920/21

Brisbane (1)
169	E.H.Hendren	Australia	1928/29

Brisbane (2)
138	I.T.Botham	Australia	1986/87
126	M.Leyland	Australia	1936/37
110	A.W.Greig	Australia	1974/75

Perth
162	B.C.Broad	Australia	1986/87
136	D.I.Gower	Australia	1986/87
133	C.J.Richards	Australia	1986/87
131	B.W.Luckhurst	Australia	1970/71
123	G.P.Thorpe	Australia	1994/95

SOUTH AFRICA

Port Elizabeth
136*	F.G.Mann	South Africa	1948/49
117	C.P.Mead	South Africa	1913/14
117	G.Boycott	South Africa	1964/65

Cape Town
187	J.B.Hobbs	South Africa	1909/10
181	W.R.Hammond	South Africa	1938/39
134*	H.Wood	South Africa	1891/92
124	A.J.L.Hill	South Africa	1895/96
121	M.J.K.Smith	South Africa	1964/65

Johannesburg (1)
152	W.Rhodes	South Africa	1913/14
143	F.L.Fane	South Africa	1905/06
132*	P.F.Warner	South Africa	1898/99
122	T.W.Hayward	South Africa	1895/96
122	G.E.Tyldesley	South Africa	1927/28

Durban (1)
119	J.W.H.T.Douglas	South Africa	1913/14

Durban (2)
243	E.Paynter	South Africa	1938/39
219	W.J.Edrich	South Africa	1938/39
181	C.P.Mead	South Africa	1922/23
148*	K.F.Barrington	South Africa	1964/65
140	C.A.G.Russell	South Africa	1922/23
140	W.R.Hammond	South Africa	1938/39

Johannesburg (2)
195	C.Washbrook	South Africa	1948/49
158	L.Hutton	South Africa	1948/49
123	L.Hutton	South Africa	1948/49
114	D.C.S.Compton	South Africa	1948/49

| 111 | A.J.Watkins | South Africa | 1948/49 |

Johannesburg (3)

185*	M.A.Atherton	South Africa	1995/96
172	E.R.Dexter	South Africa	1964/65
122*	P.H.Parfitt	South Africa	1964/65
121	K.F.Barrington	South Africa	1964/65
117	P.E.Richardson	South Africa	1956/57

Centurion

| 141 | G.A.Hick | South Africa | 1995/96 |

WEST INDIES

Bridgetown

152	A.Sandham	West Indies	1929/30
148	A.W.Greig	West Indies	1973/74
146	J.H.Edrich	West Indies	1967/68
143	A.J.Stewart	West Indies	1993/94
136*	E.R.Dexter	West Indies	1959/60

Port-of-Spain

205*	E.H.Hendren	West Indies	1929/30
174	D.L.Amiss	West Indies	1973/74
148	M.C.Cowdrey	West Indies	1967/68
143	K.F.Barrington	West Indies	1967/68
140	S.C.Griffith	West Indies	1947/48

Georgetown

169	L.Hutton	West Indies	1953/54
144	M.A.Atherton	West Indies	1993/94
123	E.H.Hendren	West Indies	1929/30
121	A.W.Greig	West Indies	1973/74
118	D.L.Amiss	West Indies	1973/74

Kingston

325	A.Sandham	West Indies	1929/30
262*	D.L.Amiss	West Indies	1973/74
205	L.Hutton	West Indies	1953/54
154*	D.I.Gower	West Indies	1980/81
153	G.A.Gooch	West Indies	1980/81

St John's

175	R.A.Smith	West Indies	1993/94
135	M.A.Atherton	West Indies	1993/94
104*	G.Boycott	West Indies	1980/81
102*	P.Willey	West Indies	1980/81

NEW ZEALAND

Christchurch

227	W.R.Hammond	New Zealand	1932/33
164*	D.L.Amiss	New Zealand	1974/75
148	A.J.Stewart	New Zealand	1991/92
141	E.R.Dexter	New Zealand	1958/59
134*	T.E.Bailey	New Zealand	1950/51

Wellington

164	D.W.Randall	New Zealand	1983/84
142	A.J.Lamb	New Zealand	1991/92
138	I.T.Botham	New Zealand	1983/84
128*	M.C.Cowdrey	New Zealand	1962/63
107	A.J.Stewart	New Zealand	1991/92

Auckland

336*	W.R.Hammond	New Zealand	1932/33
216	K.W.R.Fletcher	New Zealand	1974/75
196	G.B.Legge	New Zealand	1929/30
181	M.H.Denness	New Zealand	1974/75
158	C.T.Radley	New Zealand	1977/78

Dunedin

| 89* | M.C.Cowdrey | New Zealand | 1965/66 |

INDIA

Bombay (1)

136	B.H.Valentine	India	1933/34

Calcutta

107	M.C.Cowdrey	India	1963/64
103	A.W.Greig	India	1976/77

Madras (1)

207	M.W.Gatting	India	1984/85
201	G.Fowler	India	1984/85
127	G.A.Gooch	India	1981/82
117	C.C.Lewis	India	1992/93
102	C.F.Walters	India	1933/34

Delhi

179	D.L.Amiss	India	1976/77
160	R.T.Robinson	India	1984/85
151	M.C.Cowdrey	India	1963/64
149	C.J.Tavare	India	1981/82
137*	A.J.Watkins	India	1951/52

Bombay (2)

175	T.W.Graveney	India	1951/52
151*	K.F.Barrington	India	1961/62
148	A.W.Greig	India	1972/73
113	K.W.R.Fletcher	India	1972/73

Kanpur

172	K.F.Barrington	India	1961/62
142	I.T.Botham	India	1981/82
127	B.R.Knight	India	1963/64
126*	E.R.Dexter	India	1961/62
125	A.R.Lewis	India	1972/73

Madras (2)

88	J.B.Bolus	India	1963/64

Bangalore

82	D.L.Amiss	India	1976/77
82	D.I.Gower	India	1981/82

Bombay (3)

178	G.A.Hick	India	1992/93
136	M.W.Gatting	India	1984/85
114	I.T.Botham	India	1979/80

PAKISTAN

Dacca

165	G.Pullar	Pakistan	1961/62
114*	B.L.D'Oliveira	Pakistan	1968/69

Karachi (1)

205	E.R.Dexter	Pakistan	1961/62
139	C.Milburn	Pakistan	1968/69
111	P.H.Parfitt	Pakistan	1961/62
105	T.W.Graveney	Pakistan	1968/69

Lahore (2)

173*	D.I.Gower	Pakistan	1983/84
139	K.F.Barrington	Pakistan	1961/62
112	D.L.Amiss	Pakistan	1972/73
100	M.C.Cowdrey	Pakistan	1968/69

Hyderabad

158	D.L.Amiss	Pakistan	1972/73
100*	G.Boycott	Pakistan	1978/79

Faisalabad

152	D.I.Gower	Pakistan	1983/84
116	B.C.Broad	Pakistan	1987/88

SRI LANKA

Colombo (1)
89   D.I.Gower   Sri Lanka   1981/82

Colombo (2)
128   R.A.Smith   Sri Lanka   1992/93

CENTURIES PER PLAYER (592)

W.R.Hammond (22)

1	251	Australia	Sydney	1928/29
2	200	Australia	Melbourne	1928/29
3	119*	Australia	Adelaide	1928/29
4	177	Australia	Adelaide	1928/29
5	138*	South Africa	Edgbaston	1929
6	101*	South Africa	The Oval	1929
7	113	Australia	Headingley	1930
8	136*	South Africa	Durban (2)	1930/31
9	100*	New Zealand	The Oval	1931
10	112	Australia	Sydney	1932/33
11	101	Australia	Sydney	1932/33
12	227	New Zealand	Christchurch	1932/33
13	336*	New Zealand	Auckland	1932/33
14	167	India	Old Trafford	1936
15	217	India	The Oval	1936
16	231*	Australia	Sydney	1936/37
17	140	New Zealand	Lord's	1937
18	240	Australia	Lord's	1938
19	181	South Africa	Cape Town	1938/39
20	120	South Africa	Durban (2)	1938/39
21	140	South Africa	Durban (2)	1938/39
22	138	West Indies	The Oval	1939

M.C.Cowdrey (22)

1	102	Australia	Melbourne	1954/55
2	101	South Africa	Cape Town	1956/57
3	154	West Indies	Edgbaston	1957
4	152	West Indies	Lord's	1957
5	100*	Australia	Sydney	1958/59
6	160	India	Headingley	1959
7	114	West Indies	Kingston	1959/60
8	119	West Indies	Port-of-Spain	1959/60
9	155	South Africa	The Oval	1960
10	159	Pakistan	Edgbaston	1962
11	182	Pakistan	The Oval	1962
12	113	Australia	Melbourne	1962/63
13	128*	New Zealand	Wellington	1962/63
14	107	India	Calcutta	1963/64
15	151	India	Delhi	1963/64
16	119	New Zealand	Lord's	1965
17	105	South Africa	Trent Bridge	1965
18	104	Australia	Melbourne	1965/66
19	101	West Indies	Kingston	1967/68
20	148	West Indies	Port-of-Spain	1967/68
21	104	Australia	Edgbaston	1968
22	100	Pakistan	Lahore (2)	1968/69

G.Boycott (22)

1	113	Australia	The Oval	1964
2	117	South Africa	Port Elizabeth	1964/65
3	246*	India	Headingley	1967
4	116	West Indies	Georgetown	1967/68
5	128	West Indies	Old Trafford	1969
6	106	West Indies	Lord's	1969
7	142*	Australia	Sydney	1970/71
8	119*	Australia	Adelaide	1970/71
9	121*	Pakistan	Lord's	1971
10	112	Pakistan	Headingley	1971
11	115	New Zealand	Headingley	1973
12	112	West Indies	Port-of-Spain	1973/74
13	107	Australia	Trent Bridge	1977
14	191	Australia	Headingley	1977
15	100*	Pakistan	Hyderabad	1977/78
16	131	New Zealand	Trent Bridge	1978

17	155	India	Edgbaston	1979
18	125	India	The Oval	1979
19	128*	Australia	Lord's	1980
20	104*	West Indies	St John's	1980/81
21	137	Australia	The Oval	1981
22	105	India	Delhi	1981/82

K.F.Barrington (20)

1	128	West Indies	Bridgetown	1959/60
2	121	West Indies	Port-of-Spain	1959/60
3	139	Pakistan	Lahore (2)	1961/62
4	151*	India	Bombay (2)	1961/62
5	172	India	Kanpur	1961/62
6	113*	India	Delhi	1961/62
7	132*	Australia	Adelaide	1962/63
8	101	Australia	Sydney	1962/63
9	126	New Zealand	Auckland	1962/63
10	256	Australia	Old Trafford	1964
11	148*	South Africa	Durban (2)	1964/65
12	121	South Africa	Johannesburg (3)	1964/65
13	137	New Zealand	Edgbaston	1965
14	163	New Zealand	Headingley	1965
15	102	Australia	Adelaide	1965/66
16	115	Australia	Melbourne	1965/66
17	148	Pakistan	Lord's	1967
18	109*	Pakistan	Trent Bridge	1967
19	142	Pakistan	The Oval	1967
20	143	West Indies	Port-of-Spain	1967/68

G.A.Gooch (20)

1	123	West Indies	Lord's	1980
2	116	West Indies	Bridgetown	1980/81
3	153	West Indies	Kingston	1980/81
4	127	India	Madras (1)	1981/82
5	196	Australia	The Oval	1985
6	114	India	Lord's	1986
7	183	New Zealand	Lord's	1986
8	146	West Indies	Trent Bridge	1988
9	154	New Zealand	Edgbaston	1990
10	333	India	Lord's	1990
11	123	India	Lord's	1990
12	116	India	Old Trafford	1990
13	117	Australia	Adelaide	1990/91
14	154*	West Indies	Headingley	1991
15	174	Sri Lanka	Lord's	1991
16	114	New Zealand	Auckland	1991/92
17	135	Pakistan	Headingley	1992
18	133	Australia	Old Trafford	1993
19	120	Australia	Trent Bridge	1993
20	210	New Zealand	Trent Bridge	1994

L.Hutton (19)

1	100	New Zealand	Old Trafford	1937
2	100	Australia	Trent Bridge	1938
3	364	Australia	The Oval	1938
4	196	West Indies	Lord's	1939
5	165*	West Indies	The Oval	1939
6	122*	Australia	Sydney	1946/47
7	100	South Africa	Headingley	1947
8	158	South Africa	Johannesburg (2)	1948/49
9	123	South Africa	Johannesburg (2)	1948/49
10	101	New Zealand	Headingley	1949
11	206	New Zealand	The Oval	1949
12	202*	West Indies	The Oval	1950
13	156*	Australia	Adelaide	1950/51
14	100	South Africa	Headingley	1951
15	150	India	Lord's	1952
16	104	India	Old Trafford	1952
17	145	Australia	Lord's	1953
18	169	West Indies	Georgetown	1953/54
19	205	West Indies	Kingston	1953/54

D.I.Gower (18)

1	111	New Zealand	The Oval	1978
2	102	Australia	Perth	1978/79

3	200*	India	Edgbaston	1979
4	154*	West Indies	Kingston	1980/81
5	114	Australia	Adelaide	1982/83
6	112*	New Zealand	Headingley	1983
7	108	New Zealand	Lord's	1983
8	152	Pakistan	Faisalabad	1983/84
9	173*	Pakistan	Lahore (2)	1983/84
10	166	Australia	Trent Bridge	1985
11	215	Australia	Edgbaston	1985
12	157	Australia	The Oval	1985
13	131	New Zealand	The Oval	1986
14	136	Australia	Perth	1986/87
15	106	Australia	Lord's	1989
16	157*	India	The Oval	1990
17	100	Australia	Melbourne	1990/91
18	123	Australia	Sydney	1990/91

D.C.S.Compton (17)

1	102	Australia	Trent Bridge	1938
2	120	West Indies	Lord's	1939
3	147	Australia	Adelaide	1946/47
4	103*	Australia	Adelaide	1946/47
5	163	South Africa	Trent Bridge	1947
6	208	South Africa	Lord's	1947
7	115	South Africa	Old Trafford	1947
8	113	South Africa	The Oval	1947
9	184	Australia	Trent Bridge	1948
10	145*	Australia	Old Trafford	1948
11	114	South Africa	Johannesburg (2)	1948/49
12	114	New Zealand	Headingley	1949
13	116	New Zealand	Lord's	1949
14	112	South Africa	Trent Bridge	1951
15	133	West Indies	Port-of-Spain	1953/54
16	278	Pakistan	Trent Bridge	1954
17	158	South Africa	Old Trafford	1955

H.Sutcliffe (16)

1	122	South Africa	Lord's	1924
2	115	Australia	Sydney	1924/25
3	176	Australia	Melbourne	1924/25
4	127	Australia	Melbourne	1924/25
5	143	Australia	Melbourne	1924/25
6	161	Australia	The Oval	1926
7	102	South Africa	Johannesburg (1)	1927/28
8	135	Australia	Melbourne	1928/29
9	114	South Africa	Edgbaston	1929
10	100	South Africa	Lord's	1929
11	104	South Africa	The Oval	1929
12	109*	South Africa	The Oval	1929
13	161	Australia	The Oval	1930
14	117	New Zealand	The Oval	1931
15	109*	New Zealand	Old Trafford	1931
16	194	Australia	Sydney	1932/33

J.B.Hobbs (15)

1	187	South Africa	Cape Town	1909/10
2	126*	Australia	Melbourne	1911/12
3	187	Australia	Adelaide	1911/12
4	178	Australia	Melbourne	1911/12
5	107	Australia	Lord's	1912
6	122	Australia	Melbourne	1920/21
7	123	Australia	Adelaide	1920/21
8	211	South Africa	Lord's	1924
9	115	Australia	Sydney	1924/25
10	154	Australia	Melbourne	1924/25
11	119	Australia	Adelaide	1924/25
12	119	Australia	Lord's	1926
13	100	Australia	The Oval	1926
14	159	West Indies	The Oval	1928
15	142	Australia	Melbourne	1928/29

I.T.Botham (14)

1	103	New Zealand	Christchurch	1977/78
2	100	Pakistan	Edgbaston	1978
3	108	Pakistan	Lord's	1978

4	137	India	Headingley	1979
5	119*	Australia	Melbourne	1979/80
6	114	India	Bombay (3)	1979/80
7	149*	Australia	Headingley	1981
8	118	Australia	Old Trafford	1981
9	142	India	Kanpur	1981/82
10	128	India	Old Trafford	1982
11	208	India	The Oval	1982
12	103	New Zealand	Trent Bridge	1983
13	138	New Zealand	Wellington	1983/84
14	138	Australia	Brisbane (2)	1986/87

A.J.Lamb (14)

1	107	India	The Oval	1982
2	102*	New Zealand	The Oval	1983
3	137*	New Zealand	Trent Bridge	1983
4	110	West Indies	Lord's	1984
5	100	West Indies	Headingley	1984
6	100*	West Indies	Old Trafford	1984
7	107	Sri Lanka	Lord's	1984
8	113	West Indies	Lord's	1988
9	125	Australia	Headingley	1989
10	132	West Indies	Kingston	1989/90
11	119	West Indies	Bridgetown	1989/90
12	139	India	Lord's	1990
13	109	India	Old Trafford	1990
14	142	New Zealand	Wellington	1991/92

P.B.H.May (13)

1	138	South Africa	Headingley	1951
2	135	West Indies	Port-of-Spain	1953/54
3	104	Australia	Sydney	1954/55
4	112	South Africa	Lord's	1955
5	117	South Africa	Old Trafford	1955
6	101	Australia	Headingley	1956
7	285*	West Indies	Edgbaston	1957
8	104	West Indies	Trent Bridge	1957
9	113*	New Zealand	Headingley	1958
10	101	New Zealand	Old Trafford	1958
11	113	Australia	Melbourne	1958/59
12	124*	New Zealand	Auckland	1958/59
13	106	India	Trent Bridge	1959

J.H.Edrich (12)

1	120	Australia	Lord's	1964
2	310*	New Zealand	Headingley	1965
3	109	Australia	Melbourne	1965/66
4	103	Australia	Sydney	1965/66
5	146	West Indies	Bridgetown	1967/68
6	164	Australia	The Oval	1968
7	115	New Zealand	Lord's	1969
8	155	New Zealand	Trent Bridge	1969
9	115*	Australia	Perth	1970/71
10	130	Australia	Adelaide	1970/71
11	100*	India	Old Trafford	1974
12	175	Australia	Lord's	1975

D.L.Amiss (11)

1	112	Pakistan	Lahore (2)	1972/73
2	158	Pakistan	Hyderabad	1972/73
3	138*	New Zealand	Trent Bridge	1973
4	174	West Indies	Port-of-Spain	1973/74
5	262*	West Indies	Kingston	1973/74
6	118	West Indies	Georgetown	1973/74
7	188	India	Lord's	1974
8	183	Pakistan	The Oval	1974
9	164*	New Zealand	Christchurch	1974/75
10	203	West Indies	The Oval	1976
11	179	India	Delhi	1976/77

T.W.Graveney (11)

1	175	India	Bombay (2)	1951/52
2	111	Australia	Sydney	1954/55
3	258	West Indies	Trent Bridge	1957
4	164	West Indies	The Oval	1957

5	153	Pakistan	Lord's	1962
6	114	Pakistan	Trent Bridge	1962
7	109	West Indies	Trent Bridge	1966
8	165	West Indies	The Oval	1966
9	151	India	Lord's	1967
10	118	West Indies	Port-of-Spain	1967/68
11	105	Pakistan	Karachi (1)	1968/69

M.W.Gatting (10)

1	136	India	Bombay (3)	1984/85
2	207	India	Madras (1)	1984/85
3	160	Australia	Old Trafford	1985
4	100*	Australia	Edgbaston	1985
5	183*	India	Edgbaston	1986
6	121	New Zealand	The Oval	1986
7	100	Australia	Adelaide	1986/87
8	124	Pakistan	Edgbaston	1987
9	150*	Pakistan	The Oval	1987
10	117	Australia	Adelaide	1994/95

M.A.Atherton (10)

1	151	New Zealand	Trent Bridge	1990
2	131	India	Old Trafford	1990
3	105	Australia	Sydney	1990/91
4	144	West Indies	Georgetown	1993/94
5	135	West Indies	St John's	1993/94
6	101	New Zealand	Trent Bridge	1994
7	111	New Zealand	Old Trafford	1994
8	113	West Indies	Trent Bridge	1995
9	185*	South Africa	Johannesburg (3)	1995/96
10	160	India	Trent Bridge	1996

M.Leyland (9)

1	137	Australia	Melbourne	1928/29
2	102	South Africa	Lord's	1929
3	109	Australia	Lord's	1934
4	153	Australia	Old Trafford	1934
5	110	Australia	The Oval	1934
6	161	South Africa	The Oval	1935
7	126	Australia	Brisbane (2)	1936/37
8	111*	Australia	Melbourne	1936/37
9	187	Australia	The Oval	1938

E.R.Dexter (9)

1	141	New Zealand	Christchurch	1958/59
2	136*	West Indies	Bridgetown	1959/60
3	110	West Indies	Georgetown	1959/60
4	180	Australia	Edgbaston	1961
5	126*	India	Kanpur	1961/62
6	205	Pakistan	Karachi (1)	1961/62
7	172	Pakistan	The Oval	1962
8	174	Australia	Old Trafford	1964
9	172	South Africa	Johannesburg (3)	1964/65

R.A.Smith (9)

1	143	Australia	Old Trafford	1989
2	101	Australia	Trent Bridge	1989
3	100*	India	Lord's	1990
4	121*	India	Old Trafford	1990
5	148*	West Indies	Lord's	1991
6	109	West Indies	The Oval	1991
7	127	Pakistan	Edgbaston	1992
8	128	Sri Lanka	Colombo (2)	1992/93
9	175	West Indies	St John's	1993/94

L.E.G.Ames (8)

1	105	West Indies	Port-of-Spain	1929/30
2	149	West Indies	Kingston	1929/30
3	137	New Zealand	Lord's	1931
4	103	New Zealand	Christchurch	1932/33
5	120	Australia	Lord's	1934
6	126	West Indies	Kingston	1934/35
7	148*	South Africa	The Oval	1935
8	115	South Africa	Cape Town	1938/39

A.W.Greig (8)

1	148	India	Bombay (2)	1972/73
2	139	New Zealand	Trent Bridge	1973
3	148	West Indies	Bridgetown	1973/74
4	121	West Indies	Georgetown	1973/74
5	106	India	Lord's	1974
6	110	Australia	Brisbane (2)	1974/75
7	116	West Indies	Headingley	1976
8	103	India	Calcutta	1976/77

A.J.Stewart (8)

1	113*	Sri Lanka	Lord's	1991
2	148	New Zealand	Christchurch	1991/92
3	107	New Zealand	Wellington	1991/92
4	190	Pakistan	Edgbaston	1992
5	118	West Indies	Bridgetown	1993/94
6	143	West Indies	Bridgetown	1993/94
7	119	New Zealand	Lord's	1994
8	170	Pakistan	Headingley	1996

E.H.Hendren (7)

1	132	South Africa	Headingley	1924
2	142	South Africa	The Oval	1924
3	127*	Australia	Lord's	1926
4	169	Australia	Brisbane (1)	1928/29
5	205*	West Indies	Port-of-Spain	1929/30
6	123	West Indies	Georgetown	1929/30
7	132	Australia	Old Trafford	1934

P.H.Parfitt (7)

1	111	Pakistan	Karachi (1)	1961/62
2	101*	Pakistan	Edgbaston	1962
3	119	Pakistan	Headingley	1962
4	101*	Pakistan	Trent Bridge	1962
5	131*	New Zealand	Auckland	1962/63
6	121	India	Kanpur	1963/64
7	122*	South Africa	Johannesburg (3)	1964/65

K.W.R.Fletcher (7)

1	113	India	Bombay (2)	1972/73
2	178	New Zealand	Lord's	1973
3	129*	West Indies	Bridgetown	1973/74
4	123*	India	Old Trafford	1974
5	122	Pakistan	The Oval	1974
6	146	Australia	Melbourne	1974/75
7	216	New Zealand	Auckland	1974/75

D.W.Randall (7)

1	174	Australia	Melbourne	1976/77
2	150	Australia	Sydney	1978/79
3	126	India	Lord's	1982
4	105	Pakistan	Edgbaston	1982
5	115	Australia	Perth	1982/83
6	164	New Zealand	Wellington	1983/84
7	104	New Zealand	Auckland	1983/84

W.J.Edrich (6)

1	219	South Africa	Durban (2)	1938/39
2	119	Australia	Sydney	1946/47
3	189	South Africa	Lord's	1947
4	191	South Africa	Old Trafford	1947
5	111	Australia	Headingley	1948
6	100	New Zealand	The Oval	1949

C.Washbrook (6)

1	112	Australia	Melbourne	1946/47
2	143	Australia	Headingley	1948
3	195	South Africa	Johannesburg (2)	1948/49
4	103*	New Zealand	Headingley	1949
5	114	West Indies	Lord's	1950
6	102	West Indies	Trent Bridge	1950

B.C.Broad (6)

1	162	Australia	Perth	1986/87
2	116	Australia	Adelaide	1986/87

3	112	Australia	Melbourne	1986/87
4	116	Pakistan	Faisalabad	1987/88
5	139	Australia	Sydney	1987/88
6	114	New Zealand	Christchurch	1987/88

Hon.F.S.Jackson (5)

1	103	Australia	The Oval	1893
2	118	Australia	The Oval	1899
3	128	Australia	Old Trafford	1902
4	144*	Australia	Headingley	1905
5	113	Australia	Old Trafford	1905

A.C.MacLaren (5)

1	120	Australia	Melbourne	1894/95
2	109	Australia	Sydney	1897/98
3	124	Australia	Adelaide	1897/98
4	116	Australia	Sydney	1901/02
5	140	Australia	Trent Bridge	1905

F.E.Woolley (5)

1	133*	Australia	Sydney	1911/12
2	115*	South Africa	Johannesburg (1)	1922/23
3	134*	South Africa	Lord's	1924
4	123	Australia	Sydney	1924/25
5	154	South Africa	Old Trafford	1929

C.A.G.Russell (5)

1	135*	Australia	Adelaide	1920/21
2	101	Australia	Old Trafford	1921
3	102*	Australia	The Oval	1921
4	140	South Africa	Durban (2)	1922/23
5	111	South Africa	Durban (2)	1922/23

P.E.Richardson (5)

1	104	Australia	Old Trafford	1956
2	117	South Africa	Johannesburg (3)	1956/57
3	126	West Indies	Trent Bridge	1957
4	107	West Indies	The Oval	1957
5	100	New Zealand	Edgbaston	1958

B.L.D'Oliveira (5)

1	109	India	Headingley	1967
2	158	Australia	The Oval	1968
3	114*	Pakistan	Dacca	1968/69
4	117	Australia	Melbourne	1970/71
5	100	New Zealand	Christchurch	1970/71

A.P.E.Knott (5)

1	101	New Zealand	Auckland	1970/71
2	116	Pakistan	Edgbaston	1971
3	106*	Australia	Adelaide	1974/75
4	116	West Indies	Headingley	1976
5	135	Australia	Trent Bridge	1977

J.T.Tyldesley (4)

1	112	South Africa	Cape Town	1898/99
2	138	Australia	Edgbaston	1902
3	100	Australia	Headingley	1905
4	112*	Australia	The Oval	1905

C.P.Mead (4)

1	102	South Africa	Johannesburg (1)	1913/14
2	117	South Africa	Port Elizabeth	1913/14
3	182*	Australia	The Oval	1921
4	181	South Africa	Durban (2)	1922/23

E.Paynter (4)

1	216*	Australia	Trent Bridge	1938
2	117	South Africa	Johannesburg (1)	1938/39
3	100	South Africa	Johannesburg (1)	1938/39
4	243	South Africa	Durban (2)	1938/39

J.Hardstaff jnr (4)

1	114	New Zealand	Lord's	1937
2	103	New Zealand	The Oval	1937

3	169*	Australia	The Oval	1938
4	205*	India	Lord's	1946

R.T.Simpson (4)

1	103	New Zealand	Old Trafford	1949
2	156*	Australia	Melbourne	1950/51
3	137	South Africa	Trent Bridge	1951
4	101	Pakistan	Trent Bridge	1954

G.Pullar (4)

1	131	India	Old Trafford	1959
2	175	South Africa	The Oval	1960
3	119	India	Kanpur	1961/62
4	165	Pakistan	Dacca	1961/62

B.W.Luckhurst (4)

1	131	Australia	Perth	1970/71
2	109	Australia	Melbourne	1970/71
3	108*	Pakistan	Edgbaston	1971
4	101	India	Old Trafford	1971

M.H.Denness (4)

1	118	India	Lord's	1974
2	100	India	Edgbaston	1974
3	188	Australia	Melbourne	1974/75
4	181	New Zealand	Auckland	1974/75

R.T.Robinson (4)

1	160	India	Delhi	1984/85
2	175	Australia	Headingley	1985
3	148	Australia	Edgbaston	1985
4	166	Pakistan	Old Trafford	1987

G.A.Hick (4)

1	178	India	Bombay (3)	1992/93
2	110	South Africa	Headingley	1994
3	118*	West Indies	Trent Bridge	1995
4	141	South Africa	Centurion	1995/96

A.Shrewsbury (3)

1	105*	Australia	Melbourne	1884/85
2	164	Australia	Lord's	1886
3	106	Australia	Lord's	1893

T.W.Hayward (3)

1	122	South Africa	Johannesburg (1)	1895/96
2	130	Australia	Old Trafford	1899
3	137	Australia	The Oval	1899

L.C.Braund (3)

1	103*	Australia	Adelaide	1901/02
2	102	Australia	Sydney	1903/04
3	104	South Africa	Lord's	1907

G.E.Tyldesley (3)

1	122	South Africa	Johannesburg (1)	1927/28
2	100	South Africa	Durban (2)	1927/28
3	122	West Indies	Lord's	1928

K.S.Duleepsinhji (3)

1	117	New Zealand	Auckland	1929/30
2	173	Australia	Lord's	1930
3	109	New Zealand	The Oval	1931

Rev.D.S.Sheppard (3)

1	119	India	The Oval	1952
2	113	Australia	Old Trafford	1956
3	113	Australia	Melbourne	1962/63

M.J.K.Smith (3)

1	100	India	Old Trafford	1959
2	108	West Indies	Port-of-Spain	1959/60
3	121	South Africa	Cape Town	1964/65

R.Subba Row (3)

1	100	West Indies	Georgetown	1959/60
2	112	Australia	Edgbaston	1961
3	137	Australia	The Oval	1961

R.A.Woolmer (3)

1	149	Australia	The Oval	1975
2	120	Australia	Lord's	1977
3	137	Australia	Old Trafford	1977

G.Fowler (3)

1	105	New Zealand	The Oval	1983
2	106	West Indies	Lord's	1984
3	201	India	Madras (1)	1984/85

W.G.Grace (2)

1	152	Australia	The Oval	1880
2	170	Australia	The Oval	1886

A.G.Steel (2)

1	135*	Australia	Sydney	1882/83
2	148	Australia	Lord's	1884

R.Abel (2)

1	120	South Africa	Cape Town	1888/89
2	132*	Australia	Sydney	1891/92

A.E.Stoddart (2)

1	134	Australia	Adelaide	1891/92
2	173	Australia	Melbourne	1894/95

K.S.Ranjitsinhji (2)

1	154*	Australia	Old Trafford	1896
2	175	Australia	Sydney	1897/98

C.B.Fry (2)

1	144	Australia	The Oval	1905
2	129	South Africa	The Oval	1907

G.Gunn (2)

1	119	Australia	Sydney	1907/08
2	122*	Australia	Sydney	1907/08

W.Rhodes (2)

1	179	Australia	Melbourne	1911/12
2	152	South Africa	Johannesburg (1)	1913/14

R.E.S.Wyatt (2)

1	113	South Africa	Old Trafford	1929
2	149	South Africa	Trent Bridge	1935

A.Sandham (2)

1	152	West Indies	Bridgetown	1929/30
2	325	West Indies	Kingston	1929/30

B.H.Valentine (2)

1	136	India	Bombay (1)	1933/34
2	112	South Africa	Cape Town	1938/39

C.J.Barnett (2)

1	129	Australia	Adelaide	1936/37
2	126	Australia	Trent Bridge	1938

P.A.Gibb (2)

1	106	South Africa	Johannesburg (1)	1938/39
2	120	South Africa	Durban (2)	1938/39

J.D.B.Robertson (2)

1	133	West Indies	Port-of-Spain	1947/48
2	121	New Zealand	Lord's	1949

A.J.Watkins (2)

1	111	South Africa	Johannesburg (2)	1948/49
2	137*	India	Delhi	1951/52

T.G.Evans (2)

1	104	West Indies	Old Trafford	1950
2	104	India	Lord's	1952

W.Watson (2)

1	109	Australia	Lord's	1953
2	116	West Indies	Kingston	1953/54

J.M.Parks (2)

1	101*	West Indies	Port-of-Spain	1959/60
2	108*	South Africa	Durban (2)	1964/65

B.R.Knight (2)

1	125	New Zealand	Auckland	1962/63
2	127	India	Kanpur	1963/64

C.Milburn (2)

1	126*	West Indies	Lord's	1966
2	139	Pakistan	Karachi (1)	1968/69

R.Illingworth (2)

1	113	West Indies	Lord's	1969
2	107	India	Old Trafford	1971

C.T.Radley (2)

1	158	New Zealand	Auckland	1977/78
2	106	Pakistan	Edgbaston	1978

P.Willey (2)

1	100*	West Indies	The Oval	1980
2	102*	West Indies	St John's	1980/81

C.J.Tavare (2)

1	149	India	Delhi	1981/82
2	109	New Zealand	The Oval	1983

R.C.Russell (2)

1	128*	Australia	Old Trafford	1989
2	124	India	Lord's	1996

G.P.Thorpe (2)

1	114*	Australia	Trent Bridge	1993
2	123	Australia	Perth	1994/95

N.Hussain (2)

1	128	India	Edgbaston	1996
2	107*	India	Trent Bridge	1996

G.Ulyett (1)

1	149	Australia	Melbourne	1881/82

W.W.Read (1)

1	117	Australia	The Oval	1884

W.Barnes (1)

1	134	Australia	Adelaide	1884/85

J.Briggs (1)

1	121	Australia	Melbourne	1884/85

H.Wood (1)

1	134*	South Africa	Cape Town	1891/92

W.Gunn (1)

1	102*	Australia	Old Trafford	1893

Albert Ward (1)

1	117	Australia	Sydney	1894/95

J.T.Brown (1)

1	140	Australia	Melbourne	1894/95

A.J.L.Hill (1)

1	124	South Africa	Cape Town	1895/96

P.F.Warner (1)
1   132*   South Africa   Johannesburg (1)   1898/99

G.L.Jessop (1)
1   104   Australia   The Oval   1902

R.E.Foster (1)
1   287   Australia   Sydney   1903/04

F.L.Fane (1)
1   143   South Africa   Johannesburg (1)   1905/06

K.L.Hutchings (1)
1   126   Australia   Melbourne   1907/08

J.Sharp (1)
1   105   Australia   The Oval   1909

D.Denton (1)
1   104   South Africa   Johannesburg (1)   1909/10

J.W.Hearne (1)
1   114   Australia   Melbourne   1911/12

R.H.Spooner (1)
1   119   South Africa   Lord's   1912

J.W.H.T.Douglas (1)
1   119   South Africa   Durban (1)   1913/14

J.W.H.Makepeace (1)
1   117   Australia   Melbourne   1920/21

M.W.Tate (1)
1   100*   South Africa   Lord's   1929

E.H.Bowley (1)
1   109   New Zealand   Auckland   1929/30

G.B.Legge (1)
1   196   New Zealand   Auckland   1929/30

A.P.F.Chapman (1)
1   121   Australia   Lord's   1930

G.O.B.Allen (1)
1   122   New Zealand   Lord's   1931

Nawab of Pataudi snr (1)
1   102   Australia   Sydney   1932/33

D.R.Jardine (1)
1   127   West Indies   Old Trafford   1933

A.H.Bakewell (1)
1   107   West Indies   The Oval   1933

C.F.Walters (1)
1   102   India   Madras (1)   1933/34

R.W.V.Robins (1)
1   108   South Africa   Old Trafford   1935

T.S.Worthington (1)
1   128   India   The Oval   1936

S.C.Griffith (1)
1   140   West Indies   Port-of-Spain   1947/48

W.Place (1)
1   107   West Indies   Kingston   1947/48

F.G.Mann (1)
1   136*   South Africa   Port Elizabeth   1948/49

T.E.Bailey (1)
1   134*   New Zealand   Christchurch   1950/51

D.J.Insole (1)
1   110*   South Africa   Durban (2))   1956/57

C.A.Milton (1)
1   104*   New Zealand   Headingley   1958

R.W.Barber (1)
1   185   Australia   Sydney   1965/66

J.T.Murray (1)
1   112   West Indies   The Oval   1966

J.H.Hampshire (1)
1   107   West Indies   Lord's   1969

P.J.Sharpe (1)
1   111   New Zealand   Trent Bridge   1969

A.R.Lewis (1)
1   125   India   Kanpur   1972/73

F.C.Hayes (1)
1   106*   West Indies   The Oval   1973

D.Lloyd (1)
1   214*   India   Edgbaston   1974

D.S.Steele (1)
1   106   West Indies   Trent Bridge   1976

C.J.Richards (1)
1   133   Australia   Perth   1986/87

C.W.J.Athey (1)
1   123   Pakistan   Lord's   1987

C.C.Lewis (1)
1   117   India   Madras (1)   1992/93

N.V.Knight (1)
1   113   Pakistan   Headingley   1996

J.P.Crawley (1)
1   106   Pakistan   The Oval   1996

CENTURIES AGAINST EACH OPPOSITION

Australia	201
South Africa	90
West Indies	95
New Zealand	79
India	76
Pakistan	47
Sri Lanka	4

CENTURIES PER VENUE

England (313)

The Oval	76
Old Trafford	49
Lord's	77
Trent Bridge	44
Headingley	37
Edgbaston	30

Australia (108)

Melbourne	39
Sydney	33
Adelaide	24
Brisbane (1)	1
Brisbane (2)	3
Perth	8

South Africa (50)

Port Elizabeth	3
Cape Town	10
Johannesburg (1)	12
Durban (1)	1
Durban (2)	13
Johannesburg (2)	5
Johannesburg (3)	5
Centurion	1

West Indies (49)

Bridgetown	10
Port-of-Spain	15
Georgetown	8
Kingston	12
St John's	4

New Zealand (28)

Christchurch	9
Wellington	5
Auckland	14

India (29)

Bombay (1)	1
Calcutta	2
Madras (1)	5
Delhi	7
Bombay (2)	4
Kanpur	7
Bombay (3)	3

Pakistan (14)

Dacca	2
Karachi (1)	4
Lahore (2)	4
Hyderabad	2
Faisalabad	2

Sri Lanka (1)

Colombo (2)	1

FIFTIES PER PLAYER (1501)

G.A.Gooch (46)

1	54	Pakistan	Lord's	1978
2	91*	New Zealand	The Oval	1978
3	55	New Zealand	Trent Bridge	1978
4	74	Australia	Sydney	1978/79
5	83	India	Edgbaston	1979
6	79	India	The Oval	1979
7	99	Australia	Melbourne	1979/80
8	51	Australia	Melbourne	1979/80
9	83	West Indies	The Oval	1980
10	55	West Indies	Headingley	1980
11	83	West Indies	St John's	1980/81
12	58	India	Bangalore	1981/82
13	71	India	Delhi	1981/82
14	63	India	Calcutta	1981/82
15	58	India	Kanpur	1981/82
16	70	Australia	Trent Bridge	1985
17	74	Australia	Old Trafford	1985
18	51	West Indies	Kingston	1985/86
19	53	West Indies	Bridgetown	1985/86
20	51	West Indies	St John's	1985/86
21	51	West Indies	St John's	1985/86
22	65	Pakistan	Faisalabad	1987/88
23	93	Pakistan	Karachi (1)	1987/88
24	73	West Indies	Trent Bridge	1988
25	50	West Indies	Headingley	1988
26	84	West Indies	The Oval	1988
27	75	Sri Lanka	Lord's	1988
28	68	Australia	Headingley	1989
29	60	Australia	Lord's	1989
30	84	West Indies	Port-of-Spain	1989/90
31	85	New Zealand	Lord's	1990

32	85	India	The Oval	1990
33	88	India	The Oval	1990
34	58	Australia	Melbourne	1990/91
35	59	Australia	Sydney	1990/91
36	54	Australia	Sydney	1990/91
37	87	Australia	Adelaide	1990/91
38	68	West Indies	Trent Bridge	1991
39	60	West Indies	The Oval	1991
40	69	Pakistan	Lord's	1992
41	78	Pakistan	Old Trafford	1992
42	65	Australia	Old Trafford	1993
43	59	Australia	Headingley	1993
44	56	Australia	The Oval	1993
45	79	Australia	The Oval	1993
46	56	Australia	Brisbane (2)	1994/95

G.Boycott (42)

1	58	Australia	Old Trafford	1964
2	73	South Africa	Durban (2)	1964/65
3	76*	South Africa	Johannesburg (3)	1964/65
4	76	New Zealand	Lord's	1965
5	63*	Australia	Brisbane (2)	1965/66
6	51	Australia	Melbourne	1965/66
7	84	Australia	Sydney	1965/66
8	60	West Indies	Lord's	1966
9	71	West Indies	Trent Bridge	1966
10	68	West Indies	Port-of-Spain	1967/68
11	90	West Indies	Bridgetown	1967/68
12	62	West Indies	Port-of-Spain	1967/68
13	80*	West Indies	Port-of-Spain	1967/68
14	70	Australia	Perth	1970/71
15	50	Australia	Perth	1970/71
16	77	Australia	Sydney	1970/71
17	76*	Australia	Melbourne	1970/71
18	58	Australia	Adelaide	1970/71
19	51	New Zealand	Trent Bridge	1973
20	61	New Zealand	Lord's	1973
21	92	New Zealand	Lord's	1973
22	97	West Indies	The Oval	1973
23	56*	West Indies	Edgbaston	1973
24	93	West Indies	Port-of-Spain	1973/74
25	68	West Indies	Kingston	1973/74
26	99	West Indies	Port-of-Spain	1973/74
27	80*	Australia	Trent Bridge	1977
28	63	Pakistan	Lahore (2)	1977/78
29	79	Pakistan	Hyderabad	1977/78
30	56	Pakistan	Karachi (1)	1977/78
31	77	New Zealand	Wellington	1977/78
32	54	New Zealand	Auckland	1977/78
33	77	Australia	Perth	1978/79
34	99*	Australia	Perth	1979/80
35	75	West Indies	Trent Bridge	1980
36	86	West Indies	Old Trafford	1980
37	53	West Indies	The Oval	1980
38	62	Australia	Lord's	1980
39	70	West Indies	Port-of-Spain	1980/81
40	60	Australia	Lord's	1981
41	60	India	Bombay (3)	1981/82
42	50	India	Bangalore	1981/82

D.I.Gower (39)

1	58	Pakistan	Edgbaston	1978
2	56	Pakistan	Lord's	1978
3	71	New Zealand	Lord's	1978
4	65	Australia	Sydney	1978/79
5	82	India	Lord's	1979
6	98*	Australia	Sydney	1979/80
7	54	West Indies	Bridgetown	1980/81
8	89	Australia	Lord's	1981
9	82	India	Bangalore	1981/82
10	74	India	Calcutta	1981/82
11	64	India	Madras (1)	1981/82
12	85	India	Kanpur	1981/82
13	89	Sri Lanka	Colombo (1)	1981/82
14	74	Pakistan	Edgbaston	1982

15	74	Pakistan	Headingley	1982
16	72	Australia	Perth	1982/83
17	60	Australia	Adelaide	1982/83
18	70	Australia	Sydney	1982/83
19	72	New Zealand	Trent Bridge	1983
20	58	Pakistan	Karachi (1)	1983/84
21	57	Pakistan	Karachi (1)	1983/84
22	57*	West Indies	Old Trafford	1984
23	55	Sri Lanka	Lord's	1984
24	78	India	Kanpur	1984/85
25	86	Australia	Lord's	1985
26	66	West Indies	Port-of-Spain	1985/86
27	66	West Indies	Bridgetown	1985/86
28	90	West Indies	St John's	1985/86
29	62	New Zealand	Lord's	1986
30	71	New Zealand	Trent Bridge	1986
31	51	Australia	Brisbane (2)	1986/87
32	72	Australia	Sydney	1986/87
33	55	Pakistan	Headingley	1987
34	61	Pakistan	Edgbaston	1987
35	88*	West Indies	Trent Bridge	1988
36	57	Australia	Lord's	1989
37	79	Australia	The Oval	1989
38	61	Australia	Brisbane (2)	1990/91
39	73	Pakistan	Old Trafford	1992

M.C.Cowdrey (38)

1	54	Australia	Sydney	1954/55
2	79	Australia	Adelaide	1954/55
3	50	South Africa	Old Trafford	1955
4	81	Australia	Trent Bridge	1956
5	80	Australia	Old Trafford	1956
6	59	South Africa	Johannesburg (3)	1956/57
7	61	South Africa	Cape Town	1956/57
8	55	South Africa	Johannesburg (3)	1956/57
9	55	West Indies	Trent Bridge	1957
10	68	West Indies	Headingley	1957
11	81	New Zealand	Edgbaston	1958
12	70	New Zealand	Edgbaston	1958
13	65	New Zealand	Lord's	1958
14	84	Australia	Adelaide	1958/59
15	63*	India	Lord's	1959
16	67	India	Old Trafford	1959
17	97	West Indies	Kingston	1959/60
18	65	West Indies	Georgetown	1959/60
19	67	South Africa	Trent Bridge	1960
20	93	Australia	Headingley	1961
21	58*	Australia	Melbourne	1962/63
22	85	Australia	Sydney	1962/63
23	53	Australia	Sydney	1962/63
24	86	New Zealand	Auckland	1962/63
25	93*	Australia	The Oval	1964
26	85	New Zealand	Edgbaston	1965
27	58	South Africa	The Oval	1965
28	78*	South Africa	The Oval	1965
29	79	Australia	Melbourne	1965/66
30	89*	New Zealand	Dunedin	1965/66
31	59	New Zealand	Auckland	1965/66
32	69	West Indies	Old Trafford	1966
33	96	West Indies	Trent Bridge	1966
34	72	West Indies	Port-of-Spain	1967/68
35	71	West Indies	Port-of-Spain	1967/68
36	59	West Indies	Georgetown	1967/68
37	82	West Indies	Georgetown	1967/68
38	54	New Zealand	Auckland	1970/71

K.F.Barrington (35)

1	56	India	Trent Bridge	1959
2	80	India	Lord's	1959
3	80	India	Headingley	1959
4	87	India	Old Trafford	1959
5	69	West Indies	Port-of-Spain	1959/60
6	80	South Africa	Trent Bridge	1960
7	76	South Africa	Old Trafford	1960
8	66	Australia	Lord's	1961

9	78	Australia	Old Trafford	1961
10	53	Australia	The Oval	1961
11	83	Australia	The Oval	1961
12	52*	India	Bombay (2)	1961/62
13	84	Pakistan	Dacca	1961/62
14	50*	Pakistan	The Oval	1962
15	78	Australia	Brisbane (2)	1962/63
16	63	Australia	Adelaide	1962/63
17	94	Australia	Sydney	1962/63
18	76	New Zealand	Wellington	1962/63
19	80	West Indies	Lord's	1963
20	60	West Indies	Lord's	1963
21	80	India	Madras (2)	1963/64
22	85	Australia	Headingley	1964
23	54*	Australia	The Oval	1964
24	93	South Africa	Johannesburg (3)	1964/65
25	72	South Africa	Port Elizabeth	1964/65
26	91	South Africa	Lord's	1965
27	73	South Africa	The Oval	1965
28	53	Australia	Brisbane (2)	1965/66
29	63	Australia	Melbourne	1965/66
30	60	Australia	Adelaide	1965/66
31	93	India	Headingley	1967
32	97	India	Lord's	1967
33	75	India	Edgbaston	1967
34	63	West Indies	Kingston	1967/68
35	75	Australia	Lord's	1968

L.Hutton (33)

1	92	South Africa	Johannesburg (1)	1938/39
2	55	South Africa	Durban (2)	1938/39
3	73	West Indies	The Oval	1939
4	67	India	Old Trafford	1946
5	94	Australia	Adelaide	1946/47
6	76	Australia	Adelaide	1946/47
7	83	South Africa	The Oval	1947
8	56	West Indies	Kingston	1947/48
9	60	West Indies	Kingston	1947/48
10	74	Australia	Trent Bridge	1948
11	81	Australia	Headingley	1948
12	57	Australia	Headingley	1948
13	64	Australia	The Oval	1948
14	83	South Africa	Durban (2)	1948/49
15	87	South Africa	Cape Town	1948/49
16	66	New Zealand	Lord's	1949
17	73	New Zealand	Old Trafford	1949
18	62*	Australia	Brisbane (2)	1950/51
19	62	Australia	Sydney	1950/51
20	79	Australia	Melbourne	1950/51
21	60*	Australia	Melbourne	1950/51
22	57	New Zealand	Wellington	1950/51
23	63	South Africa	Trent Bridge	1951
24	98*	South Africa	Old Trafford	1951
25	86	India	The Oval	1952
26	60*	Australia	Trent Bridge	1953
27	66	Australia	Old Trafford	1953
28	82	Australia	The Oval	1953
29	56	West Indies	Kingston	1953/54
30	72	West Indies	Bridgetown	1953/54
31	77	West Indies	Bridgetown	1953/54
32	80	Australia	Adelaide	1954/55
33	53	New Zealand	Auckland	1954/55

A.P.E.Knott (30)

1	69*	West Indies	Port-of-Spain	1967/68
2	73*	West Indies	Georgetown	1967/68
3	52	Pakistan	Lahore (2)	1968/69
4	96*	Pakistan	Karachi (1)	1968/69
5	53	West Indies	Lord's	1969
6	73	Australia	Brisbane (2)	1970/71
7	96	New Zealand	Auckland	1970/71
8	67	India	Lord's	1971
9	90	India	The Oval	1971
10	92	Australia	The Oval	1972
11	63	Australia	The Oval	1972

12	56	India	Bombay (2)	1972/73
13	71	Pakistan	Hyderabad	1972/73
14	63*	Pakistan	Hyderabad	1972/73
15	87	West Indies	Bridgetown	1973/74
16	67	West Indies	Bridgetown	1973/74
17	61	West Indies	Georgetown	1973/74
18	83	Pakistan	Lord's	1974
19	51	Australia	Perth	1974/75
20	52	Australia	Melbourne	1974/75
21	82	Australia	Sydney	1974/75
22	69	Australia	Lord's	1975
23	64	Australia	The Oval	1975
24	50	West Indies	The Oval	1976
25	57	West Indies	The Oval	1976
26	75	India	Delhi	1976/77
27	81*	India	Bangalore	1976/77
28	57	Australia	Headingley	1977
29	59	Australia	Old Trafford	1981
30	70*	Australia	The Oval	1981

M.A.Atherton (29)

1	54	New Zealand	Lord's	1990
2	82	New Zealand	Edgbaston	1990
3	70	New Zealand	Edgbaston	1990
4	72	India	Lord's	1990
5	74	India	Old Trafford	1990
6	86	India	The Oval	1990
7	87	Australia	Adelaide	1990/91
8	76	Pakistan	Headingley	1992
9	60	Pakistan	The Oval	1992
10	80	Australia	Lord's	1993
11	99	Australia	Lord's	1993
12	55	Australia	Headingley	1993
13	63	Australia	Headingley	1993
14	72	Australia	Edgbaston	1993
15	50	Australia	The Oval	1993
16	55	West Indies	Kingston	1993/94
17	85	West Indies	Bridgetown	1993/94
18	99	South Africa	Headingley	1994
19	63	South Africa	The Oval	1994
20	54	Australia	Brisbane (2)	1994/95
21	88	Australia	Sydney	1994/95
22	67	Australia	Sydney	1994/95
23	80	Australia	Adelaide	1994/95
24	81	West Indies	Headingley	1995
25	95	West Indies	The Oval	1995
26	78	South Africa	Centurion	1995/96
27	72	South Africa	Port Elizabeth	1995/96
28	53*	India	Edgbaston	1996
29	64	Pakistan	Lord's	1996

J.B.Hobbs (28)

1	83	Australia	Melbourne	1907/08
2	57	Australia	Melbourne	1907/08
3	72	Australia	Sydney	1907/08
4	62*	Australia	Edgbaston	1909
5	89	South Africa	Johannesburg (1)	1909/10
6	53	South Africa	Durban (1)	1909/10
7	70	South Africa	Durban (1)	1909/10
8	93*	South Africa	Johannesburg (1)	1909/10
9	63	Australia	Sydney	1911/12
10	55	South Africa	Headingley	1912
11	68	South Africa	The Oval	1912
12	66	Australia	The Oval	1912
13	82	South Africa	Durban (1)	1913/14
14	92	South Africa	Johannesburg (1)	1913/14
15	64	South Africa	Durban (1)	1913/14
16	97	South Africa	Durban (1)	1913/14
17	59	Australia	Sydney	1920/21
18	76	South Africa	Edgbaston	1924
19	57	Australia	Sydney	1924/25
20	66	Australia	Melbourne	1924/25
21	88	Australia	Headingley	1926
22	74	Australia	Old Trafford	1926
23	53	West Indies	Old Trafford	1928

24	74	Australia	Adelaide	1928/29
25	65	Australia	Melbourne	1928/29
26	52	South Africa	The Oval	1929
27	78	Australia	Trent Bridge	1930
28	74	Australia	Trent Bridge	1930

D.C.S.Compton (28)

1	65	New Zealand	The Oval	1937
2	76*	Australia	Lord's	1938
3	51	India	Old Trafford	1946
4	71*	India	Old Trafford	1946
5	54	Australia	Sydney	1946/47
6	76	Australia	Sydney	1946/47
7	65	South Africa	Trent Bridge	1947
8	53	South Africa	The Oval	1947
9	53	Australia	Lord's	1948
10	66	Australia	Headingley	1948
11	72	South Africa	Durban (2)	1948/49
12	51*	South Africa	Cape Town	1948/49
13	79	New Zealand	Christchurch	1950/51
14	79	South Africa	Lord's	1951
15	73	South Africa	The Oval	1951
16	57	Australia	Lord's	1953
17	61	Australia	Headingley	1953
18	93	West Indies	Bridgetown	1953/54
19	64	West Indies	Georgetown	1953/54
20	93	Pakistan	Old Trafford	1954
21	53	Pakistan	The Oval	1954
22	84	Australia	Sydney	1954/55
23	69	South Africa	Lord's	1955
24	71	South Africa	Old Trafford	1955
25	61	South Africa	Headingley	1955
26	94	Australia	The Oval	1956
27	58	South Africa	Cape Town	1956/57
28	64	South Africa	Cape Town	1956/57

R.A.Smith (28)

1	57	West Indies	The Oval	1988
2	66	Australia	Headingley	1989
3	96	Australia	Lord's	1989
4	77*	Australia	The Oval	1989
5	57	West Indies	Kingston	1989/90
6	62	West Indies	Bridgetown	1989/90
7	55	New Zealand	Trent Bridge	1990
8	64	New Zealand	Lord's	1990
9	61*	India	Old Trafford	1990
10	57	India	The Oval	1990
11	53	Australia	Adelaide	1990/91
12	58	Australia	Perth	1990/91
13	54	West Indies	Headingley	1991
14	64*	West Indies	Trent Bridge	1991
15	63*	Sri Lanka	Lord's	1991
16	96	New Zealand	Christchurch	1991/92
17	76	New Zealand	Wellington	1991/92
18	84*	Pakistan	The Oval	1992
19	56	India	Madras (1)	1992/93
20	62	India	Bombay (3)	1992/93
21	86	Australia	Trent Bridge	1993
22	50	Australia	Trent Bridge	1993
23	84	West Indies	Georgetown	1993/94
24	78	New Zealand	Trent Bridge	1994
25	61	West Indies	Lord's	1995
26	90	West Indies	Lord's	1995
27	52	South Africa	Johannesburg (3)	1995/96
28	66	South Africa	Cape Town	1995/96

E.R.Dexter (27)

1	52	New Zealand	Old Trafford	1958
2	77	West Indies	Port-of-Spain	1959/60
3	76	West Indies	Port-of-Spain	1959/60
4	52	South Africa	Edgbaston	1960
5	56	South Africa	Lord's	1960
6	76	Australia	Old Trafford	1961
7	66*	Pakistan	Lahore (2)	1961/62
8	85	India	Bombay (2)	1961/62

9	57	India	Calcutta	1961/62
10	62	India	Calcutta	1961/62
11	72	Pakistan	Edgbaston	1962
12	65	Pakistan	Lord's	1962
13	85	Pakistan	Trent Bridge	1962
14	70	Australia	Brisbane (2)	1962/63
15	99	Australia	Brisbane (2)	1962/63
16	93	Australia	Melbourne	1962/63
17	52	Australia	Melbourne	1962/63
18	61	Australia	Adelaide	1962/63
19	73	West Indies	Old Trafford	1963
20	70	West Indies	Lord's	1963
21	57	West Indies	Edgbaston	1963
22	68	Australia	Trent Bridge	1964
23	66	Australia	Headingley	1964
24	61	South Africa	Cape Town	1964/65
25	57	New Zealand	Edgbaston	1965
26	62	New Zealand	Lord's	1965
27	80*	New Zealand	Lord's	1965

W.R.Hammond (24)

1	51	South Africa	Johannesburg (1)	1927/28
2	90	South Africa	Durban (2)	1927/28
3	66	South Africa	Durban (2)	1927/28
4	63	West Indies	Old Trafford	1928
5	65	South Africa	Headingley	1929
6	60	Australia	The Oval	1930
7	63	South Africa	Johannesburg (1)	1930/31
8	57	South Africa	Cape Town	1930/31
9	65	South Africa	Cape Town	1930/31
10	75	South Africa	Johannesburg (1)	1930/31
11	85	Australia	Adelaide	1932/33
12	75*	Australia	Sydney	1932/33
13	63	South Africa	Headingley	1935
14	87*	South Africa	Headingley	1935
15	63*	South Africa	Old Trafford	1935
16	65	South Africa	The Oval	1935
17	51	Australia	Melbourne	1936/37
18	56	Australia	Melbourne	1936/37
19	76	Australia	Headingley	1938
20	59	Australia	The Oval	1938
21	58	South Africa	Johannesburg (1)	1938/39
22	61*	South Africa	Johannesburg (1)	1938/39
23	69	India	Old Trafford	1946
24	79	New Zealand	Christchurch	1946/47

J.H.Edrich (24)

1	85	Australia	Melbourne	1965/66
2	96	West Indies	Kingston	1967/68
3	88	Australia	Edgbaston	1968
4	64	Australia	Edgbaston	1968
5	62	Australia	Headingley	1968
6	65	Australia	Headingley	1968
7	54	Pakistan	Lahore (2)	1968/69
8	58	West Indies	Old Trafford	1969
9	79	West Indies	Headingley	1969
10	68	New Zealand	The Oval	1969
11	79	Australia	Brisbane (2)	1970/71
12	55	Australia	Sydney	1970/71
13	74*	Australia	Melbourne	1970/71
14	57	Australia	Sydney	1970/71
15	62	India	Lord's	1971
16	59	India	Old Trafford	1971
17	96	India	Lord's	1974
18	70	Pakistan	Headingley	1974
19	50	Australia	Sydney	1974/75
20	70	Australia	Melbourne	1974/75
21	64	New Zealand	Auckland	1974/75
22	62	Australia	Headingley	1975
23	96	Australia	The Oval	1975
24	76*	West Indies	Trent Bridge	1976

F.E.Woolley (23)

1	58*	South Africa	Johannesburg (1)	1909/10
2	69	South Africa	Cape Town	1909/10

3	64	South Africa	Cape Town	1909/10
4	56	Australia	Melbourne	1911/12
5	73	South Africa	Lord's	1912
6	57	South Africa	Headingley	1912
7	62	Australia	The Oval	1912
8	54	South Africa	Port Elizabeth	1913/14
9	52	Australia	Sydney	1920/21
10	50	Australia	Melbourne	1920/21
11	79	Australia	Adelaide	1920/21
12	53	Australia	Sydney	1920/21
13	95	Australia	Lord's	1921
14	93	Australia	Lord's	1921
15	64	South Africa	Edgbaston	1924
16	51	South Africa	The Oval	1924
17	50	Australia	Melbourne	1924/25
18	87	Australia	Lord's	1926
19	58	Australia	Old Trafford	1926
20	83	South Africa	Headingley	1929
21	95*	South Africa	Headingley	1929
22	59	New Zealand	Auckland	1929/30
23	80	New Zealand	Lord's	1931

H.Sutcliffe (23)

1	64	South Africa	Edgbaston	1924
2	83	South Africa	Headingley	1924
3	59	Australia	Sydney	1924/25
4	59	Australia	Adelaide	1924/25
5	82	Australia	Lord's	1926
6	94	Australia	Headingley	1926
7	76	Australia	The Oval	1926
8	99	South Africa	Cape Town	1927/28
9	51	South Africa	Durban (2)	1927/28
10	54	West Indies	Old Trafford	1928
11	63	West Indies	The Oval	1928
12	58	Australia	Melbourne	1928/29
13	64	Australia	Adelaide	1928/29
14	58*	Australia	Trent Bridge	1930
15	74	Australia	Old Trafford	1930
16	54	Australia	The Oval	1930
17	52	Australia	Melbourne	1932/33
18	86	Australia	Brisbane (2)	1932/33
19	56	Australia	Sydney	1932/33
20	62	Australia	Trent Bridge	1934
21	63	Australia	Old Trafford	1934
22	69*	Australia	Old Trafford	1934
23	61	South Africa	Trent Bridge	1935

P.B.H.May (22)

1	74	India	Lord's	1952
2	69	India	Old Trafford	1952
3	69	West Indies	Kingston	1953/54
4	62	West Indies	Bridgetown	1953/54
5	53	Pakistan	The Oval	1954
6	91	Australia	Melbourne	1954/55
7	79	Australia	Sydney	1954/55
8	83	South Africa	Trent Bridge	1955
9	97	South Africa	Headingley	1955
10	89*	South Africa	The Oval	1955
11	73	Australia	Trent Bridge	1956
12	63	Australia	Lord's	1956
13	53	Australia	Lord's	1956
14	83*	Australia	The Oval	1956
15	61	South Africa	Johannesburg (3)	1956/57
16	69	West Indies	Headingley	1957
17	84	New Zealand	Edgbaston	1958
18	92	Australia	Sydney	1958/59
19	59	Australia	Adelaide	1958/59
20	71	New Zealand	Christchurch	1958/59
21	95	Australia	Old Trafford	1961
22	71	Australia	The Oval	1961

I.T.Botham (22)

1	53	New Zealand	Auckland	1977/78
2	59	Australia	Sydney	1978/79
3	74	Australia	Adelaide	1978/79

4	57	West Indies	Trent Bridge	1980
5	50	Australia	Headingley	1981
6	55	India	Bangalore	1981/82
7	66	India	Delhi	1981/82
8	58	India	Calcutta	1981/82
9	52	India	Madras (1)	1981/82
10	67	India	Lord's	1982
11	69	Pakistan	Lord's	1982
12	57	Pakistan	Headingley	1982
13	58	Australia	Adelaide	1982/83
14	61	New Zealand	Lord's	1983
15	70	New Zealand	Auckland	1983/84
16	64	West Indies	Edgbaston	1984
17	81	West Indies	Lord's	1984
18	54	West Indies	The Oval	1984
19	60	Australia	Headingley	1985
20	85	Australia	Lord's	1985
21	59*	New Zealand	The Oval	1986
22	51*	Pakistan	The Oval	1987

E.H.Hendren (21)

1	56	Australia	Sydney	1920/21
2	67	Australia	Melbourne	1920/21
3	51	Australia	Adelaide	1920/21
4	74	South Africa	Edgbaston	1924
5	50*	South Africa	Lord's	1924
6	74*	Australia	Sydney	1924/25
7	92	Australia	Adelaide	1924/25
8	65	Australia	Melbourne	1924/25
9	74	Australia	Sydney	1928/29
10	95	Australia	Melbourne	1928/29
11	70	South Africa	Edgbaston	1929
12	80	West Indies	Bridgetown	1929/30
13	77	West Indies	Port-of-Spain	1929/30
14	56	West Indies	Georgetown	1929/30
15	61	West Indies	Kingston	1929/30
16	55	West Indies	Kingston	1929/30
17	72	Australia	Trent Bridge	1930
18	93	South Africa	Cape Town	1930/31
19	86	South Africa	Cape Town	1930/31
20	64	South Africa	Johannesburg (1)	1930/31
21	79	Australia	Trent Bridge	1934

M.W.Gatting (21)

1	56	West Indies	Old Trafford	1980
2	51*	Australia	Lord's	1980
3	52	Australia	Trent Bridge	1981
4	59	Australia	Lord's	1981
5	53	Australia	The Oval	1981
6	56	Australia	The Oval	1981
7	81	New Zealand	Lord's	1983
8	75	Pakistan	Faisalabad	1983/84
9	53	Pakistan	Lahore (2)	1983/84
10	62	India	Kanpur	1984/85
11	53	Australia	Headingley	1985
12	75*	Australia	Lord's	1985
13	74	Australia	Trent Bridge	1985
14	61	Australia	Brisbane (2)	1986/87
15	96	Australia	Sydney	1986/87
16	70	Australia	Perth	1986/87
17	61	Pakistan	The Oval	1987
18	79	Pakistan	Faisalabad	1987/88
19	81	India	Calcutta	1992/93
20	61	India	Bombay (3)	1992/93
21	59	Australia	Lord's	1993

T.W.Graveney (20)

1	71	India	Headingley	1952
2	73	India	Lord's	1952
3	78	Australia	Lord's	1953
4	55	Australia	Headingley	1953
5	64*	West Indies	Bridgetown	1953/54
6	92	West Indies	Port-of-Spain	1953/54
7	84	Pakistan	Trent Bridge	1954
8	65	Pakistan	Old Trafford	1954

9	60	South Africa	Lord's	1955
10	53*	Australia	Adelaide	1958/59
11	54	Australia	Melbourne	1958/59
12	97	Pakistan	Edgbaston	1962
13	96	West Indies	Lord's	1966
14	59	India	Headingley	1967
15	81	Pakistan	Lord's	1967
16	77	Pakistan	The Oval	1967
17	55	West Indies	Bridgetown	1967/68
18	96	Australia	Edgbaston	1968
19	63	Australia	The Oval	1968
20	75	West Indies	Old Trafford	1969

A.W.Greig (20)

1	57	Australia	Old Trafford	1972
2	62	Australia	Old Trafford	1972
3	54	Australia	Lord's	1972
4	68*	India	Delhi	1972/73
5	67	India	Calcutta	1972/73
6	72	Pakistan	Lahore (2)	1972/73
7	64	Pakistan	Hyderabad	1972/73
8	63	New Zealand	Lord's	1973
9	53	India	Old Trafford	1974
10	60	Australia	Melbourne	1974/75
11	54	Australia	Sydney	1974/75
12	89	Australia	Melbourne	1974/75
13	51	New Zealand	Auckland	1974/75
14	96	Australia	Lord's	1975
15	51	Australia	Headingley	1975
16	76*	West Indies	Headingley	1976
17	76	India	Bombay (3)	1976/77
18	54	India	Madras (1)	1976/77
19	91	Australia	Lord's	1977
20	76	Australia	Old Trafford	1977

A.J.Stewart (20)

1	54	New Zealand	Lord's	1990
2	79	Australia	Melbourne	1990/91
3	91	Australia	Sydney	1990/91
4	63	New Zealand	Wellington	1991/92
5	74	Pakistan	Lord's	1992
6	69*	Pakistan	Lord's	1992
7	74	India	Madras (1)	1992/93
8	63	Sri Lanka	Colombo (2)	1992/93
9	62	Australia	Lord's	1993
10	78	Australia	Headingley	1993
11	76	Australia	The Oval	1993
12	70	West Indies	Kingston	1993/94
13	79	West Indies	Georgetown	1993/94
14	89	South Africa	Headingley	1994
15	62	South Africa	The Oval	1994
16	81	South Africa	Port Elizabeth	1995/96
17	66	India	Lord's	1996
18	50	India	Trent Bridge	1996
19	89	Pakistan	Lord's	1996
20	54	Pakistan	The Oval	1996

K.W.R.Fletcher (19)

1	83	Pakistan	Lahore (2)	1968/69
2	80	Australia	Adelaide	1970/71
3	97*	India	Madras (1)	1972/73
4	58	India	Kanpur	1972/73
5	55	Pakistan	Lahore (2)	1972/73
6	78	Pakistan	Hyderabad	1972/73
7	54	Pakistan	Karachi (1)	1972/73
8	81	New Zealand	Headingley	1973
9	52	West Indies	Edgbaston	1973
10	68	West Indies	Lord's	1973
11	86*	West Indies	Lord's	1973
12	51*	India	Edgbaston	1974
13	67*	Pakistan	Headingley	1974
14	63	Australia	Adelaide	1974/75
15	51	Australia	Edgbaston	1975
16	58*	India	Bombay (3)	1976/77
17	51	India	Delhi	1981/82

| 18 | 69 | India | Calcutta | 1981/82 |
| 19 | 60* | India | Calcutta | 1981/82 |

A.J.Lamb (18)

1	56	Australia	Perth	1982/83
2	72	Australia	Brisbane (2)	1982/83
3	82	Australia	Adelaide	1982/83
4	83	Australia	Melbourne	1982/83
5	58	New Zealand	Headingley	1983
6	52	India	Delhi	1984/85
7	67	India	Calcutta	1984/85
8	62	India	Madras (1)	1984/85
9	67	Australia	Old Trafford	1985
10	62	West Indies	Port-of-Spain	1985/86
11	64*	West Indies	Headingley	1988
12	63	Sri Lanka	Lord's	1988
13	84*	New Zealand	Lord's	1990
14	52	India	The Oval	1990
15	53	Australia	Adelaide	1990/91
16	91	Australia	Perth	1990/91
17	93	New Zealand	Christchurch	1991/92
18	60	New Zealand	Auckland	1991/92

G.P.Thorpe (18)

1	60	Australia	Edgbaston	1993
2	86	West Indies	Port-of-Spain	1993/94
3	84	West Indies	Bridgetown	1993/94
4	72	South Africa	Headingley	1994
5	73	South Africa	Headingley	1994
6	79	South Africa	The Oval	1994
7	67	Australia	Brisbane (2)	1994/95
8	51	Australia	Melbourne	1994/95
9	83	Australia	Adelaide	1994/95
10	61	West Indies	Headingley	1995
11	52	West Indies	Lord's	1995
12	94	West Indies	Old Trafford	1995
13	76	West Indies	Trent Bridge	1995
14	74	West Indies	The Oval	1995
15	59	South Africa	Cape Town	1995/96
16	89	India	Lord's	1996
17	77	Pakistan	Lord's	1996
18	54	Pakistan	The Oval	1996

B.L.D'Oliveira (15)

1	76	West Indies	Trent Bridge	1966
2	54	West Indies	Trent Bridge	1966
3	88	West Indies	Headingley	1966
4	59	Pakistan	Lord's	1967
5	81*	Pakistan	Lord's	1967
6	51	West Indies	Bridgetown	1967/68
7	87*	Australia	Old Trafford	1968
8	57	West Indies	Old Trafford	1969
9	57	Australia	Brisbane (2)	1970/71
10	56	Australia	Sydney	1970/71
11	58	New Zealand	Auckland	1970/71
12	73	Pakistan	Edgbaston	1971
13	74	Pakistan	Headingley	1971
14	72	Pakistan	Headingley	1971
15	50*	Australia	Trent Bridge	1972

G.A.Hick (15)

1	51	Pakistan	Edgbaston	1992
2	64	India	Madras (1)	1992/93
3	68	Sri Lanka	Colombo (2)	1992/93
4	64	Australia	Lord's	1993
5	80	Australia	The Oval	1993
6	96	West Indies	Kingston	1993/94
7	59	West Indies	Bridgetown	1993/94
8	58	New Zealand	Lord's	1994
9	81*	South Africa	The Oval	1994
10	80	Australia	Brisbane (2)	1994/95
11	98*	Australia	Sydney	1994/95
12	67	West Indies	Lord's	1995
13	96	West Indies	The Oval	1995
14	51*	West Indies	The Oval	1995
15	62	South Africa	Port Elizabeth	1995/96

W.J.Edrich (13)

1	71	Australia	Sydney	1946/47
2	89	Australia	Melbourne	1946/47
3	60	Australia	Sydney	1946/47
4	57	South Africa	Trent Bridge	1947
5	50	South Africa	Trent Bridge	1947
6	53	Australia	Old Trafford	1948
7	54	Australia	Headingley	1948
8	70	New Zealand	Headingley	1949
9	78	New Zealand	Old Trafford	1949
10	71	West Indies	Old Trafford	1950
11	64	Australia	Headingley	1953
12	55*	Australia	The Oval	1953
13	88	Australia	Brisbane (2)	1954/55

T.W.Hayward (12)

1	72	Australia	Sydney	1897/98
2	70	Australia	Adelaide	1897/98
3	77	Australia	Lord's	1899
4	69	Australia	Sydney	1901/02
5	90	Australia	Adelaide	1901/02
6	91	Australia	Sydney	1903/04
7	58	Australia	Melbourne	1903/04
8	67	Australia	Adelaide	1903/04
9	52	Australia	Sydney	1903/04
10	60	Australia	Headingley	1905
11	82	Australia	Old Trafford	1905
12	59	Australia	The Oval	1905

R.E.S.Wyatt (12)

1	91	South Africa	Cape Town	1927/28
2	58	South Africa	Johannesburg (1)	1927/28
3	58	West Indies	Kingston	1929/30
4	64	Australia	The Oval	1930
5	54	South Africa	Durban (2)	1930/31
6	78	Australia	Adelaide	1932/33
7	51	Australia	Sydney	1932/33
8	61*	Australia	Sydney	1932/33
9	60	New Zealand	Auckland	1932/33
10	71	West Indies	Georgetown	1934/35
11	53	South Africa	Lord's	1935
12	50	Australia	Adelaide	1936/37

C.Washbrook (12)

1	52	India	Old Trafford	1946
2	62	Australia	Melbourne	1946/47
3	65	Australia	Adelaide	1946/47
4	59	South Africa	Trent Bridge	1947
5	65	South Africa	Lord's	1947
6	75	South Africa	Headingley	1947
7	85*	Australia	Old Trafford	1948
8	65	Australia	Headingley	1948
9	74	South Africa	Cape Town	1948/49
10	97	South Africa	Johannesburg (2)	1948/49
11	58	New Zealand	Christchurch	1950/51
12	98	Australia	Headingley	1956

G.Pullar (12)

1	75	India	Headingley	1959
2	65	West Indies	Bridgetown	1959/60
3	66	West Indies	Kingston	1959/60
4	54	West Indies	Port-of-Spain	1959/60
5	59	South Africa	The Oval	1960
6	53	Australia	Headingley	1961
7	63	Australia	Old Trafford	1961
8	83	India	Bombay (2)	1161/62
9	89	India	Delhi	1961/62
10	60	Pakistan	Karachi (1)	1961/62
11	56	Australia	Brisbane (2)	1962/63
12	53	Australia	Sydney	1962/63

D.W.Randall (12)

1	53	Australia	Lord's	1977
2	79	Australia	Old Trafford	1977
3	55	Pakistan	Karachi (1)	1977/78

4	75	Australia	Brisbane (2)	1978/79
5	74*	Australia	Brisbane (2)	1978/79
6	57	India	Lord's	1979
7	95	India	The Oval	1982
8	78	Australia	Perth	1982/83
9	70	Australia	Sydney	1982/83
10	75*	New Zealand	The Oval	1983
11	83	New Zealand	Trent Bridge	1983
12	65	Pakistan	Faisalabad	1983/84

C.J.Tavare (12)

1	69	Australia	Old Trafford	1981
2	78	Australia	Old Trafford	1981
3	56	India	Bombay (3)	1981/82
4	85	Sri Lanka	Colombo (1)	1981/82
5	57	India	Old Trafford	1982
6	75*	India	The Oval	1982
7	54	Pakistan	Edgbaston	1982
8	82	Pakistan	Lord's	1982
9	89	Australia	Perth	1982/83
10	89	Australia	Melbourne	1982/83
11	69	New Zealand	Headingley	1983
12	51	New Zealand	Lord's	1983

W.Rhodes (11)

1	69	Australia	Sydney	1907/08
2	66	Australia	The Oval	1909
3	54	Australia	The Oval	1909
4	66	South Africa	Johannesburg (1)	1909/10
5	77	South Africa	Cape Town	1909/10
6	61	Australia	Melbourne	1911/12
7	59	Australia	Adelaide	1911/12
8	57*	Australia	Adelaide	1911/12
9	59	Australia	Lord's	1912
10	92	Australia	Old Trafford	1912
11	73	Australia	Melbourne	1920/21

M.J.K.Smith (11)

1	98	India	The Oval	1959
2	96	West Indies	Port-of-Spain	1959/60
3	54	South Africa	Edgbaston	1960
4	99	South Africa	Lord's	1960
5	99	Pakistan	Lahore (2)	1961/62
6	73	India	Madras (2)	1961/62
7	56	Pakistan	Karachi (1)	1961/62
8	57	India	Madras (2)	1963/64
9	75*	India	Calcutta	1963/64
10	54	New Zealand	Christchurch	1965/66
11	87	New Zealand	Christchurch	1965/66

D.L.Amiss (11)

1	56	Pakistan	Headingley	1971
2	99	Pakistan	Karachi (1)	1972/73
3	53	New Zealand	Lord's	1973
4	56	West Indies	Edgbaston	1973
5	86*	West Indies	Edgbaston	1973
6	56	India	Old Trafford	1974
7	79	India	Edgbaston	1974
8	90	Australia	Melbourne	1974/75
9	82	India	Bangalore	1976/77
10	50	India	Bombay (3)	1976/77
11	64	Australia	Melbourne	1976/77

D.R.Jardine (10)

1	83	West Indies	Old Trafford	1928
2	65*	Australia	Brisbane (1)	1928/29
3	62	Australia	Melbourne	1928/29
4	98	Australia	Adelaide	1928/29
5	79	India	Lord's	1932
6	85*	India	Lord's	1932
7	56	Australia	Adelaide	1932/33
8	60	India	Bombay (1)	1933/34
9	61	India	Calcutta	1933/34
10	65	India	Madras (1)	1933/34

M.Leyland (10)

1	53*	Australia	Melbourne	1928/29
2	73	South Africa	Lord's	1929
3	55	South Africa	Old Trafford	1929
4	52	South Africa	Cape Town	1930/31
5	91	South Africa	Johannesburg (1)	1930/31
6	83	Australia	Adelaide	1932/33
7	86	Australia	Brisbane (2)	1932/33
8	69	South Africa	Trent Bridge	1935
9	53	South Africa	Old Trafford	1935
10	60	India	Lord's	1936

J.Hardstaff jnr (10)

1	94	India	Old Trafford	1936
2	83	Australia	Melbourne	1936/37
3	64	New Zealand	Lord's	1937
4	58	New Zealand	Old Trafford	1937
5	76	West Indies	Old Trafford	1939
6	94	West Indies	The Oval	1939
7	67	Australia	Adelaide	1946/47
8	98	West Indies	Bridgetown	1947/48
9	63	West Indies	Georgetown	1947/48
10	64	West Indies	Kingston	1947/48

T.E.Bailey (10)

1	93	New Zealand	Lord's	1949
2	72*	New Zealand	Old Trafford	1949
3	82*	West Indies	Old Trafford	1950
4	95	South Africa	Headingley	1951
5	71	Australia	Lord's	1953
6	64	Australia	The Oval	1953
7	88	Australia	Brisbane (2)	1954/55
8	72	Australia	Sydney	1954/55
9	80	South Africa	Durban (2)	1956/57
10	68	Australia	Brisbane (2)	1958/59

F.J.Titmus (10)

1	59*	Australia	Adelaide	1962/63
2	52*	West Indies	Lord's	1963
3	84*	India	Bombay (2)	1963/64
4	56	Australia	The Oval	1964
5	59	South Africa	Lord's	1965
6	60	Australia	Brisbane (2)	1965/66
7	56*	Australia	Melbourne	1965/66
8	53	Australia	Adelaide	1965/66
9	65	Pakistan	The Oval	1967
10	61	Australia	Perth	1974/75

J.E.Emburey (10)

1	57	Australia	Old Trafford	1981
2	75	New Zealand	Trent Bridge	1986
3	69	Australia	Sydney	1986/87
4	58	Pakistan	Edgbaston	1987
5	53	Pakistan	The Oval	1987
6	70	Pakistan	Karachi (1)	1987/88
7	74*	Pakistan	Karachi (1)	1987/88
8	64	Australia	Old Trafford	1989
9	59	Sri Lanka	Colombo (2)	1992/93
10	55*	Australia	Edgbaston	1993

J.T.Tyldesley (9)

1	66	Australia	Melbourne	1901/02
2	79	Australia	Sydney	1901/02
3	53	Australia	Sydney	1903/04
4	97	Australia	Melbourne	1903/04
5	62	Australia	Melbourne	1903/04
6	56	Australia	Trent Bridge	1905
7	61	Australia	Trent Bridge	1905
8	52	South Africa	Lord's	1907
9	55	Australia	Headingley	1909

P.E.Richardson (9)

1	81	Australia	Trent Bridge	1956
2	73	Australia	Trent Bridge	1956
3	68	South Africa	Durban (2)	1956/57

4	76	West Indies	Lord's	1957
5	74	New Zealand	Old Trafford	1958
6	68	Australia	Melbourne	1958/59
7	67	New Zealand	Auckland	1958/59
8	71	India	Bombay (2)	1961/62
9	62	India	Calcutta	1961/62

R.W.Barber (9)

1	69*	India	Kanpur	1961/62
2	86	Pakistan	Dacca	1961/62
3	74	South Africa	Durban (2)	1964/65
4	97	South Africa	Johannesburg (3)	1964/65
5	58	South Africa	Cape Town	1964/65
6	61	South Africa	Johannesburg (3)	1964/65
7	51	New Zealand	Edgbaston	1965
8	56	South Africa	Lord's	1965
9	55	West Indies	Headingley	1966

J.M.Parks (9)

1	57	West Indies	Headingley	1963
2	51*	India	Kanpur	1963/64
3	68	Australia	Headingley	1964
4	60	Australia	Old Trafford	1964
5	59	South Africa	Cape Town	1964/65
6	52	Australia	Brisbane (2)	1965/66
7	71	Australia	Melbourne	1965/66
8	89	Australia	Melbourne	1965/66
9	91	West Indies	Lord's	1966

J.M.Brearley (9)

1	59	India	Madras (1)	1976/77
2	91	India	Bombay (3)	1976/77
3	81	Australia	Trent Bridge	1977
4	74	Pakistan	Hyderabad	1977/78
5	50	New Zealand	Trent Bridge	1978
6	53	Australia	Sydney	1978/79
7	64	Australia	Perth	1979/80
8	60*	Australia	Melbourne	1979/80
9	51	Australia	The Oval	1981

A.C.MacLaren (8)

1	50*	Australia	Sydney	1897/98
2	65	Australia	Sydney	1897/98
3	88*	Australia	Lord's	1899
4	67	Australia	Adelaide	1901/02
5	92	Australia	Sydney	1901/02
6	63	Australia	Bramall Lane	1902
7	56	Australia	Lord's	1905
8	79	Australia	Lord's	1905

T.G.Evans (8)

1	74	South Africa	Trent Bridge	1947
2	50	Australia	Trent Bridge	1948
3	63	West Indies	Trent Bridge	1950
4	66	India	Headingley	1952
5	71	India	Old Trafford	1952
6	62	South Africa	Cape Town	1956/57
7	82	West Indies	Lord's	1957
8	73	India	Trent Bridge	1959

G.Fowler (8)

1	86	Pakistan	Headingley	1982
2	83	Australia	Brisbane (2)	1982/83
3	65	Australia	Melbourne	1982/83
4	57	Pakistan	Faisalabad	1983/84
5	58	Pakistan	Lahore (2)	1983/84
6	50	West Indies	Headingley	1984
7	55	India	Bombay (3)	1984/85
8	69	India	Kanpur	1984/85

G.Ulyett (7)

1	52	Australia	Melbourne	1876/77
2	63	Australia	Melbourne	1876/77
3	87	Australia	Melbourne	1881/82
4	67	Australia	Sydney	1881/82

5	64	Australia	Melbourne	1881/82
6	68	Australia	Adelaide	1884/85
7	74	Australia	Lord's	1890

C.B.Fry (7)

1	64	South Africa	Johannesburg (1)	1895/96
2	50	Australia	Trent Bridge	1899
3	60	Australia	The Oval	1899
4	73	Australia	Lord's	1905
5	54	South Africa	Headingley	1907
6	62	Australia	The Oval	1909
7	79	Australia	The Oval	1912

G.Gunn (7)

1	74	Australia	Sydney	1907/08
2	65	Australia	Adelaide	1907/08
3	62	Australia	Sydney	1911/12
4	75	Australia	Melbourne	1911/12
5	52	Australia	Sydney	1911/12
6	61	Australia	Sydney	1911/12
7	85	West Indies	Kingston	1929/30

L.E.G.Ames (7)

1	65	India	Lord's	1932
2	69	Australia	Adelaide	1932/33
3	83*	West Indies	Lord's	1933
4	72	Australia	Old Trafford	1934
5	52	Australia	Adelaide	1936/37
6	83	Australia	Lord's	1938
7	84	South Africa	Durban (2)	1938/39

E.Paynter (7)

1	54	India	Lord's	1932
2	77	Australia	Adelaide	1932/33
3	83	Australia	Brisbane (2)	1932/33
4	74	New Zealand	Lord's	1937
5	99	Australia	Lord's	1938
6	62	South Africa	Durban (2)	1938/39
7	75	South Africa	Durban (2)	1938/39

C.F.Walters (7)

1	51	West Indies	Lord's	1933
2	78	India	Bombay (1)	1933/34
3	59	India	Madras (1)	1933/34
4	82	Australia	Lord's	1934
5	52	Australia	Old Trafford	1934
6	50*	Australia	Old Trafford	1934
7	64	Australia	The Oval	1934

M.H.Denness (7)

1	55*	New Zealand	The Oval	1969
2	76	India	Madras (1)	1972/73
3	50	Pakistan	Lahore (2)	1972/73
4	68	Pakistan	Lahore (2)	1972/73
5	67	West Indies	Kingston	1973/74
6	51	Australia	Adelaide	1974/75
7	59*	New Zealand	Christchurch	1974/75

G.R.J.Roope (7)

1	56	New Zealand	Lord's	1973
2	51	New Zealand	Lord's	1973
3	77	Australia	The Oval	1975
4	56	Pakistan	Karachi (1)	1977/78
5	50	New Zealand	Christchurch	1977/78
6	68	New Zealand	Auckland	1977/78
7	69	Pakistan	Lord's	1978

G.Miller (7)

1	98*	Pakistan	Lahore (2)	1977/78
2	89	New Zealand	Christchurch	1977/78
3	64	Australia	Adelaide	1978/79
4	63*	India	Edgbaston	1979
5	62	India	Lord's	1979
6	98	India	Old Trafford	1982
7	60	Australia	Brisbane (2)	1982/83

K.S.Ranjitsinhji (6)

1	62	Australia	Old Trafford	1896
2	71	Australia	Melbourne	1897/98
3	77	Australia	Adelaide	1897/98
4	55	Australia	Melbourne	1897/98
5	93*	Australia	Trent Bridge	1899
6	54	Australia	The Oval	1899

Hon.F.S.Jackson (6)

1	91	Australia	Lord's	1893
2	73	Australia	Lord's	1899
3	53	Australia	Edgbaston	1902
4	55*	Australia	Lord's	1902
5	82*	Australia	Trent Bridge	1905
6	76	Australia	The Oval	1905

J.W.H.T.Douglas (6)

1	77	South Africa	Johannesburg (1)	1913/14
2	60	Australia	Adelaide	1920/21
3	50	Australia	Melbourne	1920/21
4	60	Australia	Melbourne	1920/21
5	68	Australia	Sydney	1920/21
6	75	Australia	Headingley	1921

G.E.Tyldesley (6)

1	78*	Australia	Old Trafford	1921
2	81	Australia	Old Trafford	1926
3	87	South Africa	Cape Town	1927/28
4	78	South Africa	Durban (2)	1927/28
5	62*	South Africa	Durban (2)	1927/28
6	73	West Indies	The Oval	1928

J.D.B.Robertson (6)

1	80	West Indies	Bridgetown	1947/48
2	51*	West Indies	Bridgetown	1947/48
3	64	West Indies	Kingston	1947/48
4	50	India	Delhi	1951/52
5	77	India	Madras (1)	1951/52
6	56	India	Madras (1)	1951/52

R.T.Simpson (6)

1	68	New Zealand	The Oval	1949
2	94	West Indies	Trent Bridge	1950
3	61	Australia	Adelaide	1950/51
4	81	New Zealand	Christchurch	1950/51
5	51	India	Headingley	1952
6	53	India	Lord's	1952

Rev.D.S.Sheppard (6)

1	62	Australia	The Oval	1956
2	68	West Indies	Headingley	1957
3	83	Pakistan	Trent Bridge	1962
4	57	Pakistan	The Oval	1962
5	53	Australia	Brisbane (2)	1962/63
6	68	Australia	Sydney	1962/63

P.H.Parfitt (6)

1	80	Australia	Brisbane (2)	1962/63
2	67	India	Delhi	1963/64
3	52	South Africa	Johannesburg (3)	1964/65
4	86	South Africa	Trent Bridge	1965
5	54	New Zealand	Christchurch	1965/66
6	51	Australia	The Oval	1972

B.C.Broad (6)

1	55	West Indies	Lord's	1984
2	86	Sri Lanka	Lord's	1984
3	55	Pakistan	Lord's	1987
4	54	Pakistan	Edgbaston	1987
5	61	New Zealand	Wellington	1987/88
6	54	West Indies	Trent Bridge	1988

R.T.Robinson (6)

1	74	India	Madras (1)	1984/85
2	96	India	Kanpur	1984/85

3	77*	Australia	Trent Bridge	1985
4	80	Pakistan	Edgbaston	1987
5	70	New Zealand	Christchurch	1987/88
6	54	New Zealand	Auckland	1987/88

R.C.Russell (6)

1	94	Sri Lanka	Lord's	1988
2	64*	Australia	Lord's	1989
3	55	West Indies	Bridgetown	1989/90
4	62	West Indies	St John's	1993/94
5	91	West Indies	The Oval	1995
6	50*	South Africa	Centurion	1995/96

W.Bates (5)

1	58	Australia	Melbourne	1881/82
2	52*	Australia	Melbourne	1881/82
3	55	Australia	Melbourne	1882/83
4	64	Australia	Sydney	1884/85
5	61	Australia	Melbourne	1884/85

W.W.Read (5)

1	75	Australia	Melbourne	1882/83
2	66	Australia	Sydney	1882/83
3	51	Australia	Old Trafford	1886
4	94	Australia	The Oval	1886
5	52	Australia	The Oval	1893

W.Barnes (5)

1	58	Australia	Melbourne	1884/85
2	50	Australia	Sydney	1884/85
3	74	Australia	Melbourne	1884/85
4	58	Australia	Lord's	1886
5	62	Australia	The Oval	1888

W.G.Grace (5)

1	75*	Australia	Lord's	1890
2	50	Australia	Melbourne	1891/92
3	58	Australia	Adelaide	1891/92
4	68	Australia	The Oval	1893
5	66	Australia	Lord's	1896

G.H.Hirst (5)

1	62	Australia	Sydney	1897/98
2	85	Australia	Adelaide	1897/98
3	58*	Australia	The Oval	1902
4	60*	Australia	Sydney	1903/04
5	58	Australia	Adelaide	1903/04

M.W.Tate (5)

1	50	South Africa	The Oval	1924
2	54	West Indies	The Oval	1928
3	54	Australia	Melbourne	1928/29
4	54	Australia	Lord's	1930
5	50	South Africa	Durban (2)	1930/31

A.P.F.Chapman (5)

1	58	Australia	Adelaide	1924/25
2	50*	Australia	Lord's	1926
3	50	West Indies	Lord's	1928
4	50	Australia	Brisbane (1)	1928/29
5	52	Australia	Trent Bridge	1930

K.S.Duleepsinhji (5)

1	56*	New Zealand	Wellington	1929/30
2	63	New Zealand	Auckland	1929/30
3	54	Australia	Old Trafford	1930
4	50	Australia	The Oval	1930
5	63	New Zealand	Old Trafford	1931

F.R.Brown (5)

1	74	New Zealand	Christchurch	1932/33
2	57	New Zealand	Old Trafford	1937
3	62	Australia	Melbourne	1950/51
4	79	Australia	Sydney	1950/51
5	62	New Zealand	Christchurch	1950/51

C.J.Barnett (5)

1	52	West Indies	The Oval	1933
2	69	Australia	Brisbane (2)	1936/37
3	57	Australia	Sydney	1936/37
4	83*	New Zealand	Lord's	1937
5	62	New Zealand	Old Trafford	1937

R.Illingworth (5)

1	50	India	The Oval	1959
2	53	New Zealand	Lord's	1969
3	53	Australia	Sydney	1970/71
4	57	Australia	Headingley	1972
5	65	New Zealand	Headingley	1973

D.A.Allen (5)

1	55	West Indies	Georgetown	1959/60
2	79*	Pakistan	Edgbaston	1962
3	62	Pakistan	Headingley	1962
4	50*	Australia	Sydney	1965/66
5	88	New Zealand	Christchurch	1965/66

B.W.Luckhurst (5)

1	74	Australia	Brisbane (2)	1970/71
2	59	Australia	Sydney	1970/71
3	53*	Pakistan	Lord's	1971
4	78	India	Old Trafford	1971
5	96	Australia	Trent Bridge	1972

D.S.Steele (5)

1	50	Australia	Lord's	1975
2	73	Australia	Headingley	1975
3	92	Australia	Headingley	1975
4	66	Australia	The Oval	1975
5	64	West Indies	Lord's	1976

P.Willey (5)

1	52	India	The Oval	1979
2	62*	West Indies	Old Trafford	1980
3	67	West Indies	Kingston	1980/81
4	82	Australia	Lord's	1981
5	71	West Indies	Kingston	1985/86

A.Shrewsbury (4)

1	82	Australia	Sydney	1881/82
2	72	Australia	Melbourne	1884/85
3	81	Australia	Lord's	1893
4	66	Australia	The Oval	1893

A.F.A.Lilley (4)

1	65*	Australia	Old Trafford	1896
2	55	Australia	Headingley	1899
3	58	Australia	Old Trafford	1899
4	84	Australia	Sydney	1901/02

R.H.Spooner (4)

1	52	Australia	Old Trafford	1905
2	79	Australia	The Oval	1905
3	58	Australia	Old Trafford	1909
4	82	South Africa	Headingley	1912

Hon.L.H.Tennyson (4)

1	52	South Africa	Durban (1)	1913/14
2	74*	Australia	Lord's	1921
3	63	Australia	Headingley	1921
4	51	Australia	The Oval	1921

P.Holmes (4)

1	88	South Africa	Cape Town	1927/28
2	70	South Africa	Durban (2)	1927/28
3	56	South Africa	Durban (2)	1927/28
4	63	South Africa	Johannesburg (1)	1927/28

R.W.V.Robins (4)

1	50*	Australia	Trent Bridge	1930
2	55	West Indies	Old Trafford	1933

3	76	India	Old Trafford	1936
4	61	Australia	Melbourne	1936/37

N.W.D.Yardley (4)

1	61	Australia	Melbourne	1946/47
2	53*	Australia	Melbourne	1946/47
3	99	South Africa	Trent Bridge	1947
4	59	South Africa	The Oval	1947

A.J.Watkins (4)

1	64*	South Africa	Cape Town	1948/49
2	80	India	Bombay (2)	1951/52
3	68	India	Calcutta	1951/52
4	66	India	Kanpur	1951/52

R.Subba Row (4)

1	94	India	The Oval	1959
2	56	South Africa	Edgbaston	1960
3	90	South Africa	Lord's	1960
4	59	Australia	Edgbaston	1961

P.J.Sharpe (4)

1	85*	West Indies	Edgbaston	1963
2	63	West Indies	The Oval	1963
3	83	West Indies	The Oval	1963
4	86	West Indies	Lord's	1969

D.B.Close (4)

1	70	West Indies	Lord's	1963
2	55	West Indies	Edgbaston	1963
3	56	West Indies	Headingley	1963
4	60	West Indies	Lord's	1976

J.B.Bolus (4)

1	88	India	Madras (2)	1963/64
2	57	India	Bombay (2)	1963/64
3	58	India	Delhi	1963/64
4	67	India	Kanpur	1963/64

P.R.Downton (4)

1	56	West Indies	Edgbaston	1984
2	62	India	Bombay (3)	1984/85
3	74	India	Delhi	1984/85
4	54	Australia	Headingley	1985

C.W.J.Athey (4)

1	55	New Zealand	Trent Bridge	1986
2	76	Australia	Brisbane (2)	1986/87
3	96	Australia	Perth	1986/87
4	55	Australia	Adelaide	1986/87

P.A.J.DeFreitas (4)

1	55*	West Indies	Trent Bridge	1991
2	51*	New Zealand	Trent Bridge	1994
3	69	New Zealand	Old Trafford	1994
4	88	Australia	Adelaide	1994/95

C.C.Lewis (4)

1	65	West Indies	Edgbaston	1991
2	70	New Zealand	Christchurch	1991/92
3	55	Pakistan	Old Trafford	1992
4	75*	West Indies	St John's	1993/94

J.P.Crawley (4)

1	72	Australia	Sydney	1994/95
2	71	Australia	Adelaide	1994/95
3	50	West Indies	The Oval	1995
4	53	Pakistan	Headingley	1996

W.H.Scotton (3)

1	50*	Australia	Melbourne	1881/82
2	90	Australia	The Oval	1884
3	82	Australia	Adelaide	1884/85

A.E.Stoddart (3)

1	69	Australia	Sydney	1891/92
2	83	Australia	The Oval	1893
3	68	Australia	Melbourne	1894/95

R.Peel (3)

1	83	Australia	Adelaide	1891/92
2	73	Australia	Melbourne	1894/95
3	53	Australia	Melbourne	1894/95

Albert Ward (3)

1	55	Australia	The Oval	1893
2	75	Australia	Sydney	1894/95
3	93	Australia	Melbourne	1894/95

G.L.Jessop (3)

1	51	Australia	Lord's	1899
2	55	Australia	Bramall Lane	1902
3	93	South Africa	Lord's	1907

P.F.Warner (3)

1	68	Australia	Melbourne	1903/04
2	79	Australia	Adelaide	1903/04
3	51	South Africa	Johannesburg (1)	1905/06

F.L.Fane (3)

1	65	South Africa	Johannesburg (1)	1905/06
2	66*	South Africa	Cape Town	1905/06
3	50	Australia	Melbourne	1907/08

J.Hardstaff snr (3)

1	63	Australia	Sydney	1907/08
2	61	Australia	Adelaide	1907/08
3	72	Australia	Adelaide	1907/08

F.R.Foster (3)

1	56	Australia	Sydney	1911/12
2	71	Australia	Adelaide	1911/12
3	50	Australia	Melbourne	1911/12

C.P.Mead (3)

1	86	South Africa	Johannesburg (1)	1913/14
2	66	South Africa	Durban (2)	1922/23
3	73	Australia	Brisbane (1)	1928/29

A.Sandham (3)

1	58	South Africa	Johannesburg (1)	1922/23
2	51	West Indies	Bridgetown	1929/30
3	50	West Indies	Kingston	1929/30

H.Verity (3)

1	55*	India	Calcutta	1933/34
2	60*	Australia	Old Trafford	1934
3	66*	India	Old Trafford	1936

G.O.B.Allen (3)

1	57	Australia	Lord's	1930
2	61	Australia	Old Trafford	1934
3	68	Australia	Brisbane (2)	1936/37

A.H.Bakewell (3)

1	85	India	Madras (1)	1933/34
2	63	South Africa	Old Trafford	1935
3	54	South Africa	Old Trafford	1935

P.A.Gibb (3)

1	93	South Africa	Johannesburg (1)	1938/39
2	58	South Africa	Cape Town	1938/39
3	60	India	Lord's	1946

J.T.Ikin (3)

1	60	Australia	Sydney	1946/47
2	51	South Africa	Lord's	1951
3	53	India	The Oval	1952

J.F.Crapp (3)

1	56	South Africa	Johannesburg (2)	1948/49
2	54	South Africa	Cape Town	1948/49
3	51	South Africa	Johannesburg (2)	1948/49

W.Watson (3)

1	57	South Africa	Trent Bridge	1951
2	79	South Africa	Lord's	1951
3	66	New Zealand	Old Trafford	1958

R.T.Spooner (3)

1	71	India	Calcutta	1951/52
2	92	India	Calcutta	1951/52
3	66	India	Madras (1)	1951/52

G.A.R.Lock (3)

1	56	West Indies	Edgbaston	1963
2	53	West Indies	Headingley	1963
3	89	West Indies	Georgetown	1967/68

A.R.Lewis (3)

1	70*	India	Delhi	1972/73
2	74	Pakistan	Lahore (2)	1972/73
3	88	Pakistan	Karachi (1)	1972/73

R.W.Taylor (3)

1	97	Australia	Adelaide	1978/79
2	64	India	Lord's	1979
3	54	Pakistan	Edgbaston	1982

V.J.Marks (3)

1	83	Pakistan	Faisalabad	1983/84
2	74	Pakistan	Lahore (2)	1983/84
3	55	Pakistan	Lahore (2)	1983/84

M.D.Moxon (3)

1	74	New Zealand	Lord's	1986
2	99	New Zealand	Auckland	1987/88
3	81*	New Zealand	Wellington	1987/88

W.Larkins (3)

1	54	West Indies	Port-of-Spain	1989/90
2	64	Australia	Melbourne	1990/91
3	54	Australia	Melbourne	1990/91

J.Selby (2)

1	55	Australia	Melbourne	1881/82
2	70	Australia	Melbourne	1881/82

R.G.Barlow (2)

1	62	Australia	Sydney	1881/82
2	56	Australia	Melbourne	1881/82

J.M.Read (2)

1	56	Australia	Sydney	1884/85
2	57	Australia	Adelaide	1891/92

J.Briggs (2)

1	53	Australia	The Oval	1886
2	57	Australia	Sydney	1894/95

R.Abel (2)

1	70	Australia	The Oval	1888
2	94	Australia	Lord's	1896

L.C.Braund (2)

1	58	Australia	Sydney	1901/02
2	65	Australia	Old Trafford	1902

J.N.Crawford (2)

1	74	South Africa	Cape Town	1905/06
2	62	Australia	Adelaide	1907/08

G.J.Thompson (2)
1	63	South Africa	Johannesburg (1)	1909/10
2	51	South Africa	Cape Town	1909/10

M.C.Bird (2)
1	57	South Africa	Cape Town	1909/10
2	61	South Africa	Durban (1)	1913/14

J.W.Hearne (2)
1	76	Australia	Sydney	1911/12
2	57	Australia	Sydney	1920/21

J.W.H.Makepeace (2)
1	60	Australia	Adelaide	1920/21
2	54	Australia	Melbourne	1920/21

C.A.G.Russell (2)
1	59	Australia	Adelaide	1920/21
2	96	South Africa	Johannesburg (1)	1922/23

P.G.H.Fender (2)
1	59	Australia	Melbourne	1920/21
2	60	South Africa	Durban (2)	1922/23

G.Brown (2)
1	57	Australia	Headingley	1921
2	84	Australia	The Oval	1921

F.T.Mann (2)
1	84	South Africa	Durban (2)	1922/23
2	59	South Africa	Johannesburg (1)	1922/23

R.Kilner (2)
1	59	South Africa	Edgbaston	1924
2	74	Australia	Melbourne	1924/25

W.W.Whysall (2)
1	75	Australia	Adelaide	1924/25
2	76	Australia	Melbourne	1924/25

H.Larwood (2)
1	70	Australia	Brisbane (1)	1928/29
2	98	Australia	Sydney	1932/33

M.S.Nichols (2)
1	78*	New Zealand	Wellington	1929/30
2	75	New Zealand	Auckland	1929/30

G.Geary (2)
1	66	Australia	Sydney	1928/29
2	53	Australia	Trent Bridge	1934

J.Iddon (2)
1	73	West Indies	Port-of-Spain	1934/35
2	54	West Indies	Kingston	1934/35

A.Mitchell (2)
1	58	South Africa	Headingley	1935
2	72	South Africa	Headingley	1935

J.C.Laker (2)
1	55	West Indies	Port-of-Spain	1947/48
2	63	Australia	Trent Bridge	1948

W.G.A.Parkhouse (2)
1	69	West Indies	Trent Bridge	1950
2	78	India	Headingley	1959

F.A.Lowson (2)
1	58	South Africa	Headingley	1951
2	68	India	Delhi	1951/52

C.J.Poole (2)
1	55	India	Calcutta	1951/52
2	69*	India	Calcutta	1951/52

J.H.Wardle (2)

1	66	West Indies	Kingston	1953/54
2	54	Pakistan	Old Trafford	1954

M.J.Stewart (2)

1	86	Pakistan	Headingley	1962
2	87	West Indies	Old Trafford	1963

W.E.Russell (2)

1	70	South Africa	The Oval	1965
2	56	New Zealand	Auckland	1965/66

J.T.Murray (2)

1	50	New Zealand	Dunedin	1965/66
2	77	India	Edgbaston	1967

C.Milburn (2)

1	94	West Indies	Old Trafford	1966
2	83	Australia	Lord's	1968

J.A.Snow (2)

1	59*	West Indies	The Oval	1966
2	73	India	Lord's	1971

J.H.Hampshire (2)

1	55	Australia	Adelaide	1970/71
2	51*	New Zealand	Christchurch	1970/71

P.Lever (2)

1	64	New Zealand	Auckland	1970/71
2	88*	India	Old Trafford	1971

R.A.Hutton (2)

1	58*	Pakistan	Lord's	1971
2	81	India	The Oval	1971

B.Wood (2)

1	90	Australia	The Oval	1972
2	52	Australia	Lord's	1975

C.M.Old (2)

1	65	Pakistan	The Oval	1974
2	52	India	Calcutta	1976/77

R.A.Woolmer (2)

1	82	West Indies	Trent Bridge	1976
2	79	Australia	Lord's	1977

C.T.Radley (2)

1	59	New Zealand	Trent Bridge	1978
2	77	New Zealand	Lord's	1978

B.C.Rose (2)

1	70	West Indies	Old Trafford	1980
2	50	West Indies	The Oval	1980

G.R.Dilley (2)

1	56	Australia	Headingley	1981
2	52	India	Bangalore	1981/82

P.H.Edmonds (2)

1	50	New Zealand	Christchurch	1977/78
2	64	India	Lord's	1982

G.Cook (2)

1	66	India	Old Trafford	1982
2	50	India	The Oval	1982

E.E.Hemmings (2)

1	95	Australia	Sydney	1982/83
2	51	India	The Oval	1990

C.L.Smith (2)

1	91	New Zealand	Auckland	1983/84
2	66	Pakistan	Faisalabad	1983/84

D.J.Capel (2)

1	53	Pakistan	Headingley	1987
2	98	Pakistan	Karachi (1)	1987/88

K.J.Barnett (2)

1	66	Sri Lanka	Lord's	1988
2	80	Australia	Headingley	1989

N.Hussain (2)

1	71	Australia	Trent Bridge	1993
2	51	Pakistan	The Oval	1996

M.R.Ramprakash (2)

1	64	Australia	The Oval	1993
2	72	Australia	Perth	1994/95

D.Gough (2)

1	65	New Zealand	Old Trafford	1994
2	51	Australia	Sydney	1994/95

N.V.Knight (2)

1	57	West Indies	Trent Bridge	1995
2	51	Pakistan	Lord's	1996

H.Jupp (1)

1	63	Australia	Melbourne	1876/77

C.A.Absolom (1)

1	52	Australia	Melbourne	1878/79

A.P.Lucas (1)

1	55	Australia	The Oval	1880

Lord Harris (1)

1	52	Australia	The Oval	1880

C.F.H.Leslie (1)

1	54	Australia	Melbourne	1882/83

E.F.S.Tylecote (1)

1	66	Australia	Sydney	1882/83

W.Flowers (1)

1	56	Australia	Sydney	1884/85

G.A.Lohmann (1)

1	62*	Australia	The Oval	1888

H.Wood (1)

1	59	South Africa	Cape Town	1888/89

G.Bean (1)

1	50	Australia	Melbourne	1891/92

W.Gunn (1)

1	77	Australia	Lord's	1893

J.T.Brown (1)

1	53	Australia	Sydney	1894/95

S.M.J.Woods (1)

1	53	South Africa	Port Elizabeth	1895/96

A.J.L.Hill (1)

1	65	South Africa	Johannesburg (1)	1895/96

C.W.Wright (1)

1	71	South Africa	Johannesburg (1)	1895/96

H.R.Bromley-Davenport (1)

1	84	South Africa	Johannesburg (1)	1895/96

W.Storer (1)

1	51	Australia	Melbourne	1897/98

N.F.Druce (1)
1   64   Australia   Sydney   1897/98

W.G.Quaife (1)
1   68   Australia   Adelaide   1901/02

W.H.Lockwood (1)
1   52*   Australia   Edgbaston   1902

A.E.Knight (1)
1   70*   Australia   Sydney   1903/04

D.Denton (1)
1   61   South Africa   Johannesburg (1) 1905/06

R.E.Foster (1)
1   51   South Africa   The Oval   1907

J.H.King (1)
1   60   Australia   Lord's   1909

J.Sharp (1)
1   61   Australia   Headingley   1909

K.L.Hutchings (1)
1   59   Australia   The Oval   1909

A.E.Relf (1)
1   63   South Africa   Johannesburg (1) 1913/14

J.W.Hitch (1)
1   51*   Australia   The Oval   1921

A.W.Carr (1)
1   63   South Africa   Johannesburg (1) 1922/23

A.P.Freeman (1)
1   50*   Australia   Sydney   1924/25

G.G.Macaulay (1)
1   76   Australia   Headingley   1926

G.T.S.Stevens (1)
1   69   South Africa   Durban (2)   1927/28

E.W.Dawson (1)
1   55   New Zealand   Auckland   1929/30

J.O'Connor (1)
1   51   West Indies   Kingston   1929/30

M.J.L.Turnbull (1)
1   61   South Africa   Johannesburg (1) 1930/31

W.Voce (1)
1   66   New Zealand   Christchurch   1932/33

James Langridge (1)
1   70   India   Calcutta   1933/34

E.R.T.Holmes (1)
1   85*   West Indies   Port-of-Spain   1934/35

D.Smith (1)
1   57   South Africa   Headingley   1935

H.Gimblett (1)
1   67*   India   Lord's   1936

T.S.Worthington (1)
1   87   India   Old Trafford   1936

A.Wood (1)
1   53   Australia   The Oval   1938

B.H.Valentine (1)
1   97   South Africa   Johannesburg (1)   1938/39

N.Oldfield (1)
1   80   West Indies   The Oval   1939

C.Gladwin (1)
1   51*   South Africa   The Oval   1947

A.V.Bedser (1)
1   79   Australia   Headingley   1948

J.G.Dewes (1)
1   67   West Indies   Trent Bridge   1950

D.B.Carr (1)
1   76   India   Delhi   1951/52

D.Kenyon (1)
1   87   South Africa   Trent Bridge   1955

D.J.Insole (1)
1   68   South Africa   Johannesburg (3)   1956/57

M.J.Horton (1)
1   58   India   Trent Bridge   1959

R.Swetman (1)
1   65   India   The Oval   1959

P.M.Walker (1)
1   52   South Africa   Lord's   1960

A.C.Smith (1)
1   69*   New Zealand   Wellington   1962/63

J.B.Mortimore (1)
1   73*   India   Madras (2)   1963/64

J.G.Binks (1)
1   55   India   Bombay (2)   1963/64

K.Higgs (1)
1   63   West Indies   The Oval   1966

G.G.Arnold (1)
1   59   Pakistan   The Oval   1967

R.M.Prideaux (1)
1   64   Australia   Headingley   1968

J.A.Jameson (1)
1   82   India   The Oval   1971

J.Birkenshaw (1)
1   64   India   Kanpur   1972/73

J.K.Lever (1)
1   53   India   Delhi   1976/77

R.W.Tolchard (1)
1   67   India   Calcutta   1976/77

D.L.Bairstow (1)
1   59   India   The Oval   1979

P.J.W.Allott (1)
1   52*   Australia   Old Trafford   1981

W.N.Slack (1)
1   52   West Indies   St John's   1985/86

D.R.Pringle (1)
1   63   India   Lord's   1986

B.N.French (1)
| 1 | 59 | Pakistan | Old Trafford | 1987 |

G.C.Small (1)
| 1 | 59 | Australia | The Oval | 1989 |

D.A.Reeve (1)
| 1 | 59 | New Zealand | Christchurch | 1991/92 |

I.D.K.Salisbury (1)
| 1 | 50 | Pakistan | Old Trafford | 1992 |

N.H.Fairbrother (1)
| 1 | 83 | India | Madras (1) | 1992/93 |

C.White (1)
| 1 | 51 | New Zealand | Lord's | 1994 |

S.J.Rhodes (1)
| 1 | 65* | South Africa | Headingley | 1994 |

D.G.Cork (1)
| 1 | 56* | West Indies | Old Trafford | 1995 |

M.Watkinson (1)
| 1 | 82* | West Indies | Trent Bridge | 1995 |

M.A.Ealham (1)
| 1 | 51 | India | Trent Bridge | 1996 |

FIFTIES AGAINST EACH OPPOSITION

Australia	614
South Africa	212
West Indies	219
New Zealand	133
India	191
Pakistan	120
Sri Lanka	12

FIFTIES PER VENUE

England (744)
The Oval	164
Old Trafford	120
Lord's	194
Trent Bridge	91
Headingley	114
Edgbaston	59
Bramall Lane	2

Australia (337)
Melbourne	102
Sydney	103
Adelaide	76
Brisbane (1)	4
Brisbane (2)	36
Perth	16

South Africa (116)
Port Elizabeth	6
Cape Town	32
Johannesburg (1)	33
Durban (1)	7
Durban (2)	23
Johannesburg (2)	3
Johannesburg (3)	10
Centurion	2

West Indies (95)
Bridgetown	24
Port-of-Spain	24
Georgetown	13
Kingston	27
St John's	7

New Zealand (58)

Christchurch	22
Wellington	10
Auckland	24
Dunedin	2

India (100)

Bombay (1)	2
Calcutta	22
Madras (1)	18
Delhi	15
Bombay (2)	9
Kanpur	12
Madras (2)	5
Bangalore	7
Bombay (3)	10

Pakistan (46)

Dacca	2
Karachi (1)	15
Lahore (2)	16
Hyderabad	6
Faisalabad	7

Sri Lanka (5)

Colombo (1)	2
Colombo (2)	3

NINETY-NINES

Score	Batsman	Opposition	Venue	Date	Dismissal
99*	G.Boycott	Australia	Perth	1979/80	Not Out
99	H.Sutcliffe	South Africa	Cape Town	1927/28	Bowled
99	E.Paynter	Australia	Lord's	1938	LBW
99	N.W.D.Yardley	South Africa	Trent Bridge	1947	Caught
99	M.J.K.Smith	South Africa	Lord's	1960	Caught
99	M.J.K.Smith	Pakistan	Lahore (2)	1961/62	Run out
99	E.R.Dexter	Australia	Brisbane (2)	1962/63	Bowled
99	D.L.Amiss	Pakistan	Karachi (1)	1972/73	Caught
99	G.Boycott	West Indies	Port-of-Spain	1973/74	Caught
99	G.A.Gooch	Australia	Melbourne	1979/80	Run out
99	M.D.Moxon	New Zealand	Auckland	1987/88	Caught
99	M.A.Atherton	Australia	Lord's	1993	Run out
99	M.A.Atherton	South Africa	Headingley	1994	Caught

CENTURY IN EACH INNINGS

Batsman	1st	2nd	Opposition	Venue	Date
C.A.G.Russell	140	111	South Africa	Durban (2)	1922/23
H.Sutcliffe	176	127	Australia	Melbourne	1924/25
W.R.Hammond	119*	177	Australia	Adelaide	1928/29
H.Sutcliffe	104	109*	South Africa	The Oval	1929
E.Paynter	117	100	South Africa	Johannesburg (1)	1938/39
D.C.S.Compton	147	103*	Australia	Adelaide	1946/47
G.A.Gooch	333	123	India	Lord's	1990
A.J.Stewart	118	143	West Indies	Bridgetown	1993/94

CENTURY AND FIFTY IN A MATCH

Batsman	1st	2nd	Opposition	Venue	Date
G.Ulyett	149	64	Australia	Melbourne	1881/82
A.Shrewsbury	106	81	Australia	Lord's	1893
Albert Ward	75	117	Australia	Sydney	1894/95
K.S.Ranjitsinhji	62	154*	Australia	Old Trafford	1896
A.C.MacLaren	109	50*	Australia	Sydney	1897/98
G.Gunn	119	74	Australia	Sydney	1907/08
C.A.G.Russell	135*	59	Australia	Adelaide	1920/21
J.W.H.Makepeace	117	54	Australia	Melbourne	1920/21
J.B.Hobbs	115	57	Australia	Sydney	1924/25
H.Sutcliffe	59	115	Australia	Sydney	1924/25
H.Sutcliffe	76	161	Australia	The Oval	1926
H.Sutcliffe	58	135	Australia	Melbourne	1928/29
J.B.Hobbs	142	65	Australia	Melbourne	1928/29
M.Leyland	137	53*	Australia	Melbourne	1928/29
M.Leyland	73	102	South Africa	Lord's	1929
A.Sandham	152	51	West Indies	Bridgetown	1929/30

Batsman	1st	2nd	Opposition	Venue	Date
E.H.Hendren	77	205*	West Indies	Port-of-Spain	1929/30
E.H.Hendren	56	123	West Indies	Georgetown	1929/30
A.Sandham	325	50	West Indies	Kingston	1929/30
H.Sutcliffe	161	54	Australia	The Oval	1930
W.R.Hammond	101	75*	Australia	Sydney	1932/33
C.F.Walters	59	102	India	Madras (1)	1933/34
J.Hardstaff jnr	114	64	New Zealand	Lord's	1937
P.A.Gibb	93	106	South Africa	Johannesburg (1)	1938/39
L.Hutton	73	165*	West Indies	The Oval	1939
W.J.Edrich	71	119	Australia	Sydney	1946/47
C.Washbrook	62	112	Australia	Melbourne	1946/47
D.C.S.Compton	65	163	South Africa	Trent Bridge	1947
D.C.S.Compton	53	113	South Africa	The Oval	1947
C.Washbrook	143	65	Australia	Headingley	1948
W.J.Edrich	111	54	Australia	Headingley	1948
D.C.S.Compton	158	71	South Africa	Old Trafford	1955
M.C.Cowdrey	101	61	South Africa	Cape Town	1956/57
M.C.Cowdrey	114	97	West Indies	Kingston	1959/60
G.Pullar	59	175	South Africa	The Oval	1960
R.Subba Row	59	112	Australia	Edgbaston	1961
K.F.Barrington	151*	52*	India	Bombay (2)	1961/62
M.C.Cowdrey	113	58*	Australia	Melbourne	1962/63
K.F.Barrington	63	132*	Australia	Adelaide	1962/63
K.F.Barrington	101	94	Australia	Sydney	1962/63
K.F.Barrington	60	102	Australia	Adelaide	1965/66
M.C.Cowdrey	148	71	West Indies	Port-of-Spain	1967/68
G.Boycott	77	142*	Australia	Sydney	1970/71
G.Boycott	58	119*	Australia	Adelaide	1970/71
A.P.E.Knott	101	96	New Zealand	Auckland	1970/71
B.W.Luckhurst	78	101	India	Old Trafford	1971
G.Boycott	99	112	West Indies	Port-of-Spain	1973/74
A.W.Greig	116	76*	West Indies	Headingley	1976
R.A.Woolmer	79	120	Australia	Lord's	1977
G.Boycott	107	80*	Australia	Trent Bridge	1977
G.Boycott	79	100*	Pakistan	Hyderabad	1977/78
G.Boycott	62	128*	Australia	Lord's	1980
I.T.Botham	50	149*	Australia	Headingley	1981
D.W.Randall	78	115	Australia	Perth	1982/83
D.I.Gower	60	114	Australia	Adelaide	1982/83
M.W.Gatting	61	150*	Pakistan	The Oval	1987
G.A.Gooch	73	146	West Indies	Trent Bridge	1988
D.I.Gower	57	106	Australia	Lord's	1989
M.A.Atherton	131	74	India	Old Trafford	1990
R.A.Smith	121*	61*	India	Old Trafford	1990
G.A.Gooch	87	117	Australia	Adelaide	1990/91
A.J.Stewart	107	63	New Zealand	Wellington	1991/92
G.A.Gooch	65	133	Australia	Old Trafford	1993

FIFTY IN EACH INNINGS

Batsman	1st	2nd	Opposition	Venue	Date
G.Ulyett	52	63	Australia	Melbourne	1876/77
J.Selby	55	70	Australia	Melbourne	1881/82
J.T.Tyldesley	97	62	Australia	Melbourne	1903/04
J.T.Tyldesley	56	61	Australia	Trent Bridge	1905
A.C.MacLaren	56	79	Australia	Lord's	1905
J.Hardstaff snr	61	72	Australia	Adelaide	1907/08
W.Rhodes	66	54	Australia	The Oval	1909
J.B.Hobbs	53	70	South Africa	Durban (1)	1909/10
F.E.Woolley	69	64	South Africa	Cape Town	1909/10
W.Rhodes	59	57*	Australia	Adelaide	1911/12
G.Gunn	52	61	Australia	Sydney	1911/12
J.B.Hobbs	64	97	South Africa	Durban (1)	1913/14
J.W.H.T.Douglas	50	60	Australia	Melbourne	1920/21
F.E.Woolley	95	93	Australia	Lord's	1921
P.Holmes	70	56	South Africa	Durban (2)	1927/28
G.E.Tyldesley	78	62*	South Africa	Durban (2)	1927/28
F.E.Woolley	83	95*	South Africa	Headingley	1929
E.H.Hendren	61	55	West Indies	Kingston	1929/30
J.B.Hobbs	78	74	Australia	Trent Bridge	1930
W.R.Hammond	57	65	South Africa	Cape Town	1930/31
E.H.Hendren	93	86	South Africa	Cape Town	1930/31
D.R.Jardine	79	85*	India	Lord's	1932
R.E.S.Wyatt	51	61*	Australia	Sydney	1932/33
C.F.Walters	52	50*	Australia	Old Trafford	1934

Batsman	1st	2nd	Opposition	Venue	Date
H.Sutcliffe	63	69*	Australia	Old Trafford	1934
W.R.Hammond	63	87*	South Africa	Headingley	1935
A.Mitchell	58	72	South Africa	Headingley	1935
A.H.Bakewell	63	54	South Africa	Old Trafford	1935
E.Paynter	62	75	South Africa	Durban (2)	1938/39
D.C.S.Compton	51	71*	India	Old Trafford	1946
N.W.D.Yardley	61	53*	Australia	Melbourne	1946/47
L.Hutton	94	76	Australia	Adelaide	1946/47
W.J.Edrich	57	50	South Africa	Trent Bridge	1947
J.D.B.Robertson	80	51*	West Indies	Bridgetown	1947/48
L.Hutton	56	60	West Indies	Kingston	1947/48
L.Hutton	81	57	Australia	Headingley	1948
L.Hutton	79	60*	Australia	Melbourne	1950/51
R.T.Spooner	71	92	India	Calcutta	1951/52
C.J.Poole	55	69*	India	Calcutta	1951/52
J.D.B.Robertson	77	56	India	Madras (1)	1951/52
L.Hutton	72	77	West Indies	Bridgetown	1953/54
P.E.Richardson	81	73	Australia	Trent Bridge	1956
P.B.H.May	63	53	Australia	Lord's	1956
D.C.S.Compton	58	64	South Africa	Cape Town	1956/57
M.C.Cowdrey	81	70	New Zealand	Edgbaston	1958
K.F.Barrington	53	83	Australia	The Oval	1961
E.R.Dexter	57	62	India	Calcutta	1961/62
E.R.Dexter	70	99	Australia	Brisbane (2)	1962/63
E.R.Dexter	93	52	Australia	Melbourne	1962/63
K.F.Barrington	80	60	West Indies	Lord's	1963
P.J.Sharpe	63	83	West Indies	The Oval	1963
E.R.Dexter	62	80*	New Zealand	Lord's	1965
M.C.Cowdrey	58	78*	South Africa	The Oval	1965
M.J.K.Smith	54	87	New Zealand	Christchurch	1965/66
B.L.D'Oliveira	76	54	West Indies	Trent Bridge	1966
B.L.D'Oliveira	59	81*	Pakistan	Lord's	1967
G.Boycott	62	80*	West Indies	Port-of-Spain	1967/68
M.C.Cowdrey	59	82	West Indies	Georgetown	1967/68
J.H.Edrich	88	64	Australia	Edgbaston	1968
J.H.Edrich	62	65	Australia	Headingley	1968
G.Boycott	70	50	Australia	Perth	1970/71
B.L.D'Oliveira	74	72	Pakistan	Headingley	1971
A.W.Greig	57	62	Australia	Old Trafford	1972
A.P.E.Knott	92	63	Australia	The Oval	1972
M.H.Denness	50	68	Pakistan	Lahore (2)	1972/73
A.P.E.Knott	71	63*	Pakistan	Hyderabad	1972/73
G.Boycott	61	92	New Zealand	Lord's	1973
G.R.J.Roope	56	51	New Zealand	Lord's	1973
D.L.Amiss	56	86*	West Indies	Edgbaston	1973
K.W.R.Fletcher	68	86*	West Indies	Lord's	1973
A.P.E.Knott	87	67	West Indies	Bridgetown	1973/74
D.S.Steele	73	92	Australia	Headingley	1975
A.P.E.Knott	50	57	West Indies	The Oval	1976
D.W.Randall	75	74*	Australia	Brisbane (2)	1978/79
G.A.Gooch	99	51	Australia	Melbourne	1979/80
C.J.Tavare	69	78	Australia	Old Trafford	1981
M.W.Gatting	53	56	Australia	The Oval	1981
K.W.R.Fletcher	69	60*	India	Calcutta	1981/82
D.I.Gower	58	57	Pakistan	Karachi (1)	1983/84
V.J.Marks	74	55	Pakistan	Lahore (2)	1983/84
G.A.Gooch	51	51	West Indies	St John's	1985/86
J.E.Emburey	70	74*	Pakistan	Karachi (1)	1987/88
M.A.Atherton	82	70	New Zealand	Edgbaston	1990
G.A.Gooch	85	88	India	The Oval	1990
W.Larkins	64	54	Australia	Melbourne	1990/91
G.A.Gooch	59	54	Australia	Sydney	1990/91
A.J.Stewart	74	69*	Pakistan	Lord's	1992
M.A.Atherton	80	99	Australia	Lord's	1993
R.A.Smith	86	50	Australia	Trent Bridge	1993
M.A.Atherton	55	63	Australia	Headingley	1993
G.A.Gooch	56	79	Australia	The Oval	1993
G.P.Thorpe	72	73	South Africa	Headingley	1994
M.A.Atherton	88	67	Australia	Sydney	1994/95
R.A.Smith	61	90	West Indies	Lord's	1995
G.A.Hick	96	51*	West Indies	The Oval	1995

MOST RUNS IN A MATCH

G.A.Gooch	456	(333 & 123)	India	Lord's	1990
A.Sandham	375	(325 & 50)	West Indies	Kingston	1929/30
L.Hutton	364	(364 & DNB)	Australia	The Oval	1938
W.R.Hammond	336	(336* & DNB)	New Zealand	Auckland	1932/33
P.B.H.May	315	(30 & 285*)	West Indies	Edgbaston	1957
J.H.Edrich	310	(310* & DNB)	New Zealand	Headingley	1965
R.E.Foster	306	(287 & 19)	Australia	Sydney	1903/04
H.Sutcliffe	303	(176 & 127)	Australia	Melbourne	1924/25

BATSMAN CARRYING HIS BAT THROUGH A COMPLETED TEST INNINGS

Batsman	Score	Total	Opposition	Venue	Date
R.Abel	132*	307	Australia	Sydney	1891/92
P.F.Warner	132*	237	South Africa	Johannesburg (1)	1898/99
L.Hutton	202*	344	West Indies	The Oval	1950
L.Hutton	156*	272	Australia	Adelaide	1950/51
G.Boycott	99*	215	Australia	Perth	1979/80
G.A.Gooch	154*	252	West Indies	Headingley	1991
A.J.Stewart	69*	175	Pakistan	Lord's	1992

MOST RUNS IN A SERIES (1)

Single match

G.A.Gooch	212 runs	Sri Lanka	1991	(38, 174)

Two match series

W.R.Hammond	563 runs	New Zealand	1932/33	(227, 336*)

Three match series

G.A.Gooch	752 runs	India	1990	(333, 123, 116, 7, 85, 88)

Four match series

E.H.Hendren	693 runs	West Indies	1929/30	(80, 36*, 77, 205*, 56, 123, 61, 55)

Five match series

W.R.Hammond	905 runs	Australia	1928/29	(44, 28, 251, 200, 32, 119, 177, 38, 16)

Six match series

D.I.Gower	732 runs	Australia	1985	(17, 5, 86, 22, 166, 17, 47, 215, 157)

MOST RUNS IN A SERIES (2)

Batsman	Opposition	Date	Mat	Inn	NO	Runs	Avg	H/S	100	50
W.R.Hammond	Australia	1928/29	5	9	1	905	113.12	251	4	0
D.C.S.Compton	South Africa	1947	5	8	0	753	94.12	208	4	2
G.A.Gooch	India	1990	3	6	0	752	125.33	333	3	2
H.Sutcliffe	Australia	1924/25	5	9	0	734	81.56	176	4	2
D.I.Gower	Australia	1985	6	9	0	732	81.33	215	3	1
E.H.Hendren	West Indies	1929/30	4	8	2	693	115.50	205*	2	5
G.A.Gooch	Australia	1993	6	12	0	673	56.08	133	2	4
L.Hutton	West Indies	1953/54	5	8	1	667	96.71	205	2	3
D.L.Amiss	West Indies	1973/74	5	9	1	663	82.87	262*	3	0
J.B.Hobbs	Australia	1911/12	5	9	1	662	82.75	187	3	1
G.Boycott	Australia	1970/71	5	10	3	657	93.85	142*	2	5
E.Paynter	South Africa	1938/39	5	8	0	653	81.62	243	3	2
J.H.Edrich	Australia	1970/71	6	11	2	648	72.00	130	2	4
W.R.Hammond	South Africa	1938/39	5	8	1	609	87.00	181	3	2
K.F.Barrington	India	1961/62	5	9	3	594	99.00	172	3	1
A.Sandham	West Indies	1929/30	4	8	0	592	74.00	325	2	2
K.F.Barrington	Australia	1962/63	5	10	2	582	72.75	132	2	3
P.B.H.May	South Africa	1955	5	9	1	582	72.75	117	2	3
L.Hutton	South Africa	1948/49	5	9	0	577	64.11	158	2	2
M.W.Gatting	India	1984/85	5	9	3	575	95.83	207	2	1
J.B.Hobbs	Australia	1924/25	5	9	0	573	63.66	154	3	2
W.R.Hammond	New Zealand	1932/33	2	2	1	563	563.00	336*	2	0
D.C.S.Compton	Australia	1948	5	10	1	562	62.44	184	2	2
J.H.Edrich	Australia	1968	5	9	0	554	61.55	164	1	4
R.A.Smith	Australia	1989	5	10	1	553	61.44	143	2	3
M.A.Atherton	Australia	1993	6	12	0	553	46.08	99	0	6
W.J.Edrich	South Africa	1947	4	6	1	552	110.40	191	2	2
C.Washbrook	South Africa	1948/49	5	9	0	542	60.22	195	1	2
J.B.Hobbs	South Africa	1909/10	5	9	1	539	67.37	187	1	4
M.C.Cowdrey	West Indies	1967/68	5	8	0	534	66.75	148	2	4

L.Hutton	Australia	1950/51	5	10	4	533	88.83	156*	1	4
K.F.Barrington	Australia	1964	5	8	1	531	75.85	256	1	2
M.W.Gatting	Australia	1985	6	9	3	527	87.83	160	2	3
E.R.Dexter	West Indies	1959/60	5	9	1	526	65.75	136*	2	2
G.E.Tyldesley	South Africa	1927/28	5	9	1	520	65.00	122	2	3
W.R.Hammond	South Africa	1930/31	5	9	1	517	64.62	136*	1	4
H.Sutcliffe	Australia	1929	5	9	1	513	64.12	114	4	0
M.A.Atherton	West Indies	1993/94	5	9	0	510	56.66	144	2	2
K.F.Barrington	South Africa	1964/65	5	7	2	508	101.60	148*	2	2
G.P.Thorpe	West Indies	1995	6	12	0	506	42.16	94	0	5
J.B.Hobbs	Australia	1920/21	5	10	0	505	50.50	123	2	1

1000 RUNS IN A CALENDAR YEAR

Batsman	Year	Mat	Inn	NO	Runs	Avg	H/S	100
D.C.S.Compton	1947	9	15	1	1159	82.78	208	6
K.F.Barrington	1961	10	17	4	1032	79.38	172	4
E.R.Dexter	1962	11	15	1	1038	74.14	205	2
K.F.Barrington	1963	12	22	2	1039	51.95	132*	3
K.W.R.Fletcher	1973	13	22	4	1090	60.55	178	2
D.L.Amiss	1974	13	22	2	1379	68.95	262*	5
D.I.Gower	1982	14	25	2	1061	46.13	114	1
I.T.Botham	1982	14	22	0	1095	49.77	208	3
D.I.Gower	1986	14	25	1	1059	44.12	136	2
G.A.Gooch	1990	9	17	1	1264	79.00	333	4
G.A.Gooch	1991	9	17	1	1040	65.00	174	3
M.A.Atherton	1994	13	23	0	1136	49.39	144	4
M.A.Atherton	1995	13	24	1	1129	49.08	185*	2

MOST RUNS IN AN ENGLISH SUMMER

			SERIES ONE			SERIES TWO		
Batsman	Runs	Date	Opposition	Tests	Runs	Opposition	Tests	Runs
G.A.Gooch	1058	1990	New Zealand	3	306	India	3	752

CENTURY ON DEBUT

Batsman	1st Inns	2nd Inns	Opposition	Venue	Date
W.G.Grace	152	9*	Australia	The Oval	1880
K.S.Ranjitsinhji	62	154*	Australia	Old Trafford	1896
P.F.Warner	21	132*	South Africa	Johannesburg (1)	1898/99
R.E.Foster	287	19	Australia	Sydney	1903/04
G.Gunn	119	74	Australia	Sydney	1907/08
Nawab of Pataudi	102	DNB	Australia	Sydney	1932/33
B.H.Valentine	136	DNB	India	Bombay (1)	1933/34
P.A.Gibb	93	106	South Africa	Johannesburg (1)	1938/39
S.C.Griffith	140	4	West Indies	Port-of-Spain	1947/48
P.B.H.May	138	DNB	South Africa	Headingley	1951
C.A.Milton	104*	DNB	New Zealand	Headingley	1958
J.H.Hampshire	107	5	West Indies	Lord's	1969
F.C.Hayes	16	106*	West Indies	The Oval	1973
G.P.Thorpe	6	114*	Australia	Trent Bridge	1993

MOST CENTURIES IN A SERIES

Four

H.Sutcliffe	Australia	1924/25
W.R.Hammond	Australia	1928/29
H.Sutcliffe	South Africa	1929
D.C.S.Compton	South Africa	1947

Three

J.B.Hobbs	Australia	1911/12
J.B.Hobbs	Australia	1924/25
W.R.Hammond	South Africa	1938/39
E.Paynter	South Africa	1938/39
K.F.Barrington	India	1961/62
P.H.Parfitt	Pakistan	1962
K.F.Barrington	Pakistan	1967
D.L.Amiss	West Indies	1973/74
A.J.Lamb	West Indies	1984
D.I.Gower	Australia	1985
B.C.Broad	Australia	1986/87
G.A.Gooch	India	1990

MOST CENTURIES IN AN ENGLISH SUMMER

Four

H.Sutcliffe	South Africa (4)	1929
D.C.S.Compton	South Africa (4)	1947
A.J.Lamb	West Indies (3), Sri Lanka (1)	1984
G.A.Gooch	New Zealand (1), India (3)	1990

CENTURIES IN CONSECUTIVE INNINGS

THREE

H.Sutcliffe

115	Australia	Sydney	1924/25
176	Australia	Melbourne	1924/25
127	Australia	Melbourne	1924/25

D.C.S.Compton

163	South Africa	Trent Bridge	1947
208	South Africa	Lord's	1947
115	South Africa	Old Trafford	1947

G.Boycott

119*	Australia	Adelaide	1970/71
121*	Pakistan	Lords	1971
112	Pakistan	Headingley	1971

G.A.Gooch

333	India	Lord's	1990
123	India	Lord's	1990
116	India	Old Trafford	1990

CENTURIES IN CONSECUTIVE MATCHES

FOUR

K.F.Barrington

139 & 6	Pakistan	Lahore (2)	1961/62
151* & 52*	India	Bombay (2)	1961/62
21 & 172	India	Kanpur	1961/62
113*	India	Delhi	1961/62

K.F.Barrington

148 & 14	Pakistan	Lord's	1967
109*	Pakistan	Trent Bridge	1967
142 & 13*	Pakistan	The Oval	1967
143	West Indies	Port-of-Spain	1967/68

THREE

J.B.Hobbs

6 & 126*	Australia	Melbourne	1911/12
187 & 3	Australia	Adelaide	1911/12
178	Australia	Melbourne	1911/12

J.B.Hobbs

115 & 57	Australia	Sydney	1924/25
154 & 22	Australia	Melbourne	1924/25
119 & 27	Australia	Adelaide	1924/24

W.R.Hammond

251	Australia	Sydney	1928/29
200 & 32	Australia	Melbourne	1928/29
119* & 177	Australia	Adelaide	1928/29

H.Sutcliffe

161 & 54	Australia	The Oval	1930
117	New Zealand	The Oval	1931
109*	New Zealand	Old Trafford	1931

W.R.Hammond

101 & 75*	Australia	Sydney	1932/33
227	New Zealand	Christchurch	1932/33
336*	New Zealand	Auckland	1932/33

D.C.S.Compton

65 & 163	South Africa	Trent Bridge	1947
208	South Africa	Lord's	1947
115 & 6	South Africa	Old Trafford	1947

K.F.Barrington

63 & 132*	Australia	Adelaide	1962/63
101 & 94	Australia	Sydney	1962/63
126	New Zealand	Auckland	1962/63

G.Boycott

58 & 119*	Australia	Adelaide	1970/71
121*	Pakistan	Lords	1971
112 & 13	Pakistan	Headingley	1971

A.J.Lamb

23 & 110	West Indies	Lord's	1984
100 & 3	West Indies	Headingley	1984
100* & 9	West Indies	Old Trafford	1984

B.C.Broad

162 & 16	Australia	Perth	1986/87
116 & 15*	Australia	Adelaide	1986/87
112	Australia	Melbourne	1986/87

G.A.Gooch

154 & 30	New Zealand	Edgbaston	1990
333 & 123	India	Lord's	1990
116 & 7	India	Old Trafford	1990

MOST NOT OUTS

Batsman	Mat	Inns	NO	% NO
R.G.D.Willis	90	128	55	42.96
D.L.Underwood	86	116	35	30.17
J.B.Statham	70	87	28	32.18
G.Boycott	108	193	23	11.91
W.Rhodes	58	98	21	21.42
J.E.Emburey	64	96	20	20.83
G.R.Dilley	41	58	19	32.75
D.E.Malcolm	36	53	18	33.96
D.I.Gower	117	204	18	8.82
P.C.R.Tufnell	22	32	17	53.12
W.R.Hammond	85	140	16	11.42
W.Voce	27	38	15	39.47
M.Hendrick	30	35	15	42.85
D.A.Allen	39	51	15	29.41
J.C.Laker	46	63	15	23.80
R.C.Russell	49	77	15	19.48
A.V.Bedser	51	71	15	21.12
P.H.Edmonds	51	65	15	23.07
R.A.Smith	62	112	15	13.39
D.C.S.Compton	78	131	15	11.45
L.Hutton	79	138	15	10.86
K.F.Barrington	82	131	15	11.45
A.P.E.Knott	95	149	15	10.06
M.C.Cowdrey	114	188	15	7.97
J.A.Snow	49	71	14	19.71
K.W.R.Fletcher	59	96	14	14.58
T.E.Bailey	61	91	14	15.38
F.S.Trueman	67	85	14	16.47
M.W.Gatting	79	138	14	10.14
T.G.Evans	91	133	14	10.52
H.Strudwick	28	42	13	30.95
D.V.P.Wright	34	39	13	33.33
T.W.Graveney	79	123	13	10.56
C.Blythe	19	31	12	38.70
G.Duckworth	24	28	12	42.85
H.Verity	40	44	12	27.27
L.E.G.Ames	47	72	12	16.66
R.W.Taylor	57	83	12	14.45
G.G.Arnold	34	46	11	23.91
F.J.Titmus	53	76	11	14.47
R.Illingworth	61	90	11	12.22
D.L.Amiss	50	88	10	11.36

A.J.Lamb	79	139	10	7.19
A.R.C.Fraser	32	46	10	21.73

MOST DUCKS

Batsman	Mat	Inns	Ducks	% Ducks
D.L.Underwood	86	116	19	16.37
J.A.Snow	49	71	17	23.94
T.G.Evans	91	133	17	12.78
J.E.Emburey	64	96	16	16.66
M.W.Gatting	79	138	16	11.59
D.W.Randall	47	79	14	17.72
I.T.Botham	102	161	14	8.69
D.E.Malcolm	36	53	13	24.52
F.E.Woolley	64	98	13	13.26
J.B.Statham	70	87	13	14.94
G.A.Gooch	118	215	13	6.04
M.A.Atherton	62	114	12	10.52
R.G.D.Willis	90	128	12	9.37
M.J.K.Smith	50	78	11	14.10
A.V.Bedser	51	71	11	15.49
F.S.Trueman	67	85	11	12.94
P.I.Pocock	25	37	10	27.02
J.Briggs	33	50	10	20.00
A.F.A.Lilley	35	52	10	19.23
G.R.Dilley	41	58	10	17.24
P.A.J.DeFreitas	44	68	10	14.70
C.M.Old	46	66	10	15.15
D.L.Amiss	50	88	10	11.36
R.W.Taylor	57	83	10	12.04
D.C.S.Compton	78	131	10	7.63
G.Boycott	108	193	10	5.18

MOST CONSECUTIVE INNINGS WITHOUT A DUCK

Batsman	Inns	Matches without a duck		
D.I.Gower	119	Pakistan	1982 – Australia	1990/91
K.F.Barrington	78	Pakistan	1962 – West Indies	1967/68
W.R.Hammond	67	South Africa	1929 – India	1936
G.Boycott	67	New Zealand	1969 – Australia	1978/79

MOST PAIRS

THREE

R.Peel

Australia	Adelaide	1894/95	Bowled	Caught
Australia	Sydney	1894/95	Stumped	Stumped
Australia	The Oval	1896	Bowled	Bowled

D.L.Underwood

West Indies	Headingley	1966	Caught	Caught
Australia	Adelaide	1974/75	Caught	Caught
West Indies	Old Trafford	1976	Bowled	Caught

TWO

A.V.Bedser

Australia	The Oval	1948	Bowled	Bowled
West Indies	The Oval	1950	LBW	Caught

D.L.Amiss

Australia	Old Trafford	1968	Caught	Bowled
Australia	Adelaide	1974/75	Caught	Caught

P.I.Pocock

West Indies	Old Trafford	1984	Bowled	Caught
West Indies	The Oval	1984	Caught	Caught

N.A.Foster

West Indies	Bridgetown	1985/86	LBW	Caught
Pakistan	Faisalabad	1987/88	Caught	Caught

D.E.Malcolm

New Zealand	Edgbaston	1990	Bowled	Bowled
Pakistan	Lord's	1992	LBW	Bowled

ONE

G.F.Grace	Australia	The Oval	1880	Caught	Bowled
W.Attewell	Australia	Sydney	1891/92	Bowled	Caught
G.A.Lohmann	South Africa	Port Elizabeth	1895/96	Caught	Bowled
E.G.Arnold	Australia	Sydney	1903/04	LBW	Caught
A.E.Knight	Australia	Melbourne	1903/04	Bowled	Caught
E.G.Hayes	South Africa	Cape Town	1905/06	LBW	Bowled
M.C.Bird	South Africa	Cape Town	1909/10	Bowled	Caught
H.Strudwick	Australia	Trent Bridge	1921	Caught	Bowled
P.Holmes	South Africa	Durban (2)	1927/28	Caught	LBW
C.I.J.Smith	West Indies	Bridgetown	1934/35	Caught	Caught
J.T.Ikin	Australia	Sydney	1946/47	Bowled	Stumped
J.J.Warr	Australia	Adelaide	1950/51	Bowled	Bowled
F.Ridgway	India	Madras (1)	1951/52	LBW	Bowled
R.T.Spooner	South Africa	The Oval	1955	Bowled	Bowled
J.H.Wardle	Australia	Lord's	1956	Caught	Bowled
F.S.Trueman	Australia	Adelaide	1958/59	Caught	Caught
T.E.Bailey	Australia	Melbourne	1958/59	Caught	Bowled
G.Pullar	Pakistan	Lahore (2)	1961/62	Caught	Bowled
M.J.K.Smith	India	Kanpur	1961/62	Caught	LBW
J.T.Murray	Pakistan	Lord's	1967	Bowled	Caught
B.W.Luckhurst	Pakistan	Headingley	1971	Caught	Caught
A.P.E.Knott	New Zealand	Lord's	1973	Bowled	Caught
G.G.Arnold	Australia	Adelaide	1974/75	Bowled	Bowled
G.A.Gooch	Australia	Edgbaston	1975	Caught	Caught
Alan Ward	West Indies	Headingley	1976	LBW	Caught
J.C.Balderstone	West Indies	The Oval	1976	Bowled	Bowled
M.Hendrick	New Zealand	Wellington	1977/78	LBW	Caught
R.A.Woolmer	Australia	Trent Bridge	1981	Caught	Caught
I.T.Botham	Australia	Lord's	1981	LBW	Bowled
E.E.Hemmings	Australia	Adelaide	1982/83	Bowled	Caught
N.G.Cowans	India	Bombay (3)	1984/85	Caught	Caught
D.J.Capel	Pakistan	Lahore (2)	1987/88	Caught	Caught
R.J.Bailey	West Indies	Port-of-Spain	1989/90	Caught	Bowled
W.Larkins	West Indies	Bridgetown	1989/90	Caught	Caught
C.C.Lewis	Australia	Lord's	1993	LBW	Stumped
P.C.R.Tufnell	Australia	Melbourne	1994/95	Run Out	Caught
J.P.Crawley	Australia	Perth	1994/95	Caught	Caught
P.A.J.DeFreitas	Australia	Perth	1994/95	Bowled	Caught
M.R.Ramprakash	West Indies	Lord's	1995	Caught	Caught
R.K.Illingworth	West Indies	Edgbaston	1995	Bowled	Caught

HIGHEST PARTNERSHIPS FOR EACH WICKET

Wkt	Runs	Opposition	Venue	Date	Batsmen
1	359	South Africa	Johannesburg (2)	1948/49	L.Hutton & C.Washbrook
2	382	Australia	The Oval	1938	L.Hutton & M.Leyland
3	370	South Africa	Lord's	1947	W.J.Edrich & D.C.S.Compton
4	411	West Indies	Edgbaston	1957	P.B.H.May & M.C.Cowdrey
5	254	India	Bombay (2)	1972/73	K.W.R.Fletcher & A.W.Greig
6	240	New Zealand	Auckland	1962/63	P.H.Parfitt & B.R.Knight
7	197	West Indies	Port-of-Spain	1959/60	M.J.K.Smith & J.M.Parks
8	246	New Zealand	Lord's	1931	L.E.G.Ames & G.O.B.Allen
9	163*	New Zealand	Wellington	1962/63	M.C.Cowdrey & A.C.Smith
10	130	Australia	Sydney	1903/04	R.E.Foster & W.Rhodes

HIGHEST 1ST WICKET PARTNERSHIPS

No.	Runs	Opposition	Venue	Date	Batsmen
1	359	South Africa	Johannesburg (2)	1948/49	L.Hutton & C.Washbrook
2	323	Australia	Melbourne	1911/12	J.B.Hobbs & W.Rhodes
3	290	South Africa	The Oval	1960	G.Pullar & M.C.Cowdrey
4	283	Australia	Melbourne	1924/25	J.B.Hobbs & H.Sutcliffe
5	268	South Africa	Lord's	1924	J.B.Hobbs & H.Sutcliffe
6	234	Australia	Sydney	1965/66	G.Boycott & R.W.Barber
7	225	India	Old Trafford	1990	G.A.Gooch & M.A.Atherton
8=	223	New Zealand	The Oval	1983	G.Fowler & C.J.Tavare
8=	223	Australia	Perth	1986/87	B.C.Broad & C.W.J.Athey
10	221	South Africa	Cape Town	1909/10	J.B.Hobbs & W.Rhodes

HIGHEST 2ND WICKET PARTNERSHIPS

No.	Runs	Opposition	Venue	Date	Batsmen
1	382	Australia	The Oval	1938	L.Hutton & M.Leyland
2	369	New Zealand	Headingley	1965	J.H.Edrich & K.F.Barrington

3	351	Australia	The Oval	1985	G.A.Gooch & D.I.Gower
4	331	Australia	Edgbaston	1985	R.T.Robinson & D.I.Gower
5	280	South Africa	Durban (2)	1938/39	P.A.Gibb & W.J.Edrich
6	266	West Indies	Trent Bridge	1957	P.E.Richardson & T.W.Graveney
7	263	New Zealand	Trent Bridge	1994	M.A.Atherton & G.A.Gooch
8	249	New Zealand	Trent Bridge	1969	J.H.Edrich & P.J.Sharpe
9	248	Pakistan	The Oval	1962	M.C.Cowdrey & E.R.Dexter
10	241	India	Madras (1)	1984/85	G.Fowler & M.W.Gatting

HIGHEST 3RD WICKET PARTNERSHIPS

No.	Runs	Opposition	Venue	Date	Batsmen
1	370	South Africa	Lord's	1947	W.J.Edrich & D.C.S.Compton
2	308	India	Lord's	1990	G.A.Gooch & A.J.Lamb
3	303	West Indies	St John's	1993/94	M.A.Atherton & R.A.Smith
4	264	West Indies	The Oval	1939	L.Hutton & W.R.Hammond
5	262	Australia	Adelaide	1928/29	W.R.Hammond & D.R.Jardine
6	246	Australia	Old Trafford	1964	E.R.Dexter & K.F.Barrington
7=	245	South Africa	Old Trafford	1929	R.E.S.Wyatt & F.E.Woolley
7=	245	New Zealand	Lord's	1937	J.Hardstaff jnr & W.R.Hammond
9	242	South Africa	Durban (2)	1938/39	E.Paynter & W.R.Hammond
10	228	South Africa	Old Trafford	1947	W.J.Edrich & D.C.S.Compton

HIGHEST 4TH WICKET PARTNERSHIPS

No.	Runs	Opposition	Venue	Date	Batsmen
1	411	West Indies	Edgbaston	1957	P.B.H.May & M.C.Cowdrey
2=	266	India	The Oval	1936	W.R.Hammond & T.S.Worthington
2=	266	New Zealand	Auckland	1974/75	M.H.Denness & K.W.R.Fletcher
4	252	India	Headingley	1967	G.Boycott & B.L.D'Oliveira
5	249	West Indies	Kingston	1929/30	A.Sandham & L.E.G.Ames
6	248	West Indies	Lord's	1939	L.Hutton & D.C.S.Compton
7	237	West Indies	Port-of-Spain	1929/30	E.H.Hendren & L.E.G.Ames
8	223	New Zealand	The Oval	1986	D.I.Gower & M.W.Gatting
9	222	Australia	Lord's	1938	W.R.Hammond & E.Paynter
10	206	India	Kanpur	1961/62	K.F.Barrington & E.R.Dexter

HIGHEST 5TH WICKET PARTNERSHIPS

No.	Runs	Opposition	Venue	Date	Batsmen
1	254	India	Bombay (2)	1972/73	K.W.R.Fletcher & A.W.Greig
2	242	New Zealand	Christchurch	1932/33	W.R.Hammond & L.E.G.Ames
3	237	South Africa	Trent Bridge	1947	D.C.S.Compton & N.W.D.Yardley
4	210	New Zealand	Trent Bridge	1973	D.L.Amiss & A.W.Greig
5	206	Australia	Trent Bridge	1938	E.Paynter & D.C.S.Compton
6	202	India	Lord's	1974	M.H.Denness & A.W.Greig
7=	192	Australia	Sydney	1903/04	R.E.Foster & L.C.Braund
7=	192	Pakistan	Trent Bridge	1954	D.C.S.Compton & T.E.Bailey
9	191	Australia	Old Trafford	1934	E.H.Hendren & M.Leyland
10	184	New Zealand	Auckland	1929/30	G.B.Legge & M.S.Nichols

HIGHEST 6TH WICKET PARTNERSHIPS

No.	Runs	Opposition	Venue	Date	Batsmen
1	240	New Zealand	Auckland	1962/63	P.H.Parfitt & B.R.Knight
2	232	New Zealand	Wellington	1984	I.T.Botham & D.W.Randall
3=	215	Australia	The Oval	1938	L.Hutton & J.Hardstaff jnr
3=	215	Australia	Trent Bridge	1977	G.Boycott & A.P.E.Knott
5	207	Australia	Perth	1986/87	D.I.Gower & C.J.Richards
6	206*	South Africa	Durban (2)	1964/65	K.F.Barrington & J.M.Parks
7	189	New Zealand	Lord's	1949	D.C.S.Compton & T.E.Bailey
8=	186	Australia	Lord's	1938	W.R.Hammond & L.E.G.Ames
8=	186	New Zealand	Trent Bridge	1983	I.T.Botham & D.W.Randall
10	171	India	Bombay (3)	1979/80	I.T.Botham & R.W.Taylor

HIGHEST 7TH WICKET PARTNERSHIPS

No.	Runs	Opposition	Venue	Date	Batsmen
1	197	West Indies	Port-of-Spain	1959/60	M.J.K.Smith & J.M.Parks
2	174	West Indies	Lord's	1957	M.C.Cowdrey & T.G.Evans
3	167	Pakistan	Faisalabad	1983/84	D.I.Gower & V.J.Marks
4	159	Pakistan	Edgbaston	1971	A.P.E.Knott & P.Lever
5	149	New Zealand	Auckland	1970/71	A.P.E.Knott & P.Lever
6=	143	Australia	Sydney	1911/12	F.E.Woolley & J.Vine
6=	143	Pakistan	Edgbaston	1987	M.W.Gatting & J.E.Emburey

8=	142	Australia	The Oval	1909	J.Sharp & K.L.Hutchings
8=	142	Australia	Old Trafford	1989	R.C.Russell & J.E.Emburey
10	140	West Indies	Old Trafford	1933	D.R.Jardine & R.W.V.Robins

HIGHEST 8TH WICKET PARTNERSHIPS

No.	Runs	Opposition	Venue	Date	Batsmen
1	246	New Zealand	Lord's	1931	L.E.G.Ames & G.O.B.Allen
2	217	West Indies	The Oval	1966	T.W.Graveney & J.T.Murray
3	168	India	Old Trafford	1971	R.Illingworth & P.Lever
4	154	South Africa	Johannesburg (1)	1895/96	C.W.Wright & H.R.Bromley-Davenport
5	138	India	Old Trafford	1936	R.W.V.Robins & H.Verity
6	130	New Zealand	Old Trafford	1994	P.A.J.DeFreitas & D.Gough
7	124	Australia	Brisbane (1)	1928/29	E.H.Hendren & H.Larwood
8	121	Australia	Old Trafford	1948	D.C.S.Compton & A.V.Bedser
9	117	Australia	Headingley	1981	I.T.Botham & G.R.Dilley
10	107	New Zealand	Christchurch	1965/66	D.A.Allen & D.J.Brown

HIGHEST 9TH WICKET PARTNERSHIPS

No.	Runs	Opposition	Venue	Date	Batsmen
1	163*	New Zealand	Wellington	1962/63	M.C.Cowdrey & A.C.Smith
2	151	Australia	The Oval	1884	W.H.Scotton & W.W.Read
3	128	Australia	Sydney	1924/25	F.E.Woolley & A.P.Freeman
4	117	New Zealand	Christchurch	1950/51	T.E.Bailey & D.V.P.Wright
5	115	Australia	Sydney	1903/04	R.E.Foster & A.E.Relf
6	109	West Indies	Georgetown	1967/68	G.A.R.Lock & P.I.Pocock
7	108	Australia	Headingley	1926	G.Geary & G.G.Macaulay
8	95	Australia	Old Trafford	1934	G.O.B.Allen & H.Verity
9=	92	Australia	Brisbane (2)	1932/33	E.Paynter & H.Verity
9=	92	New Zealand	Lord's	1973	K.W.R.Fletcher & G.G.Arnold
9=	92	West Indies	Edgbaston	1991	D.R.Pringle & C.C.Lewis

HIGHEST 10TH WICKET PARTNERSHIPS

No.	Runs	Opposition	Venue	Date	Batsmen
1	130	Australia	Sydney	1903/04	R.E.Foster & W.Rhodes
2	128	West Indies	The Oval	1966	K.Higgs & J.A.Snow
3	117*	West Indies	The Oval	1980	P.Willey & R.G.D.Willis
4	98	Australia	Melbourne	1884/85	J.Briggs & J.Hunter
5	92	South Africa	Durban (2)	1922/23	C.A.G.Russell & A.E.R.Gilligan
6	83	West Indies	Lord's	1969	R.Illingworth & J.A.Snow
7	81*	Australia	Edgbaston	1902	W.H.Lockwood & W.Rhodes
8	79	Pakistan	Edgbaston	1982	R.W.Taylor & R.G.D.Willis
9=	74	Australia	Adelaide	1891/92	H.Wood & F.Martin
9=	74	Australia	Sydney	1897/98	K.S.Ranjitsinhji & T.Richardson
9=	74	Australia	Melbourne	1950/51	R.T.Simpson & R.Tattersall

TOTAL CENTURY PARTNERSHIPS (695)

Runs	Wkt	Opposition	Venue	Date	Batsmen
411	4	West Indies	Edgbaston	1957	P.B.H.May & M.C.Cowdrey
382	2	Australia	The Oval	1938	L.Hutton & M.Leyland
370	3	South Africa	Lord's	1947	W.J.Edrich & D.C.S.Compton
369	2	New Zealand	Headingley	1965	J.H.Edrich & K.F.Barrington
359	1	South Africa	Johannesburg (2)	1948/49	L.Hutton & C.Washbrook
351	2	Australia	The Oval	1985	G.A.Gooch & D.I.Gower
331	2	Australia	Edgbaston	1985	R.T.Robinson & D.I.Gower
323	1	Australia	Melbourne	1911/12	J.B.Hobbs & W.Rhodes
308	3	India	Lord's	1990	G.A.Gooch & A.J.Lamb
303	3	West Indies	St John's	1993/94	M.A.Atherton & R.A.Smith
290	1	South Africa	The Oval	1960	G.Pullar & M.C.Cowdrey
283	1	Australia	Melbourne	1924/25	J.B.Hobbs & H.Sutcliffe
280	2	South Africa	Durban (2)	1938/39	P.A.Gibb & W.J.Edrich
268	1	South Africa	Lord's	1924	J.B.Hobbs & H.Sutcliffe
266	4	India	The Oval	1936	W.R.Hammond & T.S.Worthington
266	2	West Indies	Trent Bridge	1957	P.E.Richardson & T.W.Graveney
266	4	New Zealand	Auckland	1974/75	M.H.Denness & K.W.R.Fletcher
264	3	West Indies	The Oval	1939	L.Hutton & W.R.Hammond
263	2	New Zealand	Trent Bridge	1994	M.A.Atherton & G.A.Gooch
262	3	Australia	Adelaide	1928/29	W.R.Hammond & D.R.Jardine
254	5	India	Bombay (2)	1972/73	K.W.R.Fletcher & A.W.Greig
252	4	India	Headingley	1967	G.Boycott & B.L.D'Oliveira
249	4	West Indies	Kingston	1929/30	A.Sandham & L.E.G.Ames
249	2	New Zealand	Trent Bridge	1969	J.H.Edrich & P.J.Sharpe

Runs	Wkt	Opposition	Venue	Date	Batsmen
248	4	West Indies	Lord's	1939	L.Hutton & D.C.S.Compton
248	2	Pakistan	The Oval	1962	M.C.Cowdrey & E.R.Dexter
246	8	New Zealand	Lord's	1931	L.E.G.Ames & G.O.B.Allen
246	3	Australia	Old Trafford	1964	E.R.Dexter & K.F.Barrington
245	3	South Africa	Old Trafford	1929	R.E.S.Wyatt & F.E.Woolley
245	3	New Zealand	Lord's	1937	J.Hardstaff jnr & W.R.Hammond
242	5	New Zealand	Christchurch	1932/33	W.R.Hammond & L.E.G.Ames
242	3	South Africa	Durban (2)	1938/39	E.Paynter & W.R.Hammond
241	2	India	Madras (1)	1984/85	G.Fowler & M.W.Gatting
240	6	New Zealand	Auckland	1962/63	P.H.Parfitt & B.R.Knight
237	4	West Indies	Port-of-Spain	1929/30	E.H.Hendren & L.E.G.Ames
237	5	South Africa	Trent Bridge	1947	D.C.S.Compton & N.W.D.Yardley
234	1	Australia	Sydney	1965/66	G.Boycott & R.W.Barber
232	6	New Zealand	Wellington	1983/84	I.T.Botham & D.W.Randall
230	2	South Africa	Johannesburg (1)	1927/28	H.Sutcliffe & G.E.Tyldesley
230+	2	India	Trent Bridge	1996	M.A.Atherton & N.Hussain (192)
					M.A.Atherton & G.P.Thorpe (38)
228	3	South Africa	Old Trafford	1947	W.J.Edrich & D.C.S.Compton
227	3	Pakistan	Edgbaston	1992	A.J.Stewart & R.A.Smith
225	1	India	Old Trafford	1990	G.A.Gooch & M.A.Atherton
223	1	New Zealand	The Oval	1983	G.Fowler & C.J.Tavare
223	4	New Zealand	The Oval	1986	D.I.Gower & M.W.Gatting
223	1	Australia	Perth	1986/87	B.C.Broad & C.W.J.Athey
222	4	Australia	Lord's	1938	W.R.Hammond & E.Paynter
221	1	South Africa	Cape Town	1909/10	J.B.Hobbs & W.Rhodes
221	2	South Africa	Edgbaston	1929	H.Sutcliffe & W.R.Hammond
221	2	India	Lord's	1974	D.L.Amiss & J.H.Edrich
219	1	Australia	Trent Bridge	1938	C.J.Barnett & L.Hutton
218	2	New Zealand	The Oval	1949	L.Hutton & W.J.Edrich
217	8	West Indies	The Oval	1966	T.W.Graveney & J.T.Murray
215	6	Australia	The Oval	1938	L.Hutton & J.Hardstaff jnr
215	6	Australia	Trent Bridge	1977	G.Boycott & A.P.E.Knott
212	1	West Indies	Trent Bridge	1950	C.Washbrook & R.T.Simpson
211	2	India	Edgbaston	1974	D.Lloyd & M.H.Denness
210	3	Australia	Melbourne	1894/95	Albert Ward & J.T.Brown
210	5	New Zealand	Trent Bridge	1973	D.L.Amiss & A.W.Greig
209	1	West Indies	Port-of-Spain	1973/74	G.Boycott & D.L.Amiss
207	3	West Indies	Trent Bridge	1957	T.W.Graveney & P.B.H.May
207	6	Australia	Perth	1986/87	D.I.Gower & C.J.Richards
206*	6	South Africa	Durban (2)	1964/65	K.F.Barrington & J.M.Parks
206	5	Australia	Trent Bridge	1938	E.Paynter & D.C.S.Compton
206	4	India	Kanpur	1961/62	K.F.Barrington & E.R.Dexter
204	1	India	Lord's	1990	G.A.Gooch & M.A.Atherton
203	1	Australia	Adelaide	1990/91	G.A.Gooch & M.A.Atherton
202	5	India	Lord's	1974	M.H.Denness & A.W.Greig
201	3	Pakistan	Lord's	1967	K.F.Barrington & T.W.Graveney
198	1	Pakistan	Dacca	1961/62	G.Pullar & R.W.Barber
197	4	South Africa	Cape Town	1938/39	W.R.Hammond & L.E.G.Ames
197	7	West Indies	Port-of-Spain	1959/60	M.J.K.Smith & J.M.Parks
194*	3	New Zealand	Headingley	1958	C.A.Milton & P.B.H.May
193	4	India	Headingley	1959	M.C.Cowdrey & K.F.Barrington
193	4	West Indies	Bridgetown	1989/90	A.J.Lamb & R.A.Smith
192	5	Australia	Sydney	1903/04	R.E.Foster & L.C.Braund
192	5	Pakistan	Trent Bridge	1954	D.C.S.Compton & T.E.Bailey
192	3	Pakistan	Lahore (2)	1961/62	K.F.Barrington & M.J.K.Smith
192	4	Australia	Melbourne	1974/75	M.H.Denness & K.W.R.Fletcher
192	4	India	Lord's	1990	G.A.Gooch & R.A.Smith
191	5	Australia	Old Trafford	1934	E.H.Hendren & M.Leyland
191	2	West Indies	Port-of-Spain	1959/60	M.C.Cowdrey & E.R.Dexter
191	4	India	Kanpur	1963/64	B.R.Knight & P.H.Parfitt
191	3	South Africa	Johannesburg (3)	1964/65	E.R.Dexter & K.F.Barrington
191	4	India	Edgbaston	1979	G.Boycott & D.I.Gower
189	6	New Zealand	Lord's	1949	D.C.S.Compton & T.E.Bailey
188	2	Australia	Sydney	1932/33	H.Sutcliffe & W.R.Hammond
188	4	Pakistan	Karachi (1)	1961/62	E.R.Dexter & P.H.Parfitt
188	4	West Indies	Port-of-Spain	1967/68	K.F.Barrington & T.W.Graveney
187*	2	South Africa	The Oval	1929	H.Sutcliffe & W.R.Hammond
187	4	Australia	Headingley	1956	P.B.H.May & C.Washbrook
187	3	Australia	Trent Bridge	1985	D.I.Gower & M.W.Gatting
186	6	Australia	Lord's	1938	W.R.Hammond & L.E.G.Ames
186	6	New Zealand	Trent Bridge	1983	I.T.Botham & D.W.Randall
185	1	Australia	The Oval	1899	T.W.Hayward & Hon.F.S.Jackson
185	1	Pakistan	Hyderabad	1977/78	G.Boycott & J.M.Brearley
184	5	New Zealand	Auckland	1929/30	G.B.Legge & M.S.Nichols

Runs	Wkt	Opposition	Venue	Date	Batsmen
184	2	South Africa	Johannesburg (1)	1938/39	P.A.Gibb & E.Paynter
184	4	Pakistan	Trent Bridge	1962	T.W.Graveney & P.H.Parfitt
182	1	Australia	Lord's	1926	J.B.Hobbs & H.Sutcliffe
182	5	India	Lord's	1946	J.Hardstaff jnr & P.A.Gibb
182	2	Australia	Sydney	1954/55	T.W.Graveney & P.B.H.May
182	4	Australia	Sydney	1958/59	P.B.H.May & M.C.Cowdrey
179	5	South Africa	The Oval	1935	M.Leyland & L.E.G.Ames
179	3	New Zealand	Christchurch	1991/92	A.J.Stewart & R.A.Smith
178	2	New Zealand	The Oval	1931	H.Sutcliffe & K.S.Duleepsinhji
178	3	Australia	Melbourne	1965/66	J.H.Edrich & K.F.Barrington
178	1	India	Madras (1)	1984/85	G.Fowler & R.T.Robinson
177	1	West Indies	Kingston	1959/60	M.C.Cowdrey & G.Pullar
176*	5	Pakistan	The Oval	1987	M.W.Gatting & I.T.Botham
176	4	India	The Oval	1982	A.J.Lamb & I.T.Botham
176	1	India	The Oval	1990	G.A.Gooch & M.A.Atherton
175	3	Australia	Adelaide	1884/85	W.H.Scotton & W.Barnes
175	3	Australia	Melbourne	1962/63	E.R.Dexter & M.C.Cowdrey
174	1	Australia	Old Trafford	1956	P.E.Richardson & M.C.Cowdrey
174	7	West Indies	Lord's	1957	M.C.Cowdrey & T.G.Evans
174	4	Australia	Sydney	1994/95	M.A.Atherton & J.P.Crawley
173	1	West Indies	Kingston	1929/30	G.Gunn & A.Sandham
172	1	Australia	The Oval	1926	J.B.Hobbs & H.Sutcliffe
172	5	Australia	The Oval	1961	R.Subba Row & K.F.Barrington
172	1	West Indies	Bridgetown	1967/68	J.H.Edrich & G.Boycott
172	2	West Indies	Georgetown	1967/68	G.Boycott & M.C.Cowdrey
172	4	West Indies	Kingston	1989/90	A.J.Lamb & R.A.Smith
171	1	Australia	Perth	1970/71	G.Boycott & B.W.Luckhurst
171	6	India	Bombay (3)	1979/80	I.T.Botham & R.W.Taylor
171	3	West Indies	Georgetown	1993/94	M.A.Atherton & R.A.Smith
171	1	West Indies	Bridgetown	1993/94	M.A.Atherton & A.J.Stewart
170	1	Australia	The Oval	1886	W.G.Grace & W.H.Scotton
170	6	Australia	The Oval	1930	H.Sutcliffe & R.E.S.Wyatt
170	1	New Zealand	Edgbaston	1990	G.A.Gooch & M.A.Atherton
169	3	India	The Oval	1959	R.Subba Row & M.J.K.Smith
169	4	West Indies	Trent Bridge	1966	T.W.Graveney & M.C.Cowdrey
169	2	Australia	Adelaide	1970/71	J.H.Edrich & K.W.R.Fletcher
169	6	India	Old Trafford	1982	I.T.Botham & G.Miller
168	3	West Indies	Bridgetown	1929/30	A.Sandham & E.H.Hendren
168	2	South Africa	Johannesburg (1)	1938/39	P.A.Gibb & E.Paynter
168	1	Australia	Headingley	1948	L.Hutton & C.Washbrook
168	2	Australia	Lord's	1953	L.Hutton & T.W.Graveney
168	8	India	Old Trafford	1971	R.Illingworth & P.Lever
168	2	Pakistan	Hyderabad	1972/73	D.L.Amiss & K.W.R.Fletcher
168	2	New Zealand	Christchurch	1987/88	B.C.Broad & R.T.Robinson
168	1	Pakistan	Headingley	1992	G.A.Gooch & M.A.Atherton
167	7	Pakistan	Faisalabad	1983/84	D.I.Gower & V.J.Marks
166	3	West Indies	Port-of-Spain	1953/54	P.B.H.May & D.C.S.Compton
166	2	Pakistan	Edgbaston	1962	M.C.Cowdrey & E.R.Dexter
166	4	New Zealand	Auckland	1962/63	K.F.Barrington & M.C.Cowdrey
166	3	Australia	Melbourne	1976/77	D.W.Randall & D.L.Amiss
165*	6	India	Edgbaston	1979	D.I.Gower & G.Miller
164	4	South Africa	Durban (2)	1938/39	W.R.Hammond & E.Paynter
164	2	India	Delhi	1961/62	G.Pullar & K.F.Barrington
163*	9	New Zealand	Wellington	1962/63	M.C.Cowdrey & A.C.Smith
163	5	Australia	Lord's	1953	W.Watson & T.E.Bailey
163	6	West Indies	Bridgetown	1973/74	A.W.Greig & A.P.E.Knott
162	5	Australia	Melbourne	1894/95	A.C.MacLaren & R.Peel
161*	1	Australia	Melbourne	1970/71	G.Boycott & J.H.Edrich
161	5	Australia	Lord's	1886	A.Shrewsbury & W.Barnes
161	6	West Indies	Old Trafford	1950	T.E.Bailey & T.G.Evans
161	4	Australia	Edgbaston	1961	E.R.Dexter & K.F.Barrington
161	4	India	Bombay (2)	1961/62	K.F.Barrington & E.R.Dexter
161	2	Pakistan	Trent Bridge	1962	Rev.D.S.Sheppard & E.R.Dexter
161	4	Australia	Melbourne	1982/83	C.J.Tavare & A.J.Lamb
161	2	Australia	Adelaide	1986/87	B.C.Broad & M.W.Gatting
161	3	West Indies	Trent Bridge	1988	G.A.Gooch & D.I.Gower
160	1	South Africa	Durban (2)	1930/31	R.E.S.Wyatt & W.R.Hammond
160	4	Australia	Old Trafford	1977	R.A.Woolmer & A.W.Greig
160	6	New Zealand	Christchurch	1977/78	I.T.Botham & R.W.Taylor
160	3	Australia	Brisbane (2)	1994/95	G.A.Hick & G.P.Thorpe
159	1	South Africa	Johannesburg (1)	1909/10	J.B.Hobbs & W.Rhodes
159	6	India	Lord's	1952	T.W.Graveney & T.G.Evans
159	1	India	Bombay (2)	1961/62	P.E.Richardson & G.Pullar
159	7	Pakistan	Edgbaston	1971	A.P.E.Knott & P.Lever

Runs	Wkt	Opposition	Venue	Date	Batsmen
158	6	Australia	The Oval	1905	J.T.Tyldesley & R.H.Spooner
158	1	Australia	The Oval	1921	C.A.G.Russell & G.Brown
158	4	India	Delhi	1951/52	A.J.Watkins & D.B.Carr
158	2	India	Lord's	1952	L.Hutton & P.B.H.May
158	4	Australia	Perth	1978/79	G.Boycott & D.I.Gower
158	5	Australia	Perth	1994/95	G.P.Thorpe & M.R.Ramprakash
157	1	Australia	Sydney	1924/25	J.B.Hobbs & H.Sutcliffe
157	6	West Indies	Kingston	1934/35	L.E.G.Ames & J.Iddon
157	4	South Africa	Port Elizabeth	1964/65	G.Boycott & K.F.Barrington
157	1	India	Edgbaston	1974	D.L.Amiss & D.Lloyd
156	6	South Africa	Durban (2)	1922/23	C.P.Mead & F.T.Mann
156	1	Australia	Headingley	1926	J.B.Hobbs & H.Sutcliffe
156	5	Australia	Adelaide	1932/33	M.Leyland & R.E.S.Wyatt
156	4	Australia	The Oval	1956	P.B.H.May & D.C.S.Compton
156	2	Pakistan	Karachi (1)	1968/69	C.Milburn & T.W.Graveney
156	1	India	Kanpur	1984/85	G.Fowler & R.T.Robinson
156	4	Australia	Old Trafford	1985	M.W.Gatting & A.J.Lamb
155	1	West Indies	The Oval	1928	J.B.Hobbs & H.Sutcliffe
155	3	Australia	Headingley	1948	W.J.Edrich & A.V.Bedser
155+	1	West Indies	The Oval	1980	G.A.Gooch & G.Boycott (9)
					G.A.Gooch & B.C.Rose (146)
155	1	India	Madras (1)	1981/82	G.A.Gooch & C.J.Tavare
154	8	South Africa	Johannesburg (1)	1895/96	C.W.Wright & H.R.Bromley-Davenport
154	1	Australia	Sydney	1901/02	A.C.MacLaren & T.W.Hayward
154	5	South Africa	Durban (2)	1922/23	C.P.Mead & P.G.H.Fender
154	4	Pakistan	Trent Bridge	1954	D.C.S.Compton & T.W.Graveney
154	1	Australia	Trent Bridge	1977	J.M.Brearley & G.Boycott
154	2	Pakistan	Lord's	1996	M.A.Atherton & A.J.Stewart
153*	6	Pakistan	Edgbaston	1962	P.H.Parfitt & D.A.Allen
153	1	South Africa	Johannesburg (1)	1922/23	A.Sandham & C.A.G.Russell
152	2	Australia	Lord's	1893	A.Shrewsbury & W.Gunn
152	3	South Africa	Johannesburg (1)	1913/14	W.Rhodes & C.P.Mead
152	6	West Indies	Headingley	1976	A.W.Greig & A.P.E.Knott
151*	3	New Zealand	Christchurch	1974/75	D.L.Amiss & M.H.Denness
151	9	Australia	The Oval	1884	W.H.Scotton & W.W.Read
151	1	Australia	The Oval	1893	W.G.Grace & A.E.Stoddart
151	4	Australia	The Oval	1905	C.B.Fry & Hon.F.S.Jackson
151	4	South Africa	The Oval	1935	W.R.Hammond & M.Leyland
151	1	Australia	Trent Bridge	1956	P.E.Richardson & M.C.Cowdrey
151	6	Australia	The Oval	1975	R.A.Woolmer & A.P.E.Knott
151	5	India	The Oval	1982	I.T.Botham & D.W.Randall
150	2	Australia	Sydney	1946/47	L.Hutton & W.J.Edrich
150	3	South Africa	Johannesburg (2)	1948/49	J.F.Crapp & D.C.S.Compton
150	3	West Indies	Georgetown	1953/54	L.Hutton & D.C.S.Compton
150	6	Australia	Trent Bridge	1993	G.A.Gooch & G.P.Thorpe
150	5	West Indies	Bridgetown	1993/94	A.J.Stewart & G.P.Thorpe
149	1	Australia	Adelaide	1901/02	T.W.Hayward & A.C.MacLaren
149	3	New Zealand	Auckland	1932/33	W.R.Hammond & E.Paynter
149	7	New Zealand	Auckland	1970/71	A.P.E.Knott & P.Lever
149	3	Australia	Melbourne	1974/75	J.H.Edrich & M.H.Denness
149	6	Australia	Old Trafford	1981	C.J.Tavare & I.T.Botham
149	2	New Zealand	Lord's	1983	C.J.Tavare & D.I.Gower
148	1	Australia	Adelaide	1903/04	T.W.Hayward & P.F.Warner
148	2	West Indies	Kingston	1929/30	A.Sandham & R.E.S.Wyatt
148	5	India	Bombay (2)	1951/52	T.W.Graveney & A.J.Watkins
148	3	West Indies	Georgetown	1959/60	E.R.Dexter & R.Subba Row
148	5	Australia	Melbourne	1974/75	K.W.R.Fletcher & A.W.Greig
148	2	New Zealand	Lord's	1990	G.A.Gooch & A.J.Stewart
148	1	West Indies	Trent Bridge	1995	N.V.Knight & M.A.Atherton
147	1	Australia	Adelaide	1911/12	J.B.Hobbs & W.Rhodes
147	2	Australia	Melbourne	1946/47	C.Washbrook & W.J.Edrich
147	1	New Zealand	The Oval	1949	L.Hutton & R.T.Simpson
147	2	Pakistan	Dacca	1961/62	G.Pullar & K.F.Barrington
147	5	India	Lord's	1986	G.A.Gooch & D.R.Pringle
146	2	West Indies	The Oval	1957	P.E.Richardson & T.W.Graveney
146	1	India	Headingley	1959	W.G.A.Parkhouse & G.Pullar
146	1	India	Bombay (3)	1976/77	D.L.Amiss & J.M.Brearley
145+	3	Australia	Melbourne	1903/04	J.T.Tyldesley & R.E.Foster (89*)
					J.T.Tyldesley & L.C.Braund (56)
145	1	Australia	Trent Bridge	1905	T.W.Hayward & A.C.MacLaren
145	6	South Africa	Lord's	1907	L.C.Braund & G.L.Jessop
145	4	Australia	Sydney	1928/29	W.R.Hammond & E.H.Hendren
145	5	India	Bombay (1)	1933/34	D.R.Jardine & B.H.Valentine
145	3	India	Edgbaston	1979	G.Boycott & G.A.Gooch

Runs	Wkt	Opposition	Venue	Date	Batsmen
145	2	West Indies	Lord's	1980	G.A.Gooch & C.J.Tavare
144	2	South Africa	Trent Bridge	1951	L.Hutton & R.T.Simpson
144	5	South Africa	Old Trafford	1955	D.C.S.Compton & T.E.Bailey
144	4	India	Kanpur	1972/73	A.R.Lewis & K.W.R.Fletcher
144	1	West Indies	St John's	1980/81	G.A.Gooch & G.Boycott
144	3	India	Madras (1)	1984/85	M.W.Gatting & A.J.Lamb
144	6	West Indies	The Oval	1995	G.A.Hick & R.C.Russell
143	7	Australia	Sydney	1911/12	F.E.Woolley & J.Vine
143	1	Australia	Adelaide	1928/29	J.B.Hobbs & H.Sutcliffe
143	1	New Zealand	Lord's	1949	L.Hutton & J.D.B.Robertson
143	1	India	The Oval	1952	L.Hutton & Rev.D.S.Sheppard
143	3	Pakistan	Karachi (1)	1961/62	E.R.Dexter & M.J.K.Smith
143	5	Australia	Old Trafford	1964	K.F.Barrington & J.M.Parks
143	7	Pakistan	Edgbaston	1987	M.W.Gatting & J.E.Emburey
142	2	Australia	Adelaide	1897/98	A.C.MacLaren & K.S.Ranjitsinhji
142	7	Australia	The Oval	1909	J.Sharp & K.L.Hutchings
142	3	Australia	Melbourne	1920/21	J.B.Hobbs & E.H.Hendren
142	2	South Africa	Lord's	1924	J.B.Hobbs & F.E.Woolley
142	6	Australia	Old Trafford	1934	M.Leyland & L.E.G.Ames
142	4	West Indies	Port-of-Spain	1959/60	K.F.Barrington & E.R.Dexter
142	6	West Indies	Bridgetown	1973/74	K.W.R.Fletcher & A.P.E.Knott
142	5	India	Calcutta	1976/77	R.W.Tolchard & A.W.Greig
142	3	Australia	Old Trafford	1977	R.A.Woolmer & D.W.Randall
142	7	Australia	Old Trafford	1989	R.C.Russell & J.E.Emburey
142	3	South Africa	Headingley	1994	M.A.Atherton & G.P.Thorpe
142	4	South Africa	Centurion	1995/96	M.A.Atherton & G.A.Hick
141	6	Australia	Old Trafford	1902	Hon.F.S.Jackson & L.C.Braund
141	1	South Africa	Johannesburg (1)	1913/14	W.Rhodes & A.E.Relf
141	1	South Africa	Headingley	1947	L.Hutton & C.Washbrook
141	4	South Africa	Trent Bridge	1951	D.C.S.Compton & W.Watson
141	3	Pakistan	The Oval	1967	K.F.Barrington & T.W.Graveney
141	3	Australia	Perth	1990/91	A.J.Lamb & R.A.Smith
140	3	Australia	Lord's	1926	F.E.Woolley & E.H.Hendren
140	1	South Africa	Cape Town	1927/28	P.Holmes & H.Sutcliffe
140	6	Australia	Melbourne	1928/29	E.H.Hendren & M.Leyland
140	7	West Indies	Old Trafford	1933	D.R.Jardine & R.W.V.Robins
140	4	Australia	Melbourne	1970/71	B.W.Luckhurst & B.L.D'Oliveira
139	3	South Africa	Durban (2)	1922/23	C.A.G.Russell & C.P.Mead
139	4	South Africa	Trent Bridge	1935	R.E.S.Wyatt & M.Leyland
139	2	India	Kanpur	1961/62	G.Pullar & K.F.Barrington
139	2	India	Headingley	1967	G.Boycott & K.F.Barrington
139+	5	Pakistan	The Oval	1974	K.W.R.Fletcher & D.L.Amiss (61*)
					K.W.R.Fletcher & A.W.Greig (78)
139	3	New Zealand	Auckland	1977/78	C.T.Radley & G.R.J.Roope
139	5	Australia	Lord's	1989	D.I.Gower & R.A.Smith
139	4	Australia	Sydney	1990/91	M.A.Atherton & D.I.Gower
139	2	Sri Lanka	Lord's	1991	G.A.Gooch & A.J.Stewart
138	8	India	Old Trafford	1936	R.W.V.Robins & H.Verity
138	1	Australia	Melbourne	1946/47	L.Hutton & C.Washbrook
138	6	Australia	Melbourne	1965/66	M.C.Cowdrey & J.M.Parks
137	2	Australia	Melbourne	1881/82	G.Ulyett & J.Selby
137	3	Australia	Lord's	1893	A.Shrewsbury & Hon.F.S.Jackson
137	1	Australia	Adelaide	1946/47	L.Hutton & C.Washbrook
137	3	Pakistan	Lahore (2)	1983/84	M.W.Gatting & D.I.Gower
136	2	Australia	Sydney	1897/98	A.C.MacLaren & T.W.Hayward
136	1	South Africa	Edgbaston	1924	J.B.Hobbs & H.Sutcliffe
136	2	South Africa	Johannesburg (3)	1964/65	R.W.Barber & E.R.Dexter
136	4	New Zealand	Edgbaston	1965	K.F.Barrington & M.C.Cowdrey
136	4	West Indies	Kingston	1980/81	D.I.Gower & P.Willey
136	3	Australia	Headingley	1985	R.T.Robinson & M.W.Gatting
136	6	India	Lord's	1996	G.P.Thorpe & R.C.Russell
135	3	Australia	The Oval	1938	L.Hutton & W.R.Hammond
135	4	South Africa	The Oval	1965	K.F.Barrington & M.C.Cowdrey
135	4	Pakistan	Headingley	1971	G.Boycott & B.L.D'Oliveira
135	7	Australia	Adelaide	1978/79	G.Miller & R.W.Taylor
135	2	India	Bombay (3)	1984/85	G.Fowler & M.W.Gatting
134	2	Australia	Sydney	1907/08	J.B.Hobbs & G.Gunn
134	2	India	Old Trafford	1936	A.E.Fagg & W.R.Hammond
134	2	South Africa	Cape Town	1948/49	L.Hutton & J.F.Crapp
134	5	Australia	Sydney	1954/55	D.C.S.Compton & T.E.Bailey
134	3	West Indies	Port-of-Spain	1967/68	M.C.Cowdrey & K.F.Barrington
134	3	India	Old Trafford	1990	M.A.Atherton & A.J.Lamb
133	1	South Africa	Durban (1)	1913/14	J.B.Hobbs & W.Rhodes
133	7	Australia	Melbourne	1924/25	W.W.Whysall & R.Kilner

Runs	Wkt	Opposition	Venue	Date	Batsmen
133	2	Australia	Melbourne	1928/29	H.Sutcliffe & W.R.Hammond
133	3	West Indies	Port-of-Spain	1967/68	M.C.Cowdrey & K.F.Barrington
133	4	Australia	Sydney	1970/71	G.Boycott & B.L.D'Oliveira
133	3	South Africa	Headingley	1994	G.A.Hick & G.P.Thorpe
132	2	South Africa	Lord's	1955	T.W.Graveney & P.B.H.May
132	2	Australia	Lord's	1968	G.Boycott & C.Milburn
132	2	Australia	Lord's	1977	J.M.Brearley & R.A.Woolmer
132	1	India	Delhi	1981/82	G.A.Gooch & G.Boycott
131	6	Australia	The Oval	1893	W.W.Read & Hon.F.S.Jackson
131	2	Australia	The Oval	1899	T.W.Hayward & K.S.Ranjitsinhji
131	2	West Indies	The Oval	1939	L.Hutton & N.Oldfield
131	2	Australia	Melbourne	1950/51	L.Hutton & R.T.Simpson
131	2	India	Old Trafford	1959	G.Pullar & M.C.Cowdrey
131	7	Australia	Lord's	1985	M.W.Gatting & I.T.Botham
131	6	Australia	Sydney	1986/87	M.W.Gatting & C.J.Richards
131	2	Sri Lanka	Lord's	1988	G.A.Gooch & R.C.Russell
130*	5	West Indies	Lord's	1966	C.Milburn & T.W.Graveney
130	10	Australia	Sydney	1903/04	R.E.Foster & W.Rhodes
130	2	South Africa	Durban (2)	1927/28	H.Sutcliffe & G.E.Tyldesley
130	4	New Zealand	The Oval	1931	W.R.Hammond & L.E.G.Ames
130	1	West Indies	Kingston	1953/54	L.Hutton & W.Watson
130	2	Pakistan	Karachi (1)	1972/73	D.L.Amiss & K.W.R.Fletcher
130	7	Pakistan	The Oval	1974	K.W.R.Fletcher & C.M.Old
130	8	New Zealand	Old Trafford	1994	P.A.J.DeFreitas & D.Gough
130	1	India	Trent Bridge	1996	M.A.Atherton & A.J.Stewart
129	2	West Indies	The Oval	1928	J.B.Hobbs & G.E.Tyldesley
129	6	South Africa	Lord's	1929	M.Leyland & M.W.Tate
129	6	Australia	Lord's	1934	M.Leyland & L.E.G.Ames
129	4	South Africa	Headingley	1935	W.R.Hammond & R.E.S.Wyatt
129	3	Australia	Sydney	1936/37	W.R.Hammond & M.Leyland
129	1	West Indies	Kingston	1947/48	L.Hutton & J.D.B.Robertson
129	1	Australia	Headingley	1948	L.Hutton & C.Washbrook
129	3	New Zealand	Christchurch	1950/51	R.T.Simpson & D.C.S.Compton
129	2	South Africa	Headingley	1951	L.Hutton & P.B.H.May
129	2	West Indies	Kingston	1967/68	J.H.Edrich & M.C.Cowdrey
129	2	Pakistan	The Oval	1974	D.L.Amiss & D.L.Underwood
129	2	New Zealand	Trent Bridge	1978	G.Boycott & C.T.Radley
129	1	New Zealand	Wellington	1987/88	B.C.Broad & M.D.Moxon
129	4	India	The Oval	1990	D.I.Gower & A.J.Lamb
128	9	Australia	Sydney	1924/25	F.E.Woolley & A.P.Freeman
128	1	South Africa	Headingley	1935	D.Smith & A.Mitchell
128	2	New Zealand	Old Trafford	1937	L.Hutton & J.Hardstaff jnr
128	10	West Indies	The Oval	1966	K.Higgs & J.A.Snow
128	3	West Indies	Old Trafford	1969	G.Boycott & T.W.Graveney
128	6	West Indies	Lord's	1969	J.H.Hampshire & A.P.E.Knott
128	4	West Indies	The Oval	1976	D.L.Amiss & P.Willey
128	5	West Indies	Lord's	1984	A.J.Lamb & I.T.Botham
127	2	Australia	Melbourne	1911/12	W.Rhodes & J.W.Hearne
127	3	South Africa	Durban (2)	1927/28	G.E.Tyldesley & W.R.Hammond
127	3	India	Old Trafford	1936	W.R.Hammond & T.S.Worthington
127	6	West Indies	Georgetown	1967/68	M.C.Cowdrey & A.P.E.Knott
127	4	India	Kanpur	1981/82	D.I.Gower & I.T.Botham
127	3	Pakistan	Edgbaston	1982	C.J.Tavare & D.I.Gower
127	1	Pakistan	Faisalabad	1983/84	C.L.Smith & M.W.Gatting
127	1	West Indies	St John's	1985/86	G.A.Gooch & W.N.Slack
127	2	India	Lord's	1990	G.A.Gooch & D.I.Gower
127	3	Australia	Adelaide	1990/91	G.A.Gooch & R.A.Smith
126*	5	Australia	The Oval	1964	M.C.Cowdrey & K.F.Barrington
126	1	Australia	Melbourne	1924/25	J.B.Hobbs & H.Sutcliffe
126	5	Australia	Melbourne	1928/29	W.R.Hammond & D.R.Jardine
126	2	New Zealand	Old Trafford	1931	H.Sutcliffe & K.S.Duleepsinhji
126	1	New Zealand	Old Trafford	1958	P.E.Richardson & W.Watson
126	3	New Zealand	Lord's	1965	G.Boycott & E.R.Dexter
126	4	West Indies	Lord's	1969	G.Boycott & P.J.Sharpe
126	5	New Zealand	Lord's	1986	G.A.Gooch & P.Willey
125*	3	Australia	Sydney	1932/33	R.E.S.Wyatt & W.R.Hammond
125	5	Australia	Old Trafford	1905	Hon.F.S.Jackson & R.H.Spooner
125	1	Australia	Trent Bridge	1930	J.B.Hobbs & H.Sutcliffe
125	6	Australia	Lord's	1930	A.P.F.Chapman & G.O.B.Allen
125	4	New Zealand	The Oval	1937	D.C.S.Compton & J.Hardstaff jnr
125	4	India	Trent Bridge	1959	P.B.H.May & K.F.Barrington
125	1	India	Bombay (2)	1963/64	J.B.Bolus & J.G.Binks
125	5	New Zealand	Christchurch	1965/66	M.J.K.Smith & P.H.Parfitt
125	4	Australia	The Oval	1968	J.H.Edrich & T.W.Graveney

Runs	Wkt	Opposition	Venue	Date	Batsmen
125	1	New Zealand	Lord's	1969	G.Boycott & J.H.Edrich
125	2	Australia	The Oval	1975	J.H.Edrich & D.S.Steele
125	7	India	Lord's	1982	D.W.Randall & P.H.Edmonds
125	1	West Indies	Trent Bridge	1988	G.A.Gooch & B.C.Broad
124	6	Australia	Sydney	1897/98	G.H.Hirst & K.S.Ranjitsinhji
124	7	Australia	Sydney	1901/02	A.F.A.Lilley & L.C.Braund
124	2	South Africa	Lord's	1912	W.Rhodes & R.H.Spooner
124	6	Australia	Adelaide	1920/21	C.A.G.Russell & J.W.H.T.Douglas
124	6	South Africa	Johannesburg (1)	1922/23	F.E.Woolley & F.T.Mann
124	8	Australia	Brisbane (1)	1928/29	E.H.Hendren & H.Larwood
124	2	Australia	Old Trafford	1948	C.Washbrook & W.J.Edrich
124	3	Australia	Brisbane (2)	1954/55	W.J.Edrich & P.B.H.May
124	3	South Africa	Old Trafford	1955	P.B.H.May & D.C.S.Compton
124	2	Australia	Melbourne	1962/63	Rev.D.S.Sheppard & E.R.Dexter
124	1	Pakistan	Lord's	1971	G.Boycott & B.W.Luckhurst
124	2	South Africa	The Oval	1994	M.A.Atherton & G.A.Hick
123*	1	Australia	Old Trafford	1934	C.F.Walters & H.Sutcliffe
123	3	Australia	Sydney	1932/33	H.Sutcliffe & Nawab of Pataudi snr
123	7	West Indies	Bridgetown	1959/60	E.R.Dexter & R.Swetman
123	1	Australia	Headingley	1968	J.H.Edrich & R.M.Prideaux
123	2	India	Old Trafford	1971	B.W.Luckhurst & J.H.Edrich
123	6	Australia	Headingley	1977	G.Boycott & A.P.E.Knott
123	6	Pakistan	Edgbaston	1978	G.Miller & I.T.Botham
123	3	Australia	Lord's	1981	G.Boycott & D.I.Gower
123	1	Pakistan	Lord's	1992	G.A.Gooch & A.J.Stewart
122	1	Australia	Sydney	1881/82	G.Ulyett & R.G.Barlow
122	4	South Africa	Johannesburg (1)	1895/96	T.W.Hayward & A.J.L.Hill
122	1	Australia	Melbourne	1903/04	P.F.Warner & T.W.Hayward
122	2	Australia	Sydney	1932/33	H.Sutcliffe & W.R.Hammond
122	4	South Africa	Lord's	1951	D.C.S.Compton & W.Watson
122	4	India	Lord's	1967	T.W.Graveney & B.L.D'Oliveira
122	4	Australia	The Oval	1975	G.R.J.Roope & R.A.Woolmer
122	4	Australia	Sydney	1982/83	D.I.Gower & D.W.Randall
122	5	Australia	Melbourne	1990/91	D.I.Gower & A.J.Stewart
122	4	New Zealand	Wellington	1991/92	R.A.Smith & A.J.Lamb
122	4	Sri Lanka	Colombo (2)	1992/93	R.A.Smith & A.J.Stewart
121*	3	South Africa	Lord's	1924	F.E.Woolley & E.H.Hendren
121	6	Australia	The Oval	1921	C.P.Mead & Hon.L.H.Tennyson
121+	6	Australia	The Oval	1934	M.Leyland & L.E.G.Ames (85*) M.Leyland & G.O.B.Allen (36)
121	8	Australia	Old Trafford	1948	D.C.S.Compton & A.V.Bedser
121	1	South Africa	Old Trafford	1951	L.Hutton & J.T.Ikin
121	4	South Africa	Johannesburg (3)	1956/57	P.E.Richardson & M.C.Cowdrey
121	4	New Zealand	Edgbaston	1958	P.B.H.May & M.C.Cowdrey
121	5	Australia	The Oval	1968	J.H.Edrich & B.L.D'Oliveira
121	4	West Indies	Trent Bridge	1976	D.S.Steele & R.A.Woolmer
121	2	Australia	Old Trafford	1985	G.A.Gooch & D.I.Gower
121	4	India	Bombay (3)	1992/93	R.A.Smith & M.W.Gatting
121	1	West Indies	Kingston	1993/94	M.A.Atherton & A.J.Stewart
120*	4	Australia	Lord's	1980	G.Boycott & M.W.Gatting
120	2	Australia	The Oval	1880	W.G.Grace & A.P.Lucas
120	4	West Indies	Old Trafford	1928	W.R.Hammond & D.R.Jardine
120	2	South Africa	Johannesburg (2)	1948/49	C.Washbrook & J.F.Crapp
120	6	South Africa	Lord's	1960	M.J.K.Smith & P.M.Walker
120	1	South Africa	Durban (2)	1964/65	G.Boycott & R.W.Barber
120	3	West Indies	Bridgetown	1980/81	G.A.Gooch & D.I.Gower
120	4	India	Delhi	1981/82	C.J.Tavare & K.W.R.Fletcher
120	6	Pakistan	Lahore (2)	1983/84	G.Fowler & V.J.Marks
120	2	West Indies	Bridgetown	1985/86	G.A.Gooch & D.I.Gower
119*	6	South Africa	Johannesburg (3)	1995/96	M.A.Atherton & R.C.Russell
119	3	South Africa	Johannesburg (1)	1895/96	T.W.Hayward & C.B.Fry
119	1	West Indies	Old Trafford	1928	J.B.Hobbs & H.Sutcliffe
119	3	South Africa	Johannesburg (1)	1930/31	W.R.Hammond & E.H.Hendren
119	4	India	Madras (2)	1963/64	J.B.Bolus & K.F.Barrington
119	3	New Zealand	Headingley	1973	G.Boycott & K.W.R.Fletcher
119+	1	West Indies	Edgbaston	1973	G.Boycott & D.L.Amiss (105*) D.L.Amiss & B.W.Luckhurst (14)
119	2	West Indies	Port-of-Spain	1973/74	D.L.Amiss & M.H.Denness
119	6	West Indies	Georgetown	1973/74	A.W.Greig & A.P.E.Knott
119	3	Australia	Adelaide	1982/83	D.I.Gower & A.J.Lamb
119	6	Pakistan	Lahore (2)	1983/84	D.I.Gower & V.J.Marks
119	1	Pakistan	Edgbaston	1987	B.C.Broad & R.T.Robinson
118	1	South Africa	Trent Bridge	1935	H.Sutcliffe & R.E.S.Wyatt
118	5	Australia	Adelaide	1946/47	D.C.S.Compton & J.Hardstaff jnr

Runs	Wkt	Opposition	Venue	Date	Batsmen
118	2	New Zealand	Headingley	1949	C.Washbrook & W.J.Edrich
118	2	India	The Oval	1952	Rev.D.S.Sheppard & J.T.Ikin
118	5	Australia	Melbourne	1958/59	P.B.H.May & M.C.Cowdrey
118	3	Australia	Melbourne	1965/66	J.H.Edrich & K.F.Barrington
118	2	New Zealand	Auckland	1965/66	W.E.Russell & M.C.Cowdrey
118	2	West Indies	Port-of-Spain	1967/68	G.Boycott & M.C.Cowdrey
118	6	Pakistan	Lord's	1978	G.R.J.Roope & I.T.Botham
118	4	Australia	Adelaide	1982/83	D.I.Gower & I.T.Botham
118	5	Australia	Brisbane (2)	1986/87	D.I.Gower & I.T.Botham
118	7	West Indies	St John's	1993/94	R.C.Russell & C.C.Lewis
117*	1	Pakistan	Lord's	1971	B.W.Luckhurst & R.A.Hutton
117*	10	West Indies	The Oval	1980	P.Willey & R.G.D.Willis
117	4	Australia	Sydney	1907/08	G.Gunn & L.C.Braund
117	7	Australia	Adelaide	1924/25	J.B.Hobbs & E.H.Hendren
117	9	New Zealand	Christchurch	1950/51	T.E.Bailey & D.V.P.Wright
117	1	Pakistan	The Oval	1962	Rev.D.S.Sheppard & M.C.Cowdrey
117	6	South Africa	Cape Town	1964/65	M.J.K.Smith & J.M.Parks
117	2	Australia	Trent Bridge	1972	B.W.Luckhurst & P.H.Parfitt
117	3	New Zealand	Auckland	1974/75	J.H.Edrich & M.H.Denness
117	8	Australia	Headingley	1981	I.T.Botham & G.R.Dilley
117	3	Pakistan	Faisalabad	1987/88	B.C.Broad & M.W.Gatting
116*	4	Australia	Lord's	1926	E.H.Hendren & A.P.F.Chapman
116	6	Australia	Sydney	1882/83	W.W.Read & E.F.S.Tylecote
116	2	Australia	Melbourne	1884/85	A.Shrewsbury & W.Barnes
116	4	Australia	Sydney	1954/55	P.B.H.May & M.C.Cowdrey
116	1	Australia	Sydney	1970/71	G.Boycott & B.W.Luckhurst
116	1	India	Lord's	1974	D.L.Amiss & D.Lloyd
116	3	New Zealand	The Oval	1978	C.T.Radley & D.I.Gower
116	1	Australia	Melbourne	1979/80	G.A.Gooch & G.Boycott
116	2	India	Delhi	1981/82	G.Boycott & C.J.Tavare
116	5	Pakistan	Faisalabad	1983/84	D.I.Gower & G.Fowler
116	2	Australia	Trent Bridge	1985	G.A.Gooch & D.I.Gower
115+	5	Australia	Melbourne	1884/85	A.Shrewsbury & W.Bates (73*)
					A.Shrewsbury & W.Flowers (42)
115	9	Australia	Sydney	1903/04	R.E.Foster & A.E.Relf
115	7	South Africa	Durban (1)	1913/14	J.W.H.T.Douglas & M.C.Bird
115	2	South Africa	Durban (2)	1938/39	P.A.Gibb & E.Paynter
115	1	South Africa	Durban (2)	1956/57	P.E.Richardson & T.E.Bailey
115	5	India	Delhi	1963/64	P.H.Parfitt & M.C.Cowdrey
115	2	West Indies	Lord's	1966	G.Boycott & T.W.Graveney
115	1	Australia	Melbourne	1974/75	D.L.Amiss & D.Lloyd
115	3	Australia	The Oval	1981	G.Boycott & M.W.Gatting
115	4	West Indies	Bridgetown	1993/94	A.J.Stewart & G.A.Hick
115	5	South Africa	Headingley	1994	A.J.Stewart & J.P.Crawley
114	1	Australia	Brisbane (2)	1932/33	H.Sutcliffe & D.R.Jardine
114	1	Australia	Brisbane (2)	1962/63	Rev.D.S.Sheppard & G.Pullar
114	3	New Zealand	Lord's	1978	C.T.Radley & D.I.Gower
114	4	India	Lord's	1979	D.I.Gower & D.W.Randall
114	7	Pakistan	Karachi (1)	1987/88	D.J.Capel & J.E.Emburey
114	3	Australia	Headingley	1989	K.J.Barnett & A.J.Lamb
113*	6	Australia	Trent Bridge	1905	Hon.F.S.Jackson & W.Rhodes
113*	7	Australia	Trent Bridge	1993	G.P.Thorpe & N.Hussain
113	7	Australia	Old Trafford	1899	T.W.Hayward & A.F.A.Lilley
113	4	Australia	Sydney	1907/08	G.Gunn & J.Hardstaff snr
113	4	Australia	Adelaide	1907/08	L.C.Braund & J.Hardstaff snr
113	5	South Africa	Lord's	1912	P.F.Warner & F.E.Woolley
113	2	Australia	Melbourne	1920/21	W.Rhodes & J.W.H.Makepeace
113	6	Australia	Melbourne	1946/47	J.T.Ikin & N.W.D.Yardley
113	3	West Indies	Kingston	1947/48	W.Place & J.Hardstaff jnr
113	5	New Zealand	Christchurch	1965/66	M.J.K.Smith & P.H.Parfitt
113	6	West Indies	Port-of-Spain	1967/68	M.C.Cowdrey & A.P.E.Knott
113	6	Pakistan	Old Trafford	1987	R.T.Robinson & B.N.French
112	5	Australia	The Oval	1888	R.Abel & W.Barnes
112	2	Australia	Melbourne	1911/12	J.B.Hobbs & G.Gunn
112	1	Australia	Lord's	1912	J.B.Hobbs & W.Rhodes
112	1	Australia	Sydney	1932/33	H.Sutcliffe & R.E.S.Wyatt
112	1	West Indies	Old Trafford	1969	J.H.Edrich & G.Boycott
112	6	Pakistan	Hyderabad	1972/73	A.W.Greig & A.P.E.Knott
112	1	New Zealand	Lord's	1973	G.Boycott & D.L.Amiss
112	2	Australia	Headingley	1975	J.H.Edrich & D.S.Steele
112	4	Pakistan	Lord's	1982	C.J.Tavare & I.T.Botham
112	1	Australia	Adelaide	1986/87	B.C.Broad & C.W.J.Athey
112	1	West Indies	Port-of-Spain	1989/90	G.A.Gooch & W.Larkins
112	1	West Indies	The Oval	1991	G.A.Gooch & H.Morris

Runs	Wkt	Opposition	Venue	Date	Batsmen
112	3	Sri Lanka	Colombo (2)	1992/93	R.A.Smith & G.A.Hick
111*	4	South Africa	Cape Town	1948/49	D.C.S.Compton & A.J.Watkins
111	1	Australia	Sydney	1897/98	A.C.MacLaren & E.Wainwright
111	5	South Africa	Headingley	1912	J.W.Hearne & F.E.Woolley
111	2	New Zealand	Auckland	1929/30	E.H.Bowley & K.S.Duleepsinhji
111	1	India	Madras (1)	1933/34	A.H.Bakewell & C.F.Walters
111	7	Australia	Melbourne	1936/37	M.Leyland & R.W.V.Robins
111	3	Australia	Trent Bridge	1948	L.Hutton & D.C.S.Compton
111	3	Australia	Old Trafford	1961	G.Pullar & P.B.H.May
111	2	Australia	Old Trafford	1964	G.Boycott & E.R.Dexter
111	1	Australia	Lord's	1975	B.Wood & J.H.Edrich
111+	4	India	Madras (1)	1976/77	J.M.Brearley & R.W.Tolchard (2)
					J.M.Brearley & A.W.Greig (109)
111	1	New Zealand	Trent Bridge	1978	G.A.Gooch & G.Boycott
111	2	Australia	Sydney	1978/79	J.M.Brearley & D.W.Randall
111	2	India	Madras (1)	1992/93	A.J.Stewart & G.A.Hick
111	4	West Indies	Lord's	1995	G.P.Thorpe & R.A.Smith
110*	7	New Zealand	The Oval	1983	A.J.Lamb & P.H.Edmonds
110	4	Australia	The Oval	1899	C.B.Fry & A.C.MacLaren
110	1	Australia	Sydney	1924/25	J.B.Hobbs & H.Sutcliffe
110	5	West Indies	Port-of-Spain	1953/54	D.C.S.Compton & T.W.Graveney
110	2	Australia	Old Trafford	1961	R.Subba Row & E.R.Dexter
110	3	India	Delhi	1984/85	R.T.Robinson & A.J.Lamb
109*	4	India	Old Trafford	1974	J.H.Edrich & M.H.Denness
109	6	Australia	The Oval	1902	Hon.F.S.Jackson & G.L.Jessop
109	3	South Africa	Cape Town	1938/39	P.A.Gibb & W.R.Hammond
109	3	West Indies	The Oval	1950	L.Hutton & D.C.S.Compton
109	4	India	Old Trafford	1959	M.J.K.Smith & K.F.Barrington
109	2	Australia	Edgbaston	1961	R.Subba Row & E.R.Dexter
109	4	New Zealand	Headingley	1965	J.H.Edrich & P.H.Parfitt
109	4	West Indies	Bridgetown	1967/68	J.H.Edrich & T.W.Graveney
109	9	West Indies	Georgetown	1967/68	G.A.R.Lock & P.I.Pocock
109	3	Australia	Brisbane (2)	1970/71	A.P.E.Knott & J.H.Edrich
109	4	Australia	Edgbaston	1985	M.W.Gatting & A.J.Lamb
108*	2	India	Lord's	1936	H.Gimblett & M.J.L.Turnbull
108	6	Australia	Adelaide	1901/02	W.G.Quaife & L.C.Braund
108	4	Australia	Melbourne	1907/08	K.L.Hutchings & L.C.Braund
108	9	Australia	Headingley	1926	G.Geary & G.G.Macaulay
108	1	Australia	Old Trafford	1930	J.B.Hobbs & H.Sutcliffe
108	7	New Zealand	Christchurch	1932/33	F.R.Brown & W.Voce
108	6	West Indies	Kingston	1953/54	L.Hutton & T.G.Evans
108	4	South Africa	Old Trafford	1955	P.B.H.May & M.C.Cowdrey
108	3	Australia	Trent Bridge	1956	P.E.Richardson & P.B.H.May
108	2	Australia	Edgbaston	1968	J.H.Edrich & M.C.Cowdrey
108	2	New Zealand	Auckland	1987/88	M.D.Moxon & R.T.Robinson
108	1	West Indies	Trent Bridge	1991	G.A.Gooch & M.A.Atherton
108	4	Australia	Headingley	1993	M.A.Atherton & G.A.Gooch
108	5	Pakistan	Headingley	1996	A.J.Stewart & N.V.Knight
107	1	Australia	The Oval	1912	J.B.Hobbs & W.Rhodes
107	5	India	Calcutta	1951/52	A.J.Watkins & C.J.Poole
107	2	West Indies	Bridgetown	1953/54	L.Hutton & P.B.H.May
107	3	Pakistan	Edgbaston	1962	M.C.Cowdrey & T.W.Graveney
107	8	New Zealand	Christchurch	1965/66	D.A.Allen & D.J.Brown
107	3	India	Headingley	1967	G.Boycott & T.W.Graveney
107	1	Australia	Adelaide	1970/71	G.Boycott & J.H.Edrich
107	2	Pakistan	Headingley	1996	A.J.Stewart & N.Hussain
106	2	Australia	Sydney	1901/02	A.C.MacLaren & J.T.Tyldesley
106	3	Australia	Headingley	1909	J.T.Tyldesley & J.Sharp
106	5	Australia	Melbourne	1920/21	J.W.H.Makepeace & J.W.H.T.Douglas
106	2	Australia	Melbourne	1924/25	H.Sutcliffe & J.W.Hearne
106	6	South Africa	Headingley	1929	F.E.Woolley & M.Leyland
106	7	Australia	The Oval	1938	J.Hardstaff jnr & A.Wood
106	3	South Africa	Trent Bridge	1947	W.J.Edrich & D.C.S.Compton
106	3	West Indies	Trent Bridge	1950	W.G.A.Parkhouse & J.G.Dewes
106	1	India	Lord's	1952	L.Hutton & R.T.Simpson
106	6	India	Trent Bridge	1959	M.J.Horton & T.G.Evans
106	6	Pakistan	Headingley	1971	B.L.D'Oliveira & R.Illingworth
106	2	India	The Oval	1971	J.A.Jameson & J.H.Edrich
106	3	West Indies	Trent Bridge	1980	G.Boycott & R.A.Woolmer
106	1	India	Old Trafford	1982	G.Cook & C.J.Tavare
106	6	India	Delhi	1984/85	R.T.Robinson & P.R.Downton
106*	4	West Indies	Port-of-Spain	1985/86	D.I.Gower & A.J.Lamb
105*	1	Australia	Edgbaston	1909	J.B.Hobbs & C.B.Fry
105	5	South Africa	Cape Town	1888/89	R.Abel & H.Wood

Runs	Wkt	Opposition	Venue	Date	Batsmen
105	2	Australia	Lord's	1896	W.G.Grace & R.Abel
105	2	Australia	Adelaide	1920/21	J.B.Hobbs & J.W.H.Makepeace
105	1	Australia	Melbourne	1928/29	J.B.Hobbs & H.Sutcliffe
105	6	South Africa	Old Trafford	1935	M.Leyland & R.W.V.Robins
105	5	New Zealand	Old Trafford	1949	R.T.Simpson & T.E.Bailey
105	7	West Indies	Kingston	1953/54	L.Hutton & J.H.Wardle
105	5	New Zealand	Lord's	1965	M.C.Cowdrey & M.J.K.Smith
105	4	Australia	Melbourne	1965/66	J.H.Edrich & M.C.Cowdrey
105	1	Pakistan	Lahore (2)	1972/73	M.H.Denness & D.L.Amiss
105	5	India	Calcutta	1981/82	D.I.Gower & K.W.R.Fletcher
105	2	Australia	Melbourne	1986/87	B.C.Broad & M.W.Gatting
105	3	Sri Lanka	Lord's	1991	G.A.Gooch & R.A.Smith
105	7	New Zealand	Wellington	1991/92	A.J.Lamb & R.C.Russell
104	2	Australia	Melbourne	1894/95	Albert Ward & A.E.Stoddart
104	3	Australia	The Oval	1909	W.Rhodes & C.B.Fry
104	5	South Africa	Port Elizabeth	1913/14	C.P.Mead & F.E.Woolley
104	6	Australia	Melbourne	1920/21	J.W.H.T.Douglas & P.G.H.Fender
104	4	Australia	Lord's	1930	K.S.Duleepsinhji & E.H.Hendren
104	1	Australia	The Oval	1934	C.F.Walters & H.Sutcliffe
104	4	Australia	Sydney	1936/37	W.R.Hammond & L.E.G.Ames
104	3	New Zealand	Lord's	1937	J.Hardstaff jnr & C.J.Barnett
104	4	New Zealand	Edgbaston	1958	P.E.Richardson & M.C.Cowdrey
104	3	Australia	Melbourne	1962/63	Rev.D.S.Sheppard & M.C.Cowdrey
104	5	Pakistan	Lord's	1967	B.L.D'Oliveira & D.B.Close
104	8	Australia	Headingley	1972	R.Illingworth & J.A.Snow
104	6	India	Old Trafford	1974	K.W.R.Fletcher & A.W.Greig
104	2	Australia	Lord's	1975	J.H.Edrich & D.S.Steele
104	2	Australia	Lord's	1993	M.A.Atherton & M.W.Gatting
104	7	Australia	Edgbaston	1993	G.P.Thorpe & J.E.Emburey
104	2	Australia	Sydney	1994/95	M.A.Atherton & G.A.Hick
104	4	West Indies	Old Trafford	1995	G.P.Thorpe & R.A.Smith
103	4	Australia	The Oval	1893	A.Shrewsbury & Albert Ward
103	3	Australia	Headingley	1948	W.J.Edrich & D.C.S.Compton
103	1	New Zealand	Old Trafford	1949	L.Hutton & C.Washbrook
103	2	West Indies	Bridgetown	1959/60	G.Pullar & K.F.Barrington
103	1	Australia	Adelaide	1970/71	G.Boycott & J.H.Edrich
103	7	India	The Oval	1971	A.P.E.Knott & R.A.Hutton
103+	5	Pakistan	Karachi (1)	1972/73	A.R.Lewis & P.I.Pocock (3*) A.R.Lewis & A.W.Greig (100)
103	8	India	Lord's	1979	G.Miller & R.W.Taylor
103	1	Pakistan	Headingley	1982	C.J.Tavare & G.Fowler
103+	5	West Indies	Headingley	1988	A.J.Lamb & R.A.Smith (103*) R.A.Smith & C.S.Cowdrey (0)
102*	3	Australia	Lord's	1902	A.C.MacLaren & Hon.F.S.Jackson
102*	5	Australia	Old Trafford	1921	G.E.Tyldesley & P.G.H.Fender
102	7	Australia	Sydney	1884/85	W.Flowers & J.M.Read
102	3	Australia	Sydney	1894/95	Albert Ward & J.T.Brown
102	2	Australia	Melbourne	1911/12	W.Rhodes & G.Gunn
102	2	South Africa	Durban (2)	1927/28	P.Holmes & G.E.Tyldesley
102	3	Australia	Sydney	1946/47	W.J.Edrich & D.C.S.Compton
102	3	New Zealand	Headingley	1949	L.Hutton & D.C.S.Compton
102	3	Australia	Lord's	1953	L.Hutton & D.C.S.Compton
102	7	India	The Oval	1959	R.Illingworth & R.Swetman
102	4	Pakistan	Lord's	1987	C.W.J.Athey & M.W.Gatting
102	2	Pakistan	Headingley	1992	G.A.Gooch & R.A.Smith
101*	6	Pakistan	Lahore (2)	1961/62	E.R.Dexter & R.W.Barber
101*	5	Australia	Adelaide	1962/63	K.F.Barrington & T.W.Graveney
101*	5	India	Delhi	1972/73	A.R.Lewis & A.W.Greig
101*	3	West Indies	Trent Bridge	1976	J.H.Edrich & D.B.Close
101	5	South Africa	The Oval	1924	A.Sandham & E.H.Hendren
101	4	South Africa	Johannesburg (1)	1930/31	W.R.Hammond & M.J.L.Turnbull
101	7	Australia	Trent Bridge	1934	E.H.Hendren & G.Geary
101	3	South Africa	Headingley	1955	P.B.H.May & D.J.Insole
101	5	West Indies	Edgbaston	1963	E.R.Dexter & P.J.Sharpe
101	5	West Indies	The Oval	1963	D.B.Close & P.J.Sharpe
101	1	India	Delhi	1963/64	J.B.Bolus & J.H.Edrich
101	3	West Indies	Kingston	1967/68	M.C.Cowdrey & K.F.Barrington
101	3	West Indies	Port-of-Spain	1973/74	G.Boycott & K.W.R.Fletcher
101	6	India	Delhi	1976/77	D.L.Amiss & A.P.E.Knott
101+	4	New Zealand	Christchurch	1977/78	G.R.J.Roope & G.Miller (77*) G.R.J.Roope & C.T.Radley (24)
101	3	Pakistan	Lord's	1978	G.A.Gooch & D.I.Gower
101	5	India	Kanpur	1981/82	I.T.Botham & M.W.Gatting
101	1	West Indies	Lord's	1984	G.Fowler & B.C.Broad

Runs	Wkt	Opposition	Venue	Date	Batsmen
101	2	Australia	Brisbane (2)	1986/87	C.W.J.Athey & M.W.Gatting
100	3	Australia	The Oval	1905	T.W.Hayward & C.B.Fry
100	4	South Africa	Cape Town	1909/10	F.L.Fane & F.E.Woolley
100	1	South Africa	Johannesburg (1)	1913/14	J.B.Hobbs & W.Rhodes
100	2	Australia	Sydney	1920/21	J.B.Hobbs & J.W.Hearne
100	1	New Zealand	Old Trafford	1937	L.Hutton & C.J.Barnett
100	1	Australia	Adelaide	1946/47	L.Hutton & C.Washbrook
100	2	Australia	Headingley	1948	C.Washbrook & W.J.Edrich
100	6	South Africa	Port Elizabeth	1948/49	F.G.Mann & R.O.Jenkins
100	2	Australia	The Oval	1953	L.Hutton & P.B.H.May
100	4	South Africa	Johannesburg (3)	1964/65	K.F.Barrington & P.H.Parfitt
100	3	West Indies	Georgetown	1973/74	D.L.Amiss & K.W.R.Fletcher
100	2	West Indies	The Oval	1976	D.L.Amiss & D.S.Steele
100	5	Australia	Perth	1982/83	C.J.Tavare & D.W.Randall
100	3	New Zealand	Headingley	1983	C.J.Tavare & A.J.Lamb
100	7	India	Kanpur	1984/85	D.I.Gower & P.H.Edmonds

+ Three batsmen sharing in partnership

CENTURY PARTNERSHIPS PER WICKET

1st Wicket	135
2nd Wicket	132
3rd Wicket	116
4th Wicket	111
5th Wicket	72
6th Wicket	72
7th Wicket	35
8th Wicket	12
9th Wicket	7
10th Wicket	3

HIGHEST PARTNERSHIPS AGAINST EACH OPPOSITION

Australia
382	L.Hutton & M.Leyland	2nd wicket	The Oval	1938
351	G.A.Gooch & D.I.Gower	2nd wicket	The Oval	1985
331	R.T.Robinson & D.I.Gower	2nd wicket	Edgbaston	1985
323	J.B.Hobbs & W.Rhodes	1st wicket	Melbourne	1911/12
283	J.B.Hobbs & H.Sutcliffe	1st wicket	Melbourne	1924/25

South Africa
370	W.J.Edrich & D.C.S.Compton	3rd wicket	Lord's	1947
359	L.Hutton & C.Washbrook	1st wicket	Johannesburg (2)	1948/49
290	G.Pullar & M.C.Cowdrey	1st wicket	The Oval	1960
280	P.A.Gibb & W.J.Edrich	2nd wicket	Durban (2)	1938/39
268	J.B.Hobbs & H.Sutcliffe	1st wicket	Lord's	1924

West Indies
411	P.B.H.May & M.C.Cowdrey	4th wicket	Edgbaston	1957
303	M.A.Atherton & R.A.Smith	3rd wicket	St John's	1993/94
264	L.Hutton & W.R.Hammond	3rd wicket	The Oval	1939
266	P.E.Richardson & T.W.Graveney	2nd wicket	Trent Bridge	1957
249	A.Sandham & L.E.G.Ames	4th wicket	Kingston	1929/30

New Zealand
369	J.H.Edrich & K.F.Barrington	2nd wicket	Headingley	1965
266	M.H.Denness & K.W.R.Fletcher	4th wicket	Auckland	1974/75
263	M.A.Atherton & G.A.Gooch	2nd wicket	Trent Bridge	1994
249	J.H.Edrich & P.J.Sharpe	2nd wicket	Trent Bridge	1969
246	L.E.G.Ames & G.O.B.Allen	8th wicket	Lord's	1931

India
308	G.A.Gooch & A.J.Lamb	3rd wicket	Lord's	1990
266	W.R.Hammond & T.S.Worthington	4th wicket	The Oval	1936
254	K.W.R.Fletcher & A.W.Greig	5th wicket	Bombay (2)	1972/73
252	G.Boycott & B.L.D'Oliveira	4th wicket	Headingley	1967
241	G.Fowler & M.W.Gatting	2nd wicket	Madras (1)	1984/85

Pakistan
248	M.C.Cowdrey & E.R.Dexter	2nd wicket	The Oval	1962
227	A.J.Stewart & R.A.Smith	3rd wicket	Edgbaston	1992
201	K.F.Barrington & T.W.Graveney	3rd wicket	Lord's	1967
198	G.Pullar & R.W.Barber	1st wicket	Dacca	1961/62

| 192 | D.C.S.Compton & T.E.Bailey | 5th wicket | Trent Bridge | 1954 |
| 192 | K.F.Barrington & M.J.K.Smith | 3rd wicket | Lahore (2) | 1961/62 |

Sri Lanka

139	G.A.Gooch & A.J.Stewart	2nd wicket	Lord's	1991
131	G.A.Gooch & R.C.Russell	2nd wicket	Lord's	1988
122	R.A.Smith & A.J.Stewart	4th wicket	Colombo (2)	1992/93
112	R.A.Smith & G.A.Hick	3rd wicket	Colombo (2)	1992/93
105	G.A.Gooch & R.A.Smith	3rd wicket	Lord's	1991

TOTAL CENTURY PARTNERSHIPS AGAINST EACH OPPOSITION

Australia	261
South Africa	94
West Indies	106
New Zealand	74
India	96
Pakistan	59
Sri Lanka	5

HIGHEST PARTNERSHIPS PER VENUE

ENGLAND

The Oval

| 382 | L.Hutton & M.Leyland | 2nd wicket | Australia | 1938 |

Old Trafford

| 246 | E.R.Dexter & K.F.Barrington | 3rd wicket | Australia | 1964 |

Lord's

| 370 | W.J.Edrich & D.C.S.Compton | 3rd wicket | South Africa | 1947 |

Trent Bridge

| 266 | P.E.Richardson & T.W.Graveney | 2nd wicket | West Indies | 1957 |

Headingley

| 369 | J.H.Edrich & K.F.Barrington | 2nd wicket | New Zealand | 1965 |

Edgbaston

| 411 | P.B.H.May & M.C.Cowdrey | 4th wicket | West Indies | 1957 |

Bramall Lane

| 64 | G.L.Jessop & A.C.MacLaren | 5th wicket | Australia | 1902 |

AUSTRALIA

Melbourne

| 323 | J.B.Hobbs & W.Rhodes | 1st wicket | Australia | 1911/12 |

Sydney

| 234 | G.Boycott & R.W.Barber | 1st wicket | Australia | 1965/66 |

Adelaide

| 262 | W.R.Hammond & D.R.Jardine | 3rd wicket | Australia | 1928/29 |

Brisbane (1)

| 124 | E.H.Hendren & H.Larwood | 8th wicket | Australia | 1928/29 |

Brisbane (2)

| 160 | G.A.Hick & G.P.Thorpe | 3rd wicket | Australia | 1994/95 |

Perth

| 223 | B.C.Broad & C.W.J.Athey | 1st wicket | Australia | 1986/87 |

SOUTH AFRICA

Port Elizabeth

| 157 | G.Boycott & K.F.Barrington | 4th wicket | South Africa | 1964/65 |

Cape Town

| 221 | J.B.Hobbs & W.Rhodes | 1st wicket | South Africa | 1909/10 |

Johannesburg (1)

| 230 | H.Sutcliffe & G.E.Tyldesley | 2nd wicket | South Africa | 1927/28 |

Durban (1)
133 J.B.Hobbs & W.Rhodes | 1st wicket | South Africa | 1913/14

Durban (2)
280 P.A.Gibb & W.J.Edrich | 2nd wicket | South Africa | 1938/39

Johannesburg (2)
359 L.Hutton & C.Washbrook | 1st wicket | South Africa | 1948/49

Johannesburg (3)
191 E.R.Dexter & K.F.Barrington | 3rd wicket | South Africa | 1964/65

Centurion
142 M.A.Atherton & G.A.Hick | 4th wicket | South Africa | 1995/96

WEST INDIES

Bridgetown
193 A.J.Lamb & R.A.Smith | 4th wicket | West Indies | 1989/90

Port-of-Spain
237 E.H.Hendren & L.E.G.Ames | 4th wicket | West Indies | 1929/30

Georgetown
172 G.Boycott & M.C.Cowdrey | 2nd wicket | West Indies | 1967/68

Kingston
249 A.Sandham & L.E.G.Ames | 4th wicket | West Indies | 1929/30

St John's
303 M.A.Atherton & R.A.Smith | 3rd wicket | West Indies | 1993/94

NEW ZEALAND

Christchurch
242 W.R.Hammond & L.E.G.Ames | 5th wicket | New Zealand | 1932/33

Wellington
232 I.T.Botham & D.W.Randall | 6th wicket | New Zealand | 1983/84

Auckland
266 M.H.Denness & K.W.R.Fletcher | 4th wicket | New Zealand | 1974/75

Dunedin
81 M.C.Cowdrey & J.T.Murray | 6th wicket | New Zealand | 1965/66

INDIA

Bombay (1)
145 D.R.Jardine & B.H.Valentine | 5th wicket | India | 1933/34

Calcutta
142 R.W.Tolchard & A.W.Greig | 5th wicket | India | 1976/77

Madras (1)
241 G.Fowler & M.W.Gatting | 2nd wicket | India | 1984/85

Delhi
164 G.Pullar & K.F.Barrington | 2nd wicket | India | 1961/62

Bombay (2)
254 K.W.R.Fletcher & A.W.Greig | 5th wicket | India | 1972/73

Kanpur
206 K.F.Barrington & E.R.Dexter | 4th wicket | India | 1961/62

Madras (2)
119 J.B.Bolus & K.F.Barrington | 4th wicket | India | 1963/64

Bangalore
88 G.A.Gooch & G.Boycott | 1st wicket | India | 1981/82

Bombay (3)
171 I.T.Botham & R.W.Taylor | 6th wicket | India | 1979/80

PAKISTAN

Dacca
198	G.Pullar & R.W.Barber	1st wicket	Pakistan	1961/62

Karachi (1)
188	E.R.Dexter & P.H.Parfitt	4th wicket	Pakistan	1961/62

Lahore (2)
192	K.F.Barrington & M.J.K.Smith	3rd wicket	Pakistan	1961/62

Hyderabad
185	G.Boycott & J.M.Brearley	1st wicket	Pakistan	1977/78

Faisalabad
167	D.I.Gower & V.J.Marks	7th wicket	Pakistan	1983/84

SRI LANKA

Colombo (1)
83	C.J.Tavare & D.I.Gower	3rd wicket	Sri Lanka	1981/82

Colombo (2)
122	R.A.Smith & A.J.Stewart	4th wicket	Sri Lanka	1992/93

TOTAL CENTURY PARTNERSHIPS PER VENUE

England (361)
The Oval	87
Old Trafford	57
Lord's	91
Trent Bridge	48
Headingley	48
Edgbaston	30

Australia (135)
Melbourne	49
Sydney	44
Adelaide	27
Brisbane (1)	1
Brisbane (2)	7
Perth	7

South Africa (51)
Port Elizabeth	3
Cape Town	9
Johannesburg (1)	14
Durban (1)	2
Durban (2)	14
Johannesburg (2)	3
Johannesburg (3)	5
Centurion	1

West Indies (57)
Bridgetown	14
Port-of-Spain	16
Georgetown	8
Kingston	15
St John's	4

New Zealand (28)
Christchurch	12
Wellington	5
Auckland	11

India (40)
Bombay (1)	1
Calcutta	3
Madras (1)	7
Delhi	11
Bombay (2)	5
Kanpur	8
Madras (2)	1
Bombay (3)	4

Pakistan (21)

Dacca	2
Karachi (1)	6
Lahore (2)	6
Hyderabad	3
Faisalabad	4

Sri Lanka (2)

Colombo (2)	2

CENTURY PARTNERSHIPS PER BATSMAN

G.Boycott (48)

1	111	2	58	Australia	Old Trafford	1964	E.R.Dexter
2	120	1	73	South Africa	Durban (2)	1964/65	R.W.Barber
3	157	4	117	South Africa	Port Elizabeth	1964/65	K.F.Barrington
4	126	3	76	New Zealand	Lord's	1965	E.R.Dexter
5	234	1	84	Australia	Sydney	1965/66	R.W.Barber
6	115	2	60	West Indies	Lord's	1966	T.W.Graveney
7	139	2	246*	India	Headingley	1967	K.F.Barrington
8	107	3	246*	India	Headingley	1967	T.W.Graveney
9	252	4	246*	India	Headingley	1967	B.L.D'Oliveira
10	172	1	90	West Indies	Bridgetown	1967/68	J.H.Edrich
11	118	2	80*	West Indies	Port-of-Spain	1967/68	M.C.Cowdrey
12	172	2	116	West Indies	Georgetown	1967/68	M.C.Cowdrey
13	132	2	49	Australia	Lord's	1968	C.Milburn
14	112	1	128	West Indies	Old Trafford	1969	J.H.Edrich
15	128	3	128	West Indies	Old Trafford	1969	T.W.Graveney
16	126	4	106	West Indies	Lord's	1969	P.J.Sharpe
17	125	1	47	New Zealand	Lord's	1969	J.H.Edrich
18	171	1	70	Australia	Perth	1970/71	B.W.Luckhurst
19	116	1	77	Australia	Sydney	1970/71	B.W.Luckhurst
20	133	4	142*	Australia	Sydney	1970/71	B.L.D'Oliveira
21	161*	1	76*	Australia	Melbourne	1970/71	J.H.Edrich
22	107	1	58	Australia	Adelaide	1970/71	J.H.Edrich
23	103	1	119*	Australia	Adelaide	1970/71	J.H.Edrich
24	124	1	121*	Pakistan	Lord's	1971	B.W.Luckhurst
25	135	4	112	Pakistan	Headingley	1971	B.L.D'Oliveira
26	112	1	92	New Zealand	Lord's	1973	D.L.Amiss
27	119	3	115	New Zealand	Headingley	1973	K.W.R.Fletcher
28	119+	1	56*	West Indies	Edgbaston	1973	D.L.Amiss & B.W.Luckhurst
29	209	1	93	West Indies	Port-of-Spain	1973/74	D.L.Amiss
30	101	3	112	West Indies	Port-of-Spain	1973/74	K.W.R.Fletcher
31	215	6	107	Australia	Trent Bridge	1977	A.P.E.Knott
32	154	1	80*	Australia	Trent Bridge	1977	J.M.Brearley
33	123	6	191	Australia	Headingley	1977	A.P.E.Knott
34	185	1	100*	Pakistan	Hyderabad	1977/78	J.M.Brearley
35	111	1	131	New Zealand	Trent Bridge	1978	G.A.Gooch
36	129	2	131	New Zealand	Trent Bridge	1978	C.T.Radley
37	158	4	77	Australia	Perth	1978/79	D.I.Gower
38	145	3	155	India	Edgbaston	1979	G.A.Gooch
39	191	4	155	India	Edgbaston	1979	D.I.Gower
40	116	1	44	Australia	Melbourne	1979/80	G.A.Gooch
41	106	3	75	West Indies	Trent Bridge	1980	R.A.Woolmer
42	155+	1	53	West Indies	The Oval	1980	G.A.Gooch & B.C.Rose
43	120*	4	128*	Australia	Lord's	1980	M.W.Gatting
44	144	1	104*	West Indies	St John's	1980/81	G.A.Gooch
45	123	3	60	Australia	Lord's	1981	D.I.Gower
46	115	3	137	Australia	The Oval	1981	M.W.Gatting
47	132	1	105	India	Delhi	1981/82	G.A.Gooch
48	116	2	105	India	Delhi	1981/82	C.J.Tavare

M.C.Cowdrey (42)

1	116	4	54	Australia	Sydney	1954/55	P.B.H.May
2	108	4	50	South Africa	Old Trafford	1955	P.B.H.May
3	151	1	81	Australia	Trent Bridge	1956	P.E.Richardson
4	174	1	80	Australia	Old Trafford	1956	P.E.Richardson
5	121	4	59	South Africa	Johannesburg (3)	1956/57	P.E.Richardson
6	411	4	154	West Indies	Edgbaston	1957	P.B.H.May
7	174	7	152	West Indies	Lord's	1957	T.G.Evans
8	121	4	81	New Zealand	Edgbaston	1958	P.B.H.May
9	104	4	70	New Zealand	Edgbaston	1958	P.E.Richardson
10	118	5	44	Australia	Melbourne	1958/59	P.B.H.May
11	182	4	100*	Australia	Sydney	1958/59	P.B.H.May
12	193	4	160	India	Headingley	1959	K.F.Barrington

13	131	2	67	India	Old Trafford	1959	G.Pullar
14	177	1	97	West Indies	Kingston	1959/60	G.Pullar
15	191	2	119	West Indies	Port-of-Spain	1959/60	E.R.Dexter
16	290	1	155	South Africa	The Oval	1960	G.Pullar
17	166	2	159	Pakistan	Edgbaston	1962	E.R.Dexter
18	107	3	159	Pakistan	Edgbaston	1962	T.W.Graveney
19	117	1	182	Pakistan	The Oval	1962	Rev.D.S.Sheppard
20	248	2	182	Pakistan	The Oval	1962	E.R.Dexter
21	175	3	113	Australia	Melbourne	1962/63	E.R.Dexter
22	104	3	58*	Australia	Melbourne	1962/63	Rev.D.S.Sheppard
23	166	4	86	New Zealand	Auckland	1962/63	K.F.Barrington
24	163*	9	128*	New Zealand	Wellington	1962/63	A.C.Smith
25	115	5	151	India	Delhi	1963/64	P.H.Parfitt
26	126*	5	93*	Australia	The Oval	1964	K.F.Barrington
27	136	4	85	New Zealand	Edgbaston	1965	K.F.Barrington
28	105	5	119	New Zealand	Lord's	1965	M.J.K.Smith
29	135	4	78*	South Africa	The Oval	1965	K.F.Barrington
30	105	4	104	Australia	Melbourne	1965/66	J.H.Edrich
31	138	6	79	Australia	Melbourne	1965/66	J.M.Parks
32	118	2	59	New Zealand	Auckland	1965/66	W.E.Russell
33	169	4	96	West Indies	Trent Bridge	1966	T.W.Graveney
34	134	3	72	West Indies	Port-of-Spain	1967/68	K.F.Barrington
35	129	2	101	West Indies	Kingston	1967/68	J.H.Edrich
36	101	3	101	West Indies	Kingston	1967/68	K.F.Barrington
37	133	3	148	West Indies	Port-of-Spain	1967/68	K.F.Barrington
38	113	6	148	West Indies	Port-of-Spain	1967/68	A.P.E.Knott
39	118	2	71	West Indies	Port-of-Spain	1967/68	G.Boycott
40	172	2	59	West Indies	Georgetown	1967/68	G.Boycott
41	127	6	82	West Indies	Georgetown	1967/68	A.P.E.Knott
42	108	2	104	Australia	Edgbaston	1968	J.H.Edrich

L.Hutton (41)

1	100	1	100	New Zealand	Old Trafford	1937	C.J.Barnett
2	128	2	100	New Zealand	Old Trafford	1937	J.Hardstaff jnr
3	219	1	100	Australia	Trent Bridge	1938	C.J.Barnett
4	382	2	364	Australia	The Oval	1938	M.Leyland
5	135	3	364	Australia	The Oval	1938	W.R.Hammond
6	215	6	364	Australia	The Oval	1938	J.Hardstaff jnr
7	248	4	196	West Indies	Lord's	1939	D.C.S.Compton
8	131	2	73	West Indies	The Oval	1939	N.Oldfield
9	264	3	165*	West Indies	The Oval	1939	W.R.Hammond
10	138	1	40	Australia	Melbourne	1946/47	C.Washbrook
11	137	1	94	Australia	Adelaide	1946/47	C.Washbrook
12	100	1	76	Australia	Adelaide	1946/47	C.Washbrook
13	150	2	122*	Australia	Sydney	1946/47	W.J.Edrich
14	141	1	100	South Africa	Headingley	1947	C.Washbrook
15	129	1	56	West Indies	Kingston	1947/48	J.D.B.Robertson
16	111	3	74	Australia	Trent Bridge	1948	D.C.S.Compton
17	168	1	81	Australia	Headingley	1948	C.Washbrook
18	129	1	57	Australia	Headingley	1948	C.Washbrook
19	359	1	158	South Africa	Johannesburg (2)	1948/49	C.Washbrook
20	134	2	87	South Africa	Cape Town	1948/49	J.F.Crapp
21	102	3	101	New Zealand	Headingley	1949	D.C.S.Compton
22	143	1	66	New Zealand	Lord's	1949	J.D.B.Robertson
23	103	1	73	New Zealand	Old Trafford	1949	C.Washbrook
24	147	1	206	New Zealand	The Oval	1949	R.T.Simpson
25	218	2	206	New Zealand	The Oval	1949	W.J.Edrich
26	109	3	202*	West Indies	The Oval	1950	D.C.S.Compton
27	131	2	79	Australia	Melbourne	1950/51	R.T.Simpson
28	144	2	63	South Africa	Trent Bridge	1951	R.T.Simpson
29	121	1	98*	South Africa	Old Trafford	1951	J.T.Ikin
30	129	2	100	South Africa	Headingley	1951	P.B.H.May
31	106	1	150	India	Lord's	1952	R.T.Simpson
32	158	2	150	India	Lord's	1952	P.B.H.May
33	143	1	86	India	The Oval	1952	Rev.D.S.Sheppard
34	168	2	145	Australia	Lord's	1953	T.W.Graveney
35	102	3	145	Australia	Lord's	1953	D.C.S.Compton
36	100	2	82	Australia	The Oval	1953	P.B.H.May
37	130	1	56	West Indies	Kingston	1953/54	W.Watson
38	107	2	77	West Indies	Bridgetown	1953/54	P.B.H.May
39	150	3	169	West Indies	Georgetown	1953/54	D.C.S.Compton
40	108	6	205	West Indies	Kingston	1953/54	T.G.Evans
41	105	7	205	West Indies	Kingston	1953/54	J.H.Wardle

G.A.Gooch (41)

1	101	3	54	Pakistan	Lord's	1978	D.I.Gower
2	111	1	55	New Zealand	Trent Bridge	1978	G.Boycott
3	145	3	83	India	Edgbaston	1979	G.Boycott
4	116	1	99	Australia	Melbourne	1979/80	G.Boycott
5	145	2	123	West Indies	Lord's	1980	C.J.Tavare
6	155+	1	83	West Indies	The Oval	1980	G.Boycott & B.C.Rose
7	120	3	116	West Indies	Bridgetown	1980/81	D.I.Gower
8	144	1	83	West Indies	St John's	1980/81	G.Boycott
9	132	1	71	India	Delhi	1981/82	G.Boycott
10	155	1	127	India	Madras (1)	1981/82	C.J.Tavare
11	116	2	70	Australia	Trent Bridge	1985	D.I.Gower
12	121	2	74	Australia	Old Trafford	1985	D.I.Gower
13	351	2	196	Australia	The Oval	1985	D.I.Gower
14	120	2	53	West Indies	Bridgetown	1985/86	D.I.Gower
15	127	1	51	West Indies	St John's	1985/86	W.N.Slack
16	147	5	114	India	Lord's	1986	D.R.Pringle
17	126	5	183	New Zealand	Lord's	1986	P.Willey
18	125	1	73	West Indies	Trent Bridge	1988	B.C.Broad
19	161	3	146	West Indies	Trent Bridge	1988	D.I.Gower
20	131	2	75	Sri Lanka	Lord's	1988	R.C.Russell
21	112	1	84	West Indies	Port-of-Spain	1989/90	W.Larkins
22	148	2	85	New Zealand	Lord's	1990	A.J.Stewart
23	170	1	154	New Zealand	Edgbaston	1990	M.A.Atherton
24	127	2	333	India	Lord's	1990	D.I.Gower
25	308	3	333	India	Lord's	1990	A.J.Lamb
26	192	4	333	India	Lord's	1990	R.A.Smith
27	204	1	123	India	Lord's	1990	M.A.Atherton
28	225	1	116	India	Old Trafford	1990	M.A.Atherton
29	176	1	88	India	The Oval	1990	M.A.Atherton
30	127	3	87	Australia	Adelaide	1990/91	R.A.Smith
31	203	1	117	Australia	Adelaide	1990/91	M.A.Atherton
32	108	1	68	West Indies	Trent Bridge	1991	M.A.Atherton
33	112	1	60	West Indies	The Oval	1991	H.Morris
34	139	2	174	Sri Lanka	Lord's	1991	A.J.Stewart
35	105	3	174	Sri Lanka	Lord's	1991	R.A.Smith
36	123	1	69	Pakistan	Lord's	1992	A.J.Stewart
37	168	1	135	Pakistan	Headingley	1992	M.A.Atherton
38	102	2	135	Pakistan	Headingley	1992	R.A.Smith
39	150	6	120	Australia	Trent Bridge	1993	G.P.Thorpe
40	108	4	59	Australia	Headingley	1993	M.A.Atherton
41	263	2	210	New Zealand	Trent Bridge	1994	M.A.Atherton

D.I.Gower (38)

1	101	3	56	Pakistan	Lord's	1978	G.A.Gooch
2	116	3	111	New Zealand	The Oval	1978	C.T.Radley
3	114	3	71	New Zealand	Lord's	1978	C.T.Radley
4	158	4	102	Australia	Perth	1978/79	G.Boycott
5	191	4	200*	India	Edgbaston	1979	G.Boycott
6	165*	6	200*	India	Edgbaston	1979	G.Miller
7	114	4	82	India	Lord's	1979	D.W.Randall
8	120	3	54	West Indies	Bridgetown	1980/81	G.A.Gooch
9	136	4	154*	West Indies	Kingston	1980/81	P.Willey
10	123	3	89	Australia	Lord's	1981	G.Boycott
11	105	5	74	India	Calcutta	1981/82	K.W.R.Fletcher
12	127	4	85	India	Kanpur	1981/82	I.T.Botham
13	127	3	74	Pakistan	Edgbaston	1982	C.J.Tavare
14	119	3	60	Australia	Adelaide	1982/83	A.J.Lamb
15	118	4	114	Australia	Adelaide	1982/83	I.T.Botham
16	122	4	70	Australia	Sydney	1982/83	D.W.Randall
17	149	2	108	New Zealand	Lord's	1983	C.J.Tavare
18	116	5	152	Pakistan	Faisalabad	1983/84	G.Fowler
19	167	7	152	Pakistan	Faisalabad	1983/84	V.J.Marks
20	137	3	173*	Pakistan	Lahore (2)	1983/84	M.W.Gatting
21	119	6	173*	Pakistan	Lahore (2)	1983/84	V.J.Marks
22	100	7	78	India	Kanpur	1984/85	P.H.Edmonds
23	116	2	166	Australia	Trent Bridge	1985	G.A.Gooch
24	187	3	166	Australia	Trent Bridge	1985	M.W.Gatting
25	121	2	47	Australia	Old Trafford	1985	G.A.Gooch
26	331	2	215	Australia	Edgbaston	1985	R.T.Robinson
27	351	2	157	Australia	The Oval	1985	G.A.Gooch
28	106	4	66	West Indies	Port-of-Spain	1985/86	A.J.Lamb
29	120	2	66	West Indies	Bridgetown	1985/86	G.A.Gooch
30	223	4	131	New Zealand	The Oval	1986	M.W.Gatting
31	118	5	51	Australia	Brisbane (2)	1986/87	I.T.Botham

32	207	6	136	Australia	Perth	1986/87	C.J.Richards
33	161	3	88*	West Indies	Trent Bridge	1988	G.A.Gooch
34	139	5	106	Australia	Lord's	1989	R.A.Smith
35	127	2	40	India	Lord's	1990	G.A.Gooch
36	129	4	157*	India	The Oval	1990	A.J.Lamb
37	122	5	100	Australia	Melbourne	1990/91	A.J.Stewart
38	139	4	123	Australia	Sydney	1990/91	M.A.Atherton

K.F.Barrington (35)

1	125	4	56	India	Trent Bridge	1959	P.B.H.May
2	193	4	80	India	Headingley	1959	M.C.Cowdrey
3	109	4	87	India	Old Trafford	1959	M.J.K.Smith
4	103	2	128	West Indies	Bridgetown	1959/60	G.Pullar
5	142	4	121	West Indies	Port-of-Spain	1959/60	E.R.Dexter
6	161	4	48*	Australia	Edgbaston	1961	E.R.Dexter
7	172	5	83	Australia	The Oval	1961	R.Subba Row
8	192	3	139	Pakistan	Lahore (2)	1961/62	M.J.K.Smith
9	161	4	151*	India	Bombay (2)	1961/62	E.R.Dexter
10	139	2	172	India	Kanpur	1961/62	G.Pullar
11	206	4	172	India	Kanpur	1961/62	E.R.Dexter
12	164	2	113*	India	Delhi	1961/62	G.Pullar
13	147	2	84	Pakistan	Dacca	1961/62	G.Pullar
14	101*	5	132*	Australia	Adelaide	1962/63	T.W.Graveney
15	166	4	126	New Zealand	Auckland	1962/63	M.C.Cowdrey
16	119	4	80	India	Madras (2)	1963/64	J.B.Bolus
17	246	3	256	Australia	Old Trafford	1964	E.R.Dexter
18	143	5	256	Australia	Old Trafford	1964	J.M.Parks
19	126*	5	54*	Australia	The Oval	1964	M.C.Cowdrey
20	206*	6	148*	South Africa	Durban (2)	1964/65	J.M.Parks
21	191	3	121	South Africa	Johannesburg (3)	1964/65	E.R.Dexter
22	100	4	93	South Africa	Johannesburg (3)	1964/65	P.H.Parfitt
23	157	4	72	South Africa	Port Elizabeth	1964/65	G.Boycott
24	136	4	137	New Zealand	Edgbaston	1965	M.C.Cowdrey
25	369	2	163	New Zealand	Headingley	1965	J.H.Edrich
26	135	4	73	South Africa	The Oval	1965	M.C.Cowdrey
27	118	3	63	Australia	Melbourne	1965/66	J.H.Edrich
28	178	3	115	Australia	Melbourne	1965/66	J.H.Edrich
29	139	2	93	India	Headingley	1967	G.Boycott
30	201	3	148	Pakistan	Lord's	1967	T.W.Graveney
31	141	3	142	Pakistan	The Oval	1967	T.W.Graveney
32	134	3	143	West Indies	Port-of-Spain	1967/68	M.C.Cowdrey
33	188	4	143	West Indies	Port-of-Spain	1967/68	T.W.Graveney
34	101	3	63	West Indies	Kingston	1967/68	M.C.Cowdrey
35	133	3	48	West Indies	Port-of-Spain	1967/68	M.C.Cowdrey

H.Sutcliffe (33)

1	136	1	64	South Africa	Edgbaston	1924	J.B.Hobbs
2	268	1	122	South Africa	Lord's	1924	J.B.Hobbs
3	157	1	59	Australia	Sydney	1924/25	J.B.Hobbs
4	110	1	115	Australia	Sydney	1924/25	J.B.Hobbs
5	283	1	176	Australia	Melbourne	1924/25	J.B.Hobbs
6	126	1	143	Australia	Melbourne	1924/25	J.B.Hobbs
7	106	2	143	Australia	Melbourne	1924/25	J.W.Hearne
8	182	1	82	Australia	Lord's	1926	J.B.Hobbs
9	156	1	94	Australia	Headingley	1926	J.B.Hobbs
10	172	1	161	Australia	The Oval	1926	J.B.Hobbs
11	230	2	102	South Africa	Johannesburg (1)	1927/28	G.E.Tyldesley
12	140	1	99	South Africa	Cape Town	1927/28	P.Holmes
13	130	2	51	South Africa	Durban (2)	1927/28	G.E.Tyldesley
14	119	1	54	West Indies	Old Trafford	1928	J.B.Hobbs
15	155	1	63	West Indies	The Oval	1928	J.B.Hobbs
16	133	2	58	Australia	Melbourne	1928/29	W.R.Hammond
17	105	1	135	Australia	Melbourne	1928/29	J.B.Hobbs
18	143	1	64	Australia	Adelaide	1928/29	J.B.Hobbs
19	221	2	114	South Africa	Edgbaston	1929	W.R.Hammond
20	187*	2	109*	South Africa	The Oval	1929	W.R.Hammond
21	125	1	58*	Australia	Trent Bridge	1930	J.B.Hobbs
22	108	1	74	Australia	Old Trafford	1930	J.B.Hobbs
23	170	6	161	Australia	The Oval	1930	R.E.S.Wyatt
24	178	2	117	New Zealand	The Oval	1931	K.S.Duleepsinhji
25	126	2	109*	New Zealand	Old Trafford	1931	K.S.Duleepsinhji
26	112	1	194	Australia	Sydney	1932/33	R.E.S.Wyatt
27	188	2	194	Australia	Sydney	1932/33	W.R.Hammond
28	123	3	194	Australia	Sydney	1932/33	Nawab of Pataudi snr
29	114	1	86	Australia	Brisbane (2)	1932/33	D.R.Jardine

30	122	2	56	Australia	Sydney	1932/33	W.R.Hammond
31	123*	1	69*	Australia	Old Trafford	1934	C.F.Walters
32	104	1	38	Australia	The Oval	1934	C.F.Walters
33	118	1	61	South Africa	Trent Bridge	1935	R.E.S.Wyatt

W.R.Hammond (33)

1	127	3	90	South Africa	Durban (2)	1927/28	G.E.Tyldesley
2	120	4	63	West Indies	Old Trafford	1928	D.R.Jardine
3	145	4	251	Australia	Sydney	1928/29	E.H.Hendren
4	133	2	200	Australia	Melbourne	1928/29	H.Sutcliffe
5	126	5	200	Australia	Melbourne	1928/29	D.R.Jardine
6	262	3	177	Australia	Adelaide	1928/29	D.R.Jardine
7	221	2	138*	South Africa	Edgbaston	1929	H.Sutcliffe
8	187*	2	101*	South Africa	The Oval	1929	H.Sutcliffe
9	101	4	63	South Africa	Johannesburg (1)	1930/31	M.J.L.Turnbull
10	160	1	136*	South Africa	Durban (2)	1930/31	R.E.S.Wyatt
11	119	3	75	South Africa	Johannesburg (1)	1930/31	E.H.Hendren
12	130	4	100*	New Zealand	The Oval	1931	L.E.G.Ames
13	188	2	112	Australia	Sydney	1932/33	H.Sutcliffe
14	122	2	101	Australia	Sydney	1932/33	H.Sutcliffe
15	125*	3	75*	Australia	Sydney	1932/33	R.E.S.Wyatt
16	242	5	227	New Zealand	Christchurch	1932/33	L.E.G.Ames
17	149	3	336*	New Zealand	Auckland	1932/33	E.Paynter
18	129	4	87*	South Africa	Headingley	1935	R.E.S.Wyatt
19	151	4	65	South Africa	The Oval	1935	M.Leyland
20	134	2	167	India	Old Trafford	1936	A.E.Fagg
21	127	3	167	India	Old Trafford	1936	T.S.Worthington
22	266	4	217	India	The Oval	1936	T.S.Worthington
23	129	3	231*	Australia	Sydney	1936/37	M.Leyland
24	104	4	231*	Australia	Sydney	1936/37	L.E.G.Ames
25	245	3	140	New Zealand	Lord's	1937	J.Hardstaff jnr
26	222	4	240	Australia	Lord's	1938	E.Paynter
27	186	6	240	Australia	Lord's	1938	L.E.G.Ames
28	135	3	59	Australia	The Oval	1938	L.Hutton
29	109	3	181	South Africa	Cape Town	1938/39	P.A.Gibb
30	197	4	181	South Africa	Cape Town	1938/39	L.E.G.Ames
31	242	3	120	South Africa	Durban (2)	1938/39	E.Paynter
32	164	4	140	South Africa	Durban (2)	1938/39	E.Paynter
33	264	3	138	West Indies	The Oval	1939	L.Hutton

J.B.Hobbs (32)

1	134	2	72	Australia	Sydney	1907/08	G.Gunn
2	105*	1	62*	Australia	Edgbaston	1909	C.B.Fry
3	159	1	89	South Africa	Johannesburg (1)	1909/10	W.Rhodes
4	221	1	187	South Africa	Cape Town	1909/10	W.Rhodes
5	112	2	126*	Australia	Melbourne	1911/12	G.Gunn
6	147	1	187	Australia	Adelaide	1911/12	W.Rhodes
7	323	1	178	Australia	Melbourne	1911/12	W.Rhodes
8	112	1	107	Australia	Lord's	1912	W.Rhodes
9	107	1	66	Australia	The Oval	1912	W.Rhodes
10	100	1	92	South Africa	Johannesburg (1)	1913/14	W.Rhodes
11	133	1	97	South Africa	Durban (1)	1913/14	W.Rhodes
12	100	2	59	Australia	Sydney	1920/21	J.W.Hearne
13	142	3	122	Australia	Melbourne	1920/21	E.H.Hendren
14	105	2	123	Australia	Adelaide	1920/21	J.W.H.Makepeace
15	136	1	76	South Africa	Edgbaston	1924	H.Sutcliffe
16	268	1	211	South Africa	Lord's	1924	H.Sutcliffe
17	142	2	211	South Africa	Lord's	1924	F.E.Woolley
18	157	1	115	Australia	Sydney	1924/25	H.Sutcliffe
19	110	1	57	Australia	Sydney	1924/25	H.Sutcliffe
20	283	1	154	Australia	Melbourne	1924/25	H.Sutcliffe
21	117	7	119	Australia	Adelaide	1924/25	E.H.Hendren
22	126	1	66	Australia	Melbourne	1924/25	H.Sutcliffe
23	182	1	119	Australia	Lord's	1926	H.Sutcliffe
24	156	1	88	Australia	Headingley	1926	H.Sutcliffe
25	172	1	100	Australia	The Oval	1926	H.Sutcliffe
26	119	1	53	West Indies	Old Trafford	1928	H.Sutcliffe
27	155	1	159	West Indies	The Oval	1928	H.Sutcliffe
28	129	2	159	West Indies	The Oval	1928	G.E.Tyldesley
29	105	1	49	Australia	Melbourne	1928/29	H.Sutcliffe
30	143	1	74	Australia	Adelaide	1928/29	H.Sutcliffe
31	125	1	74	Australia	Trent Bridge	1930	H.Sutcliffe
32	108	1	31	Australia	Old Trafford	1930	H.Sutcliffe

J.H.Edrich (32)

1	101	1	41	India	Delhi	1963/64	J.B.Bolus
2	369	2	310*	New Zealand	Headingley	1965	K.F.Barrington
3	109	4	310*	New Zealand	Headingley	1965	P.H.Parfitt
4	118	3	109	Australia	Melbourne	1965/66	K.F.Barrington
5	105	4	109	Australia	Melbourne	1965/66	M.C.Cowdrey
6	178	3	85	Australia	Melbourne	1965/66	K.F.Barrington
7	129	2	96	West Indies	Kingston	1967/68	M.C.Cowdrey
8	172	1	146	West Indies	Bridgetown	1967/68	G.Boycott
9	109	4	146	West Indies	Bridgetown	1967/68	T.W.Graveney
10	108	2	88	Australia	Edgbaston	1968	M.C.Cowdrey
11	123	1	62	Australia	Headingley	1968	R.M.Prideaux
12	125	4	164	Australia	The Oval	1968	T.W.Graveney
13	121	5	164	Australia	The Oval	1968	B.L.D'Oliveira
14	112	1	58	West Indies	Old Trafford	1969	G.Boycott
15	125	1	115	New Zealand	Lord's	1969	G.Boycott
16	249	2	155	New Zealand	Trent Bridge	1969	P.J.Sharpe
17	109	3	79	Australia	Brisbane (2)	1970/71	A.P.E.Knott
18	161*	1	74*	Australia	Melbourne	1970/71	G.Boycott
19	107	1	130	Australia	Adelaide	1970/71	G.Boycott
20	169	2	130	Australia	Adelaide	1970/71	K.W.R.Fletcher
21	103	1	40	Australia	Adelaide	1970/71	G.Boycott
22	123	2	59	India	Old Trafford	1971	B.W.Luckhurst
23	106	2	41	India	The Oval	1971	J.A.Jameson
24	109*	4	100*	India	Old Trafford	1974	M.H.Denness
25	221	2	96	India	Lord's	1974	D.L.Amiss
26	149	3	70	Australia	Melbourne	1974/75	M.H.Denness
27	117	3	64	New Zealand	Auckland	1974/75	M.H.Denness
28	111	1	175	Australia	Lord's	1975	B.Wood
29	104	2	175	Australia	Lord's	1975	D.S.Steele
30	112	2	62	Australia	Headingley	1975	D.S.Steele
31	125	2	96	Australia	The Oval	1975	D.S.Steele
32	101*	3	76*	West Indies	Trent Bridge	1976	D.B.Close

D.C.S.Compton (30)

1	125	4	65	New Zealand	The Oval	1937	J.Hardstaff jnr
2	206	5	102	Australia	Trent Bridge	1938	E.Paynter
3	248	4	120	West Indies	Lord's	1939	L.Hutton
4	118	4	147	Australia	Adelaide	1946/47	J.Hardstaff jnr
5	102	3	54	Australia	Sydney	1946/47	W.J.Edrich
6	106	3	65	South Africa	Trent Bridge	1947	W.J.Edrich
7	237	3	163	South Africa	Trent Bridge	1947	N.W.D.Yardley
8	370	3	208	South Africa	Lord's	1947	W.J.Edrich
9	228	3	115	South Africa	Old Trafford	1947	W.J.Edrich
10	111	3	184	Australia	Trent Bridge	1948	L.Hutton
11	121	8	145*	Australia	Old Trafford	1948	A.V.Bedser
12	103	3	66	Australia	Headingley	1948	W.J.Edrich
13	150	3	114	South Africa	Johannesburg (2)	1948/49	J.F.Crapp
14	111*	4	51*	South Africa	Cape Town	1948/49	A.J.Watkins
15	102	3	114	New Zealand	Headingley	1949	L.Hutton
16	189	6	116	New Zealand	Lord's	1949	T.E.Bailey
17	109	4	44	West Indies	The Oval	1950	L.Hutton
18	129	3	79	New Zealand	Christchurch	1950/51	R.T.Simpson
19	141	4	112	South Africa	Trent Bridge	1951	W.Watson
20	122	4	79	South Africa	Lord's	1951	W.Watson
21	102	3	57	Australia	Lord's	1953	L.Hutton
22	150	3	64	West Indies	Georgetown	1953/54	L.Hutton
23	166	3	133	West Indies	Port-of-Spain	1953/54	P.B.H.May
24	110	5	133	West Indies	Port-of-Spain	1953/54	T.W.Graveney
25	154	4	278	Pakistan	Trent Bridge	1954	T.W.Graveney
26	192	5	278	Pakistan	Trent Bridge	1954	T.E.Bailey
27	134	5	84	Australia	Sydney	1954/55	T.E.Bailey
28	144	5	158	South Africa	Old Trafford	1955	T.E.Bailey
29	124	3	71	South Africa	Old Trafford	1955	P.B.H.May
30	156	4	94	Australia	The Oval	1956	P.B.H.May

T.W.Graveney (26)

1	148	5	175	India	Bombay (2)	1951/52	A.J.Watkins
2	159	6	73	India	Lord's	1952	T.G.Evans
3	168	2	78	Australia	Lord's	1953	L.Hutton
4	110	5	92	West Indies	Port-of-Spain	1953/54	D.C.S.Compton
5	154	4	84	Pakistan	Trent Bridge	1954	D.C.S.Compton
6	182	2	111	Australia	Sydney	1954/55	P.B.H.May
7	132	2	60	South Africa	Lord's	1955	P.B.H.May
8	266	2	258	West Indies	Trent Bridge	1957	P.E.Richardson

9	207	3	258	West Indies	Trent Bridge	1957	P.B.H.May
10	146	2	164	West Indies	The Oval	1957	P.E.Richardson
11	107	3	97	Pakistan	Edgbaston	1962	M.C.Cowdrey
12	184	4	114	Pakistan	Trent Bridge	1962	P.H.Parfitt
13	101*	5	36*	Australia	Adelaide	1962/63	K.F.Barrington
14	115	2	96	West Indies	Lord's	1966	G.Boycott
15	130*	5	30*	West Indies	Lord's	1966	C.Milburn
16	169	4	109	West Indies	Trent Bridge	1966	M.C.Cowdrey
17	217	8	165	West Indies	The Oval	1966	J.T.Murray
18	107	3	59	India	Headingley	1967	G.Boycott
19	122	4	151	India	Lord's	1967	B.L.D'Oliveira
20	201	3	81	Pakistan	Lord's	1967	K.F.Barrington
21	141	3	77	Pakistan	The Oval	1967	K.F.Barrington
22	188	4	118	West Indies	Port-of-Spain	1967/68	K.F.Barrington
23	109	4	55	West Indies	Bridgetown	1967/68	J.H.Edrich
24	125	4	63	Australia	The Oval	1968	J.H.Edrich
25	156	2	105	Pakistan	Karachi (1)	1968/69	C.Milburn
26	128	3	75	West Indies	Old Trafford	1969	G.Boycott

M.A.Atherton (26)

1	170	1	82	New Zealand	Edgbaston	1990	G.A.Gooch
2	204	1	72	India	Lord's	1990	G.A.Gooch
3	225	1	131	India	Old Trafford	1990	G.A.Gooch
4	134	3	74	India	Old Trafford	1990	A.J.Lamb
5	176	1	86	India	The Oval	1990	G.A.Gooch
6	139	4	105	Australia	Sydney	1990/91	D.I.Gower
7	203	1	87	Australia	Adelaide	1990/91	G.A.Gooch
8	108	1	32	West Indies	Trent Bridge	1991	G.A.Gooch
9	168	1	76	Pakistan	Headingley	1992	G.A.Gooch
10	104	2	99	Australia	Lord's	1993	M.W.Gatting
11	108	4	55	Australia	Headingley	1993	G.A.Gooch
12	121	1	55	West Indies	Kingston	1993/94	A.J.Stewart
13	171	3	144	West Indies	Georgetown	1993/94	R.A.Smith
14	171	1	85	West Indies	Bridgetown	1993/94	A.J.Stewart
15	303	3	135	West Indies	St John's	1993/94	R.A.Smith
16	263	2	101	New Zealand	Trent Bridge	1994	G.A.Gooch
17	142	3	99	South Africa	Headingley	1994	G.P.Thorpe
18	124	2	63	South Africa	The Oval	1994	G.A.Hick
19	174	4	88	Australia	Sydney	1994/95	J.P.Crawley
20	104	2	67	Australia	Sydney	1994/95	G.A.Hick
21	148	1	113	West Indies	Trent Bridge	1995	N.V.Knight
22	142	4	78	South Africa	Centurion	1995/96	G.A.Hick
23	119*	6	185*	South Africa	Johannesburg (3)	1995/96	R.C.Russell
24	130	1	160	India	Trent Bridge	1996	A.J.Stewart
25	230+	2	160	India	Trent Bridge	1996	N.Hussain & G.P.Thorpe
26	154	2	64	Pakistan	Lord's	1996	A.J.Stewart

M.W.Gatting (24)

1	120*	4	51*	Australia	Lord's	1980	G.Boycott
2	115	3	53	Australia	The Oval	1981	G.Boycott
3	101	5	32	India	Kanpur	1981/82	I.T.Botham
4	127	1	75	Pakistan	Faisalabad	1983/84	C.L.Smith
5	137	3	53	Pakistan	Lahore (2)	1983/84	D.I.Gower
6	135	2	136	India	Bombay (3)	1984/85	G.Fowler
7	241	2	207	India	Madras (1)	1984/85	G.Fowler
8	144	3	207	India	Madras (1)	1984/85	A.J.Lamb
9	136	3	53	Australia	Headingley	1985	R.T.Robinson
10	131	7	75*	Australia	Lord's	1985	I.T.Botham
11	187	3	74	Australia	Trent Bridge	1985	D.I.Gower
12	156	4	160	Australia	Old Trafford	1985	A.J.Lamb
13	109	4	100*	Australia	Edgbaston	1985	A.J.Lamb
14	223	4	121	New Zealand	The Oval	1986	D.I.Gower
15	101	2	61	Australia	Brisbane (2)	1986/87	C.W.J.Athey
16	161	2	100	Australia	Adelaide	1986/87	B.C.Broad
17	105	2	40	Australia	Melbourne	1986/87	B.C.Broad
18	131	6	96	Australia	Sydney	1986/87	C.J.Richards
19	102	2	43	Pakistan	Lord's	1987	C.W.J.Athey
20	143	7	124	Pakistan	Edgbaston	1987	J.E.Emburey
21	176*	1	150*	Pakistan	The Oval	1987	I.T.Botham
22	117	3	79	Pakistan	Faisalabad	1987/88	B.C.Broad
23	121	4	61	India	Bombay (3)	1992/93	R.A.Smith
24	104	2	59	Australia	Lord's	1993	M.A.Atherton

P.B.H.May (23)

1	129	2	138	South Africa	Headingley	1951	L.Hutton

2	158	2	74	India	Lord's	1952	L.Hutton
3	100	2	39	Australia	The Oval	1953	L.Hutton
4	107	2	62	West Indies	Bridgetown	1953/54	L.Hutton
5	166	3	135	West Indies	Port-of-Spain	1953/54	D.C.S.Compton
6	124	3	44	Australia	Brisbane (2)	1954/55	W.J.Edrich
7	116	4	104	Australia	Sydney	1954/55	M.C.Cowdrey
8	182	4	79	Australia	Sydney	1954/55	T.W.Graveney
9	132	2	112	South Africa	Lord's	1955	T.W.Graveney
10	124	3	117	South Africa	Old Trafford	1955	D.C.S.Compton
11	108	4	117	South Africa	Old Trafford	1955	M.C.Cowdrey
12	101	3	97	South Africa	Headingley	1955	D.J.Insole
13	108	3	73	Australia	Trent Bridge	1956	P.E.Richardson
14	187	4	101	Australia	Headingley	1956	C.Washbrook
15	156	4	83*	Australia	The Oval	1956	D.C.S.Compton
16	411	4	285*	West Indies	Edgbaston	1957	M.C.Cowdrey
17	207	3	104	West Indies	Trent Bridge	1957	T.W.Graveney
18	121	4	84	New Zealand	Edgbaston	1958	M.C.Cowdrey
19	194*	3	113*	New Zealand	Headingley	1958	C.A.Milton
20	118	5	113	Australia	Melbourne	1958/59	M.C.Cowdrey
21	182	4	92	Australia	Sydney	1958/59	M.C.Cowdrey
22	125	4	106	India	Trent Bridge	1959	K.F.Barrington
23	111	3	95	Australia	Old Trafford	1961	G.Pullar

E.R.Dexter (23)

1	123	7	136*	West Indies	Bridgetown	1959/60	R.Swetman
2	142	4	77	West Indies	Port-of-Spain	1959/60	K.F.Barrington
3	148	3	110	West Indies	Georgetown	1959/60	R.Subba Row
4	191	2	76	West Indies	Port-of-Spain	1959/60	M.C.Cowdrey
5	109	2	180	Australia	Edgbaston	1961	R.Subba Row
6	161	4	180	Australia	Edgbaston	1961	K.F.Barrington
7	110	2	76	Australia	Old Trafford	1961	R.Subba Row
8	101*	6	66*	Pakistan	Lahore (2)	1961/62	R.W.Barber
9	161	4	85	India	Bombay (2)	1961/62	K.F.Barrington
10	206	4	126*	India	Kanpur	1961/62	K.F.Barrington
11	143	3	205	Pakistan	Karachi (1)	1961/62	M.J.K.Smith
12	188	4	205	Pakistan	Karachi (1)	1961/62	P.H.Parfitt
13	166	2	72	Pakistan	Edgbaston	1962	M.C.Cowdrey
14	161	4	85	Pakistan	Trent Bridge	1962	Rev.D.S.Sheppard
15	248	2	172	Pakistan	The Oval	1962	M.C.Cowdrey
16	175	3	93	Australia	Melbourne	1962/63	M.C.Cowdrey
17	124	2	52	Australia	Melbourne	1962/63	Rev.D.S.Sheppard
18	101	5	57	West Indies	Edgbaston	1963	P.J.Sharpe
19	111	2	174	Australia	Old Trafford	1964	G.Boycott
20	246	3	174	Australia	Old Trafford	1964	K.F.Barrington
21	136	2	172	South Africa	Johannesburg (3)	1964/65	R.W.Barber
22	191	3	172	South Africa	Johannesburg (3)	1964/65	K.F.Barrington
23	126	3	80*	New Zealand	Lord's	1965	G.Boycott

D.L.Amiss (21)

1	105	1	112	Pakistan	Lahore (2)	1972/73	M.H.Denness
2	168	2	158	Pakistan	Hyderabad	1972/73	K.W.R.Fletcher
3	130	2	99	Pakistan	Karachi (1)	1972/73	K.W.R.Fletcher
4	210	5	138*	New Zealand	Trent Bridge	1973	A.W.Greig
5	112	1	53	New Zealand	Lord's	1973	G.Boycott
6	119+	1	56	West Indies	Edgbaston	1973	G.Boycott & B.W.Luckhurst
7	209	1	174	West Indies	Port-of-Spain	1973/74	G.Boycott
8	119	2	174	West Indies	Port-of-Spain	1973/74	M.H.Denness
9	100	3	118	West Indies	Georgetown	1973/74	K.W.R.Fletcher
10	116	1	188	India	Lord's	1974	D.Lloyd
11	221	2	188	India	Lord's	1974	J.H.Edrich
12	157	1	79	India	Edgbaston	1974	D.Lloyd
13	129	4	183	Pakistan	The Oval	1974	D.L.Underwood
14	139+	5	183	Pakistan	The Oval	1974	K.W.R.Fletcher & A.W.Greig
15	115	1	90	Australia	Melbourne	1974/75	D.Lloyd
16	151*	3	164*	New Zealand	Christchurch	1974/75	M.H.Denness
17	100	2	203	West Indies	The Oval	1976	D.S.Steele
18	128	4	203	West Indies	The Oval	1976	P.Willey
19	101	6	179	India	Delhi	1976/77	A.P.E.Knott
20	146	1	50	India	Bombay (3)	1976/77	J.M.Brearley
21	166	3	64	Australia	Melbourne	1976/77	D.W.Randall

A.J.Lamb (21)

1	176	4	107	India	The Oval	1982	I.T.Botham
2	119	3	82	Australia	Adelaide	1982/83	D.I.Gower
3	161	4	83	Australia	Melbourne	1982/83	C.J.Tavare

4	110*	7	102*	New Zealand	The Oval	1983	P.H.Edmonds
5	100	3	58	New Zealand	Headingley	1983	C.J.Tavare
6	128	5	110	West Indies	Lord's	1984	I.T.Botham
7	110	3	52	India	Delhi	1984/85	R.T.Robinson
8	144	3	62	India	Madras (1)	1984/85	M.W.Gatting
9	156	4	67	Australia	Old Trafford	1985	M.W.Gatting
10	109	4	46	Australia	Edgbaston	1985	M.W.Gatting
11	106	4	62	West Indies	Port-of-Spain	1985/86	D.I.Gower
12	103+	5	64*	West Indies	Headingley	1988	R.A.Smith & C.S.Cowdrey
13	114	3	125	Australia	Headingley	1989	K.J.Barnett
14	172	4	132	West Indies	Kingston	1989/90	R.A.Smith
15	193	4	119	West Indies	Bridgetown	1989/90	R.A.Smith
16	308	3	139	India	Lord's	1990	G.A.Gooch
17	134	3	109	India	Old Trafford	1990	M.A.Atherton
18	129	4	52	India	The Oval	1990	D.I.Gower
19	141	4	91	Australia	Perth	1990/91	R.A.Smith
20	122	4	142	New Zealand	Wellington	1991/92	R.A.Smith
21	105	7	142	New Zealand	Wellington	1991/92	R.C.Russell

I.T.Botham (19)

1	160	6	103	New Zealand	Christchurch	1977/78	R.W.Taylor
2	123	6	100	Pakistan	Edgbaston	1978	G.Miller
3	118	6	108	Pakistan	Lord's	1978	G.R.J.Roope
4	171	6	114	India	Bombay (3)	1979/80	R.W.Taylor
5	117	8	149*	Australia	Headingley	1981	G.R.Dilley
6	149	6	118	Australia	Old Trafford	1981	C.J.Tavare
7	127	4	142	India	Kanpur	1981/82	D.I.Gower
8	101	5	142	India	Kanpur	1981/82	M.W.Gatting
9	169	6	128	India	Old Trafford	1982	G.Miller
10	176	4	208	India	The Oval	1982	A.J.Lamb
11	151	5	208	India	The Oval	1982	D.W.Randall
12	112	4	69	Pakistan	Lord's	1982	C.J.Tavare
13	118	4	58	Australia	Adelaide	1982/83	D.I.Gower
14	186	6	103	New Zealand	Trent Bridge	1983	D.W.Randall
15	232	6	138	New Zealand	Wellington	1983/84	D.W.Randall
16	128	5	81	West Indies	Lord's	1984	A.J.Lamb
17	131	7	85	Australia	Lord's	1985	M.W.Gatting
18	118	5	138	Australia	Brisbane (2)	1986/87	D.I.Gower
19	176*	5	51*	Pakistan	The Oval	1987	M.W.Gatting

R.A.Smith (19)

1	103+	5	38	West Indies	Headingley	1988	A.J.Lamb & C.S.Cowdrey
2	139	5	96	Australia	Lord's	1989	D.I.Gower
3	172	4	57	West Indies	Kingston	1989/90	A.J.Lamb
4	193	4	62	West Indies	Bridgetown	1989/90	A.J.Lamb
5	192	4	100*	India	Lord's	1990	G.A.Gooch
6	127	3	53	Australia	Adelaide	1990/91	G.A.Gooch
7	141	3	58	Australia	Perth	1990/91	A.J.Lamb
8	105	3	63*	Sri Lanka	Lord's	1991	G.A.Gooch
9	179	3	96	New Zealand	Christchurch	1991/92	A.J.Stewart
10	122	4	76	New Zealand	Wellington	1991/92	A.J.Lamb
11	227	3	127	Pakistan	Edgbaston	1992	A.J.Stewart
12	102	2	42	Pakistan	Headingley	1992	G.A.Gooch
13	121	4	62	India	Bombay (3)	1992/93	M.W.Gatting
14	112	3	128	Sri Lanka	Colombo (2)	1992/93	G.A.Hick
15	122	4	128	Sri Lanka	Colombo (2)	1992/93	A.J.Stewart
16	171	3	84	West Indies	Georgetown	1993/94	M.A.Atherton
17	303	3	175	West Indies	St John's	1993/94	M.A.Atherton
18	111	4	61	West Indies	Lord's	1995	G.P.Thorpe
19	104	4	44	West Indies	Old Trafford	1995	G.P.Thorpe

W.Rhodes (17)

1	130	10	40*	Australia	Sydney	1903/04	R.E.Foster
2	113*	6	39*	Australia	Trent Bridge	1905	Hon.F.S.Jackson
3	104	3	66	Australia	The Oval	1909	C.B.Fry
4	159	1	66	South Africa	Johannesburg (1)	1909/10	J.B.Hobbs
5	221	1	77	South Africa	Cape Town	1909/10	J.B.Hobbs
6	127	2	61	Australia	Melbourne	1911/12	J.W.Hearne
7	147	1	59	Australia	Adelaide	1911/12	J.B.Hobbs
8	323	1	179	Australia	Melbourne	1911/12	J.B.Hobbs
9	102	2	179	Australia	Melbourne	1911/12	G.Gunn
10	124	2	36	South Africa	Lord's	1912	R.H.Spooner
11	112	1	59	Australia	Lord's	1912	J.B.Hobbs
12	107	1	49	Australia	The Oval	1912	J.B.Hobbs
13	141	1	152	South Africa	Johannesburg (1)	1913/14	A.E.Relf

14	152	3	152	South Africa	Johannesburg (1)	1913/14	C.P.Mead
15	100	1	35	South Africa	Johannesburg (1)	1913/14	J.B.Hobbs
16	133	1	35	South Africa	Durban (1)	1913/14	J.B.Hobbs
17	113	2	73	Australia	Melbourne	1920/21	J.W.H.Makepeace

K.W.R.Fletcher (17)

1	169	2	80	Australia	Adelaide	1970/71	J.H.Edrich
2	144	4	58	India	Kanpur	1972/73	A.R.Lewis
3	254	5	113	India	Bombay (2)	1972/73	A.W.Greig
4	168	2	78	Pakistan	Hyderabad	1972/73	D.L.Amiss
5	130	2	54	Pakistan	Karachi (1)	1972/73	D.L.Amiss
6	119	3	81	New Zealand	Headingley	1973	G.Boycott
7	142	6	129*	West Indies	Bridgetown	1973/74	A.P.E.Knott
8	100	3	41	West Indies	Georgetown	1973/74	D.L.Amiss
9	101	3	45	West Indies	Port-of-Spain	1973/74	G.Boycott
10	104	6	123*	India	Old Trafford	1974	A.W.Greig
11	139+	5	122	Pakistan	The Oval	1974	D.L.Amiss & A.W.Greig
12	130	7	122	Pakistan	The Oval	1974	C.M.Old
13	192	4	146	Australia	Melbourne	1974/75	M.H.Denness
14	148	5	146	Australia	Melbourne	1974/75	A.W.Greig
15	266	4	216	New Zealand	Auckland	1974/75	M.H.Denness
16	120	4	51	India	Delhi	1981/82	C.J.Tavare
17	105	5	60*	India	Calcutta	1981/82	D.I.Gower

A.J.Stewart (17)

1	148	2	54	New Zealand	Lord's	1990	G.A.Gooch
2	122	5	79	Australia	Melbourne	1990/91	D.I.Gower
3	139	2	43	Sri Lanka	Lord's	1991	G.A.Gooch
4	179	3	148	New Zealand	Christchurch	1991/92	R.A.Smith
5	227	3	190	Pakistan	Edgbaston	1992	R.A.Smith
6	123	1	74	Pakistan	Lord's	1992	G.A.Gooch
7	111	2	74	India	Madras (1)	1992/93	G.A.Hick
8	122	4	63	Sri Lanka	Colombo (2)	1992/93	R.A.Smith
9	121	1	70	West Indies	Kingston	1993/94	M.A.Atherton
10	171	1	118	West Indies	Bridgetown	1993/94	M.A.Atherton
11	115	4	143	West Indies	Bridgetown	1993/94	G.A.Hick
12	150	5	143	West Indies	Bridgetown	1993/94	G.P.Thorpe
13	115	5	89	South Africa	Headingley	1994	J.P.Crawley
14	130	1	50	India	Trent Bridge	1996	M.A.Atherton
15	154	2	89	Pakistan	Lord's	1996	M.A.Atherton
16	107	2	170	Pakistan	Headingley	1996	N.Hussain
17	108	5	170	Pakistan	Headingley	1996	N.V.Knight

A.P.E.Knott (16)

1	113	6	69*	West Indies	Port-of-Spain	1967/68	M.C.Cowdrey
2	127	6	73*	West Indies	Georgetown	1967/68	M.C.Cowdrey
3	128	6	53	West Indies	Lord's	1969	J.H.Hampshire
4	109	3	73	Australia	Brisbane (2)	1970/71	J.H.Edrich
5	149	7	101	New Zealand	Auckland	1970/71	P.Lever
6	159	7	116	Pakistan	Edgbaston	1971	P.Lever
7	103	7	90	India	The Oval	1971	R.A.Hutton
8	112	6	63*	Pakistan	Hyderabad	1972/73	A.W.Greig
9	163	6	87	West Indies	Bridgetown	1973/74	A.W.Greig
10	142	6	67	West Indies	Bridgetown	1973/74	K.W.R.Fletcher
11	119	6	61	West Indies	Georgetown	1973/74	A.W.Greig
12	151	6	64	Australia	The Oval	1975	R.A.Woolmer
13	152	6	116	West Indies	Headingley	1976	A.W.Greig
14	101	6	75	India	Delhi	1976/77	D.L.Amiss
15	215	6	135	Australia	Trent Bridge	1977	G.Boycott
16	123	6	57	Australia	Headingley	1977	G.Boycott

E.H.Hendren (15)

1	142	3	67	Australia	Melbourne	1920/21	J.B.Hobbs
2	121*	3	50*	South Africa	Lord's	1924	F.E.Woolley
3	101	5	142	South Africa	The Oval	1924	A.Sandham
4	117	7	92	Australia	Adelaide	1924/25	J.B.Hobbs
5	140	3	127*	Australia	Lord's	1926	F.E.Woolley
6	116*	4	127*	Australia	Lord's	1926	A.P.F.Chapman
7	124	8	169	Australia	Brisbane (1)	1928/29	H.Larwood
8	145	4	74	Australia	Sydney	1928/29	W.R.Hammond
9	140	6	95	Australia	Melbourne	1928/29	M.Leyland
10	168	3	80	West Indies	Bridgetown	1929/30	A.Sandham
11	237	4	205*	West Indies	Port-of-Spain	1929/30	L.E.G.Ames
12	104	4	48	Australia	Lord's	1930	K.S.Duleepsinhji
13	119	3	64	South Africa	Johannesburg (1)	1930/31	W.R.Hammond

| 14 | 101 | 7 | 79 | Australia | Trent Bridge | 1934 | G.Geary |
| 15 | 191 | 5 | 132 | Australia | Old Trafford | 1934 | M.Leyland |

M.Leyland (15)

1	140	6	137	Australia	Melbourne	1928/29	E.H.Hendren
2	129	6	102	South Africa	Lord's	1929	M.W.Tate
3	106	6	45	South Africa	Headingley	1929	F.E.Woolley
4	156	5	83	Australia	Adelaide	1932/33	R.E.S.Wyatt
5	129	5	109	Australia	Lord's	1934	L.E.G.Ames
6	191	5	153	Australia	Old Trafford	1934	E.H.Hendren
7	142	6	153	Australia	Old Trafford	1934	L.E.G.Ames
8	121+	6	110	Australia	The Oval	1934	L.E.G.Ames & G.O.B.Allen
9	139	4	69	South Africa	Trent Bridge	1935	R.E.S.Wyatt
10	105	6	53	South Africa	Old Trafford	1935	R.W.V.Robins
11	151	4	161	South Africa	The Oval	1935	W.R.Hammond
12	179	5	161	South Africa	The Oval	1935	L.E.G.Ames
13	129	3	42	Australia	Sydney	1936/37	W.R.Hammond
14	111	7	111*	Australia	Melbourne	1936/37	R.W.V.Robins
15	382	2	187	Australia	The Oval	1938	L.Hutton

C.Washbrook (15)

1	147	2	62	Australia	Melbourne	1946/47	W.J.Edrich
2	138	1	112	Australia	Melbourne	1946/47	L.Hutton
3	137	1	65	Australia	Adelaide	1946/47	L.Hutton
4	100	1	39	Australia	Adelaide	1946/47	L.Hutton
5	141	1	75	South Africa	Headingley	1947	L.Hutton
6	124	2	85*	Australia	Old Trafford	1948	W.J.Edrich
7	168	1	143	Australia	Headingley	1948	L.Hutton
8	100	2	143	Australia	Headingley	1948	W.J.Edrich
9	129	1	65	Australia	Headingley	1948	L.Hutton
10	359	1	195	South Africa	Johannesburg (2)	1948/49	L.Hutton
11	120	2	97	South Africa	Johannesburg (2)	1948/49	J.F.Crapp
12	118	2	103*	New Zealand	Headingley	1949	W.J.Edrich
13	103	1	44	New Zealand	Old Trafford	1949	L.Hutton
14	212	1	102	West Indies	Trent Bridge	1950	R.T.Simpson
15	187	4	98	Australia	Headingley	1956	P.B.H.May

A.W.Greig (15)

1	101*	5	40*	India	Delhi	1972/73	A.R.Lewis
2	254	5	148	India	Bombay (2)	1972/73	K.W.R.Fletcher
3	112	6	64	Pakistan	Hyderabad	1972/73	A.P.E.Knott
4	103+	5	48	Pakistan	Karachi (1)	1972/73	A.R.Lewis & P.I.Pocock
5	210	5	139	New Zealand	Trent Bridge	1973	D.L.Amiss
6	163	6	148	West Indies	Bridgetown	1973/74	A.P.E.Knott
7	119	6	121	West Indies	Georgetown	1973/74	A.P.E.Knott
8	104	6	53	India	Old Trafford	1974	K.W.R.Fletcher
9	202	5	106	India	Lord's	1974	M.H.Denness
10	139+	6	32	Pakistan	The Oval	1974	K.W.R.Fletcher & D.L.Amiss
11	148	5	89	Australia	Melbourne	1974/75	K.W.R.Fletcher
12	152	6	116	West Indies	Headingley	1976	A.P.E.Knott
13	142	5	103	India	Calcutta	1976/77	R.W.Tolchard
14	111+	4	54	India	Madras (1)	1976/77	J.M.Brearley & R.W.Tolchard
15	160	4	76	Australia	Old Trafford	1977	R.A.Woolmer

W.J.Edrich (14)

1	280	2	219	South Africa	Durban (2)	1938/39	P.A.Gibb
2	102	2	119	Australia	Sydney	1946/47	D.C.S.Compton
3	147	2	89	Australia	Melbourne	1946/47	C.Washbrook
4	150	2	60	Australia	Sydney	1946/47	L.Hutton
5	106	3	57	South Africa	Trent Bridge	1947	D.C.S.Compton
6	370	3	189	South Africa	Lord's	1947	D.C.S.Compton
7	228	3	191	South Africa	Old Trafford	1947	D.C.S.Compton
8	124	2	53	Australia	Old Trafford	1948	C.Washbrook
9	100	2	111	Australia	Headingley	1948	C.Washbrook
10	155	3	111	Australia	Headingley	1948	A.V.Bedser
11	103	3	54	Australia	Headingley	1948	D.C.S.Compton
12	118	2	70	New Zealand	Headingley	1949	C.Washbrook
13	218	2	100	New Zealand	The Oval	1949	L.Hutton
14	124	3	88	Australia	Brisbane (2)	1954/55	P.B.H.May

C.J.Tavare (14)

1	145	2	42	West Indies	Lord's	1980	G.A.Gooch
2	149	6	78	Australia	Old Trafford	1981	I.T.Botham
3	116	2	149	India	Delhi	1981/82	G.Boycott
4	120	4	149	India	Delhi	1981/82	K.W.R.Fletcher

5	155	1	35	India	Madras (1)	1981/82	G.A.Gooch
6	106	1	57	India	Old Trafford	1982	G.Cook
7	127	3	54	Pakistan	Edgbaston	1982	D.I.Gower
8	112	4	82	Pakistan	Lord's	1982	I.T.Botham
9	103	1	33	Pakistan	Headingley	1982	G.Fowler
10	100	5	89	Australia	Perth	1982/83	D.W.Randall
11	161	4	89	Australia	Melbourne	1982/83	A.J.Lamb
12	223	1	109	New Zealand	The Oval	1983	G.Fowler
13	100	3	69	New Zealand	Headingley	1983	A.J.Lamb
14	149	2	51	New Zealand	Lord's	1983	D.I.Gower

L.E.G.Ames (13)

1	237	4	105	West Indies	Port-of-Spain	1929/30	E.H.Hendren
2	249	4	149	West Indies	Kingston	1929/30	A.Sandham
3	246	8	137	New Zealand	Lord's	1931	G.O.B.Allen
4	130	4	41	New Zealand	The Oval	1931	W.R.Hammond
5	242	5	103	New Zealand	Christchurch	1932/33	W.R.Hammond
6	129	6	120	Australia	Lord's	1934	M.Leyland
7	142	6	72	Australia	Old Trafford	1934	M.Leyland
8	121+	6	33*	Australia	The Oval	1934	M.Leyland & G.O.B.Allen
9	157	6	126	West Indies	Kingston	1934/35	J.Iddon
10	179	5	148*	South Africa	The Oval	1935	M.Leyland
11	104	4	29	Australia	Sydney	1936/37	W.R.Hammond
12	186	6	83	Australia	Lord's	1938	W.R.Hammond
13	197	4	115	South Africa	Cape Town	1938/39	W.R.Hammond

T.W.Hayward (12)

1	119	3	122	South Africa	Johannesburg (1)	1895/96	C.B.Fry
2	122	4	122	South Africa	Johannesburg (1)	1895/96	A.J.L.Hill
3	136	2	72	Australia	Sydney	1897/98	A.C.MacLaren
4	113	7	130	Australia	Old Trafford	1899	A.F.A.Lilley
5	185	1	137	Australia	The Oval	1899	Hon.F.S.Jackson
6	131	2	137	Australia	The Oval	1899	K.S.Ranjitsinhji
7	154	1	69	Australia	Sydney	1901/02	A.C.MacLaren
8	149	1	90	Australia	Adelaide	1901/02	A.C.MacLaren
9	122	1	58	Australia	Melbourne	1903/04	P.F.Warner
10	148	1	67	Australia	Adelaide	1903/04	P.F.Warner
11	145	1	47	Australia	Trent Bridge	1905	A.C.MacLaren
12	100	3	59	Australia	The Oval	1905	C.B.Fry

F.E.Woolley (12)

1	100	4	64	South Africa	Cape Town	1909/10	F.L.Fane
2	143	7	133*	Australia	Sydney	1911/12	J.Vine
3	113	5	73	South Africa	Lord's	1912	P.F.Warner
4	111	5	57	South Africa	Headingley	1912	J.W.Hearne
5	104	5	54	South Africa	Port Elizabeth	1913/14	C.P.Mead
6	124	6	115*	South Africa	Johannesburg (1)	1922/23	F.T.Mann
7	142	4	134*	South Africa	Lord's	1924	J.B.Hobbs
8	121*	3	134*	South Africa	Lord's	1924	E.H.Hendren
9	128	9	123	Australia	Sydney	1924/25	A.P.Freeman
10	140	3	87	Australia	Lord's	1926	E.H.Hendren
11	106	6	83	South Africa	Headingley	1929	M.Leyland
12	245	3	154	South Africa	Old Trafford	1929	R.E.S.Wyatt

G.Pullar (12)

1	146	1	75	India	Headingley	1959	W.G.A.Parkhouse
2	131	2	131	India	Old Trafford	1959	M.C.Cowdrey
3	103	2	65	West Indies	Bridgetown	1959/60	K.F.Barrington
4	177	1	66	West Indies	Kingston	1959/60	M.C.Cowdrey
5	290	1	175	South Africa	The Oval	1960	M.C.Cowdrey
6	111	3	63	Australia	Old Trafford	1961	P.B.H.May
7	159	1	83	India	Bombay (2)	1961/62	P.E.Richardson
8	139	2	119	India	Kanpur	1961/62	K.F.Barrington
9	164	2	89	India	Delhi	1961/62	K.F.Barrington
10	198	1	165	Pakistan	Dacca	1961/62	R.W.Barber
11	147	2	165	Pakistan	Dacca	1961/62	K.F.Barrington
12	114	1	56	Australia	Brisbane (2)	1962/63	Rev.D.S.Sheppard

G.P.Thorpe (12)

1	150	6	114*	Australia	Trent Bridge	1993	G.A.Gooch
2	113*	7	114*	Australia	Trent Bridge	1993	N.Hussain
3	104	7	60	Australia	Edgbaston	1993	J.E.Emburey
4	150	5	84	West Indies	Bridgetown	1993/94	A.J.Stewart
5	142	3	72	South Africa	Headingley	1994	M.A.Atherton
6	133	3	73	South Africa	Headingley	1994	G.A.Hick

7	160	3	67	Australia	Brisbane (2)	1994/95	G.A.Hick
8	158	5	123	Australia	Perth	1994/95	M.R.Ramprakash
9	111	4	52	West Indies	Lord's	1995	R.A.Smith
10	104	4	94	West Indies	Old Trafford	1995	R.A.Smith
11	136	6	89	India	Lord's	1996	R.C.Russell
12	230+	2	45	India	Trent Bridge	1996	M.A.Atherton & N.Hussain

P.H.Parfitt (11)

1	188	4	111	Pakistan	Karachi (1)	1961/62	E.R.Dexter
2	153*	6	101*	Pakistan	Edgbaston	1962	D.A.Allen
3	184	4	101*	Pakistan	Trent Bridge	1962	T.W.Graveney
4	240	6	131*	New Zealand	Auckland	1962/63	B.R.Knight
5	115	5	67	India	Delhi	1963/64	M.C.Cowdrey
6	191	4	121	India	Kanpur	1963/64	B.R.Knight
7	100	4	122*	South Africa	Johannesburg (3)	1964/65	K.F.Barrington
8	109	4	32	New Zealand	Headingley	1965	J.H.Edrich
9	113	5	54	New Zealand	Christchurch	1965/66	M.J.K.Smith
10	125	5	46*	New Zealand	Christchurch	1965/66	M.J.K.Smith
11	117	2	46	Australia	Trent Bridge	1972	B.W.Luckhurst

A.C.MacLaren (10)

1	162	5	120	Australia	Melbourne	1894/95	R.Peel
2	136	2	109	Australia	Sydney	1897/98	T.W.Hayward
3	142	2	124	Australia	Adelaide	1897/98	K.S.Ranjitsinhji
4	111	1	65	Australia	Sydney	1897/98	E.Wainwright
5	110	4	49	Australia	The Oval	1899	C.B.Fry
6	154	1	116	Australia	Sydney	1901/02	T.W.Hayward
7	149	1	67	Australia	Adelaide	1901/02	T.W.Hayward
8	106	2	92	Australia	Sydney	1901/02	J.T.Tyldesley
9	102*	3	47*	Australia	Lord's	1902	Hon.F.S.Jackson
10	145	1	140	Australia	Trent Bridge	1905	T.W.Hayward

R.E.S.Wyatt (10)

1	245	3	113	South Africa	Old Trafford	1929	F.E.Woolley
2	148	2	58	West Indies	Kingston	1929/30	A.Sandham
3	170	6	64	Australia	The Oval	1930	H.Sutcliffe
4	160	1	54	South Africa	Durban (2)	1930/31	W.R.Hammond
5	112	1	38	Australia	Sydney	1932/33	H.Sutcliffe
6	156	5	78	Australia	Adelaide	1932/33	M.Leyland
7	125*	3	61*	Australia	Sydney	1932/33	W.R.Hammond
8	118	1	149	South Africa	Trent Bridge	1935	H.Sutcliffe
9	139	4	149	South Africa	Trent Bridge	1935	M.Leyland
10	129	4	44	South Africa	Headingley	1935	W.R.Hammond

P.E.Richardson (10)

1	108	3	81	Australia	Trent Bridge	1956	P.B.H.May
2	151	1	73	Australia	Trent Bridge	1956	M.C.Cowdrey
3	174	1	104	Australia	Old Trafford	1956	M.C.Cowdrey
4	121	4	117	South Africa	Johannesburg (3)	1956/57	M.C.Cowdrey
5	115	1	68	South Africa	Durban (2)	1956/57	T.E.Bailey
6	266	2	126	West Indies	Trent Bridge	1957	T.W.Graveney
7	146	2	107	West Indies	The Oval	1957	T.W.Graveney
8	104	4	100	New Zealand	Edgbaston	1958	M.C.Cowdrey
9	126	1	74	New Zealand	Old Trafford	1958	W.Watson
10	159	1	71	India	Bombay (2)	1961/62	G.Pullar

M.J.K.Smith (10)

1	109	4	100	India	Old Trafford	1959	K.F.Barrington
2	169	3	98	India	The Oval	1959	R.Subba Row
3	197	7	96	West Indies	Port-of-Spain	1959/60	J.M.Parks
4	120	6	99	South Africa	Lord's	1960	P.M.Walker
5	192	3	99	Pakistan	Lahore (2)	1961/62	K.F.Barrington
6	143	3	56	Pakistan	Karachi (1)	1961/62	E.R.Dexter
7	117	6	121	South Africa	Cape Town	1964/65	J.M.Parks
8	105	5	44	New Zealand	Lord's	1965	M.C.Cowdrey
9	113	5	54	New Zealand	Christchurch	1965/66	P.H.Parfitt
10	125	5	87	New Zealand	Christchurch	1965/66	P.H.Parfitt

M.H.Denness (10)

1	105	1	50	Pakistan	Lahore (2)	1972/73	D.L.Amiss
2	119	2	44	West Indies	Port-of-Spain	1973/74	D.L.Amiss
3	109*	4	45*	India	Old Trafford	1974	J.H.Edrich
4	202	5	118	India	Lord's	1974	A.W.Greig
5	211	2	100	India	Edgbaston	1974	D.Lloyd
6	149	3	188	Australia	Melbourne	1974/75	J.H.Edrich

7	192	4	188	Australia	Melbourne	1974/75	K.W.R.Fletcher
8	117	3	181	New Zealand	Auckland	1974/75	J.H.Edrich
9	266	4	181	New Zealand	Auckland	1974/75	K.W.R.Fletcher
10	151*	3	59*	New Zealand	Christchurch	1974/75	D.L.Amiss

D.W.Randall (10)

1	166	3	174	Australia	Melbourne	1976/77	D.L.Amiss
2	142	3	79	Australia	Old Trafford	1977	R.A.Woolmer
3	111	2	150	Australia	Sydney	1978/79	J.M.Brearley
4	114	4	57	India	Lord's	1979	D.I.Gower
5	125	7	126	India	Lord's	1982	P.H.Edmonds
6	151	5	95	India	The Oval	1982	I.T.Botham
7	100	5	78	Australia	Perth	1982/83	C.J.Tavare
8	122	4	70	Australia	Sydney	1982/83	D.I.Gower
9	186	6	83	New Zealand	Trent Bridge	1983	I.T.Botham
10	232	6	164	New Zealand	Wellington	1983/84	I.T.Botham

B.C.Broad (10)

1	101	1	55	West Indies	Lord's	1984	G.Fowler
2	223	1	162	Australia	Perth	1986/87	C.W.J.Athey
3	112	1	116	Australia	Adelaide	1986/87	C.W.J.Athey
4	161	2	116	Australia	Adelaide	1986/87	M.W.Gatting
5	105	2	112	Australia	Melbourne	1986/87	M.W.Gatting
6	119	1	54	Pakistan	Edgbaston	1987	R.T.Robinson
7	117	3	116	Pakistan	Faisalabad	1987/88	M.W.Gatting
8	168	2	114	New Zealand	Christchurch	1987/88	R.T.Robinson
9	129	1	61	New Zealand	Wellington	1987/88	M.D.Moxon
10	125	1	54	West Indies	Trent Bridge	1988	G.A.Gooch

R.T.Robinson (10)

1	110	3	160	India	Delhi	1984/85	A.J.Lamb
2	106	6	160	India	Delhi	1984/85	P.R.Downton
3	178	1	74	India	Madras (1)	1984/85	G.Fowler
4	156	1	96	India	Kanpur	1984/85	G.Fowler
5	136	3	175	Australia	Headingley	1985	M.W.Gatting
6	331	2	148	Australia	Edgbaston	1985	D.I.Gower
7	113	4	166	Pakistan	Old Trafford	1987	B.N.French
8	119	1	80	Pakistan	Edgbaston	1987	B.C.Broad
9	168	2	70	New Zealand	Christchurch	1987/88	B.C.Broad
10	108	2	54	New Zealand	Auckland	1987/88	M.D.Moxon

Hon.F.S.Jackson (9)

1	137	3	91	Australia	Lord's	1893	A.Shrewsbury
2	131	6	103	Australia	The Oval	1893	W.W.Read
3	185	1	118	Australia	The Oval	1899	T.W.Hayward
4	102*	3	55*	Australia	Lord's	1902	A.C.MacLaren
5	141	6	128	Australia	Old Trafford	1902	L.C.Braund
6	109	6	49	Australia	The Oval	1902	G.L.Jessop
7	113*	6	82*	Australia	Trent Bridge	1905	W.Rhodes
8	125	5	113	Australia	Old Trafford	1905	R.H.Spooner
9	151	4	76	Australia	The Oval	1905	C.B.Fry

L.C.Braund (9)

1	124	7	58	Australia	Sydney	1901/02	A.F.A.Lilley
2	108	6	103*	Australia	Adelaide	1901/02	W.G.Quaife
3	141	6	65	Australia	Old Trafford	1902	Hon.F.S.Jackson
4	192	5	102	Australia	Sydney	1903/04	R.E.Foster
5	145+	3	20	Australia	Melbourne	1903/04	J.T.Tyldesley & R.E.Foster
6	145	6	104	South Africa	Lord's	1907	G.L.Jessop
7	117	4	30	Australia	Sydney	1907/08	G.Gunn
8	108	4	49	Australia	Melbourne	1907/08	K.L.Hutchings
9	113	4	47	Australia	Adelaide	1907/08	J.Hardstaff snr

J.Hardstaff jnr (9)

1	245	3	114	New Zealand	Lord's	1937	W.R.Hammond
2	104	3	64	New Zealand	Lord's	1937	C.J.Barnett
3	128	2	58	New Zealand	Old Trafford	1937	L.Hutton
4	125	4	103	New Zealand	The Oval	1937	D.C.S.Compton
5	215	6	169*	Australia	The Oval	1938	L.Hutton
6	106	7	169*	Australia	The Oval	1938	A.Wood
7	182	5	205*	India	Lord's	1946	P.A.Gibb
8	118	5	67	Australia	Adelaide	1946/47	D.C.S.Compton
9	113	3	64	West Indies	Kingston	1947/48	W.Place

T.E.Bailey (9)

1	189	6	93	New Zealand	Lord's	1949	D.C.S.Compton
2	105	5	72*	New Zealand	Old Trafford	1949	R.T.Simpson
3	161	6	82*	West Indies	Old Trafford	1950	T.G.Evans
4	117	9	134*	New Zealand	Christchurch	1950/51	D.V.P.Wright
5	163	5	71	Australia	Lord's	1953	W.Watson
6	192	5	36*	Pakistan	Trent Bridge	1954	D.C.S.Compton
7	134	5	72	Australia	Sydney	1954/55	D.C.S.Compton
8	144	5	44	South Africa	Old Trafford	1955	D.C.S.Compton
9	115	1	80	South Africa	Durban (2)	1956/57	P.E.Richardson

G.Fowler (9)

1	103	1	86	Pakistan	Headingley	1982	C.J.Tavare
2	223	1	105	New Zealand	The Oval	1983	C.J.Tavare
3	116	5	57	Pakistan	Faisalabad	1983/84	D.I.Gower
4	120	6	58	Pakistan	Lahore (2)	1983/84	V.J.Marks
5	101	1	106	West Indies	Lord's	1984	B.C.Broad
6	135	2	55	India	Bombay (3)	1984/85	M.W.Gatting
7	178	1	201	India	Madras (1)	1984/85	R.T.Robinson
8	241	2	201	India	Madras (1)	1984/85	M.W.Gatting
9	156	1	69	India	Kanpur	1984/85	R.T.Robinson

G.A.Hick (9)

1	111	2	64	India	Madras (1)	1992/93	A.J.Stewart
2	112	3	68	Sri Lanka	Colombo (2)	1992/93	R.A.Smith
3	115	4	59	West Indies	Bridgetown	1993/94	A.J.Stewart
4	133	3	110	South Africa	Headingley	1994	G.P.Thorpe
5	124	2	81*	South Africa	The Oval	1994	M.A.Atherton
6	160	3	80	Australia	Brisbane (2)	1994/95	G.P.Thorpe
7	104	2	98*	Australia	Sydney	1994/95	M.A.Atherton
8	144	6	96	West Indies	The Oval	1995	R.C.Russell
9	142	4	141	South Africa	Centurion	1995/96	M.A.Atherton

E.Paynter (8)

1	149	3	36	New Zealand	Auckland	1932/33	W.R.Hammond
2	206	5	216*	Australia	Trent Bridge	1938	D.C.S.Compton
3	222	4	99	Australia	Lord's	1938	W.R.Hammond
4	184	2	117	South Africa	Johannesburg (1)	1938/39	P.A.Gibb
5	168	2	100	South Africa	Johannesburg (1)	1938/39	P.A.Gibb
6	115	2	243	South Africa	Durban (2)	1938/39	P.A.Gibb
7	242	3	243	South Africa	Durban (2)	1938/39	W.R.Hammond
8	164	4	75	South Africa	Durban (2)	1938/39	W.R.Hammond

B.L.D'Oliveira (8)

1	252	4	109	India	Headingley	1967	G.Boycott
2	122	4	33	India	Lord's	1967	T.W.Graveney
3	104	5	81*	Pakistan	Lord's	1967	D.B.Close
4	121	4	158	Australia	The Oval	1968	J.H.Edrich
5	133	4	56	Australia	Sydney	1970/71	G.Boycott
6	140	4	117	Australia	Melbourne	1970/71	B.W.Luckhurst
7	135	4	74	Pakistan	Headingley	1971	G.Boycott
8	106	6	72	Pakistan	Headingley	1971	R.Illingworth

B.W.Luckhurst (8)

1	171	1	131	Australia	Perth	1970/71	G.Boycott
2	116	1	38	Australia	Sydney	1970/71	G.Boycott
3	140	4	109	Australia	Melbourne	1970/71	B.L.D'Oliveira
4	124	1	46	Pakistan	Lord's	1971	G.Boycott
5	117*	1	53*	Pakistan	Lord's	1971	R.A.Hutton
6	123	2	101	India	Old Trafford	1971	J.H.Edrich
7	117	2	96	Australia	Trent Bridge	1972	P.H.Parfitt
8	119+	1	12	West Indies	Edgbaston	1973	G.Boycott & D.L.Amiss

R.T.Simpson (7)

1	105	5	103	New Zealand	Old Trafford	1949	T.E.Bailey
2	147	1	68	New Zealand	The Oval	1949	L.Hutton
3	212	1	94	West Indies	Trent Bridge	1950	C.Washbrook
4	131	2	156*	Australia	Melbourne	1950/51	L.Hutton
5	129	3	81	New Zealand	Christchurch	1950/51	D.C.S.Compton
6	144	2	137	South Africa	Trent Bridge	1951	L.Hutton
7	106	2	53	India	Lord's	1952	L.Hutton

Rev.D.S.Sheppard (7)

1	143	1	119	India	The Oval	1952	L.Hutton
2	118	2	119	India	The Oval	1952	J.T.Ikin

3	161	2	83	Pakistan	Trent Bridge	1962	E.R.Dexter
4	117	1	57	Pakistan	The Oval	1962	M.C.Cowdrey
5	114	1	53	Australia	Brisbane (2)	1962/63	G.Pullar
6	124	2	113	Australia	Melbourne	1962/63	E.R.Dexter
7	104	3	113	Australia	Melbourne	1962/63	M.C.Cowdrey

R.A.Woolmer (7)

1	122	4	149	Australia	The Oval	1975	G.R.J.Roope
2	151	6	149	Australia	The Oval	1975	A.P.E.Knott
3	121	4	82	West Indies	Trent Bridge	1976	D.S.Steele
4	132	2	120	Australia	Lord's	1977	J.M.Brearley
5	142	3	137	Australia	Old Trafford	1977	D.W.Randall
6	160	4	137	Australia	Old Trafford	1977	A.W.Greig
7	106	3	29	West Indies	Trent Bridge	1980	G.Boycott

R.C.Russell (7)

1	131	2	94	Sri Lanka	Lord's	1988	G.A.Gooch
2	142	7	128*	Australia	Old Trafford	1989	J.E.Emburey
3	105	7	24*	New Zealand	Wellington	1991/92	A.J.Lamb
4	118	7	62	West Indies	St John's	1993/94	C.C.Lewis
5	144	6	91	West Indies	The Oval	1995	G.A.Hick
6	119*	6	29*	South Africa	Johannesburg (3)	1995/96	M.A.Atherton
7	136	6	124	India	Lord's	1996	G.P.Thorpe

A.Shrewsbury (6)

1	116	2	72	Australia	Melbourne	1884/85	W.Barnes
2	115+	5	105*	Australia	Melbourne	1884/85	W.Bates & W.Flowers
3	161	5	164	Australia	Lord's	1886	W.Barnes
4	137	3	106	Australia	Lord's	1893	Hon.F.S.Jackson
5	152	2	81	Australia	Lord's	1893	W.Gunn
6	103	4	66	Australia	The Oval	1893	Albert Ward

C.B.Fry (6)

1	119	3	64	South Africa	Johannesburg (1)	1895/96	T.W.Hayward
2	110	4	60	Australia	The Oval	1899	A.C.MacLaren
3	100	3	144	Australia	The Oval	1905	T.W.Hayward
4	151	4	144	Australia	The Oval	1905	Hon.F.S.Jackson
5	105*	1	35*	Australia	Edgbaston	1909	J.B.Hobbs
6	104	3	62	Australia	The Oval	1909	W.Rhodes

G.Gunn (6)

1	117	4	119	Australia	Sydney	1907/08	L.C.Braund
2	113	4	74	Australia	Sydney	1907/08	J.Hardstaff snr
3	134	2	122*	Australia	Sydney	1907/08	J.B.Hobbs
4	112	2	43	Australia	Melbourne	1911/12	J.B.Hobbs
5	102	2	75	Australia	Melbourne	1911/12	W.Rhodes
6	173	1	85	West Indies	Kingston	1929/30	A.Sandham

C.P.Mead (6)

1	152	3	102	South Africa	Johannesburg (1)	1913/14	W.Rhodes
2	104	5	117	South Africa	Port Elizabeth	1913/14	F.E.Woolley
3	121	6	182*	Australia	The Oval	1921	Hon.L.H.Tennyson
4	154	5	181	South Africa	Durban (2)	1922/23	P.G.H.Fender
5	156	6	181	South Africa	Durban (2)	1922/23	F.T.Mann
6	139	3	66	South Africa	Durban (2)	1922/23	C.A.G.Russell

G.E.Tyldesley (6)

1	102*	5	78*	Australia	Old Trafford	1921	P.G.H.Fender
2	230	2	122	South Africa	Johannesburg (1)	1927/28	H.Sutcliffe
3	127	3	78	South Africa	Durban (2)	1927/28	W.R.Hammond
4	102	2	62*	South Africa	Durban (2)	1927/28	P.Holmes
5	130	2	100	South Africa	Durban (2)	1927/28	H.Sutcliffe
6	129	2	73	West Indies	The Oval	1928	J.B.Hobbs

A.Sandham (6)

1	153	1	58	South Africa	Johannesburg (1)	1922/23	C.A.G.Russell
2	101	5	46	South Africa	The Oval	1924	E.H.Hendren
3	168	3	152	West Indies	Bridgetown	1929/30	E.H.Hendren
4	173	1	325	West Indies	Kingston	1929/30	G.Gunn
5	148	2	325	West Indies	Kingston	1929/30	R.E.S.Wyatt
6	249	4	325	West Indies	Kingston	1929/30	L.E.G.Ames

D.R.Jardine (6)

1	120	4	83	West Indies	Old Trafford	1928	W.R.Hammond
2	126	5	62	Australia	Melbourne	1928/29	W.R.Hammond

3	262	3	98	Australia	Adelaide	1928/29	W.R.Hammond
4	114	1	46	Australia	Brisbane (2)	1932/33	H.Sutcliffe
5	140	7	127	West Indies	Old Trafford	1933	R.W.V.Robins
6	145	5	60	India	Bombay (1)	1933/34	B.H.Valentine

P.A.Gibb (6)

1	184	2	93	South Africa	Johannesburg (1)	1938/39	E.Paynter
2	168	2	106	South Africa	Johannesburg (1)	1938/39	E.Paynter
3	109	3	58	South Africa	Cape Town	1938/39	W.R.Hammond
4	115	2	38	South Africa	Durban (2)	1938/39	E.Paynter
5	280	2	120	South Africa	Durban (2)	1938/39	W.J.Edrich
6	182	5	60	India	Lord's	1946	J.Hardstaff jnr

J.M.Brearley (6)

1	111+	4	59	India	Madras (1)	1976/77	R.W.Tolchard & A.W.Greig
2	146	1	91	India	Bombay (3)	1976/77	D.L.Amiss
3	132	2	49	Australia	Lord's	1977	R.A.Woolmer
4	154	1	81	Australia	Trent Bridge	1977	G.Boycott
5	185	1	74	Pakistan	Hyderabad	1977/78	G.Boycott
6	111	2	53	Australia	Sydney	1978/79	D.W.Randall

G.Miller (6)

1	101+	4	89	New Zealand	Christchurch	1977/78	G.R.J.Roope & C.T.Radley
2	123	6	48	Pakistan	Edgbaston	1978	I.T.Botham
3	135	7	64	Australia	Adelaide	1978/79	R.W.Taylor
4	165*	6	63*	India	Edgbaston	1979	D.I.Gower
5	103	8	62	India	Lord's	1979	R.W.Taylor
6	169	6	98	India	Old Trafford	1982	I.T.Botham

T.G.Evans (5)

1	161	6	104	West Indies	Old Trafford	1950	T.E.Bailey
2	159	6	104	India	Lord's	1952	T.W.Graveney
3	108	6	28	West Indies	Kingston	1953/54	L.Hutton
4	174	7	82	West Indies	Lord's	1957	M.C.Cowdrey
5	106	6	73	India	Trent Bridge	1959	M.J.Horton

W.Watson (5)

1	141	4	57	South Africa	Trent Bridge	1951	D.C.S.Compton
2	122	4	79	South Africa	Lord's	1951	D.C.S.Compton
3	163	5	109	Australia	Lord's	1953	T.E.Bailey
4	130	1	116	West Indies	Kingston	1953/54	L.Hutton
5	126	1	66	New Zealand	Old Trafford	1958	P.E.Richardson

R.Subba Row (5)

1	169	3	94	India	The Oval	1959	M.J.K.Smith
2	148	3	100	West Indies	Georgetown	1959/60	E.R.Dexter
3	109	2	112	Australia	Edgbaston	1961	E.R.Dexter
4	110	2	49	Australia	Old Trafford	1961	E.R.Dexter
5	172	5	137	Australia	The Oval	1961	K.F.Barrington

J.M.Parks (5)

1	197	7	101*	West Indies	Port-of-Spain	1959/60	M.J.K.Smith
2	143	6	60	Australia	Old Trafford	1964	K.F.Barrington
3	206*	6	108*	South Africa	Durban (2)	1964/65	K.F.Barrington
4	117	6	59	South Africa	Cape Town	1964/65	M.J.K.Smith
5	138	6	89	Australia	Melbourne	1965/66	M.C.Cowdrey

R.W.Barber (5)

1	101*	6	39*	Pakistan	Lahore (2)	1961/62	E.R.Dexter
2	198	1	86	Pakistan	Dacca	1961/62	G.Pullar
3	120	1	74	South Africa	Durban (2)	1964/65	G.Boycott
4	136	2	97	South Africa	Johannesburg (3)	1964/65	E.R.Dexter
5	234	1	185	Australia	Sydney	1965/66	G.Boycott

D.S.Steele (5)

1	104	2	45	Australia	Lord's	1975	J.H.Edrich
2	112	2	73	Australia	Headingley	1975	J.H.Edrich
3	125	2	66	Australia	The Oval	1975	J.H.Edrich
4	121	4	106	West Indies	Trent Bridge	1976	R.A.Woolmer
5	100	2	44	West Indies	The Oval	1976	D.L.Amiss

C.T.Radley (5)

1	101+	4	15	New Zealand	Christchurch	1977/78	G.R.J.Roope & G.Miller
2	139	3	158	New Zealand	Auckland	1977/78	G.R.J.Roope
3	116	3	49	New Zealand	The Oval	1978	D.I.Gower

4	129	2	59	New Zealand	Trent Bridge	1978	G.Boycott
5	114	3	77	New Zealand	Lord's	1978	D.I.Gower

W.G.Grace (4)

1	120	2	152	Australia	The Oval	1880	A.P.Lucas
2	170	1	170	Australia	The Oval	1886	W.H.Scotton
3	151	1	68	Australia	The Oval	1893	A.E.Stoddart
4	105	2	66	Australia	Lord's	1896	R.Abel

W.Barnes (4)

1	175	3	134	Australia	Adelaide	1884/85	W.H.Scotton
2	116	2	58	Australia	Melbourne	1884/85	A.Shrewsbury
3	161	5	58	Australia	Lord's	1886	A.Shrewsbury
4	112	5	62	Australia	The Oval	1888	R.Abel

Albert Ward (4)

1	103	4	55	Australia	The Oval	1893	A.Shrewsbury
2	102	3	117	Australia	Sydney	1894/95	J.T.Brown
3	104	2	32	Australia	Melbourne	1894/95	A.E.Stoddart
4	210	3	93	Australia	Melbourne	1894/95	J.T.Brown

J.T.Tyldesley (4)

1	106	2	79	Australia	Sydney	1901/02	A.C.MacLaren
2	145+	3	97	Australia	Melbourne	1903/04	R.E.Foster & L.C.Braund
3	158	6	112*	Australia	The Oval	1905	R.H.Spooner
4	106	3	55	Australia	Headingley	1909	J.Sharp

R.E.Foster (4)

1	192	5	287	Australia	Sydney	1903/04	L.C.Braund
2	115	9	287	Australia	Sydney	1903/04	A.E.Relf
3	130	10	287	Australia	Sydney	1903/04	W.Rhodes
4	145+	3	49*	Australia	Melbourne	1903/04	J.T.Tyldesley & L.C.Braund

J.W.Hearne (4)

1	127	2	114	Australia	Melbourne	1911/12	W.Rhodes
2	111	5	45	South Africa	Headingley	1912	F.E.Woolley
3	100	5	57	Australia	Sydney	1920/21	J.B.Hobbs
4	106	2	44	Australia	Melbourne	1924/25	H.Sutcliffe

J.W.H.T.Douglas (4)

1	115	7	119	South Africa	Durban (1)	1913/14	M.C.Bird
2	124	6	60	Australia	Adelaide	1920/21	C.A.G.Russell
3	106	5	50	Australia	Melbourne	1920/21	J.W.H.Makepeace
4	104	6	60	Australia	Melbourne	1920/21	P.G.H.Fender

C.A.G.Russell (4)

1	124	6	135*	Australia	Adelaide	1920/21	J.W.H.T.Douglas
2	158	1	102*	Australia	The Oval	1921	G.Brown
3	153	1	96	South Africa	Johannesburg (1)	1922/23	A.Sandham
4	139	3	140	South Africa	Durban (2)	1922/23	C.P.Mead

K.S.Duleepsinhji (4)

1	111	2	117	New Zealand	Auckland	1929/30	E.H.Bowley
2	104	4	173	Australia	Lord's	1930	E.H.Hendren
3	178	2	109	New Zealand	The Oval	1931	H.Sutcliffe
4	126	2	63	New Zealand	Old Trafford	1931	H.Sutcliffe

R.W.V.Robins (4)

1	140	7	55	West Indies	Old Trafford	1933	D.R.Jardine
2	105	6	108	South Africa	Old Trafford	1935	M.Leyland
3	138	8	76	India	Old Trafford	1936	H.Verity
4	111	7	61	Australia	Melbourne	1936/37	M.Leyland

A.J.Watkins (4)

1	111*	4	64*	South Africa	Cape Town	1948/49	D.C.S.Compton
2	158	4	137*	India	Delhi	1951/52	D.B.Carr
3	148	5	80	India	Bombay (2)	1951/52	T.W.Graveney
4	107	5	68	India	Calcutta	1951/52	C.J.Poole

R.Illingworth (4)

1	102	7	50	India	The Oval	1959	R.Swetman
2	106	6	45	Pakistan	Headingley	1971	B.L.D'Oliveira
3	168	8	107	India	Old Trafford	1971	P.Lever
4	104	8	57	Australia	Headingley	1972	J.A.Snow

P.J.Sharpe (4)

1	101	5	85*	West Indies	Edgbaston	1963	E.R.Dexter
2	101	5	63	West Indies	The Oval	1963	D.B.Close
3	126	4	86	West Indies	Lord's	1969	G.Boycott
4	249	2	111	New Zealand	Trent Bridge	1969	J.H.Edrich

D.Lloyd (4)

1	116	1	46	India	Lord's	1974	D.L.Amiss
2	157	1	214*	India	Edgbaston	1974	D.L.Amiss
3	211	2	214*	India	Edgbaston	1974	M.H.Denness
4	115	1	44	Australia	Melbourne	1974/75	D.L.Amiss

G.R.J.Roope (4)

1	122	4	77	Australia	The Oval	1975	R.A.Woolmer
2	101+	4	50	New Zealand	Christchurch	1977/78	G.Miller & C.T.Radley
3	139	3	68	New Zealand	Auckland	1977/78	C.T.Radley
4	118	6	69	Pakistan	Lord's	1978	I.T.Botham

P.Willey (4)

1	128	4	33	West Indies	The Oval	1976	D.L.Amiss
2	117*	10	100*	West Indies	The Oval	1980	R.G.D.Willis
3	136	4	67	West Indies	Kingston	1980/81	D.I.Gower
4	126	5	42	New Zealand	Lord's	1986	G.A.Gooch

R.W.Taylor (4)

1	160	6	45	New Zealand	Christchurch	1977/78	I.T.Botham
2	135	7	97	Australia	Adelaide	1978/79	G.Miller
3	103	8	64	India	Lord's	1979	G.Miller
4	171	6	43	India	Bombay (3)	1979/80	I.T.Botham

C.W.J.Athey (4)

1	101	2	76	Australia	Brisbane (2)	1986/87	M.W.Gatting
2	223	1	96	Australia	Perth	1986/87	B.C.Broad
3	112	1	55	Australia	Adelaide	1986/87	B.C.Broad
4	102	4	123	Pakistan	Lord's	1987	M.W.Gatting

J.E.Emburey (4)

1	143	7	58	Pakistan	Edgbaston	1987	M.W.Gatting
2	114	7	70	Pakistan	Karachi (1)	1987/88	D.J.Capel
3	142	7	64	Australia	Old Trafford	1989	R.C.Russell
4	104	7	37	Australia	Edgbaston	1993	G.P.Thorpe

W.W.Read (3)

1	116	6	66	Australia	Sydney	1882/83	E.F.S.Tylecote
2	151	9	117	Australia	The Oval	1884	W.H.Scotton
3	131	6	52	Australia	The Oval	1893	Hon.F.S.Jackson

W.H.Scotton (3)

1	151	9	90	Australia	The Oval	1884	W.W.Read
2	175	3	82	Australia	Adelaide	1884/85	W.Barnes
3	170	1	34	Australia	The Oval	1886	W.G.Grace

R.Abel (3)

1	112	5	70	Australia	The Oval	1888	W.Barnes
2	105	5	120	South Africa	Cape Town	1888/89	H.Wood
3	105	2	94	Australia	Lord's	1896	W.G.Grace

K.S.Ranjitsinhji (3)

1	124	6	175	Australia	Sydney	1897/98	G.H.Hirst
2	142	2	77	Australia	Adelaide	1897/98	A.C.MacLaren
3	131	2	54	Australia	The Oval	1899	T.W.Hayward

P.F.Warner (3)

1	122	1	68	Australia	Melbourne	1903/04	T.W.Hayward
2	148	1	79	Australia	Adelaide	1903/04	T.W.Hayward
3	113	5	39	South Africa	Lord's	1912	F.E.Woolley

R.H.Spooner (3)

1	125	5	52	Australia	Old Trafford	1905	Hon.F.S.Jackson
2	158	6	79	Australia	The Oval	1905	J.T.Tyldesley
3	124	2	119	South Africa	Lord's	1912	W.Rhodes

J.W.H.Makepeace (3)

1	105	2	30	Australia	Adelaide	1920/21	J.B.Hobbs
2	106	5	117	Australia	Melbourne	1920/21	J.W.H.T.Douglas

| 3 | 113 | 2 | 54 | Australia | Melbourne | 1920/21 | W.Rhodes |

P.G.H.Fender (3)

1	104	6	59	Australia	Melbourne	1920/21	J.W.H.T.Douglas
2	102*	5	44*	Australia	Old Trafford	1921	G.E.Tyldesley
3	154	5	60	South Africa	Durban (2)	1922/23	C.P.Mead

G.O.B.Allen (3)

1	125	6	57	Australia	Lord's	1930	A.P.F.Chapman
2	246	8	122	New Zealand	Lord's	1931	L.E.G.Ames
3	121+	6	19	Australia	The Oval	1934	M.Leyland & L.E.G.Ames

C.F.Walters (3)

1	111	1	59	India	Madras (1)	1933/34	A.H.Bakewell
2	123*	1	50*	Australia	Old Trafford	1934	H.Sutcliffe
3	104	1	64	Australia	The Oval	1934	H.Sutcliffe

C.J.Barnett (3)

1	104	3	83*	New Zealand	Lord's	1937	J.Hardstaff jnr
2	100	1	62	New Zealand	Old Trafford	1937	L.Hutton
3	219	1	126	Australia	Trent Bridge	1938	L.Hutton

J.T.Ikin (3)

1	113	6	48	Australia	Melbourne	1946/47	N.W.D.Yardley
2	121	1	38	South Africa	Old Trafford	1951	L.Hutton
3	118	2	53	India	The Oval	1952	Rev.D.S.Sheppard

J.F.Crapp (3)

1	150	3	56	South Africa	Johannesburg (2)	1948/49	D.C.S.Compton
2	134	2	54	South Africa	Cape Town	1948/49	L.Hutton
3	120	2	51	South Africa	Johannesburg (2)	1948/49	C.Washbrook

D.B.Close (3)

1	101	5	46	West Indies	The Oval	1963	P.J.Sharpe
2	104	5	36	Pakistan	Lord's	1967	B.L.D'Oliveira
3	101*	3	36*	West Indies	Trent Bridge	1976	J.H.Edrich

J.B.Bolus (3)

1	119	4	88	India	Madras (2)	1963/64	K.F.Barrington
2	125	1	57	India	Bombay (2)	1963/64	J.G.Binks
3	101	1	58	India	Delhi	1963/64	J.H.Edrich

C.Milburn (3)

1	130*	5	126*	West Indies	Lord's	1966	T.W.Graveney
2	132	2	83	Australia	Lord's	1968	G.Boycott
3	156	2	139	Pakistan	Karachi (1)	1968/69	T.W.Graveney

P.Lever (3)

1	149	7	64	New Zealand	Auckland	1970/71	A.P.E.Knott
2	159	7	47	Pakistan	Edgbaston	1971	A.P.E.Knott
3	168	8	88*	India	Old Trafford	1971	R.Illingworth

A.R.Lewis (3)

1	101*	5	70*	India	Delhi	1972/73	A.W.Greig
2	144	4	125	India	Kanpur	1972/73	K.W.R.Fletcher
3	103+	5	88	Pakistan	Karachi (1)	1972/73	P.I.Pocock & A.W.Greig

P.H.Edmonds (3)

1	125	7	64	India	Lord's	1982	D.W.Randall
2	110*	7	43*	New Zealand	The Oval	1983	A.J.Lamb
3	100	7	49	India	Kanpur	1984/85	D.I.Gower

V.J.Marks (3)

1	167	7	83	Pakistan	Faisalabad	1983/84	D.I.Gower
2	120	6	74	Pakistan	Lahore (2)	1983/84	G.Fowler
3	119	6	55	Pakistan	Lahore (2)	1983/84	D.I.Gower

N.Hussain (3)

1	113*	7	47*	Australia	Trent Bridge	1993	G.P.Thorpe
2	230+	2	107*	India	Trent Bridge	1996	M.A.Atherton & G.P.Thorpe
3	107	2	48	Pakistan	Headingley	1996	A.J.Stewart

G.Ulyett (2)

| 1 | 137 | 2 | 87 | Australia | Melbourne | 1881/82 | J.Selby |
| 2 | 122 | 1 | 67 | Australia | Sydney | 1881/82 | R.G.Barlow |

W.Flowers (2)

1	102	7	56	Australia	Sydney	1884/85	J.M.Read
2	115+	5	16	Australia	Melbourne	1884/85	A.Shrewsbury & W.Bates

A.E.Stoddart (2)

1	151	1	83	Australia	The Oval	1893	W.G.Grace
2	104	2	68	Australia	Melbourne	1894/95	Albert Ward

J.T.Brown (2)

1	102	3	53	Australia	Sydney	1894/95	Albert Ward
2	210	3	140	Australia	Melbourne	1894/95	Albert Ward

A.F.A.Lilley (2)

1	113	7	58	Australia	Old Trafford	1899	T.W.Hayward
2	124	7	84	Australia	Sydney	1901/02	L.C.Braund

G.L.Jessop (2)

1	109	6	104	Australia	The Oval	1902	Hon.F.S.Jackson
2	145	6	93	South Africa	Lord's	1907	L.C.Braund

A.E.Relf (2)

1	115	9	31	Australia	Sydney	1903/04	R.E.Foster
2	141	1	63	South Africa	Johannesburg (1)	1913/14	W.Rhodes

K.L.Hutchings (2)

1	108	4	126	Australia	Melbourne	1907/08	L.C.Braund
2	142	7	59	Australia	The Oval	1909	J.Sharp

J.Hardstaff snr (2)

1	113	4	63	Australia	Sydney	1907/08	G.Gunn
2	113	4	72	Australia	Adelaide	1907/08	L.C.Braund

J.Sharp (2)

1	106	3	61	Australia	Headingley	1909	J.T.Tyldesley
2	142	7	105	Australia	The Oval	1909	K.L.Hutchings

F.T.Mann (2)

1	156	6	84	South Africa	Durban (2)	1922/23	C.P.Mead
2	124	6	59	South Africa	Johannesburg (1)	1922/23	F.E.Woolley

A.P.F.Chapman (2)

1	116*	4	50*	Australia	Lord's	1926	E.H.Hendren
2	125	6	121	Australia	Lord's	1930	G.O.B.Allen

G.Geary (2)

1	108	9	35*	Australia	Headingley	1926	G.G.Macaulay
2	101	7	53	Australia	Trent Bridge	1934	E.H.Hendren

P.Holmes (2)

1	140	1	88	South Africa	Cape Town	1927/28	H.Sutcliffe
2	102	2	56	South Africa	Durban (2)	1927/28	G.E.Tyldesley

M.J.L.Turnbull (2)

1	101	4	61	South Africa	Johannesburg (1)	1930/31	W.R.Hammond
2	108*	2	37*	India	Lord's	1936	H.Gimblett

T.S.Worthington (2)

1	127	3	87	India	Old Trafford	1936	W.R.Hammond
2	266	4	128	India	The Oval	1936	W.R.Hammond

N.W.D.Yardley (2)

1	113	6	61	Australia	Melbourne	1946/47	J.T.Ikin
2	237	5	99	South Africa	Trent Bridge	1947	D.C.S.Compton

J.D.B.Robertson (2)

1	129	1	64	West Indies	Kingston	1947/48	L.Hutton
2	143	1	121	New Zealand	Lord's	1949	L.Hutton

A.V.Bedser (2)

1	121	8	37	Australia	Old Trafford	1948	D.C.S.Compton
2	155	3	79	Australia	Headingley	1948	W.J.Edrich

W.G.A.Parkhouse (2)

1	106	3	69	West Indies	Trent Bridge	1950	J.G.Dewes
2	146	1	78	India	Headingley	1959	G.Pullar

R.Swetman (2)

| 1 | 102 | 7 | 65 | India | The Oval | 1959 | R.Illingworth |
| 2 | 123 | 7 | 45 | West Indies | Bridgetown | 1959/60 | E.R.Dexter |

D.A.Allen (2)

| 1 | 153* | 6 | 79* | Pakistan | Edgbaston | 1962 | P.H.Parfitt |
| 2 | 107 | 8 | 88 | New Zealand | Christchurch | 1965/66 | D.J.Brown |

B.R.Knight (2)

| 1 | 240 | 6 | 125 | New Zealand | Auckland | 1962/63 | P.H.Parfitt |
| 2 | 191 | 4 | 127 | India | Kanpur | 1963/64 | P.H.Parfitt |

J.A.Snow (2)

| 1 | 128 | 10 | 59* | West Indies | The Oval | 1966 | K.Higgs |
| 2 | 104 | 8 | 48 | Australia | Headingley | 1972 | R.Illingworth |

P.I.Pocock (2)

| 1 | 109 | 9 | 13 | West Indies | Georgetown | 1967/68 | G.A.R.Lock |
| 2 | 103+ | 5 | 4 | Pakistan | Karachi (1) | 1972/73 | A.R.Lewis & A.W.Greig |

R.A.Hutton (2)

| 1 | 117* | 1 | 58* | Pakistan | Lord's | 1971 | B.W.Luckhurst |
| 2 | 103 | 7 | 81 | India | The Oval | 1971 | A.P.E.Knott |

R.W.Tolchard (2)

| 1 | 142 | 5 | 67 | India | Calcutta | 1976/77 | A.W.Greig |
| 2 | 111+ | 4 | 8* | India | Madras (1) | 1976/77 | J.M.Brearley & A.W.Greig |

C.J.Richards (2)

| 1 | 207 | 6 | 133 | Australia | Perth | 1986/87 | D.I.Gower |
| 2 | 131 | 6 | 38 | Australia | Sydney | 1986/87 | M.W.Gatting |

M.D.Moxon (2)

| 1 | 108 | 2 | 99 | New Zealand | Auckland | 1987/88 | R.T.Robinson |
| 2 | 129 | 1 | 81* | New Zealand | Wellington | 1987/88 | B.C.Broad |

J.P.Crawley (2)

| 1 | 115 | 5 | 38 | South Africa | Headingley | 1994 | A.J.Stewart |
| 2 | 174 | 4 | 72 | Australia | Sydney | 1994/95 | M.A.Atherton |

N.V.Knight (2)

| 1 | 148 | 1 | 57 | West Indies | Trent Bridge | 1995 | M.A.Atherton |
| 2 | 108 | 5 | 113 | Pakistan | Headingley | 1996 | A.J.Stewart |

A.P.Lucas (1)

| 1 | 120 | 2 | 55 | Australia | The Oval | 1880 | W.G.Grace |

R.G.Barlow (1)

| 1 | 122 | 1 | 62 | Australia | Sydney | 1881/82 | G.Ulyett |

J.Selby (1)

| 1 | 137 | 2 | 55 | Australia | Melbourne | 1881/82 | G.Ulyett |

E.F.S.Tylecote (1)

| 1 | 116 | 6 | 66 | Australia | Sydney | 1882/83 | W.W.Read |

W.Bates (1)

| 1 | 115+ | 5 | 61 | Australia | Melbourne | 1884/85 | A.Shrewsbury & W.Flowers |

J.M.Read (1)

| 1 | 102 | 7 | 56 | Australia | Sydney | 1884/85 | W.Flowers |

H.Wood (1)

| 1 | 105 | 5 | 59 | South Africa | Cape Town | 1888/89 | R.Abel |

W.Gunn (1)

| 1 | 152 | 2 | 77 | Australia | Lord's | 1893 | A.Shrewsbury |

R.Peel (1)

| 1 | 162 | 5 | 73 | Australia | Melbourne | 1894/95 | A.C.MacLaren |

A.J.L.Hill (1)

| 1 | 122 | 4 | 65 | South Africa | Johannesburg (1) | 1895/96 | T.W.Hayward |

C.W.Wright (1)
1   154   8   71   South Africa   Johannesburg (1) 1895/96   H.R.Bromley-Davenport

H.R.Bromley-Davenport (1)
1   154   8   84   South Africa   Johannesburg (1) 1895/96   C.W.Wright

G.H.Hirst (1)
1   124   6   62   Australia   Sydney   1897/98   K.S.Ranjitsinhji

E.Wainwright (1)
1   111   1   49   Australia   Sydney   1897/98   A.C.MacLaren

W.G.Quaife (1)
1   108   6   68   Australia   Adelaide   1901/02   L.C.Braund

F.L.Fane (1)
1   100   4   37   South Africa   Cape Town   1909/10   F.E.Woolley

J.Vine (1)
1   143   7   36   Australia   Sydney   1911/12   F.E.Woolley

M.C.Bird (1)
1   115   7   61   South Africa   Durban (1)   1913/14   J.W.H.T.Douglas

G.Brown (1)
1   158   1   84   Australia   The Oval   1921   C.A.G.Russell

Hon.L.H.Tennyson (1)
1   121   6   51   Australia   The Oval   1921   C.P.Mead

A.P.Freeman (1)
1   128   9   50*   Australia   Sydney   1924/25   F.E.Woolley

W.W.Whysall (1)
1   133   7   76   Australia   Melbourne   1924/25   R.Kilner

R.Kilner (1)
1   133   7   74   Australia   Melbourne   1924/25   W.W.Whysall

G.G.Macaulay (1)
1   108   9   76   Australia   Headingley   1926   G.Geary

H.Larwood (1)
1   124   8   70   Australia   Brisbane (1)   1928/29   E.H.Hendren

M.W.Tate (1)
1   129   6   100*   South Africa   Lord's   1929   M.Leyland

E.H.Bowley (1)
1   111   2   109   New Zealand   Auckland   1929/30   K.S.Duleepsinhji

G.B.Legge (1)
1   184   5   196   New Zealand   Auckland   1929/30   M.S.Nichols

M.S.Nichols (1)
1   184   5   75   New Zealand   Auckland   1929/30   G.B.Legge

Nawab of Pataudi snr (1)
1   123   3   102   Australia   Sydney   1932/33   H.Sutcliffe

F.R.Brown (1)
1   108   7   74   New Zealand   Christchurch   1932/33   W.Voce

W.Voce (1)
1   108   7   66   New Zealand   Christchurch   1932/33   F.R.Brown

B.H.Valentine (1)
1   145   5   136   India   Bombay (1)   1933/34   D.R.Jardine

A.H.Bakewell (1)
1   111   1   85   India   Madras (1)   1933/34   C.F.Walters

J.Iddon (1)
1   157   6   54   West Indies   Kingston   1934/35   L.E.G.Ames

D.Smith (1)
1   128   1   57   South Africa   Headingley   1935   A.Mitchell

A.Mitchell (1)
1   128   1   72   South Africa   Headingley   1935   D.Smith

H.Gimblett (1)
1   108*   2   67*   India   Lord's   1936   M.J.L.Turnbull

A.E.Fagg (1)
1   134   2   39   India   Old Trafford   1936   W.R.Hammond

H.Verity (1)
1   138   8   66*   India   Old Trafford   1936   R.W.V.Robins

A.Wood (1)
1   106   7   53   Australia   The Oval   1938   J.Hardstaff jnr

N.Oldfield (1)
1   131   2   80   West Indies   The Oval   1939   L.Hutton

W.Place (1)
1   113   3   107   West Indies   Kingston   1947/48   J.Hardstaff jnr

F.G.Mann (1)
1   100   6   136*   South Africa   Port Elizabeth   1948/49   R.O.Jenkins

R.O.Jenkins (1)
1   100   6   29   South Africa   Port Elizabeth   1948/49   F.G.Mann

J.G.Dewes (1)
1   106   3   67   West Indies   Trent Bridge   1950   W.G.A.Parkhouse

D.V.P.Wright (1)
1   117   9   45   New Zealand   Christchurch   1950/51   T.E.Bailey

D.B.Carr (1)
1   158   4   76   India   Delhi   1951/52   A.J.Watkins

C.J.Poole (1)
1   107   5   55   India   Calcutta   1951/52   A.J.Watkins

J.H.Wardle (1)
1   105   7   66   West Indies   Kingston   1953/54   L.Hutton

D.J.Insole (1)
1   101   3   47   South Africa   Headingley   1955   P.B.H.May

C.A.Milton (1)
1   194*   3   104*   New Zealand   Headingley   1958   P.B.H.May

M.J.Horton (1)
1   106   6   58   India   Trent Bridge   1959   T.G.Evans

P.M.Walker (1)
1   120   6   52   South Africa   Lord's   1960   M.J.K.Smith

A.C.Smith (1)
1   163*   9   69*   New Zealand   Wellington   1962/63   M.C.Cowdrey

J.G.Binks (1)
1   125   1   55   India   Bombay (2)   1963/64   J.B.Bolus

D.J.Brown (1)
1   107   8   44   New Zealand   Christchurch   1965/66   D.A.Allen

W.E.Russell (1)
1   118   2   56   New Zealand   Auckland   1965/66   M.C.Cowdrey

K.Higgs (1)
1   128   10   63   West Indies   The Oval   1966   J.A.Snow

J.T.Murray (1)
1   217   8   112   West Indies   The Oval   1966   T.W.Graveney

G.A.R.Lock (1)
| 1 | 109 | 9 | 89 | West Indies | Georgetown | 1967/68 | P.I.Pocock |

R.M.Prideaux (1)
| 1 | 123 | 1 | 64 | Australia | Headingley | 1968 | J.H.Edrich |

J.H.Hampshire (1)
| 1 | 128 | 6 | 107 | West Indies | Lord's | 1969 | A.P.E.Knott |

J.A.Jameson (1)
| 1 | 106 | 2 | 82 | India | The Oval | 1971 | J.H.Edrich |

D.L.Underwood (1)
| 1 | 129 | 2 | 43 | Pakistan | The Oval | 1974 | D.L.Amiss |

C.M.Old (1)
| 1 | 130 | 7 | 65 | Pakistan | The Oval | 1974 | K.W.R.Fletcher |

B.Wood (1)
| 1 | 111 | 1 | 52 | Australia | Lord's | 1975 | J.H.Edrich |

B.C.Rose (1)
| 1 | 155+ | 1 | 50 | West Indies | The Oval | 1980 | G.A.Gooch & G.Boycott |

R.G.D.Willis (1)
| 1 | 117* | 10 | 24* | West Indies | The Oval | 1980 | P.Willey |

G.R.Dilley (1)
| 1 | 117 | 8 | 56 | Australia | Headingley | 1981 | I.T.Botham |

G.Cook (1)
| 1 | 106 | 1 | 66 | India | Old Trafford | 1982 | C.J.Tavare |

C.L.Smith (1)
| 1 | 127 | 1 | 66 | Pakistan | Faisalabad | 1983/84 | M.W.Gatting |

P.R.Downton (1)
| 1 | 106 | 6 | 74 | India | Delhi | 1984/85 | R.T.Robinson |

W.N.Slack (1)
| 1 | 127 | 1 | 52 | West Indies | St John's | 1985/86 | G.A.Gooch |

D.R.Pringle (1)
| 1 | 147 | 5 | 63 | India | Lord's | 1986 | G.A.Gooch |

B.N.French (1)
| 1 | 113 | 4 | 59 | Pakistan | Old Trafford | 1987 | R.T.Robinson |

D.J.Capel (1)
| 1 | 114 | 7 | 98 | Pakistan | Karachi (1) | 1987/88 | J.E.Emburey |

C.S.Cowdrey (1)
| 1 | 103+ | 5 | 0 | West Indies | Headingley | 1988 | A.J.Lamb & R.A.Smith |

K.J.Barnett (1)
| 1 | 114 | 3 | 80 | Australia | Headingley | 1989 | A.J.Lamb |

W.Larkins (1)
| 1 | 112 | 1 | 54 | West Indies | Port-of-Spain | 1989/90 | G.A.Gooch |

H.Morris (1)
| 1 | 112 | 1 | 44 | West Indies | The Oval | 1991 | G.A.Gooch |

C.C.Lewis (1)
| 1 | 118 | 7 | 75* | West Indies | St John's | 1993/94 | R.C.Russell |

P.A.J.DeFreitas (1)
| 1 | 130 | 8 | 69 | New Zealand | Old Trafford | 1994 | D.Gough |

D.Gough (1)
| 1 | 130 | 8 | 65 | New Zealand | Old Trafford | 1994 | P.A.J.DeFreitas |

M.R.Ramprakash (1)
| 1 | 158 | 5 | 72 | Australia | Perth | 1994/95 | G.P.Thorpe |

+ Three batsmen sharing in partnership

MOST SUCCESSFUL PARTNERSHIPS

Batsmen	Century Partnerships
J.B.Hobbs & H.Sutcliffe	15
G.A.Gooch & M.A.Atherton	9
J.B.Hobbs & W.Rhodes	8
L.Hutton & C.Washbrook	8
K.F.Barrington & M.C.Cowdrey	8
G.A.Gooch & D.I.Gower	8

Bowling Records

LEADING WICKET TAKERS

Bowler	Balls	Runs	Wkts	Avg	Best	5WI	10WM	S/R
I.T.Botham	21815	10878	383	28.40	8-34	27	4	56.95
R.G.D.Willis	17357	8190	325	25.20	8-43	16	0	53.40
F.S.Trueman	15178	6625	307	21.57	8-31	17	3	49.43
D.L.Underwood	21862	7674	297	25.83	8-51	17	6	73.60
J.B.Statham	16056	6261	252	24.84	7-39	9	1	63.71
A.V.Bedser	15918	5876	236	24.89	7-44	15	5	67.44
J.A.Snow	12021	5387	202	26.66	7-40	8	1	59.50
J.C.Laker	12027	4101	193	21.24	10-53	9	3	62.31
S.F.Barnes	7873	3106	189	16.43	9-103	24	7	41.65
G.A.R.Lock	13147	4451	174	25.58	7-35	9	3	75.55
M.W.Tate	12523	4055	155	26.16	6-42	7	1	80.79
F.J.Titmus	15118	4931	153	32.22	7-79	7	0	98.81
J.E.Emburey	15391	5646	147	38.40	7-78	6	0	104.70
H.Verity	11173	3510	144	24.37	8-43	5	2	77.59
C.M.Old	8858	4020	143	28.11	7-50	4	0	61.94
A.W.Greig	9802	4541	141	32.20	8-86	6	2	69.51
P.A.J.DeFreitas	9838	4700	140	33.57	7-70	4	0	70.27
G.R.Dilley	8192	4107	138	29.76	6-38	6	0	59.36
T.E.Bailey	9712	3856	132	29.21	7-34	5	1	73.57
W.Rhodes	8231	3425	127	26.96	8-68	6	1	64.81
P.H.Edmonds	12028	4273	125	34.18	7-66	2	0	96.22
D.A.Allen	11297	3779	122	30.97	5-30	4	0	92.59
R.Illingworth	11934	3807	122	31.20	6-29	3	0	97.81
D.E.Malcolm	7922	4441	122	36.40	9-57	5	2	64.93
A.R.C.Fraser	7967	3509	119	29.48	8-75	8	0	66.94
J.Briggs	5332	2094	118	17.74	8-11	9	4	45.18
G.G.Arnold	7650	3254	115	28.29	6-45	6	0	66.52
G.A.Lohmann	3821	1205	112	10.75	9-28	9	5	34.11
D.V.P.Wright	8135	4224	108	39.11	7-105	6	1	75.32
R.Peel	5216	1715	102	16.81	7-31	6	2	51.13
J.H.Wardle	6597	2080	102	20.39	7-36	5	1	64.67
C.Blythe	4546	1863	100	18.63	8-59	9	4	45.46
W.Voce	6360	2733	98	27.88	7-70	3	2	64.89
C.C.Lewis	6852	3490	93	37.52	6-111	3	0	73.67
T.Richardson	4497	2220	88	25.22	8-94	11	4	51.10
N.A.Foster	6261	2891	88	32.85	8-107	5	1	71.14
M.Hendrick	6208	2248	87	25.83	4-28	0	0	71.35
F.E.Woolley	6495	2815	83	33.91	7-76	4	1	78.25
W.R.Hammond	7969	3138	83	37.80	5-36	2	0	96.01
G.O.B.Allen	4386	2379	81	29.37	7-80	5	1	54.14
D.J.Brown	5098	2237	79	28.31	5-42	2	0	64.53
H.Larwood	4969	2212	78	28.35	6-32	4	1	63.70
F.H.Tyson	3452	1411	76	18.56	7-27	4	1	45.42
J.K.Lever	4433	1951	73	26.72	7-46	3	1	60.72
K.Higgs	4112	1473	71	20.74	6-91	2	0	57.91
B.R.Knight	5377	2223	70	31.75	4-38	0	0	76.81
D.R.Pringle	5287	2518	70	35.97	5-95	3	0	75.52
W.E.Bowes	3655	1519	68	22.33	6-33	6	0	53.75
P.C.R.Tufnell	6378	2671	68	39.27	7-47	4	1	93.79
P.I.Pocock	6650	2976	67	44.41	6-79	3	0	99.25
D.G.Cork	3752	1949	67	29.08	7-43	3	0	56.00
A.P.Freeman	3732	1707	66	25.86	7-71	5	3	56.54
E.R.Dexter	5317	2306	66	34.93	4-10	0	0	80.56
R.W.V.Robins	3318	1758	64	27.46	6-32	1	0	51.84
K.Farnes	3932	1719	60	28.65	6-96	3	1	65.53
G.Miller	5149	1859	60	30.98	5-44	1	0	85.81

Bowler	Balls	Runs	Wkts	Avg	Best	5WI	10WM	S/R
G.H.Hirst	3967	1770	59	30.00	5-48	3	0	67.23
R.Tattersall	4228	1513	58	26.08	7-52	4	1	72.89
G.C.Small	3927	1871	55	34.01	5-48	2	0	71.40
N.G.B.Cook	4174	1689	52	32.48	6-65	4	1	80.26
N.G.Cowans	3452	2003	51	39.27	6-77	2	0	67.68
W.Barnes	2289	793	51	15.54	6-28	3	0	44.88
W.Bates	2364	821	50	16.42	7-28	4	1	47.28
G.Ulyett	2627	1020	50	20.40	7-36	1	0	52.54
J.T.Hearne	2976	1082	49	22.08	6-41	4	1	60.73
J.C.White	4801	1581	49	32.26	8-126	3	1	97.97
L.C.Braund	3803	1810	47	38.51	8-81	3	0	80.91
B.L.D'Oliveira	5706	1859	47	39.55	3-46	0	0	121.40
G.Geary	3810	1353	46	29.41	7-70	4	1	82.82
F.R.Foster	2447	926	45	20.57	6-91	4	0	54.37
I.A.R.Peebles	2882	1391	45	30.91	6-63	3	0	64.04
F.R.Brown	3260	1398	45	31.06	5-49	1	0	72.44
J.W.H.T.Douglas	2812	1486	45	33.02	5-46	1	0	62.48
W.E.Hollies	3554	1332	44	30.27	7-50	5	0	80.77
I.J.Jones	3546	1769	44	40.20	6-118	1	0	80.59
W.H.Lockwood	1970	884	43	20.55	7-71	5	1	45.81
E.E.Hemmings	4437	1825	43	42.44	6-58	1	0	103.18
D.Gough	2521	1358	43	31.58	6-49	1	0	58.62
R.W.Barber	3426	1806	42	43.00	4-132	0	0	81.57
M.S.Nichols	2565	1152	41	28.09	6-35	2	0	62.56
P.Lever	3571	1509	41	36.80	6-38	2	0	87.09
W.J.Edrich	3234	1693	41	41.29	4-68	0	0	78.87
J.S.E.Price	2724	1401	40	35.02	5-73	1	0	68.10

LOWEST BOWLING AVERAGES

(Minimum qualification: 10 wickets)

Bowler	Avg	Runs	Wkts
J.J.Ferris	7.00	91	13
C.S.Marriott	8.72	96	11
F.Martin	10.07	141	14
G.A.Lohmann	10.75	1205	112
A.E.Trott	11.64	198	17
H.Dean	13.90	153	11
W.Barnes	15.54	793	51
W.Bates	16.42	821	50
S.F.Barnes	16.43	3106	189
R.Peel	16.81	1715	102
J.Briggs	17.74	2094	118
R.Appleyard	17.87	554	31
H.J.Butler	17.91	215	12
W.S.Lees	17.96	467	26
G.H.T.Simpson-Hayward	18.26	420	23
F.Morley	18.50	296	16
F.H.Tyson	18.56	1411	76
C.Blythe	18.63	1863	100
M.J.C.Allom	18.92	265	14
A.S.Kennedy	19.32	599	31
W.H.Copson	19.80	297	15
J.H.Wardle	20.39	2080	102
G.Ulyett	20.40	1020	50
W.H.Lockwood	20.55	884	43
F.R.Foster	20.57	926	45
K.Higgs	20.74	1473	71
A.G.Steel	20.86	605	29
W.Brearley	21.11	359	17
W.Flowers	21.14	296	14
J.C.Laker	21.24	4101	193
J.R.Gunn	21.50	387	18
N.A.Mallender	21.50	215	10
F.S.Trueman	21.57	6625	307
James Langridge	21.73	413	19
H.I.Young	21.83	262	12
V.W.C.Jupp	22.00	616	28
E.Peate	22.00	682	31
J.T.Hearne	22.08	1082	49
T.Greenhough	22.31	357	16
W.E.Bowes	22.33	1519	68
P.J.Loader	22.51	878	39
R.G.Barlow	22.55	767	34

Bowler	Avg	Runs	Wkts
W.Attewell	23.18	626	27
R.M.H.Cottam	23.35	327	14
A.Shaw	23.75	285	12
B.J.T.Bosanquet	24.16	604	25
H.Verity	24.37	3510	144
J.B.Statham	24.84	6261	252
A.V.Bedser	24.89	5876	236
A.E.Relf	24.96	624	25

GREATEST STRIKE RATES

(Deliveries per wicket – minimum qualification: 10 wickets)

Bowler	S/R	Balls	Wkts
J.J.Ferris	20.92	272	13
C.S.Marriott	22.45	247	11
A.E.Trott	27.88	474	17
F.Martin	29.28	410	14
G.A.Lohmann	34.11	3821	112
B.J.T.Bosanquet	38.80	970	25
G.H.T.Simpson-Hayward	39.04	898	23
H.Dean	40.63	447	11
W.Brearley	41.47	705	17
S.F.Barnes	41.65	7873	189
W.Barnes	44.88	2289	51
N.A.Mallender	44.90	449	10
J.Briggs	45.18	5332	118
F.H.Tyson	45.42	3452	76
C.Blythe	45.46	4546	100
W.H.Lockwood	45.81	1970	43
H.J.Butler	46.00	552	12
H.I.Young	46.33	556	12
V.W.C.Jupp	46.46	1301	28
A.G.Steel	47.03	1364	29
W.Bates	47.28	2364	50
W.S.Lees	48.30	1256	26
S.L.Watkin	48.54	534	11
F.S.Trueman	49.43	15178	307
W.H.Copson	50.80	762	15
T.Richardson	51.10	4497	88
R.Peel	51.13	5216	102
R.Appleyard	51.48	1596	31
R.W.V.Robins	51.84	3318	64
G.Ulyett	52.54	2627	50
R.G.D.Willis	53.40	17357	325
W.E.Bowes	53.75	3655	68
S.Haigh	53.91	1294	24
G.O.B.Allen	54.14	4386	81
E.G.Arnold	54.29	1683	31
A.S.Kennedy	54.29	1683	31
Alan Ward	54.35	761	14
F.R.Foster	54.37	2447	45
J.R.Gunn	55.50	999	18
D.G.Cork	56.00	3752	67
K.Cranston	56.11	1010	18
C.P.Buckenham	56.28	1182	21
J.N.Crawford	56.48	2203	39
James Langridge	56.52	1074	19
A.P.Freeman	56.54	3732	66
I.T.Botham	56.95	21815	383
A.Fielder	57.34	1491	26
K.Higgs	57.91	4112	71
M.J.C.Allom	58.35	817	14
D.Gough	58.62	2521	43
J.D.F.Larter	58.70	2172	37
G.T.S.Stevens	59.30	1186	20
G.R.Dilley	59.36	8192	138
G.J.Thompson	59.43	1367	23
J.A.Snow	59.50	12021	202

BEST BOWLING

Score	Bowler	Opposition	Venue	Date	No
10–53	J.C.Laker	Australia	Old Trafford	1956	280

Score	Bowler	Opposition	Venue	Date	No
9–28	G.A.Lohmann	South Africa	Johannesburg (1)	1895/96	52
9–37	J.C.Laker	Australia	Old Trafford	1956	279
9–57	D.E.Malcolm	South Africa	The Oval	1994	500
9–103	S.F.Barnes	South Africa	Johannesburg (1)	1913/14	139
8–7	G.A.Lohmann	South Africa	Port Elizabeth	1895/96	51
8–11	J.Briggs	South Africa	Cape Town	1888/89	31
8–29	S.F.Barnes	South Africa	The Oval	1912	132
8–31	F.S.Trueman	India	Old Trafford	1952	256
8–34	I.T.Botham	Pakistan	Lord's	1978	409
8–35	G.A.Lohmann	Australia	Sydney	1886/87	22
8–43	H.Verity	Australia	Lord's	1934	199
8–43	R.G.D.Willis	Australia	Headingley	1981	425
8–51	D.L.Underwood	Pakistan	Lord's	1974	381
8–56	S.F.Barnes	South Africa	Johannesburg (1)	1913/14	138
8–58	G.A.Lohmann	Australia	Sydney	1891/92	35
8–59	C.Blythe	South Africa	Headingley	1907	97
8–68	W.Rhodes	Australia	Melbourne	1903/04	84
8–75	A.R.C.Fraser	West Indies	Bridgetown	1992/93	497
8–81	L.C.Braund	Australia	Melbourne	1903/04	86
8–86	A.W.Greig	West Indies	Port–of–Spain	1973/74	377
8–94	T.Richardson	Australia	Sydney	1897/98	64
8–103	I.T.Botham	West Indies	Lord's	1984	446
8–107	B.J.T.Bosanquet	Australia	Trent Bridge	1905	89
8–107	N.A.Foster	Pakistan	Headingley	1987	465
8–126	J.C.White	Australia	Adelaide	1928/29	168
7–17	J.Briggs	South Africa	Cape Town	1888/89	30
7–17	W.Rhodes	Australia	Edgbaston	1902	75
7–27	F.H.Tyson	Australia	Melbourne	1954/55	271
7–28	W.Bates	Australia	Melbourne	1882/83	6
7–31	R.Peel	Australia	Old Trafford	1888	28
7–32	D.L.Underwood	New Zealand	Lord's	1969	352
7–34	T.E.Bailey	West Indies	Kingston	1953/54	266
7–35	G.A.R.Lock	New Zealand	Old Trafford	1958	296
7–36	G.Ulyett	Australia	Lord's	1884	10
7–36	G.A.Lohmann	Australia	The Oval	1886	19
7–36	J.H.Wardle	South Africa	Cape Town	1956/57	283
7–37	J.J.Ferris	South Africa	Cape Town	1891/92	39
7–38	G.A.Lohmann	South Africa	Port Elizabeth	1895/96	50
7–39	J.B.Statham	South Africa	Lord's	1955	274
7–40	R.G.Barlow	Australia	Sydney	1882/83	8
7–40	C.Blythe	South Africa	Headingley	1907	98
7–40	J.A.Snow	Australia	Sydney	1970/71	357
7–42	G.A.Lohmann	South Africa	Cape Town	1895/96	54
7–43	D.G.Cork	West Indies	Lord's	1996	504
7–44	R.G.Barlow	Australia	Old Trafford	1886	16
7–44	A.V.Bedser	Australia	Trent Bridge	1953	261
7–44	T.E.Bailey	West Indies	Lord's	1957	286
7–44	F.S.Trueman	West Indies	Edgbaston	1963	323
7–46	C.Blythe	South Africa	Cape Town	1909/10	118
7–46	J.K.Lever	India	Delhi	1976/77	391
7–47	P.C.R.Tufnell	New Zealand	Christchurch	1991/92	490
7–48	I.T.Botham	India	Bombay (3)	1979/80	421
7–49	H.Verity	India	Madras (1)	1933/34	194
7–49	A.V.Bedser	India	Lord's	1946	223
7–49	J.A.Snow	West Indies	Kingston	1967/68	343
7–50	W.E.Hollies	West Indies	Georgetown	1934/35	204
7–50	D.L.Underwood	Australia	The Oval	1968	349
7–50	C.M.Old	Pakistan	Edgbaston	1978	407
7–51	G.A.R.Lock	New Zealand	Headingley	1958	295
7–52	A.V.Bedser	India	Old Trafford	1946	225
7–52	R.Tattersall	South Africa	Lord's	1951	249
7–55	A.V.Bedser	Australia	Trent Bridge	1953	260
7–56	W.Rhodes	Australia	Melbourne	1903/04	83
7–56	S.F.Barnes	South Africa	Durban (1)	1913/14	142
7–56	James Langridge	West Indies	Old Trafford	1933	190
7–56	J.H.Wardle	Pakistan	The Oval	1954	268
7–57	J.B.Statham	Australia	Melbourne	1958/59	297
7–58	A.V.Bedser	South Africa	Old Trafford	1951	251
7–60	S.F.Barnes	Australia	Sydney	1907/08	104
7–61	H.Verity	Australia	Lord's	1934	198
7–66	P.H.Edmonds	Pakistan	Karachi (1)	1977/78	402
7–68	T.Emmett	Australia	Melbourne	1878/79	2
7–70	G.Geary	South Africa	Johannesburg (1)	1927/28	159
7–70	W.Voce	West Indies	Port–of–Spain	1929/30	178

Score	Bowler	Opposition	Venue	Date	No
7–70	P.A.J.DeFreitas	Sri Lanka	Lord's	1991	488
7–71	W.H.Lockwood	Australia	The Oval	1899	68
7–71	A.P.Freeman	South Africa	Old Trafford	1929	172
7–74	W.Bates	Australia	Melbourne	1882/83	7
7–75	F.S.Trueman	New Zealand	Christchurch	1962/63	319
7–76	F.E.Woolley	New Zealand	Wellington	1929/30	175
7–78	R.G.D.Willis	Australia	Lord's	1977	396
7–78	J.E.Emburey	Australia	Sydney	1986/87	464
7–79	F.J.Titmus	Australia	Sydney	1962/63	317
7–80	G.O.B.Allen	India	The Oval	1936	211
7–88	S.F.Barnes	South Africa	Durban (1)	1913/14	143
7–103	J.C.Laker	West Indies	Bridgetown	1947/48	231
7–105	D.V.P.Wright	Australia	Sydney	1946/47	227
7–113	D.L.Underwood	Australia	Adelaide	1974/75	384
7–115	A.P.Freeman	South Africa	Headingley	1929	171
7–121	S.F.Barnes	Australia	Melbourne	1901/02	72
7–168	T.Richardson	Australia	Old Trafford	1896	58
6–7	A.E.R.Gilligan	South Africa	Edgbaston	1924	151
6–11	S.Haigh	South Africa	Cape Town	1898/99	66
6–12	D.L.Underwood	New Zealand	Christchurch	1970/71	358
6–20	G.A.R.Lock	West Indies	The Oval	1957	291
6–23	R.Peel	Australia	The Oval	1896	61
6–25	P.C.R.Tufnell	West Indies	The Oval	1991	486
6–28	W.Barnes	Australia	Sydney	1886/87	21
6–28	F.H.Tyson	South Africa	Trent Bridge	1955	273
6–29	T.W.J.Goddard	New Zealand	Old Trafford	1937	216
6–29	R.Illingworth	India	Lord's	1967	339
6–30	F.S.Trueman	Australia	Headingley	1961	308
6–31	W.Barnes	Australia	Melbourne	1884/85	13
6–31	F.S.Trueman	Pakistan	Lord's	1962	313
6–32	H.Larwood	Australia	Brisbane (1)	1928/29	164
6–32	R.W.V.Robins	West Indies	Lord's	1933	189
6–33	W.E.Bowes	West Indies	Old Trafford	1939	221
6–33	J.E.Emburey	Sri Lanka	Colombo (1)	1981/82	431
6–34	W.E.Bowes	New Zealand	Auckland	1932/33	188
6–34	I.T.Botham	New Zealand	Trent Bridge	1978	411
6–35	M.S.Nichols	South Africa	Trent Bridge	1935	206
6–36	P.J.Loader	West Indies	Headingley	1957	289
6–37	A.V.Bedser	South Africa	Trent Bridge	1951	248
6–38	P.Lever	Australia	Melbourne	1974/75	385
6–38	G.R.Dilley	New Zealand	Christchurch	1987/88	469
6–39	T.Richardson	Australia	Lord's	1896	55
6–40	F.H.Tyson	South Africa	Port Elizabeth	1956/57	285
6–41	J.T.Hearne	Australia	The Oval	1896	60
6–41	W.Voce	Australia	Brisbane (2)	1936/37	212
6–41	D.L.Underwood	New Zealand	The Oval	1969	353
6–42	S.F.Barnes	Australia	Melbourne	1901/02	71
6–42	M.W.Tate	South Africa	Headingley	1924	153
6–43	G.H.T.Simpson–Hayward	South Africa	Johannesburg (1)	1909/10	115
6–44	C.Blythe	Australia	Edgbaston	1909	106
6–44	R.Tattersall	New Zealand	Wellington	1950/51	247
6–45	J.Briggs	Australia	Lord's	1886	18
6–45	D.L.Underwood	Australia	Headingley	1972	365
6–45	G.G.Arnold	India	Delhi	1972/73	366
6–48	W.H.Lockwood	Australia	Old Trafford	1902	78
6–48	R.Tattersall	India	Kanpur	1951/52	254
6–49	J.Briggs	Australia	Adelaide	1891/92	36
6–49	S.F.Barnes	Australia	Bramall Lane	1902	76
6–49	D.Gough	Australia	Sydney	1994/95	501
6–50	F.Martin	Australia	The Oval	1890	32
6–51	B.J.T.Bosanquet	Australia	Sydney	1903/04	85
6–52	F.Martin	Australia	The Oval	1890	33
6–52	S.F.Barnes	South Africa	Headingley	1912	129
6–53	G.A.R.Lock	New Zealand	Christchurch	1958/59	300
6–53	R.G.D.Willis	India	Bangalore	1976/77	394
6–54	J.J.Ferris	South Africa	Cape Town	1891/92	38
6–54	C.M.Old	New Zealand	Wellington	1977/78	403
6–55	J.C.Laker	South Africa	The Oval	1951	253
6–55	J.C.Laker	Australia	Headingley	1956	278
6–58	I.T.Botham	India	Bombay (3)	1979/80	420
6–58	E.E.Hemmings	New Zealand	Edgbaston	1990	478
6–59	C.S.Marriott	West Indies	The Oval	1933	192
6–60	J.A.Snow	West Indies	Georgetown	1967/68	345
6–60	D.L.Underwood	New Zealand	The Oval	1969	354

Score	Bowler	Opposition	Venue	Date	No
7–70	W.Voce	West Indies	Port–of–Spain	1929/30	178
6–61	P.J.W.Allott	West Indies	Headingley	1984	447
6–63	S.F.Barnes	Australia	Headingley	1909	110
6–63	I.A.R.Peebles	South Africa	Johannesburg (1)	1930/31	182
6–63	J.B.Statham	South Africa	Lord's	1960	304
6–65	G.A.R.Lock	India	Madras (2)	1961/62	311
6–65	N.G.B.Cook	Pakistan	Karachi (1)	1983/84	441
6–65	A.R.Caddick	West Indies	Port–of–Spain	1993/94	496
6–66	D.L.Underwood	Australia	Old Trafford	1977	397
6–67	R.Peel	Australia	Sydney	1894/95	46
6–67	P.M.Such	Australia	Old Trafford	1993	494
6–68	C.Blythe	South Africa	Cape Town	1905/06	94
6–73	F.J.Titmus	India	Kanpur	1963/64	326
6–76	T.Richardson	Australia	Old Trafford	1896	59
6–77	N.G.Cowans	Australia	Melbourne	1982/83	436
6–77	R.M.Ellison	Australia	Edgbaston	1985	454
6–77	D.E.Malcolm	West Indies	Port–of–Spain	1989/90	475
6–78	W.S.Lees	South Africa	Johannesburg (1)	1905/06	93
6–78	I.T.Botham	Australia	Perth	1979/80	418
6–79	P.I.Pocock	Australia	Old Trafford	1968	346
6–82	A.Fielder	Australia	Sydney	1907/08	100
6–82	A.R.C.Fraser	Australia	Melbourne	1990/91	482
6–84	J.W.Sharpe	Australia	Melbourne	1891/92	34
6–84	T.E.Bailey	New Zealand	Old Trafford	1949	237
6–85	E.Peate	Australia	Lord's	1884	9
6–85	S.F.Barnes	South Africa	Lord's	1912	128
6–85	F.H.Tyson	Australia	Sydney	1954/55	269
6–85	L.J.Coldwell	Pakistan	Lord's	1962	314
6–85	D.L.Underwood	New Zealand	Christchurch	1970/71	359
6–87	J.Briggs	Australia	Adelaide	1891/92	37
6–87	R.Illingworth	Australia	Headingley	1968	348
6–90	I.T.Botham	Sri Lanka	Lord's	1984	449
6–91	F.R.Foster	Australia	Melbourne	1911/12	121
6–91	K.Higgs	West Indies	Lord's	1966	338
6–94	T.W.Cartwright	South Africa	Trent Bridge	1965	331
6–95	A.V.Bedser	Australia	Headingley	1953	264
6–95	I.T.Botham	Australia	Headingley	1981	424
6–96	K.Farnes	Australia	Melbourne	1936/37	215
6–98	J.T.Hearne	Australia	Melbourne	1897/98	63
6–99	M.W.Tate	Australia	Melbourne	1924/25	156
6–100	F.S.Trueman	West Indies	Lord's	1963	320
6–101	W.H.Lockwood	Australia	Lord's	1893	40
6–101	I.T.Botham	New Zealand	Lord's	1978	412
6–101	R.G.D.Willis	India	Lord's	1982	433
6–104	T.Richardson	Australia	Melbourne	1894/95	49
6–104	N.A.Foster	India	Madras (1)	1984/85	450
6–111	C.C.Lewis	West Indies	Edgbaston	1991	485
6–114	J.A.Snow	Australia	Brisbane (2)	1970/71	355
6–118	T.E.Bailey	New Zealand	Headingley	1949	235
6–118	I.J.Jones	Australia	Adelaide	1965/66	335
6–124	R.Howorth	West Indies	Bridgetown	1947/48	232
6–125	I.T.Botham	Australia	The Oval	1981	427
6–130	M.W.Tate	Australia	Sydney	1924/25	154
6–142	W.E.Bowes	Australia	Headingley	1934	200
6–154	G.R.Dilley	Pakistan	The Oval	1987	467
6–164	A.W.Greig	West Indies	Bridgetown	1973/74	376
6–204	I.A.R.Peebles	Australia	The Oval	1930	180
5–11	I.T.Botham	Australia	Edgbaston	1981	426
5–14	G.O.B.Allen	New Zealand	The Oval	1931	184
5–16	F.R.Foster	South Africa	Lord's	1912	127
5–16	C.I.J.Smith	West Indies	Bridgetown	1934/35	203
5–17	G.A.Lohmann	Australia	Sydney	1887/88	23
5–17	G.A.R.Lock	New Zealand	Lord's	1958	293
5–17	J.C.Laker	New Zealand	Headingley	1958	294
5–18	R.Peel	Australia	Sydney	1887/88	24
5–18	N.G.B.Cook	Pakistan	Karachi (1)	1983/84	442
5–19	R.G.Barlow	Australia	The Oval	1882	5
5–19	C.A.Smith	South Africa	Port Elizabeth	1888/89	29
5–19	F.J.Titmus	New Zealand	Headingley	1965	330
5–20	F.E.Woolley	Australia	The Oval	1912	135
5–20	T.E.Bailey	South Africa	Johannesburg (3)	1956/57	281
5–20	D.L.Underwood	Pakistan	Lord's	1974	380
5–21	C.M.Old	India	Lord's	1974	379
5–21	I.T.Botham	Australia	Headingley	1977	400

Score	Bowler	Opposition	Venue	Date	No
5–24	W.Bates	Australia	Sydney	1884/85	15
5–24	R.Pollard	India	Old Trafford	1946	224
5–24	A.W.Greig	India	Calcutta	1972/73	367
5–25	J.Briggs	Australia	The Oval	1888	26
5–25	S.F.Barnes	South Africa	Lord's	1912	126
5–27	A.V.Bedser	India	Old Trafford	1952	257
5–27	F.S.Trueman	South Africa	Trent Bridge	1960	306
5–27	G.G.Arnold	New Zealand	Headingley	1973	373
5–27	R.G.D.Willis	India	Calcutta	1976/77	392
5–28	W.H.Lockwood	Australia	Old Trafford	1902	79
5–28	S.F.Barnes	South Africa	The Oval	1912	130
5–28	H.Larwood	Australia	Sydney	1932/33	186
5–28	G.A.R.Lock	West Indies	The Oval	1957	290
5–28	P.H.Edmonds	Australia	Headingley	1975	388
5–28	D.L.Underwood	Sri Lanka	Colombo (1)	1981/82	430
5–28	A.R.C.Fraser	West Indies	Kingston	1989/90	474
5–29	J.Briggs	Australia	Lord's	1886	17
5–29	F.E.Woolley	Australia	The Oval	1912	134
5–30	S.F.Barnes	Australia	The Oval	1912	133
5–30	D.A.Allen	Pakistan	Dacca	1961/62	312
5–31	W.Bates	Australia	Adelaide	1884/85	11
5–31	F.S.Trueman	New Zealand	Edgbaston	1958	292
5–31	G.A.R.Lock	New Zealand	Christchurch	1958/59	299
5–31	J.B.Statham	India	Trent Bridge	1959	301
5–31	C.C.Lewis	New Zealand	Auckland	1991/92	491
5–32	W.Barnes	Australia	The Oval	1888	27
5–32	R.G.D.Willis	New Zealand	Wellington	1977/78	404
5–33	H.Verity	Australia	Sydney	1932/33	187
5–34	J.Briggs	Australia	The Oval	1893	41
5–34	W.S.Lees	South Africa	Johannesburg (1)	1905/06	92
5–34	J.B.Statham	South Africa	Lord's	1960	305
5–35	G.Geary	Australia	Sydney	1928/29	165
5–35	G.O.B.Allen	India	Lord's	1936	208
5–35	T.Greenhough	India	Lord's	1959	302
5–35	F.S.Trueman	West Indies	Port-of-Spain	1959/60	303
5–35	I.T.Botham	India	Lord's	1979	417
5–35	R.G.D.Willis	New Zealand	Headingley	1983	437
5–35	N.G.B.Cook	New Zealand	Lord's	1983	438
5–36	F.R.Foster	Australia	Adelaide	1911/12	122
5–36	W.R.Hammond	South Africa	Johannesburg (1)	1927/28	161
5–36	G.O.B.Allen	Australia	Brisbane (2)	1936/37	213
5–37	E.G.Arnold	South Africa	Lord's	1907	96
5–37	C.S.Marriott	West Indies	The Oval	1933	191
5–38	A.Shaw	Australia	Melbourne	1876/77	1
5–38	C.Heseltine	South Africa	Johannesburg (1)	1895/96	53
5–38	C.H.Parkin	Australia	Old Trafford	1921	147
5–38	M.J.C.Allom	New Zealand	Christchurch	1929/30	174
5–39	A.P.Freeman	West Indies	Old Trafford	1928	163
5–39	D.L.Underwood	West Indies	Lord's	1976	389
5–39	I.T.Botham	New Zealand	Lord's	1978	413
5–40	R.Peel	Australia	Sydney	1887/88	25
5–40	J.B.Statham	South Africa	The Oval	1965	333
5–41	F.E.Woolley	South Africa	The Oval	1912	131
5–41	A.V.Bedser	India	The Oval	1952	259
5–41	D.A.Allen	South Africa	Durban (2)	1964/65	328
5–41	I.T.Botham	Australia	Melbourne	1986/87	461
5–42	J.T.Hearne	Australia	Sydney	1897/98	62
5–42	D.J.Brown	Australia	Lord's	1968	347
5–42	R.G.D.Willis	West Indies	Headingley	1976	390
5–42	R.G.D.Willis	New Zealand	The Oval	1978	410
5–42	N.G.Cowans	Pakistan	Lahore (2)	1983/84	444
5–43	E.Peate	Australia	Sydney	1881/82	4
5–43	G.O.B.Allen	India	Lord's	1936	209
5–44	S.F.Barnes	Australia	Melbourne	1911/12	120
5–44	R.G.D.Willis	Australia	Perth	1978/79	414
5–44	G.Miller	Australia	Sydney	1978/79	415
5–45	W.H.Lockwood	Australia	The Oval	1902	81
5–45	G.A.R.Lock	Australia	The Oval	1953	265
5–46	W.Flowers	Australia	Melbourne	1884/85	14
5–46	J.W.H.T.Douglas	Australia	Melbourne	1911/12	125
5–46	A.V.Bedser	Australia	Melbourne	1950/51	243
5–46	I.T.Botham	India	Lord's	1982	432
5–46	R.M.Ellison	Australia	The Oval	1985	455
5–46	D.E.Malcolm	New Zealand	Edgbaston	1990	479

Score	Bowler	Opposition	Venue	Date	No
5–47	K.Shuttleworth	Australia	Brisbane (2)	1970/71	356
5–47	R.G.D.Willis	Pakistan	Lord's	1978	408
5–48	G.H.Hirst	Australia	Melbourne	1903/04	87
5–48	J.N.Crawford	Australia	Melbourne	1907/08	103
5–48	S.F.Barnes	South Africa	Durban (1)	1913/14	137
5–48	D.V.P.Wright	New Zealand	Wellington	1950/51	246
5–48	F.S.Trueman	India	The Oval	1952	258
5–48	F.S.Trueman	Australia	Lord's	1964	327
5–48	G.C.Small	Australia	Melbourne	1986/87	462
5–49	T.Richardson	Australia	Old Trafford	1893	43
5–49	A.E.Trott	South Africa	Johannesburg (1)	1898/99	65
5–49	J.W.Hearne	South Africa	Johannesburg (1)	1913/14	140
5–49	W.E.Bowes	Australia	The Oval	1938	217
5–49	F.R.Brown	Australia	Melbourne	1950/51	244
5–49	R.Tattersall	South Africa	Lord's	1951	250
5–50	C.Blythe	South Africa	Cape Town	1905/06	95
5–50	N.A.Mallender	Pakistan	Headingley	1992	492
5–51	R.Peel	Australia	Adelaide	1884/85	12
5–51	R.Appleyard	Pakistan	Trent Bridge	1954	267
5–51	A.W.Greig	New Zealand	Auckland	1974/75	387
5–52	Hon.F.S.Jackson	Australia	Trent Bridge	1905	88
5–52	F.S.Trueman	West Indies	Lord's	1963	321
5–52	D.L.Underwood	Pakistan	Trent Bridge	1967	340
5–53	J.H.Wardle	South Africa	Cape Town	1956/57	282
5–53	J.B.Statham	Australia	Old Trafford	1961	309
5–53	P.A.J.DeFreitas	New Zealand	Trent Bridge	1990	476
5–54	A.P.Freeman	West Indies	Old Trafford	1928	162
5–54	A.V.Bedser	South Africa	Old Trafford	1951	252
5–55	M.S.Nichols	India	Bombay (1)	1933/34	193
5–55	W.E.Bowes	Australia	The Oval	1934	202
5–55	N.Gifford	Pakistan	Karachi (1)	1972/73	369
5–55	G.R.Dilley	West Indies	Lord's	1988	471
5–56	F.Morley	Australia	The Oval	1880	3
5–56	S.F.Barnes	Australia	Old Trafford	1909	111
5–56	J.C.Laker	South Africa	The Oval	1955	275
5–57	T.Richardson	Australia	Melbourne	1894/95	47
5–57	A.Warren	Australia	Headingley	1905	90
5–57	S.F.Barnes	South Africa	Durban (1)	1913/14	136
5–57	H.Larwood	South Africa	Edgbaston	1929	170
5–57	W.R.Hammond	Australia	Adelaide	1936/37	214
5–57	J.D.F.Larter	Pakistan	The Oval	1962	315
5–57	J.A.Snow	Australia	Lord's	1972	363
5–57	J.Birkenshaw	Pakistan	Karachi (1)	1972/73	370
5–58	C.Blythe	Australia	Edgbaston	1909	107
5–58	G.H.Hirst	Australia	Edgbaston	1909	108
5–58	W.Voce	South Africa	Durban (2)	1930/31	181
5–58	J.C.Laker	Australia	Headingley	1956	277
5–58	F.S.Trueman	Australia	Headingley	1961	307
5–58	G.G.Arnold	Pakistan	The Oval	1967	341
5–58	K.Higgs	Pakistan	The Oval	1967	342
5–59	A.V.Bedser	Australia	Melbourne	1950/51	245
5–59	J.K.Lever	India	Madras (1)	1976/77	393
5–59	I.T.Botham	New Zealand	Wellington	1983/84	440
5–59	N.A.Foster	India	Madras (1)	1984/85	451
5–60	C.H.Parkin	Australia	Adelaide	1920/21	144
5–60	G.Geary	South Africa	Johannesburg (1)	1927/28	160
5–60	J.B.Statham	Australia	Melbourne	1954/55	270
5–60	G.R.Dilley	New Zealand	Auckland	1987/88	470
5–61	L.C.Braund	Australia	Sydney	1901/02	70
5–61	C.Blythe	South Africa	The Oval	1907	99
5–61	M.J.Hilton	India	Kanpur	1951/52	255
5–61	J.H.Wardle	South Africa	Durban (2)	1956/57	284
5–61	R.G.D.Willis	Australia	Melbourne	1974/75	382
5–61	I.T.Botham	India	Bombay (3)	1981/82	428
5–61	P.C.R.Tufnell	Australia	Sydney	1990/91	483
5–62	F.S.Trueman	Australia	Melbourne	1962/63	316
5–63	W.Rhodes	Australia	Bramall Lane	1902	77
5–63	C.Blythe	Australia	Old Trafford	1909	112
5–63	James Langridge	India	Madras (1)	1933/34	195
5–63	R.Berry	West Indies	Old Trafford	1950	238
5–63	W.E.Hollies	West Indies	Old Trafford	1950	239
5–63	F.S.Trueman	West Indies	Trent Bridge	1957	287
5–63	D.J.Brown	Australia	Sydney	1965/66	334
5–63	N.G.B.Cook	New Zealand	Trent Bridge	1983	439

Score	Bowler	Opposition	Venue	Date	No
5–63	A.R.Caddick	West Indies	Bridgetown	1993/94	498
5–64	G.G.Macaulay	South Africa	Cape Town	1922/23	148
5–64	N.A.Foster	West Indies	The Oval	1988	473
5–65	S.F.Barnes	Australia	Sydney	1901/02	69
5–65	R.G.D.Willis	West Indies	Trent Bridge	1980	422
5–66	F.J.Titmus	South Africa	Durban (2)	1964/65	329
5–66	R.G.D.Willis	Australia	Brisbane (2)	1982/83	435
5–66	A.R.C.Fraser	West Indies	Lord's	1995	503
5–67	W.M.Bradley	Australia	Old Trafford	1899	67
5–67	D.A.Allen	India	Calcutta	1961/62	310
5–67	N.A.Foster	Pakistan	Lahore (2)	1983/84	443
5–68	G.A.Lohmann	Australia	The Oval	1886	20
5–68	J.D.F.Larter	South Africa	Trent Bridge	1965	332
5–68	G.R.Dilley	Australia	Brisbane (2)	1986/87	459
5–69	G.H.T.Simpson-Hayward	South Africa	Johannesburg (1)	1909/10	117
5–70	H.Verity	South Africa	Cape Town	1938/39	218
5–70	D.C.S.Compton	South Africa	Cape Town	1948/49	234
5–70	P.Lever	India	Old Trafford	1971	361
5–70	R.Illingworth	India	The Oval	1971	362
5–70	A.W.Greig	West Indies	Port-of-Spain	1973/74	378
5–70	I.T.Botham	India	Edgbaston	1979	416
5–71	I.T.Botham	West Indies	Bridgetown	1985/86	458
5–71	P.A.J.DeFreitas	New Zealand	Trent Bridge	1994	499
5–72	S.F.Barnes	Australia	Melbourne	1907/08	102
5–72	I.T.Botham	West Indies	The Oval	1984	448
5–72	C.C.Lewis	India	Edgbaston	1996	506
5–73	J.M.Sims	India	The Oval	1936	210
5–73	J.S.E.Price	India	Calcutta	1963/64	325
5–73	I.T.Botham	New Zealand	Christchurch	1977/78	405
5–73	A.R.C.Fraser	Australia	Sydney	1994/95	502
5–74	S.F.Barnes	Australia	Melbourne	1911/12	124
5–74	I.T.Botham	Australia	Trent Bridge	1977	398
5–74	I.T.Botham	Pakistan	Lord's	1982	434
5–75	T.Richardson	Australia	Adelaide	1894/95	48
5–75	M.W.Tate	Australia	Melbourne	1924/25	157
5–75	F.S.Trueman	West Indies	Edgbaston	1963	322
5–75	G.C.Small	Australia	Sydney	1986/87	463
5–76	J.T.Hearne	Australia	Lord's	1896	57
5–76	J.R.Gunn	Australia	Adelaide	1901/02	73
5–76	A.S.Kennedy	South Africa	Durban (2)	1922/23	150
5–77	G.H.Hirst	Australia	The Oval	1902	80
5–77	I.A.R.Peebles	New Zealand	Lord's	1931	183
5–77	K.Farnes	Australia	Trent Bridge	1934	197
5–78	R.M.Ellison	West Indies	Kingston	1985/86	456
5–78	J.E.Emburey	West Indies	Port-of-Spain	1985/86	457
5–79	J.N.Crawford	Australia	Melbourne	1907/08	101
5–79	J.H.Wardle	Australia	Sydney	1954/55	272
5–80	D.V.P.Wright	South Africa	Lord's	1947	230
5–80	J.E.Emburey	Australia	Brisbane (2)	1986/87	460
5–82	J.E.Emburey	Australia	Headingley	1985	452
5–83	W.Rhodes	Australia	Old Trafford	1909	113
5–83	A.E.R.Gilligan	South Africa	Edgbaston	1924	152
5–83	F.J.Titmus	West Indies	Old Trafford	1966	337
5–84	D.L.Underwood	India	Bombay (3)	1976/77	395
5–84	D.G.Cork	South Africa	Johannesburg (3)	1995/96	505
5–85	A.E.Relf	Australia	Lord's	1909	109
5–85	W.H.Copson	West Indies	Lord's	1939	220
5–86	J.A.Snow	West Indies	Bridgetown	1967/68	344
5–86	G.G.Arnold	Australia	Sydney	1974/75	383
5–86	P.A.J.DeFreitas	Pakistan	Karachi (1)	1987/88	468
5–87	A.R.C.Fraser	Australia	The Oval	1993	495
5–88	A.S.Kennedy	South Africa	Durban (2)	1922/23	149
5–88	R.G.D.Willis	Australia	Trent Bridge	1977	399
5–90	P.G.H.Fender	Australia	Sydney	1920/21	146
5–90	G.T.S.Stevens	West Indies	Bridgetown	1929/30	177
5–90	F.S.Trueman	Australia	Lord's	1956	276
5–92	F.R.Foster	Australia	Sydney	1911/12	119
5–92	J.A.Snow	Australia	Trent Bridge	1972	364
5–92	G.R.Dilley	Pakistan	Edgbaston	1987	466
5–94	W.Rhodes	Australia	Sydney	1903/04	82
5–94	D.L.Underwood	Pakistan	Dacca	1968/69	350
5–94	D.E.Malcolm	New Zealand	Lord's	1990	477
5–94	P.C.R.Tufnell	Sri Lanka	Lord's	1991	489
5–94	D.E.Malcolm	Pakistan	The Oval	1992	493

Score	Bowler	Opposition	Venue	Date	No
5–95	L.C.Braund	Australia	Melbourne	1901/02	74
5–95	D.V.P.Wright	South Africa	Lord's	1947	229
5–95	D.R.Pringle	West Indies	Headingley	1988	472
5–96	H.Larwood	Australia	Sydney	1932/33	185
5–98	M.W.Tate	Australia	Sydney	1924/25	155
5–98	E.W.Clark	Australia	The Oval	1934	201
5–98	A.W.Greig	New Zealand	Auckland	1974/75	386
5–98	I.T.Botham	Australia	Perth	1979/80	419
5–100	A.P.Freeman	South Africa	Old Trafford	1929	173
5–100	W.E.Bowes	South Africa	Old Trafford	1935	207
5–100	R.T.D.Perks	South Africa	Durban (2)	1938/39	219
5–100	J.K.Lever	India	Bangalore	1981/82	429
5–100	D.R.Pringle	West Indies	Lord's	1991	484
5–102	S.F.Barnes	South Africa	Johannesburg (1)	1913/14	141
5–102	K.Farnes	Australia	Trent Bridge	1934	196
5–102	R.G.D.Willis	Australia	The Oval	1977	401
5–103	F.J.Titmus	Australia	Sydney	1962/63	318
5–104	A.R.C.Fraser	India	Lord's	1990	480
5–105	S.F.Barnes	Australia	Adelaide	1911/12	123
5–105	G.Geary	Australia	Melbourne	1928/29	169
5–105	G.T.S.Stevens	West Indies	Bridgetown	1929/30	176
5–105	A.V.Bedser	Australia	Lord's	1953	262
5–106	D.V.Lawrence	West Indies	The Oval	1991	487
5–107	T.Richardson	Australia	Old Trafford	1893	44
5–107	J.C.White	Australia	Melbourne	1928/29	166
5–107	J.C.Laker	Australia	Sydney	1958/59	298
5–108	D.L.Underwood	New Zealand	Auckland	1970/71	360
5–108	D.R.Pringle	West Indies	Edgbaston	1984	445
5–109	I.T.Botham	New Zealand	Auckland	1977/78	406
5–109	I.T.Botham	Australia	Lord's	1985	453
5–110	W.Brearley	Australia	The Oval	1905	91
5–110	P.I.Pocock	West Indies	Port–of–Spain	1973/74	375
5–113	C.M.Old	New Zealand	Lord's	1973	372
5–113	G.G.Arnold	West Indies	The Oval	1973	374
5–113	D.G.Cork	Pakistan	Headingley	1996	507
5–114	J.Briggs	Australia	The Oval	1893	42
5–114	J.A.Snow	West Indies	Lord's	1969	351
5–115	C.P.Buckenham	South Africa	Johannesburg (1)	1909/10	116
5–115	M.W.Tate	Australia	Sydney	1924/25	158
5–115	A.V.Bedser	Australia	Old Trafford	1953	263
5–116	R.O.Jenkins	West Indies	Lord's	1950	240
5–116	F.J.Titmus	India	Madras (2)	1963/64	324
5–118	J.B.Statham	West Indies	Trent Bridge	1957	288
5–122	P.G.H.Fender	Australia	Melbourne	1920/21	145
5–123	W.E.Hollies	South Africa	Trent Bridge	1947	228
5–123	D.A.Allen	New Zealand	Auckland	1965/66	336
5–124	M.W.Tate	Australia	Headingley	1930	179
5–124	J.E.Emburey	West Indies	Port–of–Spain	1980/81	423
5–124	A.R.C.Fraser	India	Old Trafford	1990	481
5–127	A.V.Bedser	West Indies	Trent Bridge	1950	241
5–130	J.C.White	Australia	Adelaide	1928/29	167
5–131	W.E.Hollies	Australia	The Oval	1948	233
5–131	G.G.Arnold	New Zealand	Trent Bridge	1973	371
5–133	W.E.Hollies	New Zealand	Lord's	1949	236
5–134	T.Richardson	Australia	Lord's	1896	56
5–141	J.N.Crawford	Australia	Sydney	1907/08	105
5–141	D.V.P.Wright	West Indies	The Oval	1950	242
5–146	D.W.Carr	Australia	The Oval	1909	114
5–156	R.T.D.Perks	West Indies	The Oval	1939	222
5–167	D.V.P.Wright	Australia	Brisbane (2)	1946/47	226
5–168	G.A.E.Paine	West Indies	Kingston	1934/35	205
5–169	P.I.Pocock	Pakistan	Hyderabad	1972/73	368
5–181	T.Richardson	Australia	Sydney	1894/95	45

BEST BOWLING AGAINST EACH OPPOSITION

Australia

10–53	J.C.Laker	Old Trafford	1956
9–37	J.C.Laker	Old Trafford	1956
8–35	G.A.Lohmann	Sydney	1886/87
8–43	H.Verity	Lord's	1934
8–43	R.G.D.Willis	Headingley	1981

South Africa

9-28	G.A.Lohmann	Johannesburg (1)	1895/96
9-57	D.E.Malcolm	The Oval	1994
9-103	S.F.Barnes	Johannesburg (1)	1913/14
8-7	G.A.Lohmann	Port Elizabeth	1895/96
8-11	J.Briggs	Cape Town	1888/89

West Indies

8-75	A.R.C.Fraser	Bridgetown	1992/93
8-86	A.W.Greig	Port-of-Spain	1973/74
8-103	I.T.Botham	Lord's	1984
7-34	T.E.Bailey	Kingston	1953/54
7-43	D.G.Cork	Lord's	1996

New Zealand

7-32	D.L.Underwood	Lord's	1969
7-35	G.A.R.Lock	Old Trafford	1958
7-47	P.C.R.Tufnell	Christchurch	1991/92
7-51	G.A.R.Lock	Headingley	1958
7-75	F.S.Trueman	Christchurch	1962/63

India

8-31	F.S.Trueman	Old Trafford	1952
7-46	J.K.Lever	Delhi	1976/77
7-48	I.T.Botham	Bombay (3)	1979/80
7-49	H.Verity	Madras (1)	1933/34
7-49	A.V.Bedser	Lord's	1946

Pakistan

8-34	I.T.Botham	Lord's	1978
8-51	D.L.Underwood	Lord's	1974
8-107	N.A.Foster	Headingley	1987
7-50	C.M.Old	Edgbaston	1978
7-56	J.H.Wardle	The Oval	1954

Sri Lanka

7-70	P.A.J.DeFreitas	Lord's	1991
6-33	J.E.Emburey	Colombo (1)	1981/82
6-90	I.T.Botham	Lord's	1984
5-28	D.L.Underwood	Colombo (1)	1981/82
5-94	P.C.R.Tufnell	Lord's	1991

BEST BOWLING PER VENUE

ENGLAND

The Oval

9-57	D.E.Malcolm	South Africa	1994
8-29	S.F.Barnes	South Africa	1912
7-36	G.A.Lohmann	Australia	1886
7-50	D.L.Underwood	Australia	1968
7-56	J.H.Wardle	Pakistan	1954

Old Trafford

10-53	J.C.Laker	Australia	1956
9-37	J.C.Laker	Australia	1956
8-31	F.S.Trueman	India	1952
7-31	R.Peel	Australia	1888
7-35	G.A.R.Lock	New Zealand	1958

Lord's

8-34	I.T.Botham	Pakistan	1978
8-43	H.Verity	Australia	1934
8-51	D.L.Underwood	Pakistan	1974
8-103	I.T.Botham	West Indies	1984
7-32	D.L.Underwood	New Zealand	1969

Trent Bridge

8-107	B.J.T.Bosanquet	Australia	1905
7-44	A.V.Bedser	Australia	1953
7-55	A.V.Bedser	Australia	1953
6-28	F.H.Tyson	South Africa	1955
6-34	I.T.Botham	New Zealand	1978

Headingley

8-43	R.G.D.Willis	Australia	1981
8-59	C.Blythe	South Africa	1907
8-107	N.A.Foster	Pakistan	1987
7-40	C.Blythe	South Africa	1907
7-51	G.A.R.Lock	New Zealand	1958

Edgbaston

7-17	W.Rhodes	Australia	1902
7-44	F.S.Trueman	West Indies	1963
7-50	C.M.Old	Pakistan	1978
6-7	A.E.R.Gilligan	South Africa	1924
6-44	C.Blythe	Australia	1909

Bramall Lane

6-49	S.F.Barnes	Australia	1902
5-63	W.Rhodes	Australia	1902

AUSTRALIA

Melbourne

8-68	W.Rhodes	Australia	1903/04
8-81	L.C.Braund	Australia	1903/04
7-27	F.H.Tyson	Australia	1954/55
7-28	W.Bates	Australia	1882/83
7-56	W.Rhodes	Australia	1903/04

Sydney

8-35	G.A.Lohmann	Australia	1886/87
8-58	G.A.Lohmann	Australia	1891/92
8-94	T.Richardson	Australia	1897/98
7-40	R.G.Barlow	Australia	1882/83
7-40	J.A.Snow	Australia	1970/71

Adelaide

8-126	J.C.White	Australia	1928/29
7-113	D.L.Underwood	Australia	1974/75
6-49	J.Briggs	Australia	1891/92
6-87	J.Briggs	Australia	1891/92
6-118	I.J.Jones	Australia	1965/66

Brisbane (1)

6-32	H.Larwood	Australia	1928/29

Brisbane (2)

6-41	W.Voce	Australia	1936/37
6-114	J.A.Snow	Australia	1970/71
5-36	G.O.B.Allen	Australia	1936/37
5-47	K.Shuttleworth	Australia	1970/71
5-66	R.G.D.Willis	Australia	1982/83

Perth

6-78	I.T.Botham	Australia	1979/80
5-44	R.G.D.Willis	Australia	1978/79
5-98	I.T.Botham	Australia	1979/80

SOUTH AFRICA

Port Elizabeth

8-7	G.A.Lohmann	South Africa	1895/96
7-38	G.A.Lohmann	South Africa	1895/96
6-40	F.H.Tyson	South Africa	1956/57
5-19	C.A.Smith	South Africa	1888/89

Cape Town

8-11	J.Briggs	South Africa	1888/89
7-17	J.Briggs	South Africa	1888/89
7-36	J.H.Wardle	South Africa	1956/57
7-37	J.J.Ferris	South Africa	1891/92
7-42	G.A.Lohmann	South Africa	1895/96

Johannesburg (1)

9-28	G.A.Lohmann	South Africa	1895/96
9-103	S.F.Barnes	South Africa	1913/14
8-56	S.F.Barnes	South Africa	1913/14

| 7-70 | G.Geary | South Africa | 1927/28 |
| 6-43 | G.H.T.Simpson-Hayward | South Africa | 1909/10 |

Durban (1)

7-56	S.F.Barnes	South Africa	1913/14
7-88	S.F.Barnes	South Africa	1913/14
5-48	S.F.Barnes	South Africa	1913/14
5-57	S.F.Barnes	South Africa	1913/14

Durban (2)

5-41	D.A.Allen	South Africa	1964/65
5-58	W.Voce	South Africa	1930/31
5-61	J.H.Wardle	South Africa	1956/57
5-66	F.J.Titmus	South Africa	1964/65
5-76	A.S.Kennedy	South Africa	1922/23

Johannesburg (2)

| 3-88 | R.O.Jenkins | South Africa | 1948/49 |

Johannesburg (3)

| 5-20 | T.E.Bailey | South Africa | 1956/57 |
| 5-84 | D.G.Cork | South Africa | 1995/96 |

Centurion
England have not bowled at Centurion

WEST INDIES

Bridgetown

8-75	A.R.C.Fraser	West Indies	1992/93
7-103	J.C.Laker	West Indies	1947/48
6-124	R.Howorth	West Indies	1947/48
6-164	A.W.Greig	West Indies	1973/74
5-16	C.I.J.Smith	West Indies	1934/35

Port-of-Spain

8-86	A.W.Greig	West Indies	1973/74
7-70	W.Voce	West Indies	1929/30
6-65	A.R.Caddick	West Indies	1993/94
6-77	D.E.Malcolm	West Indies	1989/90
5-35	F.S.Trueman	West Indies	1959/60

Georgetown

| 7-50 | W.E.Hollies | West Indies | 1934/35 |
| 6-60 | J.A.Snow | West Indies | 1967/68 |

Kingston

7-34	T.E.Bailey	West Indies	1953/54
7-49	J.A.Snow	West Indies	1967/68
5-28	A.R.C.Fraser	West Indies	1989/90
5-78	R.M.Ellison	West Indies	1985/86
5-168	G.A.E.Paine	West Indies	1934/35

St John's

| 4-126 | D.E.Malcolm | West Indies | 1989/90 |

NEW ZEALAND

Christchurch

7-47	P.C.R.Tufnell	New Zealand	1991/92
7-75	F.S.Trueman	New Zealand	1962/63
6-12	D.L.Underwood	New Zealand	1970/71
6-38	G.R.Dilley	New Zealand	1987/88
6-53	G.A.R.Lock	New Zealand	1958/59

Wellington

7-76	F.E.Woolley	New Zealand	1929/30
6-44	R.Tattersall	New Zealand	1950/51
6-54	C.M.Old	New Zealand	1977/78
5-32	R.G.D.Willis	New Zealand	1977/78
5-48	D.V.P.Wright	New Zealand	1950/51

Auckland

| 6-34 | W.E.Bowes | New Zealand | 1932/33 |
| 5-31 | C.C.Lewis | New Zealand | 1991/92 |

5-51	A.W.Greig	New Zealand	1974/75
5-60	G.R.Dilley	New Zealand	1987/88
5-98	A.W.Greig	New Zealand	1974/75

Dunedin

| 4-16 | F.H.Tyson | New Zealand | 1954/55 |

INDIA

Bombay (1)

| 5-55 | M.S.Nichols | India | 1933/34 |

Calcutta

5-24	A.W.Greig	India	1972/73
5-27	R.G.D.Willis	India	1976/77
5-67	D.A.Allen	India	1961/62
5-73	J.S.E.Price	India	1963/64

Madras (1)

7-49	H.Verity	India	1933/34
6-104	N.A.Foster	India	1984/85
5-59	J.K.Lever	India	1976/77
5-59	N.A.Foster	India	1984/85
5-63	James Langridge	India	1933/34

Delhi

| 7-46 | J.K.Lever | India | 1976/77 |
| 6-45 | G.G.Arnold | India | 1972/73 |

Bombay (2)

| 4-74 | G.A.R.Lock | India | 1961/62 |

Kanpur

6-48	R.Tattersall	India	1951/52
6-73	F.J.Titmus	India	1963/64
5-61	M.J.Hilton	India	1951/52

Madras (2)

| 6-65 | G.A.R.Lock | India | 1961/62 |
| 5-116 | F.J.Titmus | India | 1963/64 |

Bangalore

| 6-53 | R.G.D.Willis | India | 1976/77 |
| 5-100 | J.K.Lever | India | 1981/82 |

Bombay (3)

7-48	I.T.Botham	India	1979/80
6-58	I.T.Botham	India	1979/80
5-61	I.T.Botham	India	1981/82
5-84	D.L.Underwood	India	1976/77

PAKISTAN

Dacca

| 5-30 | D.A.Allen | Pakistan | 1961/62 |
| 5-94 | D.L.Underwood | Pakistan | 1968/69 |

Karachi (1)

7-66	P.H.Edmonds	Pakistan	1977/78
6-65	N.G.B.Cook	Pakistan	1983/84
5-18	N.G.B.Cook	Pakistan	1983/84
5-55	N.Gifford	Pakistan	1972/73
5-57	J.Birkenshaw	Pakistan	1972/73

Lahore (2)

| 5-42 | N.G.Cowans | Pakistan | 1983/84 |
| 5-67 | N.A.Foster | Pakistan | 1983/84 |

Hyderabad

| 5-169 | P.I.Pocock | Pakistan | 1972/73 |

Faisalabad

| 4-42 | N.A.Foster | Pakistan | 1987/88 |

SRI LANKA

Colombo (1)
6-33	J.E.Emburey	Sri Lanka	1981/82
5-28	D.L.Underwood	Sri Lanka	1981/82

Colombo (2)
4-66	C.C.Lewis	Sri Lanka	1992/93

FIVE WICKET INNINGS PER BOWLER (507)

I.T.Botham (27)
1	5-74	Australia	Trent Bridge	1977
2	5-21	Australia	Headingley	1977
3	5-73	New Zealand	Christchurch	1977/78
4	5-109	New Zealand	Auckland	1977/78
5	8-34	Pakistan	Lord's	1978
6	6-34	New Zealand	Trent Bridge	1978
7	6-101	New Zealand	Lord's	1978
8	5-39	New Zealand	Lord's	1978
9	5-70	India	Edgbaston	1979
10	5-35	India	Lord's	1979
11	6-78	Australia	Perth	1979/80
12	5-98	Australia	Perth	1979/80
13	6-58	India	Bombay (3)	1979/80
14	7-48	India	Bombay (3)	1979/80
15	6-95	Australia	Headingley	1981
16	5-11	Australia	Edgbaston	1981
17	6-125	Australia	The Oval	1981
18	5-61	India	Bombay (3)	1981/82
19	5-46	India	Lord's	1982
20	5-74	Pakistan	Lord's	1982
21	5-59	New Zealand	Wellington	1983/84
22	8-103	West Indies	Lord's	1984
23	5-72	West Indies	The Oval	1984
24	6-90	Sri Lanka	Lord's	1984
25	5-109	Australia	Lord's	1985
26	5-71	West Indies	Bridgetown	1985/86
27	5-41	Australia	Melbourne	1986/87

S.F.Barnes (24)
1	5-65	Australia	Sydney	1901/02
2	6-42	Australia	Melbourne	1901/02
3	7-121	Australia	Melbourne	1901/02
4	6-49	Australia	Bramall Lane	1902
5	5-72	Australia	Melbourne	1907/08
6	7-60	Australia	Sydney	1907/08
7	6-63	Australia	Headingley	1909
8	5-56	Australia	Old Trafford	1909
9	5-44	Australia	Melbourne	1911/12
10	5-105	Australia	Adelaide	1911/12
11	5-74	Australia	Melbourne	1911/12
12	5-25	South Africa	Lord's	1912
13	6-85	South Africa	Lord's	1912
14	6-52	South Africa	Headingley	1912
15	5-28	South Africa	The Oval	1912
16	8-29	South Africa	The Oval	1912
17	5-30	Australia	The Oval	1912
18	5-57	South Africa	Durban (1)	1913/14
19	5-48	South Africa	Durban (1)	1913/14
20	8-56	South Africa	Johannesburg (1)	1913/14
21	9-103	South Africa	Johannesburg (1)	1913/14
22	5-102	South Africa	Johannesburg (1)	1913/14
23	7-56	South Africa	Durban (1)	1913/14
24	7-88	South Africa	Durban (1)	1913/14

F.S.Trueman (17)
1	8-31	India	Old Trafford	1952
2	5-48	India	The Oval	1952
3	5-90	Australia	Lord's	1956
4	5-63	West Indies	Trent Bridge	1957
5	5-31	New Zealand	Edgbaston	1958
6	5-35	West Indies	Port-of-Spain	1959/60
7	5-27	South Africa	Trent Bridge	1960
8	5-58	Australia	Headingley	1961

9	6-30	Australia	Headingley	1961
10	6-31	Pakistan	Lord's	1962
11	5-62	Australia	Melbourne	1962/63
12	7-75	New Zealand	Christchurch	1962/63
13	6-100	West Indies	Lord's	1963
14	5-52	West Indies	Lord's	1963
15	5-75	West Indies	Edgbaston	1963
16	7-44	West Indies	Edgbaston	1963
17	5-48	Australia	Lord's	1964

D.L.Underwood (17)

1	5-52	Pakistan	Trent Bridge	1967
2	7-50	Australia	The Oval	1968
3	5-94	Pakistan	Dacca	1968/69
4	7-32	New Zealand	Lord's	1969
5	6-41	New Zealand	The Oval	1969
6	6-60	New Zealand	The Oval	1969
7	6-12	New Zealand	Christchurch	1970/71
8	6-85	New Zealand	Christchurch	1970/71
9	5-108	New Zealand	Auckland	1970/71
10	6-45	Australia	Headingley	1972
11	5-20	Pakistan	Lord's	1974
12	8-51	Pakistan	Lord's	1974
13	7-113	Australia	Adelaide	1974/75
14	5-39	West Indies	Lord's	1976
15	5-84	India	Bombay (3)	1976/77
16	6-66	Australia	Old Trafford	1977
17	5-28	Sri Lanka	Colombo (1)	1981/82

R.G.D.Willis (16)

1	5-61	Australia	Melbourne	1974/75
2	5-42	West Indies	Headingley	1976
3	5-27	India	Calcutta	1976/77
4	6-53	India	Bangalore	1976/77
5	7-78	Australia	Lord's	1977
6	5-88	Australia	Trent Bridge	1977
7	5-102	Australia	The Oval	1977
8	5-32	New Zealand	Wellington	1977/78
9	5-47	Pakistan	Lord's	1978
10	5-42	New Zealand	The Oval	1978
11	5-44	Australia	Perth	1978/79
12	5-65	West Indies	Trent Bridge	1980
13	8-43	Australia	Headingley	1981
14	6-101	India	Lord's	1982
15	5-66	Australia	Brisbane (2)	1982/83
16	5-35	New Zealand	Headingley	1983

A.V.Bedser (15)

1	7-49	India	Lord's	1946
2	7-52	India	Old Trafford	1946
3	5-127	West Indies	Trent Bridge	1950
4	5-46	Australia	Melbourne	1950/51
5	5-59	Australia	Melbourne	1950/51
6	6-37	South Africa	Trent Bridge	1951
7	7-58	South Africa	Old Trafford	1951
8	5-54	South Africa	Old Trafford	1951
9	5-27	India	Old Trafford	1952
10	5-41	India	The Oval	1952
11	7-55	Australia	Trent Bridge	1953
12	7-44	Australia	Trent Bridge	1953
13	5-105	Australia	Lord's	1953
14	5-115	Australia	Old Trafford	1953
15	6-95	Australia	Headingley	1953

T.Richardson (11)

1	5-49	Australia	Old Trafford	1893
2	5-107	Australia	Old Trafford	1893
3	5-181	Australia	Sydney	1894/95
4	5-57	Australia	Melbourne	1894/95
5	5-75	Australia	Adelaide	1894/95
6	6-104	Australia	Melbourne	1894/95
7	6-39	Australia	Lord's	1896
8	5-134	Australia	Lord's	1896
9	7-168	Australia	Old Trafford	1896
10	6-76	Australia	Old Trafford	1896

11	8-94	Australia	Sydney	1897/98

J.Briggs (9)

1	5-29	Australia	Lord's	1886
2	6-45	Australia	Lord's	1886
3	5-25	Australia	The Oval	1888
4	7-17	South Africa	Cape Town	1888/89
5	8-11	South Africa	Cape Town	1888/89
6	6-49	Australia	Adelaide	1891/92
7	6-87	Australia	Adelaide	1891/92
8	5-34	Australia	The Oval	1893
9	5-114	Australia	The Oval	1893

G.A.Lohmann (9)

1	7-36	Australia	The Oval	1886
2	5-68	Australia	The Oval	1886
3	8-35	Australia	Sydney	1886/87
4	5-17	Australia	Sydney	1887/88
5	8-58	Australia	Sydney	1891/92
6	7-38	South Africa	Port Elizabeth	1895/96
7	8-7	South Africa	Port Elizabeth	1895/96
8	9-28	South Africa	Johannesburg (1)	1895/96
9	7-42	South Africa	Cape Town	1895/96

C.Blythe (9)

1	6-68	South Africa	Cape Town	1905/06
2	5-50	South Africa	Cape Town	1905/06
3	8-59	South Africa	Headingley	1907
4	7-40	South Africa	Headingley	1907
5	5-61	South Africa	The Oval	1907
6	6-44	Australia	Edgbaston	1909
7	5-58	Australia	Edgbaston	1909
8	5-63	Australia	Old Trafford	1909
9	7-46	South Africa	Cape Town	1909/10

J.C.Laker (9)

1	7-103	West Indies	Bridgetown	1947/48
2	6-55	South Africa	The Oval	1951
3	5-56	South Africa	The Oval	1955
4	5-58	Australia	Headingley	1956
5	6-55	Australia	Headingley	1956
6	9-37	Australia	Old Trafford	1956
7	10-53	Australia	Old Trafford	1956
8	5-17	New Zealand	Headingley	1958
9	5-107	Australia	Sydney	1958/59

G.A.R.Lock (9)

1	5-45	Australia	The Oval	1953
2	5-28	West Indies	The Oval	1957
3	6-20	West Indies	The Oval	1957
4	5-17	New Zealand	Lord's	1958
5	7-51	New Zealand	Headingley	1958
6	7-35	New Zealand	Old Trafford	1958
7	5-31	New Zealand	Christchurch	1958/59
8	6-53	New Zealand	Christchurch	1958/59
9	6-65	India	Madras (2)	1961/62

J.B.Statham (9)

1	5-60	Australia	Melbourne	1954/55
2	7-39	South Africa	Lord's	1955
3	5-118	West Indies	Trent Bridge	1957
4	7-57	Australia	Melbourne	1958/59
5	5-31	India	Trent Bridge	1959
6	6-63	South Africa	Lord's	1960
7	5-34	South Africa	Lord's	1960
8	5-53	Australia	Old Trafford	1961
9	5-40	South Africa	The Oval	1965

J.A.Snow (8)

1	7-49	West Indies	Kingston	1967/68
2	5-86	West Indies	Bridgetown	1967/68
3	6-60	West Indies	Georgetown	1967/68
4	5-114	West Indies	Lord's	1969
5	6-114	Australia	Brisbane (2)	1970/71
6	7-40	Australia	Sydney	1970/71

7	5-57	Australia	Lord's	1972
8	5-92	Australia	Trent Bridge	1972

A.R.C.Fraser (8)

1	5-28	West Indies	Kingston	1989/90
2	5-104	India	Lord's	1990
3	5-124	India	Old Trafford	1990
4	6-82	Australia	Melbourne	1990/91
5	5-87	Australia	The Oval	1993
6	8-75	West Indies	Bridgetown	1993/94
7	5-73	Australia	Sydney	1994/95
8	5-66	West Indies	Lord's	1995

M.W.Tate (7)

1	6-42	South Africa	Headingley	1924
2	6-130	Australia	Sydney	1924/25
3	5-98	Australia	Sydney	1924/25
4	6-99	Australia	Melbourne	1924/25
5	5-75	Australia	Melbourne	1924/25
6	5-115	Australia	Sydney	1924/25
7	5-124	Australia	Headingley	1930

F.J.Titmus (7)

1	7-79	Australia	Sydney	1962/63
2	5-103	Australia	Sydney	1962/63
3	5-116	India	Madras (2)	1963/64
4	6-73	India	Kanpur	1963/64
5	5-66	South Africa	Durban (2)	1964/65
6	5-19	New Zealand	Headingley	1965
7	5-83	West Indies	Old Trafford	1966

R.Peel (6)

1	5-51	Australia	Adelaide	1884/85
2	5-18	Australia	Sydney	1887/88
3	5-40	Australia	Sydney	1887/88
4	7-31	Australia	Old Trafford	1888
5	6-67	Australia	Sydney	1894/95
6	6-23	Australia	The Oval	1896

W.Rhodes (6)

1	7-17	Australia	Edgbaston	1902
2	5-63	Australia	Bramall Lane	1902
3	5-94	Australia	Sydney	1903/04
4	7-56	Australia	Melbourne	1903/04
5	8-68	Australia	Melbourne	1903/04
6	5-83	Australia	Old Trafford	1909

W.E.Bowes (6)

1	6-34	New Zealand	Auckland	1932/33
2	6-142	Australia	Headingley	1934
3	5-55	Australia	The Oval	1934
4	5-100	South Africa	Old Trafford	1935
5	5-49	Australia	The Oval	1938
6	6-33	West Indies	Old Trafford	1939

D.V.P.Wright (6)

1	5-167	Australia	Brisbane (2)	1946/47
2	7-105	Australia	Sydney	1946/47
3	5-95	South Africa	Lord's	1947
4	5-80	South Africa	Lord's	1947
5	5-141	West Indies	The Oval	1950
6	5-48	New Zealand	Wellington	1950/51

G.G.Arnold (6)

1	5-58	Pakistan	The Oval	1967
2	6-45	India	Delhi	1972/73
3	5-131	New Zealand	Trent Bridge	1973
4	5-27	New Zealand	Headingley	1973
5	5-113	West Indies	The Oval	1973
6	5-86	Australia	Sydney	1974/75

A.W.Greig (6)

1	5-24	India	Calcutta	1972/73
2	6-164	West Indies	Bridgetown	1973/74
3	8-86	West Indies	Port-of-Spain	1973/74

4	5-70	West Indies	Port-of-Spain	1973/74
5	5-98	New Zealand	Auckland	1974/75
6	5-51	New Zealand	Auckland	1974/75

J.E.Emburey (6)

1	5-124	West Indies	Port-of-Spain	1980/81
2	6-33	Sri Lanka	Colombo (1)	1981/82
3	5-82	Australia	Headingley	1985
4	5-78	West Indies	Port-of-Spain	1985/86
5	5-80	Australia	Brisbane (2)	1986/87
6	7-78	Australia	Sydney	1986/87

G.R.Dilley (6)

1	5-68	Australia	Brisbane (2)	1986/87
2	5-92	Pakistan	Edgbaston	1987
3	6-154	Pakistan	The Oval	1987
4	6-38	New Zealand	Christchurch	1987/88
5	5-60	New Zealand	Auckland	1987/88
6	5-55	West Indies	Lord's	1988

W.H.Lockwood (5)

1	6-101	Australia	Lord's	1893
2	7-71	Australia	The Oval	1899
3	6-48	Australia	Old Trafford	1902
4	5-28	Australia	Old Trafford	1902
5	5-45	Australia	The Oval	1902

A.P.Freeman (5)

1	5-54	West Indies	Old Trafford	1928
2	5-39	West Indies	Old Trafford	1928
3	7-115	South Africa	Headingley	1929
4	7-71	South Africa	Old Trafford	1929
5	5-100	South Africa	Old Trafford	1929

G.O.B.Allen (5)

1	5-14	New Zealand	The Oval	1931
2	5-35	India	Lord's	1936
3	5-43	India	Lord's	1936
4	7-80	India	The Oval	1936
5	5-36	Australia	Brisbane (2)	1936/37

H.Verity (5)

1	5-33	Australia	Sydney	1932/33
2	7-49	India	Madras (1)	1933/34
3	7-61	Australia	Lord's	1934
4	8-43	Australia	Lord's	1934
5	5-70	South Africa	Cape Town	1938/39

W.E.Hollies (5)

1	7-50	West Indies	Georgetown	1934/35
2	5-123	South Africa	Trent Bridge	1947
3	5-131	Australia	The Oval	1948
4	5-133	New Zealand	Lord's	1949
5	5-63	West Indies	Old Trafford	1950

T.E.Bailey (5)

1	6-118	New Zealand	Headingley	1949
2	6-84	New Zealand	Old Trafford	1949
3	7-34	West Indies	Kingston	1953/54
4	5-20	South Africa	Johannesburg (3)	1956/57
5	7-44	West Indies	Lord's	1957

J.H.Wardle (5)

1	7-56	Pakistan	The Oval	1954
2	5-79	Australia	Sydney	1954/55
3	5-53	South Africa	Cape Town	1956/57
4	7-36	South Africa	Cape Town	1956/57
5	5-61	South Africa	Durban (2)	1956/57

N.A.Foster (5)

1	5-67	Pakistan	Lahore (2)	1983/84
2	6-104	India	Madras (1)	1984/85
3	5-59	India	Madras (1)	1984/85
4	8-107	Pakistan	Headingley	1987
5	5-64	West Indies	The Oval	1988

D.E.Malcolm (5)

1	6-77	West Indies	Port-of-Spain	1989/90
2	5-94	New Zealand	Lord's	1990
3	5-46	New Zealand	Edgbaston	1990
4	5-94	Pakistan	The Oval	1992
5	9-57	South Africa	The Oval	1994

W.Bates (4)

1	7-28	Australia	Melbourne	1882/83
2	7-74	Australia	Melbourne	1882/83
3	5-31	Australia	Adelaide	1884/85
4	5-24	Australia	Sydney	1884/85

J.T.Hearne (4)

1	5-76	Australia	Lord's	1896
2	6-41	Australia	The Oval	1896
3	5-42	Australia	Sydney	1897/98
4	6-98	Australia	Melbourne	1897/98

F.R.Foster (4)

1	5-92	Australia	Sydney	1911/12
2	6-91	Australia	Melbourne	1911/12
3	5-36	Australia	Adelaide	1911/12
4	5-16	South Africa	Lord's	1912

F.E.Woolley (4)

1	5-41	South Africa	The Oval	1912
2	5-29	Australia	The Oval	1912
3	5-20	Australia	The Oval	1912
4	7-76	New Zealand	Wellington	1929/30

G.Geary (4)

1	7-70	South Africa	Johannesburg (1)	1927/28
2	5-60	South Africa	Johannesburg (1)	1927/28
3	5-35	Australia	Sydney	1928/29
4	5-105	Australia	Melbourne	1928/29

H.Larwood (4)

1	6-32	Australia	Brisbane (1)	1928/29
2	5-57	South Africa	Edgbaston	1929
3	5-96	Australia	Sydney	1932/33
4	5-28	Australia	Sydney	1932/33

R.Tattersall (4)

1	6-44	New Zealand	Wellington	1950/51
2	7-52	South Africa	Lord's	1951
3	5-49	South Africa	Lord's	1951
4	6-48	India	Kanpur	1951/52

F.H.Tyson (4)

1	6-85	Australia	Sydney	1954/55
2	7-27	Australia	Melbourne	1954/55
3	6-28	South Africa	Trent Bridge	1955
4	6-40	South Africa	Port Elizabeth	1956/57

D.A.Allen (4)

1	5-67	India	Calcutta	1961/62
2	5-30	Pakistan	Dacca	1961/62
3	5-41	South Africa	Durban (2)	1964/65
4	5-123	New Zealand	Auckland	1965/66

C.M.Old (4)

1	5-113	New Zealand	Lord's	1973
2	5-21	India	Lord's	1974
3	6-54	New Zealand	Wellington	1977/78
4	7-50	Pakistan	Edgbaston	1978

N.G.B.Cook (4)

1	5-35	New Zealand	Lord's	1983
2	5-63	New Zealand	Trent Bridge	1983
3	6-65	Pakistan	Karachi (1)	1983/84
4	5-18	Pakistan	Karachi (1)	1983/84

P.A.J.DeFreitas (4)

1	5-86	Pakistan	Karachi (1)	1987/88

2	5-53	New Zealand	Trent Bridge	1990
3	7-70	Sri Lanka	Lord's	1991
4	5-71	New Zealand	Trent Bridge	1994

P.C.R.Tufnell (4)

1	5-61	Australia	Sydney	1990/91
2	6-25	West Indies	The Oval	1991
3	5-94	Sri Lanka	Lord's	1991
4	7-47	New Zealand	Christchurch	1991/92

R.G.Barlow (3)

1	5-19	Australia	The Oval	1882
2	7-40	Australia	Sydney	1882/83
3	7-44	Australia	Old Trafford	1886

W.Barnes (3)

1	6-31	Australia	Melbourne	1884/85
2	6-28	Australia	Sydney	1886/87
3	5-32	Australia	The Oval	1888

L.C.Braund (3)

1	5-61	Australia	Sydney	1901/02
2	5-95	Australia	Melbourne	1901/02
3	8-81	Australia	Melbourne	1903/04

G.H.Hirst (3)

1	5-77	Australia	The Oval	1902
2	5-48	Australia	Melbourne	1903/04
3	5-58	Australia	Edgbaston	1909

J.N.Crawford (3)

1	5-79	Australia	Melbourne	1907/08
2	5-48	Australia	Melbourne	1907/08
3	5-141	Australia	Sydney	1907/08

J.C.White (3)

1	5-107	Australia	Melbourne	1928/29
2	5-130	Australia	Adelaide	1928/29
3	8-126	Australia	Adelaide	1928/29

W.Voce (3)

1	7-70	West Indies	Port-of-Spain	1929/30
2	5-58	South Africa	Durban (2)	1930/31
3	6-41	Australia	Brisbane (2)	1936/37

I.A.R.Peebles (3)

1	6-204	Australia	The Oval	1930
2	6-63	South Africa	Johannesburg (1)	1930/31
3	5-77	New Zealand	Lord's	1931

K.Farnes (3)

1	5-102	Australia	Trent Bridge	1934
2	5-77	Australia	Trent Bridge	1934
3	6-96	Australia	Melbourne	1936/37

R.Illingworth (3)

1	6-29	India	Lord's	1967
2	6-87	Australia	Headingley	1968
3	5-70	India	The Oval	1971

P.I.Pocock (3)

1	6-79	Australia	Old Trafford	1968
2	5-169	Pakistan	Hyderabad	1972/73
3	5-110	West Indies	Port-of-Spain	1973/74

J.K.Lever (3)

1	7-46	India	Delhi	1976/77
2	5-59	India	Madras (1)	1976/77
3	5-100	India	Bangalore	1981/82

D.R.Pringle (3)

1	5-108	West Indies	Edgbaston	1984
2	5-95	West Indies	Headingley	1988
3	5-100	West Indies	Lord's	1991

R.M.Ellison (3)

1	6-77	Australia	Edgbaston	1985
2	5-46	Australia	The Oval	1985
3	5-78	West Indies	Kingston	1985/86

C.C.Lewis (3)

1	6-111	West Indies	Edgbaston	1991
2	5-31	New Zealand	Auckland	1991/92
3	5-72	India	Edgbaston	1996

D.G.Cork (3)

1	7-43	West Indies	Lord's	1995
2	5-84	South Africa	Johannesburg (3)	1995/96
3	5-113	Pakistan	Headingley	1996

E.Peate (2)

1	5-43	Australia	Sydney	1881/82
2	6-85	Australia	Lord's	1884

F.Martin (2)

1	6-50	Australia	The Oval	1890
2	6-52	Australia	The Oval	1890

J.J.Ferris (2)

1	6-54	South Africa	Cape Town	1891/92
2	7-37	South Africa	Cape Town	1891/92

B.J.T.Bosanquet (2)

1	6-51	Australia	Sydney	1903/04
2	8-107	Australia	Trent Bridge	1905

W.S.Lees (2)

1	5-34	South Africa	Johannesburg (1)	1905/06
2	6-78	South Africa	Johannesburg (1)	1905/06

G.H.T.Simpson-Hayward (2)

1	6-43	South Africa	Johannesburg (1)	1909/10
2	5-69	South Africa	Johannesburg (1)	1909/10

C.H.Parkin (2)

1	5-60	Australia	Adelaide	1920/21
2	5-38	Australia	Old Trafford	1921

P.G.H.Fender (2)

1	5-122	Australia	Melbourne	1920/21
2	5-90	Australia	Sydney	1920/21

A.S.Kennedy (2)

1	5-88	South Africa	Durban (2)	1922/23
2	5-76	South Africa	Durban (2)	1922/23

A.E.R.Gilligan (2)

1	6-7	South Africa	Edgbaston	1924
2	5-83	South Africa	Edgbaston	1924

W.R.Hammond (2)

1	5-36	South Africa	Johannesburg (1)	1927/28
2	5-57	Australia	Adelaide	1936/37

G.T.S.Stevens (2)

1	5-105	West Indies	Bridgetown	1929/30
2	5-90	West Indies	Bridgetown	1929/30

James Langridge (2)

1	7-56	West Indies	Old Trafford	1933
2	5-63	India	Madras (1)	1933/34

C.S.Marriott (2)

1	5-37	West Indies	The Oval	1933
2	6-59	West Indies	The Oval	1933

M.S.Nichols (2)

1	5-55	India	Bombay (1)	1933/34
2	6-35	South Africa	Trent Bridge	1935

R.T.D.Perks (2)
1	5-100	South Africa	Durban (2)	1938/39
2	5-156	West Indies	The Oval	1939

J.D.F.Larter (2)
1	5-57	Pakistan	The Oval	1962
2	5-68	South Africa	Trent Bridge	1965

D.J.Brown (2)
1	5-63	Australia	Sydney	1965/66
2	5-42	Australia	Lord's	1968

K.Higgs (2)
1	6-91	West Indies	Lord's	1966
2	5-58	Pakistan	The Oval	1967

P.Lever (2)
1	5-70	India	Old Trafford	1971
2	6-38	Australia	Melbourne	1974/75

P.H.Edmonds (2)
1	5-28	Australia	Headingley	1975
2	7-66	Pakistan	Karachi (1)	1977/78

N.G.Cowans (2)
1	6-77	Australia	Melbourne	1982/83
2	5-42	Pakistan	Lahore (2)	1983/84

G.C.Small (2)
1	5-48	Australia	Melbourne	1986/87
2	5-75	Australia	Sydney	1986/87

A.R.Caddick (2)
1	6-65	West Indies	Port-of-Spain	1993/94
2	5-63	West Indies	Bridgetown	1993/94

A.Shaw (1)
1	5-38	Australia	Melbourne	1876/77

T.Emmett (1)
1	7-68	Australia	Melbourne	1878/79

F.Morley (1)
1	5-56	Australia	The Oval	1880

G.Ulyett (1)
1	7-36	Australia	Lord's	1884

W.Flowers (1)
1	5-46	Australia	Melbourne	1884/85

C.A.Smith (1)
1	5-19	South Africa	Port Elizabeth	1888/89

J.W.Sharpe (1)
1	6-84	Australia	Melbourne	1891/92

C.Heseltine (1)
1	5-38	South Africa	Johannesburg (1)	1895/96

S.Haigh (1)
1	6-11	South Africa	Cape Town	1898/99

A.E.Trott (1)
1	5-49	South Africa	Johannesburg (1)	1898/99

W.M.Bradley (1)
1	5-67	Australia	Old Trafford	1899

J.R.Gunn (1)
1	5-76	Australia	Adelaide	1901/02

Hon.F.S.Jackson (1)
1	5-52	Australia	Trent Bridge	1905

A.Warren (1)
1   5-57   Australia   Headingley   1905

W.Brearley (1)
1   5-110   Australia   The Oval   1905

E.G.Arnold (1)
1   5-37   South Africa   Lord's   1907

A.Fielder (1)
1   6-82   Australia   Sydney   1907/08

A.E.Relf (1)
1   5-85   Australia   Lord's   1909

D.W.Carr (1)
1   5-146   Australia   The Oval   1909

C.P.Buckenham (1)
1   5-115   South Africa   Johannesburg (1)   1909/10

J.W.H.T.Douglas (1)
1   5-46   Australia   Melbourne   1911/12

J.W.Hearne (1)
1   5-49   South Africa   Johannesburg (1)   1913/14

G.G.Macaulay (1)
1   5-64   South Africa   Cape Town   1922/23

M.J.C.Allom (1)
1   5-38   New Zealand   Christchurch   1929/30

R.W.V.Robins (1)
1   6-32   West Indies   Lord's   1933

E.W.Clark (1)
1   5-98   Australia   The Oval   1934

G.A.E.Paine (1)
1   5-168   West Indies   Kingston   1934/35

C.I.J.Smith (1)
1   5-16   West Indies   Bridgetown   1934/35

J.M.Sims (1)
1   5-73   India   The Oval   1936

T.W.J.Goddard (1)
1   6-29   New Zealand   Old Trafford   1937

W.H.Copson (1)
1   5-85   West Indies   Lord's   1939

R.Pollard (1)
1   5-24   India   Old Trafford   1946

R.Howorth (1)
1   6-124   West Indies   Bridgetown   1947/48

D.C.S.Compton (1)
1   5-70   South Africa   Cape Town   1948/49

R.O.Jenkins (1)
1   5-116   West Indies   Lord's   1950

R.Berry (1)
1   5-63   West Indies   Old Trafford   1950

F.R.Brown (1)
1   5-49   Australia   Melbourne   1950/51

M.J.Hilton (1)
1   5-61   India   Kanpur   1951/52

R.Appleyard (1)

1	5-51	Pakistan	Trent Bridge	1954

P.J.Loader (1)

1	6-36	West Indies	Headingley	1957

T.Greenhough (1)

1	5-35	India	Lord's	1959

L.J.Coldwell (1)

1	6-85	Pakistan	Lord's	1962

J.S.E.Price (1)

1	5-73	India	Calcutta	1963/64

T.W.Cartwright (1)

1	6-94	South Africa	Trent Bridge	1965

I.J.Jones (1)

1	6-118	Australia	Adelaide	1965/66

K.Shuttleworth (1)

1	5-47	Australia	Brisbane (2)	1970/71

J.Birkenshaw (1)

1	5-57	Pakistan	Karachi (1)	1972/73

N.Gifford (1)

1	5-55	Pakistan	Karachi (1)	1972/73

G.Miller (1)

1	5-44	Australia	Sydney	1978/79

P.J.W.Allott (1)

1	6-61	West Indies	Headingley	1984

E.E.Hemmings (1)

1	6-58	New Zealand	Edgbaston	1990

D.V.Lawrence (1)

1	5-106	West Indies	The Oval	1991

N.A.Mallender (1)

1	5-50	Pakistan	Headingley	1992

P.M.Such (1)

1	6-67	Australia	Old Trafford	1993

D.Gough (1)

1	6-49	Australia	Sydney	1994/95

FIVE WICKET INNINGS AGAINST EACH OPPOSITION

Australia	215
South Africa	86
West Indies	70
New Zealand	53
India	47
Pakistan	31
Sri Lanka	5

FIVE WICKET INNINGS PER VENUE

England (262)

The Oval	65
Old Trafford	41
Lords	72
Trent Bridge	28
Headingley	34
Edgbaston	20
Bramall Lane	2

Australia (113)

Melbourne	43
Sydney	44

Adelaide	14
Brisbane (1)	1
Brisbane (2)	8
Perth	3

South Africa (47)

Port Elizabeth	4
Cape Town	14
Johannesburg (1)	16
Durban (1)	4
Durban (2)	7
Johannesburg (3)	2

West Indies (26)

Bridgetown	10
Port-of-Spain	9
Georgetown	2
Kingston	5

New Zealand (23)

Christchurch	9
Wellington	6
Auckland	8

India (23)

Bombay (1)	1
Calcutta	4
Madras (1)	5
Delhi	2
Kanpur	3
Madras (2)	2
Bangalore	2
Bombay (3)	4

Pakistan (11)

Dacca	2
Karachi (1)	6
Lahore (2)	2
Hyderabad	1

Sri Lanka (2)

Colombo (1)	2

BEST BOWLING IN A MATCH

Match	1st & 2nd inns	Bowler	Opposition	Venue	Date	
19-90	9-37 & 10-53	J.C.Laker	Australia	Old Trafford	1956	60
17-159	8-56 & 9-103	S.F.Barnes	South Africa	Johannesburg (1)	1913/14	32
15-28	7-17 & 8-11	J.Briggs	South Africa	Cape Town	1888/89	7
15-45	7-38 & 8-7	G.A.Lohmann	South Africa	Port Elizabeth	1895/96	14
15-99	8-59 & 7-40	C.Blythe	South Africa	Headingley	1907	24
15-104	7-61 & 8-43	H.Verity	Australia	Lord's	1934	47
15-124	7-56 & 8-68	W.Rhodes	Australia	Melbourne	1903/04	22
14-99	7-55 & 7-44	A.V.Bedser	Australia	Trent Bridge	1953	57
14-102	7-28 & 7-74	W.Bates	Australia	Melbourne	1882/83	1
14-144	7-56 & 7-88	S.F.Barnes	South Africa	Durban (1)	1913/14	33
13-57	5-28 & 8-29	S.F.Barnes	South Africa	The Oval	1912	29
13-71	5-20 & 8-51	D.L.Underwood	Pakistan	Lord's	1974	76
13-91	6-54 & 7-37	J.J.Ferris	South Africa	Cape Town	1891/92	11
13-106	6-58 & 7-48	I.T.Botham	India	Bombay (3)	1979/80	82
13-156	8-86 & 5-70	A.W.Greig	West Indies	Port-of-Spain	1973/74	75
13-163	6-42 & 7-121	S.F.Barnes	Australia	Melbourne	1901/02	20
13-244	7-168 & 6-76	T.Richardson	Australia	Old Trafford	1896	17
13-256	5-130 & 8-126	J.C.White	Australia	Adelaide	1928/29	38
12-71	9-28 & 3-43	G.A.Lohmann	South Africa	Johannesburg (1)	1895/96	15
12-89	5-53 & 7-36	J.H.Wardle	South Africa	Cape Town	1956/57	61
12-97	6-12 & 6-85	D.L.Underwood	New Zealand	Christchurch	1970/71	73
12-101	7-52 & 5-49	R.Tattersall	South Africa	Lord's	1951	54
12-101	6-41 & 6-60	D.L.Underwood	New Zealand	The Oval	1969	72
12-102	6-50 & 6-52	F.Martin	Australia	The Oval	1890	8
12-104	7-36 & 5-68	G.A.Lohmann	Australia	The Oval	1886	3
12-112	7-58 & 5-54	A.V.Bedser	South Africa	Old Trafford	1951	55
12-119	5-75 & 7-44	F.S.Trueman	West Indies	Edgbaston	1963	69
12-130	7-70 & 5-60	G.Geary	South Africa	Johannesburg (1)	1927/28	36
12-136	6-49 & 6-87	J.Briggs	Australia	Adelaide	1891/92	10

Match	1st & 2nd inns	Bowler	Opposition	Venue	Date	
12-171	7-71 & 5-100	A.P.Freeman	South Africa	Old Trafford	1929	40
11-48	5-28 & 6-20	G.A.R.Lock	West Indies	The Oval	1957	63
11-65	4-14 & 7-51	G.A.R.Lock	New Zealand	Headingley	1958	64
11-68	7-31 & 4-37	R.Peel	Australia	Old Trafford	1888	6
11-70	4-38 & 7-32	D.L.Underwood	New Zealand	Lord's	1969	71
11-74	5-29 & 6-45	J.Briggs	Australia	Lord's	1886	2
11-76	6-48 & 5-28	W.H.Lockwood	Australia	Old Trafford	1902	21
11-83	6-65 & 5-18	N.G.B.Cook	Pakistan	Karachi (1)	1983/84	84
11-84	5-31 & 6-53	G.A.R.Lock	New Zealand	Christchurch	1958/59	65
11-88	5-58 & 6-30	F.S.Trueman	Australia	Headingley	1961	67
11-90	6-7 & 5-83	A.E.R.Gilligan	South Africa	Edgbaston	1924	34
11-93	4-41 & 7-52	A.V.Bedser	India	Old Trafford	1946	51
11-96	5-37 & 6-59	C.S.Marriott	West Indies	The Oval	1933	44
11-97	6-63 & 5-34	J.B.Statham	South Africa	Lord's	1960	66
11-98	7-44 & 4-54	T.E.Bailey	West Indies	Lord's	1957	62
11-102	6-44 & 5-58	C.Blythe	Australia	Edgbaston	1909	25
11-110	5-25 & 6-85	S.F.Barnes	South Africa	Lord's	1912	27
11-113	5-58 & 6-55	J.C.Laker	Australia	Headingley	1956	59
11-118	6-68 & 5-50	C.Blythe	South Africa	Cape Town	1905/06	23
11-140	6-101 & 5-39	I.T.Botham	New Zealand	Lord's	1978	80
11-145	7-49 & 4-96	A.V.Bedser	India	Lord's	1946	50
11-147	4-100 & 7-47	P.C.R.Tufnell	New Zealand	Christchurch	1991/92	88
11-149	4-79 & 7-70	W.Voce	West Indies	Port-of-Spain	1929/30	42
11-152	6-100 & 5-52	F.S.Trueman	West Indies	Lord's	1963	68
11-153	7-49 & 4-104	H.Verity	India	Madras (1)	1933/34	45
11-163	6-104 & 5-59	N.A.Foster	India	Madras (1)	1984/85	85
11-173	6-39 & 5-134	T.Richardson	Australia	Lord's	1896	16
11-176	6-78 & 5-98	I.T.Botham	Australia	Perth	1979/80	81
11-215	7-113 & 4-102	D.L.Underwood	Australia	Adelaide	1974/75	77
11-228	6-130 & 5-98	M.W.Tate	Australia	Sydney	1924/25	35
10-49	5-29 & 5-20	F.E.Woolley	Australia	The Oval	1912	30
10-57	6-41 & 4-16	W.Voce	Australia	Brisbane (2)	1936/37	49
10-58	5-18 & 5-40	R.Peel	Australia	Sydney	1887/88	5
10-60	6-41 & 4-19	J.T.Hearne	Australia	The Oval	1896	18
10-70	7-46 & 3-24	J.K.Lever	India	Delhi	1976/77	79
10-78	5-35 & 5-43	G.O.B.Allen	India	Lord's	1936	48
10-82	4-37 & 6-45	D.L.Underwood	Australia	Headingley	1972	74
10-87	8-35 & 2-52	G.A.Lohmann	Australia	Sydney	1886/87	4
10-93	5-54 & 5-39	A.P.Freeman	West Indies	Old Trafford	1928	37
10-104	7-46 & 3-58	C.Blythe	South Africa	Cape Town	1909/10	26
10-104	6-77 & 4-27	R.M.Ellison	Australia	Edgbaston	1985	86
10-105	5-57 & 5-48	S.F.Barnes	South Africa	Durban (1)	1913/14	31
10-105	5-46 & 5-59	A.V.Bedser	Australia	Melbourne	1950/51	53
10-115	6-52 & 4-63	S.F.Barnes	South Africa	Headingley	1912	28
10-119	4-64 & 6-55	J.C.Laker	South Africa	The Oval	1951	56
10-124	5-96 & 5-28	H.Larwood	Australia	Sydney	1932/33	43
10-130	4-45 & 6-85	F.H.Tyson	Australia	Sydney	1954/55	58
10-137	4-60 & 6-77	D.E.Malcolm	West Indies	Port-of-Spain	1989/90	87
10-138	1-81 & 9-57	D.E.Malcolm	South Africa	The Oval	1994	89
10-142	8-58 & 2-84	G.A.Lohmann	Australia	Sydney	1891/92	9
10-142	4-82 & 6-60	J.A.Snow	West Indies	Georgetown	1967/68	70
10-148	5-34 & 5-114	J.Briggs	Australia	The Oval	1893	12
10-149	5-98 & 5-51	A.W.Greig	New Zealand	Auckland	1974/75	78
10-156	5-49 & 5-107	T.Richardson	Australia	Old Trafford	1893	13
10-175	5-95 & 5-80	D.V.P.Wright	South Africa	Lord's	1947	52
10-179	5-102 & 5-77	K.Farnes	Australia	Trent Bridge	1934	46
10-195	5-105 & 5-90	G.T.S.Stevens	West Indies	Bridgetown	1929/30	41
10-204	8-94 & 2-110	T.Richardson	Australia	Sydney	1897/98	19
10-207	7-115 & 3-92	A.P.Freeman	South Africa	Headingley	1929	39
10-253	6-125 & 4-128	I.T.Botham	Australia	The Oval	1981	83

BEST BOWLING IN A MATCH AGAINST EACH OPPOSITION

Australia

19-90	9-37 & 10-53	J.C.Laker	Old Trafford	1956
15-104	7-61 & 8-43	H.Verity	Lord's	1934
15-124	7-56 & 8-68	W.Rhodes	Melbourne	1903/04
14-99	7-55 & 7-44	A.V.Bedser	Trent Bridge	1953
14-102	7-28 & 7-74	W.Bates	Melbourne	1882/83

South Africa

17-159	8-56 & 9-103	S.F.Barnes	Johannesburg (1)	1913/14
15-28	7-17 & 8-11	J.Briggs	Cape Town	1888/89
15-45	7-38 & 8-7	G.A.Lohmann	Port Elizabeth	1895/96

| 15-99 | 8-59 & 7-40 | C.Blythe | Headingley | 1907 |
| 14-144 | 7-56 & 7-88 | S.F.Barnes | Durban (1) | 1913/14 |

West Indies
13-156	8-86 & 5-70	A.W.Greig	Port-of-Spain	1973/74
12-119	5-75 & 7-44	F.S.Trueman	Edgbaston	1963
11-48	5-28 & 6-20	G.A.R.Lock	The Oval	1957
11-96	5-37 & 6-59	C.S.Marriott	The Oval	1933
11-98	7-44 & 4-54	T.E.Bailey	Lord's	1957

New Zealand
12-97	6-12 & 6-85	D.L.Underwood	Christchurch	1970/71
12-101	6-41 & 6-60	D.L.Underwood	The Oval	1969
11-65	4-14 & 7-51	G.A.R.Lock	Headingley	1958
11-70	4-38 & 7-32	D.L.Underwood	Lord's	1969
11-84	5-31 & 6-53	G.A.R.Lock	Christchurch	1958/59

India
13-106	6-58 & 7-48	I.T.Botham	Bombay (3)	1979/80
11-93	4-41 & 7-52	A.V.Bedser	Old Trafford	1946
11-145	7-49 & 4-96	A.V.Bedser	Lord's	1946
11-153	7-49 & 4-104	H.Verity	Madras (1)	1933/34
11-163	6-104 & 5-59	N.A.Foster	Madras (1)	1984/85

Pakistan
13-71	5-20 & 8-51	D.L.Underwood	Lord's	1974
11-83	6-65 & 5-18	N.G.B.Cook	Karachi (1)	1983/84
9-110	3-25 & 6-85	L.J.Coldwell	Lord's	1962
9-116	6-31 & 3-85	F.S.Trueman	Lord's	1962
9-144	4-70 & 5-74	I.T.Botham	Headingley	1982

Sri Lanka
8-95	5-28 & 3-67	D.L.Underwood	Colombo (1)	1981/82
8-115	7-70 & 1-45	P.A.J.DeFreitas	Lord's	1991
7-164	3-77 & 4-87	P.J.Newport	Lord's	1988
7-204	1-114 & 6-90	I.T.Botham	Lord's	1984
6-88	0-55 & 6-33	J.E.Emburey	Colombo (1)	1981/82

BEST BOWLING IN A MATCH PER VENUE

ENGLAND

The Oval
13-57	5-28 & 8-29	S.F.Barnes	South Africa	1912
12-101	6-41 & 6-60	D.L.Underwood	New Zealand	1969
12-102	6-50 & 6-52	F.Martin	Australia	1890
12-104	7-36 & 5-68	G.A.Lohmann	Australia	1886
11-48	5-28 & 6-20	G.A.R.Lock	West Indies	1957

Old Trafford
19-90	9-37 & 10-53	J.C.Laker	Australia	1956
13-244	7-168 & 6-76	T.Richardson	Australia	1896
12-112	7-58 & 5-54	A.V.Bedser	South Africa	1951
12-171	7-71 & 5-100	A.P.Freeman	South Africa	1929
11-68	7-31 & 4-37	R.Peel	Australia	1888

Lord's
15-104	7-61 & 8-43	H.Verity	Australia	1934
13-71	5-20 & 8-51	D.L.Underwood	Pakistan	1974
12-101	7-52 & 5-49	R.Tattersall	South Africa	1951
11-70	4-38 & 7-32	D.L.Underwood	New Zealand	1969
11-74	5-29 & 6-45	J.Briggs	Australia	1886

Trent Bridge
| 14-99 | 7-55 & 7-44 | A.V.Bedser | Australia | 1953 |
| 10-179 | 5-102 & 5-77 | K.Farnes | Australia | 1934 |

Headingley
15-99	8-59 & 7-40	C.Blythe	South Africa	1907
11-65	4-14 & 7-51	G.A.R.Lock	New Zealand	1958
11-88	5-58 & 6-30	F.S.Trueman	Australia	1961
11-113	5-58 & 6-55	J.C.Laker	Australia	1956
10-82	4-37 & 6-45	D.L.Underwood	Australia	1972

Edgbaston

12-119	5-75 & 7-44	F.S.Trueman	West Indies	1963
11-90	6-7 & 5-83	A.E.R.Gilligan	South Africa	1924
11-102	6-44 & 5-58	C.Blythe	Australia	1909
10-104	6-77 & 4-27	R.M.Ellison	Australia	1985

Bramall Lane

7-99	6-49 & 1-50	S.F.Barnes	Australia	1902

AUSTRALIA

Melbourne

15-124	7-56 & 8-68	W.Rhodes	Australia	1903/04
14-102	7-28 & 7-74	W.Bates	Australia	1882/83
13-163	6-42 & 7-121	S.F.Barnes	Australia	1901/02
10-105	5-46 & 5-59	A.V.Bedser	Australia	1950/51

Sydney

11-228	6-130 & 5-98	M.W.Tate	Australia	1924/25
10-58	5-18 & 5-40	R.Peel	Australia	1887/88
10-87	8-35 & 2-52	G.A.Lohmann	Australia	1886/87
10-124	5-96 & 5-28	H.Larwood	Australia	1932/33
10-130	4-45 & 6-85	F.H.Tyson	Australia	1954/55

Adelaide

13-256	5-130 & 8-126	J.C.White	Australia	1928/29
12-136	6-49 & 6-87	J.Briggs	Australia	1891/92
11-215	7-113 & 4-102	D.L.Underwood	Australia	1974/75

Brisbane (1)

8-62	6-32 & 2-30	H.Larwood	Australia	1928/29

Brisbane (2)

10-57	6-41 & 4-16	W.Voce	Australia	1936/37

Perth

11-176	6-78 & 5-98	I.T.Botham	Australia	1979/80

SOUTH AFRICA

Port Elizabeth

15-45	7-38 & 8-7	G.A.Lohmann	South Africa	1895/96

Cape Town

15-28	7-17 & 8-11	J.Briggs	South Africa	1888/89
13-91	6-54 & 7-37	J.J.Ferris	South Africa	1891/92
12-89	5-53 & 7-36	J.H.Wardle	South Africa	1956/57
11-118	6-68 & 5-50	C.Blythe	South Africa	1905/06
10-104	7-46 & 3-58	C.Blythe	South Africa	1909/10

Johannesburg (1)

17-159	8-56 & 9-103	S.F.Barnes	South Africa	1913/14
12-71	9-28 & 3-43	G.A.Lohmann	South Africa	1895/96
12-130	7-70 & 5-60	G.Geary	South Africa	1927/28

Durban (1)

14-144	7-56 & 7-88	S.F.Barnes	South Africa	1913/14
10-105	5-57 & 5-48	S.F.Barnes	South Africa	1913/14

Durban (2)

7-103	5-61 & 2-42	J.H.Wardle	South Africa	1956/57

Johannesburg (2)

4-139	3-104 & 1-35	D.V.P.Wright	South Africa	1948/49

Johannesburg (3)

9-162	5-84 & 4-78	D.G.Cork	South Africa	1995/96

Centurion
England have not bowled at Centurion

WEST INDIES

Bridgetown

10-195	5-105 & 5-90	G.T.S.Stevens	West Indies	1929/30

Port-of-Spain

13-156	8-86 & 5-70	A.W.Greig	West Indies	1973/74
11-149	4-79 & 7-70	W.Voce	West Indies	1929/30
10-137	4-60 & 6-77	D.E.Malcolm	West Indies	1989/90

Georgetown

10-142	4-82 & 6-60	J.A.Snow	West Indies	1967/68

Kingston

8-88	7-34 & 1-54	T.E.Bailey	West Indies	1953/54

St John's

4-126	4-126 & DNB	D.E.Malcolm	West Indies	1989/90

NEW ZEALAND

Christchurch

12-97	6-12 & 6-85	D.L.Underwood	New Zealand	1970/71
11-84	5-31 & 6-53	G.A.R.Lock	New Zealand	1958/59
11-147	4-100 & 7-47	P.C.R.Tufnell	New Zealand	1991/92

Wellington

9-124	7-76 & 2-48	F.E.Woolley	New Zealand	1929/30

Auckland

10-149	5-98 & 5-51	A.W.Greig	New Zealand	1974/75

Dunedin

7-39	3-23 & 4-16	F.H.Tyson	New Zealand	1954/55

INDIA

Bombay (1)

8-108	3-53 & 5-55	M.S.Nichols	India	1933/34

Calcutta

9-162	5-67 & 4-95	D.A.Allen	India	1961/62

Madras (1)

11-153	7-49 & 4-104	H.Verity	India	1933/34
11-163	6-104 & 5-59	N.A.Foster	India	1984/85

Delhi

10-70	7-46 & 3-24	J.K.Lever	India	1976/77

Bombay (2)

5-107	4-74 & 1-33	G.A.R.Lock	India	1961/62

Kanpur

9-93	4-32 & 5-61	M.J.Hilton	India	1951/52

Madras (2)

9-162	5-116 & 4-46	F.J.Titmus	India	1963/64

Bangalore

8-100	6-53 & 2-47	R.G.D.Willis	India	1976/77

Bombay (3)

13-106	6-58 & 7-48	I.T.Botham	India	1979/80

PAKISTAN

Dacca

8-225	4-155 & 4-70	G.A.R.Lock	Pakistan	1961/62

Karachi (1)

11-83	6-65 & 5-18	N.G.B.Cook	Pakistan	1983/84

Lahore (2)

7-131	2-89 & 5-42	N.G.Cowans	Pakistan	1983/84

Hyderabad

5-169	5-169 & DNB	P.I.Pocock	Pakistan	1972/73

Faisalabad

5-142	3-101 & 2-41	G.R.Dilley	Pakistan	1983/84

SRI LANKA

Colombo (1)

8-95	5-28 & 3-67	D.L.Underwood	Sri Lanka	1981/82

Colombo (2)

5-87	4-66 & 1-21	C.C.Lewis	Sri Lanka	1992/93

TEN WICKET MATCHES PER BOWLER (89)

S.F.Barnes (7)

1	13-163	6-42 & 7-121	Australia	Melbourne	1901/02
2	11-110	5-25 & 6-85	South Africa	Lord's	1912
3	10-115	6-52 & 4-63	South Africa	Headingley	1912
4	13-57	5-28 & 8-29	South Africa	The Oval	1912
5	10-105	5-57 & 5-48	South Africa	Durban (1)	1913/14
6	17-159	8-56 & 9-103	South Africa	Johannesburg (1)	1913/14
7	14-144	7-56 & 7-88	South Africa	Durban (1)	1913/14

D.L.Underwood (6)

1	11-70	4-38 & 7-32	New Zealand	Lord's	1969
2	12-101	6-41 & 6-60	New Zealand	The Oval	1969
3	12-97	6-12 & 6-85	New Zealand	Christchurch	1970/71
4	10-82	4-37 & 6-45	Australia	Headingley	1972
5	13-71	5-20 & 8-51	Pakistan	Lord's	1974
6	11-215	7-113 & 4-102	Australia	Adelaide	1974/75

G.A.Lohmann (5)

1	12-104	7-36 & 5-68	Australia	The Oval	1886
2	10-87	8-35 & 2-52	Australia	Sydney	1886/87
3	10-142	8-58 & 2-84	Australia	Sydney	1891/92
4	15-45	7-38 & 8-7	South Africa	Port Elizabeth	1895/96
5	12-71	9-28 & 3-43	South Africa	Johannesburg (1)	1895/96

A.V.Bedser (5)

1	11-145	7-49 & 4-96	India	Lord's	1946
2	11-93	4-41 & 7-52	India	Old Trafford	1946
3	10-105	5-46 & 5-59	Australia	Melbourne	1950/51
4	12-112	7-58 & 5-54	South Africa	Old Trafford	1951
5	14-99	7-55 & 7-44	Australia	Trent Bridge	1953

J.Briggs (4)

1	11-74	5-29 & 6-45	Australia	Lord's	1886
2	15-28	7-17 & 8-11	South Africa	Cape Town	1888/89
3	12-136	6-49 & 6-87	Australia	Adelaide	1891/92
4	10-148	5-34 & 5-114	Australia	The Oval	1893

T.Richardson (4)

1	10-156	5-49 & 5-107	Australia	Old Trafford	1893
2	11-173	6-39 & 5-134	Australia	Lord's	1896
3	13-244	7-168 & 6-76	Australia	Old Trafford	1896
4	10-204	8-94 & 2-110	Australia	Sydney	1897/98

C.Blythe (4)

1	11-118	6-68 & 5-50	South Africa	Cape Town	1905/06
2	15-99	8-59 & 7-40	South Africa	Headingley	1907
3	11-102	6-44 & 5-58	Australia	Edgbaston	1909
4	10-104	7-46 & 3-58	South Africa	Cape Town	1909/10

I.T.Botham (4)

1	11-140	6-101 & 5-39	New Zealand	Lord's	1978
2	11-176	6-78 & 5-98	Australia	Perth	1979/80
3	13-106	6-58 & 7-48	India	Bombay (3)	1979/80
4	10-253	6-125 & 4-128	Australia	The Oval	1981

A.P.Freeman (3)

1	10-93	5-54 & 5-39	West Indies	Old Trafford	1928
2	10-207	7-115 & 3-92	South Africa	Headingley	1929
3	12-171	7-71 & 5-100	South Africa	Old Trafford	1929

J.C.Laker (3)

1	10-119	4-64 & 6-55	South Africa	The Oval	1951

| 2 | 11-113 | 5-58 & 6-55 | Australia | Headingley | 1956 |
| 3 | 19-90 | 9-37 & 10-53 | Australia | Old Trafford | 1956 |

G.A.R.Lock (3)

1	11-48	5-28 & 6-20	West Indies	The Oval	1957
2	11-65	4-14 & 7-51	New Zealand	Headingley	1958
3	11-84	5-31 & 6-53	New Zealand	Christchurch	1958/59

F.S.Trueman (3)

1	11-88	5-58 & 6-30	Australia	Headingley	1961
2	11-152	6-100 & 5-52	West Indies	Lord's	1963
3	12-119	5-75 & 7-44	West Indies	Edgbaston	1963

R.Peel (2)

| 1 | 10-58 | 5-18 & 5-40 | Australia | Sydney | 1887/88 |
| 2 | 11-68 | 7-31 & 4-37 | Australia | Old Trafford | 1888 |

W.Voce (2)

| 1 | 11-149 | 4-79 & 7-70 | West Indies | Port-of-Spain | 1929/30 |
| 2 | 10-57 | 6-41 & 4-16 | Australia | Brisbane (2) | 1936/37 |

H.Verity (2)

| 1 | 11-153 | 7-49 & 4-104 | India | Madras (1) | 1933/34 |
| 2 | 15-104 | 7-61 & 8-43 | Australia | Lord's | 1934 |

A.W.Greig (2)

| 1 | 13-156 | 8-86 & 5-70 | West Indies | Port-of-Spain | 1973/74 |
| 2 | 10-149 | 5-98 & 5-51 | New Zealand | Auckland | 1974/75 |

D.E.Malcolm (2)

| 1 | 10-137 | 4-60 & 6-77 | West Indies | Port-of-Spain | 1989/90 |
| 2 | 10-138 | 1-81 & 9-57 | South Africa | The Oval | 1994 |

W.Bates (1)

| 1 | 14-102 | 7-28 & 7-74 | Australia | Melbourne | 1882/83 |

F.Martin (1)

| 1 | 12-102 | 6-50 & 6-52 | Australia | The Oval | 1890 |

J.J.Ferris (1)

| 1 | 13-91 | 6-54 & 7-37 | South Africa | Cape Town | 1891/92 |

J.T.Hearne (1)

| 1 | 10-60 | 6-41 & 4-19 | Australia | The Oval | 1896 |

W.H.Lockwood (1)

| 1 | 11-76 | 6-48 & 5-28 | Australia | Old Trafford | 1902 |

W.Rhodes (1)

| 1 | 15-124 | 7-56 & 8-68 | Australia | Melbourne | 1903/04 |

F.E.Woolley (1)

| 1 | 10-49 | 5-29 & 5-20 | Australia | The Oval | 1912 |

A.E.R.Gilligan (1)

| 1 | 11-90 | 6-7 & 5-83 | South Africa | Edgbaston | 1924 |

M.W.Tate (1)

| 1 | 11-228 | 6-130 & 5-98 | Australia | Sydney | 1924/25 |

G.Geary (1)

| 1 | 12-130 | 7-70 & 5-60 | South Africa | Johannesburg (1) | 1927/28 |

J.C.White (1)

| 1 | 13-256 | 5-130 & 8-126 | Australia | Adelaide | 1928/29 |

G.T.S.Stevens (1)

| 1 | 10-195 | 5-105 & 5-90 | West Indies | Bridgetown | 1929/30 |

H.Larwood (1)

| 1 | 10-124 | 5-96 & 5-28 | Australia | Sydney | 1932/33 |

C.S.Marriott (1)

| 1 | 11-96 | 5-37 & 6-59 | West Indies | The Oval | 1933 |

K.Farnes (1)
1	10-179	5-102 & 5-77	Australia	Trent Bridge	1934

G.O.B.Allen (1)
1	10-78	5-35 & 5-43	India	Lord's	1936

D.V.P.Wright (1)
1	10-175	5-95 & 5-80	South Africa	Lord's	1947

R.Tattersall (1)
1	12-101	7-52 & 5-49	South Africa	Lord's	1951

F.H.Tyson (1)
1	10-130	4-45 & 6-85	Australia	Sydney	1954/55

J.H.Wardle (1)
1	12-89	5-53 & 7-36	South Africa	Cape Town	1956/57

T.E.Bailey (1)
1	11-98	7-44 & 4-54	West Indies	Lord's	1957

J.B.Statham (1)
1	11-97	6-63 & 5-34	South Africa	Lord's	1960

J.A.Snow (1)
1	10-142	4-82 & 6-60	West Indies	Georgetown	1967/68

J.K.Lever (1)
1	10-70	7-46 & 3-24	India	Delhi	1976/77

N.G.B.Cook (1)
1	11-83	6-65 & 5-18	Pakistan	Karachi (1)	1983/84

N.A.Foster (1)
1	11-163	6-104 & 5-59	India	Madras (1)	1984/85

R.M.Ellison (1)
1	10-104	6-77 & 4-27	Australia	Edgbaston	1985

P.C.R.Tufnell (1)
1	11-147	4-100 & 7-47	New Zealand	Christchurch	1991/92

TEN WICKET MATCHES AGAINST EACH OPPOSITION

Australia	37
South Africa	24
West Indies	11
New Zealand	8
India	7
Pakistan	2

TEN WICKET MATCHES PER VENUE

England (48)
The Oval	12
Old Trafford	9
Lord's	14
Trent Bridge	2
Headingley	7
Edgbaston	4

Australia (16)
Melbourne	4
Sydney	7
Adelaide	3
Brisbane (2)	1
Perth	1

South Africa (11)
Port Elizabeth	1
Cape Town	5
Johannesburg (1)	3
Durban (1)	2

West Indies (5)
Bridgetown   1
Port-of-Spain   3
Georgetown   1

New Zealand (4)
Christchurch   3
Auckland   1

India (4)
Madras (1)   2
Delhi   1
Bombay (3)   1

Pakistan (1)
Karachi (1)   1

MOST WICKETS IN A SERIES (1)

Single match
J.J.Ferris   13 wickets   South Africa   1891/92
I.T.Botham   13 wickets   India   1979/80

Two match series
J.Briggs   21 wickets   South Africa   1888/89

Three match series
G.A.Lohmann   35 wickets   South Africa   1895/96

Four match series
F.S.Trueman   29 wickets   India   1952

Five match series
S.F.Barnes*   49 wickets   South Africa   1913/14

Six match series
I.T.Botham   34 wickets   Australia   1981

* Played in four matches of a five match series

MOST WICKETS IN A SERIES (2)

Bowler	Opposition	Date	Mat	Balls	Runs	Wkts	Avg	B/B	5WI	10WM	S/R
S.F.Barnes	South Africa	1913/14	4	1356	536	49	10.93	9-103	7	3	27.67
J.C.Laker	Australia	1956	5	1703	442	46	9.60	10-53	4	2	37.02
A.V.Bedser	Australia	1953	5	1591	682	39	17.48	7-44	5	1	40.79
M.W.Tate	Australia	1924/25	5	2528	881	38	23.18	6-99	5	1	66.52
G.A.Lohmann	South Africa	1895/96	3	520	203	35	5.80	9-28	4	2	14.85
S.F.Barnes	Australia	1911/12	5	1782	778	34	22.88	5-44	3	0	52.41
S.F.Barnes	South Africa	1912	3	768	282	34	8.29	8-29	5	3	22.58
G.A.R.Lock	New Zealand	1958	5	1056	254	34	7.47	7-35	3	1	31.05
F.S.Trueman	West Indies	1963	5	1420	594	34	17.47	7-44	4	2	41.76
I.T.Botham	Australia	1981	6	1635	700	34	20.58	6-95	3	1	48.08
H.Larwood	Australia	1932/33	5	1322	644	33	19.51	5-28	2	1	40.06
T.Richardson	Australia	1894/95	5	1747	849	32	26.53	6-104	4	0	54.59
F.R.Foster	Australia	1911/12	5	1660	692	32	21.62	6-91	3	0	51.87
W.Rhodes	Australia	1903/04	5	1032	488	31	15.74	8-68	3	1	33.29
A.S.Kennedy	South Africa	1922/23	5	1683	599	31	19.32	5-76	2	0	54.29
J.A.Snow	Australia	1970/71	6	1805	708	31	22.83	7-40	2	0	58.22
I.T.Botham	Australia	1985	6	1510	855	31	27.58	5-109	1	0	48.70
J.N.Crawford	Australia	1907/08	5	1426	742	30	24.73	5-48	3	0	47.53
A.V.Bedser	Australia	1950/51	5	1560	482	30	16.06	5-46	2	1	52.00
A.V.Bedser	South Africa	1951	5	1655	517	30	17.23	7-58	3	1	55.16
F.S.Trueman	India	1952	4	718	386	29	13.31	8-31	2	0	24.75
D.Underwood	India	1976/77	5	1517	509	29	17.55	5-84	1	0	52.31
R.G.D.Willis	Australia	1981	6	1516	666	29	22.96	8-43	1	0	52.27
F.H.Tyson	Australia	1954/55	5	1208	583	28	20.82	7-27	2	1	43.14
R.Peel	Australia	1894/95	5	1831	721	27	26.70	6-67	1	0	67.81
M.W.Tate	South Africa	1924	5	1304	424	27	15.70	6-42	1	0	48.29
J.B.Statham	South Africa	1960	5	1218	491	27	18.18	6-63	2	1	45.11
F.J.Titmus	India	1963/64	5	2393	747	27	27.66	6-73	2	0	88.62
J.A.Snow	West Indies	1967/68	4	990	504	27	18.66	7-49	3	1	36.66
R.G.D.Willis	Australia	1977	5	1000	534	27	19.77	7-78	3	0	37.03
W.S.Lees	South Africa	1905/06	5	1256	467	26	17.96	6-78	2	0	48.30

Bowler	Opposition	Date	Mat	Balls	Runs	Wkts	Avg	B/B	5WI	10WM	S/R
C.Blythe	South Africa	1907	3	603	270	26	10.38	8-59	3	1	23.19
W.Voce	Australia	1936/37	5	1297	560	26	21.53	6-41	1	1	49.88
J.H.Wardle	South Africa	1956/57	4	1118	359	26	13.80	7-36	3	1	43.00
J.K.Lever	India	1976/77	5	898	380	26	14.61	7-46	2	1	34.53
D.G.Cork	West Indies	1995	5	1106	661	26	25.42	7-43	1	0	42.53
A.Fielder	Australia	1907/08	4	1299	627	25	25.08	6-82	1	0	51.96
J.C.White	Australia	1928/29	5	2440	760	25	30.40	8-126	3	1	97.60
F.S.Trueman	South Africa	1960	5	1083	508	25	20.32	5-27	1	0	43.32

HAT-TRICKS

W.Bates – Australia – Melbourne – 1882/83

1st wicket	P.S.McDonnell	Bowled
2nd wicket	G.Giffen	Caught & Bowled
3rd wicket	G.J.Bonnor	Caught W.W.Read

J.Briggs – Australia – Sydney – 1891/92

1st wicket	W.F.Giffen	Bowled
2nd wicket	S.T.Callaway	Caught W.G.Grace
3rd wicket	J.M.Blackham	LBW

G.A.Lohmann – South Africa – Port Elizabeth – 1895/96

1st wicket	F.J.Cook	Bowled
2nd wicket	J.Middleton	Bowled
3rd wicket	J.T.Willoughby	Caught T.W.Hayward

J.T.Hearne – Australia – Headingley – 1899

1st wicket	C.Hill	Bowled
2nd wicket	S.E.Gregory	Caught A.C.MacLaren
3rd wicket	M.A.Noble	Caught K.S.Ranjitsinhji

M.J.C.Allom – New Zealand – Christchurch – 1929/30

1st wicket	T.C.Lowry	LBW
2nd wicket	K.C.James	Caught W.L.Cornford
3rd wicket	F.T.Badcock	Bowled

T.W.J.Goddard – South Africa – Johannesburg (1) – 1938/39

1st wicket	A.D.Nourse	Caught & Bowled
2nd wicket	N.Gordon	Stumped L.E.G.Ames
3rd wicket	W.W.Wade	Bowled

P.J.Loader – West Indies – Headingley – 1957

1st wicket	J.D.C.Goddard	Bowled
2nd wicket	S.Ramadhin	Caught F.S.Trueman
3rd wicket	R.Gilchrist	Bowled

D.G.Cork – West Indies – Old Trafford – 1996

1st wicket	R.B.Richardson (5)	Bowled
2nd wicket	J.R.Murray (6)	LBW
3rd wicket	C.L.Hooper (7)	LBW

FOUR WICKETS IN FIVE BALLS

M.J.C.Allom	W-WWW	New Zealand	Christchurch	1929/30
C.M.Old*	WW-WW	Pakistan	Edgbaston	1978

* Four wickets in four legitimate balls, the third delivery was a no-ball

WICKET WITH FIRST BALL IN TEST CRICKET

Bowler	Batsman	Dismissal	Opposition	Venue	Date
W.M.Bradley	F.J.Laver	Caught A.F.A.Lilley	Australia	Old Trafford	1899
E.G.Arnold	V.T.Trumper	Caught R.E.Foster	Australia	Sydney	1903/04
G.G.Macaulay	G.A.L.Hearne	Caught P.G.H.Fender	South Africa	Cape Town	1922/23
M.W.Tate	M.J.Susskind	Caught R.Kilner	South Africa	Edgbaston	1924
R.Howorth	D.V.Dyer	Caught C.Gladwin	South Africa	The Oval	1947
R.K.Illingworth	P.V.Simmons	Bowled	West Indies	Trent Bridge	1991

FIVE WICKETS IN AN INNINGS ON DEBUT

Bowler		Inns	Opposition	Venue	Date
J.J.Ferris*	7-37	2nd	South Africa	Cape Town	1891/92

Bowler		Inns	Opposition	Venue	Date
D.G.Cork	7-43	2nd	West Indies	Lord's	1995
J.K.Lever	7-46	1st	India	Delhi	1976/77
A.V.Bedser	7-49	1st	India	Lord's	1946
James Langridge	7-56	2nd	West Indies	Old Trafford	1933
J.C.Laker	7-103	1st	West Indies	Bridgetown	1947/48
G.H.T.Simpson-Hayward	6-43	1st	South Africa	Johannesburg (1)	1909/10
F.Martin	6-50	1st	Australia	The Oval	1890
F.Martin	6-52	2nd	Australia	The Oval	1890
J.J.Ferris*	6-54	1st	South Africa	Cape Town	1891/92
C.S.Marriott	6-59	2nd	West Indies	The Oval	1933
P.M.Such	6-67	1st	Australia	Old Trafford	1993
W.H.Lockwood	6-101	1st	Australia	Lord's	1893
T.E.Bailey	6-118	1st	New Zealand	Headingley	1949
C.I.J.Smith	5-16	2nd	West Indies	Bridgetown	1934/35
C.A.Smith	5-19	1st	South Africa	Port Elizabeth	1888/89
R.Pollard	5-24	1st	India	Old Trafford	1946
P.H.Edmonds	5-28	1st	Australia	Headingley	1975
W.S.Lees	5-34	1st	South Africa	Johannesburg (1)	1905/06
N.G.B.Cook	5-35	1st	New Zealand	Lord's	1983
W.R.Hammond	5-36	2nd	South Africa	Johannesburg (1)	1927/28
C.S.Marriott	5-37	1st	West Indies	The Oval	1933
A.Shaw	5-38	2nd	Australia	Melbourne	1876/77
M.J.C.Allom	5-38	1st	New Zealand	Christchurch	1929/30
K.Shuttleworth	5-47	2nd	Australia	Brisbane (2)	1970/71
A.E.Trott	5-49	2nd	South Africa	Johannesburg (1)	1898/89
T.Richardson	5-49	1st	Australia	Old Trafford	1893
N.A.Mallender	5-50	2nd	Pakistan	Headingley	1992
R.Peel	5-51	2nd	Australia	Adelaide	1884/85
R.Appleyard	5-51	1st	Pakistan	Trent Bridge	1954
F.Morley	5-56	1st	Australia	The Oval	1880
J.D.F.Larter	5-57	1st	Pakistan	The Oval	1962
R.Berry	5-63	1st	West Indies	Old Trafford	1950
G.G.Macaulay	5-64	2nd	South Africa	Cape Town	1922/23
S.F.Barnes	5-65	1st	Australia	Sydney	1901/02
I.T.Botham	5-74	1st	Australia	Trent Bridge	1977
K.Farnes	5-77	2nd	Australia	Trent Bridge	1934
W.H.Copson	5-85	1st	West Indies	Lord's	1939
F.R.Foster	5-92	2nd	Australia	Sydney	1911/12
K.Farnes	5-102	1st	Australia	Trent Bridge	1934
T.Richardson	5-107	2nd	Australia	Old Trafford	1893
D.W.Carr	5-146	1st	Australia	The Oval	1909

* England debut having already played for Australia

TEN WICKETS IN A MATCH ON DEBUT

13-91*	6-54 & 7-37	J.J.Ferris	South Africa	Cape Town	1891/92
12-102	6-50 & 6-52	F.Martin	Australia	The Oval	1890
11-96	5-37 & 6-59	C.S.Marriott	West Indies	The Oval	1933
11-145	7-49 & 4-96	A.V.Bedser	India	Lord's	1946
10-70	7-46 & 3-24	J.K.Lever	India	Delhi	1976/77
10-156	5-49 & 5-107	T.Richardson	Australia	Old Trafford	1893
10-179	5-102 & 5-77	K.Farnes	Australia	Trent Bridge	1934

* England debut having already played for Australia

Wicket-Keeping Records

MOST CAREER DISMISSALS

Wicket-keeper	Dis	Cat	St	Mat	DPM
A.P.E.Knott	269	250	19	95	2.83
T.G.Evans	219	173	46	91	2.40
R.W.Taylor	174	167	7	57	3.05
R.C.Russell	152	141	11	49	3.10
J.M.Parks	114*	103	11	46	2.47
L.E.G.Ames	97*	74	23	47	2.06
A.F.A.Lilley	92	70	22	35	2.62
P.R.Downton	75	70	5	30	2.50

Wicket-keeper	Dis	Cat	St	Mat	DPM
A.J.Stewart	75*	70	5	58	1.29
H.Strudwick	72	60	12	28	2.57
G.Duckworth	60	45	15	24	2.50
J.T.Murray	55	52	3	21	2.61
S.J.Rhodes	49	46	3	11	4.45
B.N.French	39	38	1	16	2.43

* Both J.M.Parks and L.E.G.Ames took two catches in three Tests when not keeping wicket. A.J.Stewart has taken 27 catches in the 41 Tests that he has been used solely as a batsman.

MOST CAREER CATCHES

Wicket-keeper	Cat	Mat	CPM
A.P.E.Knott	250	95	2.63
T.G.Evans	173	91	1.90
R.W.Taylor	167	57	2.92
R.C.Russell	141	49	2.87
J.M.Parks	103	46	2.23
L.E.G.Ames	74	47	1.57
A.F.A.Lilley	70	35	2.00
A.J.Stewart	70	58	1.20
P.R.Downton	70	30	2.33
H.Strudwick	60	28	2.14
J.T.Murray	52	21	2.47
S.J.Rhodes	46	11	4.18
G.Duckworth	45	24	1.87
B.N.French	38	16	2.37

MOST CAREER STUMPINGS

Wicket-keeper	St	Mat	SPM
T.G.Evans	46	91	.50
L.E.G.Ames	23	47	.48
A.F.A.Lilley	22	35	.62
A.P.E.Knott	19	95	.20
G.Duckworth	15	24	.62
H.Strudwick	12	28	.42
J.M.Parks	11	46	.23
R.C.Russell	11	49	.22

MOST DISMISSALS IN A MATCH

Wicket-keeper	Dis	1st	2nd	Opposition	Venue	Date
R.C.Russell	11	6 + 0	5 + 0	South Africa	Johannesburg (3)	1995/96
R.W.Taylor	10	7 + 0	3 + 0	India	Bombay (3)	1979/80
R.C.Russell	9	4 + 1	3 + 1	South Africa	Port Elizabeth	1995/96
L.E.G.Ames	8	2 + 2	4 + 0	West Indies	The Oval	1933
J.M.Parks	8	5 + 0	3 + 0	New Zealand	Christchurch	1965/66
H.Strudwick	7	2 + 2	2 + 1	South Africa	Johannesburg (1)	1913/14
T.G.Evans	7	3 + 1	3 + 0	South Africa	Lord's	1955
T.G.Evans	7	2 + 1	4 + 0	Australia	Lord's	1956
T.G.Evans	7	3 + 0	4 + 0	West Indies	Trent Bridge	1957
J.T.Murray	7	3 + 0	4 + 0	Australia	Old Trafford	1961
A.P.E.Knott	7	3 + 0	4 + 0	Pakistan	Trent Bridge	1967
A.P.E.Knott	7	4 + 0	2 + 1	Pakistan	Headingley	1971
A.P.E.Knott	7	2 + 0	4 + 1	India	Old Trafford	1974
R.W.Taylor	7	3 + 0	3 + 1	Australia	Perth	1979/80
R.W.Taylor	7	3 + 0	4 + 0	Australia	Headingley	1981
R.W.Taylor	7	4 + 0	3 + 0	India	Bombay (3)	1981/82
S.J.Rhodes	7	4 + 0	3 + 0	Australia	Adelaide	1994/95

MOST CATCHES IN A MATCH

Wicket-keeper	Cat	1st/2nd	Opposition	Venue	Date
R.C.Russell	11	6 + 5	South Africa	Johannesburg (3)	1995/96
R.W.Taylor	10	7 + 3	India	Bombay (3)	1979/80
J.M.Parks	8	5 + 3	New Zealand	Christchurch	1965/66
T.G.Evans	7	3 + 4	West Indies	Trent Bridge	1957
J.T.Murray	7	3 + 4	Australia	Old Trafford	1961
A.P.E.Knott	7	3 + 4	Pakistan	Trent Bridge	1967
R.W.Taylor	7	3 + 4	Australia	Headingley	1981
R.W.Taylor	7	4 + 3	India	Bombay (3)	1981/82
S.J.Rhodes	7	4 + 3	Australia	Adelaide	1994/95
R.C.Russell	7	4 + 3	South Africa	Port Elizabeth	1995/96

MOST STUMPINGS IN A MATCH

Wicket-keeper	St	1st/2nd	Opposition	Venue	Date
A.F.A.Lilley	3	0 + 3	Australia	Sydney	1903/04
H.Strudwick	3	2 + 1	South Africa	Johannesburg (1)	1913/14
A.F.A.Lilley	3	1 + 2	Australia	Trent Bridge	1905
G.Duckworth	3	1 + 2	South Africa	Old Trafford	1929
L.E.G.Ames	3	2 + 1	West Indies	Georgetown	1929/30
T.G.Evans	3	1 + 2	South Africa	Cape Town	1948/49
T.G.Evans	3	1 + 2	New Zealand	Old Trafford	1949
T.G.Evans	3	1 + 2	West Indies	Old Trafford	1950
T.G.Evans	3	1 + 2	India	Headingley	1952
T.G.Evans	3	1 + 2	Australia	Old Trafford	1953
A.P.E.Knott	3	0 + 3	Australia	Headingley	1968

MOST DISMISSALS IN AN INNINGS

Wicket-keeper	Dis	C/S	Inns	Opposition	Venue	Date
R.W.Taylor	7	7 + 0	1st	India	Bombay (3)	1979/80
J.T.Murray	6	6 + 0	1st	India	Lord's	1967
R.C.Russell	6	6 + 0	1st	Australia	Melbourne	1990/91
R.C.Russell	6	6 + 0	1st	South Africa	Johannesburg (3)	1995/96
J.G.Binks	5	5 + 0	1st	India	Calcutta	1963/64
J.M.Parks	5	3 + 2	1st	Australia	Sydney	1965/66
J.M.Parks	5	5 + 0	1st	New Zealand	Christchurch	1965/66
A.P.E.Knott	5	4 + 1	2nd	India	Old Trafford	1974
R.W.Taylor	5	5 + 0	1st	New Zealand	Trent Bridge	1978
R.W.Taylor	5	5 + 0	1st	Australia	Brisbane (2)	1978/79
C.J.Richards	5	5 + 0	1st	Australia	Melbourne	1986/87
R.C.Russell	5	5 + 0	1st	West Indies	Bridgetown	1989/90
R.C.Russell	5	5 + 0	2nd	South Africa	Johannesburg (3)	1995/96
R.C.Russell	5	4 + 1	1st	South Africa	Port Elizabeth	1995/96

MOST CATCHES IN AN INNINGS

Wicket-keeper	Cat	Inns	Opposition	Venue	Date
R.W.Taylor	7	1st	India	Bombay (3)	1979/80
J.T.Murray	6	1st	India	Lord's	1967
R.C.Russell	6	1st	Australia	Melbourne	1990/91
R.C.Russell	6	1st	South Africa	Johannesburg (3)	1995/96
J.G.Binks	5	1st	India	Calcutta	1963/64
J.M.Parks	5	1st	New Zealand	Christchurch	1965/66
R.W.Taylor	5	1st	New Zealand	Trent Bridge	1978
R.W.Taylor	5	1st	Australia	Brisbane (2)	1978/79
C.J.Richards	5	1st	Australia	Melbourne	1986/87
R.C.Russell	5	1st	West Indies	Bridgetown	1989/90
R.C.Russell	5	2nd	South Africa	Johannesburg (3)	1995/96

MOST STUMPINGS IN AN INNINGS

Wicket-keeper	St	Inns	Opposition	Venue	Date
A.F.A.Lilley	3	2nd	Australia	Sydney	1903/04
A.P.E.Knott	3	2nd	Australia	Headingley	1968

MOST DISMISSALS IN A SERIES

Wicket-keeper	Dis	Cat	St	Mat	Opposition	Date
R.C.Russell	27	25	2	5*	South Africa	1995/96
A.P.E.Knott	24	21	3	6	Australia	1970/71
A.P.E.Knott	23	22	1	6	Australia	1974/75
H.Strudwick	21	21	0	5	South Africa	1913/14
S.J.Rhodes	21	20	1	5	Australia	1994/95
T.G.Evans	20	20	0	5	South Africa	1956/57
R.W.Taylor	20	18	2	6	Australia	1978/79
P.R.Downton	20	19	1	6	Australia	1985

* Fielded in four matches only

ZERO BYES CONCEDED IN A TOTAL ABOVE 500

Wicket-keeper	Total Conceded	Opposition	Venue	Date
T.G.Evans	659 for 8 declared	Australia	Sydney	1946/47
A.J.Stewart	632 for 4 declared	Australia	Lord's	1993
R.C.Russell	601 for 7 declared	Australia	Headingley	1989
R.C.Russell	593 for 5 declared	West Indies	St John's	1993/94

Wicket-keeper	Total Conceded	Opposition	Venue	Date
R.J.Blakey	560 for 6 declared	India	Madras (1)	1992/93
A.P.E.Knott	551 for 9 declared	New Zealand	Lord's	1973
A.P.E.Knott	532 for 9 declared	Australia	The Oval	1975
R.C.Russell	528	Australia	Lord's	1989
A.P.E.Knott	526 for 7 declared	West Indies	Port-of-Spain	1967/68
C.J.Richards	514 for 5 declared	Australia	Adelaide	1986/87
B.N.French	512 for 6 declared	New Zealand	Wellington	1987/88

Fielding Records

MOST CAREER CATCHES

Fielder	Mat	Cat	CPM	Aus	SA	WI	NZ	IND	PAK	SL
M.C.Cowdrey	114	120	1.05	40	22	21	15	11	11	–
I.T.Botham	102	120	1.17	57	–	19	14	14	14	2
W.R.Hammond	85	110	1.29	43	30	22	9	6	–	–
G.A.Gooch	118	103	.87	29	1	28	13	21	7	4
A.W.Greig	58	87	1.50	37	–	18	2	16	14	–
T.W.Graveney	79	80	1.01	24	9	24	6	5	12	–
A.J.Lamb	79	75	.94	20	–	20	15	13	5	2
D.I.Gower	117	74	.63	26	–	11	11	13	8	5
F.E.Woolley	64	64	1.00	36	28	–	–	–	–	–
F.S.Trueman	67	64	.95	21	4	16	11	6	6	–
G.A.Hick	46	62	1.34	9	6	16	13	7	11	–
W.Rhodes	58	60	1.03	36	21	3	–	–	–	–
G.A.R.Lock	49	59	1.20	15	2	17	10	9	6	–
M.W.Gatting	79	59	.74	19	–	7	9	8	14	2
K.F.Barrington	82	58	.70	19	8	7	8	9	7	–
L.Hutton	79	57	.72	22	18	9	5	3	–	–
K.W.R.Fletcher	59	54	.91	10	–	6	12	17	6	3
M.J.K.Smith	50	53	1.06	8	16	5	14	6	4	–
J.M.Brearley	39	52	1.33	20	–	1	5	17	9	–
D.C.S.Compton	78	49	.62	17	14	5	5	3	5	–
R.Illingworth	61	45	.73	16	1	7	10	11	–	–
D.L.Underwood	86	44	.51	14	–	12	4	12	2	–
M.A.Atherton	62	44	.70	11	3	9	5	7	8	1
J.H.Edrich	77	43	.55	16	1	11	6	5	4	–
P.H.Parfitt	37	42	1.13	12	5	–	9	8	8	–
P.B.H.May	66	42	.63	10	10	5	6	8	3	–
P.H.Edmonds	51	42	.82	11	–	2	17	3	9	–

MOST CATCHES IN A MATCH

Fielder	Cat	1st/2nd	Opposition	Venue	Date
A.Shrewsbury	6	3 + 3	Australia	Sydney	1887/88
F.E.Woolley	6	2 + 4	Australia	Sydney	1911/12
M.C.Cowdrey	6	3 + 3	West Indies	Lord's	1963
A.W.Greig	6	2 + 4	Pakistan	Headingley	1974
A.J.Lamb	6	4 + 2	New Zealand	Lord's	1983
G.A.Hick	6	4 + 2	Pakistan	Headingley	1992
W.Barnes	5	2 + 3	Australia	Melbourne	1884/85
W.G.Grace	5	2 + 3	Australia	Sydney	1891/92
L.C.Braund	5	4 + 1	Australia	Bramall Lane	1902
W.Rhodes	5	1 + 4	Australia	Old Trafford	1905
H.Sutcliffe	5	2 + 3	Australia	Lord's	1926
D.R.Jardine	5	3 + 2	India	Calcutta	1933/34
W.R.Hammond	5	2 + 3	Australia	Trent Bridge	1934
W.R.Hammond	5	3 + 2	South Africa	Durban (2)	1938/39
J.T.Ikin	5	3 + 2	South Africa	Old Trafford	1951
A.S.M.Oakman	5	2 + 3	Australia	Old Trafford	1956
P.H.Parfitt	5	3 + 2	New Zealand	Christchurch	1962/63
A.W.Greig	5	3 + 2	India	Delhi	1972/73
K.W.R.Fletcher	5	2 + 3	New Zealand	Auckland	1974/75
J.M.Brearley	5	2 + 3	India	Madras (1)	1976/77
P.H.Edmonds	5	3 + 2	Pakistan	Hyderabad	1977/78
P.H.Edmonds	5	4 + 1	New Zealand	Christchurch	1977/78
I.T.Botham	5	3 + 2	Australia	Sydney	1978/79
I.T.Botham	5	2 + 3	Australia	Sydney	1982/83
A.J.Lamb	5	3 + 2	West Indies	Port-of-Spain	1989/90

MOST CATCHES IN AN INNINGS

Fielder	Cat	Inns	Opposition	Venue	Date
L.C.Braund	4	1st	Australia	Bramall Lane	1902
W.Rhodes	4	2nd	Australia	Old Trafford	1905
L.C.Braund	4	1st	Australia	Sydney	1907/08
F.E.Woolley	4	2nd	Australia	Sydney	1911/12
A.P.F.Chapman	4	1st	West Indies	The Oval	1928
H.Larwood	4	2nd	Australia	Brisbane (1)	1928/29
J.E.McConnon	4	1st	Pakistan	Old Trafford	1954
P.B.H.May	4	1st	Australia	Adelaide	1954/55
P.H.Parfitt	4	1st	Australia	Trent Bridge	1972
A.W.Greig	4	2nd	Pakistan	Headingley	1974
P.H.Edmonds	4	1st	New Zealand	Christchurch	1977/78
A.J.Lamb	4	1st	New Zealand	Lord's	1983
G.A.Hick	4	1st	Pakistan	Headingley	1992
G.A.Hick	4	1st	India	Calcutta	1992/93
G.A.Hick	4	1st	New Zealand	Trent Bridge	1994
T.Emmett	3	2nd	Australia	Melbourne	1876/77
A.Shrewsbury	3	1st	Australia	Sydney	1881/82
G.B.Studd	3	1st	Australia	Sydney	1882/83
W.Barnes	3	2nd	Australia	Melbourne	1884/85
A.Shrewsbury	3	1st	Australia	Sydney	1887/88
A.Shrewsbury	3	2nd	Australia	Sydney	1887/88
G.A.Lohmann	3	1st	Australia	Lord's	1888
W.G.Grace	3	2nd	Australia	Old Trafford	1888
R.Abel	3	1st	South Africa	Port Elizabeth	1888/89
G.Ulyett	3	2nd	South Africa	Port Elizabeth	1888/89
W.G.Grace	3	2nd	Australia	Sydney	1891/92
S.M.J.Woods	3	1st	South Africa	Cape Town	1895/96
L.C.Braund	3	1st	Australia	Melbourne	1903/04
J.N.Crawford	3	1st	South Africa	Cape Town	1906
J.N.Crawford	3	1st	Australia	Sydney	1907/08
W.Rhodes	3	1st	Australia	The Oval	1909
F.E.Woolley	3	1st	South Africa	Johannesburg (1)	1909/10
J.W.H.T.Douglas	3	2nd	Australia	The Oval	1912
M.C.Bird	3	1st	South Africa	Port Elizabeth	1913/14
F.E.Woolley	3	1st	South Africa	Durban (2)	1922/23
C.A.G.Russell	3	1st	South Africa	Johannesburg (1)	1922/23
H.Sutcliffe	3	2nd	Australia	Lord's	1926
W.R.Hammond	3	2nd	South Africa	Cape Town	1927/28
W.R.Hammond	3	2nd	West Indies	Old Trafford	1928
W.R.Hammond	3	2nd	West Indies	The Oval	1928
A.P.F.Chapman	3	2nd	Australia	Brisbane (1)	1928/29
D.R.Jardine	3	1st	Australia	Melbourne	1928/29
W.R.Hammond	3	2nd	Australia	Trent Bridge	1930
W.R.Hammond	3	2nd	South Africa	Johannesburg (1)	1930/31
A.P.F.Chapman	3	2nd	South Africa	Durban (2)	1930/31
W.R.Hammond	3	1st	New Zealand	Lord's	1931
R.W.V.Robins	3	1st	India	Lord's	1932
D.R.Jardine	3	1st	India	Calcutta	1933/34
W.R.Hammond	3	2nd	Australia	Trent Bridge	1934
W.R.Hammond	3	2nd	Australia	The Oval	1934
J.M.Sims	3	1st	Australia	Sydney	1936/37
W.R.Hammond	3	2nd	Australia	Adelaide	1936/37
W.R.Hammond	3	1st	South Africa	Durban (2)	1938/39
W.J.Edrich	3	2nd	South Africa	Lord's	1947
L.Hutton	3	2nd	West Indies	Kingston	1947/48
L.Hutton	3	1st	Australia	Lord's	1948
W.J.Edrich	3	1st	New Zealand	Headingley	1949
W.J.Edrich	3	1st	New Zealand	The Oval	1949
J.T.Ikin	3	1st	South Africa	Old Trafford	1951
A.J.Watkins	3	1st	India	Headingley	1952
G.A.R.Lock	3	1st	Australia	Headingley	1953
J.H.Wardle	3	2nd	Pakistan	The Oval	1954
A.S.M.Oakman	3	2nd	Australia	Old Trafford	1956
M.C.Cowdrey	3	1st	South Africa	Johannesburg (3)	1956/57
D.J.Insole	3	2nd	South Africa	Johannesburg (3)	1956/57
M.C.Cowdrey	3	1st	Australia	Melbourne	1958/59
F.S.Trueman	3	1st	Australia	Melbourne	1958/59
G.A.R.Lock	3	1st	New Zealand	Christchurch	1958/59
D.B.Close	3	2nd	India	Headingley	1959
R.Illingworth	3	2nd	India	Old Trafford	1959
P.H.Parfitt	3	2nd	India	Madras (2)	1961/62
M.C.Cowdrey	3	1st	Pakistan	Lord's	1962

Fielder	Cat	Inns	Opposition	Venue	Date
T.W.Graveney	3	2nd	Pakistan	Lord's	1962
T.W.Graveney	3	1st	Australia	Sydney	1962/63
K.F.Barrington	3	2nd	New Zealand	Wellington	1962/63
P.H.Parfitt	3	1st	New Zealand	Christchurch	1962/63
M.C.Cowdrey	3	1st	West Indies	Lord's	1963
M.C.Cowdrey	3	2nd	West Indies	Lord's	1963
M.J.K.Smith	3	2nd	Australia	Sydney	1965/66
T.W.Graveney	3	1st	West Indies	The Oval	1966
T.W.Graveney	3	1st	West Indies	Port-of-Spain	1967/68
M.C.Cowdrey	3	1st	Australia	Lord's	1968
B.L.D'Oliveira	3	1st	Pakistan	Lahore (2)	1968/69
D.L.Underwood	3	1st	New Zealand	Auckland	1970/71
R.Illingworth	3	1st	India	Lord's	1971
R.Illingworth	3	1st	Australia	Headingley	1972
A.W.Greig	3	1st	India	Delhi	1972/73
K.W.R.Fletcher	3	2nd	India	Calcutta	1972/73
P.I.Pocock	3	1st	West Indies	Port-of-Spain	1973/74
K.W.R.Fletcher	3	2nd	West Indies	Port-of-Spain	1973/74
D.Lloyd	3	2nd	Pakistan	Lord's	1974
K.W.R.Fletcher	3	2nd	New Zealand	Auckland	1974/75
J.M.Brearley	3	2nd	India	Madras (1)	1976/77
A.W.Greig	3	1st	Australia	Melbourne	1976/77
M.Hendrick	3	1st	Australia	Trent Bridge	1977
P.H.Edmonds	3	1st	Pakistan	Hyderabad	1977/78
G.R.J.Roope	3	2nd	New Zealand	Wellington	1977/78
P.H.Edmonds	3	2nd	New Zealand	Wellington	1977/78
I.T.Botham	3	2nd	New Zealand	Christchurch	1977/78
G.R.J.Roope	3	2nd	Pakistan	Lord's	1978
I.T.Botham	3	1st	Australia	Sydney	1978/79
I.T.Botham	3	1st	India	Edgbaston	1979
I.T.Botham	3	1st	Australia	Old Trafford	1981
D.I.Gower	3	1st	Sri Lanka	Colombo (1)	1981/82
I.T.Botham	3	2nd	Australia	Sydney	1982/83
I.T.Botham	3	1st	Australia	Adelaide	1982/83
D.I.Gower	3	1st	Pakistan	Lahore (2)	1983/84
M.W.Gatting	3	2nd	Pakistan	Lahore (2)	1983/84
A.J.Lamb	3	1st	India	Bombay (3)	1984/85
A.J.Lamb	3	2nd	India	Delhi	1984/85
P.H.Edmonds	3	1st	Australia	Edgbaston	1985
G.A.Gooch	3	1st	New Zealand	The Oval	1986
I.T.Botham	3	1st	Australia	Perth	1986/87
I.T.Botham	3	1st	Australia	Melbourne	1986/87
A.J.Lamb	3	2nd	Australia	Sydney	1986/87
M.D.Moxon	3	1st	Pakistan	The Oval	1987
A.J.Lamb	3	1st	West Indies	Port-of-Spain	1989/90
A.J.Lamb	3	1st	West Indies	Lord's	1991
I.T.Botham	3	1st	West Indies	The Oval	1991
R.A.Smith	3	2nd	New Zealand	Christchurch	1991/92
G.A.Hick	3	1st	Australia	Brisbane (2)	1994/95
G.A.Hick	3	1st	Australia	Melbourne	1994/95
N.V.Knight	3	1st	India	Edgbaston	1996
M.A.Atherton	3	1st	Pakistan	Headingley	1996

MOST CATCHES IN A SERIES

Fielder	Cat	Tests	Opposition	Date
L.C.Braund	12	5	Australia	1901/02
W.R.Hammond	12	5	Australia	1934
J.T.Ikin	12	3	South Africa	1951
A.W.Greig	12	6	Australia	1974/75
I.T.Botham	12	6	Australia	1981

All-round Records

1000 RUNS & 100 WICKETS

Player	Runs	Wkts	Tests	No. of Tests for each double		
				1000/100	2000/200	3000/300
I.T.Botham	5200	383	102	21	41	72
M.W.Tate	1198	155	39	33		
A.W.Greig	3599	141	58	37		

1000 RUNS & 100 WICKETS

Player	Runs	Wkts	Tests	No. of Tests for each double		
				1000/100	2000/200	3000/300
F.J.Titmus	1449	153	53	40		
W.Rhodes	2325	127	58	44		
J.E.Emburey	1713	147	64	46		
T.E.Bailey	2290	132	61	47		
R.Illingworth	1836	122	61	47		

1000 RUNS & 50 WICKETS

Player	Runs	Wkts	Tests
W.R.Hammond	7249	83	85
E.R.Dexter	4502	66	62
C.C.Lewis	1105	93	32
F.E.Woolley	3283	83	64
G.Miller	1213	60	34

500 RUNS & 100 WICKETS

Player	Runs	Wkts	Tests
F.S.Trueman	981	307	67
D.L.Underwood	937	297	86
P.A.J.DeFreitas	934	140	44
D.A.Allen	918	122	39
P.H.Edmonds	875	125	51
C.M.Old	845	143	46
R.G.D.Willis	840	325	90
J.Briggs	815	118	33
J.A.Snow	772	202	49
G.A.R.Lock	742	174	49
A.V.Bedser	714	236	51
J.C.Laker	676	193	46
J.B.Statham	675	252	70
H.Verity	669	144	40
J.H.Wardle	653	102	28
G.R.Dilley	521	138	41

1000 RUNS & 50 DISMISSALS

Wicket-keeper	Runs	Dis	Mat
A.P.E.Knott	4389	269	95
A.J.Stewart	3935	75*	58
T.G.Evans	2439	219	91
L.E.G.Ames	2434	97	47
J.M.Parks	1962	114*	46
R.C.Russell	1807	152	49
R.W.Taylor	1156	174	57

* J.M.Parks took two catches in three Tests when not keeping wicket. A.J.Stewart has taken 27 catches in the 41 Tests that he has been used solely as a batsman.

1000 RUNS & 50 CATCHES

Player	Runs	Cat	Tests
G.A.Gooch	8900	103	118
D.I.Gower	8231	74	117
M.C.Cowdrey	7624	120	114
W.R.Hammond	7249	110	85
L.Hutton	6971	57	79
K.F.Barrington	6806	58	82
I.T.Botham	5200	120	102
T.W.Graveney	4882	80	79
A.J.Lamb	4656	75	79
M.W.Gatting	4409	59	79
A.W.Greig	3599	87	58
F.E.Woolley	3283	64	64
K.W.R.Fletcher	3272	54	59
G.A.Hick	2672	62	46
W.Rhodes	2325	60	58
M.J.K.Smith	2278	53	50
J.M.Brearley	1442	52	39

CENTURY & TEN WICKETS IN A MATCH

Player	Runs & Wickets	Opposition	Venue	Date
I.T.Botham	114 & 13-106 (6-58 & 7-48)	India	Bombay (3)	1979/80

FIFTY & TEN WICKETS IN A MATCH

Player	Runs & Wickets	Opposition	Venue	Date
W.Bates	55 & 14-102 (7-28 & 7-74)	Australia	Melbourne	1882/83
F.E.Woolley	62 & 10-49 (5-29 & 5-20)	Australia	The Oval	1912
J.K.Lever+	53 & 10-70 (7-46 & 3-24)	India	Delhi	1976/77
A.W.Greig	51 & 10-149 (5-98 & 5-51)	New Zealand	Auckland	1974/75

+ achieved on debut

CENTURY & FIVE WICKETS IN AN INNINGS

Player	Runs & Wickets	Opposition	Venue	Date
I.T.Botham	108 & 8-34	Pakistan	Lord's	1978
I.T.Botham	114 & 7-48	India	Bombay (3)	1979/80
I.T.Botham	149* & 6-95	Australia	Headingley	1981
A.W.Greig	148 & 6-164	West Indies	Bridgetown	1973/74
I.T.Botham	114 & 6-58	India	Bombay (3)	1979/80
I.T.Botham	138 & 5-59	New Zealand	Wellington	1983/84
I.T.Botham	103 & 5-73	New Zealand	Christchurch	1977/78

FIFTY & FIVE WICKETS IN AN INNINGS

Player	Runs & Wickets	Opposition	Venue	Date
I.T.Botham	81 & 8-103	West Indies	Lord's	1984
J.E.Emburey	69 & 7-78	Australia	Sydney	1986/87
J.K.Lever+	53 & 7-46	India	Delhi	1976/77
T.E.Bailey	72* & 6-84	New Zealand	Old Trafford	1947
H.Larwood	70 & 6-32	Australia	Brisbane (1)	1928/29
C.C.Lewis	65 & 6-111	West Indies	Edgbaston	1991
W.Barnes	58 & 6-31	Australia	Melbourne	1884/85
D.Gough	51 & 6-49	Australia	Sydney	1994/95
I.T.Botham	50 & 6-95	Australia	Headingley	1981
P.Lever	88* & 5-70	India	Old Trafford	1971
I.T.Botham	85 & 5-109	Australia	Lord's	1985
Hon.F.S.Jackson	82* & 5-52	Australia	Trent Bridge	1905
F.R.Foster	71 & 5-36	Australia	Adelaide	1911/12
G.O.B.Allen	68 & 5-36	Australia	Brisbane (2)	1936/37
A.W.Greig	67 & 5-24	India	Calcutta	1972/73
I.T.Botham	67 & 5-46	India	Lord's	1982
G.Geary	66 & 5-35	Australia	Sydney	1928/29
W.Barnes	62 & 5-32	Australia	The Oval	1888
P.G.H.Fender	59 & 5-122	Australia	Melbourne	1920/21
G.G.Arnold	59 & 5-58	Pakistan	The Oval	1967
G.H.Hirst	58* & 5-77	Australia	The Oval	1902
L.C.Braund	58 & 5-61	Australia	Sydney	1901/02
I.T.Botham	57 & 5-74	Pakistan	Headingley	1982
W.Flowers	56 & 5-46	Australia	Sydney	1884/85
F.R.Foster+	56 & 5-92	Australia	Sydney	1911/12
I.T.Botham	54 & 5-72	West Indies	The Oval	1984
I.T.Botham	53 & 5-109	New Zealand	Auckland	1977/78
W.R.Hammond+	51 & 5-36	South Africa	Johannesburg (1)	1927/28
D.C.S.Compton	51* & 5-70	South Africa	Cape Town	1948/49
P.A.J.DeFreitas	51* & 5-71	New Zealand	Trent Bridge	1994

+ achieved on debut

FIFTY & FIVE DISMISSALS IN AN INNINGS

Wicket-keeper	Runs & Dis	Opposition	Venue	Date
A.J.Stewart	76 & 6	Australia	The Oval	1993
P.R.Downton	74 & 6	India	Delhi	1984/85
A.J.Stewart	63 & 6	Sri Lanka	Colombo (2)	1992/93
J.M.Parks	91 & 5	West Indies	Lord's	1966
A.F.A.Lilley	84 & 5	Australia	Sydney	1901/02
A.P.E.Knott	73 & 5	Australia	Brisbane (2)	1970/71
T.G.Evans	66 & 5	India	Headingley	1952
A.F.A.Lilley	65* & 5	Australia	Old Trafford	1896
T.G.Evans	62 & 5	South Africa	Cape Town	1956/57
A.P.E.Knott	59 & 5	Australia	Old Trafford	1981
R.C.Russell	55 & 5	West Indies	Bridgetown	1989/90
R.W.Taylor	54 & 5	Pakistan	Edgbaston	1982
P.R.Downton	54 & 5	Australia	Headingley	1985
L.E.G.Ames	52 & 5	Australia	Adelaide	1936/37

250 RUNS & 20 WICKETS IN A SERIES

Player	Runs	Wkts	Tests	Opposition	Date
A.W.Greig	430	24	5	West Indies	1973/74
I.T.Botham	399	34	6	Australia	1981
I.T.Botham	291	23	6	Australia	1978/79
G.J.Thompson	267	23	5	South Africa	1909/10
L.C.Braund	256	21	5	Australia	1901/02
I.T.Botham	250	31	6	Australia	1985

250 RUNS & 20 DISMISSALS IN A SERIES

Wicket-keeper	Runs	Dis	Tests
A.P.E.Knott	364	23	6

Captaincy Records

ENGLAND CAPTAINS 1877-1996

Test		Captain	Date	Opposition	Venue	Result	Toss
1	1	James Lillywhite (1)	1876/77	Australia	Melbourne	Lost	Lost
2		James Lillywhite (2)	1876/77	Australia	Melbourne	Won	Lost
3	2	Lord Harris (1)	1878/79	Australia	Melbourne	Lost	Won
4		Lord Harris (2)	1880	Australia	The Oval	Won	Won
5	3	A.Shaw (1)	1881/82	Australia	Melbourne	Drew	Won
6		A.Shaw (2)	1881/82	Australia	Sydney	Lost	Won
7		A.Shaw (3)	1881/82	Australia	Sydney	Lost	Won
8		A.Shaw (4)	1881/82	Australia	Melbourne	Drew	Won
9	4	A.N.Hornby (1)	1882	Australia	The Oval	Lost	Lost
10	5	Hon.I.F.W.Bligh (1)	1882/83	Australia	Melbourne	Lost	Lost
11		Hon.I.F.W.Bligh (2)	1882/83	Australia	Melbourne	Won	Won
12		Hon.I.F.W.Bligh (3)	1882/83	Australia	Sydney	Won	Won
13		Hon.I.F.W.Bligh (4)	1882/83	Australia	Sydney	Lost	Won
14		A.N.Hornby (2)	1884	Australia	Old Trafford	Drew	Won
15		Lord Harris (3)	1884	Australia	Lord's	Won	Lost
16		Lord Harris (4)	1884	Australia	The Oval	Drew	Lost
17	6	A.Shrewsbury (1)	1884/85	Australia	Adelaide	Won	Lost
18		A.Shrewsbury (2)	1884/85	Australia	Melbourne	Won	Won
19		A.Shrewsbury (3)	1884/85	Australia	Sydney	Lost	Lost
20		A.Shrewsbury (4)	1884/85	Australia	Sydney	Lost	Won
21		A.Shrewsbury (5)	1884/85	Australia	Melbourne	Won	Lost
22	7	A.G.Steel (1)	1886	Australia	Old Trafford	Won	Lost
23		A.G.Steel (2)	1886	Australia	Lord's	Won	Won
24		A.G.Steel (3)	1886	Australia	The Oval	Won	Won
25		A.Shrewsbury (6)	1886/87	Australia	Sydney	Won	Lost
26		A.Shrewsbury (7)	1886/87	Australia	Sydney	Won	Won
27	8	W.W.Read (1)	1887/88	Australia	Sydney	Won	Lost
28		A.G.Steel (4)	1888	Australia	Lord's	Lost	Lost
29	9	W.G.Grace (1)	1888	Australia	The Oval	Won	Lost
30		W.G.Grace (2)	1888	Australia	Old Trafford	Won	Won
31	10	C.A.Smith (1)	1888/89	South Africa	Port Elizabeth	Won	Lost
32	11	M.P.Bowden (1)	1888/89	South Africa	Cape Town	Won	Won
33		W.G.Grace (3)	1890	Australia	Lord's	Won	Lost
34		W.G.Grace (4)	1890	Australia	The Oval	Won	Lost
35		W.G.Grace (5)	1891/92	Australia	Melbourne	Lost	Lost
36		W.G.Grace (6)	1891/92	Australia	Sydney	Lost	Lost
37		W.G.Grace (7)	1891/92	Australia	Adelaide	Won	Won
38		W.W.Read (2)	1891/92	South Africa	Cape Town	Won	Lost
39	12	A.E.Stoddart (1)	1893	Australia	Lord's	Drew	Won
40		W.G.Grace (8)	1893	Australia	The Oval	Won	Won
41		W.G.Grace (9)	1893	Australia	Old Trafford	Drew	Lost
42		A.E.Stoddart (2)	1894/95	Australia	Sydney	Won	Lost
43		A.E.Stoddart (3)	1894/95	Australia	Melbourne	Won	Lost
44		A.E.Stoddart (4)	1894/95	Australia	Adelaide	Lost	Lost
45		A.E.Stoddart (5)	1894/95	Australia	Sydney	Lost	Won
46		A.E.Stoddart (6)	1894/95	Australia	Melbourne	Won	Lost
47	13	Sir T.C.O'Brien (1)	1895/96	South Africa	Port Elizabeth	Won	Lost
48	14	Lord Hawke (1)	1895/96	South Africa	Johannesburg (1)	Won	Won
49		Lord Hawke (2)	1895/96	South Africa	Cape Town	Won	Won
50		W.G.Grace (10)	1896	Australia	Lord's	Won	Lost
51		W.G.Grace (11)	1896	Australia	Old Trafford	Lost	Lost
52		W.G.Grace (12)	1896	Australia	The Oval	Won	Won
53	15	A.C.MacLaren (1)	1897/98	Australia	Sydney	Won	Won

Test		Captain	Date	Opposition	Venue	Result	Toss
54		A.C.MacLaren (2)	1897/98	Australia	Melbourne	Lost	Lost
55		A.E.Stoddart (7)	1897/98	Australia	Adelaide	Lost	Lost
56		A.E.Stoddart (8)	1897/98	Australia	Melbourne	Lost	Lost
57		A.C.MacLaren (3)	1897/98	Australia	Sydney	Lost	Won
58		Lord Hawke (3)	1898/99	South Africa	Johannesburg (1)	Won	Won
59		Lord Hawke (4)	1898/99	South Africa	Cape Town	Won	Won
60		W.G.Grace (13)	1899	Australia	Trent Bridge	Drew	Lost
61		A.C.MacLaren (4)	1899	Australia	Lord's	Lost	Won
62		A.C.MacLaren (5)	1899	Australia	Headingley	Drew	Lost
63		A.C.MacLaren (6)	1899	Australia	Old Trafford	Drew	Won
64		A.C.MacLaren (7)	1899	Australia	The Oval	Drew	Won
65		A.C.MacLaren (8)	1901/02	Australia	Sydney	Won	Won
66		A.C.MacLaren (9)	1901/02	Australia	Melbourne	Lost	Won
67		A.C.MacLaren (10)	1901/02	Australia	Adelaide	Lost	Won
68		A.C.MacLaren (11)	1901/02	Australia	Sydney	Lost	Won
69		A.C.MacLaren (12)	1901/02	Australia	Melbourne	Lost	Lost
70		A.C.MacLaren (13)	1902	Australia	Edgbaston	Drew	Won
71		A.C.MacLaren (14)	1902	Australia	Lord's	Drew	Won
72		A.C.MacLaren (15)	1902	Australia	Bramall Lane	Lost	Lost
73		A.C.MacLaren (16)	1902	Australia	Old Trafford	Lost	Lost
74		A.C.MacLaren (17)	1902	Australia	The Oval	Won	Lost
75	16	P.F.Warner (1)	1903/04	Australia	Sydney	Won	Lost
76		P.F.Warner (2)	1903/04	Australia	Melbourne	Won	Won
77		P.F.Warner (3)	1903/04	Australia	Adelaide	Lost	Lost
78		P.F.Warner (4)	1903/04	Australia	Sydney	Won	Won
79		P.F.Warner (5)	1903/04	Australia	Melbourne	Lost	Lost
80	17	Hon.F.S.Jackson (1)	1905	Australia	Trent Bridge	Won	Won
81		Hon.F.S.Jackson (2)	1905	Australia	Lord's	Drew	Won
82		Hon.F.S.Jackson (3)	1905	Australia	Headingley	Drew	Won
83		Hon.F.S.Jackson (4)	1905	Australia	Old Trafford	Won	Won
84		Hon.F.S.Jackson (5)	1905	Australia	The Oval	Drew	Won
85		P.F.Warner (6)	1905/06	South Africa	Johannesburg (1)	Lost	Won
86		P.F.Warner (7)	1905/06	South Africa	Johannesburg (1)	Lost	Won
87		P.F.Warner (8)	1905/06	South Africa	Johannesburg (1)	Lost	Lost
88		P.F.Warner (9)	1905/06	South Africa	Cape Town	Won	Lost
89		P.F.Warner (10)	1905/06	South Africa	Cape Town	Lost	Won
90	18	R.E.Foster (1)	1907	South Africa	Lord's	Drew	Won
91		R.E.Foster (2)	1907	South Africa	Headingley	Won	Won
92		R.E.Foster (3)	1907	South Africa	The Oval	Drew	Won
93	19	F.L.Fane (1)	1907/08	Australia	Sydney	Lost	Won
94		F.L.Fane (2)	1907/08	Australia	Melbourne	Won	Lost
95		F.L.Fane (3)	1907/08	Australia	Adelaide	Lost	Lost
96	20	A.O.Jones (1)	1907/08	Australia	Melbourne	Lost	Lost
97		A.O.Jones (2)	1907/08	Australia	Sydney	Lost	Won
98		A.C.MacLaren (18)	1909	Australia	Edgbaston	Won	Lost
99		A.C.MacLaren (19)	1909	Australia	Lord's	Lost	Lost
100		A.C.MacLaren (20)	1909	Australia	Headingley	Lost	Lost
101		A.C.MacLaren (21)	1909	Australia	Old Trafford	Drew	Lost
102		A.C.MacLaren (22)	1909	Australia	The Oval	Drew	Lost
103	21	H.D.G.Leveson Gower (1)	1909/10	South Africa	Johannesburg (1)	Lost	Lost
104		H.D.G.Leveson Gower (2)	1909/10	South Africa	Durban (1)	Lost	Lost
105		H.D.G.Leveson Gower (3)	1909/10	South Africa	Johannesburg (1)	Won	Lost
106		F.L.Fane (4)	1909/10	South Africa	Cape Town	Lost	Won
107		F.L.Fane (5)	1909/10	South Africa	Cape Town	Won	Won
108	22	J.W.H.T.Douglas (1)	1911/12	Australia	Sydney	Lost	Lost
109		J.W.H.T.Douglas (2)	1911/12	Australia	Melbourne	Won	Lost
110		J.W.H.T.Douglas (3)	1911/12	Australia	Adelaide	Won	Lost
111		J.W.H.T.Douglas (4)	1911/12	Australia	Melbourne	Won	Won
112		J.W.H.T.Douglas (5)	1911/12	Australia	Sydney	Won	Won
113	23	C.B.Fry (1)	1912	South Africa	Lord's	Won	Lost
114		C.B.Fry (2)	1912	Australia	Lord's	Drew	Won
115		C.B.Fry (3)	1912	South Africa	Headingley	Won	Won
116		C.B.Fry (4)	1912	Australia	Old Trafford	Drew	Won
117		C.B.Fry (5)	1912	South Africa	The Oval	Won	Lost
118		C.B.Fry (6)	1912	Australia	The Oval	Won	Won
119		J.W.H.T.Douglas (6)	1913/14	South Africa	Durban (1)	Won	Lost
120		J.W.H.T.Douglas (7)	1913/14	South Africa	Johannesburg (1)	Won	Lost
121		J.W.H.T.Douglas (8)	1913/14	South Africa	Johannesburg (1)	Won	Won
122		J.W.H.T.Douglas (9)	1913/14	South Africa	Durban (1)	Drew	Lost
123		J.W.H.T.Douglas (10)	1913/14	South Africa	Port Elizabeth	Won	Lost
124		J.W.H.T.Douglas (11)	1920/21	Australia	Sydney	Lost	Lost
125		J.W.H.T.Douglas (12)	1920/21	Australia	Melbourne	Lost	Lost
126		J.W.H.T.Douglas (13)	1920/21	Australia	Adelaide	Lost	Lost
127		J.W.H.T.Douglas (14)	1920/21	Australia	Melbourne	Lost	Won

Test		Captain	Date	Opposition	Venue	Result	Toss
128		J.W.H.T.Douglas (15)	1920/21	Australia	Sydney	Lost	Won
129		J.W.H.T.Douglas (16)	1921	Australia	Trent Bridge	Lost	Won
130		J.W.H.T.Douglas (17)	1921	Australia	Lord's	Lost	Won
131	24	Hon.L.H.Tennyson (1)	1921	Australia	Headingley	Lost	Lost
132		Hon.L.H.Tennyson (2)	1921	Australia	Old Trafford	Drew	Won
133		Hon.L.H.Tennyson (3)	1921	Australia	The Oval	Drew	Won
134	25	F.T.Mann (1)	1922/23	South Africa	Johannesburg (1)	Lost	Lost
135		F.T.Mann (2)	1922/23	South Africa	Cape Town	Won	Lost
136		F.T.Mann (3)	1922/23	South Africa	Durban (2)	Drew	Won
137		F.T.Mann (4)	1922/23	South Africa	Johannesburg (1)	Drew	Won
138		F.T.Mann (5)	1922/23	South Africa	Durban (2)	Won	Won
139	26	A.E.R.Gilligan (1)	1924	South Africa	Edgbaston	Won	Lost
140		A.E.R.Gilligan (2)	1924	South Africa	Lord's	Won	Lost
141		A.E.R.Gilligan (3)	1924	South Africa	Headingley	Won	Won
142		J.W.H.T.Douglas (18)	1924	South Africa	Old Trafford	Drew	Lost
143		A.E.R.Gilligan (4)	1924	South Africa	The Oval	Drew	Lost
144		A.E.R.Gilligan (5)	1924/25	Australia	Sydney	Lost	Lost
145		A.E.R.Gilligan (6)	1924/25	Australia	Melbourne	Lost	Lost
146		A.E.R.Gilligan (7)	1924/25	Australia	Adelaide	Lost	Lost
147		A.E.R.Gilligan (8)	1924/25	Australia	Melbourne	Won	Won
148		A.E.R.Gilligan (9)	1924/25	Australia	Sydney	Lost	Lost
149	27	A.W.Carr (1)	1926	Australia	Trent Bridge	Drew	Won
150		A.W.Carr (2)	1926	Australia	Lord's	Drew	Lost
151		A.W.Carr (3)	1926	Australia	Headingley	Drew	Won
152		A.W.Carr (4)	1926	Australia	Old Trafford	Drew	Lost
153	28	A.P.F.Chapman (1)	1926	Australia	The Oval	Won	Won
154	29	R.T.Stanyforth (1)	1927/28	South Africa	Johannesburg (1)	Won	Lost
155		R.T.Stanyforth (2)	1927/28	South Africa	Cape Town	Won	Lost
156		R.T.Stanyforth (3)	1927/28	South Africa	Durban (2)	Drew	Lost
157		R.T.Stanyforth (4)	1927/28	South Africa	Johannesburg (1)	Lost	Lost
158	30	G.T.S.Stevens (1)	1927/28	South Africa	Durban (2)	Lost	Won
159		A.P.F.Chapman (2)	1928	West Indies	Lord's	Won	Won
160		A.P.F.Chapman (3)	1928	West Indies	Old Trafford	Won	Lost
161		A.P.F.Chapman (4)	1928	West Indies	The Oval	Won	Lost
162		A.P.F.Chapman (5)	1928/29	Australia	Brisbane (1)	Won	Won
163		A.P.F.Chapman (6)	1928/29	Australia	Sydney	Won	Lost
164		A.P.F.Chapman (7)	1928/29	Australia	Melbourne	Won	Lost
165		A.P.F.Chapman (8)	1928/29	Australia	Adelaide	Won	Won
166	31	J.C.White (1)	1928/29	Australia	Melbourne	Lost	Won
167		J.C.White (2)	1929	South Africa	Edgbaston	Drew	Won
168		J.C.White (3)	1929	South Africa	Lord's	Drew	Won
169		J.C.White (4)	1929	South Africa	Headingley	Won	Lost
170		A.W.Carr (5)	1929	South Africa	Old Trafford	Won	Won
171		A.W.Carr (6)	1929	South Africa	The Oval	Drew	Lost
172	32	A.H.H.Gilligan (1)	1929/30	New Zealand	Christchurch	Won	Lost
173		A.H.H.Gilligan (2)	1929/30	New Zealand	Wellington	Drew	Lost
174		A.H.H.Gilligan (3)	1929/30	New Zealand	Auckland	Drew	Lost
175		A.H.H.Gilligan (4)	1929/30	New Zealand	Auckland	Drew	Won
176	33	Hon.F.S.G.Calthorpe (1)	1929/30	West Indies	Bridgetown	Drew	Lost
177		Hon.F.S.G.Calthorpe (2)	1929/30	West Indies	Port-of-Spain	Won	Won
178		Hon.F.S.G.Calthorpe (3)	1929/30	West Indies	Georgetown	Lost	Lost
179		Hon.F.S.G.Calthorpe (4)	1929/30	West Indies	Kingston	Drew	Won
180		A.P.F.Chapman (9)	1930	Australia	Trent Bridge	Won	Won
181		A.P.F.Chapman (10)	1930	Australia	Lord's	Lost	Won
182		A.P.F.Chapman (11)	1930	Australia	Headingley	Drew	Lost
183		A.P.F.Chapman (12)	1930	Australia	Old Trafford	Drew	Lost
184	34	R.E.S.Wyatt (1)	1930	Australia	The Oval	Lost	Won
185		A.P.F.Chapman (13)	1930/31	South Africa	Johannesburg (1)	Lost	Won
186		A.P.F.Chapman (14)	1930/31	South Africa	Cape Town	Drew	Lost
187		A.P.F.Chapman (15)	1930/31	South Africa	Durban (2)	Drew	Lost
188		A.P.F.Chapman (16)	1930/31	South Africa	Johannesburg (1)	Drew	Lost
189		A.P.F.Chapman (17)	1930/31	South Africa	Durban (2)	Drew	Won
190		D.R.Jardine (1)	1931	New Zealand	Lord's	Drew	Lost
191	35	D.R.Jardine (2)	1931	New Zealand	The Oval	Won	Won
192		D.R.Jardine (3)	1931	New Zealand	Old Trafford	Drew	Lost
193		D.R.Jardine (4)	1932	India	Lord's	Won	Won
194		D.R.Jardine (5)	1932/33	Australia	Sydney	Won	Lost
195		D.R.Jardine (6)	1932/33	Australia	Melbourne	Lost	Lost
196		D.R.Jardine (7)	1932/33	Australia	Adelaide	Won	Lost
197		D.R.Jardine (8)	1932/33	Australia	Brisbane (2)	Won	Won
198		D.R.Jardine (9)	1932/33	Australia	Sydney	Won	Lost
199		D.R.Jardine (10)	1932/33	New Zealand	Christchurch	Drew	Won
200		R.E.S.Wyatt (2)	1932/33	New Zealand	Auckland	Drew	Lost
201		D.R.Jardine (11)	1933	West Indies	Lord's	Won	Won

Test		Captain	Date	Opposition	Venue	Result	Toss
202		D.R.Jardine (12)	1933	West Indies	Old Trafford	Drew	Lost
203		R.E.S.Wyatt (3)	1933	West Indies	The Oval	Won	Won
204		D.R.Jardine (13)	1933/34	India	Bombay (1)	Won	Lost
205		D.R.Jardine (14)	1933/34	India	Calcutta	Drew	Won
206		D.R.Jardine (15)	1933/34	India	Madras (1)	Won	Won
207	36	C.F.Walters (1)	1934	Australia	Trent Bridge	Lost	Lost
208		R.E.S.Wyatt (4)	1934	Australia	Lord's	Won	Won
209		R.E.S.Wyatt (5)	1934	Australia	Old Trafford	Drew	Won
210		R.E.S.Wyatt (6)	1934	Australia	Headingley	Drew	Won
211		R.E.S.Wyatt (7)	1934	Australia	The Oval	Lost	Lost
212		R.E.S.Wyatt (8)	1934/35	West Indies	Bridgetown	Won	Won
213		R.E.S.Wyatt (9)	1934/35	West Indies	Port-of-Spain	Lost	Won
214		R.E.S.Wyatt (10)	1934/35	West Indies	Georgetown	Drew	Won
215		R.E.S.Wyatt (11)	1934/35	West Indies	Kingston	Lost	Lost
216		R.E.S.Wyatt (12)	1935	South Africa	Trent Bridge	Drew	Won
217		R.E.S.Wyatt (13)	1935	South Africa	Lord's	Lost	Lost
218		R.E.S.Wyatt (14)	1935	South Africa	Headingley	Drew	Won
219		R.E.S.Wyatt (15)	1935	South Africa	Old Trafford	Drew	Won
220		R.E.S.Wyatt (16)	1935	South Africa	The Oval	Drew	Won
221	37	G.O.B.Allen (1)	1936	India	Lord's	Won	Won
222		G.O.B.Allen (2)	1936	India	Old Trafford	Drew	Lost
223		G.O.B.Allen (3)	1936	India	The Oval	Won	Won
224		G.O.B.Allen (4)	1936/37	Australia	Brisbane (2)	Won	Won
225		G.O.B.Allen (5)	1936/37	Australia	Sydney	Won	Won
226		G.O.B.Allen (6)	1936/37	Australia	Melbourne	Lost	Lost
227		G.O.B.Allen (7)	1936/37	Australia	Adelaide	Lost	Lost
228		G.O.B.Allen (8)	1936/37	Australia	Melbourne	Lost	Lost
229	38	R.W.V.Robins (1)	1937	New Zealand	Lord's	Drew	Won
230		R.W.V.Robins (2)	1937	New Zealand	Old Trafford	Won	Won
231		R.W.V.Robins (3)	1937	New Zealand	The Oval	Drew	Lost
232	39	W.R.Hammond (1)	1938	Australia	Trent Bridge	Drew	Won
233		W.R.Hammond (2)	1938	Australia	Lord's	Drew	Won
234		W.R.Hammond (3)	1938	Australia	Headingley	Lost	Won
235		W.R.Hammond (4)	1938	Australia	The Oval	Won	Won
236		W.R.Hammond (5)	1938/39	South Africa	Johannesburg (1)	Drew	Won
237		W.R.Hammond (6)	1938/39	South Africa	Cape Town	Drew	Won
238		W.R.Hammond (7)	1938/39	South Africa	Durban (2)	Won	Won
239		W.R.Hammond (8)	1938/39	South Africa	Johannesburg (1)	Drew	Won
240		W.R.Hammond (9)	1938/39	South Africa	Durban (2)	Drew	Lost
241		W.R.Hammond (10)	1939	West Indies	Lord's	Won	Lost
242		W.R.Hammond (11)	1939	West Indies	Old Trafford	Drew	Lost
243		W.R.Hammond (12)	1939	West Indies	The Oval	Drew	Won
244		W.R.Hammond (13)	1946	India	Lord's	Won	Lost
245		W.R.Hammond (14)	1946	India	Old Trafford	Drew	Lost
246		W.R.Hammond (15)	1946	India	The Oval	Drew	Lost
247		W.R.Hammond (16)	1946/47	Australia	Brisbane (2)	Lost	Lost
248		W.R.Hammond (17)	1946/47	Australia	Sydney	Lost	Won
249		W.R.Hammond (18)	1946/47	Australia	Melbourne	Drew	Lost
250		W.R.Hammond (19)	1946/47	Australia	Adelaide	Drew	Won
251	40	N.W.D.Yardley (1)	1946/47	Australia	Sydney	Lost	Won
252		W.R.Hammond (20)	1946/47	New Zealand	Christchurch	Drew	Won
253		N.W.D.Yardley (2)	1947	South Africa	Trent Bridge	Drew	Lost
254		N.W.D.Yardley (3)	1947	South Africa	Lord's	Won	Won
255		N.W.D.Yardley (4)	1947	South Africa	Old Trafford	Won	Lost
256		N.W.D.Yardley (5)	1947	South Africa	Headingley	Won	Lost
257		N.W.D.Yardley (6)	1947	South Africa	The Oval	Drew	Won
258	41	K.Cranston (1)	1947/48	West Indies	Bridgetown	Drew	Lost
259		G.O.B.Allen (9)	1947/48	West Indies	Port-of-Spain	Drew	Won
260		G.O.B.Allen (10)	1947/48	West Indies	Georgetown	Lost	Lost
261		G.O.B.Allen (11)	1947/48	West Indies	Kingston	Lost	Lost
262		N.W.D.Yardley (7)	1948	Australia	Trent Bridge	Lost	Won
263		N.W.D.Yardley (8)	1948	Australia	Lord's	Lost	Lost
264		N.W.D.Yardley (9)	1948	Australia	Old Trafford	Drew	Won
265		N.W.D.Yardley (10)	1948	Australia	Headingley	Lost	Won
266		N.W.D.Yardley (11)	1948	Australia	The Oval	Lost	Won
267	42	F.G.Mann (1)	1948/49	South Africa	Durban (2)	Won	Lost
268		F.G.Mann (2)	1948/49	South Africa	Johannesburg (2)	Drew	Won
269		F.G.Mann (3)	1948/49	South Africa	Cape Town	Drew	Won
270		F.G.Mann (4)	1948/49	South Africa	Johannesburg (2)	Drew	Won
271		F.G.Mann (5)	1948/49	South Africa	Port Elizabeth	Won	Lost
272		F.G.Mann (6)	1949	New Zealand	Headingley	Drew	Won
273		F.G.Mann (7)	1949	New Zealand	Lord's	Drew	Won
274	43	F.R.Brown (1)	1949	New Zealand	Old Trafford	Drew	Won
275		F.R.Brown (2)	1949	New Zealand	The Oval	Drew	Lost

Test	Captain	Date	Opposition	Venue	Result	Toss
276	N.W.D.Yardley (12)	1950	West Indies	Old Trafford	Won	Won
277	N.W.D.Yardley (13)	1950	West Indies	Lord's	Lost	Lost
278	N.W.D.Yardley (14)	1950	West Indies	Trent Bridge	Lost	Won
279	F.R.Brown (3)	1950	West Indies	The Oval	Lost	Lost
280	F.R.Brown (4)	1950/51	Australia	Brisbane (2)	Lost	Lost
281	F.R.Brown (5)	1950/51	Australia	Melbourne	Lost	Lost
282	F.R.Brown (6)	1950/51	Australia	Sydney	Lost	Won
283	F.R.Brown (7)	1950/51	Australia	Adelaide	Lost	Lost
284	F.R.Brown (8)	1950/51	Australia	Melbourne	Won	Lost
285	F.R.Brown (9)	1950/51	New Zealand	Christchurch	Drew	Lost
286	F.R.Brown (10)	1950/51	New Zealand	Wellington	Won	Lost
287	F.R.Brown (11)	1951	South Africa	Trent Bridge	Lost	Lost
288	F.R.Brown (12)	1951	South Africa	Lord's	Won	Won
289	F.R.Brown (13)	1951	South Africa	Old Trafford	Won	Lost
290	F.R.Brown (14)	1951	South Africa	Headingley	Drew	Lost
291	F.R.Brown (15)	1951	South Africa	The Oval	Won	Lost
292 44	N.D.Howard (1)	1951/52	India	Delhi	Drew	Won
293	N.D.Howard (2)	1951/52	India	Bombay (2)	Drew	Lost
294	N.D.Howard (3)	1951/52	India	Calcutta	Drew	Won
295	N.D.Howard (4)	1951/52	India	Kanpur	Won	Lost
296 45	D.B.Carr (1)	1951/52	India	Madras (1)	Lost	Won
297 46	L.Hutton (1)	1952	India	Headingley	Won	Lost
298	L.Hutton (2)	1952	India	Lord's	Won	Lost
299	L.Hutton (3)	1952	India	Old Trafford	Won	Won
300	L.Hutton (4)	1952	India	The Oval	Drew	Won
301	L.Hutton (5)	1953	Australia	Trent Bridge	Drew	Lost
302	L.Hutton (6)	1953	Australia	Lord's	Drew	Lost
303	L.Hutton (7)	1953	Australia	Old Trafford	Drew	Lost
304	L.Hutton (8)	1953	Australia	Headingley	Drew	Lost
305	L.Hutton (9)	1953	Australia	The Oval	Won	Lost
306	L.Hutton (10)	1953/54	West Indies	Kingston	Lost	Lost
307	L.Hutton (11)	1953/54	West Indies	Bridgetown	Lost	Lost
308	L.Hutton (12)	1953/54	West Indies	Georgetown	Won	Won
309	L.Hutton (13)	1953/54	West Indies	Port-of-Spain	Drew	Lost
310	L.Hutton (14)	1953/54	West Indies	Kingston	Won	Lost
311	L.Hutton (15)	1954	Pakistan	Lord's	Drew	Won
312 47	Rev.D.S.Sheppard (1)	1954	Pakistan	Trent Bridge	Won	Lost
313	Rev.D.S.Sheppard (2)	1954	Pakistan	Old Trafford	Drew	Won
314	L.Hutton (16)	1954	Pakistan	The Oval	Lost	Lost
315	L.Hutton (17)	1954/55	Australia	Brisbane (2)	Lost	Won
316	L.Hutton (18)	1954/55	Australia	Sydney	Won	Lost
317	L.Hutton (19)	1954/55	Australia	Melbourne	Won	Won
318	L.Hutton (20)	1954/55	Australia	Adelaide	Won	Lost
319	L.Hutton (21)	1954/55	Australia	Sydney	Drew	Lost
320	L.Hutton (22)	1954/55	New Zealand	Dunedin	Won	Won
321	L.Hutton (23)	1954/55	New Zealand	Auckland	Won	Won
322 48	P.B.H.May (1)	1955	South Africa	Trent Bridge	Won	Won
323	P.B.H.May (2)	1955	South Africa	Lord's	Won	Won
324	P.B.H.May (3)	1955	South Africa	Old Trafford	Lost	Won
325	P.B.H.May (4)	1955	South Africa	Headingley	Lost	Won
326	P.B.H.May (5)	1955	South Africa	The Oval	Won	Won
327	P.B.H.May (6)	1956	Australia	Trent Bridge	Drew	Won
328	P.B.H.May (7)	1956	Australia	Lord's	Lost	Lost
329	P.B.H.May (8)	1956	Australia	Headingley	Won	Won
330	P.B.H.May (9)	1956	Australia	Old Trafford	Won	Won
331	P.B.H.May (10)	1956	Australia	The Oval	Drew	Won
332	P.B.H.May (11)	1956/57	South Africa	Johannesburg (3)	Won	Won
333	P.B.H.May (12)	1956/57	South Africa	Cape Town	Won	Won
334	P.B.H.May (13)	1956/57	South Africa	Durban (2)	Drew	Won
335	P.B.H.May (14)	1956/57	South Africa	Johannesburg (3)	Lost	Won
336	P.B.H.May (15)	1956/57	South Africa	Port Elizabeth	Lost	Lost
337	P.B.H.May (16)	1957	West Indies	Edgbaston	Drew	Won
338	P.B.H.May (17)	1957	West Indies	Lord's	Won	Lost
339	P.B.H.May (18)	1957	West Indies	Trent Bridge	Drew	Won
340	P.B.H.May (19)	1957	West Indies	Headingley	Won	Lost
341	P.B.H.May (20)	1957	West Indies	The Oval	Won	Lost
342	P.B.H.May (21)	1958	New Zealand	Edgbaston	Won	Won
343	P.B.H.May (22)	1958	New Zealand	Lord's	Won	Won
344	P.B.H.May (23)	1958	New Zealand	Headingley	Won	Lost
345	P.B.H.May (24)	1958	New Zealand	Old Trafford	Won	Won
346	P.B.H.May (25)	1958	New Zealand	The Oval	Drew	Lost
347	P.B.H.May (26)	1958/59	Australia	Brisbane (2)	Lost	Won
348	P.B.H.May (27)	1958/59	Australia	Melbourne	Lost	Won
349	P.B.H.May (28)	1958/59	Australia	Sydney	Drew	Won

Test		Captain	Date	Opposition	Venue	Result	Toss
350		P.B.H.May (29)	1958/59	Australia	Adelaide	Lost	Won
351		P.B.H.May (30)	1958/59	Australia	Melbourne	Lost	Lost
352		P.B.H.May (31)	1958/59	New Zealand	Christchurch	Won	Won
353		P.B.H.May (32)	1958/59	New Zealand	Auckland	Drew	Lost
354		P.B.H.May (33)	1959	India	Trent Bridge	Won	Won
355		P.B.H.May (34)	1959	India	Lord's	Won	Lost
356		P.B.H.May (35)	1959	India	Headingley	Won	Lost
357	49	M.C.Cowdrey (1)	1959	India	Old Trafford	Won	Won
358		M.C.Cowdrey (2)	1959	India	The Oval	Won	Lost
359		P.B.H.May (36)	1959/60	West Indies	Bridgetown	Drew	Won
360		P.B.H.May (37)	1959/60	West Indies	Port-of-Spain	Won	Won
361		P.B.H.May (38)	1959/60	West Indies	Kingston	Drew	Won
362		M.C.Cowdrey (3)	1959/60	West Indies	Georgetown	Drew	Won
363		M.C.Cowdrey (4)	1959/60	West Indies	Port-of-Spain	Drew	Won
364		M.C.Cowdrey (5)	1960	South Africa	Edgbaston	Won	Won
365		M.C.Cowdrey (6)	1960	South Africa	Lord's	Won	Won
366		M.C.Cowdrey (7)	1960	South Africa	Trent Bridge	Won	Won
367		M.C.Cowdrey (8)	1960	South Africa	Old Trafford	Drew	Won
368		M.C.Cowdrey (9)	1960	South Africa	The Oval	Drew	Won
369		M.C.Cowdrey (10)	1961	Australia	Edgbaston	Drew	Won
370		M.C.Cowdrey (11)	1961	Australia	Lord's	Lost	Won
371		P.B.H.May (39)	1961	Australia	Headingley	Won	Lost
372		P.B.H.May (40)	1961	Australia	Old Trafford	Lost	Lost
373		P.B.H.May (41)	1961	Australia	The Oval	Drew	Won
374	50	E.R.Dexter (1)	1961/62	Pakistan	Lahore (2)	Won	Lost
375		E.R.Dexter (2)	1961/62	India	Bombay (2)	Drew	Won
376		E.R.Dexter (3)	1961/62	India	Kanpur	Drew	Lost
377		E.R.Dexter (4)	1961/62	India	Delhi	Drew	Lost
378		E.R.Dexter (5)	1961/62	India	Calcutta	Lost	Lost
379		E.R.Dexter (6)	1961/62	India	Madras (2)	Lost	Lost
380		E.R.Dexter (7)	1961/62	Pakistan	Dacca	Drew	Lost
381		E.R.Dexter (8)	1961/62	Pakistan	Karachi (1)	Drew	Lost
382		E.R.Dexter (9)	1962	Pakistan	Edgbaston	Won	Lost
383		E.R.Dexter (10)	1962	Pakistan	Lord's	Won	Lost
384		M.C.Cowdrey (12)	1962	Pakistan	Headingley	Won	Lost
385		E.R.Dexter (11)	1962	Pakistan	Trent Bridge	Drew	Lost
386		E.R.Dexter (12)	1962	Pakistan	The Oval	Won	Won
387		E.R.Dexter (13)	1962/63	Australia	Brisbane (2)	Drew	Lost
388		E.R.Dexter (14)	1962/63	Australia	Melbourne	Won	Lost
389		E.R.Dexter (15)	1962/63	Australia	Sydney	Lost	Won
390		E.R.Dexter (16)	1962/63	Australia	Adelaide	Drew	Lost
391		E.R.Dexter (17)	1962/63	Australia	Sydney	Drew	Won
392		E.R.Dexter (18)	1962/63	New Zealand	Auckland	Won	Won
393		E.R.Dexter (19)	1962/63	New Zealand	Wellington	Won	Won
394		E.R.Dexter (20)	1962/63	New Zealand	Christchurch	Won	Won
395		E.R.Dexter (21)	1963	West Indies	Old Trafford	Lost	Lost
396		E.R.Dexter (22)	1963	West Indies	Lord's	Drew	Lost
397		E.R.Dexter (23)	1963	West Indies	Edgbaston	Won	Won
398		E.R.Dexter (24)	1963	West Indies	Headingley	Lost	Lost
399		E.R.Dexter (25)	1963	West Indies	The Oval	Lost	Won
400	51	M.J.K.Smith (1)	1963/64	India	Madras (2)	Drew	Lost
401		M.J.K.Smith (2)	1963/64	India	Bombay (2)	Drew	Lost
402		M.J.K.Smith (3)	1963/64	India	Calcutta	Drew	Lost
403		M.J.K.Smith (4)	1963/64	India	Delhi	Drew	Lost
404		M.J.K.Smith (5)	1963/64	India	Kanpur	Drew	Lost
405		E.R.Dexter (26)	1964	Australia	Trent Bridge	Drew	Won
406		E.R.Dexter (27)	1964	Australia	Lord's	Drew	Won
407		E.R.Dexter (28)	1964	Australia	Headingley	Lost	Lost
408		E.R.Dexter (29)	1964	Australia	Old Trafford	Drew	Lost
409		E.R.Dexter (30)	1964	Australia	The Oval	Drew	Lost
410		M.J.K.Smith (6)	1964/65	South Africa	Durban (2)	Won	Won
411		M.J.K.Smith (7)	1964/65	South Africa	Johannesburg (3)	Drew	Won
412		M.J.K.Smith (8)	1964/65	South Africa	Cape Town	Drew	Won
413		M.J.K.Smith (9)	1964/65	South Africa	Johannesburg (3)	Drew	Won
414		M.J.K.Smith (10)	1964/65	South Africa	Port Elizabeth	Drew	Lost
415		M.J.K.Smith (11)	1965	New Zealand	Edgbaston	Won	Won
416		M.J.K.Smith (12)	1965	New Zealand	Lord's	Won	Lost
417		M.J.K.Smith (13)	1965	New Zealand	Headingley	Won	Won
418		M.J.K.Smith (14)	1965	South Africa	Lord's	Drew	Lost
419		M.J.K.Smith (15)	1965	South Africa	Trent Bridge	Lost	Lost
420		M.J.K.Smith (16)	1965	South Africa	The Oval	Drew	Won
421		M.J.K.Smith (17)	1965/66	Australia	Brisbane (2)	Drew	Lost
422		M.J.K.Smith (18)	1965/66	Australia	Melbourne	Drew	Lost
423		M.J.K.Smith (19)	1965/66	Australia	Sydney	Won	Won

Test	Captain	Date	Opposition	Venue	Result	Toss
424	M.J.K.Smith (20)	1965/66	Australia	Adelaide	Lost	Won
425	M.J.K.Smith (21)	1965/66	Australia	Melbourne	Drew	Won
426	M.J.K.Smith (22)	1965/66	New Zealand	Christchurch	Drew	Won
427	M.J.K.Smith (23)	1965/66	New Zealand	Dunedin	Drew	Lost
428	M.J.K.Smith (24)	1965/66	New Zealand	Auckland	Drew	Lost
429	M.J.K.Smith (25)	1966	West Indies	Old Trafford	Lost	Lost
430	M.C.Cowdrey (13)	1966	West Indies	Lord's	Drew	Lost
431	M.C.Cowdrey (14)	1966	West Indies	Trent Bridge	Lost	Lost
432	M.C.Cowdrey (15)	1966	West Indies	Headingley	Lost	Lost
433 52	D.B.Close (1)	1966	West Indies	The Oval	Won	Lost
434	D.B.Close (2)	1967	India	Headingley	Won	Won
435	D.B.Close (3)	1967	India	Lord's	Won	Lost
436	D.B.Close (4)	1967	India	Edgbaston	Won	Won
437	D.B.Close (5)	1967	Pakistan	Lord's	Drew	Won
438	D.B.Close (6)	1967	Pakistan	Trent Bridge	Won	Lost
439	D.B.Close (7)	1967	Pakistan	The Oval	Won	Won
440	M.C.Cowdrey (16)	1967/68	West Indies	Port-of-Spain	Drew	Won
441	M.C.Cowdrey (17)	1967/68	West Indies	Kingston	Drew	Won
442	M.C.Cowdrey (18)	1967/68	West Indies	Bridgetown	Drew	Lost
443	M.C.Cowdrey (19)	1967/68	West Indies	Port-of-Spain	Won	Lost
444	M.C.Cowdrey (20)	1967/68	West Indies	Georgetown	Drew	Lost
445	M.C.Cowdrey (21)	1968	Australia	Old Trafford	Lost	Lost
446	M.C.Cowdrey (22)	1968	Australia	Lord's	Drew	Won
447	M.C.Cowdrey (23)	1968	Australia	Edgbaston	Drew	Won
448 53	T.W.Graveney (1)	1968	Australia	Headingley	Drew	Lost
449	M.C.Cowdrey (24)	1968	Australia	The Oval	Won	Won
450	M.C.Cowdrey (25)	1968/69	Pakistan	Lahore (2)	Drew	Won
451	M.C.Cowdrey (26)	1968/69	Pakistan	Dacca	Drew	Lost
452	M.C.Cowdrey (27)	1968/69	Pakistan	Karachi (1)	Drew	Won
453 54	R.Illingworth (1)	1969	West Indies	Old Trafford	Won	Won
454	R.Illingworth (2)	1969	West Indies	Lord's	Drew	Lost
455	R.Illingworth (3)	1969	West Indies	Headingley	Won	Won
456	R.Illingworth (4)	1969	New Zealand	Lord's	Won	Won
457	R.Illingworth (5)	1969	New Zealand	Trent Bridge	Drew	Lost
458	R.Illingworth (6)	1969	New Zealand	The Oval	Won	Lost
459	R.Illingworth (7)	1970/71	Australia	Brisbane (2)	Drew	Lost
460	R.Illingworth (8)	1970/71	Australia	Perth	Drew	Lost
461	R.Illingworth (9)	1970/71	Australia	Sydney	Won	Won
462	R.Illingworth (10)	1970/71	Australia	Melbourne	Drew	Lost
463	R.Illingworth (11)	1970/71	Australia	Adelaide	Drew	Won
464	R.Illingworth (12)	1970/71	Australia	Sydney	Won	Lost
465	R.Illingworth (13)	1970/71	New Zealand	Christchurch	Won	Lost
466	R.Illingworth (14)	1970/71	New Zealand	Auckland	Drew	Lost
467	R.Illingworth (15)	1971	Pakistan	Edgbaston	Drew	Lost
468	R.Illingworth (16)	1971	Pakistan	Lord's	Drew	Won
469	R.Illingworth (17)	1971	Pakistan	Headingley	Won	Won
470	R.Illingworth (18)	1971	India	Lord's	Drew	Won
471	R.Illingworth (19)	1971	India	Old Trafford	Drew	Won
472	R.Illingworth (20)	1971	India	The Oval	Lost	Won
473	R.Illingworth (21)	1972	Australia	Old Trafford	Won	Won
474	R.Illingworth (22)	1972	Australia	Lord's	Lost	Won
475	R.Illingworth (23)	1972	Australia	Trent Bridge	Drew	Won
476	R.Illingworth (24)	1972	Australia	Headingley	Won	Lost
477	R.Illingworth (25)	1972	Australia	The Oval	Lost	Won
478 55	A.R.Lewis (1)	1972/73	India	Delhi	Won	Lost
479	A.R.Lewis (2)	1972/73	India	Calcutta	Lost	Lost
480	A.R.Lewis (3)	1972/73	India	Madras (1)	Lost	Won
481	A.R.Lewis (4)	1972/73	India	Kanpur	Drew	Lost
482	A.R.Lewis (5)	1972/73	India	Bombay (2)	Drew	Lost
483	A.R.Lewis (6)	1972/73	Pakistan	Lahore (2)	Drew.	Won
484	A.R.Lewis (7)	1972/73	Pakistan	Hyderabad	Drew	Won
485	A.R.Lewis (8)	1972/73	Pakistan	Karachi (1)	Drew	Lost
486	R.Illingworth (26)	1973	New Zealand	Trent Bridge	Won	Won
487	R.Illingworth (27)	1973	New Zealand	Lord's	Drew	Lost
488	R.Illingworth (28)	1973	New Zealand	Headingley	Won	Lost
489	R.Illingworth (29)	1973	West Indies	The Oval	Lost	Lost
490	R.Illingworth (30)	1973	West Indies	Edgbaston	Drew	Lost
491	R.Illingworth (31)	1973	West Indies	Lord's	Lost	Lost
492 56	M.H.Denness (1)	1973/74	West Indies	Port-of-Spain	Lost	Lost
493	M.H.Denness (2)	1973/74	West Indies	Kingston	Drew	Won
494	M.H.Denness (3)	1973/74	West Indies	Bridgetown	Drew	Lost
495	M.H.Denness (4)	1973/74	West Indies	Georgetown	Drew	Won
496	M.H.Denness (5)	1973/74	West Indies	Port-of-Spain	Won	Won
497	M.H.Denness (6)	1974	India	Old Trafford	Won	Won

Test		Captain	Date	Opposition	Venue	Result	Toss
498		M.H.Denness (7)	1974	India	Lord's	Won	Won
499		M.H.Denness (8)	1974	India	Edgbaston	Won	Lost
500		M.H.Denness (9)	1974	Pakistan	Headingley	Drew	Lost
501		M.H.Denness (10)	1974	Pakistan	Lord's	Drew	Lost
502		M.H.Denness (11)	1974	Pakistan	The Oval	Drew	Lost
503		M.H.Denness (12)	1974/75	Australia	Brisbane (2)	Lost	Lost
504		M.H.Denness (13)	1974/75	Australia	Perth	Lost	Lost
505		M.H.Denness (14)	1974/75	Australia	Melbourne	Drew	Lost
506	57	J.H.Edrich (1)	1974/75	Australia	Sydney	Lost	Lost
507		M.H.Denness (15)	1974/75	Australia	Adelaide	Lost	Won
508		M.H.Denness (16)	1974/75	Australia	Melbourne	Won	Lost
509		M.H.Denness (17)	1974/75	New Zealand	Auckland	Won	Won
510		M.H.Denness (18)	1974/75	New Zealand	Christchurch	Drew	Won
511		M.H.Denness (19)	1975	Australia	Edgbaston	Lost	Won
512	58	A.W.Greig (1)	1975	Australia	Lord's	Drew	Won
513		A.W.Greig (2)	1975	Australia	Headingley	Drew	Won
514		A.W.Greig (3)	1975	Australia	The Oval	Drew	Lost
515		A.W.Greig (4)	1976	West Indies	Trent Bridge	Drew	Lost
516		A.W.Greig (5)	1976	West Indies	Lord's	Drew	Won
517		A.W.Greig (6)	1976	West Indies	Old Trafford	Lost	Lost
518		A.W.Greig (7)	1976	West Indies	Headingley	Lost	Lost
519		A.W.Greig (8)	1976	West Indies	The Oval	Lost	Lost
520		A.W.Greig (9)	1976/77	India	Delhi	Won	Won
521		A.W.Greig (10)	1976/77	India	Calcutta	Won	Lost
522		A.W.Greig (11)	1976/77	India	Madras (1)	Won	Won
523		A.W.Greig (12)	1976/77	India	Bangalore	Lost	Lost
524		A.W.Greig (13)	1976/77	India	Bombay (3)	Drew	Lost
525		A.W.Greig (14)	1976/77	Australia	Melbourne	Lost	Won
526	59	J.M.Brearley (1)	1977	Australia	Lord's	Drew	Won
527		J.M.Brearley (2)	1977	Australia	Old Trafford	Won	Lost
528		J.M.Brearley (3)	1977	Australia	Trent Bridge	Won	Lost
529		J.M.Brearley (4)	1977	Australia	Headingley	Won	Won
530		J.M.Brearley (5)	1977	Australia	The Oval	Drew	Lost
531		J.M.Brearley (6)	1977/78	Pakistan	Lahore (2)	Drew	Lost
532		J.M.Brearley (7)	1977/78	Pakistan	Hyderabad	Drew	Lost
533	60	G.Boycott (1)	1977/78	Pakistan	Karachi (1)	Drew	Won
534		G.Boycott (2)	1977/78	New Zealand	Wellington	Lost	Won
535		G.Boycott (3)	1977/78	New Zealand	Christchurch	Won	Won
536		G.Boycott (4)	1977/78	New Zealand	Auckland	Drew	Lost
537		J.M.Brearley (8)	1978	Pakistan	Edgbaston	Won	Won
538		J.M.Brearley (9)	1978	Pakistan	Lord's	Won	Won
539		J.M.Brearley (10)	1978	Pakistan	Headingley	Drew	Lost
540		J.M.Brearley (11)	1978	New Zealand	The Oval	Won	Lost
541		J.M.Brearley (12)	1978	New Zealand	Trent Bridge	Won	Won
542		J.M.Brearley (13)	1978	New Zealand	Lord's	Won	Lost
543		J.M.Brearley (14)	1978/79	Australia	Brisbane (2)	Won	Lost
544		J.M.Brearley (15)	1978/79	Australia	Perth	Won	Lost
545		J.M.Brearley (16)	1978/79	Australia	Melbourne	Lost	Lost
546		J.M.Brearley (17)	1978/79	Australia	Sydney	Won	Won
547		J.M.Brearley (18)	1978/79	Australia	Adelaide	Won	Lost
548		J.M.Brearley (19)	1978/79	Australia	Sydney	Won	Lost
549		J.M.Brearley (20)	1979	India	Edgbaston	Won	Won
550		J.M.Brearley (21)	1979	India	Lord's	Drew	Lost
551		J.M.Brearley (22)	1979	India	Headingley	Drew	Won
552		J.M.Brearley (23)	1979	India	The Oval	Drew	Won
553		J.M.Brearley (24)	1979/80	Australia	Perth	Lost	Won
554		J.M.Brearley (25)	1979/80	Australia	Sydney	Lost	Lost
555		J.M.Brearley (26)	1979/80	Australia	Melbourne	Lost	Won
556		J.M.Brearley (27)	1979/80	India	Bombay (3)	Won	Lost
557	61	I.T.Botham (1)	1980	West Indies	Trent Bridge	Lost	Won
558		I.T.Botham (2)	1980	West Indies	Lord's	Drew	Lost
559		I.T.Botham (3)	1980	West Indies	Old Trafford	Drew	Lost
560		I.T.Botham (4)	1980	West Indies	The Oval	Drew	Lost
561		I.T.Botham (5)	1980	West Indies	Headingley	Drew	Lost
562		I.T.Botham (6)	1980	Australia	Lord's	Drew	Lost
563		I.T.Botham (7)	1980/81	West Indies	Port-of-Spain	Lost	Won
564		I.T.Botham (8)	1980/81	West Indies	Bridgetown	Lost	Won
565		I.T.Botham (9)	1980/81	West Indies	St John's	Drew	Won
566		I.T.Botham (10)	1980/81	West Indies	Kingston	Drew	Lost
567		I.T.Botham (11)	1981	Australia	Trent Bridge	Lost	Lost
568		I.T.Botham (12)	1981	Australia	Lord's	Drew	Lost
569		J.M.Brearley (28)	1981	Australia	Headingley	Won	Lost
570		J.M.Brearley (29)	1981	Australia	Edgbaston	Won	Won
571		J.M.Brearley (30)	1981	Australia	Old Trafford	Won	Won

Test		Captain	Date	Opposition	Venue	Result	Toss
572		J.M.Brearley (31)	1981	Australia	The Oval	Drew	Won
573	62	K.W.R.Fletcher (1)	1981/82	India	Bombay (3)	Lost	Lost
574		K.W.R.Fletcher (2)	1981/82	India	Bangalore	Drew	Won
575		K.W.R.Fletcher (3)	1981/82	India	Delhi	Drew	Won
576		K.W.R.Fletcher (4)	1981/82	India	Calcutta	Drew	Won
577		K.W.R.Fletcher (5)	1981/82	India	Madras (1)	Drew	Won
578		K.W.R.Fletcher (6)	1981/82	India	Kanpur	Drew	Won
579		K.W.R.Fletcher (7)	1981/82	Sri Lanka	Colombo (1)	Won	Lost
580	63	R.G.D.Willis (1)	1982	India	Lord's	Won	Won
581		R.G.D.Willis (2)	1982	India	Old Trafford	Drew	Won
582		R.G.D.Willis (3)	1982	India	The Oval	Drew	Won
583		R.G.D.Willis (4)	1982	Pakistan	Edgbaston	Won	Won
584	64	D.I.Gower (1)	1982	Pakistan	Lord's	Lost	Lost
585		R.G.D.Willis (5)	1982	Pakistan	Headingley	Won	Lost
586		R.G.D.Willis (6)	1982/83	Australia	Perth	Drew	Lost
587		R.G.D.Willis (7)	1982/83	Australia	Brisbane (2)	Lost	Lost
588		R.G.D.Willis (8)	1982/83	Australia	Adelaide	Lost	Won
589		R.G.D.Willis (9)	1982/83	Australia	Melbourne	Won	Lost
590		R.G.D.Willis (10)	1982/83	Australia	Sydney	Drew	Lost
591		R.G.D.Willis (11)	1983	New Zealand	The Oval	Won	Won
592		R.G.D.Willis (12)	1983	New Zealand	Headingley	Lost	Lost
593		R.G.D.Willis (13)	1983	New Zealand	Lord's	Won	Lost
594		R.G.D.Willis (14)	1983	New Zealand	Trent Bridge	Won	Won
595		R.G.D.Willis (15)	1983/84	New Zealand	Wellington	Drew	Lost
596		R.G.D.Willis (16)	1983/84	New Zealand	Christchurch	Lost	Lost
597		R.G.D.Willis (17)	1983/84	New Zealand	Auckland	Drew	Lost
598		R.G.D.Willis (18)	1983/84	Pakistan	Karachi (1)	Lost	Won
599		D.I.Gower (2)	1983/84	Pakistan	Faisalabad	Drew	Lost
600		D.I.Gower (3)	1983/84	Pakistan	Lahore (2)	Drew	Lost
601		D.I.Gower (4)	1984	West Indies	Edgbaston	Lost	Won
602		D.I.Gower (5)	1984	West Indies	Lord's	Lost	Lost
603		D.I.Gower (6)	1984	West Indies	Headingley	Lost	Won
604		D.I.Gower (7)	1984	West Indies	Old Trafford	Lost	Lost
605		D.I.Gower (8)	1984	West Indies	The Oval	Lost	Won
606		D.I.Gower (9)	1984	Sri Lanka	Lord's	Drew	Won
607		D.I.Gower (10)	1984/85	India	Bombay (3)	Lost	Won
608		D.I.Gower (11)	1984/85	India	Delhi	Won	Lost
609		D.I.Gower (12)	1984/85	India	Calcutta	Drew	Lost
610		D.I.Gower (13)	1984/85	India	Madras (1)	Won	Lost
611		D.I.Gower (14)	1984/85	India	Kanpur	Drew	Lost
612		D.I.Gower (15)	1985	Australia	Headingley	Won	Lost
613		D.I.Gower (16)	1985	Australia	Lord's	Lost	Lost
614		D.I.Gower (17)	1985	Australia	Trent Bridge	Drew	Won
615		D.I.Gower (18)	1985	Australia	Old Trafford	Drew	Won
616		D.I.Gower (19)	1985	Australia	Edgbaston	Won	Won
617		D.I.Gower (20)	1985	Australia	The Oval	Won	Won
618		D.I.Gower (21)	1985/86	West Indies	Kingston	Lost	Won
619		D.I.Gower (22)	1985/86	West Indies	Port-of-Spain	Lost	Lost
620		D.I.Gower (23)	1985/86	West Indies	Bridgetown	Lost	Won
621		D.I.Gower (24)	1985/86	West Indies	Port-of-Spain	Lost	Lost
622		D.I.Gower (25)	1985/86	West Indies	St John's	Lost	Won
623		D.I.Gower (26)	1986	India	Lord's	Lost	Lost
624	65	M.W.Gatting (1)	1986	India	Headingley	Lost	Lost
625		M.W.Gatting (2)	1986	India	Edgbaston	Drew	Won
626		M.W.Gatting (3)	1986	New Zealand	Lord's	Drew	Won
627		M.W.Gatting (4)	1986	New Zealand	Trent Bridge	Lost	Won
628		M.W.Gatting (5)	1986	New Zealand	The Oval	Drew	Won
629		M.W.Gatting (6)	1986/87	Australia	Brisbane (2)	Won	Lost
630		M.W.Gatting (7)	1986/87	Australia	Perth	Drew	Won
631		M.W.Gatting (8)	1986/87	Australia	Adelaide	Drew	Lost
632		M.W.Gatting (9)	1986/87	Australia	Melbourne	Won	Won
633		M.W.Gatting (10)	1986/87	Australia	Sydney	Lost	Won
634		M.W.Gatting (11)	1987	Pakistan	Old Trafford	Drew	Lost
635		M.W.Gatting (12)	1987	Pakistan	Lord's	Drew	Won
636		M.W.Gatting (13)	1987	Pakistan	Headingley	Lost	Won
637		M.W.Gatting (14)	1987	Pakistan	Edgbaston	Drew	Won
638		M.W.Gatting (15)	1987	Pakistan	The Oval	Drew	Lost
639		M.W.Gatting (16)	1987/88	Pakistan	Lahore (2)	Lost	Won
640		M.W.Gatting (17)	1987/88	Pakistan	Faisalabad	Drew	Won
641		M.W.Gatting (18)	1987/88	Pakistan	Karachi (1)	Drew	Won
642		M.W.Gatting (19)	1987/88	Australia	Sydney	Drew	Won
643		M.W.Gatting (20)	1987/88	New Zealand	Christchurch	Drew	Lost
644		M.W.Gatting (21)	1987/88	New Zealand	Auckland	Drew	Won
645		M.W.Gatting (22)	1987/88	New Zealand	Wellington	Drew	Lost

Test		Captain	Date	Opposition	Venue	Result	Toss
646		M.W.Gatting (23)	1988	West Indies	Trent Bridge	Drew	Won
647	66	J.E.Emburey (1)	1988	West Indies	Lord's	Lost	Lost
648		J.E.Emburey (2)	1988	West Indies	Old Trafford	Lost	Won
649	67	C.S.Cowdrey (1)	1988	West Indies	Headingley	Lost	Lost
650	68	G.A.Gooch (1)	1988	West Indies	The Oval	Lost	Won
651		G.A.Gooch (2)	1988	Sri Lanka	Lord's	Won	Won
652		D.I.Gower (27)	1989	Australia	Headingley	Lost	Won
653		D.I.Gower (28)	1989	Australia	Lord's	Lost	Won
654		D.I.Gower (29)	1989	Australia	Edgbaston	Drew	Lost
655		D.I.Gower (30)	1989	Australia	Old Trafford	Lost	Won
656		D.I.Gower (31)	1989	Australia	Trent Bridge	Lost	Lost
657		D.I.Gower (32)	1989	Australia	The Oval	Drew	Lost
658		G.A.Gooch (3)	1989/90	West Indies	Kingston	Won	Lost
659		G.A.Gooch (4)	1989/90	West Indies	Port-of-Spain	Drew	Lost
660	69	A.J.Lamb (1)	1989/90	West Indies	Bridgetown	Lost	Won
661		A.J.Lamb (2)	1989/90	West Indies	St John's	Lost	Won
662		G.A.Gooch (5)	1990	New Zealand	Trent Bridge	Drew	Lost
663		G.A.Gooch (6)	1990	New Zealand	Lord's	Drew	Lost
664		G.A.Gooch (7)	1990	New Zealand	Edgbaston	Won	Lost
665		G.A.Gooch (8)	1990	India	Lord's	Won	Lost
666		G.A.Gooch (9)	1990	India	Old Trafford	Drew	Won
667		G.A.Gooch (10)	1990	India	The Oval	Drew	Lost
668		A.J.Lamb (3)	1990/91	Australia	Brisbane (2)	Lost	Lost
669		G.A.Gooch (11)	1990/91	Australia	Melbourne	Lost	Won
670		G.A.Gooch (12)	1990/91	Australia	Sydney	Drew	Lost
671		G.A.Gooch (13)	1990/91	Australia	Adelaide	Drew	Lost
672		G.A.Gooch (14)	1990/91	Australia	Perth	Lost	Won
673		G.A.Gooch (15)	1991	West Indies	Headingley	Won	Lost
674		G.A.Gooch (16)	1991	West Indies	Lord's	Drew	Won
675		G.A.Gooch (17)	1991	West Indies	Trent Bridge	Lost	Won
676		G.A.Gooch (18)	1991	West Indies	Edgbaston	Lost	Lost
677		G.A.Gooch (19)	1991	West Indies	The Oval	Won	Won
678		G.A.Gooch (20)	1991	Sri Lanka	Lord's	Won	Won
679		G.A.Gooch (21)	1991/92	New Zealand	Christchurch	Won	Lost
680		G.A.Gooch (22)	1991/92	New Zealand	Auckland	Won	Lost
681		G.A.Gooch (23)	1991/92	New Zealand	Wellington	Drew	Won
682		G.A.Gooch (24)	1992	Pakistan	Edgbaston	Drew	Won
683		G.A.Gooch (25)	1992	Pakistan	Lord's	Lost	Won
684		G.A.Gooch (26)	1992	Pakistan	Old Trafford	Drew	Lost
685		G.A.Gooch (27)	1992	Pakistan	Headingley	Won	Lost
686		G.A.Gooch (28)	1992	Pakistan	The Oval	Lost	Won
687		G.A.Gooch (29)	1992/93	India	Calcutta	Lost	Lost
688	70	A.J.Stewart (1)	1992/93	India	Madras (1)	Lost	Lost
689		G.A.Gooch (30)	1992/93	India	Bombay (3)	Lost	Won
690		A.J.Stewart (2)	1992/93	Sri Lanka	Colombo (2)	Lost	Won
691		G.A.Gooch (31)	1993	Australia	Old Trafford	Lost	Won
692		G.A.Gooch (32)	1993	Australia	Lord's	Lost	Lost
693		G.A.Gooch (33)	1993	Australia	Trent Bridge	Drew	Won
694		G.A.Gooch (34)	1993	Australia	Headingley	Lost	Lost
695	71	M.A.Atherton (1)	1993	Australia	Edgbaston	Lost	Won
696		M.A.Atherton (2)	1993	Australia	The Oval	Won	Won
697		M.A.Atherton (3)	1993/94	West Indies	Kingston	Lost	Won
698		M.A.Atherton (4)	1993/94	West Indies	Georgetown	Lost	Lost
699		M.A.Atherton (5)	1993/94	West Indies	Port-of-Spain	Lost	Lost
700		M.A.Atherton (6)	1993/94	West Indies	Bridgetown	Won	Lost
701		M.A.Atherton (7)	1993/94	West Indies	St John's	Drew	Lost
702		M.A.Atherton (8)	1994	New Zealand	Trent Bridge	Won	Lost
703		M.A.Atherton (9)	1994	New Zealand	Lord's	Drew	Lost
704		M.A.Atherton (10)	1994	New Zealand	Old Trafford	Drew	Won
705		M.A.Atherton (11)	1994	South Africa	Lord's	Lost	Lost
706		M.A.Atherton (12)	1994	South Africa	Headingley	Drew	Won
707		M.A.Atherton (13)	1994	South Africa	The Oval	Won	Won
708		M.A.Atherton (14)	1994/95	Australia	Brisbane (2)	Lost	Lost
709		M.A.Atherton (15)	1994/95	Australia	Melbourne	Lost	Won
710		M.A.Atherton (16)	1994/95	Australia	Sydney	Drew	Won
711		M.A.Atherton (17)	1994/95	Australia	Adelaide	Won	Won
712		M.A.Atherton (18)	1994/95	Australia	Perth	Lost	Lost
713		M.A.Atherton (19)	1995	West Indies	Headingley	Lost	Won
714		M.A.Atherton (20)	1995	West Indies	Lord's	Won	Won
715		M.A.Atherton (21)	1995	West Indies	Edgbaston	Lost	Won
716		M.A.Atherton (22)	1995	West Indies	Old Trafford	Won	Lost
717		M.A.Atherton (23)	1995	West Indies	Trent Bridge	Drew	Won
718		M.A.Atherton (24)	1995	West Indies	The Oval	Drew	Won
719		M.A.Atherton (25)	1995/96	South Africa	Centurion	Drew	Lost

Test	Captain	Date	Opposition	Venue	Result	Toss
720	M.A.Atherton (26)	1995/96	South Africa	Johannesburg (3)	Drew	Won
721	M.A.Atherton (27)	1995/96	South Africa	Durban (2)	Drew	Lost
722	M.A.Atherton (28)	1995/96	South Africa	Port Elizabeth	Drew	Lost
723	M.A.Atherton (29)	1995/96	South Africa	Cape Town	Lost	Won
724	M.A.Atherton (30)	1996	India	Edgbaston	Won	Lost
725	M.A.Atherton (31)	1996	India	Lord's	Drew	Lost
726	M.A.Atherton (32)	1996	India	Trent Bridge	Drew	Lost
727	M.A.Atherton (33)	1996	Pakistan	Lord's	Lost	Lost
728	M.A.Atherton (34)	1996	Pakistan	Headingley	Drew	Won
729	M.A.Atherton (35)	1996	Pakistan	The Oval	Lost	Won

RESULTS PER CAPTAIN

Captain	Mat	Won	Drawn	Lost	% Won	% Drawn	% Lost
P.B.H.May	41	20	11	10	48.78	26.82	24.39
M.A.Atherton	35	8	14	13	22.85	40.00	37.14
G.A.Gooch	34	10	12	12	29.41	35.29	35.29
D.I.Gower	32	5	9	18	15.62	28.12	56.25
R.Illingworth	31	12	14	5	38.70	45.16	16.12
J.M.Brearley	31	18	9	4	58.06	29.03	12.90
E.R.Dexter	30	9	14	7	30.00	46.66	23.33
M.C.Cowdrey	27	8	15	4	29.62	55.55	14.81
M.J.K.Smith	25	5	17	3	20.00	68.00	12.00
L.Hutton	23	11	8	4	47.82	34.78	17.39
M.W.Gatting	23	2	16	5	8.69	69.56	21.73
A.C.MacLaren	22	4	7	11	18.18	31.81	50.00
W.R.Hammond	20	4	13	3	20.00	65.00	15.00
M.H.Denness	19	6	8	5	31.57	42.10	26.31
J.W.H.T.Douglas	18	8	2	8	44.44	11.11	44.44
R.G.D.Willis	18	7	6	5	38.88	33.33	27.77
A.P.F.Chapman	17	9	6	2	52.94	35.29	11.76
R.E.S.Wyatt	16	3	8	5	18.75	50.00	31.25
F.R.Brown	15	5	4	6	33.33	26.66	40.00
D.R.Jardine	15	9	5	1	60.00	33.33	6.66
N.W.D.Yardley	14	4	3	7	28.57	21.42	50.00
A.W.Greig	14	3	6	5	21.42	42.85	35.71
W.G.Grace	13	8	2	3	61.53	15.38	23.07
I.T.Botham	12	0	8	4	0.00	66.66	33.33
G.O.B.Allen	11	4	2	5	36.36	18.18	45.45
P.F.Warner	10	4	0	6	40.00	0.00	60.00
A.E.R.Gilligan	9	4	1	4	44.44	11.11	44.44
A.E.Stoddart	8	3	1	4	37.50	12.50	50.00
A.R.Lewis	8	1	5	2	12.50	62.50	25.00
A.Shrewsbury	7	5	0	2	71.42	0.00	28.57
F.G.Mann	7	2	5	0	28.57	71.42	0.00
D.B.Close	7	6	1	0	85.71	14.28	0.00
K.W.R.Fletcher	7	1	5	1	14.28	71.42	14.28
C.B.Fry	6	4	2	0	66.66	33.33	0.00
A.W.Carr	6	1	5	0	16.66	83.33	0.00
Hon.F.S.Jackson	5	2	3	0	40.00	60.00	0.00
F.L.Fane	5	2	0	3	40.00	0.00	60.00
F.T.Mann	5	2	2	1	40.00	40.00	20.00
Lord Harris	4	2	1	1	50.00	25.00	25.00
A.Shaw	4	0	2	2	0.00	50.00	50.00
Hon.I.F.W.Bligh	4	2	0	2	50.00	0.00	50.00
A.G.Steel	4	3	0	1	75.00	0.00	25.00
Lord Hawke	4	4	0	0	100.00	0.00	0.00
R.T.Stanyforth	4	2	1	1	50.00	25.00	25.00
J.C.White	4	1	2	1	25.00	50.00	25.00
A.H.H.Gilligan	4	1	3	0	25.00	75.00	0.00
Hon.F.S.G.Calthorpe	4	1	2	1	25.00	50.00	25.00
N.D.Howard	4	1	3	0	25.00	75.00	0.00
G.Boycott	4	1	2	1	25.00	50.00	25.00
R.E.Foster	3	1	2	0	33.33	66.66	0.00
H.D.G.Leveson Gower	3	1	0	2	33.33	0.00	66.66
Hon.L.H.Tennyson	3	0	2	1	0.00	66.66	33.33
R.W.V.Robins	3	1	2	0	33.33	66.66	0.00
A.J.Lamb	3	0	0	3	0.00	0.00	100.00
James Lillywhite	2	1	0	1	50.00	0.00	50.00
A.N.Hornby	2	0	1	1	0.00	50.00	50.00
W.W.Read	2	2	0	0	100.00	0.00	0.00
A.O.Jones	2	0	0	2	0.00	0.00	100.00
Rev.D.S.Sheppard	2	1	1	0	50.00	50.00	0.00
J.E.Emburey	2	0	0	2	0.00	0.00	100.00

Captain	Mat	Won	Drawn	Lost	% Won	% Drawn	% Lost
A.J.Stewart	2	0	0	2	0.00	0.00	100.00
C.A.Smith	1	1	0	0	100.00	0.00	0.00
M.P.Bowden	1	1	0	0	100.00	0.00	0.00
Sir T.C.O'Brien	1	1	0	0	100.00	0.00	0.00
G.T.S.Stevens	1	0	0	1	0.00	0.00	100.00
C.F.Walters	1	0	0	1	0.00	0.00	100.00
K.Cranston	1	0	1	0	0.00	100.00	0.00
D.B.Carr	1	0	0	1	0.00	0.00	100.00
T.W.Graveney	1	0	1	0	0.00	100.00	0.00
J.H.Edrich	1	0	0	1	0.00	0.00	100.00
C.S.Cowdrey	1	0	0	1	0.00	0.00	100.00
TOTAL	**729**	**247**	**275**	**207**	**33.88**	**37.72**	**28.39**

RESULTS OF TOSS PER CAPTAIN

Captain	Mat	Won	Lost	% Won	% Lost
P.B.H.May	41	26	15	63.41	36.58
M.A.Atherton	35	16	19	45.71	54.28
G.A.Gooch	34	16	18	47.05	52.94
D.I.Gower	32	14	18	43.75	56.25
R.Illingworth	31	15	16	48.38	51.61
J.M.Brearley	31	13	18	41.93	58.06
E.R.Dexter	30	13	17	43.33	56.66
M.C.Cowdrey	27	17	10	62.96	37.03
M.J.K.Smith	25	10	15	40.00	60.00
L.Hutton	23	7	16	30.43	69.56
M.W.Gatting	23	14	9	60.86	39.13
A.C.MacLaren	22	11	11	50.00	50.00
W.R.Hammond	20	12	8	60.00	40.00
M.H.Denness	19	9	10	47.36	52.63
J.W.H.T.Douglas	18	7	11	38.88	61.11
R.G.D.Willis	18	8	10	44.44	55.55
A.P.F.Chapman	17	9	8	52.94	47.05
R.E.S.Wyatt	16	12	4	75.00	25.00
F.R.Brown	15	3	12	20.00	80.00
D.R.Jardine	15	7	8	46.66	53.33
N.W.D.Yardley	14	9	5	64.28	35.71
A.W.Greig	14	6	8	42.85	57.14
W.G.Grace	13	4	9	30.76	69.23
I.T.Botham	12	6	6	50.00	50.00
G.O.B.Allen	11	6	5	54.54	45.45
P.F.Warner	10	5	5	50.00	50.00
A.E.R.Gilligan	9	2	7	22.22	77.77
A.E.Stoddart	8	2	6	25.00	75.00
A.R.Lewis	8	3	5	37.50	62.50
A.Shrewsbury	7	3	4	42.85	57.14
F.G.Mann	7	5	2	71.42	28.57
D.B.Close	7	4	3	57.14	42.85
K.W.R.Fletcher	7	5	2	71.42	28.57
C.B.Fry	6	4	2	66.66	33.33
A.W.Carr	6	3	3	50.00	50.00
Hon.F.S.Jackson	5	5	0	100.00	0.00
F.L.Fane	5	3	2	60.00	40.00
F.T.Mann	5	3	2	60.00	40.00
Lord Harris	4	2	2	50.00	50.00
A.Shaw	4	4	0	100.00	0.00
Hon.I.F.W.Bligh	4	3	1	75.00	25.00
A.G.Steel	4	2	2	50.00	50.00
Lord Hawke	4	4	0	100.00	0.00
R.T.Stanyforth	4	4	0	100.00	0.00
J.C.White	4	3	1	75.00	25.00
A.H.H.Gilligan	4	1	3	25.00	75.00
Hon.F.S.G.Calthorpe	4	2	2	50.00	50.00
N.D.Howard	4	2	2	50.00	50.00
G.Boycott	4	3	1	75.00	25.00
R.E.Foster	3	3	0	100.00	0.00
H.D.G.Leveson Gower	3	0	3	0.00	100.00
Hon.L.H.Tennyson	3	2	1	66.66	33.33
R.W.V.Robins	3	2	1	66.66	33.33
A.J.Lamb	3	2	1	66.66	33.33
James Lillywhite	2	0	2	0.00	100.00
A.N.Hornby	2	1	1	50.00	50.00
W.W.Read	2	0	2	0.00	100.00
A.O.Jones	2	1	1	50.00	50.00

Captain	Mat	Won	Lost	% Won	% Lost
Rev.D.S.Sheppard	2	1	1	50.00	50.00
J.E.Emburey	2	1	1	50.00	50.00
A.J.Stewart	2	1	1	50.00	50.00
C.A.Smith	1	0	1	0.00	100.00
M.P.Bowden	1	1	0	100.00	0.00
Sir T.C.O'Brien	1	0	1	0.00	100.00
G.T.S.Stevens	1	0	1	0.00	100.00
C.F.Walters	1	0	1	0.00	100.00
K.Cranston	1	0	1	0.00	100.00
D.B.Carr	1	1	0	100.00	0.00
T.W.Graveney	1	0	1	0.00	100.00
J.H.Edrich	1	0	1	0.00	100.00
C.S.Cowdrey	1	0	1	0.00	100.00
TOTAL	**729**	**363**	**366**	**49.79**	**50.20**

World Test Match Records

TEST MATCH RESULTS PER COUNTRY

AUSTRALIA

Opposition	First Match	Tests	Won	Drew	Lost	Tied
England	1877	285	111	84	90	0
South Africa	1902	59	31	15	13	0
West Indies	1930	81	32	21	27	1
New Zealand	1946	32	13	12	7	0
India	1947	50	24	17	8	1
Pakistan	1956	40	14	15	11	0
Sri Lanka	1983	10	7	3	0	0
Total		**557**	**232**	**167**	**156**	**2**

ENGLAND

Opposition	First Match	Tests	Won	Drew	Lost	Tied
Australia	1877	285	90	84	111	0
South Africa	1889	110	47	43	20	0
West Indies	1928	115	27	40	48	0
New Zealand	1930	75	34	37	4	0
India	1932	84	32	38	14	0
Pakistan	1954	55	14	32	9	0
Sri Lanka	1982	5	3	1	1	0
Total		**729**	**247**	**275**	**207**	**0**

SOUTH AFRICA

Opposition	First Match	Tests	Won	Drew	Lost	Tied
England	1889	110	20	43	47	0
Australia	1902	59	13	15	31	0
New Zealand	1932	21	12	6	3	0
West Indies	1992	1	0	0	1	0
India	1992	4	1	3	0	0
Sri Lanka	1993	3	1	2	0	0
Pakistan	1995	1	1	0	0	0
Zimbabwe	1995	1	1	0	0	0
Total		**200**	**49**	**69**	**82**	**0**

WEST INDIES

Opposition	First Match	Tests	Won	Drew	Lost	Tied
England	1928	115	48	40	27	0
Australia	1930	81	27	21	32	1
India	1948	65	27	31	7	0
New Zealand	1952	28	10	14	4	0
Pakistan	1958	31	12	12	7	0
South Africa	1992	1	1	0	0	0
Sri Lanka	1993	1	0	1	0	0
Total		**322**	**125**	**119**	**77**	**1**

NEW ZEALAND

Opposition	First Match	Tests	Won	Drew	Lost	Tied
England	1930	75	4	37	34	0
South Africa	1932	21	3	6	12	0
Australia	1946	32	7	12	13	0
West Indies	1952	28	4	14	10	0
Pakistan	1955	37	4	16	17	0
India	1955	35	6	16	13	0
Sri Lanka	1983	13	4	7	2	0
Zimbabwe	1992	4	1	3	0	0
Total		**245**	**33**	**111**	**101**	**0**

INDIA

Opposition	First Match	Tests	Won	Drew	Lost	Tied
England	1932	84	14	38	32	0
Australia	1947	50	8	17	24	1
West Indies	1948	65	7	31	27	0
Pakistan	1952	44	4	33	7	0
New Zealand	1955	35	13	16	6	0
Sri Lanka	1982	14	7	6	1	0
Zimbabwe	1992	2	1	1	0	0
South Africa	1992	4	0	3	1	0
Total		**298**	**54**	**145**	**98**	**1**

PAKISTAN

Opposition	First Match	Tests	Won	Drew	Lost	Tied
India	1952	44	7	33	4	0
England	1954	55	9	32	14	0
New Zealand	1955	37	17	16	4	0
Australia	1956	40	11	15	14	0
West Indies	1958	31	7	12	12	0
Sri Lanka	1982	17	9	5	3	0
Zimbabwe	1993	6	4	1	1	0
South Africa	1995	1	0	0	1	0
Total		**231**	**64**	**114**	**53**	**0**

SRI LANKA

Opposition	First Match	Tests	Won	Drew	Lost	Tied
England	1982	5	1	1	3	0
Pakistan	1982	17	3	5	9	0
India	1982	14	1	6	7	0
New Zealand	1983	13	2	7	4	0
Australia	1983	10	0	3	7	0
South Africa	1993	3	0	2	1	0
West Indies	1993	1	0	1	0	0
Zimbabwe	1994	3	0	3	0	0
Total		**66**	**7**	**28**	**31**	**0**

ZIMBABWE

Opposition	First Match	Tests	Won	Drew	Lost	Tied
India	1992	2	0	1	1	0
New Zealand	1992	4	0	3	1	0
Pakistan	1993	6	1	1	4	0
Sri Lanka	1994	3	0	3	0	0
South Africa	1995	1	0	0	1	0
Total		**16**	**1**	**8**	**7**	**0**

GREATEST VICTORIES

Victory by an innings and 200 or more runs

Margin of victory	Country	Opposition	Venue	Date
Innings & 579 runs	England	Australia	The Oval	1938
Innings & 336 runs	West Indies	India	Calcutta	1958/59
Innings & 332 runs	Australia	England	Brisbane (2)	1946/47
Innings & 322 runs	West Indies	New Zealand	Wellington	1994/95
Innings & 285 runs	England	India	Lord's	1974
Innings & 259 runs	Australia	South Africa	Port Elizabeth	1949/50
Innings & 237 runs	England	West Indies	The Oval	1957
Innings & 230 runs	England	Australia	Adelaide	1891/92
Innings & 226 runs	Australia	India	Brisbane (2)	1947/48
Innings & 226 runs	West Indies	England	Lord's	1973
Innings & 225 runs	England	Australia	Melbourne	1911/12
Innings & 222 runs	Australia	New Zealand	Hobart	1993/94
Innings & 217 runs	England	Australia	The Oval	1886
Innings & 217 runs	Australia	West Indies	Brisbane (1)	1930/31
Innings & 215 runs	England	New Zealand	Auckland	1962/63
Innings & 208 runs	South Africa	Sri Lanka	Colombo (2)	1993/94
Innings & 207 runs	England	India	Old Trafford	1952
Innings & 202 runs	England	South Africa	Cape Town	1888/89
Innings & 200 runs	Australia	England	Melbourne	1936/37

Victory by 300 or more runs

Margin	Country	Opposition	Venue	Date
675 runs	England	Australia	Brisbane (1)	1928/29
562 runs	Australia	England	The Oval	1934
530 runs	Australia	South Africa	Melbourne	1910/11
425 runs	West Indies	England	Old Trafford	1976
409 runs	Australia	England	Lord's	1948
408 runs	West Indies	Australia	Adelaide	1979/80
382 runs	Australia	England	Adelaide	1894/95
382 runs	Australia	West Indies	Sydney	1968/69
377 runs	Australia	England	Sydney	1920/21
365 runs	Australia	England	Melbourne	1936/37

Margin	Country	Opposition	Venue	Date
356 runs	South Africa	England	Lord's	1994
348 runs	Australia	Pakistan	Melbourne	1976/77
343 runs	West Indies	Australia	Bridgetown	1990/91
338 runs	England	Australia	Adelaide	1932/33
329 runs	Australia	England	Perth	1994/95
326 runs	West Indies	England	Lord's	1950
324 runs	South Africa	Pakistan	Johannesburg (3)	1994/95
323 runs	South Africa	Australia	Port Elizabeth	1969/70
322 runs	England	Australia	Brisbane (2)	1936/37
312 runs	England	South Africa	Cape Town	1956/57
308 runs	Australia	England	Melbourne	1907/08
307 runs	Australia	England	Sydney	1924/25
307 runs	South Africa	Australia	Johannesburg (3)	1969/70
301 runs	Pakistan	Sri Lanka	Colombo (1)	1994/95
300 runs	Australia	India	Perth	1991/92

NARROWEST VICTORIES
Victory by less than 20 runs

Margin	Country	Opposition	Venue	Date
1 run	West Indies	Australia	Adelaide	1992/93
3 runs	Australia	England	Old Trafford	1902
3 runs	England	Australia	Melbourne	1982/83
5 runs	South Africa	Australia	Sydney	1993/94
6 runs	Australia	England	Sydney	1884/85
7 runs	Australia	England	The Oval	1882
10 runs	England	Australia	Sydney	1894/95
11 runs	Australia	England	Adelaide	1924/25
12 runs	England	Australia	Adelaide	1928/29
13 runs	England	Australia	Sydney	1886/87
16 runs	Australia	India	Brisbane (2)	1977/78
16 runs	Pakistan	India	Bangalore	1986/87
16 runs	Australia	Sri Lanka	Colombo (2)	1992/93
17 runs	South Africa	England	Johannesburg (3)	1956/57
18 runs	England	Australia	Headingley	1981
19 runs	South Africa	England	Johannesburg (1)	1909/10

One wicket victories

Country	Opposition	Venue	Date		10th wicket partnership
England	Australia	The Oval	1902	15*	G.H.Hirst & W.Rhodes
South Africa	England	Johannesburg (1)	1905/06	48*	A.W.Nourse & P.W.Sherwell
England	Australia	Melbourne	1907/08	39*	S.F.Barnes & A.Fielder
England	South Africa	Cape Town	1922/23	5*	A.S.Kennedy & G.G.Macaulay
Australia	West Indies	Melbourne	1951/52	38*	D.T.Ring & W.A.Johnston
New Zealand	West Indies	Dunedin	1979/80	4*	G.B.Troup & S.L.Boock
Pakistan	Australia	Karachi (1)	1994/95	57*	Inzamam-ul-Haq & Mushtaq Ahmed

Two wicket victories

Country	Opposition	Venue	Date		9th wicket partnership
England	Australia	The Oval	1890	2*	G.MacGregor & J.W.Sharpe
Australia	England	Sydney	1907/08	56*	G.R.Hazlitt & A.Cotter
England	South Africa	Durban (2)	1948/49	12*	A.V.Bedser & C.Gladwin
Australia	West Indies	Melbourne	1960/61	2*	K.D.Mackay & J.W.Martin
India	Australia	Bombay (2)	1964/65	32*	C.G.Borde & B.S.Chandrasekhar
Australia	India	Perth	1977/78	12*	W.M.Clark & J.R.Thomson
West Indies	England	Trent Bridge	1980	4*	A.M.E.Roberts & M.A.Holding
New Zealand	Pakistan	Dunedin	1984/85	50*	J.V.Coney & E.J.Chatfield
West Indies	Pakistan	Bridgetown	1987/88	61*	P.J.L.Dujon & W.K.M.Benjamin
Pakistan	England	Lord's	1992	46*	Wasim Akram & Waqar Younis

Tied matches

Country	Opposition	Venue	Date
Australia	West Indies	Brisbane (2)	1960/61
India	Australia	Madras (1)	1986/87

HIGHEST TOTALS

Total	Country	Opposition	Venue	Date
903 for 7 declared	England	Australia	The Oval	1938
849	England	West Indies	Kingston	1929/30
790 for 3 declared	West Indies	Pakistan	Kingston	1957/58
758 for 8 declared	Australia	West Indies	Kingston	1954/55

Total	Country	Opposition	Venue	Date
729 for 6 declared	Australia	England	Lord's	1930
708	Pakistan	England	The Oval	1987
701	Australia	England	The Oval	1934
699 for 5	Pakistan	India	Lahore (2)	1989/90
695	Australia	England	The Oval	1930
692 for 8 declared	West Indies	England	The Oval	1995
687 for 8 declared	West Indies	England	The Oval	1976
681 for 8 declared	West Indies	England	Port-of-Spain	1953/54
676 for 7	India	Sri Lanka	Kanpur	1986/87
674 for 6	Pakistan	India	Faisalabad	1984/85
674	Australia	India	Adelaide	1947/48
671 for 4	New Zealand	Sri Lanka	Wellington	1990/91
668	Australia	West Indies	Bridgetown	1954/55
660 for 5 declared	West Indies	New Zealand	Wellington	1994/95
659 for 8 declared	Australia	England	Sydney	1946/47
658 for 8 declared	England	Australia	Trent Bridge	1938
657 for 8 declared	Pakistan	West Indies	Bridgetown	1957/58
656 for 8 declared	Australia	England	Old Trafford	1964
654 for 5	England	South Africa	Durban (2)	1938/39
653 for 4 declared	England	India	Lord's	1990
653 for 4 declared	Australia	England	Headingley	1993
652 for 7 declared	England	India	Madras (1)	1984/85
652 for 8 declared	West Indies	England	Lord's	1973
652	Pakistan	India	Faisalabad	1982/83
650 for 6 declared	Australia	West Indies	Bridgetown	1964/65
645	Australia	England	Brisbane (2)	1946/47
644 for 7 declared	India	West Indies	Kanpur	1978/79
644 for 8 declared	West Indies	India	Delhi	1958/59
636	England	Australia	Sydney	1928/29
633 for 5 declared	England	India	Edgbaston	1979
632 for 4 declared	Australia	England	Lord's	1993
631 for 8 declared	West Indies	India	Kingston	1961/62
631	West Indies	India	Delhi	1948/49
629 for 6 declared	West Indies	India	Bombay (2)	1948/49
629	England	India	Lord's	1974
627 for 9 declared	England	Australia	Old Trafford	1934
624	Pakistan	Australia	Adelaide	1983/84
622 for 9 declared	South Africa	Australia	Durban (2)	1969/70
620	South Africa	Australia	Johannesburg (3)	1966/67
619 for 6 declared	England	West Indies	Trent Bridge	1957
619	Australia	West Indies	Sydney	1968/69
617 for 5 declared	Australia	Sri Lanka	Perth	1995/95
617	Australia	Pakistan	Faisalabad	1979/80
616 for 5 declared	Pakistan	New Zealand	Auckland	1988/89
616	West Indies	Australia	Adelaide	1968/69
614 for 5 declared	West Indies	India	Calcutta	1958/59
611	England	Australia	Old Trafford	1964
608 for 7 declared	Pakistan	England	Edgbaston	1971
608	England	South Africa	Johannesburg (2)	1948/49
607 for 6 declared	Australia	New Zealand	Brisbane (2)	1993/94
606 for 9 declared	India	England	The Oval	1990
606	West Indies	England	Edgbaston	1984
606	West Indies	Australia	Sydney	1992/93
604 for 6 declared	West Indies	India	Bombay (3)	1974/75
604	Australia	England	Melbourne	1936/37
602 for 6 declared	Australia	England	Trent Bridge	1989
601 for 7 declared	Australia	England	Headingley	1989
601 for 8 declared	Australia	England	Brisbane (2)	1954/55
600 for 4 declared	India	Australia	Sydney	1985/86
600 for 7 declared	Pakistan	England	The Oval	1974
600 for 9 declared	Australia	West Indies	Port-of-Spain	1954/55
600	Australia	England	Melbourne	1924/25

LOWEST COMPLETED TOTALS

Total	Country	Opposition	Venue	Date
26	New Zealand	England	Auckland	1954/55
30	South Africa	England	Port Elizabeth	1895/96
30	South Africa	England	Edgbaston	1924
35	South Africa	England	Cape Town	1898/99
36	Australia	England	Edgbaston	1902
36	South Africa	Australia	Melbourne	1931/32
42	Australia	England	Sydney	1887/88
42	New Zealand	Australia	Wellington	1945/46

Total	Country	Opposition	Venue	Date
42*	India	England	Lord's	1974
43	South Africa	England	Cape Town	1888/89
44	Australia	England	The Oval	1896
45	England	Australia	Sydney	1886/87
45	South Africa	Australia	Melbourne	1931/32
46	England	West Indies	Port-of-Spain	1993/94
47	South Africa	England	Cape Town	1888/89
47	New Zealand	England	Lord's	1958

* One batsman absent hurt

MOST APPEARANCES

Player	Country	Tests	Aus	Eng	SA	WI	NZ	Ind	Pak	SL	Zim
A.R.Border	Australia	156	–	47	6	31	23	20	22	7	–
Kapil Dev	India	131	20	27	4	25	10	–	29	14	2
S.M.Gavaskar	India	125	20	38	–	27	9	–	24	7	–
Javed Miandad	Pakistan	124	25	22	–	16	18	28	–	12	3
I.V.A.Richards	West Indies	121	34	36	–	–	7	28	16	–	–
G.A.Gooch	England	118	42	–	3	26	15	19	10	3	–
D.I.Gower	England	117	42	–	–	19	13	24	17	2	–
D.L.Haynes	West Indies	116	33	36	1	–	10	19	16	1	–
D.B.Vengsarkar	India	116	24	26	–	25	11	–	22	8	–
M.C.Cowdrey	England	114	43	–	14	21	18	8	10	–	–
C.H.Lloyd	West Indies	110	29	34	–	–	8	28	11	–	–
G.Boycott	England	108	38	–	7	29	15	13	6	–	–
C.G.Greenidge	West Indies	108	29	32	–	–	10	23	14	–	–
D.C.Boon	Australia	107	–	31	6	22	17	11	11	9	–
I.T.Botham	England	102	36	–	–	20	15	14	14	3	–
R.W.Marsh	Australia	96	–	42	–	17	14	3	20	–	–
A.P.E.Knott	England	95	34	–	–	22	9	16	14	–	–
G.St A.Sobers	West Indies	93	19	36	–	–	12	18	8	–	–
T.G.Evans	England	91	31	–	19	16	14	7	4	–	–
G.R.Viswanath	India	91	18	30	–	18	9	–	15	1	–
R.G.D.Willis	England	90	35	–	–	13	14	17	10	1	–
Salim Malik	Pakistan	90	12	19	1	7	16	19	–	13	3
Imran Khan	Pakistan	88	18	12	–	18	7	23	–	10	–
S.M.H.Kirmani	India	88	17	20	–	21	9	–	20	1	–
G.S.Chappell	Australia	87	–	35	–	17	14	3	17	1	–
D.L.Underwood	England	86	29	–	–	17	8	20	11	1	–
R.B.Richardson	West Indies	86	29	27	1	–	7	9	12	1	–
R.J.Hadlee	New Zealand	86	23	21	–	10	–	14	12	6	–
W.R.Hammond	England	85	33	–	24	13	9	6	–	–	–
K.F.Barrington	England	82	23	–	14	17	5	14	9	–	–
C.A.Walsh	West Indies	82	24	25	1	–	8	11	12	1	–
J.G.Wright	New Zealand	82	19	23	–	10	–	9	11	10	–
S.R.Waugh	Australia	81	–	26	4	16	14	5	11	5	–
P.J.L.Dujon	West Indies	81	23	23	–	–	7	19	9	–	–
M.D.Marshall	West Indies	81	19	26	–	–	7	17	12	–	–
Wasim Bari	Pakistan	81	19	24	–	9	11	18	–	–	–
R.J.Shastri	India	80	9	20	3	19	6	–	15	7	1
T.W.Graveney	England	79	22	–	6	19	8	11	13	–	–
L.Hutton	England	79	27	–	19	13	11	7	2	–	–
M.W.Gatting	England	79	27	–	–	9	11	16	15	1	–
A.J.Lamb	England	79	20	–	–	22	14	13	8	2	–
R.N.Harvey	Australia	79	–	37	14	14	–	10	4	–	–
L.R.Gibbs	West Indies	79	24	26	–	–	5	15	9	–	–
R.B.Kanhai	West Indies	79	20	33	–	–	–	18	8	–	–
I.A.Healy	Australia	79	–	22	6	19	8	5	11	8	–
D.C.S.Compton	England	78	28	–	24	9	8	5	4	–	–
Zaheer Abbas	Pakistan	78	20	14	–	8	14	19	–	3	–
J.H.Edrich	England	77	32	–	1	14	11	10	9	–	–
M.D.Crowe	New Zealand	77	17	22	4	7	–	6	11	8	2
Mudassar Nazar	Pakistan	76	19	18	–	5	9	18	–	7	–
I.M.Chappell	Australia	75	–	30	9	17	6	9	4	–	–

LEADING RUN SCORERS

Batsman	Country	Mat	Inn	NO	Runs	H/S	Avg	100	50
A.R.Border	Australia	156	265	44	11174	205	50.56	27	63
S.M.Gavaskar	India	125	214	16	10122	236*	51.12	34	45
G.A.Gooch	England	118	215	6	8900	333	42.58	20	46
Javed Miandad	Pakistan	124	189	21	8832	280*	52.57	23	43
I.V.A.Richards	West Indies	121	182	12	8540	291	50.23	24	45
D.I.Gower	England	117	204	18	8231	215	44.25	18	39
G.Boycott	England	108	193	23	8114	246*	47.72	22	42

Batsman	Country	Mat	Inn	NO	Runs	H/S	Avg	100	50
G.St A.Sobers	West Indies	93	160	21	8032	365*	57.78	26	30
M.C.Cowdrey	England	114	188	15	7624	182	44.06	22	38
C.G.Greenidge	West Indies	108	185	16	7558	226	44.72	19	34
C.H.Lloyd	West Indies	110	175	14	7515	242*	46.67	19	39
D.L.Haynes	West Indies	116	202	25	7487	184	42.29	18	39
D.C.Boon	Australia	107	190	20	7422	200	43.65	21	32
W.R.Hammond	England	85	140	16	7249	336*	58.45	22	24
G.S.Chappell	Australia	87	151	19	7110	247*	53.86	24	31
D.G.Bradman	Australia	52	80	10	6996	334	99.94	29	13
L.Hutton	England	79	138	15	6971	364	56.67	19	33
D.B.Vengsarkar	India	116	185	22	6868	166	42.13	17	35
K.F.Barrington	England	82	131	15	6806	256	58.67	20	35
R.B.Kanhai	West Indies	79	137	6	6227	256	47.53	15	28
R.N.Harvey	Australia	79	137	10	6149	205	48.41	21	24
G.R.Viswanath	India	91	155	10	6080	222	41.93	14	35
R.B.Richardson	West Indies	86	146	12	5949	194	44.39	16	27
D.C.S.Compton	England	78	131	15	5807	278	50.06	17	28
M.A.Taylor	Australia	72	129	9	5502	219	45.85	14	33
M.D.Crowe	New Zealand	77	131	11	5444	299	45.36	17	18
J.B.Hobbs	England	61	102	7	5410	211	56.94	15	28
K.D.Walters	Australia	74	125	14	5357	250	48.26	15	33
I.M.Chappell	Australia	75	136	10	5345	196	42.42	14	26
J.G.Wright	New Zealand	82	148	7	5334	185	37.82	12	23
Kapil Dev	India	131	184	15	5248	163	31.05	8	27
W.M.Lawry	Australia	67	123	12	5234	210	47.15	13	27
I.T.Botham	England	102	161	6	5200	208	33.54	14	22
J.H.Edrich	England	77	127	9	5138	310*	43.54	12	24
Salim Malik	Pakistan	90	134	21	5101	237	45.14	14	25
Zaheer Abbas	Pakistan	78	124	11	5062	274	44.79	12	20
S.R.Waugh	Australia	81	125	26	5002	200	50.52	11	28
T.W.Graveney	England	79	123	13	4882	258	44.38	11	20
R.B.Simpson	Australia	62	111	7	4869	311	46.81	10	27
I.R.Redpath	Australia	66	120	11	4737	171	43.45	8	31
A.J.Lamb	England	79	139	10	4656	142	36.09	14	18
M.A.Atherton	England	62	114	3	4627	185*	41.68	10	29
H.Sutcliffe	England	54	84	9	4555	194	60.73	16	23
P.B.H.May	England	66	106	9	4537	285*	46.77	13	22
E.R.Dexter	England	62	102	8	4502	205	47.89	9	27
E.de C.Weekes	West Indies	48	81	5	4455	207	58.61	15	19
K.J.Hughes	Australia	70	124	6	4415	213	37.41	9	22
M.W.Gatting	England	79	138	14	4409	207	35.55	10	21
A.I.Kallicharran	West Indies	66	109	10	4399	187	44.43	12	21
A.P.E.Knott	England	95	149	15	4389	135	32.75	5	30
M.Amarnath	India	69	113	10	4378	138	42.50	11	24
M.Azharuddin	India	71	101	4	4362	199	44.96	14	15
R.C.Fredericks	West Indies	59	109	7	4334	169	42.49	8	26
R.A.Smith	England	62	112	15	4236	175	43.67	9	28
Mudassar Nazar	Pakistan	76	116	8	4114	231	38.09	10	17

HIGHEST INDIVIDUAL SCORES

Batsman	Score	Country	Opposition	Venue	Date
B.C.Lara	375	West Indies	England	St John's	1993/94
G.St A.Sobers	365*	West Indies	Pakistan	Kingston	1957/58
L.Hutton	364	England	Australia	The Oval	1938
Hanif Mohammad	337	Pakistan	West Indies	Bridgetown	1957/58
W.R.Hammond	336*	England	New Zealand	Auckland	1932/33
D.G.Bradman	334	Australia	England	Headingley	1930
G.A.Gooch	333	England	India	Lord's	1990
A.Sandham	325	England	West Indies	Kingston	1929/30
R.B.Simpson	311	Australia	England	Old Trafford	1964
J.H.Edrich	310*	England	New Zealand	Headingley	1965
R.M.Cowper	307	Australia	England	Melbourne	1965/66
D.G.Bradman	304	Australia	England	Headingley	1934
L.G.Rowe	302	West Indies	England	Bridgetown	1973/74
D.G.Bradman	299*	Australia	South Africa	Adelaide	1931/32
M.D.Crowe	299	New Zealand	Sri Lanka	Wellington	1990/91
I.V.A.Richards	291	West Indies	England	The Oval	1976
R.E.Foster	287	England	Australia	Sydney	1903/04
P.B.H.May	285*	England	West Indies	Edgbaston	1957
Javed Miandad	280*	Pakistan	India	Hyderabad	1982/83
D.C.S.Compton	278	England	Pakistan	Trent Bridge	1954
B.C.Lara	277	West Indies	Australia	Sydney	1992/93
R.G.Pollock	274	South Africa	Australia	Durban (2)	1969/70

Batsman	Score	Country	Opposition	Venue	Date
Zaheer Abbas	274	Pakistan	England	Edgbaston	1971
Javed Miandad	271	Pakistan	New Zealand	Auckland	1988/89
G.A.Headley	270*	West Indies	England	Kingston	1934/35
D.G.Bradman	270	Australia	England	Melbourne	1936/37
G.N.Yallop	268	Australia	Pakistan	Melbourne	1983/84
P.A.de Silva	267	Sri Lanka	New Zealand	Wellington	1990/91
W.H.Ponsford	266	Australia	England	The Oval	1934
D.L.Houghton	266	Zimbabwe	Sri Lanka	Bulawayo (2)	1994/95
D.L.Amiss	262*	England	West Indies	Kingston	1973/74
F.M.M.Worrell	261	West Indies	England	Trent Bridge	1950
C.C.Hunte	260	West Indies	Pakistan	Kingston	1957/58
Javed Miandad	260	Pakistan	England	The Oval	1987
G.M.Turner	259	New Zealand	West Indies	Georgetown	1971/72
T.W.Graveney	258	England	West Indies	Trent Bridge	1957
S.M.Nurse	258	West Indies	New Zealand	Christchurch	1968/69
R.B.Kanhai	256	West Indies	India	Calcutta	1958/59
K.F.Barrington	256	England	Australia	Old Trafford	1964
D.J.McGlew	255*	South Africa	New Zealand	Wellington	1952/53
D.G.Bradman	254	Australia	England	Lord's	1930
W.R.Hammond	251	England	Australia	Sydney	1928/29
K.D.Walters	250	Australia	New Zealand	Christchurch	1976/77
S.F.A.F.Bacchus	250	West Indies	India	Kanpur	1978/79

MOST CENTURIES

Batsman	Country	100s	Tests	Matches for each 100
S.M.Gavaskar	India	34	125	3.67
D.G.Bradman	Australia	29	52	1.79
A.R.Border	Australia	27	156	5.77
G.St A.Sobers	West Indies	26	93	3.57
G.S.Chappell	Australia	24	87	3.62
I.V.A.Richards	West Indies	24	121	5.04
Javed Miandad	Pakistan	23	124	5.39
W.R.Hammond	England	22	85	3.86
M.C.Cowdrey	England	22	114	5.18
G.Boycott	England	22	108	4.90
R.N.Harvey	Australia	21	79	3.76
D.C.Boon	Australia	21	107	5.09
K.F.Barrington	England	20	82	4.10
G.A.Gooch	England	20	118	5.90
L.Hutton	England	19	79	4.15
C.H.Lloyd	West Indies	19	110	5.78
C.G.Greenidge	West Indies	19	108	5.68
D.L.Haynes	West Indies	18	116	6.44
D.I.Gower	England	18	117	6.50
M.D.Crowe	New Zealand	17	77	4.52
D.C.S.Compton	England	17	78	4.58
D.B.Vengsarkar	India	17	116	6.82
H.Sutcliffe	England	16	54	3.37
R.B.Richardson	West Indies	16	86	5.37
C.L.Walcott	West Indies	15	44	2.93
E.de C.Weekes	West Indies	15	48	3.20
J.B.Hobbs	England	15	61	4.06
K.D.Walters	Australia	15	74	4.93
R.B.Kanhai	West Indies	15	79	5.26
M.Azharuddin	India	14	71	5.07
M.A.Taylor	Australia	14	72	5.14
I.M.Chappell	Australia	14	75	5.35
A.J.Lamb	England	14	79	5.64
Salim Malik	Pakistan	14	90	6.42
G.R.Viswanath	India	14	91	6.50
I.T.Botham	England	14	102	7.28
P.B.H.May	England	13	66	5.07
W.M.Lawry	Australia	13	67	5.15
A.R.Morris	Australia	12	46	3.83
Hanif Mohammad	Pakistan	12	55	4.58
P.R.Umrigar	India	12	59	4.91
A.I.Kallicharran	West Indies	12	66	5.50
J.H.Edrich	England	12	77	6.41
Zaheer Abbas	Pakistan	12	78	6.50
J.G.Wright	New Zealand	12	82	6.83
D.L.Amiss	England	11	50	4.54
D.M.Jones	Australia	11	52	4.72
Asif Iqbal	Pakistan	11	58	5.27

Batsman	Country	100s	Tests	Matches for each 100
M.Amarnath	India	11	69	6.27
T.W.Graveney	England	11	79	7.18
R.J.Shastri	India	11	80	7.27
S.R.Waugh	Australia	11	81	7.36
G.A.Headley	West Indies	10	22	2.20
S.R.Tendulkar	India	10	41	4.10
A.L.Hassett	Australia	10	43	4.30
M.E.Waugh	Australia	10	54	5.40
Mushtaq Mohammad	Pakistan	10	57	5.70
R.B.Simpson	Australia	10	62	6.20
M.A.Atherton	England	10	62	6.20
Mudassar Nazar	Pakistan	10	76	7.60
M.W.Gatting	England	10	79	7.90

HIGHEST PARTNERSHIPS FOR EACH WICKET

Wkt	Runs	Country	Opposition	Venue	Date	Batsmen
1st	413	India	New Zealand	Madras (2)	1955/56	M.H.Mankad (231)
						Pankaj Roy (173)
2nd	451	Australia	England	The Oval	1934	W.H.Ponsford (266)
						D.G.Bradman (244)
3rd	467	New Zealand	Sri Lanka	Wellington	1990/91	A.H.Jones (186)
						M.D.Crowe (299)
4th	411	England	West Indies	Edgbaston	1957	P.B.H.May (285*)
						M.C.Cowdrey (154)
5th	405	Australia	England	Sydney	1946/47	S.G.Barnes (234)
						D.G.Bradman (234)
6th	346	Australia	England	Melbourne	1936/37	J.H.W.Fingleton (136)
						D.G.Bradman (270)
7th	347	West Indies	Australia	Bridgetown	1954/55	D.St E.Atkinson (219)
						C.C.Depeiza (122)
8th	246	England	New Zealand	Lord's	1931	L.E.G.Ames (137)
						G.O.B.Allen (122)
9th	190	Pakistan	England	The Oval	1967	Asif Iqbal (146)
						Intikhab Alam (51)
10th	151	New Zealand	Pakistan	Auckland	1972/73	B.F.Hastings (110)
						R.O.Collinge (68*)

TOTAL HIGHEST PARTNERSHIPS

Runs	Wkt	Country	Opposition	Venue	Date	Batsmen
467	3rd	New Zealand	Sri Lanka	Wellington	1990/91	A.H.Jones (186)
						M.D.Crowe (299)
451	2nd	Australia	England	The Oval	1934	W.H.Ponsford (266)
						D.G.Bradman (244)
451	3rd	Pakistan	India	Hyderabad	1982/83	Mudassar Nazar (231)
						Javed Miandad (280*)
446	2nd	West Indies	Pakistan	Kingston	1957/58	C.C.Hunte (260)
						G.St A.Sobers (365*)
415+	3rd	India	England	Madras (1)	1981/82	D.B.Vengsarkar (71*)
						G.R.Viswanath (222)
						Yashpal Sharma (140)
413	1st	India	New Zealand	Madras (2)	1955/56	M.H.Mankad (231)
						Pankaj Roy (173)
411	4th	England	West Indies	Edgbaston	1957	P.B.H.May (285*)
						M.C.Cowdrey (154)
405	5th	Australia	England	Sydney	1946/47	S.G.Barnes (234)
						D.G.Bradman (234)
399	4th	West Indies	England	Bridgetown	1959/60	G.St A.Sobers (226)
						F.M.M.Worrell (197*)
397	3rd	Pakistan	Sri Lanka	Faisalabad	1985/86	Qasim Omar (206)
						Javed Miandad (203*)
388	4th	Australia	England	Headingley	1934	W.H.Ponsford (181)
						D.G.Bradman (304)
387	1st	New Zealand	West Indies	Georgetown	1971/72	G.M.Turner (259)
						T.W.Jarvis (182)
382	2nd	England	Australia	The Oval	1938	L.Hutton (364)
						M.Leyland (187)
382	1st	Australia	West Indies	Bridgetown	1964/65	W.M.Lawry (210)
						R.B.Simpson (201)
370	3rd	England	South Africa	Lord's	1947	W.J.Edrich (189)
						D.C.S.Compton (208)
369	2nd	England	New Zealand	Headingley	1965	J.H.Edrich (310*)
						K.F.Barrington (163)

Wkt	Runs	Country	Opposition	Venue	Date	Batsmen
359	1st	England	South Africa	Johannesburg (2)	1948/49	L.Hutton (158) C.Washbrook (195)
351	2nd	England	Australia	The Oval	1985	G.A.Gooch (196) D.I.Gower (157)
350	4th	Pakistan	New Zealand	Dunedin	1972/73	Mushtaq Mohammad (201) Asif Iqbal (175)
347	7th	West Indies	Australia	Bridgetown	1954/55	D.St E.Atkinson (219) C.C.Depeiza (122)
346	6th	Australia	England	Melbourne	1936/37	J.H.W.Fingleton (136) D.G.Bradman (270)
344*	2nd	India	West Indies	Calcutta	1978/79	S.M.Gavaskar (182*) D.B.Vengsarkar (157*)
341	3rd	South Africa	Australia	Adelaide	1963/64	E.J.Barlow (201) R.G.Pollock (175)
338	3rd	West Indies	England	Port-of-Spain	1953/54	E.de C.Weekes (206) F.M.M.Worrell (167)
336	4th	Australia	West Indies	Sydney	1968/69	W.M.Lawry (151) K.D.Walters (242)
332*	5th	Australia	England	Headingley	1993	A.R.Border (200*) S.R.Waugh (157*)
331	2nd	England	Australia	Edgbaston	1985	R.T.Robinson (148) D.I.Gower (215)
329	1st	Australia	England	Trent Bridge	1989	G.R.Marsh (138) M.A.Taylor (219)
323	1st	England	Australia	Melbourne	1911/12	J.B.Hobbs (178) W.Rhodes (179)
322	4th	Pakistan	England	Edgbaston	1992	Javed Miandad (153*) Salim Malik (165)
319	3rd	South Africa	England	Trent Bridge	1947	A.Melville (189) A.D.Nourse (149)
308	7th	Pakistan	New Zealand	Lahore (1)	1955/56	Waqar Hassan (189) Imtiaz Ahmed (209)
308	3rd	West Indies	Australia	St John's	1983/84	R.B.Richardson (154) I.V.A.Richards (178)
308	3rd	England	India	Lord's	1990	G.A.Gooch (333) A.J.Lamb (139)
303	3rd	West Indies	England	Trent Bridge	1976	I.V.A.Richards (232) A.I.Kallicharran (97)
303	3rd	England	West Indies	St John's	1993/94	M.A.Atherton (135) R.A.Smith (175)
301	2nd	Australia	England	Headingley	1948	A.R.Morris (182) D.G.Bradman (173*)

+ D.B.Vengsarkar retired hurt and was succeeded by Yashpal Sharma with the score on 99.

LEADING WICKET TAKERS

Bowler	Country	Balls	Runs	Wkts	Avg	Best	5WI	10WM	S/R
Kapil Dev	India	27740	12867	434	29.64	9-83	23	2	63.91
R.J.Hadlee	New Zealand	21918	9611	431	22.29	9-52	36	9	50.85
I.T.Botham	England	21815	10878	383	28.40	8-34	27	4	56.95
M.D.Marshall	West Indies	17584	7876	376	20.94	7-22	22	4	46.76
Imran Khan	Pakistan	19458	8258	362	22.81	8-58	23	6	53.75
D.K.Lillee	Australia	18467	8493	355	23.92	7-83	23	7	52.01
R.G.D.Willis	England	17357	8190	325	25.20	8-43	16	0	53.40
L.R.Gibbs	West Indies	27115	8989	309	29.09	8-38	18	2	87.75
C.A.Walsh	West Indies	17578	7738	309	25.04	7-37	11	2	56.88
F.S.Trueman	England	15178	6625	307	21.57	8-31	17	3	49.43
Wasim Akram	Pakistan	16034	6874	300	22.91	7-119	20	3	53.44
D.L.Underwood	England	21862	7674	297	25.83	8-51	17	6	73.60
C.J.McDermott	Australia	16586	8332	291	28.63	8-97	14	2	56.99
C.E.L.Ambrose	West Indies	14319	5658	266	21.27	8-45	14	3	53.83
B.S.Bedi	India	21364	7637	266	28.71	7-98	14	1	80.31
J.Garner	West Indies	13169	5433	259	20.97	6-56	7	0	50.84
J.B.Statham	England	16056	6261	252	24.84	7-39	9	1	63.71
M.A.Holding	West Indies	12680	5898	249	23.68	8-92	13	2	50.92
R.Benaud	Australia	19108	6704	248	27.03	7-72	16	1	77.04
G.D.McKenzie	Australia	17681	7328	246	29.78	8-71	16	3	71.87
B.S.Chandrasekhar	India	15963	7199	242	29.74	8-79	16	2	65.96
A.V.Bedser	England	15918	5876	236	24.89	7-44	15	5	67.44
Abdul Qadir	Pakistan	17126	7742	236	32.80	9-56	15	5	72.56
G.St A.Sobers	West Indies	21599	7999	235	34.03	6-73	6	0	91.91
R.R.Lindwall	Australia	13650	5251	228	23.03	7-38	12	0	59.86
C.V.Grimmett	Australia	14513	5231	216	24.21	7-40	21	7	67.18

Bowler	Country	Balls	Runs	Wkts	Avg	Best	5WI	10WM	S/R
Waqar Younis	Pakistan	8483	4553	216	21.07	7-76	19	4	39.27
M.G.Hughes	Australia	12285	6017	212	28.38	8-87	7	1	57.94
S.K.Warne	Australia	13118	4870	207	23.52	8-71	10	3	63.37
J.A.Snow	England	12021	5387	202	26.66	7-40	8	1	59.50
A.M.E.Roberts	West Indies	11136	5174	202	25.61	7-54	11	2	55.12
J.R.Thomson	Australia	10535	5601	200	28.00	6-46	8	0	52.67
J.C.Laker	England	12027	4101	193	21.24	10-53	9	3	62.31
W.W.Hall	West Indies	10421	5066	192	26.38	7-69	9	1	54.27
S.F.Barnes	England	7873	3106	189	16.43	9-103	24	7	41.65
E.A.S.Prasanna	India	14353	5742	189	30.38	8-76	10	2	75.94
A.K.Davidson	Australia	11587	3819	186	20.53	7-93	14	2	62.29
G.F.Lawson	Australia	11118	5501	180	30.56	8-112	11	2	61.76
Sarfraz Nawaz	Pakistan	13927	5798	177	32.75	9-86	4	1	78.68
G.A.R.Lock	England	13147	4451	174	25.58	7-35	9	3	75.55
Iqbal Qasim	Pakistan	13019	4807	171	28.11	7-49	8	2	76.13
H.J.Tayfield	South Africa	13568	4405	170	25.91	9-113	14	2	79.81
T.M.Alderman	Australia	10181	4616	170	27.15	6-47	14	1	59.88
K.R.Miller	Australia	10461	3906	170	22.97	7-60	7	1	61.53
M.H.Mankad	India	14686	5236	162	32.32	8-52	8	2	90.65
W.A.Johnston	Australia	11048	3826	160	23.91	6-44	7	0	69.05
S.Ramadhin	West Indies	13939	4579	158	28.98	7-49	10	1	88.22
D.K.Morrison	New Zealand	9916	5445	157	34.68	7-89	10	0	63.15
S.Venkataraghavan	India	14877	5634	156	36.11	8-72	3	1	95.36
M.W.Tate	England	12523	4055	155	26.16	6-42	7	1	80.79
F.J.Titmus	England	15118	4931	153	32.22	7-79	7	0	98.81
R.J.Shastri	India	15751	6185	151	40.96	5-75	2	0	104.31

BEST BOWLING

Bowler	10WM	Country	Opposition	Venue	Date
J.C.Laker	10-53	England	Australia	Old Trafford	1956
G.A.Lohmann	9-28	England	South Africa	Johannesburg (1)	1895/96
J.C.Laker	9-37	England	Australia	Old Trafford	1956
R.J.Hadlee	9-52	New Zealand	Australia	Brisbane (2)	1985/86
Abdul Qadir	9-56	Pakistan	England	Lahore (2)	1987/88
D.E.Malcolm	9-57	England	South Africa	The Oval	1994
J.M.Patel	9-69	India	Australia	Kanpur	1959/60
Kapil Dev	9-83	India	West Indies	Ahmedabad	1983/84
Sarfraz Nawaz	9-86	Pakistan	Australia	Melbourne	1978/79
J.M.Noreiga	9-95	West Indies	India	Port-of-Spain	1970/71
S.P.Gupte	9-102	India	West Indies	Kanpur	1958/59
S.F.Barnes	9-103	England	South Africa	Johannesburg (1)	1913/14
H.J.Tayfield	9-113	South Africa	England	Johannesburg (3)	1956/57
A.A.Mailey	9-121	Australia	England	Melbourne	1920/21
G.A.Lohmann	8-7	England	South Africa	Port Elizabeth	1895/96
J.Briggs	8-11	England	South Africa	Cape Town	1888/89
S.F.Barnes	8-29	England	South Africa	The Oval	1912
C.E.H.Croft	8-29	West Indies	Pakistan	Port-of-Spain	1976/77
F.Laver	8-31	Australia	England	Old Trafford	1909
F.S.Trueman	8-31	England	India	Old Trafford	1952
I.T.Botham	8-34	England	Pakistan	Lord's	1978
G.A.Lohmann	8-35	England	Australia	Sydney	1886/87
L.R.Gibbs	8-38	West Indies	India	Bridgetown	1961/62
A.E.Trott	8-43	Australia	England	Adelaide	1894/95
H.Verity	8-43	England	Australia	Lord's	1934
R.G.D.Willis	8-43	England	Australia	Headingley	1981
C.E.L.Ambrose	8-45	West Indies	England	Bridgetown	1989/90
D.L.Underwood	8-51	England	Pakistan	Lord's	1974
M.H.Mankad	8-52	India	Pakistan	Delhi	1952/53
G.B.Lawrence	8-53	South Africa	New Zealand	Johannesburg (3)	1961/62
R.A.L.Massie	8-53	Australia	England	Lord's	1972
M.H.Mankad	8-55	India	England	Madras (1)	1951/52
S.F.Barnes	8-56	England	South Africa	Johannesburg (1)	1913/14
G.A.Lohmann	8-58	England	Australia	Sydney	1891/92
Imran Khan	8-58	Pakistan	Sri Lanka	Lahore (2)	1981/82
C.Blythe	8-59	England	South Africa	Headingley	1907
A.A.Mallett	8-59	Australia	Pakistan	Adelaide	1972/73
Imran Khan	8-60	Pakistan	India	Karachi (1)	1982/83
N.D.Hirwani	8-61	India	West Indies	Madras (1)	1987/88
H.Trumble	8-65	Australia	England	The Oval	1902
W.Rhodes	8-68	England	Australia	Melbourne	1903/04
H.J.Tayfield	8-69	South Africa	England	Durban (2)	1956/57
Sikander Bakht	8-69	Pakistan	India	Delhi	1979/80
S.J.Snooke	8-70	South Africa	England	Johannesburg (1)	1905/06

Bowler	10WM	Country	Opposition	Venue	Date
G.D.McKenzie	8-71	Australia	West Indies	Melbourne	1968/69
S.K.Warne	8-71	Australia	England	Brisbane (2)	1994/95
A.A.Donald	8-71	South Africa	Zimbabwe	Harare	1995/96
S.Venkataraghavan	8-72	India	New Zealand	Delhi	1964/65
N.D.Hirwani	8-75	India	West Indies	Madras (1)	1987/88
A.R.C.Fraser	8-75	England	West Indies	Bridgetown	1993/94
E.A.S.Prasanna	8-76	India	New Zealand	Auckland	1975/76
B.S.Chandrasekhar	8-79	India	England	Delhi	1972/73
L.C.Braund	8-81	England	Australia	Melbourne	1903/04
J.R.Ratnayeke	8-83	Sri Lanka	Pakistan	Sialkot	1985/86
R.A.L.Massie	8-84	Australia	England	Lord's	1972
Kapil Dev	8-85	India	Pakistan	Lahore (2)	1982/83
A.W.Greig	8-86	England	West Indies	Port-of-Spain	1973/74
M.G.Hughes	8-87	Australia	West Indies	Perth	1988/89
M.A.Holding	8-92	West Indies	England	The Oval	1976
T.Richardson	8-94	England	Australia	Sydney	1897/98
C.J.McDermott	8-97	Australia	England	Perth	1990/91
I.T.Botham	8-103	England	West Indies	Lord's	1984
A.L.Valentine	8-104	West Indies	England	Old Trafford	1950
Kapil Dev	8-106	India	Australia	Adelaide	1985/86
B.J.T.Bosanquet	8-107	England	Australia	Trent Bridge	1905
N.A.Foster	8-107	England	Pakistan	Headingley	1987
G.F.Lawson	8-112	Australia	West Indies	Adelaide	1984/85
J.C.White	8-126	England	Australia	Adelaide	1928/29
C.J.McDermott	8-141	Australia	England	Old Trafford	1985
M.H.N.Walker	8-143	Australia	England	Melbourne	1974/75

BEST BOWLING IN A MATCH

Bowler		Country	Opposition	Venue	Date
J.C.Laker	19-90	England	Australia	Old Trafford	1956
S.F.Barnes	17-159	England	South Africa	Johannesburg (1)	1913/14
N.D.Hirwani	16-136	India	West Indies	Madras (1)	1987/88
R.A.L.Massie	16-137	Australia	England	Lord's	1972
J.Briggs	15-28	England	South Africa	Cape Town	1888/89
G.A.Lohmann	15-45	England	South Africa	Port Elizabeth	1895/96
C.Blythe	15-99	England	South Africa	Headingley	1907
H.Verity	15-104	England	Australia	Lord's	1934
R.J.Hadlee	15-123	New Zealand	Australia	Brisbane (2)	1985/86
W.Rhodes	15-124	England	Australia	Melbourne	1903/04
F.R.Spofforth	14-90	Australia	England	The Oval	1882
A.V.Bedser	14-99	England	Australia	Trent Bridge	1953
W.Bates	14-102	England	Australia	Melbourne	1882/83
Imran Khan	14-116	Pakistan	Sri Lanka	Lahore (2)	1981/82
J.M.Patel	14-124	India	Australia	Kanpur	1959/60
S.F.Barnes	14-144	England	South Africa	Durban (1)	1913/14
M.A.Holding	14-149	West Indies	England	The Oval	1976
C.V.Grimmett	14-199	Australia	South Africa	Adelaide	1931/32
C.A.Walsh	13-55	West Indies	New Zealand	Wellington	1994/95
S.F.Barnes	13-57	England	South Africa	The Oval	1912
D.L.Underwood	13-71	England	Pakistan	Lord's	1974
M.A.Noble	13-77	Australia	England	Melbourne	1901/02
J.J.Ferris	13-91	England	South Africa	Cape Town	1891/92
Abdul Qadir	13-101	Pakistan	England	Lahore (2)	1987/88
I.T.Botham	13-106	England	India	Bombay (3)	1979/80
F.R.Spofforth	13-110	Australia	England	Melbourne	1878/79
Fazal Mahmood	13-114	Pakistan	Australia	Karachi (1)	1956/57
M.H.Mankad	13-131	India	Pakistan	Delhi	1952/53
Waqar Younis	13-135	Pakistan	Zimbabwe	Karachi (2)	1993/94
B.A.Reid	13-148	Australia	England	Melbourne	1990/91
A.W.Greig	13-156	England	West Indies	Port-of-Spain	1973/74
S.F.Barnes	13-163	England	Australia	Melbourne	1901/02
H.J.Tayfield	13-165	South Africa	Australia	Melbourne	1952/53
C.V.Grimmett	13-173	Australia	South Africa	Durban (2)	1935/36
H.J.Tayfield	13-192	South Africa	England	Johannesburg (3)	1956/57
M.G.Hughes	13-217	Australia	West Indies	Perth	1988/89
A.A.Mailey	13-236	Australia	England	Melbourne	1920/21
T.Richardson	13-244	England	Australia	Old Trafford	1896
J.C.White	13-256	England	Australia	Adelaide	1928/29
G.A.Lohmann	12-71	England	South Africa	Johannesburg (1)	1895/96
C.T.B.Turner	12-87	Australia	England	Sydney	1887/88
H.Trumble	12-89	Australia	England	The Oval	1896
J.H.Wardle	12-89	England	South Africa	Cape Town	1956/57
Fazal Mahmood	12-94	Pakistan	India	Lucknow	1952/53

Bowler	10WM	Country	Opposition	Venue	Date
D.L.Underwood	12-97	England	New Zealand	Christchurch	1970/71
Fazal Mahmood	12-99	Pakistan	England	The Oval	1954
Fazal Mahmood	12-100	Pakistan	West Indies	Dacca	1958/59
R.Tattersall	12-101	England	South Africa	Lord's	1951
D.L.Underwood	12-101	England	New Zealand	The Oval	1969
F.Martin	12-102	England	Australia	The Oval	1890
G.A.Lohmann	12-104	England	Australia	The Oval	1886
B.S.Chandrasekhar	12-104	India	Australia	Melbourne	1977/78
M.H.Mankad	12-108	India	England	Madras (1)	1951/52
A.V.Bedser	12-112	England	South Africa	Old Trafford	1951
F.S.Trueman	12-119	England	West Indies	Edgbaston	1963
A.M.E.Roberts	12-121	West Indies	India	Madras (1)	1974/75
A.K.Davidson	12-124	Australia	India	Kanpur	1959/60
B.A.Reid	12-126	Australia	India	Melbourne	1991/92
S.J.Snooke	12-127	South Africa	England	Johannesburg (1)	1905/06
S.K.Warne	12-128	Australia	South Africa	Sydney	1993/94
G.Geary	12-130	England	South Africa	Johannesburg (1)	1927/28
Waqar Younis	12-130	Pakistan	New Zealand	Faisalabad	1990/91
J.Briggs	12-136	England	Australia	Adelaide	1891/92
A.A.Donald	12-139	South Africa	India	Port Elizabeth	1992/93
S.Venkataraghavan	12-152	India	New Zealand	Delhi	1964/65
Imran Khan	12-165	Pakistan	Australia	Sydney	1976/77
G.Dymock	12-166	Australia	India	Kanpur	1979/80
A.P.Freeman	12-171	England	South Africa	Old Trafford	1929
H.Trumble	12-173	Australia	England	The Oval	1902
H.V.Hordern	12-175	Australia	England	Sydney	1911/12
A.E.E.Vogler	12-181	South Africa	England	Johannesburg (1)	1909/10
L.Sivaramakrishnan	12-181	India	England	Bombay (3)	1984/85

MOST FIVE WICKET INNINGS

Bowler	Country	5WI	Tests	Matches for each 5 wkt inns
R.J.Hadlee	New Zealand	36	86	2.38
I.T.Botham	England	27	102	3.77
S.F.Barnes	England	24	27	1.12
D.K.Lillee	Australia	23	70	3.04
Imran Khan	Pakistan	23	88	3.82
Kapil Dev	India	23	131	5.69
M.D.Marshall	West Indies	22	81	3.68
C.V.Grimmett	Australia	21	37	1.76
Wasim Akram	Pakistan	20	70	3.50
Waqar Younis	Pakistan	19	41	2.15
L.R.Gibbs	West Indies	18	79	4.38
F.S.Trueman	England	17	67	3.94
D.L.Underwood	England	17	86	5.05
B.S.Chandrasekhar	India	16	58	3.62
G.D.McKenzie	Australia	16	60	3.75
R.Benaud	Australia	16	63	3.93
R.G.D.Willis	England	16	90	5.62
A.V.Bedser	England	15	51	3.40
Abdul Qadir	Pakistan	15	67	4.46
H.J.Tayfield	South Africa	14	37	2.64
T.M.Alderman	Australia	14	41	2.92
A.K.Davidson	Australia	14	44	3.14
B.S.Bedi	India	14	67	4.78
C.J.McDermott	Australia	14	71	5.07
C.E.L.Ambrose	West Indies	14	61	4.35
Fazal Mahmood	Pakistan	13	34	2.61
M.A.Holding	West Indies	13	60	4.61
S.P.Gupte	India	12	36	3.00
R.R.Lindwall	Australia	12	61	5.08
T.Richardson	England	11	14	1.27
C.T.B.Turner	Australia	11	17	1.54
W.J.O'Reilly	Australia	11	27	2.45
G.F.Lawson	Australia	11	46	4.18
A.M.E.Roberts	West Indies	11	47	4.27
C.A.Walsh	West Indies	11	82	7.45
E.A.S.Prasanna	India	10	49	4.90
S.Ramadhin	West Indies	10	43	4.30
S.K.Warne	Australia	10	44	4.40
D.K.Morrison	New Zealand	10	47	4.70

MOST TEN WICKET MATCHES

Bowler	Country	10WM	Tests	Matches for each 10 wkt match
R.J.Hadlee	New Zealand	9	86	9.55
S.F.Barnes	England	7	27	3.85
C.V.Grimmett	Australia	7	37	5.28
D.K.Lillee	Australia	7	70	10.00
D.L.Underwood	England	6	86	14.33
Imran Khan	Pakistan	6	88	14.66
G.A.Lohmann	England	5	18	3.60
A.V.Bedser	England	5	51	10.20
Abdul Qadir	Pakistan	5	67	13.40
T.Richardson	England	4	14	3.50
F.R.Spofforth	Australia	4	18	4.50
C.Blythe	England	4	19	4.75
J.Briggs	England	4	33	8.25
Fazal Mahmood	Pakistan	4	34	8.50
I.T.Botham	England	4	102	25.50
M.D.Marshall	West Indies	4	81	20.25
Waqar Younis	Pakistan	4	41	10.25

MOST CAREER DISMISSALS

Wicket-keeper	Country	Dis	Cat	St	Mat	DPM
R.W.Marsh	Australia	355	343	12	96	3.69
I.A.Healy	Australia	275	255	20	79	3.48
P.J.L.Dujon	West Indies	272*	267	5	81	3.35
A.P.E.Knott	England	269	250	19	95	2.83
Wasim Bari	Pakistan	228	201	27	81	2.81
T.G.Evans	England	219	173	46	91	2.40
S.M.H.Kirmani	India	198	160	38	88	2.25
D.L.Murray	West Indies	189	181	8	62	3.04
A.T.W.Grout	Australia	187	163	24	51	3.66
I.D.S.Smith	New Zealand	176	168	8	63	2.79
R.W.Taylor	England	174	167	7	57	3.05
R.C.Russell	England	152	141	11	49	3.10
J.H.B.Waite	South Africa	141	124	17	50	2.82
K.S.More	India	130	110	20	49	2.65
W.A.S.Oldfield	Australia	130	78	52	54	2.40
J.M.Parks	England	114*	103	11	46	2.47
D.J.Richardson	South Africa	107	107	0	28	3.82
Salim Yousuf	Pakistan	104	91	13	32	3.25

* Both P.J.L.Dujon and J.M.Parks took two catches in two and three tests respectively when not keeping wicket.

MOST DISMISSALS IN A MATCH

Wicket-keeper	Country	Dis	1st	2nd	Opposition	Venue	Date
R.C.Russell	England	11	6 + 0	5 + 0	South Africa	Johannesburg (3)	1995/96
R.W.Taylor	England	10	7 + 0	3 + 0	India	Bombay (3)	1979/80
G.R.A.Langley	Australia	9	3 + 1	5 + 0	England	Lord's	1956
D.A.Murray	West Indies	9	5 + 0	4 + 0	Australia	Melbourne	1981/82
R.W.Marsh	Australia	9	3 + 0	6 + 0	England	Brisbane (2)	1982/83
S.A.R.Silva	Sri Lanka	9	6 + 0	3 + 0	India	Colombo (2)	1985/86
S.A.R.Silva	Sri Lanka	9	3 + 1	5 + 0	India	Colombo (1)	1985/86
D.J.Richardson	South Africa	9	4 + 0	5 + 0	India	Port Elizabeth	1992/93
Rashid Latif	Pakistan	9	4 + 0	5 + 0	New Zealand	Auckland	1993/94
I.A.Healy	Australia	9	5 + 0	4 + 0	England	Brisbane (2)	1994/95
C.O.Browne	West Indies	9	4 + 0	5 + 0	England	Trent Bridge	1995
R.C.Russell	England	9	4 + 1	3 + 1	South Africa	Port Elizabeth	1995/96

MOST DISMISSALS IN AN INNINGS

Wicket-keeper	Country	Dis	C/S	Inns	Opposition	Venue	Date
Wasim Bari	Pakistan	7	7 + 0	1st	New Zealand	Auckland	1978/79
R.W.Taylor	England	7	7 + 0	1st	India	Bombay (3)	1979/80
I.D.S.Smith	New Zealand	7	7 + 0	1st	Sri Lanka	Hamilton	1990/91
A.T.W.Grout	Australia	6	6 + 0	2nd	South Africa	Johannesburg (3)	1957/58
D.T.Lindsay	South Africa	6	6 + 0	1st	Australia	Johannesburg (3)	1966/67
J.T.Murray	England	6	6 + 0	1st	India	Lord's	1967
S.M.H.Kirmani	India	6	5 + 1	1st	New Zealand	Christchurch	1975/76
R.W.Marsh	Australia	6	6 + 0	2nd	England	Brisbane (2)	1982/83
S.A.R.Silva	Sri Lanka	6	6 + 0	1st	India	Colombo (2)	1985/86
R.C.Russell	England	6	6 + 0	1st	Australia	Melbourne	1990/91
R.C.Russell	England	6	6 + 0	1st	South Africa	Johannesburg (3)	1995/96

MOST CAREER CATCHES

Fielder	Country	Mat	Cat	CPM	Aus	Eng	SA	WI	NZ	IND	PAK	SL	Zim
A.R.Border	Australia	156	156	1.00	–	57	5	19	31	14	22	8	–
G.S.Chappell	Australia	87	122	1.40	–	61	–	16	18	5	22	–	–
I.V.A.Richards	West Indies	121	122	1.00	24	29	–	–	7	39	23	–	–
M.C.Cowdrey	England	114	120	1.05	40	–	22	21	15	11	11	–	–
I.T.Botham	England	102	120	1.17	57	–	–	19	14	14	14	2	–
W.R.Hammond	England	85	110	1.29	43	–	30	22	9	6	–	–	–
R.B.Simpson	Australia	62	110	1.77	–	30	27	29	–	21	3	–	–
G.St A.Sobers	West Indies	93	109	1.17	27	40	–	–	11	27	4	–	–
S.M.Gavaskar	India	125	108	0.86	19	35	–	17	11	–	19	7	–
I.M.Chappell	Australia	75	105	1.40	–	31	11	24	16	17	6	–	–
M.A.Taylor	Australia	72	105	1.45	–	31	6	19	15	7	16	11	–
G.A.Gooch	England	118	103	0.87	29	–	1	28	13	21	7	4	–
D.C.Boon	Australia	107	99	0.92	–	25	4	21	16	10	17	6	–
C.G.Greenidge	West Indies	108	96	0.88	22	29	–	–	8	18	19	–	–
Javed Miandad	Pakistan	124	93	0.75	12	20	–	12	20	18	–	11	–
C.H.Lloyd	West Indies	110	90	0.81	24	32	–	–	3	20	11	–	–
R.B.Richardson	West Indies	86	90	1.04	26	26	–	–	10	11	16	1	–
A.W.Greig	England	58	87	1.50	37	–	–	18	2	16	14	–	–
I.R.Redpath	Australia	66	83	1.25	–	29	6	22	1	17	8	–	–
T.W.Graveney	England	79	80	1.01	24	–	9	24	6	5	12	–	–
D.B.Vengsarkar	India	116	78	0.67	18	15	–	13	13	–	13	6	–
A.J.Lamb	England	79	75	0.94	20	–	–	20	15	13	5	2	–
D.I.Gower	England	117	74	0.63	26	–	–	11	11	13	8	5	–
M.D.Crowe	New Zealand	77	71	0.92	10	19	7	12	–	2	16	4	1
Majid Khan	Pakistan	63	70	1.11	13	14	–	14	19	9	–	1	–
M.Azharuddin	India	71	70	0.98	6	9	6	11	4	–	12	20	2

1000 RUNS & 100 WICKETS

Player	Country	Runs	Wkts	Tests	No. of Tests for each double			
					1000/100	2000/200	3000/300	4000/400
I.T.Botham	England	5200	383	102	21	41	72	
V.Mankad	India	2109	162	44	23			
Kapil Dev	India	5248	434	131	25	50	83	115
M.A.Noble	Australia	1997	121	42	27			
R.J.Hadlee	New Zealand	3124	431	86	28	54	83	
G.Giffen	Australia	1238	103	31	30			
Imran Khan	Pakistan	3807	362	88	30	50	75	
R.Benaud	Australia	2201	248	63	32	60		
M.W.Tate	England	1198	155	39	33			
K.R.Miller	Australia	2958	170	55	33			
A.K.Davidson	Australia	1328	186	44	34			
T.L.Goddard	South Africa	2516	123	41	36			
A.W.Greig	England	3599	141	58	37			
R.R.Lindwall	Australia	1502	228	61	38			
F.J.Titmus	England	1449	153	53	40			
Intikhab Alam	Pakistan	1493	125	47	41			
J.G.Bracewell	New Zealand	1001	102	41	41			
W.Rhodes	England	2325	127	58	44			
R.J.Shastri	India	3830	151	80	44			
I.W.Johnson	Australia	1000	109	45	45			
Wasim Akram	Pakistan	1652	300	70	45			
J.E.Emburey	England	1713	147	64	46			
T.E.Bailey	England	2290	132	61	47			
R.Illingworth	England	1836	122	61	47			
G.St S.Sobers	West Indies	8032	235	93	48	80		
M.D.Marshall	West Indies	1810	376	81	49			
M.G.Hughes	Australia	1032	212	53	52			
Sarfraz Nawaz	Pakistan	1045	177	55	55			
Abdul Qadir	Pakistan	1029	236	67	62			

CENTURY & TEN WICKETS IN A MATCH

Player	Country	Runs & Wickets		Opposition	Venue	Date
I.T.Botham	England	114 & 13-106	(6-58 & 7-48)	India	Bombay (3)	1979/80
Imran Khan	Pakistan	117 & 11-180	(6-98 & 5-82)	India	Faisalabad	1982/83

CENTURY & FIVE WICKETS IN AN INNINGS

Player	Country	Runs & Wickets	Opposition	Venue	Date
I.T.Botham	England	108 & 8-34	Pakistan	Lord's	1978
I.T.Botham	England	114 & 7-48	India	Bombay (3)	1979/80

Player	Country	Runs & Wickets	Opposition	Venue	Date
J.M.Gregory	Australia	100 & 7-69	England	Melbourne	1920/21
I.T.Botham	England	149* & 6-95	Australia	Headingley	1981
A.W.Greig	England	148 & 6-164	West Indies	Bridgetown	1973/74
Imran Khan	Pakistan	117 & 6-98	India	Faisalabad	1982/83
I.T.Botham	England	114 & 6-58	India	Bombay (3)	1979/80
K.R.Miller	Australia	109 & 6-107	West Indies	Kingston	1954/55
J.H.Sinclair	South Africa	106 & 6-26	England	Cape Town	1898/99
D.St E.Atkinson	West Indies	219 & 5-56	Australia	Bridgetown	1954/55
Mushtaq Mohammad	Pakistan	201 & 5-49	New Zealand	Dunedin	1972/73
V.Mankad	India	184 & 5-196	England	Lord's	1952
G.S.Sobers	West Indies	174 & 5-41	England	Headingley	1966
P.R.Umrigar	India	172* & 5-107	West Indies	Port-of-Spain	1961/62
I.T.Botham	England	138 & 5-59	New Zealand	Wellington	1983/84
G.A.Faulkner	South Africa	123 & 5-120	England	Johannesburg (1)	1909/10
Wasim Akram	Pakistan	123 & 5-100	Australia	Adelaide	1989/90
Mushtaq Mohammad	Pakistan	121 & 5-28	West Indies	Port-of-Spain	1976/77
Imran Khan	Pakistan	117 & 5-82	India	Faisalabad	1982/83
C.Kelleway	Australia	114 & 5-33	South Africa	Old Trafford	1912
B.R.Taylor	New Zealand	105 & 5-86	India	Calcutta	1964/65
G.S.Sobers	West Indies	104 & 5-63	India	Kingston	1961/62
I.T.Botham	England	103 & 5-73	New Zealand	Christchurch	1977/78
R.Benaud	Australia	100 & 5-84	South Africa	Johannesburg (3)	1957/58
O.G.Smith	West Indies	100 & 5-90	India	Delhi	1958/59

MOST APPEARANCES AS CAPTAIN

Captain	Country	Tests	Won	Drew	Lost	Tied
A.R.Border	Australia	93	32	38	22	1
C.H.Lloyd	West Indies	74	36	26	12	0
I.V.A.Richards	West Indies	50	27	15	8	0
G.S.Chappell	Australia	48	21	14	13	0
Imran Khan	Pakistan	48	14	26	8	0
S.M.Gavaskar	India	47	9	30	8	0
P.B.H.May	England	41	20	11	10	0
Nawab of Pataudi jnr	India	40	9	12	19	0
R.B.Simpson	Australia	39	12	15	12	0
G.St A.Sobers	West Indies	39	9	20	10	0
M.Azharuddin	India	37	11	17	9	0
M.A.Atherton	England	35	8	14	13	0
G.A.Gooch	England	34	10	12	12	0
Javed Miandad	Pakistan	34	14	14	6	0
Kapil Dev	India	34	4	22	7	1
J.R.Reid	New Zealand	34	3	13	18	0
A.Ranatunga	Sri Lanka	33	5	16	12	0
D.I.Gower	England	32	5	9	18	0
R.Illingworth	England	31	12	14	5	0
J.M.Brearley	England	31	18	9	4	0
E.R.Dexter	England	30	9	14	7	0
I.M.Chappell	Australia	30	15	10	5	0
G.P.Howarth	New Zealand	30	11	12	7	0